**DO NOT REMOVE
CARDS FROM POCKET**

**ALLEN COUNTY PUBLIC LIBRARY
FORT WAYNE, INDIANA 46802**

You may return this book to any agency, branch,

or bookmobile of the Allen County Public Library.

DEMCO

Encyclopedia of British Humorists

GARLAND REFERENCE LIBRARY OF THE HUMANITIES (VOL. 906)

Encyclopedia of British Humorists
Geoffrey Chaucer to John Cleese

Volume 2 L–W

Edited by
Steven H. Gale

GARLAND PUBLISHING, INC.
New York & London
1996

Library of Congress Cataloging-in-Publication Data

Encyclopedia of British humorists : Geoffrey Chaucer to John Cleese / edited by
   Steven H. Gale.
       p.   cm. — (Garland reference library of the humanities ;
vol. 906)
   Includes bibliographical references and index.
   ISBN 0-8240-5990-5
   1. English wit and humor—Bio-bibliography.   2. Humorists, English—Biog-
raphy—Dictionaries.   3. English wit and humor—Dictionaries.   I. Gale,
Steven H.   II. Series.
PR931.E54   1996
827.009—dc20
[B]
                                                  95-2282
                                                   CIP

Cover photograph: Gertrude Lawrence and Noel Coward. Courtesy of the Bettmann
Archive. Photo researcher Marjorie Trenk.

Cover design by Larry Wolfson Design, NY

Printed on acid-free, 250-year-life paper
Manufactured in the United States of America

To Kathy, Shannon, Ashley, Kristin,
my father, Norman A. Gale, and Linda,
the Goodwins, the Johnsons, the Corums,
and in memory of my mother, Mary Wilder
Haase, and my brother, Bill, as always,
with all my love and thanks

Contents

xi   Acknowledgments

xiii   Preface

xix   Chronological Index

xxxi   Pseudonyms

Volume 1

3   Ackerley, J. R.

6   Adams, Douglas

10   Addison, Joseph

14   Amis, Kingsley

22   Amis, Martin Louis

26   Anderson, Lindsay Gordon

35   Anstey, F.

38   Armin, Robert

41   Armstrong, John

45   Auden, W. H.

59   Austen, Jane

66   Ayckbourn, Alan

73   Bagnold, Enid Algerine

77   Barnes, Peter

85   Barrie, James Matthew

89   Bashford, Henry Howarth

92   Beaumont, Francis

99   Beckett, Samuel

114	Beerbohm, Max	307	Dickens, Charles
118	Behan, Brendan	315	D'Israeli, Isaac
128	Belloc, Joseph Peter René Hilaire	319	Donne, John
132	Benson, E. F.	329	Douglas, Norman
138	Bentley, E. C.	333	Dryden, John
142	The Beowulf Poet	337	Du Maurier, George
146	Betjeman, John	340	Dunbar, William
151	Bradbury, Malcolm Stanley	345	Ewart, Gavin
157	Browning, Robert	351	Farquhar, George
164	Bunbury, Henry William	355	Fergusson, Robert
168	Burnand, Francis Cowley	358	Fielding, Henry
172	Burney, Frances "Fanny"	365	Finch, Anne
177	Burns, Robert	369	Firbank, Ronald
185	Butler, Samuel	371	Fletcher, John
190	Byron, Lord George Gordon	378	Foote, Samuel
203	Calverley, Charles Stuart	382	Ford, Ford Madox
206	Carey, Henry	389	Forster, E. M.
209	Carlyle, Thomas	398	Frayn, Michael
213	Carroll, Lewis	404	Friel, Brian
219	Cary, Joyce	409	Fry, Christopher
223	Chapman, George	429	The Gawain/Pearl Poet
228	Chaucer, Geoffrey	434	Gay, John
243	Chesterton, G. K.	440	Gibbons, Stella Dorothea
248	Churchill, Winston S.	445	Gilbert, W. S.
252	Cleese, John	452	Goldsmith, Oliver
256	Coleridge, Samuel Taylor	458	Grahame, Kenneth
262	Collier, John Henry Noyes	465	Gray, Simon
264	Congreve, William	473	Greene, Graham
274	Coren, Alan	485	Greene, Robert
278	Coward, Noel Pierce	491	Grossmith, George
289	Crisp, Quentin	491	Grossmith, Walter Weedon
293	Dahl, Roald	495	Haliburton, Thomas Chandler
296	D'Arcy, Ella	499	Hall, John
302	Deloney, Thomas	503	Hall, Joseph

511	Hankin, St. John	704	Lovelace, Richard
513	Hardy, Thomas	711	Macdonell, Archibald Gordon
518	Herbert, A. P.	714	Mankowitz, Wolf
522	Herbert, George	719	Marlowe, Christopher
525	Hoffnung, Gerard	725	Marryat, Frederick
529	Hogg, James	728	Marston, John
531	Hone, William	733	Marvell, Andrew
535	Hood, Thomas	738	Maugham, W. Somerset
540	Hook, Theodore Edward	744	Maurice, Thomas
543	Hope, Anthony	747	Mayhew, Henry
546	Housman, A. E.	752	Meredith, George
550	Howleglas	757	Middleton, Thomas
552	Huxley, Aldous Leonard	763	Mikes, George
557	Isherwood, Christopher	764	Milligan, Spike
565	Jacobs, W. W.	770	Milne, A. A.
568	Jellicoe, Ann	775	Mitford, Nancy
573	Jerome, Jerome Klapka	781	Nashe, Thomas
579	Jerrold, Douglas William	787	O'Casey, Sean
585	Johnson, Samuel	798	O'Nolan, Brian
594	Jonson, Ben	803	Orton, Joe
608	Joyce, James	807	Orwell, George
621	Kempe, William	829	Pain, Barry Eric Odell
624	Kipling, Rudyard	832	Peacock, Thomas Love
		841	Peele, George
	Volume 2	844	Philips, John
		847	Pinter, Harold
635	Lamb, Charles	862	Planche, James Robinson
642	Lear, Edward	865	Pope, Alexander
650	Lemon, Mark	871	Potter, Stephen Meredith
656	Levy, Benn Wolfe	875	Prior, Matthew
661	Lewis, C. S.	889	Pritchett, V. S.
671	Lewis, Wyndham	894	Pym, Barbara
684	Livings, Henry	901	Ralegh, Walter
691	Lodge, David	904	Rattigan, Terence Mervyn
701	Lonsdale, Frederick		

908	Russell, Bertrand Arthur
912	Russell, Willy
919	Saki
922	Scoggin, John
924	Seaman, Owen
926	Secombe, Harry Donald
931	Shaffer, Peter Levin
938	Shakespeare, William
950	Sharpe, Tom
957	Shaw, George Bernard
967	Shenstone, William
969	Sheridan, Richard Brinsley
974	Shirley, James
980	Sidney, Philip
984	Sillitoe, Alan
994	Simple, Peter (joint pseudonym)
	Wharton, Michael
	Welch, Colin
1000	Simpson, N. F.
1007	Sitwell, Edith
1013	Skelton, John
1018	Smith, Sydney
1026	Smollett, Tobias George
1034	Somerville and Ross (joint pseudonym)
	Somerville, Edith Anna Oenone
	Martin, Violet Florence
1041	Southey, Robert
1046	Spark, Muriel Sarah
1050	Steele, Richard

1057	Sterne, Laurence
1067	Stoppard, Tom
1075	Strachey, Lytton
1080	Suckling, John
1085	Swift, Jonathan
1093	Symons, Arthur William
1103	Tarlton, Richard
1106	Taylor, John
1113	Thomas, Dylan
1118	Tinniswood, Peter
1122	Tolkien, J. R. R.
1132	Townsend, Sue
1136	Travers, Ben
1141	Trollope, Anthony
1153	Ustinov, Peter
1163	Vajda, Albert
1165	Wakefield Master
1168	Waller, Edmund
1173	Waterhouse, Keith Spencer
1183	Waugh, Auberon Alexander
1189	Waugh, Evelyn Arthur St. John
1195	Wells, H. G.
1199	Wilde, Oscar
1207	Willans, Geoffrey
1212	Wilson, Sandy
1217	Wodehouse, P. G.
1227	Wycherley, William
1233	Contributors
1253	Index

L

Lamb, Charles

Born: London, February 10, 1775
Education: Christ's Hospital, 1782–1789
Died: Edmonton, December 27, 1834

Biography

Born at No. 2 Crown Office Row, the Temple, London, on February 10, 1775, Charles Lamb was the youngest child of John Lamb, who was about fifty years old at Charles's birth, and Elizabeth (Field) Lamb, who was thirty-eight. When Charles was in his eighth year he entered Christ's Hospital, an excellent school established for poor boys, where he studied under Matthew Field (no relation of Lamb's mother). In his seven years there Lamb obtained a strong foundation in the classics, especially Latin, which he mastered so fully that in adulthood he could compose letters in that language, and he learned to write clear English prose. In *Biographia Literaria* (1817), Samuel Taylor Coleridge, whom Lamb met at school and who became a lifelong friend, describes his own training in this regard under James Boyer; presumably Lamb's was similar.

Because a stutter barred Lamb from a career in the church, he did not continue his education after leaving Christ's Hospital, though he had pursued the college preparatory rather than the commercial curriculum. Bookish by nature—Charles Valentine Le Grice, a classmate, recalled the boy as "quiet, gentle, studious . . . a looker on rather than a participant in the frolics of others" (Courtney, 40)—Lamb lamented in 1820 that he had "been defrauded . . . of the sweet food of academic institution" ("Oxford in the Vacation"). His university would be his beloved London, with its bookstalls and theaters, as well as conversations with friends such

as Coleridge, William Hazlitt, William Godwin, John Keats, and Henry Crabb Robinson. Upon leaving Christ's Hospital he became a clerk to Joseph Paice. Paice continued Lamb's education in books (Paice was devoted to the Elizabethans, an enthusiasm that Lamb would share) and life. In "Modern Gallantry" Lamb describes Paice's gentlemanly treatment of women, another of Paice's characteristics that he would adopt. Together with Samuel Salt, the employer of Lamb's father, Paice secured Lamb his post with the East India House, where he served as clerk for thirty-three years (1792–1825).

On September 22, 1796, Charles's sister, Mary, killed their mother in a fit of insanity. Their older brother, John, favored confining Mary for life, but Charles resolved to care for her. He thus put aside for many years any hope of marriage and, temporarily, all thoughts of literature. Like Lamb's repeated farewells to tobacco, this rejection of writing proved short-lived. He already had published four sonnets in Coleridge's *Poems on Several Subjects* (1796), and another of his pieces, "The Grandame," appeared in Charles Lloyd's *Poems on the Death of Priscilla Farmer* (1796). Lamb was collecting excerpts for his *Specimens of the English Dramatic Poets Who Lived about the Time of Shakespeare* (1808) and, inspired perhaps by William Henry Ireland's Shakespearean forgeries, he helped with, perhaps contributed to, *Original Letters of Sir John Falstaff* (1796) by his Christ's Hospital schoolmate James White (later celebrated in "The Praise of Chimney-Sweepers").

To supplement his income Lamb wrote for various magazines and newspapers, and throughout his life he tried to write for the theater. Only one of his pieces was staged: *Mr. H—* opened on December 10, 1806, and closed the same night. Many in the audience, including the author, hissed during the performance. More successful were his works for children—often Mary served as his co-author—published by William Godwin's Juvenile Library. Lamb's *Works* appeared in 1818, and though the two volumes contain a number of fine poems and essays, his best writing lay ahead of him. From 1820 to 1825 he contributed to the *London Magazine*. These pieces, collected in *Elia, Essays which have Appeared under that Signature in the London Magazine* (1823) and *The Last Essays of Elia* (Philadelphia, 1828; London, 1833), earned him an important place in the annals of the familiar essay. In 1820, the Lambs met the eleven-year-old Emma Isola. After her father died in 1823 the Lambs adopted her; she married Edward Moxon in 1833. Lamb died at Edmonton on December 27, 1834 and is buried there.

Literary Analysis

Lamb's strength and weakness as an author lie in the autobiographical nature of his work; with Montaigne he might have said, "It is myself that I portray." Hence, he was less successful in those genres that require the writer to move beyond himself. As much as he loved the stage, as good a critic of the theater as he was, he could not create a stageworthy plot. *Mr. H—*, the best of his efforts, depends upon the thin device of Mr. Hogsflesh's efforts to conceal his name. *John Woodvil* (1802) reveals Lamb's penchant for writing "for antiquity" (as he wrote to B.W. Proctor on January 22, 1829), with its Elizabethan verse and seventeenth-century setting. The play fails, however, not because of its language—Lamb could write effective dialogue—but because it offers little character development or story. The eponymous hero, John, accidentally reveals where his father, Sir Walter Woodvil, is hiding from the Royalist forces of King Charles II. Sir Walter is captured and dies; Simon, John's younger brother, goes abroad; John repents and so wins back the love of Margaret. Had the play provided better characterization, more action, and more tension, even such a thin plot might have succeeded, but the drama lacks all of these ingredients.

Lamb's one novelistic effort, *A Tale of Rosamund Gray* (1798), while weak as fiction, is fascinating precisely because of its autobio-graphical element. In this work Lamb recounts his love for Ann Simmons of Blenheim, whom he met during one of his visits to Hertfordshire where his grandmother, Mary Field, cared for the deserted estate of Blakesware. This failed love affair deeply affected Lamb's life and writing. In 1795, he went mad for six weeks and had to be confined in an asylum; the likely cause of his illness was the realization that he could not marry Ann. After she married John Thomas Bartrum (or Bartram), Lamb reportedly would walk back and forth in front of her husband's pawn shop near Leicester Square to catch a glimpse of her. Apparently, he was successful occasionally, for in May 1799, he told Robert Southey that he had recently dined with her twice. Many of his poems were inspired by her, and in his poignant essay "Dream Children" he imagines that he has married Ann (called Alice W—n in the essay). The dream children toll him back to his sole self when they announce, "The children of Alice call Bartrum father. We are nothing, less than nothing . . . We are only what might have been."

In the novel Ann is the title character, Lamb becomes Allan Clare, and his thinly disguised sister is Elinor. The work is set near Blakesware, where Lamb met Ann, and he supplies her cottage with his own favorite books: Isaak Walton's *The Compleat Angler*, John Bunyan's *The Pilgrim's Progress*, George Wither's *Emblems*, and the Bible. His naming the villain Matrevis suggests that he had read Christopher Marlowe's *Edward II*, where Matrevis is the evil follower of young Mortimer, and, as does *John Woodvil*, indicates how early in life he was imbued with the Elizabethan spirit.

For students of Lamb, then, *A Tale of Rosamund Gray* is worth reading. The story, though, is contrived. Matrevis rapes Rosamund, who dies soon afterward; within a few chapters Lamb also dispatches Elinor and then the villain, whom Allan forgives as Matrevis is dying of a wound received in a duel. The denouement derives from Samuel Richardson's *Clarissa* (1747–1748), as do the rape and the use of letters in chapter 7. Unhappily, Lamb's characters lack the complexity of Richardson's. In "Detached Thoughts on Books and Reading," Lamb expressed his impatience with modern fiction, and in a letter to John Dibdin he remarked, "I naturally take little interest in story" (July 28, 1824). The novel was not his genre.

Lamb may have been temperamentally incapable of the sustained effort that a long prose narrative or a play requires. As a conversationalist, he was noted for his pithy remarks rather than for lengthy monologues. His stutter may have been partly responsible, but the tendency may indicate a habit of mind as well. Lamb's work for the East India House also limited his time; he complained of losing at least six hours a day, and in the evenings he longed for company. When he tried to secrete himself by renting a room or by creating a study removed from visitors, he could not long tolerate the isolation.

The writer succeeded, therefore, with short works that thrive on personal revelation. In the year that *Rosamund Gray* appeared, he published "The Old Familiar Faces," which conveyed the same sense of loss as the novel but more concisely and so more powerfully:

> I loved a love once, fairest among
>   women;
> Closed are her doors on me, I must not
>   see her—
> All, all are gone, the old familiar faces.
> How some they have died, and some
>   they have left me,
> And some are taken from me; all are departed;
> All, all are gone, the old familiar faces.

The sonnets inspired by Ann also rise to the level of real literature. Especially noteworthy is the one beginning:

> Was it some sweet device of Faery
> That mocked my steps with many a
>   lonely glade,
> And fancied wanderings with a fair-
>   hair'd maid?
> Have these things been?

As with Keats's questioning conclusion of "Ode to a Nightingale," in the poem Lamb indicates the elusive nature of reality, the difficulty of distinguishing between the actual and the imagined. "Written at Cambridge" arises from the sense of another loss, that of a college education. "We Were Two Pretty Babes" and "The Gypsy's Malison" speak of the death of youthful innocence. By looking at his own heart the author produced verse with universal appeal.

Lamb's reputation rests on his prose, though, particularly his literary criticism, let-

ters, and essays. Like so much other Romantic criticism, Lamb's depends on personal responses to his reading. *Specimens of English Dramatic Poets* is essentially a commonplace book of favorite passages, enriched with his reactions to them. Thus, of a passage in Cyril Tourneur's *The Revenger's Tragedy* he writes:

> The reality and life of this Dialogue
> passes any scenical illusion I ever felt. I
> never read it but my ears tingle, and I
> feel a hot blush spread my cheeks, as if I
> were presently about to "proclaim"
> some such "malefactions" of myself, as
> the Brothers here rebuke in their unnatural parent; in words more keen and dagger-like than those which Hamlet speaks
> to his mother.

He makes a fine distinction among the witches of William Shakespeare's *The Tragedy of Macbeth*, Thomas Middleton's *The Witch*, and Mother Sawyer in Thomas Dekker's *The Witch of Edmonton* by noting the type of reaction that each elicits. He was a reader-response theorist well before the twentieth-century critic Stanley Fish.

A lifelong devotee of the theater from the time he saw his first play (Thomas Arne's *Artaxerxes*) at the age of five, Lamb was a particularly astute critic of drama. Among his most provocative pieces are those treating Shakespeare's tragedies and Restoration comedy. In the former he argues that Shakespeare's plays lose much when translated to the stage, a point also made by Coleridge and Hazlitt, who may well have gotten this idea from their friend Lamb. Seeing Lear alone in the storm, Lamb writes:

> We want to take him into shelter and
> relieve him. That is all the feeling which
> the acting of Lear ever produced in me.
> But the Lear of Shakespeare cannot be
> acted. The contemptible machinery by
> which they mimic the storm which he
> goes out in, is not more inadequate to
> represent the horrors of the real elements, than any actor can be to represent
> Lear; they might more easily propose to
> personate the Satan of Milton upon
> stage, or one of Michael Angelo's terrible
> figures. ("On the Tragedies of Shakespeare")

L

Lamb is not criticizing the lack of stage illusion or the acting. Even the best production will pale compared to the imaginings of a sensitive mind. One detects here the Platonism of the Romantics. Just as for Percy Bysshe Shelley or Coleridge the poem on the page is so much less than the envisioned work, so for Lamb the stage cannot rival the theater of the imagination.

The writer's response to Restoration comedy is similarly subjective:

> I do not know how it is with others, but I feel the better always for the perusal of one of Congreve's—nay, why should I not add even of Wycherley's—comedies. I am the gayer at least for it; and I could never connect those sports of a witty fancy in any shape with any result to be drawn from them to imitation in real life. ("On the Artificial Comedy of the Last Century")

The theatrical artificiality that diminishes Shakespeare heightens Congreve. In real life such actions as are depicted in Restoration comedy would shock, but on the stage they delight. Hence, Lamb praises John Palmer (1742–1798) for his "highly artificial manner."

Lamb brought to his criticism a keen intelligence, exquisite taste, independence, and a solid grounding in both classical and English literature acquired at Christ's Hospital and through his extensive reading. He praised Keats's poetry when almost all other reviewers damned it; when Robert Southey objected to Coleridge's *Rime of the Ancient Mariner*, Lamb defended the work. He did, however, urge Coleridge to pursue simplicity, and he warned William Wordsworth to curb his didacticism. In both cases he was offering good counsel.

The qualities that make him a first-rate critic similarly assure him a place among the best of correspondents. The medium suited him: he could write letters at work and could record his ideas as they came to him. Hazlitt commented on the excellence of Lamb's conversation; his letters served as discussions on paper. As in his conversations, he suited the matter to the recipient. B.W. Proctor observed that Lamb spoke to different people in different ways:

> With Hazlitt he talked as though they met the subject in discussion on equal terms; with Leigh Hunt he exchanged repartees; to Wordsworth he was almost respectful; with Coleridge he was sometimes jocose, sometimes deferring; with Martin Burney fraternally familiar; with Manning affectionate; with Godwin merely courteous; or if friendly, then in a minor degree. (Proctor, 173–74)

The same distinction appears in the letters. Though he thought about his readers' interests, and though the crossings out in the manuscripts show concern for language as well as content, in his letters Lamb was not writing for posterity. He never kept copies. Approximately 1,150 of his letters survive because the recipients thought them worthy of preservation.

The letters are interesting in a number of ways. They serve as an excellent biography, a recording of thoughts as well as actions. Much sound criticism of his contemporaries appears in them, as does his reaction to earlier works. Thus, he tells Coleridge on October 28, 1796, that *The Compleat Angler* "breathes the very spirit of innocence, purity, and simplicity of heart; . . . it would sweeten a man's temper at any time to read it." The letters frequently entertain, too. Wordsworth, in "Extempore Effusion on the Death of the Ettrick Shepherd" (1835), refers to "Lamb, the frolic and the gentle." Lamb enjoyed frolicking in his letters. On Christmas Day, 1815, he wrote to Thomas Manning, who was then in China, that all of Manning's friends, including Coleridge, Wordsworth, Godwin, and Mary Lamb were dead, St. Paul's reduced to ruins, and the Monument to the Great Fire of London shrunk to less than half its former height. This same delight in practical joking is evident in a letter that he sent to his landlord and former schoolmate James Matthew Gutch sometime in 1800. While Gutch was in Birmingham, Lamb wrote that a clerk had stolen all of Gutch's money and that his partner had fled. On the back of the sheet Lamb added that he had been teasing, but Gutch must have experienced some uneasy moments.

Another facet of Lamb's humor is the use of hyperbole. His justly famous "Dissertation on Roast Pig" plays on the notion that the dish is so delectable that people would burn down their houses to enjoy the taste. "Mrs. Battle's Opinions on Whist" elevates the card game to life's primary concern. Whist is Mrs. Battle's "duty, the thing she came into the world to do,—and she did it." Those failing to take cards seriously are "insufferable triflers," a title one might ordinarily apply to people of the opposite persuasion. Lamb appreciated James White's annual feast for chimney sweepers because the poor children were addressed as gentlemen, the dinner served as though to London's wealthiest inhabitants, "the small ale [offered] as if it were wine." White's behavior delights Lamb because it smacks of the same exaggeration that he himself practiced in his writing.

This playfulness also manifests itself in Lamb's handling of language. The writer said that he hoped to inhale his last breath through a pipe and exhale it with a pun. The wordplay for which he was so noted in conversation sometimes enriches his letters, which, he claimed, consisted of "news, sentiment, and puns" ("Distant Correspondents"). Shortly before he proposed to the actress Fanny Kelly (her gentle refusal did nothing to impair their friendship), he wrote to ask her for theater passes, then often made of bone. "If your Bones are not engaged on Monday night, will you favor us with the use of them? I know, if you can oblige us, you will make no bones of it." He proceeded in this fashion until he concluded, "I am almost at the end of my bon-mots" (July 9, 1819). Playing on the name of his correspondent, he wrote to Thomas Hood in 1823, "And what dost thou at the Priory? *Cuculus not facit Monachum*" (a hood does not make a monk). Later in the same letter he spoke of the pleasures of fishing and ascribed to that occupation the designation of ancient Britons as East and West Angles.

Wit, sincerity, and sympathy—the qualities that great letters require—characterize Lamb's. They delighted and informed—or misinformed—their recipients, as they have later readers. Through them one can still encounter the essential Lamb and experience the pleasure that his friends must have taken in his company.

Excellent as a critic and correspondent, as a familiar essayist Lamb has no peers. Even in his twenties he had attempted this genre, but the *Morning Post* rejected his efforts. John Scott and his successor, John Taylor, more astutely placed no restrictions on Lamb's writing, and the essays that they published under the name of Elia earned the admiration of Lamb's contemporaries together with the love and gratitude of posterity.

The familiar essay perfectly suited the author's autobiographical propensities and his habits of composition. A number of the Elia manuscripts are written on East India House paper and so may have been completed on company time, though Lamb did take quills and paper home from work. Many of his contributions to the *London Magazine* began in other forms, as George L. Barnett has demonstrated in detail in *Charles Lamb: The Evolution of Elia*. A careful craftsman, Lamb meticulously revised these essays and did not hesitate to alter reality to suit his needs. Barnett points out, for example, that when Lamb first wrote to Mrs. Hazlitt about George Dyer's encounter with the New River, he attributed the rescue to others (November 1823). By the time he finished "Amicus Redidivus," Lamb had become the Aeneas who bore aged Anchises on his shoulders. The one-eyed doctor who attended Dyer receives the name Monoculus, and the brief description of him in the letter grew to a full seventeenth-century character sketch.

"Amicus Redidivus" reflects the seventeenth-century style, particularly Sir Thomas Browne's, that was second nature to Lamb. It also reflects Lamb's wide reading. Toward the end of the piece he speaks of the nightmares which the episode has occasioned. Undoubtedly embroidering reality as is his wont, he speaks of Clarence's liquid dream (Shakespeare, *Richard III*), Christian's sinking and crying to Hopeful (*The Pilgrim's Progress*), and the death of Palinurus (Virgil's *Aeneid*). Despite the near-tragic nature of the event that he describes, his characteristic humor keeps breaking in. He compliments Monoculus for tasting the brandy and water that he has prescribed for Dyer: "It addeth confidence to the patient, to see his medical adviser go hand and hand with himself in the remedy." The artificiality of the style distances the potential tragedy and converts it to comedy, and Dyer's recalling earlier mishaps narrowly averted is presented in the rhythm of Richard III's speech on the death of princes in act 3, scene 2, of Shakespeare's play. The implied comparison between Dyer's escaping the "carelessness of nurses" and monarchs "poisoned by their wives" helps place the episode in perspective.

In one respect "Amicus Redidivus" differs from most of the Elia essays: it describes a recent event. Especially in the earlier essays of this series a strong nostalgia pervades the writing. Of the twenty-eight pieces in the 1823 collection, more than half deal with the essayist's past, particularly his childhood. In the Preface to *The Last Essays of Elia* he describes himself as one on whom "the *toga virilis* never sate gracefully ... The impressions of infancy had burnt into him, and he resented the impertinence of manhood." Is he too sentimental when he mourns the death of James, his friend from Christ's Hospital days and founder of the annual feast for London's chimney sweeps ("The Praise of Chimney-Sweepers")? Is he too lachrymose when, after the death of his brother, John, he thinks of all of the familiar faces that have vanished ("Dream Children: A Reverie")? Before condemning him, one must recall that throughout his life Lamb put others ahead of himself. In his youth he played whist with his senile father when friends and books so alluringly beckoned. He assumed responsibility for his sister when even his older, and richer, brother refused, and so resigned himself to bachelorhood, limited company, and frequent moves, despite how much he hated moving, when neighbors learned of Mary's illness or when depression rendered an address no longer tolerable to her. For over thirty years he worked at a job he hated until he felt that the wood of his desk had entered his very soul. He bore his lot like a man; if occasionally he showed that he also felt it like a man, one should not judge him too harshly.

Furthermore, it is not a black but a white melancholy that colors these essays. When Coleridge referred to him as "gentle-hearted" in "This Lime-Tree Bower My Prison," Lamb objected: "Substitute drunken dog, ragged head, seld-shaven, odd-eyed, stuttering, or any other epithet which truly and properly belongs to the Gentleman in question" (August 14, 1800). If he indulged himself with the might-have-been, even "Dream Children" ends matter-of-factly with the speaker awake in his chair and Bridget/Mary by his side. His reflections on the ideal past or the non-existent present are of a piece with the great Romantic imaginings such as Shelley's *Hellas*, but, as did the saner Romantics, Lamb sadly recognized that time, chance, and mutability rule the human condition. Generous, compassionate, companionable in life, so he was in his essays. As E.V. Lucas has commented, "There is more friendliness in a page of Lamb than in all Hazlitt's writings" (1:344).

Summary

Except for his partiality to London rather than the sylvan retreats of Wordsworth and Coleridge, Charles Lamb exemplifies the Romantic movement. His essays, his works for Godwin's Juvenile Library, and his adoption of Emma Isola reflect the early nineteenth-century belief in and worship of childhood innocence. In an age that venerated Shakespeare, he was among the chief admirers. While he called attention to other Elizabethan dramatists, he did so in part to show "how far in his divine mind and manners [Shakespeare] surpassed them and all mankind" ("Preface" to *Specimens of the English Dramatic Poets Who Lived about the Time of Shakespeare*). His subjective criticism and focus on self in everything he wrote bears the unmistakable stamp of his personality: whimsical, tolerant, sympathetic. After Lamb retired from the East India House he wrote to Wordsworth, "It was like passing from life into eternity" (April 6, 1825). His letters and essays truly did grant immortality to a life well lived. With his beloved Shakespeare he might have said of these works, "So long as men can breathe, or eyes can see, / So long lives this, and this gives life to thee."

Selected Bibliography

Primary Sources

Works. Ed. E.V. Lucas. 7 vols. New York: Putnam, 1903–1905.

Novels

A Tale of Rosamund Gray and Old Blind Margaret. London: Lee and Hurst, 1798.
John Woodvil, a Tragedy. London: G. and J. Robinson, 1802.

Poetry

Blank Verse, by Charles Lloyd and Charles Lamb. London: Bensley, 1798.
The Works of Charles Lamb. 2 vols. London: Ollier, 1818. Includes prose as well.
Album Verses. London: Edward Moxon, 1830.

Essays

Elia, Essays which have Appeared under that Signature in the London Magazine. London: Taylor and Hessey, 1823.
The Last Essays of Elia. London: Moxon, 1833.
Essays of Elia. New York: Oxford University Press, 1987. Includes *The Last Essays of Elia*.

Criticism

Specimens of the English Dramatic Poets Who Lived about the Time of Shakespeare. London: Longmans, 1808.

Children's Books

With Mary Lamb. *Mrs. Leicester's School.* London: M.J. Godwin, 1807; London: Dent, 1899.

With Mary Lamb. *Tales from Shakespeare.* London: Thomas Hodgkins, 1807; New York: Macmillan, 1958.

The Adventures of Ulysses. London: Juvenile Library, 1808; New York: Frederick A. Stokes, 1926.

Poetry for Children. London: M.J. Godwin, 1809.

Secondary Sources

Biographies

Blunden, Edmund. *Charles Lamb and His Contemporaries.* Cambridge: Cambridge University Press, 1933. The Clark Lectures Blunden delivered at Trinity College, Cambridge, in 1932. Blunden had intended a more extensive book, but he condensed many sound observations into a highly readable 200 pages. A good introduction to Lamb and his writings.

Courtney, Winifred F. *Young Charles Lamb 1775–1802.* New York: New York University Press, 1982. Good account of the early life. Argues, not totally convincingly, that Lamb was politically radical in this period.

Lucas, Edward V. *The Life of Charles Lamb.* London: Methuen, 1905. The standard biography, as well written as it is detailed. Frequently allows Lamb to speak for himself through letters and other writings.

Proctor, Bryan W. (Barry Cornwall, pseud.). *Charles Lamb: A Memoir.* Boston: Roberts Brothers, 1866. Sympathetic revelations by a close friend. Includes some fascinating anecdotes.

Books

Barnett, George L. *Charles Lamb.* Boston: Twayne, 1976. After a brief biography, Barnett surveys Lamb's poetry, drama, fiction, his letters, essays of Elia, and criticism. Includes a useful bibliography.

———. *Charles Lamb: The Evolution of Elia.* Bloomington: Indiana University Press, 1964; Haskell House, 1973. Examination in detail of the genesis and evolution of Lamb's Elia essays, tracing them back to earlier pieces, especially the letters.

McKenna, Wayne. *Charles Lamb and the Theatre.* Gerrards Cross, Buckinghamshire: Colin Smythe, 1978. McKenna begins with a survey of the British theater, then discusses Lamb as critic and dramatist.

Monsman, Gerald. *Confessions of a Prosaic Dreamer.* Durham, NC: Duke University Press, 1984. In this pleasant little book Monsman offers a psychological exploration of Lamb's use of personae, especially Elia, to cope with the terrors of his life.

Randel, Fred V. *The World of Elia: Charles Lamb's Essayistic Romanticism.* Port Washington, NY: Kennikat Press, 1975. Randel argues for the enduring greatness of Lamb's essays.

Articles

Boas, F.S. "Charles Lamb and the Elizabethan Dramatists." *Essays and Studies by Members of the English Association*, 29 (1944): 62–81. Boas examines Lamb's criticism, which, despite some reservations, Boas regards as essentially sound.

Haven, Richard. "The Romantic Art of Charles Lamb." *English Literary History*, 30 (June 1963): 137–46. Haven analyzes "Old China" and "The Old Benchers of the Inner Temple" to show the similarities between Lamb's Elia essays and the Romantic lyric.

Henderson, Arnold. "Some Constants of Charles Lamb's Criticism." *Studies in Romanticism*, 7 (Winter 1963): 104–16. Henderson notes Lamb's personal response to literature but also his historical sense; both of these elements characterize Romantic criticism in general. Claims that Lamb's "touchstones for excellence [are] depth of feeling, moral worth, and truth to nature" (109).

Jessup, Bertram. "The Mind of Elia." *Journal of the History of Ideas*, 15 (April 1954): 246–59. Jessup sees Elia as a character distinct from Lamb. Drawing on the essays for the *London Magazine*, Jessup constructs a philosophy of judging life aesthetically, empirically, individually.

Scoggins, James. "Images of Eden in the Essays of Elia." *Journal of English and Germanic Philology*, 71 (1972): 198–210. Discussion of the way Lamb's essays view childhood as an age of inno-

L

cence, an Eden removed from the fallen world of adulthood.

Tillotson, Geoffrey. "The Historical Importance of Certain *Essays of Elia.*" In *Some British Romantics*, ed. James Logan et al. Columbus: Ohio State University Press, 1966, pp. 89–116. Tillotson explores the debt that Victorian novelists owe to Lamb's essays.

Joseph Rosenblum

Lear, Edward

Born: Holloway, London, May 12, 1812
Education: Tutored privately by his sister Ann; briefly to school at age eleven; attended Sass's School of Art, Bloomsbury, 1835 but did not complete the course; returned to Sass's, 1849; probationer and then full student at the Royal Academy from 1849 to 1850
Died: San Remo, Italy, January 29, 1888

Biography

Edward Lear was born to Jeremiah and Cordelia Lear on May 12, 1812, in Holloway, London, the twentieth of their twenty-one children. The Regency was in its second year, Charles Dickens had been born a few months earlier, Alfred Tennyson was two years old, and Lord Byron in his mid-twenties. A Dorset family which had prospered in eighteenth-century London as sugar refiners, by 1816 the Lears fell on hard times as a consequence of switching from sugar to the stock market. Rescued from the loss of "Bowman's Lodge," their Holloway home, by a bank loan, they continued for a time in sharply reduced circumstances. As in so many large Victorian families, the mother was a distant figure and most of Edward's education was supplied in makeshift form by older sisters: Eleanor gave him drawing lessons; Harriett taught him social demeanor; Ann seems to have had almost complete charge of the child from his infancy and total responsibility after 1827 when Jeremiah retired to Gravesend with his wife and one daughter, Florence. At about that time Ann inherited a small income, making her independent without the necessity of marriage, and thus she was able to devote the remainder of her life to rearing Edward. When his father died in 1833 and his mother in 1844, their demise is mentioned only briefly in Lear's diary.

Unfortunately, unlike the case in many large Victorian families, there was little security

afforded the growing boy. In his diary, Lear referred to his secret illness of epilepsy (seemingly petit mal seizures, sometimes three a day) as "the demon," and the manic-depressiveness that he shared with so many of his contemporaries, as "the morbids." Ann took the ailing child to Margate for his health, the place that John Keats went for the same reason. She probably used *Magnall's Questions* and *The Child Guide* for his elementary education, but she read him many Classical myths and much from the Bible as well. When Edward was ten or eleven, like Alfred, Lord Tennyson, he wept at the news of Lord Byron's death. It was also Ann who encouraged Edward's proclivity to paint flowers, butterflies, and birds, an activity that he had begun with her sister Eleanor. He may have attended school briefly in 1823.

The diary records two "evils" that had been done to him by "F.H." and "C." It now seems likely that these were homosexual assaults by a cousin, Frederick Harding, who had been bought out of his regiment and was staying with the Lears during the spring of 1822 and by someone identified in the diary as "C," possibly the brother Charles who had earlier bullied him. At any rate, Lear always assumed that it was these pederastic experiences that made normal sexual orientation difficult.

When his sister Sarah married Charles Street and moved to Arundel, Edward spent much time with them in the South Downs so beloved of Samuel Palmer and the Pre-Raphaelite Brotherhood. It was in this outdoor world of Sussex and amidst the warm congeniality of a young married couple that Lear discovered his gift for nonsense that made him seem "three-parts crazy" and wholly affectionate, a boy who could do "nothing like other people" (Letter to Fanny Combe, July 15, 1832). It was here that he penned his first poems, "Ode to a Chinaman," "Miss Maniac," and "Peppering Roads," all dedicated to Eliza Drewitt. Of great importance to his art, it was here, too, that he met the Earl of Egremont (who lived in the great country house, Petworth), Walter Fawkes, and Lord de Tabley.

At the age of fifteen, living with Ann in rooms on Gray's Inn Road, Lear started to earn his own living by drawings and colored work for shops ("uncommon queer shop-sketches") and medical illustrations ("morbid disease drawings"). Fortunately for the youth, the current vogue for illustrated books on botany and zoology meshed immediately with his own artistic preferences. So, at sixteen, through an introduction made by Mrs. Godfrey Wentworth, he was employed on the Selby and Jardine *Illustrations of British Ornithology*. Largely by his own initiative, he produced a visitors' guide, *The Gardens of the Zoological Society Delineated*. Drawing parrots from life, he prepared two of fourteen folios, *Illustrations of the Family of Psittacidae, or Parrots* and on November 30, 1830, at the ripe age of eighteen, he was made an associate of the Linnean Society.

As a consequence, the president of the Society, Lord Stanley, Earl of Derby, became Lear's patron and invited the young man to visit his estate at Knowsley, just outside of Liverpool, where he had one of the best private menageries in Europe. Moving with Ann to the east side of Regent's Park to be near the zoo, Lear finished folios three through twelve by April 1832. The youngest of his close friends, Hubert Congreve, then only seventeen, made a searching comment on his paintings and his sketchings: "Whatever may be the final verdict on his 'Topographies' [the way that both Lear and Congreve referred to his oils and watercolors] no one can deny the great cleverness and power of his artist's sketches. They were always done in pencil on the ground, and then inked in in sepia and brush-washed with color in the winter evenings" (Chitty, 241). At this point Lear described himself as a tall, ugly twenty-year-old, sufficiently normal to have caroused with Bernard Nevill among barmaids and domestics and to have contracted syphilis. Of greater significance, he was dabbling in verse—imitations of Byron describing a Greece that Lear had never visited, pastoral celebrations of the South Downs, and brief Romantic lyrics.

When he went to Knowsley, where he remained until 1837, to draw Lord Stanley's zoo, he began his long career as court jester in the great country houses of England. His success was great with the Stanley children and his first "nonsenses" were received with "uproarious delight and welcome," but in a letter to Miss Combe, with the harsh judgment of youth, he complained that "the uniform apathetic tone assumed by lofty society irks me *dreadfully*." During the next ten years, he added to, perfected, and published his first *Book of Nonsense* as a vehicle not only to amuse the children and please his hosts but also to mock fashionable life upstairs (odd people, going odd places, and doing odd things), sometimes ending the sing-song rhythms with a soothing refrain, but occasionally with a farcical bump.

Realizing that his sketches were more skillful for ornithology than for landscape or the human figure, he sensibly enrolled in Sass's School of Art in Bloomsbury, in 1835, but he could not afford the entire course. A fateful 1835 summer walking trip with Arthur Stanley (later Dean of Westminster) in Ireland and William Wordsworth's Lake District established tendencies which dominated his later life: he decided to become an itinerant landscape painter and the Stanleys gave him some commissions to sketch and paint Roman antiquities. Thus, at twenty-five years of age, the young man accepted the patronage of the great to seek a climate kinder to weak eyes, asthma, and bronchitis. Another tendency was always to seek the companionship of a male friend to irradiate the landscape studies with good fellowship. At the end of July, Lear left England for Brussels; this would be the first of many departures and returns. Although Ann accompanied him on his first trip to Brussels and they often wrote to each other, she lived the remainder of her life alone, not seeing Lear for four years.

An essay on Lear, the painter of huge oil landscapes, multitudinous drawings, and watercolor sketches, would contain an itinerary which included Luxembourg, the German Alps, Florence, Rome, Sicily, Abruzzi, the Adriatic coast, Corfu, the Greek islands, Egypt, the Holy Land, India, and the Balkans. An artistic pattern fell into place: the wandering topographical landscape painter of wild landscapes which were suffused with light and vivid with color and which the artist then turned into dark stilted lithographs. Later in life he was to develop a system that he called "tyrants" by which he would set out as many as 240 sketches, line them out in ink, and apply a watercolor wash, doing the rose in all of the copies and then the ochre, and so on. His vast landscapes in oil now sell better than then, although he did receive 500 guineas for a large landscape of the village of Ascension on Corfu and his nine-foot "Cedars of Lebanon" was sold for 200 guineas. His artistic recognition was such that in 1846 he gave twelve drawing lessons to Queen Victoria at Osborne House and Buckingham Palace, and in February 1864 he sold ten colored sketches to the Prince of Wales.

Lear's large landscapes, after the manner of Claude Lorrain, were competent and dramatic, but somehow disappointing. The foreground

L

would be too detailed and the mountains slip into obscurity, the perspective was frequently awkward, and with all of his interest in people, his human figures were positively clumsy stiff puppets, almost stick-men, as if he preferred the landscape to carry its own intrinsic drama, empty of human life.

From a period of profound depression, he was rescued by the Pre-Raphaelite Brotherhood (P.R.B.). Fascinated by their rich sense of color, he admired the meticulous naturalism of their work. When they exhibited in the summer of 1850, one of Lear's oils hung along with those of other members and admirers of the P.R.B. Although this admiration provided him with a fresh look at art, the public fury and disgust with the exhibition did him little good financially or in terms of his artistic standing. He had the privilege of spending ten days sketching and painting with Holman Hunt, who in turn introduced him to William Rossetti and John Everett Millais. Hunt never thought very highly of Lear's painting, but they became lifelong friends, and it was at this point (in 1852) that Lear started to set Tennyson lyrics to music and decided to illustrate the Laureate's poems, a project to which he returned frequently and which occupied the last decade of his life. After a stag party Wilkie Collins gave for Millais, who was about to marry Effie Ruskin, Lear wrote to Tennyson: "I feel woundily like a spectator—all through my life—of what goes on amongst those I know—very little an actor." His personal outlook remained dismal: no wife, no lover, little fame and fortune, always on the edge of poverty. When his mother died in May 1844 he invited Ann to live with him, but considering his wandering life, endlessly in and out of England, she wisely decided to remain at home.

At precisely this low point in his life, Lear met Chichester Fortescue, who, along with Franklin Lushington and Hubert Congreve, became one of the three great loves of his life. Lear met Fortescue in Rome in 1845 and immediately became one of his closest friends. Fortescue was elected MP for Louth in 1847, Chief Secretary for Ireland in 1865, and Lord of the Privy Seal in 1881. When he married Frances, Lady Waldegrave in 1871, Lear was desolated, although Fortescue had been devoted to her for the preceding twenty years during which she had been married three times. She was always condescending to Lear but commissioned seven of his large paintings, and her niece

Lady Strachey edited the *Letters* and *Later Letters of Edward Lear*, as well as two of his nonsense volumes.

Lushington was Lear's closest friend and his literary executor. They had met in Malta in 1849 and that spring they traveled together in southern Greece for several weeks, which Lear always considered the happiest and most carefree period of his life. However, when in 1855 Lushington was appointed judge to the Supreme Court of Justice in the Ionian Islands and Lear accompanied him to live on Corfu, it was apparent that the Justice's taciturn and withdrawn formalism and the demands of his political life made the continuation of those halcyon weeks impossible. Lear, who was godfather to all of Lushington's children, was described thus by the grateful father: "I have never known a man who deserved more love for his goodness of heart and his determination to do right . . . There never was a more generous or more unselfish soul." Unfortunately, Lear left all his papers to his friend, who destroyed almost all of them, and his own correspondence with Lear has not survived.

Congreve was another matter. In December 1876, after a fortnight visit from Lushington at his villa in San Remo, Lear found himself becoming very fond of Hubert, the son of his neighbor Walter Congreve. He gave the youth drawing lessons and hoped that he might become an artist. When, in February 1877, Lear's servant and constant companion Giorgio asked to return to the island of Corfu, Lear and eighteen-year-old Hubert accompanied him as far as Brindisi and then made a leisurely way back through Naples and Rome. For Lear, it was a winter repeat of his 1849 spring romance with Lushington. Back in England he visited with Emily Tennyson, always sensitive and understanding, and his sister Ellen, who was now nearly blind and deaf. Then the news arrived that Hubert was leaving San Remo to study in London. Lear wrote in his diary: "In vain I work for an hour—tears blind me. In vain I play on the Piano—and I get convulsed; in vain I pace the large room—or try to sleep. True, all these symptoms happened also in 1855—but there was not the finality there is now . . . God help me. I was never nearer to utter and total madness than now."

Interestingly, Lear almost proposed to women three times: to Helena Cortazzi in 1855 and to Gussie Bethell in 1864 and again in 1888. However, these were calmer, more sympathetic, almost domestic attachments. In his diary he recorded: "I see life as basically tragic and futile and the only thing that matters is making little jokes." On May 12, 1883, his birthday, he summed up: "So ends seventy-one years of my very silly life." These sad and silly remarks bring us to the central topic of this biographical essay—Nonsense. William Blake had an aphorism: "If the fool would persist in his folly, he would become wise." Did Edward Lear persist in nonsense?

During the summer of 1845, on Lear's second trip back to England, he was busily assembling two books, one about his travels in the Abruzzi and the other a collection of limericks. On February 10, Thomas McLean, who had been the publisher for his *Views in Rome* of 1841, published *A Book of Nonsense* in two volumes, with seventy limericks in all, under the nom de plume "Derry down Derry." Even though McLean was not a publisher of children's books, it had moderate sales. However, when a new edition was issued in 1854 with some format changes, the reviews were bad and the sales poor, so in 1861 Routledge, Warne and Routledge, specialists in children's books, were able to buy the rights for only £125, and then the work began to sell briskly. It was a bad deal for the rhymester: *A Book of Nonsense* went through nineteen editions and Lear received not a penny. In the third 1861 edition of *A Book of Nonsense* Lear dropped the pseudonym and used his own name. "The History of the Seven Families of the Lake Pipple-Popple," written in February 1864 as a gift to the young son of Lord and Lady Fitzwilliam, was published in book form in 1865 and sold very well. It was in Cannes, during the winter of 1867, that the author wrote the first of his nonsense songs, "The Owl and the Pussy-Cat," which was included in his *Nonsense Songs, Stories, Botany and Alphabets*, published in December 1871. Two years later, in December 1872, *More Nonsense* was published and the last of his books, *Laughable Lyrics*, was published in December of 1877. Amazingly, in a listing of favorite authors in the *Pall Mall Gazette* for February 1886, John Ruskin placed Lear at the head of his own list.

While he was busily painting his "tyrants" and the monstrous nine-foot oils in his new rooms at Stratford Place, Ann, who was now seventy, came to sit with Lear as he worked. On March 11, 1861, she died, leaving her brother to wander from one friend to another lamenting,

"I now have no sister Ann to love and think of me." His sister appears to have been the very model of the self-sacrificing Victorian spinster who lives only to render loving service. Lear often seems to have returned meager dividends for her devotion, although a regular correspondence was maintained during his travels, and he had invited Ann to live with him after his mother's death. In 1867, the *Cedars of Lebanon* was sold to Louisa, Lady Ashburton, for £200, less than a third of its original price, and in 1869, *Journal of a Landscape Painter in Corsica*, the last of his travel books, was published.

In 1870, Lear decided that it was time to have a place of his own and bought land in San Remo on the Italian Riviera, near Nice. Villa Emily (named either after a niece in New Zealand or Emily Tennyson) was everything that he desired for his art and for the entertainment of friends. Unfortunately, a hotel was built just below his property, blocking the view and reflecting glaring light into his studio from its whitewashed walls. He built a replica of the first house on a new plot of land, by virtue of generous loans from his friends, and called it unequivocally Villa Tennyson. The relationship with Emily was an interesting one. She was always his confidant and sympathetic friend, but her husband, Alfred, was another matter. When he visited the Tennysons at their home at Aldsworth, Lear wrote in his diary: "The evening was very pleasant in many ways, and he was less violent than often." The fact of the matter was that Lear and Tennyson never really liked each other. Perhaps the Laureate disapproved of the closeness of Lear's friendship with his wife. Certainly he was annoyed by Lear's tendency to see everything as nonsense and by the liberal bias of his politics. Lear confided in his diary that he deplored the poet's "slovenliness, selfishness, and morbid folly."

Thomas George Baring, the Earl of Northbrook, from the time he was introduced by Fortescue in 1848, became one of Lear's most faithful and appreciative friends. When Baring served as Viceroy of India (1873–1875), Lear was his honored guest. Sensing the earl's genuine admiration for his work, Lear gave him several hundred of his travel watercolors, but sadly almost all of Lear's letters to Baring, still in existence during the 1930s, seem to have been destroyed.

The 1880s were a period of necrology: Giorgio, his faithful attendant, died in 1883. When Lord Derby invited Lear to Knowsley in

January 1883, he felt too old and feeble to go. When Gussie Bethell passed through with two nieces in tow, she was widowed, but Lear could not raise the courage to ask for her hand. When he prepared the site for his own grave, he erected a stone next to it in commemoration of the long service and friendship of Giorgio. He made lists of what items he wished to leave to various friends, and he sold the Villa Emily for a third of the asking price. Although from January through April 1886 he spent weeks in bed with bronchitis, in March he was able to make the final repayment to his friends of the debt incurred in building Villa Tennyson.

The friends of former years gathered around. Fortescue visited and almost immediately came down with chills and fever. Lear lost the sight of his right eye; rheumatism made his right side more or less useless. Lushington came to stay in November. Bedridden, Lear wrote to Gussie and she came immediately, took a room in a neighboring hotel, and visited him daily. After Gussie left, the Barings came to stay for a few weeks and Hallam Tennyson arranged for an American publisher to visit the villa and look over the Tennyson drawings with the idea of using them in a new edition of his father's poems. He bought a painting for himself, but from the massive Tennyson project there issued only a small edition of one hundred copies of "The Daisy," "The Princess," and "The Palace of Art," with only a few illustrations from the more than 200 drawings that Lear had finished.

On Sunday, January 29, 1888, Lear asked his servant Guiseppe to convey his final greetings to Lushington, Baring, and Fortescue, explaining: "I did not answer their letters because I could not write, as no sooner did I take a pen in my hand than I felt as if I were dying." Two hours later, he was dead.

Literary Analysis

One afternoon in 1879, Lear made a social call at the home of the British Vice-Consul at San Remo. The time was actually spent, however, in visiting with the Vice-Consul's daughter, the charming Miss Bevan. Finding her younger brothers and sisters at tea with her, Lear started to sing, entertain, compose nonsense verse, and generally strip away the barrier of the years between himself and his youthful audience. This was the "Adopty Duncle" with hundreds of little folks, the "uncLE ARly" who was most at home with the young and who loved to "see little folks merry." This same Miss Bevan, evi-

dently a witty, vivacious young woman, collaborated with Lear on the important poem "How Pleasant to Know Mr. Lear!" In the eight quatrains, the authors admit that Lear has written "volumes of stuff," that his nose is remarkably large, and that his face is more or less hideous and framed by a beard which resembles a wig. It is noted that although some may consider him "queer," he has the perfectly normal number of ears, eyes, and fingers. His parlor is beautiful; he has a splendid library; he drinks copiously of Marsala, but it does not make him tipsy. His cat and his many friends complete the inventory of self-description. All of this seems merely superficial, but underneath there are morbid depths. Some people think him ill-tempered, some find him pleasant; the natives of San Remo refer to him as "that crazy old Englishman." His self-pity makes him weep at the seashore as well as on the mountain top; he used to be a "singer" but now he is "dumb" and his life, which can only be described as a "pilgrimage," is now about to "vanish."

From the early days when Lear was drawing the birds in the Earl of Derby's private menagerie, he had entertained the children of the estate by composing and illustrating poems in the then uncommon form of the limerick. Concerning these verses, William Baring-Gould, in *The Lure of the Limerick*, claims that even "Sumer is i-cumen in" (ca. 1300) was a limerick and finds other examples in the works of William Shakespeare, Ben Jonson, and Robert Herrick. Other authorities find them in the comedies of Aristophanes. Although Lear never referred to these poems in the limerick format as limericks, certainly he adopted the form from John Harris's *The Adventures of Fifteen Young Ladies*, its sequel, *The History of Sixteen Wonderful Old Women* (published in London, 1821), and in what seems to be a parody of these, *Anecdotes and Adventures of Fifteen Gentlemen*, published in 1822 by John Marshall—the parody contained the "sick man of Tobago" limerick mentioned by Dickens in chapter 2 of *Our Mutual Friend*. In the preface to his *More Nonsense* Lear confesses that this limerick in particular was the inspiration for his own "There Was a Sick Man of Tobago." Indeed, almost all of the limericks contain a cast of characters and a geography in the sense that it is always an Old Man or a Young Lady of a particular town, city, or country.

Lear wrote two series of limericks, the first an expanded version of *A Book of Nonsense*, published in final form in 1861, which ultimately went through twenty-seven editions. The second appeared as his third nonsense book, *More Nonsense*. All of these limericks have very firm poetic structure: the first two lines are in amphibrachic trimeter (unaccented, accented, unaccented); lines three and four are in anapaestic diameter (in the early limericks a single tetrameter with internal rhyme and a regular caesura); and a fifth line repeating the first line with only minor variations of syntax or vocabulary. Lear has a regular stock cast of characters: Old Man, Young Lady, Old Person, Young Person, followed by a place-name. The repetition of a refrain tends to make the limerick sound like a ballad, the seesaw rhythm like a nursery rhyme. The basic absurdity of character and action creates the aura of nonsense.

It would be interesting to know if Lear intended any particular sequence. Probably the first edition was arranged by the publisher; Lear may have had a hand in the organization of the Routledge reissue of 1861. There are 112 limericks in the first book (begun when Lear was in his twenties and completed when he was in his late forties) and one hundred in the second. The second series was written when he was in his fifties, in the same decade that Lewis Carroll was writing the *Alice* books. The first series came at the beginning of the Victorian vogue for nonsense books and the second right at the height of the fashion.

Although there seems to be little serial arrangement, the limericks do fall into topical groupings. At the beginning the Old Man is almost always victimized and the Young Lady is serenely in charge of all situations. In the second series, the Old Man may well be furious, frenzied, or threatening whereas the Young Lady has aged sharply and has lost her earlier ability to entrance. But, both stereotypes, male and female, play out their brief comedic roles against the disapproving backdrop of "They"— the dismaying Victorian ogre of "But what will THEY think?" We begin to understand the urgency of Lear's insistence that although some people found him ill-natured, he had all the normal number of ears, eyes, and fingers.

There is also a sense in which Lear's limericks form a Victorian bestiary, with the beasts at first either menacing or charmed but later becoming the poet, or more likely becoming a bird. It is notable that although the author seems always to have been an extremely popular guest in great English country houses, he actually hated snobs, philistines, and idlers and felt that upper-class Englishmen were too often all of these. Therefore, it was always the children who became his easiest friends—he supplied them with nonsense alphabet letters each morning at breakfast, kicked chestnut burrs and called them "yonghy-bonghy-bos," or sang "The Owl and the Pussy-cat" in a "funny little crooning tune." From the observation of birds and animals in the Knowsley menagerie, he was at home with creatures, so the limericks mention ravens, larks, wrens, crows, parrots, ducklings, geese, cranes, owls, hens, carps, pigs, frogs, Bluebottle flies, bears, mice, rabbits, apes, cats, horses, cows, and calves—but not dogs, since Lear seems to have feared them all his life.

Congreve had called attention to the recognizable expertise of Lear's sketches. However, although many seem to enhance and illustrate the limericks, often the sketches seem to indicate pain, alienation, uncertainty, and unhappiness that were not specifically mentioned in the text. The Old Man in a boat, the Old Man of Ibreem, and the Old Man who screamed out all depict a mood evoked by an illumination darker in tone than the poem that it supposedly illustrates.

Each limerick in itself may seem trifling and inconsequential. The odd foods, the eccentric behavior, the outlandish locales, the absurd dilemmas, and the outrageous solutions seem to indicate a view of a world which has scarcely emerged from the nursery. From the child's point of view the adult world often seems overwhelming, full of violence and meaningless rules. The limericks are eminently successful in conveying the wonder of a child, the absurdity of human behavior, and the inflexibility of adult regulation.

Nevertheless, a quite different and larger picture emerges once we consider the limerick as a *persona* behind which the poet's heart bleeds. If Lear was convinced that he was incapable of normal sexuality, that in some strange sense he had never outgrown his own childhood, that the preponderance of public opinion would always disapprove of his inner nature, that his art was somehow inadequate, and that his endless wanderings upon the face of the picturesque were pointless—then the nonsensical richly informs the biographical.

It is also important to recall the loci of Lear's wanderings. His essentially Romantic art led him always to ruined temples, holy mountains, and the picturesque—the dramatic and overwhelming. As he sought spiritual meaning in outward nature, perhaps the limerick technique of paring away the ordinary and common-sensical from human behavior might reveal an inner landscape of sublimity. These slight but intense verses, illustrated with secret meanings, contribute an arresting urgency to the search for meaning. They challenge all stock responses and require the wonder and honesty of a little child. The fact that almost all of the human figures, and many animal and bird figures as well, are portrayed on their tiptoes suggests that the limericks are meant to get us up high enough on tiptoe that we can look over the omnipresent walls and confining institutions of the Victorian world into a mysterious but wonderfully fulfilling life across the sea, through the night, to lands far, far away.

In the spring of 1871, Lear was almost sixty, his sight was failing in his good eye, and his energy could no longer be depended on. Although he traveled to India in 1873 and 1874, his incessant wandering was about over and San Remo increasingly became the perimeter of his activities. He sketched, painted, tended his garden, entertained his multitude of friends and even made new ones. Chiefly, though, he tended to turn inward to his verses and their illustrative sketches. Revising some old and some recent poems, he put together a botany and three alphabets and called it *Nonsense Songs, Stories, Botany and Alphabets*. This was his second nonsense book. Five years later the fourth and last nonsense book, *Laughable Lyrics*, was published. The poems in the collection are longer and the versifying more mature, but the topics are few to the point of obsession. There are ten poems about courtship voyages, three about family life, three about the bliss of paradise, and a scattering about clothes, autobiography, and an incomplete sonnet.

Lear's most famous nonsense poem, "The Owl and the Pussy-cat," was written in 1867 for Janet, the daughter of John Addington Symonds. Set to his own music, he often played and sang it as court jester in the country houses where he was guest. Each eleven-line stanza alternates rhyming iambic tetrameter and trimeter for the first eight lines, followed by a trimeter refrain, two short single iambic lines, and a repetition of the trimeter refrain. The song expresses romantic love, the quest for married bliss, and the wedding ceremony. The verbal paraphernalia of nonsense is carried over from the limericks, but the central oddity is easy to miss. Obviously the Owl should be the groom and the Cat the bride; but it is the female who steers the boat while the male sits in the bow serenading flatteringly; she proposes, he gets the ring bashfully from a pig's nose while she glares balefully at his ineptitude. Still, the romance is consummated, the turkey presides magisterially, and the couple's marital bliss is depicted in their dancing hand in hand on the sand in the silver light of the moon.

In "The Duck and the Kangaroo," composed in tetrameters and trimeters, the poet has once again an ill-matched pair with the male fastidious and hypochondriacal and the cigar-smoking female duck resourceful and decisive. The quest—"three times round the world"—seems frantic and excessive, but the duck is rescued from domestic boredom and the kangaroo seems only mildly uncomfortable.

In "The Daddy Long-legs," the voyagers are not lovers but male companions, reminding us of the many voyages and hikes that Lear took with male friends young and old. Both of the friends are deformed and ill-matching and the issue of the journey is not shared love but the playing of endless games.

Three more of the *Nonsense Songs* concern courtship voyage. The reductionism is marked; landscape shrinks to small domestic settings, the animals and birds diminish to insects in "Daddy Long-legs." Living creatures become only household utensils in "The Nutcrackers and the Table and the Chair." In the first of these three poems the utensils break out of boring domestic confinement into a mad ride around the stables and the town—never to return. In the second they take a decorous ride in the Park, interrupted by a violent quarrel which finally simmers down to the domestic banality of a cup of tea. The ill-matched pair in the third poem desperately longs for a walk and gets lost in an alley, only to be rescued by a duck, a mouse, and a beetle. The first poem celebrates escape, the second and third dolefully admit to retreat.

Although *Laughable Lyrics, a Fourth Book of Nonsense Poems, Songs, Botany, Music, etc.* includes family and cloth poems, the four which continue the courtship voyage theme are far more significant. They are still in the ballad form, but more intricate, lyrical, dramatic, and narrative.

"The Dong with a Luminous Nose" contains only barely concealed sexual innuendo. Strangely, it is a flashback, set in Paradise, the Gromboolian Plain where the Dong has gone to seek the Jumbly girl. But, even Paradise is lonely without love, so the Dong weaves a luminous nose, ever seeking, never finding. This is Lear's most desperate poetic version of his alienated plight.

"The Courtship of the Yonghy-Bonghy-Bo" is once again set in Paradise. The verse is metrically similar to Tennyson's "Row Us Out From Desenzano." The Bo proposes to the Lady Jingly Jones, but while she responds to his courtship, she already has a mate and must decline (perhaps a biographical reference to Gussie Bethell, married to a crippled, older husband, Adamson Parker). If the Lady will not have him, a male friend will have to do, so he flees to sea on the back of a turtle. Lear, however, never worked up the courage to propose; in poetry the swain can accept a rejection never given in real life and dash off boldly and decisively rather than hole up at San Remo.

"The Pobble Who Has No Toes" (which survives in two versions) is a sad and resigned poem about deprivation. The Pobble is a wonderfully daring adventurer who sets off to fish for Aunt Jobiska's Runcible Cat. He is brought back, toeless, to the consolation of his Aunt's insistence that everybody knows a Pobble is happier without his toes. But, does the Pobble know that?

As Thomas Byrom points out, "The Pelican Chorus" is a happy sort of nonsense-epithalamium. The Pelicans are a happily married couple whose daughter Dell marries the Crane King and is carried off to the great Gromboolian Plain. Although the parents know that they will see her no more, they were happy before the nuptial flight and they still consider that there are "no Birds so happy as we." When Lear was able to move from sexual fears and his personal sense of deformity to imagining that the difficult courtship is past and a beloved child is now moving out into normal domestic bliss, "violently loved," then at last the darkness lifts and contentment settles.

Summary

Edward Lear's sketches were admired and sold well. His vast Romantic oils with tiny, poorly delineated humans, are now prized, but during his lifetime they were largely ignored.

However, he seems to have found his metier in the limericks and nonsense songs where he could combine his artistic, poetic, and musical talents. Like many productions seemingly for children—the Grimm brothers' collections, the *Alice* books—these sparkling, child-like jingles express the wandering bachelor's criticism of Mrs. Grundy (They), his sense that his art was only moderately successful, and the growing realization that his personal ugliness and sexual abnormalities condemned him to a life of laughing about loneliness, alienation, and homelessness.

Selected Bibliography

Primary Sources

Edward Lear's Diary is in the Houghton Library at Harvard University.

Lear's Journals, mostly in relation to painting excursions

Journals of a Landscape Painter in Greece and Albania, etc. London: Richard Bentley, 1851.

Journals of a Landscape Painter in Southern Calabria and the Kingdom of Naples. London: Richard Bentley, 1852.

Journal of a Landscape Painter in Corsica. London: Bush, 1870.

Lear in Sicily. Intro. Granville Proby. London: Duckworth, 1938.

Edward Lear's Journals: A Selection. Ed. H. Van Thal. London: Arthur Barker, 1952.

Edward Lear's Indian Journal. Ed. Ray Murphy. London: Jarrolds, 1953.

Edward Lear in Southern Italy. Intro. Peter Quennell. London: William Kimber, 1964.

Letters

Letters of Edward Lear. Ed. Lady Strachey. London: T. Fisher Unwin, 1907. Selections from Lear's voluminous correspondence with Chichester Fortescue, Lord Carlingford; and Frances, Countess Waldegrave.

Later Letters of Edward Lear. Ed. Lady Strachey. London: T. Fisher Unwin, 1911. A sequel to the 1907 volume, this collection continues correspondence from 1864 to Lear's death in 1888. Estimated volume of correspondence: seventy-six per month, 408 per year. Introduction by Lady Strachey; Preface by Hubert Congreve.

Edward Lear: Selected Letters. Ed. Vivien Noakes. Oxford: Clarendon, 1988. Good apparatus of Chronology (in which Noakes is the acknowledged expert), Biographical Register and Notes.

Wherever possible, the copies of Lear's illustrations by Mrs. Bowen are included.

Works by Edward Lear
A Book of Nonsense, by Derry Down Derry (Edward Lear). London: Thomas McLean, 1846.
A Book of Nonsense. London: Routledge, Warne and Routledge. Enl. ed. 1861.
Edward Lear's "Nonsense Songs" and "Laughable Lyrics." Mt. Vernon, NY: Peter Pauper Press, n.d. Nineteen of the longer poems with excellent authentic illustrations and no commentary.
Nonsense Songs, Stories, Botany and Alphabets. London: Bush, 1871.
More Nonsense, Pictures, Rhymes, Botany, etc. London: Bush, 1872.
Laughable Lyrics, a Fourth Book of Nonsense Poems, Songs, Botany, Music, etc. London: Bush, 1877.
Nonsense Songs and Stories. Intro. Sir Edward Strachey. London: Warne, 1895.
Queery Leary Nonsense. Ed. Lady Strachey. London: Mills & Boon, 1911.
The Lear Colored Bird Book for Children. Foreword, J. St. Loe Strachey. London: Mills & Boon, 1912.
The Complete Nonsense of Edward Lear. Ed. Holbrook Jackson. London: Faber & Faber, 1947; New York: Dover, 1951.
Teapots and Quails. Ed. Angus Davidson and Philip Hofer. London: John Murray, 1953.

Secondary Sources
Byrom, Thomas. *Nonsense and Wonder: The Poems and Cartoons of Edward Lear*. New York: Dutton, 1977. Byron admits total indebtedness to Noakes for biographical chronology but is excellent on analysis of limericks, ballads, and cartoons.
Chitty, Susan. *That Singular Person Called Lear*. New York: Atheneum, 1989. In her introduction Lady Chitty claims as the reason for a third biography (after the works of Angus Davidson and Vivien Noakes) that more is now known of his "immensely complicated personality . . . in particular . . . his homosexuality." Weak on literary or art criticism, the sexual inversion is often pushed beyond any documentation.
Croft-Cooke, Rupert. *Feasting with Panthers:*

A New Consideration of Some Late Victorian Writers. New York, Chicago, San Francisco: Holt, Rinehart and Winston, 1967. Very well-written discussion of John Addington Symonds, Lefroy, Lear, and Lewis Carroll in chapter 7. Excellent photographs, little literary or art criticism.
Davidson, Angus. *Edward Lear: Landscape Painter and Nonsense Poet*. London: John Murray, 1938. Carefully researched from journals, diaries, and letters, the events of Lear's life are clear and authoritative. Weak on interpretation of poetry and the artist's mental and emotional crises.
Lehmann, John. *Edward Lear and His World*. New York: Charles Scribner's Sons, 1977. A pleasant pictorial biography with more emphasis on the oils, watercolors, and sketches than on any literary analysis of the verse.
Noakes, Vivien. *Edward Lear, the Life of a Wanderer*. London: Collins, 1968. Biographically more factual and exact than Davidson, but not so well written. Adds a good deal of information on venereal disease and sexual abnormalities. Probably the standard book of biography referred to most frequently by later writers.
Quennell, Peter. *The Singular Preference: Portraits and Essays*. New York: Viking Press, 1953. Collection of articles published in monthly or weekly journals across twenty years. Elegant, brief article on Lear under "Victorians," pp. 95–101.
Sewell, Elizabeth. *The Field of Nonsense*. London: Chatto and Windus, 1952. Valuable comparative study of Lewis Carroll and Lear in order to establish a literary definition of nonsense. Good literary analysis. No notes or index.

Elton E. Smith

Lemon, Mark

Born: London, November 30, 1809
Education: Cheam School, Surrey
Marriage: Helen (Nelly) Romer, September 28, 1839; ten children
Died: Crawley, May 23, 1870

Biography

Mark Lemon was born in London on November 30, 1809, the son of Martin Lemon, a hops merchant, and Alice Collis Lemon of Oxford Street. Though Lemon was often attacked later in life for being of Jewish ancestry, there is no evidence that the claim was true.[1] His father died when Lemon was eight, and Mark went to live with his paternal grandparents in the village of Hendon. (His mother remained in London and opened a millinery shop.) Sometime during this period he attended Cheam School in Surrey. At fourteen, after both of his grandparents died, Lemon went to Boston, in Lincolnshire, to learn the hops business from his maternal uncle.

By 1836, Lemon was living in London. He worked for a time at a brewery managed by a step-uncle, as evidenced when, at the time of his marriage to Helen (Nelly) Romer on September 28, 1839, Lemon listed his occupation as "brewer." After this business closed in 1840, he took charge of the Shakespeare's Head, a Drury Lane tavern popular with theater people and journalists. Though proprietorship was brief, this period ensured that he would be ridiculed as "The Literary Pot Boy" or "Mine Host" for years to come.

Throughout this time, Lemon was also attempting to make a career out of writing. As early as 1834, he was asked for more contributions for *Leigh Hunt's London Journal*, and some of his early efforts in prose and verse were published in both the *New Sporting Magazine* and *Bentley's Miscellany*. He directed his greatest energies toward the theater. A dozen Lemon farces, melodramas, and operas were staged between 1836 and 1839, and his pace picked up after he married Helen, the sister of his composer-collaborator for the 1838 opera *Rob of the Fen*. Fourteen more dramatic works appeared in 1840 alone. Despite his tremendous output, a need to support his growing family (ten children born to the Lemons over the next eighteen years) meant that Lemon would always be struggling for financial security.

He found some relief, and all of his fame, in a comic weekly called *Punch*. Though the actual sequence of events is hotly disputed,[2] and Lemon was almost certainly not involved in the very earliest stages, the prospectus manuscript is in his hand, his signature is one of the five appearing on the Articles of Agreement, and "The Moral of Punch," an essay in the first number (July 17, 1841) which sets out the paper's intentions and principles, is his work. The first few years were difficult. The third number appeared only after Lemon turned over the proceeds from one of his dramas to the publisher, and increasing financial troubles led some of the principals to abandon ship and others to find themselves nudged overboard.

Joseph Last, the printer, went first, selling his share to the engraver, Ebenezer Landells. When the publishers Bradbury and Evans, largely at Lemon's instigation, took over *Punch* in late 1842, Landells (to his surprise) lost the engraving duties that he had assumed would continue after the sale. Lemon's co-editors soon followed. Joseph Stirling Coyne was dismissed. Henry Mayhew, bitter after the new owners elevated Lemon to editor and declared Mayhew "suggester-in-chief," left of his own accord in 1845. Years later, Lemon would sum up this process by explaining that "The editorship *became* centralized." Though bad feelings and charges of betrayal lingered on, it is, however, undeniable that by early 1843 Lemon had become *Punch*'s editor and its guiding spirit— roles that he played until his death.

While *Punch* remained at the center of his professional and social life, Lemon still pursued other literary ventures. Fifty more stage pieces appeared during the 1840s. He took on editing assignments for friend Herbert Ingram, including the Christmas supplements for the *Illustrated London News* (1842). Lemon also shared a passion for acting with his friend Charles Dickens, and from 1845 on, they often appeared together in amateur theatricals, including the farce *Mr. Nightingale's Diary* (1851), which both men had some hand in writing.[3] Though Lemon frequently led or dragged the *Punch* staff onstage with them, Dickens's 1858 separation from his wife—Lemon represented Catherine Dickens in the negotiations— unhappily ended these collaborations.

In the 1860s, the editor of *Punch* made many public appearances in his own right. His 1862 lectures on the history of London were later published as *Up and Down the London Streets* (1867). He turned his 1849 play *Hearts Are Trumps* into a prose tale and gave public readings of it in 1863. And in 1868 and 1869, Lemon toured as William Shakespeare's Falstaff, a role that he had played in an 1848 production of *The Merry Wives of Windsor* and one for which his own massive bulk and famous conviviality ideally suited him.[4]

Tales, collections, and novels appeared as well. His children's books and folklore anthologies included *The Enchanted Doll* (1849), *The Legends of Number Nip* (1864), *Fairy Tales* (1868), and *Tinykin's Transformations* (1869).

L

Prose and Verse (1852) was a sampling of his early periodical writing, *A Christmas Hamper* (1860) was composed of reprints of his seasonal pieces, and *Tom Moody's Tales* (1863) was a gathering together his writing on sporting and country life. *The Jest Book* (1864) provided a home (or, perhaps more accurately, a mausoleum) for hundreds of old jokes and witty anecdotes, all appearing with "their faces washed and all uncleanness removed."[5] Lemon also completed six novels: *Wait for the End* (1864), *Loved at Last* (1864), *Faulkner Lyle* (1866), *Leyton Hall and Other Tales* (1867), *Golden Fetters* (1867), and *The Taffeta Petticoat* (which was never published).

As the sheer number of later publications suggests, Lemon was doing whatever he could to raise money. Though his annual *Punch* salary at his death was £1,500—the largest amount then paid to any English editor—family expenses, his famous generosity, and a talent for bad investments kept him in financial trouble. A move to Crawley, Sussex, in 1858 turned Lemon into a very public benefactor. He organized and often funded clubs and exhibitions, established public lighting and fire brigades, and even restored coach service—though he made his own frequent commutes to London by train. He died in Crawley on May 23, 1870, and was buried at St. Margaret's Church, Ifield.

Literary Analysis

Lemon himself made probably the most astute comment on his literary achievement. "I was made for *Punch* and *Punch* for me," he once remarked, "I should never have succeeded in any other way."[6] His writing is generally undistinguished. His eighty plays, farces, melodramas, burlettas, and operas were products of the popular theater of the time, which was hardly a great era of English drama. As for his other writing, *Punch* contributor Douglas Jerrold dubbed *Prose and Verse* "Prose and Worse," and Lemon wrote his novels simply to provide for his children.[7]

At the time of *Punch*'s birth in 1841 his reputation was virtually non-existent. Arthur Prager describes him then as "a literary dabbler, a hack playwright, a brewer's clerk, and a failed tavern-keeper"—a harsh but reasonably accurate assessment which leads Prager to speculate that some secret financial backing from Lemon's relatives might account for his prominence in *Punch*'s early stages. His own contributions to *Punch* were neither numerous nor notable. A very early series, a number of verses, some short bits, and almost nothing written during the entire 1850s lend support to Prager's claim that "Lemon knew he was a third-rate writer and wrote little."[8]

What he did write for *Punch* tended to be light, pleasant, and forgettable. In his humorous verse, a farcical close always deflates the high-flown and misleading rhetoric of the poem's opening. One sonnet, for example, begins with a lyric account of a young woman "taking the veil":

—'twas at the vesper hour,
When day was gently melting into night,
When Earth's fair features fade from human sight,
'Twas then she took the veil.

This action does not, however, lead to a convent, as the final lines reveal:

She saw not him who fixed his glaring eye
Upon her every motion anxiously;
Silently awhile she stood. She took the veil!
Then loud he cried, "Policeman, here's a wench
Shoplifting, take the customer to jail."[9]

Lemon's "Songs for the Sentimental," which appeared early in the 1840s, were a series of variations on the same literary joke. In one "Song," a young man passionately assures his love that his refusal to dance has nothing to do with jealousy or the fading of his passion. His explanation comes at the end:

Canst still thy faithful Edwin doubt?
Know then the truth: I've broke my braces![10]

Such efforts are certainly intended to raise "the evanescent smile of a harmless satire"— Lemon's description of the effect which *Punch*'s lightest material should have. More commonly, though, his writing is oppressively hearty, jolly, and sententious. We can be grateful that *Punch* only intermittently sounded like the article Lemon wrote for its first issue:

As we hope, gentle public, to pass many happy hours in your society, we think it right that you should know something of our character and intentions. Our title, at a first glance, may have misled you into a belief that we have no other intention than the amusement of a thoughtless crowd, and the collection of pence. We have a higher object. Few of the admirers of our prototype, merry Master Punch, have looked upon his vagaries but as the practical outpourings of a rude and boisterous mirth. We have considered him a teacher of no mean pretensions, and have, therefore, adopted him as the sponsor for our weekly sheet of pleasant instruction.[11]

Such prose was typical of the middling comic literature of Lemon's day, and perhaps the greatest single reason for his eventual success was his awareness that scores of authors could write such material better.

Lemon's genius lay in his editorial skills, and *Punch* demanded all of them. As its subtitle, *The London Charivari*, indicates, *Punch* was modeled on Charles Philipon's hugely successful Paris daily, which boasted political satire, broad humor, and engravings by such superb artists as Honore Daumier and Gustave Dore. *Punch* began even more ambitiously. Its prospectus promised that in addition to providing an "asylum" for "thousands of orphan jokes" and "millions of perishing puns," *Punch* would comment regularly on politics, fashion, books, the fine arts, music and the drama, the police, and sports. Of course, everything would be "embellished with cuts and caricatures."[12] In the first issue, "The Moral of Punch" further promised not only "trifles that have no other object than the moment's approbation" but "pleasant instruction" on such subjects as debtors' prisons, capital punishment, and the gap between worldly success and virtue.[13]

Many of these plans fell by the wayside, but to paraphrase his favorite character, Falstaff, though not especially witty himself, as *Punch*'s editor Lemon still had to be "the cause that wit is in other men." He began by freeing his contributors from the endless busy work that any periodical entails. Though Spielmann observes that to Lemon "fell the organisation, administration, and practical making-up of the paper," it would be more accurate to say that he seized these duties.[14] He also recruited contributors, transacted all business with the publishers, visited his artists and engravers to ensure that their work was done on time, and orga-

nized the special issues, staff dinners, and rambles. At all times, he fought for his publication. Lemon once said that he believed in one God, one woman, and one paper, and he proved a faithful champion to all three.

Creating harmony among his talented and diverse staff was also a challenge. Within six years of its first issue, *Punch* boasted a stable of contributors probably unsurpassed by any later comic publication. Though Queen Victoria, Prince Albert, the Duke of Wellington, and many other favorite *Punch* targets may stand in the foreground of "Mr. Punch's Fancy Ball," an 1847 double-page cartoon by John Leech, the orchestra members shown playing in the background were in their own way just as illustrious. Lemon is conducting. His musicians include Jerrold, *Punch*'s first star contributor; William Makepeace Thackeray, on the verge of becoming one of England's greatest novelists; Gilbert A. Beckett, *Punch*'s most prolific contributor and a veteran of comic papers; and Percival Leigh, Tom Taylor, and Horace Mayhew. *Punch*'s artists are playing as well—Leech himself, whose drawings carried *Punch* during its first years, Richard "Dicky" Doyle, who would sever his connection in 1850 over *Punch*'s anti-Catholic bias, and the journeyman William Newman.

As these contributors resigned or died, Lemon often managed to recruit artists and writers of equal or superior talent. The art improved. Replacing Doyle was John Tenniel, famous for his illustrations of Lewis Carroll's *Alice* books. The year 1851 brought Charles Keene, perhaps *Punch*'s most talented artist. George du Maurier, whose social cuts came to define the image of late-Victorian England, first contributed in the early 1860s and took his place on the regular staff when Leech died in 1864. All three men served *Punch* loyally—du Maurier for thirty-six years, Keene for thirty-eight, and Tenniel for fifty-one! The writing recruits often proved as reliable. Shirley Brooks began contributing in 1851 and served as editor from Lemon's death until his own in 1874. F.C. Burnand joined the staff in 1863; he would edit *Punch* from 1880 until he unwillingly retired in 1906.

Especially for a comic publication, naturally such longevity has its dangers. But as R.G.G. Price notes, for any paper "to begin with continuity" is "a rare and invaluable advantage," and Lemon's twenty-nine years with Punch gave it a firm foundation.[15] He had the

L

rare gift of being able to recognize his own limitations. "All better men than I am," he once said about the *Punch* staff, and his faith in his star contributors was most obvious in his practice of letting them send their weekly assignments directly to the printers.[16] In this way, Lemon not only granted his writers artistic independence but for a time kept *Punch* from assuming a single political or social perspective.

A sense of staff unity did develop, thanks to the tradition of the *Punch* dinner which combined determining the subject for each week's big political cartoon with the pleasures of good talk and company. Though the business side of the operation attended the dinners, Lemon always insisted on the creative side's autonomy. On the only occasion when the financial backers tried to force certain materials into *Punch*, Lemon proclaimed, "Boys, follow me!" The staff prepared to leave, and Bradbury and Evans backed down.[17]

Lemon's personality matched the character of his publication. Though Prager notes that some of Lemon's contemporaries considered him "a mealy-mouth sycophant" and "one of the most accomplished humbugs of his time" and R.G.G. Price refers to Lemon's "ruthlessness and his unctuous manner, with his continual smiling and hand-shaking and handwashing," in the *Dictionary of National Biography*'s sketch of him he is represented as "in person robust, handsome, and jovial, humorous rather than witty in his conversation, indefatigable and prolific in production," which probably comes closer to the general impression.[18] As for the *Punch* staff, even those who felt that they were Lemon's social superiors generally had a sincere affection for the editor whom they called "Uncle Mark," and when the artists drew Father Christmas or John Bull they often used him as their model.

Lemon would, however, overrule his "better men" if he thought that the situation demanded it. He published Thomas Hood's "The Song of the Shirt" in 1843 over everyone's objections—and tripled the paper's circulation. Perhaps the best example of Lemon's eye for talent and his editorial powers is found in the story of how he recruited Burnand. In 1863, Burnand was working for *Fun*, a rival comic publication. When its editor refused to publish Burnand's parody of the sensation literature then appearing in the *London Journal*, the author took the piece to Lemon, who not only recognized Burnand's promise and accepted his work but also persuaded the original artists to parody their own illustrations. (Two of them, du Maurier and Keene, conveniently worked for *Punch*, but Sir John Millais, John Gilbert, and "Phiz" [Hablot Knight Browne] agreed as well.) Since the *London Journal* was published by Bradbury and Evans, Lemon even managed to reproduce the same format and type. The result, *Mokeanna, or the White Witness,* was a *Punch* triumph and undoubtedly hastened Burnand's arrival on the staff.

Lemon's lasting achievement, though, was the one that William Gladstone identified when awarding Nelly Lemon a Civil List pension in 1872: lifting comic journalism out of political vendetta and scurrility and up to the level of universal humor. As the editor of *Punch*, Lemon was the acknowledged legislator of comic propriety in Victorian England. Violently cruel humor, libelous attacks, and smut were banned from the start, and while his paper's anti-Semitic and anti-Catholic bent faded only gradually, it was Lemon who for better *and* worse successfully aimed *Punch* at the drawing rooms and the entire families which occupied them.

Summary

Though not a great, or even a notable humorist in his own right, as editor of Britain's premier comic publication through its formative years, Mark Lemon exerted a force over English humorous writing that has been virtually unequaled. From 1841 until his death, his history was his paper's history—a fact that its staff acknowledged with the words they placed on his coffin: "Mark Lemon Esq., Editor of *Punch*, died May 23, 1870, aged 60 years."[19]

Notes

1. For further discussion of Lemon's ancestry, see Arthur A. Adrian, *Mark Lemon: First Editor of "Punch"* (London: Oxford University Press, 1966), p. 3.

2. Each of the early participants has his supporters for the honor of creating *Punch*, and all of the major biographies and histories try to reconstruct this history. See Adrian, pp. 29–32; Arthur Prager, *The Mahogany Tree: An Informal History of PUNCH* (New York: Hawthorn Books, 1979), pp. 33–37; R.G.G. Price, *A History of PUNCH* (London: Collins, 1957), pp. 19–22 and 353–55; and M.H. Spielmann, *The His-*

tory of "PUNCH" (New York: Cassell, 1895), pp. 10–28.

3. A detailed discussion of authorship, the English theater, and the text itself, appears in Leona Weaver Fisher, *Lemon, Dickens, and Mr. Nightingale's Diary* (Victoria, BC: English Literary Studies, 1988).

4. See Adrian, pp. 177–91, for an account of Lemon's later performances.

5. *Ibid,* p. 164.

6. *Ibid,* p. 176.

7. *Ibid.*

8. Prager, pp. 48–49.

9. Adrian, pp. 50–51; originally in *Punch,* April 8, 1843.

10. Prager, p. 49.

11. *Ibid,* pp. 50–52; originally in *Punch,* July 17, 1841.

12. Spielmann, p. 23.

13. Prager, pp. 51–53.

14. Spielmann, p. 257.

15. Price, p. 87.

16. Adrian, p. 47.

17. *Ibid,* p. 36.

18. Prager, pp. 48–49; Price, p. 29.

19. Adrian, p. 206.

Selected Bibliography

Primary Sources

Periodicals
Punch, or The London Charivari. July 17, 1841 to May 1870.

Editions
Fisher, Leona Weaver. *Lemon, Dickens, and Mr. Nightingale's Diary: A Victorian Farce.* Victoria, BC: English Literary Studies, 1988. Edition of the manuscript and published versions, with extensive discussion of composition.

Collections
The Enchanted Doll. London: Bradbury and Evans, 1849.
Prose and Verse. London: Bradbury and Evans, 1852.
A Christmas Hamper. London: Routledge, Warne, and Routledge, 1860.
The Jest Book. London: Macmillan, 1864.
Up and Down the London Streets. London: Chapman and Hall, 1867.
Also five novels, other collections, and eighty plays and operas: see Adrian, pp. 209–15 for an extensive bibliography.

Secondary Sources

Biographies
Adrian, Arthur A. *Mark Lemon: First Editor of "Punch."* London: Oxford University Press, 1966. The major biography to date. Positive but discriminating, especially when evaluating Lemon's writing. An extensive bibliography.

Hamilton, John Andrew, Lord Sumber of Ibstone. "Mark Lemon." *The Dictionary of National Biography: From Earliest Times to 1900.* Ed. Sir Leslie Stephen and Sir Sidney Lee. 21 vols. Oxford: Oxford University Press, 1921–1922. Vol. 11, pp. 909–10.

Books and Articles
Fisher, Leona Weaver. "Mark Lemon's Farces on the 'Woman Question.'" *Studies in English Literature, 1500–1900,* 28 (1988): 649–70. Fisher argues that *The Ladies Club* (1840), *The House of Ladies* (1840), and *The Petticoat Parliament* (1867) not only express conventional Victorian ideas on women's rights but as farces deconstruct these ideas as well.

Prager, Arthur. *The Mahogany Tree: An Informal History of PUNCH.* New York: Hawthorn Books, 1979. Heavily anecdotal history from the beginnings to 1979.

Price, R.G.G. *A History of PUNCH.* London: Collins, 1957. The best history, and by a *Punch* contributor. Unlike Spielmann, Price is sharply evaluative, and even dismissive, of certain periods and contributors. Very useful appendices on the origins of *Punch* and on "Drawing and Reproduction," by Kenneth Bird.

Savory, Jerold J. "Punch." In *British Literary Magazines: The Victorian and Edwardian Age, 1837–1913.* Ed. Alvin Sullivan. Westport, CT: Greenwood, 1984, pp. 325–29. Historical overview.

Spielmann, M.H. *The History of "Punch."* New York: Cassell, 1895. The most detailed source of information about *Punch*'s first fifty years. Heavily illustrated, with information about virtually every contributor. The major weakness is Spielmann's genial and uncritical approval of almost everyone and everything connected with *Punch*.

Craig Howes

Levy, Benn Wolfe

Born: London, January 1, 1900
Education: Repton School, Derbyshire,
  1914–1918; University College, Oxford
  University, 1919–1922
Marriage: Constance Cummings, 1933; two
  children
Died: Oxford, December 7, 1973

Biography

From 1925, when his first comedy, *This Woman Business*, was produced, until 1966, when his last play, *Public and Confidential*, premiered, Benn Levy wrote more than twenty stage plays, mostly in the prevailing West End styles—traditional comedies, farces, melodramas, and social problem plays. A political activist as well, he divided his time and energies between the theater and liberal causes such as the abolition of theater censorship, nuclear disarmament, and legal injustices.

Born in London to Octave and Nannie Joseph Levy and the grandson of the Honorable J. Levy of New South Wales, Levy was educated at Repton School in Derbyshire (1914–1918), following which he served in the Royal Air Force (1918) and then in the Royal Navy during World War II. Wounded in the Adriatic, he received the M.B.E. (Member, Order of the British Empire) in 1944.

Between the two World Wars, he attended University College, Oxford (1919–1922), after which he entered publishing and rose to the managing editorship at Jarrolds Publishing, Ltd., of London. He also wrote film scripts, one, co-authored with Charles Bennett, reputed to be the first British talkie (*Blackmail*, 1929). Later he wrote a radio play, *Anniversary* (broadcast 1941), and a television trilogy—*Triple Bill: The Great Healer, The Island of Cipango*, and *The Truth About the Truth* (broadcast 1952). In addition, Levy frequently directed his own plays as well as those by other dramatists.

In 1933, Levy married the American-born actress Constance Cummings. In the tradition of Anton Chekhov's wife, Olga Knipper, Cummings played successfully in her husband's dramas, among these *Young Madame Conti* (1936), *Madame Bovary* (1937), *The Jealous God* (1939), *Clutterbuck* (1946), *Return to Tyassi* (1950), *The Rape of the Belt* (1957), and *Public and Confidential*, later published as *The Member for Gaza*.

The American connection in Levy's career is an important one. Some of his plays, such as *Springtime for Henry* (1931), were premiered in New York. After its successful American run of 198 performances (with a British cast), it ran in London for 108 performances. Then a second American production toured the country for nearly eighteen years, concluding upon its return to Broadway and providing its leading actor, Edward Everett Horton, with a near-career in the tradition of Eugene O'Neill's father and *The Count of Monte Cristo*. The drama's success in America is partly the reason that Levy was occasionally mistaken for an American.

Levy's most popular play with a London audience was an Edwardian farce, *Clutterbuck* (1946), which ran for 366 performances, with its American run (1949) totaling 218 performances. The sea-difference in the popularity of Levy's two best-known farces reflects the different types of humor to which the respective national audiences respond.

The writer's theater career was interrupted by a five-year term in Parliament, 1945–1950, when he represented the Labour Party for the normally Conservative Eton-Slough constituency. While an MP, he was an eloquent spokesman for liberal causes, championing, in particular, abolition of the stage censorship that had been in effect since the Licensing Act was instituted in 1737. The Levy Bill, as it was known, was in the final stages of passage when, for personal reasons, he chose not to run for a second term. It died then, and it was not until 1968 that the Theaters Bill passed when, as an outsider, Levy, along with other prominent dramatists such as John Osborne and John Mortimer, once more took up oratorical cudgels in its defense.

Levy died in Oxford on December 7, 1973, and is survived by his wife; two children, Jemima and Jonathan; and six grandchildren.

Literary Analysis

Representing a spectrum of prevailing comic modes in the tradition of George Bernard Shaw and Noel Coward, four of Levy's plays demonstrate stylistic and thematic considerations found throughout his work: *This Woman Business*, *Springtime for Henry*, *Clutterbuck*, and *The Rape of the Belt*.

Within a structure resembling William Shakespeare's *Love Labours Lost*, in *This Woman Business* Levy launched a wittily Shavian debate style that continued, not only in his subsequent comedies, but also in his serious plays such as *The Devil* (1930), where healthy laughter is replaced by a sometimes corrosive irony. In *This Woman Business*, a group of misogynists of various ages and from various professions gather for respite from the demands of women in their lives. The comedy also launched a theme, the battle of the sexes, that permeates the rest of the playwright's work.

In this, Levy's first play, he depicts the misogynists' male bonding slowly disintegrating under attacks by a female intruder who with Shavian aplomb punctures male pomposities, especially those of the young would-be poet, Honey, the youngest member of the group who seems a satiric variation on the poet, Eugene Marchbanks, of Shaw's *Candida*. The dry wit of the eldest, Judge Bingham, on occasion suggests Shaw's Captain Overshot in his reference, for example, to his profession as legalized malevolence, a phrase evoking Shaw's definition of marriage as legalized prostitution.

More to the Shavian point, however, is the intruder, a female thief named Crawford who defends her thievery, saying that a little poverty can make one dare a great deal. Like Ann Whitefield, who pursues John Tanner in Shaw's *Man and Superman*, Crawford manages to snare Hodges, the strongest misogynist. She does so in the name of the convention of the moment: "to succumb to men who don't TRY to conquer us: to clever men, and, more particularly, ugly men." She admits to unashamed usage of three weapons of her sex—the flaunting of her sex, lying, and cajolery—woman's only weapons in a male-created morality in which force is not considered as immoral as fraud.

In reaction to this successful first play, critics called attention to Levy's talent for witty repartee and debate, one reviewer commenting on his "universally keen eye for people" and "an almost exhaustible flow of wit and humour."[1]

The playwright's middle-class comedy of manners changes to a kind of Restoration farce in *Springtime for Henry*, a play about two rakes who are also business associates with old-school ties. Levy turns conventional morality upside down in a delightfully amoral world in which romance and business, standard farce fare, conflict and then unite in a happy return to an accustomed lifestyle, despite a brief period of reformation into which one of them, Henry Dewlip, temporarily strays. Brooks Atkinson described the play as "enjoyably unscrupulous" and "hilariously impudent," a comedy with humor that much of the time stems from the manner in which "well-bred Englishmen can insult each other with a perfect sense of decorum and without any sign of human emotion. It is high art."[2]

Levy's humor stems, as well, from a plot pattern built around sets of interlocking relationships. If Dewlip's problems consist of his affair with Jelliwell's wife, Julia, and of Julia's temporary replacement by his new secretary, a Miss Smith who is bent on doing the "decent thing," Jelliwell, too, has his share of problems in both business and love. Only when Dewlip resumes his affair with Julia and when Jelliwell, in full knowledge of the past of Miss Smith (who is actually Madame Tantpis, a French husband-murderer), establishes a liaison with her, do both men prosper once more in affairs of both business and the heart. Sophisticated farce at its best, the romp of the two rakes contains its own inevitability that courses its way to a happy conclusion for all.

The dramatist's use of sets of relationships reaches technical heights in *Clutterbuck*, in which geometric patterns of behavior between two apparently mismatched couples are similar to those of Coward's *Private Lives*. One pair consists of a novelist with a wife who is less than intellectually acute, the other a Wodehousian bumbler with an intelligent wife. Their witty conversations and humorous situations stem from their respective qualities, one husband a straight man to the other, and similarly one wife to the other. The convention of farcical doubling is exquisite. On a cruise, the foursome are soon beset with boredom and irritation with one another.

The catalyst for a welcome relief is an ingenious twist involving a third couple, Clutterbuck and Melissa, who are recognized by the Pughs (Julian and Jane) and the Pomfrets (Arthur and Deborah), each of whom attempts to disguise that recognition from the other three. The twist, disclosed in the course of the play, is that Julian and Arthur, unknown one to the other, had been involved with Melissa before their respective marriages, as have Deborah and Jane with Clutterbuck. The parallels provide Levy with possibilities for additional farcical doublings. For the wives, Clutterbuck ex-

L

ists only in their wishful thinking, and he walks on stage a few times but says nothing. For the husbands, Melissa provides some respite from the boredom that has set in. When the ship docks for a brief time, she spends the night in a room between the rooms of Julian and Arthur, each of whom, like their wives, entertains the possibility of a romantic interlude. Farcical confusions lead to complications that are eventually cleared in a conventional recognition scene. As the two husbands resume their bickering, this time over who sits where in which chairs, their wives reprimand them, sighing: "Why are women never quarrelsome and cantankerous like men?"

The author keeps the realism of the marital relationships well in balance with the farcical actions so that, as in *Springtime for Henry*, the return to normality is inevitable. What sets *Clutterbuck* off from Levy's other plays are the speech habits by which each character repeatedly stamps himself/herself. Arthur's is the fumbling slang of the Edwardian dandy. He has difficulty starting, to say nothing of finishing, a thought, and in the best Wodehousian tradition he relies on the mannered idiom of the time. Julian's ironic barbs at Arthur's fatheadedness consistently go unnoticed by the latter. Melissa engages in the fashionable schoolgirl's habit of adding certain syllables to words. She attempts to settle one of the many quibbles between Julian and Arthur—each disgustedly accusing the other of taking advantage of Melissa: "Now, now, now, now now! Peace upon earthle and good willikins among millikens! That's not a nice way to talk, Artle. I think you ought to apologize." In the end, as Deborah and Jane sigh as they sail off once more, Deborah resorts to her customary literary quotations: "How beauteous the morn!" and Jane, responding to the same view, issues her verdict in the stylish slang of the day: "Crikey, what a view!"

If *This Woman Business* is a Shavian comedy, *Springtime for Henry* a Restoration comedy of manners with farcical overtones, and *Clutterbuck* a Cowardian-Wodehousian farce, it is in *The Rape of the Belt* that Levy elevates the comic genre to the high comedy of ideas with mythic proportions not present in his earlier plays. Again there is a geometry in the three sets of relationships: Zeus and Hera, Theseus and Hippolyte, and Heracles and Antiope. Each couple is hostage to history and myth, as the couples in the other comedies and farces are hostage to the laws of their genres. This comedy is not about the narrowly defined areas of male-female warrings, male enclaves, male business associates, or shipboard romances. Rather, as with Aristophanes's *Lysistrata*, females confront males on issues of war and peace and on the relative merits of civilized and so-called barbarian values as these are translated into political entities of patriarchy and matriarchy.

As with his other comedies, Levy has great fun in exposing male ideals for their shabbiness and in accommodating the more humane ideals of a matriarchy. The intended use of force by Heracles and Theseus is a profound version of Crawford's accusing males of using force to achieve their ends in *This Woman Business*.

For context, Levy uses Zeus and Hera as spectators of the actions of Heracles and Theseus in carrying out Heracles' ninth labor: the wresting of her girdle from Antiope, Queen of the Amazons. Intermittently, the actions are interrupted by the gods' comments on the goings-on, but especially by their own continuing feud about Zeus's infidelities, particularly his impersonation of Amphitryon, which resulted in the birth of Heracles. Their verbal interruptions develop into action when Hera changes the peaceful Amazons into a warring army. She does so by entering the lightning-struck body of Hippolyte, who, upon awakening, immediately calls for *more* staff, only to be reminded ironically by Antiope that they hadn't *any* staff. Hera's intrusion results in the Amazons' loss of the war, the direct opposite of her intentions. The play expresses the author's disillusionment about Western civilization, in the tradition of Shaw's *Heartbreak House*. Both the plot and the debates proceed by clever incremental reversal of Western ideals and practices.

The situational wit begins immediately as Theseus, in his attempt to scale the walls of Themiscyra, is mistaken for a stud kept for reproduction purposes who has escaped from one of the hygienic sheds of the Farm. Painfully pinning his hand to the wall, Hippobomene (her name suggests her size and strength) sets in motion a series of Levy's putdowns of the Western world. Later the Greek heroes are informed by Thalestris, the Minister of Maternity, that "the men at the Farm are all properly labelled and numbered. And our girls MUST make a note of who they are mating with."

Heracles and Theseus, attracted to Antiope and Hippolyte, are frustrated and weakened by their inability to deal with their "enemies" on the latter's terms. To Heracles' chagrin, Antiope does not recognize the heroes, and she further discomfits him by returning his compliment on her beauty. She seems, moreover, more impressed by the telling of his deeds than by the deeds themselves. When the men propose conditions for the conduct of the war, Antiope is not in the least attracted by the idea of slaughter, no matter how civilized the manner in which it is conducted. Heracles tries out his Western male logic on her—that she cannot both refuse a challenge and refuse to surrender. She continues to do both until she makes the mistake of choosing Hera as a goddess to replace Ashtoreth—just for a change, she claims.

One by one Western myths are exploded, as, for example, the popularly held view of the Amazons' one-breastedness. The Greeks are told that a great-Aunt Euphemia, realizing that "nothing is too wild for masculine credulity," created the myth of right-breast amputation "so as to further our skill with the bow and arrow." The women giggle at stories about their fierce, warlike natures, perpetuated in the West. Even the belt that Heracles seeks is not kept under lock and key, since there is no need to keep it safe from thieves even though those thieves (like the current intruders) be heroes by profession. When, finally, in a sham single combat between Heracles and Antiope, the former wins, he is inclined to return the belt, an offer that she refuses for, "even if I took it, it would no longer be ours. We have betrayed it." In a Shavian-style farewell, Antiope addresses Heracles as a "true man" who must be brave in his world of fear, and he, in turn, declares her a "true woman" who must be faithful in her world of hope. He prays that someday the gods will unite their two half-worlds.

Some of the most comic scenes are those in which Heracles and Theseus are frustrated by their inability to provoke the Amazons when it is clear that there is no will or intent to fight on the part of their hostesses. In an anachronistically burlesque turn, they resort to the use of the medieval ritual of the glove to challenge Antiope to battle. After a male quibble (in the manner of Julian and Arthur in *Clutterbuck*) about which of the two will enact the challenge, Theseus wins the dubious honor, unsuccessfully explaining his action as his duty, as he confesses that he has loved her from the moment that he first saw her and asserts his need to protect her. She gleefully mocks him: "By clouting me with a glove?" He is reduced to inarticulateness. Her acceptance of his love as a matter of course,

since she claims that he should love everyone, wrings from him a confession that he loathes most people. Accused of being a "horrid little man," he explains: "Everybody loathes most people. If everybody loved everybody else, it would be a nice mix-up. It wouldn't be decent. Do you suppose I feel the same about that blacksmith creature [Hippobomene] that I feel about you?"

The debate of ideas is Levy's means of exploring the problems and contradictions of his own time. His skill in debate, exercised so strongly in and out of Parliament, is wickedly directed at both gods and men. For instance, fine legal points come into play in Hera's questioning of the legitimacy of Zeus's claim as father of Heracles. Zeus responds: "You raise a novel legal point. You mean to say, when I borrow Amphitryon's body to woo his wife, is the resulting progeny fathered by the body or the body's occupant, by the ground-landlord, as it were, or by the tenant? Fascinating. It should keep the lawyers busy." Many years later, Zeus's argument continues to resonate familiarly in the unprecedented complications of parentage created by rapid scientific developments involving sperm banks and in-vitro births.

In addition to the kinds of humor found in these four plays, there are examples of humor throughout Levy's canon. Less profound in its subject matter than *The Rape of the Belt*, *Cupid and Psyche* (1952) is a farcical romp by a group of young artists enjoying the freedom of the latest ideas of the times. The debates seem an excuse for the prankish situations, one piled on another by means of the farce contrivances of well-timed exits and entrances, withheld secrets, recognition scenes, and so forth. Feminist, but without the matriarchal thrust of *The Rape of the Belt*, the seriousness of the debates is outflanked by hilarious complications that are eventually unraveled by the unexpected appearance of a middle-aged feminist in the Pankhurst tradition. Having entered the male profession of men's tailoring and (the big secret of the play) having given birth to an illegitimate son, she is accused by that son, now a biologist, of having emulated rather than repudiated male standards.

In an earlier play, *Hollywood Holiday* (1931), written during Levy's script-writing days, his farcical kaleidoscope takes a burlesque plunge. A most unaccomplished governess, Miss Pinnet, finds herself transported from her chintzy Bayswater boardinghouse to Holly-

L

wood by movie moguls who are unable to control the tantrums of a temperamental actress, Hedda Maelstrom. In desperation, they had decided to unearth an English governess constantly invoked by Hedda in support of her contentions of superiority over her Hollywood compatriots. The burlesque turns on the misunderstandings created as a result of Miss Pinnet's own aspiration to fame, which consists of having her script, *Bitter Willows*, made into a movie.

Caricatures of Hollywood denizens and of the gullible Miss Pinnets of this world are accomplished riotously by distinctive speech characteristics of the types so skillfully realized in the later *Clutterbuck*. Also caricatured is the process of script changes; any resemblance of the final film product to the original script has disappeared completely. The most hilarious moment of the farce is when Miss Pinnet ineptly reads aloud her tenth-rate script, and the climactic moment in the farce is her physical tussle with Hedda, following which she returns to her Bayswater boardinghouse, a celebrity of sorts to her fellow boarders.

In yet another very popular early play, *Mrs. Moonlight* (1928), Levy, intending to satirize the sentimental fantasy of James Barrie's "what-if" plays, succeeded only in making even the most cynical critics of the genre admit to shedding a tear or two. In this story about a woman who is given a wish-granting necklace to remain forever young, the irony takes on a seriousness that is the premise for his later Ibsen-like social problem plays *The Jealous God* and *Public and Confidential* (which is about a politician whose morality defeats him in the end). In a group of plays such as *The Devil*, subtitled *A Religious Comedy*, humor takes the form of irony, as a shadowy figure shows up at a country-house gathering of artists and intellectuals, his mission being to tempt each with a way to become famous. One of these incidents involves the discovery of an unfinished Joseph Conrad novel that is offered to a thus-far unsuccessful novelist. A variation on Luka in Maxim Gorki's *The Lower Depths*, the Mephistophelean character exits at the end, bent on continuing his mission in life, to create an awareness of morality in those who could easily succumb to shabby and immoral conduct. Levy's ironic plays are modern moralities.

His experimentation with styles includes an expressionistic play, *The Poet's Heart* (1937), based on the Don Juan legend and evocative of the "Don Juan in Hell" portion of Shaw's *Man and Superman*. Another genre that Levy experimented with early in his career is the gothic horror melodrama, *A Man With Red Hair* (1928), adapted from Hugh Walpole's chilling novel. Tinges of the gothic similarly color of some of his other plays such as *Mud and Treacle* (also 1928), about a country-house fortnight that ends with a murder. The murder, however, in one of Levy's plot twists, is silently dramatized in the prologue in order to do away with the requisite suspense of a mystery story and focus on the sociopsychological problems. In an uneven mixture, a comic secondary debate is carried on between a literate butler, who writes secretly for a London newspaper, and a farcical character, who lectures the butler on matters of class discriminations, the latter is reminiscent of Snobby Price in Shaw's *Major Barbara*. Levy's most chilling psychodrama is an adapted courtroom melodrama, *Young Madame Conti*, also about a murder. The focus is a play-long interior debate within the murderer as she anticipates and responds to the questions that she will face from an all-male court. To an audience of the end of the twentieth century, Levy's corrosive irony echoes the real-life melodrama of the Clarence Thomas–Anita Hill hearings held by the United States Senate. Finally, written after the famous scandal involving British Cabinet minister John Profumo, fittingly *Public and Confidential* is about the public and private life of a politician, the influence of the press, and the disillusionment of the young. Like *Young Madame Conti*, the work resonates with echoes of real-life events many years later and merits revival, according to Alan Strachan, for its "virtues of solid craftsmanship as well as its understanding of political realities."

Summary

Most successful with his comedies and farces that reflect the styles of his contemporaries—Shaw, Coward, J.B. Priestley, and Terence Rattigan—Benn Levy was less effective in those plays in which he mixes genres. His serious dramas were frequently faulted for their looseness of plot and, consequently, the diminishing hold of a play on an audience. Led too often more by his head than his heart, according to his own statement, he loved a good debate, and it is the witty dialogue with which his characters are endowed and the distinctive speech habits of each character for which Levy was constantly lauded by the critics.

Described by Michael Foot, a fellow Parliamentarian, as "the best polemicist of the post-1945 period,"[3] Levy translated his polemics into what Strachan calls a "comedy of genuine style," whose "symmetry and sense of form . . ., happiest in his favourite quartet relationship . . ., is allied to an elegance and wit not usually found in combination on the English stage."[4] His historical importance is that of a highly literate, socially conscious dramatist whose sharp wit of both mind and language resulted in the writing in a variety of dramatic genres whose styles and thematic concerns are a mirror of their age, an age that embraced the so-called twilight of the Shaw era and the English stage revolution that began in 1956.

Notes

1. *Observer*, October 25, 1925, n.p.
2. Brooks Atkinson, *New York Times*, March 15, 1961, p. 36.
3. Michael Foot, *Tribune*, December 14, 1973, n.p.
4. Alan Strachan, "Benn Wolfe Levy," in *Contemporary Dramatists* (New York: St. Martin's Press, 1973), pp. 477–78.

Selected Bibliography
Primary Sources

Plays
This Woman Business. London: Benn, and New York: French, 1925.
A Man with Red Hair (adapted from Hugh Walpole's novel). London: Macmillan, 1928.
Mud and Treacle. London: Gollancz, 1928.
Mrs. Moonlight. London: Gollancz, 1929.
Art and Mrs. Bottle. London: Secker, 1929; New York: French, 1931.
The Devil. London: Secker, 1930; republished as *The Devil Passes*, New York: French, 1932.
Hollywood Holiday, with John Van Druten. London: Secker, 1931.
Springtime for Henry. New York and London: French, 1932; London: Secker, 1932.
The Poet's Heart. London: Cresset Press, 1937.
Young Madame Conti (adapted with Hubert Griffith from Bruno Frank's play). London: French, 1938.
The Jealous God. London: Secker and Warburg, 1939.
Clutterbuck. London: Heinemann, 1947; New York: Dramatists Play Service, 1950.
Return to Tyassi. London: Gollancz, 1951.
Cupid and Psyche. London: Gollancz, 1952.
The Rape of the Belt. London: MacGibbon & Kee, 1957.
The Member for Gaza. London: Evans, 1968.

Television Plays
The Great Healer and The Island of Cipango. London: French, 1954.

Secondary Sources
Clark, Barrett H., and George Freedley. *A History of Modern Drama*. New York: Appleton Century, 1947, pp. 196–208.
Mantle, Robert Burns. *The Best Plays of 1931–32*. New York: Dodd, Mead, 1932, p. ix.
Rusinko, Susan. "Benn Wolfe Levy." In *British Dramatists Since World War II*, ed. Stanley Weintraub. Detroit: Gale Research, 1982. Vol. 13, pp. 291–98. An overview of Levy's plays, with specific emphasis on his traditional style.
———. *The Plays of Benn Levy: Between Shaw and Coward*. Rutherford, NJ: Fairleigh Dickinson University Press; London and Toronto: Associated University Presses, 1994. A critical assessment of Levy's complete works and his eclectic significance as a mirror of his age and to the styles and themes of his more famous contemporaries.
Strahan, Alan. "Benn Wolfe Levy." In *Contemporary Dramatists*, ed. James Vinson. New York: St. Martin's Press, 1973, pp. 75–478. An incisive if brief evaluation of Levy's work, preceded by a short statement by Levy.

Susan Rusinko

L

Lewis, C[live] S[taples]
Born: Belfast, Northern Ireland, November 29, 1898
Education: Wynard School, Watford, England, 1908–1910; Cherbourg School, Malvern, 1911–1913; Malvern College, 1913–1914; private tutor, 1914–1917; University College, Oxford University, 1917–1923, B.A.
Marriage: Helen Joy Davidman Gresham, April 23, 1956; no children
Died: November 22, 1963

Biography

Clive Staples Lewis was born in Belfast, Northern Ireland, on November 29, 1898, the second son of well-educated, upper-middle-class parents. His father, Albert James Lewis, was a successful solicitor, and his mother, Flora Hamilton Lewis, took a degree in mathematics and logic at Queen's University, Belfast.

Lewis's education began at home, where he was tutored by a governess and his mother, until the latter's death in 1908, an event shown by recent biographers to have affected him deeply.[1] The rest of his schooling took place in England, at Wynard School in Watford (1908–1910), Cherbourg School in Malvern (1911–1913), Malvern College (1913–1914), under a private tutor, W.T. Kirkpatrick (1914–1917); and, with a break for war service until he was wounded, University College, Oxford (1917–1923), where he earned firsts in Honor Moderations (Greek and Latin), Greats (classical philosophy and history), and English Language and Literature.

After filling a one-year term (1924–1925) as tutor in philosophy at University College, in 1925 Lewis was appointed to a Fellowship in English at Magdalen College, Oxford. He held that position until he was elected Professor of Medieval and Renaissance Literature at Cambridge University in 1954. He lived in Oxford from his university days onward, sharing his home with Jamie King Askins Moore, the mother of a friend killed in World War I who became a sort of surrogate mother to Lewis, and with his brother Warren after the latter retired from his military career.

Although Lewis's parents were Christians and he was confirmed in his parish church when he was sixteen, Lewis had by then already drifted away from the faith and considered himself an atheist for almost a decade and a half. In the mid- to late-1920s, he found himself drawn back toward Christianity through the logical force of his belief in moral law (as explained in "Right and Wrong as a Clue to the Meaning of the Universe" [*Broadcast Talks*, 1942; in revised form, part 1 of *Mere Christianity*, 1952]), through response to the romantic longings he called "Joy" (described first in *The Pilgrim's Regress* [1933] and later in *Surprised by Joy* [1955]), through the appeal of Christian themes in the literature that he was studying, and through the influence of Christian friends such as J.R.R. Tolkien. In 1929, he converted to theism and in 1931 to Christianity. Eventually he became more widely known for his religious writings than for his literary scholarship.

A bachelor for most of his life, he was married in 1956 to Helen Joy Davidman Gresham, an American divorcée converted to Christianity through Lewis's books. Lewis agreed to marry her in a civil ceremony on April 23, 1956 to enable her to stay in England when the Home Office refused to renew her visa. When, shortly thereafter, she was diagnosed as having terminal cancer, they were married by a clergyman in her hospital room on March 21, 1957. He also became legal guardian of her two children. Joy was taken to Lewis's home to die, but the cancer went into remission; they spent three very happy years together before the cancer returned. She died in July 1960; his moving book *A Grief Observed* (1961), published under the name N.W. Clerk, is based on his efforts to deal with his sorrow. The 1993 movie, *Shadowlands,* is an account of their relationship.

By this time Lewis himself was not well. His health continued to fail over the next couple of years. He was forced to resign from his Professorship in August, 1963. He died in Oxford on November 22, 1963, the same day as Aldous Huxley and John F. Kennedy.

Literary Analysis

From his earliest years Lewis seemed destined to be a writer. He had learned to read by the time he was three, and by the age of seven he was writing plays and stories. Lewis and his brother turned an attic room into their "study" where they wrote and illustrated stories about "Animal-land" and "India" which eventually were combined into the world of "Boxen." Some of Lewis's stories have been published in *Boxen: The Imaginary World of the Young C.S. Lewis* (1985).

His chief desire, however, was to be a poet. Throughout his teens he composed verse, narrative as well as lyric. His earliest publication was a collection of lyric poems, *Spirits in Bondage* (1919), followed by a long narrative poem, *Dymer* (1926). Both volumes were published under the pseudonym Clive Hamilton. His preference for poetry written with meter and rhyme, however, was out of step with contemporary poetry, such as that of Ezra Pound and T.S. Eliot. Despite many positive reviews, the low sales of the books convinced Lewis that he would not earn a living as a poet. Still, he did continue to write poems, sufficient to fill two volumes, *Poems* (1964) and *Narrative Poems* (1969), after his death.

By the time that *Dymer* was published, Lewis was already pursuing the first of three major paths that his subsequent literary career would take (literary scholar, exponent of Christianity, and fiction writer). His emphasis as a scholar was historical, particularly in making works of the Middle Ages and the Renaissance more accessible to twentieth-century readers by explaining the literary and ideological backgrounds. His earliest scholarly book, *The Allegory of Love: A Study in Medieval Tradition* (1936), described the nature and characteristics of allegory and courtly love, traced the history of allegory, and examined a number of major allegorical works, concluding with Edmund Spenser's *The Faerie Queene*. Although some parts of the book have been questioned or superseded, it remains an important study, and it was influential in the revival of interest in Spenser's poetry.

Other works of literary history include *A Preface to Paradise Lost* (1942), in which he studies the characteristics of the epic and the Christian ideas familiar to John Milton's first readers though not to most readers in the twentieth century. Lewis's *English Literature in the Sixteenth Century Excluding Drama* (1954) is a massive, chronological study of the intellectual and literary background of the "Renaissance" in Scotland and England (although he argues against the usefulness of that term) and a survey of minor and major poets, divided into "Drab" and "Golden," a classification which has proved controversial as well as lively and provocative. *The Discarded Image: An Introduction to Medieval and Renaissance Literature* (1964) was based on two series of lectures popular at Oxford for many years; in the volume Lewis endeavors to clarify unfamiliar details about medieval thought and history and to enable his readers to experience the cosmos through medieval eyes.

An Experiment in Criticism (1961) is more theoretical in tone. In this volume Lewis proposes that books should be judged by the way people read them: books that "permit and invite" reading, and especially rereading, for enjoyment and enlargement of one's being are "good books"; books that can be read only for "what happens" or to stimulate daydreams or pornographic fantasies are "bad books."[2] His motivation for this proposal was, in part, critics' denigration of the Romance, which he loved and defended throughout his life (his essay "On Stories" [1947] is one of the best available defenses of "story," or narrative art).[3] Despite a theoretical orientation, Lewis's preference for literary history is evident: his aim is to help readers "receive" works—whether medieval romance, Elizabethan tragedy or nineteenth-century lyric poem—more fully by placing the works in their setting and enabling readers to enter "the frame of mind of those to whom they were addressed."[4] Such was the purpose also of his lectures on Spenser, published posthumously as *Spenser's Images of Life* (1967), and of numerous essays published throughout his life and collected in *Studies in Medieval and Renaissance Literature* (1966) and *Selected Literary Essays* (1969).

Although his scholarly work made Lewis well known in academic circles, a second literary path gave him much wider recognition. Beginning with *The Problem of Pain* in 1940, and throughout the rest of his life he published books defending and clarifying the Christian faith. *The Screwtape Letters* (1942) was a bestseller in Britain and the United States. Screwtape, a senior bureaucrat in Hell, writes these imaginary letters to his nephew, Wormwood, a lower ranking tempter, advising him about how to lead his "patient" to damnation. The strength of the book lies in the combination of its wit and satire with keen psychological and theological insights that Lewis affords into human beings and relationships.

Four series of broadcast talks on the BBC during World War II increased Lewis's fame in Britain, and then throughout the world when they were published individually and later collected as *Mere Christianity* (1952—"mere" signifying "basic" or "essential"). In addition to books such as *Miracles* (1947), *Reflections on the Psalms* (1958), *The Four Loves* (1960), and *Letters to Malcolm: Chiefly on Prayer* (1964), there are several collections of sermons, lectures, and essays that he contributed to religious periodicals, some of which were published during his life and some since his death.

A third literary path combined the other two, as Lewis drew on the Romance form that he loved to write stories informed by the Christian ideas that he believed in. The earliest was *Out of the Silent Planet* (1938), an H.G. Wells-type science-fiction tale in which Elwin Ransom, a character resembling Lewis or his friend J.R.R. Tolkien, is taken to the planet Malacandra (Mars). Here he finds an ancient,

L

unfallen utopia which exposes by contrast the self-centeredness and materialism of our fallen world ("silent" because it is cut off from the unfallen heavens). A sequel, *Perelandra* (1943), is a reworking of the Garden of Eden story, as Ransom goes to Venus, to help the "Eve" of that newly inhabited world resist the temptation to evil. This seems to have been Lewis's favorite of his own stories, as the abundant detail filled him with longing for the lush beauty of the world that he created. In *That Hideous Strength* (1945), Ransom confronts, and with supernatural help defeats, a world-threatening totalitarian power headquartered in a small university town (a smaller Oxford). The book, often compared to George Orwell's *Nineteen Eighty Four* which was published a few years later, is a powerful warning against the threat posed to freedom and civilization by tyrants backed by the new resources of the sciences and social sciences.

In 1945, Lewis published *The Great Divorce*, a brief fantasy on Heaven and Hell which reflects his interest in medieval literature. On a deeper level, it is a Dantesque exploration of moral and spiritual choices and their effects, beginning in this life and extending into the next.

The medieval Romance also informs the Chronicles of Narnia, the seven fairy stories for which he is now, and possibly will remain, most famous. In *The Lion, the Witch and the Wardrobe* (1950), the four Pevensie children, Peter, Susan, Edmund, and Lucy, go through the back of a magical wardrobe and enter the land of Narnia where they help the animal inhabitants and other mythical creatures defeat the evil White Witch. In *Prince Caspian* (1951), they are brought back to Narnia to help restore Caspian to the throne that has been usurped by his evil Uncle, Miraz; in *The Voyage of the "Dawn Treader"* (1952), Edmund, Lucy, and their cousin Eustace Scrubb accompany Caspian on a quest to the end of the earth in search of the Seven Lost Lords; and in *The Silver Chair* (1953), Eustace and Jill Pole rescue Caspian's son from underworld imprisonment. In *The Horse and His Boy* (1954), two horses and two children save Archenland and Narnia from attack by the evil king of Calormene. Lewis describes the creation of Narnia in *The Magician's Nephew* (1955), and in *The Last Battle* (1956) he tells about its destruction by the Calormenes and about the entry of the children and good animals into the "New Narnia."

The Chronicles of Narnia have become enormously successful, selling millions of copies in English and several translations. Their success can be attributed to the characteristics about "story" which the author discussed in "On Stories."[5] They appeal to readers, young and old, first, because they are well-told romances. They are full of action, excitement, adventure, and suspense. Lewis skillfully uses detail to give them atmosphere, a distinctive blend of the familiar (human children, British foods, ordinary animals) with the unfamiliar (a world separate from ours, animals who think and talk, mythical characters actually existing), of the ideal (an egalitarian pastoral paradise unspoiled by factories and cities) with the reality of evil forces and characters. He preserves the "animalness" of the animal characters and creates intriguing creatures such as the dour but good-natured Marshwiggles in *The Silver Chair*.

The success of the Chronicles is also due in part to Christian themes woven more or less obviously through them. Narnia is protected by the great lion, Aslan, who in *The Lion, the Witch and the Wardrobe* sacrifices his life to rescue the traitor Edmund from the White Witch. Aslan creates Narnia by his voice in *The Magician's Nephew* and brings the children and other good creatures to his Country in *The Last Battle*. The books clearly have allegorical strains and often are called allegories, but Lewis insisted that they are not. For him allegories are stories in which concrete actions and characters are used to represent abstract qualities. He argued that in his stories the characters and actions were important for themselves, not as representations of "meanings." He wanted readers to "receive"[6] the stories, enjoying the action, atmosphere, and excitement, not to use them as puzzles for finding biblical parallels or as vehicles for conveying Christian morals and messages.

Lewis regarded his final work of fiction, *Till We Have Faces* (1956), as his best story. It is also his most difficult and it was not well received by readers and reviewers. In it the writer retells the myth of Cupid and Psyche from the viewpoint of one of Psyche's sisters. Orual is unaware that her deep love for Psyche is self-centered and possessive; through her jealousy, she destroys Psyche's happiness. She masks her real nature from others and herself until near the end of her life when she comes to self-realization and learns the true meaning of love. The story is carefully crafted and subtle: Christian love and sacrifice are central to its meaning, but they are conveyed indirectly, through action and symbol, not with the explicitness of his earlier fiction. In *Till We Have Faces* Lewis's Christian faith, his love of romance and myth, and his interest in the historical—in bringing to life the world and literature of the past—are synthesized creatively.

No work of Lewis's is primarily humorous in purpose, but humor was an important characteristic of his life and literary style. From his father he inherited a love of what his family called "wheezes,"[7] or anecdotes; throughout his life he loved conversation which involved either intense discussion of ideas or telling of humorous stories (never small talk or chit-chat). Lewis the raconteur comes through vividly in *Surprised by Joy* as he describes his first schoolmaster, Oldie (one can almost hear him imitate the different voices and see him imitate Oldie's grimaces and gestures [32–35]), and in the accounts of his and Warren's interactions with their father in chapter 8 and the descriptions of his tutor W.T. Kirkpatrick in chapter 9. His friend Owen Barfield describes Lewis's "irrepressible feeling for comedy" in his conversation, without which "one would miss altogether the typical flavor of his company" (34).

Comic storytelling is a central characteristic of Lewis as humorist. His command of techniques was sure—his ear for dialogue, his eye for the absurd detail, his timing, and his ability to build to a climax all contribute their parts. The early chapters of *The Great Divorce* are a good illustration, as in the tale of the disillusioned ghost who was sure that all of the many places he has visited—Peking, Niagara Falls, the Pyramids, Salt Lake City, the Taj Mahal, and most recently Hell—are tourist traps, all advertisement stunts, all run by the same people: "There's a combine, you know, a World Combine, that just takes an Atlas and decides where they'll have a Sight. Doesn't matter what they choose: anything'll do as long as the publicity's properly managed."[8] His ability to spin yarns appears also in his depiction of the Marshwiggles in *The Silver Chair* (Puddleglum is able to find a dark center in any cloud, no matter how bright and silver-lined it seems) and of the Dufflepuds in *The Voyage of the "Dawn Treader."*

Wit is equally characteristic of Lewisian humor. It is an important ingredient in his poetry, especially in his epigrams:

Erected by her sorrowing brothers

In memory of Martha Clay.
Here lies one who lived for others;
Now she has peace. And so have they.[9]

It appears frequently in his fiction. One thinks immediately, for example, of the opening line of *The Voyage of the "Dawn Treader"*: "There was a boy called Eustace Clarence Scrubb, and he almost deserved it."[10] Wit appears occasionally in his moral and religious writings ("A man who was merely a man and said the sort of things Jesus said wouldn't be a great moral teacher. He'd either be a lunatic—on a level with the man who say's he's a poached egg—or else he'd be the Devil of Hell. You must make your choice"[11]) and is one of the delightful ingredients in his literary criticism: "The *Mirror for Magistrates* continued to be a running sore in English poetry"; "no one lays [it] down without a sense of relief."[12]

Lewis uses irony effectively as a humorous technique. There is the dramatic irony of *The Great Divorce*, as readers understand the situation of the damned ghosts more fully than do they. This combines tellingly with verbal irony:

"But they'll *see* me."
"What does it matter if they do?"
"I'd rather die."
"But you've died already. There's no
good trying to go back to that."[13]

The Chronicles of Narnia are filled with gentle—and sometimes not so gentle—ironies. Edmund, instead of becoming a prince and the White Witch's heir, is seized as her prisoner. Eustace, who values himself very highly, finds that he cannot even be given away as a slave: "Though no one would want to be sold as a slave, it is perhaps even more galling to be a sort of utility slave whom no one will buy."[14]

Much of the humor in Lewis's books is satiric.[15] Satire appears in his earliest stories and continues throughout his career. There are the jibes at and disparaging descriptions of the flappers of the 1920s in *The Pilgrim's Regress*. There is Ransom's difficulty in translating Weston's unreasonable philosophy into the language of Malacandra in *Out of the Silent Planet*, a passage modeled on Gulliver's struggle to make the Houyhnhnms understand English life in part 4 of *Gulliver's Travels*. There is humorous satire on modern thought and values throughout *That Hideous Strength*, not least in the acronym N.I.C.E. for the diabolical National Institute for Co-ordinated Experiments. *The Great Divorce* is replete with ironic humor, typified by the satire on the liberal theology of the bishop who laments that the Crucifixion was a disaster—"What a tragic waste . . . so much promise cut short"—and decides not to remain in Heaven because it lacks "an atmosphere of free inquiry" and because he has to be back in Hell that Friday to read a paper to a theological society on what Jesus's mature views would have been if he had not died so young (42–43). And there is the satire on schools in chapter 14 of *Prince Caspian*, on economic development in chapter 4 of *The Voyage of the "Dawn Treader,"* and on socialism and liberal theology in chapter 3 of *The Last Battle*.

Lewis's place as a humorist is most firmly established by *The Screwtape Letters*, which contains all of the characteristics and techniques described above. Its humor grows out of the satiric depiction of Hell as a gigantic bureaucracy, modern and tyrannical, with its own "Lowerarchy," Training College, Records Office, Research Department, and Secret Police. Screwtape carries on a correspondence with Wormwood, advising him on the best means of tempting his "patient." There is humor in the ironic reversal that results from using Screwtape's viewpoint ("Of course a war is entertaining. The immediate fear and suffering of the humans is a legitimate and pleasing refreshment for our myriads of toiling workers. But what permanent good does it do us unless we make use of it for bringing souls to Our Father Below?" [30]) and in the detail that Screwtape employs, as when he tells Wormwood that having the patient attend his parish church can be helpful: "When he goes inside, he sees the local grocer with rather an oily expression on his face bustling up to offer him one shiny little book containing a liturgy which neither of them understands, and one shabby little book containing corrupt texts of a number of religious lyrics, mostly bad, and in very small print. When he gets to his pew and looks round him he sees just that selection of his neighbours whom he has hitherto avoided. You want to lean pretty heavily on those neighbours" (15–16).

There is much wit, and even occasional self-satire on Lewis's part, as in this bit of Screwtape's counsel: "As long as [the patient] does not convert it into action, it does not matter how much he thinks about this new repentance. Let the little brute wallow in it. Let him, if he has any bent that way, write a book about it; that is often an excellent way of sterilising the seeds which the Enemy plants in a human soul" (69–70). Letter Eleven makes the connection to humor even more explicit by exploring human laughter, which Screwtape disparages as "disgusting and a direct insult to the realism, dignity, and austerity of Hell" (58). While Joy and Fun belong to the Enemy (God), Screwtape believes that Jokes and Flippancy can be of value, especially among the English, "who take their 'sense of humour' so seriously that a deficiency in this sense is almost the only deficiency at which they feel shame" (59). *The Screwtape Letters* has held up well and exemplifies Lewis's ability to employ wit, satire, and humor in developing moral and religious themes—and even after fifty years can be read with enjoyment.

Summary

C.S. Lewis's importance as a writer is difficult to assess at this point. He was one of the foremost literary scholars of his generation, and the depth and breadth of his learning continue to be admired, but his kind of scholarship—historical and moral—is currently out of fashion. His religious writings, though widely read and influential among conservative (particularly American) Christians, are regarded in a larger Christian context as overly simplified and old-fashioned. As a writer of fantasy and romance, he seems to merit a secure place "in the canon of worthwhile minor writers of twentieth-century British fiction,"[16] especially for *Perelandra*, the Narnian Chronicles, and *Till We Have Faces*. And finally, although *The Screwtape Letters* and the comic or satiric portions of other writings do not reach the levels of his contemporaries Max Beerbohm and P.G. Wodehouse, Lewis does deserve recognition as a notable minor writer in the humoristic tradition.

Notes

1. George Sayer, *Jack: C.S. Lewis and His Times* (London: Macmillan, 1988), pp. 22, 30, 87–89; A.N. Wilson, *C.S. Lewis: A Biography* (London: Collins, 1990), pp. xi, 19–20, 22, 47, 59, 210, 214, 224.
2. Lewis, *An Experiment in Criticism* (Cambridge: Cambridge University Press, 1961), p. 113.
3. "On Stories" is reprinted in *Of Other Worlds* (1966) and *On Stories* (1982). For discussions of Lewis's contributions to narrative theory and practice, see the

essays in part 2 of *Word and Story in C.S. Lewis*, ed. Peter J. Schakel and Charles A. Huttar (Columbia: University of Missouri Press, 1991).

4. *An Experiment in Criticism*, pp. 121–22.
5. See Schakel, "Elusive Birds and Narrative Nets: The Appeal of Story in C.S. Lewis' Chronicles of Narnia," in *A Christian for All Christians: Essays in Honour of C.S. Lewis*, ed. Andrew Walker and James Patrick (London: Hodder and Stoughton, 1990), pp. 116–31.
6. *An Experiment in Criticism*, p. 19.
7. Lewis, *Surprised by Joy* (London: Geoffrey Bles, 1955), p. 12.
8. Lewis, *The Great Divorce* (London: Geoffrey Bles, 1945), p. 50.
9. Lewis, *Poems*, ed. Walter Hooper (London: Geoffrey Bles, 1964), p. 134.
10. Lewis, *The Voyage of the "Dawn Treader"* (London: Geoffrey Bles, 1952), p. 9.
11. *Broadcast Talks* (London: Geoffrey Bles—The Centenary Press, 1942), pp. 50–51. *Mere Christianity* (London: Geoffrey Bles, 1952), book 2, chapter 3.
12. Lewis, *English Literature in the Sixteenth Century Excluding Drama*, Vol. 3 of *The Oxford History of English Literature,* ed. F.P. Wilson and Bonamy Dobree (Oxford: Clarendon, 1954), pp. 467, 246 (quoted by Margaret Patterson Hannay, *C.S. Lewis* [New York: Ungar, 1981], p. 163).
13. *The Great Divorce*, pp. 56–57.
14. *The Voyage of the "Dawn Treader,"* p. 62.
15. See Schakel, "The Satiric Imagination of C.S. Lewis," *Studies in the Literary Imagination*, 22 (1989): 129–48.
16. Corbin S. Carnell, "C.S. Lewis as a Novelist," *CSL: The Bulletin of the New York C.S. Lewis Society*, 21 (May 1990): 4.

Selected Bibliography
Primary Sources

Literary History and Criticism
The Allegory of Love: A Study in Medieval Tradition. Oxford: Clarendon, 1936. Rev. ed. 1938.
A Preface to Paradise Lost. London: Oxford University Press, 1942.

English Literature in the Sixteenth Century Excluding Drama. Vol. 3 of *The Oxford History of English Literature*. Ed. F.P. Wilson and Bonamy Dobree. Oxford: Clarendon, 1954.
Studies in Words. Cambridge: Cambridge University Press, 1960.
An Experiment in Criticism. Cambridge: Cambridge University Press, 1961.
The Discarded Image: An Introduction to Medieval and Renaissance Literature. Cambridge: Cambridge University Press, 1964.
Studies in Medieval and Renaissance Literature. Ed. Walter Hooper. Cambridge: Cambridge University Press, 1966.
Of Other Worlds: Essays and Stories. Ed. Walter Hooper. London: Geoffrey Bles, 1966.
Spenser's Images of Life. Ed. Alastair Fowler. Cambridge: Cambridge University Press, 1967.
Selected Literary Essays. Ed. Walter Hooper. Cambridge: Cambridge University Press, 1969.
Of This and Other Worlds. Ed. Walter Hooper. London: Collins, 1982. American Title: *On Stories, and Other Essays in Literature*.

Religious and Ethical Writings
The Problem of Pain. London: Geoffrey Bles, 1940.
The Screwtape Letters. London: Geoffrey Bles, 1942. Expanded as *The Screwtape Letters and Screwtape Proposes a Toast*. London: Geoffrey Bles, 1961.
The Abolition of Man: or, Reflections on Education with Special Reference to the Teaching of English in the Upper Forms of Schools. London: Oxford University Press, 1943.
Miracles: A Preliminary Study. London: Geoffrey Bles, 1947. With a revised third chapter, London: Fontana, 1960.
Mere Christianity. London: Geoffrey Bles, 1952. A revised version of *Broadcast Talks* (1942), *Christian Behaviour* (1943), and *Beyond Personality* (1944).
Reflections on the Psalms. London: Geoffrey Bles, 1958.
The Four Loves. London: Geoffrey Bles, 1960.
Letters to Malcolm: Chiefly on Prayer. London: Geoffrey Bles, 1964.

Christian Reflections. Ed. Walter Hooper. London: Geoffrey Bles, 1967.

God in the Dock: *Essays on Theology and Ethics*. Ed. Walter Hooper. Grand Rapids, MI: Eerdmans, 1970. British title: *Undeceptions: Essays on Theology and Ethics*. Ed. Walter Hooper. London: Geoffrey Bles, 1971.

Autobiographies

All My Road Before Me: The Diary of C.S. Lewis 1922–1927. Ed. Walter Hooper. London: Harper Collins, 1991.

Surprised by Joy: The Shape of My Early Life. London: Geoffrey Bles, 1955.

N.W. Clerk, pseud. *A Grief Observed*. London: Faber & Faber, 1961.

Letters

Letters of C.S. Lewis. Ed. W.H. Lewis. London: Geoffrey Bles, 1966. Rev. and enl. ed. Ed. Walter Hooper. London: Fount, 1988.

Letters to an American Lady. Ed. Clyde S. Kilby. Grand Rapids, MI: Eerdmans, 1967.

They Stand Together: The Letters of C.S. Lewis to Arthur Greeves (1914–1963). Ed. Walter Hooper. London: Collins, 1979.

Letters to Children. Ed. Lyle W. Dorsett and Marjorie Lamp Mead. New York: Macmillan, 1985.

Poetry

Clive Hamilton, pseud. *Spirits in Bondage: A Cycle of Lyrics*. London: William Heinemann, 1919.

Clive Hamilton, pseud. *Dymer*. London: J. M. Dent, 1926.

Poems. Ed. Walter Hooper. London: Geoffrey Bles, 1964.

Narrative Poems. Ed. Walter Hooper. London: Geoffrey Bles, 1969.

Fiction

The Pilgrim's Regress: An Allegorical Apology for Christianity, Reason and Romanticism. London: J.M. Dent, 1933; London: Sheed and Ward, 1935. With new preface and notes by author, London: Geoffrey Bles, 1943.

Out of the Silent Planet. London: John Lane, Bodley Head, 1938.

Perelandra. London: John Lane, Bodley Head, 1943.

That Hideous Strength: A Modern Fairy-Tale for Grown-Ups. London: John Lane, Bodley Head, 1945.

The Great Divorce: A Dream. London: Geoffrey Bles, Centenary Press, 1945.

The Lion, the Witch and the Wardrobe. London: Geoffrey Bles, 1950.

Prince Caspian: The Return to Narnia. London: Geoffrey Bles, 1951.

The Voyage of the "Dawn Treader." London: Geoffrey Bles, 1952.

The Silver Chair. London: Geoffrey Bles, 1953.

The Horse and His Boy. London: Geoffrey Bles, 1954.

The Magician's Nephew. London: Bodley Head, 1955.

The Last Battle. London: Bodley Head, 1956.

Till We Have Faces: A Myth Retold. London: Geoffrey Bles, 1956.

The Dark Tower and Other Stories. Ed. Walter Hooper. London: Collins, 1977.

Boxen: The Imaginary World of the Young C.S. Lewis. Ed. Walter Hooper. London: Collins, 1985.

Secondary Sources

Biographies

Carpenter, Humphrey. *The Inklings: C.S. Lewis, J.R R. Tolkien, Charles Williams, and Their Friends*. London: Allen and Unwin, 1979. Very readable, unsentimentalized account of Lewis's life, in the context of his friendships.

Como, James T., ed. *C.S. Lewis at the Breakfast Table and Other Reminiscences*. New York: Macmillan, 1979. Twenty-four notes and essays by persons having a variety of relationships with Lewis.

Green, Roger Lancelyn, and Walter Hooper. *C.S. Lewis: A Biography*. London: Collins, 1974. Good source of information about Lewis's life and the writing of his books.

Griffin, William. *Clive Staples Lewis: A Dramatic Life*. San Francisco: Harper and Row, 1986. Lively reading, but regarded by many readers as unreliable on details and sources.

Sayer, George. *Jack: C.S. Lewis and His Times*. London: Macmillan, 1988. Written by a student and longtime friend of Lewis's; thorough, reliable, conveys a good sense of Lewis as a person; strong on three women important in Lewis's life—his mother, Mrs. Moore, and Joy Davidman.

Wilson, A.N. *C.S. Lewis: A Biography*. London: Collins, 1989. Well-written, useful, but occasionally wrong on details and highly controversial in its use of psychoanalytic interpretation.

Bibliographies

Christopher, Joe R., and Joan K. Ostling. *C.S. Lewis: An Annotated Checklist of Items about Him and His Works*. Kent, OH: Kent State University Press, 1974. Annotated list of secondary materials through June 1972.

Hooper, Walter. "A Bibliography of the Writings of C.S. Lewis: Revised and Enlarged." In *C.S. Lewis at the Breakfast Table and Other Essays*. Ed. James T. Como. New York: Macmillan, 1979, pp. 245–88. A thorough, accessible listing of Lewis's works.

General Studies

Carnell, Corbin S. *Bright Shadow of Reality*: *C.S. Lewis and the Feeling Intellect*. Grand Rapids, MI: Eerdmans, 1974. The basic work on *Sehnsucht*, or "longing," in Lewis.

Christopher, Joe R. *C.S. Lewis*. Boston: Twayne, 1987. Twayne's English Authors Series. Concise, insightful survey of Lewis's works by genres; strong on Lewis's use of Dante.

Gibb, Jocelyn, ed. *Light on C.S. Lewis*. London: Geoffrey Bles, 1965. Seven essays written shortly after Lewis's death on different aspects of his career; valuable introduction by Owen Barfield.

Hannay, Margaret Patterson. *C.S. Lewis*. New York: Ungar, 1981. Summaries of Lewis's works with helpful critical analyses of them.

Hart, Dabney A. *Through the Open Door*: *A New Look at C.S. Lewis*. University, AL: University of Alabama Press, 1984. On Lewis as a teacher who challenged uncritical acceptance of modern views, and on myth as the key to his critical and imaginative writings.

Kilby, Clyde S. *The Christian World of C.S. Lewis*. Grand Rapids, MI: Eerdmans, 1964. Overview of Lewis's career with

an emphasis on religious themes.

Walsh, Chad. *C.S. Lewis: Apostle to the Skeptics*. New York: Macmillan, 1949. A still-interesting study of Lewis's early works.

———. *The Literary Legacy of C.S. Lewis*. New York: Harcourt Brace Jovanovich, 1979. A readable survey of Lewis's fiction, with more summary and less analysis than one might wish.

Books, on His Religious and Philosophical Writings

Adey, Lionel. *C.S. Lewis's "Great War" with Owen Barfield*. British Columbia: University of Victoria, 1978. English Literary Studies Monograph Series, no. 14. Adey examines the philosophical disputes between Lewis and Barfield in the 1920s.

Beversluis, John. *C.S. Lewis and the Search for Rational Religion*. Grand Rapids, MI: Eerdmans, 1985. Beversluis challenges Lewis's rationalistic approach to and arguments in defense of Christianity.

Cunningham, Richard B. *C.S. Lewis: Defender of the Faith*. Philadelphia: Westminster Press, 1967. A survey of Lewis's writings, fiction and non-fiction, as apologetics.

Meilaender, Gilbert. *The Taste for the Other*: *The Social and Ethical Thought of C.S. Lewis*. Grand Rapids, MI: Eerdmans, 1978. A valuable examination of Lewis's social and ethical ideas, with useful glances at his theology and fiction.

Purtill, Richard L. *C.S. Lewis's Case for the Christian Faith*. San Francisco: Harper and Row, 1981. An overview and summary of Lewis's positions.

Smith, Robert H. *Patches of Godlight*: *The Pattern of Thought of C.S. Lewis*. Athens, GA: University of Georgia Press, 1981. The "pattern" traced is the Platonic and medieval model which underlies much of Lewis's work; a helpful general study.

White, William. *The Image of Man in C.S. Lewis*. Nashville, TN: Abingdon Press, 1969. White explores Lewis's doctrines about humankind—Creation, Fall, Redemption, Immortality—as expressed in his apologetic writings and fiction.

Books on Literary Criticism and Theory

Edwards, Bruce L., Jr. *A Rhetoric of Reading*:

C.S. Lewis's Defense of Western Literacy. Provo, UT: Center for the Study of Christian Values in Literature, 1986. An examination of Lewis's literary criticism and theory of literature, particularly his attention to the process of reading.

———, ed. The Taste of the Pineapple: Essays on C.S. Lewis as Reader, Critic, and Imaginative Writer. Bowling Green, OH: Bowling Green State University Popular Press, 1988. Fourteen essays on Lewis's critical practice, rhetorical strategies, the relation of his criticism to his imaginative writings, and his influences and contemporaries.

Books on His Fiction

Downing, David C. Planets in Peril: A Critical Study of C.S. Lewis's Ransom Trilogy. Amherst: University of Massachusetts Press, 1991. A thorough consideration of the personal background, intellectual concepts, and theological themes of the trilogy, with an assessment of its achievement.

Filmer, Kath. The Fiction of C.S. Lewis: Mask and Mirror. New York: St. Martin's Press, 1993. A study of the supernatural, good and evil, political beliefs, and attitude toward women in Lewis's fiction.

Ford, Paul F. Companion to Narnia. San Francisco: Harper and Row, 1980. A thorough, valuable handbook, alphabetically arranged, identifying and illuminating names, places, and themes in the Narnian Chronicles.

Gibson, Evan K. C.S. Lewis, Spinner of Tales: A Guide to His Fiction. Washington, D.C.: Christian University Press, 1980. Interesting and insightful formalistic close readings of Lewis's fiction.

Glover, Donald E. C.S. Lewis: The Art of Enchantment. Athens, OH: Ohio University Press, 1981. Excellent studies of Lewis's fiction, based on theories of fiction expressed in his own letters and critical writings.

Holbrook, David. The Skeleton in the Wardrobe: C.S. Lewis's Fantasies—A Phenomenological Study. Lewisburg, PA: Bucknell University Press, 1991. Controversial discussion, based on Freudian readings, of what Holbrook considers disturbing elements in and a coercive approach to religion in the Chronicles of Narnia and the Ransom Trilogy.

Howard, Thomas. The Achievement of C.S. Lewis: A Reading of His Fiction. Wheaton, IL: Harold Shaw, 1980. Thematic studies of the Chronicles of Narnia, the Ransom Trilogy, and Till We Have Faces.

Lindskoog, Kathryn. The Lion of Judah in Never-Never Land. Grand Rapids, MI: Eerdmans, 1973. Lindskoog brings out religious themes in the Narnian Chronicles; relates them to other works by Lewis.

Manlove, C.N. C.S. Lewis: His Literary Achievement. London: Macmillan, 1987. A study of theme, structure, symbols, and style in Lewis's fictional works.

Schakel, Peter J. Reading with the Heart: The Way into Narnia. Grand Rapids, MI: Eerdmans, 1979. Studies literary features in each of the seven Chronicles and notes relationships to images in Mere Christianity.

———. Reason and Imagination in C.S. Lewis: A Study of Till We Have Faces. Grand Rapids, MI: Eerdmans, 1984. The first half is a close reading of Till We Have Faces; the second half places it in the context of Lewis's movement from reliance on reason to fuller acceptance of imagination.

———, ed. The Longing for a Form: Essays on the Fiction of C.S. Lewis. Kent, OH: Kent State University Press, 1977. Fourteen essays on the Ransom Trilogy, the Chronicles of Narnia, and Till We Have Faces as literature.

———, and Charles A. Huttar, eds. Word and Story in C.S. Lewis. Columbia: University of Missouri Press, 1991. Sixteen essays exploring Lewis's ideas about language and narrative, both in theory and practice.

Urang, Gunnar. Shadows of Heaven: Religion and Fantasy in the Writings of C.S. Lewis, Charles Williams, and J.R.R. Tolkien. Philadelphia: Pilgrim Press, 1971. Urang considers Lewis's use of fantasy in conveying religious emphases in the Ransom Trilogy, The Great Divorce, and Till We Have Faces.

Peter J. Schakel

Lewis, [Percy] Wyndham

Born: On his father's yacht off Amherst, Nova Scotia, Canada, November 18, 1882

Education: Educated at a succession of private schools; Rugby School, 1897–1898; the Slade School of Art, London, 1898–1901

Marriage: Gladys Anne Hoskyns, October 9, 1930; five illegitimate children

Died: March 7, 1957

Biography

The only child of an American father, Captain Charles Edward Lewis, and a British mother, Anne (nee Prickett) Lewis, Percy Wyndham Lewis was born on his father's yacht off Amherst in the Bay of Fundy, Nova Scotia, on November 18, 1882. His parents permanently separated when he was eleven years old and he settled in England with his mother in 1893 where they existed precariously in the London suburbs. His unsettled adolescence was marked by education at a succession of private schools culminating in attendance with the help from his estranged father's family at Rugby School where he was bottom of his class from 1897 to 1898. He won a scholarship to study (with Henry Tonks) at the Slade School of Art, London, between 1898 and 1901 but left without completing his course.

Despite his father's urgings that he should complete his formal education, ideally at Cornell University, for the next eight years Lewis lived for lengthy periods variously in Germany, Spain, and Holland, but mostly in Brittany or Paris where he practiced painting, preferring the bohemian life of what he called the "vaster alma maters of Paris, or Munich." In this period he fathered the first of his five illegitimate children and contracted the first of several venereal infections. While living in Paris he fell under the influence of the anti-Romantic group of writers and also attended the lectures at the College de France of the famous French philosopher Henri Bergson whose vitalist ideas he was later to vilify in his satirical writings.

Lewis returned to London in 1909 with the all but announced intention of becoming a major figure in contemporary arts and letters. With the help of Ford Madox Ford and Ezra Pound and their literary circle and in association with the painters Augustus John and Spencer Gore in the art world, he rapidly established himself as a revolutionary artist, avant-garde polemicist, and writer. Ford, as editor of the *English Review*, accepted three short stories by Lewis for publication in 1909, the most notable being "Les Saltambiques," which is set in Brittany and involves a visiting circus troupe. From this time until the outbreak of World War I he concentrated on earning a reputation as an avant-garde painter and draftsman. He exhibited his paintings and drawings (which were done under the influence of Cubism as co-founder of the Camden Group) in London in 1911 and in 1912 in the Post-Impressionist exhibition organized by Roger Fry, an influential art critic and impresario. In July 1915, Lewis briefly joined the latter's Omega Workshop, which was dedicated to producing various arts and crafts after the manner of William Morris.

On publicly breaking with Fry after a bitter quarrel, Lewis exhibited his work in Frank Rutter's Post-Impressionist and Futurist Exhibition and with the new London Group before becoming Director of the Rebel Art Centre in the Spring of 1914. By now Lewis had arrived at an original Abstract style of avant-garde painting which constituted the first sustained body of such work to be produced in England. His works of art, in which he emphasized hardness, rigidity, intensity, and force, were derived from a synthesis of Expressionist, Cubist, and Futurist ideas that was subsequently called "Vorticism," a term invented by Ezra Pound. With Pound, Lewis co-edited the flamboyant review *BLAST: Review of the Great English Vortex*, the official journal of the movement which survived only two volumes (1914 and 1915) but marked in its manifestoes, intended to shake up the English Art establishment (to "Kill John Bull With Art"), the beginnings of Lewis's revolutionary activity as a leader of the English "Futurists" in literature as well as painting. Lewis, T.S. Eliot, James Joyce, and Ford became known as "The Men of 1914." In 1915, he organized the first and only English Vorticist Exhibition at the Dore Galleries in London.

The outbreak of World War I in 1914 a few weeks after the appearance of BLAST ended any revolution in the arts, and in March 1916 Lewis enlisted for military service in the Garrison Artillery. By August he was a bombardier (noncommissioned) and by Christmas a battery officer. He served in France, seeing heavy action as a gunner at the front; after recovering from trench fever he was seconded as an official war artist with the Canadian War Memorials Scheme (1917–1919). A particularly fine example of his figurative but tightly organized paintings of this period is *A Battery Shelled* (1919), which is in the Imperial War Museum in London. In his autobiography appropriately titled *Blasting and Bombardiering* (1937; rev. 1967), Lewis vividly describes his experiences in France and Flanders which provided him with a "political education." His new understanding of the relationship between art, architecture, and politics is evident in his writings entitled *The Caliph's Design: Architects! Where Is Your Vortex?* (1919).

Lewis resettled in London after his war service, and his first and highly comical literary masterpiece with tragic implications, *Tarr*, was published in 1918 (rev. 1928). He had begun work on the novel about 1910 and it was not finished until 1914, first appearing as a serial in Eliot's magazine *The Egoist* in 1917. The work was based on his life in pre-war Paris and in it he dealt dramatically from a polemical stance with a group of students of mixed nationalities. In February 1919, he held his first one-man exhibition, entitled "Guns," at the Goupil Galleries in London. The exhibition included pictures completed during his tenure as a war artist. Lewis attempted to revive Vorticism later in the same year under the name of the X Group, which held one exhibition at the Mansard Gallery in London in 1920, but when the Vorticist painters merged with the London Group he disengaged himself. He never approached total abstraction in his paintings again apart from his 1921 exhibition, "Tyros and Portraits," in which he created a set of fashionably attired grotesques and caricatures (in his telling words, "these laughing Elementals are at once satires, pictures and stories") which he acknowledged as being inspired by the English caricaturist William Hogarth. The years from 1918 to 1926 were marked "strictly private" for Lewis; during this time he devoted himself to intensive reading and research and published little. Toward the end of this period he entered a phase as a polemical and quarrelsome critic of culture and society starting, editing, and largely writing in a confrontational style the angry periodicals *The Tyro: A Review of the Arts of Painting, Sculpture and Design* (two volumes, 1921 and 1922) and *The Enemy: A Review of Art and Literature* (three volumes, 1927 to 1929). Beginning in 1924 he also worked as a free-lance journalist, and on October 9, 1930, he secretly married Gladys Anne Hoskyns, an art student with a German mother and British father.

In 1927, Lewis published a collection of short stories entitled *The Wild Body*; a key essay, "The Meaning of the Wild Body," displays his particular brand of tough, satirical humor for the first time. It also outlines the comic aesthetic and method of that collection as well as his theory of laughter as something "primitive, hard, and unchangeable." In 1928, he published the first volume (*The Childermass*) of what was to form a massive tetralogy, *The Human Age*. *The Apes of God* was published in 1930, a savage attack on the cultural life of London and its luminaries, especially the Bloomsbury Group, in the 1920s. Simultaneously with this in his sixty-page pamphlet "Satire and Fiction" Lewis explains most fully his theory of satire, which was followed by his most complete statement on the aesthetic of satire and laughter in *Men Without Art* (1934).

Lewis's fourth novel, *The Snooty Baronet* (1932), was denied a wide readership by the actions of the Boots/Smiths circulating libraries (an important source of revenue for authors), which refused to put the book on their shelves on the grounds of erotic coarseness and obscene language. His one book of verse, titled *Engine-Fight Talk* (*One-Way Song*) and published in 1933, while cast in the same vigorous, aggressive, and satiric mold of "comic pyrotechnics" or "gusting humour" (Symons), has been seen by critics as difficult to accept as poetry and being at best prose poetry or "flat pamphleteering in verse" (Bridson). *The Roaring Queen*, written in 1936, was an enjoyable satirical novel in which Lewis caricatured several celebrated literary figures, most notably Arnold Bennett and Virginia Woolf, and which was withdrawn before publication for fear of libel but eventually published in 1973. Once again the posturing behavior of the Bloomsbury Group and the Chelsea Left-wing intelligentsia are energetically ridiculed in the true Lewisian style of savage and outrageous comedy, which is further exemplified in *The Revenge for Love* (1937), a political satire set against the background of the Spanish Civil War and Bolshevik conspiracies.

The interwar years, despite Lewis's persistent illness and being under constant pressure of poverty and debt, were frantically productive years, although by the beginning of the 1930s the author had become a largely neglected and isolated figure in the British literary scene and was relegated to the status of an "unreadable eccentric" (Schenker). With his wife, Lewis made several visits abroad to the Continent and briefly to America before revisiting North Africa in 1931, where he rode "all over the Atlas" mountains on mules. His visits to Nazi Germany in 1930 and 1931 occasioned his notorious panegyric revealing a protofascist leaning in *Hitler* (1931), which grew out of a series of ephemeral journalistic articles in the periodical *Time and Tide*. Two successful libel actions brought against him in 1932 made publishers wary of Lewis although he was put under contract to Cassell for three novels to be published at the unrealistic rate of one volume every six months. Despite his subsequent recantation in *The Hitler Cult and How It Will End* (1939), he failed to wipe out the hostility and ostracism that he incurred from British and American intellectuals in the build-up to the Second World War. The ostensively anti-Semitic title of his book *The Jews: Are They Human?* (also published in 1939) hastened the departure of Lewis and his wife (who were deep in debt) from England on the day before war was declared.

The Lewises spent the next six years of the war first in New York City but mainly in Canada where Lewis survived penuriously on pot-boiling portraits and occasional articles and lectures. *America I Presume* (1940) consisted of lightweight, mostly lighthearted sketches of the United States, one such product of his brief sojourn in that country. At one time an adviser to the Library of Congress in Washington, D.C., Lewis found some solace in his appointment in 1943–1944 to the faculty of Assumption College, Windsor, Ontario during his friendless sojourn in Toronto, Canada from 1940 to 1945—most of which was spent living in a dilapidated hotel. This experience provided subject matter for his last major and semiautobiographical novel, *Self Condemned* (1954). Despite his liking of individual Americans and Canadians as well as his belief in the melting-pot of the United States in turning its back on "race, caste, and all that pertains to the rooted state," his deep feelings about his largely friendless exile throughout this period are revealed in his numerous letters published in 1963.

By September 1945, Lewis and his wife were back in England, settling in Notting Hill Gate, London, where he soon reestablished himself when, in 1946, he was appointed art

critic to the BBC weekly magazine *The Listener*, a post which he occupied until 1950. He began to receive belated acclaim both as a writer and as a painter, in the latter case in 1949 when he was given a retrospective exhibition at the Redfern Gallery in London. A major retrospective exhibition entitled "Wyndham Lewis and Vorticism" was held in the Tate Gallery, London in 1956. The second volume of his autobiography, *Rude Assignment: A Narrative of My Career Up-to-Date*, was published in 1950 and a further collection of semifactual satirical stories, *Rotting Hill*, attacked a degenerate Britain in the form of the Welfare State of Clement Attlee's first post-war Labor Government. In 1952, Lewis was granted a Civil List pension and in the same year he received an Honorary Doctorate of Letters from the University of Leeds. In spite of the onset of blindness in 1949 (Lewis's eyes had first troubled him in 1941) and following the discovery of a brain tumor, in 1951 the BBC commissioned and presented a radio play version of Lewis's novel *The Childermass* and subsidized its sequels (written with D.G. Bridson), *Monstre Gai* and *Malign Fiesta*, which together were published as *The Human Age* (1955–1956), a title that Lewis assigned to the whole trilogy. He was totally blind by 1954 and died in London on March 7, 1957.

Literary Analysis

While there is clear evidence of Lewis's appreciation of the "comedy of existence" and his recognition of the absurdities in the relationship between artists and society from his earliest writings, it was his political education in the First World War trenches that transformed him into the social critic and satiric novelist of the 1920s and 1930s. Thus, in his autobiography *Blasting and Bombardiering* (1937) he writes, "That we were all on a fool's errand had become plain to many of us" (187). The proclamatory aesthetic tone of the manifestoes of *BLAST* represented a satire upon its own audience (i.e., leaving the readers, especially the intellectually lazy public, less passive observers than villains and victims). This displays Lewis's desire to establish himself and his like-minded colleagues as a new revolutionary cultural elite (the English "Futurists") while at the same time expressing resentment at having to explain the obvious fact of their superiority to a backward-looking audience, especially the English educated middle class, whom he knows that he does not really need. The "blasts" as proclamations were aimed at a wide range of Victorian and Edwardian sociocultural residues, and the "blesses" (including English humor) were proclamations supportive of the Vorticists and their new beliefs and attitudes toward society and culture.

The confrontational and polemical style of the vitriolic satirist that Lewis developed in the interwar years, however, was increasingly more focused and deliberately directed at such targets as fellow intellectuals whose ideas the author profoundly rejected as well as physical objects and subjects offensive to his aesthetic eye and sensibilities. After the war Lewis approached the public as though it was a dynamic force to be reckoned with which needed to be confronted and made conscious of the consequences of modernity in their lives. His first novel, *Tarr*, is essentially both an intellectual comedy of art and a comedy of sex set in the bohemian and cosmopolitan student life of pre-1914 Paris. Thus, his title figure, Tarr, as narrator adopts the contemplative and sardonic stance of the detached observer who ridicules the other major male character, Kreisler, a wild bourgeois bohemian figure who is depicted as a would-be artist with no talent. He is seen as a comic automaton spasmodically embodying the ideas of Teutonic Romanticism and militarism which is counterposed to the piercing intelligence of Tarr, who embodies Lewis's neoclassical leanings and whose message is that the "only escape from modern man's ridiculous predicament is through art, intellect and will" (Phelps, 317). In his alternation of focus between his two central women characters, Bertha and Anastasya, Lewis gives comic expression (if not his overt intention) to his own misogynist and sexist leanings albeit, as Frederick Jameson has perceptively noted, prefiguring the interpersonal or dialogical narrative form of literary expression elaborated by Mikhail Bakhtin.

For example, Tarr, at the quarrelsome end of a sumptuous meal and conversation with Anastasya in a Paris restaurant as a prelude to her seduction, ironically reflects as follows:

She had recovered from the effects of the drinks completely and was sitting up and talking briskly, looking at him with the same serious rather flattered face she had had during their argument on Art and Death.

"I know you are a famous whore, who becomes rather acid in her cups!—when you showed me your legs this evening, I suppose I was meant—"

"Assez! Assez!!" She struck the table with her fist. "Let's get to business." He put his hat on and leant towards her.

"It's getting late. Twenty-five francs, I'm afraid, is all I can manage."

"Twenty-five francs for what? With you—it would be robbery! Twenty-five francs to be your audience while you drivel about art? Keep your money and buy Bertha an—efficient chimpanzee! She will need it if she mames you!" Her mouth drawn tight and her hands in her overcoat pockets, she walked out of the door of the cafe.

Tarr ordered another drink.

"It's like a moral tale told on behalf of Bertha," he thought. That was the temper of Paradise! The morality, in pointing to Bertha, did her no good, but caused her to receive the trop-plein of his discontent. (Tarr [1973], p. 323)

Lewis's anti-Romantic satirizing represented his complete rejection of the then fashionable genre in modernist fiction of the "stream of consciousness" novel (later his satirizing was to be turned against a central "stream of consciousness" exponent, Joyce, a one-time friend and collaborator) and the Bergsonian concepts of time with its primacy of inward feeling which Lewis saw as a new form of sloppy and vulgar Romanticism. As such, the author's first novel seemed "notably experimental both in form and content, based, in part, on application of vorticist thought to fiction with the end of creating through satire or at least irony externalist art" (Jones, 66). Behind all of this the intensely biographical nature of his style of narrative which marks all of his writing is brought out in Lewis's remarks in the preface to *Tarr* where he self-revealingly notes that, "if you look closely at my grin, you will perceive that it is a very logical and deliberate grimace" (viii). His narrative method of self-tormenting introspection has been likened by critics to that of Feodor Dostoyevsky, a writer whom he admired greatly.

The "paradox of Lewisian satire" (Schenker, 73) is best illustrated in the writer's epic tetralogy *The Human Age,* comprising *The Childermass, Monstre Gai,* and *Malign Fiesta,* an intended fourth part, *The Trial of Man,* existing only in the form of a synopsis and a draft of the first chapter. *The Childermass* and its companion volumes represent his most remarkable work and his best fictional satire written from a surrealistic and obscure style of a philosophical extravaganza dealing with a journey through a fantastic and macabre Heaven.

Earning the sobriquet from Jameson of "theological science fiction" (6), the first volume is set in the afterlife on a wasteland outside the gate of this fictional Heaven where the "emigrant mass" of humanity awaits interrogation by the Bailiff. This permits Lewis to parade his ethical and aesthetic phobias and antipathies about the nature of the personality or of individuality in brilliant dialectical debate between characters and powerful narrative. This is achieved through the mouthpiece of Hyperides, a pseudo-Greek philosopher in the process of interrogation and assignment of deceased souls marshaled before his adversary, the celestial and cynical Bailiff who is a representative of reality. The book's intellectual hero, Pullman, and his emotionally underdeveloped companion and former schoolfellow, Satherwaite, as anti-heroes, are new arrivals representing two ordinary souls (a "pseudo-couple," according to Jameson [58]). Pullman and Satherwaite take a stroll before the day's session outside Magnetic City begins and display their "neurotic dependency" (Jameson, 58) in conversing in highly and deliberately flourished anglicisms and then current English colloquial language ("fuss," "toddle," "beastly," "strapping"). Pullman has been seen primarily as a model of the kind of intellectual that Lewis rejected, being overtly modeled on Joyce with whom the writer had enjoyed an interlude of friendship (although for a year or two before *The Childermass* they had been verbally caricaturing each other).

In the novel Lewis satirized practitioners of the stream-of-consciousness technique of writing, which he saw as barbaric, and characteristically presented thinly disguised vindictive portrayals of individuals whom he personally despised. The dominant stylistic device and narrative structure employed in this novel presupposes the reader's preliminary familiarity with the then current stereotypical epithets and appositions, as well as visual and verbal clichés employed by his principal characters in their "ready-made, free-floating bits of speech" (Jameson, 71). Jameson notes the novelist's figural use of pre-existing, conventionalized roles (Keystone Cops, Jack the Giantkiller), along with the archetypal circus clowns and Pierrots used in his earliest works to illustrate the comic "obedience" of reality to its own archetypes.

This style, or what Jameson calls Lewis's "satire-collage," has been attributed to his earlier Vorticist association with T.E. Hulme and the other imagists. Such stylistic devices enable Lewis to achieve the effect of a painter transferring impressions to canvas or of creating explicitly "painterly" and technical signals in certain descriptive passages through startling similes and unfamiliar collocations of words to produce a riotous comic and satiric effect in depicting the surreal afterworld of the novel. The consequent "wild phantasmagoria of broad farce, poetic symbolism and philosophical subtlety" (Stevenson, 172) of the work is further heightened by the Bailiff, a cartoon character acting as the household bogeyman (as Jameson describes him). The Bailiff conducts his inquisition from a Punch-and-Judy booth, evoking roars of laughter from the mob of working-class peons (or "herd," as Lewis dismissingly calls them—the "sham-puppet victims of his satire" (Jameson, 161). If the book can be seen as a theological and ethical epic concerned centrally with sin and virtue, Lewis is following in the footsteps of *The Divine Comedy,* and *The Childermass* is, indeed, full of Dantean echoes. Such ancestry is reinforced by "The hallucinatory atmosphere, the grotesquerie, the power and conviction of the narrative, the ritualistic and symbolic overtones of meaning, which together make this novel sequence something unique in modern literature" (Daiches, 317).

The subsequent parts of *The Human Age—Monstre Gai,* and *Malign Fiesta*—while closely connected with *The Childermass* also display a separate, prose poetic element which Lewis had virtually abandoned for almost twenty years. In reviewing the complete work in 1957, Julian Symons notes, therefore, that "The targets at which Mr. Lewis aimed in the 1920s are no longer visible, or they no longer interest him; changes in the human situation over a quarter of a century have dictated the altered style and attitude of *The Human Age*'s later books" (Gross, 114). The later books better cross-reference with the then emerging New

Wave science fiction, and Lewis's handling and criticism of his philosophical and religious attitudes and rhetoric is very different from those of *The Childermass* in volume 1. Similarly, the nature of his employment of the satiric aesthetic of otherness and "insistently satiric eye" (Symons, 114) of externality shows transformations from the earlier 1930s influence of Swiftian satire, fully acknowledged by Lewis in *Satire and Fiction* (1930). In the depiction of life as hell in *The Human Age*, the presentation itself may be said to transcend satire (as Jonathan Swift could and did) because at last Lewis is able through the "tandem treatment" of his characters (Jameson, 58) to see himself as "involved in the fabric of the hellishness" (Seymour-Smith, 211).

The novelist evokes this grotesque hellishness in one of the most powerful scenes in *Monstre Gai* in which Sammael (the Devil) gives Pullman a tour of Dis (Hell) in his car with a captive French woman who is to be dispatched to the beasts:

> He flung the door open, getting bitten in the hand by one of the ravening beasts. There burst into the car the fearful stench, there was a scarlet flash of sexual monstrosity, the whining and snorting of a score of faces—the beasts leaping on one another's backs, so that several appeared to be about to spring on to the roof of the car.—Scores of sinewy arms terminating in claws shot into the car, and snatched the woman out of it.

> There was her body, shoulder-high, for the fraction of a second, in the midst of the stinking pack—the sickening odour increasing in intensity. Just for that fractional speck of time a dozen claws could be seen defiling her person. The most terrible scream Pullman had ever heard filled aurally that speck of time. The car gathered speed, the door was violently closed, and that was that. The silence was tremendous and Pullman was alone—more alone than he had ever been with anyone in his life—with the lord Sammael. (From *The Human Age* in Symons, *The Essential Wyndham Lewis*, p. 371)

The satiric apparatus which Lewis evolves appears designed to show that his satire never

killed anyone and could never do so (Jameson, 162). Furthermore, in contradistinction to his mentor, as Symons observes, "Mr. Lewis's style sometimes gets in the way of his satire, there is so much style that one can see nothing else. With Swift this is never so" (Gross, 113).

Lewis's other major and perhaps best-known imaginative and immense work (625 pages) of nonmoralistic satire—"his most complex and reflexive satiric construction" (Jameson, 174)—came from his most productive writing period when he was at the height of his literary powers. *The Apes of God* caused a furor in literary London. Lewis described this novel as his one "pure" satire. In it he savagely scourged wealthy dilettantes, or "Apes" of art, and the frivolous self-indulgent lifestyle in the hothouse environment of bourgeois-bohemian London and its luminaries, the leading members of the Bloomsbury Group. Thus, this saturnine Jonsonian comedy of "Humours" (Stevenson, 183) is essentially a *roman à clef* representing an "episodic cage-by-cage exhibition" (Jameson, 174) and portraying types rather than individuals as Lilliputian caricatures (literary forms of his earlier-drawn Tyros) or "galvanized puppets" (Gross, 109) of satiric representation. This is reinforced by the author's narrative style of savage diatribe in which he insists upon exact physical description and external detail. Virtually every character in *The Apes of God* is described somewhere as an "animal," a "machine," a "robot," or a "dummy," or above all as a "split-man" deemed to be "alienated from their true selves by the pressure of 'group-rhythm' and drifting with the flux of contemporary fads" (Stevenson, 176–77). Chief antagonists Lewis denounced as "romantics." Among those contemporaries satirized and reduced to such grotesque stereotypes as totems of a sick and dying culture were Joyce, Woolf, the Sitwells, and the Bloomsbury painter Vanessa Bell.

Principal among the social practices and cultural fads which are the objects of his most vitriolic satiric attacks are homosexuality (especially lesbianism), burgeoning feminism, militarism, nationalism, the cult of youth, the pose of political radicalism (especially leftist), the pose of adulation for the colored races, and the pervasive interest among the bourgeois best-circles of Freudian theories of the unconscious. He reserved particular scorn, given his artistic talents, for the invasion of the arts by pretentious and mediocre bourgeois amateurs posing as would-be painters and writers who thereby aped the genuine power and example of the God-like artist with his superior intellect and genius.

Once again Lewis presents the reader with a gallery of rogues and monsters (Pritchard, 69) in a picaresque plot which, according to Daniel Schenker, parallels Swift's satirical intentions as well as owing something to Swift's prose or at least to the philosophical assumptions behind it. Lewis's Lilliputians are a "community of upper-middle-class bohemians who conspire to destroy the talented persons whom they cannot exploit for their own petty ends" (Pritchard, 76). Among these is Dan Boleyn (Lewis's Gulliver), an imbecilic, juvenile, would-be poet and apprentice ape-hunter who is initiated into the world of "Apes" peopling the household of the aristocratic family of his mysterious patron, Sir Horace Zagreus, an androgynous non- and anti-ape. Sir Horace is a loquacious character who makes a career of staging elaborate practical jokes for his friends, and in the second half of *The Apes of God* Dan accompanies his middle-aged mentor to the country estate of Lord Osmund Finian-Shaw (a thinly disguised caricature of Osbert Sitwell). The latter is tellingly characterized with his painterly eye by Lewis as follows:

> In colour Lord Osmund was a pale coral, with flaxen hair brushed tightly back, his blond pencilled pap rising straight from his sloping forehead: galb-like wings to his nostrils—the goat-like profile of Edward the Peacemaker. The lips were curved. They were thickly profiled as though belonging to a moslem portrait of a stark-lipped sultan. His eyes, vacillating and easily discomfited, slanted down to the heavy curved nose. Eyes, nose and lips contributed to one effect, so that they seemed one feature. It was the effect of the jouissant animal—the licking, eating, fat-muzzled machine—dedicated to Wine, Womanry, and Free Verse-cum-soda water. (From *The Apes of God* in Symons, *The Essential Wyndham Lewis*, p. 308)

Zagreus has been commissioned by Lord Osmund, an aesthete and showman for all of the puppet figures that go through their mechanical gesticulations in the story. Lewis's most sympathetic character portrayal is that of Bertram Starr-Smith, a proto-fascist, who is suggestive of an authorial alter-ego, as is the absent protagonist of the novel, the mysterious painter-philosopher Pierpoint whose mouthpiece is Zagreus. Singled out for particular satirical demolition is the figure of a self-promoting author, James-Julius Ratner, who is a palpable caricature of Joyce.

In his recourse to corrosive satire in which he displays a mixture of verbal burlesque and grotesque combined with sheer volubility, Lewis is attempting to force complacent people to sit up and take notice of the central political and cultural issues and developments creating the mechanization of self and decay of the European vision of life which preoccupied him in the post–World War I period. Thus, he employs a comic and ultraempirical style that "denotes a whole society of Gullivers who have surrendered themselves to mechanical metaphors for thought and action" (Schenker, 78). The distinctive prose style of the novel led Eliot to claim Lewis as the greatest master of style of his generation and Symons to emphasize the novelist's genius for writing lifelike dialogue. A contemporary reviewer, Orlo Williams, graphically described *The Apes of God* as "one of the steppes or tundra of modern literature" (quoted in Gross, 104). Jameson, however, sees the extraordinary prolixity of the work as a kind of ambiguous monument to Lewis's "illimitable sentence-producing capacity" (32), adding that the polemical and intransigent style of unremitting malice (Stevenson, 177) in his writing make some of the experimental texts virtually unreadable for any sustained length of time—which coupled with its slow-moving narrative are not likely to endear him to the contemporary reader. Symons also critically suggests that *The Apes of God* is little more than a tour of Bloomsbury and its celebrated inhabitants and that such parochialism must diminish its effectiveness.

Much the same can be said of the satiric effect which inevitably must suffer from the contemporary reader's missing time-specific (i.e., 1920s and 1930s) allusions to events, persons, objects, and lifestyles that are unfamiliar today, not to mention the English middle-class vernacular language of the time which Lewis liberally employs for comic purposes and satire. His highly idiosyncratic style thereby departs from classical satire which was written in a language that reflected universally acknowledged, if rarely attended to, rational standards and moral values by which the world as a modern inferno, as vividly portrayed by Lewis in his novels, can ultimately be judged as worthy of vilification and contempt by the reader. Schenker suggests that the evidence in such a profoundly anarchic book as *The Apes of God* confirms that the writer did not see himself laughing with his readers but instead laughing at his literary creations and his readers with the consequence that the contemporary reader "will feel that he, too, has been the victim of an elaborate literary confidence trick."

Lewis's fourth novel, *The Snooty Baronet*, is labeled by Schenker a "Religious Satire." The book, which approximates the conventional form of novel more closely than its two predecessors, has been seen as a masterpiece of Hogarthian comedy and the author's nearest approach to a "comic romp" (Stevenson, 178) containing wonderful comic scenes (Symons, 316). Until recently, however, critics in general have seen it as a minor work which is less than satisfactory as a novel. In the mid-1970s, though, Timothy Materer proposed that the book should be reinterpreted as an ironic affirmation of human values, and Schenker has recently pointed up the "self-consuming ironies" of *The Snooty Baronet*. Bernard Lafourcade, a leading Lewisian revivalist, also has argued recently that this novel, with all its attendant existential anxieties about the disappearance of the subject, is a precursor to postmodern fiction. Readers should, therefore, despite the book's being intensely biographical and autoreferential, carefully distinguish between the persona of the sardonic and ironical first-person narrator, Sir Kell-Imrie (nicknamed Snooty), a war veteran with a silver plate in his skull and an artificial leg, and Lewis as author. The monologue form in the novel's parodic interplay of literature and existence, according to Lafourcade, permits Lewis, through the mouthpiece of Snooty with his brutally mechanistic assumptions, to digress into his familiar phobias, including his central interest in expressing his ideas on a vast range of literary monuments, philosophical icons, and even the French painter Rousseau the Douanier. There are numerous parodies of various forms of then contemporary subliteratures (e.g., the cheap novelette) accompanied by a massive use of chatty and impulsive dialogue replete with anonymous quotations and allusions (including songs, nursery rhymes, limericks, puns, and popular sayings of the day) used to telling comic and satiric effect.

Although the book is not a *roman à clef*, Lewis modeled Humph, the central character's literary agent, on Rupert Grayson, a member of the publishing firm which had already published the cheap edition of *The Apes of God* and was to publish his travel book, *Filibusters in Barbary*. The figure of the mild McPhail was based on his friend, the poet Roy Campbell, with whom he had stayed in the South of France in mid-1930. The narrator, Snooty (a self-portrait), is constantly butting in, commenting on his "Life and Opinions" in the present tense, and his unique contradictory nature personifies Lewis's deriding of psychological behaviorism as advanced by John B. Watson. The protagonist's lunatic, puppet-like actions equate self and impulse by abandoning reflection as a prisoner of the moment. In the chapter "The Hatter's Automaton," Snooty is identified with the Automaton in a London hatter's shop window. Lewis also intrudes on this fictional world (an ironic inversion of Joyce's authorial method) with amusing cameo appearances under a flimsy disguise (clownishly involving "the ghost in the machine," the artificially absentee author, according to Lafourcade, which can be taken as a self-conscious belittling of authorial authority [Schenker, 88]). Snooty thus compares himself at one time with William Windham, an eighteenth-century English politician renowned for his independence, extremism, and powerful resentments—characteristics not unlike those of the other Wyndham! Likewise, the author punningly involves Sinclair Lewis and I.N. Lewis, of machine-gun fame, as two favorites of the Lewis (Wyndham) Circus.

The Snooty Baronet is about the attempt of the boorish Humph to arrange a fake kidnap and ransom demand by bandits during Snooty's travels in Persia to research the Mithraic significance of bullfighting—as part of a bizarre publicity stunt devised by Humph on his behalf. In Lafourcade's opinion, unlike *The Apes of God* with its slow-moving narrative, in *The Snooty Baronet* Lewis achieves some of the fast-paced, picaresque qualities of Evelyn Waugh's early novels, writing in the style of the diary or picaresque travelogue, with Snooty being transported from New York to Persia via Mayfair and Martigues, in the South of France. It is the writer's employment of this comic genre that leads Lafourcade to suggest that there is a conspicuous structural analogy between *The Snooty Baronet* and Laurence Sterne's *Tristram Shandy* despite the huge differences in background and personality between the two literary characters. These two literary works not only share the great Anglo-

Saxon tradition of nonsense but their absurdist systems also share two of its fundamental ingredients, viz. philosophy and obscenity. Lewis's dualistic and fertile inventiveness, however, is seen by Lafourcade as more diverse, entertaining, and disquieting than Sterne's work, "with the pendulum swinging madly between desire and disgust in its discovery of mechanical sex as the arch expression of behaviourism" (264). Nowhere is this better exemplified than in comic scenes involving Snooty unscrewing his artificial leg before having sex with his aging mistress Val. In this regard the distinct feature of what Lafourcade calls "existential farce" (264) in Lewis's intensity of description of the mechanical gyrations of sex in which the principal character is both butt and medium of the satire is well illustrated as follows:

She grappled with me at once, before the words were well out of my mouth, with the self-conscious gusto of a Chatterly-taught expert. But as I spoke I went to meet her—as I started my mechanical leg giving out an ominous creak (I had omitted to oil it, like watches and clocks these things require lubrication). I seized her stiffly round the body. All of her still passably lisson person—on the slight side—gave. It was the human willow, more or less. It fled into the hard argument of my muscular pressures. Her waist broke off and vanished into me as I took her over in waspish segments, an upper and a nether. The bosoms and head settled like a trio of hefty birds upon the upper slopes of my militant trunk: a headless nautilus on the other hand settled upon my middle, and attacked my hams with its horrid tentacles—I could feel the monster of the slimy submarine-bottoms grinding away beneath, headless and ravenous. (*The Snooty Baronet* [1984], p. 48)

However, it is the comedy and black humor associated with the disgust and nausea graphically described throughout the book as much as the obscenity of utterance and language which for Lafourcade marks the crucial break with the Shandyan tradition to establish *The Snooty Baronet* as a "dehumanized-machine-age version of the comedy of manners, Behaviourism" (265). Similarly, the tragicomedy of Humph's murder (committed as a kind

of joke) at the hands of Snooty and the latter's desertion of his dying mistress suggests to Stevenson that the novel's action lapses into a sort of farcical melodrama reminiscent of George Bernard Shaw (178).

Taking up the Celtic literary tradition of poetic invective and its linguistic identification of satire and magic spells which he sees as akin to the angry words of *The Snooty Baronet*, Schenker's reinterpretation of this work confirms for him Lewis's claim that this novel represented a "metaphysical" satire whose mission was more properly religious than moral. Symons refers to the "rich philosophical comedy" made by Lewis out of such scenes in "The Hatter's Automaton" which, together with what Lafourcade calls its "metaphysical casuistry," leads the latter to suggest that "The collision of Berkeley and Watson turns *The Snooty Baronet* into an existential farce concerned with the phantasmal disappearance of the subject" (*The Essential Wyndham Lewis*, 264). If Lewis is to be thought of as an anti-novelist, for Lafourcade *The Snooty Baronet* is possibly his funniest, lightest, yet most complex novel which for better or for worse marks the apex of his literary career.

As a literary critic and essayist, Lewis was concerned also with explicating his idiosyncratic theory of satiric humor and laughter which he set down in his important "Satire and Fiction," published to coincide with the publication of *The Apes of God*. Building on his earlier "Wildboy" (1927) essay which explicates his comic aesthetic and theory of laughter, Lewis presents a contrary view to that of the classical satirist as essentially a moralist attacking his enemies from a position that his readers recognize as normative. In contrast, he further argues in *Men Without Art* (1934) that the greatest satire would be nonmoralistic and consequently such a satirist would always find himself the enemy of society. In acknowledging the preeminence of Swift, John Dryden, and Alexander Pope, and in contradistinction to Shakespearean comedy, Lewis concludes that "there is laughter and laughter, and that of true satire is as it were tragic laughter" (113). As the antithesis of humor, satire as an attack on complacency must be brutal and destructive in telling the truth about contemporary vices. While he shares with all true satirists the purpose of reform, unlike his distinguished predecessors Lewis does not seek to operate didactically within the established normative frameworks of society to preserve tradition. Alternatively, he seeks to achieve reform through displaying the unvarnished truth, without compunction (Stevenson, 175), despite the distinct risk of thereby ironically becoming, with his persistent display of malice, bile, and misanthropy, cast as R.C. Elliot suggests, "the satirist satirized."[1]

Lewis's most complete statement on his aesthetic of satire is found in *Men Without Art* in which he reasserts that his satiric writing is not produced in the service of morality but rather as art reflecting his belief that the artistic impulse is more primitive than ethical. Indeed, he asserts that "the greatest satire cannot be moralistic at all: if for no other reason, because no mind of the first order, expressing itself in art, has ever itself been taken in, nor consented to take in others, by the crude injunctions of any purely moral code." Again in explicating his comic aesthetic while admitting that perfect laughter, if there could be such a thing, would be inhuman, he claims that our deepest laughter is at the same time non-personal and nonmoral, not the "natural," "bubbling" laughter of William Shakespeare but rather a "healthy clatter" or the tragic laughter of true satire.

If nothing else, Lewis's enormous output of fifty books and 360 essays means that he is too massive a writer to be ignored. He is a unique figure in twentieth-century letters as the only writer of the age to be distinguished in another art—painting—besides literature, although he has been likened to Jean Cocteau as a man who spread his genius over a number of artistic occupations and thereby diluted his talents. Nevertheless, this uniquely enabled him to bring a painter's eye to his writing to the extent that "he offered in place of stream-of-consciousness not traditionalism but a glittering mineral prose based on his practice as a painter" (Seymour-Smith, 175). The versatility of his writing, the assumption of numerous literary personae, and the omniscient subject matter of his works have earned Lewis the title of the "modern Diogenes." He has also justifiably been confirmed in Jameson's judgment as "the most European and least insular of all the great contemporary British writers" (quoted in Seymour-Smith, 88) as well as "one of the most original critics in the English language to emerge since the death of Matthew Arnold" (Quennell, 496). Each of his books contains dazzling strokes of wit along with extraordinary insights and valuable passages of critical analysis—even if these are wholly individual and offer an analysis of a writer's work linked to his own interests and attitudes. Few would deny the summation of his biographer, Jeffrey Meyers, that Lewis was an independent, courageous artist and a "brilliant and original" observer of contemporary mass society and modern civilization (Marshall McCluhan accurately dubbed him "an avant-garde by himself"[2]) as well as one of the most lively and stimulating forces in modern English literature.

Despite his undoubted genius, critical appreciation of his writings remains divided, one supporter (Seymour-Smith) claiming that *The Human Age* will come to be recognized as the greatest single imaginative prose work in English in the twentieth century with Lewis being without question the greatest English-language writer of the century and one of the greatest in world literature. His detractors, however, suggest that the author let his neoclassical prejudices vitiate his talent and then complain that he seemingly lacked the discipline to write an important novel (Wagner) and that he may not survive as one of the major novelists even of his own age (Stevenson). Still, the most recent critical appraisals of his work by Jameson, Lafourcade, and Schenker confirm the view that Lewis's art uses and transcends its ideological raw materials and forms the foundation for a much overdue reevaluation of his canon.

Although he rejected many of the techniques of modernism developed by his literary contemporaries (most notably Joyce), Lewis must be seen as "one of the most prodigiously talented modernists, whose freshness and astringency may deter us from too complete absorption in so-called post-modernism" (Jones, 67). According to Schenker, as an "arch-modernist" and avant-garde polemicist striving to make people confront the consequences of modernity in their lives, "Lewis endures as a portraitist of the violence within 20th-century people and their words, ideas, and actions, and as an auger of the apocalyptic doom of mass civilization bereft of those strong personalities whose will and common decency are necessary to prevent the apocalypse" (Jones, 67).

Stevenson likewise regards Lewis as an exemplary spokesman of the social and moral cataclysm of World War I which split his career in two: "its explosive force, obliterated the sophisticated aloofness of his Edwardian predecessors, and on the flattened bombsites the postwar generation of satirists constructed their new version of disillusioned disdain" (Stevenson, 183).

In spite of Lewis's blistering 1952 attack on Sartrean engagement and the concept of a political vocation for literature, it is of interest to note Jameson's observation that in *A Soldier of Humour* (with the satiric tone of his description of workers as "cogs," "bobbins," or "puppets" in the context of the dynamics of group praxis) Lewis prefigured Jean-Paul Sartre's *Critique of Dialectical Reason*. In the preface to *Time and Western Man* (1927) his discussion of being and non-being (or of self and not-self) and laughter as becoming a hysterical attempt to bridge the gap clearly anticipates the later existential concerns of Sartre's *Being and Nothing,* and his comedic treatment of nausea in *The Snooty Baronet* predates that of *La Nausée* (Lafourcade, 264). A classical outsider and marginal man himself, Lewis expounded a philosophical attitude toward violence that prefigured Albert Camus, post–World War II *L'Etranger*, and the Angry Young Men of 1950s British literature and paralleled his earlier generational polemical attack on British bourgeois complacency and regressive social vision. Jameson also draws attention to the kinship between Lewis's much earlier style of verbal production and that of the openly schizophrenic discontinuities and flux of postmodernist works such as Samuel Beckett's *Watt*, an opinion which is further echoed by Lafourcade's reference to the "Beckettian touch" or "evasiveness" of Lewis's narrative in sections of *The Snooty Baronet.*

Likewise, *Tarr* may have been more influential on Joyce than is generally supposed. Ironically, given his vehement attacks on Joyce's stream-of-consciousness techniques, Lewis's *Tarr* is the best representative of this genre while Joyce's *Ulysses* is more accurately seen, in contrast, as a "stream-of-unconsciousness" novel. Indicative also of his contradictory nature is the fact that while most of the writers whom he attacked were expressionists (an attack motivated by the violence that he saw as inherent in their expressionism), Lewis paradoxically produced energetically expressionist creative works in his three major novels.

If Lewis's philosophical and political opinions are so uniquely his own that they can hardly be elucidated except by reading him (Kunitz and Haycraft, 824), and if approaching his prose work for the first time is to be confronted with a bewildering variety from which to choose (Tomlin, 740), Lewis is obviously not an easy writer for the present-day reader to relate to and comprehend. According to even as sympathetic a critic as Lafourcade, he was not a born novelist despite Tomlin's claim that the two later volumes of *The Human Age* constitute the best novel to come out of the Cold War. Thus, as summarized by Bergonzi, "His prose is abrasive, angular, and not always easy to read but it is a magnificent medium for de-familiarizing the habitual" (413). This latter propensity is at the heart of all forms of comic writing, especially satire, which is the principal genre of Lewis's literary canon. While it is commonly agreed that his works contain passages of good writing and are punctuated with flashes of sudden insight of deadly shrewdness, this is balanced by the fact that "Lewis never achieved sustained greatness in any work: he was a master of the sentence, the paragraph, even the scene; but never the whole book" (Bertram, 628). In further confirming that his later works especially conform to no definable category, Kunitz and Haycraft suggest that "they are part novel, part essay, part prose poem, but all satire" (823).

If Lewis's comic vision is bleak but bracing (Bergonzi), his satires were based on the conviction that "the root of the comic is . . . in the sensations resulting from the observations of a thing behaving like a person." His view that men are really machines pretending to be humans (his concept of the "wild body") is a peculiar inversion of Bergson's influential theory of laughter, expressed in *Le Rire*, and a misreading of this aspect of Bergsonianism in that Lewis paradoxically "celebrates the mechanization of the human subject which Bergson seeks to deny" (Ayers, 19). In laughing at his satiric creations and his English middle-class readers of the 1920s and 1930s rather than with them, Lewis no doubt will mystify many present-day readers unaware of the significance of his allusions and the butts of his vernacular satires. Many of his pungently expressed beliefs and ideas will also be alien to firm beliefs in the social and cultural institutions (not the least of which is the Welfare State that he vilified in *Rotting Hill*) with their humane and sympathetic approach to individual needs in a modern society. Satire of the absolutized, externalized, nonromantic, and nonmoralistic forms expressed in Lewis's mature aesthetic was for him the very essence of art and in his literary works assume something of this genre's primitive power and its archaic vocation of malediction and revolt (Jameson, 136–38).

Accordingly, while in the tradition of Swiftian prose writing, his central problem as a novelist is seen by Materer as being how to reconcile his satiric and his tragic visions of the world which (coupled with his insistence on particularities, on assailing our time—the perpetual present and not all time) robs his satire of universality (Wagner, 310–11). In contrast, then, with the works of such distinguished forbears as Pope, Dryden, and Swift with whom admiring critics equate him, Lewis is seen as lacking "the compensating nobility of vision that elevates these works above invective into universal masterpieces" (Stevenson, 183). If, however, we see the sociological emergence of and force of satire at the end of an era and in an age of crisis in a society and its culture, we can perhaps best see Lewis as a major twentieth-century contributor to radical bourgeois revolutionary literature (Metscher). In its subversive form, especially satire, this genre invades the dominant culture as a powerful medium of social criticism of the sedimented, regressive social vision of that culture. The post–World War I and interwar years in Britain in particular were a period that afforded the author full scope for his particular satiric vision in his major novels and essays.

As an integral part of his theory of human nature, Lewis clearly saw laughter as an aggressive weapon and a profoundly human expression of consciousness (as opposed to Freudian unconsciousness) and will against the unconsciousness of the mass or "herd." As something "primitive, hard and unchangeable, laughter however transcends the individual subject as a terrifying and impersonal force which sweeps the surface of a two-dimensional planet" (Jameson, 137). True laughter for Lewis is an expression only of the fully conscious, true "person" who "sees all satirically, externally, nonromantically, in a perpetual present" (Wagner, 310). In personifying and practicing this precept he not only laughed at the intellectual implications of D.H. Lawrence and his "Mithraic Gods" or "Dark Demons" but with characteristic and uncomfortable honesty in recognizing his own animality he saw the precept as comic. Ahead of his time and generation of writers, a feature of his writing is its comic objectivity about the existence of such physicality.[3]

While much of Lewis's sardonic diatribes on his contemporaries and their ideas and beliefs was extreme and dated, today the interest in him and his works centers more on the prophetic nature of his writings and ideas as a consequence of that earlier twentieth-century generation's social practices and beliefs and their forms of individual behavior. If, as Jameson avers, Lewis cannot be fully assimilated in the contemporary textual aesthetic without anachronism, we can equally subscribe to the critical reevaluation that "the approach of a postindustrialistic age argues powerfully for the discovery of Lewis's kinship with us" (20). On a more mundane level Symons reminds us that "it is startling, sixty years later, to see how prophetically right he was in relation to the demise of the family, the standardization of clothing and its unisexual nature, the rise of feminism and homosexuality, the immense growth of what he called 'associational life' through the development of specialized interests, and the control exerted over all our lives by gigantic international cartels and the press. He was dramatically wrong about the fading of national feelings, the elimination of national boundaries, and the acceptance of an international world order" (7).

Summary

Both as a remarkable and leading forerunner of a properly postmodernist or "schizophrenic conception of the cultural artefact" (Jameson, 20) and as a masterly varied exponent of British humorous writing in the twentieth century, Wyndham Lewis is that "the Great Outsider, whose jokes and satires angered his enemies, [and who] should find no agreement after his death among his friends" (Jameson, 374) regarding his place in British literary history—as either the major satirist of his age or as a novelist of limited appeal.

Notes

1. Eliot, Robert C. *The Power of Satire,* Princeton: Princeton University Press, 1968. As cited in Jameson, p. 138.
2. McCluhan, Marshall. "Lewis's Prose Style," *Wyndham Lewis: A Reevaluation,* Jeffrey Meyers, ed. Montreal: McGill-Queens University Press; London: Athlone Press, 1980, p. 64.
3. Seymour-Smith, Martin. "Wyndham Lewis as Imaginative Writer," *Agenda,* Vol. 17 (1969–1970), p. 10.

Selected Bibliography

Primary Sources
Tarr. London: The Egoist, 1918; rev. ed. London: Methuen, 1928; New York: Jubilee Books, 1973.

The Wild Body, A Soldier of Humour, and Other Stories. London: Chatto & Windus, 1927; New York: New American Library, 1966.

The Human Age: Vol. 1. The Childermass. London: Chatto & Windus, 1927; rev. ed. London: Methuen, 1956; London: J. Calder, 1965; Vol. 2. *Monstre Gai*. Co-authored with D.G. Bridson. London: Methuen, 1956; London: J. Calder, 1965; Vol. 3. *Malign Fiesta*. Co-authored with D.G. Bridson. London: Methuen, 1955; London: J. Calder, 1966.

The Apes of God. London: Nash & Grayson, 1930; London: Penguin Books, 1965.

Satire and Fiction. London: Arthur Press, 1930.

The Snooty Baronet. London: Cassell, 1932; Santa Barbara: Black Sparrow Press, 1984.

Men Without Art. London: Cassell, 1934; Santa Barbara: Black Sparrow Press, 1987.

Blasting and Bombardiering. London: Eyre and Spottiswoode, 1937; rev. ed. Berkeley: University of California Press, 1967. Autobiography.

Rude Assignment: A Narrative of My Career Up-to-Date. London: Hutchinson, 1950; Santa Barbara: Black Sparrow Press, 1984.

Rotting Hill. London: Methuen, 1951; Santa Barbara: Black Sparrow Press, 1986.

Collections

The Letters of Wyndham Lewis. Ed. W.K. Rose. Norfolk: New Directions, 1963.

A Soldier of Humour and Selected Writings. Ed. Raymond Rosenthal. New York: New American Library, 1966.

Lewis: An Anthology of His Prose. Ed. Eric W.F. Tomlin. London: Methuen, 1969.

Pound/Lewis: the letters of Ezra Pound and Wyndham Lewis. Ed. Timothy Materer. London: Faber, 1985.

The Essential Wyndham Lewis: An Introduction to his Works. Ed. Julian Symons. London: Vintage, 1991.

Secondary Sources

Books

Ayers, David. *Wyndham Lewis and Western Man*. Basingstoke: Macmillan, 1992.

Bridson, Gavin. *The Filibuster, A Study of the Political Ideas of Wyndham Lewis*. London: Cassell, 1972.

Chapman, Robert. *Wyndham Lewis: Fiction and Satires*. London: Vision Press, 1973.

Grigson, Geoffrey. *A Master of Our Time: A Study of Wyndham Lewis*. London, 1951; New York: Haskell House, 1972.

Jameson, Frederic. *Fables of Aggression: Wyndham Lewis, the Modernist as Fascist*. Berkeley: University of California Press, 1979.

Kenner, Hugh. *Wyndham Lewis*. Norfolk: New Directions, 1954.

Materer, Timothy. *Wyndham Lewis the Novelist*. Detroit: Wayne State University Press, 1976.

Meyers, Jeffrey, ed. *Wyndham Lewis: A Re-evaluation*. Montreal: McGill-Queens University Press; London: The Athlone Press, 1980.

———. *The Enemy: A Biography of Wyndham Lewis*. London: Routledge & Kegan Paul, 1980.

Porteus, Hugh Gordan. *Wyndham Lewis: A Discursive Exposition*. London: Desmond Harmsworth, 1932.

Pound, Omar S., and Phillip Grover. *Lewis: A Descriptive Bibliography*. Folkestone: Dawson, 1978.

Pritchard, William H. *Wyndham Lewis*. New York: Twayne, 1968.

Schenker, Daniel. *Wyndham Lewis: Religion and Modernism*. Tuscaloosa: Alabama University Press, 1992.

Wagner, Geoffrey. *Wyndham Lewis: A Portrait of the Artist as the Enemy*. New Haven: Yale University Press, and London: Routledge & Kegan Paul, 1957.

Articles and Chapters of Books

Bergonzi, Bernard. "Late Victorian to Modernist: 1870–1930." In *The Oxford Illustrated History of English Literature*. Ed. Pat Rogers. Oxford and New York: Oxford University Press, 1987, pp. 412–14.

Bertram, Anthony. "Lewis, Percy Wyndham." *Dictionary of National Biography*. Oxford: Oxford University Press, 1971, pp. 626–29.

Daiches, David. "Lewis, (Percy) Wyndham." In *The Penguin Companion to Literature: Britain and the Commonwealth*.

London: Penguin Books, 1971, pp. 316–17.

Gross, John, ed. *The Modern Movement*. (A *Time Literary Supplement* Companion). London: Harvill, 1992, pp. 101–14.

Henkle, Roger B. "The 'Advertised Self': Wyndham Lewis's Satire," *Novel*, 13 (1979): 95–108.

Jones, Edward T. "Wyndham Lewis." In *Encyclopedia of World Literature in the 20th Century*. Ed. Leonard S. Klein. Vol. 13 (rev. ed.). New York: Frederick Unger, 1983, pp. 65–69.

Kunitz, Stanley, and Howard Haycraft, eds. *Twentieth Century Authors: A Biographical Dictionary of Twentieth-Century Authors: A Biographical Dictionary of Modern Literature*. New York: H.W. Wilson, 1942, pp. 823–24.

Lafourcade, Bernard. "Afterword" in *The Snooty Baronet*. Santa Barbara: Black Sparrow Press, 1984.

Metscher, T. "Subversive, Radical and Revolutionary Traditions in European Literature between 1300 and the Age of Bunyan," *Zeitschrift fur Anglistik und Amerikanistik*, 1981.

Moretti, Franco. *Signs Taken for Wonders: Essays in the Sociology of Literary Forms*. London: Verso, 1983.

Phelps, Gilbert. *A Short Guide to the World Novel*. London: The Folio Society, 1987, p. 317.

Quennell, Peter. *A History of English Literature*. London: Weidenfeld and Nicholson, 1973, pp. 210–12.

Seymour-Smith, Martin, ed. *Novels and Novelists: A Guide to the World of Fiction*. London: Windward, 1980, pp. 174–75.

———. *Who's Who in Twentieth Century Literature*. London: Weidenfeld and Nicholson, 1973.

Stevenson, Lionel. *The History of the English Novel. Vol. XI—Yesterday and After*. New York: Barnes & Noble, 1967, pp. 163–83.

Symons, Julian. "The Thirties Novels," *Agenda* (Wyndham Lewis issue), 7/3–8/1 (Autumn–Winter 1969): 37–48.

Tomlin, Eric Walter Frederick. "Wyndham Lewis." In *Novelists and Prose Writers*. Ed. James Vinson. Great Writers of the English Language Series. London: Macmillan, 1979, pp. 738–41.

George E.C. Paton

Livings, Henry

Born: Prestwich, Lancashire, September 20, 1929

Education: University of Liverpool, 1948–1950

Marriage: Judith Frances Carter, April 2, 1957; two children

Biography

Henry Livings's entrance into life was nowhere as controversial as his entrance into a career as a dramatist. He was born in Prestwich, Lancashire on September 20, 1929, the son of George Livings (a shop manager) and Dorothy Buckley Livings. He attended Park View Primary School from 1935 to 1939 and Stand Grammar School from 1940 to 1945, where he won a scholarship to the University of Liverpool. Livings concentrated on Hispanic studies while at Liverpool from 1948 to 1950. After leaving the university, he spent two years (1950 to 1952) fulfilling his National Service obligation as a member of the Royal Air Force, during which time he served as a cook. He was engaged in a series of varied jobs until he became interested in the theater; his first experience as an actor was in the roles of Curio and Sebastian in William Shakespeare's *Twelfth Night* at the Century Mobile theater in Hinckley, Leicestershire, in February 1954. In May 1956, as a member of Joan Littlewood's Theater Workshop company at the Theatre Royal, Stratford, East London, Livings played Prisoner C in Brendan Behan's *The Quare Fellow*.

The dramatist-to-be's first London theatrical experience was to have a large impact on his life, for Littlewood introduced him to a new perspective on the theater, and the influence of Behan's writing would be seen in Livings's own work. As he says, "Littlewood opened out my understanding of the art more than any other has done. Her illuminations of the relevance of the theater to life and society (they coincide), and to the basic teaching of [Konstantin] Stanislavsky, are still fundamental to me." Another influence on Livings's life was also drawn from Littlewood's troupe—Judith Frances "Franny" Carter, a fellow actress with the company whom the writer married on April 2, 1957. The couple has a son, Toby, and a daughter, Maria.

Livings's first play, *Jack's Horrible Luck*, was written in 1958, but it was not produced until 1961 when it was televised by the BBC. In the meantime, the dramatist's *Stop It, Whoever You Are* was produced at the Arts Theatre in London on February 15, 1961. There was a considerable amount of critical bickering about the value of the play, but Livings received the *Evening Standard* Award in 1961 for the work. This encouraged him to actively pursue a profession as a writer, and *Big Soft Nellie*, originally entitled *Thacred Nit*, was produced on September 18, 1961. Then, *Nil Carborundum*, a play based on the author's RAF experiences, attracted considerable attention when it was produced by the Royal Shakespeare Company as part of an experimental season at the Arts Theatre on April 12, 1962. Ironically, *Kelly's Eye*, mounted at the Royal Court Theatre on June 12, 1963, was a straightforward drama and some critics, Kenneth Tynan among them, who had applauded Livings's farces up to that time were disappointed by the seriousness of this piece (which won the Britannica Award, given by *Encyclopedia Britannica*, for 1965).

On October 29, 1964, *Eh?* opened at the Aldwych Theatre in London with David Warner in the lead role. The drama subsequently was staged at the Circle in the Square in New York beginning October 16, 1966, and starring Dustin Hoffman. Livings won the 1966 Obie Award for the play. This off-Broadway run (232 performances) brought Livings to the attention of American audiences. A number of plays followed: *The Little Mrs. Foster Show* (November 8, 1966; Liverpool); *Good Grief!*, a collection of one-acts and sketches including: *After the Last Lamp*, *You're Free*, *Variable Lengths*, *Pie-Eating Contest*, *Does It Make Your Cheeks Ache?* and *The Reasons for Flying* (July 18, 1967; Manchester); *Honour and Offer* (November 21, 1968; Playhouse in the Park, Cincinnati); *The Gamecock* (October 1969; Manchester); *Rattel* (October 1969; Manchester); *Conciliation* (March 1970; Lincoln); *The Boggart* (1970; Birmingham); *Beewine* (1970; Birmingham); *The Rifle Volunteer* (1970; Birmingham); *The ffinest ffamily in the Land* (June 16, 1970; Lincoln); *Tiddles* (November 1970; Birmingham); *Mushrooms and Toadstools* (1970; London); *Brainscrew* (1971; Birmingham); *This Jockey Drives Late Nights* (January 27, 1972; Birmingham); *The Rent Man* (April 1972; Stoke-on-Trent); *Cinderella* (September 1972; Stoke-on-Trent); *The Tailor's Britches* (January 1973; Stoke-on-Trent); *Jug* (November 1975; Nottingham); *Shuttlecock* (May 1976; London); and *Tom Thumb* (December 1979; London). Many of these plays have been published.

Livings has also been very active in writing for television and radio, and he has produced a screenplay version of *Eh?* (*Work Is a Four-Letter Word*, Cavalcade Films-Universal, 1968), some nonfiction, and more recently some short fiction.

Literary Analysis

Livings has been variously described as an Absurdist, an Angry Young Man, and a member of the "kitchen sink" school. His plays are about the British working class, and the dramatist tends to pay little attention to the traditional elements of plot and character development. His prime intent seems to be to make his audience laugh, and the vices of the farce are the means by which he attains his goal. Furthermore, the author captures the language patterns of the working class, and he shares with his contemporaries Samuel Beckett and Harold Pinter a distrust of the simple, overblown exposition of the well-made play and Shavian comedies.

Although not performed until after *Stop It, Whoever You Are*, the televised *Jack's Horrible Luck* is a picaresque tale of Jack, a naive young sailor on shore leave in Liverpool. A combination of broad farce and fantasy, the comedy is a series of episodes strung together in what John Russell Taylor has called a "parable-in-farce-technique" which takes the form of Jack's quest for a semimythical cafe called Uncle Joe's. Interestingly, even this slight framework was not included in the original, as the plot was added at the suggestion of the BBC.

Stop It, Whoever You Are, Livings's first successful theatrical venture, exemplifies his approach to playwriting. As he has said, "I had entirely theatrical tools to use. I chose simple stories and corny situations because I didn't want to be wasting time going forward along a single track when I could see a way of covering St. Pancras Station. And I broke down the story into 'units' of about ten minutes each—about as long, I reckoned, as you can hold a new situation clearly and totally in mind."

The play is divided into five scenes, each of which is a self-contained, though related, farcical skit. The protagonist, William Perkin Warbeck, whose name derives from that of an unsuccessful late-fifteenth-century pretender to the English throne, works as a lavatory attendant in a factory. The plot, such as it is, unfolds as Warbeck is beaten up by two young apprentices whom he thinks are homosexuals, and then he is raped by a local Lolita (a buxom fourteen-year-old named Marilyn Arbuckle). Caught by the police during this latter act, he is arrested. Meanwhile, alderman Michael Oglethorpe is in charge of the dedication ceremony of a nearby municipal library and arts complex. Warbeck attempts to exact revenge on Oglethorpe, his detested landlord, but accidentally soaks his employer and one-time military commander Captain Bootl, a person whom he regards highly. In the final scene, Warbeck arrives home and drops dead at his wife's feet. A mystical Mrs. Arbuckle, played by the same actor who played Warbeck, enters and, looking "like Warbeck in drag," serves as a vehicle through which the dead Warbeck speaks to his wife: "You can do whatever you've a fancy to do. I've been a nuisance all my life. To you, me, and everybody—and I haven't had much joy of it, I can tell you—But I might have gone down to the grave not knowing what a hairy old baboon I was. I didn't. I did it. I'm entirely dead now, and you can heap words on me. You can heap six foot of dirt on me, for that matter. But I shall have been entirely alive." Warbeck's wife, Rose, shouts, "I can't stand it! You're driving me out of my mind; it's enough! Shut up shut up shut up! Whoever you are, stop it!" The play ends when everything is blown up with the explosion of a leaky gas pipe.

Taylor has pointed out that in *Big Soft Nellie,* another plotless farce, Livings comes close to the work of Ann Jellicoe. *Big Soft Nellie* is about Stanley, a mother's boy who is the butt of jokes played by the employees of an electrical appliances shop. Livings's ability to capture working-class cadences and the irony of his humor is demonstrated in an exchange between Marris, the shop owner, and a police sargeant:

> MARRIS: Do you ever get those anxieties coming on unexpectedly? No, I don't suppose you do.
> SARGEANT: Don't you be surprised.
> MARRIS: So we can expect you to grace the British Legion very shortly?
> SARGEANT: Thank you. I think I'd better just talk to the staff to wind this business up. Don't want to leave them with the idea that they've got away with everything. [*He turns to the door where Benny and Stanley stand pale and resigned.*] Ouf!

> MARRIS: Yes, they gave me a bit of a start I'll admit.
> SARGEANT: They'd gone clean out of my mind. Why don't they go and do something?
> MARRIS: I don't know. Perhaps they can't think of anything suitable.
> SARGEANT: Eerie, aren't they? That's how I imagine condemned men look, on the morning.
> MARRIS: Funny how these anxieties come on unexpectedly, isn't it?

Nil Carborundum, Livings's comedy about life in the peacetime armed services, followed. Staged at the Arts Theatre immediately after Arnold Wesker's *Chips With Everything, Nil Carborundum* provides an interesting contrast. In the Wesker play, peacetime service life is a microcosm of the outside world; for Livings, peacetime service life is a means of escaping from reality into fantasy. In the Livings play Harrison, a new cook, comes into contact with stereotyped servicemen. The commanding officer and Harrison appear to be the only sane men among the bunch.

While some critics consider *Nil Carborundum* to be the dramatist's best work, others argue that *Eh?* is superior. Like Charlie Chaplin in *Modern Times,* the hero of *Eh?*, Valentine Brose, is literally caught up in the machinery of a large, modern factory. The farce grows out of the character of this boiler-room attendant, and once again there is virtually no plot line. Val becomes more concerned with his hallucinogenic mushrooms than with the boilers, and the play ends explosively. As in the works of N.F. Simpson, farce and fantasy fuse in Livings.

Most of the techniques that Livings uses to create humor in his plays can be found in *Eh?* An obvious starting point is with characterization. In his cast of characters, Livings describes Valentine as: "pale and totally lacking in human fire. He behaves excitedly on occasion, even frenetically, and he wears gaudy cheap clothes with some dash; but he himself stays still and unaffected in the core of the fireworks. It's as if he were giving a performance of some character he's dreamed up, and his pale eyes wander in search of effect even in his apparently wildest moments."

Throughout the farce Valentine's actions support the author's description—his mushroom-growing activities, his relationship with

Betty, his behavior with his co-workers are all of a piece. For example, in act 1 Valentine is interviewed for a position by Price, the works manager:

> PRICE: Are you some kind of a nit?
> VAL: Erm, yes, I think so.
> PRICE: That gear, for instance, you'd a fooled me if you'd said you'd left your guitar outside.
> VAL: I came, didn't I? Oh, I don't mind you calling me a nit that's all right. That is, I don't mind so long as I get the post. Of course, if I don't I'll half-murder you.
> PRICE (stares): You what?
> He turns to draw MRS MURRAY to one side, gazing vaguely at VAL, who continues calmly.
> VAL: I'll get you, don't you worry. Some night when you're going for your bus. Scuffle, then clunk. There won't be much blood to speak of, just an agony and an aching, and not being able to drag yourself along the wet pavement. (10)

The humor comes from the casualness of the non sequitur, coupled with the absolute shocking inappropriateness of the reply.

Elsewhere Mrs. Murray and Price discuss Valentine's thirty-four references. One of the references is purportedly by a Mr. Frint who says that Valentine is "forsaking a brilliant academic future for a career in the Foreign Office" (30). An examination of the letter suggests that Valentine has erased the word "satisfactory" and substituted the word "brilliant." Furthermore, when contacted, Mr. Frint admits to having had a student named Valentine Brose at one time, but he also claims not to have the "faintest recollection" of him. Another reference, one related to Mr. Oliver Broad, J.P., consists of two newspaper clippings. The first is a disclaimer: Mr. V. Brose of 2 Holy Bones is not the V. Brose whose prosecution for vagrancy was reported in the previous day's news. The audience can assume that the V. Brose of 2 Holy Bones is not Valentine. The second clipping is a report on the failure of the police to establish a case against V. Brose for depositing offensive matter in a public thoroughfare, though Brose was fined for obstruction by Broad, the Justice of the Peace. Here the humor lies in the invalidity of the references and what the references reveal about Valentine—apparently revelations the nature of which he is unaware.

The play opens with an announcement over the factory loudspeaker that sets the tone for what is to follow. "I have a message here from the bleach croft," says the speaker, "Bleach croft say will all workers look out for a black cat, or maybe white" ([9]). The humor obviously comes from the understated, and seemingly tacked on, logical twist at the end of the announcement. The surprise is enhanced by the straight-faced assumption of an unspoken, unlikely, and perhaps even impossible event—that the cat may have gotten into the croft and been bleached white.

A sense of the ludicrous is evident in Livings's humor. At one point Val complains about the Labor Exchange: "it's just this getting up in the morning. I've missed my dole for the last twelve weeks because of that. They put my time for eleven o'clock. Dirty trick" (16). He is upset because he is expected to be at the labor office at such an early hour to collect his unemployment. Of course, if he were working, he would have had to be at work hours earlier.

Then, when Price observes that Val would be able to get there on time with his new job because it is at night, Val thinks that such an arrangement might be to his benefit since he could use two unemployment cards. After all, he says, "I shall want something behind me in case I can't get up in the morning at night as well." This statement is followed immediately by his noticing the words "Starter button" on the boiler. "What does it start?" he asks. On the one hand the answer to the question is patently obvious—it starts the boiler. On the other hand, in the world that Valentine inhabits, nothing can be taken for granted, as he has already demonstrated in his conversation with Price. In fact, he admits that he is "not very keen on work," as though that concept had not already been made clear (18). Valentine is serious when he informs Price about his attitude toward work.

Valentine also displays a sense of humor. When Price discovers the box of mushrooms, Valentine denies that they are mushrooms: "No. That's the maker's name. Capitals. Capital M, capital U, SHROOMS: Mervyn Uhlrich Shrooms, seed merchant" (23). The ridiculousness of his contention that the word is actually a name is compounded by the name that he pretends that it represents.

As is typical in a farce, some of the humor is physically based, slapstick in fact: "VAL tries again to see that gauge from ground level. No good. He races to the ladder and places it in a better position. The safety valve splutters and then begins to give off a ferocious blast of steam. VAL mounts the ladder at a fair lick and then straight down and then up again. . . . The ladder slides away, leaving him spread-eagled on the top. He leaps to his feet and hops frantically from one foot to the other as each hots up on the man-hole. He turns about, strips off his jacket, toboggans down . . . "(25). On a similar note, Valentine plays a good portion of act 2 wearing a false nose. Another bit of schtick, right out of the English music hall and burlesque, comes when Betty tries to remove Valentine's clothes while he tries to remain dressed, a scene that is sure to have the audience laughing, in part because of the reversal of stereotypical male/female sexual roles and in part because of the sight of the flying fingers:

> [Betty] *undoes the bottom button of his shirt and pulls it open a little.*
> VAL: Well, it's the best part really, isn't it?
> *He does up the bottom button of his shirt and tucks it in.*
> BETTY (*undoing the next button*): Is there?
> VAL (*doing it up*): Yes.
> BETTY: This'll do me.
> *Undoes the third button.*
> VAL: I've thought of everything.
> *Does up the third button.*
> BETTY (*undoing the fourth button*): I'll bet you have.
> VAL (*doing up the fourth button*): I'm thinking of everything now.
> BETTY (*down to the bottom button again*): So am I. (48)

Livings uses physical actions to startle his audience as well. In act 2, just as the Reverend Mort reaches a climactic statement about tyrannosaurus in his declamation on evolution, "A great saurian roar reverberates through the auditorium" (53). Moments later, with Valentine having declared "I believe in God!" the roar is heard again and then "A door swings and bangs in the auditorium" (54).

Finally, there are elements of wit and word play in *Eh?* too. When Mrs. Murray mentions the subconscious, Valentine exhibits his knowledge of Freudianism, but as might be expected with Livings, he goes beyond the norm. First,

Valentine notes that the subconscious is called the Id. Then he offers his analysis of the word's derivation: "Latin: id, meaning 'that.' Hence 'id-iot,' meaning 'that idiot.' Also 'idio-tic': that twitching idiot" (63).

The writer is also known for his twelve *Pongo Plays*, most of which have been staged outside London. Based on folk tales and Japanese Kyogen plays, these dramas are essentially short sketches about Sam Pongo, a simple, sharp-witted weaver from Lancashire who is reminiscent of Charles Dickens's Sam Weller, the wily servant of Mr. Pickwick. Typically portrayed as a foil for blustering masters and *milos glorioso* military types, Pongo survives Sancho Panza-like by employing his common sense. Michael J. Weimer calls Pongo Livings's "most fertile creation."

Summary

Henry Livings's works have been the source of great critical disagreement. Nearing the end of his playwriting career, he has become noted, especially in the regional theaters of England, for his farces. In these plays he portrays members of the English working class interacting in humorous ways but at the same time demonstrating that they are a hard-working, proud, and robust people who are content with being themselves. Livings's goal has been to present his characters in ways that would bring laughter, and in this he has succeeded admirably.

Selected Bibliography

Primary Sources

Plays
Stop It, Whoever You Are, produced 1961. In *New English Dramatists 5*, Harmondsworth: Penguin Books, 1962.
Big Soft Nellie, produced 1961; London: Methuen, 1961; New York: Hill & Wang, 1964.
Nil Carborundum, produced 1962. In *New English Dramatists 6*, Harmondsworth: Penguin Books, 1963.
Kelly's Eye, produced 1963; London: Methuen, 1963; New York: Hill & Wang, 1964.
Kelly's Eye and Other Plays. London: Methuen, 1964. Includes *Big Soft Nellie*.
Eh? produced 1964; London: Eyre-Methuen, 1964; London: Methuen, 1965; New York: Hill & Wang, 1967.
The Little Mrs. Foster Show, produced 1966;

London: Methuen, 1969.

Good Grief! produced 1967; London: Methuen, 1968. One-acts and sketches: *After the Last Lamp, You're Free, Variable Lengths, Pie-Eating Contest, Does It Make Your Cheeks Ache?,* and *The Reasons for Flying.*

Honour and Offer, produced 1968; London: Methuen, 1969.

The Gamecock, produced 1969. In *Pongo Plays 1–6: Six Short Plays.* London: Methuen, 1971.

Rattel, produced 1969. In *Pongo Plays 1–6: Six Short Plays.* London: Methuen, 1971.

Variable Lengths and Longer: An Hour of Embarrassment, produced 1969. In *Good Grief!* London: Methuen, 1968. Includes *The Reasons for Flying* and *Does It Make Your Cheeks Ache?*

The Boggart, produced 1970. In *Pongo Plays 1–6: Six Short Plays.* London: Methuen, 1971.

Conciliation, produced 1970. In *Pongo Plays 1–6: Six Short Plays.* London: Methuen, 1971.

The Rifle Volunteer, produced 1970. In *Pongo Plays 1–6: Six Short Plays.* London: Methuen, 1971.

Beewine, produced 1970. In *Pongo Plays 1–6: Six Short Plays.* London: Methuen, 1971.

The ffinest ffamily in the Land, produced 1970; London: Methuen, 1973.

You're Free, produced 1970.

Mushrooms and Toadstools, produced 1970. In *Six More Pongo Plays (Including Two for Children).* London: Methuen, 1974.

Tiddles, produced 1970. In *Six More Pongo Plays (Including Two for Children).* London: Methuen, 1974.

Brainscrew, produced 1971. In *Second Playbill 3.* Ed. Alan Durband. London: Hutchinson, 1973.

Pongo Plays 1–6: Six Short Plays. London: Methuen, 1971; rev. ed. 1976. Includes *The Gamecock, Rattel, The Boggart, Beewine, The Rifle Volunteer,* and *Conciliation.*

This Jockey Drives Late Nights: a play from The Power of Darkness by Leo Tolstoy, produced 1972; London: Methuen, 1972, 1976. Adaptation of Leo Tolstoy's play *The Power of Darkness.*

Daft Sam, produced 1972 (televised); produced 1976. In *Six More Pongo Plays (Including Two for Children).* London: Eyre Methuen, 1974.

The Rent Man, produced 1972. In *Six More Pongo Plays (Including Two for Children).* London: Methuen, 1974.

Cinderella: A Likely Tale, produced 1972; published 1976. Adaptation of Charles Perrault's story.

The Tailor's Britches, produced 1973. In *Six More Pongo Plays (Including Two for Children).* London: Methuen, 1974.

Glorious Miles, produced 1973 (televised); produced 1975.

Jonah, produced 1974; published 1975.

Six More Pongo Plays (Including Two for Children). London: Methuen, 1974. Includes *Tiddles, The Rent Man, The Ink-Smeared Lady, The Tailor's Britches, Daft Sam,* and *Mushrooms and Toadstools.*

Jack and the Beanstalk, produced 1974. Music by Alan Glasgow.

Jug, produced 1975. Adaptation of Heinrich von Kleist's play *The Broken Jug.*

Shuttlecock, produced 1976.

The Astounding Adventures of Tom Thumb, produced 1979. Children's play.

Radio Plays

The Day Dumbfounded Got His Pylon, produced 1963; staged 1965; published 1967.

Worth a Hearing: A Collection of Radio Plays, 1967.

"After the Last Lamp." Adaptations of Hauptmann's "The Weavers" and Ibsen's "An Enemy of the People."

Screenplays

Work Is a Four-Letter Word. Cavalcade Films-Universal, 1968. Adaptation of *Eh?*

Teleplays

The Arson Squad, 1961.

Jack's Horrible Luck, 1961.

There's No Room for You Here for a Start, 1963.

A Right Crusader, 1963.

Brainscrew, 1966.

GRUP, 1970.

Shuttlecock, 1976.

The Game, 1977. Adaptation of Harold Brighouse's play.

The Mayor's Charity, 1977.
Two Days That Shook the Branch, 1978.
We Had Some Happy Hours, 1981.

Fiction

Big Soft Nellie. London: Methuen, 1961; New York: Hill & Wang, 1964.

Kelly's Eye. London: Methuen, 1963; New York: Hill & Wang, 1964.

Eh? London: Methuen, 1965; New York: Hill & Wang, 1967.

Good Grief! London: Methuen, 1968. Includes *After the Last Lamp, You're Free, Variable Lengths, Pie-Eating Contest, Does It Make Your Cheeks Ache?* and *The Reasons for Flying*.

The Little Mrs. Foster Show. London: Methuen, 1969.

Honour and Offer. London: Methuen, 1969.

Pongo Plays 1–6: Six Short Plays. London: Methuen, 1971; rev. ed. 1976. Includes *The Gamecock, Rattel, Conciliation, The Boggart, Beewine,* and *The Rifle Volunteer*.

This Jockey Drives Late Nights: A Play from The Power of Darkness by Leo Tolstoy. London: Methuen, 1972.

The ffinest ffamily in the Land. London: Methuen, 1973.

Six More Pongo Plays (Including Two for Children). London: Methuen, 1974. Includes *Tiddles, The Rent Man, The Ink-Smeared Lady, The Tailor's Britches, Daft Sam,* and *Mushrooms and Toadstools*.

Non-Fiction

That the medals and the baton be put on view: The story of a village band, 1875–1975. London: David & Charles, 1975.

Short Fiction
Pennine Tales, 1983.

Secondary Sources

Anonymous. "Henry Livings." In *Contemporary Authors*. Ed. Clare Kinsman. Detroit: Gale, 1975. Vol. 13–16, p. 271.

Barnes, Philip. *A Companion to Post-War British Theatre*. New York: Barnes & Noble, 1986, pp. 141–72. Brief summary of life and works.

Bigsby, C.W.E. "Henry Livings." In *Contemporary Dramatists*. Ed. James Vinson. New York: St. Martin's Press, 1982.

Ferris, Paul. "Finding Fresh Writers." *Observer* (London, October 13, 1963): 23.

Giannetti, Louis D. "Henry Livings: A Neglected Voice in the New Drama." *Modern Drama*, 12 (1969): 38–48.

Glover, William. "No 'Protest' Plays: Dramatist Makes Points With Laughs." *Newark Sunday News* (August 7, 1966): VI: E4.

Hunt, Hugh, et al., eds. *The Revels History of Drama in English, Volume VII, 1880 to the Present Day*. Ed. Clifford Leech and T.W. Craik. New York: Harper and Row, 1979.

Nightingale, Benedict. "Rough Justice." *New Statesman* (November 21, 1975): 651–52. Review of *Jug*.

Pasolli, Robert. "Non-Brooding Mr. Livings: The Eccentric Is the Real." *Village Voice* (July 14, 1966): 19–20.

Rusinko, Susan. *British Drama 1950 to the Present: A Critical History*. Boston: Twayne, 1989, pp. 169–72. Includes Livings in her chapter on working-class writers.

Taylor, John Russell. *The Angry Theatre: New British Drama*. New York: Hill & Wang, 1969, pp. 286–300. An early, serious look at Livings's work by a major critic.

———. "The Human Dilemma." *Plays and Players*, 10 (June 1963): 24–26.

Taylor, Thomas J. "Henry Livings." In *Critical Survey of Drama*. Ed. Frank N. Magill. Englewood Cliffs, NJ: Salem Press, 1985, pp. 1151–57. Brief overview of life and works.

Thomson, Peter, ed. "Henry Livings and the Accessible Theatre." In *Western popular theater: the proceedings of a symposium sponsored by the Manchester University Department of Drama*. Ed. David Mayer and Kenneth Richards. London: Methuen, 1980.

Wakeman, John, ed. *World Authors 1950–1970*. New York: H.W. Wilson, 1975.

Weimer, Michael J. "Henry Livings." In *Dictionary of Literary Biography, Volume XIII: British Dramatists Since World War II, Part 1*, 1982, pp. 305–10. Overview and analysis of canon in a biographical context.

Steven H. Gale

Lodge, David

Born: London, January 28, 1935

Education: St. Joseph's Academy, Blackheath; University College, University of London, B.A. (First-class Honours), 1955; M.A., 1959; University of Birmingham, Ph.D., 1967

Marriage: Mary Frances Jacob, May 16, 1959; three children

Biography

David Lodge was born in London on January 28, 1935, the son of William Frederick Lodge, a professional musician who played in dance bands (during the war he was an Air Force musician), and Rosalie Marie Murphy Lodge, a Roman Catholic of Irish-Belgian descent. He has described his family as "lower-middle-class-London-suburban."[1] He belonged to that generation of Englishmen and women whose childhood and adolescence were influenced by the Second World War and the following years of austerity. He is a spokesman for both his generation and for a specific subset of it, the minority Roman Catholic population that in the decades following the war experienced changes in its religious life which were as far-reaching as those experienced in the national life. On a yet more personal level Lodge has experienced other significant changes: born in a lower-middle-class family with limited financial resources, he has, by virtue of his scholarship and writing ability—and by the happenstance of coming of age in the flush years of the British meritocracy—brought himself to the forefront of the academic and artistic worlds. These changes in the social and personal aspects of his life, which themselves reflect changes in the British national life, lie behind the attitudes that he expresses in his novels.

Like so many children of his generation, Lodge was an evacuee during the war years, and his consistent schooling only began in 1945 when he was ten years old and was enrolled in St. Joseph's Academy, Blackheath, a grant-aided grammar school taught by members of the Roman Catholic order of the Delasalles. His academic success there won him a place in 1952 at University College of the University of London, where he was one of the youngest and most brilliant of his entering class. He was a student in the English language and literature program and earned a First-Class Honours B.A. in 1955.

As an undergraduate, Lodge was an active member of the Roman Catholic student group where a fellow student was Mary Frances Jacob. They married on May 16, 1959. Between his graduation and marriage, Lodge served his compulsory two years—from 1955 to 1957—of military service in the Royal Armored Corps; he returned to University College, London, in 1957 for the two-year M.A. program in English literature. At that time the M.A. at the University of London was a research degree. Lodge wrote a thesis entitled "Catholic Fiction Since the Oxford Movement: Its Literary Form and Religious Content." He drew upon this work for several of his later professional writings. From 1959 to 1960, Lodge worked for the British Council's Overseas Students Center in London. In 1960, the University of Birmingham gave him a teaching appointment in the English Department as Lecturer. He remained there for his entire professional career. In 1967, Birmingham awarded him a Ph.D. He was advanced to Senior Lecturer in 1971 and to Reader in 1973. He was named Professor of Modern English Literature in 1976 and retired in 1987. During his professional career, he received many honors and served as a visiting professor at other British and American universities. Of particular importance to his fiction were the visits that he made to the United States from 1964 through 1965 as the Harkness Commonwealth Fellow and 1968 through 1969 as a visiting Associate Professor at the University of California (Berkeley), where he saw at first hand the student revolution. During the 1970s and '80s, he was a frequent speaker at literary conferences as well as in university courses.

Literary Analysis

Lodge has been one of the most prolific writers of his generation. His literary output (which continues in his retirement) falls into two main categories, scholarly writings and creative work in both fiction and drama. As a scholar of English literature he has published in many academic forms. He is the author of important critical essays, monographs, and book-length studies, including *Language of Fiction: Essays in Criticism and Verbal Analysis of the English Novel* (1966), *The Novelist at the Crossroads and Other Essays on Fiction and Criticism* (1971), *The Modes of Modern Writing: Metaphor, Metonymy, and the Typology of Modern Literature* (1977), *Working with Structuralism: Essays and Reviews on Nineteenth and Twentieth-Century Literature* (1981), *Write On: Occasional Essays, 1965–1985* (1986), *After*

Bakhtin: Essays on Fiction and Criticism (1990), and *The Art of Fiction* (1993). He has written about writers in the Catholic tradition in *About Catholic Authors* (1957), *Graham Greene* (1966), and *Evelyn Waugh* (1971). He has edited *Jane Austen's Emma: A Casebook* (1968), *Twentieth Century Literary Criticism* (1972), and *Modern Criticism and Theory* (1988). He has specialized in the study of fiction and perhaps knows as much—or more—about the multiple forms of literary theory as anyone alive.

In his role as creative artist he has published eight novels (several of them have been televised), and he has also written plays and collaborated on other theatrical productions. Since his writings for the theater and television have not been published, they are not included in this survey. Although his academic work appears to lie outside the narrow consideration of him as a "humorist," the student of his fiction will find that he often writes his novels so that they embody the critical theories which he discusses in his professional writings and he bases the comedy in his humorous novels on his specialized knowledge of English literature which stands behind his scholarly works. Because he is one of the foremost critics of fiction in his generation, students of his novels and stories must always be uncertain as to whether they can understand a given work solely in terms of what it appears to be, or whether they must look for a secondary motive, some insidious subtext that alters the meaning of the work.

Lodge's novels include *The Picturegoers* (1960), *Ginger, You're Barmy* (1962), *The British Museum Is Falling Down* (1965), *Out of the Shelter* (1970), *Changing Places: A Tale of Two Campuses* (1975), *How Far Can You Go?* (1980; published in America under the title *Souls and Bodies*), *Small World* (1984), *Nice Work* (1988), and *Paradise News* (1991). Although they are linked by their recognizable origins in Lodge's personal experiences, the novels fall into two groups. The author himself defined the first of these in 1989, specifying that *The Picturegoers*, *Ginger, You're Barmy*, and *Out of the Shelter* are "'serious' realistic novel[s] in which comedy is an incidental rather than a structural element, and metafictional games and stylistic experiment are not allowed to disturb the illusion of life."[2] His latest novels, *Nice Work* and *Paradise News*, also belong to this group.

In those novels Lodge asserts his position as a novelist in the realistic tradition, making use of humor only when it is pertinent to the real life situations that concern him. In *The Picturegoers* he centers his story upon the spiritual development of a lapsed Catholic, Mark Underwood, a youthful student of English literature. Mark boards with a Roman Catholic family, the Mallorys, who live in a South London suburb. The novel begins with Mark lusting for the devout Clare Mallory; it concludes with the two young people in opposite roles, Clare willing to accept Mark, but he now resolved to enter the priesthood. These realistic characters define themselves through their reactions to the cinema which along with the local Catholic church forms the center of their lives. The writing is polished and the manipulation of the narrative reflects a skill that is not often found in a first novel.

The Picturegoers and *Ginger, You're Barmy* are essentially taken from Lodge's own experiences and are structured around the personal development of their main characters, while Lodge's later and more successfully organized novels take their structure from exterior forms, generally other literary works. *Ginger, You're Barmy* also represents the specific manifestation of the *Bildungsroman* among male British writers in the fifteen years following the end of World War II, for it is an account of the military service that was then required of almost all young Britons. While some of these military tales are humorous—Auberon Waugh, for example, took over his father's techniques and attitudes and managed to create a pastiche of Evelyn Waugh's satire in *The Foxglove Saga* (1960)—Lodge's novel rarely goes beyond a realistic treatment of the material derived from his period of National Service.

His surrogate persona in *Ginger, You're Barmy* is Jon Browne, a young intellectual who has just received his First-Class B.A. and who must now fulfill his military obligation. Working from his own experiences, the novelist describes the inanities of military training and the tensions that arise when different classes of young men are forced to live together. Browne forms a friendship with another University man, although he ultimately takes the other's girl and even betrays him. Lodge's interest is in developing the character of Browne from that of a cynical, unattached intellectual into that of a caring human being, but unfortunately the manipulation of the plot and the actions of the main characters rob the development of its credibility. Critics have called attention to the similarities between this novel and various works by Graham Greene, *The Quiet American* offering the closest parallels. Lodge's most important accomplishment in the book is the depiction of the mood of England in the 1950s and of its young men as they reluctantly fulfill their National Service obligations. But since the mood of the period was as austere as its economics, the novel is perhaps the most depressing of all of the author's fiction and gives little suggestion that the novelist might achieve fame as a humorist.

Lodge points out in his "Introduction" to the revised edition of *Out of the Shelter*, his fourth novel, that it "is probably the most autobiographical" of his volumes (ix). In it he uses personal experiences that predate his time at the university and in the military. The novel concerns the not-often-commented-upon situation of the American and British civilians who were employed by the American Army of Occupation in Germany in the decade or so following World War II. The writer specifically contrasts the daily life of the average Englishman in 1951 with that of the Americans living in occupied Germany; the novel provides accurate documentation concerning post-war European life and the role which the Army of Occupation and its civilian personnel played in that life. As in the earlier novels, Lodge demonstrates his ability not only to observe the social situation accurately but also to re-create the public attitudes of the time. He tells the story through the consciousness of the central character Timothy, a rapidly maturing sixteen-year-old. Although Timothy's observations often call forth a wry or sardonic smile from the reader, they spring from the novelist's desire to create a realistic character and not from any attempt to be funny at the character's expense.

Yet, *Out of the Shelter* was written after Lodge had discovered in his third novel, *The British Museum Is Falling Down*, how his academic knowledge might be incorporated in his fictional creations. By his own testimony he consciously combined "the *Bildungsroman* . . . and the Jamesian 'international' novel of conflicting ethical and cultural codes. James Joyce's *A Portrait of the Artist as a Young Man* and Henry James's *The Ambassadors* are its most obvious literary models."[3] Relying upon these literary antecedents, Lodge did not strive to create humor—indeed, he deliberately controlled the comedy in the work by rigidly holding to the point of view of the central character—but the contrast between the innocent, sheltered sixteen-year-old narrator and the situations in which he finds himself allows Lodge to express his comic view of life. He sympathetically describes Timothy's sexual encounters with the older American secretary and with the teen-aged Gloria Jean; and while never allowing the reader to laugh at Timothy, he draws a convincing and amusing image of the teenage male body with its seemingly uncontrollable ejaculations.

These realistic novels continued in 1988 with *Nice Work,* which, like many other contemporary post-war novels in which realistic views of English life are presented, is set in the industrial north. Again Lodge presents characters who are thrust into an unfamiliar world and must adapt to the new situation: their reactions provide the reader with a fresh insight into both their personalities and the social situation that the novelist is investigating. Thus, Robyn Penrose, a female lecturer in the English Department of the local university, is given the dubious honor of being the government-mandated link between the educational establishment and the local industry. She is asked to be the "shadow" of Victor Wilcox, the Managing Director of J. Pringle & Sons, a local foundry, and for several months she spends one day a week with him as part of the government-sponsored scheme. Then the situation is reversed, and the executive becomes her shadow, staying at her side as she lectures, conducts tutorials, and interviews students. The contrasting attitudes of the academic in the workplace and the businessman in the academy offer considerable opportunities for humor, but, like any traditional English novelist, in *Nice Work* Lodge is primarily concerned with the evolving personalities of the two main characters. He makes them into well-rounded figures, with a strong supporting cast of flat, but believable characters, and essentially the novel provides a thoughtful, even insightful consideration of contemporary British life.

Paradise News offers further evidence of Lodge's desire to write novels with a larger frame of reference than that of his comedies of university life. Again his protagonist is a Roman Catholic male with religious doubts. Bernard Walsh is an excommunicated priest who has left the priesthood after Daphne, a thirty-five-year-old nurse, falls in love with him, and his religious doubts grow stronger than his faith. But he is physically unable to consummate their relationship. He has lost his faith, yet he supports himself by lecturing on theology at a training college. He receives a phone call from his father's sister Ursula, a divorced G.I. bride whose Irish family has turned its back upon her and who, now in her seventies and dying of cancer in Hawaii, wants to be reconciled with them. She pays for Bernard and his father to fly out to her. Since the cheapest flight to Hawaii is part of a package tour, Lodge can set up his paradoxical situation: the Walshes go to visit a dying woman who longs for a heavenly paradise in the company of tourists who are seeking the joys of an earthly paradise.

Although true to life, *Paradise News* is shaped by the novelist's comic vision of life. He painstakingly resolves the problems of all of the characters—both major and minor—on the tour: Bernard finds fulfilling love and a sexual relationship with Yolande, the soon-to-be-divorced wife of a university professor; Ursula dies at peace with the world and her family, and in the physical comfort that a single share of IBM stock, purchased in 1952 and never drawn upon, can provide; and her family profits from the IBM largesse which Ursula leaves to them.

As he does in so many of his other novels, Lodge structures *Paradise News* upon a basic literary device, in this case, the pilgrimage. Sheldrake, the anthropologist on the tour, explains, "'sightseeing is a substitute for religious ritual. The sightseeing tour [can be seen] as secular pilgrimage.'"[4] Lodge employs traditional storytelling tactics that are found in his previous novels: the diary that reveals the story which could not otherwise be plausibly reported, excerpts from letters, as well as miscellaneous notes and reports. Underlying the interesting characters and well-plotted incidents is his constant preoccupation with man's journey through life and hope of a paradise in the afterlife. *Paradise News* is essentially a moral tale in which the author attempts to communicate a meaningful story to the general reading public.

These realistic novels indicate that Lodge, who knows that the mainstream British novelists have made their reputations by writing within such traditional forms, wishes to join their ranks and intends to do so by mastering this particular form. These novels also show his skill in his chosen genre, and they are, if only incidentally, informed by his genial sense of humor. Still, excellent as they are, it is not these novels which justify his being included in the present study—it is the second group, composed of *The British Museum Is Falling Down, Changing Places, How Far Can You Go?* and *Small World,* which establish him as an important British humorist. These comedies have several characteristics in common: they are all set in the academic world that he knows from firsthand experience; they increasingly employ "metafictional games and stylistic experiments;"[5] and each one owes its structure, as well as many of its details, to one or more works from the canon of English literature. Based on academic situations and characters, they are to be explained by their references to academic (specifically literary) materials, and their greatest appeal is to an academic audience.

In the earliest of these novels, *The British Museum Is Falling Down,* several characteristics of Lodge's comedies are illustrated. Foremost among these is the structuring of the novel. Having written two conventional novels, Lodge realized that his comic vision of life could not be expressed through the point of view of the naive, realistic writer and that to achieve comedy he had to write self-consciously, never letting the reader forget that while each novel may have believable characters who are involved in real-life situations, it is also the conscious work of a writer who is preoccupied by the act of writing and who invokes, through parody or allusion, the entire English literary tradition. These humorous novels are cast in the form of metafiction, for Lodge the comic novelist takes his inspiration from the work of Lodge the literary critic and historian.

Readers quickly see that *The British Museum Is Falling Down* is a sort of lighthearted autobiography, for the author obviously draws upon his own personal experience as he creates an immediately recognizable picture of the London research student of the 1950s and 1960s, portraying the persons who were then to be seen daily in the Reading Room of the British Museum (many of these characters appear in Angus Wilson's *Hemlock and After* [1952] too). There is also a photographic verisimilitude in such stage props as the setting of the London townscape and traffic, the cafes and social attitudes of the period. But, increasingly the attentive reader becomes aware that Lodge is parodying different writers from the British (and American) novel tradition and that the structure of the book is based upon that of Joyce's *Ulysses.* The story of Appleby, a Ph.D. candidate in English literature who is writing his dissertation in the British Museum Reading Room (but whose thoughts are generally focused on his and his wife's sexual life within their Roman Catholic marriage), is highly entertaining; yet the turns of plot and the amusing characters pale in significance beside the stylistic tours de force and presentation of Appleby as a modern-day Leopold Bloom. This literary ambiance, expressed through the "in-jokes" of the writing, suggests that the novel is directed more toward the professional literary student than toward the general reader. In some metafictional sense Appleby might have written the novel for his fellow literary researchers since only they could appreciate his arcane literary knowledge (such as the Kafka-fantasy in chapter 3 when Adam renews his Reading Room Ticket) and the parallels between his and Bloom's life. As in *Ulysses,* the action of the novel occupies almost a twenty-four-hour period in a restricted geographical area, and Appleby, like Bloom, constantly thinks of his wife during the day, although he is concerned not with impotence, but fecundity. Barbara Appleby, like Molly, remains fixed at home during her husband's wanderings, and the novel concludes with her monologue which is a parody of the Penelope section of Joyce's mock-epic.

Lodge's allusions to *Ulysses* begin in the first chapter as the Applebys awaken and Barbara asks Adam to "Make a cup of tea."[6] When he finds that she has washed his underpants, he attempts to dry a pair in the grill-pan of the electric stove, only to burn them, just as Leopold burned the kidney he was preparing for his breakfast. And, like Leopold considering the *Titbits* literary competition, so Adam tries to complete a rhyming couplet in an advertising scheme: for the line "I always choose a Brown-long chair" he offers, "Whenever I relax *au pair*" or "For laying girls with long brown hair" (19). But, unlike Bloom, Adam, although only twenty-five, has three children and as a practicing Roman Catholic worries at the likely prospect that soon there will be more. Later in the day when his fellow students accuse him of "no longer [being] able to distinguish between life and literature"—an interesting metafictional joke that Lodge makes at his own expense— Adam wittily defends himself by saying that "Literature is mostly about having sex and not much about having children. Life is the other way round" (50). The Joycean allusions continue as Adam wanders round London, the novel ending with four pages of Barbara's unpunctuated monologue. Significantly, the affirmative "yes" that Molly pronounces on her life is replaced by the more equivocal "perhaps": "by the way how many children are we going to have as many as you like he said it'll be wonderful you'll see perhaps it will I said perhaps it will be wonderful perhaps even though it won't be like you think perhaps that won't matter perhaps" (140).

In the "Introduction" which Lodge wrote for the 1981 edition of *The British Museum Is Falling Down,* he names the ten authors whom he parodies in the work, as well as some of the other incidental literary references. In addition to Joyce these include Baron Corvo, Virginia Woolf, Graham Greene, and especially Henry James (most of chapter 7 is a parody in both style and subject matter of "The Aspern Papers").[7] Thus, although the novel provides amusing characters and action that smacks of late nineteenth-century French farce (Adam escapes the seductive teenager in a bedroom scene that might have been written by Georges Feydeau), readers are deliberately challenged by literary allusions that constantly remind us that we are reading a novel about the novel and that the style is as important as the characters and action.

The common denominator of Lodge's humorous novels is the fact that they concern academic life and are addressed to an academic audience. Unlike Kingsley Amis's broadly drawn professorial types in *Lucky Jim* (1954), Lodge's university types are individuals whose comic eccentricities are mainly appreciated by those who have actually known their prototypes. Indeed, they are most amusing for members of their own department of the university, for only their fellow English department colleagues will be able to understand their in-jokes and, increasingly through the group of novels, the metafictional ploys of the author as he makes his characters live out the literary works which are the subjects of their studies. This contrast between *Lucky Jim* and Lodge's novels suggests a basic distinction between Amis's and Lodge's approaches: Amis is the classical satirist who tries to reform a general situation by mocking stereotypes; Lodge accepts what he finds and is content merely to laugh and to make his reader laugh at specific characters and the situations in which they are presented. Lodge is a humorist who enjoys the antics of his fellow human beings too much for him to wish to change them or even to ask them to be other than what they are.

Lodge's other two university novels are *Changing Places: A Tale of Two Campuses* and *Small World: An Academic Romance. How Far Can You Go?* is related to this group of novels because its characters share a common university background and also appear to come from the author's professional, academic life. All three books increasingly reflect his interest in metafiction and use of literary texts: Lodge always tries to entertain the reader by playfully manipulating an older literary text as he tells his "new" story. Naturally, this tactic further focuses the audience to which he addresses his writing, for such an approach is generally more interesting to the academic rather than the general reader, particularly since Lodge sometimes uses scholarly works for his theoretical mode. Thus, in *Changing Places* the primary allusion is to E.M. Forster's *Aspects of the Novel* (1927). Lodge uses this critical study because it allows him, even as he puts his fictional characters into action, to make their story into an implicit comment upon various critical theories concerning literature.

The story of *Changing Places* comes from a situation in which persons in the same profession temporarily exchange their jobs. Here the exchange is between the Englishman Philip Swallow from the University of Rummidge ("a large, graceless industrial city sprawled over the English Midlands at the intersection of three motorways, twenty-six railway lines and a half-a-dozen stagnant canals") and the American Morris J. Zapp from the State University of Euphoria, located in "Plotinus" (Berkeley) across the bay from the city of "Esseph" (San Francisco). This plotting device logically justifies the author's presenting an Englishman's view of the American scene and vice versa. Although this structure appears to have been derived from the author's own experiences as a visiting professor at the University of California, it was actually anticipated in Forster's description of Anatole France's novel *Thais* in *Aspects of the Novel*. Forster describes *Thais* as having "the shape of an hour-glass" because the two main characters "converge, cross, and recede with mathematical precision," precisely the movement of Lodge's characters.[8]

Lodge does not attempt to conceal his use of Forster. Rather, like the detective-story writer who prides himself on his ability to put forward clues even as he puzzles the reader, Lodge supplies references to the all-important text. Early in the novel the Englishman is asked to teach a course in creative writing. In desperation he asks his wife in England to send him a book entitled *Let's Write a Novel*. The visiting American professor locates the book in the Englishman's office, so we first see it through his hypercritical eyes: "It had been published in 1927 . . . 'Every novel must tell a story,' it began, 'Oh, dear, yes,' Morris commented sardonically" (87). The author of this work is named as A.J. Beamish. Readers of Forster's colloquially written study immediately hear the parody of the older writer's voice; they note the similarity in publication dates; and in comparing the initials "A.J.B." with those of "E.M.F." they recognize the mathematical basis of the transformation from the real name to the fictional: four letters back, three back, and four back).

Lodge structures his text after Forster's work in other places in the novel too. At one point the Englishman's wife observes of *Let's Write a Novel* that it has "a whole chapter on how to write an epistolary novel, but surely nobody's done that since the eighteenth century?" (130). This observation comes in the middle of a chapter entitled "Corresponding," which is composed of letters between the two husbands and the two wives—who "correspond" to one another in their different situations. Similarly, when the long-awaited book arrives in California it has been "Damaged by Sea Water" and the pages are stuck together. Philip manages "to prise it open in the middle, however, and read: 'Flashbacks should be used sparingly, if at all. They slow down the progress of the story and confuse the reader . . .'" (186). At once the narrative shifts into a sequence of flashbacks, their importance noted by the italics with which each begins.

At every point in the novel the text provides a comment upon itself. Like a typically realistic novel, *Changing Places* begins with exposition describing the simultaneous journey of the two professors to their new positions: the flight west and the flight east allow the novelist to balance the information that he supplies about each man. Likewise, the ending describes the trips of the two professors, each with the consort of the other, to a meeting in New York. Since Lodge wishes to distance himself from their situations and to tease the reader with the problem of how fictional characters might resolve their problems, he shifts into the format of a movie scenario. He absolves himself of any responsibility for a conclusion by providing as a last line, "PHILIP shrugs. The camera stops, freezing him in mid-gesture" (251).

Changing Places is more a caricature of academic life than a satire of it. Lodge's models of the places and the people about whom he writes can always be identified (unfortunately, fears of libel have effectively prevented critics from publishing the names of these persons), yet these places and people have been so transformed that we are forced to see them as the novelist does and to share his value judgments. Because he is a humanist who holds the traditional values associated with a practicing member of a conservative religious faith and because he writes with a genuine sympathy for his subjects, few readers will be offended by his judgments. He is an internationalist who sees little difference between British and American students and who knows that while academic behavior may differ, it is equally ridiculous whether in California or in England. Indeed, although for the past two centuries most British writers who have visited the United States have written negative reports of their experiences, Lodge has too much appreciation for all types of experience to dismiss any way of life on merely national grounds. His positive attitude lies behind the meditation in which Philip Sparrow brings his (and we suspect the author's) American experience into focus:

> [H]e saw himself, too, as part of a great historical process—a reversal of that cultural Gulf Stream which had in the past swept so many Americans to Europe in search of Experience. Now it was not Europe but the West Coast of America that was the furthest rim of experiment in life and art, to which one made one's pilgrimage in search of liberation and enlightenment; and so it was to American literature that the European now looked for a mirror-image of his quest. (194–95)

Even as he muses, Sparrow, like a good teacher, provides examples from the expatriates Henry James and Henry Miller; he realizes that he now understands "American Literature . . . its prodigality couldn't have explained it to his students, some thoughts do often lie too deep for seminars" (195). In such passages Lodge infuses his creation of character and development of plot with his characteristic verbal humor.

Lodge's 1980 publication *How Far Can You Go?* poses several problems for the critic, not least being the question of its form. In the work he provides an account of what a group of young Catholic students at the University of London do with their lives between 1952 and 1975. It is a social history that allows the novelist to tell the story of the changes within the Roman Catholic church by showing how they affect the lives of these individuals. He focuses upon two primary subjects: the attitude of the Church toward sexuality and the definition of religious faith. The humor in the work arises chiefly from the sexual dilemmas of these devout Catholics. He assembles his characters much as a social scientist might seek out a representative population, bringing together a group of young people whose sexual inclinations are wide ranging, although they all share one thing: the inhibitions instilled in them by the priest-directed Church. By detailing their experiences over a quarter-century of enormous religious change, the author can draw upon an immediate source of humor: the stark contrast between sexual attitudes of 1950 and 1975.

In the course of this narration Lodge creates believable characters and makes a significant evaluation of the moral life of England. In short, all of the ingredients of the traditional novel are present, except for plot and the usual assumption by the novelist that he is creating fiction. Lodge writes as the omniscient narrator, yet he does not hesitate to speak in the first person, projecting the image of a persona whose experiences are almost identical to those of David Lodge. Thus, when he begins to describe the married life of his characters and their futile attempts to follow the teaching of the Church on birth control, he reminds the reader how he has "written about this before, a novel about a penurious young Catholic couple whose attempts to apply the Safe Method have produced three children in as many years . . . It was intended to be a comic novel and most Catholic readers seemed to find it funny, especially priests, who were perhaps pleased to learn that the sex life they had renounced for a higher good wasn't so very marvelous after all."[9] He remembers that a Czech reader wrote in appreciation, commenting that "Den zkazy v Britskem museu" is "an extraordinary smiling book," and he suggests that the present work "is not a comic novel, exactly, but I have tried to make it smile as much as possible" (74). Later, when he has to record the birth of a

Downs' syndrome baby to one of the couples he comments, "I did say this wasn't a comic novel, exactly" (112). And at the end of the novel as he accounts for each character, he writes of himself (even though he has neither appeared in the work nor identified himself as one of the characters), "I teach English literature at a redbrick university and write novels in my spare time, slowly, and hustled by history" (243). *How Far Can You Go?*, like the humorous academic novels, is yet another example of metafiction, an experiment which in this case takes its model not so much from earlier literary works as from the case studies popular in the social sciences.

In this novel, perhaps more than in any of the others, Lodge appears as the English Catholic humorist, following in the tradition of those writers long familiar to him from his academic studies. Combining eccentric figures and (to the general reader) esoteric doctrines, he creates scenes and incidents that may be considered by many readers to be more genuinely humorous than those in the university novels because he works here with the ordinary, daily world of reality rather than the restricted life of the academy. He describes the wedding night in 1958 of one of the virginal Catholic couples; inexperienced and inhibited, they are unable to consummate the relationship until the husband realizes that some ointment is needed:

> She did, as it happened, have some Vaseline with her, which she used for the prevention of chapped lips. Applied to her nether lips it produced almost magical results. Afterwards, Michael put his hands behind his head and smiled beatifically at the ceiling.
>
> "From now on," he said, "I'm always going to give Vaseline for wedding presents." (64)

Since the focus of *How Far Can You Go?* is on sexual license within the changing Roman Catholic church, Lodge legitimately describes a variety of sexual scenes, but always his sense of humor takes away any lascivious or pornographic element. Indeed, his emphasis upon religious values gives a sense of depth and meaning to events that would otherwise be ridiculous. The character Ruth, who enters a convent, finds herself caught up in the changes within the institutions of the Church; she se-

cures permission to visit other orders and ultimately finds herself in California. She participates in strikes by exploited workers and refers to the police as "Mean-looking mothers" because this "term of abuse, which she privately interpreted as a contraction of 'Mother Superior,' had rather caught her fancy, and she continued to use it freely until enlightened as to its true derivation by an amused Franciscan friar during a sit-in at a napalm factory" (140). At a Charismatic Day of Renewal she is overcome by "a profound sense of bliss" and is finally able to send a wire to her Mother Superior: "'BY THE WATERS OF DISNEYLAND I SAT DOWN AND WEPT STOP HAVE FOUND WHAT IVE BEEN LOOKING FOR STOP RETURNING IMMEDIATELY'" (179). Throughout the novel Lodge offers a serious consideration of the religious issues involved, issues which are familiar to readers of Evelyn Waugh, Graham Greene, and G.K. Chesterton —even though these writers would themselves have been shocked by the freedom of subject and of language allowed to the post–Vatican II writer.

The high point of Lodge's academic comedy is found in *Small World*. Subtitled "An Academic Romance," it describes the academic jet set of the 1970s and '80s. Many of the characters are carried over from *Changing Places*, the most important being Swallow and Zapp, along with their spouses. Here they figure in the international world of literary specialists who spend their time attending conferences at which they present theoretical propositions which move further and further away from traditional literary concerns. The writer pointedly mocks the academic handling of literature early in the novel when the traditionally oriented Swallow asks the avant-garde Zapp, after the latter has given a highly controversial lecture on the nature of literary studies, "Then what in God's name is the point of it all?" Zapp responds: "The point, of course, is to uphold the institution of academic literary studies. We maintain our position in society by publicly performing a certain ritual, just like any other group of workers in the realm of discourse—lawyers, politicians, journalists" (29).

Again Lodge addresses his novel to a specific audience, and very probably only English Department academics will realize that *Small World* encapsulates a history of literary criticism in the late twentieth century, and that the characters depicted in it represent both actual persons and the major critical movements in literary theory. Lodge places his history within one of the forms which have proved to be of particular interest to the literary theorists, that of the romance. The subtitle of the novel is to be taken at full value, for *Small World* is truly an "academic *romance*." The novelist carries his parody of the accepted canon of English literature to its extreme, for every detail and twist of the plot, even the names of the characters, are taken from romance literature. The most important of these sources is Edmund Spenser's *The Faerie Queene*, and Lodge creates characters and plotting for *Small World* which parallel those of its model. The novel is held together by the quest of Persse McGarrigle, a virginal Irish Roman Catholic, poet, and university lecturer on English language and literature, for the girl of his dreams. His pursuit leads him from literary conference to literary conference, in whatever parts of the globe they may be held, his journeys expedited by an American Express card. As in the earlier novels, Lodge draws upon his academic colleagues for models, although here their eccentricities are further complicated by the fact that they also represent different schools of literary theory. In this volume, too, Lodge indulges in various metafictional devices: shifts of point of view, authorial intrusions, cinematic techniques—indeed, there is hardly a technique in the British novelist's 300-year-old stockpile that he does not employ at one point or another. *Small World* is certainly a comedy which, in its wealth of characters and events, will amuse any reader. However, the more pointed jokes represented by these characters, as well as the humorous significances of their adventures, are, like the other academic comedies, available only to those with a considerable background in English literature and, more particularly, an awareness of the writings and attitudes of the professional teachers of English literature in the late twentieth century.

Nevertheless, Lodge aspires to be more than a writer for his fellow academics, as his earlier realistic novels show. In so far as his own feelings about literary theory can be deduced from his novels, he believes in the reality of the world outside literature and in the sanctity of the individual and the individual's art. It is for this reason that his considerable gift for satire is always found in the context of academic life for he appears to find a particular pleasure in dealing with academics and critics who value their criticism more highly than they do the work of the writers of the accepted literary canon.

Summary

Although he has achieved an international reputation as a critic, David Lodge is also attempting to earn what he appears to consider a more valuable title, that of traditional British novelist. To this end he has written serious, realistic novels that deal with the life of late twentieth-century Britain, as well as humorous, satiric novels that demonstrate his wide-ranging knowledge of British literature and of its critics. Because they are set in university surroundings and create memorable pictures of academic types, they are read with more interest and profit by those who are familiar with the characters and scenes described in them, but their humor is available to the general reader who can accept the stereotypes if not the specific details.

Notes

1. David Lodge, "Introduction," *Out of the Shelter* [rev. ed.] (New York: Penguin Books, 1989), p. viii.
2. *Ibid.*, p. xii.
3. *Ibid.*, p. ix.
4. Lodge, *Paradise News* (New York: Viking Press, 1992), p. 61.
5. *Out of the Shelter*, p. xii.
6. Lodge, *The British Museum Is Falling Down* (London: Panther Books Ltd., 1967), p. 11. Subsequent references to the text are to this edition.
7. See also Robert T. Levine, "The 'Dangerous Quest': Echoes of *The Aspern Papers* in Lodge's *The British Museum Is Falling Down*." *The Comparatist*, 13 (May 1989): 53–59.
8. E.M. Forster, *Aspects of the Novel* (New York: Harcourt, Brace and World, 1954), p. 150.
9. Lodge, *How Far Can You Go?* (Harmondsworth: Penguin, 1985), pp. 73–74. Subsequent references in the text are to this edition.

Selected Bibliography

Primary Sources
About Catholic Authors. London: St. Paul Press, 1957.
The Picturegoers. London: MacGibbon and Kee, 1960; Garden City: Doubleday, 1965.

L

Ginger, You're Barmy. London: MacGibbon and Kee, 1962; New York: Doubleday, 1965. London: Secker & Warburg, 1982.

The British Museum Is Falling Down. London: MacGibbon and Kee, 1965; New York: Holt Rinehart and Winston, 1967; London: Secker & Warburg, 1981.

Language of Fiction: Essays in Criticism and Verbal Analysis of the English Novel. London: Routledge and Kegan Paul, and New York: Columbia University Press, 1966.

Graham Greene. New York and London: Columbia University Press, 1966. Columbia Essays on Modern Writers, No. 17.

Out of the Shelter. London: Macmillan, 1970. Rev. ed. London: Secker & Warburg, 1985; New York: Viking Penguin, 1989.

The Novelist at the Crossroads and Other Essays on Fiction and Criticism. London: Routledge and Kegan Paul, and Ithaca: Cornell University Press, 1971.

Evelyn Waugh. New York and London: Columbia University Press, 1971. Columbia Essays on Modern Writers, No. 58.

Changing Places: A Tale of Two Campuses. London: Secker & Warburg, 1975; New York: Penguin Books, 1978.

The Modes of Modern Writing: Metaphor, Metonymy, and the Typology of Modern Literature. Ithaca: Cornell University Press; London: Arnold, 1977.

Modernism, Antimodernism and Postmodernism. Birmingham: University of Birmingham, 1977.

How Far Can You Go? London: Secker & Warburg, 1980; Harmondsworth: Penguin, 1985. Published as *Souls and Bodies*. New York: William Morrow, 1982.

Working with Structuralism: Essays and Reviews on Nineteenth and Twentieth-Century Literature. London and Boston: Routledge and Kegan Paul, 1981.

Small World: An Academic Romance. London: Secker & Warburg, and New York: Macmillan, 1984.

Write On. Occasional Essays, 1965–1985. London: Secker & Warburg, 1986.

Nice Work. London: Secker & Warburg, 1988; New York: Viking Penguin, 1989.

After Bakhtin. Essays on Fiction and Criticism. London: Routledge, 1990.

Paradise News. London: Secker & Warburg,

1991; New York: Viking Press, 1992.

The Art of Fiction. New York: Viking Press, 1993.

Secondary Sources

Students of David Lodge's humor should note that the author has made significant comments on his novels in the following editions: "Introduction" to *The British Museum Is Falling Down* (London: Secker & Warburg, 1981); "Afterword" in *Ginger, You're Barmy* (London: Secker & Warburg, 1982); and "Introduction" to *Out of the Shelter* (London: Secker & Warburg, 1985). The novels, as well as Lodge's literary studies, have been widely reviewed in both Great Britain and the United States (journals with a Roman Catholic connection have been particularly attentive to his work); the interested reader will find these reviews listed in the standard annual bibliographies of periodicals. By the early 1990s, Lodge's fiction was increasingly being studied by academics; their theses and critical essays can be located through the *Dissertation Abstracts International* and the *Modern Language Association Bibliography*.

Bergonzi, Bernard. "David Lodge Interviewed." *Month*, 229 (February 1970): 108–16. Lodge discusses the literary origins and Catholic orientation of his first three novels.

Bradbury, Malcolm. "Donswapping." *New Review*, 1 (February 1975): 65–66. A review of *Changing Places* in which Bradbury summarizes the story with much praise for the author.

Honon, Park. "Review Essay: David Lodge and the Cinematic Novel in England." *Novel: A Forum on Fiction*, 5 (Winter 1972): 167–73. Enthusiastic study of Lodge's narrative technique in the first four novels.

Holmes, Frederick M. "The Reader as Discoverer in David Lodge's *Small World*." *Critique: Studies in Contemporary Fiction*, 32 (Fall 1990): 47–57. Intensive study of *Small World* as a self-reflexive romance written from the deconstructionist perspective.

Jackson, Dennis. "David Lodge." *Dictionary of Literary Biography, Volume 14: British Novelists Since 1960, Pt. 2*. Detroit:

Gale, 1983), pp. 469–481. Judicious, comprehensive survey of Lodge's life and writings (academic and fictional) through 1981.

Levine, Robert T. "The 'Dangerous Quest': Echoes of *The Aspern Papers* in Lodge's *The British Museum Is Falling Down.*" *The Comparatist*, 13 (May 1989): 53–59. A close (and convincing) reading of the two texts to illustrate Lodge's parody of James.

Marecki, Joan E. "David Lodge." *Contemporary Authors. New Revision Series, Vol. 19.* Detroit: Gale, 1987, pp. 297–303. Comprehensive survey of Lodge's fiction with important comments by the author on his writing. Includes useful list of reviews of the novels.

Marowski, Daniel G., ed. "David Lodge." *Contemporary Literary Criticism, Vol. 36.* Detroit: Gale, 1986, pp. 266–78. Quotations from twenty-four significant reviews of Lodge's criticism and fiction.

Mews, Siegfried. "The Professor's Novel: David Lodge's *Small World.*" *Modern Language Notes*, 104 (April 1989): 713–26. Consideration of *Small World* and *Changing Places* as examples of the "campus novel" and as a "serious questioning of the purpose of literary studies and of the institution of academic criticism itself."

Morace, Robert A. *The Dialogic Novels of Malcolm Bradbury and David Lodge.* Carbondale and Edwardsville, IL: Southern Illinois University Press, 1989, pp. [xx], 222. Crosscurrents/Modern Critiques, Third Series. In his first chapter, "Critical Assumptions," Morace acknowledges his critical debts to Mikhail Bakhtin; in chapters 6 through 11 (pp. 109–208) he considers Lodge's novels up to and including *Small World.* Writing as an academic, Morace uses Lodge's critical writings to help illuminate the novels as he argues his Bakhtin theory. Includes a useful list of "Works Cited" (pp. 211–17).

Reckwitz, Erhard. "Literaturprofessoren als Romanciers—die Romane von David Lodge und Malcolm Bradbury." *Germanisch-Romanische Monatsschrift* N.F. 37 (1987): 199–217. Study of *Changing Places* and *How Far Can You Go?* as expressions of an advanced theorist and as revelations of English cultural attitudes. In German.

Widdowson, Peter. "The Anti-History Men: Malcolm Bradbury and David Lodge." *Critical Quarterly*, 26, 4 (Winter 1984): 5–32. An essentially hostile study of the two authors' criticism and fiction as examples of the realistic, liberal-humanist tradition, divorced from political concerns.

Wilson, A.N. "Square-bashing." *Spectator*, 249 (July 31, 1982): 23–24. Detailed review of the reissue of *Ginger, You're Barmy* with lengthy comments on Lodge's other fiction.

Elgin W. Mellown

L

Lonsdale, Frederick

Born: St. Helier, Jersey, Channel Islands, February 5, 1881
Education: Self-educated
Marriage: Leslie Brook Hoggan, 1904; three children
Died: London, April 4, 1954

Biography

Frederick Lonsdale was born in the town of St. Helier on the Channel Island of Jersey on February 5, 1881, and was christened Lionel Frederick Leonard. (He changed his name in 1908, apparently to avoid payment of debts.) His father, Frederick Leonard, owned and operated a tobacco shop while his mother, Susan Belford Leonard, worked in their two-room cottage doing odd jobs and caring for her three boys. Young Frederick distinguished himself as a willful, rebellious child from his earliest years. Each time he was dragged kicking and screaming to school, he would sneak away and vow never to return. His parents, unable to overcome this attitude, soon released Frederick to his own devices. Although he had no formal education, by the time he was twenty he had cultivated the accent and manner of an Oxford man.

While he was still an adolescent, Lonsdale sometimes worked in his father's shop; however, he joined the army as a private at eighteen in order to escape his small home island. Eventually he was discharged with a certificate stating that he had heart problems—a condition which he later denied. After his release from the service, he worked as a respondent to passengers' travel questions for the South-Western Railway, a job that bored him. He had fallen in love with a Canadian girl who visited the area, so he took a job as a steward aboard a liner cruising to Canada. This employment must not have appealed to him either because he traveled as a passenger on the return voyage. After his short stay in Canada, he moved to Southampton as a dock worker. This career did not suit him either, so he moved back to Jersey.

The island was more exciting upon his return, since a Miss Leslie Hoggan had moved there with her family. Lonsdale fell in love with her and the two were married in 1904 after a brief courtship. Their union produced three daughters. The family moved about England, living in poverty much of the time while Lonsdale continued to learn the craft of writing romantic comedies.

From 1906 to the late 1940s, at least thirty of Lonsdale's comedies were staged, and he wrote the screenplays for four films as well (most notably *The Private Life of Don Juan,* 1934, directed by Alexander Korda and starring Douglas Fairbanks). Particularly in the first couple of decades of his career, the writer's works were very popular with audiences and critics alike. Lonsdale died in London on April 4, 1954.

Literary Analysis

By the time he was twenty-seven, Lonsdale's plays filled London theaters; three of his plays, *The Early Worm, The King of Cadonia,* and *The Best People* were produced in that year alone. Lonsdale was successful almost as soon as he began writing his drawing room comedies which were composed in a style reminiscent of Oscar Wilde's comedies of manners. The plots are slight, but the plays are tightly constructed and the dialogue is witty enough to sustain interest.

The Maid of the Mountain (1917), co-authored with Harold Fraser-Simson and Harry Graham, was a hit during the First World War primarily because British troops on leave in London adopted it as their own and went to see the show repeatedly. After this production, the dramatist's reputation was secured; he simply continued to write comedies, often musicals, about matrimony, aristocratic negligence, and the flighty upper-middle class until the public tired of them many years later. His plays contain tightly structured, light, mostly far-fetched plots laced with witty, satirical dialogue. Usually a pair of lovers misunderstand each other but end up reconciled or married.

Lonsdale's comedies of the 1920s survived better than most other plays of the period, but still they are dated, especially since they were written almost entirely with commercial success in mind. His work is often compared with that of W. Somerset Maugham, but Lonsdale's lacked the strong, astringent satire and seriousness of Maugham's plays. Still, in his time, Lonsdale's works about politeness and good social behavior were big box office hits of London's West End theater district.

Staged at the St. James Theatre, his best-remembered play is *The Last of Mrs. Cheyney* (1925), a satire of human nature starring Gerald du Maurier and Gladys Cooper which perfectly showcases Lonsdale's natural wit. This work is memorable, standing out from his others because of its strong plot. Mrs. Cheyney, a beautiful, seemingly rich Australian woman, is accepted into London society, but by the end of the first act the audience realizes that she is part of the criminal gang that is pretending to be her servants. Mrs. Cheyney intends to steal the pearl strands of the wealthy Mrs. Ebley. The plan is foiled by Lord Dilling, who recognizes one of the crooks and is also in love with Mrs. Cheyney. He forces Mrs. Cheyney to admit her criminal intentions to the other characters, but the police are not notified because she has a letter which can be used to blackmail the others. They write her a check to buy her silence, but Mrs. Cheyney destroys the check and the letter—thereby turning honorable enough to become Lady Dilling.

This comedy is a bit melodramatic, but it has swift action, many unexpected twists, and some wonderfully satirical lines concerning the lifestyles of the rich. For example, there is a conversation between two servants working at a garden party which takes place during the first act:

> Charles: He was my Lord Elton—a rich, eligible bachelor, an intimate friend of royalty—and a man of considerable importance. Dukes open their doors personally when he calls upon them—the aspirants to the higher life leave theirs open in the hope that it might rain and he might be driven in for shelter!
>
> George: He sounds great!
>
> Charles: To have got him here today is a triumph—he so seldom goes anywhere!
>
> George: What do you think brought him here?
>
> Charles: You've heard the singing at this charity concert, so the intelligent

assumption is he finds your mistress a very attractive young lady!

George: She's a knock-out. The feller who couldn't do the card trick—I like him—he made me laugh. Who was he?

Charles: He? He's quite of another kind! He's my Lord Dilling. Young, rich, attractive, clever. Had he been born a poor man, he might have died a great one! But he has allowed life to spoil him! He has a reputation with women that is extremely bad, consequently as hope is a quality possessed by all women, women ask him everywhere. I would describe him as a man who has kept more husbands at home than any other man of modern times.

This play was turned into a Hollywood film in 1927.

Lonsdale's next hit was the more biting *On Approval* (1926), which is distinguished, along with *Canaries Sometimes Sing* (1929), by having only four characters. *On Approval* shows the playwright's greatest merits—sparkling dialogue and brilliant construction—to their best advantage. The title refers to two trial marriages in which people are treated like commercial products to be returned when found lacking. Mrs. Wislake, a terribly selfish creature, wants to be positive that her second husband will be more content to be her lackey than was her first. She takes her suitor, Richard Halton, to her home in Scotland to try him out for a month. The pompous Duke of Bristol, who wishes to sell his title for cash in marriage to a rich woman, follows the other couple to Scotland with his intended partner, Helen Hayle, the daughter of a pickle millionaire. Richard and Helen discover not only how selfish their partners are but also that they love one another; they run away to be married, leaving the pompous Duke and catty Mrs. Wislake to be hateful only to each other.

Unlikely as it seems, this play is in no way concerned with premarital sexual relations. Its witty banter seems intended only to show proper human behavior through Lonsdale's superb craftsmanship, a style which depends upon suspense and somewhat titillating situations. This is exactly opposite to the style of Jane Austen, an earlier novelist who also wrote constantly about matrimony; her ideas of weddings creating the bedrock of good society—if all married according to their stations—is mocked by Lonsdale's portrayal of courtship as an outrageous game where various levels of society mix (with the aristocracy often looking either silly or terribly cynical). This democratic flair made him popular in the United States, and many of his plays were produced on New York stages after they had played in London.

By the mid-1930s, Lonsdale's style was considered old-fashioned, his epigrammatic wittiness dated. Perhaps he had so saturated the theater market with his many great successes that audiences and critics were simply tired of singing his praises. The problem may have been that his light comedies were no longer interesting enough in a time when the world was on the brink of another great war; the idea that he may have been a Nazi sympathizer did nothing to help his popularity. Lonsdale wrote little after the 1930s, and what he did write was so similar to his early work that it can easily be confused with his plays of 1908.

Summary

During his career as a playwright of romantic comedies, Frederick Lonsdale poked fun at wealthy individuals, an approach that had been timely earlier when the English were beginning to doubt the assumed superiority of the aristocracy. Middle-class audiences between 1908 and 1930 enjoyed his satirical observations about the upper-class mode of living. Lonsdale was an accomplished craftsman who could make a mere trifle of a plot sparkle with his brilliant dialogue—his technique is always more outstanding than the plays' contents. These lightweight comedies about courtship and marriage were intended to amuse and entertain rather than to instruct. Lonsdale's polished style earned him much money, but little real respect. He always insisted on engaging the best actors and actresses to star in his works, a ploy that greatly aided the advancement of his box office sales. His themes were rarely fresh; he simply rewrote old ideas amusingly, with exciting dialogue and thrilling twists in a manner which made all audience members feel comfortable, as well as momentarily engrossed in the theater.

Selected Bibliography

Primary Sources

Plays
Who's Hamilton, 1903, New Theatre, Ealing.
The Early Worm, 1908.

The King of Cadonia (Co-authored with
    Sidney Jones), 1908; produced by Frank
    Curzon at Prince of Wales Theatre, Lon-
    don.
The Best People, 1908.
Aren't We All, 1909; 1923, Globe Theatre,
    New York (with director Charles
    Dillingham and starring Cyril Maude).
The Balkan Princess (Co-authored with
    Frank Curzon and P.A. Rubens), 1910.
The Woman of It, 1913.
Betty (Co-authored with Gladys Unger and
    P.A. Unger), 1914.
The Patriot, 1915.
High Jinks (from a play by P. Bilhaud and M.
    Hennequin), 1916.
Waiting at the Church, 1916.
The Maid of the Mountain (Co-authored
    with Harold Fraser-Simson and Harry
    Graham), 1916, Daly's Theatre, London;
    London and New York: French, 1949.
Monsieur Beaucaire (Co-authored with
    Andre Messager, from the novel by
    Booth Tarkington), 1919.
The Lady of the Rose (Co-authored with J.
    Gilbert, from a work by R. Schanzer and
    E. Welisch), 1921.
Spring Cleaning, 1923 (starring Edna Best).
    London: Gollancz, 1925.
Madame Pompadour (Co-authored with
    Harry Graham and Leo Fall), 1923.
The Street Singer (Co-authored with H.
    Fraser Simon and P. Greenbank), 1924;
    London and New York: French, 1929.
The Fake, 1924, Apollo Theatre (starring
    Godfrey Tearle and Allan Jeayes); Lon-
    don and New York: French, 1927.
Katja the Dancer (Co-authored with Harry
    Graham and J. Gilbert, from a work by
    L. Jacobsohn and R. Osterreicher), 1924.
The Last of Mrs. Cheyney, 1925, St. James
    Theatre, London (starring Gerald du
    Maurier and Gladys Cooper); New
    York: French, 1929.
On Approval, 1926 (starring Roland
    Moorwood); New York: Samuel French,
    1927; televised 1982.
The High Road, 1927; London: Collins, 1927.
Lady Mary (Co-authored with J. Hastings
    Turner and A. Sirmay), 1928.
Canaries Sometimes Sing, 1929; London:
    Methuen, 1929.
Never Come Back, 1932.
Once Is Enough, 1938, Henry Miller's The-
    ater, New York (starring Ina Claire and

Hugh Williams); London: Samuel
    French, 1938.
The Foreigners, 1939.
Another Love Story, 1943, Fulton Theater,
    New York (starring Roland Young);
    London: English Theatre Guild, 1948.
But for the Grace of God, 1946 (directed by
    Peter Daubeney).
The Way Things Go, 1950—revised as *Day
    After Tomorrow*; London: French, 1951.
Let Them Eat Cake, 1959, Cambridge The-
    atre, London; London: Evans, 1961 (re-
    vision of *Once Is Enough*).
Half a Loaf, 1958, Royal Theatre, Windsor.

Screenplays
The Last of Mrs. Cheyney, 1927.
The Devil to Pay, 1930.
Lovers Courageous, 1932.
The Private Life of Don Juan (with Lajos
    Baro), 1934; (directed by Alexander
    Korda and starring Douglas Fairbanks).
Forever and a Day, 1943 (with Charles
    Bennett, C.S. Forester, John van Druten).

Secondary Sources
Agate, James. *The Contemporary Theater*,
    1925. New York: Benjamin Bloom,
    1969. Review of Lonsdale's *The Fake* as
    it was being performed at the Apollo.
Donaldson, Frances. *Freddy Lonsdale*. New
    York: J.B. Lippincott, 1957. A primarily
    biographical account of Lonsdale's life
    and times with some smattering of liter-
    ary criticism.
Elson, John. "Faulty Goods," *The Listener*,
    95, p. 26. Elson compares Lonsdale to
    other contemporary playwrights, indicat-
    ing that *On Approval* has been under-
    rated by critics.

Laura Lambdin

Lovelace, Richard

Born: Woolwich, Kent, 1618
*Education: Charterhouse School, 1629–1634;
    Oxford University, 1634–1636, M.A.;
    Cambridge University, 1637*
Died: London, 1657

Biography

Richard Lovelace was born in Woolwich, Kent
in 1618. His family owned a considerable
amount of property, the revenues from which
allowed them to live quite comfortably. Love-

lace's mother was named Anne, and his father, William, was a colonel in the army and was knighted in 1609 by King James I. By seeking a career in the military, Lovelace's father continued a family tradition, which he then passed on to his own children. Richard and his siblings eventually joined the army as well.

Lovelace's education was lengthy. In 1629, his mother petitioned for a scholarship for him to attend Charterhouse School in London where he remained until 1634. During this time, he was introduced at the court (1631), and he wrote his first play *The Scholars* (1634), initiating a career as a dramatist that continued for the remainder of the decade. After he left Charterhouse, he attended Oxford University and was awarded a Master of Arts degree in 1636. The next year he attended Cambridge University for two months.

Following the completion of his education, Lovelace concentrated all of his talent, resources, and energy in defense of King Charles I in the sovereign's ill-fated dispute with the Puritan Parliament. Lovelace joined the army to support the King's unsuccessful campaigns into Scotland in 1639 and 1640. During this time, he wrote his tragedy *The Soldier* (1640). While the tensions mounted between the King and his legislature, Lovelace delivered a pro-royalist petition to the Parliament in 1642, urging a cessation of hostilities toward the king. Lovelace was jailed for his labors. He spent seven weeks incarcerated, during which he wrote his most memorable lyric, "To Althea, From Prison." After a while, he sued for release on the grounds that he wished to help the king in his Irish expedition. Although he was released, he was forbidden to join the military.

When the civil war broke out in 1643, Lovelace, unable to assist in the fighting because of the Parliamentary ruling, sold his lands in order to generate money and supplies for the king's troops. At this time, the poet left the country for two years, keeping residence in both Holland and France. He continued to help the king's efforts, financially assisting his brothers who were taking part in the fighting. After he returned to England, Lovelace was once again arrested when he attempted to thwart the plundering of his home by Parliamentary forces. This time he spent six months in jail.

With the king defeated and all of Lovelace's wealth and property lost in the war effort, the poet was financially ruined. Thus, he published his first volume of poems (*Lucasta*, 1649), hoping to gain new revenues. He lived out the remainder of his life in poverty and died in London of consumption in 1657. Some of his acquaintances published a second volume of the poet's work (*Lucasta/Posthume Poems*, 1659), which included poems that Lovelace had considered unworthy of inclusion in the previous volume along with elegies written in his memory.

Literary Analysis

At least one scholar of Lovelace's poetry has argued that the man was not notable for his humor, and it is true that the jocular moments in the poet's work are rare. However, this position may be generated by a twentieth-century perception of what is funny. Although it is difficult to conjure from the past an outline of those methods, subjects, behaviors, or rhetorical flourishes that may or may not have made a seventeenth-century audience laugh, there are identifiable moments when the poet becomes playfully abusive or excessive in the development of his topic, and these moments are almost exclusively at the expense of women. As is the case with John Donne, Lovelace is the most humorous when he assumes the pose of a young womanizing rogue whose overwhelming objective is to glut his libidinous appetite or when his exuberant praise for his mistress oversteps the bounds of modesty in terms of either its eroticism or its frivolity. Possibly the evaluation of Lovelace's humor lies in the desensitization of the twentieth-century audience to the erotic and also, paradoxically, in the growing sensitivity to the abuse and exploitation of women in literature. Therefore, the quips that may be regarded by many in this century as mild, only marginally humorous and yet somewhat vulgar and insensitive may have roused a chuckle and a blush in a seventeenth-century audience.

Perhaps in imitation of Donne's poem "The Indifferent," Lovelace's "The Scrutinie" involves a witty and familiar argument against monogamy among lovers. The poem is an aubade in which an amorous young rogue attempts to extricate himself from a promise of devotion made during the heat of passion the night before. As is the case with works by the metaphysical poets, the poem becomes the speaker's elaborate demonstration of the value of variety in sexual partners. He begins by asserting that his lady is unreasonable in her efforts to hold him to a pledge of loyalty made twelve hours before, and he attempts to invoke her sense of gratitude by reminding her that he has worked for many hours to please her. The subtext of his commentary is that twelve hours of labor should be sufficient to fulfill his promise of eternal love. Doubtlessly incurring his lady's derision, the desperate speaker appeals to his partner's sense of justice and vanity. Immodestly, he argues that he would deprive other women of his company if he were to maintain his pledge of fidelity, and he indicates that it is his responsibility to seek out beauty, just as a "minerallist" searches for treasure. The speaker pays his mistress the same compliment with which he honors himself, perhaps hoping to avoid the odium of conceit. He very generously offers to withdraw so that he does not deprive the lady of the other sexual partners who long to "dote upon her face." However, before he departs, the magnanimous speaker offers to return when he has completed his study of the region's beauties, suggesting that he will be more capable of recognizing his current mistress's admirable attributes once he has enjoyed the amorous embraces of other ladies. He will have other experiences with which to compare the present one, and he promises that his roving spirit will be "sated with variety." The situation in which the young man attempts to escape from the promises that he made to seduce his mistress is the premise of many comic masterpieces, and the young rake's desperation coupled with the young woman's clinging devotion and expectations constitutes a comic tension capable of delighting audiences of any time.

The inconstant young man of "The Scrutinie" is similar to the unfaithful lady described in "The Apostacy of One, and but One Lady." In this poem the speaker satirizes his mistress's mutable passions. He employs irony by appearing to compliment while actually undermining her integrity through comparison. For example, he says that her love is as hard as "Ice in the Sun's Eye" and as permanent as a reflection in a mirror after the subject passes. He says that she remains as calm as lightning, as "constant as the wind," as "certain" as the paths of "the blind," and as "gentle as chaines." Finally, in a brief moment of honesty, the speaker admits that the lady is "as the devil not half so true." The fickleness of women's desires was an occasional subject of the humorous love lyrics of the age, as in Donne's "Woman's Constancy" and "Go and Catch a Falling Star." These poems are an ironic reversal of the traditional pose of the young rake who seeks to weasel out of his commitment after a single night of pleasure, and they are amusing because of their freshness and originality.

Lovelace's work also includes bawdy seduction poems whose playful and entertaining wickedness is the source of much delight. In "Depose Your Finger," the poet pleads with his lady to surrender her ring; he then compares it to her maidenhead, explaining that her momentary loss has not harmed the ring and, by the same token, if she concedes her virginity, her flesh will not be sullied and her honor will not be damaged. In the second stanza the poet asserts that the surrender of her virginity will have no graver consequence. Paradoxically, he argues that her "chaste treasure" will be increased through lending, both by pleasure and by childbirth, and he immodestly maintains that her joys will be even greater than his own. Appealing to her altruistic sensibilities, he contends that she has an obligation to resign herself, since she can do him much good and remain unblemished herself: "Not to save others is a curse / The Blackest, when y'are none the worse." The humor of this roguish and clearly duplicitous appeal is intensified by the certainty that following the maiden's surrender, the young rake will energetically and scornfully protest his desire to withdraw.

On the surface the poem "The Faire Begger" constitutes an amusing reversal of the traditional male and female roles. Here, the mistress is the lascivious partner and the speaker is the one who craves love and commitment. The speaker indicates that he would be willing to satiate her carnal appetite, if she would proclaim her love for him. Thus, he hopes to strike a bargain that involves a concession by both parties. He chastises the lady, insinuating that her beauty and appeal are diminished by her lack of emotional depth, and he generously promises to embrace her, if she will concede that she loves him:

> If thou wilt promise me imbrac't;
> Wee'l ransack neither Chest nor Shelfe,
> I'll cover thee with mine own selfe.

The poem is the speaker's ploy to seduce the reluctant mistress by suggesting that their union is a foregone conclusion and to conceal his own sexually insidious designs by accusing the mistress of the same faults. The wit of this maneuver is the fountainhead of humor in the poem.

In "You Are Deceiv'd," Lovelace continues the pose of the rascal who mistreats women, and indeed the poem is quite unkind at the same time that it is hysterically funny. The poem was supposedly written in response to a lady's request for adoration. Because the speaker does not admire the lady's appearance, he finds her wishes impossible to fulfill, so he writes a poem of dispraise, revealing the several reasons why he cannot applaud her beauty in verse and urging her to forsake any pretenses to attractiveness. Initially, he reveals the impossibility of dedicating the "bright hue of verse" to this woman, arguing that he could dull the constellations or sweeten the stench of death with as much ease. His role is to recognize and celebrate beauty; only heaven can create it. In the second stanza the speaker maintains that he would diminish the honor of deserving ladies if he were to hail so foul a woman. His concern is for the truth; he would have as much difficulty calling Lucasta (his paragon of virtue) an infidel, Castara "impure," or Saccarisa unfaithful. Approaching the issue from every angle, the speaker shows the woman that his refusal saves her from the odium of attention. He reminds her that she currently dwells in blissful obscurity, yet his verse would reveal faults that might otherwise remain unnoticed. Of course, the comic irony of his claim rests in the realization that the current poem draws more attention to her negative attributes than any polite poem would. Finally, the speaker demonstrates that true praise is unnatural to this woman. He unkindly describes her as "A wicked Owl in Cloth of Gold . . . / Or the ridiculous Ape, / In sacred Vesta's Shape." He says that no poet's pen can amend the flaws that her birth bestowed upon her. The roguishness of this abusive verse is the source of its humor. Certainly the poem is unkind, but, like William Shakespeare's "My Mistress' Eyes," "You Are Deceiv'd" is a welcome relief from the tedious sentimentality of the sixteenth- and seventeenth-century love lyric. It is a marvelously funny parody of the Petrarchan pose.

Lovelace is not only comic when he chooses to satirize literary conventions; even those poems that fully comply with tradition can be quite humorous. Several of his Petrarchan-style poems become hilariously excessive and consequently absurd. In "Lucasta, taking the waters at Tunbridge," the poet assumes the pose of the Petrarchan amorist who regards his mistress as heavenly and who becomes jealous of her free interaction with inanimate objects. In this poem the author's theme revolves around Lucasta's decision to bathe in mineral springs. The poet envies the good fortune of those waters that pass the gates of Lucasta's womb. Elaborating on this conceit, he decides that the waters are purified through this contact with her heavenly body: they thus become holy water. Addressing the baths, the poet asks if they have ever smelled as sweet a scent as that of Lucasta's womb, and he attributes the bubbling of the bath to the heat of passion that the waters must feel in their close encounter with the lady. The portrait of Lucasta blessing the waters with her womb can hardly be regarded as a sober tribute to the mistress. Clearly, the poet hopes to amuse himself and his readers at the lady's expense.

Another poem in which he pretends to attempt to praise Lucasta but swiftly lapses into absurdity is "A Black Patch on Lucasta's Face." Here the poet explains the origin of the mole on the lady's visage. He maintains that a fly flew too near her eyes and was scorched by their brightness. Therefore, "the black patch" is a monument, honoring the insect's suicidal devotion to beauty. The fly had mistaken her face for paradise because of the various aromatic cosmetics employed by Lucasta to "emulate the gay / Daughter of Day." Now that the insect has expired, the same sweets that lured it to its death act as a floral cover for its tomb. Despite the clever tribute to the devastating beauty of Lucasta's face, it is unlikely that the mistress was flattered by this vulgar account explaining the origin of her mole, and it is also doubtful that true praise was the purpose behind the work. Instead, the poet clearly hoped to advance a clever joke.

Another poem that utilizes this device of Petrarchan excess is "Elinda's Glove." In this short lyric the author eases his frustrations by bestowing his affections on one of Elinda's possessions. She has discarded her glove while gathering flowers and admirers, and the poet retrieves this new object of devotion, lavishing praise on it as though it were a holy relic. He compares it to the tenement house owned but not currently occupied by the lady. He observes that the dwelling is particularly fashioned to house only the mistress's alabaster hand, but he, nevertheless, decides to leave his rent of "five kisses." In the final image of the poem he compares the glove to an empty lute case, implying that although he is too base to finger the instrument itself, he can at least fondle its case. This portrayal of a frustrated lover driven to the extreme of caressing and praising his mistress's glove cannot be regarded with complete seriousness. The exaggerated devotion and desperation of the amorist become the object of considerable mirth.

Summary

The humor of Richard Lovelace's poetry is sometimes rather subtle, and, often, recognizing and appreciating it involves making an assessment of the poet's seriousness. Some of the writer's most sober moments involve a playful excess that causes the reader to doubt the implicit intentions of the work. At times, he goes too far in his praise or his abuse to avoid the suggestion of parody, and this parody is often aimed at the various poses of men and women caught up in sexual contestation. Of course, in a largely male-dominated society such as that of the seventeenth century, the woman as object of the duplicitous young suitor's rhetorical acrobatics was probably the subject of much jest. However, the caricature of the presumptuous, desperate, immodest, and roguish male amorist must have been equally amusing and, at times, the target of much ridicule.

Selected Bibliography

Primary Sources
The Poems of Richard Lovelace. Ed. C.H. Wilkinson. Oxford: Clarendon, 1930. Includes all of Lovelace's poetry as well as a brief biography.

Secondary Sources
Anselment, Raymond A. "'Clouded Majesty': Richard Lovelace, Sir Peter Lely, and the Royalist Spirit." *Studies in Philology*, 86 (1989): 367–87. Anselment examines Lovelace's poetic interpretation of a painting by Lely.
———. "'Griefe Triumphant' and 'Victorious Sorrow': A Reading of Richard Lovelace's 'The Falcon.'" *Journal of English and Germanic Philology*, 70 (1971): 404–17. "The Falcon" is an allegory representing the defeat of the royalist cause.
Berry, Herbert, and E.K. Timings. "Lovelace at Court and a Version of Part of His 'The Scrutinie.'" MLN, 60 (1954): 396–98.
Clayton, Thomas. "Lovelace's Cupid Far Gone." *Explicator*, 33 (1974).
———. "Some Versions, Texts, and Readings of 'To Althea From Prison.'" *Papers of the Bibliographical Society of America*, 68 (1974): 225–35.
Cutts, John D. "John Wilson and Lovelace's 'The Rose.'" *Notes & Queries*, 198 (1953): 153–54.
Duncan-Jones, E.E. "Lovelace and the Great Eclipse of 1652." *Notes & Queries*, 4 (1957): 456.
———. "Two Allusions in Lovelace's Poems." *Modern Language Review*, 51 (1956): 107–09.
Evans, Willa McClung. "An Early Lovelace Text." *Publications of the Modern Language Association of America*, 60 (1945): 382–85. Evans discusses alterations in one of Lovelace's poems.
———. "Lovelace's Concept of Prison Life in 'The Vintage to the Dungeon.'" *Philological Quarterly*, 26 (1947): 62–63. Evans argues that Lovelace's poems are carefully crafted works.
———. "Richard Lovelace's 'Mock Song.'" *Philological Quarterly*, 24 (1945): 317–28. A discussion of changes made in various copies of Lovelace's poem.
———. "'The Rose': A Song by Wilson and Lovelace." *Modern Language Quarterly*, 7 (1946): 269–78.
———. "To Amathea." *Philological Quarterly*, 23 (1944): 129–34. Evans maintains that the poem was written by Lovelace.
———. "Tormenting Fires." *Modern Language Quarterly*, 9 (1948): 11–16. Evans indicates that the work named in the article's title is a companion poem to Lovelace's "To Elinda."
Gosse, Edmund. *The English Poets*. 1887. Gosse indicts the poet for his sloppy style.
Grierson, Herbert J.C. *Metaphysical Lyrics and Poems of the Seventeenth Century*. 1921. Grierson criticizes the poet's reckless style.
Hartmann, Cyril Hughes. *The Cavalier Spirit*. New York: Haskell House, 1973. The critic demonstrates that Lovelace was the embodiment of the Cavalier Royalist and that his poetry reflected his interest in this cause.
Jones, G.F. "'Lov'd I not Honour More': The Durability of a Literary Motif." *Com-

parative Literature, 11 (1959): 131–43. Jones discusses the idea of "honor" in Lovelace's "To Lucasta, Going to the Warres."

Judkins, David C. "Recent Studies in the Cavalier Poets: Thomas Carew, Richard Lovelace, John Suckling, and Edmund Waller." *English Literary Renaissance*, 7 (1977). A bibliography of secondary criticism on each of the cavaliers named in the title. My own bibliography owes a heavy debt to Judkins's scholarship.

McChesney, John. "Lovelace's 'The Grasshopper.'" *Explicator*, 9 (1951).

Mcguire, Mary Ann C. "The Cavalier Country-House Poem: Mutations on a Jonsonian Tradition." The critic discusses the Jonsonian tradition in Carew's "To Saxham" and Lovelace's "Amyntor's Grove."

Nathan, Norman. "Lovelace's 'Flie.'" *Notes & Queries* (1955): 428–9.

Palmer, Paulina. "Lovelace: Some Unnoticed Allusions to Carew." *Notes & Queries*, 14 (1967): 96–98.

———. "Lovelace's Treatment of Some Marinesque Motifs." *Contemporary Literature*, 29 (1977): 300–12. Palmer discusses the influence of the Italian poet Marino on Lovelace's work.

Pearson, Norman Holmes. "Lovelace's 'To Lucasta, Going to the Warres.'" *Explicator*, 7 (1949).

Skelton, Robin. *The Cavalier Poets*. London: Longmans, Green, 1960. Skelton addresses Lovelace's strengths as a poet.

Wadsworth, Randolph L. "On 'The Snayl' by Richard Lovelace." *Modern Language Review*, 65 (1970): 750–60. Wadsworth contends that the poem is an allegory of Puritan England's politics.

Wall, L.N. "Some Notes on Marvell's Sources." *Notes & Queries*, 202 (1957): 70–73. Wall discusses the influence of Lovelace on Andrew Marvell.

Wedgewood, C.V. "Cavalier Poetry and Cavalier Politics." In *Velvet Studies*. London: Jonathan Cape, 1946.

Weidhorn, Manfred. *Richard Lovelace*. New York: Twayne, 1970. This is a comprehensive analysis of the body of Lovelace's work in a biographical context.

Williamson, C.F. "Two Notes on the Poems of Richard Lovelace." *Modern Language Review*, 52 (1957): 227–29.

James R. Keller

L

M

Macdonell, Archibald Gordon

Born: Aberdeen, Scotland, November 3, 1895
Education: Winchester public school
Marriage: Mona Mann, 1926; one child;
*   Rosie Paul-Schiff*
Died: Oxford, England, January 16, 1941

Biography

A son of William Robert Macdonell, LL.D., and Alice Elizabeth (White) Macdonell, Archie Macdonell was born at Aberdeen in northeast Scotland on November 3, 1895. His secondary education was at one of England's best-known public schools, Winchester. During World War I, he served as a lieutenant in the Royal Field artillery of the 51st Highland Division (Territorial Forces), from 1916 to 1918. From 1922 to 1927, Macdonell was a member of the headquarters staff of the League of Nations Union. In both 1923 and 1924, he stood as a Liberal candidate for Parliament at Lincoln; he was not even close to being elected but did not lose interest in politics, for he served as chairman of the Guildford Liberal Association in the mid-1930s.

Macdonell was twice married. His first father-in-law was the Glasgow-born artist, Harrington Mann, who lived in fashionable Eaton Square, London. His marriage to Mona Mann in 1926, however, did not last long, being dissolved the next year. The couple produced a daughter. At his death, he was survived by his second wife, a Viennese woman, Rosie Paul-Schiff, who had fled Austria just before the Anschluss.

From the late 1920s onward, Macdonell must have been a busy man, for in addition to an impressive output of books and journalism, he seems to have been a social fellow, a member of Princes club, and an enthusiastic sportsman who listed his recreations in *Who's Who* (1936) as gold, cricket, tennis, squash racquets, badminton, gardening, and talking.

He contributed essays to newspapers and periodicals, among them the *Observer*, the *London Mercury*, and the *Strand Magazine*; he reviewed books for the *Bystander*. In the late 1930s, he made many broadcasts on the BBC's overseas' network, often satirizing enemy propaganda.

A decade of industrious writing was brought to a premature close on January 16, 1941. Macdonell's death in his forty-sixth year at his home in Broad Street, Oxford, is a puzzle. Hugo Vickers says that the author "died suddenly in his bath." But, according to Stanley J. Kunitz, he was "killed in an air-raid at Oxford," a fact that has proved difficult to substantiate and probability makes it difficult to believe. His obituary in the *Oxford Times* makes no mention of the cause of death. It may be that wartime reporting restrictions ensured silence.

Literary Analysis

Living in and around London, Macdonell wrote voluminously and quickly established himself as a minor man of letters. In the late 1920s, he began writing detective stories, several of which were reprinted by New York's The Crime Club series; their appeal, however, seems to have faded, and copies are now difficult to find. For his crime novels Macdonell used two pseudonyms, John Cameron and Neil Gordon. Among these books, his best-known is *The Shakespeare Murders* (1933). His interest in such fiction was probably genuine because for a while he served as secretary of the Sherlock Holmes Society of London and visited the

American branch for a New York banquet in 1934, a trip which formed the basis of his *A Visit to America* (1935).

Macdonell wrote a wide range of books, of which humor forms only a small portion. Apart from nine detective stories, he penned half-a-dozen novels, a collection of short stories (*The Spanish Pistol*), a patriotic piece of non-fiction (*My Scotland*), one serious historical study (*Napoleon and His Marshals*) which was translated into German (1941), and two plays.

At least four of his books are of interest to the student of literary humor. In *How Like an Angel!* (1934) he uses humor throughout and pokes fun at English conventions, domestic and national. *Lords and Masters* (1936) is fiction infused with satire against the background of European rearmament; it introduces a Waugh-like Jack Crawford, the cavalry officer-cum-super-cad. He is more successful as a creation than the coldly calculating hero, Edward Percival Fox-Ingleby, who complains of his father: "he developed a painful knack of espousing lost causes, and, worse, of subscribing to them." Though it enjoyed some success (it was translated into both Italian and German and is still readable), *The Autobiography of a Cad* (1938) has its ponderous moments.

Macdonell is deservedly best known for *England, Their England* (1933). Initially the novel was met by widespread approval on both sides of the Atlantic. By the outbreak of World War II, it had gone into its eleventh impression, and an illustrated edition was produced during the war when nostalgia for a more innocent England of leisurely cricket matches on the village green probably boosted its stock. During the last eight years of his life, the author published eleven books, but none matched the success of his major humorous work.

The book is thinly veiled autobiography (Macdonell is clearly Donald Cameron) but works much better than *Cad*. Here the Scot was able to incorporate a rich and often critical experience of English life and English personalities to good effect. It probably no longer matters that the reader does not know that the fictional editor, William Hodge, is based on Sir John Squire, or that Mr. Huggins is a sketch of "Beachcomber" (the pseudonym of J.B. Morton), or even that Alec Waugh is depicted in Bobby Southcott. Nor is it essential to be aware of the Cliveden set behind Macdonell's depiction of Ormerode Towers. The characteristic writing is of that kind which pleased J.B. Priestley: "thinking in fun, while feeling in earnest."

The theme of the book is the English at work and at play, and often one is aware of a satiric edge to the writing. Macdonell's premise is that these self-proclaimed practical people are really poets. The work begins with some serious passages illuminating military leadership during World War I. A newspaperman's apprenticeship in the provinces culminates with a metropolitan job on the *London Weekly*, which introduces Donald to Hodge and the "poets" of his circle. Macdonell uses the Mark Twain innocent character to good effect as Donald is introduced to the social and sporting niceties of his new life. A chance commission to write a book on England allows Donald further license to explore the arcane rituals and cant of dinner parties, country-house weekends, and so forth.

The episodic structure makes for much comic incident and allows for many comic characters. At its less inspired the humor hinges on a schoolboy sense of fun, which probably owes a nod to P.G. Wodehouse—the wife of an American stockbroker is Mrs. O.K. Poop. There are caricature upper-class twits and politicians, even a trio of young diplomats all combining double-barrel names and the aplomb of a Rolls-Royce. Some of the names are reminiscent of the virtues of William Makepeace Thackeray.

The structure is workable, but some critics have rightly observed that there is a falling off after the sustained humor of the cricket match (chapter 7) and the golf game (chapter 8). The closing dream-ending, where Donald has succumbed to the medieval spell of Winchester, is curious and uncertain in tone. By that point the probing of national character has been left behind, and Macdonell opts for a conclusion that cozily praises scant virtues and forgives frailties; it is a fudged cadence which never returns to the main key of the book.

At his best Macdonell displays a fertile invention and a firm sense of the rampant snobbery and vacuous conversation. Exaggeration can be deftly employed, as in the cricket match, and often at the expense of literary pretenders and book reviewers; indeed, Macdonell has a gift for parody. The portrayal of the British delegation to Geneva has the freshness of a script for *Yes, Minister*. Furthermore, Macdonell's amused look at the political hustings and personalities has an impressive timelessness. Overall, Macdonell takes his place with that strand of comedy in the English novel which is used to comment on the reasonable and simple in human conduct via a comic, even iconoclastic, eye—which eventually leads to the angry young men of the 1950s.

Summary

Archibald G. Macdonell's *England, Their England* is his humorous masterpiece and, for all its uncertainties, is well worth the attention of everyone interested in literary humor. Reasonably well-known to two generations of English schoolboys, regrettably this book seems to have faded from general awareness, perhaps because the better-known novelists and poets of the interwar period have made more serious claims upon those interested in English literature. More jovial in tone than *Autobiography of a Cad*, *England, Their England* is likely to be read as the best of Macdonell's humorous writing in years to come, for it is here that overlooking the unevenness, we see him able to move occasionally beyond the satirical toward that whimsical nonsense that induces a gale of laughter in readers.

Selected Bibliography

Primary Sources

England, Their England. London: Macmillan, 1933; 1935; 1941; with foreword by Christopher D. Morley, New York: Macmillan, 1933, 1934; Hamburg: The Albatross, 1934; illust. ed. with prefatory note by Sir John Squire, London: Macmillan, 1942; London: Pan Books, 1949; New York: Macmillan (St. Martin's Press), 1964; London: Macmillan, 1967; London: The Folio Society, 1986.

How like an Angel! London: Macmillan, 1934; New York: Macmillan, 1935.

Napoleon and his Marshals. London and New York: Macmillan, 1934.

A Visit to America. London and New York: Macmillan, 1935.

Lords and Masters. London: Macmillan, 1936; New York: Macmillan, 1937.

My Scotland. In *My Country* series, London: Jarrolds, and New York and London: Funk & Wagnalls, 1937.

Autobiography of a Cad. London: Macmillan, 1938; New York and London: Harper, 1939; London: Macmillan, 1951.

Flight from a Lady. London: Macmillan, 1939.

The Spanish Pistol, and Other Stories. London: Macmillan, 1939.

What Next, Baby? or, *Shall I go to Tanganyika?* (play). London: Macmillan, 1939.

The Crew of the Anaconda. London: Macmillan, 1940; London: Pan Books, 1950.

The Fur Coat (play). London: Macmillan, 1943.

The Village Cricket Match. [Excerpt from *England, Their England*]. London: St. Hugh's Press, 1950.

Detective Works under pseudonym John Cameron

The Seven Stabs. London: Gollancz, 1929; 1931; New York: Doubleday, Doran (for The Crime Club), 1930.

Body Found Stabbed. London: Methuen, 1932.

Detective Works under pseudonym Neil Gordon

The Factory on the Cliff. London: Longmans, 1928.

The New Gun Runners. New York: Harcourt Brace, 1928.

The Professor's Poison. London: Longmans, and New York: Harcourt Brace, 1928.

The Silent Murders. London: Longmans, and New York: Longmans, Green, 1929; New York: Doubleday, Doran (for The Crime Club), 1930.

The Big Ben Alibi. London: John Lane, 1930.

Murder in Earl's Court. London: John Lane, 1931.

The Shakespeare Murders. London: Arthur Barker, and New York: H. Holt, 1933.

Secondary Sources

Anonymous. "Scotsman Humorously Portrays the English." *The Springfield Sunday Union and Republican* (August 6, 1933): 7E. Review of humorous sketches of social and sporting life; brightly amusing if not new; wit with an ironically intellectual edge; the book as a whole is not quite so good as the sum even of its better parts.

Anonymous. "The Uses of Comic Vision: A Concealed Social Point in Playing for Laughs," *Times Literary Supplement*, 3054 (September 9, 1960): ix. In a special number devoted to the British Imagi-

M

nation, this article deals with the use of humor by English novelists during the previous fifty years; no mention of Macdonell, but the stress on humor as "natural situation" is useful.

Anonymous. *New York Times* (January 18, 1941): 15. Macdonell placed "among the leaders of the younger school of satirical novelists."

Anonymous. *Wilson Library Bulletin,* 15, 8 (April, 1941): 614. *England, Their England* created a considerable stir both at home and abroad; "of the generation that succeeded Chesterton, no more picturesque, dashing and talented figure appeared."

Howarth, Patrick. *Squire, Most Generous of Men.* London: Hutchinson, 1963, pp. 154–57, 205–18, 240–41. Useful background on Macdonell as a colleague and journalist, including the publication of *England, Their England* by Macmillan, whose reader (Squire) found it "esoteric."

Kunitz, Stanley J., and Howard Haycraft. *Twentieth-Century Authors.* New York: H.W. Wilson, 1942, pp. 871–72. Brief overview.

Moran, Helen. Review of *England, Their England,* in *The London Mercury.* "A test of your friends, for if they do not enjoy it, you are distinctly disappointed in them."

Pound, Reginald. *Mirror of the Century: The Strand Magazine, 1891–1950.* South Brunswick, NJ: A.S. Barnes, 1967, pp. 161–62. Generally an account of the magazine which emphasized fiction and nurtured numerous well-known writers, including Macdonell.

Pritchett, V.S. "The Comic Element in the English Novel: 5. The Last Forty Years." *Listener,* LI, 1320 (June 17, 1954): 1047–49, 1053. Pritchett argues for the centrality of a comic sensibility in English literature; though Macdonell is not a feature, Pritchett notes the emphasis on the "exorbitant," and gives a good context for *England, Their England* and *Autobiography of a Cad.*

Squire, Sir John Collings. *The Honeysuckle and the Bee.* London and Toronto: Heinemann, 1937. Very casual reminiscences about his literary circle and friends; useful for seeing why Macdonell portrays Squire as "Hodge" in *England, Their England.*

Vickers, Hugo. "Introduction." In *England, Their England.* London: The Folio Society, 1986, pp. vii–xvi. Amid the humor, the spirit of England is captured.

John S. Batts

Mankowitz, Wolf

Born: London, November 7, 1924
Education: East Ham Grammar School, London; Downing College, Cambridge University, M.A., 1946
Marriage: Ann Margaret Seligmann, August 2, 1944; four children

Biography

Like a character in his novel *!Abracadabra!* Wolf Mankowitz might be described as "an undoubtedly Jewish gentleman of the English persuasion." In the case of the character Solomon Hakoen, the phrase turns out to be inaccurate; in the case of Mankowitz himself, the description is merely insufficient. He was born in London's East End on November 7, 1924, to Solomon and Rebecca (Brick) Mankowitz, Russian-Jewish immigrants. Solomon was a used book and antique dealer, and Mankowitz has made a career of careering from china to literature to film and back again. As a result, the peripatetic Mankowitz has often been accused of spreading himself too thin. In truth, though, he has always been a "specialist," to borrow a term from his first novel, *Make Me an Offer.* He simply has a vast number of specialties and has been successful at most. By his own account in the introduction to *The Blue Arabian Nights,* Mankowitz has been "a shop-keeper and a gallery-owner, a film-writer and a theatrical producer, an impresario and a television performer, a night-club owner and an inveterate night-walker, a musical librettist and a newspaper columnist, a restaurateur, a ceramic encyclopaedist and a Wedgwood historian." But above all, as Malcolm Muggeridge, then editor of *Punch,* noted early in Mankowitz's career, "he is, essentially, a humorist."[1]

Educated at East Ham Grammar School in London and Downing College, Cambridge (where he took an M.A. in English and earned an award for poetry in 1946), Mankowitz married Ann Margaret Seligmann on August 2, 1944 (the couple had four children). He first applied his personal talents and energies to Wedgwood china. By the mid-1950s, he had parlayed his interest into a profitable business in antique and modern ceramics, as well as three volumes on Wedgwood and related subjects. Not coincidentally, his career as a novelist was launched at the same time with *Make Me an Offer* (1952), the unexpectedly funny tale of a Wedgwood dealer. At about that time, too, Mankowitz became a regular contributor of social and political satire to various newspapers and magazines, including *Punch*. His subsequent fiction retains ties to Mankowitz's background in the East End and to the small shops and market stalls where his father worked and where he himself got his start in china. His second novel, the mildly grim *A Kid for Two Farthings* (1953), is set in Fashion Street where Mankowitz grew up. Though his third novel, *Laugh Till You Cry* (1955), is set on a tropical island, its protagonist is a small-time salesman, and *My Old Man's a Dustman* (1956) is a tale of quixotic existence at a rubbish dump. As a predictable variation, the narrator of *The Mendelman Fire* (1957) mentions books and "Chinese blue and white porcelain" as among the things that never interested him.

Though traces of his background continue to recur in more recent fiction—the narrator's parents in *!Abracadabra!* (1980) are Jewish booksellers—Mankowitz's growing involvement in theater, cinema, and television was quickly reflected in both the genre and subject-matter of his works. He adapted *Make Me an Offer* for television the same year that it was published and followed that with a series of original plays, some of which were collected in *Five One-Act Plays* (1955). Many of his early plays and fictions were also recycled as movies and television productions, making the author seem something of a literary version of the second-hand dealers and scavengers that populate his work. *The Bespoke Overcoat* (1954), the first of Mankowitz's original plays, earned him the 1957 Academy Award, among other prizes, when he adapted it for the screen. Besides adaptations of his own work, according to Judy Cooke, "the films to which he has contributed range in their appeal from the glamorous (*The Millionairess* [1960]) to the horrific (*The Two Faces of Dr. Jekyll* [1960]), from adventure (*The Day the Earth Caught Fire* [1962]) to schmaltz (*Black Beauty* [1971])."[2] Other films with screenplays in whole or in part by Mankowitz include *Trapeze* (1956) and *Casino Royale* (1967).

Mankowitz's growing fascination during the 1950s with the world of entertainment can be seen in his non-fiction *ABC of Show Business* (1956), but it is his disgust with show-business types which seems clearest in his fiction of the period. "Expresso Bongo" (1958), a story later turned into a musical, is a satiric exposé of the pre-Beatles British equivalent of Tin Pan Alley. *Cockatrice* (1963), his first novel in seven years, is full of Mankowitz's increasingly bitter humor about the exploitative and cynical film industry.

Cockatrice is also, to date, the last of Mankowitz's fictions to be published in the United States and his only novel to appear in the twenty-three years between *My Old Man's a Dustman* and *Raspberry Reich* (1979), excepting only the short, separately published novella, *The Biggest Pig in Barbados* (1965). These years were filled with numerous plays and screenplays, a book of poems, several collections of short fiction, and biographies of Charles Dickens and Edgar Allen Poe. Nevertheless, Mankowitz's almost complete disappearance from the American literary scene after 1963 is rather surprising, especially considering that there was sufficient interest in his work in 1961 for an American anthology of his novels, stories, and plays to be published (under the title *Expresso Bongo: A Wolf Mankowitz Reader*). Moreover, Mankowitz has been an increasingly frequent visitor to the United States in the last two decades and has recently written several novels set in America—all, apparently, without renewing the interest of an American publisher.

Changes in locale seem to spark Mankowitz's creativity as much as changes in occupation. Beginning in 1961, for example, the author and his family wintered in Barbados and, four years later, he published the fable, *The Biggest Pig in Barbados*. Then, for tax reasons, Mankowitz moved to Ireland in 1971, settling in County Cork, where he continues to reside. He entered into the public life of his adopted home sufficiently to become the Honorary Consul to the Republic of Panama in Dublin his first year in residence, and he used Irish history in his one-act play, *The Irish-Hebrew Lesson* (1977), set in 1921, in which a young Irish revolutionary and an elderly Jewish scholar exchange wisdom about the preservation of one's culture.[3] Having returned to the novel at first with works set in contemporary Europe—*Raspberry Reich* (1979)—and an England of the past and future—*!Abracadabra!* (1980)—Mankowitz has focused on America for much of the last decade.

From 1982 to 1986 he was Adjunct Professor of English at the University of New Mexico, where he returned for the academic year 1987–1988 as Adjunct Professor of Theater Arts. His interest in the United States is also evident in several novels over the past decade, all of which mix American locales and occult plots: *The Devil in Texas* (1984); *The Magic Cabinet of Professor Smucker* (1988), which takes place in Los Angeles; and most recently *Exquisite Cadaver* (1990), set in an unnamed region of the American Southwest.

Literary Analysis

Though Mankowitz often chose Jewish characters and neighborhoods for his early fiction, there is little to justify Cooke's contention that "Wolf Mankowitz writes in the tradition of the Yiddish storyteller."[4] In fact, there is little in the way of traditional Jewish culture or traditions in Mankowitz's work at all, except perhaps for the tales set in Russia and collected in the section entitled "A Village Like Yours" in *The Mendelman Fire and Other Stories*. The title of *A Kid for Two Farthings*, for example, comes from the refrain of a Passover song in Aramaic called "Had Gadya" ("One Kid"), but there is no more of the song's cycle of violence and retribution in this novel than there is a father-and-son relationship in the equally misleading title of *My Old Man's a Dustman* which was taken from a popular English song. In *A Kid* Mankowitz uses the familiar Fashion Street setting and, like the subsequent *The Bespoke Overcoat*, the novel has a Jewish tailor as one of its main characters. Kandinsky, the tailor of *A Kid*, is also a surrogate father for young Joe, whose own father is off trying to strike it rich in "the Kaffir business" in Africa. Kandinsky chants the last round of the Passover song when Joe comes home with a young, sickly, one-horned goat, but the images of the novel are drawn less from the Haggada than they are from Kandinsky's fables about unicorns and Africa. Balanced by Mankowitz's realistic portrayal of the poverty and desperation of their lives, *A Kid* is the work of an author familiar with the milieu of lower-class Jewish life in the East End, not one interested in drawing on more traditional Jewish sources.

The same can be said of Mankowitz's first novel, *Make Me an Offer*, narrated in a hard-boiled style that owes more to Dashiell Hammett and Damon Runyon than to Sholem Aleichem. The narrator, a literally hungry Wedgwood dealer in post-war London, is as obsessed with an early green Wedgwood copy of the Portland vase as Hammett's characters are with the Maltese falcon. As does Hammett, Mankowitz too creates a strange circle of characters all of whom are involved in a convoluted plot to fix the auction of a room, the contents of which are known by the narrator to be nearly worthless. As the narrator sums up his day at the end of the novel, "I sold a room. Then I didn't buy it. Then I did. Then I sold it again. Then I bought a green vase." The story is buoyed by Mankowitz's deft handling of the details of a china dealer's business and turns hilarious when the narrator finally acquires the coveted vase by cheating a man too old and sick to protest. Deaf and nearly paralyzed, the old man is in the care of his beautiful granddaughter, who has no idea of the vase's value. At the narrator's instigation, she asks her grandfather if he would like to sell what both men know is a nearly priceless piece.

> The old boy was doing his best to have a stroke. But she understood him and knew he was pleased.
>
> "What is it worth?" she asked.
>
> "Well," I said, "there are all sorts of vases of this pattern, but this one is nicely made and I like the color. I might pay a very good price for it."
>
> The old man was shaking away, trying to tell her to throw me out. But I held on to the vase and kept smiling. Ninety pounds had fallen into my pocket that day. "I'll give you eighty pounds for it," I said.
>
> When she recovered, she told the old man and he jerked for a while, trying to tell her, "No."
>
> "He's trying to say he's very grateful," she said to me, "Mister . . . I don't even know your name."
>
> "Drage," I said. "Name of Drage." I was looking at the old man. He made a convulsive effort and rose up shaking upon his feet.
>
> I counted out sixteen fivers, smiling at him the while.

"Thank Mr. Drage, Grandfather," the girl said.

He moved and pushed the table over, scattering the five-pound notes.

"He's so excited, Mr. Drage," the girl said, and she put him carefully back in the chair.

The real Drage, long dead, is the man from whom the grandfather probably stole the Wedgwood vase. The narrator mentions it to remind us that, if the scene's black humor makes us uncomfortable, he is only cheating a thief. Indeed, discomfort and dubious morality are often part of Mankowitz's funniest work, and *Make Me an Offer* has all of the elements of Mankowitz at his best: a Dickensian cast of curious minor characters, an expertly portrayed and closely observed social setting, and humor as unlikely as it is funny.

One of the best-received of Mankowitz's fictions is *My Old Man's a Dustman*, a bittersweet post-war comedy about Arp, a shell-shocked, mute, garbage-dump scavenger with no identity and a name borrowed from the Air Raid Precautions insignia on his second-hand jacket, and Old Cock, the blustering but kindly watchman at the rubbish heap. The image of society here is bleak—for Arp, "the whole world was nothing but these rubbish dumps." And, by lodging Arp on the dilapidated sets of an abandoned movie studio, Mankowitz extends his wasteland metaphor from society's reality to its dreams. But, when the representatives of that soulless society attempt to evict the pair from the studio and dump, Old Cock plays a cockney Don Quixote to Arp's silent Sancho Panza; the two tilt at bureaucratic windmills and, somehow, win. Writing in *The Atlantic*, John Metcalf described Old Cock as "one of the most remarkable characters in modern English fiction" and claimed that the novel finally established Mankowitz "as something more, considerably more, than a facile genre writer with promise."[5]

Metcalf was wrong, however, in suggesting that *My Old Man's a Dustman* is achieved "without recourse to semi-autobiographical background," since Mankowitz was certainly familiar with the economic relationship between rubbish-picker and second-hand dealer (the latter represented in the novel by the obviously Jewish character Rambam, whose name

is the traditional acronym for Maimonides). By the time his next novel appeared in 1963, Mankowitz had also become familiar with the world of show business, but he seems to have responded less sympathetically to the affluent yet obnoxious personalities of the film industry than to the impoverished and quirky ones of the marketplace of his youth. At any rate, *Cockatrice*, which recounts the amoral adventures of an underling who usurps a major producer's place while the impresario is out of town, is told with a strident humor on the level of its protagonist's name, Danny Pisarov. Indeed, Mankowitz's humor can be seen as progressively less subtle in its development from *Make Me an Offer* to *Cockatrice*, a fact that might be attributed to the differing requirements of fiction and stage or screen, in both of which he became increasingly active during this period. Whatever the reason, *Cockatrice* was poorly received, especially in the United States where Mankowitz has not subsequently published another volume of fiction.

The Oscar-winning *The Bespoke Overcoat* is Mankowitz's most celebrated play and screenplay, the story of a poor, drunken tailor whose even poorer friend, Fender, has died but still haunts his memory. In a note written for the publication of the work in *Five One-Act Plays*, Mankowitz credits the original director, Alec Clunes, with understanding "that this story was not a ghost-story; he understood that *The Bespoke Overcoat* was a sustained, typically over-long Jewish joke—than which there is no sadder and no funnier story." The humor and pathos of the play come from the tailor's continuing commitment to his friend, now dead, and the dead Fender's feeling that, all things considered, he would rather be alive. The play is witty and touching, very much the product of Mankowitz's early period and in sharp contrast to the shrill tones of his later fiction. Among the author's later writings only another play, *The Irish-Hebrew Lesson*, approaches the achievement of his earliest work—possibly an indication that Mankowitz's humor is most subtle and successful when his sympathies are engaged by struggling visionaries, usually of the impoverished and Jewish varieties.

The same qualities are to be found in some of Mankowitz's other endeavors, most notably his documentary on pre-war Yiddish movies, *Almonds and Raisins* (the title is a rendering of a line from a traditional Yiddish lullaby). In *Almonds and Raisins*, Mankowitz mixes poi-

M

gnant footage of Yiddish films from a culture now destroyed with hilarious scenes from early Hollywood-produced Westerns in Yiddish complete with gunslingers and cowboys.

Mankowitz returned to the novel with *Raspberry Reich*, its title taken from an epigraph supplied by Ulrike Meinhof, hardly the stuff of comedy. Far from the sources of Mankowitz's humor, the novel has less to do with recent German terrorism than with the cynicism and indifference of Europe's upper classes. The writer's sarcasm becomes tedious by the time that Clio, the novel's most positive character (in part, one suspects, because she is "a quarter Jewish" and has "surprisingly large breasts"), is shot dead at the end by her roommate with multiple personalities. In contrast, Mankowitz's next effort, *!Abracadabra!*, is his best novel of recent years. Narrated by a crazed geriatric case in the year 2013, when England has converted to Islam and is patrolled by agents of the Inland Revenue, the central story of *!Abracadabra!* recounts the narrator's adventures as a boy evacuated from London during the Blitz and billeted in the unlikely town of Sodbury with the more unlikely Solomon Hakoen, "last of the alchemists and pseudo-Jew."

Mankowitz has continued to use the occult to humorous effect in more recent novels, though with an American setting. *The Devil in Texas* seems at first conventional in its use of a cultured Englishman as a stranger in the strange land of the western United States; yet Dr. Stanley is in Texas not only to satirize American excesses, but to search for vampires, when the woman he loves becomes possessed. *The Magic Cabinet of Professor Smucker* shifts the setting to a very contemporary Los Angeles, still mixing in large doses of illusion and magic. And, *Exquisite Cadaver*, narrated by a ghostly Dadaist stuck in a New Mexico-like locale, though "an almost entirely traditional contribution to a genre of the fantastic in fiction which has been designated posthumous fantasy," according to John Clute, is nonetheless "canny and extreme, sour and airy."[6]

Summary

Wolf Mankowitz has only occasionally matched the originality and energy of his earliest work in a career now spanning more than four decades, but he has continued to make important contributions to contemporary English literature and art in such a variety of genres and media that it would be hard to overestimate his influence. Despite this, and despite his recently frequent residence in and use of America as the setting for his novels, Mankowitz's fiction and plays have not been published in the United States for nearly thirty years and have received so little critical attention here that his name has never even appeared in the annual *MLA International Bibliography of Books and Articles on the Modern Languages and Literatures*.

Mankowitz's lack of success in the United States is the more remarkable when one considers the reception of American-Jewish writers such as Saul Bellow, Bernard Malamud, and Philip Roth who, like Mankowitz, came to prominence in the post-war years. Though Mankowitz has never employed the theme of the Jew as representative victim which was favored by those American writers especially in the first decades after the Holocaust, his best work combines poignant and funny views of the milieu of impoverished East End Jews and their little victories in a seemingly indifferent universe.

Notes

1. Malcolm Muggeridge, in his foreword to Wolf Mankowitz, *Laugh Till You Cry* (New York: Dutton, 1955), p. 5.
2. Judy Cooke in James Vinson, ed. *Contemporary Dramatists*, 3rd ed. (New York: St. Martin's Press, 1982), p. 514.
3. The history of *The Irish-Hebrew Lesson* is a good example of Mankowitz's reworking of his own material in various forms. Originally entitled *The Hebrew Lesson*, it began as a screenplay for a film that Mankowitz directed in 1972; rewritten for the stage, it retained that title when first published in 1977. But, Mankowitz changed the title to *The Irish-Hebrew Lesson* when the play was first produced, in London in 1978. Since then, it has appeared in print under that title, in Ed Berman, ed. *Ten of the Best: British Short Plays* (New York: Interaction Inprint, 1979).
4. Cooke in D. Kirkpatrick, ed. *Contemporary Novelists*, 4th ed. (New York: St. Martin's Press, 1986), p. 573.
5. Metcalf was reviewing the American publication of the novel, retitled *Old Soldiers Never Die*, in "Wolf Mankowitz," *The Atlantic*, 198 (October 1956): 86–87.

6. John Clute, "Fakeries," review of *Exquisite Cadaver*, *Times Literary Supplement* (August 17, 1990): 868.

Selected Bibliography
Primary Sources

Fiction
Make Me an Offer. London: Deutsch, and New York: Dutton, 1952.
A Kid for Two Farthings. London: Deutsch, 1953; New York: Dutton, 1954.
Laugh Till You Cry: An Advertisement. New York: Dutton, 1955.
My Old Man's a Dustman. London: Deutsch, 1956; in America under the title *Old Soldiers Never Die*, Boston: Little, Brown, 1956.
The Mendelman Fire and Other Stories. London: Deutsch, and Boston: Little, Brown, 1957.
Expresso Bongo: A Wolf Mankowitz Reader. New York: Yoseloff, 1961.
Cockatrice. London: Longmans, Green, 1963; New York: Putnam, 1965.
The Biggest Pig in Barbados: A Fable. London: Longmans, Green, 1965.
The Penguin Wolf Mankowitz. Harmondsworth: Penguin Books, 1967.
The Blue Arabian Nights: Tales of a London Decade. London: Mitchell, 1973.
The Day of the Women and the Night of the Men. London: Robson, 1977.
Raspberry Reich. Dublin: Gill and Macmillan, 1979.
!Abracadabra! Dublin: Gill and Macmillan, 1980.
The Devil in Texas. London: Royce, 1984.
Gioconda. London: Allen, 1987.
The Magic Cabinet of Professor Smucker. London: Allen, 1988.
Exquisite Cadaver. London: Deutsch, 1990.

Plays
The Bespoke Overcoat. London: Evans, 1954; New York: French, n.d.
Five One-Act Plays. London: Evans, 1955; New York: French, n.d.
Expresso Bongo. London: Evans, 1960.
The Samson Riddle: An Essay and a Play, with the Text of the Original Story of Samson. London: Mitchell, 1972.
The Hebrew Lesson. London: Evans, 1977; rpt. as *The Irish-Hebrew Lesson*. New York: French, n.d.

Miscellaneous
The Portland Vase and the Wedgwood Copies. London: Deutsch, 1952.
Wedgwood. London: Batsford, and New York: Dutton, 1953.
Majollika and Company. London: Deutsch, 1955.
ABC of Show Business. London: Oldbourne Press, 1956.
A Concise Encyclopedia of English Pottery and Porcelain. London: Deutsch, and New York: Hawthorn, 1957.
XII Poems. London: Workshop Press, 1971.
Dickens of London. London: Weidenfeld and Nicolson, 1976; New York: Macmillan, 1977.
The Extraordinary Mr. Poe: A Biography of Edgar Allan Poe. London: Weidenfeld and Nicolson, and New York: Summit, 1978.
Mazeppa: The Lives, Loves, and Legends of Adah Isaacs Menken; A Biographical Quest. London: Blond and Briggs, and New York: Stein and Day, 1982.

Secondary Sources
Duprey, Richard A. "Wolf Mankowitz." *Dictionary of Literary Biography*. *British Novelists, 1930–1959*. Vol. 15. Part 2. Ed. Bernard Oldsey. Detroit: Gale Research, 1983, pp. 351–57.
Cooke, Judy. "Wolf Mankowitz." *Contemporary Dramatists*. Ed. James Vinson. New York: St. Martin's Press, 1982. 3rd ed, pp. 514–20.
———. "Wolf Mankowitz." *Contemporary Novelists*. Ed. D. Kirkpatrick. New York: St. Martin's Press, 1986. 4th ed, pp. 572–73.
Metcalf, John. "Wolf Mankowitz." *The Atlantic*, 198 (October 1956): 86–88.
Wilson, Michaela Swart. "Wolf Mankowitz." *Contemporary Authors*. Ed. Ann Evory. New Rev. Ser. Vol. 5. Detroit: Gale Research, 1982, pp. 346–49.

David Mesher

M

Marlowe, Christopher

Born: Canterbury, England, February 1564
Education: King's School, Canterbury; Corpus Christi College, Cambridge University, B.A., 1584; M.A., 1587
Died: Deptford, June 1, 1593

Biography

Christopher Marlowe was born in Canterbury in February 1564 (he was baptized on the 26th), two months before his major dramatic rival, William Shakespeare. His father, John Marlowe, was a fairly prosperous Canterbury shoemaker—successful enough to employ at least four apprentices in his shop. One of nine children, Christopher distinguished himself academically by winning two scholarships, first to the King's School in Canterbury, and later a Matthew Parker scholarship to Corpus Christi College, Cambridge. The Parker scholarship, established by and named after the Archbishop of Canterbury, was designed for students planning to enter the ministry. Marlowe held the scholarship six years, earning a B.A. in 1584 and M.A. in 1587, though for reasons unknown he never entered the clergy.

Marlowe encountered some difficulties in securing his M.A. degree, apparently because of a lack of attendance at Cambridge University and the suspicion that he had spent time at a Catholic seminary in Rheims. He was awarded the degree only after the Queen's Privy Council wrote a letter to university authorities assuring them that Marlowe "deserved to be rewarded for his faithful dealings" for he had been employed in "matters touching the benefit of his country." No evidence exists for the sort of service Marlowe performed. However, if he did spend time at the seminary in Rheims, he may have worked as a government agent, spying on Catholic exiles who posed threats against Protestant England. The possibility of employment as a government spy is also suggested by Marlowe's friendship with Thomas Walsingham, the brother of Francis Walsingham who was Minister of Security.

After receiving his M.A., Marlowe moved to London and began a career as a playwright. His major plays include *Tamburlaine The Great, I, Tamburlaine The Great, II, The Jew of Malta, The Tragedy of Edward II,* and *The Tragical History of Dr. Faustus,* along with *Dido, Queen of Carthage* (heavily dependent on Virgil's *Aeneid*) and *The Massacre at Paris* (which survives only in a mangled and abbreviated form). He also wrote a narrative poem, *Hero and Leander,* as well as translations of the Roman poets, Ovid and Lucan. There is little firm evidence or scholarly consensus on the dating of his works.

While in London, Marlowe carried on a troubled relationship with city authorities. In 1589, he was imprisoned on charges of murder. According to the investigation report, Marlowe was engaged in a street fight with William Bradley, when Thomas Watson, a poet and friend of Marlowe's, intervened and fatally stabbed Bradley. Watson was imprisoned for five months and then acquitted, but Marlowe spent only one week in prison—perhaps due to his connections at Court. In 1592, Marlowe was issued a warrant to keep the peace after two London constables reported that they were in fear of their lives from him. The following year, he was accused of atheism after his friend and fellow dramatist, Thomas Kyd, was arrested, and authorities found an atheistic tract in the search of his chambers. Under torture Kyd claimed that the tract belonged to Marlowe, with whom he had shared a room two years earlier. Kyd also accused Marlowe of being "intemperate and of a cruel heart," and claimed that his former roommate would often "jest at the divine scriptures, gibe at prayers, and strive in argument to frustrate and confute what hath been spoke or writ by prophets and such holy men." The Queen's Privy Council issued a warrant for Marlowe's arrest, but instead of prison and torture Marlowe was only required to report daily to the Council until his case could be heard—such lenient treatment would again suggest connections in high places.

Before his case was heard, Marlowe was dead. According to the official report, Marlowe traveled to Deptford, outside London, to meet with three men: Ingram Frizer, Nicholas Skeres, and Robert Poley. On June 1, 1593, they dined at a local inn, spent the afternoon strolling in the garden, and later returned to the inn for supper, after which Frizer and Marlowe argued over the bill. The investigators report that Marlowe seized Frizer's dagger, and in self-defense Frizer grabbed Marlowe's hand and turned the dagger against him, inflicting a "mortal wound over his right eye of the depth of two inches and of the width of one inch" from which he "then and there instantly died." The account appears suspicious, since modern medical experts claim that such a wound might lead to a coma but not instant death. Moreover, Frizer was fully acquitted (and lived to a ripe old age as a church warden) and later came into the employ of Thomas Walsingham, the brother of the Minister of Security. Though no firm evidence exists, Marlowe's death may have been a planned assassination. Government authorities may have had much to fear from Marlowe:

perhaps he knew too much about secret operations, or perhaps his atheistical ideas posed a threat of scandal for his associates at Court.

Between Kyd's arrest and Marlowe's death, Richard Baines, a professional informer, was hired by the Privy Council to gather information on Marlowe. According to Baines's report, Marlowe habitually scorned God and religion and lured men into atheism ("atheism" in the sixteenth century could mean virtually any departure from orthodox religion). On "the testimony of many honest men," Baines accused Marlowe of uttering these and other blasphemies: "Moses was but a juggler"; "the first beginning of religion was only to keep men in awe"; "Christ was a bastard and his mother dishonest"; "if there be any God or any good religion, then it is in the papists', because the service of God is performed with more ceremonies, as elevation of the mass, organs, singing men, shaven crowns, etc."; "all protestants are hypocritical asses"; "St. John the Baptist was bedfellow to Christ"; "they that love not tobacco and boys were fools." There is no telling how accurate Baines's account was, but such remarks at least roughly corroborate the accusations of Kyd, as well as others such as Robert Greene, who referred to Marlowe as "daring God out of heaven with the atheist Tamburlaine," and Thomas Beard, who claimed that Marlowe "cursed and blasphemed to his last gasp."

Literary Analysis

In his prologue to *Tamburlaine The Great, I* (ca. 1587), Marlowe claims to surpass the "clownage" of early Elizabethan drama, aspiring to a more stately and sophisticated "tragic glass." Yet, much in the play is reminiscent of the comic antics of the conventional Vice figure of medieval morality plays. As the conventional Vice derives his humor from irreverent mockery of Christian morality, Tamburlaine lashes out at the religious and political values of Elizabethan culture. Much of the humor in the play lies in the technique of reversal which is found in Tamburlaine's outrageous assaults on orthodox values, treating the serious frivolously, the reverent irreverently, the sacred indecently—comically turning the world upside down.

The earliest text of *Tamburlaine The Great, I* includes a preface by the printer in which he claims to have "left out some fond and frivolous gestures" that some playgoers had "fondly gaped at." The preface implies that the original play included additional comic scenes. Even so, the abbreviated text that survives includes plenty of material worth gaping at. Marlowe often resorts to outrageous stage spectacles. Perhaps the most prominent example is when Bajazeth, the Emperor of the Turks, is captured and placed in a cage to be carried about by Tamburlaine's soldiers. Though Tamburlaine is merely the son of a lowly Scythian shepherd, he readily defeats and publicly humiliates an emperor. Caged like a beast, Bajazeth soon degenerates in royal dignity as he threatens Tamburlaine: "I could willingly feed upon thy blood-raw heart" (4.4. 11–12). Tamburlaine responds by securing a piece of meat to the tip of his sword and taunting the miserable Turk, after which Bajazeth "takes the food, and stamps upon it" (stage direction). The Turkish emperor is quickly reduced from ruler to beast to pouting infant. Bajazeth ultimately resorts to suicide as "He brains himself against the cage" (stage direction). His wife Zabina arrives to offer a vivid comment on the bloody mess: "His skull all riven in twain! his brains dash'd out" (5.2.243). She then proceeds to follow her husband's example and "runs against the cage, and brains herself" (stage direction). Surely the spectacular excesses of such scenes would have provoked amusement in the audience (at least among those with a sufficiently hearty sense of humor), especially if the double suicide was enacted with the aide of sheep or pig brains splattered about the stage. The effect was probably not unlike that of a modern horror film—distasteful to some, gut-busting humor to others.

Such episodes in Marlowe's plays suggest a kinship with popular forms of Elizabethan entertainment such as bear-baiting in which bears would be chained to a stake and then attacked by dogs to the bloody amusement of the crowd. In *Tamburlaine The Great, I*, we find something not altogether different, but instead of a bear tied to a stake we find an emperor in a cage. Elizabethan theaters were often located in the vicinity of bear-baiting amphitheaters, were architecturally modeled on such amphitheaters, and most likely could provide an atmosphere as raucous and irreverent. In fact, fights between members of the theater audience and actors on stage were not uncommon, and during play performances beer, wine, nuts, apples, and tobacco were readily consumed by the playgoers. Considering the atmosphere of communal merrymaking, what might seem disturbing in the

M

study would more likely seem humorous on the Elizabethan stage.

In *Tamburlaine The Great, II* (ca. 1588), the Scythian conqueror continues with similar antics, this time defeating assorted kings, placing horse bits in their mouths, and forcing them to draw him about in his chariot, as he whips them and feeds them raw meat. In a comic inversion of the natural order, Marlowe presents a spectacle of kings made beasts by a shepherd made king.

In addition to his savage mockery of royal blood and traditional hierarchy, the dramatist undermines a Christian view of cosmic order. While early Elizabethan tragedies typically abide by the Fall of Princes tradition in which the hero proudly rises but inevitably falls in accordance with a dependable moral order, Marlowe repeatedly teases the audience with expectations of Tamburlaine's fall only to frustrate such traditional expectations. Instead of behaving according to formula, Tamburlaine makes it to the top of Fortune's Wheel and refuses to budge. When he finally dies, the circumstances of his death do not confirm but rather undermine the traditional Christian moral order. After a career of unrestrained blasphemy, Tamburlaine is brought low not by the Christian God but by the prophet of Islam. After ordering his soldiers to burn the Koran, he defies Mohamet:

> Now, Mohamet, if thou have any power,
> Come down thyself and work a miracle.
> Thou art not worthy to be worshipped
> That suffers flames of fire to burn the
>   writ
> Wherein the sum of thy religion rests.
>   (5.2.185–89)

Within moments, Tamburlaine falls ill: "I feel myself distemper'd suddenly" (5.2.216). The timing of his sickness and death implies that if there is any moral order it must be Islamic. Soon, though, the Islamic order is also undermined when a physician who has examined Tamburlaine's urine gives an elaborate medical description of the causes of his illness—implying that Tamburlaine dies not from divine wrath of any sort but from purely naturalistic causes. Marlowe momentarily affirms Islam in order to satirize Christianity, only to then turn around and satirize Islam.

In *The Jew of Malta* (ca. 1590), Marlowe aims his black humor even more directly at Christianity. Although the prologue refers to the play as the "tragedy of a Jew," it is tragic only in the limited sense of depicting a character's rise and fall. Modeled on the medieval Vice figure, Barabas the Jew is far too inhuman, too vicious, too much a caricature, to elicit our engagement. The stage actions, like those in *Tamburlaine the Great, I* and *II*, are often wildly exaggerated and sensational—in fact, even more than in the earlier plays. T.S. Eliot aptly called the play a farce.

Unlike Shakespeare's Shylock, Marlowe's Barabas is depicted free of troubling ambiguity. He is an uncomplicated and unrelenting subhuman Machiavellian schemer. What keeps the play from degenerating into mere Jew-baiting is that Marlowe baits the Christians with equal savagery. As it soon becomes evident, the Christians are every bit as greedy and malicious as Barabas, only not so clever. Much of the humor in the play is in Marlowe's emphasis on Christian hypocrisy, usually with the implication that if any character can lay claim to moral superiority, it must be Barabas, since his unabashed greed is more straightforward; it is not masked by pious hypocrisies. Entirely disillusioned and cynical, Barabas boldly recognizes, and even flaunts, his sinister and cunning evil.

The play begins with Ferneze, the Christian Duke of Malta, seizing half of the property of the Jews in order to pay his debts to the Turks. Barabas responds to the scheme with biting irony: "Is theft the ground of your religion?" (1.2.99). When all of his property is seized because of his protest, Barabas replies: "Your extreme right does me exceeding wrong" (1.2.157). With subversive and ironic wit, Barabas often adopts the very logic of Christian thought in order to turn it against itself:

> It's no sin to deceive a Christian;
> For they themselves hold it a principle.
> Faith is not to be held with heretics.
> But all are heretics that are not Jews.
>   (2.3.314–17)

Along with Barabas's witty assaults at Christian hypocrisy, the play amuses with scene after scene of outrageous Machiavellian cunning. When Barabas purchases the slave Ithamore, the two men compete in telling anecdotes of their clever and sensational misdeeds:

Barabas: As for myself, I walk abroad a-
    nights,

And kill sick people groaning under
    walls.
Sometimes I go about and poison
    wells . . .
     . . . . .
But tell me now, how hast thou spent thy
    time?
Ithamore: Faith, master.
In setting Christian villages on fire,
Chaining of eunuchs, binding galley
    slaves.
     . . . . .
Once at Jerusalem, where the pilgrims
    kneel'd
I strewed powder on the marble stones,
And therewithal their knees would
    rankle so,
That I have laugh'd a-good to see the
    cripples
Go limping home to Christendom on
    stilts. (2.3.179–218)

As in Shakespeare's *Titus Andronicus*, villainy is so overdone that it soon turns unreal and comic. Moreover, the net effect of such outrageous acts of villainy seems not merely comic but parodic. Marlowe wildly exaggerates Renaissance stereotypes of Jews so that he is parodying not Jews but Christian concepts of Jews.

Like *Tamburlaine the Great, I* and *II, The Jew of Malta* (ca. 1590) also has its share of stage spectacle. After poisoning an entire convent of nuns, Barabas provokes two friars into a heated competition for his soul and the money that would come with it. In an exquisitely cunning scheme, he strangles one friar, sets the corpse upright against a wall, and waits for the rival friar to arrive and beat the already dead corpse until "his brains drop out on's nose" (4.2.179–80). As is often the case in Marlowe's plays, what might seem horrible turns comic in its grisly and sensational excess—not to mention that friars may not be the most sympathetic characters in the eyes of a Protestant English audience.

Barabas ultimately perishes, not by the operations of a moral order, but by his own overly subtle trickery. As in *Tamburlaine the Great, I* and *II*, the playwright hints at the structure of a conventional tragedy only to thwart such expectations. Barabas sets up an elaborate trap door with a burning cauldron below in a scheme to kill Calymath the Turk, but in an unguarded moment Barabas is outwitted by Ferneze and falls into the cauldron him-self—and survives long enough to heartily curse them all. Ferneze, the Christian governor, regains power in Malta, and in the final lines of the play he voices the conventional ending of a Christian tragedy: "let due praise be given, / Neither to Fate nor Fortune, but to Heaven" (5.5.130–31). Though Ferneze affirms an orthodox moral order, the context of his persistently un-Christian behavior provides an overwhelming sense of irony, reducing his concluding remark to a hollow piety. The ending may seem orthodox, in that a blaspheming Jew is justly slain by his own treachery, but the ironic tone of the play persistently defies such orthodoxies.

The Tragical History of Dr. Faustus (ca. 1592) and *The Tragedy of Edward II* (ca. 1592) are the two plays by Marlowe that most approximate tragedy, and thus are on the whole least humorous. In *The Tragical History of Dr. Faustus*, comedy is mostly confined to the subplot of Wagner, Robin, and Dick (though there is no scholarly consensus on how much of the subplot Marlowe actually wrote). Throughout the play, the comic subplot tends to function as an ironic inversion of the tragic main plot. Faustus, for example, uses his magic book to conjure the devil, Mephostophilis, and in exchange for his soul he is granted twenty-four years of magical power. In the following scene, his servant Wagner manages to conjure devils as well, thus suggesting that Faustus's special power to conjure devils is merely an illusion. Later, Faustus uses his magic to play tricks on the Pope. He snatches dishes and cups, steals the triple crown, and then boxes the Pope on the ears and flings fireworks among several friars—all of this to the delight of a Protestant audience. The scene is followed by Robin and Dick stealing a cup from a vintner, and then being transformed by Mephostophilis into an ape and dog. Again, the subplot undermines the heroic dignity of Faustus, reducing his theft of the triple crown to the level of common thievery, transforming him, at least metaphorically, into an ape or dog. As the play proceeds, the tragic and comic plots tend to converge, as Faustus himself engages in farcical trickery. He sells a horse to a man but when the buyer rides it in water it turns into a bottle of hay. The man returns (all wet) to find Faustus sleeping, tries to wake him by tugging at his leg, but finds that the leg comes off in his hand—a fine stage trick, perhaps, but virtually indistinguishable from the clownage of Robin and Dick and hardly worth the price of Faustus's soul. Ironically, Faustus's longing for superhuman knowledge and power debases him into a subhuman clown.

The Tragedy of Edward II contains none of the clownage found in *The Tragical History of Dr. Faustus*, but instead a more sophisticated and subtle dark humor. King Edward—profligate, ineffectual, and entirely given over to homosexual love for his minion Gaveston—orders the punishment and imprisonment of Gaveston's principle enemy, the Bishop of Coventry: "Throw off his golden mitre, rend his stole, / And in the channel christen him anew!" (1.1.187–88). The play takes place in medieval Catholic England, so dunking the bishop's head in a sewer would almost assuredly provoke laughter. Still, the ultimate effect of such scenes may be more subtle and subversive. Marlowe seems intent not merely to humiliate particular characters, but to violate and degrade the very principles of religious and political hierarchy.

King Edward is subjected to an abuse so savage that it exceeds anything like just retribution. The drama does not merely degrade Edward but degrades the very principles of kingship and royal blood. After the king is defeated and captured by his enemies, he is imprisoned "up to the knees" in the castle sewer (5.5.2). When, Christ-like in his "tatter'd robes," he requests "water, gentle friends, to cool my thirst," the guards offer him not water or even vinegar, but "puddle-water" (5.5.69; 5.3.25–30). In a perverse baptism, the guards wash the king in the sewer and shave his beard. Still worse, he is executed with supreme Machiavellian cunning by Lightborn, who crushes him between a table and feather-bed and in a gesture of Dantesque retribution penetrates the king's "fundament" with a "red-hot" "spit" (5.5.32). The scene, though perhaps the most tragic in all of Marlowe's plays, falls short of full tragic stature, as our sympathy for the king is thwarted by the degrading spectacle of suffering and humiliation. In its untempered excess, the punishment of the king, like that of the bishop, seems not merely just retribution but a sardonic undermining of the most essential and sacred principles of Elizabethan culture.

Summary

All of Christopher Marlowe's plays contain humor, though usually that humor has a bitter and sardonic edge. Marlowe typically exploits characters whom his audiences would find loathesome and alien—blasphemers, infidels, necromancers, deviants—as objects of scorn but also as scorners of the values that Elizabethan culture (or at least the state and church) held out as sacred and inviolable.

Selected Bibliography

Primary Sources

The Complete Plays. Ed. J.B. Steane. New York: Penguin Books, 1969. All quotes from Marlowe's plays are from this edition.

The Complete Poems and Translations. Ed. Stephen Orgel. New York: Penguin Books, 1971.

Secondary Sources

Dollimore, Jonathan. *Radical Tragedy.* Chicago: University of Chicago Press, 1984. Includes chapters on radical skepticism in Renaissance England and a chapter on *The Tragical History of Dr. Faustus.*

Eliot, T.S. "Christopher Marlowe." *Selected Essays 1917–1932.* New York: Harcourt Brace, 1932. Eliot characterizes Marlowe's plays as written in a tone of "terribly serious, even savage comic humour" (p. 105).

Greenblatt, Stephen. *Renaissance Self-fashioning.* Chicago: University of Chicago Press, 1980. Includes a highly insightful chapter on Marlowe, covering the major plays.

Gurr, Andrew. *Playgoing in Shakespeare's London.* Cambridge: Cambridge University Press, 1987. A thorough study of the atmosphere and audiences of theaters in Renaissance London.

Kocher, Paul H. *Christopher Marlowe: A Study of His Thought, Learning, and Character.* Chapel Hill: University of North Carolina Press, 1946. Includes a chapter on Marlowe's humor.

Leech, Clifford. *Christopher Marlowe: Poet for the Stage.* Ed. Anne Lancashire. New York: AMS Press, 1986. Leech writes chapters on all of Marlowe's plays, often with an eye for humor.

Steane, J.B. *Marlowe: A Critical Study.* Cambridge: Cambridge University Press, 1964. Analyzes all of Marlowe's works and includes a thorough biographical chapter and an appendix with a reprint of the Baines note.

Stephen J. Lynch

Marryat, Frederick

Born: London, July 10, 1792
Education: Formal education concluded at
  the age of fourteen
Marriage: Catherine Shairp, January 21,
  1819; separated, 1839; eleven children
Died: Langham, Norfolk, August 9, 1848

Biography

Frederick Marryat was born on July 10, 1792, in London, to Charlotte von Geyer, the daughter of American loyalists, and Joseph Marryat, the member of Parliament for Sandwich, chairman of the board of Lloyds, and colonial agent for Grenada and Trinidad. Marryat's formal education ended when he was allowed to join the Royal Navy in 1806. His first captain, the benevolent Lord Cochrane of the *Imperieuse*, served as the model for portraits of many officers in Marryat's novels.

Marryat served in the West Indies, the Mediterranean, and the North Atlantic, and he was frequently commended for his bravery. Some entries from his private log of 1807 give an example of the exciting life that Marryat led:

> Jan. 2—Stove the cutter, and Henry Christian drowned.

> Jan. 4—Anchored, and stormed a battery.

> Jan. 6—Took a galliot; blew up ditto.

> Jan. 8—Trying to get a prize off that was ashore, lost five men.

Marryat was promoted to captain in 1820. That same year he was made a member of the Royal Society at the recommendation of his friend, mathematician Charles Babbage. In 1824, Marryat fought in the war against the King of Burma, and he was the first British officer to command a steam ship. He achieved the rank of Post-Captain in 1826 and was made Companion of the Bath.

The success of Marryat's first novel, the semi-autobiographical *The Naval Officer: or, Scenes and Adventures in the Life of Frank Mildmay* (often referred to simply as *Frank Mildmay*) published in 1829, helped prompt him to resign from the Navy. This decision was also influenced by the lack of opportunities for promotion and by the powerful enemies (including King William IV) that Marryat made because of a pamphlet that he had written against impressment.

Once out of the Navy, Marryat soon became a fashionable man in London society. He became part of Lady Blessington's circle (and later Charles Dickens's) and was a good friend of the Duke of Sussex. In 1833, he stood in the reform interest for Parliament from the Tower Hamlets, but his narrow focus on naval issues resulted in his being soundly defeated.

Marryat was editor of the *Metropolitan Magazine* (1832–1836) where many of his works were published wholly or in part. In 1835, Marryat went on a tour of the Continent with his family. He then set out on a trip to America (1837–1838), at least in part to avoid his unhappy marriage. Marryat separated from his wife Catherine in 1839. He had married her on January 21, 1819, and despite their having eleven children, seven of whom survived to adulthood, the union was always precarious.

An extravagant spender, Marryat was ever in need of money. In an attempt to meet this need he wrote a series of lucrative children's books in the 1840s. He moved to Langham, Norfolk, in 1843, where he tried unsuccessfully to make a living as a gentleman farmer. Habitually a highly volatile man, he died at Langham on August 9, 1848, of a ruptured blood vessel, an ailment that he had first suffered during his time in the Navy.

Literary Analysis

Captain Marryat, although generally neglected in recent years, was the greatest English writer of sea tales between the time of Tobias Smollett and Joseph Conrad, and he was the first nineteenth-century writer to publish his novels serially in his own magazine, the *Metropolitan*, an important precedent for later novelists such as Dickens and William Makepeace Thackeray. Although he was a popular writer, he was not, however, just a novelist for the masses. His work was enjoyed by, among others, Samuel Taylor Coleridge, Dickens, Washington Irving, Edward Bulwer-Lytton, Thackeray, Herman Melville, John Ruskin, and Robert Louis Stevenson. Many twentieth-century writers have also praised his work highly. Conrad considered Marryat to be one of his chief influences and thought that "[h]is greatness is undeniable" (54). The title work in Virginia Woolf's *The Captain's Deathbed and Other Essays* is a laudatory piece on Marryat. Ernest Hemingway, D.H. Lawrence,

C.S. Forester, and William Styron praised him. Ford Madox Ford even said that Marryat was England's greatest novelist. Perhaps Woolf's assessment of him is best: "Captain Marryat had in embryo at least most of the gifts that go to make a master" (42).

Marryat's novels are all loosely connected series of adventures which are often based on his experiences at sea. They reflect the harsh life that he led, where death could come at any moment. As a result, there can be a grim side to the humor in his novels. In *The Naval Officer,* for example, while a well-dressed man is walking along on a distant beach, a captain orders a gun fired as a test. The gunners aim at the man but never expect to hit him; unfortunately, the ball strikes the man and cuts him in two. Frank Mildmay, the protagonist, dryly tells us the man had been reading a book before being hit— Ovid's *Metamorphoses.*

In *Peter Simple* (1834), considered the author's best work, Marryat tells the story of a naive boy who becomes educated during his time in the Navy. Peter says, "It has been from time immemorial the heathenish custom to sacrifice the greatest fool of the family to the prosperity and naval superiority of the country, and, at the age of fourteen, I was selected as the victim" (chapter 1).[1]

Peter's innocence is the source of humor through much of the novel. This humor often has a ribald side, for which Marryat sometimes was condemned by his contemporaries. In one scene, for instance, Peter encounters a prostitute but is unaware of her profession:

> I had arrived opposite a place called Sally Port, when a young lady, very nicely dressed, looked at me very hard and said, "Well, Reefer, how are you off for soap?" I was astonished at the question, and more so at the interest she seemed to take in my affairs. I answered, "Thank you, I am very well off; I have four cakes of Windsor, and two bars of yellow for washing . . . "

> Just as we passed the admiral's house, I perceived my captain walking with two of the admiral's daughters. I was not a little proud to let him see that I had female acquaintances as well as he had, and, as I passed him with the young lady under my protection, I took off my hat, and made a low bow. To my surprise,

not only did he not return the salute, but he looked at me with a very stern countenance. (chapter 4)

As with all Marryat's heroes, things eventually work out well for Peter. He becomes heir to the large estate of his snobbish uncle Lord Privilege, but only after he has endured a number of misfortunes, including a twenty-month period in an asylum.

Woolf says that "perhaps the Captain's greatest gift was his power of drawing character" (43). Peter's friend Mr. Chucks, who aspires to be a gentleman, exemplifies the novelist's ability to create a memorable character. Chucks would "rather be the bye-blow of a gentleman, than the 'gitimate offspring of a boatswain and his wife" (chapter 14). Eventually Chucks, who it is believed had been killed in battle, returns as Count Shucksen, a war hero who has married a Swedish countess.

Although Marryat is generally thought of as a sea novelist, in two of his best works he abandons this setting. He chooses the London riverside as the locale for his own favorite work, *Jacob Faithful* (1834). The theme is ostensibly about the need for sublimating one's individuality to a larger whole. As is often the case in Marryat's work, one gets conflicting messages; the quest for independence, if done in moderation, is also praised.

Japhet, in Search of a Father (1836), also set on land, was written at breakneck speed, as much as sixty-five pages in one day, yet it was one of Marryat's best-selling works and has sections that are splendidly written. Japhet, abandoned by his parents, is left at the Foundling Hospital. He becomes an apprentice to an apothecary, Mr. Cophagus, who speaks with the halting speech demonstrated by Dickens's Mr. Jingle in *The Posthumous Papers of the Pickwick Club* (1836–1837): "Read—write—spell—good, and *so on.* Bring him up—rudiments, spatula—write labels—um—M.D. one of these days—make a man of him, and so on" (chapter 1).

Japhet's monomania in seeking his father often leads him on false quests. For instance, he pursues a bishop whose nose resembles his own on the assumption that the man is his father. Japhet eventually does find his father, a wealthy retired general from India, and after a farcical argument between the two, Japhet wins him over.

In Marryat's most popular work, *Mr. Midshipman Easy* (1836), the author deals, as he does in so many of his novels, with the education of its hero. Jack Easy is raised by an eccentric father who believes in the doctrine of equality, extending it so far that his tenants pay no rent. The boy, once at sea, learns that his father's ideas are ludicrous. Yet, even though Jack dismisses the notion of equality, he remains influenced by some of his father's beliefs as is evidenced by his befriending the African-born cook, Mesty.

The book abounds in lighthearted humor and puns: "Mr. Nicodemus Easy was a gentleman who lived down in Hampshire: he was a married man, and in very easy circumstances. Most couples find it very easy to have a family, but not always quite so easy to maintain them" (chapter 1).

There are delightful attacks on prudery. When a young woman is brought in to be the nurse for young Jack, it is discovered that she is an unmarried mother. The horrified Mrs. Easy cries, "Not a married woman, and she has a child!" The woman simply curtsies and says, "If you please, ma'am, it was a very little one" (chapter 3). Unfortunately, once Jack abandons his father's philosophy, the book loses much of its humor and its charm.

Marryat traveled to America in 1837 and 1838. He soon made enemies over his position in favor of a copyright law and his toast to a captain who sank an American ship during an insurrection in Canada. Indeed, he aroused so much ire that he was burned in effigy twice. Despite Marryat's lofty claims about the intentions of his travel account, *A Diary in America* (1839), the work is merely a rambling, albeit often entertaining, series of anecdotes and attacks on America and its institutions.

The novels after Marryat's American visit have less humor than his earlier works, although in *Poor Jack* (1840) and *Percival Keene* (1842) flashes of Marryat's old genius still are noticeable. In the latter novel, for example, Keene's cruel teacher always threatens his students with a "blow-up" if they anger him. Ironically, he suffers this fate himself when Keene sets fire to a cache of fireworks near the teacher.

Seeing that interest in his sea novels was waning, Marryat turned to writing children's novels, including *Masterman Ready* (1841–1842) and *The Children of the New Forest* (1847). These remained standard reading for children for many years.

Summary
Captain Frederick Marryat's works often are flawed. He wrote rapidly and published more frequently than he should have. The plots are often weakly constructed, overly melodramatic and sentimental, and too reliant upon farce. However, he can relate a lively story, provide vivid characterization, and establish a warm bond between his narrator and the reader; moreover, as Woolf says, "he can create a world" (43). In the words of another of his admirers, Conrad, the loss of his work "would be irreparable" (53). For these reasons, it is hoped that he will not be completely forgotten by future readers.

Notes
1. There are many editions of Marryat's novels; therefore, I have used chapter rather than page numbers. All quotations are from *The Novels of Captain Marryat*. 24 vols. Ed. and intro. by R[eginald] Brimley Johnson. London: J.M. Dent; New York: Little, Brown, 1895–1896.

Selected Bibliography
Primary Sources
The Naval Officer: or, *Scenes and Adventures in the Life of Frank Mildmay*. 3 vols. London: Colburn, 1829.
The King's Own. 3 vols. London: Colburn & Bentley, 1830.
Newton Forster: or, *the Merchant Service*. 3 vols. London: Cochrane, 1832.
Peter Simple. 3 vols. London: Saunders & Otley, 1834. Chapters 1–42 serialized in the *Metropolitan Magazine* from June 1832–September 1833; remaining twenty-three chapters not in serial.
Jacob Faithful. 3 vols. London: Saunders & Otley, 1834. Serialized in the *Metropolitan Magazine* from September 1833–October 1834.
Japhet, in Search of a Father. 3 vols. London: Saunders & Otley, 1836. Serialized in the *Metropolitan Magazine* from November 1834–January 1836.
Mr. Midshipman Easy. 3 vols. London: Saunders & Otley, 1836.
Snarleyyow: or, *the Dog Fiend*. 3 vols. London: Colburn, 1837. Serialized in the *Metropolitan Magazine* from January 1836–July 1837.
The Phantom Ship. 3 vols. London: Colburn,

1839; 1 vol. Boston: Weeks, Jordan, 1839. Serialized in the *New Monthly Magazine* from March 1837–August 1839.

A Diary in America, with Remarks on Its Institutions. 6 vols. London: Longman, Orme, Brown, Green, and Longmans, 1839; 1 vol. New York: Appleton, 1839.

Poor Jack. London: Longman, Orme, Brown, Green, and Longmans, 1840. 12 monthly parts.

Masterman Ready: or, the Wreck of the Pacific. 3 vols. London: Longman, Orme, Brown, Green, and Longmans, 1841–1842.

Percival Keene. 3 vols. London: Colburn, 1842.

The Settlers in Canada. 2 vols. London: Longman, Orme, Brown, Green, and Longmans, 1844.

The Privateer's-Man: One Hundred Years Ago. 2 vols. London: Longman, Orme, Brown, Green, and Longmans, 1846; 1 vol. Boston: Roberts, 1866. Serialized in the *New Monthly Magazine* from August 1845–June 1846.

The Children of the New Forest. 2 vols. London: Hurst, 1847.

Secondary Sources

Brantlinger, Patrick. *Rule of Darkness: British Literature and Imperialism, 1830–1914.* Ithaca: Cornell University Press, 1988, pp. 47–70. Marryat's work is seen as imperialistic doctrine.

Conrad, Joseph. "Tales of the Sea" (1898). In *Notes on Life and Letters.* Garden City, NY: Doubleday, 1921, pp. 53–55. The merits of Marryat and James Fenimore Cooper are discussed.

Engel, Elliot, and Margaret F. King. *The Victorian Novel before Victoria: British Fiction during the Reign of William IV, 1830–37.* New York: St. Martin's Press, 1984, pp. 19–38. A useful if overly critical look at Marryat's early fiction.

Gautier, Maurice-Paul. *Captain Marryat: L'homme et l'oeuvre.* Montreal: Didier, 1973. Meticulously researched, more biographical than sustained literary criticism. In French.

Hannay, David. *Life of Frederick Marryat.* London: Walter Scott, 1889. A distillation of Florence Marryat's work (see below).

Hawes, Donald. "Marryat and Dickens." *Dickens Studies Annual,* 1971, pp. 39–68. Examination of the literary relationship between the two authors as well as an overview of Marryat's work.

Lloyd, Christopher. *Captain Marryat and the Old Navy.* London: Longmans, Green, 1939. Lloyd concentrates on Marryat's years in the Royal Navy with one chapter on the novels.

Marryat, Florence. *Life and Letters of Captain Marryat.* 2 vols. New York: D. Appleton, 1872. Not a probing examination, but the main source for most biographical material on Marryat, including his letters.

Stokes, Roy B. "Frederick Marryat." *Victorian Novelists before 1885.* Vol. 21 of *The Dictionary of Literary Biography.* Ed. Ira B. Nadel and William E. Fredeman. Detroit: Gale, 1983, pp. 222–27. Overview of Marryat's life and work.

Warner, Oliver. *Captain Marryat: A Rediscovery.* London: Constable, 1953. Largely biographical with some critical commentary on the novels.

Woolf, Virginia. *The Captain's Deathbed and Other Essays.* Originally published in the *Times Literary Supplement,* September 26, 1935; New York: Harcourt Brace Jovanovich, 1950, pp. 37–47. This is a succinct, well-balanced look at the Captain and his work.

Louis Parascandola

Marston, John

Born: October 1576, in Wardington, Oxfordshire
Education: Brasenose College, Oxford University, B.A. February 1594
Marriage: Mary Wilkes, 1605(?); one child
Died: London, June 25, 1634

Biography

A Wardington, Oxfordshire, baptism record dated October 7, 1576, serves as the notice of birth for John Marston, son of John Marston, a lawyer and member of the Middle Temple, and Marie Guarsi Marston, the daughter of an Italian physician. Although little is known of his early education, it is likely that young John lived and attended school in Coventry (though even this has been questioned), where his father owned property and served as steward of the city from 1588 to 1599. John Marston, Sr., expected his son to follow in his footsteps as a lawyer and to that end entered him as a member of the Middle Temple (where the elder Marston was a reader) in August 1592. Young John graduated from Brasenose College, Oxford University, in February 1594 and assumed residency in November 1595 at Middle Temple, where he shared his father's chambers and for a time shared his desire to study law, despite being expelled in 1601 (he was reinstated later that year).

It was at Middle Temple that Marston's writing career began in 1598 with the publication of two books of verse satire, issued anonymously, although one, *The Scourge of Villanie*, contains an address to the reader signed by "W. Kinsayder." Soon after these publications Marston embarked on a career as a playwright. He gave up his chamber at Middle Temple in 1606 (holding on to the chamber some seven years after the death of his father) and continued to write for the theater until 1608, when he was committed to Newgate prison for the performance of an offensive play.[1]

Other than the fact that his father-in-law, the Reverend William Wilkes, supported his family financially, little is known of Marston's marriage to Mary Wilkes. In fact, the exact date of Marston's marriage is unknown, though it may have been in 1605. Some sources suggest that Marston was never officially married, others fail to mention his child, and still others dispense with a marriage date altogether (stating simply that Marston was married sometime in his life). On September 24, 1609, he was ordained as a deacon in the parish church of Stanton Harcourt, Oxfordshire, and he became a priest on December 24. He spent the rest of his life as a clergyman, becoming incumbent of Christchurch, Hampshire, on October 10, 1616, where he stayed until September 13, 1631, when he quit his living at Christchurch. His only child, John, died in infancy in 1624. In 1633, William Sheares issued a collection of Marston's work, but the playwright did not approve and ordered his name removed from all copies. Marston died on June 25, 1634, at his home in Aldermanbury, London, and was buried next to his father in Middle Temple.

Literary Analysis

At Middle Temple, Marston was a proficient wit in a closed society of highly educated, leisured, and wealthy men trained to debate, argue, and satirize. Marston and his peers reveled in the writing of satire, excoriating the people,

institutions, and function of society from a seemingly privileged distance. This milieu nurtured Marston's style and personality as a writer and led to his first publications in 1598: *The Metamorphosis of Pigmalions Image and Certaine Satyres* and *The Scourge of Villanie. Three Books of Satyres*. In these books Marston is seen to be a creator of satires both serious and comical (as a playwright he would write mostly comedies, some tragedies, and many combinations of both); in "Satire XI" of *The Scourge of Villanie*, for example, the narrator presents himself as a humorist with a "jocund Muse." *The Metamorphosis of Pigmalions Image* demonstrates the author's propensity for parodying the rhetorical practices of his day, particularly the ever-popular Petrarchan sonnet, even though some critics read this satire as a botched attempt at an Ovidian epyllion. Attacks on the literary and societal fancies of his age became a comic trademark for Marston: in *Histriomastix, or the Player Whipt* (ca. 1598–99),[2] he parodies acting companies and the theater in general; in *Jacke Drums Entertainment* (1600), he lampoons the heightened language of young gallants: Pasquil's "When I turne fickle, vertue shall be vice" is answered by Katherine's "When I prove false, Hell shall be Paradise," an exchange of rhymed couplets that serves to highlight their bloated rhetoric; *The Fawn* is also titled *Parasitaster*, an obvious reference to Ben Jonson's *Poetaster* (1601), which contains a lampoon of Marston in the character of Crispinus; in *The History of Antonio and Mellida* (1600) Marston pokes fun at Marlovian rhetoric, especially that of *Tamburlaine* (1587), as well as all types of love poetry and the lovers it portrays; *Antonio's Revenge* (1600) is often viewed as a satire of revenge tragedy, especially as represented in the popular and influential play by Thomas Kyd, *The Spanish Tragedy* (ca. 1587); *The Dutch Courtezan* (1605) is labeled a city comedy, a genre in which tradesmen, merchants, and other urban inhabitants are lampooned. In addition, Marston's plays were written for children's companies (primarily the Children of Paul's until 1604, when the author bought a managing share of the Children of the Queen's Revels), in which young boys played all of the adult roles, male or female. This fact has led some to believe that the presence of boy actors served as a further means of burlesquing the adult world, even in speeches of relative weight, such as in *Antonio's Revenge* when Pandulpho observes, "Why, all this time I ha' but play'd a part, / Like to some boy that acts a tragedy."

Because of the frequency with which satirical stances can be found in Marston's work, there has been a critical tendency to search for satire in every Marston play. Many argue that his drama is merely a direct offshoot of his verse satire transplanted to a new venue (a transfer that Marston may have been forced to make because of the ban on satire in June 1599 decreed by the Bishops of Canterbury and York).[3] There is some merit to this argument: in *The Scourge of Villanie* the narrator announces, "I hate no man, but mens impietie," a stance that Marston returns to often in his plays and that he ultimately embodies in the title character of his most famous play, *The Malcontent* (1602–1603). Similarly, in *What You Will* (1601) the character of Quadratus is, like William Shakespeare's Falstaff (a character to whom he is often compared, although Falstaff is a much more complex creation), a self-centered clown, both the perpetrator and the victim of practical jokes as well as the wise fool whose judgments on those who inhabit the world with him are particularly astute. Quadratus's asides set him apart from the action as a commentator, a role, according to some scholars, that Marston has merely transplanted from verse to the stage. The ironic stance of the narrator of *The Metamorphosis of Pigmalions Image*, as R.C. Horne argues, observes "the sheer silliness of the situation" in which Pigmalion cannot see the absurdity of his worship of the statue (18), thus making him the forerunner of Quadratus, in spite of the fact that he does not possess Quadratus's humor. Another early Marston satirist/commentator, Chrisoganus of the undistinguished *Histriomastix, or The Player Whipt*, also lacks the raillery of Quadratus.

This quest for the satirical, however, has come at the expense of focusing on Marston's talent to create comedy, often for comedy's sake. The energy and gaiety found in most of the dramatist's work help to develop an atmosphere so varied in comic style and tone that the plays themselves take on the characteristics of revue sketches or burlesques (in the more modern sense of the word). Such designations suggest that plot and character become a secondary concern for a playwright more mindful of tone, mood, and scenes. Indeed, Marston was; his plays remain generally weak in plot structure and are populated by a variety of fools, fops, buffoons, and clowns—one-dimensional

characters all. However, those who are willing to overlook Marston's weaknesses in plot and character development are more accepting of Marston as a comic innovator. The character of Lampatho in *What You Will* is but one example of the critical tension that has characterized literary analysis of Marston's canon. Solemn satire-seekers remark that this character is meant to be a mockery of the author's rival and sometime friend, Ben Jonson. Philip Finkelpearl, however, describes Lampatho as a mockery of Marston himself (164). The writer's ability to caricature himself, then, may have been too often overlooked, making it another casualty in the war between the theatrical and the literary.

Jacke Drums Entertainment and *What You Will* are festive comedies primarily and satires secondarily. The titles of each announce the atmosphere that Marston will create through the action, but in some cases the characters rather metatheatrically elaborate upon the implications of the title: "*What You Will*, a slight toye, lightly composed, to swiftly finisht, ill plotted, worse written, I feare me worst acted, and indeed *What You Will*" (still another example of Marston's self-satire). Both plays involve singing, dancing, pantomime, puns, mistaken identity, farcical characters, and practical jokes. Neither play is particularly dependent on plot or, in some instances, narrative; scenes begin for no apparent reason and narrative line is often interrupted by song or dance, such as Mamon's comic "Dittie" about coins in *Jacke Drums Entertainment*:

> Chunck, chunck, chunck, chunck, his
>   bagges do ring
> A merry note with chuncks to sing:
> Those that are farre more yong and
>   wittie,
> Are wide from singing such a Dittie
> As Chunck, chunck, chunck.

In short, while Marston's satirical stance is ever present—the plays lampoon absurdities of inflated language, foppery, and pretentiousness found in both the world of the stage and the society that Marston inhabited—his sense of fun and festivity operates as a more powerful force. Indeed, both plays are considered artistic failures, but no critic has been able to dismiss the intensity and variety of Marston's comic vision.

Other comic devices used by Marston include disguise and stereotyping. In both *The*

Malcontent and *The Fawn* (1604), the heroes disguise themselves in order to observe and ultimately ridicule the fashionable pretentiousness of their respective courts. Marston's court satire in these instances is unmistakable, but it is the comic/theatrical technique of disguise that distinguishes his use of satire. *Antonio and Mellida* contains a subplot involving buffoonish Italian characters with attributive names such as Balurdo ("fool," according to a 1598 Italian/English dictionary) and Dildo. Fittingly, Dildo corrects Balurdo's "I'll mount my courser and most gallantly prick . . ." with "'Gallantly prick' is too long, and stands hardly in the verse sir." The characters of *The Fawne* possess similarly representative names, especially Sir Amoroso Debile-Dosso, whose rhyming name literally means "lover with a weak back" (and therefore impotent). *The Dutch Courtezan* is about Franceschina, the title character, who speaks in an exaggerated Dutch dialect: "O mine aderliver love, vat sall me do to requit dis your mush affection?" (some scholars have viewed Franceschina to be a parody of Thomas Dekker's Bellafront in *The Honest Whore* [1604]). Similarly, in *What You Will* Albano's nervousness translates into a sterotypical (but hilarious) stutter: "I will be even *What you will*, do, do, do, k, k, k, kisse my wife be, be, be, be, fore . . ." (note also the self-conscious reference to the play's title). Although satire of such presentations is obvious and not particularly refined, it nevertheless makes up a small part of Marston's propensity to use comic techniques to his advantage as warranted by the situations in his plays.

Because his comic scenes often alternate with the more serious workings of his plots, Marston is credited with exploring a crude form of tragicomedy (the Stationers' Register labeled *The Malcontent* as such). His plays often combine the aforementioned comic devices with Senecan horror (a very popular convention in Marston's time), philosophizing, and perceptive commentary. In *The Malcontent* such combinations turn rhetorical:

> *Pietro:* Let heaven unclasp itself, vomit
>   forth flames!
> *Malevole:* O do not rant, do not turn
>   player—there's more of them than
>   can well live one by another already.

While some critics see this shifting between the serious and the comic as evidence of Marston's inconsistencies as a writer, it is more accurate to view them as the work of a playwright unafraid to experiment with comic technique.

Marston also distinguishes himself as a bold comic experimenter through a type of theatrical self-consciousness. The above quoted response by Malevole calls attention to the artifice of theater, a technique that Marston returned to again and again: in the induction of *The Malcontent* Sly asks Condell, "I would know how you cam by this play"; in *Antonio's Revenge* the fool Balurdo comes onstage with only half his costume beard attached to his face and calling attention to it; *Antonio and Mellida* contains actors who comment on their roles ("The necessity of the play forceth me to play two parts"); Quadratus of *What You Will* concludes act 2 with "So ends our chat: sound music for the Act." Marston's goal was to keep the audience from truly believing in the action onstage. Rather, even in his so-called tragedies *The Malcontent* and the Antonio plays, through tomfoolery and absurdism the writer creates a dream-like world that is devoid of sense and order but that is nevertheless a world of fun and festivity. In this regard, as in so many others, Marston is a most modern playwright whose comic devices are every bit as Brechtian, Pirandellian, and Beckettian as they are Elizabethan.

Summary

As a humorist, poet, and playwright, John Marston is best remembered for his biting satires on the foolishness of his day and for his festive plays. A cunning theatrical experimenter, he worked within and among genres, fashioning joyous comedies, tragicomedies, and even revenge tragedies featuring a heavy dose of fooling. However, his importance as a humorist has yet to be fully recognized. The tendency to dismiss his work on the grounds of its detectable lack of artistry and/or his alleged cynicism (a charge often unfairly used to define both the man and the artist) has led him to enjoy a respectable but not enthusiastic reputation. Scholars today are as sharply divided as to the purpose, artistry, and ultimate merit of his output as were the critics of his own day. Those eager to dismiss his work as inferior (especially in an unfair comparison to his contemporary Shakespeare) view the cynical debunking of literary and societal norms so prevalent in his plays and poetry as the work of a poor writer, unskilled, undisciplined, and quick on the attack. A more

M

open-minded approach finds Marston praised for his iconoclastic tendencies, a writer whose skill in satire and stage entertainments deserves recognition. It is the latter group of critics who see Marston as a humorist, albeit a hard-edged one.

Marston may still earn a higher place in English letters if there is a greater scholarly emphasis on his value as an influence upon modern drama rather than upon the drama of his own day. If his use of comedy (with or without the emphasis on satire) is limited to his festive, revue-like plays, he will be seen solely as a product of a time that delighted in such entertainments. However, Marston's age was one of great theatrical innovation (as his own work demonstrates) which has influenced writers of the present day. When his lampooning is seen as visionary, that is, identifying the inanities of the world beyond that of the stage, he may be viewed as a worthy predecessor to the modern absurdist movement, and he will earn the reputation as a writer equally comfortable with high, low, light, or black comedy.

Notes

1. There is speculation that the play that caused offense was *The Fawn*, which was said to contain a not too subtle attack on James I. However, it has not been proven that Marston was responsible for offending the king. Incidentally, in Marston's time the title was usually spelled with an "e"; modern editors normally delete the "e."

2. Dates following titles of plays represent the year of first performance.

3. Another explanation for Marston's sudden turn to the stage is that he favored plays and the theater. His father's will contained the following statement (later deleted): "god blesse hym and give hym trewe knowledge of hymself and to foregoe his delighte in playes vayne studdyes and fooleryes."

Selected Bibliography
Primary Sources

Verse Satire
The Metamorphosis of Pigmalions Image. And Certaine Satyres. London: J. Roberts, 1598.
The Scourge of Villanie. Three Books of Satyres. London: J. Roberts, 1598.

Plays
Jacke Drums Entertainment: Or, The Comedie of Pasquill and Katherine. London: T. Creede, 1601.
The History of Antonio and Mellida. London: R. Bradock, 1602.
Antonio's Revenge. London: R. Bradock, 1602.
The Malcontent. London: V. Simmes, 1604.
The Dutch Courtezan. London: T. Purfoote, 1605.
Parasitaster, or The Fawne. London: T. Purfoote, 1606.
The Wonder of Women, or The Tragedie of Sophonisba. London: J. Windet, 1606.
What You Will. London: G. Eld, 1607.
Histriomastix, or The Player Whipt. London: G. Eld, 1610.

Collaborations
Eastward Hoe. With Ben Jonson and George Chapman. London: G. Eld, 1605.
The Insatiate Countesse. With William Barksted. London: T. Snodham, 1613.
Lust's Dominion, or The Lascivious Queen. With Thomas Dekker, John Day, and William Haughton. London, 1657.

Editions
The Poems of John Marston. Ed. Arnold Davenport. Liverpool: Liverpool University Press, 1961.
Antonio and Mellida: The First Part. Ed. G.K. Hunter. Lincoln: University of Nebraska Press, 1965.
Antonio's Revenge: The Second Part of Antonio and Mellida. Ed. G.K. Hunter. Lincoln: University of Nebraska Press, 1965.
The Dutch Courtesan. Ed. M.L. Wine. Lincoln: University of Nebraska Press, 1965.
The Fawn. Ed. Gerald A. Smith. Lincoln: University of Nebraska Press, 1965.
Histriomastix. Tudor Facsimile Texts. Old English Plays 128. New York: AMS Press, 1970. Rpt. of 1912 ed.
Jack Drum's Entertainment. Tudor Facsimile Texts. Old English Plays 93. New York: AMS Press, 1974. Rpt. of 1912 ed.
The Scourge of Villanie. English Literature Series 33. New York: S.G. Haskell, 1974.
The Malcontent. Ed. Bernard Harris. New York: W.W. Norton, 1976.
Parasitaster or The Fawn. Ed. David A. Blostein. Baltimore: Johns Hopkins Uni-

versity Press, 1979.

The Wonder of Women or The Tragedy of Sophonisba. Ed. William Kemp. New York: Garland Press, 1979.

The Insatiate Countess. Ed. Giorgio Melchiori. New York: St. Martin's Press, 1988.

The Malcontent. Ed. George K. Hunter. New York: St. Martin's Press, 1988.

The Plays of John Marston. Ed. H. Harvey Wood. 3 vols. 1934. Somerset Publishing, 1988.

Antonio and Mellida. Eds. W. Reavley Gair et al. New York: St. Martin's Press, 1992.

Secondary Sources

Bibliographies
Tucker, Kenneth. *John Marston: A Reference Guide*. Boston: G.K. Hall, 1985. Chronological listing (1598–1981) of books, articles, and editions. References to Marston's place in dramatic and/or literary history are included.

Books
Caputi, Anthony. *John Marston: Satirist*. New York: Cornell University Press, 1960. Caputi emphasizes parody and burlesque in Marston's work.

Colley, John Scott. *John Marston's Theatrical Drama*. Salzburg Studies in English Literature, Jacobean Drama Studies 33. Salzburg, Austria: 1974. Colley attempts to explain the "oddities" found in the plays through an emphasis on Marston's theatricality.

Finkelpearl, Philip J. *John Marston of the Middle Temple: An Elizabethan Dramatist in His Social Setting*. Cambridge, MA: Harvard University Press, 1969. The influence of Marston's Middle Temple years on his literary output is emphasized.

Foakes, R.A. *Marston and Tourneur*. Essex: Longman Group, 1978. Short but incisive study of both playwrights.

Wharton, T.F. *The Critical Rise and Fall of John Marston*. Columbia, SC: Camden House, 1994. Analyzes the critical reception of Marston's works.

Articles
Foakes, R.A. "John Marston and Cyril Tourneur." *British Writers*. Vol. 2. New York: Charles Scribner's Sons, 1979, pp. 24–41. Reprint of Foakes's book (see above). Includes detailed bibliography.

Geckle, George L. "John Marston." *Dictionary of Literary Biography*, Vol. 58. Detroit: Gale Research, 1987, pp. 139–68. Excellent study of Marston's career. Includes biographical information and an extensive bibliography.

Horne, R.C. "Voices of Alienation: The Moral Significance of Marston's Satiric Strategy." *Modern Language Review*, 81, 1 (January 1986): 18.

Geckle, George L. *John Marston's Drama: Themes, Images, Sources*. Rutherford, NJ: Fairleigh Dickinson University Press, 1980. An excellent study of Marston's career, in which Geckle argues for a reappraisal of the dramatist's work.

Ingram, R.W. *John Marston*. Twayne's English Authors Series 216. Boston: Twayne, 1978. A good study of Marston's entire body of work with Ingram focusing on each play as it represents a point in Marston's life.

Scott, Michael. *John Marston's Plays: Theme, Structure and Performance*. London: Macmillan, 1978. Scott stresses the theatricality of Marston's plays as well as their literary worth. He suggests Marston's link to absurdist theater.

Robert Cooperman

Marvell, Andrew

Born: Winestead-in-Holderness, March 31, 1621
Education: Hull Grammar School; Trinity College, Cambridge University, B.A., 1639
Died: London, August 16, 1678

Biography
The son of Andrew Marvell and Anne Pease, Andrew Marvell was born on March 31, 1621, in Winestead-in-Holderness, near Hull, where his father was a clergyman. In 1624, the family moved to Hull where Marvell senior was appointed lecturer in Holy Trinity Church and later elected to the Mastership of the Charterhouse, an almshouse. Marvell received his early education at the Hull Grammar School, proceeding to Cambridge as sizar of Trinity College in 1633, and receiving his B.A. in 1639. He left Cambridge in 1641 and his

movements over the next few years are uncertain, with some of this time being spent in travels abroad.

Marvell returned to England around 1647 and began moving in London literary circles, contributing verses to two volumes of poetry published in 1649. On returning to England he appears to have sought the patronage of persons in power with a view toward gaining employment, addressing poems to Oliver Cromwell (1650, 1653) and Oliver St. John (1651), and writing about political topics such as the war with the Dutch (1653) and diplomatic negotiations with Sweden (1653–1654). Between 1650 and 1652, he served as tutor to Maria Fairfax, the daughter of Sir Thomas Fairfax, on the family's Yorkshire estate, and it is thought that many of his lyrics date from this period, including his tribute to Fairfax, "Upon Appleton House." In February 1653, John Milton wrote to John Bradshaw recommending Marvell for government employment. From 1653 to 1656/1657 he was employed by Cromwell as tutor to his *de facto* ward William Dutton, with whom Marvell resided at Eton until departing the country with Dutton for travels abroad. They were reported to be in France in 1656. In 1657, he finally secured civil employment as Latin Secretary to Secretary of State John Thurloe.

In 1659, Marvell was elected Member of Parliament for Hull and, while losing his seat briefly after the Restoration, was re-elected in April 1660 and served as parliamentarian until his death in 1678. His parliamentary career is marked by opposition to the Stuart court, particularly in opposition to pro-French foreign policy and advocacy of political and religious liberty, causes espoused inside the House and outside in his writings over the next twenty years. An early target of his ire was Edward Hyde, Earl of Clarendon, whom he attacked in works such as "Clarendon's House-Warming" and "The Last Instruction to a Painter." Marvell participated in Clarendon's impeachment in November 1667. In 1672, he entered the famous controversy with Samuel Parker which produced some of his finest satirical humor, writing *The Rehearsal Transpros'd* Parts I and II between 1672 and 1673. His parodic "His Majesty's Most Gracious Speech to Both Houses of Parliament" was written in April 1675. In 1676, he again entered the arena of ecclesiastical controversy, this time against Francis Turner, with the publication of *Mr.*

Smirke, or The Divine in Mode. In 1677, he published anonymously *An Account of the Growth of Popery and Arbitrary Government in England,* for whose author an arrest warrant was issued. Marvell died in London on August 16, 1678 after falling ill on a journey from Hull to London. He was buried in the church of St. Giles-in-the-Fields. In 1681, his *Miscellaneous Poems* appeared, published by Mary Palmer, alias Marvell, who claimed to be the writer's wife.

Literary Analysis

Marvell's writing covers a wide range of seventeenth-century genres: lyrical, occasional, and satirical verses and controversial prose. His work as a humorist may be seen in all of these genres, but particularly in his satirical writings in verse and prose. His humor ranges from the highly intellectual wit of the lyrics to the burlesque, bawdy, and sometimes savage humor of his satires. Marvell's contemporary reputation was as an incorruptible patriot and a scathing wit who used his literary powers and humor in the defense of religious and political liberty. This reputation persisted into the twentieth century, when it was eclipsed by admiration of his lyric poetry (not widely known during his life as the poems were published posthumously in 1681) and as an exponent of the conceited wit of the school known as the metaphysical poets.

While most of Marvell's humorous and satirical writing dates from after the Restoration of King Charles II when he participated in the political opposition to the Stuart court, early examples of the blend of humor and satire on which his contemporary reputation was based may be found in poems of the late 1640s and 1650s such as "Fleckno, an English Priest at Rome" (ca. 1648–1649), "Tom May's Death" (1650), and "The Character of Holland" (1653). In these three verses, Marvell combines the conceited wit of the metaphysical school with stylistic features that are closer to the Augustan, such as experimentation with the couplet form.

While it is arguable exactly what influence Marvell exerted on writers such as John Dryden and Alexander Pope, it is certain that his work represents an important stage in the development of English satirical humor. "Fleckno" reveals the poet's skill at burlesque and comic exaggeration, providing a parodic portrait of the literary pretensions of the expatriate priest living in Rome. The humor of the poem is highly visual, particularly in the author's description of the physical appearance of the poetic hack who has neglected the material world in pursuit of his art and appears swaddled in drafts of his own poetry, wearing a "jacket of poetic buff, / With which he does his third dimension stuff."[1] In "Tom May's Death" the ghost of Ben Jonson is resurrected to provide a humorous but vitriolic attack on May, whose reputed death after a night of drinking provides the opening attack on the excesses of his life: "As one put drunk into a packet-boat, / Tom May was hurry'd hence, and did not know't."[2] May, the historian of the Long Parliament, is attacked by Marvell for his venality and mediocrity as a writer.

"The Character of Holland," written during the course of the First Anglo-Dutch War (1652–1654), is an energetic piece of burlesque and exaggeration which effectively draws on decades of anti-Dutch sentiment in English writing, playing on and refining many of the stocks-in-trade of English abuse of the Dutch—the Dutch language, the inundation of their land by water, their religious toleration and quest for trade, their reputed drunkenness and boorishness, and so on. Marvell's Holland becomes less than the conventional swamp or marsh of other writers such as Owen Felltham[3] and is reduced to simply the accumulated effluvia of the waters which daily threaten it with flooding:

> Holland, that scarce deserves the name
> of land,
> As but th' off-scouring of the British
> sand,
> And so much earth as was contributed
> By English pilots when they heav'd the
> lead,
> Or what by the ocean's slow alluvion fell
> Of shipwrackt cockle and the muscle-
> shell:
> This indigested vomit of the sea
> Fell to the Dutch by just propriety.[4]

Marvell's Dutch are more fish than men, absurd amphibians whose pretensions on land and sea are lampooned without mercy. The success of the poem in giving humorous vent to national rivalries and animosities is attested to by the fact that it was twice revived in the seventeenth century, coinciding with further outbreaks of Anglo-Dutch hostilities in 1665 and 1672. As late as the nineteenth century, the poem was still able to hit its mark, as evidenced

in the comments of Leigh Hunt who recalls how he and Charles Lamb were reduced to "laughing immeasurably" on reading its opening lines.[5]

Consideration of Marvell's works after the Restoration of Charles II is complicated by uncertainty concerning the canon. His reputation as one of the drollest wits of his time resulted in his name acquiring vendibility exploited by booksellers attributing to him pieces which are of uncertain authorship. Of the satirical verse most certainly by Marvell, the strongest include "Clarendon's House-Warming," "The Last Instructions to a Painter" (1667), and "The Loyal Scot" (1667, 1669–1673). "Clarendon's House-Warming" takes the occasion of the completion of Clarendon's grand house (the building of which commenced in 1664) to launch a stinging attack on the arrogance and avarice of the Chancellor. In "The Last Instructions to a Painter," for satiric purposes Marvell adapts the Italian advice-to-a-painter genre, introduced into England in Admiral Waller's panegyric verse on the Duke of York (published in December 1666). Under the pretext of instructing an artist in painting a portrait of the Stuart court, Marvell provides a rambling and in parts very funny satirical expose of courtly manners and vice, political corruption, and ineptitude. In the poem his range is wide and while stylistically he is somewhat inconsistent, the work has some very fine moments of satirical humor, including the lines admired by Jonathan Swift on the relief of Clarendon at the proroguing of Parliament:

> Blither than hare that hath escap'd the
> hounds,
> The House prorogu'd, the Chancellor
> rebounds, . . .
> What frosts to fruit, what arsnick to the
> Rat,
> What to fair Denham mortal chocolat,
> What an account to Carteret; that and
> more,
> A Parliament is to the Chancellor.[6]

Also of great interest is the poet's treatment of the aftermath of the Medway disaster and the search for a scapegoat onto whom the blame for the English defeat was to be dumped. A scapegoat was found in the person of a hapless officer of the Admiralty, Peter Pett, whose name is made to "answer all" in a witty display of proficiency in the couplet form with the poet devising a sequence of more than a dozen questions all of which are answered in rhyme with Pett's name. In "The Loyall Scot," Marvell once more adapts a model provided by another writer, in this instance John Cleveland's "The Rebel Scot," and again he provides a satiric attack on the government's vicious ineptitude in the handling of the Second Dutch War. The method of this work is largely mock-heroic with the figure of Captain Douglas, the loyal Scot of the title, in the heroic role in defense of the *Royal Oak*.

Marvell's reputation as a writer of humor in prose rests largely on two works, *The Rehearsal Transpros'd* (1672) and its continuation, *The Rehearsal Transpros'd, the Second Part* (1673), and to a lesser extent on the later piece *Mr. Smirke, or The Divine in Mode* (1676), another foray into ecclesiastical satire in the same vein as the earlier works. The title *The Rehearsal Transpros'd* alludes to George Villiers's, First Duke of Buckingham's, satirical farce, *The Rehearsal*, and Marvell exploits the great success of this play in his refutation of Parker's attacks on the principle of freedom of conscience in religious matters in such works as *A Defense and Continuation of the Ecclesiastical Politie* (1671). In taking on Parker, Marvell entered a controversy of some years standing in the defense of religious nonconformity. In Marvell's work, Parker, the ambitious Anglican divine, becomes a version of Mr. Bayes, the character of the pedantic and verbose hack playwright in Buckingham's play.

The great success of *The Rehearsal Transpros'd* lies in the energy of the author's attack on Parker. Several strategies may be seen at work here. Throughout most of the work, Marvell adopts the method of the animadversion, using Parker's own words to condemn him, pulling him up for verbosity, reductively summarizing his arguments in absurd aphorisms, using the structure and argument of Parker's work as the basis for his attack. Elsewhere, Marvell adopts the persona of the naive narrator or commentator, as when he embarks on a fictional biography of Parker in an attempt to account for the peculiar distemper of his brain, finally diagnosed as lycanthropy, by pointing to, amongst other things, the evil influence on him of reading Miguel de Cervantes's *Don Quixote* too early and the Bible too late. Marvell concludes his potted biography with the comment: "Alas, that a sweet gentleman, and so hopeful, should miscarry!"[7]

The continuation of the controversy with Parker, *The Rehearsal Transpros'd, the Second Part,* was written in response to Parker's *Reproof* to his first tract and is similar in many respects to the earlier work. The political and ecclesiastical issues at stake in Marvell's controversy with Parker pale alongside the robust humor directed against the man himself. In both pieces, Marvell works to discredit Parker; refutation of Parker's ecclesiastical position relies on the discrediting of the man himself through unrelenting and often lampooning attack. Every opportunity is seized to fire broadsides at Parker. Even a discussion of the literary decorum appropriate in such controversial writing is turned to advantage as Marvell, seeking the reader's tolerance for his humor, writes that he will not commit the absurdity of writing gravely of a buffoon.[8]

Marvell's skill at parody, evident in his comic portrait of Fleckno and his animadversions on the writings of Parker are again evident in his parodic version of the speech with which Charles II opened the thirteenth session of the Cavalier Parliament in 1675, "His Majesty's Most Gracious Speech to Both houses of Parliament." The writer adopts the persona of Charles II speaking from the throne for satiric purposes; the mock-speech at once skillfully characterizes and damns the king. Marvell's Charles is condemned through his own mouth as a selfish, willful child, far more concerned with the gratification of his sensual appetites than the welfare of the realm. Marvell deftly reproduces the habits and cadences of the king's speech as he complains of his over-burdened economic circumstances and the demands of both his "harlots in service" and the "reformado concubines" who lie heavy upon him. He acknowledges that he has a "passable good estate" but exclaims, "God's-fish, I have a great charge upon't."[9]

While the style and method of Marvell's humorous writings are diverse, his humor is characterized by an acute observation of and play on detail which is often both highly visual and concrete. Marvell's reductive and often parodic humor works most effectively with personality, character, manners, physical description—details of which become indicators of, or metaphors for, the moral economy of the subject. While ostensibly political, many of his satirical writings are based on character or personality, the character of Clarendon, Parker, or Charles II, even the physical character of the

Netherlands in "The Character of Holland," and attention to the details comprising character frequently takes the place of direct comment on the political situation.

Marvell's humorous writing is richly allusive, drawing on his knowledge of history and classical and modern languages. Puns and other witty wordplay are features of his work, along with a characteristic use of metaphoric language whereby metaphors are frequently literalized. "The Character of Holland" provides plentiful examples of his characteristic punning wordplay. The water-logged Dutch literally become so many fish, indistinguishable from the fish that form the staple of their diet, as in the following lines:

> The fish ofttimes the burger dispossessed
> And sat not as a meat but as a guest
> And oft the tritons and the sea-nymphs saw
> Whole shoals of Dutch served up for cabillau
> Or as they over the new level ranged
> For pickled herring, pickled Heeren changed.

The fish-like Dutch worship herring as a God and confuse "Poor John" (or dried hake) with St. John the Evangelist. The poetic voice in this poem is characterized by an easy sense of English superiority in which the reader is invited to share at the expense of the Dutch, the "Half-anders" (as distinct from Hollanders/Whole-anders) lampooned in the poem. Elsewhere in his satirical writings Marvell employs a comparable voice, using colloquialisms and references to familiar London landmarks to enhance the sense of a shared culture between himself and his readers.

Summary

Andrew Marvell's vigorous blend of humor and satire in verse and prose represents an important contribution to the development of English literary humor, particularly in demonstrating the efficacy of humor in the arsenal of the writer bent on exposing folly, vice, and corruption in the corridors of power.

Notes

1. Andrew Marvell, *Complete Works*, 4 vols., ed. Alexander B. Grosart (1872–1875; New York: AMS Press, 1966), Vol. I, p. 231. With the exception of the mock-speech, all references to Marvell's work are from this edition.
2. *Ibid.*, Vol. I, p. 37.
3. See Owen Felltham, *A Brief Character of the Low-Countries Under the States Being Three Weeks Observations of the Vices and Virtues of the Inhabitants.* London, 1652.
4. Marvell, Vol. I, p. 242.
5. Leigh Hunt, "Andrew Marvell" in *Wit and Humor Selected from the English Poets* (1846), rpt. in Elizabeth Story Donno, ed., *Andrew Marvell: The Critical Heritage* (London: Routledge & Kegan Paul, 1978), p. 137.
6. *Ibid.*, Vol. I, p. 265.
7. *Ibid.*, Vol. III, p. 51.
8. *Ibid.*, Vol. III, p. 78.
9. The text of this speech, first attributed to Marvell in 1704, may be found in Robert Wilcher, ed. *Selected Poetry and Prose* (London: Methuen, 1986), pp. 160–63.

Selected Bibliography

Primary Sources

The Rehearsal Transpros'd. London: Printed by A.B., 1672.

The Rehearsal Transpros'd, the Second Part. London: Printed for Nathaniel Ponder, 1673.

Mr. Smirke, or the Divine in Mode. London: n.p., 1676.

Miscellaneous Poems. London, 1681.

Complete Works. 4 vols. Ed. Alexander B. Grosart. London, 1872–1875; New York: AMS Press, 1966.

Poems and Letters. 2 vols. 3rd rev. ed. Ed. H.M. Margoliouth; rev. Pierre Legouis and E.E. Duncan-Jones. Oxford: Clarendon, 1971.

The Rehearsal Transpros'd and *The Rehearsal Transpros'd, the Second Part.* Ed. D.I.B. Smith. Oxford: Clarendon, 1971.

Selected Poetry and Prose. Ed. Robert Wilcher. London: Methuen, 1986.

Secondary Sources

Chernaik, Warren. *The Poet's Time: Politics and Religion in the Works of Andrew Marvell.* Cambridge: Cambridge University Press, 1983. A study of Marvell's satirical writings addressing questions of method and form.

Coolidge, John S. "Martin Marprelate, Marvell, and *Decorum Personae* as a Satirical Theme." *Publications of the*

Modern Language Association, 74 (1959): 526–32. Coolidge draws links between Marvell's method in the controversy with Parker and the earlier Marprelate controversies.

Donno, Elizabeth Story, ed. *Andrew Marvell: The Critical Heritage*. London: Routledge & Kegan Paul, 1978. Very useful for tracing Marvell's reputation from seventeenth century to the present—of particular interest in revealing how his reputation as humorist preceded admiration for his other literary skills.

Farley-Hills, David. *The Benevolence of Laughter: Comic Poetry of the Commonwealth and Restoration*. London and Basingstoke: Macmillan, 1974. Pages 72–98 include a useful discussion of "Last Instructions" in relation to the developing Augustan aesthetic.

Feltham, Owen. *A Brief Character of the Low-Countries Under the States Being Three Weeks Observations of the Vices and Virtues of the Inhabitants*. London, 1652.

Kelliher, Hilton. *Andrew Marvell: Poet and Politician*. British Museum Publications, 1978. Catalogue of the British Library's tercentenary exhibition—a very useful reference on the life and writings.

Legouis, Pierre. *Andrew Marvell: Poet, Puritan, Patriot*. Oxford: Clarendon, 1965. An abridged translation of the author's massive work published in France in 1928, still the most authoritative work on the life of the subject.

Denise Cuthbert

Maugham, William Somerset

Born: Paris, January 25, 1874
Education: King's School, Canterbury, 1885–1889; St. Thomas's Hospital, London, 1892–1897
Marriage: Gwendolyn Syrie Barnardo Wellcome, May 26, 1917; one child
Died: Villa Mauresque, Cap Ferrat, France, December 16, 1965

Biography

William Somerset Maugham was born January 25, 1874, in the British Embassy at Paris. His father, Robert Ormond Maugham, was an attorney with offices in Paris and was at that time a legal attache to the embassy. Somerset's mother, Edith Mary Snell Maugham, suffered from tuberculosis. Some physicians then apparently believed pregnancy to be good for tubercular women, and, although Somerset was to be the last of her four surviving children, all sons, she was to endure two more pregnancies, dying shortly after the birth of the second dead child in 1882. Until his own death, Somerset was to recall his mother's death as the most traumatic event of his life. Maugham's father died in 1884.

The future author was more fluent in French than English when he was shipped to England to be raised by his father's only surviving brother, Henry MacDonald Maugham, vicar of Whitstable, and his wife. Somerset's older brothers, one of whom would become Lord Chancellor of England, were away in school, and the ten-year-old child felt isolated. Before this time, apparently no one had commented on his stutter; after this move and the abrupt dismissal of the nurse who had raised him, the stutter became a serious handicap and was in part responsible for the boy's acute discomfort at King's School, Canterbury, which he left in 1889. From Canterbury, he went to Heidelberg, Germany. He was not enrolled at the university there, but he attended lectures and was exposed to a more sophisticated culture than before, including the theater of Henrik Ibsen.

Returning to Whitstable in 1892, Maugham was encouraged by his guardian to find a career. He tried accounting; he was unhappy. A local physician suggested medicine; Maugham enrolled at St. Thomas's Hospital, where he studied from 1892 to 1897, qualifying as physician and surgeon. A modest inheritance allowed him to study by day and write by night with occasional traveling. His final months of medical training, during which he delivered babies in squalid London slums, gave him material for the first of his novels, *Liza of Lambeth* (1897), a naturalistic study that brought him condemnation from would-be censors. The praise of American novelist Theodore Dreiser helped assure substantial sales, but Maugham's next ten years were a struggle. Although determined to write rather than to practice medicine, he was unable to get his plays staged, and his fiction was either rejected or unsuccessful.

The turning point came in 1907, however, when because of an emergency his play *Lady Frederick* was presented by the Court Theatre. This comedy of manners was so successful that within months Maugham became the first playwright to have four plays running simultaneously in London: *Lady Frederick*, *Mrs. Dot*, *Jack Straw*, and *The Explorer*. This brought him financial security, and he turned to the novel, publishing *Of Human Bondage* in 1915. He read proofs of that novel while serving with the ambulance corps in France where he served at the beginning of World War I despite his age. Before the war ended, he would father a daughter by Gwendolyn Syrie Barnardo (Mrs. Henry Wellcome), be named in newspaper headlines about her divorce, be sent on intelligence missions to Switzerland and Russia, marry Wellcome (on May 26, 1917), and be hospitalized with tuberculosis.

His intelligence service duties curtailed, certainly, by his health and, perhaps, because of the newspaper headlines, Maugham in 1916 sailed from San Francisco on a voyage that would introduce him to the characters who provided material for his most famous short story, "Rain," and the background for his novel, *The Moon and Sixpence*, based on the life of French painter Paul Gauguin, as well as notes on many other scenes and characters that would form the South Sea tales for which he is justly famous. Finding that such material stimulated his writing, Maugham was to become perhaps the most traveled writer of the early twentieth century. The series of novels, plays, and stories that would follow, although inevitably uneven in quality, made Maugham one of the best-known writers of his age. His success brought him invitations into the fashionable world of London.

Although Maugham's marriage and his involvements with other women reflected his attempts to adjust to a life that his world considered normal, increasingly he came to terms with his homosexuality. His marriage failed in 1927. By then he had chosen Gerald Haxton, whom he met while with the ambulance corps in France, as his companion. Haxton had been arrested in England and could not reenter the country where until 1967 homosexual behavior could still be punished with scandal and prison terms. In 1926, Maugham bought the Villa Mauresque on the French Riviera; there he maintained a rigorous morning writing routine and, assisted by Haxton, entertained lavishly later in the day with guests who ranged from students at King's School to celebrities such as H.G. Wells, George Bernard Shaw, and Noel Coward. After Haxton's death in 1944, Alan Searle, who survived Maugham, became the author's companion. Apart from extensive trav-

els in search of materials and to see friends, Maugham's life in France was interrupted only by World War II, when, forced from France, he was sent by the British Government on a propaganda and possibly intelligence mission to the United States.

Although Maugham's literary outpourings were prolific, as he aged he gave up his literary genres one by one. His drawing room comedies remained successful, though between 1928 and 1933 he determined to end his career as playwright with three serious plays: *The Sacred Flame* (1928), which is about euthanasia; *For Services Rendered* (1932), an anti-war play; and *Sheppey* (1933), the subject of which is the then-popular topic of what would happen if a Christ-like figure returned to earth in the twentieth century. *Creatures of Circumstance* (1947) was his last short-story collection, while his final novel, *Catalina*, appeared in 1948.

In his old age Maugham was recipient of many honors and became a media celebrity. In 1948, he overcame his stutter to provide narration for a film of four of his short stories, *Quartet*, and he followed this with *Trio* in 1958 and *Encore* in 1951. He appeared in opening and closing moments of "The Somerset Maugham Theatre" produced by CBS in 1950. He received a number of honorary degrees, including those from Oxford and Heidelberg, and he was honored on his eightieth birthday with a dinner at the Garrick Club, which had similarly honored only three other writers—Charles Dickens, William Makepeace Thackeray, and Anthony Trollope.

Unfortunately, during the last several years of his life, Maugham slowly lapsed into senile dementia, producing "Looking Back" (1962), a tactless unpublished account of his life with Syrie Maugham, by then dead, that was to destroy friendships of many years. As his brain disintegrated, increasing paranoia led to court fights with his daughter Liza, by then married to Lord John Hope, and the publicity of these later years contaminated the memory of Maugham's early productive years and shadowed critical evaluations of his achievements. During the last two years of his life, he was rarely lucid for sustained periods of time; he died at Villa Mauresque on December 16, 1965.

Literary Analysis
Somerset Maugham was master of four literary genres and as many prose styles. He was also versatile in his ability to use wit and humor:

verbal wit flashes through his non-fiction; aphorisms reminiscent of Oscar Wilde's illumine his comedies of manners; and sardonic twists of plot and character make his fiction memorable. Consistent throughout his writing, however, is his principal theme: the entrapment of man and woman in an environment of social codes and institutions and their attempts to escape. Sometimes those attempts meet with success, but often the grim—sometimes grimly humorous—tone of the stories reflects the characters' need for the very codes and institutions that imprison them; they cannot cope with freedom, with liberation from bourgeois rules.

Maugham's short stories probably will remain his most lasting contribution to literature, although they have met with little praise from academic critics or critics belonging to the English or American intelligentsia. Maugham is a consummate teller of tales in an age in which such critics tend to value experiments in form more than Maugham's gift of simple story telling. Still, his talent brought him great popularity with the general public. His style is lucid in the manner of French author Guy de Maupassant, who influenced him, as did Voltaire. His pacing is fast. Even in the many stories that are primarily accounts of the unraveling of characters when bourgeois colonial British are placed in alien cultures where familiar rules do not apply, the unfolding of the characters' disintegration is so compellingly developed that the stories are difficult to put down. The narrators are usually objective, cool, aloof, Maugham-like, and, with them, the reader watches improbable events unfolding as if on a movie screen.

The best of his stories are those with a background in his intelligence work, collected in *Ashenden; or, The British Agent* (1928), and those, such as "Rain" (*The Trembling of a Leaf*, 1921), with settings outside England. What is humorous in these stories is grimly, ironically humorous.

"Mr. Harrington's Washing," from the *Ashenden* collection, exemplifies both the ironies of these tales and the theme of freedom and imprisonment. Ashenden, the secret agent, finds himself in Petrograd at the time that Aleksandr Kerensky's forces are overpowered by the Bolshevik forces of V.I. Lenin and Leon Trotsky. The city is in chaos, and Ashenden and his Russian friend Anastasia Alexandrovna do well to survive. Ashenden has traveled into the tumultuous city with John Quincy Harrington, a tidy New Englander imprisoned by his hab-

its. A compulsive talker and devoted family man, Harrington reads great speeches from history, oblivious to the history being made around him. In Ashenden's eyes, Harrington becomes almost heroic in his refusal to let the Russian revolution interfere with his proper breakfast, his seat on a train, and his clean laundry. As soldiers randomly shoot in the street, Harrington fusses because the hotel has not returned his washing. He goes after it, and Ashenden and his Russian friend follow, anxious to see the helplessly conventional man safely out of Russia. They find him: "He lay on his face, in a pool of blood . . . But his hand was clenched tight on the parcel that contained four shirts, two union suits, a pair of pyjamas and four collars. Mr. Harrington had not let his washing go."[1]

A more complex attitude toward freedom and convention, but an equally sardonic twist underlies "Rain"—the victory of a prostitute over a self-righteous missionary. (This story has been filmed several times, starring Gloria Swanson, Joan Crawford, and Rita Hayworth, and was staged in both dramatic and musical versions.) The Reverend Davidson is among the many Maugham characters whose code of social behavior collapses in the freedom of the tropics; attempting to convert the prostitute, he succumbs to her. Unable to tolerate freedom, he kills himself, and the prostitute is permanently embittered. Again, the humor is grimly ironic, as when the Reverend Davidson boasts, on the eve of his seduction, that "Last night I was privileged to bring a lost soul to the loving arms of Jesus."[2]

Similarly ironic twists give wit to his novels, although only one of the four important novels can be considered comic. Maugham's first novel was the autobiographical *Of Human Bondage*, a coming-of-age novel in the style of Samuel Butler's *Ernest Pontifex, or The Way of All Flesh* (1903). Often considered his best work, this novel tells the story of Philip Carey, crippled by a club foot instead of a stutter but in all other ways resembling his author. In this novel the protagonist is bound by the narrowness of his upbringing, by his physical handicap, and by his debasing love for Mildred Rogers, whom he seeks out although she is stupid, greedy, and conventional. Maugham's second significant novel, *The Moon and Sixpence*, is serious, as is *The Razor's Edge*, published in 1944 when Maugham had explored with authors Gerald Heard, Christopher Isherwood, and Aldous Huxley the Indian mysticism that had preoccupied them in their Hollywood years. The novel tells of Larry Darrell's quest to find an acceptable way of life and to free himself from the materialism of the post-war world and the American dream. The novel has been said to foreshadow the flower children and dropouts of the 1960s and 1970s, but in many ways it is a summing up, in fiction, of his own life. *Cakes and Ale* (1930), however, is both a deliberately comic and scandalous fiction.

Cakes and Ale takes many of the same events recorded in *Of Human Bondage*, but treats them more mildly. The novel records the life of Edward Driffield, a figure said to have been modeled on Thomas Hardy, and his first wife Rosie, one of Maugham's exuberantly earthy women. As in the spy stories, the narrator of this novel is Ashenden—Willie Ashenden—who has been asked to provide information for a biography of Driffield. The book is to be written by Alroy Kear, a figure unflatteringly modeled on British popular novelist Hugh Walpole, the reason for the scandal. The biography has been commissioned by Driffield's conventional second wife. Ashenden's reminiscences are filled with a contrast of convention and freedom, careerism and creativity, genuine women and artificial ones. The humor here, which is considerable, resides in those contrasts, in the narrator's dry irony, and the satiric portraits of such figures as Kear. At the center of the story is Rosie, whose marriage to Driffield and whose elopement from him must be concealed by his second wife and members of the London literary establishment, but Rosie's life-enhancing qualities are precisely those lacking in the careerists of literary London whose self-serving concern with propriety is rendered comic by contrast with Rosie's vibrant energy.

A broader, more obvious comedy governs the stage dramas that made Maugham famous. While his few serious plays reflect the theater of Ibsen, the comedies echo the style of Wilde, although themes sometimes suggest Shaw. Of Maugham's many plays, the most important are *Lady Frederick*, first produced in England in 1907; *The Circle*, 1920; *Our Betters*, 1923; and *The Constant Wife*, 1927.

The Constant Wife typifies the best of Maugham's comedy. Early dialogue is in the epigrammatic style of Wilde, until, mid-play, the heroine takes control and forces the serious theme to the surface, a theme close to that taken up in Shaw's highly controversial *Mrs. Warren's Profession* (censored, but privately produced in 1902): marriage, as practiced by the upper classes of England, is little more than legalized prostitution, but nonetheless it is the only trade open to most of the women in those classes. Maugham had always understood women to be imprisoned by their economic helplessness; in his first novel, *Liza of Lambeth*, for instance, his heroine is the victim of her environment, and poverty is her enemy. At the beginning of *The Constant Wife*, Constance Middleton is met by her sister, who is eager to inform her of Constance's husband's adultery with her best friend. (The sister is one of the idle, bored, manipulative women that Maugham detested.) As it happens, Connie is aware of her husband's folly, but has been trying to conceal it from her mother, her sister, and her friend's husband. She fails and suddenly realizes that she is "tired of being the modern wife," which she defines as "a prostitute who doesn't deliver the goods."[3]

These seemingly melodramatic events become comic through a technique often used by Shaw. As Connie tires of her idleness, she takes on the roles, responsibilities, and stage dialogue of a man. She goes into a friend's business, earns enough money to pay her husband for her last year's room and board, and takes off for a six-week trip to Italy with a man who once proposed to her. Her husband is reduced to the drooling conventional inanities of a melodramatic heroine, but Constance has escaped her prison and is unrepentant. As she leaves, her husband is more aware of her attractions than when she was a conventional woman, and he urges her to return when her trip is over.

Equally strong female roles exist in *Lady Frederick* and *The Circle*, in which Maugham celebrates women able to overcome the conditioning of their age. In *Lady Frederick*, for example, a middle-aged adventuress heroine is tempted to rid herself of debt by marrying an innocent young nobleman. Again, comic qualities emerge from the reversal of male and female roles. In the play's most famous scene, often associated with the satire of Jonathan Swift, Lady Frederick, repenting of her proposed seduction of the innocent, allows him to see her without makeup and in early morning disarray. He is disillusioned by her artificiality, and she, having successfully maneuvered her way through a minefield of would-be bribers, blackmailers, and suitors, ends with an appropriate marriage with an equal. Strong female roles exist also in Maugham's serious drama, as in *The Sacred Flame*, in which the mother of a helplessly paralyzed war veteran overcomes the voice of conventional morality in order to provide her son with a merciful death.

The author's fourth genre was non-fiction prose, which includes his highly readable essays ranging from travel studies (*The Gentleman in the Parlour*, 1935, and others), to literary criticism. Two volumes remain essential reading for writers and students of writing: *The Summing Up* (1938) and *A Writer's Notebook* (1949). Neither are personal autobiographies. They are occasionally witty rather than comic writings; both illumine not only Maugham's writing but the nature of writing itself, the former by frank discussion of his experiences and the conclusions at which he arrived and the latter by showing how a writer's eye works as it records the sights and sounds that lead to stories.

Summary

W. Somerset Maugham's attitudes and prose styles were formed during the Victorian and Edwardian eras, in which story-telling was of more importance than experimental form. In spite of the modern period's proclivity for stylistic experimentation, he achieved great popular success among an international audience for his story-telling gifts, although his talents have generally been ignored by American and British academicians and professional critics. Further, some biographers have tended to let the errors of his senile last years and his public confrontations with his family, as well as his homosexuality, contaminate their picture of his literary achievements. A fairer picture would be that of a writer's writer, whose stories exemplify luminously clear, lucid, terse, story-telling, whose non-fiction is usually entertaining and often witty, and, in two cases, provides textbook material on writing, and whose plays, although somewhat dated, still are playable and, in fact, illumine ideas that remain topical many decades after his death. As a humorist, he demonstrates an unusually great range of techniques: aphorisms and turns of phrase that evoke the memory of Wilde or of the Enlightenment, ironies of situation and character that evoke memories of the Greeks, and social satire purely modern in its force and directness. There is an irony that Maugham himself must have appreciated in the fact that while critics were condemning him for pandering to the tastes of the common man or woman, censors on both sides of the Atlantic were busily attempting to ensure that the common man or woman would not see or read his work. This kind of muddle still clouds Maugham's reputation, and his ability as an English prose stylist is not yet fully recognized.

Notes

1. W. Somerset Maugham. "Mr. Harrington's Washing," in *East and West*, Vol. 1 of *The Complete Short Stories of W. Somerset Maugham* (Garden City, NY: Doubleday, 1952), p. 640.
2. Maugham, "Rain," *East and West*, p. 33.
3. Maugham, *The Constant Wife*, in *Representative Modern Plays: British*, ed. Robert Warnock (Glenview: Scott, 1953), p. 478.

Selected Bibliography
Primary Sources

Autobiography and Essays
On A Chinese Screen. London: Heinemann, 1935.
The Gentleman in the Parlour. London: Heinemann, 1935; Garden City, NY: Doubleday, 1935; rev. 1950.
The Summing Up. London: Heinemann, 1938; Garden City, NY: Doubleday, 1938.
A Writer's Notebook. London: Heinemann, 1949; Garden City, NY: Doubleday, 1949.
The Vagrant Mood. London: Heinemann, 1952; Garden City, NY: Doubleday, 1953.
Selected Prefaces and Introductions of W. Somerset Maugham. London: Heinemann, 1963; Garden City, NY: Doubleday, 1963.
A Traveller in Romance: Uncollected Writings, 1901–1964. Ed. John Whitehead. London: Blond, and New York: Clarkson, 1984.

Novels
Liza of Lambeth. London: Unwin, 1897.
Mrs. Craddock. London: Heinemann, 1902; rev. 1928.
Of Human Bondage. London: Heinemann, and New York: Doran, 1915.
The Moon and Sixpence. London: Heinemann, and New York: Doran,

1919.

The Painted Veil. London: Heinemann, and New York: Doran, 1925.

Cakes and Ale. London: Heinemann, and Garden City, NY: Doubleday, 1930.

The Narrow Corner. London: Heinemann, and Garden City, NY: Doubleday, 1932.

Theatre. London: Heinemann, and Garden City, NY: Doubleday, 1937.

Christmas Holiday. London: Heinemann, 1941.

The Razor's Edge. London: Heinemann, and Garden City, NY: Doubleday, 1944.

Then and Now. London: Heinemann, and Garden City, NY: Doubleday, 1946.

Catalina. London: Heinemann, and Garden City, NY: Doubleday, 1948.

Plays

Collected Plays. Vol. 1. London: Heinemann, 1931. Contains *Lady Frederick, Mrs. Dot,* and *Jack Straw.*

Collected Plays. Vol. 2. London: Heinemann, 1931. Contains *Penelope, Smith,* and *The Land of Promise.*

Collected Plays. Vol. 3. London: Heinemann, 1932. Contains *Our Betters, The Unattainable,* and *Home and Beauty.*

Collected Plays. Vol. 4. London: Heinemann, 1932. Contains *The Circle, The Constant Wife,* and *The Breadwinner.*

Collected Plays. Vol. 5. London: Heinemann, 1934. Contains *Caesar's Wife, East of Suez,* and *The Sacred Flame.*

Collected Plays. Vol. 6. London: Heinemann, 1934. Contains *The Unknown, For Services Rendered,* and *Sheppey.*

Six Comedies. Garden City, NY: Doubleday, 1937. Contains *The Unattainable (Caroline), Home and Beauty, The Circle, Our Betters, The Constant Wife,* and *The Breadwinner.*

Representative Modern Plays: British. Ed. Robert Warnock. Glenview: Scott, 1953. Contains *The Constant Wife.*

Short Story Collections

The Trembling of a Leaf. London: Heinemann, and New York: Doran, 1921.

The Casuarina Tree. London: Heinemann, and New York: Doran, 1926.

Ashenden; or, The British Agent. London: Heinemann, and New York: Doran, 1928.

Six Stories in the First Person Singular. London: Heinemann, and Garden City, NY: Doubleday, 1931.

Ah King. London: Heinemann, and Garden City, NY: Doubleday, 1933.

Cosmopolitans. London: Heinemann, and Garden City, NY: Doubleday, 1936.

The Mixture as Before. London: Heinemann, and Garden City, NY: Doubleday, 1940.

Creatures of Circumstance. London: Heinemann, and Garden City, NY: Doubleday, 1947.

Quartet: Stories by Somerset Maugham; Screen-Plays by R.C. Sherriff. Garden City, NY: Doubleday, 1949.

The Complete Short Stories of W. Somerset Maugham. 2 vols. Garden City, NY: Doubleday, 1952.

Secondary Sources

Bibliographies

Sanders, Charles, comp. and ed. *W. Somerset Maugham: An Annotated Bibliography of Writings About Him.* De Kalb: Northern Illinois University Press, 1970. Includes abstracts, many of them from non-English sources.

Stott, Raymond Toole. *A Bibliography of the Works of W. Somerset Maugham.* London: Kaye and Ward, 1973. Considered definitive, but now, like Sanders above, needs updating.

Biographies

Burt, Forrest D. *W. Somerset Maugham.* Twayne's English Authors Series 399. Boston: Twayne, 1986. Good introduction for beginning student.

Calder, Robert. *Willie: The Life of W. Somerset Maugham.* London: Heinemann, and New York: St. Martin's Press, 1989. Definitive.

Curtis, Anthony. *Somerset Maugham.* New York: Macmillan, 1977. Excellently illustrated biography.

Kanin, Garson. *Remembering Mr. Maugham.* New York: Atheneum, 1966. Sympathetic reminiscences by a theatrical figure who, with his wife Ruth Gordon, was a friend and frequent visitor for many years.

Maugham, Robin. *Somerset and All the Maughams.* London: Longman and Heinemann, and New York: New American Library, 1966. Reminiscences and much about Maugham ancestry.

Morgan, Ted. *Maugham*. New York: Simon and Schuster, 1980. Well researched but generally unsympathetic.

Criticism

Barnes, Ronald. *The Dramatic Comedy of William Somerset Maugham*. The Hague: Mouton, 1968. Difficult scholarly study of structure and society in Maugham's plays.

Brander, Laurence. *Somerset Maugham: A Guide*. London: Oliver, 1963. Simply written introduction.

Calder, Robert L. *Somerset Maugham and the Quest for Freedom*. New York: Doubleday, 1973. Study of Maugham's main themes by his most sensitive biographer and critic.

Cordell, Richard A. *Somerset Maugham: A Writer for All Seasons*. Bloomington: Indiana University Press, 1969. Sound introductory biographical and critical study.

Curtis, Anthony. *The Pattern of Maugham: A Critical Portrait*. New York: Taplinger, 1974. General overview.

———, ed. *W. Somerset Maugham: The Critical Heritage*. London: Routledge & Kegan Paul, 1987. Historical cross-section showing changing views toward Maugham, his theater, and his fiction.

Jonas, Klaus W., ed. *The Maugham Enigma*. New York: Citadel, 1954. A collection of reviews and criticisms that includes material by Theodore Dreiser, Malcolm Cowley, and Graham Greene, among others.

———, ed. *The World of Somerset Maugham*. Westport: Greenwood, 1972. Includes essays by Frank Swinnerton, St. John Ervine, and Glenway Wescott.

Loss, Archie. *W. Somerset Maugham*. New York: Ungar, 1988.

Mander, Raymond, and Joe Mitchenson. *Theatrical Companion to Maugham*. London: Rockliff, 1955. Contains synopsis of every Maugham play, precise information as to plays and films adapted from his writing; includes information concerning first stage productions, casts.

Menard, Wilmon. *The Two Worlds of Somerset Maugham*. Los Angeles: Sherbourne, 1965. Readable study depicting Hawaii and the South Seas as Maugham and his generation would have perceived them; studies of originals of some Maugham characters.

Raphael, Frederic. *W. Somerset Maugham and His World*. New York: Charles Scribner's Sons, 1974. Illustrated biographical and critical introduction.

Betty Richardson

Maurice, Thomas

Born: Hertford, 1754
Education: Christ's Hospital; Ealing; Kingswood School, Bath; Inner Temple; St. John's College, Oxford University; University College, Oxford University; B.A., 1778; M.A., 1808
Marriage: To the daughter of Thomas Pearce, 1786
Died: London, March 30, 1824

Biography

The Reverend Thomas Maurice lived a life of replication and accumulation. Born in Hertford in 1754, the second child of six in the family of a schoolmaster formerly in the West India trade, he followed in his father's footsteps, pursuing a pedagogical and research career through a mapful of institutions. From Christ's Hospital, he proceeded through Ealing, the Kingswood School of Bath, the Inner Temple (where he was an unusually neglectful student, bypassing the prescribed courses in law for the perusal of the classics), St. John's College, Oxford, and, at long last, came to rest at University College, Oxford, where he took two degrees (a B.A. in 1778 and an M.A. in 1808). Over the twenty-odd years between his bachelor's degree and the turn of the century, Maurice accumulated no fewer than seven ecclesiastical livings and sinecures, only one of which he ever resigned. After his first post as Curate of Woodford (1778), he compiled a folio of benefices comprised of the Chaplaincy of Epping (1785), the Chaplaincy of the 97th Regiment (1785), the Vicarage of Wormleighton (1798), the Assistant Keepership of Manuscripts in the British Museum (1798), William Cowper's vacated Royal Pension (1800), and the Vicarage of Cudham (1804). From these holdings Maurice drew substantial revenues, the only worldly distraction from his studies being his one brief marriage in 1786 to the daughter of Thomas Pearce, an East

India Company merchant. The marriage ended in 1790 with her untimely death. Maurice was, in any case, disinclined toward the pursuit of domestic recreations. His own family had never been keen on family life. His father acquired his fortune by marrying an elderly, short-lived widow, got his children from a young and hastily acquired second wife, died, and left the children to his former spouse and later her second husband, a rather cruel Irish lord. So preoccupied was Maurice by his scholarly lucubrations that he eventually died with dignity, reading in the British Museum in London on March 30, 1824.

Literary Analysis

Maurice's credentials as a humorist derive from two early poems, published in 1775 and 1778, "The Schoolboy" and "The Oxonian." The remainder of his works have long since retired to the deposit area of the British Library, from whence they are seldom fetched. Aside from these two comic delights, Maurice's habit of sycophancy extended to the landscape. His second favorite genre was the laudatory topographical poem (his verses on Richmond Hill drew the attention but not the approval of Lord Byron). Maurice's prose writings pertain mostly to oriental studies, whether mystical speculations on "Indian Trinities" or sober histories of Hindustan. These scholarly works occupy over fifteen massive tomes. In conjunction with his eastern investigations, Maurice penned a translation of *Oedipus Tyrannus* (done while at Oxford) and a tragedy on the "Fall of the Mogul" (1806). His *Oedipus* established some important social connections, probably because it included prefatory remarks from Dr. Samuel Johnson. Maurice never achieved general public recognition, but he is remembered in journals and literary remains as a frequent visitor to salons and a favorite of contemporary literati.

Although his output of humorous verse scarcely exceeds 500 lines, compilation and repetition are the keys to understanding his frail comedy. Seventy years before Maurice, John Philips had made a career out of mock-heroic imitations of John Milton, the renowned Puritan author of *Paradise Lost* and other epics on Christian themes. Philips's mock-epic caprices turned on the incongruity between the noble Miltonic mode and the ignoble matter of urban life—or, sometimes, the ignobility and incompetence of Philips himself. It would seem that Philips, who penned five mock-Miltonic excursions, would have exhausted the mode, but the indefatigable Maurice compiles still more Miltonisms. He self-consciously imitates Philips's imitations of Milton's emulations of antiquity, pointing out through title and preface that he aspires to duplicate the techniques of *The Splendid Shilling* (1701). Maurice thus strikes a poignantly paradoxical pose, one curiously combining nostalgia, envy, a sense of inferiority, respect, emulation, zeal, and aplomb. Whereas Philips, as the first person to hit on the idea of mocking Milton, wrote in the character of an original imitator, Maurice sings out as a semi-sentimental idolater of Philips, a good-natured pedant yearning for the good old days of Augustan coffeehouses filled with men of wit.

"The Schoolboy" and "The Oxonian" are remembrances of English education. The first covers childhood days spent under the domineering headmasters in boys' school. The second celebrates the terrors and traumas of life in an Oxford college. Both poems belong to the tradition of college miscellany verse. The renowned *The Oxford Sausage*, one compilation of popular college poems, is cited as a source in "The Oxonian."

Although Maurice's verse is always spritely (to the extent that Miltonic language can manage merriment), the stories that he tells are somewhat unpleasant. "The Schoolboy" renders the terrors of a scholar about to be switched by the master; "The Oxonian" chronicles the disobedience and confinement of rambunctious collegiate youths. We laugh when we think of Milton's angels fighting in a rural classroom, but we shudder when we pass—and bypass—Maurice's slightly sadistic account of a thrashing: "He [the headmaster] shakes his Sceptre, and th' impending Scourge / Brandishes high; / nor Tears nor Shrieks avail; / But with impetuous Fury it descends, / Imprinting horrid Wounds, with fatal Flow / Of Blood attended, and convulsive Pangs" ("The Schoolboy," 6). Maurice's description of the English pedant, on the other hand, is pure—and purely delightful—domesticated Milton: "When lo! with haughty Stride (in Size like him / Who erst extended on the burning Lake, / Lay floating many a Rood;) his sullen Brow, / With low-ring Frowns and fearful Glooms o'ercast, / Enters the Paedagogue; terrific Sight!" ("The Schoolboy," 4).

Maurice had little staying power as a poet. In "The Schoolboy" he defined his mode while in "The Oxonian" he perfected and concluded it. In "The Schoolboy" Philips's mock-Miltonism—and hence Milton—is reduced to a flawless formula. Maurice makes Milton into mannerism; he masters the conversion of adjectives into verbs ("the blushing Morn / Purples the East"), the elaborate extension of comparisons ("as in full Career / With Horns, and Hounds, and thund'ring Shouts he drives / The flying Stag"), and the Philips-style reduction of thundering orations to anti-climaxes (the foregoing lines terminate "in sprightly Bumpers, and the mantling Bowl"). Particularly accomplished with the Miltonic close-up shot—he offers a chilling portrait of the pedagogue's "fiery Eyeballs, like two blazing Stars"—Maurice brings out in detail the overlooked absurdity of the bombastic Milton. He enjoys injecting overly derivative, absurdly archaic words like "conn" (would not the more familiar "know" suffice?) into familiar settings such as that of the tight ranks of pews in a classroom. The amalgamative Maurice never fears boldly to go where even the universe-encompassing Milton had not dared go. He concocts outrageous, Augustanized, pseudo-Miltonic periphrases ("Chronologic Page" replaces "history book"); he whimsically expresses his envy of fish, who can skinny-dip any time they please. Maurice also goes where Milton would *refuse* to go. Midway through "The Schoolboy" he inserts a panegyric to "Illustrious George" (King George III) for no apparent reason other than to curry favor.

The poet's second Miltonic production, "The Oxonian," lacks the verve of "The Schoolboy" but outperforms its predecessor in both intellectual breadth and rhetorical variety. Now imitating himself imitating Philips imitating Milton imitating the ancients, Maurice is hard put to maintain the precisely measured distance between himself, Philips, and Milton that energized earlier mock-Miltonic verse. Yet, he is also free to borrow more liberally and inventively from his predecessors. He apes Milton's broad learning in the oriental arts, doffing invocations to "*Phoebus*, or *Mithras*," by way of demonstrating his own polycultural acumen. Geometry is lassoed into the writer's comprehensive ken when the Miltonizing muse leads him through "Mysterious studies" of "Figures and lines," "Oblique or square, and time, and mode, and space." Unfortunately, "Logic, rugged maid," foils his mathematical adventures when she decides to "perplex" his

"brains." Combing the Miltonic universe and discovering the catalogue of devils in Pandaemonium, Maurice offers up a series of verse "characters," capsule descriptions of notable figures in his college, especially the "*Proctors*" with "sleeves of ominous sweep, / of *Genoa*'s looms the fam'd produce, well-known, / And dreaded." All the familiar archaisms echo through Maurice's Oxonian halls; we get the expected sputtering of "Ycleped" as he spoofs Edmund Spenser, Geoffrey Chaucer, and the yeomanry. Still, his tone is noticeably softer than in his first mock-Miltonic venture. Abstract expressions of "Frantic joy" replace lurid scenes of whipping and fighting. One new twist introduced in "The Oxonian" is the use of direct transcriptions from Milton. The comic effect of these passages comes straight from England's greatest epic bard and is thus all the more ridiculous when imported into the little red schoolhouse. Maurice also imports poetical riffs wholesale from Philips, probably not with intellectual theft in mind but rather to startle, excite, wrestle with, and, in sum, entertain his reader. His obvious borrowing of Philips' idea (in *The Splendid Shilling*) for a paean to tobacco is perhaps the ultimate tribute to his mentor, for Maurice treats Philips as just as much an original writer as Milton himself. He extrapolates from and mocks the author of *Cyder* in exactly the same way that Philips had roasted England's regicidal bard.

Maurice's poems are, if nothing else, a monument to the durability of the Miltonic tradition. That that monument should be a comic one is all the greater a tribute to Milton, for it suggests that devoted writers were willing to try almost any stratagem, even travesty, to keep Miltonian discourse going. In perfecting the mock-Miltonic mannerism seven decades too late and in applying it to startlingly original subjects pressed into the form, Maurice, as the Earl of Rochester might say, took Milton beyond the limits of Milton's bounded universe. Overextended, Maurice was to become the last mock-Miltonist of the Miltonizing multitude, himself a monument to the avidity of Augustan satire and an important juncture joining the comic Miltonolatry of Philips and the reverential Miltonianism of Samuel Taylor Coleridge and William Wordsworth.

Summary

Thomas Maurice practiced accumulation in every aspect of his life, from the organization of his career to his scholarly pursuits and on to his latter-day compilations of mock-Miltonic verse. An imitator of an imitator of Milton, he specialized in the wringing out of a fading verse tradition, making the futility and oddity of his project into a (short-lived) genre of its own. Maurice's expansive idiom compels him to take his poems into uncharted, sometimes frightening territory, but even his most hideous scenes are accompanied with a reassuring sense of absurdity, bungling, and limitation.

Selected Bibliography
Primary Sources
"The Schoolboy, A Poem in Imitation of Mr. Philips's Splendid Shilling." London: Kearsley, 1775.
"The Oxonian: A Poem. In Imitation of the Splendid Shilling." London: Kearsley, 1778.

Secondary Sources
There are no secondary writings on Thomas Maurice other than a short entry in the *Dictionary of National Biography* and spotty references in obsolete encyclopedias.

Kevin L. Cope

Mayhew, Henry
Born: London, November 25, 1812
Education: Westminster School, 1822–1827
Marriage: Jane Douglas, 1844; two children
Died: London, July 25, 1887

Biography
Henry Mayhew, the fourth son of seventeen children, was born on November 25, 1812, in London. Although little is known of Mayhew's mother, Mary Ann Mayhew, his father, Joshua Mayhew, was a prosperous and prominent London solicitor. Joshua was, by all accounts, a stern man with little patience for what he considered the irresponsible behavior of his five literary sons, Henry in particular.

Mayhew was admitted to the prestigious Westminster School on January 14, 1822, in the hope that he would eventually join the family firm. While at Westminster School, he made a lifelong friendship with future journalist and farceur, Gilbert A'Beckett. Mayhew and A' Beckett established their rebellious natures early by running away from Westminster School on at least one occasion in 1827.

After this escapade, Mayhew was sent as midshipman to Calcutta, but he proved unsuited to the sea as well and was dismissed for disciplinary reasons upon the ship's return to England. When he returned to England, probably at the end of the 1820s, he joined his father's law firm as an articled clerk.

In 1835, however, Mayhew was abruptly dismissed from his father's employ after neglecting to deliver important papers to the Chancery on Joshua's behalf. The incident not only almost resulted in his father's imprisonment for contempt of court but also added to Henry's increasing reputation as a wayward son.

Henry went off in disgrace to Paris with an allowance of only one pound per week. In Paris, he met up with his old music master, John Barnett, and through Barnett he became acquainted with the successful dramatist and his future father-in-law, Douglas Jerrold. William Makepeace Thackeray was also in Paris during 1835, and the men frequently gathered in the evenings to discuss literary ideas, journalism, and theater.[1] Mayhew had something in common with his new acquaintances by 1835. He had already authored a successful farce, *The Wandering Minstrel*, and collaborated in the creation of several comic periodicals. The most successful of these was *Figaro in London,* which he established in 1831 with his boyhood friend A'Beckett.

Mayhew's son, Athol, reports that his father returned to England, sometime in 1836, and he lived until 1838 in Wales. While living on the banks of the Wye, Mayhew reportedly spent his time reading and preparing to embark on a literary career. By the summer of 1838, Mayhew had returned to London where he began his work as a journalist.[2] He married Jane Douglas in 1844 and they had two children, Amy and Athol.

Fortunately, Mayhew had been able to establish some financial independence from his father through his writing during the 1830s. In 1841, he co-founded *Punch*, the most successful nineteenth-century comic journal. But always irresponsible in money matters, Mayhew began spending far more than he earned during the early 1840s and by 1846 he was forced to declare bankruptcy. The bankruptcy was a tremendous personal and family disgrace for which his father never forgave him. Henry was eventually cut off from his father's very substantial estate with only a pound per week allowance as punishment for his continued financial irresponsibility.

M

Mayhew wrote prolifically during the 1840s and 1850s. In addition to contributing to literary journals, Henry and his brother Augustus wrote two didactic fairy tales and four comic novels for family entertainment.[3]

During the late 1840s and early 1850s, Mayhew wrote a series of articles for the *Morning Chronicle* which he later compiled into a four-volume series entitled *London Labour and the London Poor*. It is that work for which he is primarily remembered today.

Although his name does not appear in dramatic lists during the 1840s, he remained active in the theatrical community. In 1845, he was a member of Charles Dickens's production of *Every Man in His Humour*. In 1847, he was among the strolling players who performed Ben Jonson's comedy, *Paul Pry*, in Manchester and Liverpool. Other members of the cast included Mark Lemon, Jerrold, and George Cruikshank ("Phiz").[4]

In the 1850s and 1860s, Mayhew wrote four popular didactic biographies for boys, several of which remained in print into the 1890s. Fulfilling the expectations of adult buyers who expected certain morals and values to be expressed in works for their children, the biographies were a critical success and were published in the United States and Germany as well as England. Also during the 1850s and 1860s, he contributed to the well-established literary tradition of travel books. He wrote several popular travel books about Germany in which he satirized popular German customs.

During the last years of his life, Mayhew edited a variety of journals and continued to pursue his interest in science. He died in London on July 25, 1887.

Literary Analysis

Mayhew is best remembered today for his investigative journalistic work for the *Morning Chronicle* that helped bring to light the poor conditions of the working class in London and which culminated in the four-volume series, *London Labour and the London Poor*. He was much more than an investigative journalist, however. He was also an editor of comic magazines and a popular writer of comic novels for adults and fairy tales for family enjoyment and moral edification. In addition, he wrote successful travel books, highly successful juvenile biographies for boys, and popular farce and burlesque.

Mayhew's writing career began auspiciously during the 1830s when he and A'Beckett started several comic journals. In 1831, the men hit a great success with *Figaro in London*, a one-penny, four-page quarto published every Saturday. The journal was first edited by A'Beckett (1831–1834) and then by Mayhew (1835–1838).

Figaro in London was one of the most commercially successful satirical journals of the decade. A comparison of the circulation figures of other popular periodicals during this period illustrates *Figaro*'s success. By 1837, the average circulation of *The Examiner* was 3,900 and circulation of *The Bell's Life in London* reached 16,400 in 1837. At a high point during its existence, however, the circulation of *Figaro in London* reached 70,000—an astounding figure in comparison. Weekly issues of *Figaro in London* were often reprinted due to high demand, and half-year and yearly bound volumes became a tradition.

Unlike that in its often short-lived and highly partisan competitors, the satire contained in *Figaro in London* was focused on politics as a whole, thus appealing to a wider audience than those of the other comic journals. In addition to satirizing political events, the contributors to *Figaro in London* also poked fun at the pomposity of the aristocracy and the concern with appearances of the upper-middle class. An example of the comic technique used most often in the periodical, a play on words, comes from a weekly section called "Brevities." Under the title "Candour of the Times" the author responds to the editorial opinion of the *Times* regarding the issuance of paper currency. The *Figaro* editor writes: "The *Times* is opposed to a paper issue, which it calls a depreciated currency. It is at least candid of our contemporary to admit, that it believes no good can arise to the country from a *large paper circulation*." A quarter of the magazine's space was dedicated to theater reviews, which makes it a valuable source of information for details regarding theatrical events between 1831 and 1838. The popularity of *Figaro in London* paved the way for *Punch*.

Mayhew's most enduring contribution to English humor was the co-founding of *Punch* in 1841. Legend has it that the idea for *Punch* was born in Paris in 1835 when Mayhew, Jerrold, and Thackeray spent their evenings together discussing the need for a good comic journal along the lines of the Parisian *Charivari*. Unlike the sardonic satire in the Parisian comic paper, the satire in the early issues of *Punch* was of a genial nature. The weekly magazine focused on topical issues in society and government, and the contributors attempted to point out through humor the absurdity of pompous political figures or ineffective institutions.

Representative of the type of humor found in *Punch* during the 1840s is the joke that Mayhew is credited with having written for the January *Punch Almanack* of 1845:

Worthy of Attention
Advice to Persons About Marry—Don't[5]

Because of the incredible success and longevity of *Punch* (which unfortunately stopped publication in 1992, over 150 years later), there began a rather heated debate at the end of the nineteenth century regarding who played what role in the founding of the journal. It is, however, generally accepted that Mayhew was a co-founder of the journal. He is credited with giving the journal its original genial tone and pleasant and philosophical wit.[6]

When *Punch* was sold to the publishing firm Bradbury and Evans in December 1842, Lemon became sole editor of the journal. After that time Mayhew grew increasingly less involved with the magazine for reasons which remain unclear.[7] At any rate, Mayhew continued to contribute to *Punch* until 1845.

In 1850 and 1851, Mayhew edited *The Comic Almanack*, a highly successful monthly established in 1835 and illustrated by Cruikshank. With good-humored satire, the monthly publication dealt comically with topical events and issues. Blue-stockings were a favorite target of ridicule, as was the pomposity of the upper-middle class. Contributors to *The Comic Almanack* included some of the most popular comic writers of the day—Thackeray, Albert Smith, Henry and Horace Mayhew, and Robert Brough.

Mayhew's comic talents also appear in his writings for the stage. In January 1834, his first play, *The Wandering Minstrel*, was produced at the Fitzroy Theatre (also known as the Theatre Royal) in London. On the surface *The Wandering Minstrel* is a farce of mistaken identity and courtship intrigue fulfilling the traditional expectations of the genre: after various misunderstandings and witty wordplay, a young girl overcomes her guardian's disapproval of her choice of lover and a crucial mistake in identity is discovered. *The Wandering Minstrel* departs from the conventions of farce by seriously questioning the overt classism of early Victorian England.

The play begins with Julia arguing with her upper-class Aunt, Mrs. Crincum, about the suitability of her professional-class lover, Herbert Carol. Julia's love for Herbert, a solicitor, threatens her aunt's aspirations to raise her own social position. Mrs. Crincum hopes to arrange a marriage between Julia and the aristocrat who, according to the local newspaper, may soon be seen "travelling through the country under the guise of a wandering minstrel" (scene 1, p. 16).

In her mad desire to improve her social position, Mrs. Crincum mistakes a vagabond, Jem Baggs, who is playing a violin outside her house, for the aristocrat. Mr. and Mrs. Crincum come to the front of the house, the former very much annoyed by the noise:

JEM. B. I knew they couldn't stand that wery long.

MRS. C. See ther, Mr. C?—there he is—there's the Wandering Minstrel!—oh, the dear melodious creature.

JEM. B. She says I'm a hodious screecher—I sartinly must ax em a shilling!

MRS. C. And now, Mr. C. you go and place your house at the disposal of the tilted votary of Apollo—assuring him your constant study shall be to endow it with all the comfort of a home.

JEM. B. Vell!—if she isn't a talking about the comforts of a home—now, there arn't no one sets a higher "walley" on the comforts of a home, than I does—I couldn't think of moving on under a shilling.

Baggs's responses to Mrs. Crincum represent more than mere punning for the amusement of the audience. The inability of the tramp and the upper-class woman to communicate is clearly indicative of the great distance between their classes. Although they are from the same country and the same town, one cannot even understand the words of the other. Their worlds are too different and their frames of reference too unrelated. Furthermore, the tramp is aware that his presence is so "hodious" to members of the upper class that he is prepared to cash in on their distaste and charge them for going away.

Baggs eventually catches on to the error and, deciding to get in on the fun, agrees to play that evening for a party at the Crincums' house. Mistaking him for a member of the nobility, guests at the party hang onto his every word with deference, undisturbed by Baggs's strange responses in conversation. Herbert challenges Baggs to a singing duel that evening at the party, forcing Mrs. Crincum to see that Baggs is a tramp and demonstrating through his music that he (Herbert) has the cultural and linguistic qualities requisite for good society.

The main source of humor in *The Wandering Minstrel* comes from Mayhew's exploitation of the different languages spoken by the varying classes. Baggs's vulgar speech is the target of ridicule, and when he is brought in contact with the upper-class Crincums, who speak well, the cultural and linguistic distance between the characters incites laughter. Furthermore, the comedy is enhanced by the fact that Mrs. Crincum and her upper-class friends, who put such store in social standing, are unable to recognize that Baggs is a tramp rather than an aristocrat. The audience laughs not only at Mrs. Crincum's human imperfections, but also because they can recognize her snobbishness either in themselves or in people they know. In his first successful work, Mayhew begins what will be a lifelong career of challenging fashionable opinion and calling for change, if only moderate change, through laughter.

At a time when similar plays typically disappeared without a trace after a few performances and were rarely published, *The Wandering Minstrel* remained on stage for more than half a century and in print for sixty-three years. Because Mayhew's farce exploited popular interests in a familiar form, he was successful in keeping the public ear in his challenge to classism against the professional and middle class in Victorian England.

In 1838, Mayhew wrote his second successful farce, *But however—*, in collaboration with Henry Baylis. As in *The Wandering Minstrel*, the main plot of *But however—* revolves around mistaken identity. In this case, members of the upper-middle class and landed gentry are unable to tell the difference between a common thief and a squire who is expected to arrive from India any day to claim his recently inherited estate and his bride.

Like Mrs. Crincum in *The Wandering Minstrel*, the characters in *But however—* accept and show deference to a man beneath them in the social hierarchy, not because he is good or has proven himself worthy of respect, but because he is believed to be a member of the upper class.

But however— is in many respects a more conventional farce than *The Wandering Minstrel*; the punning in the farce is clearly intended more for a bawdy laugh than for social commentary. In one scene the two-bit swindler, Chizzler, sees the silly case of his mistaken identity as another opportunity to make some quick cash. Without waiting to case the situation carefully, he quickly pounces upon a respectable woman, Mrs. Juniper, as an easy victim:

> CHIZ: What, doesn't your own heart tell you? A friend Mrs. Juniper—a buzzum friend—that would console you and mind the bar—look after your interests and keep the key of the till,—love you sincerely and receive your dividends half yearly—counsel—protect—comfort you, and larrup the pot-boy. Mrs. J. you are a lone unprotected female,—I a private single gentle-man—you endowed with every charm—I not particulary bad looking—you possessed of a snug little income—and I—but however—,
> MRS. JUN: Lord, sir, I don't understand you, what do you take me for?
> CHIZ: Take you for, Mrs. J.? Why, to look at you, I'd take you for—better or worse with a great deal of pleasure.
> MRS. JUN: You take me for better or worse, sir; you who are engaged to Miss Julia of the Grange—oh, you shocking man. (scene 1, p. 12)

But however— is a much more physical farce than *The Wandering Minstrel*—characters hide in closets and stumble over furniture—and its physicality cannot be explained as easily in terms of plot or character as can the few physical scenes in *The Wandering Minstrel*. Although *But however—* did not have the enduring appeal with Victorian audiences that *The Wandering Minstrel* had, it offers valuable insight into the expectations and social values of Victorian audiences.[8]

In addition to writing farces and comic journalism, during the 1840s and 1850s Mayhew wrote several comic novels in collaboration with his brother Augustus. The novels gently satirize the attitudes and customs of the middle and upper-middle classes in a manner that asks the reader to laugh at himself. As with his farce, Mayhew used humor to suggest a moderate change in social attitudes.

Representative of the comic novels by the Brothers Mayhew are *The Greatest Plague of Life; or, the Adventures of a Lady in Search of a Good Servant* (1847) and *Whom to Marry and How to Get Married! or, the Adventures of a Lady in Search of a Good Husband* (1848). The narrator of *The Greatest Plague of Life* is a young, middle-class wife in search of a reliable servant. The novel satirizes the stereotypically sweet naiveté of a young Victorian housewife whose empty-headedness finally causes her more sophisticated husband to take matters into his own hands after he becomes fed up with the uncomfortable condition of his house. The novel, illustrated by Cruikshank, remained in print until 1892.

As in *The Greatest Plague of Life*, the narrator of *Whom to Marry and How to Get Married* is a woman. Each chapter in the novel centers on a different memory of the woman's younger years and silly thoughts of love and marriage. Reflecting Victorian sentiments, the heroine learns through a series of amusing adventures and observances about the wretchedness that befalls young women who do not obey their fathers or abide by the wishes of their mothers. In the end the heroine learns her lesson well when she marries an older man against her father's will, and her husband turns out to be mean and selfish and miserly. As is typical in novels by the Brothers Mayhew, the story ends on a sweetly sentimental note. Despite the heroine's wayward behavior, her father's love never fails. Sustaining fundamental Victorian domestic values, the novels were both critically and commercially successful.

Summary

Henry Mayhew's long-lived success as a comic writer can be attributed to his having had his finger firmly on the pulse of Victorian sensibilities. It was by connecting with the beliefs and attitudes of his many readers that Mayhew was able to covertly challenge those beliefs in order to bring about change in his society. Whether satirizing social institutions in his comic novels, mocking ineffectual political institutions in the journals *Figaro in London* and *Punch*, or questioning social hierarchy in his farce, Mayhew's humor was not offensively irreverent nor did it overtly question the basic values of Victorian society. With his first works in the 1830s, Mayhew began a lifelong career of calling for moderate social change through laughter.

Notes

1. Athol Mayhew, *A Jorum of Punch*. London: Downey, 1895, p. 10.
2. *Ibid.*, p. 26.
3. Also see *1851; or, The Adventures of Mr. and Mrs. Sandboys and Family, who came up to London to 'enjoy themselves,' and to see the Great Exhibition* (London: Bogue, 1851). Mayhew wrote the comic novel in 1851 in honor of the Great Exhibition. The novel, illustrated by George Cruikshank, deals with the comic mishaps of the Sandboys family while they were in London to see the Great Exhibition. It was a moderate success primarily due to Cruikshank's illustrations.
4. S.J. Adair Fitz-Gerald, *Dickens and the Drama: being an account of Charles Dickens's connection with the stage and the stage's connection with him* (London: Chapman & Hall, 1910), pp. 19–20.
5. M.H. Spielmann, *The History of "Punch"* (New York: Cassell, 1895), p. 270.
6. *Ibid.*, pp. 17, 28.
7. Anne Humpherys suggests that Mayhew was pushed out of the editorship under unpleasant circumstances. *Punch* scholar R.G.G. Price, on the other hand, suggests that it was Mayhew's decision to remove himself because he was not pleased with the hard-edged satire towards which his father-in-law, Douglas Jerrold, was leading the journal.
8. In 1838, Mayhew published "Peter Punctilio: The Gentleman in Black" in *Bentley's Miscellany*. In 1840, a farce called *The Gentleman in Black* by Mark Lemon was performed in London. The farce is almost entirely a word-for-word stage version of Mayhew's story. According to Mayhew's bankruptcy trial, he sold the short story to Lemon for £200 but was never paid. For further reference to Mayhew's dramatic collaborations during the 1830s, see the account of his bankruptcy trial in *The Times* (London).

Selected Bibliography

Primary Sources

Farce
The Wandering Minstrel. London: J. Miller, 1834.

But however—. London: Chapman & Hall, 1838.
"Peter Punctilio: The Gentleman in Black." *Bentley's Miscellany*, 4 (1838): 609–626.

Comic Novels by The Brothers Mayhew
The Greatest Plague of Life; or, the Adventures of a Lady in Search of a Good Servant. London: David Bogue, 1847.
Whom to Marry and How to Get Married! or, the Adventures of a Lady in Search of a Good Husband. London: David Bogue, 1848.

Secondary Sources

Book and Parts of Books
Bradley, John L. "Introduction." *Selections from "London Labour and the London Poor."* London: Oxford University Press, 1965. Biography and brief analysis of Mayhew's literary career including his writing of burlesque.
Humpherys, Anne. *Travels into the Poor Man's Country: The Work of Henry Mayhew.* Athens: University of Georgia Press, 1977. First book-length study of Mayhew's social surveys.
———. *Henry Mayhew.* Boston: Twayne, 1984. Broad analysis of Mayhew's literary career concentrating on his social surveys. Extensive bibliography of works by and about Mayhew.
Mayhew, Athol. *A Jorum of Punch.* London: Downey, 1895. Anecdotal account of the founding of *Punch* by Mayhew's son.
Price, R.G.G. *A History of PUNCH.* London: Collins, 1957.
Spielmann, M.H. *The History of "Punch."* New York: Cassell, 1895.
Thompson, E.P. *The Unknown Mayhew.* Ed. E.P. Thompson and Eileen Yeo. New York: Pantheon, 1971. An early study of Mayhew biased in favor of his social journalism.

Articles
Account of Mayhew's bankruptcy. *The Times* (London), February 12, 1847, p. 8.
Bradley, John L. "Henry Mayhew: Farce Writer of the 1830's." *Victorian Newsletter*, 23 (1963): 21–23. Discussion of Mayhew's farce from the 1830s concentrating on *The Wandering Minstrel*.

Rebekah N. Galbreath

Meredith, George

Born: Portsmouth, February 12, 1828
Education: St. Paul's School, Southsea, and the Moravian School at Neuwied on the Rhine (1843–1844); apprenticed to Richard Charnock, a solicitor, in 1845 (?)
Marriage: Mary Ellen Nicolls, April 9, 1849; one child; Marie Vuilliamy, September 20, 1864; two children
Died: London, May 9, 1909

Biography

George Meredith was born in Portsmouth on February 12, 1828, the only son of Augustus and Jane Macnamara Meredith. His mother died when he was five; his father, a tailor, struggled to provide Meredith with an education despite financial difficulties that caused him to file for bankruptcy in 1838. Augustus Meredith's insolvency, his occupation, and his eventual marriage to the family housekeeper, Matilda Buckett, embarrassed and alienated his son.

Educated in England at St. Paul's School in Southsea and then at the Moravian School at Neuwied on the Rhine, Germany, from 1843 to 1844, Meredith was apprenticed at the age of seventeen to Richard Charnock, a London solicitor with an affinity for literature and a set of witty, sophisticated friends which included Mary Ellen Nicolls, the widowed daughter of Thomas Love Peacock. On April 9, 1849, Meredith married Mary Ellen; they had one son, Arthur, in 1853. Anxious to establish himself as an author, Meredith published his first book of poems in 1851 and his first prose work, *The Shaving of Shagpat*, in 1855.

Meredith's early adulthood was marred by personal crisis: his wife had an affair with the artist Henry Wallis and left England with Wallis after giving birth to a son (probably Wallis's) in 1858. Mary Ellen Meredith later returned to England, where she died in 1861. Facing financial difficulties, Meredith became publisher's reader for Chapman & Hall, a position that he held from 1860 through 1894. He also contributed essays and reviews to a number of periodicals. Despite his liberal sympathies, he wrote leading articles and a weekly news commentary for the conservative *Ipswich Journal* from 1858 through 1868. He also was associated with the *Westminster Review* (1857–1858) and *Once a Week* (1860).

On September 20, 1864, Meredith married Marie Vuilliamy; the couple had two children.

The author contributed to the *Morning Post* and in 1866 served as a special correspondent during the war between Italy and Austria. Beginning in 1867, he, too, wrote for the *Fortnightly Review*, briefly taking over the editorship while his friend John Morley traveled in North America.

In 1872 and 1873, Meredith contributed a series of sketches to the *Graphic*. His literary reputation began to take hold in the late 1870s, especially after his novel *Beauchamp's Career* (1876) garnered some favorable reviews. His well-known lecture "On the Idea of Comedy and the Uses of the Comic Spirit," delivered on February 1, 1877, at the London Institution, informed both the series of short stories he published in the *New Quarterly Magazine* (1877–1879) and his most famous novel, *The Egoist* (1879).

In the 1880s, Meredith experienced the onset of the neurological problems and deafness that plagued his later years. His second wife, Marie, died in 1885, and in 1890 his son Arthur died of tuberculosis. Meredith's recognition as England's leading writer was commemorated by his election as President of the Society of Authors in 1892, the same year that he was granted an honorary degree from St. Andrew's University in Scotland. In 1895, he changed publishers, moving from Chapman & Hall to Constable; his son William, who worked for Constable, became Meredith's literary agent. Meredith received the Order of Merit in 1905. He died in London on May 9, 1909.

Literary Analysis

Meredith began his literary career as a poet with *Poems* (1851), published at his own expense. His fiction was, at least initially, written in an effort to make money. Although he published a second book of poetry, *Modern Love and Poems of the English Roadside*, in 1862, Meredith did not bring out another book of poems until *Poems and Lyrics of the Joy of Earth* (1883). His reputation as a comic writer rests on the fiction and essays that he had written in the meantime.

Many of Meredith's themes and ideas about comedy are evident in *The Shaving of Shagpat*, a parody of Oriental romances inspired by *The Arabian Nights* (Meredith's favorite childhood reading) and the works of Thomas Carlyle. *The Shaving of Shagpat* features a barber, Shibli Bagarag, who embarks on a heroic quest to shave the head of Shagpat, a

tailor who owes his wealth and power to a single, magical hair. Like many of Meredith's later characters, Shibli is a naive, egotistical hero who can only accomplish his goal by enduring difficulties ("thwackings") and by learning to recognize his own foolishness. Comedy contributes to Shibli's enlightenment: trapped in the Palace of Aklis, Shibli is freed when he sees himself in a mirror and laughs. Shibli also benefits from the wisdom of Noorna bin Noorka, a woman who aids him in return for his promise of marriage. In the author's insistence that character is shaped by circumstances, his presentation of the protagonist's struggle against his own vanity and pretension, and his representation of women's strength and intelligence, *The Shaving of Shagpat* anticipates the major themes of much of his later work.

In his first major novel, *The Ordeal of Richard Feverel* (1859), Meredith explores the link between comedy and tragedy. Although he touches on contemporary scientific, educational, and social debates, he is mainly concerned with illustrating the psychological responses of his main characters. Both Austin Feverel's educational experiment and his son Richard's efforts at social heroism are directly related to their internal conflicts. Embittered by his own failed marriage, Austin Feverel's "system" for Richard's education consists primarily of isolating Richard from other children, especially girls. Richard falls in love with Lucy Desbrough, the daughter of a neighboring farmer, and marries her in spite of his father's attempts to separate the young lovers.

Like Shagpat, Richard Feverel is another would-be-hero whose ordeal has comic moments. Prior to his marriage, the novel refers to itself as a comedy (as when an episode in which Richard sets fire to a farm is designated as the "Bakewell Comedy"), and it has followed an essentially comic plot. But the title of the chapter in which Lucy and Richard are married— "In Which the Last Act of a Comedy takes the Place of the First"—signals an inversion of the expected pattern. Drawing as it does upon Meredith's bitter experience with his first wife, Mary, *The Ordeal of Richard Feverel* is not a novel in which marriage can provide a happy ending. The aftereffects of Austin Feverel's disappointment continue to poison his relationship with his son; combined with Richard's own pride and misguided attempts at heroism, they ensure that the son's marriage will end as disastrously as the father's.

M

Though not comic in the usual sense, *The Ordeal of Richard Feverel* is the first of his novels in which Meredith illustrates the consequences of ignoring the comic perspective. In the novelist's view, comedy could have corrected Austin Feverel's arrogance and self-delusion; as the writer comments, "a good wind of laughter had relieved him of much of the blight of self-deception, and oddness, and extravagance; had given a healthier view of our atmosphere of life; but he had it not."[1] Richard also suffers because he cannot see that his humanitarianism is rooted in pride. He takes to the streets of London as a modern knight-errant on a quest to rescue prostitutes only to become the victim of one of the women whom he had hoped to rehabilitate. Victorian readers were baffled by his subtle irony and psychological sophistication. They were also offended by his frank treatment of Richard's seduction. Mudie's circulating library dropped the book, and Meredith's reputation suffered from the accusation of impropriety.

Meredith's next novels, *Evan Harrington* (1860) and *Emilia in England* (1864; later renamed *Sandra Belloni*), are more purely and conventionally comic in design, and his satire against social pretension and sentimentality is more decisively demonstrated. *Evan Harrington*'s subtitle, *He Would Be a Gentleman*, places it with other mid-Victorian efforts (such as Dinah Mulock's *John Halifax, Gentleman*, 1856) to define the gentleman according to character instead of birth. Meredith's novel also shows the influence of Carlyle's *Sartor Resartus* in that Meredith, like Carlyle, uses the motif of clothing and tailoring to explore social and personal imposture. In doing so, Meredith drew upon his family background. Evan's father, "The Great Mel," is a flamboyant, socially ambitious tailor much like Melchizedec Meredith, the novelist's grandfather, while Evan's sisters, all of whom have distanced themselves from their origins through advantageous marriages, are modeled after Meredith's aunts.

Evan, like the protagonists of Meredith's previous works, must endure an ordeal, which consists of choosing between marrying the aristocratic Rose Jocelyn or carrying on his late father's tailoring business. Evan's sister, the Countess de Saldar, schemes tirelessly and ingeniously for her own and Evan's social advancement; she encourages Evan to marry Rose, and thus to secure a place among the landed gentry. The Countess is one of Meredith's finest comic characters. Like Thackeray's Becky Sharp, her manipulations are so outrageous that the reader is compelled to admire her. Opposed to the Countess is Evan's mother, who straightforwardly reminds him of his duty towards his family. Meredith contrives the plot so that Evan's true gentlemanliness is demonstrated by his choice of work and duty, and rewarded by Rose's insistence upon marrying him.

Sandra Belloni, the title character of which was described by the author as "a contrast of a girl of simplicity and passion and our English sentimental, socially-aspiring damsels,"[2] was his first novel with a female protagonist. Emilia Alessandra Belloni, a half-Italian musical genius, is Meredith's "simple" heroine whom he contrasts with the members of the Pole family. Arabella, Adela, Cornelia, and Wilfrid Pole, along with their father, a wealthy London merchant on the brink of financial ruin, are the targets of Meredith's most direct attack on middle-class hypocrisy. The Pole daughters are, by his definition, "sentimentalists" who display a veneer of refinement and sensitivity that only thinly disguises their commonplace snobbery and social ambition. Though they look down upon Emilia's lack of sophistication, they are not above exploiting her musical talent to gain social preeminence. Meredith attacks both male egoism and the Victorian marriage market in Wilfrid Pole, who cannot choose between Emilia and a wealthy, titled widow.

Meredith's most important comic writings were those of the 1870s. He began the decade with *The Adventures of Harry Richmond* (1871; a *Bildungsroman* in the tradition of Charles Dickens's *David Copperfield*) in which the title character is all but displaced by his audacious father, Richmond Roy. Roy, an indefatigable schemer akin to *Evan Harrington*'s Countess de Saldar, claims to be an illegitimate son of royalty. The novel never reveals whether Roy's claims are valid, focusing instead on Harry's struggle to come to terms with his father's recklessness.

Meredith articulated his ideas about comedy in a lecture, "On the Idea of Comedy and the Uses of the Comic Spirit" (later published as *An Essay on Comedy*), delivered on February 1, 1877, at the London Institution. In the *Essay*, he insists that comedy can only flourish in a cultivated society: one that is based on common sense and one in which women and men are social equals. The relationship that Meredith perceived between comedy and the emancipation of women led him to recommend the comic perspective to his female readers. Holding out William Congreve's Millamant and especially Jean Baptiste Molière's Celimene as exemplary heroines because of their wit, intelligence, and command of language, Meredith suggests that comedy not only provides women with a weapon in the battle of the sexes but that it also helps to lessen the cultural influences which fuel that battle.

He personifies his idea of comedy in the Comic Spirit, an entity that acts as a detached observer of human irrationality, sentimentalism, and pretension:

> Its common aspect is one of unsolicitous observation, as if surveying a full field and having leisure to dart on its chosen morsels, without any fluttering eagerness. Men's future upon earth does not attract it; their honesty and shapeliness in the present does; and whenever they wax out of proportion, overblown, affected, pretentious, bombastical, hypocritical, pedantic, fantastically delicate; whenever it sees them self-deceived or hoodwinked, given to run riot in idolatries, drifting into vanities, congregating in absurdities, planning shortsightedly, plotting dementedly; whenever they are at variance with their professions, and violate the unwritten but perceptible laws binding them in consideration one to another; whenever they offend sound reason, fair justice; are false in humility or mined with conceit . . . the Spirit overhead will look humanely malign, and cast an oblique light on them, followed by volleys of silvery laughter.[3]

The impersonal attitude of the Comic Spirit separates it from humor and satire, forms of comedy that appeal to the emotions. Meredith's comedy is primarily intellectual, a way of looking at the world without contempt and without illusions. It is also a form of social vigilance by which the values of a civilized society can be identified and maintained.

The ideas expressed in his *Essay* informed the writer's most famous comic novel, *The Egoist*. The novel begins with a "Prelude" in which Meredith again affirms that the purpose of comedy is to illuminate the world of civilized men and women, and he identifies the Egoist as an English gentleman surrounded by "imps" that wait for him to reveal himself as a comic target.

Since the *Essay on Comedy* drew most of its examples from the stage, *The Egoist*'s dramatic elements (the temporal and spatial confines of the plot and its reliance upon dialogue) provide another link to his theoretical writing.

The Egoist in Meredith's novel is Sir Willoughby Patterne, the heir of Patterne Hall. Once jilted, Willoughby has recently become engaged to Clara Middleton, the young, intelligent, but inexperienced daughter of a classical scholar. To Willoughby, Clara is "a parasite and a chalice," a dependent vessel which he immediately attempts to fill with "knowledge of himself."[4] Meredith had read John Stuart Mill's *On the Subjection of Women* (1869), which may have shaped his depiction of Willoughby's sexism. His treatment of Clara's quandary reinforced the relationship between feminism and comedy that he had written about in the *Essay*.

In the "Prelude," Meredith implies that Willoughby's self-love will bring about self-destruction, and in fact, Willoughby engineers his downfall with only minimal assistance from other characters. Although the novelist had argued that the Comic Spirit approached its objects without contempt, Willoughby's torment and eventual defeat receive an emphasis that seems to contradict Meredith's vaunted objectivity. The novel's greatest emphasis, however, is on Clara's psychological development. Her gradual perception of Willoughby's narcissism is skillfully represented, as is her struggle to discover a way to break her engagement without compromising her integrity.

In his subsequent novels, *The Tragic Comedians* (1880), *Diana of the Crossways* (1885), *One of Our Conquerors* (1891), *Lord Ormont and His Aminta* (1894), and *The Amazing Marriage* (1895), Meredith extends *The Egoist*'s feminist critique of Victorian marriage and sexuality. He also returns to poetry, beginning with *Poems and Lyrics of the Joy of Earth* in 1883.

Among the writers who most strongly influenced Meredith are his father-in-law, Thomas Love Peacock, whose satirical novels provided plots and characters that Meredith later adapted. In his rhetorical style, his emphasis on work, and his belief in the healing potential of laughter, Meredith echoes Carlyle, who knew and approved of the younger writer's work. Several of Meredith's early novels, particularly *Evan Harrington*, present Dickensian characters. Other influences surface in the *Essay on Comedy*, where Meredith makes particular ref-

M

erence to Continental writers such as Heinrich Heine, Johann Goethe, Miguel de Cervantes, and Molière.

As a publisher's reader for Chapman & Hall, Meredith provided advice and encouragement to several young writers, most notably Thomas Hardy and George Gissing. His circle of friends included Robert Louis Stevenson and J.M. Barrie. The influence of his emphasis on psychological development of characters and of his narrative experimentation can be seen in novelists such as Henry James, James Joyce, and Virginia Woolf.

Summary

Both George Meredith's *Essay on Comedy* and his novel *The Egoist* established him as the exponent of a highly sophisticated comedy that took self-absorption as its primary target and frequently championed women against male selfishness. Meredith is known for his emphasis on the psychological development of his characters and for plots that reveal the importance of seemingly minor incidents. Despite the difficulty of his writing style, his works were highly influential in the late nineteenth and early twentieth centuries.

Notes

1. George Meredith, *The Ordeal of Richard Feverel*, Vol. 2 of *The Works of George Meredith* (New York: Charles Scribner's Sons, 1910), p. 189.
2. Meredith, *The Collected Letters of George Meredith*, ed. C.L. Cline (Oxford: Clarendon, 1970), vol. 1, p. 236.
3. Meredith, "Essay: On the Idea of Comedy and the Uses of the Comic Spirit," in *Works*, Vol. 23, p. 47.
4. Meredith, *The Egoist*, in *Works*, Vol. 11, p. 50.

Selected Bibliography

Primary Sources

Letters

The Collected Letters of George Meredith. Ed. C.L. Cline. 3 vols. Oxford: Clarendon, 1970.

Novels

The Shaving of Shagpat. London: Chapman & Hall, 1856.
Farina. London: Smith, Elder, 1857.
The Ordeal of Richard Feverel. London: Chapman & Hall, 1859; rev. ed., London: C. Kegan Paul, 1878.
Evan Harrington. New York: Harper and Brothers, 1860; London: Bradbury and Evans, 1861.
Emilia in England. London: Chapman & Hall, 1864. Published in 1885 under the title *Sandra Belloni*.
Rhoda Fleming. London: Tinsely Brothers, 1865.
The Adventures of Harry Richmond. London: Smith, Elder, 1871.
Beauchamp's Career. London: Chapman & Hall, 1876.
The Egoist. London: C. Kegan Paul, 1879.
The Tragic Comedians. London: Chapman & Hall, 1880.
Diana of the Crossways. London: Chapman & Hall, 1885.
One of Our Conquerors. London: Chapman & Hall, 1891.
Lord Ormont and His Aminta. London: Chapman & Hall, 1894.
The Tale of Chloe. London: Ward, Lock and Bowden, 1894.
The Amazing Marriage. Westminster: Archibald Constable, and New York: Charles Scribner's Sons, 1895.

Poems

Poems. London: John W. Parker, 1851.
Modern Love and Poems of the English Roadside. London: Chapman & Hall, 1862.
Poems and Lyrics of the Joy of Earth. London: Macmillan, 1883.
Ballads and Poems of Tragic Life. London and New York: Macmillan, 1887.
A Reading of Earth. London and New York: Macmillan, 1888.
Poems: The Empty Purse. London: Macmillan, and Boston: Roberts Brothers, 1892.
Odes in Contribution to the Song of French History. Westminster: Archibald Constable, 1898.
A Reading of Life. Westminster: Archibald Constable, 1901.
Last Poems. London: Constable, and New York: Charles Scribner's Sons, 1909.

Collected Works

The Works of George Meredith. 27 vols. London: Constable, and New York: Charles Scribner's Sons, 1909–1911. Memorial Edition.

Secondary Sources

Biographies

Stevenson, Lionel. *The Ordeal of George Meredith*. New York: Charles Scribner's Sons, 1953.

Bibliographies

Collie, Michael. *George Meredith: A Bibliography*. Toronto: University of Buffalo Press, 1974.

Forman, Maurice Buxton. *A Bibliography of the Writings in Prose and Verse of George Meredith*. Edinburgh: The Bibliographical Society, 1922.

———. *Meredithiana, Being a Supplement to the Bibliography of Meredith*. Edinburgh: The Bibliographical Society, 1924.

Olmsted, John. *George Meredith: An Annotated Bibliography of Criticism, 1925–1975*. New York: Garland, 1978.

Books

Beer, Gillian. *Meredith: A Change of Masks*. London: Athlone, 1970.

Fletcher, Ian, ed. *Meredith Now: Some Critical Essays*. New York: Barnes & Noble, 1971.

Moses, Joseph. *The Novelist as Comedian: George Meredith and the Ironic Sensibility*. New York: Schocken, 1983.

Wilt, Judith. *The Readable People of George Meredith*. Princeton: Princeton University Press, 1975.

Articles and Chapters in Books

Henkle, Roger B. "Meredith and Butler: Comedy as Lyric, High Culture, and the Bourgeois Trap." In *Comedy and Culture: England 1820–1900*. Princeton: Princeton University Press, 1980, pp. 238–95.

Martin, Robert Bernard. "George Eliot, Leslie Stephen, and George Meredith." In *The Triumph of Wit: A Study of Victorian Comic Theory*. Oxford: Clarendon, 1974, pp. 82–100.

Stevenson, Lionel. "Carlyle and Meredith." In *Carlyle and His Contemporaries*. Ed. J. Clubbe. Durham: Duke University Press, 1976, pp. 257–79.

Maura Ives

Middleton, Thomas

Born: London, April 1580
Education: Matriculated at Queens College, Oxford University, 1598
Marriage: Mary Marbeck, 1602 or 1603; one child
Died: Newington Butts, Surrey, July 4, 1627

Biography

Thomas Middleton was born in London in 1580. The exact date of his birth is not known, though he was baptized on April 18. His father, William, was a bricklayer who died in 1586 leaving a fairly substantial sum of land to his next of kin. The legal battle over this land between his sister Avis's husband, Allan Waterer, and his mother Anne's new husband, the ne'er-do-well Thomas Harvey, may have formed an impression on the young Thomas, providing a source for his later portrayal of middle-class greed and family disputes over land and inheritance.

Middleton did begin an academic career at Queens College, Oxford, on April 7, 1598, but there is no record of him completing his degree and a legal document dated February 8, 1601, in what should have been the final months of his education, states "nowe [Middleton] remaynethe heare in London daylie accompaninge the players."[1] It may have been during this initial involvement in the theater that Middleton met his future wife, Mary Marbeck, as one of her brothers was an actor with the company The Admiral's Men. The couple married in 1602 or 1603; a son was born to them in 1603 or 1604.

Middleton began his writing career at the end of the sixteenth century when he wrote two poems: *The Wisdom of Solomon Paraphrased* (1597) and *Micro-Cynicon* (1599). Neither of these works is of great merit, and they are considered tedious and dull. In 1602, he began his playwriting career when he wrote a number of unpublished plays for Philip Henslowe's commercially motivated company. After serving this apprenticeship Middleton began to write plays of his own, the first two on record being *The Family of Love* (ca. 1602) and *The Phoenix* (1603–1604). During the period 1604 to 1606, he wrote four comedies: *Your Five Gallants*, *Michaelmas Term*, *A Mad World My Masters*, and *A Tricke to Catch the Old One*. These plays were written for The Children of St. Pauls company. The collapse of the company in 1606 led to the publication of the dramas. In 1608, he wrote *The Roaring Girl* with Thomas Dekker, and around 1611 he wrote *A Chaste Maid in Cheapside*. Middleton did not confine himself to writing for one company and he wrote for both children's and adult's companies, including the reputable King's Men, the company of William Shakespeare and John Fletcher.

In 1613 and 1614, he began work on a pageant for the Lord Mayor's entry into London and this was followed by several similar commissions culminating in his appointment in 1620 as Chronologer to the City of London, a post that he held until his death. Towards the end of his career Middleton wrote two great tragedies: *The Changeling* (with William Rowley) in 1622 and *Women Beware Women* sometime between 1613 and 1621. His last comedy, *A Game at Chesse*, was extremely successful; a satire based on the unease of the public at the proposed marriage of Prince Charles to a Spanish Infanta, the play expressed the people's distrust of the Spanish and the popular belief that the Roman Catholic church intended world domination. Middleton was called before the Privy Council for his part in this play and he may have spent some time in prison. At the end of his life Middleton's talent appears to have declined and he produced several masques and pageants for which he was criticized. He died on July 4, 1627, and is buried at Newington Butts.

Literary Analysis

Middleton is primarily remembered for his tragedies *The Changeling*, written with Rowley, and *Women Beware Women*. A third tragedy, *The Revenger's Tragedy* (1606–1607), is also attributed to him, although many scholars believe it to be the work of Cyril Tourneur. It is on these works that Middleton's reputation in the nineteenth and twentieth centuries has come to be based. However, while the tragedies are indisputably fine works, we should not forget that the playwright also wrote some of the funniest comedies of the Jacobean period and in recent years there has been an increased interest in these previously neglected works. That interest is focused chiefly on the works produced between 1604 and 1611, the works that fall into the sub-genre of city comedy.

City comedy has its roots in several literary genres, both dramatic and non-dramatic. One of these sources was the medieval morality play which contained exempla in tableaux form featuring stock characters such as Vice and Avarice. The Jacobean playwright took this form and combined it with other dramatic forms such as the Roman intrigue plays of Terence and Plautus. The intrigue plays and the

commedia dell'arte which they influenced featured episodes of trickery, or *lazzi*, combined with standard characters and plots. Many of these earlier plays were concerned with the conflict between young lovers and strict parents, and the plot was structured around ways of overcoming parental restrictions. These dramatic forms were combined with other literary forms such as the coney-catching pamphlets of Greene which sought to expose trickery and deception by the representation of fictitious and non-fictitious characters in a recognizable urban setting. The ancient tradition of debate and invective was also drawn upon and verse satirists such as Ben Jonson began to use this form in drama. Jonson, Marston, and Middleton are considered the three main exponents of city comedy.

Drama does not exist in a vacuum, though, and the amalgamation of these literary forms served to create a new form which became an adequate way of expressing and commenting on the corruption and vice which was seen to be characteristic of the early seventeenth century. The exclusion of fairy-tale romance and magic from city comedy and the sharp representation of folly, vice, and human corruption can be seen as a definition of the genre. City comedy involves the exposition and portrayal of man's baseness and inherent sinfulness. The characters are not fully rounded psychological portraits and their names (Allwit, Penitent Brothel, Epicure Mammon, and Sir Walter Whorehound) are an indication of the vice that they embody. The characters are not wholly emblematic either, and they scheme and plot, each character dependent on others both for his living (moral or immoral) and his comic effect. The characters are set against a background, usually London, and so finely depicted are the settings that critics such as T.S. Eliot have been led to call Middleton's comedy "photographic."[2] Social realism, however, is not the purpose of city comedy, and the combination of realistic settings and stylized characterization enables the playwright to make a moral comment on a general level while grounding it in a recognizable environment. The audience is drawn in and engaged by familiarity and yet distanced from the less realistic characters. Middleton has often been criticized as lacking in moral judgment and it is true that many of his characters are not punished by the judiciary or by divine intervention. Instead, the characters are punished by the forces of their own corruption; plots are set up and fail, schemes backfire, and the last words of *A Tricke to Catch the Old One* serves as a moral: "Who seem most crafty prove oft-times most fools." In *Your Five Gallants*, the first of his plays that can be considered as a city comedy, the dramatist portrays characters who seem to embody every vice possible set against a background of depravity. In this play, though, Middleton ends with the gallants being officially punished for their crime. The ending does not appear to have been in keeping with the playwright's developing dramatic form because he does not repeat it—his future characters will be punished by their own folly.

In *Michaelmas Term* he portrays the aspirations of the middle classes, a subject popular with Middleton. In the play the social climbing of the nouveau riche merchant class involves the search for land in an attempt to buy into the old order of tradition and history of the English gentry. The principal character Quomodo believes that the acquisition of an estate will bring him a new respectability which he also hopes to enhance by marrying his daughter to a "good" man and by the entrance of his son into a profession, preferably the law. Unfortunately for Quomodo, his initial success leads to final disaster when, through overweening pride, he tests his family's opinion of him by feigning death. Instead of hearing his praises sung, he is cheated by his employees, his daughter marries the wrong man, and his wife marries Easy, the gentleman whom he has tricked out of his estate.

Although these two plays are not the author's greatest, they show through the beginnings of change in the dramatic form that he is rejecting romantic comedy in favor of a social comedy in which the humor is found in the portrayal of the breakdown and disorder of society, a society in which standards, established hierarchies, and morals are mixed up, and in which love is replaced by sex—a marketable commodity—in a world of materialism and crime.

A Mad World My Masters, *A Tricke to Catch the Old One*, and *A Chaste Maid in Cheapside*—the three plays which can be considered the greatest of Middleton's city comedies—build on his earlier experiments in this form and he manages to create plays in which his social observation, ironic detachment, and sharp wit combine to produce three fast-moving dramas exposing trickery, vice, and corruption. The success of these comedies can only be appreciated when seen or read as a whole, as the humor is dependent on the interaction of the characters and the brilliant and ironic manipulation and corruption of language. Ironic humor relies on context for its effectiveness and in many ways the multiple layers of language lose vitality in isolation. *A Chaste Maid* is particularly dependent on double meaning and the whole play is built on the equation of sex with money. In many instances the word "meat," or variants of it, are used not only to mean actual meat but also sex as a saleable commodity. The whole community operates within this corrupt framework and all of the relationships are built on it. The play can almost be read on two levels: that in which meat is required to live, a day-to-day struggle for food and existence; and the bawdy second meaning where sex is the only coinage and means of sustenance.

That the play is set in the period of Lent adds a further dimension as both the sale and consumption of meat and sex are banned during this period and thus the characters defy civil and religious law. The plot centers on various triangular and sexual relationships. Sir Yellowhammer and his wife wish to make a good marriage for their children and therefore have betrothed their daughter to Sir Walter Whorehound and their son to a Welsh widow, who turns out to be an ex-mistress of Sir Walter. Sir Walter is a good match because he stands to inherit the fortune of Lord and Lady Kix, a rich but barren couple. Sir Walter, who is central to the plot, is also maintaining the household of the Allwits. Mistress Allwit is his whore and he has fathered several illegitimate children by her. Her husband brags about the situation and is happy to have Sir Walter maintain him and his wife. Touchwood senior provides a contrast to the Kixes since he is poor but excessively fertile, which leads him to separate from his wife as they cannot afford more children. He cons Lord Kix into believing that he has a secret fertility potion and proves this by getting Lady Kix pregnant! Because of this Sir Walter is disinherited, which allows the Yellowhammers' daughter to marry Touchwood junior, whom she secretly loves. Sir Walter eventually learns the error of his ways and reforms, leaving the Allwits to support themselves. Still, they are not deterred and decide to set up a brothel.

Some of the scenes contain elements of romance comedy, as, for example, in the wedding of the Yellowhammers' daughter and the junior Touchwood. These scenes are often paro-

M

dies of romance comedies, and depravity and corruption enter even here.

One of the funniest scenes in this play is the christening of Allwit's/Sir Walter's latest child. At the christening several gossips and two Puritans gather round the bed. Allwit is cross because he suspects that they have only come for the food and drink. His suspicions are proved correct when, after making a number of pious comments, the Puritans become more and more drunk and eventually call to the nurse, "Bring hither that same cup, nurse, I would fain drive away this (hup!) anti-christian grief" (3.2.91). This satire of Puritans may seem strange when we consider that Middleton himself had Puritanical beliefs; however, what he is exposing is false belief and irreligious behavior. Sir Walter, ironically, speaks the moral of the play when he says:

> When man turns base, out goes his soul's
>   pure flame,
> The fat of ease o'erthrows the eyes of
>   shame. (2.2.40–41)

This moral is not hammered home in a didactic manner, but Middleton leaves the audience in their detachment to make their own judgment.

Sex and money are equated in Middleton's earlier play, *A Mad World My Masters*, although on a less obvious level. Two plots form the structure of the play: the main plot concerns the tricking of an old, rich man, Sir Bounteous Progress, by the ingenious plotting of his grandson Follywit; the subject that is focused on in the secondary plot is the possessive jealousy of Harebrain for his wife, who he treats as a piece of property. In the story line it is the brilliance and skill of the cunning plots that provide the comic element of the play. Follywit stands to inherit a fortune on his grandfather's death, but, even though Sir Bounteous is a generous and hospitable man, he will not release the money before this time. Follywit thus devises a series of tricks to obtain money from his grandfather. In the first plot he disguises himself as Lord Owemuch and comes to sample Bounteous's renowned hospitality. Follywit and his men then rob the house before tying themselves up to make it seem as though they are also victims (leaving one to escape with the booty).

Follywit's next plot is to disguise himself as his grandfather's mistress, Frank Gullman. Sir Bounteous is somewhat puzzled by this and re-

marks, "I gave her a kiss at bottom o' th' stairs, and by th' mass, methought her breath had much ado to be sweet, like a thing compounded, methought of wine, beer, and tobacco" (4.3.53–55). Follywit gets away with his crime, stealing the jewels from the house, yet his success has its counter side when he actually falls in love with Frank Gullman himself. He does not realize that her position is his grandfather's mistress and, planning to marry her, he tells her mother of his coming inheritance:

> Follywit: My estate is yet but sickly; but
>   I've a grandsire will make me thou-
>   sands on his death.
> Mother: I know your grandsire well; she
>   knows him better. (4.5.94–96)

Here the humor lies in the pun on the word know—to be familiar with, and to know sexually. Comedy is also derived from the dramatic irony of the situation in which the audience knows what is happening but certain characters are not so enlightened.

Follywit's final trickery takes the part of a play at his grandfather's house. Disguised as an actor, he asks for certain articles, including a watch, to be used as props. These are then passed backstage and his accomplices carry them away. Unfortunately, they are apprehended by a constable who brings them back. In a stroke of genius, Follywit incorporates the constable into the play and proceeds to tie him up. It appears that yet again Follywit has escaped punishment. His undoing follows, however, when he is dressed back in his own clothes as Follywit and the watch goes off in his pocket. This hilarious scene is farce-like in its construction and depends greatly on speed and vitality for its comic effect. Follywit does not seem an inherently bad character, and we admire his clever scheming, perhaps feeling that he is simply a boyish rogue.

The subplot contains less admirable characters such as the mean Harebrain, who keeps his wife locked up with only a chaste companion for counsel. Ironically, this companion turns out to be Frank Gullman, who leads Mistress Harebrain into an affair with Penitent Brothel, who (disguised as a doctor) visits the sick woman and makes love to her while Frank carries out an imaginary conversation to conceal their noise from the listening husband.

Penitent Brothel, as his oxymoronic name suggests, is both lecherous and repentant and his experience with a succubus leads him to see the error of his ways (rather like Sir Walter). The introduction of this repentance is the only element of moral good that Middleton allows to enter into the play's construction and its presence highlights the complete immorality of the other characters. If there is a moral to the play, it is spoken in the final lines by Sir Bounteous:

> Who lives by cunning, mark it, his fate's
>   cast
> When he has gull'd all, then is himself
>   the last.

This moral in the context of the play is rather weak as Follywit, although finding himself the fiancé of his grandfather's whore, at the same time receives a thousand marks for his pains.

Punishment is not obviously meted out in *A Tricke To Catch the Old One*, considered by many to be Middleton's finest city comedy. This play has a greater unity of plot than the two discussed above, and it centers on the character of Witgood, who has been swindled out of his estate by his uncle, the usurer Pecunious Lucre. We learn that Witgood's misfortune is mainly his own doing and that his debts are chiefly caused by his depraved lifestyle. Witgood hatches a plot to trick his uncle into making him heir by pretending that he is about to marry a rich widow. The widow is, in fact, Witgood's mistress. Assisted by his intermediary—the Host, a skillful character who has learned to play the world at its own game—Witgood's plan succeeds. Lucre falls for the plot and, seeing a chance to make more money, reinstates his nephew. Witgood's creditors also release their claim on him in the belief that each will be the beneficiary of his increased generosity to them in the future. The plot is complicated when Lucre's enemy and rival, Walkadine Hoard, falls in love with the widow and through trickery seemingly gets her away from Witgood in a secret marriage. What Hoard does not know is that Witgood has planned this with his compliant mistress's consent. Witgood has also secretly married Hoard's niece Joyce. Lucre is furious when he learns that he has reinstated Witgood only for his rival to marry the rich widow. Still, he has the last laugh at the wedding reception when Hoard's brother recognizes the widow as Witgood's mistress. The play ends with both Witgood and the widow repenting. This repentance is delivered in lines so contrived and regular in comparison to the rest of the

play's easy dialogue that we suspect insincerity if not parody here. The play's moral seems to lie in the pun on the words "cozen," which means to swindle, and "cousin," which is used for any family relative. This and the double meaning of aunt—a relative and a prostitute—imply that kinship counts for very little in this corrupt society and the audience is left with the impression that while one vice is punished by its own folly another thrives on the misfortune. Alone in the play in terms of virtue are the three women: Witgood's mistress, who stands by him and is honest with Hoard and vows to love him if he will let her; Joyce, who we hear of at second hand as being chaste; and Audrey, who tenderly cares for the appropriately named Dampit, who in the subplot drinks himself to damnation.

Of Middleton's city comedies, *A Tricke to Catch the Old One* has the most psychologically rounded characters and the comic effect is gained by the interaction of these personalities. Despite its more unified structure and realistic human characterizations, *A Tricke to Catch the Old One* remains (with the other city comedies) a play in which usury, trickery, and the equation of sex with money epitomizes a corrupt and amoral society. The dramatist does not preach to his audience, and we may find his characters and their situations funny; but, we do not sympathize with them or allow our emotions to be engaged, and it is in this way, through his ironic wit, that Middleton allows his audience to make the final judgment.

Towards the middle of the seventeenth century, before the closure of the theater due to the civil war, elements of romance began to be introduced into comedy. Nevertheless, city comedy influenced later plays such as Restoration comedy, which began with the re-opening of the theaters in the latter part of the century. These comedies of manners, sexual intrigues, and bawdy innuendoes owe much to the comedies of playwrights such as Middleton.

Summary

Thomas Middleton's contribution to comedy is most notable in the plays that fall within the sub-genre of city comedy. In these plays he portrays, with brilliant ironic wit, the folly and vice of a corrupt Jacobean society. His plots of intrigue and trickery and his characters embodying man's inherent sinfulness create a dramatic form that exposes this corruption without resorting to a forced didactic message. His skill in language and his sharp observation can be seen as both an insight into and a comment on the society in which he lived.

Notes

1. Philias, "Middleton's Early Contact with the Law," quoted in R.H. Barker. *Thomas Middleton* (New York: Columbia University Press, 1958), p. 8.
2. T.S. Eliot, *Selected Prose of T.S. Eliot*, ed. Frank Kermode (London: Faber & Faber, 1975), p. 195.

Selected Bibliography

Primary Sources

Two complete editions of Middleton's work have been published:

Middleton's Works. Ed. A. Dyce. 5 vols. London: 1840.

Middleton's Works. Ed. A.H. Bullen. 8 vols. London: 1885–1886.

Modern editions of the plays

Thomas Middleton: Five Plays. Ed. B. Loughrey and N. Taylor. Middlesex: Penguin Books, 1988. This volume includes *A Tricke to Catch the Old One*, *The Revenger's Tragedy*, *A Chaste Maid in Cheapside*, *Women Beware Women*, and *The Changeling*.

Comedies not included in the above

A Mad World My Masters. Ed. Standish Henning. Regents Renaissance Drama Series. London, 1956.

The Roaring Girl (Co-authored with Thomas Dekker). Ed. Andor Gomme. London: New Mermaids, Ernest Benn, 1976.

A Fair Quarrel (Co-authored with William Rowley). Ed. R.V. Holdsworth. London: New Mermaids, Ernest Benn, 1974.

A Game at Chesse. Ed. J.W. Harper. London: New Mermaids, Ernest Benn, 1966.

Secondary Sources

Bibliographies

Wolff, Dorothy. *Thomas Middleton: An Annotated Bibliography*. New York: Garland, 1985.

Books and Articles

Barker, R.H. *Thomas Middleton*. New York: Columbia University Press, 1958. Barker provides a chapter on Middleton's life, his first work, and then moves on to discuss the early comedies. He includes a chapter on *The Revenger's Tragedy* sometimes attributed to Middleton, and this is followed by a discussion of his later comedies. Barker ends his study with a chapter on the later tragedies and a catalogue of Middleton's works.

Brooks, John B. "Recent Studies in Middleton." *English Literary Renaissance*, 14 (1984): 114–28.

Brown, John Russell, and Bernard Harris, eds. *Jacobean Theatre*. Stratford-upon-Avon Series. London: Edward Arnold, 1965. This volume has one chapter on Middleton, an essay by R.B. Parker entitled "Middleton's experiment with comedy and judgement." There is a chapter by Arthur Brown entitled "Citizen Comedy and domestic drama" which also mentions Middleton. The plays discussed in this volume are *The Phoenix*, *Your Five Gallants*, *A Mad World My Masters*, *Michaelmas Term*, *A Chaste Maid in Cheapside*, and *Women Beware Women*.

Farley-Hills, David. *Jacobean Drama*. London: Macmillan, 1988.

Gibbons, B. *Jacobean City Comedy*. 2nd ed. London: Methuen, 1980. Gibbons discusses city comedy as a genre, looks at it in relationship to the social, political, and economic background, and then focuses on individual plays and playwrights, including Ben Jonson and John Marston. In his chapter "Money makes the world go round" he examines Middleton's *The Phoenix*, *A Mad World My Masters*, and *A Tricke to Catch the Old One* in addition to plays by Jonson and Marston. Finally, in a chapter devoted to Middleton and Jonson, he discusses *A Tricke* and *A Chaste Maid in Cheapside*.

Heinemann, Margot. *Puritanism and Theatre: Thomas Middleton and Oppositional Drama Under the Early Stuarts*. Cambridge: Cambridge University Press, 1980. Heinemann discusses Middleton's satirical plays and relates them to the social, political, and economic context in which they were written. She examines Puritanism and anti-Puritanism in his work and discusses the moral aspects of his plays and the possible political opposition to be identified in his satire. This is a key work for those interested in Middleton. It is comprehensive and covers most of his plays.

Mulryne, J.R. *Thomas Middleton: Writers and Their Work*. Harlowe: Essex, 1979. In this concise book Mulryne provides an extensive biography of Middleton before going on to discuss the city comedies *Michaelmas Term*, *A Tricke to Catch the Old One*, and *A Chaste Maid in Cheapside*. He then follows this with one chapter on the tragedies and one on the satirical comedy *A Game at Chesse*.

Rowe, G.E., Jr. *Thomas Middleton and The New Comedy Tradition*. Lincoln: University of Nebraska Press, 1979. Rowe discusses Middleton's use of new comedy focusing on seven comedies and two tragicomedies. He suggests that Middleton inverts this tradition and in so doing rejects some of its aesthetic ideals.

White, M. *Middleton and Tourneur*. London: Macmillan, 1992. In this comprehensive study White examines Middleton's work from his early prose satires to his tragedies. He devotes a chapter to the city comedies *Michaelmas Term*, *A Mad World My Masters*, and *A Tricke to Catch the Old One*. This is followed by individual studies of *The Roaring Girl* and *A Chaste Maid in Cheapside*. Middleton's satirical *A Game at Chesse* also has a single chapter devoted to it.

Alizon Brunning

Mikes, George

Born: Siklos, Hungary, February 15, 1912
Education: University of Budapest, 1930–1933
Marriage: Lea Hanak; two children
Died: London, August 30, 1987

Biography

George Mikes was a naturalized Briton. He was born on February 15, 1912, in the small town of Siklos in western Hungary and was originally called Gyorgy. His father, Alfred Mikes, was a prosperous attorney and young Gyorgy was to follow in his footsteps by taking up law at the University of Budapest and then working as a lawyer. However, George was more attracted to journalism and while contributing to various newspapers he was taken on as a member of the staffs of *Reggel (Morning)* and *8 Orai ujsag (8 a.m. News)*. In 1938, he was sent to London to represent his papers and never returned to live in Hungary. In 1946, he became a British subject. For the rest of his fairly long life, Mikes lived in London, first working for the World Service of the BBC, then as a freelance writer. He was once the President of the *Writers in exile*, *PEN*, a member of the Garrick Club, and the friend of many eminent men of letters such as Arthur Koestler, J.B. Priestley, and Andre Deutsch, who as a publisher was the architect of Mikes's success.

Mikes was a well-loved figure at the Hurlingham Club, where he played senior tennis with such gusto and humor that he often beat much younger and better players. They could not return his tricky balls for laughing.

He died on August 30, 1987, in London.

Literary Analysis

Mikes was a natural comic. Humor was in his veins, laughter in his movements; his features included a small, rotund figure and a round head with a moon-like face, large but quickly darting eyes, and a ready, engaging smile. His best work was just like him: funny, rarely sardonic; anecdotal, never long-winded. He wrote over forty books, thirty-five of them humorous, and the best of them post-war British classics. He was recognized as the blender of elements of Hungarian and English humor, the former rooted in a mixed Gentile-Jewish tradition, the latter akin to that of A.A. Milne. Mikes's best books were some of the earliest and a couple of his latest. *How to be an Alien* (1946), his first and absolute bestseller, was translated into twenty-two languages and published in thirty-nine countries. In it he depicted himself as a bumbling alien in the vast, strange but friendly *country* of London and described the habits of the natives. The result was a humorous "survival kit" of what to do and what not to do amongst the British. Phrases from this volume became conversation pieces. For example, he noted that "Continental people have sex life, British people have the hot water bottle." Elsewhere, he suggested this advice from a mother to her daughter: "I know it's disgusting, but close your eyes and think of the British Empire."

Having poked fun at the British, Mikes traveled to numerous countries and gathered a bookful of humor in most of them. Local jokes were blended into his own humor. The best examples of these travel books are *Über Alles*

(Germany), *Milk and Honey* (Israel), *How to Scrape Skies* (United States), and *The land of rising yen* (Japan). In the mid-1980s, when he was passing the seventy mark himself, he returned to England to write about Britain in his last classic, *How to be a Brit* (1987). The humor is spicy but not biting; Mikes's trademark was the wit of give and take. Nicholas Bentley, who illustrated many of his books, captured the essence of Mikes in his drawings for two of the volumes, *Milk and Honey* and *How to Be Inimitable* (1960).

Mikes's favorite comic device was to place himself, an inveterate yet vulnerable traveler, an ardent rationalist with European values, in situations where he discovers national pretensions behind proud phraseology and greed behind bourgeois attitudes. Thus, he was able to flesh out "national stereotypes" with comic characteristics. His French are "little cabbages," his Japan is that of the "rising yen," his Hungarians are among *everyone's* ancestry ("Everybody is a Hungarian, but some people don't know it yet"), his English, even the most eccentric ones, only pretend to be interested in sex.

Every now and then Mikes ventured into the territory of serious or non-humorous literature. He wrote a memorable novel called *Mortal Passion* (1963) about a man who could not stop gorging himself. He recorded his experiences of the Hungarian Revolution (which he visited as a journalist in 1956) and his friendship with Koestler. He was a good conversationalist, with a much better English than Hungarian vocabulary, his sentence structures were faultless, and his pronunciation was unique.

Summary

George Mikes was liberal and he was a Liberal. The world of his books puts his small figure on the stage, a man who cannot keep a straight face facing the foolishness of others. He did not think of life as a joke, but he thought that most of us are jokers.

Selected Bibliography

Primary Sources
How to Be an Alien. London: Allen Wingate, 1946.
How to Scrape Skies. London: Allen Wingate, 1948.
Milk and Honey. Drawings by Nicholas Bentley. London and New York: Allen Wingate, 1950.
Down with Everybody! . . . *and other stories.* Drawings by David Langdon. London: Allen Wingate, 1951.
Über Alles. London: Allen Wingate, 1953.
The Hungarian Revolution. London: Collins, 1958.
How to Be Inimitable: *coming of age in England*. Drawings by Nicholas Bentley. London: Andre Deutsch, 1960.
Tango. A solo Journey across South America. London: Andre Deutsch, 1961.
Mortal Passion. London: Andre Deutsch, 1963.
The land of rising yen. Harmondsworth: Penguin Books, 1973.
Arthur Koestler: the story. London: Andre Deutsch, 1983.
How to Be a Brit. 1987.

Secondary Sources
"George Mikes." *Who's Who* (1987): 1206.
"Mr. George Mikes." *The Times* (September 3, 1987).
Sarkozi, M. "George Mikes." *Gazette Litteraire*, Paris (October–November 1987).
                                    Thomas Kabdebo

Milligan, Spike (Terence Alan)

Born: Ahmednagar, India, April 18, 1918
Education: Roman Catholic schools in India and England; Woolwich day continuation school; courses in music at Goldsmith's College
Marriage: June Marlow (divorced 1959); Margaret Patricia Ridgeway (died 1978); Shelagh Sinclair; four children

Biography

Spike Milligan is one of the most original and influential British comic writers of the twentieth century—in fact, when you consider where his influence pops up, he may be the most influential, period. Born in Ahmednagar, India, on April 18, 1918, Milligan was the first son of Leo Alphonso Milligan, an Irish-born regimental sergeant-major in the British Army, and his wife, Florence Winifred Kettlebrand. Both parents were talented performers, and Milligan grew up around music and improvised stage shows. Young Milligan showed a talent for music, song, acting, and madcap jesting. He passed his youth and early adolescence in Poona, India, and in Rangoon, Burma.

With his family, at 16 Milligan moved, unhappily, to England. It was then the depression, and his family went from the security of army life to poverty. At the various Roman Catholic schools that he had attended in India and subsequently in England, Milligan did poorly. He spent a brief stint at Woolwich day continuation school, and he took music courses at Goldsmith's College (University of London). In the meantime, he was sent out to work at a series of poorly paying laboring jobs. At this time he joined the Harlem Club Band, a jazz group with whom he sang and played drums and double bass. This band was his first big break, doing well enough to free him from his day jobs.

Then came World War II, a turning point for Milligan in many ways. In 1940, he was conscripted into D Battery of the 56th Heavy Regiment Royal Artillery, in which he was a gunner and a trumpeter in the Battery Band. His personal brand of lunatic humor made him popular with his mates and a nightmare for his superiors ("Silence when you speak to an officer!")—and for the south coast town of Bexhill-on-Sea, near which he did his basic training.

In 1941, D Battery embarked for North Africa and thence to Italy. In January 1944, during the arduous advance toward Cassino, he was wounded while trying to establish an observation post. Though evidently he had to be dragged off the field, forever afterward he would be haunted by a sense of his own cowardice and inadequacy. Milligan had suffered a major psychological break, a bad case of battle shock that led to his reclassification as unfit for battle. Blackouts, manic mood swings, and despair punctuated his life for the next decade—indeed, the latter two never left him. He is yet another clown whose energy rose out of a catastrophic encounter with lunacy. During his recuperation, he met Harry Secombe, who would become an essential link to his future life as writer and humorist.

Postwar, Milligan played in the Bill Hall Trio, having the jobs of "trumpet player in a band for a while, then trumpet player not in a band." He lived in the same house as Secombe, whose career in radio and stand-up comedy was just starting. Milligan began his own radio career in 1949, appearing in *Opportunity Knocks*. He also met producer, writer, and bar-owner Jimmy Grafton, who in turn brought Milligan and Secombe together with Peter Sellers and Michael Bentine.

In 1951, these four began a radio show called *Crazy People*, soon rechristened *The Goon Show*, a zany comedy half-hour on the BBC with Milligan as the primary scriptwriter (Eric Sykes and Larry Stephens also wrote some episodes). Bentine left in 1952, and Sellers, Secombe, and Milligan took the Goons all the way to 1960. (All four of the original Goons went on to celebrated solo careers.) This, the most popular comedy show in BBC history, revolutionized radio comedy. During the same period, Milligan was writing for television— *A Show Called Fred, Son of Fred*—winning the TV Writer of the Year award for 1956. He also began a career as an actor, which has spanned appearances in more than 25 movies.

Predictably, the BBC resisted many of the *Goon Show* ideas, creating a running feud with Milligan that spanned more than a decade. Nevertheless, the Goons gained unprecedented freedom for their half-hour of mayhem, and they became cult figures for BBC listeners all over the world. Show business exacerbated Milligan's tendency to manic depression, and for the rest of his life he would spend intervals in psychiatric hospitals. A decade of script-per-week pressure claimed at least one casualty: Milligan's first marriage. He had married June Marlow; the couple divorced in 1959. His marriage to Margaret Patricia Ridgeway ended with her death in 1978, and he married Shelagh Sinclair. He is the father of four children.

After the final Goons series, Milligan turned to writing plays (*Oblomov, The Bedsitting Room*), children's literature (*The Bald Twit Lion*), poetry, novels (*Puckoon*), motion picture scripts (*The Postman's Knock* and *The Magnificent Seven Deadly Sins*), and, of course, humor. Along with his motion picture acting career (including roles in *The Magic Christian, The Three Musketeers*, and *Life of Brian*), he acted onstage in recurrent productions of *Treasure Island*, as well as *The Bedsitting Room, Oblomov, Son of Oblomov*, his touring one-man show *For One Week Only*, and *Ubu*. He is also an accomplished illustrator and painter. In the mid-1970s Milligan began a series of autobiographical books, the first of which was the hilarious *Adolf Hitler: My Part in His Downfall* in 1971. Two of his works—*The Bedsitting Room* and *Adolf Hitler: My Part in His Downfall*—have been turned into films. As of this writing, Milligan books are still appearing at the rate of almost one a year.

Literary Analysis
Milligan stands in a tradition of silly, anarchic, satirical humor that amounts to a great English

tradition, connecting William Shakespeare and Ben Jonson with the English pantomime, Lord Byron, Charles Dickens, vaudeville, and Monty Python. One can sense his influence in *Beyond the Fringe*; *I'm Sorry, I'll Read That Again* and its next self, *Monty Python's Flying Circus*; the funny work of John Lennon and the Beatles; and the American style of group associational humor in the 1960s and 1970s, including the Firesign Theater and the various incarnations of *Saturday Night Live*.

A typical *Goon Show* has a plot in which some dastardly villain threatens truth, justice, and the British way. Normally, this behavior is extremely silly—like knocking people's teeth out, surreptitiously shaving their heads, hitting them with batter puddings, or stealing massive Wurlitzer organs to set a new land speed record at Daytona Beach. To the rescue come a dramatis personae of *Goon Show* regulars: Eccles, the "original Goon" and all-purpose kindly idiot; Neddie Seagoon, "true blue British idiot and hero always"; Bluebottle, Seagoon's cowardly sidekick; Miss Minnie Barrister ("Spinster of the Parish"); Mr. Grytpype-Thynne (a villain) and his sidekick, the Frenchman Moriarty; and Major Denis Bloodnok, "military idiot, coward, and bar." Secombe played Seagoon, who usually solves or fails to solve the mystery; Sellers (along with Milligan) took on an amazing number of other roles.

Critics often call the *Goon Shows* "surreal," but the scripts are not as serious or as organized as that word usually implies. What they are is associational, most of those associations being in the Milligan mind, which may ricochet anywhere, generating a slew of first-, second-, and third-generation puns ("where was Seagoon's father, his four mothers, the first cook, the underfootman and the overfootman?"), perversions of homely clichés ("What has become of mother? Dear mother, she was like one of the family"), and simply unacceptable thoughts ("SEAGOON: 'How did you get back on board?'" BLOODNOK: "I was molested by a lobster with a disgusting mind."). Milligan's humor often relies on the nature of the radio medium—one can feel the Goons reveling in their power to create outlandish images in the hearer's mind. Here Bluebottle narrates his own actions: "Hurriedly wraps up captain in brown paper parcel labelled 'Explosives' and stuffs him through headquarters letter box. Jumps on to passing dustcart and exits left to buy bowler before price goes up. Thinks—that wasn't a

very big part for Bluebottle." Secombe and Sellers, very gifted impressionists, added their own zingers, all against a background of outlandish sound effects and music.

After a few minutes the rush of crazy language undoes character, setting, and theme, until all hangs by a very slender filament, as seen in a passage from "The Dreaded Batter Pudding Hurler (of Bexhill-on-Sea)":

SEAGOON. . . . Major Bloodnok?
BLOODNOK. How dare you call me Major Bloodnok.
SEAGOON. That's your name.
BLOODNOK. In that case—I forgive you.
SEAGOON. Where's [Eccles'] other boot?
BLOODNOK. Stolen.
SEAGOON. Who by?
BLOODNOK. A thief.
SEAGOON. You sure it wasn't a pickpocket?
BLOODNOK. Positive—Eccles never keeps his boots in his pocket.
SEAGOON. Damn. They all had a watertight alibi—but just to make sure I left it in a fish tank overnight.

In "The House of Teeth," Seagoon decides to stop for the night. His African chief sidekick O'Brien doesn't like the idea:

O'BRIEN. Lord Seagoon, me no like to spend the night on this pitch black road.
SEAGOON. Don't worry, you won't be noticed. Now, as we're staying the night here, unroll my brass bedstead and erect my marble wash stand. Abdul?
ABDUL. (approach) What you want, sahib?
SEAGOON. Before I retire prepare a light sixteen-course banquet.
ABDUL. I go and connect the gas stove up to the horse.
SEAGOON. Mind you get the right end this time. . . . Next hoist a small Union Jack and unveil a bust of Queen Victoria. Now I'll just make a rough "Englishman lost on the mountainside Menu." Brown Windsor soap, meat, two veg., pots., boiled rice and jam. Fair makes your mouth water.

Milligan seems to know that the unconscious is at the back of it all. What he says about *William McGonagall Meets George Gershwin*—that it is a "freefall comic fantasy in which the subconscious mind is the author"—holds true for almost all of his works. *McGonagall Meets Gershwin* ends with a Miss Muriel Body reporting for a job as a nude model. As she endures her first day's work, the scene shifts between her and—wait for it—a Zulu attack on a small British garrison. As the book draws to a close, the Zulus grow to millions and trillions, eventually overflowing into the Miss Body scene, chasing her with spears down a London street onto a number 9 bus.

From Shakespeare to the Marx Brothers to Monty Python's Flying Circus, silly humor comes round to score trenchant points against the status quo. You would expect this childish kind of free-for-all to be pointless, but, especially in Milligan, silly humor secretes a special venom against the establishment. Certainly, Milligan had run nose-to-nose against the army, the church, and the BBC; his resentments coalesce into idiot bigwig characters such as Major Bloodnok. "Essentially," Milligan has said, "it is critical comedy. It is against bureaucracy, and on the side of human beings. Its starting point is one man shouting gibberish in the face of authority, and proving by fabricated insanity that nothing could be as mad as what passes for ordinary living."

There is no question of the widespread influence of the Goons. John Cleese and other Pythons grew up listening to them. Dudley Moore and others of *Beyond the Fringe* have paid him homage. John Lennon's wordplay is often called "Joycean," when it just as well might be called "Milliganesque," and Lennon himself pointed to the influence of Milligan's "coup d'état of the mind." In America, the members of the Firesign Theater, Second City, and other comedy groups have all at one time or another credited Milligan and the other Goons.

Since the *Goon Show*, Milligan has become a constant presence in the British press. Unexpectedness is ever his ally as a journalist. Milligan the essayist is a true *bricoleur*, and his shifting, scattershot style often scores hits that "normal" essayists cannot. One essay, entitled "Sex Revolution," orchestrates personal recollection, newspaper excerpts, and imagined dialogues into an attack on the notion of a "sexual revolution." "Sad/Funny Men" is a telling reflection on the intense personal sadness in the lives of clowns.

His books tend to be miscellaneous collections of skits, drawings, jests, and verse. Calling them "uneven" is like calling a tornado "wild." He is a natural for children's literature and a surprising poet. His autobiographical books now amount to an impressive testimony on the Second World War. Like the labile Milligan mind, they are now side-splitting, now heartbreaking, now diamond-sharp in their perceptions of violence, suffering, bureaucratic idiocy, and the constant opportunity for laughter.

Summary

Spike Milligan's greatest fame will probably always derive from the *Goon Show* scripts, but that should not obscure the physically painful laughter that he can provoke. After reading as many *Goon Show* scripts as one can—and hearing the shows on record—one should read *Puckoon*, a couple of the McGonagall books, *Indefinite Articles* (for a taste of the Milligan essay), and—if one is still standing—*Milligan's War*, his collected war memoirs. That selection will give a sense of the irrepressible Milligan.

Selected Bibliography
Primary Sources

Children's Literature
Silly Verse for Kids. London: Dobson, 1959.
With Carol Baker. *The Bald Twit Lion*. London: Dobson, 1968.
A Book of Milliganimals. London: Dobson, 1968.
Badjelly the Witch. London: 1971.
Dip the Puppy. London: M. Joseph, 1974.
Narrator and co-author. *The Snow Goose*. Recording, based on the Paul Gallico novel. RCA Records, 1976.
A Book of Goblins. London: Hutchinson, 1978.
Unspun Socks from a Chicken's Laundry. London: M. Joseph, 1981.
Sir Nobunk and the Terrible, Awful, Dreadful, Naughty, Nasty Dragon. London: M. Joseph, 1982.

Novels
Puckoon. London: Anthony Blond, 1963.
The Looney: An Irish Fantasy. London: M. Joseph, 1987.

Poetry
Values. London: Offcut, 1969.

Small Dream of a Scorpion. London: M. Joseph, 1972.

Open Heart University. London: M. Joseph, 1979.

Floored Masterpieces and Worst Verse. London: Macmillan, 1985.

Mirror Running. London: M. Joseph, 1987.

One Hundred and One Best and Only Limericks of Spike Milligan. Harmondsworth: Penguin, 1988.

Hidden Words: Collected Poems. London: M. Joseph, 1993.

General

A Dustbin of Milligan. London: Dobson, 1961.

The Little Pot Boiler: A Book Based Freely on His Seasonal Overdraft. London: Dobson, 1961.

With John Antrobus. *The Bedsitting Room*. First produced, 1963; published, London: Hobbs, 1970.

A Book of Bits; or, A Bit of a Book. London: Dobson, 1965.

The Bedside Milligan; or, Read Your Way to Insomnia. London: Hobbs, 1969.

With Jack Hobbs. *Milligan's Ark*. London: Hobbs, 1971.

The Goon Show Scripts. London: Woburn, 1972; London and New York: St. Martin's, 1973.

More Goon Show Scripts. London: Woburn, 1973.

With Joseph McGrath. *The Great McGonagall*. Screenplay. Daritan Productions, 1974.

As a contributor. *Cricket's Choice*. London: Open Court, 1974.

With Jack Hobbs. *The Great McGonagall Scrapbook*. London: M. Joseph, 1975.

The Milligan Book of Records, Games, Cartoons, and Commercials. London: M. Joseph, 1975.

Transport of Delight. Harmondsworth: Penguin, 1975.

With others. *The Book of the Goons*. London: Corgi, 1975.

William McGonagall: The Truth at Last. London: M. Joseph, 1976.

With Jack Hobbs. *The Q Annual*. London: M. Joseph, 1979.

Get in the Q Annual. London: Hobbs, 1980.

Indefinite Articles and Scunthorpe. London: M. Joseph, 1981.

Goon Cartoons. London: M. Joseph, 1982.

More Goon Cartoons. London: M. Joseph, 1983.

There's a Lot of It About. London: M. Joseph, 1983.

Melting Pot. London: Robson, 1983.

Further Transports of Delight. Harmondsworth: Penguin, 1986.

The Lost Goon Shows. London: Robson, 1987.

With Jack Hobbs. *William McGonagall Meets George Gershwin*. London: M. Joseph, 1988.

That's Amazing. London: Ladybird, 1988.

It Ends with Magic; A Milligan Family Story. London: M. Joseph, 1990.

Peace Work. London: Penguin, 1992.

Motion Picture Scripts

With John Bailey, Jack Trevor Story, and George Barclay. *Postman's Knock*. 1962.

The Bedsitting Room. 1969.

With Bob Larby, John Esmond, Dave Freeman, Barry Cryer, Graham Chapman, Graham Stark, Marty Feldman, Alan Simpson, and Ray Galton. *The Magnificent Seven Deadly Sins*. 1971.

With Joseph McGrath. *The Great McGonagall*. Daritan Productions, 1974.

Memoirs

Adolf Hitler: My Part in His Downfall. London: M. Joseph, 1971.

Rommel: Gunner Who? London: M. Joseph, 1974.

Monty: His Part in My Victory. London: M. Joseph, 1976.

Mussolini: His Part in My Downfall. London: M. Joseph, 1978.

Adolf Hitler: My Part in His Downfall. Recording. Columbia Records, 1981.

Where Have All the Bullets Gone? Harmondsworth: Penguin, 1986.

Goodbye Soldier. London: M. Joseph, 1986.

Milligan's War: The Selected War Memoirs of Spike Milligan. London: M. Joseph, 1988.

Author of many unpublished scripts for radio and television, as well as of two plays, *Oblomov* and *Son of Oblomov*.

Recordings

With the Goons. "Bluebottle Blues"/"I'm Walking Backwards for Christmas." 78. Decca F 10756. 1956. [Same recording on 45: Decca 45-F 10756. 1957.]

With the Goons. "Ying Tong Song"/ "Bloodnok's Rock 'n' Roll Call." 78. Decca F 10780. 1956. [Same recording on 45: Decca 45-F 10780. Also on Decca F 13414. 1957.]

"My September Love"/"You Gotta Go Oww!!" 78. Parlophone R 4251. 1956. [Same recording on 45: Parlophone 45-R 4251.]

With the Goons. "I Love You"/"Bloodnok's Rock 'n' Roll Call." 45. Decca F 13609. 1956.

With the Goons. *The Goons*. EP. Decca DFE 6396.

With the Goons. "Eeh! Ah! Ooh!"/"I Love You." 78. Decca F 10885. 1956. [Same recording on 45: Decca 45-F 10885. 1957.]

With the Goons. "A Russian Love Song"/ "Whistle Your Cares Away." 78. Decca F 10945. 1957. [Same recording on 45: Decca 45-F 10945.]

"Will I Find My Love"/"I Wish I Knew." 78. Parlophone R 4406. 1958. [Same recording on 45: Parlophone 45-R 4405.]

With the Goons. *Best of the Goon Shows*. LP. Parlophone PMC 1108. 1959.

With the Goons. *Best of the Goon Shows*. No. 2. LP. Parlophone 1129. 1960.

"Olympic Team"/"Epilogue." 45. Pye 7N 15720. 1960.

"I'm Walking out with a Mountain"/"Sewers of the Strand." 45. Parlophone 45-R 4839. 1961.

Milligan Preserved. LP. Parlophone PMC 1148. 1961.

"Postman's Knock"/"Wormwood Scrubs Tango." 45. Parlophone 45-R 4891. 1962.

With others. *The Bridge on the River Wye*. LP. Parlophone PMC 1190. 1962.

With the Goons. *The Goons Unchained Melodies*. LP. Decca LF 1332. 1964.

With the Goons. *How to Win an Election*. LP. Philips AL 3464. 1964.

Best of Milligan's Wake. LP. Pye NPL 18104. 1964.

With others. *Rhymes and Rhythms*. LP. Argo RG 414/5. 1965.

Muses with Milligan. LP. Decca LK 4701. 1965.

"Tower Bridge"/"Silent Night." 45. Parlophone R 5543. 1966.

"Purple Aeroplane"/"Nothing at All." Parlophone 5513. 1966.

With the Goons. *Goon—but Not Forgotten*. LP. Parlophone PMC 7037. 1967.

World of Beachcomber. LP. Pye NPL 18271. 1968.

With the Goons. *Goon Again—Goon Shows*. LP. Parlophone PMC 7062. 1968.

"The Q5 Piano Tune"/"Ning Nang Nong." 45. Parlophone R 5771. 1969.

With the Goons. *World of British Comedy*. LP. Decca PA 39. 1969.

With others. *No One's Gonna Change Our World*. LP. Regal SRS 5013. 1969.

A Record Load of Rubbish. LP. BBC REB 98M. 1971.

"Girl on a Pony"/"Old Man's Protest Song." 45. Warner Brothers K 16240. 1972.

With the Goons. *The Last Goon Show of All*. LP. BBC REB 1428. 1972.

With others. *Alice's Adventures in Wonderland*. LP. Warner Brothers K 56009. 1972.

With Michael Parkinson and the Goons. LP. *Michael Parkinson Meets the Goons*. BBC REB 165M. 1973.

With others. *World of Children*. LP. Argo SPA 200. 1973.

With the Goons. "Ying Tong Song"/"I'm Walking Backwards for Christmas." 45. Decca F 13414. 1973. Reissue.

With others. "Cheese"/"Shipmates." 45. Starline PSR 367. 1974.

"On the Ning Nang Nong"/"The Silly Old Baboon." 45. Polydor 2058524. 1974.

With others. "The Wormwood Scrubs Tango"/"The Little Grey Hole in My Vest." 45. BBC RESL 18/2. 1974.

With Peter Sellers. *He's Innocent of Watergate*. LP. Decca SKL 5194. 1974.

With the Goons. *Goon Show Classics*. LP. BBC REB 177. 1974.

With others. *Treasure Island*. LP. Starline SRS 5191. 1974.

Badjelly the Witch. LP. Polydor 2460 235. 1974.

With the Goons. *The Very Best of the Goons*. LP. EMI EMC 3062. 1974.

Live at Cambridge University. LP. Spark SRLO 3001. 1974.

With the Goons. *Goon Show Classics*. Volume 2. LP. BBC REB 213. 1975.

With others. *Golden Hour of Comedy*. LP. Golden Hour GH 530. 1975.

With the Goons. *Goon Show Classics*. Volume 3. LP. BBC REB 246. 1976.

With others. *Twenty Golden Giggles*. LP.

EMI NTS 125. 1976.

With the London Symphony Orchestra. *The Snow Goose*. LP. RCA RS 1088. 1976.

With the London Symphony Orchestra. "The Snow Goose"/"Goose Walk." 45. RCA 2752. 1976.

With others. *Forty Years of Television: The Comedians Sing*. LP. BBC REB 249. 1976.

"Remember You're a Womble"/"Die Wombles Sind im Kommen." 45. Reprise K 14422. 1976.

With the Goons. *Goon Show Classics*. Volume 4. LP. BBC REB 291. 1977.

With the Goons. *Goon Show Classics*. Volume 5. LP. BBC REB 339. 1978.

With the Goons. "The Raspberry Song"/ "Rhymes." 45. Decca F 13769. 1978.

With Ed Welch. *Sing Songs from Q8*. LP. United Artists UAG 30223. 1979.

With others. *Cavalcade of London Theatre*. LP. Decca D 140D/1–4. 1979.

With the Goons. *Goon Show Classics*. Volume 6. LP. BBC REB 366. 1979.

With Ed Welch. "One Sunny Day/Woe Is Me." 45. United Artists UP 36489. 1979.

With the Goons. *World of the Goons*. LP. Decca SPA 569. 1980.

With the Goons. *Goon Show Classics*. Volume 7. LP. BBC REB 392. 1980.

Puckoon. LP. EMI SCX 6630. 1980.

Adolf Hitler: My Part in His Downfall. LP. Columbia SCX 6636. 1981.

With the Goons. *Goon Show Classics*. Volume 8. LP. BBC REB 422. 1981.

With the Goons. *Voice Behind the Mask*. LP. Guild 62002A-D. 1981.

We Are Most Amused. LP. Ronco RTD 2067A-B. 1981.

Snow Goose. LP. RCA INTS 5224. 1982. Reissue.

With the Goons. *Goon Show Classics*. Volume 9. LP. BBC REB 444. 1982.

Unspun Socks from a Chicken's Laundry. LP. Ridedrop. Spike L1. 1982.

With Ed Welch. *Wolves, Witches, and Giants*. LP. Impression MIL 2. 1984.

Secondary Sources

Behan, Dominic. *The Life and Times of Spike Milligan*. London: Mandarin, 1989.

Dear Robert, Dear Spike: The Graves-Milligan Correspondence. Ed. Pauline Scudamour. London: Sutton, 1991.

Farnes, Norma. *The Spike Milligan Letters*. London: M. Joseph, 1977.

———. *More Milligan Letters*. London: M. Joseph, 1984.

Scudamour, Pauline. *Spike Milligan: A Biography*. London: Grafton, 1987.

John Timpane

Milne, A[lan] A[lexander]

Born: Hampstead, London, January 18, 1882
Education: Henley House; Westminster, 1893–1900; Trinity College, Cambridge University, 1900–1903, B.A. (3rd class honors in the Mathematical Tripos; 1903)
Marriage: Dorothy (Daphne) de Selincourt, June 14, 1913; one child
Died: Hartfield, Sussex, January 31, 1956

Biography

Alan Alexander (A.A.) Milne was born in Hampstead on January 18, 1882, the third and youngest son of John Vine Milne, the headmaster of Henley House, a private day school for boys, and Sarah Maria Heginbotham. Alan received his early education at his father's school, where he was taught science and mathematics by H.G. Wells, who was also later to become one of Britain's leading humorous writers. He gained a scholarship to Westminster (1893–1900), where he specialized in mathematics and won a closed minor scholarship to Trinity College, Cambridge. At Cambridge (1900–1903) he appears to have lost interest in mathematics, and he began to write light verses for the Cambridge magazine *Granta* which he went on to edit in 1903.

He gained only a rather mediocre third-class degree in the Mathematical Tripos at Cambridge, and his father thought that he might be suited to a career in the British Civil Service. Milne decided instead to try to earn his living as a free-lance journalist and soon was writing regularly for *Punch*. His involvement with *Punch* led to his becoming an assistant editor for the journal in 1906. On June 14, 1913, he married Dorothy (Daphne) de Selincourt. In 1915, he took a commission in Britain's wartime army and served in France until he was invalided home with trench fever in November 1916. He then turned to writing plays and in the years after the war when the public wanted lightweight plays, he was both prolific and successful. After his son Christopher Robin was born in 1920, Milne began to write the children's books for which he is now best remembered. The book of poems *When We Were Very Young* appeared in 1924; it was followed by *Winnie-the-Pooh* in 1926, more verse in *Now We Are Six* in 1927, and *The House at Pooh Corner* in 1928, all of which were best-sellers at the time and have remained so ever since, not just in English but in nearly thirty other languages. He was the obvious person to adapt Kenneth Grahame's *The Wind in the Willows* for the stage as *Toad of Toad Hall* in 1929, and this very successful play for children, unlike his other plays, continues to be performed by professional companies.

During the 1930s, Milne continued to write plays, as well as novels, autobiography, and even a pacifist tract rooted in his experience of the First World War (but which he repudiated during the Second). After World War II, he published another novel and a number of short stories. His last years were saddened by a crippling stroke and he died in Hartfield, Sussex on January 31, 1956.

Literary Analysis

Milne was prolific as a writer of light verse and whimsical essays and, for a time, he was a very successful playwright. Yet, today he is known almost entirely as a writer of books for children, which also have an irresistible humorous appeal for adults. Although popular at the time, none of his humorous works written exclusively for adults continues to be read. He is, as indeed he feared, only remembered as the author of *When We Were Very Young* (1924), *Winnie-the-Pooh* (1926), *Now We Are Six* (1927), and *The House at Pooh Corner* (1928), which are all books described as being poems and stories "for children," and of *Toad of Toad Hall* (1929), a children's play adapted from Grahame's *The Wind in the Willows*. Like *The Wind in the Willows*, his children's works have all become classics of a distinctively British kind that work equally well for adults and children and succeed at many levels of meaning. Milne should not have feared for his literary reputation for he belongs to that small group of geniuses whose only other members are Grahame and Lewis Carroll.

Milne's stories about Christopher Robin, Pooh, Piglet, and the animals who live in Hundred Acre Wood are simple in construction and set in an ordinary landscape where nothing outrageously fabulous happens—but the familiar toy animals have the ability to talk. Hence, the stories are easily accessible to young children. What makes them distinctive is Milne's genius for understanding, manipulating, and defying the ordinary, implicit rules of communication to produce humorous nonsense. It is worth remembering that Milne, like Carroll, was a mathematician, for mathematicians live in a world of precise and explicit rules that progresses by breaking them to form new rules, by creating and then explaining paradox. For mathematicians, ideas and concepts such as irrational numbers, imaginary numbers, the division of one infinitely small entity by another, the set of things that do not belong to a set or the impossibility of completing mathematics and resolving the problem of the nature of mathematics itself, lie at the core of their work. Rules and axioms exist to be varied, a program that produced exquisite comedy when applied by Carroll to the logic and language of everyday life. Milne's comic talent likewise lay in his ability to bend subtly the uses of language and particularly the rules of bona fide communication. Sometimes he does this in a way that mocks the conventional pomposities of adults. On other occasions he mimics the way children try to use the idiosyncrasies of language to avoid a probing question or the thrust of an unwelcome fact or argument which they recognize but do not necessarily fully understand. Similarly, children are often puzzled yet fascinated when adults make a point indirectly to them that seems to be nonsense yet conceals something of meaning. Milne's son, Christopher (Robin) Milne, in his autobiography *The Enchanted Places* recalls the visit of a journalist to their house when he was expected to look neater and tidier than usual: "My father wondered gently which side I usually parted my hair these days; and I remember thinking this is odd because I had always parted it on the left" (23).

In the Pooh stories the art of meaningless, indirect prevarication to hide a defect takes the child's, or indeed the adult's, evasiveness to the point where the everyday rules of communication nearly break down. Milne is always able, though, to keep the conversation going, to stretch it one more time for the amusement of the reader, as we can see below:

> And as they went, Tigger told Roo (who wanted to know) all about the things that Tiggers could do.
>
> "Can they fly?" asked Roo.

"Yes," said Tigger, "they're very good flyers, Tiggers are. Strornry good flyers."

"Oo!" said Roo. "Can they fly as well as Owl?"

"Yes," said Tigger. "Only they don't want to."

"Why don't they want to?"

"Well they just don't like it somehow."

Roo couldn't understand this, because he thought it would be lovely to be able to fly, but Tigger said it was difficult to explain to anybody who wasn't a Tigger himself.

"Well," said Roo, "can they jump as far as Kangas?"

"Yes," said Tigger. "When they want to."

"I *love* jumping," said Roo. "Let's see who can jump furthest, you or me."

"*I* can," said Tigger. "But we mustn't stop now, or we shall be late."

"Late for what?"

"For whatever we want to be in time for," said Tigger hurrying on. ("In which it is shown that Tiggers don't climb trees")

Tigger's wish to appear omnicompetent eventually results in the two characters being stuck up in a tall tree after he has boasted that tiggers can climb trees better than bears. The real material world has intruded and added a new humorous twist to the layers of comic evasion. Owl, by contrast, has more success when challenged by Rabbit to read a notice left by Christopher Robin on the door of his house:

"Read that."

Owl took Christopher Robin's notice from Rabbit and looked at it nervously. He could spell his own name WOL, and he could spell Tuesday so that you knew it wasn't Wednesday, and he could read quite comfortably when you weren't looking over his shoulder and saying "Well?" all the time, and he could—

"Well?" said Rabbit.

"Yes," said Owl looking Wise and Thoughtful. "I see what you mean. Undoubtedly."

"Well?"

"Exactly," said Owl. "Precisely." And he added, after a little thought, "If you had not come to me, I should have come to you."

"Why?" asked Rabbit.

"For that very reason," said Owl, hoping that something helpful would happen soon. ("In which Rabbit has a busy day and we learn what Christopher Robin does in the mornings")

Owl is both the child concealing the fact that he can't yet read properly *and* a pompous adult who hides behind words. He is known for his pointless use of long-winded phrases such as "a blusterous day . . . in the late forenoon" (a phrase which amused Milne that was used by the Scotsman who taught him mathematics at Trinity) or "the Necessary Dorsal Muscles" rather in the manner of Marcel Proust's inane diplomat, M. Norpois.

Likewise, Milne from time to time plays with the language and logic of sets and classes. Indeed, *The House at Pooh Corner* begins with just such a confusion. Pooh goes to Piglet's house but Piglet isn't there, so he decides to visit Eeyore instead but first returns home for his muffler:

He hurried back to his own house, and his mind was so busy on the way with the hum he was getting ready for Eeyore that, when he suddenly saw Piglet sitting in his best arm-chair, he could only stand there rubbing his head and wondering whose house he was in.

"Hallo, Piglet," he said. "I thought you were out."

"No," said Piglet, "it's you who were out, Pooh."

"So it was," said Pooh. "I knew one of us was." ("In which a house is built at Pooh Corner for Eeyore")

The mysterious and bounciful Tigger is a particularly splendid source of such "bulls":

"When [Pooh] awoke in the morning, the first thing he saw was Tigger sitting in front of the glass and looking at himself.

"Hallo!" said Pooh.

"Hallo!" said Tigger. "I've found somebody just like me. I thought I was the only one of them . . . "

("Later at Piglet's house")

"Hallo, Pooh," said Piglet.

"Hallo, Piglet. This is Tigger."

"Oh, is it?" said Piglet, and he edged round to the other side of the table.

"I thought Tiggers were smaller than that."

"Not the big ones," said Tigger. ("In which Tigger comes to the Forest and has breakfast")

All of these conversations are ordinary, normal, plausible, and yet absurd, the very essence of a Milne paradox, the very secret of his success in appealing to children who are learning rules and adults who can still laugh when such rules are subtly defied. Even here, though, the games with rules are a gentle bending of conventions between more or less conversational equals. There are none of the almost frightening sudden transformations of reality that characterize Carroll's work, no explicit interrogations such as that administered to Alice by the formidable egg-head Humpty Dumpty. Rather, we are in the land of "Trespassers William" and Pooh living "under the name of Sanders," a reasonable if not entirely rational world for one child to inhabit and another to enter.

Milne's poems for children also involve a humorous breaking of rules, but in a different way from his stories. His poems are anti-didactic. They are told from the child's point of view, and the children in them are in control and break the rules, conventions, prudential restrictions, and obedience imposed by the adult world. Indeed, even today the censorious might well be able to inhibit the publication of such delightfully subversive verses on the grounds that they encourage bad habits and disobedience in children. (They would probably be equally unwilling to allow the publications of works like those of Milne's precursor Hilaire Belloc.) All of the rules of childhood are broken in Milne's verses and no disaster follows. Among adults only those with a sense of humor can enjoy them or recommend them to children. This humorously anti-didactic quality comes across especially well in the exercise avoiding *Teddy Bear*, who is "proud of being short and stout," and in *If I Were a King*, where a child enjoys the fantasy of being powerful enough to demolish adult restrictions. Likewise, children and adults alike can rejoice with Emmeline whose hands aren't clean and Mary Jane who obstinately refuses the rice pudding which is good for her. The very titles of the poems "Politeness," "Independence," and "Disobedience" suggest a thoroughly enjoyable reveling in an imaginary anarchic carnival.

Undoubtedly, though, Milne's subversive masterpiece is *The Dormouse and the Doctor*. The doctor, the enforcer of the modern, universal, compulsory ideal of health, forces the dormouse to switch from his bed of restful delphiniums and geraniums to one of invigorating chrysanthemums. The dormouse is, it would seem, helpless to resist, but then he turns to the most powerful means of undermining and outwitting that we have—imagination:

The Doctor next morning was rubbing
    his hands,
And saying, "There's nobody quite un-
    derstands
These cases as I do! The cure has begun!
How fresh the chrysanthemums look in
    the sun!"
The Dormouse lay happy, his eyes were
    so tight,
He could see no chrysanthemums, yellow
    or white,
And all that he felt at the back of his
    head
Were delphiniums (blue) and geraniums
    (red).

Milne's success in writing comedies that subvert the everyday rule-governed world links him in a strange way to the comic writer who had first taught him mathematics at school, H.G. Wells. Wells's own comedies, *The History of Mr. Polly, Kipps,* and *Bealby: A Holiday,* all rely on a fantasy of escape in which a powerless, lower-middle-class adult or adolescent breaks out into a more interesting, less constraining world. Milne's children and animals escape in a less dramatic way, by the use of imagination and verbal ingenuity. His appeal is not limited to children, for adults can laugh at and rejoice with his characters just as they do in the case of Wells's. It is an odd coincidence that these two English comic geniuses should have known each other at Milne's father's school, but it is not entirely surprising that in a society then noted for its orderliness, they should each in their own way have written comedies of escape and imagination.

Summary

A.A. Milne was a prolific writer of sketches, essays, plays, and novels whose work, except for his humorous writings for children, notably *Winnie-the-Pooh* and *The House at Pooh Corner,* has largely been forgotten. The appeal of these two books to adults as well as to children and the skill and subtlety with which Milne has balanced different layers of meaning and word-play have made them classics. The well-known ending to "An Enchanted Place," the last story in *The House at Pooh Corner,* is an unintended epitaph to Milne's enchanted work: "Wherever they go and whatever happens to them on the way, in that enchanted place on the top of the Forest a little boy and his Bear will always be playing."

Selected Bibliography
Primary Sources

Works for Children
When We Were Very Young. London: Methuen, 1924.
Winnie-the-Pooh. London: Methuen, 1926.
Now We Are Six. London: Methuen, 1927.
The House at Pooh Corner. London: Methuen, 1928.
Toad of Toad Hall. London: Methuen, 1929.

Other Works
Lovers in London. London: Alsten Rivers, 1905.

The Days Play. London: Methuen, 1910.
The Holiday Round. London: Methuen, 1912.
Once a Week. London: Methuen, 1914.
Happy Days. New York: George H. Doran, 1915.
Once On a Time. London: Hodder & Stoughton, 1917.
Not That It Matters. London: Methuen, 1919.
First Plays. London: Chatto & Windus, 1919.
If I May. London: Methuen, 1920.
Second Plays. London: Chatto & Windus, 1921.
Mr. Pim. London: Hodder & Stoughton, 1922.
The Sunny Side. London: Methuen, 1921.
The Red House Mystery. London: Methuen, 1922.
Three Plays. New York: Putnam, 1922.
Success. London: Chatto & Windus, 1923.
The Man in the Bowler Hat. London: French, 1924.
For the Luncheon Interval: Cricket and Other Verses. London: Methuen, 1925.
Four Plays. London: Chatto & Windus, 1926.
Miss Marlow at Play. London: French, 1926.
The Ascent of Man. London: Ernest Benn, 1928.
The Ivory Door. London: Chatto & Windus, 1929.
By Way of Introduction. London: Methuen, 1929.
The Secret and Other Stories. London: Methuen, 1929.
Those Were the Days. London: Methuen, 1929.
The Fourth Wall or the Perfect Alibi. London: French, 1929.
Michael and Mary. London: Chatto & Windus, 1930.
Two People. London: Methuen, 1931.
Four Plays. New York: Putnam, 1932.
Four Days' Wonder. London: Methuen, 1933.
Peace With Honour. London: Methuen, 1934.
More Plays. London: Chatto & Windus, 1935.
Miss Elizabeth Bennett. London: Chatto & Windus, 1936.
Four Plays. London: Penguin Books, 1939.
Behind the Lines. London: Methuen, 1940.
War With Honour. London: Macmillan, 1940.

War Aims Unlimited. London: Methuen, 1941.

The Pocket Milne. New York: Dutton, 1941.

The Ugly Duckling. London: French, 1941.

Chloe Marr. London: Methuen, 1946.

Birthday Party and Other Stories. New York: Dutton, 1948.

The Norman Church. London: Methuen, 1948.

A Table Near the Band. London: Methuen, 1950.

Before the Flood. London: French, 1951.

Year In Year Out. London: Methuen, 1952.

Autobiographies

When I Was Very Young. London: Methuen, 1930.

It's Too Late Now. London: Methuen, 1939.

Secondary Sources

Bibliographies

Haring-Smith, Tori. *A.A. Milne: A Critical Bibliography*. New York: Garland, 1982.

Payne, John R. "Four Children's Books by A.A. Milne." *Studies in Bibliography*, Vol. 23, 1970.

Sibley, Brian. *A.A. Milne: A Handlist of His Writings*. London: Henry Pootle Press, 1976.

Townsend, John Rowe. "A.A. Milne." *Twentieth-Century Children's Writers*. London: St. James, 1978, pp. 546–49. Kirkpatrick, D.L. ed.

Books

Crews, Frederick C. *The Pooh Perplex: A Freshman Casebook*. New York: Dutton, 1963; London: Arthur Barker, 1964. Milton Keynes, Robin Clark, 1979. Very funny set of parodies of literary critics trying to analyze the Pooh books.

Hoff, Benjamin. *The Tao of Pooh*. London: Methuen, 1982. The title either is or isn't self-explanatory.

Milne, Christopher. *The Enchanted Places*. London: Methuen, 1974. The autobiography of A.A. Milne's son, who was the model for Christopher Robin, with his reflections on the books for children and his father's other work.

Thwaite, Ann. *A.A. Milne: His Life*. London: Faber & Faber, 1990. The prize-winning biography. Very thorough.

Articles

Carpenter, Humphrey. *Secret Gardens: A Study of the Golden Age of Children's Literature*. London: Unwin Hyman, 1985.

Hurt, Peter. "A.A. Milne." In *Writers for Children*. Ed. Jane M. Bingham. New York: Charles Scribner's Sons, 1988.

Eugene Trivizas and Christie Davies

M

Mitford, Nancy

Born: London, November 28, 1904

Education: Very little formal education; "finishing school" at Hatherop Castle, 1921–1922

Marriage: Peter Murray Rennell Rodd, December 4, 1933

Died: Versailles, France, June 30, 1973

Biography

Nancy Mitford was born in London on November 28, 1904, the eldest daughter of David Mitford (who succeeded as second Baron Redesdale in 1916) and his wife Sydney. Nancy's birth was followed by those of a son and five more daughters. The Mitfords were an eccentric family, and almost all of the beautiful Mitford girls achieved notoriety of one sort or another: Nancy with her novels; Diana as the wife of Sir Oswald Mosley, founder of the British Union of Fascists; Unity as an outspoken Nazi sympathizer; Jessica as a prominent member of the Communist Party; and Deborah as the Duchess of Devonshire.

The family lived first at Batsford Park and subsequently at Asthall Manor and then at Swinbrook Manor (all in the Cotswolds). The children's lives were secluded, dominated by their hot-tempered, furiously philistine father. Lord Redesdale did not believe in educating women, and Nancy received only a minimal formal education, supplemented by her own extensive reading.

After a short spell at finishing school at Hatherop Castle (1921–1922) and in Europe, followed by a conventional debutante season, Mitford lived at home for several years. It was there that she decided to embark on a literary career as a means of supplementing her meager allowance. She began in 1928 with gossip and society columns in various magazines, and her first two novels, *Highland Fling* and *Christmas Pudding*, were written in 1931 and 1932. On December 4, 1933, she married the Honorable

Peter Murray Rennell Rodd, a brilliant ne'er-do-well. The marriage served the purpose of setting Mitford free from parental authority, but it was not a happy union and the Rodds separated during the war—though they did not divorce until 1958. The couple had no children.

Wigs on the Green (1935) and Pigeon Pie (1940) followed the first two novels. During the war, Mitford helped run a canteen for interned French soldiers, then became an assistant in Heywood Hill's bookshop (in which she later bought a partnership). It was at this time that she met Gaston Palewski, Charles De Gaulle's directeur du cabinet, with whom she was to be in love for the rest of her life.

After the war Mitford moved permanently to Paris, partly to be near Palewski. She became an ardent francophile, though it was in France that she was to write her most quintessentially English novels. The Pursuit of Love appeared in 1945, followed by Love in a Cold Climate (1949), The Blessing (1951), and Don't Tell Alfred (1960); all of these novels were bestsellers. In 1956, she outraged and amused the English-speaking world with her article, "The English Aristocracy," followed by Noblesse Oblige. She also wrote several biographies, as well as continuing her journalistic work with a weekly Paris letter for the Sunday Times.

Mitford contracted Hodgkins' Disease in 1969; after several years of painful illness, she died at home in Versailles, France, on June 30, 1973.

Literary Analysis

In 1962, Mitford wrote that the English regarded her as "their chief purveyor of fairy tales."[1] In a period encompassing depression, increasing social awareness, war, and European reconstruction, her novels continued to describe an enchanted never-never land of rich, witty aristocrats, truly the stuff of fairy tales. Though many have classified her as a satirist, it is really the element of romantic fantasy that makes her books so appealing.

Mitford's first three novels, while amusing in a brittle, self-conscious manner, show little of the power that would mark her later work. Highland Fling and Christmas Pudding deal with her own milieu, and their principal theme is the clash of the Edwardian, philistine life of the country aristocracy with the younger generation, usually represented by effete Oxford aesthetes and bright young people. These books

achieved a certain coterie success. The influence of Evelyn Waugh's early novels, especially Vile Bodies (1930), is evident. Though Mitford could not be said to belong to any "school" of literature, she was friends with a group of writers that included Waugh, Robert Byron, John Betjeman, Harold Acton, and Raymond Mortimer. The friendship with Waugh was especially influential upon her work, and she looked on him as something of a mentor, receiving (though not always following) a great deal of advice.

Wigs on the Green has a certain historical interest, for in it Mitford lampoons the growing Fascist movement. Her brother-in-law, Sir Oswald Mosley, appears as Captain Jack, leader of the Union Jack Movement, and her sister Unity as the beautiful but mad Eugenia Malmains, who makes impassioned Union Jack speeches from her soapbox on the village green. Mitford was never politically passionate (even though she voted as a Socialist), but her dislike of Fascism was real enough, and in this novel she hoped to emphasize its absurdities.

Pigeon Pie is the last of the "essentially ephemeral novels so much a part of the fashion and idiom of the thirties;"[2] in it Mitford deals with the period of the "phoney war," and the novel's commercial failure was largely due to the fact that its publication coincided with the real war, making it a period piece before it had even appeared.

The foundation of Mitford's reputation is formed by her post-war novels. With The Pursuit of Love, Mitford found her real subject—her own family in its intractable Englishness. The book is narrated by a young girl, Fanny Logan, and concerns Fanny's cousins the Radletts—especially the beautiful and romantic Linda. The Radletts are very firmly based on the Mitfords themselves, and Lord Redesdale, fictionalized as the roaring and raging Uncle Matthew, comes into his own as a classic figure of comedy. He is the quintessential backwoods peer, philistine (the only book he has ever read was Jack London's White Fang), obsessed with blood sports and warfare: over his chimney-piece hangs "an entrenching tool, with which, in 1915, Uncle Matthew had whacked to death eight Germans one by one as they crawled out of a dug-out."[3] Among his other eccentricities, he "had four magnificent bloodhounds, with which he used to hunt his children. Two of us would go off with a good start to lay the trail, and Uncle Matthew and the rest would follow the hounds on horseback . . . This caused the most tremendous stir locally, the Kentish weekenders on their way to church were appalled by the sight of four great hounds in full cry after two little girls." Uncle Matthew is also the most insular of jingos. "Abroad," he says, "is unutterably bloody, and foreigners are fiends."[4]

While Mitford claimed to feel much resentment towards her father, her portrait of Uncle Matthew is ultimately a deeply sympathetic one. He is made somehow representative of all that is English, and Fanny voices this feeling: "Much as we feared, much as we disapproved of, passionately as we sometimes hated Uncle Matthew, he still remained for us a sort of criterion of English manhood; there seemed something not quite right about any man who greatly differed from him."[5]

Against this background Mitford places, by contrast, the charm and sophistication of the French, personified by Linda's lover Fabrice de Sauveterre (an idealized version of Palewski). Fabrice—romantic, passionate, cosmopolitan, frivolous but erudite—is the entire French nation (which Mitford idolized) rolled into one character.

As much as she loved things French, Mitford's French characters have a stagey quality that is never evident in her English creations. However, the overt romanticism released by her love for France gave a new dimension to the brittle humor of the pre-war novels and provided a real level of human compassion for the post-war ones, beginning with *The Pursuit of Love*. That novel was followed by sequels, *Love in a Cold Climate*, which displays an even greater virtuosity, *Don't Tell Alfred,* and *The Blessing.* Narrated again by Fanny, the story focuses on the very rich and grand Lord and Lady Montdore and their beautiful but self-contained daughter Polly. Tragedy seems to strike when Polly makes a grotesquely unsuitable marriage, and the Montdores console themselves with a visit from their unknown Canadian heir. They expect a hulking Colonial, but Cedric is a surprise: "A glitter of blue and gold crossed the parquet, and a human dragonfly was kneeling on the fur rug in front of the Montdores, one long white hand extended towards each."[6] It transpires that he lives in a French chateau—"I was sent to Paris by my guardian, a banker, to learn some horrid sort of job, I quite forget what, as I never had to go near it. It is not really necessary to have jobs in Paris, one's friends are so very very kind." As

for Canada, "I am very very happy to say that kindly Nature has allowed a great sea-fog of oblivion to rise between me and Nova Scotia so that I hardly remember one single thing about it." The charming Cedric effects the complete transformation of the formidable, monstrously dowdy Lady Montdore into a vision of thin, blue-haired *chic*; Polly leaves her old-maidish husband, Boy Dougdale, and marries a local duke; Boy, Cedric, and Lady Montdore ride off into the sunset in the Montdores' big Daimler, and all ends happily.

In this novel Mitford created two exquisitely comic characters. Lady Montdore is awfulness personified ("I think I may say we put India on the map. Hardly any of one's friends in England had ever even heard of India before we went there, you know'"[7]). With Cedric, Mitford brought the homosexuality which had gone unstated in many of her characters, from *Highland Fling* on, out of the closet—indeed, Harold Acton found the novel most original in having a homosexual as "beneficent rather than as a pernicious influence" (76). Many of Mitford's friends were homosexual, and her novels were among the first to capture their idiom and humor in fiction.

The Blessing is even more of a fairy tale than Mitford's other novels for in it she wove the story of what she would have liked her own life to be: the very English Grace, Mitford's alter-ego, is married to Charles-Edouard de Valhubert (Palewski again), and the novel is the story of Grace's coming-to-terms with her husband's incurable infidelity. This infidelity is presented by Mitford as inseparable from the vitality and free spirits of French manhood, and in the end the couple is happily reunited with Grace determined to turn a blind eye on Charles-Edouard's peccadilloes. Seen in the light of Mitford's own life—Palewski, as well as having many love-affairs, had no interest in marrying Mitford—this novel has a particular pathos. Like its predecessors, though, it is wildly funny, especially when the author emphasizes the unyielding Englishness of the characters who have been uprooted to France, like the Valhubert child's nanny when confronted with a delicious cheese: "I wish you could have smelt it dear, awful it was, and still covered with bits of straw . . . Funny-looking bread here, too, all crust and holes, I don't know how you'd made a nice bit of damp toast with that."

Mitford abandoned the first-person technique in *The Blessing*, but, realizing that it had

M

given her work a special focus and force, re-sumed the voice of Fanny in her final novel, *Don't Tell Alfred*.

Mitford wrote light journalism throughout her life; her Paris letter for the *Sunday Times* usually contained, it is said, something to offend everyone. This was also the case with *Noblesse Oblige*, a book of essays (by Mitford herself, Waugh, Betjeman, and others) which she edited around a scholarly essay by Professor Alan Ross called "U and Non-U: An Essay in Sociological Linguistics." This teased the class-conscious British by mapping out the differences between "U" (upper-class) and "Non-U" linguistic usage (i.e., Non-U "wealthy" versus U "rich"); the book became a national obsession, with everyone scanning his own and his neighbor's conversation for tell-tale non-U markers. Mitford's own essay, "The English Aristocracy," teases both aristocrats and bourgeois: "The English nobleman, whose forebears were such lovers of beauty, seems to have lost all aesthetic sense . . . Should one of his guests perceive that a blackened square of canvas in a spare bedroom is a genuine Caravaggio, that picture will appear at Christies before you can say Jack Robinson, though there is no necessity whatever for such a sale . . . Divest, divest, is the order of the day."

The writer's forays into biography were popular but not critical successes: as A.J.P. Taylor kindly put it, "no historian could write a novel half as good as Miss Mitford's work of history."[8] Her wild generalizations and frothy style were unsuited to historical precision. Waugh pointed out that she wrote as though she were babbling into a telephone; perhaps this is the secret of the novels' chatty, conversational charm.

Summary
Nancy Mitford's early books are interesting but frivolous documents of the 1930s. Her real reputation rests on her last four novels, *The Pursuit of Love*, *Love in a Cold Climate*, *The Blessing*, and *Don't Tell Alfred*. In them she brings to life what she knows best: the foibles of the British aristocracy. Though her feelings toward that milieu are ambiguous, the portrait that she ultimately paints is affectionate, confirming the validity and even the superiority of the upper classes.

Notes
1. *The Water Beetle*, p. 144.
2. Selina Hastings, *Nancy Mitford: A Biography* (London: Hamish Hamilton, 1985), p. 128.
3. *The Pursuit of Love* (Modern Library edition), p. 3.
4. *Ibid.*, p. 100.
5. *Ibid.*, p. 33.
6. *Love in a Cold Climate* (Modern Library edition), p. 476.
7. *Ibid.*, p. 476.
8. A.J.P. Taylor, *Manchester Guardian* (March 12, 1954): 6.

Selected Bibliography
Primary Sources

Novels
Highland Fling. London: Thornton Butterworth, 1931.
Christmas Pudding. London: Thornton Butterworth, 1932.
Wigs on the Green. London: Thornton Butterworth, 1935.
Pigeon Pie: a Wartime Receipt. London: Hamish Hamilton, 1940.
The Pursuit of Love. London: Hamish Hamilton, 1945.
Love in a Cold Climate. London: Hamish Hamilton, 1949.
The Blessing. London: Hamish Hamilton, 1951.
Don't Tell Alfred. London: Hamish Hamilton, 1960.

Biographies
Madame de Pompadour. London: Hamish Hamilton, 1954.
Voltaire in Love. London: Hamish Hamilton, 1957.
The Sun King: Louis IV at Versailles. London: Hamish Hamilton, 1966.
Frederick the Great. London: Hamish Hamilton, 1957.

Works Edited by Nancy Mitford
The Ladies of Alderley: being the letters between Maria Josepha, Lady Stanley of Alderley, and her daughter-in-law, Henrietta Maria Stanley. London: Chapman & Hall, 1939.
The Stanleys of Alderley: Their Letters Between the Years 1851–1865. London: Chapman & Hall, 1939.
Noblesse Oblige. London: Hamish Hamilton, 1956.

Translations

La Fayette, Marie Madeleine (Madame de). *The Princess of Cleves*. London: Euphorion Books, 1950.

Roussin, A. *The Little Hut*. London: Hamish Hamilton, 1951.

Collections and Omnibuses

The Nancy Mitford Omnibus. London: Hamish Hamilton, 1956.

The Water Beetle. London: Hamish Hamilton, 1962.

The Best Novels of Nancy Mitford. London: Hamish Hamilton, 1974.

Pursuit of Love/Love in a Cold Climate. New York: Modern Library, 1982.

Mosley, Charlotte, ed. *A Talent to Annoy: Essays, Articles and Reviews 1929–1968*. London: Hamish Hamilton, 1986.

Secondary Sources

Biographies

Acton, Harold. *Nancy Mitford: A Memoir*. London: Hamish Hamilton, 1975. A friend's account of Mitford's life, based largely upon excerpts from her letters.

Hastings, Selina. *Nancy Mitford: A Biography*. London: Hamish Hamilton, 1985. The most complete treatment of Mitford's life and work.

Guinness, Jonathan, with Catherine Guinness. *The House of Mitford*. London: Hutchinson, 1984. The most comprehensive of the several books on the Mitford family—written by family members, however, and thus not without its prejudices.

Bibliographies

Parise, Marina Patta. "Nancy Mitford: A Bibliography." *Bulletin of Bibliography*, 46, 1 (March 1989): 3–9.

Articles and Chapters in Books

Atkins, John Alfred. "Nancy Mitford: The Uncrossable Bridge." *Six Novelists Look At Society: An Enquiry Into the Social Views of Elizabeth Bowen, L.P. Hartley, Rosamund Lehman, Christopher Isherwood, Nancy Mitford, and C.P. Snow*. London: John Calder Publishers, 1977, pp. 166–99. Atkins examines Mitford's politics and High Tory background, and looks at her fiction within its social context.

Hastings, Selina. "The Pursuit of Nancy Mitford." In *Essays by Divers Hands: Being the Transactions of the Royal Society of Literature*. Ed. Richard Faber. Wolfeboro, NH: Boydell, 1988. New Series, Vol. 45, pp. 91–102. An account of Hastings's research for her biography of Mitford.

Highet, G. "English Shibboleths." *Talents and Geniuses: The Pleasures of Appreciation*. New York: Oxford University Press, 1957, pp. 207–14. An amusing discussion of *Noblesse Oblige* and the U and Non-U mania.

Brooke Allen

N

Nashe, Thomas

Born: Lowestoft, Suffolk, England, 1567
Education: St. John's College, Cambridge
  University, B.A., 1586
Died: Yarmouth, Norfolk (?) 1599 to 1601 (?)

Biography

Thomas Nashe was born in Lowestoft, Suffolk, England, in the fall of 1567 to William Nashe and his second wife. In 1573, the family moved to West Harling, Norfolk, where Thomas most likely remained until his departure for Cambridge. An October 13, 1582, entry in the Cambridge University Register lists him as a sizar (a student receiving an allowance from his college toward his expenses) at St. John's. After receiving his B.A. in 1586, he stayed on in Cambridge but left the University before taking an M.A.

Nashe was in London by the fall of 1588; on September 19, 1588, he registered *The Anatomie of Absurditie*. Between the time that he registered that work and 1589, Nashe became one of "the University Wits"—a small group of university-educated poets, playwrights, and pamphleteers who lived by their wits and pens—John Lyly, George Peele, and Robert Greene among them. Of chief importance to Nashe was his friendship with Greene. Greene had Nashe write the preface to his 1589 prose romance *Menaphon*. G.R. Hibbard assumes that Greene, an already established author, provided Nashe his entry into the literary world. From that point on, Nashe's life became closely intertwined with Greene's literary activities.

In the preface to *Menaphon*, Nashe took on the contemporary literary world as a satirical critic. While the preface pointed out the literary follies of the day, Nashe also praised a number of contemporary writers, including Gabriel Harvey, among those who wrote good Latin verse. Harvey was a Cambridge tutor at Pembroke and later a fellow of Trinity; ironically, that praise led Nashe into one of the more famous literary quarrels of that contentious age—the Nashe–Harvey quarrel. Greene was at odds with Harvey, and for one of Greene's cronies to include Harvey in a work both satirical and praising must have seemed ironic, to say the least. Only two months after *Menaphon* appeared, Richard Harvey, Gabriel's brother, published *A Theological Discourse on the Lamb of God and His Enemies* which contained an attack on Nashe. While Nashe did not respond immediately, he did not forget the attack. He rounded out 1589 by pursuing his literary criticism in *The Anatomie of Absurditie*.

The age was one of controversy—over politics, literature, personal affairs, and religion. Nashe shied from none that affected him. His early prose style brought him to the attention of Archbishop Whitgift, who employed Nashe and Lyly as anti-Martinist pamphleteers in the Martin Marprelate controversy. A strong advocate of the English Church, Nashe may have written several of the anti-Martinist papers, but given that they were published anonymously, we cannot attribute with precision those that Nashe wrote. His experience in the Marprelate affair cemented his friendship with Whitgift.

In 1592, three years after Richard Harvey's *A Theological Discourse* appeared, Nashe published *Pierce Penilesse his Supplication to the Divell*, a satirical counter. He followed this with *Strange Newes, of the Intercepting certaine Letters*, another satire, this time on Gabriel Harvey. Harvey had attacked the now-dead Greene and Nashe in *Four Letters*, and Nashe retaliated.

The quarrel between Nashe and Harvey then lay dormant for four years. In 1592, plague broke out. Nashe took refuge with Whitgift when the latter repaired to Croydon to wait out the disease's ravages. Sometime during 1592–1593 Nashe wrote the play *Summers Last Will and Testament*. Although this work was not published until 1600, internal evidence clearly links it to the plague years.

From Croydon, Nashe traveled to the Isle of Wight in the company of Sir George and Lady Elizabeth Carey. In 1593, Nashe dedicated his religious meditation, *Christs Teares over Jerusalem*, to Lady Elizabeth, and in 1594 he dedicated *The Terrors of the Night*, a treatise on dreams and nightmares, to Lady Elizabeth's daughter. In this same year *The Unfortunate Traveller. Or, the life of Jacke Wilton*, his most well-known and influential work, appeared, dedicated to the Earl of Southampton.

In 1596, Nashe resumed his quarrel with Gabriel Harvey with the publication of *Have with You to Saffron-walden. Or, Gabriell Harveys Hunt is up*. The appearance of this volume escalated tensions between the two and signaled a reissuing of the mens' attacks on one another.

One controversy never seemed enough for Nashe. Soon he was at work with Ben Jonson on the lost satirical play, *Isle of Dogs*. Staged in the summer of 1597, this work so stirred the wrath of the authorities that Jonson ended up in prison. Whether that was to have been Nashe's fate as well remains uncertain. It is known, however, that he left London and took up residence in Great Yarmouth.

During his sojourn in Great Yarmouth, Nashe produced his final work, *Nashe's Lenten Stuffe*. Even here, despite the controversies that his chosen path as satirist led him into and the brushes with authority that resulted, he held the course. *Lenten Stuffe* appeared in 1599. Although milder than his earlier works, *Lenten Stuffe* became the final faggot in the fire of Nashe's controversies, for in 1599 Whitgift ordered his works suppressed.

The exact date and circumstances of Nashe's death have yet to be discovered. He probably died in Yarmouth, Norfolk; that he was dead by 1601 is certain, for in that year Charles Fitzgeffrey, in *Affaniae*, offered a Latin epigram on Nashe's death praising him as a satirist.

Literary Analysis

While not a major figure in the English Renaissance, Nashe is important. His prose style, un-doubtedly influenced by Greene and others of the University Wits, has become a hallmark for invective and satire. At the same time, his works for the Carey women show his non-humorous side.

His prefaces to *Menaphon* and *The Anatomie of Absurditie* are parallel pieces. In both he decries the state of learning, the decline in the quality of literature, and the participation of the universities in that decline. What may be perceived as an oddity is the fact that Nashe speaks against the romance in the preface to *Menaphon*; he was, after all, introducing Greene's romance. However, Greene's reputation was established; whatever Nashe wrote here could attract readers to his own work. The preface may have served as an advertisement for *The Anatomie*.

Nashe begins the "Preface" by addressing the gentlemen students. Expressing his opinions on both the current state of university education and the literary scene, he intermingles satire, invective, and irony along with praise. It is a model of the vituperation that characterizes the pamphlet wars of the era. While contemporaries such as Sir Philip Sidney, Edmund Spenser, George Peele, Roger Ascham, George Gascoigne, and others receive praise, Nashe lashes out at university-educated poetasters. He complains against those who through their education choose "inkhorn" and "tapsterly terms" to "the English [they were] born to." He attacks hexameral verse with parody, asking the reader to judge the "description of a tempest, which is thus 'Then did he make, heavens vault to rebounde, with rounce robble hobble / Of ruffe raffe roaring, with thwick thwack thurley bouncing.'" He concludes by asking readers to judge this work accordingly—that is, as a work that restores art to its proper place.

The Anatomie, a slight work by literary standards, does show the beginnings of Nashe's satiric style. He opens the work with a satire on the failings of womankind, a common subject of the day. He complains that authors and poets try to "repair the ruinous walls of Venus's court, to restore to the world that forgotten legendary license of lying" as they blazon forth "women's slender praises." Noting that there are far more bad women than good, he reminds the reader that regarding marriage Diogenes said that the proper time "for the young man [was] not yet, and the old man never." From there Nashe moves on to an appraisal of the follies of the age. Those afflicted with false learning are mocked for knowing authors only through a translator's work. Zealots make but a "pretence of purity." He also attacks the failings of contemporary literature, crying out against the "babbling ballads" that every drunkard composes and contrasts the current state of poetry with the work of the ancients. Thriftless youth is satirized for not pursuing learning and for "casting that away at a cast at dice, which cost their dads a year's toil," a complaint not dissimilar to ones lodged against today's college students. He ends the work in praise of proper learning.

In *Pierce Penilesse*, a more ambitious work, Nashe again calls attention to the failures of the universities and the lack of elegance in or quality of current literature. At the same time there is an elegance present here that was lacking in his own earlier writing. The writer establishes a clear, engaging, narrative voice. While the work includes personal attacks on the living, its quality—satire, invective, alliteration, wit—transcends topicality. Indulging himself again in self-mockery, Nashe laments the writer's fate. He has "spent many years in studying how to live . . . without money" due to ungrateful patrons and will, therefore, submit a supplication to the Devil. The supplication proper gives an account of the seven deadly sins as they currently exist in London. He complains of the pride of the "greasy son of a clothier" who has ambitions for a title, for example, and takes the opportunity to satirize the Spaniard, the Italian, the Frenchman, and the Dane for their pride. Nashe also fires his first salvo in the Harvey-Nashe quarrel with this work. He calls Richard Harvey a "great baboon," a "Pygmy braggart," and a "pamphleteer of nothing." After concluding with the seven deadly sins, Pierce questions the nature of the Devil and the extent of his dominion. Nashe ends the work by asking the "gentle reader" to consider his volume worth buying and by taking one last slap at patronage, for all he can hope for from his "young master" is a "blush."

When *Pierce Penilesse* appeared, Gabriel Harvey was engaged in writing his *Four Letters*, an attack on Greene. Nashe's work sufficiently incensed Harvey that he devoted the third letter to Nashe. Nashe retaliated with *Strange Newes, of the intercepting Certaine Letters*. He immediately attacks Harvey in the "epistle dedicatory" as "a Doctor and his fart that have kept a foul stinking stir in Paul's churchyard" whom Nashe will "trounce." The author's purpose is to confute Harvey word for word. He begins by commending *Four Letters* "because all men dislike it." Nashe defends the now-dead Greene as a better poet than Harvey, whose hexameral "verses run hobbling like a brewer's cart upon the stones, and observe no length in their feet." By quoting Harvey and commenting on the quotations, Nashe ridicules him throughout. While Nashe admits that hexameral verse is appropriate in Greek and Latin, Harvey "goes twitching and hopping in our language like a man running upon quagmires, up the hill in one syllable, and down the dale in another." And for condemning Greene, Nashe calls him "a wisp, a wisp, a wisp, rip, rip, you kitchenstuff wrangler." At length Nashe grows tired of confuting and closes by letting Harvey "be an ass still."

Summer's Last Will and Testament is Nashe's only attempt at dramatic comedy. In it Summer interviews his potential heirs only to find that the ensuing seasons are either profligate or niggardly. Despite their errors, Summer leaves his crown to Autumn and Winter. Though written as drama, the play is more monologic than dramatic as each character is called on stage to reveal his nature. The comedy arises from the presence of Will Summers, who not only introduces and closes the play but also comments on the deficiencies or excesses of each character. Nashe employs self-mockery by having Will open the play speaking "in the person of the Idiot our Playmaker [who] like a fop and an ass, must be making himself a public laughing stock, and have no thank for his labor." When Harvest exits, Will plays on his "thatch suit," noting that if he could have kept him until the play's end, Will would have put him to practical use as a doormat to his lodgings. After Bacchus knights Will as "Sir Robert Tosspot," Nashe satirizes the Dutch by having Will observe that his clothes are so drenched with beer that any "Dutchman within twenty miles . . . [will] claim kindred of him." Nashe also satirizes learning. After Winter discusses the evil nature of poets, historians, and grammarians, Will asks, "Who would be a scholar? . . . this learning was such a filthy thing, which made me hate it." This work is not successful as theater due to its monologic nature, yet it is unquestionably comic.

The Unfortunate Traveller is Nashe's best-known work. In it Jack Wilton takes us from the wars engulfing Europe to a one-man-view of worldly imperfections and static beauty. The humor in this piece arises from Wilton's cavalier attitude as well as his wit. He satirizes war by speaking plainly of its "wonderful spectacle" replete with people "wallowing in their gore" which results in "a peace concluded." After condemning the German Anabaptists for their false learning, Jack meets with the Earl of Surrey, his former master, and eventually arrives in Italy. This portion of the narrative, the most adventuresome, also proves the most comic. While jailed in Venice, Jack impregnates a fellow prisoner falsely accused of adultery, thus giving proof to the lie. She proves to be his benefactor, and they travel to Florence. When the Earl of Surrey arrives and provokes a tournament, Nashe has Jack describe the elegant excesses of knightly attire which contrasts with the clumsiness of the tourney itself. Only the Earl of Surrey possesses elegance.

Jack next moves to Rome where Nashe examines beauty and excess once again. While Rome's artifice may create a second "gorgeous gallery of gallant devices," it is also home to the pope, under whose aegis bandits break into the homes of supposed plague victims. Jack witnesses the rape and suicide of a chaste matron and is accused of her murder. A fellow Englishman testifies on Jack's behalf. After Jack's release, his countryman questions why Jack travels, since travel brings nothing but evil. Nashe rehearses the bad national characteristics that one will learn from travel: the Italians are bloody minded, the French false, the Spanish braggarts, the Dutch and Danes drunkards. The lesson, however, is "worse than an upbraiding . . . after a birching" to Jack, and he falls into one last adventure.

One Zadoch seizes Jack as a bondsman and sells him to the pope's Jewish doctor for the annual anatomy. Jack ironically allows "there's no such ready way to make a man a true Christian" as to turn him into an anatomy lesson. Jack's benefactor had also fallen victim to Zadoch (Nashe does not reveal how), and through various plot twists liberates Jack. Nashe ends this work with the deaths of Zadoch and Cutwolf. Jack marries his benefactor and performs "many alms deed" before returning to the English king in France.

Nashe's war with the Harveys is continued in *Have with You to Saffron-walden*. The comic hallmark of this work is Nashe's use of invective. The Harveys are "two blockheads, two blunderkins, having their brains stuffed with nought but balderdash." Casting the work in the form of a dialogue, Nashe examines Harvey's lineage, his birth, education, and life. Then, as in *Strange Newes*, Nashe cites his reasons for defending himself against Harvey's attacks and proceeds to confute his target's writing through quotation and response. He concludes that should Harvey respond he has "More battering engines" at his disposal.

Nashes Lenten Stuffe is a mock encomium in praise of the red herring. He opens the work with a topical allusion to his involvement in *The Isle of Dogs* and his having sought safety in Great Yarmouth. From there he presents a lengthy parodic history of the town. He reminds us of Great Yarmouth's 600 years only to cover himself: "let me not be taken with a lie, five hundred ninety eight, that wants but a pair of years to make me a true man." To make his "history" accurate he reminds us that "Henry the fifth [was] the fifth of the Henrys that ruled over us." Moving from Great Yarmouth proper to the importance of the fishing industry, Nashe rehearses the mythical history of the red herring before turning to his parodic version of Christopher Marlowe's *Hero and Leander*. Noting the irony in Hero's being a "chaste vestal priest to Venus, the queen of unchastity," Nashe observes that since her parents showed no chastity in begetting her, Hero "must prove herself a bastard, or show herself like them." Upon their deaths the gods assign them watery graves from whence they produce the ling and the herring. Even their baud accompanies them "in the heel of the week at the best men's tables" in the form of mustard. From there Nashe moves to an allegory that traces the rise of the red herring to be king of fishes. As he moves to the end, Nashe turns to a little hidden defense of *Pierce Penilesse*, a critique of the law as currently practiced, and a final request that his "godchildren" take his part in his quarrel should they hear him "mangled and torn in men's mouths." Obviously he wishes to keep his quarrel with Harvey alive. This last work is more than a mere mock encomium. It is, in fact, Nashe's own "red herring." Unfortunately, much of the personal and political satire is lost to us through time.

Summary

While he is not a major figure in the English Renaissance, Thomas Nashe is important. His work shows the changes taking place in the literary world. His involvement in the Marprelate controversy signifies a value, both economic and political, placed on writing. Some of his later work—i.e., for the Carey women—shows the importance of patronage to someone who oft railed against it. And, in *The unfortunate traveller* Nashe shows an advance in English narrative technique.

Selected Bibliography

Primary Sources

"Preface." *Menaphon Camillas Alarum to slumbering Euphues.* 1589.

An Almond for a Parrat, or Cuthbert Curry-knaues almes. Fit for the knaue Martin. 1589.

The Anatomie of Absurditie: contayning a breefe confutation of the slender imputed prayses to feminine perfection. 1589.

Pierce Penilesse his Supplication to the Divell. 1592.

Strange Newes, of the Intercepting certaine Letters. 1592.

Christs Teares over Jerusalem. 1593.

The Terrors of the Night or, a discourse on apparitions. 1594.

The Unfortunate Traveller. Or, the life of Jacke Wilton. 1594.

Haue with You to Saffron-walden. Or, Gabriell Harveys Hunt is up. 1596.

Nashes Lenten Stuffe, containing, the description of Great Yarmouth with a new play of the praises of the red herring. 1599.

A pleasant comedie, called Summers Last Will and Testament. 1600.

Editions

McKerrow, R.B., ed. *The Works of Thomas Nashe.* 5 vols. London: Bullen, 1904–1910; Oxford: Blackwell, 1958. Contains all the primary materials, including some questionable works. Detailed and valuable source material.

Secondary Sources

Best, Michael. "Nashe, Lyly, and *Summers Last Will and Testament.*" *Philological Quarterly*, 48 (January 1696): 1–11. Best suggests that the work was originally a brief "show" written by Lyly. Nashe later found the piece, expanded it, and introduced Summers into it to poke fun at both Lyly and the child actors for whom Lyly wrote the original.

Fehrenbach, Robert J. "Recent Studies in Nashe (1968–1979)." *English Literary Renaissance*, 11, 3 (Autumn 1981): 344–50. An annotated bibliography.

Ferguson, Margaret. "Nashe's *The Unfortu-nate Traveller*: The 'Newes of the Maker' Game." *English Literary Renaissance*, 11, 2 (Spring 1981): 165–82. Beginning with the second preface, Ferguson examines who and what create the game, the sense of play versus reality. Ferguson sees Jack as a maker who moves from potency to impotency. In trying to achieve mastery over others (verbally or physically), we can lose our sense of self-reflection on the consequence of our "making." The tortures create for Jack "self-chastisement" by which he repents his "play."

Friedenreich, Kenneth. "Nashe's Strange News and the Case for Professional Writers." *Studies in Philology*, 74 (1974): 451–72. Examines the Nashe-Harvey quarrel in terms of the differences between literary and professional writing.

Harrington, Susan Marie, and Michael Nahor Bond. "'Good Sir Be Ruld by Me': Patterns of the Domination and Manipulation in Thomas Nashe's *The Unfortunate Traveller.*" *Studies in Short Fiction*, 24, 3 (Summer 1987): 243–50. Through a series of episodes of control and exploitation, Nashe creates a world that empowers the reader to establish the work's coherence.

Hibbard, G.R. *Thomas Nashe.* Cambridge, MA: Harvard University Press, 1962. Study of Nashe's life and works.

Hutson, Lorna. *Thomas Nashe in Context.* London: Oxford University Press, 1991.

Jones, Ann Rosalind. "Inside the Outsider: Nashe's *The Unfortunate Traveller* and Bakhtin's Polyphonic Novel." *English Literary History*, 50, 1 (Spring 1983): 61–81. Jones sees the work as an example of the polyphonic novel arising in time of cultural upheaval. It exemplifies intertextuality. Jones observes that Jack is hardly "unfortunate" but profits instead. Nashe deliberately jars the reader with multiplicity.

Kaula, David. "The Low Style in Nashe's *The Unfortunate Traveller.*" *Studies in English Literature*, 6, 1 (Winter 1966): 43–57. Kaula sees Wilton's world divided into paradise, purgatory, and hades. Through his style Nashe then uses Wilton to point to the world's follies about him via parody of language, clothing, and genres. He forces us to a different way of perceiving the world and ourselves in relationship to it.

Lanham, Richard. "Tom Nashe and Jack Wilton: Personality as Structure in *The Unfortunate Traveller*." *Studies in Short Fiction*, 4, 3 (Spring 1967): 201–16. Lanham finds the critical methodology [formalism] inadequate to the work's nature. He sees Jack's personality as key to understanding the work as an artistic whole—Jack is perceived as the embodiment of neurosis expressed in the antisocial violence of the piece.

Larson, Charles. "The Comedy of Violence in Nashe's *The Unfortunate Traveller*." *Cahiers Elisabethains*, 8 (1976): 15–29. Examination of the use of violent farce as a means of artistic distancing which creates comic release.

Leggatt, Alexander. "Artistic Coherence in *The Unfortunate Traveller*." *Studies in English Literature*, 14, 1 (Winter 1974): 31–46. Leggatt argues for coherence in the latter part of the work, using the pleasure garden in Rome as the metaphor for contrived order, an order that Nashe imposed toward the work's end and in contrast to the earlier episodic parts.

Mallard, Barbara. "Thomas Nashe and the Functional Grotesque in Elizabethan Prose Fiction." *Studies in Short Fiction*, 15, 1 (Winter 1978): 39–48. Mallard examines the grotesque in relationship to the picaresque and how the grotesque becomes the center of the picaresque. She shows the grotesque as one mode of Elizabethan expression.

McGinn, Donald J. *Thomas Nashe*. Boston: Twayne, 1981. A study of Nashe's life and works.

Simons, Louise. "Rerouting *The Unfortunate Traveller*: Strategies for Coherence and Direction." *Studies in English Literature*, 28, 1 (Winter 1988): 17–38. Simons sees the work as "proto-*postmodernist*-novel" and less episodic and picaresque than past critics have viewed it. Coherence comes from the education that Jack undergoes and the rhetorical strategy that ties the seemingly disparate elements together.

Stephenson, Raymond. "The Epistemological Challenge of Nashe's *The Unfortunate Traveller*." *Studies in English Literature*, 23, 1 (Winter 1983): 21–36. To condemn Nashe for incoherence overlooks his purpose, which is to show the world as it is: chaotic. Man tries to impose the order that he wishes on the world, but the world will not let him. Deliberate distortion is his purpose.

Stevenson, Ruth M. "The Roman Banketting House: Nashe's Forsaken Image of Art." *Studies in Short Fiction*, 17, 3 (Summer 1980): 291–301. The controlled art of the house is contrasted with the chaotic world of reality through five geographical centers. Nashe moves us from the edenic vision that the artistic illusion gives to the reality and brutality of the world's evil, the antithesis of the artistic illusion.

Sulfridge, Cynthia. "*The Unfortunate Traveller*: Nashe's Narrative in a 'Cleane Different Vaine.'" *Journal of Narrative Technique*, 10, 1 (Winter 1980): 1–15. Nashe establishes a double narrative voice which engages the reader by means of its orality. This results in blending "textual time and reader time"—creating the eccentric nature of the narrative. The oral Jack is our friend, the literary Jack someone who repels us for this insensitivity, hence the work's failure to be popular.

Summersgill, Travis L. "The Influence of the Marprelate Controversy upon the Style of Thomas Nashe." *Studies in Philology*, 48 (1948): 145–60. From the Marprelate controversy Nashe adopted the wit of invective, extemporaneousness, satiric posturing, imaginary dialogue, epithet—all of which became hallmarks of his style.

Wells, Stanley. "Thomas Nashe and the Satirical Stance." *Cahiers Elisabethains*, 9 (April 1976): 1–7. The genre creates the public stance, yet Wells argues that the feud, which produced some of Nashe's best writing, resulted from personal feeling. He deals with *Pierce Penilesse* and Nashe's ability to produce superior satire by his balance between the particular and the general.

Mary Free

O'Casey, Sean

Born: Dublin, Ireland, March 30, 1880
Education: Grammar school; largely self-educated
Marriage: Eileen Carey Reynolds, September 23, 1927; three children
Died: Torquay, England, September 18, 1964

Biography

Sean O'Casey was born as John Casey in Dublin on March 30, 1880. The thirteenth child (eight of whom died in infancy) of Protestant parents, Michael and Susan Casey, he experienced a childhood marked by frequent illnesses—croup and a recurrent eye ailment that required continual medical attention. He grew up in a working-class tenement area of north Dublin, a setting that he was to immortalize in his most famous plays.

His being Protestant in an overwhelmingly Catholic environment was an alienating element and one of the sources of O'Casey's lifelong battle with clericalism and Catholic pietism. His father died in 1886 when Sean was very young, and the child formed an intense bond with his mother, who championed him through a difficult childhood. This and other stages of O'Casey's life are vividly chronicled in his autobiography, *Mirror in My House: The Autobiographies of Sean O'Casey* (1956).

O'Casey's education was fitful. Largely self-taught, he read voraciously when his eyes permitted and, when they didn't, he had others read to him. He read widely, especially writers such as William Butler Yeats who were trying to promote the Irish literary revival. By 1898, O'Casey was earning his living as a manual laborer, and for nine years he worked for the Great Northern Railway of Ireland (his longest stint as a laborer, 1902 to 1911). He remained a laborer until he became a full-time writer after *Juno and the Paycock* won the Hawthornden Prize in 1924.

O'Casey was deeply influenced by James Larkin's attempt to unionize Dublin laborers, which led to the walkout of transport workers in 1913. He also joined James Connolly's Irish Citizen Army and became its secretary, but he left the organization after quarrels with members over appropriate strategies. As a result, during the 1916 Easter uprising, O'Casey did not participate in the events. The conflict of socialism and nationalism had produced a split in O'Casey, and he was to perceive the nationalist struggle of the uprising, the Anglo-Irish guerrilla war of 1918 to 1921, and the civil war that followed the treaty in 1921 as flawed efforts at a general social revolution. These events form the core background of O'Casey's most famous plays, *The Shadow of a Gunman*, *Juno and the Paycock*, and *The Plough and the Stars*.

The dramatist's theater apprenticeship was almost as long and spotted as his informal education. He played the role of Father Dolan in Dion Boucicault's *The Shaughraun*; before *The Shadow of a Gunman* was accepted in 1923, he wrote several plays—among them *The Frost in the Flower*, *The Harvest Festival*, a revision of *The Frost in the Flower*, and *The Crimson in Tricolour*—all of which were rejected by the Abbey Theater.

Combining a passion for William Shakespeare and nineteenth-century Irish sentimental comedy and melodrama (Boucicault in particular), O'Casey chose as his subject the vivid life of the Dublin tenements and the characters who people the cities, streets, and pubs. While a modicum of method and a cast of characters were chosen by the author, Irish history was evolving in a way that would guarantee O'Casey's subject matter for his best-known plays.

Other apprentice works included a 1907 essay on the Irish education system, published in *The Present and Ireland*, and essays in *Irish Worker*, founded in 1911 as the trade newspaper for the Irish Transport and General Workers Union. The union's strike, the Great Walkout, lasted for seven months (August 15, 1913, until March 1914) and became the materia poetica for both *A Star Turns Red* and *Red Roses For Me*. The Irish Citizen Army was formed in October 1913 to protect the workers from police brutality and was reorganized with O'Casey as secretary after the strikes. His anti-war ballad "The Grand Oul' Dame Britannia" (1916) and his 1918 publication of *The Story of the Irish Citizen Army* are likewise germane to his theater apprenticeship.

The writer's search for a name is closely related to this apprenticeship. He became fluent in Gaelic and was involved with national movements such as the Irish Ireland movement and the Gaelic League (founded by Douglas Hyde for the revival of the Irish language) by the early 1900s, when he assumed a Gaelic version of his name, Sean O'Cathasaigh, probably in 1906. He had become Sean O'Casey by the time *The Shadow of a Gunman* was accepted for production by the Abbey Theater in 1923. He retained this name until Sean O'Casside and the O'Casside clan became personae/masks in the six volumes of his autobiography (published 1913–1954).

O'Casey was fortunate that a theater was ready to present his plays, works that would not have had much chance in the standard commercial theater of the time. The Abbey Theater had evolved by stages through the efforts of Lady Gregory and Yeats into a world-famous organization. Some of its notoriety came from the controversies surrounding J.M. Synge's ironic peasant comedies (especially *The Playboy of the Western World*) but also from the folk comedies of Lady Gregory and experiments in the poetic drama of Yeats.

At the beginning of the 1920s, when the plays that O'Casey submitted were rejected, he was encouraged by Lennox Robinson and by Lady Gregory, who was especially charmed by his skills at portraying character.

Finally, *The Shadow of a Gunman* was accepted. This play was successful and appealed to a segment of the Dublin audience not much attracted to the more culturally challenging experiments at the Abbey. *The Shadow of a Gunman* was quickly followed by *Juno and the Paycock* (1934; the dates given here and later are of first performances), generally considered O'Casey's most famous and successful drama. Now regarded as a major talent on the rise, O'Casey saw produced at the Abbey *The Plough and the Stars* (1926), the third of what has come to be called, however, loosely, his Dublin trilogy. This piece presented the Dublin Easter Monday uprising to an audience some of whose members had taken part in the rising only a decade before. Riots broke out in protest, and the premiere received international attention. *The Plough and the Stars* represents the peak of O'Casey's Irish success.

His next play, *The Silver Tassie* (1929), an expression of protest against the carnage of World War I, was rejected for the Abbey by Yeats in 1928, and a bitter controversy followed. O'Casey left Ireland and settled in England, where he lived for the rest of his life. From *The Silver Tassie* onward, the author's plays varied in their level of success and audience acceptance, but they never quite measured up to the level of the Dublin trilogy. He continued to write and engage in controversies into old age. Some of his post-war plays, attacking Catholic clericalism in Ireland, had controversial premieres, and *The Drums of Father Ned* was withdrawn from a Dublin film festival. O'Casey retaliated by banning all performances of his plays in Ireland until 1984. His autobiography was mainly well-received as it appeared in single volumes and also when it appeared in a collected edition. Parts of this autobiography, particularly those dealing with O'Casey's childhood, were successfully staged.

On September 23, 1927, O'Casey married an actress, Eileen Carey Reynolds, who would write of their marriage in *Sean* following O'Casey's death. After his marriage, which produced two sons and a daughter, at the end of the 1930s he settled down in Devon in the south of England, and he died at Torquay on September 18, 1964.

Literary Analysis

After his apprenticeship of more than a quarter of a century, O'Casey was an instant success when the Abbey group produced what some critics call his Irish plays: *Shadow*, *Juno*, and *Plough*. These three tragedies treat the materials of less than a decade (1916–1922) in twentieth-century Ireland's struggle to become an independent nation. Aside from being superior drama—tragedies in which both humor and comedy are present—the plays are historically important because they brought a new audience of workers and tenement dwellers, O'Casey's people, to the theater. With *The Shadow of a Gunman*, for the first time, the House Full sign was used at the Abbey Theater. It was used again with *Juno and the Paycock*.

O'Casey's plays defy exact categorization. "Tragi-comedy" is a loose term that somewhat covers their violent and melodramatic plots and, especially in the Dublin trilogy, the virtuoso verbal sparring of the tenement dwellers. O'Casey was an inclusive artist, not much worried about creating internal contradictions of mood or theme; he wrote about troubled times, and, except for a few doctrinaire dramas such as *The Star Turns Red* (1940), it is not always easy to trace a coherent political trend through his plays. His special genius, most notably in the Dublin trilogy, was to show how humble people survived when the world collapsed around them. If his major comic heroes have one fundamental trait, it is the ability to foster a grandiose illusion of themselves, despite the evidence of their squalid lives and the doubts of their friends and the outrage of their families.

O'Casey's style of humor reminds one of the cliché about Ireland as "the land of the tear and the smile," and also of Richard Brinsley Sheridan's quip about Ireland as "the land of merry wars and sad love songs." In O'Casey's canon the sentimental is forever at war with the hilarious. When the characters think that they are rising to heights of eloquence, they are usually making utter fools of themselves. But when the shock of war and political violence strikes down the brave and innocent, the laughter evaporates like fog before the sun, although not for long. The vitality of his characters wins out, and the wheel of fortune and O'Casey's tragedy/comedy alternation bring on the clowns.

Much of the dramatist's stage humor is related in one way or another to the tradition of the "stage Irishman." This is an instantly recognizable version of Irishness, the distinctive speech (the brogue), the power of eloquence (the blarney), with an admixture of emotional extravagance, boastfulness, and some degree of wit and charm (the twinkle in the eye). The Saint Patrick's Day industry in the United States is almost completely dependent upon this stereotype, and the stage Irishman is still a stock figure of fun on British television in a way that might be considered offensive in America. In Ireland, the concept is controversial, as one might expect. Some see it as an English imperial invention, the creation of an underclass that need not be taken seriously; others see it as partially an Irish screen erected to distract the foreigner from real Irish motives. Like most stereotypes, the image is an oversimplified exaggeration of real traits. A national literature cannot be created without some distinctive traits already existing among a people. Visitors to Ireland immediately perceive what they think is a distinctive national character and the Irish Tourist Board fervently offers it for sale. The Irish tend to deplore the stage Irishman as a denigration of their national character, but given a grotesquely overdrawn Irishman in the right context, the Irish enjoy the joke.

O'Casey was deeply influenced by the actor-playwright Boucicault, who was responsible for a stage codification of the leading traits of the stage Irishman. The character of Myles na Coppaleen in the play *The Colleen Bawn, or the Brides of Garryowen*, is frequently cited as a classic stage Irishman. According to critic David Krause, Boucicault's version is a kind of Robin Goodfellow, a master of revels, a quick-witted master of anarchy who can as easily talk his way into any female heart as out of any dramatic crisis . . . in short, "a fine broth of a boy" (Krause, 58–59).

While O'Casey's plays do not contain any characters quite like Myles na Coppaleen or Conn (who is described in the play *The Shaughraun* as "the soul of every fair, the life of every funeral, the first fiddle at all weddings and patterns"), there are several comic characters who give O'Casey's plays what he liked in Boucicault, the "color and stir." Fluther Good in *The Plough and the Stars* is a prime example, as is the Joxer Daly–Captain Boyle combination in *Juno and the Paycock*. These characters have most of the major traits of the stage Irishman, including vainglory, exaggeration, and the comic repetition of tag lines or words. Fluther has his "derogatory" and Joxer has his "daarlin," for instance. If they are too old or ugly to exude much romantic charm, Fluther can at least give a parody of it in his encounter with the prostitute in the second act of *Plough*.

O'Casey has much fun with Boucicault-like Irish tricksters in *Purple Dust* (1940), a play in which Englishmen escaping the blitz in World

War II are conned and victimized by the wily, cunning, yet smooth-talking local Irishmen. On the more romantic side of the traditional stage Irishman, Ayamonn Breydon of *Red Roses for Me* (1943) is one of the playwright's more egregious examples of pure blarney, perhaps in this case not intended as comic exaggeration but coming across as an unintended parody of Irish verbal inflation.

O'Casey's men tend to be self-deluded fools or rogues. There is a singular absence of heroes, particularly in the famous plays. But there is no shortage of heroines, from Minnie Powell in *The Shadow of a Gunman* to the faithful Juno, suffering the follies of her family, to Bessie Burgess, standing like a rock of working-class common sense only to be cut down by a cruel fate.

The Shadow of a Gunman is set in May 1920 during the time of the Troubles (when the Irish became masters of hit-and-run and propaganda warfare and the English authorities looked increasingly ridiculous); *Juno and the Paycock* is set during the Irish Civil War in 1922 after the declaration of the Irish Free State; *The Plough and the Stars* is set during the Easter Rising when Padraic Pearse and other Irish leaders raised the Irish flag over the General Post Office in Dublin and Pearse proclaimed the existence of the Irish Republic. Great Britain, despite deep involvement in World War I, had to deal with the Irish. Using machines and weapons of war, the British crushed the rebellion and publicly executed most of its leaders. Those not executed became the leaders and planners of the Troubles and then of the Irish Civil War.

The O'Casey who brought a new audience to the theater and whose plays permitted the House Full sign to be used was a skilled craftsman, a satirist, and a humorist. Laughter and tears are never far apart, either in life or in O'Casey's plays, and O'Casey, the master humorist, uses laughter as a weapon to unmask and ridicule pretense and to attack evil in all its forms.

The Shadow of a Gunman, the writer's first major success, introduces one of his primary themes, the gap between patriotic rhetoric of the "Dyin' for Ireland" variety and the grim realities of political violence. This collision of romantic dream and tawdry and brutal fact runs through all three plays of the Dublin trilogy, but it is most solidly at the core of *Shadow*. The anti-hero, Donal Davoren, a poet and a dreamer in the Percy Shelley mold, finds himself in a working-class tenement where, by a chain of accidents, he is thought to be an IRA gunman.

Davoren is dubious at first about his fame and respect, but he soon finds that it suits his ego projections, especially when it involves the hero worshiping of the pretty Minnie Powell. Davoren's roommate, a lazy peddler named Seumas Shields, offers a comic and cynical commentary on the inflation and deflation of patriotic rhetoric and terrorist fact. Shields has brought into the room a sack of bombs that he is keeping for a *real* gunman. At the climax, Donal and Seumas are less than heroic, but Minnie sacrifices herself by taking the bombs, and she is killed.

This early play reveals O'Casey's ability to inhabit his stage with characters of great comic vitality. The canvas is less broad than *Juno* or *Plough*, but in the character of Davoren, the playwright draws something of a self-portrait, the imaginative man of literary ambitions pulled into a whirlpool of real political violence that he cannot shape or control.

Much of the humor is verbal. Shields is congenitally slovenly: "I don't think I need to wash myself this morning; do I look all right" (*Collected Plays*, 1, 97). He is contemptuous of Maguire, the IRA man on the run, and attributes to Maguire his own faults. Maguire is late, and just before he arrives Seumas proclaims him to be "almost too lazy to wash himself" (*Collected Plays*, 1, 98). He is also superstitious: "I knew things ud go wrong when I missed Mass this morning'" (*Collected Plays*, 1, 145).

Adolphus Grigson is an important coward and a drinker who never gets enough to drink. According to Mrs. Grigson, "No matter how much he may have taken, when he's taken more he'll always say, 'Here's the first to-day.'" She describes her husband as "far gone in the horns," "always fumblin'," and asks, when he misses curfew, "Do the insurance companies pay if a man is shot after curfew?" Mrs. Henderson describes Mr. Gallagher's letter "as good a letter as was decomposed by a scholar" (*Collected Plays*, 1, 116). The dramatist treats life in the inner city humorously, life that includes people who take themselves too seriously and death that comes unasked and, in the case of Minnie, undeserved.

In *Juno and the Paycock*, O'Casey presents his most memorable Dublin slum family. Headed by vainglorious, drunken (when he can be) "Captain" Jack Boyle, the family is a collection of disasters waiting to happen. Only Juno, the sorely tried mother, holds things together. She is there to mourn when she has to, to sustain her daughter when she is "ruined," and to bear up under the follies of her husband. Less overtly political than *Shadow* and *Plough*, *Juno* sets the comic antics and tragic destinies of the Boyle family in starkly parallel paths. The setting is the early years of Free State Government and IRA defiance of the Anglo-Irish Treaty. The son, Johnny Boyle, wounded in a nationalist struggle, has apparently betrayed a comrade and awaits, near the final curtain, the furies of an IRA execution squad.

The tragic emotion of the play centers on Juno, whose flaw is Greek in the simplicity of its hubris. She has not mourned the death of Mrs. Tancred's son, a "die-hard" who has resisted the treaty. When Juno's turn comes with the death of her son Johnny, she learns the ultimate futility of violence, and she sees how shallow her reaction was to the death of the other young man: "Maybe I didn't feel sorry enough for Mrs. Tancred when her poor son was found as Johnny's been found now—because he was a Die-hard! Ah, why didn't I remember that then he wasn't a Die-hard or a Stater, but only a poor dead son. . . . Sacred Heart o' Jesus, take away our heart o' stone, and give us hearts o' flesh! Take away this murdherin' hate, an' give us Thine own eternal love!"

The comic side of the drama is sustained by the goings on of Captain Boyle, whose legs, if not his back, prevent him from taking any of the jobs that well-meaning friends and the local priests are continually finding for him. Boyle is a classic case of a controlling illusion isolating a character from a cruel reality. He pretends to be the "Ancient Mariner" himself, though the only evidence of his seamanship from any reliable witness is that he made voyages to Liverpool on coal boats.

Following Boyle as a pilot fish, much like the clever ironic slave of Roman drama, is Joxer, whose function it is to echo the vainglorious monologues of his comrade and to feed the Captain cue lines to flesh out his heroic fantasies. Each of them has his own tag lines, and the play ends with a final reprise, or encore, of their favorite clichés. For Joxer, it is the ever-obliging, ever-cringing line, "D'jever rade Willie Reilly an' his own Colleen Bawn? It's a darlin' story, a daarlin' story." For the Captain, it is the portentous line, "I'm telling you, Joxer, the whole worl's in a terrible state o' chassis!" Although the pair seems to enact the roles of master and follower, Joxer is not stupid. He can echo the Captain's bombastic line, "What is the stars?" but he can also fire the line back at the Captain after he is temporarily rejected by his leader.

The engine of the comic side of the plot is the news that the Boyle's family penury is over, thanks to a bequest from a distant, wealthy relative. The Boyles believe themselves to have been the darlings of the gods, and the promise of money brings out the worst in them, changing their working-class directness and simplicity into petty bourgeois extravagance and pretension. The second act displays the folly, and the third act brings on the retribution. Mary is pregnant by a man who deserts her; Johnny is executed by his former comrades; Juno leaves the Captain. And, after Juno's great final speech (quoted above), the dramatist does something very daring. He works directly against the tragic emotion that he has aroused by bringing on the Captain and Joxer for one last drunken, comic romp. The effect is ambiguous: Is this a tragicomic comment on the folly of it all or, especially from the point of view of Dublin tenement dwellers, is it one last comic turn by these lovable fools?

Ultimately, O'Casey loved his carousing fools too much to subject them to a final ironic judgment. It is that doubleness of vision, the acceptance of human frailty on one side of the balance and the protest against the cruelty of evil social conditions, which gives his best plays their sometimes bewilderingly rich texture.

In *Juno and the Paycock*, O'Casey uses stock characters: the universal mother (Juno), braggart soldier (Captain Jack), wronged daughter (Mary), parasite (Joxer), and others. Again, the humor is largely, but not entirely, verbal. Reflecting his parasitical role, Joxer utters every line as a cliché or the repetition of something just said by another character, as in "When the cat's away, the mice can play!" (*Collected Plays*, 1, 10), "Wanse bitten twice shy," and "Ah, affter all, an honest man's the noblest work o' God." Joxer's favorite adjective is "darlin'" or "daaarlin'," as in darlin' man, darlin' thing, or—for emphasis—"Ah, a cup o' tay's a darlin' thing, a daaarlin' thing."

Captain Boyle, Joxer's "oul' butty," claims "pains in me legs," "a little pride left in me still," and joins the establishment when he thinks that he has gotten an inheritance. He becomes greatly concerned for his reputation and is the moralistic, vindictive father when he learns that Mary is pregnant. "Amn't I afther goin' through enough without havin' to go through this!" Then, when he realizes that there is no inheritance after all, he observes, "The boyo that's afther doin' it to Mary done it to me as well."

O'Casey's humor is not used in an attempt to hide the terrible destruction wrought by people at war. In a strangely effective way, the humor of the slums emphasizes the carnage, as sons lose hips and arms, are killed and buried, or executed for treason; it also lends a continuing emphasis to human nature as survivors acclimate to what is left for them.

Juno is the voice for the major concern, for the main theme of the play. With her son dead, she observes, "These things have nothing to do with the Will o' God. Ah, what can God do agen the stupidity o' men!" (*Collected Plays*, 1, 86).

In some ways *The Plough and the Stars* is the most ambitious, powerful, and perhaps puzzling O'Casey play in its effect. The plot is composed of the actions of those living in one tenement in the time up to and during the Easter Monday uprising. Jack Clitheroe is an officer in the Irish Citizen Army; his wife Nora is deeply opposed to his paramilitary activities. In the turmoil of the rising, Jack is killed and Nora, after miscarrying, goes mad. In the Dublin plays, one can usually expect the most fervent patriots to turn out to be windbags or worse. "Dying for Ireland" is the besetting rhetorical sin of such people; at the first hint of violence, bravado usually turns to revulsion and cowardice.

Among the characters, the middle-class aspirations (or uppitiness) of the Clitheroes is matched by the working-class antics of Fluther Good (the carpenter), Bessie Burgess (the loudmouth loyalist), and Jinny Gogan (a Catholic antagonist of Bessie's, with a babe in one hand and a ball of malt in the other).

The main force of O'Casey's play tends toward exposing the suicidal folly of the nationalist rebels. Jack's participation in the Citizen Army is presented as mainly a matter of personal vanity and ambition, and he is not alone. The charge is made that one of the major forces keeping the rising in motion is the fear of being branded a coward, an unrebutted charge. And, what do the "Plain People of Ireland" do after the rebellion breaks out? On the street that

O'Casey offers as a microcosm, the uppermost urge of Fluther and Bessie is to loot. The ultimate irony of the play is that loyalist Bessie is shot by a British soldier who thinks she is a sniper. The drama's final image is of a group of British soldiers brewing tea and singing "Keep the 'Ome Fires Burning" as Dublin burns in the background.

As one might imagine, many things in this play did not sit well with men and women who had been involved in the struggle just ten years earlier, an event that had been inflated into the major turning point in modern Irish history. The spark that set off the rioting at the Abbey Theatre was a memorable scene in act 2 in which a nationalist speaker delivers a violent speech praising the shedding of blood while within a pub we see considerably less heroic goings-on—a whore plying her trade and loud and vulgar brawls. The speaker is modeled on Pearse, and the words calling for blood are indeed those of a well-known utterance by Pearse, a leader of the uprising and one of those shot by the British. Then Clitheroe and a comrade come into the pub to slake their thirst, bringing with them the flag of the Citizen Army, the plough and the stars. This presumed desecration set off the rioting.

This play has entered the canon of masterpieces of modern Irish drama and now has enormous impact for Irish audiences who no longer look for one-sided versions of their national past. Even so, the play lacks an ideological base; in the midst of raving patriots, ordinary people turned looters, and sane British tommies trying to survive, what would have been a *proper* reaction to the uprising? By the end of the play, we are offered many extremes but little middle, not even Yeats's ambiguous "A terrible beauty is born."

Here, as earlier, the humor is mostly, though not entirely, verbal. The cowering postures and Minnie's immature romanticism in *The Shadow of a Gunman* and the procession of gramophone, clothes, and other material goods in *Juno* are humorous. The prepared shopping lists, the use of prams, and Mrs. Gogan's search for Cuban shoes with pointy heels during the looting scenes in *The Plough and the Stars* are hilarious, almost hysterical, in view of the carnage around the characters and the poverty in which the looters live.

O'Casey also uses the standard fare of earlier and later Irish comedy: the drinker's recurrent temperance pledge. Fluther says, "No more dhrink for Fluther. It's three days now since I've touched a dhrop, an' I feel a new man already." Yet, when he feels dizzy, he said, "I hope I didn't give up th' beer too suddenly." On a darker note, when Fluther is urged to "spread that out, an' thry to keep a sup for to-morrow," he responds, "Spread it out? Keep a sup for to-morrow? How th' hell does a fella know there'll be any tomorrow? If I'm goin' to be whipped away, let me be whipped away when it's empty, an' not when it's half full!" Another stock subject in Irish drama is religion and Fluther observes, "I think we ought to have as great a regard for religion as we can, so as to keep it out of as many things as possible" (*Collected Plays*, 1, 170).

On nationality, Covey says, "There's no such thing as an Irishman, or an Englishman, or a German or a Turk; we're all only human bein's. Scientifically speakin', it's all a question of the accidental gatherin' together of mollycewels an' atoms" (*Collected Plays*, 1, 170).

The Plough and the Stars brought laborers, revolutionaries, and rioters to the Abbey Theater. The rioters said that they were opposed to the references to sexual immorality though, so far as O'Casey was concerned, they rioted because he satirized the motives and the performances of national heroes during Easter Week. Yeats tried to speak reasonably to the Irish ("You have disgraced yourselves again") but O'Casey decided to leave Ireland. He later described the riots at the Abbey and his decision in *Inishfallen, Fare Thee Well*, volume 4 of his autobiography.

With *The Plough and the Stars* O'Casey left, for the most part, the Dublin world of his youth and early manhood as subject matter. In all those years, from 1926 to *The Drums of Father Ned* (which was withdrawn from production in 1958), O'Casey wrote plays on a wide variety of subject matter and modes of treatment and saw them produced under varied circumstances.

From his beginnings as a dramatist, he was an experimenter, testing his own mastery as a craftsman and stretching the limits of existing dramaturgical devices. The plays immediately following *The Plough and the Stars* are not particularly noted for their humor. *The Silver Tassie*, an expressionistic anti-war play of deadly seriousness, was rejected by Yeats largely because he thought that the author's feelings about the Great War lacked the authenticity of his reactions to recent Irish history. This controversy led O'Casey to break with the Abbey and ultimately with Ireland. *The Silver Tassie* presents symbolically and dramatically O'Casey's commitment to life but includes little of the humor that gives vitality to his Irish plays. *Within the Gates* (1933) is expressionist poetic drama in mode and Shavian in its efforts to talk about a myriad of world problems. It is a sequel to *The Silver Tassie*, a morality play about humankind's quest from beginning to end. Some of the characters are defeated, beaten, or fragmented in one way or another (the down-and-outs, attendants, evangelists, and arguers). Others (the bishop, the dreamer, and the young whore) reveal the basic theme of *Within the Gates* to be a "cry for vigorous and effective life" ("The Cutting of an Agate," p. 48). *Within the Gates* is not a lighthearted play, and there is little humor, except in the irony of circumstance.

The Star Turns Red is the writer's most Marxist play, a paean of praise to a labor organizer, the character "Red Jim," based on James Larkin, who attempted to organize the Dublin Transport Workers. Such movements and the events of the famous general strike and lockout of 1913 serve as background to the touching *Red Roses for Me*, in some ways the later O'Casey's most effective return to his mid-1920s manner and subject.

In *Red Roses for Me*, however, the dramatist moves further in his experimental quest and the play contains expressionistic and symbolic, as well as fantastic, elements. Action begets miracles. Down-and-outs are momentarily transformed into vital, concerned people. As in earlier plays, O'Casey's sardonic sense of humor is the foundation for every line of dialogue. The play itself is a gallery of portraits—all satiric. In an essay, "St. Patrick's Day in the Morning" (*The Green Crow*, p. 219), O'Casey describes the sardonic sense of humor as "the only thing we Irish have in full measure." Ayamonn Breydon, the labor strike leader, is a twenty-two-year-old poet and Protestant martyr, always serious. Using the power of the word, he does effect transformations, yet he has little time for humor.

Mrs. Breydon, his mother, has a better sense of perspective. Of her son's romantic relationship with Sheila, Mrs. Breydon observes, "The bigger half of Ireland would say that a man's way with a maid must be regulated by his faith an' hers, an' the other half by the way her father makes his living" (*Collected Plays*, 3,

134). O'Casey argues on several occasions that every marriage should be mixed—one woman and one man. The Catholic-Protestant touchstone is further tested by the Protestant, Brennan o' the Moor, who argues with his zealous Irish Catholic friend, Roory O'Balacaun: "I refuse to argue with a one who's no' a broad-minded mon. Abuse is no equivalent for lugic—so I say God save th' King, an' tae hull with th' Pope!" (*Collected Plays*, 3, 167). In this drama O'Casey continues to explore and refine the advantages of expressionism and fantasy and symbolic techniques.

O'Casey seems to have held the socialist view that whatever changes in political power were achieved by Irish independence, a social revolution was *not* achieved. The dominance of the Roman Catholic Church in post-treaty Ireland is one of the writer's favorite subjects, most obviously from World War II onward.

Two other full-length plays deserve attention for the humor that molds them. They are *Purple Dust* and *Cock-a-Doodle Dandy*. In *Purple Dust*, England's empire is represented by a crumbling Tudor mansion, and its people are represented by Cyril Poges and Basil Stoke, named after Stoke Poges, the country churchyard that occasioned Thomas Gray's "Elegy Written in a Country Churchyard" and that, aptly, includes his remains. Poges and Stoke are incapable of direct action and assume that they can "muddle through." They do not see clearly or hear well and are inept and impotent, as well as English. They cannot start fires but they spout frequent and recurrent cliché's about efficiency, modernism, and the backwardness of the Irish. Living in Ireland, they have lusty young women whom they lose, along with their investment, to the rural Irish men who *can* start fires and ride horses. When O'Casey attacks—with humor—any enemy, nothing is held back. In this morality play/farce/fantasy, a cow is mistaken for a bull and is shot, and a giant roller purchased for leveling the lawn goes out of control, crashing through the wall of the already crumbling mansion. When Poges questions, "Where the hell did that bull come from? Who owns her?" (*Collected Plays*, 3, 58), O'Casey's reference to John Bull is obvious. The Englishmen are gulls and fools, though in their own minds they are inherently and permanently superior to the primitive Irish.

In this juxtaposition the rural Irish are free, vital, and more concerned with the living present than the dead past. O'Killigain, a stone-mason, is a representative rural Irishman whose very name relates directly to the profit motives of Poges and Stoke. The humor of the play is both surface and deep. It is both slapstick and satiric. It bolsters the dramatist's thematic element, vividly presented by the second Workman (obviously Irish):

> There is sweet music in the land, but not for the deaf; there is wisdom too, but it is not in a desk it is, but out in th' hills, an' in the life of all things rovin' round, undher th' blue sky.

The Tudor mansion, a microcosm of the British Empire, is decrepit when the play begins. By the final curtain, all aspects of British power (cows, enterprising hens, startling cocks, bathrooms, antiques, and efficiency experts) have disappeared or have self-destructed. O'Casey appropriately subtitles *Purple Dust* "A Wayward Comedy in Three Acts."

Cock-a-Doodle Dandy, the author's favorite play, is his comic paean to the goodness of the sexual urge in the face of clerical Puritanism. The work is dedicated to James Stephens, another Irish humorist: "the jesting poet/with a radiant star/in's coxcomb." By the end of the play, Nyadnanave, the setting for the play, is turned upside down and left to the lifeless and dying. This drama, like several of O'Casey's earlier works, is a morality play and we can see ourselves and many whom we know in the various roles. As is fairly traditional in morality plays, the scenes are set progressively (morning, midday, dusk). As is also traditional, the world is microcosmic and the characters are stock characters.

In *Cock-a-Doodle Dandy* the playwright goes beyond the surreal and distorted and fantastic of *The Silver Tassie*, *Within the Gates*, and *Red Roses for Me*. He uses magic, magic that is slapstick humor at its best: religious pictures are turned to the wall; beautiful, sexy women grow devilish horns; a whiskey bottle is demonized; a hat walks; chairs collapse; geese or ducks or something transports fools away; and the hat-cock confusion becomes increasingly hilarious.

The villains and members of the establishment are basically stock villains: the religious quack (Shanaar), the life-killing priest (Father Domineer), the half-witted and half-blind (One-Eyed Larry), and the landowners and employers. These are juxtaposed with the Cock and his followers. The Cock is a mature poet, a leader, and a magician with the power of the word. His followers include Maid Marion, Robin Adair, and Loreleen. These good characters recognize that dance and song and joy are healing. They know that life is possible only for the young and the vital. Loreleen is singled out by the villains as a sinful slut, honeyed harlot, painted paramour, and shuttlecock of sin. Father Domineer refers to her "rosy rottenness of sin."

In a wonderfully ironic yielding to the powers of Domineer and the establishment, O'Casey's characters agree that if song and dance and joy and life are devil inspired, then "th' devil's not a bad fella either." This clearly anticipates the writer's later play, *The Drums of Father Ned*, wherein Father Ned (Devil) calls us to song, dance, joy, and life.

Despite the slapstick and verbal humor here, O'Casey is an angry artist. Each of the three scenes ends on a chilling note: act 1 in a mockery of ritual, sending Julia off to Lourdes to be cured; act 2 with Father Domineer striking and killing the truck driver who wanted to be with his maid; and act 3 with the revelers and life-givers being expelled from Nyadnanave.

Certainly, O'Casey continues his use of humor and satire in later plays, but the techniques are not particularly changed or modified. Microcosm becomes "Mickrocosm" and Father Ned becomes the symbol of life and caring and freedom. In *Bedtime Story*, a one-act masterpiece, Angela Nightingale represents vitality and the ability to survive. Her customer, John Jo Mulligan, is static and "constitutionally frightened." He, like the Tudor mansion in *Purple Dust*, has been reduced to total absurdity by the end of the play. Every symbol of his manhood has been taken by the wily Angela. The humor is delicious, but nothing new is used by the author.

The Bishop's Bonfire (1955) marked O'Casey's return to the Dublin stage after many decades, and his attack on what he regarded as clerical dominance aroused much of the old fury and controversy. Some Irish commentators faulted the playwright's later dramas for being "out of touch" with Irish life; O'Casey's heated replies to his critics fueled a long series of controversies. The drama is about the battle between life and death and the humor is increasingly darker. The young leave Ireland. The establishment fears art and would destroy it while simultaneously denying censoring it. Thematically, all places are sacred and those will survive who can mock their oppressors.

In *The Drums of Father Ned*, the beat of the drums is that of the human heart, the pulse beat of life. Those in charge would restrict or destroy youth and life. The drumbeats urge change and rebellion against the strictures and the lethargy of the establishment, perfectly personified by the Reverend D. Fillifogue. The theme is clearly stated by Nora McGilligan, who is running for an elective office against Bennington, an ally of Fillifogue:

> [We are fighting] Oh, not against our
>   fathers!
> We're fighting what is old and stale and
>   vicious:
> the hate, the meanness their policies
>   preach;
> and to make a way for the young and
>   thrusting. (*Drums of Father Ned*,
>   81, 82)

This statement is a fitting summary of the major theme in O'Casey's canon from beginning to end.

O'Casey was always a humorist, always a satirist, always a vigilant, angry artist lashing out against those who would destroy life, either literally or by repressing the human spirit. In his war plays, in the ongoing battle between warriors and survivors, his choice is obviously that of the "congenital pacifist" who knows the pain and sorrow and loss of the survivors. In the battle between past and present, he would destroy museums and build playing fields or libraries. The status quo is never sacred in his writing, and rituals and traditions must be questioned; nothing should be taken at face value. As a result, opinions range from the belief that just about everything that he did is defensible as showing marks of genius to the criticism that he was a seriously flawed artist, lacking in self-criticism and suffering from self-indulgent lapses in taste.

In any case, O'Casey's wonderful sense of humor informed every line that he wrote. His autobiographies, short stores, essays, poems, songs, and letters are as open, direct, and exciting as his plays. For the most part, people who know O'Casey's work praise the three Irish plays that by themselves are sufficient to earn him a permanent niche in theater's hall of fame.

Summary

The high critical reputation of Sean O'Casey's best plays has remained firm, and he is still widely regarded as one of the major figures of the Irish literary revival. But, outside the plays that are thought to be his best (largely the Dublin trilogy), controversy swirls. That he gave memorable expression to the life of Dublin's poor during one of his country's most explosive decades and that he created some unforgettable comic characters is undisputed. His tragicomic mode of expression helped push further from the center the rigid separation of the serious and the comedic.

Selected Bibliography

Primary Sources

Plays

Collected Plays. Vol. 1. London: Macmillan, 1963. Includes *Juno and the Paycock, The Shadow of a Gunman, The Plough and the Stars, The End of the Beginning,* and *A Pound on Demand.*

Collected Plays. Vol. 2. London: Macmillan, 1959. Includes *The Silver Tassie, Within the Gates,* and *The Star Turns Red.*

Collected Plays. Vol. 3. London: Macmillan, 1962. Includes *Purple Dust, Red Roses for Me,* and *Hall of Healing.*

Collected Plays. Vol. 4. London: Macmillan, 1958. Includes *Oak Leaves and Lavender, Cock-a-Doodle Dandy, Bed Time Story,* and *Time to Go.*

Five One-Act Plays. London: Macmillan, 1958. Includes *The End of the Beginning, A Pound on Demand, Hall of Healing, Bedtime Story,* and *Time to Go.*

The Drums of Father Ned. London: Macmillan, 1960.

The Bishop's Bonfire. London: Macmillan, 1961.

Three Plays by Sean O'Casey. London: Macmillan, 1961. Includes *Behind the Green Curtain, Figuro in the Night,* and *The Moon Shines on Kylenamoe.*

Three Plays: Juno and the Paycock, The Shadow of a Gunman, The Plough and the Stars. New York: St. Martin's Press, 1966.

The Harvest Festival. New York: Harcourt, Brace, Jovanovich, 1979.

Seven Plays by Sean O'Casey: A Students' Edition. Ed. Ronald Ayling. London: Macmillan, 1985.

Autobiographies

Mirror in My House: The Autobiographies of Sean O'Casey. New York: Macmillan, 1956. 2 vols.

I Knock at the Door. New York: Macmillan, 1960.

Pictures in the Hallway. New York: Macmillan, 1960.

Drums Under the Windows. New York: Macmillan, 1960.

Inishfallen, Fare Thee Well. New York: Macmillan, 1960.

Rose and Crown. New York: Macmillan, 1961.

Sunset and Evening Star. New York: Macmillan, 1961.

Essays and Miscellaneous

Windfalls: Stories, Poems, and Plays. London: Macmillan, 1934. Includes short stories "I Wanna Woman," "The Star Jazzer," "The Job," and "A Fall in a Gentle Wind."

The Flying Wasp. London, Macmillan, 1937. This is also included in *The Green Crow.*

The Green Crow. New York: George Braziller, 1956.

Feathers From the Green Crow. Ed. Robert Hogan. Columbia: University of Missouri Press, 1962.

Under a Colored Cap. New York: St. Martin's Press, 1963.

Blasts and Benedictions, Articles and Stories. Ed. Ronald Ayling. New York: St. Martin's Press, 1967.

The Sting and the Twinkle: Conversations with Sean O'Casey. Ed. E.H. Mikhail and John O'Riordan. New York: Barnes and Noble, 1974.

The Letters of Sean O'Casey. Ed. David Krause. Vol. 1, 1910–1941. New York: Macmillan, 1975; vol. 2, 1942–1954, New York: Macmillan, 1980; vol. 3, 1955–1958, Washington, DC: Catholic University of America Press, 1989; vol. 4, 1959–1964, Washington, DC: Catholic University of America Press, 1992.

Secondary Sources

Bibliographies

Ayling, Ronald and Michael J. Durkan. *Sean O'Casey, A Bibliography.* London: Macmillan, and Seattle: University of Washington Press, 1978. Details of composition as well as publication of O'Casey's works and lists of reviews are given.

Mikhail, E.H. *Sean O'Casey: A Bibliography of Criticism.* London: Macmillan, 1972.

Biographies

Fallon, Gabriel. *Sean O'Casey: The Man I Knew.* Boston: Little, Brown, 1965.

Krause, David. *Sean O'Casey: The Man and His Work.* London: MacGibbon and Kee, and New York: Macmillan, 1960; New York: Macmillan, 1975. One of the first full-length studies of O'Casey's work; Krause combines biography and full-scale critical analysis. One of the leading O'Casey scholars, Krause tends to make sound aesthetic judgments, with a decided sympathy for the author.

_____. *A Self-Portrait of the Artist as a Man.* Ireland: Dolmen Press, 1968.

_____. *Sean O'Casey and His World.* London: Thames and Hudson, 1976.

O'Casey, Eileen. *Sean.* Ed. J.C. Trewin. London: Macmillan, 1971; New York: Coward McCann & Geoghogan, 1972. Touching and intimate account of the playwright by his actress wife.

O'Connor, Garry. *Sean O'Casey, A Life.* New York: Atheneum, 1988. A full-length account, replete with fascinating details about O'Casey's life and his encounters with friends, foes, theatrical collaborators, and critics.

Criticism

Armstrong, W.A. *Experimental Drama.* London: G. Bell, 1963.

Atkinson, Brooks. *Sean O'Casey: From Times Past.* Ed. Robert G. Lowery. London: Macmillan, 1982.

Ayling, Ronald, ed. *Modern Judgments: Sean O'Casey.* Nashville: Aurora, 1985.

_____. *O'Casey: The Dublin Trilogy.* London: Macmillan, 1985.

Benstock, Bernard. *Sean O'Casey.* Lewisburg: Bucknell University Press, 1970.

_____. *Paycocks and Others: Sean O'Casey's World.* New York: Barnes and Noble, 1976.

Cowasjee, Saros. *Sean O'Casey: The Man Behind the Plays.* London: Oliver & Boyd, 1963.

Hogan, Robert. *The Experiments of Sean O'Casey.* New York: St. Martin's Press, 1960. Hogan, an expert on modern Irish drama, explains the many turns in O'Casey's style and dramaturgy after the mainly realistic plays of the Dublin trilogy.

Hogan, Robert and Richard Burnham. *The Years of O'Casey, 1921–1926: A Documentary History.* Gerrards Cross, Bucks: Colin Smythe, and Newark: University of Delaware Press, 1992. Vol. 6 of the Modern Irish Drama Series. An exhaustive account of the Dublin theatrical scene, and especially the Abbey Theater, during the years 1921 to 1926. The authors present, with commentary, evidence from these years in the form of press criticism, reports of conversations, and letters to newspapers. While O'Casey gives his name to these years, all drama in Dublin and elsewhere in Ireland is within the purview of this volume.

Howarth, Herbert. *The Irish Writers, 1880–1940.* London: Rockliff, 1958.

Koslow, Jules. *The Green and the Red: Sean O'Casey, the Man and His Plays.* New York: Golden Griffin Books, 1950.

Kosok, Heinz. *O'Casey the Dramatist.* Gerrards Cross, Bucks: Colin Smythe, and Totoway, NJ: Barnes and Noble, 1989. Irish Literary Studies 19. In this analysis of all O'Casey's plays, the critic tries to focus the attention on the plays themselves, on their individual qualities, and he tries to avoid the partisan bickering of opposing schools of O'Casey scholars, especially regarding the more controversial aspects of O'Casey's life and opinions.

Kosok, Heinz and Robert G. Lowery, eds. *Sean O'Casey Centenary Studies.* Gerrards Cross: Colin Smythe, 1980. Irish Literary Studies 7. Essays on a wide range of topics by leading O'Casey scholars. Contributions cover O'Casey's relationship with James Joyce, Yeats, Lady Gregory, and George Bernard Shaw, as well as background studies of O'Casey and the Abbey Theater and Irish history and politics. Robert Lowery, one of the most assiduous of O'Casey scholars, contributes a chronology of O'Casey's life as well as a record of performances of the author's plays at the Abbey Theater.

Lowery, Robert G. *The Sean O'Casey Review, Volumes One Through Eight.* New York: Holbrook, 1974–1982.

O

_____. *Essays on Sean O'Casey's Autobiographies*. Totowa, NJ: Barnes and Noble, 1981.

_____. *O'Casey Annual No. 1* through *O'Casey Annual No. 4*. London: Macmillan, 1982–1985.

_____. *Sean O'Casey's Autobiographies: An Annotated Index*. Westport, CT: Greenwood, 1983. Extremely helpful. Lowery guides us to specifics in O'Casey's autobiographies and includes helpful identifications, definitions, and commentary.

Mercier, Vivian. *The Irish Comic Tradition*. Oxford: Clarendon Press, 1962.

Mikhail, E.N. *Sean O'Casey and His Critics*. Metuchen, NJ: Scarecrow, 1985.

O'Riordan, John. *A Guide to O'Casey's Plays*. London: Macmillan, 1984. Macmillan Studies in Anglo-Irish Literature. Enthusiastic discussion of O'Casey's plays, with especially interesting comments on the plays' stage histories.

Smith, B.L. *O'Casey's Satiric Vision*. Kent, OH: Kent State University Press, 1978.

Staley, Thomas, ed. *James Joyce Quarterly: O'Casey Issue*. Tulsa, OK: University Press, 1970.

John P. Frayne and Bobby L. Smith

O'Nolan, Brian (Flann O'Brien; Myles na Gopaleen)

Born: Strabane, County Tyrone, Ireland, October 5, 1911

Education: At home until 1923; Christian Brothers School, Dublin, 1923–1927; Blackrock College, 1927–1929; University College, Dublin, B.A., 1932; M.A., 1935

Marriage: Evelyn McDonnell, December 2, 1948

Died: Dublin, April 1, 1966

Biography

Brian O'Nolan was born on October 5, 1911, in Strabane, County Tyrone, Ireland, the third of twelve children and the third son of Michael O'Nolan and Agnes Gormley. Brian's father, a customs and excise officer in the employ of the English government, was enough of an Irish nationalist that he insisted that Irish be spoken by the family, and the children were educated at home until Brian was twelve years old.

The children did, certainly, learn English—their mother did not speak Irish and they played with English-speaking children—and when his father was transferred, after several interim moves, to Dublin's Inland Revenue office after the establishment of the Irish Free State in 1922, the boys were at last sent to school. His father's choice of the Christian Brothers School in Synge Street, Dublin, was an unfortunate one, if O'Nolan's later reminiscences are to be trusted; he speaks of "brutality and degradation" and of the teachers as not simply "sadists, brutes, psychotics" but as actual criminals. He spent five unhappy years there, until in 1927 the family moved again, this time to Blackrock. Brian was happy in his final years at Blackrock College (1927–1929).

His university years at University College, Dublin (he received a B.A. in 1932 and an M.A. in 1935) were happy, though in later years he expressed only contempt for the quality of the education that he received. It was in this period that his brilliance as a humorist and satirist began to evidence itself, and it is worth noting that among his contemporaries there were many fine minds that would later distinguish themselves in Irish letters. He was so successful as a campus wit and debater that it is hardly an exaggeration to say that everything in his later life seemed to him anticlimactic, his early brilliant promise never achieved. He became a prominent member of an important campus institution, the Literary and Historical Society, and he won a gold medal for impromptu debate. His memorable contribution in debate was not so much in the political astuteness of his ideas as in the fact that he saw through the absurdities and pretensions of both sides. In short, from the beginning his was the satirist's stance.

O'Nolan was well-known as one of the literary undergraduates. The college magazine *Comhthrom Feinne* published articles by him, in both Irish and English, under the first of his many pseudonyms, Brother Barnabas, and he founded his own short-lived magazine, *Blather*. He wrote a parodic epic in Old Irish that was rumored to be obscene; since not even his professors knew as much Old Irish as he did, however, he escaped punishment. He took a master's degree, writing his thesis on nature poetry in Irish. Even at this stage, then, it was evident that his interests were in parody and fantasy, a talent brilliantly exhibited in 1939 in his first published work, the novel *At Swim-Two-Birds*.

By this time O'Nolan had been working in the Irish civil service for four years, an employment that continued until his retirement after fourteen more years in 1953. He was an efficient and diligent if not particularly enthusiastic civil servant, serving as private secretary to four ministers and finally becoming the chief officer for town planning. On December 2, 1948, he married Evelyn McDonnell, a typist in the Department of Local Government in which he was working. He retired from the Civil Service in 1953 for reasons that are unclear, though it is apparent that he left with no friendly feeling for the service.

O'Nolan's literary output falls naturally into two parts: he was the author of six novels (not all published in his lifetime), an uncompleted novel, three plays, and some television scripts; and he also wrote a popular column, *Cruiskeen Lawn* (Gaelic for "my full little jug"— from a traditional drinking song), which ran regularly in the *Irish Times* from 1940 to 1966.

It was in fact the *Times* column, rather than what he considered his more serious work, that made O'Nolan, known affectionately throughout the city as Myles, one of the prominent figures of the Dublin literary scene of his day, and this seeming rejection of his novels was not easy for him to accept. The initial success of *At Swim-Two-Birds* made the failure of his later novels even more bitter. *The Third Policeman*, completed in 1940 and in its way as good as *At Swim-Two-Birds* though without the hilarity of its predecessor, did not find a publisher until 1967, a year after his death, for he was so wounded by its initial rejection that he put the manuscript away and claimed that it was lost.

His single novel in Gaelic, *An Beal Bocht*, attained a small amount of success in 1941 but did not receive an English translation (by Patrick Power, as *The Poor Mouth*) until 1973, half a dozen years after O'Nolan's death. Three plays, *Faustus Kelly*, *The Insect Play*, and *Thirst*, were produced in Dublin in 1943, but were followed by a long period of frustration. Not until 1960, when *At Swim* was reissued to some critical acclaim, did he begin serious work again. Two lesser novels, *The Hard Life* (1961) and *The Dalkey Archive* (1964, a reworking of some of his favorite parts of *The Third Policeman*), were published and *A Bash in the Tunnel* was completed but not published; *Slattery's Sago Saga*, in outline by the end of 1964, remained uncompleted at the time of his death.

At the same time, he was producing his newspaper columns for the *Irish Times*. He began writing these in Gaelic, alternated Gaelic, and English for several years, then wrote entirely in English. These columns, written under the pseudonym Myles na Gopaleen, were known to most people in Dublin. (The pseudonym was borrowed from a popular nineteenth-century play by Dion Boucicault and means "Myles of the Ponies.") During his last years, he severed his connection with the *Times*, but despite ill health he continued writing, placing columns where he could in provincial newspapers.

Those last years of his life were not happy. He suffered from ill health and he drank too much (as, indeed, he had for years). His small pension from the government was not quite enough to live on, and he was constantly seeking employment or literary assignments. He wrote, not very successfully, for television in the years after 1961, including a series for the popular Irish comic Jimmy O'Dea. He died of cancer in a Dublin hospital on April 1, 1966.

Literary Analysis

O'Nolan's writing was all done pseudonymously. In his years as a member of the civil service in Dublin he sometimes signed his name as Nolan; in his student years he sometimes used the Gaelic version of his name, Brian O Nuaillain; in his major writing he employed two pseudonyms: for his novels, Flann O'Brien; for his newspaper columns, Myles na Gopaleen. Most men spend their lives under a single name: ought anything be read into this multiple naming?

Certainly one reason for the author's use of pseudonyms was the fact of his being essentially a very shy, sensitive, and private person, according to the testimony of his friends. But, it also seems to be the case that O'Nolan was preoccupied with the problem of identity all of his life. Such a preoccupation has been a regular part of the Irish experience; for centuries the country was occupied and ruled by the alien power of England, the Irish forbidden to use their own language, their own religion, their own names. Thus, although identity is not a direct theme in O'Nolan's writing, it perhaps underlies much of his preoccupation with scientific paradoxes: the dizzying meditation "Who am I?" too much indulged in leading to "Where am I?" and even, in *The Third Policeman*, "What am I, man or bicycle?"

It was during the vulnerable period of childhood that the questioning of identity might well have begun. Though County Tyrone is one of the six counties of Northern Ireland, the town of

Strabane itself lies on the border between them and the Republic of Ireland. Was he, then, Northerner or Southerner? Well, strictly, geographically speaking, Northerner. Still, he was born into a Catholic family and was thus more like a Southerner. However, his father worked as a customs and excise officer for the British crown and was thus Northerner. But, his father, though not a fanatically active nationalist, did insist that Gaelic be spoken at home—thus again a Southerner. The experience of being taught at home, pleasant though the freedom that it gave the boys was, served further, of course, to distance Brian from ordinary children. It is no wonder that he used several names.

O'Nolan's genius is particularly evident in two aspects of his writing: in parody and in the wildly fantastic. His sense of the pretentious or the ridiculous was unfailing, and he had utterly perfect pitch for reproducing the Irish voice in conversation. He was a fine linguist, competent in several languages, and his interest in language is evident in his fondness for wordplay of all kinds, particularly puns and malapropisms; it is also seen in his hatred of clichés, which misuse language by employing it without thought.

All of these talents are exhibited in *At Swim-Two-Birds* in which the various layers of the novel serve to unsettle the reader's notions of reality in what has long been seen as a typically Irish characteristic: the refusal to accept only scientific fact as fact. In the novel, O'Nolan also offers parodies of such widely divergent forms as the ancient Irish sagas and American Wild West stories. The title derives from the adventures of Mad King Sweeny, one of the characters in the novel. According to ancient Irish legend, in his madness Sweeny flies from tree to tree about Ireland; *At Swim-Two-Birds* is one of the places that he visits.

At Swim presents the first-person narrative of a college student, never named, who is writing a novel about a novelist named Dermot Trellis who is writing a novel, and the volume is at least as complicated as that brief description suggests. Trellis has a theory that characters ought not to have to be created anew for each novel. Indeed, most of his characters are borrowed or hired from other novelists.

It was also the narrator-hero's contention—and O'Nolan's as well—that it was not the novel's purpose to compel the reader's belief or to force characters to be all good or all bad. Characters should be allowed to have a private life and some say in their own destinies.

Trellis's characters rebel against him while he is asleep on the grounds that he is causing them to do immoral things, and they take him prisoner; this is another story within a story. Still another is the story written by Trellis's illegitimate son Orlick, born as the result of the rape of one of his own characters by Dermot Trellis. In Orlick's story, Dermot is made to suffer unspeakable torments as punishment for his dreadful deed.

O'Nolan's fascination with the supernatural and the Other-world, seen first in *At Swim-Two-Birds* (among the characters are the Good Fairy and the Pooka Fergus MacPhellimey, "by calling a devil") and subsequently in each of his other novels as well, is very Irish. The native Gaelic literature of Ireland—and it is a very old literature—is permeated from the earliest sagas and tales with wonders and magic. The nature of reality eludes definition; anything can happen; impossibilities abound. (The story of Mad Sweeny is just one example of many.)

The Third Policeman offers readers bicycles and their riders that exchange atomic particles over the years until it becomes more and more difficult to tell whether we are dealing with a man or a bicycle. We have to suspect that the transformation is far along when a man is frequently seen leaning with one elbow against a wall or standing propped by one foot at the curb. We have in the same book a spear with the point so thin as to be invisible and a nest of wondrously-wrought boxes most of which are too small to be seen even with the strongest magnifying glass.

Perhaps the greatest wonder in *The Hard Life*, O'Nolan's fourth novel, is the Gravid Water patented by the narrator's enterprising brother Manus, a young man rich in schemes (often bizarre) for making money. The Gravid Water has the miraculous property of curing rheumatism; unfortunately, the directions are misunderstood, the patient takes three times as much as he should, and he gains weight until he weighs over 400 pounds. What is extraordinary is that he remains the same in outward appearance.

Related to the fantasy and wonder of these incredible tales are the mad scientists of such books as *The Third Policeman* and *The Dalkey Archive*. Zany theories and inventions abound. *The Third Policeman*'s de Selby, who believes that traveling from place to place or even living a hallucination, is closely related to *The Dalkey Archive*'s almost identically named De Selby, who has invented a time machine that enables him to speak to such figures of the past as St. Augustine.

All of O'Nolan's novels gain a part of their humor from his fascination with what might be called the possibilities of infinity. In *The Third Policeman*, particularly, the mad scientist de Selby sets up mirrors in such a way that they reflect backward to infinity; by means of a powerful magnifying glass he claims to have made out his own reflection at the age of twelve. Policeman MacCruiskeen's infinitesimally small boxes are another version of this, as is his ability to hear musical notes inaudible to the human "earcup."

O'Nolan also frequently employs parody. Concurrently, with the convoluted plot of *At Swim-Two-Birds* he presents a brilliant parody of the ancient saga of the Irish hero Finn MacCool in which the novelist's thorough familiarity with both the style and the content of the old tales is manifest. He also parodies American cowboy tales, showing cowboys undergoing typical western adventures in the city of Dublin.

Experimentation with the standard forms of narration was continued in *The Third Policeman*, where again there is a first-person narrator. In this case O'Nolan takes an even more radical liberty with conventional techniques, for at the end of the novel it is discovered that the narrator actually has been dead and in hell for most of the story. Here the problematic nature of existence includes that of the storyteller himself as he discovers that he has no existence in the "real" world.

The author's later novels do not continue these originalities of narration, but the brilliant parodies of *At Swim* are continued in *The Poor Mouth*. The narrator of this story is a poor young country lad, and the tales of his adventures mock the reports of peasant life that were having a current vogue in Ireland. Such biographical narratives often painted life in the remote out-regions of western Ireland as idyllic in its simplicity; O'Nolan's hilarious novel purports to show the sordid reality. But, not only is the romanticized simple peasant being satirized, equal fun is heaped upon the earnest linguistic scholar who visits the region to make recordings of the rapidly disappearing Irish speech and ends up mistaking for Gaelic the snorts and grunts of the family pig who sleeps in the cottage with them.

Much of O'Nolan's funniest writing appeared in his newspaper column *Cruiskeen Lawn,* written under the Myles na Gopaleen pseudonym. His subject matter, ranging far and wide and frequently dealing with contemporary news items, nevertheless reveals Myles's interests as paralleling those of Flann O'Brien. The columns often chronicled the activities of what Myles called the Central Research Bureau, whose inventions were as goofily impractical as any of those of his fictional characters. One, for example, was a plan to save on fuel costs by running all Irish trains only across boglands. A device would allow them to scoop up turf, or peat, from the bogs as they steamed along, to dry it, and to burn it for fuel. Other projects of the Bureau included a plan to print the *Irish Times* in a new ink that would emit an alcoholic vapor, thus giving readers a quick pick-me-up in the morning; the development of an intoxicating ice cream; and the generation of jam for morning toast from secondhand electricity.

Another recurrent subject matter for the column was the adventures of the poet John Keats and his friend George Chapman, who were made to serve as characters in elaborate tales that always ended in a pun. In one column, for example, Myles writes that an expensive horse belonging to Keats escaped from his stable. Keats immediately began to search for the horse:

> He was like a dog looking for a trail, except that he found a trail where many a good dog would have found nothing. Immediately the poet was off cross-country following the trail. It happened that Chapman was on a solitary walking-tour in the vicinity and he was agreeably surprised to encounter the poet in a remote mountainy place. Keats was walking quickly with his eyes on the ground and looked very preoccupied. He had evidently no intention of stopping to converse with Chapman. The latter, not understanding his friend's odd behaviour, halted and cried:
>
> "What are you doing, old man?"
>
> "Dogging a fled horse," Keats said as he passed by.

Myles's interest in language is seen in his hatred of clichés, too, and many columns took the form of a Catechism of Cliché:

> Is man ever hurt in a motor smash?

No. He sustains an injury.
Does such a man ever die from his inju-
ries?
No. He succumbs to them.

As he says in another column, there are other ways of murdering the English language, and he quotes half a dozen mindless sentences of the sort that everyone mouths without thought.

The character who regales Myles (usually while they are waiting for the bus) with the adventures of the Brother is a master of such talk. The character and the Brother represent a kind of innocent world; it seems that they will believe anything. Ignorant, opinionated, and complacent, they know what's what. The Brother is a fund of medical misinformation, for instance, but he does know better than to try to treat himself; he goes to his friend Charley down the street for help when something is wrong with him—when, for example, his nose goes out of order:

> Well do you see it's like this. Listen till I tell you. Here's the way he's fixed. He starts suckin the wind in by the mouth. That's OK, there's no damper there. But now he comes along and shuts the mouth. Fair enough. He starts suckin in through the nose. AND THEN DO YOU KNOW WHAT?
>
> What?
>
> THE—WIND GOES ASTRAY SOME-WHERE. Wherever it goes it doesn't go down below. Do you understand me? There's some class of a leak above in the head somewhere. There's what they call a valve there. The brother's valve is banjaxed.

In the Irish tradition, the Brother's stories are unhampered by any slavish adherence to fact, and whatever his adventures, we hear of them in an unmistakably Dublin voice, the cocky confidence clearly rendered and the accent suggested by subtle phonetic misspellings.

Much the same voice is heard in the columns in which The Plain People of Ireland appear. In some of these columns Myles himself is the recipient of the downright common sense scorn of The Plain People of Ireland when his writing gets a bit flowery and pretentious. In others Myles and The Plain People are of one mind about the pretensions of the artistic or intellectual or political crowds.

The most devastating of Myles's satires on the citizens of Dublin is reserved for The Bore: "boring other people is his sole occupation, enjoyment, recreation." There is the man with the watch that he got for a few shillings eighteen years ago and that has never lost a minute, the man who knows how to make a tuppenny razor blade last for five years, the man who buys wholesale, the man who never gives pennies to beggars, the man who has read it in manuscript ("Ever read *Warren Peace* by T. Allstoy?" you inquire. "Ah, yes, I read that thing in manuscript years ago. Is it published yet?"), and the man who does his own carpentry.

Summary

Brian O'Nolan's humor is inescapably Irish. It is Irish in its wonderfully vivid speaking voice, in its fantasy and imagination, and in the fascination with parody and wordplay. No one had a better ear for the sound of an Irishman speaking—although O'Nolan himself gave James Joyce credit for being better able to capture Dublin dialogue than he himself. O'Nolan and Joyce were (and are) often compared, to O'Nolan's distaste; he did not want to be seen as a kind of second-rate imitator. And indeed, though they were interested in doing many of the same things, O'Nolan is more than a weakly derivative follower of Joyce. Although Joyce went beyond what O'Nolan was capable of as a novelist in the understanding of the human heart, O'Nolan's ability to see through pretension, his skill at recording human conversation in all its fatuousness and cliché, and his delight in wordplay are little less masterly than Joyce's.

Selected Bibliography

Primary Sources
At Swim-Two-Birds. London: Longmans, Green, 1939; London: MacGibbon & Kee, 1960.
The Hard Life. London: MacGibbon & Kee, 1961.
A Flann O'Brien Reader. Ed. Stephen Jones. New York: Viking Press, 1961.
The Dalkey Archive. London: MacGibbon & Kee, 1964.
An Beal Bocht. Dublin: Dolmen, 1964. Trans. Patrick Power, as *The Poor Mouth,* London: Hart-Davis, MacGibbon, 1973.

The Third Policeman. London: MacGibbon
& Kee, 1967.

The Best of Myles. London: MacGibbon &
Kee, 1968.

Stories and Plays. London: Hart-Davis,
MacGibbon, 1973.

*The Various Lives of Keats and Chapman
and the Brother.* London: Hart-Davis,
MacGibbon, 1976.

Myles Away from Dublin. London: Granada,
1985.

Secondary Sources

Clissmann, Anne. *Flann O'Brien: A Critical
Introduction to His Writing.* Dublin: Gill
& Macmillan, 1975. Brief biography
with introduction to complete works.

————, and David Powell, eds. *The Journal
of Irish Literature,* 3 (January 1974). An
edition devoted to O'Brien with essays
on several aspects of his writing.

Cronin, Anthony. *No Laughing Matter: The
Life and Times of Flann O'Brien.* Lon-
don: Grafton, 1989. Biography by one of
O'Brien's younger Dublin friends.

Imhof, Rudiger, ed. *Alive-Alive O!: Flann
O'Brien's At Swim-Two-Birds.* Dublin:
Wolfhound Press, 1985. Collection of
critical essays on O'Brien's best-known
novel.

O'Keeffe, Timothy, ed. *Myles: Portraits of
Brian O'Nolan.* London: Martin Brian
& O'Keeffe, 1973. A collection of bio-
graphical reminiscences.

Ryan, John. *Remembering How We Stood:
Bohemian Dublin at the Mid-Century.*
Dublin: Gill & Macmillan, 1975. Reminiscences by one of O'Brien's contemporaries.

Peggy Broder

O

Orton, Joe

Born: Leicester, England, January 1, 1933
Education: Clark's College, 1945–1947;
Royal Academy of Dramatic Arts, 1951–
1953
Died: London, August 9, 1967

Biography

John (Joe) Kingsley Orton was born on January 1, 1933, to parents William and Elsie Orton
in Leicester, England. His father was a mild and
ineffectual man, while his mother was an authoritative and stubborn woman who tried to
dominate Joe's life. In 1945, she insisted that he
attend Clark's College where he would learn
secretarial skills. However, her son had more
ambitious plans. Hoping to become an actor,
Orton moved to London in 1951 to attend the
Royal Academy of Dramatic Arts, and there he
met his lifetime companion and homosexual
lover Kenneth Halliwell, a highly cultivated
individual, who is credited with having nurtured Orton's writing style. After two years at
the RADA, the men quit school to devote their
full attentions to the writing of novels, none of
which were ever published. In 1962, they were
sentenced to six months in prison for defacing
library books from which they cut artwork to
adorn the walls of their small and cheerless
apartment. Upon their release, Orton began his
career as a playwright with the radio broadcast
of *Ruffian on the Stair* (1964) and the production of *Entertaining Mr. Sloane* (1964). In 1966,
Loot was staged. Three television scripts ensued: *The Erpingham Camp* (1966), *The Good
and Faithful Servant* (1967), and *Funeral
Games* (1968). His most widely read work,
What the Butler Saw (1969), was first produced
two years after his death. His accomplishments
also include a film script for the Beatles (*Up
Against It,* published in 1979 and mounted in
a stage production in 1995) and a novel called
Head to Toe, published posthumously in 1971.
A film version of *Loot,* directed by Silvio Narizzano and starring Lee Remick, Richard Attenborough, and Milo O'Shea, was released in
1972. Halliwell, who had become increasingly
despondent over Orton's success and his own
failure, beat the playwright to death in London
on August 9, 1967, and then committed suicide.

Literary Analysis

Orton's plays are remarkably funny, combining
the reckless abandon of the Roman saturnalia
with the stiff reticence of the conservative British middle class, thus creating a synthesis of
both humor and social commentary. In the chaotic world of his comedies, the dramatist introduces such socially taboo topics as homosexuality, incest, rape, and necrophilia and such
common themes as the collapse of family values, the abuse of power, the hypocrisy of religion, the insolence of public officials, and the
suffering of the individual in an industrial society. However, despite the occasional gravity of
the subject matter, Orton is able to provide the
instant gratification of a belly laugh, and much
of this humor comes from his characters' inabil-

ity to behave in a manner that is appropriate for their particular social positions. There is a husband who sympathizes with his wife's attacker, a priest who has no Christian charity, a policeman who has no respect for the law, a nurse who murders her patients for their money, and a psychiatrist who causes mental anguish rather than foster contentment. Often, the riotousness of a few disorderly individuals infects everyone, causing the dramatic action to degenerate into an amusing chaos.

The most humorous moments in Orton's *Ruffian on the Stair* involve a satire on marital responsibilities. Wilson, a young rogue posing as a potential renter, invades a private home, insisting that the owner's wife, Joyce, lease him a room. Once she refuses, he threatens to molest her and returns the next day to vandalize the property. The woman complains to her insensitive husband, Mike, who seems unconcerned and insists that she is safe from harm since she is too unattractive to inspire a rape. Becoming ever bolder, the ruffian returns while the husband is home, once again asking for a room. Joyce tries to enlist Mike's assistance, but he indifferently combs his hair while she literally wrestles with the intruder. When she finally gets her husband's attention, he apathetically attributes the entire incident to her hysteria. He advises her not to make herself any more ridiculous and insists on hearing Wilson's version of the story. The intruder virtually admits that he mistreated the man's wife. Nevertheless, the husband eventually invites the young tough to share a room. Of course, the concord between the two men is broken, not by the wife's complaints, but by the discovery of Wilson's intention to revenge himself upon Mike, who killed the intruder's brother in a hit-and-run traffic accident. Although Wilson's activities are rather grim, Mike and Joyce provide some comic relief in the drama. Mike is a parody of the indifferent husband, and the humor of the play lies in the exaggerated hiatus between his apathy and his wife's panic.

Orton's second production, *Entertaining Mr. Sloane*, demonstrates a similar humorous and irreverent disregard for conventional interactions between family members. Siblings Ed and Kath take in a tenant, Mr. Sloane, and then compete for his affections. Paradoxically, Kath, who is considered by her brother to be a loose woman, desires both to mother and to arouse Mr. Sloane, and the dialogue between her and the tenant reveals the incestuous implications of

their relationship. When Sloane impregnates Kath and then shows his displeasure over their predicament, she patronizes him, referring to the impending child as a "baby brother." When Ed becomes angered over the situation, demanding that Sloane depart and reminding his sister of the young man's indifference to her, Kath argues, "I'm his mamma and he appreciates me" (106). Furthermore, Ed's own fury is not so much righteous indignation as it is jealousy. Ed showed his homoerotic tendencies early in life; his father has not spoken to him for years because he caught Ed in bed with a young male companion, and Ed's inclinations have not subsided. He lusts after Sloane too, and this explains his exaggerated reaction to his sister's indiscretion. At the same time, like Kath, he treats Sloane as a son, admonishing the youth when he takes the car without permission and when he fraternizes with boys of questionable character. Ed's vituperative attacks on his sister are a further indication of his jealousy. He reveals that his sister once stole one of his amorous acquaintances, luring the young man away with her feminine wiles, and he is angered that she has similarly corrupted Sloane. Ed, the ironic inversion of the protective brother who looks after his sister's chastity, instead warns others of her depravity. This sibling rivalry ends when Sloane kills Ed's and Kath's father Kemp. Rather than showing concern for their abused parent, the two blackmail Sloane, persuading him to remain with them and agreeing to share him equally. The comical ending of the drama reveals the conspicuous absence of conventional values and the self-absorption of the characters who are more concerned with the pursuit of their own sensual pleasure than with the fate of the members of their own family.

Despite an initial lack of success, *Loot* has become one of Orton's most familiar works. The action of the drama involves the attempt by two young bankrobbers, Hal and Dennis, to conceal stolen money in the coffin of Hal's recently deceased mother. Naturally, the movement of the play involves their efforts to avoid being exposed by the meddling inspector Truscott, and in the midst of the resulting confusion a number of unusual characters emerge who have an irreverent disregard for conventional behavior. One of these is Hal, whose treatment of his mother's corpse is both shameful and uproariously funny. He shows no respect for his mother's memory when he removes her body from the casket, wraps it in bandages, places it in a closet, and claims that it is a sewing dummy. When his mother's glass eye falls out, he indifferently carries it around with him for much of the drama. Once the criminal activities have been exposed, inspector Truscott comments on Hal's comic insensitivity: "Your sense of detachment is terrifying, lad. Most people would at least flinch upon seeing their mother's eyes and teeth handed around like nuts at Christmas" (272), a humorously understated observation.

Hal's lack of filial deference is matched by Truscott's disregard for the law that he presumably upholds. Suspecting that the bankrobbers are hiding in the McLeavy household, Truscott enters pretending to be a representative of the water board who needs no warrant to search the premises. The humor of his behavior is derived from his desire to carry on the activities of an investigator while refusing to admit his real profession. When he tries to detain Hal, the young man protests that a member of the water board cannot make an arrest. However, Truscott insists that they can in particular situations, but that he is unwilling to reveal "the inner secrets of the water board to a member of the general public" (234). Once he confesses his genuine vocation, Truscott confines the family to the house, disconnects the phone, and claims that a policeman who has respect for the truth will never advance in the profession. After he has thoroughly thrashed and bound Dennis and has, consequently, been accused of brutality by the youth, Truscott threatens "to beat the eyes out of . . . [the young man's] head" if he ever again accuses the police of striking a prisoner. Finally, after the loot has been exposed, the inspector agrees to take a bribe and then arrests Mr. McLeavy, the only honest person in the play, because the old man threatens to report all of them. Truscott's unwillingness to embrace any of the common values of law enforcement officers and Hal's failure to display the appropriate respect for his mother's dead body provide both the humor and the social commentary of the play.

In *The Erpingham Camp*, Orton satirizes the pride and arrogance of the petty despot who abuses his power over other people. Erpingham, who owns a group of holiday camps, presides over them like a dictator, exercising regal tyranny over both his employees and his guests. When the revelers become riotous, Erpingham blames his activities director and publicly strips him of his sash and medal as though the man

were a disgraced soldier. When the mob begins to direct its anger at Erpingham himself, he neglects his responsibilities as the owner of a holiday camp, refuses to feed and shelter his guests, and vows to use "fire hoses, tear gas, boot[s]" to maintain order (315). He insists that the camp is his kingdom and that he is the lawmaker. Nevertheless, his pride abates when he plunges through the floor boards to his death. Despite this unfortunate outcome, Erpingham's exaggerated sense of his own importance is quite amusing. The play is an allegory of a political revolution and the subsequent overthrow of a tyrant, and the humor of the work is inherent in the ironic distance between the pettiness of the play's characters and events and the loftiness of their allegorical signification.

Continuing his lighthearted indictment of public servants, Orton creates the humorous portrait of a meddling social worker, Mrs. Vealfoy, in *The Good and Faithful Servant*. The plot of this particular drama is perhaps Orton's bleakest, addressing the humiliation and dehumanization of the modern industrial worker. Buchanan, who has labored diligently for the company for fifty years, is given only a cheap toaster as a retirement gift, and only a short time after his departure his employers and co-workers cannot remember him. Mrs. Vealfoy is the source of most of the humor in the piece, allowing herself to intrude in every facet of the employees' lives. She arranges the marriage of Buchanan's grandson, Ray, and his pregnant girlfriend, Debbie, but only after she has informed the young man that pregnancy is not sufficient reason to marry. She also urges Ray to join the company's work force and thereby assume responsibility. She coordinates the recreational activities of retirees like Buchanan, introducing new members, ensuring that people are socializing, and even interfering in private conversations as though she were a pre-school director. Finally, she pronounces Buchanan's eulogy at the end of the play. Although in many ways a clown because of her disregard for the employees' privacy, Mrs. Vealfoy represents industry management's attempt to control laborers; the employees spend their entire lives under the auspices of the company.

In *Funeral Games*, Orton takes aim at the clergy in his hilarious portrait of Pringle, a minister who is determined to murder his wife, Tessa, for her alleged adultery and despite an investigator's testimony to her innocence. In his efforts to kill his wife, Pringle demonstrates his complete disregard for Christian values. For example, when Caulfield reminds the minister to "love thy neighbor," Pringle remarks, "The man who said that was crucified by his" (340). Ironically, Pringle believes that he must kill his wife in order to avoid public scorn. To dissuade him from his intentions, Tessa agrees to pretend to be murdered so that her husband can appear to fulfill his duty. Paradoxically, the remainder of the drama involves the minister's attempts to prove to the world that he has, indeed, killed his wife and is, therefore, a man of integrity. This confusing reversal inspires some of Orton's most clever dialogue. When a letter accuses Pringle of having failed to kill his wife, the minister responds, "There's no end to the malice of people" (344), and the witty discussion following the proposal that Pringle shoot his wife so that he can present her body as evidence of his honesty is Orton's comic trademark:

> CAULFIELD. Kill your wife.
> PRINGLE. I've already killed her once. I couldn't do it again. I'd be a murderer.
> CAULFIELD. You are a murderer in the eyes of the world. I'm only asking you to live up to your public image.
> PRINGLE. That's a terrible thing to ask a man to do.
> CAULFIELD (*pause*). Unless you kill your wife she'll accuse you of not being her murderer . . . You're a clergyman. It's time you practiced what you preach. (353)

The farcical caricature of a clergyman devoted to the wrong principles provides for Orton's audience both a hearty laugh and a brief insight into religious hypocrisy.

What the Butler Saw, Orton's final play, was produced posthumously. In it he lampoons the medical community, depicting the hilarious confusion that follows a psychiatrist's efforts to seduce a secretarial applicant. Dr. Prentice asks Geraldine to remove her clothes on the pretense that he must examine her reactions, and the ensuing chaos results from his attempts to conceal and reclothe the woman before his wife discovers her. In this play, both Dr. Prentice and Dr. Rance exploit their powers as psychiatrists in order to manipulate others, and instead of bringing mental health to those around them, they cause other characters to experience identity crises. Dr. Prentice's wife accurately describes her husband's success as a therapist:

"The purpose of my husband's clinic isn't to cure, but liberate and exploit madness" (388). It is true that Geraldine is exploited. Prentice employs the traditional analysis of the psychiatric patients' relationship with their parents to convince Geraldine to remove her dress, and when he is finally able to reclothe her, she is forced to impersonate a male in order to avoid discovery by Mrs. Prentice. When Dr. Rance arrives at the Prentice household and attempts to assist Geraldine, he only adds to the young woman's gender confusion, which finally erupts in her plea for help: "Undress me then, Doctor! Do whatever you like only prove that I'm a girl" (414). Naturally, her masquerade results in accusations of homosexuality against both herself and Dr. Prentice, leading Dr. Rance to conclude that his colleague is a "pervert." Consequently, Mrs. Prentice tries to make her husband concede that he desires men more than women, an admission that would diminish her sense of sexual inadequacy. Needless to say, he is not willing to oblige her. Nick, the young man who is blackmailing Mrs. Prentice with pornographic photographs and insisting on a job as the doctor's secretary, also participates in the gender mayhem. He is encouraged by Prentice to impersonate Geraldine in order to escape arrest on molestation charges. Furthermore, Mrs. Prentice experiences a personality crisis when Dr. Rance insists that her "depraved appetites" have led to her husband's mental collapse, and even the constable who has come to arrest Nick ends up drugged and undressed. The anarchic situation reaches its visual climax when the two psychiatrists attempt to certify each other at gun point. As in the playwright's other dramas, the humor of *What the Butler Saw* stems from the unconventional behavior of individuals who have little regard for the ethics of their professions and who employ their arts to manipulate rather than to heal.

Summary
In his plays, Joe Orton invokes a traditional brand of humor in an untraditional way. Obviously, social satire was not invented by this twentieth-century dramatist, but he did increase the ways in which it could be accomplished. His liberated approach to sexuality allowed him to place his characters in humorous situations that may have been too bawdy for previous generations. The characters in Orton's plays are not immoral in a traditional sense; instead, they seem to be oblivious to morality, remaining

ignorant of restrictions on their behavior and offering the most immodest proposals as though they are quite common and natural. Without apology or explanation, Orton offers transvestism, incest, homosexuality, bisexuality, adultery, and other forms of illicit sex, expecting his audience either to laugh and join in the fun or to become a part of the strict and rigid culture that is being satirized. The plays involve a conflict between the forces of decadence and social liberation and those of conservatism and restraint, and often the most hilarious scenes result from the capitulation of authority figures to the amorality of the progressives.

Selected Bibliography

Primary Sources

Head To Toe. London: Anthony Blond, 1971.

Joe Orton: The Complete Plays. New York: Grove Press, 1976.

Up Against It: A Screenplay for the Beatles. London: Methuen, 1979; staged 1995.

Secondary Sources

Casmus, Mary I. "Farce and Verbal Style in the Plays of Joe Orton." *Journal of Popular Culture*, 23 (1980): 461–68. Casmus traces the progress of Orton's style from naturalism to farce.

Charney, Maurice. *Joe Orton*. New York: Grove Press, 1984. Charney's book is a collection of essays (many of which are published elsewhere) addressing all of Orton's work, including his novel and his screenplay for the Beatles.

Dean, Joan F. "Joe Orton and the Redefinition of Farce." *Theatre Journal*, 34 (December 1982): 481–92. Dean argues that Orton invents a new kind of farce, one that serves to subvert rather than sustain the status quo.

Draubt, M. "Comic, Tragic, or Absurd? On the Parallels Between the Farces of Joe Orton and Seventeenth-Century Tragedy." *ES*, 59 (1978): 202–17. As the title suggests, Draubt traces the influences of Jacobean drama on Orton's work.

Esslin, Martin. "Joe Orton: The Comedy of (Ill) Manners." In *Contemporary English Drama*. Ed. C.W.E. Bigsby. New York: Holmes and Meier, 1981, pp. 95–107. Esslin argues against Lahr's assertion that Orton is a major dramatist, focusing on the development of the playwright's style from derivative to original.

Fraser, Keath. "Joe Orton: His Brief Career." *Modern Drama*, 14 (February 1972): 413–19. The essay involves a brief explication of each of the playwright's works, mentioning his use of farce and the decadence of his characters.

Hunt, Albert. "What Joe Orton Saw." *New Society*, 32 (1975): 148–50. Hunt addresses Orton's satire of social institutions.

Lahr, John. *Prick up Your Ears*. New York: Knopf, 1978. Lahr is Orton's official biographer, and his book is based on the playwright's diary.

Shepherd, Simon. "Edna's Last Stand, or Joe Orton's Dialectic of Entertainment." *Renaissance and Modern Studies*, 22 (1978): 87–110. Shepherd discusses the self-reflexive element of Orton's plays.

Walcot, Peter. "An Acquired Taste: Joe Orton and the Greeks." In *Legacy of Thespis*. Ed. Karelisa V. Hartigan. New York: University Press of America, 1984. Vol. 4, pp. 99–123. Walcot reveals Orton's indebtedness to Greek dramatists.

James Keller

O

Orwell, George (born Eric Arthur Blair)

Born: Motihari, India, June 25, 1903

Education: St. Cyprians Private School, 1911–1916; Wellington Public School, 1917; Eton Public School, 1917–1921

Marriage: Eileen O'Shaughnessy, June 9, 1936; two children (one adopted); Sonia Brownell, October 13, 1949

Died: London, January 21, 1950

Biography

Eric Arthur Blair was born to Richard Walmesley Blair and Ida Mabel (née Limouzin) Blair in Motihari, India, on June 25, 1903. Richard Blair worked in the Opium Department of Customs and Excise in the Indian Civil Service until his retirement in 1912 when he returned to England. In 1933, at the age of thirty, Eric Blair changed his name to George Orwell. In discussing the publication of *Down and Out in Paris and London*, Orwell, who had been using the name of P.S. Burton at the time, wrote to his publisher late in 1932 saying that he was considering three pennames—"Kenneth Miles," "George Orwell," and "H. Lewis Allways." He finally settled on "George Orwell" (the Orwell is a river in Suffolk, south of his parents' home), and used this for *Down and*

Out in Paris and London (1933), and later for *Burmese Days* (1934), in order not to cause the Blair family distress. Much of the reason for the change was his belief that publishing these books under the name of Eric Blair would have caused his family to lose social respectability (Coppard and Crick, 13). Furthermore, he felt that the name of "George Orwell" was a plain, solid, and very English name (Calder, *Animal Farm and Nineteen Eighty-Four*, 1).

As a school child, Orwell was sent to St. Cyprians Private School (1911–1916), a fashionable preparatory school on the south coast of England, at considerable sacrifice to his parents. There, Orwell developed a strong inferiority complex. He did not have nearly as much spending money as the other boys. Furthermore, he did not have any of the qualities that were admired. Of this experience he said, "I had no money. I was weak. I was ugly. I was unpopular. I had a chronic cough. I was cowardly. I smelt" (Hopkinson, 275).

Despite his sense of failure, Orwell was awarded a scholarship to attend Wellington in 1917 and later a scholarship to attend Eton, which he did from 1917 to 1921. Eton was noted for its tolerant attitudes toward the individual and its promotion of intellectual freedom. Orwell said he learned nothing at Eton; however, most other schools would have expelled someone who held a scholarship but chose not to do any work. And Eton broadened Orwell's perspective and gave him an opportunity to do much reading of his own choice.

After his public school experience, Orwell went to Burma where he stayed from 1922 until 1927. He was a member of the Indian Imperial Police in Burma, and he documented his feelings of this period by writing his satirical anti-imperialist novel, *Burmese Days*; the book was not published until 1934. In *Burmese Days* the writer vividly documents the provincial and chauvinistic British community of a small, backwater village named Kyauktada, where the bored English colonials sat around the European Club recalling an idealized British Raj that had never actually existed except in their minds. This colonial society was dominated by the "pukka sahib" code which dictated that all white men had to "hang together" and forbade any kind of social relationships with the natives. This situation gave Orwell a sense of claustrophobic oppression as social and psychological as it was political. Orwell hated his police duties in Burma, and he was repelled by the authority that he himself had. But paradoxically, there was also a Kiplingesque side to Orwell's character which allowed him to romanticize the Raj and its mystique.

Nevertheless, John Flory, the protagonist of *Burmese Days*, said, "Free speech is unthinkable. All other kinds of freedom are permitted. You are free to be a drunkard, an idler, a coward, a backbiter, a fornicator; but you are not free to think for yourself. Your opinion on every subject of any conceivable importance is dictated for you by the pukka sahib's code" (Zehr, 411). Orwell's hatred for this regimentation of thought that stunts the development of internally defined values of morality and usurps the freedom of the individual would later be more fully developed in his *1984*. He was aware of the fact that freedom and power both employ the same weapons to achieve their ends. He noticed that people who want power can get this power by persuading others that they are really seeking freedom (Atkins, 2).

While in Burma, Orwell also wrote a powerful non-fiction essay entitled "Shooting an Elephant." The story is about an elephant that runs amok, describing Orwell's reactions to his duties as the British official of the district who has to take action by shooting the elephant. He borrows a rifle and follows the elephant into the fields where he finds it standing peacefully, recovered now from its attack of madness. He feels pressure from all the people around him who are determined to witness a shooting, so he does shoot the elephant. The elephant "looked suddenly stricken, shrunken, immensely old, as though the frightful impact of the bullet had paralysed him without knocking him down" (Hopkinson, 176). Then the elephant "sagged flabbily to his knees. His mouth slobbered. An enormous senility seemed to have settled upon him. One could have imagined him thousands of years old" (276). Tom Hopkinson compares Orwell's sensitivity in "Shooting an Elephant" with that in "A Hanging," which appeared in *Adelphi* in 1931. When the noose was placed around the victim's throat he began crying out to his god, "Ram! Ram! Ram! Ram!" The hangman placed a small cotton bag over the prisoner's head, but the prisoner continued to repeat "Ram! Ram! Ram! Ram!" though the sound was muffled by the cloth. There was a sort of morbid jocular relief after the hanging as "We all had a drink together, native and European alike, quite amicably. The dead man was a hundred yards away" (276).

In 1927, Orwell had become thoroughly fed up with the power and authority that he commanded as a member of the Indian Imperial Police. He felt that his life must take a different, in fact an opposite, direction. Because he felt guilty as a result of his Burmese experiences, he went to Paris where he would plunge himself into the life of poverty that he had always hated. He wanted to experience failure in its most painful form, to interact with mankind at its lowest and dirtiest level, to commit an act of public defiance against a world that was ruled by money and what money could buy. Orwell viewed the working-class life with nostalgia. He considered it a warm feather bed where all pretensions could be abandoned. His family had fought hard to bring itself into the middle class, and Orwell had fought hard to stay there, but in view of his Burma remembrances he now considered the fight to have been in vain, and he felt that the only sensible thing to do would be to relax and descend. He knew that there would be hardships, but he felt that the hardships would be compensated for by a sense of peace of mind. In the back of his mind he probably also thought that such hardships, as dramatic as they were desperate, would be the basis of a book, but he dared not say so because he did not know whether he would be able to write in these circumstances or not. He did write his first book out of these experiences, and it was entitled *Down and Out in Paris and London.*

Orwell's eighteen months in Paris were spent in abject poverty. On his best days he was able to get a job as a dishwasher in a large Paris hotel. He calculated that during the decade from 1930 to 1940 his literary earnings did not quite equal three pounds sterling per week. The publication of *Down and Out* did not make him rich; few copies were sold. But, the book received high critical acclaim and undoubtedly convinced him that he had the wherewithal to become a writer. Early in 1928, Orwell put on some old clothes and went to live in the East End of London in order to further explore the life of the impoverished and the unemployed. He did this because he had an adventurous spirit, because he wanted to become a writer, and because he wanted to break free from the bonds of his class and upbringing.

Between 1929 and 1935, Orwell earned a meager salary as a private tutor and a teacher in cheap private schools. He also worked in a book shop from 1934 to 1935. Out of this experience came *A Clergyman's Daughter* in 1935, a horrifying view of life in cheap private schools, written much in the tradition of Charles Dickens. *A Clergyman's Daughter* is a continuation of the author's exploration of the clash between individual freedoms and a repressive, middle-class society. In it Orwell tells the story of Dorothy Hare, the overworked only child of an acrimonious rector of the Church of England. The novel is written in the picaresque tradition in which the heroine moves about from place to place in a series of dramatic adventures. Much of the novel is autobiographical, including the hop-picking in Kent, being a bum in London, visiting the London doss-houses, and teaching at the gloomy private schools. The book suggests that reform is necessary.

Nineteen thirty-six was a pivotal year in Orwell's life. On June 9, he married Eileen O'Shaughnessy; the couple would have one child, a daughter born in 1949. He rented a general store in Wallington named "The Stores," and began running the store and keeping his goats. He published *Keep the Aspidistra Flying*, and he was asked by Victor Gollancz, his publisher, to investigate the unemployed and working class in the coal-mining districts of Yorkshire and Lancashire.

The Road to Wigan Pier (1936) is Orwell's first clear identification with the aims and ideals of socialism. The title is based on a North Country joke, for the word "Pier" suggests the seaside, holidays, and gaiety while "Wigan" is a forbidding inland town whose pier is a derelict wharf not on the seaside but on a canal. The expression "Wigan Pier" is therefore considered by North Country people to be an oxymoron.

Orwell was impulsive and much motivated by current events. If there was a cause which he believed in, he always threw all of his energies into the cause to learn more about it and to be able to understand it and write about it. One such cause was the Spanish Civil War which represented to Orwell the cause of individual freedom. He joined the Partido Obrero de Unificacion Marxista (POUM). Orwell explains his compulsion to join: "I had come to Spain with some notion of writing newspaper articles but I had joined the militia almost immediately, because at that time and in that atmosphere it seemed the only conceivable thing to do" (Hopkinson, 281).

The fact that the author was very grounded in the present time is ironic, because much of his writing is critical of people who do not have a sense of history or a sense of consequences. In 1942, Orwell expressed his disgust at the way that the Nazis, the Russians, and others twisted historical facts to their own purposes. He was upset that "some ruling clique, controls not only the future but *the past*. If the Leader says of such and such an event, 'It never happened'—well, it never happened. If he says that two and two are five, well, two and two are five. This prospect frightens me much more than bombs" (Zehr, 418).

John Atkins notes that Orwell looked back to the inequalities and unfairness of the past with nostalgia because it was a time of relative decency. Orwell expressed his fascination with the past in ironic and unexpected ways, as when he wrote "Decline of the English Murder," in which he deplored the declining quality of English murder! He had little patience with the new style, the Cleft Chin and Bristol Bank Manager affairs. He said that they compared badly with "the old domestic poisoning dramas, [the] product of a stable society where the all-prevailing hypocrisy did at least ensure that crimes as serious as murder should have strong emotions behind them" (4).

Tom Hopkinson suggests that Orwell was "magnificent" in the Spanish militia not because Orwell was a good soldier but rather because he was not a good soldier. The writer was not naturally a man of action, and his contacts with the physical world were always disastrous. Whenever he painted a room, the paint would smear and smudge. Whenever he cleaned a lamp, it would catch fire. Any cigarettes that he rolled would continually fall to pieces. So, he was an incompetent soldier, but he was also a soldier who was bright and who was committed. Hopkinson considers Orwell's training in the militia to have been "a brief parody of training." Orwell himself says that the odd clothes they were issued were so varied that they should have been called "multi-forms" rather than "uniforms." Furthermore, the weapons that they were assigned were rusty Mausers stamped "1896." In such array, Orwell found himself at the front near Huesca in 1937. He was hit in the throat by a bullet during this battle. One of his vocal cords was damaged leaving him with an altered voice for the rest of his life. The Spanish doctors proclaim that the bullet missed severing Orwell's windpipe and carotid artery only by a millimeter.

Homage to Catalonia (1938) is a personal memoir in which the drudgery of war, of social revolution, and of interparty political conflict are described. It is written with vigor, buoyancy, and élan, and chronicles a time in Spain when tipping had been forbidden, ceremonial forms of speech had been replaced by the term "comrade," and shops and cafes were being closed and churches systematically demolished. Orwell recognized this as a state of affairs worth fighting for, and this is why he joined the militia.

In 1939, a tubercular lesion on one of Orwell's lungs began to hemorrhage, and he spent five months in a sanatorium. The author L.H. Meyers anonymously gave him £300 to go to Marrakesh, Morocco, for his health, and this is where Orwell wrote *Coming Up for Air* (1939).

In 1940, when *Twentieth Century Authors* asked him for a short summary of his life, he mentioned each of his major achievements and then followed this with some admission of failure or weakness. He was educated at Eton, *but* he did no work there and learned very little. He served with the Indian Imperial Police in Burma, *but* the climate ruined his health, and "in any case there was no honour in having served the 'racket' of imperialism." He wrote fiction for a year-and-a-half in Paris, *but* no publisher would accept any of his work. He fought in the Spanish Civil War, *but* the experience gave him a "horror of politics" (Shelden, 2).

During the 1940s, Orwell made a number of attempts to enlist in the military service, but he was always turned down because of the lesions on his lung. He was nevertheless able to salve his patriotic conscience by joining the Home Guard (where he served as a sergeant), and by formulating his thoughts on the English cultural heritage that confirmed both his patriotism and his faith in the potential power of the common, ordinary Englishman.

In 1941 and 1942, Orwell wrote and broadcast programs for the BBC; then in 1943, he became the literary editor of the *Tribune*, which represented the left wing of the Labour Party. He was too soft-hearted to be a good literary editor; he could not turn down bad poems if he knew the poet to be poor. Still, his weekly column, "As I Please," was brilliant and dealt with such themes as love of nature, love of literature, dislike of mass production, distrust of bureaucracy, hatred of totalitarianism, detestation of censorship, praise of plain speaking, the good things from the past, and decency, fraternity, individuality, liberty, egalitarianism, and patriotism in general. Unlike other columns, it did not deal with sports, sex, crime, travel, and political or social gossip, for Orwell was, in Cyril Connolly's words, "a revolutionary who is in love with 1910." Connolly also remarked that Orwell could "hardly blow his nose without suspecting and denouncing cartels among handkerchief manufacturers" (Coppard and Crick, 15).

In 1944, Orwell and his wife adopted a son, Richard. Eileen Orwell died in 1945 during what should have been a routine surgical operation. *Animal Farm* (1945), a brilliant Swiftean satire about the Russian revolution, was at first rejected by a number of publishers in both England and America (including Faber & Faber where T.S. Eliot read the manuscript). One American publisher rejected it because "Americans were not in the mood for animal stories" (Zehr, 418). Four other publishers did not want to publish an attack on the Soviet Union since it was at the time a valuable ally of the West. Still, *Animal Farm* became one of the books used for English instruction in the training of African journalists in the Nairobi and Lagos centers of the International Press Institute. Hopkinson reports that a number of different students were convinced that Orwell must have known and been writing specifically about the African state from which they had come.

Even though Orwell was very ill in 1947, he decided to leave the comforts of London and move, with his small son and his sister, Avril Blair, to a cold, damp, isolated Scottish Hebridean house on the isle of Jura off the West coast of Scotland. He wanted to take his son and get away from the possibilities of being involved in an atomic war, so he left London and went to Jura. Hopkinson conjectures that if Orwell's earlier life can be used as evidence, Orwell was not the type of person who would leave London because of a possible atomic attack; in fact, this is the kind of thing that would have enticed him to stay in London:

> It was a rugged existence on Jura, and a long way from civilization. To many it has seemed characteristic of Orwell's dogged refusal to compromise that he should have made his life on the remotest part of a remote island, far from doctors and friends at a time when his health was so precarious. (Calder, *Animal Farm and Nineteen Eighty-Four*, 4)

That same year, Orwell said, "Every line of serious work that I have written since 1936 has been written, directly or indirectly, *against* to-talitarianism and *for* democratic Socialism" (Calder, *Chronicles*, 259). But, Orwell also said, "Socialism, at least in this island [Jura], does not smell any longer of revolution and the overthrow of tyrants; it smells of crankishness, machine workshop and the stupid cult of Russia" (Zehr, 414). Orwell lamented that the mere mention of the words "Socialism" and "Communism" have a magnetic force that automatically attracts "every fruit-juice drinker, nudist, sandal-wearer, sex-maniac, Quaker, 'Nature Cure' Quack, pacifist and feminist in England" (Zehr, 414). Socialism would remain an obsession for Orwell throughout his writing of *1984*.

1984 (written in 1948 and published in 1949) was probably a satire on post-war European life; however, so many millions of readers interpreted it to be a warning of the political enslavement of the future that 1984 became a symbolic year against which to measure the development of totalitarian systems. In 1950, E.M. Forster wrote that in *1984* Orwell "extended discomfort into agony . . . *1984* crowned his work, and it is understandably a crown of thorns" (Bal, 15).

By 1945, Orwell's tuberculosis had grown worse and the doctors at University College Hospital gave him a fifty-fifty chance to live, but only if he was well looked after and if he were willing to settle for life as a semi-invalid. In spite of this prognosis, on October 13, 1949, the author married Sonia Brownell.

When in London on January 21, 1950, he suffered a fatal tubercular hemorrhage which killed him instantly, his consultant doctor admitted that he had lied to Orwell:

> He had not, in fact, given Orwell any chance of survival, but did not see it as his business to tell anyone that Orwell was not expected to live. It is a sad irony that the great truth-teller, who set his heart on trying to be absolutely honest in literary, moral and political judgements, should have been treated in that way by a consultant. (Coppard and Crick, 17)

Three books of Orwell's essays were published posthumously. They are *Shooting an Elephant, and Other Essays* (1950), *England Your England and Other Essays* (1953), and *The Collected Essays, Journalism, and Letters of George Orwell* in four volumes (1968).

England Your England and Other Essays was first published in England and a short time later in the United States (under the title of *Such, Such Were the Joys*). It is ironic that the basic difference between the English and the American version is that the American version contains an article about England that the English version does not contain. This essay is entitled "Such, Such Were the Joys," and it is an autobiographical essay about Orwell's life in an English preparatory school. It was left out of the English edition because of the possibility of libel proceedings.

Literary Analysis

In a book entitled *The Paradox of George Orwell*, Richard Voorhees sees Orwell's life and writing as paradoxical in three important respects. First, he was a rebel with a remarkably strong sense of responsibility. His rebellion was comprehensive and sometimes violent, and because of this some of his critics considered him to be neurotic. However, Voorhees feels that Orwell's sense of responsibility was "eminently sane and practical" (11). To illustrate the point Voorhees noted that Orwell did not himself have religious feelings; he nevertheless recognized that any society which loses its sense of religion soon tends to deteriorate. Likewise, Orwell rejected all political orthodoxies; he was nevertheless closely engaged in the various political issues of his day. He was horrified also by large concentrations of power, and he was determined to resist such power concentrations. Nevertheless, he often joined these concentrations of power himself. Voorhees feels that one reason he did so was to learn more about the power system that he was attacking. Finally, Orwell crusaded for a socialistic society, yet he had strong reservations about socialism. He was confident that socialism would succeed, but he was not at all pleased with some of the corollaries of socialism. Socialism implied increased mechanization, but Orwell had an aversion to modern machinery. Socialism by its very nature would invade areas of life which capitalism does not invade. Because of this, Orwell had a nostalgia for nineteenth-century England, a time when life was simpler and freer in many ways than the society toward which he directed his energies.

Orwell complained bitterly about the "sweeping statements" that he so often found in politics. Yet his critics frequently note that he himself had the same tendencies. Stuart Hampshire writes about the author's "aggressive ex-aggeration" and "ferocious over-statements." Bolton says that Orwell's writing "encompasses most viewpoints because it avoids the specifics that might exclude many," and George Woodcock noted that Orwell's writing is influential because it is forceful, inclusive, economical, clear, fluent, and descriptively vivid, but then he adds that these are all "superficial virtues," very much tied to a particular time and place (Bolton, 17).

Mark Connelly notes that the reason for Orwell's popularity is that he took independent stands at a time which was dominated by fierce political loyalties and rigid party lines: "He wrote clearly and directly without self-censorship" (2). At times he followed standard Socialist lines that only structural reform would improve mankind, but at other times he praised the moralist position of Dickens—"Orwell's contradictions illustrate that he was working from a broader philosophy, which is variously defined as being existential, theological, or psychological in nature" (3). Reading Orwell is like looking through a kaleidoscope or a series of distorted mirrors. Connelly continues: "Catholics, anarchists, New Critics, Freudians, Marxists, and existentialists have probed Orwell's clear prose and written prolifically, each claiming Orwell as one of their own. Like Shakespeare, Orwell has become a handy source for quotes, which, taken out of context, are used to endorse almost anything" (3).

Sant Singh Bal divides Orwell's writing career into two stages. During the 1930s, Orwell was a social critic. In the 1940s, he became an essayist and a political satirist. The writings published after his death in 1950 show him to be an austere yet gentle author. It was the real world which motivated Orwell to write his satires during the 1940s: he saw troops who had never fired a shot hailed in the newspapers as heroes of imaginary victories; he saw "history being written not in terms of what happened but of what ought to have happened according to various 'party lines'" (Beadle, 13).

Because of Orwell's ambivalent social position during his formative years, the extraordinary importance of money was a prominent theme in his first four books. This also explains why Orwell developed his strong attitudes in favor of the bourgeoisie and against the privileged intelligentsia. In the conflict between the society at large and the individual, Orwell always favored the individual. His love for individual freedom is demonstrated not only in the social subjects that he chose to write about during the 1930s but also in the political subjects of his writings during the 1940s. He strongly disliked favoritism, arbitrary rules, and the omnipotence of the system. Cyril Connolly, one of Orwell's colleagues at Eton, remarked that Orwell rejected "the war, the Empire, Kipling, Sussex, and Character" (Zehr, 408).

Orwell says that a writer "should bifurcate himself, devoting one part (the citizen) to an ideology and the other part (the writer) to eternal values. John Atkins criticizes this position, saying, "Here, surely, lay the very origin of a super-Doublethink!" (Bal, 11).

Tom Hopkinson feels that the excitement of Orwell's writing far exceeded that of his real life. Hopkinson describes Orwell's writing as nervous, flexible, and lucid, and says further that writing was so much a part of Orwell's nature that many qualities can be found in his writing that did not reveal themselves in Orwell's real life. In real life, the author was rather dull and lifeless. His writings, however, especially his essays, are very witty, and his *Animal Farm* is filled with witty observation and lively vigorous expression. The success of *Animal Farm* is also the result of the fable form, the simplicity of style, and the notable absence of a narrative or authorial voice. The result is the "potential for a mythic quality that engages a deeper level of consciousness than either realist fiction or the essay" can achieve.

Orwell's *Down and Out in Paris and London* had initially been entitled "A Scullion's Diary." It was written in diary form and blended imaginative fantasy with accurate reportage. The book is buoyant and lively. The Paris part is imaginative and evocative, with a tenuous story line that bases the narrator's experiences on typical events experienced by Parisian low life. There is a sprinkling of queer tales and stories about individuals who lived "lives that were curious beyond words" (Zehr, 410). The anecdotes and experiences are told in a vigorous and individualized voice with boyish glee. The London part of the book is less imaginative and has more detachment. The narrator is no longer a raconteur; rather he is a research worker and detached social critic, and he tells an honest and objective story about tramps and the social laws that serve to perpetuate their condition. The London part also contains a three-page description of London street slang and describes the various types of hous-

ing available for the poor. This book illustrates well Orwell's schizoid desire to produce an imaginative work of art while at the same time expounding directly on the social issues and conditions that he felt so deeply about.

Burmese Days describes Burma as a multilingual country where class and language are interrelated. In Burma, a butler may be rebuked for learning his English too well, and an English woman may find it best not to learn anything more than "kitchen Urdu" (Bolton, 19). *Burmese Days* is frequently taken to be socialistic in intent, but in fact it is merely anti-imperialistic. In 1930, when Jack Common asked Orwell where he stood on this issue, he responded that he was a "Tory anarchist." Orwell was not entirely joking (Coppard and Crick, 12).

The central idea of *A Clergyman's Daughter* revolves around a play-like dialogue among tramps and beggars passing the night in Trafalgar Square. The speech of these lower-class characters is clearly distinguishable from that of the Irish whore and that of the clergyman who has fallen to become a member of the group. In *A Clergyman's Daughter*, as in *Down and Out* and in "Hop-Picking," Orwell is concerned with various non-standard varieties of English and how this dialect is related to the character and status of the individual who uses it (Bolton, 19).

At one point in the novel the clergyman's daughter finds herself homeless in Trafalgar Square on a freezing night with a bunch of characters just as lost and even more desperate than she is. Their talk is a kind of "litany of the damned." In the group there is a defrocked parson, a woman whose husband has locked her out, an old louse-infested tramp, and a bunch of children from the north who sing at the pubs for a living. To add to the pathos, every time those in the group are beginning to experience an illusion of warmth and fellowship, a policeman stops by and moves them along.

To demonstrate the grimness of the head mistress in *A Clergyman's Daughter*, Orwell has her classify all of her pupils into three categories. The first category consists of pupils who may be ill-treated to any extent. The second category consists of pupils who should be treated with some care. And, the third category consists of pupils who must not be touched for whatever reason and whose work must be constantly praised. The placement of pupils into these categories is determined by how promptly the parents pay their bills.

Keep the Aspidistra Flying (1936) is a gloomy novel about money. Gordon Comstock, the protagonist, is a struggling poet and angry young man who declares a war on money by giving up his position in an advertising firm to take a low-paying job as an assistant in a book store. He feels that by doing this he will have time for his writing. Ironically, his new poverty so dominates his thoughts that he cannot get on with his writing. Comstock has a manuscript rejected and thinks to himself, "'The Editor regrets!' Why be so bloody mealy-mouthed about it? Why not say out-right, 'We don't want your bloody poems. We only take poems from chaps we were at Cambridge with'" (Hopkinson, 275). *Keep the Aspidistra Flying* is autobiographical to the extent that Orwell himself was an assistant in a Hampstead book shop named "Booklovers Corner" for eighteen months between 1932 and 1934, during which time he published in a number of magazines including *Adelphi*. The title, *Keep the Aspidistra Flying*, is an allusion to an almost indestructible potted plant, the aspidistra. For Orwell, this plant becomes the symbol of middle-class endurance and sense of personal responsibility.

The Road to Wigan Pier is largely autobiographical. Here Orwell wrote much about his Burma experience, saying that during this time, "I had reduced everything to the simple theory that the oppressed are always right and the oppressors are always wrong: a mistaken theory, but the natural result of being one of the oppressors yourself" (Calder, *Animal Farm and Nineteen Eighty-Four*, 2). In *The Road to Wigan Pier*, Orwell shows his widely varied ability to loathe his fellow men. He hates some because they are bald, others because they are hairy. He hates some because their clothes are pretentious, others because their clothes are shabby. He hates some because they have an accent and others because they have none, or because they used to have one and gave it up. He hates some because they smell bad and others because they have abandoned the honest and simple life of the working class and as a result no longer smell bad.

Homage to Catalonia is Orwell's second clear identification with the ideals and aims of socialism, but it also demonstrates his development of a passionate distrust of communism. *Homage* is a sample of excellent reporting. It is vivid, and it is dramatic, but it did not sell well, because it was also remorselessly objective. And no one wanted to read an objective book about the Spanish Civil War. Those on the Right preferred stories about the desecration of dead nuns' bodies, and those on the left wanted a heroic picture of their unity and courage. Of the original 1,500 copies printed, 600 still had not been sold at the time of Orwell's death. Orwell went to Spain as a soldier, saying, "someone has to kill Fascists." He went not to write, but to fight; nevertheless *Homage to Catalonia* was the result. It is one of the shrewdest and most biting polemics against the Stalinist and Communist reckless and fatal attempts to use the Civil War for their own ends (Coppard and Crick, 14).

In Orwell's *Coming Up for Air*, George Bowling is the solitary, middle-aged, non-intellectual, lower-middle-class insurance-salesman protagonist. George is fat and good natured and has a ripe and easy sense of humor. Although George's life is dreary, he is not a dreary character himself, as the book is written with dash and enjoyment. George wins some money at the track and, deciding that he will visit the little country town where he was raised, conceals his winnings from his wife. In his mind his former home was the symbol of idyllic peace and natural rural beauty. But when he arrives at his old home, he discovers that the sylvan setting has been replaced by a "hellish" development. According to Hopkinson, Orwell here and in other places enjoys "rubbing the reader's nose in it." The reader must accompany George everywhere he goes as he sees what has happened to the old marketplace, to the old High Street, to the old horse trough, to the tea shop, the corn merchant's, the churchyard, to the pool where the great fish used to be, and finally to the girl he had once loved.

George wants to be able to breathe again the fresh air of a simpler time, a time when even the simplest and poorest of men could maintain a quiet dignity. But to Bowling's disgust and disillusionment, however, he discovers that Lower Binfield has become a growing industrial city filled with factories, munitions plants, choking chemical odors, polluted streams, lunatic asylums, noxious smells, nudist colonies, and miles of "straggling red suburb" (Greenblatt, 37). Furthermore, "Bowling has learned the bitter lesson that he can never come up for air, that he is condemned to live at the bottom of the foul, murky ocean of ignorance and brutality" (Greenblatt, 38). *Coming Up for Air* is about the time when the war broke out. Orwell says that Neville Chamberlain's England had problems though it was not so bad as Hitler's Germany was. Orwell believed there was some virtue in popular patriotism, yet he made the distinction between love of country and vulgar nationalism. England, he said, was "a family with the wrong members in charge" (Coppard and Crick, 14).

One vivid scene in the novel is a description of the effects of bombing. A bomb has fallen on Lower Binfield. It is ironic that the bomb has fallen by accident and during peacetime. The result is nevertheless dramatic, as the bomb has sheared away the front of a house, leaving all of its contents exposed and strangely undisturbed, like a doll's house with the door open. This scene in Orwell's 1939 novel is a warning of the imminence of war.

What frightens Bowling (and Orwell as well) is not the destruction that might be caused by war. Rather, it is the semi-anesthetic political environment of England in 1938 and the vision of what it would be like after the war in a world filled with hate, slogans, colored shirts, barbed wire, and rubber truncheons. This would be a world where electric lights burn night and day because the windows have been boarded up against the bombs, a world where detectives watch everyone while they sleep and there are processions and posters with huge faces and crowds of millions of people all cheering for and worshiping their Leader. This was prophetic.

It was in 1940 that Orwell wrote his first political pamphlet, entitled *Inside the Whale*. It was in 1941 that he wrote an even more important political pamphlet under the title of *The Lion and the Unicorn: Socialism and the English Genius*, a pamphlet in which he attempted to reconcile his conservative and radical tendencies.

Orwell's *Animal Farm* (1945) is about how power corrupts. There is a betrayal of the revolution, and there is a gradual perversion of its ideals. *Animal Farm* is a rough approximation of what had happened during Orwell's time in Spain and in the Soviet Union (Beadle, 13). It is the one book in which he was able to achieve a level of detachment and admirable good humor that was largely missing from his other books. Hopkinson suggests that one reason for this is Orwell's disillusionment with Socialism as a perfect political system. Another reason was Orwell's choice of animals rather than humans as his characters. He had a sincere love for animals, and this was one of the reasons for the detachment and good humor of *Animal Farm*.

In fact, it is his detachment in *Animal Farm* that raises the novel to a higher satiric plane than he was able to achieve in any of his previous or later writings.

Animal Farm contains humorous but biting satire and is noted for its wit and charm. It is an allegory which portrays the animals on Animal Farm as misled victims of a rising totalitarian dictatorship. Hopkinson suggests that Orwell's study of Swift in an essay entitled "Politics vs. Literature" foreshadows the novel. Orwell said that *Animal Farm* is the first book in which he successfully fused political purpose and artistic purpose into a single unity. He further said that it was the only book that he had every really sweated over. Ironically, this is the novel that shows the *fewest* signs of being sweated over, since it flows smoothly and clearly from start to finish, as though all that the author had done was copy it from another source. *Animal Farm* is written in the classic tradition of satire, the tradition of receding planes. There is a level for every reader, regardless of the reader's sophistication. Like *Gulliver's Travels* or *Aesop's Fables*, the novel can be read as a delightful children's story. But, it is also an attack on Stalinism. At still another level it is a lament on the fate of revolutions. And finally, it is a profound and moving commentary of human interactions in general.

At the beginning of the novel, which is also a fable, the animals on Manor Farm are upset at the inequality of the system where the humans enjoy all of the privileges and the animals do all of the work. Old Major is the political visionary who represents Karl Marx. He describes the plight of the animals, their lack of freedom, their misery, and their powerlessness. As he declares the principle of "Animalism," it is clear that Orwell is allegorically describing the Marxist view of the relationship between the working class and the rich, landowning class of any society.

So, the animals take over the farm with the idea of making it into a utopian society. They change the name of the farm to "Animal Farm," and they adopt as their motto, "All Animals are Equal." It is not long until the animals discover that for everyone except the pigs and their protectors, the dogs, life is exactly as hard and as painful as it had been with Mr. Jones. Although "All Animals are Equal," the pigs argue that pigs must be in positions of leadership because of their superior knowledge and intellects. They must be the leaders in order to assure that

Farmer Jones will not return and take back the farm. Furthermore, the pigs must be given the apples and the milk, not because they especially like apples and milk but because apples and milk are brain food, and sharp brains are needed for the survival of the group. Thus, although they do not especially like milk or apples, they must eat them for the good of the whole animal community.

Orwell suggests that the socialistic structure on Animal Farm fails for three fundamental reasons: the first is the perverse drive for power among those who already possess it; the second is the lack of intelligence and memory (i.e., past) among the lower animals; the third is the idea that merely altering the superficial shape of a society (without changing the internal reasoning processes) is an inadequate revolutionary goal. Because the lower animals lack a verifiable historical consciousness, they are easy prey to the manipulative uses of language and power that repeatedly falsify their sense of history and their sense of identity. During the Battle of the Cowshed, Snowball "had not paused for an instant even when the pellets from Jones's gun had wounded his back . . . Snowball fought bravely at the Battle of the Cowshed . . . Did we not give him 'Animal Hero, First Class,' immediately afterwards?" (*Animal Farm*, 80). Squealer responds simply, "That was our mistake, comrade. For we know now—it is all written down in the secret documents that we have found—that in reality he was trying to lure us to our doom" (*Animal Farm*, 80).

This is indeed dark and ironic humor, as is the abolishment of the singing of *Beasts of England*. When asked why this revolutionary song had been abolished and why it was now forbidden to sing it, Squealer said stiffly, "*Beasts of England* was the song of the Rebellion. But the Rebellion is now completed" (*Animal Farm*, 86). Again the humor is very dark. It becomes darker still later, when the animals hear guns being fired and ask what that means. "To celebrate our victory!" (*Animal Farm*, 99), cried Squealer. When Squealer is asked what victory he is referring to, he responds:

"What victory, comrade? Have we not driven the enemy off our soil—the sacred soil of Animal Farm?"

"But they have destroyed the windmill. And we had worked on it for two years!"

"What matter? We will build another windmill. We will build six windmills if we feel like it." (*Animal Farm*, 100)

The loss of historical memory is also demonstrated by the gradual rewriting of the seven commandments of Animalism. Clover thought that she had remembered the Fourth Commandment differently:

"Muriel," she said, "read me the Fourth Commandment. Does it not say something about never sleeping in a bed?" With some difficulty Muriel spelt it out. "It says, 'No animal shall sleep in a bed *with sheets*,'" she announced finally. (*Animal Farm*, 69)

After a number of animals had been executed, Clover again thought that she had remembered a commandment differently, so she asked Muriel to read the Sixth Commandment, "No animal shall kill any other animal *without cause*." The novel continues, "somehow or other, the last two words had slipped out of the animal's memory" (*Animal Farm*, 88). Toward the end of the novel, Muriel "was reading over the Seven Commandments to herself and noticed that there was yet another of them which the animals had remembered wrong. They had thought the Fifth Commandment was 'No animal shall drink alcohol,' but there were two words that they had forgotten. Actually the Commandment read, 'No animal shall drink alcohol *to excess*'" (*Animal Farm*, 103).

The great irony of *Animal Farm* is that the Pigs, who were the leaders in the rebellion against the humans, were becoming more human every day. The main followers of the Pigs were the Sheep, who bleated throughout the novel, "Four legs good, two legs bad!" (*Animal Farm*, 59), but by the end of the novel were bleating instead, "Four legs good, two legs *better*!" (*Animal Farm*, 122). Later the animals discover that the Seven Commandments have been reduced to a single Commandment: "All Animals Are Equal" has been extended to "But Some Animals Are More Equal than Others" (123). They have even lost their sense of special pride in being animals when they return from the fields one evening to discover that the pigs have taken to walking on two legs and carrying whips (*Animal Farm*, 123).

In 1946, Orwell published *Critical Essays*. This was later republished in America as

Dickens, Dali and Others (1946). David Zehr considers this to be Orwell's finest collection of essays. "The Art of Donald McGill" is about the comic postcards of Orwell's day, each of which was simply an illustration to a joke; these cards stood or fell by their ability to raise a laugh. The Donald McGill line was not only the most artistic, but it was also the most prolific and most representative of this comic tradition.

In "The Art of Donald McGill," Orwell is making an important point about the nature of humor. Obscene remarks and gestures seem to be perfectly acceptable orally and on stage, but if these same remarks and gestures are printed, there is usually a public outcry. However, the comic genre of the comic postcard seems to be an exception to this rule, since it is the only medium in which really low humor is considered to be printable: "Only in post cards and on the variety stage can the stuck-out behind, the dog and lamp-post, baby's nappy type of joke be freely exploited." Orwell suggests that these postcards give expression to what he calls the "Sancho-Panza view of life":

> The Don Quixote-Sancho Panza combination, which of course is simply the ancient dualism of body and soul in fiction form, recurs more frequently in the literature of the last four hundred years than can be explained by mere imitation. It comes up again and again, in endless variations, Bouvard and Pecuchet, Jeeves and Wooster, Bloom and Dedalus, Holmes and Watson. ("Art," in *Dickens, Dali and Others*, 135)

Orwell suggests that these representations merely reflect that in real life the two principles, noble folly and base wisdom, exist side by side in every human being ("Art," in *Dickens, Dali and Others*, 135).

McGill is our unofficial self. He is "the voice of the belly protesting against the soul. His tastes lie towards safety, soft beds, no work, pots of beer, and women with voluptuous figures":

> There is a constant world-wide conspiracy to pretend that he is not there, or at least that he doesn't matter. Codes of law and morals, or religious systems, never have much room in them for a humorous view of life. Whatever is funny is subversive, every joke is ulti-mately a custard pie, and the reason why so large a proportion of jokes centre around obscenity is simply that all societies, as the price of survival, have to insist on a fairly high standard of sexual morality. A dirty joke is not, of course, a serious attack upon morality, but it is a sort of mental rebellion, a momentary wish that things were otherwise. ("Art," in *Dickens, Dali and Others*, 136)

The McGill postcards are a kind of saturnalia, a harmless rebellion against virtue. "They express only one tendency in the human mind, but a tendency which is always there and will find its own outlet, like water. On the whole, human beings want to be good, but not too good, and not quite all the time ("Art," in *Dickens, Dali and Others*, 138).

England is the scene of *1984*, published in 1949, but England is now known as "Airstrip One" and is part of a larger nationality named "Oceania." There are three superstates; each of them is a system of oligarchical collectivism that has eliminated all intellectual freedom and privacy. During the novel, there is a ceaseless and pointless war that goes rumbling along. Sometimes Oceania is in alliance with Eastasia against Eurasia; at other times Oceania is in alliance with Eurasia against Eastasia. It does not seem to matter much who is fighting who as long as the war prevails. Everything in Oceania is controlled by the Party, which has three slogans, "War is Peace," "Freedom is Slavery," and "Ignorance is Strength." The government is divided into four ministries, the Ministry of Truth (concerned with education, news, the arts, and other propaganda), the Ministry of Love (concerned with law and order as controlled by the Thought Police), the Ministry of Plenty (concerned with rationing goods), and the Ministry of Peace (concerned with the conduct of war). Orwell uses "Doublethink" as a term to attack satirically the myopic intellectuals of his day. "Doublethink" is "the power of holding two contradictory beliefs in one's mind simultaneously and accepting them both" (Calder, *Chronicles*, 256). Orwell's protagonist, Winston Smith, works in the Ministry of Truth, and his job is to rewrite history to the benefit of the Party. But Winston is in secret revolt against the Party, and he illegally keeps a private diary in which he records his thoughts and feelings.

The choice of England as the setting of *1984* was made because Orwell wanted to emphasize that "the English-speaking races are not innately better than anyone else and that totalitarianism, if not fought against, could triumph anywhere." Gordon Beadle considers Orwell to be the Don Quixote of England "who first sensed the possibility of a totalitarian future in the land of La Mancha" (14). In Orwell's Oceania there is a perpetual state of crisis which is used as a weapon to get people to behave properly and submit to power. They are persuaded that their own individual interests are exactly the same as are the national interests, and ironically, wartime Britain at this time was making exactly the same claim (Calder, *Huxley*, 9).

1984 is written from the point of view of the working class. It is sweaty and gritty, and the unaesthetic vernacular language indicates that there is no time for considering the delicacies of phrasing or fancy rhetoric: "He has no time; he must get it all down." When he wrote *1984*, the last thing that Orwell was concerned about was literature. This is one reason why there are no credible or three-dimensional characters. Another reason is that the novelist was trying to present a world in which individuality had become obsolete and personality a crime. Nonetheless, many intellectuals feel "embarrassed before the apocalyptic desperation of the book. They begin to wonder whether it may not be just a little overdrawn and humorless; they even suspect it is tinged with the hysteria of the death-bed" (Howe, *Politics and the Novel*, 236–37). In contrast, Franz Kafka's *The Trial* is also a book of terror, but it is also a paradigm, and in some ways a puzzle where *1984* is not (235).

1984 is not a prediction but a warning. On the dust jacket of the novel, Orwell writes, "I don't believe that the kind of society I describe will arrive, but I believe something resembling it could arrive." The primary purpose of the novel is to satirically magnify the disturbing conditions, tendencies, and habits of thought that existed all around him, so that these tendencies could be recognized and arrested. What makes the novel more disturbing than Aldous Huxley's *Brave New World* or Evgeny Zamyatin's *We* is the familiarity and plausibility of the world which Orwell describes. His setting is only thirty-five years in the future. In the novel he shows the importance of an awareness of the past, a past which the Party is trying to erase from human consciousness. Smith, the protagonist, is writing a diary (a political crime) in order to give substance to his "ancestral memory." He also gathers relics of the past, such as a diary, a paperweight, and the Charrington's upstairs room, a "pocket of the past" in which he and Julia make love. This room is a place where they can escape from the present nightmarish world of Oceania into a place where they can "recover the sources of ordinary human experience" (Zehr, 421). Their obsession with the past is not merely nostalgic; rather it is a sense that the past asserts value and significance to the human consciousness and therefore to the preservation of human liberty and human heritage. In the novel, the proles, who represent 85 percent of the total population, can be oppressed because they (like the animals on *Animal Farm*) have no consciousness of their past. But, the image of a working-class woman who sings as she hangs up her clothes symbolizes for Smith the abiding human spirit that the Party has not yet extinguished.

The novel does not have a happy ending. Smith is obliterated, and the proles survive. This demonstrates Orwell's basic pessimistic nature, as expressed also in statements such as, "When you are on a sinking ship, your thoughts will be about sinking ships" (Zehr, 421).

1984 is a bitter warning of what living in a completely totalitarian world would be like. Earlier, Orwell had written an article entitled "Politics and the English Language" which foreshadowed the "Newspeak" that would later appear in *1984*. In this essay, Orwell examines political conformity in terms of language abuse. He demonstrates an intimate connection between words and thought and argues that the honest expression of clear thoughts is a necessary first step to political integrity. To this end he denounces the use of clichés, euphemisms, jargon, and foreign expressions that tend to prevent thought and lead to confused ideas or outright propaganda.

Isaac Deutscher points out that Orwell borrowed the idea, the plot, the chief characters, the symbols, and in fact the entire climate of the story of *1984* from a Russian book entitled *We*, written by Zamyatin:

> *We* is an "anti-Utopia," a nightmare vision of the shape of things to come, and a Cassandra cry. Orwell's work is a thoroughly English variation on Zamyatin's theme; and it is perhaps only the thoroughness of Orwell's English approach that gives to his work the originality that it possesses. (252)

In view of the close relationship between *We* and *1984*, it is ironic that Orwell suggested that Huxley's *Brave New World* "must be partly derived from Zamyatin's novel." Orwell wondered why this had never been pointed out (Deutscher, 253).

Hopkinson feels that the weaknesses of *1984* are two-fold. First, because Orwell was sick and dispirited at the time of writing, he imagined nothing new. His world of 1984 is merely the wartime world of 1944 except a little dirtier and more cruel. In 1944 as in 1984, totalitarianism is a series of witch hunts conducted by secret police whose charges are never clearly formulated and can therefore never be answered. The war of 1984 is fought with the weapons of 1944, rockets and tommy guns. Hopkinson feels that a second weakness of the novel is its total dystopian vision: "By amputating courage and self-sacrifice from his human beings, Orwell has removed any real tension from his story" (285). Winston Smith is a feeble creature who is incapable of any significant action, and he is also not able to draw any strength from his co-protagonist, Julie. What Winston feels for Julie is not love, and it is not lust; it is merely "a tepid mixture of attraction and contempt" (285).

There is, however, one important invention in *1984*, and that is "Newspeak," a language invented by Ingsoc (English socialism) to make all unpatriotic thoughts impossible. In Newspeak, large amounts of vocabulary were systematically eliminated and words were stripped of any unorthodox connotations. The result had the effect of diminishing the range of thought possible, so that all unconventional ideas became by definition unthinkable. Orwell gives an example of how Newspeak works: "The word *free* still existed in Newspeak, but it could only be used in such statements as 'This dog is free from lice' or 'This field is free from weeds.' It could not be used in its old sense of 'politically free' or 'intellectually free,' since political and intellectual freedom no longer existed even as concepts, and were therefore of necessity nameless" (Hopkinson, 185). Deutscher has noted that "*1984* has provided the English language with some important terminology: The title of Orwell's book is a political byword. The terms coined by him— 'Newspeak,' 'Oldspeak,' 'Mutability of the Past,' 'Big Brother,' 'Ministry of Truth,' 'Thought Police,' 'Crimethink,' "Doublethink," 'Hate Week,' etc.—have entered the political vocabulary'" (Deutscher, 250).

As soon as *1984* was written, it was claimed by the politically right, and in fact, Fredric Warburg, Orwell's publisher, said, "*1984* is worth a cool million votes to the Conservative Party; it is imaginable that it might have a preface by Winston Churchill after whom its hero is named." In an article entitled "Arguments against Orwell," D.A.N. Jones notes that such anti-Communist writers as Robert Conquest, Kingsley Amis, and Lincoln Barnett considered Orwell to be as anti-Communist as they were, and they often quoted Orwell to support their arguments in favor of the American war in Vietnam. However, American leftists such as Noam Chomsky, Norman Mailer, and Arthur Schlesinger Jr. felt that Orwell was in *their* camp and quoted him in support of their position in opposition to the United States government's war policy. Jones says, "It seems that people of almost any political persuasion can find some of their beliefs expressed in Orwell's work" (Bolton, 16). Conservatives and liberals alike agree with Orwell that "the control of language is a necessary step toward the control of minds" (Bolton, 17). Paul Chilton and Crispin Aubrey state it this way:

> In recent years key ideas and cliches from *1984* have been used by both sides in the nuclear arms debate. Alun Chalfont accuses CND of "newspeak" (*Encounter Pamphlet 13*); CND accuses its opponents of "nukespeak." In the 1983 general election a caller to a radio phone-in programme asked the Defence Minister whether acceptance of American cruise missiles and military bases did not make Great Britain look like Airstrip One—Orwell's name for Great Britain in the novel. (2)

Most British reviewers of *1984* read the book as a satiric warning against totalitarianism, but a few American reviewers "willfully misread it as an attack simply on all forms of socialism. This greatly disturbed Orwell, and he wrote a reply to those critics, warning prophetically against "the big cannibal critics that lurk in the deeper waters of American quarterly reviews" (Coppard and Crick, 17).

1984 is an ambiguous novel, and it targets bolshevism, capitalism, Nazism, catholicism, ancient slave societies, and Platonic utopias among others. Thus, readers can interpret the book in many different ways; according to

Chilton and Aubrey they "paid their money and took their pick" (2). Still, there is another ambiguity of *1984*. Many readers consider it to be a prediction or a forecast. But, it can also be read as a warning, so that the message is "If you don't do x, then y will follow." A third possible reading is that it is some sort of political theorizing concerning the nature of the totalitarian state, asking if it is "possible for naked power to sustain itself without some legitimating ideology." Still a fourth reading is as a satire or a parody—a look at the way things *could* but not necessarily *would* be. Orwell himself spoke of the novel in this last way—as a satire or parody (Chilton and Aubrey, 3).

In 1950, certain sections of *1984* were being reprinted in the American-founded German magazine *Der Monat*. T.R. Fyvel, who had spent some time working in psychological warfare against Nazi Germany, showed these German translations of *1984* to Orwell, at the same time pointing out that "Goebbels had systematically developed a totalitarian Nazi version of German 'Newspeak,' obligatory for the entire German press and radio he controlled" (2).

In 1973, the National Council of Teachers of English established the "Committee on Public Doublespeak" designed to expose the dishonest and inhumane use of language on the one hand and to promote the critical analysis of public discourse on the other hand. In 1984, the "Orwell Award" was presented to Ted Koppel, moderator of the ABC-TV program *Nightline*, for his extensive analysis of topical news, his intelligence, informed interest, social awareness, verbal fluency, and fair and rigorous questioning of controversial figures. In 1984, the ironic "Doublespeak Award" was given to the United States Department of State which arrested an estimated 1,100 Grenadians and others suspected or accused of opposing the American invasion of their island. The State Department denied that they were making arrests. "We are detaining people," they said, "They should be described as detainees." The State Department also announced in 1984 that it would no longer use the word "killing" in its official reports on the status of human rights. In the future, the word "killing" would be replaced by "unlawful or arbitrary deprivation of life."

Antony Easthope notes that by 1984 more than eleven million copies of *1984* had been sold, that it had gone through forty-one impressions, and that "more than any other novel this century this book has come to pervade general consciousness. '1984,' 'doublethink,' 'Big Brother is watching you' have become shorthand figures, collective images for the fear of bureaucratic, state-controlled totalitarianism" (264).

In an article entitled "Predicting 1984: How Did Orwell Do?—Don't Ask," Richard Friedman points out that during 1984, articles appeared in almost every publication of the popular press, and almost every columnist sometime during the year commented on how many of Orwell's "predictions" had come true. The most extensive listing may have been that by L.M. Boyd, who systematically went through the 300 odd "predictions" to see how many were in effect in 1984. Friedman suggests that all of this commentary is based on a misreading of the novel as a prediction.

Many of Orwell's critics consider the satire of *Animal Farm* and of *1984* to be very similar to that of Swift and Huxley. Orwell's writing tended to emphasize the gloomy aspects of every subject. He said that the reason *1984* turned out to be so gloomy is that he was very ill as he was writing it. Jenni Calder considers *Animal Farm* and *1984* to be a mythology in the same literary tradition as Swift's *Gulliver's Travels*, Dickens's *Posthumous Papers of the Pickwick Club*, Robert Louis Stevenson's *Strange Case of Dr. Jekyll and Mr. Hyde*, and some of Shakespeare's plays: "These are works which many of us feel we have read, even if we have not, because their message, direct or implied, has been absorbed into our cultural environment, and aspects of them have become a part of the landscape of language within which we live" (Calder, *Animal Farm and Nineteen Eighty-Four*, 5).

Audrey Coppard and Bernard Crick note that there is a close affinity between *Animal Farm* and *1984* even though they are very different in form and tone:

> The humour and lightness of *Animal Farm* masks grim implications, is darker than it seems on first reading; and *1984* is not as dark and pessimistic as it is often painted. Orwell intended it as a satire and it is full of black humour about events and institutions of his time; he probably expected people to be amused by it. (16)

Talking about *Shooting an Elephant, and Other Essays*, Jenni Calder says:

Orwell's writings are at their best in the documentary tradition in which the writer himself is the hero as observer, as in his great essays "A Hanging" and "Shooting an Elephant" which ambiguously mix fact and fiction. Almost certainly Orwell is the best polemical writer in English since Swift, and he is moreover a typically "English" writer. (Coppard and Crick, 18)

England Your England and Other Essays was republished in America as *Such, Such Were the Joys* (1953). In this attack of St. Cyprians School and its proprietors, whom he calls "Flip" and "Sambo," the writer is able to describe in detail the sour porridge clinging to the rims of the pewter bowls, the smells of sweaty stockings and dirty towels in the corridors, and the cold, loneliness, and lack of privacy. He also remembers the humiliating punishments and the pressures to conform.

He felt ugly, cowardly,. unpopular, and weak; he learned at first hand the injustice of class and snobbery. His emotions and ideals were manipulated to make him feel guilty and subservient . . . The worst source of guilt was that while inwardly loathing and fearing Flip, he found himself desperately trying to please her. (Meyers, *George Orwell*, 4)

Writing about *1984*, W.J. West says that the whole pattern of society shapes up along the same lines of fear which had been laid down in "Such, Such Were the Joys." Frederick Karl remarks that Orwell's description of his life at St. Cyprians School is very similar to the life in Oceania, and in both cases they have a Kafkaesque tone. According to Karl, both works deal with the pathos and terror which are involved when a man is caught between what he wants for himself and what the political system has to offer him. Karl sees the political matter as being secondary to the personal content (Carter, 3–4).

In a book entitled *George Orwell: An Annotated Bibliography of Criticism*, Jeffrey and Valerie Meyers give annotations for 500 critical articles relating to Orwell's work (all dissertations, all newspaper articles, and most book reviews are excluded). The books, articles, and important reviews which are included were originally written in a number of different languages—French, Italian, Spanish, German, Dutch, Norwegian, and Japanese—as well as English. *Animal Farm* has been translated into most of the major languages of the world, like Russian and Japanese, but it has also appeared in Ukrainian, Burmese, Vietnamese, and other minor languages.

It was not until *The Collected Essays, Journalism, and Letters of George Orwell* was published in 1968 that a broad range of critics could determine that John Wain had been right all along in arguing as early as 1954 that "Orwell's essays are obviously much better than his novels" (Coppard and Crick, 18).

Summary

Tongue in cheek, Lionel Trilling celebrates George Orwell for "the virtue of not being a genius." Arthur Koestler suggests that we consider Orwell to be "the only writer of genius among the litterateurs of social revolt between the two wars," and he further calls him "the missing link between Kafka and Swift" (Trilling, 1).

As an essayist, novelist, and writer of political pamphlets, Orwell was a barometer of England's popular culture during the 1930s and 1940s. Orwell hated political and literary expediency. He sympathized with the poor and the underprivileged and, therefore, challenged imperialistic, intellectual, and aristocratic privilege. During the 1940s, he was a vigorous spokesman for the bourgeois life and constantly felt a nostalgia for the order and stability of his simpler pre-1914 life. Orwell's family were servants to their King and Country, but they had been able to achieve middle-class economic status. Thus, he described himself as belonging to the "lower-upper-middle class" because of his sparse upbringing coupled with a reverence for intellectual values. One reason that he changed his name from Eric Blair to George Orwell was to show disdain for his middle-class roots. An upbringing like his has produced a disproportionate number of notable characters, and, as Hopkinson suggests, such an upbringing "does not as a rule produce characters of grace and charm, but it does produce characters" (275).

Orwell's satire can be best compared to that of Swift. It is a satire against mankind, and it is a satire against the frustrations of various personal experiences. In his essays, he tends to choose subjects that other writers overlook, like the comics which are read by schoolboys and the humorous postcards which are sold at shops along the English seaside.

Orwell was in many ways a paradox. Although he loved things British, he was sharply critical of many elements of British life such as British Imperialism. He hated socio-political control and authority, but he was fascinated by it. He made a number of incisive criticisms of socialism, yet he adamantly expressed his commitment to the ideals of socialism. He had strongly radical impulses and strongly conservative impulses as well. He reacted against the values of his upbringing, education, and class, but at the same time he valued patriotism and traditional values.

It is Orwell's ability to speak to people of widely ranging political persuasions which makes him "more widely read than perhaps any other serious writer in the twentieth century." George Woodcock says, "When people of widely differing viewpoints—Conservatives and Anarchists, Socialists and Liberals, ageing academics and young writers born old—find encouragement for their attitudes in a single author's work, we can reasonably assume that each of them is missing something, and that the work, considered as a whole, must be a good deal more complex than it appears at first sight" (Carter, 1).

Interest in Orwell has steadily increased since his death in 1950, and at present all of his books are available in paperback, including a four-volume collection of essays, articles, and letters. His *1984* has been translated into sixty-two languages and has been published continuously since 1949. In the first months of 1984, this novel sold 50,000 copies per day (1).

Emil Draitser used to write satire for Russia's best satiric publication *Krokodil*. It is therefore of special irony and interest to find on page seven of his *Forbidden Laughter* an especially appropriate statement by Orwell: "Every joke is a tiny revolution."

Selected Bibliography
Primary Sources
The major collection of primary materials (mostly letters) is the Orwell Archive at University College, London; there are additional materials at the University of Texas and the New York Public Library. No biography has been written because of a clause in the author's will.

Non-Fiction
Down and Out in Paris and London. New York: Harper, 1933. London: Secker & Warburg, 1986.
Burmese Days. New York: Harper, and London: Gollancz, 1934.

Novels
A Clergyman's Daughter. London: Gollancz, 1935; New York: Harper, 1936.
Keep the Aspidistra Flying. London: Gollancz, 1936; New York: Harcourt, Brace, 1956.
The Road to Wigan Pier. London: Gollancz, 1936; New York: Harcourt, Brace, 1958.
Homage to Catalonia. London: Secker & Warburg, 1938; New York: Harcourt, Brace, 1952.
Coming Up for Air. London: Gollancz, 1939; New York: Harcourt, Brace, 1950.
Animal Farm. London: Secker & Warburg, 1945; New York: Harcourt, Brace, 1946.
1984. London: Secker & Warburg, and New York: Harcourt, Brace, 1949.

Essays
Critical Essays. London: Secker & Warburg, 1946.
Dickens, Dali and Others. New York: Reynal and Hitchcock, 1946. Includes "The Art of Donald McGill."
Shooting an Elephant, and Other Essays. London: Secker & Warburg, 1950.
England Your England and Other Essays. London: Secker & Warburg, 1953; rpt. as *Such, Such Were the Joys.* New York: Harcourt, Brace, 1953.
The Collected Essays, Journalism, and Letters of George Orwell. 4 vols. Ed. Sonia Orwell and Ian Angus. London: Secker & Warburg, and New York: Harcourt, Brace and World, 1968.

Political Pamphlets
The Lion and the Unicorn: Socialism and the English Genius. London: Secker & Warburg, 1941.
Inside the Whale. London: Secker & Warburg, 1950.

Secondary Sources

Biographies
Bal, Sant Singh. *George Orwell: The Ethical Imagination.* New Delhi, India: Arnold-Heinemann, 1981. Bal notes that during the thirty years following Orwell's death

in 1950, more than twenty volumes and scores of critical essays and reviews were published. Orwell was admired because of his honesty of purpose, his keen observations, his humanist outlook, his wry humor, his clear and effective prose, and the power of his reportage.

Buddicom, Jacintha. *Eric and Us: A Remembrance of George Orwell*. London: Leslie Frewin, 1974. Buddicom has never met George Orwell, but she knew Eric Blair very well. They lived together in the village of Shiplake in Oxfordshire. "It was as Eric Blair he was born: it was as Eric Blair that he wished to be buried. So it is Eric Blair I would like others to remember, as I remember him" (xx).

Calder, Robert L. "George Orwell." In Robert Beum, ed. *Modern British Essayists, First Series*. Vol. 98. Detroit, MI: Gale, 1990, pp. 254–60. Calder notes that one of the essays in *The Collected Essays, Journalism, and Letters of George Orwell* (1968) entitled "Lear, Tolstoy and the Fool" is a reaction to a 1903 scathing attack of Shakespeare by the Russian, Leo Tolstoy. Shakespeare was one of Orwell's favorite authors, and in "Lear, Tolstoy and the Fool" Orwell showed what a remarkable similarity there was between King Lear and Leo Tolstoy.

Carter, Michael. *George Orwell and the Problem of Authentic Existence*. London: Croom Helm, 1985. Carter considers "authentic existence" to be important in Orwell's novels in two ways. First, it obtrudes into critical expectations to the extent that it disrupts attempts to define Orwell's literary provenance; second, it provides a conceptual unity that transcends the contradictions and paradoxes which various critics have found in Orwell's writings.

Connelly, Mark. *The Diminished Self: Orwell and the Loss of Freedom*. Pittsburgh: Duquesne University Press, 1987. The observations in Orwell's novels are more historical than political.

Coppard, Audrey, and Bernard Crick. *Orwell Remembered*. London: Ariel, 1984.

Crick, Bernard. *George Orwell: A Life*. Boston: Little, Brown, 1980. Crick indicates that Orwell made his name as a journalist by his skill at "rubbing the fur of his own cat backwards." He says that at times Orwell was "like those loyal and vociferous football supporters who are at their best when hurling complaint, sarcasm, and abuse at their own long-suffering side" (xv).

Fyvel, T.R. *George Orwell: A Personal Memoir*. New York: Macmillan, 1982. Fyvel recounts a visit to George Orwell on his deathbed. Orwell was critically ill and his body was thin and wasted. It was like the scene in *1984* when Winston Smith weeps in prison at the sight of his shrunken and tortured body. Orwell turned to Fyvel and asked with a wry smile, "Do you think one can die if one has an unwritten book in one's mind?" (2).

Gardner, Averil. *George Orwell*. Boston: Twayne, 1987. Gardner establishes the importance of *1984* by noting that in the actual year of 1984 it was extremely difficult to register that date as other than a phrase copyrighted by Orwell. She notes that "his fiction had preempted history."

Hammond, J.R. *A George Orwell Companion: A Guide to the Novels, Documentaries and Essays*. New York: St. Martin's Press. Hammond considers Orwell to be a man divided against himself, a man whose moods fluctuated throughout his career "between an engaging happiness and a profound pessimism" (xii).

Hollis, Christopher. *A Study of George Orwell: The Man and His Works*. London: Hollis and Carter, 1956. Hollis and Orwell were in school together at Eton; according to Hollis, "we had, with a somewhat curious exactness, I fancy, enough in common and enough in difference to make argument between us stimulating" (viii).

Hopkinson, Tom. "George Orwell (1903–1950)." In Ian Scott-Kilvert, ed. *British Writers*. New York: Charles Scribner's Sons, pp. 273–87. Orwell was always looking at things from a slightly different perspective. When Gandhi insisted that eating animal food is a sin, even if life is in danger, Orwell responds, "There must be some limit to what we will do in order to remain alive, and the limit is well on this side of chicken broth" (282).

Kalechofsky, Roberta. *George Orwell*. New York: Frederick Ungar, 1973.

Kalechofsky notes that Orwell wrote *Coming Up for Air* after he had experienced the Spanish Civil War.

Meyers, Jeffrey. *A Reader's Guide to George Orwell*. New Jersey: Littlefield, 1977. Meyers believes that Orwell, like Solzhenitsyn, was the "conscience of his age." Orwell's entire life and writings were a struggle against barbarism. Meyers compares George Orwell to Samuel Johnson.

Patai, Daphne. *The Orwell Mystique: A Study in Male Ideology*. Amherst: University of Massachusetts Press, 1984. The words "honesty" and "decency" have been applied to Orwell so much that his name has become a sort of "talisman, linked to a moral stature that is assumed to be unassailable . . . What is of interest is that Orwell can be used with such ease to defend opposing claims, yet this state of affairs never calls into question his moral stature and role as a touchstone of right thinking" (3).

Prasad, Shankar Narayan. *The Crystal Spirit: The Mind and Art of George Orwell*. Atlantic Highlands, NJ: Humanities Press, 1982. Orwell's work "bristles with sharp points memorably made." Orwell writes of Dickens that he is a novelist worth stealing, but Prasad points out that, ironically, this same statement is even more true of Orwell himself.

Reilly, Patrick. *George Orwell: The Age's Adversary*. London: Macmillan, 1986. Orwell had a talent for the unpalatable truth. His writing has a fierce relevance, a living presence. He is a writer who must be read, by opponents as much as by followers.

Rodden, John. *The Politics of Literary Reputation: The Making and Claiming of "St. George" Orwell*. Oxford: Oxford University Press, 1989. Even some of Orwell's staunchest supporters have had to admit that Orwell is much more important for how he lived than for what he wrote.

Shelden, Michael. *Orwell: The Authorized Biography*. London: Heinemann, 1991. Ironically, Orwell always considered himself to be a failure. When congratulated for being famous and successful, he responded, "I wonder if you know what my books sell—usually 2000! My best book, the one about the Spanish war, sold less than 1000" (1–2).

Stansky, Peter, and William Abrahams. *The Unknown Orwell*. New York: Knopf, 1972. Stansky and Abrahams explain the transformation that took place as Eric Blair became George Orwell.

———. *Orwell: The Transformation*. New York: Knopf, 1980. The publication of *Down and Out in Paris and London* "in itself was a first step—by which 'the essential second self was set free'—and what followed was a slow, arduous process of transformation" (6).

Thompson, John. *Orwell's London*. London: Fourth Estate, 1984. Eric Blair was eleven years old when World War I broke out. It was at that time that he published his first piece.

Voorhees, Richard J. *The Paradox of George Orwell*. West Lafayette, IN: Purdue University Studies, 1961. Voorhees sees Orwell's life and writing as paradoxical in three important respects.

Williams, Raymond. *George Orwell*. New York: Viking, 1971. Imperialism was one of the important targets of Orwell's satires; however, when Orwell himself was being an imperialist his response was much more complicated.

Woodcock, George. *The Crystal Spirit: A Study of George Orwell*. Boston: Little, Brown, 1966. Woodcock makes an interesting comparison between George Orwell and Don Quixote.

Wykes, David. *A Preface to Orwell*. London: Longman, 1987. Wykes considers it a paradox in a paradoxical career that Orwell is most famous for his novels but his best writing occurs in his essays, for it is in his essays that he draws on his interpretations of his life and his reading with pathos and insight.

Zehr, David Morgan. "George Orwell." In Bernard Oldsey, ed. *British Novelists, 1930–1959*. Detroit, MI: Bruccoli Clark, 1983, part 2: M–Z, pp. 407–23. Zehr feels that during the 1940s George Orwell was England's most prominent political writer and further feels that Orwell's remarkable international reputation is based primarily on his last two novels, *Animal Farm* and *1984*. Orwell had a practical and common-sense mindset and was committed to intellectual integrity, though his life was complex and paradoxical.

Bibliographies

Meyers, Jeffrey, and Valerie Meyers. *George Orwell: An Annotated Bibliography of Criticism*. New York: Garland, 1977. Jeffrey and Valerie Meyers have demonstrated that over the past fifteen years there has been an enormous increase in Orwell criticism, though most of the recent work is "derivative or polemical and generates more heat than light" (ix) and "the disparity between Orwell's lucid style and the prose of his critics is often appalling" (ix).

Books

Atkins, John. *George Orwell: A Literary Study*. London: Calder, 1954. Atkins claims that the common element running throughout George Orwell's writing is a "sense of decency." Orwell had the mind of an intellectual but the feelings of a common man, and in the conflict between the intellect and sentiment it was sentiment that usually won.

Bolton, W.F. *The Language of 1984: Orwell's English and Ours*. Oxford: Basil Blackwell, 1984. Bolton notes the effect that Orwell's language has had on twentieth-century English.

Calder, Jenni. *Chronicles of Conscience: A Study of George Orwell and Arthur Koestler*. London: Secker & Warburg, 1968. George Orwell owed his allegiance to no particular party, and he wrote as his conscience dictated. Arthur Koestler, on the other hand, was a member of the Communist Party, and he wrote as one. But, there are also similarities between Orwell and Koestler.

————. *Huxley and Orwell: "Brave New World" and "1984."* London: Edward Arnold, 1976. *Brave New World* and *1984* are usually placed into the category of anti-utopian fiction. Both Huxley and Orwell were very worried about the tendency of people to believe that an ideal is worth any sacrifice or that progress by its very nature must be good for humanity. *Brave New World* describes a time in the distant future and is more relaxed and satiric than *1984*. *1984* is more urgent, more authentic, more deeply felt, and the unelaborated prose is filled with fear and terror.

————. *Animal Farm and Nineteen Eighty-Four*. Philadelphia, PA: Open University Press, 1987.

Chilton, Paul, and Crispin Aubrey, eds. *Nineteen Eighty-Four in 1984: Autonomy, Control and Communication*. London: Comedia, 1983. Chilton and Crispin suggest that after 1066, 1984 is not only the best known date in English history but in fact that it is more important because it is symbolic of political fears and implies unsuccessful resistance because of the ultimate submission of Winston Smith to Big Brother.

Gottlieb, Erika. *The Orwell Conundrum: A Cry of Despair or Faith in the Spirit of Man?* Ottawa, Canada: Carleton University Press, 1992. Gottlieb calls *1984* a "flawed masterpiece" because there is no genuine tension or struggle since the defeat is there from the beginning. Orwell was too obsessed with "the real," and with "the process," to allow time for his imagination to take effect.

Greenblatt, Stephen Jay. *Three Modern Satirists: Waugh, Orwell, and Huxley*. New Haven: Yale University Press, 1965. Greenblatt suggests the possibility that Orwell could not have written *1984* without Evelyn Waugh's discovery of Catholicism and Aldous Huxley's discovery of the perennial philosophy of *Brave New World* and *Ape and Essence*. "Somehow one cannot imagine George Orwell settling back into a warm and cozy orthodoxy of his own" (72).

Howe, Irving. *1984 Revisited: Totalitarianism in Our Century*. New York: Harper and Row, 1983. Howe suggests that we can now look back on our time and "say unhesitatingly that its crucial sequence of events has been the rise of totalitarianism as brought to ghastly climax in the Holocaust and the Gulag" (ix).

————. *Politics and the Novel*. New York: Horizon Press, 1957. Howe contends that *1984* does not take us away from our obsession with immediate social reality. The book is appealing because its terror is particular to our century rather than being inherent in the "human condition."

Hunter, Lynette. *George Orwell: The Search*

for a Voice. Milton Keynes, England: Open University Press, 1984. In view of Orwell's clear, direct, and precise writing style, it is surprising that much Orwell criticism is concerned with the fact that he had difficulty finding a valid voice with which to express his opinions.

Jensen, Ejner J. *The Future of Nineteen Eighty-Four*. Ann Arbor: University of Michigan Press, 1984. Because *1984* is so time-bound, it is difficult to consider it a "timeless book." Jensen asks "what happens to a book set in the future when the future becomes our present?"

Kubal, David L. *Outside the Whale: George Orwell's Art and Politics*. Notre Dame: University of Notre Dame Press, 1972. Kubal discusses how author Richard Rees called Orwell a "fugitive from the camp of victory," because for Orwell, truth was more precious than the security of any particular belief system. Lies, no matter how useful to the cause, could only result in some form of totalitarianism, and this is why Orwell's fellow Socialists were no safer from his criticism and satire than were the Tories or the Fascists.

Lee, Robert A. *Orwell's Fiction*. Notre Dame: University of Notre Dame Press, 1969. Lee identifies prevailing metaphors controlling each of Orwell's novels—symbolism for *Burmese Days*, character in *Keep the Aspidistra Flying*, point of view in *Coming Up For Air*, etc.

Lewis, Peter. *George Orwell: The Road to 1984*. New York: Heinemann, 1981. In a chapter entitled "Profile of a Paradox," Lewis quotes from an unpublished preface to *Animal Farm*. One of the many paradoxes about Orwell is that thirty years after his death, Orwell is more alive than he ever was.

Lief, Ruth Ann. *Homage to Oceania: The Prophetic Vision of George Orwell*. Columbus: Ohio State University Press, 1969. In an article entitled "Why I Write," Orwell lists four reasons: "sheer egoism," "aesthetic enthusiasm," "historical impulse," and "political purpose."

Petro, Peter. *Modern Satire: Four Studies*. Berlin, Germany: Mouton, 1982. Northrop Frye classifies *1984* as a "utopian satire," together with Evgeny Zamyatin's *We* and Aldous Huxley's *Brave New World*. Some of the ideas in *1984* can be traced to Dostoyevsky's *Grand Inquisitor*, others to Shigalev's *The Possessed* and still others to *Notes from the Underground*.

Rai, Alok. *Orwell and the Politics of Despair: A Critical Study of the Writings of George Orwell*. Cambridge, MA: Cambridge University Press, 1988. Orwell called himself "someone who is a Socialist by allegiance and a Liberal by temperament." He is a liberal, but he endorses the socialist criticisms of liberalism and capitalism, and his life was devoted to resolving this paradox.

Rees, Richard. *George Orwell: Fugitive from the Camp of Victory*. London: Secker & Warburg, 1961. Both Orwell and Swift wrote highly critical satires, but Orwell's writing is not so tinged with personal bitterness as Swift's. Orwell, like Swift, was a master of plain prose with little ornamentation. "His writing went in a clean, hard line" (v).

Reilly, Patrick. *1984: Past, Present, and Future*. Boston: Twayne, 1989. Orwell was a man of principle. He once sacrificed around 40,000 pounds and refused the Book-of-the-Month Club offer to take *1984* on condition that he leave out certain sections. His response was, "What I have written I have written" (2).

Sandison, Alan. *George Orwell After 1984*. Dover, NH: Longwood Academic, 1986. Sandison says that Orwell is a chameleon on a tartan rug. In analyzing the works of Orwell we must discover the "basic shape or perspective which will allow these disparate elements to be seen as integral parts of a larger but quite distinct whole" (3).

Slater, Ian. *Orwell: The Road to Airstrip One*. New York: W.W. Norton, 1985. There was a great deal of diversity in Orwell's writing. "We need to look at more than one theme if we are to have a clear understanding of Orwell and some of his more engaging and irritating paradoxes" (16).

Small, Christopher. *The Road to Miniluv*. Pittsburgh, PA: University of Pittsburgh Press, 1975. *1984* is a dream, but dreams are important. *1984* is not just Orwell's dream; it is partly our dream as well, and that is what makes it valuable.

Steinhoff, William. *George Orwell and the Origins of 1984*. Ann Arbor: University of Michigan Press, 1975. In Burma, Orwell once read an article that he did not like in a "mildly avant-garde magazine," so he propped the magazine up at the end of his veranda and used it for target practice. "Several years later, having given up that kind of literary criticism, Orwell began appearing before the public as a left-wing writer with a mind of his own" (3).

West, W.J. *The Larger Evils: Nineteen Eighty-Four—The Truth Behind the Satire*. Edinburgh, Scotland: Canongate Press, 1992. Orwell had never had his name officially changed and at the end of his life had gone back to his real name of Eric Blair. It is ironic, then, that after Orwell's death Sonia, his second wife, took the name of Orwell. West notes that Sonia Orwell did not look after Orwell's son, as many people felt she should have, but she *did* jealously guard his literary identity.

Winnifrith, Tom, and William V. Whitehead. *1984 and All's Well?* London: Macmillan, 1984. *Animal Farm* is a fable in two important respects. First, we know that animals could not take over a farm, but second, "nobody could be both so stupid or so noble as animals like Boxer." Winston Smith, in contrast to Boxer, is neither particularly stupid nor particularly noble. He represents the average individual filled with a muddled mixture of decent altruism and selfish greed.

Zwerdling, Alex. *Orwell and the Left*. New Haven: Yale University Press, 1974. Zwerdling indicates that in reactions to communism there tend to be three stages of political development: infatuation, growing doubts, and the inevitable break. He notes that Orwell's *Animal Farm* and *1984* both represent this last stage of development.

Anthologies

Meyers, Jeffrey, ed. *George Orwell: The Critical Heritage*. London: Routledge & Kegan Paul, 1975. Orwell worked as a dishwasher, hop-picker, tutor and teacher, book dealer, farmer, shopkeeper, film critic, broadcaster, editor, columnist, war correspondent, and soldier. "Orwell deliberately sought out experience to provide material for his writing, and everything he produced is related to the events of his life" (1). Orwell had an acute eye for detail and passionate desire to inform others.

Mulvihill, Robert, ed. *Reflections on America, 1984: An Orwell Symposium*. Athens: University of Georgia Press, 1986. Orwell's essays deal with questions of liberty, justice, and decency. One of the most famous passages from his essays occurs in "A Hanging" and deals with a condemned man's effort to avoid stepping into a puddle on his way to the gallows.

Norris, Christopher, ed. *Inside the Myth: Orwell: Views from the Left*. London: Lawrence and Wishart, 1984. Norris and other authors in this anthology consider it ironic that using Orwell as the voice against everything perceived as a threat to consensus democracy is "largely manufactured—and by methods which Orwell clearly foretold."

Rose, Jonathan, ed. *The Revised Orwell*. East Lansing: Michigan State University Press, 1992. Many of the articles in Rose's anthology criticize two types of Orwellian criticism: the debate about whether or not *1984* was correctly foreseen and speculation on where Orwell would stand on certain current topics such as the Vietnam War, the 1984–1985 British coal miners' strike, and other political controversies.

Shoham, Shlomo Giora, and Francis Rosenstiel, eds. *And He Loved Big Brother: Man, State and Society in Question*. London: Macmillan, 1985. The year 1949 saw the publication of *1984* and the founding of the Council of Europe. In the novel *1984* the characters say, "War is Peace," "Freedom is Slavery," and "Ignorance is Strength." In the year 1984 the Council of Europe hosted a conference and declared, "Co-Operation is Peace," "Freedom is Pluralism," and "Access to Knowledge is Strength" in describing the condition of much of Europe in 1984.

Stansky, Peter, ed. *On Nineteen Eighty-Four*. New York: W.H. Freeman, 1983. This book is divided into four sections: "The

O

Book, The Man, The Year," "War is Peace," "Ignorance is Strength," and "Freedom is Slavery."

Wemyss, Courtney T., and Alexej Ugrinsky, eds. *George Orwell*. New York: Greenwood Press, 1987. Orwell is a much more significant figure than can be accounted for by his literary accomplishments. He is the "Patron Saint of Poverty" and the "Bard of Apocalypse."

West, W.J. *Orwell: The War Broadcasts*. London: Duckworth/BBC, 1985. It was in August of 1941 that George Orwell became the Talks Producer in the Indian Section of the BBC's Eastern Service. He remained in this position until November 1943.

Williams, Raymond, ed. *George Orwell: A Collection of Critical Essays*. Englewood Cliffs, NJ: Prentice-Hall, 1974. Orwell was not a traitor, but he was also not a liberator. He was neither a truth-teller nor a slanderer. His work is filled with contradictions and paradoxes; truth and falsehood, and humanity and inhumanity are not always clearly distinguishable.

Articles

Beadle, Gordon. "George Orwell and the Spanish Civil War." *Duquesne Review*, 16 (Spring, 1971): 3–16. Beadle notes that although Orwell's *Coming Up for Air* is set in England, "the story nevertheless reverberates with thinly-disguised verbal pictures and grim interpretations of what Orwell had seen and experienced in Spain."

Croft, Andy. "Worlds without End Foisted Upon the Future—Some Antecedents of *1984*." In Christopher Norris, ed. *Inside the Myth*: *Orwell: Views from the Left*. London: Lawrence and Wishart, 1984, pp. 183–216. In 1941, Orwell complained that English literature had failed to contribute to "the special class of literature that has arisen out of the European political struggle since the rise of fascism." Croft, however, says that Orwell misled his readers in this regard.

Deutscher, Isaac. "1984—The Mysticism of Cruelty." In Isaac Deutscher, ed. *Russia in Transition and Other Essays*. London: Hamilton, 1957, pp. 230–45. *1984* is intense and concentrated, fear-ridden and restricted in imagination. The symbolism of *1984* is crude; Orwell's story unfolds like a cheap science-fiction film.

Easthope, Antony. "Fact and Fantasy in *1984*." In Christopher Norris, ed. *Inside the Myth*: *Orwell: Views from the Left*. London: Lawrence and Wishart, 1984, pp. 263–85. Easthope evaluates the accuracy of *1984* as a prediction.

Friedman, Richard. "Predicting 1984: How Did Orwell Do?—Don't Ask." *WHIMSY*, 3 (1985): 13–14. Friedman notes that Orwell had reversed the last two numbers in 1948 (the year the novel was written) to get 1984 (the title of the novel) and suggests that Orwell was commenting on his own world and time rather than trying to describe a future one. Newspeak is discussed as further evidence for grounding the novel in the present time.

Lutz, William D. "1984 Orwell Award, and 1984 Doublespeak Award." *WHIMSY*, 3 (1985): 108–09. In 1973, the Committee on Public Doublespeak of the National Council of Teachers of English established the "Orwell Award" to recognize the author who had made an outstanding contribution to the critical analysis of public discourse, and the ironic and oxymoronic "Doublespeak Award" to "pay tribute" to language which is grossly deceptive, evasive, euphemistic, confusing, or self-contradictory.

Rahv, Philip. "The Unfuture of Utopia." *Partisan Review*, 16 (July, 1949): 743–49. Rahv suggests that *1984* inspires dread not because it is a glimpse of the future, but because "its materials are taken from the real world as Orwell knew it, from conditions prevailing in the totalitarian nations" of the day (182).

Trilling, Lionel. "Introduction." *Homage to Catalonia*. Boston: Beacon, 1952, pp. v–xxiii. Orwell was a revolutionary, but he nevertheless "clung with a kind of wry, grim pride to the old ways of the last class that had ruled the old order."

Vinz, Ruth. "1984: Intricate Corridors within a Barren World." *English Journal*, 72, 6 (1983): 39–41. Winston's paperweight in *1984* was a symbol of the past and of the future—a symbol of identity and hope.

Don L.F. Nilsen

P

Pain, Barry Eric Odell

Born: Cambridge, September 28, 1864
Education: Perse School, Cambridge, ?–1879;
Sedbergh School, 1879–1883; Corpus
Christi College, Cambridge University,
1883–1886; Third Class, Division 2 in
the Classical Tripos
Marriage: Amelia Nina Anna Lehmann,
1892; two children
Died: Watford, May 5, 1928

Biography

Born in Cambridge on September 28, 1864, Barry Pain was the youngest son of John Odell Pain, linen draper and silk mercer of 3 Sidney Street, and his wife Maria. From the Perse School, Cambridge, he transferred in 1879 to Sedbergh School and went on from there to Corpus Christi College, Cambridge, in 1883, where he joined his three lively brothers, who were also at the university. He began well with the award of a scholarship at the end of his first year; thereafter his academic career was undistinguished; he ended, in 1886, in Class III, Division 2 of the Classical Tripos. However, at both school and university he stood out as an all-round man: a keen debater, a public-spirited office-holder, a dependable footballer, and a fertile contributor to student magazines (he was a writer from the age of eight).

From 1886 to 1890 he taught classics at an army crammer's at Guildford. In 1888, *The Cambridge Fortnightly* was founded, mainly, according to British art critic and painter Roger Fry, "in order to provide an outlet for Mr. Barry Pain's writings"; the birth of *Granta* in 1889 furnished another outlet, and encouragement from the editor of *The Cornhill Magazine* inspired Pain to settle in London on New Year's Day 1890 to try his luck as a freelance writer. His first book was published in the following year, and his finances were eased in 1893 by the death of his prosperous father.

Pain contributed during the 1890s to *Black and White, Punch, The National Observer, To-Day*, and other periodicals. In 1897, he became editor of *To-Day*, succeeding Jerome K. Jerome, who had always valued him highly. For the rest of his life Pain was a prolific and popular writer, equally popular as a public speaker, bearded, hearty, but wary of interviews with the Press.

In 1892, Pain married Amelia Nina Anna Lehmann, daughter of the painter Rudolf Lehmann and sister of the composer Liza Lehmann. Bret Harte and Mrs. Oscar Wilde were among the wedding guests. The union seems to have been a happy one, and it produced two daughters. Mrs. Pain wrote fiction and plays. The family lived for the most part in places near London, then still rural or semi-rural (at Pinner, Vushey, Farnham Royal), but also for a time in St. John's Wood. Pain was a sincere Christian, a home-lover, a great walker, a keen gardener, a gifted cook, a pianist, and a singer. The friend who remembered him as a "cheery cynic" also remembered his "over-flowing good humor." "He has a host of friends," *The Ludgate Magazine* reported in March 1896, "and would never think it worth while to have what you might seriously call an enemy."

When war broke out in 1914, Pain was touring the United States, but by April 1915, he had joined the anti-aircraft section of the Royal Naval Volunteer Reserve and was helping to man a searchlight station on Parliament Hill, Hampstead Heath. He was released from these duties suffering from eye-strain and spent the rest of the war on the London Appeals Tribunal, examining conscientious objectors.

The death of his wife in 1920 (followed by the loss of his brother, Aubrey, early in the next year) was a blow from which he never recovered. He moved to a new address in Watford, over-worked, smoked too much, and became a recluse. In a late photograph he appears a haggard, tragic figure. He died at Watford on May 5, 1928.

Literary Analysis

Pain was urged by W.E. Henley to write on serious matters; he had serious interests—Georgian literature, occultism, precious stones—but humor would keep bubbling up. With Pett Ridge and Jerome he was hailed as one of the leaders of the "New Humor" (in the 1890s everything had to be "New") but was himself to declare: "The distinction between the old and the new humor is ridiculous and perfectly arbitrary." Indeed, even Holbrook Jackson, in his classic account of the decade, can only say that the new humor "probably differed from the old humor in that it was more self-conscious and less capable of laughing at itself. The New Humor when it was *new* was perhaps a little inhuman, and it reached its highest expression not in any of the works written with an eye on laughter, but in works like the plays of Bernard Shaw, which provoked laughter out of more serious business."

Certainly when Pain's first book, *In a Canadian Canoe*, appeared in 1891, his contemporaries sensed that a new note had been struck. He was in his late twenties and already at the peak of his powers, mixing lighthearted meditation, shameless puns, youthful parody, bleak naturalism, dream-sequences, and a happy surrealism.

Two books followed in 1892: *Playthings and Parodies*—he had much fun with John Ruskin, Walter Pater, and R.D. Blackmore—and *Stories and Interludes*, the interludes being in verse, sometimes serious. Unfortunately, he now went into overproduction, tempted by the vast array of middlebrow 1890s magazines and a public hungry for light fiction. *Graeme and Cyril* (1893) is an undistinguished school story; *The Kindness of the Celestial* (1894) and *Wilmay* (1898) are collections of tales that are merely competent; *The Octave of Claudius* (1897) is a readable fantasy thriller, and *The Romantic History of Robin Hood* (1898) is hack work.

However, with *Eliza* (1900) his full powers are evident. The book recalls *The Diary of a Nobody* (George and Weedon Grossmith), published eight years earlier, but has more subtlety. "I believe," writes Eliza's husband, a complacent suburban office-worker, "there are but few people who could give you an accurate description of themselves." He never doubts that he is one of those few. Eliza and her mother are aware that he is not, and their stoical patience is impressive. The book was rejected by publisher after publisher, despite Pain's popularity. When it eventually appeared it was hugely successful. Sequels were demanded, and Pain provided them: *Eliza Getting On* in 1901, *Eliza's Husband* in 1903, *Exit Eliza* in 1912, and *Eliza's Son* in 1913.

The comedy of Eliza's husband is the comedy of his self-deception; the reader sees the truth through the eyes of Eliza. There is a similar situation in the Barleys' marriage in *The One Before* (1902). Sometimes, instead of the wife, it is the servants who discern the truth, servants like the char in *Mrs. Murphy* (1913) and the gardener in *Edwards* (1915) who have their employers well summed up. In a reversal of character types, however, Constantin Dix is not self-deceived: a criminal posing as a social worker, he deceives others—Pain liked a cheeky rogue, and *Memoirs of Constantin Dix* (1905) was very successful.

The skill that Pain used to satirize people was sometimes applied to the parodying of fashionable authors such as Margot Asquith, A.S.M. Hutchinson, and Michael Arlen, and these parodies were very popular. Indeed, his writing continued to be popular in all of the sub-genres that he essayed until his death in 1928 and for a few years beyond, gladdening the vacant evenings and weekends of a public with no television and only an infant radio. Light novels, not to mention the grimly serious *Lindley Kays* (1904), and collections of tales poured from his pen with a fatal facility that did him no harm in the literary markets of the day, yet which in retrospect is rather saddening.

Pain certainly studied all social classes attentively and without sentimentality. As the son of a provincial shopkeeper, he had more early opportunities to do so than most of his college friends; in his first, impoverished days in London he lodged in a workman's flat, and he is said to have found the model for Eliza in Pinner. C.L. Hind noticed the "slow, amused, estimating look" that Pain directed at people around him, and he evidently worked hard to catch the structure and flavor of their speech. In *De Omnibus* (1901) he presents a bus conductor, in *The Confessions of Alphonse* (1917), less entertainingly, a foreign waiter.

Pain wanted to be a serious craftsman and he often succeeded. The first page of *Eliza* deserves close analysis. In 1916, he was commissioned by Martin Secker to write a little book on the short story and he used this opportunity to inveigh against "pulpy and nerveless English" and the "false, sweet story with a silly sunny ending." He pointed out that publishing is commerce and the writer must accept this if he wants to be printed, "yet within any limitations it is still possible to write clean sentences, to remember the meaning of the words you use, and to write of people whom you have made alive in your mind and not stale dummies." He sees nothing shameful in a happy ending but stresses that the art of the short story is the difficult art of compression. Still, he claims, "Difficulty is pure joy to an artist."

"In France," Alfred Noyes wrote two years after Pain's death, "he would have been recognized as a great artist." Hind was more discerning. Pain, he declared, seemed "always to be on the eve of writing a great book."

Summary

During the 1890s, Barry Pain was seen as one of the leading exponents of the New Humor. A genial, many-sided man, he was a prolific author and an extremely popular purveyor of humor and light fiction. Unfortunately, because of his popularity he developed a facility in his writing that diminished his talent. However, he aspired to be a serious artist, and he produced a number of humorous works that are eminently readable.

Selected Bibliography

Primary Sources
In a Canadian Canoe. London: Henry, 1891.
Stories and Interludes. London: Henry, 1892.
Playthings and Parodies. London: Cassell, 1892.
Graeme and Cyril. London: Hodder & Stoughton, 1893.
The Kindness of the Celestial. London: Henry, 1894.
The Octave of Claudius. London and New York: Harper, 1897.
The Romantic History of Robin Hood. London and New York: Harper, 1898.
Wilmay. London and New York: Harper, 1898.
Eliza. London: S.H. Bousfield, 1900; rpt. in *The Eliza Stories*. London: Pavilion Books (Michael Joseph), 1984.
Eliza Getting On. London: Cassell, 1901; rpt. in *The Eliza Stories*. London: Pavilion Books (Michael Joseph), 1984.
De Omnibus. London: Fisher Unwin, 1901.
Stories in the Dark. London: Grant Richards, 1901.
Another Englishwoman's Love Letters. London: Fisher Unwin, 1901.
Nothing Serious. London: Black & White, 1901.
The One Before. London: Grant Richards, 1902.
Little Entertainments. London: Fisher Unwin, 1903.
Eliza's Husband. London: Chatto & Windus, 1903; rpt. in *The Eliza Stories*. London: Pavilion Books (Michael Joseph), 1984.
Curiosities. London: Fisher Unwin, 1904.
Deals. London: Hodder & Stoughton, 1904.
Lindley Kays. London: Methuen, 1904.
Three Fantasies. London: Methuen, 1904.
The Memoirs of Constantin Dix. London: Fisher Unwin, 1905; London: Greenhill Books, 1985.
Robinson Crusoe's Return. London: Hodder & Stoughton, 1906.
Wilhelmina in London. London: John Long, 1906.
The Diary of a Baby. London: Eveleigh Nash, 1907.
The Gifted Family. London: Methuen, 1909.
Proofs before Pulping. London: Mills & Boon, 1909.
The Exiles of Faloo. London: Methuen, 1910.
An Exchange of Souls. London: Eveleigh Nash, 1911.
Here and Hereafter. London: Methuen, 1911.
Stories in Grey. London: Werner Laurie, 1911.
The New Gulliver. London: Werner Laurie, 1912.
Exit Eliza. London: Cassell, 1912; rpt. in *The Eliza Stories*. London: Pavilion Books (Michael Joseph), 1984.
Stories without Tears. London: Mills & Boon, 1912.
Eliza's Son. London: Cassell, 1913; rpt. in *The Eliza Stories*. London: Pavilion Books (Michael Joseph), 1984.

Mrs. Murphy. London: Werner Laurie, 1913.

The Confessions of Alphonse. London: Werner Laurie, 1917.

One Kind and Another. London: Martin Secker, 1914.

Futurist Fifteen. London: Werner Laurie, 1914.

Edwards. London: Werner Laurie, 1915; Bath: Cedric Chivers, 1969.

The Short Story. London: Martin Secker, 1916.

Me and Harris. London: Werner Laurie, 1916.

Innocent Amusements. London: Werner Laurie, 1918.

The Problem Club. London: W. Collins & Son, 1919.

Marge Askinforit. London: Werner Laurie, 1920.

The Death of Maurice. London: Skeffington & Son, 1920.

Going Home. London: Werner Laurie, 1922.

If Summer Don't. London: Werner Laurie, 1922.

Tamplin's Tales of His Family. London: Werner Laurie, 1924.

This Charming Green Hat-Fair. London: Werner Laurie, 1925.

Dumphry. London: Ward Lock, 1927.

The Later Years. London: Chapman & Hall, 1927.

Secondary Sources

Bowden, John Head. Introduction to Barry Pain. *More Stories.* London: Werner Laurie, 1930. Very slight.

Hind, C.L. "Barry Pain." In his *More Authors and I.* London: John Lane, 1922, pp. 260–65. A handful of memories and critical remarks.

Jones, Terry. Introduction to *The Eliza Stories.* London: Pavilion, 1984. Merely a puff by a popular entertainer for a very funny book.

Lawrence, Arthur H. "The Humour of Women: Mr. Barry Pain, his work and his views." *The Young Woman,* 6 (1897–98): 129–32. An enthusiastic appreciation of "his work and his views" with some important biographical details.

Noyes, Alfred. Introduction to Barry Pain. *Humorous Stories.* London: Werner Laurie, 1930. Very slight.

F.H.P. Introduction to *Barry Pain (Short Stories of Today).* London: Harrap & Co., 1928. A very brief appreciation.

John Adlard

Peacock, Thomas Love

Born: Weymouth, Dorset, October 18, 1785
Education: John Harris Wicks school, Englefield Green near Windsor, Berkshire, 1792–1798
Marriage: Jane Gryffydh, March 22, 1820; four children, plus one adopted child
Died: Lower Halliford, Middlesex, January 23, 1866

Biography

Thomas Love Peacock, born on October 18, 1785, in Weymouth, Dorset, was the only child of glass merchant Samuel Peacock and the former Sarah Love. Following Samuel's death (date uncertain), Sarah and young Thomas took up residence at Gogmoor Hall in Chertsey, Middlesex, with Sarah's parents, Thomas Love, a pensioned naval officer, and his wife. Peacock received his only formal education at the school of John Harris Wicks in Englefield Green near Windsor, Berkshire, during a six-year period beginning in 1792. Thereafter, he read extensively on his own, developing an impressive erudition, particularly in the Greek and Roman classics, which is evident throughout his later works.

Following the early conclusion of his formal schooling, Peacock worked as a clerk in London and began attempting poetry, with his mother, who lived with him until her death in 1833, as his ever dependable audience. With one of these attempts, a response in couplets to a question concerning the relative educational merits of history and biography, he won a contest sponsored by a young people's magazine and gained his first recognition as a writer. During the early years of the nineteenth century, Peacock dedicated himself increasingly to his reading and writing, publishing the pamphlet-length *The Monks of St. Mark* in 1804 and *Palmyra, and Other Poems* in late 1805 (but dated 1806). At about this period, too, Sarah's father died, leaving an annuity which, until it was exhausted in 1811, helped to support Sarah and her literary son, who moved back for a time to Chertsey.

By 1807, Peacock had become engaged to a Chertsey neighbor, Fanny Falkner, whose family pressured her to break off the engagement, Peacock's first in a series of amorous disappointments. More lasting and of greater importance to his literary ambitions was the friendship that he formed during this same year with Thomas and Edward Hookham, whose father, also Thomas, was a key figure in the London book trade. Ultimately, the Hookham family would publish many of Peacock's most important works.

Following a distressing several months in 1808 and 1809 as secretary to the captain of the H.M.S. *Venerable*, a period in which Peacock continued to write despite the discomforts of shipboard life, he made a walking tour of the valley of the Thames and wrote *The Genius of the Thames*, a lengthy topographical poem published in 1810 by the younger Hookhams. By 1810, too, he had moved to Wales, where he was drawn to two women, one of whom, Jane Gryffydh, after a hiatus of nearly a decade, would become his wife.

With the expiration of the family annuity, Peacock and his mother experienced a time of financial distress partially alleviated by Literary Fund grants in 1811, 1812, and 1813. The publication of *The Philosophy of Melancholy* in February 1812 encouraged him to further writing efforts, but the unsuccessful submission to Drury Lane Theatre of a series of farces in 1812 and 1813 temporarily reversed his literary fortunes. Nevertheless, he continued his walking tours of the picturesque countryside of England and Wales, again fell deeply and momentarily in love, this time with a fifteen-year-old girl, and formed the most important literary friendship of his long and rich life. His introduction to Percy Bysshe Shelley in 1812 had profound implications for both writers, providing the prodigiously learned Shelley with further recondite knowledge from Peacock's also ample store and presenting a challenge to Shelley's extreme idealism while giving the satiric Peacock access to an intellectual circle whose radical theories both fascinated and amused him.

The appearance of two poems, *Sir Hornbook* in late 1813 (but dated the following year) and *Sir Proteus* in 1814, breathed new life into Peacock's literary career, but his personal life remained troubled. An apparent engagement to longtime family acquaintance Marianne de St. Croix came to nothing, and an amorous adventure with a supposed heiress proved a further disappointment when Peacock discovered her to be penniless. His financial difficulties climaxed in 1815 at Liverpool, where he was jailed for nonpayment of debts. Shelley, whom Peacock had helped through the traumatic aftermath of his flight to the Continent with Mary Godwin, rescued his impecunious friend from further economic embarrassment by granting

him a generous annuity which Peacock used to establish his mother and himself in lodgings in the vicinity of Marlow, Buckinghamshire.

The publication of the first of his important satiric novels, *Headlong Hall*, later in 1815 (but bearing the date 1816) consolidated his change of fortune and ushered in the period of his transition from chaotic disrepute to prosperous stability. Two minor works, the poems *The Round Table* (1817) and *Rhododaphne* (1818), appeared during this time, but his second and third satiric novels, *Melincourt* (1817) and *Nightmare Abbey* (1818), among his most significant comic achievements, were also written within this dynamic period.

In May 1819, Peacock accepted a position with the East India Company, thereby becoming a colleague, among others, of utilitarian philosopher James Mill, and in November of that year, by correspondence, he asked Jane Gryffydh to marry him. Despite the long period during which they had been out of touch, Miss Gryffydh accepted his proposal, and they were married on March 22, 1820. A daughter, Mary Ellen, was born to the couple in the following year, the first of their four biological children. Despite his new professional and familial responsibilities, Peacock also found time to read the galleys of Shelley's masterpiece *Prometheus Unbound*, to write "The Four Ages of Poetry," which appeared in the January 1820 issue of *Ollier's Literary Miscellany* and inspired Shelley's magnificent "A Defence of Poetry," and to commence the writing of his fourth novel, *Maid Marian*, ultimately published in 1822.

Following Shelley's tragic drowning on July 8, 1822, Peacock became co-executor, with Lord Byron, of the Shelley estate. Shouldering most of the duties, Peacock worked diligently to assure the future of Mary Shelley, who was not a favorite with Shelley's father. Added to this demand on his time and to the continuing need to establish himself at the East India Company, Peacock was also coordinating the reconstruction of a pair of cottages in Lower Halliford, Middlesex, into one large dwelling into which he moved with his mother, his wife, and his daughter, in 1823. He maintained lodgings in London, which he occupied during the work week, but on non-work days and during the decade of his retirement, Lower Halliford was his home.

The births within the next two years of a second daughter and a son, Margaret and Edward, deepened Peacock's domesticity and help to explain the relative literary silence of this period of his life. By 1825, he had begun composing the *Paper Money Lyrics*, finally published in 1837, but his urgency to write appears to have been less intense in these than in the immediately preceding years, and the death in 1826 of Margaret and the resultant breakdown of Jane further drained his creative energies. The couple's adoption in the same year of Mary Rosewell, who reminded them of Margaret, and the birth in 1828 of Rosa Jane, the last of the Peacock children, seem to have healed some of the parental wounds, but Jane never entirely recovered from the shock of losing her daughter.

By decade's end and on into the 1830s, the more resilient Thomas was publishing articles in periodicals such as the *Westminster Review*, the *Edinburgh Review*, the *Globe*, the *Examiner*, and the *London Review* and was completing his fourth and fifth novels, *The Misfortunes of Elphin* (1829) and *Crotchet Castle* (1831). Somewhat anomalously, he was also beginning a decade-long effort to improve communication with India through the use of steamships, his primary contribution to the affairs of the East India Company. So successful were both his business and his literary ventures that in 1836 he became Chief Examiner of Correspondence for the corporation, the position previously held by Mill, and in 1837 four of his works were reissued in a combined volume of Bentley's "Standard Novels."

The death of the author's mother in 1833, however, had destroyed much of his zest for writing, as he himself admitted, and though the passing of his most appreciative reader did not put an immediate halt to his literary efforts, his productivity from the late 1830s through 1856, the year of his corporate retirement, was insignificant. Clearly, too, the heavy responsibilities of the Chief Examinership took their toll, as the more pleasant distractions of Peacock's natural conviviality never had. During his long life, Peacock numbered such luminaries as Shelley and the elder Mill, John Stuart Mill, Jeremy Bentham, John Cam Hobhouse, Benjamin Disraeli, and William Makepeace Thackeray among his friends and acquaintances, and the time that he expended in social and intellectual intercourse was an infinitely more potent stimulant to his satiric genius than were the countless hours that he dedicated to the exigencies of business.

Family problems have also been pointed to as a deterrent to Peacock's literary output. His daughter Mary Ellen's first husband, Lieutenant Edward Nicolls, drowned in 1844 within months of their marriage. His invalid wife Jane, in poor health since 1826, died in 1851. Both his son Edward and his daughter Rosa Jane, who would die in 1857, entered into marriages of which Peacock disapproved, and Mary Ellen's second marriage proved the most disastrous of all. Remarried in 1849, this time to novelist and poet George Meredith, Mary Ellen abandoned her husband in 1858 for another man, only to return to London, where she found herself alone and where ultimately she died in misery in 1861.

However, despite these various blows, Peacock experienced a last period of creative achievement. In response to three works on Shelley issued in 1858, he published his own two-part *Memoirs of Percy Bysshe Shelley*, edited some of Shelley's previously unpublished correspondence, and wrote a final "Supplementary Notice" on the poet, all of which appeared in various numbers of *Fraser's Magazine* between 1858 and 1862. From April to December of 1860, *Fraser's* also published Peacock's last novel, *Gryll Grange*, which was issued as a separate volume the following year.

Peacock died in Lower Halliford on January 23, 1866, reputedly as the traumatic aftereffect of a fire in his home. Physically unhurt but terrified, he had stubbornly remained in his beloved library despite the flames. His adopted daughter, Mary Rosewell, was his sole heir.

Literary Analysis

Peacock sought literary success from his teenage years onward, but the first decade or so of his career, dedicated almost entirely to poetry, gives little indication of the comic genius which would express itself primarily through prose fiction. *The Monks of St. Mark*, though, is an exception to the general seriousness of the author's early poetic publications, and its comic medievalism, derivative of the parodies written in reaction to the Gothic ballads of Matthew Gregory ("Monk") Lewis, Robert Southey, and others, foreshadows the farcical exuberance of his later works and contains hints of the mock Gothicism to be found in *Nightmare Abbey* and elsewhere. With its midnight opening and its references to "the *tempest-fiend*" and "the *storm-king*," the poem threatens to become a typical Lewis elemental-spirit ballad, but Peacock suddenly informs us at the end of the second stanza that the monks of the title have gathered in the refectory rather than the chapel and that their struggle will be "with Bacchus, not Satan," thereby transforming the narrative from a tale of terror into a tale of drunken revelry. The punning and unbridled slapstick of the poem's latter stanzas are typical of Peacock's love of witty buffoonery, and his use of outrageous humor to mock a literary fashion foreshadows much of the satire to come.

The Gothic ballads were inspired by the several English translations in 1796 of Gottfried August Burger's horror ballad "Lenore," a manifestation of a Germanic influence on British artistic and intellectual life which Peacock took frequent occasion to deplore, and in the third stanza of *Sir Proteus*, one of Peacock's most ambitious attempts at poetic satire and his last significant publication before the satiric novels, he directly parodies the best-known lines of the extraordinarily popular William Taylor translation of Burger's poem:

> Tramp! tramp! across the land he went;
> Splash! splash! across the sea;
> And then he gave his bragging vent—
> "Pray who can ride like me?"

Ironically dedicated to Lord Byron and full of Scriblerian annotations attacking Southey, Sir Walter Scott, William Wordsworth, Samuel Taylor Coleridge, and others, *Sir Proteus* is a lampoon of the Germanic supernaturalism, brooding egotism, insipid sentimentalism, false primitivism, and other literary barbarisms of an age bent on abandoning the Classical clarity and good sense which Peacock so emphatically prized.

Sir Proteus is a high-spirited poem, but its satiric convolutions achieved nothing like the success of the following year's *Headlong Hall*, the work in which Peacock discovered his metier. *Headlong Hall* exploits a conversational humor with which Peacock had recently been experimenting in unsuccessful farces intended for the Drury Lane Theatre. In its perfected form in this and four of the six later novels, his comic technique involves the subordination, but never the elimination, of other narrative elements to long passages of self-revelatory dialogue, generally centered on the opposing eccentricities and intellectual obsessions of the novel's cast of characters. Jonsonian in their single-mindedness, these characters are drawn together at the place referred to in the novel's title

where they speak and interact in conformity to their defining peccadilloes, thereby allowing Peacock to reveal the inadequacies of the human types, the schools of thought, or the individuals which they represent. The long-winded talk, the essence of these conversation novels, is typically strung together around a threadbare love plot, the good-humored resolution of which permits the writer to affirm the enduring joy of life while laughing at its too frequently defective manifestations.

The above description indicates the general pattern of Peacock's satiric technique in the conversation novels but suggests nothing of their topical richness, a richness which bewilders most readers who attempt to approach him without editorial assistance. Peacock deals with such timeless satiric subjects as vanity, hypocrisy, and greed, yet he more characteristically concerns himself with contemporary intellectual, political, social, and artistic pretension, and he does so with the erudition of a cultural historian. The poetic headnote to *Headlong Hall*, slightly modified from Swift, indicates the central tenet of Peacock's critique:

> All philosophers, who find
> Some favorite system to their mind,
> In every point to make it fit,
> Will force all nature to submit.

Mingled in the tale which follows are elements of the necessitarian thinking of William Godwin and the young Shelley, the primitivism of Jean Jacques Rousseau, the deteriorationism of Thomas Malthus, the vegetarianism of J.F. Newton, and the phrenological speculations of J.K. Spurzheim. Certain characters voice the landscape theories of Richard Payne Knight, Uvedale Price, Humphry Repton, and "Capability" Brown, while others are presumed, by consensus of the critics, to caricature novelist Amelia Opie, reviewer Francis Jeffrey, and poets Southey and Coleridge. And, this does not even approximate a complete list of the targets of Peacock's barbed pen.

The plot premise of *Headlong Hall* which allows Peacock to draw together these disparate elements is that the amiably self-indulgent Harry Headlong, Esquire, of ancient Welsh lineage, having added an interest in the intellectual and the aesthetic to the more usual fascinations of his class with the delights of sport and the table, has invited a group congenial to his new passions to visit him at his ancestral home. His guests include a panoply of crack-brained thinkers, writers, artists, and dilletanti, each of whom talks incessantly of his personal hobby-horse and ignores every evidence of the inadequacy and absurdity of his limited point of view. Mr. Foster, who believes that all things work toward the world's ultimate perfection, interprets every event as productive of good, but his antagonist, Mr. Escot, sees only perpetual deterioration. Mr. Jenkison, whose faith is in an eternal equivocation which maintains the status quo, denies that, when seen properly, a choice can be made between the perfectionist and the deteriorationist positions. The Reverend Doctor Gaster, on the other hand, although exhibiting a polite interest in the philosophic wranglings of his companions, sees reality, first, last, and always, in terms of gastronomy, while for Mr. Cranium, phrenology is the key to truth. Assorted additional characters argue the book's central philosophical question or some subsidiary question, particularly what constitutes beauty and good taste, with all the zeal of the dogmatic (and generally self-serving) intellectual crank.

Peacock, for whom a moderate Epicurean enjoyment and a common-sense realism were antidotes to much of the foolishness that plagued the world, deflates the pomposities of his characters, established largely through the intricate circumlocutions of their endless talk, by the time-honored comic technique of creating circumstances in which life steals away their dignity and renders their poses ridiculous. Mr. Escot falls in love with Mr. Cranium's daughter Cephalis and wrestles with the problem of how to reconcile the possibility of marital happiness with the doctrine of universal deterioration. Even more basic questions, touching upon the fundamental nature of the philosopher, trouble his thoughts: "The deteriorationist entered into a profound moral soliloquy, in which he examined *whether a philosopher ought to be in love?* Having decided this point affirmatively against Plato and Lucretius, he next examined, *whether that passion ought to have the effect of keeping a philosopher awake?* Having decided this negatively, he resolved to go to sleep immediately: not being able to accomplish this to his satisfaction, he tossed and turned like Achilles or Orlando." Surviving his insomnia, Escot successfully proposes marriage to Cephalis, but earning the consent of her father is a more difficult matter. Having delivered a lecture on skulls whose undercurrent of misanthropy is worthy of the bitterest comments of Swift, Cranium nevertheless shows his own flawed humanity by preferring a suitor with £10,000 to the suitor of his daughter's choice. Even the fact of Escot's having saved him from drowning (after an explosion set off by Mr. Milestone, an improver of landscapes through the liberal use of gunpowder, had precipitated him ignobly from a tower) is insufficient to inspire his paternal benevolence. A Godwinian argument on the mechanical inevitability of the events, including Escot's heroism, allows him to brush aside appeals to gratitude. What he cannot dismiss, however, is the bribe of the supposed skull of the great Welshman Cadwallader, and for this, he exchanges his daughter. The book ends with not one but four weddings proving the comic rightness of the world and with the incorrigible Escot speaking of the fallenness of modern marriage even as his own blissfully embraced marriage has barely begun.

Peacock followed up the success of *Headlong Hall* with the publication of a second conversation novel, *Melincourt*. Concerned more with political and social problems than *Headlong Hall*, *Melincourt* also differs from its predecessor in more clearly defining and more directly advocating its author's position on the issues with which it deals. Defining a generous liberalism in terms of a contemporary renewal of chivalric ideals, in the novel the author traces the gradual union of Anthelia Melincourt, who demands a true modern chivalry of whoever will win her hand, and Sylvan Forester, who possesses just such a chivalric nature but who must be drawn from his retired life at Redrose Abbey if he is to be united with his soulmate and achieve his life's full potential. Also on the side of chivalric good is Sir Oran Haut-ton, described by his friend and patron Forester as "a specimen of the natural and original man." An orangutan of unusual attainments (whose characterization suggests that Edgar Rice Burroughs may have read Peacock), Sir Oran is both a satiric tool for belittling the more extreme notions of the primitivists, particularly Lord Monboddo, and an embodiment of an active, instinctive heroism.

Among Anthelia's false suitors are Mr. Derrydown, a caricature of Walter Scott who is fascinated with the antiquarian shadow of chivalry rather than its substance, and Lord Anophel Achthar, a reactionary conservative who interprets Anthelia's chivalric ideal as Jacobin. Achthar unchivalrically arranges for two abductions of Anthelia, the first of which comes to nothing as a result of Sir Oran's intervention but the second of which succeeds. This leads to Forester's quest for Anthelia, her eventual rescue—again with the active assistance of Sir Oran—and her marriage to Forester. Along the way to this triumph of chivalric good over reactionary evil, Peacock introduces episodes which illustrate the need for reform of rotten boroughs, portray the exploitation of agricultural workers by wealthy landowners, protest the continuing existence of slavery in the West Indies, and (by way of Moley Mystic of Cimmerian Lodge and Mr. Feathernest and Mr. Paperstamp of Mainchance Villa) satirize the literary offenses of Coleridge's obscurity and Southey and Wordsworth's turncoat conservatism.

Nightmare Abbey, the most often studied of Peacock's works, expands the critique of his literary contemporaries, including his close friend Shelley, and indicates his amused disapproval of certain Romantic excesses. Set, with claustrophobic concentration, at the Gothic home of Christopher Glowery, Esquire, the novel is a record of the talk and the misadventures of still another gathering of cranks and crotchets who are this time imbued with the melancholy and the radicalism, both reactionary and reformist, of the early nineteenth-century English literati.

Out of natural temperament and failure in love, the senior Glowery has become subject to "those phantoms of indigestion which are commonly called *blue devils*" and has raised a son, Scythrop, named in honor of a suicidal ancestor, who outdoes his father in gloom and amorous mischance. Already betrayed by one lover as the novel begins and destined to experience further amorous agony, the Shelleyan Scythrop immerses himself in "the distempered ideas of metaphysical romance and romantic metaphysics" and simultaneously develops a *"passion for reforming the world."* The Coleridgean Mr. Flosky, on the other hand, although even more addicted to metaphysical obscurity, has lost faith in human progress and wishes to reconstruct the oppressive past. Having been "in his youth an enthusiast for liberty," he had "hailed the dawn of the French Revolution as the promise of a day that was to banish war and slavery, and every form of vice and misery, from the face of the earth," but he has since become so disillusioned by the failure of his hopes that, in illogical reaction, he wishes now "to rake the rubbish together, and rebuild it without any of those loopholes by which the light had originally crept in."

Also dissatisfied with the present state of things, though in yet another sense, is "the Manichaean Millenarian," Mr. Toobad. Modeled after Shelley's friend J.F. Newton, Mr. Toobad believes in the apocalyptic triumph of good over evil, although only at some indeterminate future date; the world of those alive at present will inevitably be dominated, in his view, by the powers of darkness. Even more negative in his outlook is the Byronic Mr. Cypress, who is destined like his real-life counterpart to an exile's hopeless quest for perfection in a fallen world and who is drawn like Childe Harold to the ruins of the past: "The mind is restless, and must persist in seeking, though to find is to be disappointed. Do you feel no aspirations toward the countries of Socrates and Cicero? No wish to wander among the venerable remains of the greatness that has passed for ever?" Summing up the fashionable enervation produced by these various visions of gloom is Mr. Listless, who uses the pervasive taste for melancholy as a convenient rationale for perpetual exhaustion and habitual inaction.

Although Peacock again employs a thin love plot as a device to pull together his satire, a love plot at the conclusion of which the doubly rejected Scythrop chooses inebriation over his original intention of sensitive suicide, the storyline is merely a means of allowing his characters to strike their defining Romantic poses. *Nightmare Abbey* is the most devastating of contemporary attacks on Romantic pretension, but it lampoons its targets with such disarming good humor that even its victims, particularly Shelley and Byron, could enjoy its exuberant wit.

Shelley, at least, was less accepting of "The Four Ages of Poetry," Peacock's next attack on his poetic contemporaries. A commentary on poetic achievement from primitive times to the present, Peacock's essay delineates an ancient and a modern cycle of poetic history, both consisting of four parts: an age of iron, an age of gold, an age of silver, and an age of brass. Poetry in the age of iron consists largely in praising those presently in power by means of language and myth steeped in savagery and superstition. In the age of gold, poetry looks backward to the glories of the age of iron and magnifies the grandeur of this misrepresented past out of a sense of present degeneration. Nevertheless, because no intellectual endeavors of real consequence exist to compete with poetic creation, poetry achieves its greatest perfection. The poetic age of silver, faced with the accomplishments of the age of gold and possessing more rational methods than the writing of poetry for discovering truth, loses itself in a civilized polish and a monotonous imitation which produce works of exquisite craftsmanship but drain poetry of its life. What follows is "the age of brass, which, by rejecting the polish and the learning of the age of silver, and taking a retrograde stride to the barbarisms and crude traditions of the age of iron, professes to return to nature and revive the age of gold. This is the second childhood of poetry." Nonnus isthe definitive poet of the ancient age of brass; Wordsworth, Coleridge, Scott, Byron, Southey, Thomas Moore, and Thomas Campbell are among his modern counterparts. Despite being spared from personal attack, Shelley responded to Peacock's essay in the posthumously published "A Defense of Poetry," an eloquent argument for the imaginative as opposed to the purely rational approach to the creation of knowledge and the establishment of human values.

Many months before the publication of "The Four Ages of Poetry," Peacock had completed considerable work on his fourth novel, *Maid Marian*, but the book was not finished and in print until 1822. Its sprightly dialogue notwithstanding, *Maid Marian* is a historical romance rather than a conversation novel, but its purpose remains satiric despite its outward form. Intended, according to Peacock himself, as an attack "on all the oppressions that are done under the sun," the novel makes heavy use of the Robin Hood lore gathered by antiquarian Joseph Ritson, who had explicitly pointed out the parallels between the anti-authoritarian ideals expressed in these medieval legends and the ideals of the French Revolution. Setting the charitable, subversive brigands of Sherwood Forest against the self-serving brigands of the world of privilege and established order, Peacock plays on the themes of egalitarian hope and resistance to tyranny throughout *Maid Marian*. In particular, he uses the motif of robbing the rich to give to the poor to explore the economic implications of strength and weakness. He implies that wealth flows from the powerless to the powerful, whether the exaction is enforced by law or by armed might, and that those who wish a redistribution of the world's riches must first seek a redistribution of the world's power. From his Sherwood Forest

stronghold, Robin Hood is unable to impose his notions of equity on the world at large, but he does alter the lives of a few in the one corner of his world where he has influence.

Economics is almost wholly the concern of *The Paper Money Lyrics,* a series of poems written by Peacock during the financial panic which began in December 1825; he published the poems during a similar panic a dozen years later. He does take the opportunity to parody several of his favorite literary targets, including Wordsworth and Coleridge, but his central subject is the suffering produced by the British financial system. Portraying the system as a flimsy structure of paper promises which is perpetually vulnerable to corruption, mismanagement, and greed, he places much of the blame for the system's defects on Scottish economists and bankers, going so far at one point as to suggest that what "Scotch steel" had failed to conquer during the many years of strife between England and her northern neighbor might instead be conquered by "Scotch paper."

In *The Misfortunes of Elphin*, the second of Peacock's historical romances, the economic theme again appears, tied in this time with an attack on entrenched bureaucracy. Set in the Wales of King Arthur and the Celts, the first segment of the story traces the causes and the consequences of a catastrophic flood. Prosperous and overly complacent, the people of the Plain of Gwaelod depend for the preservation of their comfortable lives on an embankment which holds back the sea. A commission to superintend the embankment has long been in existence, but its head, Prince Seithenyn, is a drunkard who pockets much of the commission's money, except, of course, what is pocketed by his equally corrupt underlings. A Tory to the bone, Seithenyn has such faith in what his ancestors have created that he does nothing to renovate the bureaucracy of which he is a self-serving part or to repair the crumbling structure which maintains his country's wealth and security. When the embankment inevitably gives way, those who are not literally swept off by the flood have their prosperous lives swept away, and misfortune follows misfortune. Although the abuse of established power in *The Misfortunes of Elphin* calls forth the waters of destruction rather than the wrath of a disenfranchised rebel, the warning of possible revolution, as a number of commentators have pointed out, is certainly implicit in Peacock's symbolism and, if anything, the message is more emphatic here than it was in *Maid*

Marian. Remain content with what is, do nothing to repair what has ceased to function, and prepare to witness the deluge.

In *Crotchet Castle*, Peacock returns to the novelistic form which initiated his fame. This fourth conversation novel is set largely at the home of Ebenezer Mac Crotchet, a retired businessman who, like Peacock's previous hosts, has a penchant for gathering obsessed eccentrics around him. Among others, there are Mr. Firedamp, who fears water-borne contagion, Mr. Henbane, whose experiments with poison have cost the lives of innumerable cats, Mr. Skionar, who continues Peacock's line of unflattering Coleridge portraits, Mr. Toogood, who espouses the Utopian theories of philanthropic industrialist Robert Owen, Mr. Chainmail, who wishes to revive the ways of the Middle Ages, and Mr. Mac Quedy, who judges everything in terms of profit and loss. As the presence of Mac Quedy suggests, *Crotchet Castle* is like Peacock's other recent works in being at least partially about economics, and as Mac Quedy's nationality hints, Scottish theories of political economy, which Peacock abhorred for their replacement of the personal with the numerical, are the target of his particular wrath.

Throughout the novel, Mac Quedy argues for using monetary value as the measure of all things and for making financial calculation the arbiter of every human decision, and his ledger-book mentality is shared by certain of the novel's other characters. Mac Crotchet has done very well for himself by operating under "the rational principle, of enriching himself at the expense of the rest of mankind, by all the recognized modes of accumulation on the windy side of the law," and his son is following in the paternal footsteps. As the novel opens, in fact, the younger Crotchet has very nearly landed a rich young wife, Susannah Touchandgo, only to find it necessary to dump her when her fortune evaporates. Matters of the heart, after all, must not interfere with matters of the purse. He soon finds an apparent match for his greed and ambition in Lady Clarinda, who claims to have been convinced by Mac Quedy that she is "a commodity in the market" and "ought to set [herself] at a high price." As the novel progresses, however, and the characters wander beyond the materialist confines of Crotchet Castle, Lady Clarinda is won over from the mercenary to the personal by the poor but loving Captain Fitzchrome, the abandoned Susannah finds her soulmate in the impractical but endearing Mr. Chainmail, and profit-and-loss calculation loses out to the wisdom of the heart.

Three decades after *Crotchet Castle*, Peacock published his fifth and final conversation novel, *Gryll Grange*. Serialized in 1860 and appearing in volume form in 1851, *Gryll Grange* is again set in and around a rural estate where a hospitable proprietor helps draw together an eccentric cast of characters whose interactions, romantic and otherwise, delineate the novel's satiric concerns. Gregory Gryll is a country gentleman whose satisfaction with the comforts of his present life predisposes him to resist change. His neighbor, Algernon Falconer, is even more addicted to a ritualized stability. Attended by seven virginal handmaids and surrounded in his tower home by stacks of books, Falconer lives a life whose paralytic calm is an implied critique of the cultured inaction of certain members of the Victorian intelligentsia. Although he cultivated an Epicurean tranquility and a bookish intellectualism in his own life, Peacock was not one to withdraw from the practical concerns of the world nor to advocate such a withdrawal in the lives of others. Counterpoised against Falconer is the energetic but undisciplined Lord Curryfin, whose lectures on fish before the Pantopragmatic Society are part of a misguided attempt to transform the world through a dissemination of miscellaneous knowledge, knowledge as distant from true wisdom as the "ologies" of Dickens's Gradgrind. Lord Curryfin is also associated with an impulsive inventiveness and an unreflective risk-taking that illustrate another Victorian tendency, the rush to progress uninformed by cautious forethought, particularly in science and technology.

The world produced by a Curryfin restless energy dissociated from a Gryll/Falconer stability, the world which Peacock the corporate businessman had, in fact, helped to create, whatever the qualms of Peacock the contemplative intellectual, is portrayed in chapter 28, "Aristophanes in London." There, in the speeches of a play intentionally reminiscent of ancient Greek satiric drama, Peacock describes the age of the gaslight, the steamship, and the railroad, the age of pollution and frenetic, sometimes catastrophic, motion, the agitated age embraced by the uncautious many despite the trepidations of the cautious few.

At the conclusion of his novel, Peacock matches Curryfin with a woman who moderates his imprudent activity and Falconer with a woman who lures him away from his reclusive

P

passivity, but the opposing principles which the two male characters embody are not so much combined as brought into tolerant coexistence, and the comic excessiveness of the nine marriages with which the novelist caps his plot suggests a tongue-in-cheek wish-fulfillment rather than a conviction that all will be well with the world. In this final statement of Peacock the humorist, then, the comedian speaks his message of unconquerable joy while the satirist folds his arms in skeptical amusement.

Summary

In poetry and prose published over more than half a century, Thomas Love Peacock satirized the intellectual, artistic, political, and social excesses of the nineteenth century. Adhering to standards of Classical balance and English common sense in his judgments of the contemporary scene, he attacked radical liberalism with as much relish as reactionary conservatism and found absurdity in both the cult of the primitive and the cult of progress. Particularly in his five novels of conversation, noteworthy for their dazzling erudition and topical detail, Peacock castigated the promoters of crack-brained movements and the proselytizers of irrational theories without losing his sense of the joy of life.

Selected Bibliography

Primary Sources

Poetry

The Monks of St. Mark. London: privately printed, 1804.

Sir Proteus: A Satirical Ballad. London: T. Hookham Jr., and E.T. Hookham, 1814.

The Round Table; or, King Arthur's Feast. London: John Arliss, [1817].

Rhododaphne; or, The Thessalian Spell. London: T. Hookham, Jr., and Baldwin, Craddock, & Joy, 1918.

Paper Money Lyrics and Other Poems. London: C. and W. Reynell, 1837.

Essays

"The Four Ages of Poetry." *Ollier's Literary Miscellany* I (1820): 183–200.

Novels

Headlong Hall. London: T. Hookham Jr., and E.T. Hookham, 1816.

Melincourt. London: T. Hookham Jr., and Baldwin, Craddock, & Joy, 1817.

Nightmare Abbey. London: T. Hookham Jr., and Baldwin, Craddock, & Joy, 1818.

Maid Marian. London: T. Hookham Jr., and Longman, Hurst, Rees, Orme, & Brown, 1822.

The Misfortunes of Elphin. London: T. Hookham Jr., 1829.

Crotchet Castle. London: T. Hookham Jr., 1831.

Gryll Grange. London: Parker, Son, & Bourn, 1861.

Complete Works

The Halliford Edition of the Works of Thomas Love Peacock. Ed. H.F.B. Brett-Smith and C.E. Jones. 10 vols. London: Constable, 1924–1934; New York: AMS Press, 1967.

Secondary Sources

Baron, Michael, and Michael Slater. *Headlong Hall and Gryll Grange.* New York: Oxford University Press, 1987. Introductions, a chronology of Peacock, and notes. The editorial machinery of this edition of two of Peacock's novels illustrates the kind of assistance which can render the most topical details of Peacock intelligible.

Butler, Marilyn. *Peacock Displayed: A Satirist in His Context.* Boston: Routledge & Kegan Paul, 1979. A detailed study of the intellectual and social influences on Peacock's novels and criticism.

Dawson, Carl. *His Fine Wit: A Study of Thomas Love Peacock.* Berkeley: University of California Press, 1970. A scholarly analysis of the full range of Peacock's literary accomplishment, including the minor works.

Madden, Lionel. *Thomas Love Peacock.* London: Evans Brothers, 1967. A comparatively short study of the life, ideas, and literary works of Peacock intended for the non-specialist.

Mills, Howard. *Peacock: His Circle and His Age.* Cambridge: Cambridge University Press, 1969. A discussion of *Headlong Hall*, *Melincourt*, and *Nightmare Abbey* within the contexts of Regency history and Romantic literary development.

Mulvihill, James. *Thomas Love Peacock.* Boston: Twayne, 1987. Twayne English Authors Series 456. An excellent introduction to Peacock's life and works, with insightful commentary on the novels, poems, and essays. Also includes a bibliography of the most significant

Peacock scholarship.

Stewart, J.I.M. *Thomas Love Peacock*. London: Longmans, Green, 1963. Writers and Their Work 156. A very concise overview of the life and literature.

Van Doren, Carl. *The Life of Thomas Love Peacock*. London: J.M. Dent & Sons, and New York: E.P. Dutton, 1911; New York: Russell & Russell, 1966. A pioneering biography which has yet to be superseded.

Robert H. O'Connor

Peele, George

Born: London, July 1556

Education: Christ's Hospital, London, 1562–1565; Broadgates Hall (Pembroke College), Oxford University, 1571; Christ's Church, Oxford University, B.A., 1577; Christ's Church, Oxford University, M.A., 1579

Marriage: Ann Christian, 1580; Mary Yates, 1591 (? second marriage)

Died: London, November 9, 1596

Biography

George Peele was born in London sometime before July 25, 1556, the son of James Peele, a clerk. Although merely a tradesman by Elizabethan social standards, James was educated and found work, along with modest reward, as a writer, bookkeeper, and teacher. He was employed for some time as Clerk of Christ's Hospital, and there young George began his education in 1562. From Christ's Hospital, the elder Peele sent his son first to Broadgates Hall (Pembroke College), Oxford, in 1571, then on to Christ's Church, Oxford, in 1574, doubtless in hopes that such further education would afford young George greater opportunities in life than he himself had known. Given the changes in government and the growth of bureaucracy, university education held promise for advancement.

Oddly enough, Peele's term at the university coincided with changes in admission policies and greater scholarship opportunities. Heretofore entrance to the university was primarily the privilege of the nobility. Now sons of the prospering middle class, along with those of clerks, cobblers, and bricklayers (a number of whom may have entered as sizars [scholarship students]) mingled with the nobility's sons, all pursuing the new humanism. What this produced was too many talented and capable people for the bureaucracy to absorb. The path that father Peele had hoped would be open for his son vanished before George even had a chance at it.

His stay at Oxford did not go wholly for naught. In addition to receiving a B.A. in 1577 and an M.A. in 1579, he translated *Iphigenia* while there, though as to its success, there are no testimonies. Peele remained in Oxford, marrying Ann Christian in 1580. Between then and 1583, Peele may have gone down to London. He may have married Mary Yates in 1591. In any event, he was in Oxford in 1593. In that year he received monies for dramatic works and entertainments for the Count Palentine Albert Alasco. That he returned to Oxford and was paid for his work suggests that he showed literary talent during his university days.

While Peele might have found success in Oxford, it eluded him elsewhere. In London, with its superfluity of talented university educated men, life was more difficult. Peele never achieved a secure financial posting. Talented though he was, he became yet another of the University Wits struggling for recognition and patronage. Although his circumstances became strained, he seems never to have resorted to hack-work prose or pamphleteering.

In London, Peele continued to write plays along with poetry (especially in the form of "gratulatory" verses) and, following in his father's footsteps, pageants for the annual Lord Mayor's show. While much of his work leans toward the courtly, Peele was not beneath writing for the popular theater as well.

Peele seems to have written out of economic need, despite his first wife's inheritance of roughly £250. What money he had and what money he earned through his literary efforts did not sustain him. In the last year of his life debt and illness forced him to write to Lord Burghley asking for charity. None came. Peele died in London on November 9, 1596.

Literary Analysis

Peele's work includes courtly verse as in the *Polyhymnia* (1590), a commemorative piece in which he gives a detailed account of the Ascension Day tilt when Sir Henry Lee retired as the queen's champion; gratulatory poetry such as *The Honour of the Garter* (1593) in which he specifically honors the Earl of Northumberland who had paid him to write the poem; entertainments for the Lord Mayor's shows, and plays. Peele's humorous work lies in this last category.

P

The *Araygnement of Paris* (1584) and *The Old Wives' Tale* (1595) are his most noted works. The former is an elaborate pastoral incorporating the myth of Paris and the golden apple. Peele uses the myth as a vehicle for complementing Queen Elizabeth I. When the goddesses accuse Paris of partisanship in his awarding Venus the apple, Diana becomes the arbiter. All agree to abide by her decision, and Peele then devotes the final 110 lines to praise of Elizabeth. The play ends with Diana delivering the apple to the queen herself and with Venus, Juno, and Pallas yielding to Elizabeth.

Despite the element of conflict and one death in the play, it delights. Through the goddesses' and Paris's predicaments and via the pastoralism, Peele creates a comic tone that lightens the play. The first act opens with punning references to sexual misconduct among the pastoral deities; while Pan literally has a lamb to offer the goddesses, the boneless and fat lamb is also something that he has "sacrificed" for country maids and grown thin thereby (1.1). The author explores the consequences of such misconduct throughout the play. Pointed use of ironic understatement occurs as well. As Flora describes the glory of her floral representations for each goddess, Pomona and Pan deflate her verbal excesses by noting that the yellow oxlips mirror Juno's jealousy and the red flowers represent for Pallas the blood of war, while the blue ones (which signify being true) for Venus are opposite her nature (1.3). Although Peele first presents the goddesses as regal, their conversation quickly turns to sexual indiscretion and cuckoldry. Peele further demystifies them and turns them comic in their reaction to the golden ball. As each of them claims herself the fairest, Peele reduces them to sophisticated fishwives, each one willing to sink Paris in mortal sin for her own pride (2.1–2). Nor is the writer beyond relying on visual humor. To punish Thestylis for her "murdering" Colin (he has died of a broken heart), Peele has her pursue a churl who rejects her in turn. Sexual punning occurs later in act 4, lines 1–2 where he has a nymph outwit Vulcan and Bacchus in their pursuit of her. The final comic moment comes when the Council of Gods must decide who is to receive the apple. After the goddesses depart, the gods' unease is apparent; they know that "women's wits work men's unceasing woes" regardless of whom they choose (4.4.221). From here Peele turns serious once more and concludes with the tribute and the apple both going to Elizabeth.

While *The Araygnement* is overall less comic than, say, *A Comedy of Errors* or *Gammer Gurton's Needle*, Peele employs humorous techniques typical of pastoral drama. In so doing he presents a play that both delights and functions as praise for Elizabeth. By mocking the lesser and greater mythic gods, the playwright elevates Renaissance England's greatest cult figure—Elizabeth Regina.

The Old Wives' Tale is Peele's most comic work. Although separated by some years from *The Araygnement*, *The Old Wives' Tale* bears a similarity with its predecessor, especially in its fancifulness and in its breaking of the theatrical illusion. Here, however, instead of a courtly praise of Elizabeth at the play's end the writer has his stage audience incorporate the play's audience into a form of ritual feasting to conclude the work. The play is highly romantic and incorporates numerous folk tale elements: a conjurer; a damsel in distress; magic; a ghost who aids the hero in rescuing the damsel and then demands half of her according to a bargain struck earlier. Among the humorous devices and techniques that Peele uses in this work are puns and invective along with character types like the clown and the *miles gloriosus* (the braggart soldier). The play's highly episodic nature contributes to its comedy (albeit some critics charge that its episodic nature is a flaw that proves Peele poor at plotting).

This play opens with a repetitive emphasis on the audience's being entertained, and they cannot help but be diverted as the action ensues. Beginning with an on-stage audience, Peele then introduces "actors" who come to "tell" the tale. The continual presence of and frequent interruptions by the on-stage audience directs our attention and reactions to the comedy that follows. When Huanebango, the *miles gloriosus*, first appears, for example, Madge (the titular old wife) announces that he is on his way to the conjurer. Peele then treats us to Huanebango's bombast and Booby's invective. When Huanebango and the clown next appear Madge reinforces what we have seen: he "is a choleric gentleman! All you that love your lives, keep out of the smell of his two-hand sword. Now he goes to the conjurer" (672–75). At the same time another member of the on-stage audience deems Huanebango a "fool" worthy of being placed in a "juggling-box." Should the actor be entering through the great hall sword in hand, the comments serve both verbal and visual comic purpose.

While invective is Peele's primary stock-in-trade in *The Old Wives' Tale*, in the drama he mocks religion as well in the friar and the minor church officers. Making two references to pulling down steeples, selling bells, and thatching chancels, he not only calls attention to the closing of the abbeys but to the excesses attributed to them.

The dramatist also takes on the literary conventions and debates of the day. He mocks Gabriel Harvey's work on versification and parodies Petrarchanism in Huanebango's praise of Zantippa.

The heart and culmination of the play combines the comic with the folkloric. Eumenides, the wandering knight, is well-meaning but somewhat simple. He alone can rescue Delia, but he must be guided. Following advice to give all away, Eumenides provides for a poor man's burial. As a reward, Jack, the man's ghost, accompanies the knight, puts money in his purse, and becomes the means by which the conjurer is destroyed and the fair Delia rescued. The comedy here arises from Eumenides's innocence and Jack's wit. Having promised Jack half of all he wins in his journeys, Eumenides must meet Jack's demand for half of Delia. While to modern eyes such a demand is offensive, Eumenides's preference of faith to friendship over loyalty to his lady unthinkable, and Delia's patent acceptance of her death unbelievable, the moment is not only comic in its very absurdity but also in keeping with jest-book Renaissance humor. The play is a tour de force.

Peele's other dramas are historical or biblical in nature. *Edward I* (1593), although it contains a Robin Hood element and disguisings, is more serious than comic. The plot involves treachery and violence on a major scale. *The Battle of Alcazar* (1594) takes a popular and patriotic story and presents it in a tragic vein. In *David and Fair Bethsabe* (1599) Peele dramatizes the biblical story.

Summary

While not as prolific a writer as some of his fellow University Wits, George Peele was a polished writer. His importance to the history of British literature lies in his dramatic work. Although his plots might not possess the polished structure William Shakespeare's did, Peele's verse displays an eloquence that sets him apart. This quality marks his most important contribution.

Selected Bibliography
Primary Sources

The Araygnement of Paris: A Pastorall. London: Printed by H. Marsh, 1584.

Polyhymnia: Describing the Honourable Triumph at Tylt. London: Printed by R. Jhones, 1590.

The Famous Chronicle of King Edward the 1st. London: Printed by A. Jeffes, sold by W. Barley 1593.

The Honour of the Garter: Displaied in a Poeme Gratulatorie: Entitled, To the Earle of Northumberland created Knight of that Order, and Installed Anno Regni Elizabethae. 35. die Iunij 26. London: Printed by the Widdowe Charlewood for F. Busbie, 1593.

The Battell of Alcazar. London: Printed by E. Allde for R. Bankworth, 1594.

The Old Wives' Tale. A Pleasant Conceited Comedie. London: Printed by J. Danter, sold by R. Hancocke & J. Hardie, 1595.

The Love of King David and Fair Bethsabe. London: Printed by A. Islip, 1599.

Editions

The Works of George Peele. Ed. Alexander Dyce. 2nd rev. ed. 3 vols. London: William Pickering, 1829–1839. Dated. Should be used in conjunction with Prouty.

The Life and Works of George Peele. Ed. Charles Tyler Prouty. 3 vols. New Haven: Yale University Press, 1952–1970. Best edition. Can be informed by more recent work.

Secondary Sources

General Studies

Axton, Marie. *The Queen's Two Bodies: Drama and the Elizabethan Succession.* London: Royal Historical Society, 1977. Includes a discussion of *The Battle of Alcazar* and *Edward I* and an examination of them as manifestations of the political atmosphere at this point in Elizabeth's reign.

Ball, B.W. "George Peele's Huanebango: A Caricature of Gabriel Harvey." *Renaissance Papers* (1968): 29–39. Ball argues that the knight's posturing and use of hexameters are a slap at Harvey.

Bergeron, David. *English Civic Pageantry 1558–1642.* London: Edward Arnold, 1971. Includes a discussion of Peele's

Lord Mayor pageants in this overview.

Bradbrook, M.C. "Peele's *Old Wives' Tale*: A Play of Enchantment." *English Studies*, 43 (1962): 323–30. Bradbrook sees the play as a unified work and Peele's masterpiece.

Braunmuller, A.R. *George Peele*. Boston: Twayne, 1983. A careful and well done overview.

Doebler, John. "The Tone of George Peele's *The Old Wives' Tale*." *English Studies*, 53 (1972): 412–21. Doebler sees the play as a parody of chivalric romance.

Free, Mary G. "Audience within Audience in *The Old Wives' Tale*." *Renaissance Papers* (1983): 53–61. Free sees the Induction characters as Peele's means for maintaining audience control.

Goldstone, Herbert. "Interplay in Peele's *The Old Wives' Tale*." *Boston University Studies in English*, 4 (1960): 202–13. Goldstone finds the plot "clear and logical" with the unity coming from the direct interplay of the play's different literary worlds.

Greg, W.W. *Pastoral Poetry and Pastoral Drama*. London: Bullen, 1906. Greg discusses both *The Araygnement of Paris* and *The Old Wives' Tale* as forces in the development of the pastoral tradition in England.

Jenkins, Harold. "Peele's 'Old Wives' Tale.'" *Modern Language Review*, 34 (1939): 177–85. Jenkins finds the text garbled and concludes that the text is a "mutilated" one left from the Queen's Mens' years in the provinces.

Jones, Gwenan. "The Intention of Peele's 'Old Wives' Tale.'" *Aberstwyth Studies*, 7 (1925): 79–93. Jones feels that our sense of delight comes from the folk tale elements and that as a folk play it differs from the earlier heroic romances.

Senn, Werner. *Studies in the Dramatic Construction of Robert Greene and George Peele*. Swiss Studies in English 74. Bern: Francke, 1973. Senn discusses the nature of Peele's plot structure.

Symonds, J. Addington. *Shakespeare's Predecessors in the English Drama*. 2nd ed. 1884; rpt. London: John Murray, 1924. Symonds finds *The Old Wives' Tale* to be relatively worthless save for its resemblance to *Comus* and its setting.

Mary Free

Philips, John

Born: Bampton, December 30, 1676
Education: Christ's Church, Oxford University, B.A., 1697
Died: Hereford, February 15, 1709

Biography

John Philips's brief and placid life passed without the encumbrance of notable public exploits. Born on December 30, 1676, the fourth of six sons of the Reverend Stephen Philips, D.D., of Bampton, Philips spent most of his childhood and adolescence indoors, the victim of ill health and a frail constitution. During this period of disappointing development, he gave early evidence of the whimsicality and eccentricity that would become the trademark of his later comic verse. He allowed his wispy, flaxen hair to grow to great length, whereupon he discovered his greatest pleasure, that of combing and being combed. Throughout his tenure at Christ Church, Oxford (where he received a B.A. on August 16, 1697), the only period in his life when he could have been accurately described as "employed," the budding humorist spent his free hours retired in his chambers, quietly reading the works of John Milton while attendants caressed his coiffeur. Surprisingly, Philips's most avid supporter in Oxford society was the infamous Edmund Smith, a scholar so renowned for the shabbiness of his dress and the wild profligacy of his spending that he acquired the sobriquet "Captain Rag." While under the tutelage of Captain Rag, Philips managed to cultivate a few romantic ambitions, but his habit of directing his attentions to married or promised persons precluded any abductions, trysts, or engagements. He never married.

As is appropriate for an imitator of Milton, Philips's literary career was composed of a series of fortunate pratfalls. His morbid shyness discouraged him from publishing his first and, some say, finest work, *The Splendid Shilling* (1701). Less reticent, pranking university chums, however, purloined the manuscript for this groundbreaking poem, and printed it in pirated form in a collection of assorted verse dainties by Oxford wits. *The Splendid Shilling* drew widespread plaudits immediately. Having stumbled into renown, the poet was eventually prevailed upon to print a glitzy "corrected" edition of his work some four years later. Philips's virtuous performance drew the attention of powerful political patrons, especially Robert Harley, later the Earl of Oxford, and Henry

St. John, later Viscount Bolingbroke. Harley and St. John commissioned Philips to compose *Blenheim*, a serio-Miltonic celebration of the victories of the Duke of Marlborough in the Austrian wars. Already well-off and lately pried from his closet, Philips was assured of an audience for the remainder of his life. Thenceforward his unrushed productions emerged at annual intervals.

Philips's career was cut short by a combination of chronic ill health and hypochondria. He perished of consumption and complications in Hereford, on February 15, 1709, after an attempt at a cure in the waters at Bath. He was interred at the cathedral of Hereford where a monument, raised by his mother and literary correspondents, records his achievements.

Literary Analysis

Despite his dilettantism, Philips enjoys a status in the history of English letters seldom achieved even by the elite: that of an innovator. His principle claim to literary fame rests on his invention of the mock-Miltonic mode, a specialized and indeed catalytic variety of the mock-heroic later deployed by John Gay, Alexander Pope, and countless other Augustan scribblers. Philips is also of no small importance in the development of the urban pastoral, the satiric verse description of city life that was perfected by Ambrose Philips [no relation to John] and ironized by Jonathan Swift. Comic juxtaposition of heroic, iambic pentameter, pseudo-Homeric verse against undignified subject matter had already been attempted by John Dryden in *MacFlecknoe* and Samuel Garth in *The Dispensary*, but the humorous application of Miltonic blank verse to trivial, fanciful topics originated with Philips.

The poet revolutionized the tradition of mockery in many ways. He didn't hesitate to import the subjects as well as the styles of his various rhetorical models. His mockery is never merely a matter of bilateral contrasts but a multilateral project, a continual shuffling of all of the elements of poetry into amusingly unexpected juxtapositions. When Philips reports that he "sinks found'ring in the vast Abyss," he invokes both Milton's hieratic style and one of Milton's topics, the great abyss between heaven and earth. He then turns the entire Miltonic universe upside-down by disclosing that this sublime "Abyss" is actually a tear in his trousers! When Philips appends a grandiose history of Britain to the pedigree of "Mundungus"

(a popular, cheap tobacco of his day) or when he Miltonically inverts the order of nouns and adjectives ("durance strict," "conundrum quaint"), he hyperextends a tradition—mockery—that is as much concerned with repetition and veneration as with burlesque. "To mock," after all, means "to copy" as well as "to travesty." Philips's "title," *The Splendid Shilling*, exemplifies his multivalent rhetoric, for this phrase is only the subtitle of Philips's poem. Habit alone has established it as the commonly recognized title. "An Imitation of Milton" is the title proper, suggesting that reiteration and all of its complexities are as much the concern of Philips's mocking muse as is inverting transformation.

The serious side of mockery is best exemplified by Philips's oddly somber, tediously meditative celebration, *Blenheim* (1706). *Blenheim* is an ill-conceived attempt to associate the campaigning John Churchill, later Duke of Marlborough, with assorted heroes—Adam, Christ, Raphael—from *Paradise Lost*. For those roles the ambitious general is less than the casting director's dream. Thomas Campbell tried to rescue *Blenheim* by declaring it "as completely a burlesque upon Milton as *The Splendid Shilling*, though it was written and read with gravity," but modern readers will have to stretch their imaginations in order to appreciate Campbell's sympathetic verdict. The author may have gotten the message himself, for he attempted only one other serious poem, the short panegyric "Ode ad Henricum S. John."

Philips seems much more at home in his next lightly comic release, *Cerealia* (1706), a celebration of the making of malt liquor from English grains. Here he can indulge his hard-edged, unexpectedly aggressive wit, defaming inferior continental wines while lauding homegrown brews. "Delicious Tipple! that in heav'nly Veins / Assimilated, vig'rous ICHOR bred, / Superior to *Frontiniac*, or *Bordeaux*, / Or old *Falern*, *Campania's* best Increase." *Cerealia*, with its abundant agricultural and geological imagery, allows Philips to experiment with the sarcastic, crabby comedy of dialect. He invokes salt-of-the-earth, pseudo-Spenserian, quasi-Saxon language like "Eycleeped" by way of making sport of rustics and locals. This brand of in-group comedy sounds a shattering note in sensitive modern ears, but the poet's young, citified readers delighted in it. More than a little bit of his humor concerns the quaint, rough-and-ready habits of Britannic yeomen: "'Tis to this

[beer], she [Cere] cry'd / The *British Cohorts* owe their martial Fame." At its climactically vulgar conclusion, Philips stoops to body-humor of the *Animal House* variety, to give a modern parallel. He chortles and guffaws as intoxicated college students "Night-founder'd in Town-Ditches stagnant Gurge," as "SOPH rolls on SOPH Promiscuous," and as "the Sport of fierce *Norwegian* Tempests Roar / Of loud *Euroclydon's* tumultuous Gusts."

In the last full year of his life (1708), Philips's attitude toward the countryside seems to have softened, or at least fermented. The lenitive Philips emerges in his swan-song, *Cyder,* parts I and II. *Cyder* is unlikely to draw an audience among devotees of sassy wit or slapstick, for its gentle wit harkens back to bucolic times, when "clown" meant peaceful countryman as well as colorful circus comic. Nostalgic and serene, the poem is a chronicle of the growing and harvest of apples, the pressing of juice, the fermentation of hard cider, and the merry revels that the consumption of that beverage encourages. Its comedy is simple and childlike. The whimsy of dancing elephants and Norman Rockwell-like buffoons replaces the smirking of a Henry Fielding, the wry turns of a William Shakespeare, or the tongue-lashings of a Don Rickles. The rhetorical model to which Philips's mockery makes reference is no longer that of the damnation-dispensing Milton but, rather, of Virgil's gentle series of pastorals, the *Georgics.* The setting, likewise, moves from contemporary England back to the mythical, prehistoric land of "Ariconium," an agricultural paradise alleged to have been swallowed up by the earth (perhaps out of hunger for apples).

The writer's familiar mock-Miltonic strain still echoes throughout *Cyder*—"What Soil the Apple loves, what care is due / To Orchats, timeliest when to press the Fruits, / They gift, *Pomona,* in *Miltonian* Verse / Adventrous I presume to sing"—but Milton's colossal cadences always and quickly concede to a "Verse / Nor skill'd, nor studious" from the "Native Soil" of the countryside. Although Philips always remembers the comic triviality of his subject, apple cider, he easily surrenders to the seductive power of his own song, extending his humble project from the vanished fields of Ariconium to "the utmost Bounds of this / Wide Universe" in the hope that "Silurian Cyder" "Shall please all Tastes, and triumph o'er the Vine." Much of the comedy of *Cyder* is thus either neurotic, external to the poem, or both,

with Philips's humor growing more strained and more anxious as he watches himself stretch a conceit further and further. He laughs somewhat nervously at his tendency to take his silly project, the mockery of Virgilianism, half seriously. *Cyder,* after all, is a didactic poem, giving specific instructions about fertilizing, variety selection, pest control, and overwintering. Whether out of confusion, hysteria, bungling, or premeditation, he spends many a line marveling at the capacity of humor, ribaldry, and burlesque to pass for encyclopedic learning or even epic verse.

Lightheartedly learned, Philips displays an almost miraculous skill in substituting style for substance while denying the superiority of either to the other. He perfects a mode in which every rhetorical technique comments comically on its topic, in which every topic points up a rhetorical incongruence, and in which every part of experience, every half, quarter, eighth, or infinitesimal part of anything at all, is proved, delightfully and delicately, to hold the whole of Miltonic, or Virgilian or Homeric or Drydenian, universe.

Summary

John Philips converted imitation into originality. In six celebratory pieces, he perfected the art of simultaneously revivifying and burlesquing the greatest of English epic writers, Milton. Whether in his first piece, *The Splendid Shilling,* or in his masterwork, *Cyder,* Philips aspires to a verse which laughs respectfully, which pokes fun at the triviality of modern life and its incongruity with the heroic tradition. Urbane and witty, in his verse he nevertheless treasures those nostalgic scenes and domestic curiosities that make up British life. Philips's influence was extensive (and disproportionate to his slender *oeuvre*). His example of comic but reverent mockery would be emulated by Pope, Edward Young, Oliver Goldsmith, and hundreds of Grub Street poetasters.

Selected Bibliography

Primary Sources
The Poems of John Philips. Ed. M.G. Lloyd. Oxford: Blackwell, 1927.

Note: All of Philips's poems were issued separately and are easily accessed in major rare book libraries. This edition conveniently binds together Philips's otherwise scattered works.

Secondary Sources

Bond, Richmond P. *English Burlesque Poetry, 1700–1750*. Cambridge, MA: Harvard University Press, 1932.

Chalker, John. *The English Georgic*. Baltimore: Johns Hopkins University Press, 1969.

Cope, Kevin L. "When the Past Presses the Present: Shillings, Cyder, Malts, and Wine." In *Reader Entrapment in Eighteenth-Century Literature*. Ed. Carl Kropf. New York: AMS Press, 1991, pp. 15–43.

Doody, Margaret. *The Daring Muse: Augustan Poetry Reconsidered*. Cambridge: Cambridge University Press, 1985.

Griffin, Dustin. "The Bard of Cyder-Land: John Philips and Miltonic Imitation." *Studies in English Literature*, 24 (1984): 441–60.

Haven, Raymond. *The Influence of Milton on English Poetry*. Cambridge, MA: Harvard University Press, 1922.

Kevin L. Cope

Pinter, Harold

Born: London, October 10, 1930
Education: Hackney-Downes Grammar School, 1947; attended the Royal Academy of Dramatic Art and the Central School of Speech and Drama briefly
Marriage: Vivien Merchant, September 14, 1956; divorced, 1980; one child; Lady Antonia Fraser, November 1980

Biography

Harold Pinter was born on October 10, 1930, in Hackney, a working-class section of London, the only child of a Jewish ladies' tailor, Hyman (Jack) Pinter, and his wife, Frances (née Mann). Pinter was evacuated to Cornwall when World War II broke out. In 1944, he returned to London where he experienced the German Blitz—he saw the flying bombs, and his garden was frequently in flames. The family had to evacuate their house several times, a traumatic experience that had a great impact on the youngster.

Pinter won a scholarship to the local all-boys grammar school, Hackney-Downes, where he studied until 1947. Under the direction of Joseph Brearley, his English master, he acted in Shakespearean plays. The only academic subject to interest the young man was English language and literature. He played football and cricket, ran the 100-yard dash in a school record time, and by the age of thirteen he had also had his first love affair and begun writing poetry.

Pinter applied for a grant to study acting at the Royal Academy of Dramatic Art and he received a London County Council grant on the recommendation of producer R.D. (Reggie) Smith. He found that he did not like the academy and faked a nervous breakdown in order to escape. Subsequently, he enrolled at the Central School of Speech and Drama but was not a serious student there.

Following the war, fascism began to be revived in London's East End. Pinter encountered a considerable amount of violence in the area because gangs of toughs frequented the alleys through which he walked. The thugs carried broken milk bottles and threatened to "carve up" anybody whom they did not like, especially those who looked either Jewish (as did Pinter, who wore glasses) or whom they took to be a Communist (again Pinter was a target because he carried books). The dramatist-to-be learned how important language could be as he talked his way through these frightening situations. Such encounters, plus tales of the treatment of Jews in Germany during Adolf Hitler's Third Reich, led Pinter to declare himself a conscientious objector when he turned eighteen. He refused to serve in the National Service and stood trial twice for this refusal, though he escaped imprisonment.

In 1949, Pinter began writing "Kullus," a work that reappears in several forms in his later writing. 1950 saw his first publication: the August issue of *Poetry London* contained two of his poems, "New Year in the Midlands" and "Chandeliers and Shadows." He wrote hundreds of poems during this period and started an autobiographical novel, *The Dwarfs*.

Most of his time, however, was involved with acting. Pinter's first theater-going experience was seeing Sir Donald Wolfit in the role of King Lear. Later he was to act in a production with Wolfit. Reggie Smith helped Pinter find small parts on the radio, his first professional role being in the BBC home service broadcast "Focus on Football Pools" on September 19, 1950.

In 1951, Pinter began his acting career in earnest. He appeared in the BBC's Third Programme production of William Shakespeare's *Henry VIII*. Soon afterward he answered Anew McMaster's advertisements for actors to participate in a Shakespearean tour of Ireland. Over the following eighteen-month period of one-night stands, he became friends with Alun Owen, Patrick McGee, and Barry Foster, and he met Vivien Merchant while the two were acting at the King's Theatre in Hammersmith in 1953. In 1954, Pinter assumed the stage name of David Baron and toured provincial England with a repertory company.

In 1954/1955, the prose version of "The Black and White" was written, and in 1955 he wrote the short story "The Examination," which hearkens back to "Kullus." Pinter and Merchant met again in 1956 when they played leads opposite one another and the couple was married on September 14 of that year.

Henry Wolfe, a repertory company friend, asked if Pinter would write a play for production by the drama department at Bristol University in 1957. Four days later Pinter had finished his first play, *The Room*. Directed by Wolfe, *The Room* was entered in the *Sunday Times* student drama festival. One of the judges, critic Harold Hobson, was impressed by the work and wrote an admiring review of it. As a result, Michael Codron wrote to Pinter to find out if he had written a full-length play; Pinter had just completed *The Birthday Party*. In January 1958, Pinter's son Daniel was born. Three months later, on April 28, 1958, *The Birthday Party* premiered at the Arts Theatre, Cambridge. Pinter helped in the directing. In May the production moved to the Lyric Theatre, Hammersmith, for its first London staging. It was a critical disaster.

Nevertheless, Pinter continued to write. *Something in Common*, an unperformed radio play, and *A Slight Ache* were both completed in 1958. The following year he created a group of revue sketches, "That's Your Trouble," "That's All," "Applicant," "Interview," "Dialogue For Three," and "Getting Acquainted." Also in 1959 "The Examination" was published in *Prospect*, and *The Dumb Waiter* premiered at the Frankfurt, Germany Municipal Theatre. Two of Pinter's sketches, "Trouble in the Works" and "The Black and the White," were included in Disley Jones's *One to Another*, a musical revue mounted at the Lyric Theatre in July. *A Slight Ache* was broadcast on the BBC Third Programme later that month and in September another musical revue, *Pieces of Eight*, included Pinter's "Getting Acquainted," "Last to Go," "Request Stop," and "Special Offer."

The dramatist's fortunes began to change in 1960. *The Room*, which he directed, and *The Dumb Waiter* were produced at the Hampstead Theatre Club and the BBC Third Programme broadcast *A Night Out*, with Pinter as Seeley. *The Birthday Party* was telecast by Associated Rediffusion Television and *A Night Out* was broadcast by ABC-TV. *Night School* was televised. Shortly thereafter *The Birthday Party* became Pinter's first play to be performed professionally in America when the Actors Workshop production in San Francisco opened on July 27. The BBC broadcast *The Dwarfs* on its Third Programme. Also in 1960 the prose version of "The Black and the White" was published in *The Spectator*.

The most important event for Pinter in 1960, though, was the premiere of *The Caretaker* at the Arts Theatre Club in London on April 27. In May, the production was moved to the Duchess Theatre in the West End. The play was critically acclaimed by Kenneth Tynan and other reviewers. It closed at the Duchess after 425 performances; in the meantime, it had been judged by the *Evening Standard* as the best play of 1960, and when the drama moved to the United States it was nominated for an Antoinette Perry Award and the Newspaper Guild of New York cited *The Caretaker* as the best play of the year.

Nineteen sixty-one was a busy year: "Harold Pinter Replies," an essay, was published in *New Theatre* magazine; *A Slight Ache* was mounted in London; "Afternoon Poem" and an essay, "Writing for Myself," were published in *Twentieth Century*; *The Collection* was televised; and *A Night Out* was staged. In 1962, Pinter co-directed *The Collection* with Peter Hall at London's Aldwych Theatre, "Between the Lines," an essay, was published in the *Sunday Times* (London), and the author read "The Examination" on the BBC Third Programme.

The next four years were impressive. *The Lover* was telecast in 1963 (and received the Guild of British Television Producers along with the Directors Prix Italia for Television Drama at Naples awards for Best Script). Pinter subsequently directed the first stage presentation of the play when it opened at the Arts Theatre Club in London with *The Dwarfs*. In 1963, the short story "Tea Party" was written, and Pinter won two Screenwriters Guild awards, one for a television play and one for a screenplay.

Pinter's entrance into the world of the cinema, a subject in which he had shown an interest as a student, was a propitious one. His first screenplay, *The Caretaker*, based on his own drama, was released in 1963. Directed by Clive Donner and starring Alan Bates, Robert Shaw, and Donald Pleasence, the film received a Silver Bear Award at the Berlin Film Festival and a Certificate of Merit at the Edinburgh Festival. *The Servant*, Pinter's second screenplay (based on Robin Maugham's novel and directed by Joseph Losey), was also released in 1963, and in 1964 the quality of the author's screenwriting was further recognized when the movie was the official British entry at the Venice Film Festival and the first New York Film Festival; it received awards from both the British Screenwriters Guild and the New York Film Critics.

Five of Pinter's revue sketches ("Applicant," "Dialogue for Three," "Interview," "That's All," "That's Your Trouble") were broadcast on the BBC Third Programme in 1964, and Pinter read the prose version of *Tea Party* on the BBC Third Programme and directed a revival of *The Birthday Party* as well. "Writing for the Theatre" was published in *The Evergreen Review*; "Applicant," "Dialogue for Three," "Interview," "That's All," and "That's Your Trouble" were broadcast on the BBC Third Programme; and Pinter read *Tea Party* on the Third Programme. The prose version of *Tea Party* was published in *Playboy* in 1965.

In 1965, Pinter won the British Film Academy Award for Best Screenplay for his 1964 scenario of Penelope Mortimer's *The Pumpkin Eater*. It was clear that his work in the theater carried over thematically and technically into his work in film and vice versa, just as his radio and television writing had already had an impact on his dramaturgy. The dramatic version of *Tea Party* was televised in England and throughout Europe as part of the European Broadcasting Union's 1965 "The Largest Theatre in the World" series. *The Homecoming* opened at the Aldwych under Hall's direction. Pinter also acted in a BBC Television presentation of Jean Paul Sartre's *No Exit* that year.

Pinter's script for the film *Langrishe, Go Down* was published in 1966, another reflection of the author's increasing interest in writing for the cinema. That year he was also named Commander, Order of the British Empire in the Queen's Birthday List ("the year *after* the Beatles," he noted) and *The Quiller Memorandum*, for which he wrote the screenplay (adapted from an Adam Hall novel), was released.

In 1967, two of Pinter's essays were published, "Two People in a Room: Playwriting" in the *New Yorker* and "Beckett" in the festschrift *Beckett at Sixty*. *The Homecoming* moved to New York in 1967 where it won the Antoinette Perry (Tony) Award for Best Play on Broadway, the New York Drama Critics Circle Award for the Best Play on Broadway, the Whitbread Anglo-American Award for the Best British Play on Broadway, and the American Library Association "Notable Books of 1967" award. Pinter acted in a BBC-TV telecast of *The Basement* and directed Robert Shaw's *The Man in the Glass Booth* in London as well and then took the play to New York, where he was nominated for a Tony for his directing. *Accident*, another Losey film from a Pinter screenplay, was released (Pinter played a small part in it). The film (an adaptation of Nicholas Mosley's book) was named one of the year's ten best by the National Board of Review. At dramatist Joe Orton's funeral Pinter read a poem that he had written as a eulogy.

The year 1968 proved to be a busy one for the author. *Mac*, his fond memoir of his repertory experiences with Irish actor-manager McMaster, was published, the film version of *The Birthday Party* was screened in New York, *Landscape* was broadcast, *The Basement* began a run at East Side Playhouse in New York, and the volume *Poems* was published. Additionally, much of Pinter's time was consumed in a battle with the Lord Chamberlain, who objected to several four-letter words in *Landscape*; the play was not given a license to be acted on stage. However, because radio was not subject to the Lord Chamberlain's censorship, the drama was performed on the BBC Third Programme.

In 1969, *Night* was produced, and Pinter's screenplay adaptation of L.P. Hartley's *The Go-Between* was completed. Along with Pleasence the author appeared in the award-winning NBC Experiment in Television production, *Pinter People*. World premieres of Pinter's plays in 1969 included *Night*, which opened at the Comedy Theatre, and *Landscape* and *Silence*, at the Aldwych, mounted by the Royal Shakespeare Company.

A relatively sparse year followed: "All of That," a poem, was published in the *Times Literary Supplement*, and Pinter was elected an honorary member by the Modern Language Association of America and awarded Hamburg University's Shakespeare Prize. He directed Simon Gray's *Butley* and James Joyce's *Exiles* in London. Unfortunately, at this point, although more and more movies based on his fine

P

filmscripts have been released, Pinter's other writing generally became increasingly sporadic and diminished both in quality and quantity for a period of seven or eight years.

In December 1971, "Speech: Hamburgh 1970" appeared in *Theatre Quarterly*. "Pinter on Beckett," an essay, was published in *New Theatre Magazine* and "Poem" was published in the *New York Times* magazine. Hall's production of *Old Times* opened at the Aldwych; six months later the play moved to New York. *Plays and Players* recognized *Old Times* with its Best New Play award, and the drama also was nominated for a Tony. *The Go-Between* (from L.P. Hartley's novel) was released and won the Cannes Film Festival Golden Palm Award as Best Picture and Pinter received a British Academy of Film and Television Arts Award for his screenplay. The author received a Writers Guild Award too.

In 1972, he wrote an adaptation of Marcel Proust's *A la Recherche du Temps Perdu*, an interesting literary anomaly in that the screenplay has never been filmed, yet it has been published.

The essay "Pinter on Pinter" was included in *Cinebill* in 1973, *Monologue* was performed on British television, and the film version of *The Homecoming*, directed by Hall, was released as part of the American Film Theatre series. Pinter became an associate director at the National Theatre (an association that he maintained through 1983) and directed his first film, an adaptation of Gray's *Butley*. He also received the Austrian State Prize for European Literature.

In 1974, Pinter directed John Hopkins's *Next of Kin* at the Old Vic, and "An Unpublished Speech" was published in *Theatre Quarterly*.

Hall's production of *No Man's Land*, starring Sir John Gielgud and Sir Ralph Richardson, opened in 1975, and Pinter directed Gray's *Otherwise Engaged*. He appeared in *Rogue Male* (BBC-TV) and Beckett's *Rough for Radio*. The film version of F. Scott Fitzgerald's *The Last Tycoon* was released in 1976, a recipient of the National Board of Review's Best English-Language Film Award. Pinter acted in *Two Plays* by Vaclav Havel and directed first William Archibald's *The Innocents* in New York City that year and then Noel Coward's *Blithe Spirit* in London in 1977. A year later *Langrishe, Go Down* was televised, and *Betrayal* was staged at the National. The latter received the Society of West End Theatres Award and, when it crossed the Atlantic Ocean, the New

York Drama Critics' Circle 1980 award for best foreign play. At this point Pinter seems to have lost his driving interest in writing for the theater, though he continued to direct—Gray's *The Rear Column* in 1978 and *Close of Play* in 1979. Indeed, it was 1980 before anything else of professional significance occurred; *Family Voices* was broadcast on BBC-3 Radio. This was followed by the first performance of *The Hothouse*, the original version of which had been completed in 1960, Pinter directing. Pinter was awarded the Pirandello Prize. Also in 1980 Merchant sued Pinter for divorce, naming noted biographer and novelist Lady Antonia Fraser as correspondent. In November, after the divorce, Pinter married Lady Antonia.

In 1981, *The French Lieutenant's Woman*, perhaps the author's finest film, was released and nominated for an Academy Award in the best screenplay adaptation category (John Fowles' novel was the source) and won the Ennio Flaiano Award for Screenwriting (1982) and the Donatello Prize (Italy, also 1982). The Bank of Delaware Common Wealth Award was presented to Pinter, and he directed Gray's *Quartermaine's Terms*. *Family Voices* was staged, *Victoria Station* and *A Kind of Alaska* premiered as part of a triple bill with *Family Voices* in 1982, and in 1983 *Players* was presented. The film version of *Betrayal* opened in 1982. Pinter continued directing, Robert East's *Incident at Tulsa Hill* in 1982 and Jean Giraudoux's *The Trojan War Will Not Take Place* in 1983. Meanwhile, he also continued to garner honors—another Academy Award nomination for best screenplay adaptation in 1983 (for *Betrayal*). In addition, he received the British Theatre Association Award (an honor repeated in 1985).

In 1984, *One for the Road* was published in the *New York Review of Books* and televised in 1985. *Precisely* was broadcast by the BBC in 1984. Pinter directed Gray's *The Common Pursuit* in 1984 and Tennessee Williams's *Sweet Bird of Youth* in 1985. In 1985, too, the film *Turtle Diary* (from Russell Hoban's novel) was released and the writer was honored with the Elmer Holmes Bobst Award for Arts and Letters, and his tribute to McMaster and the batsman in cricket, *Players: Mac and Arthur Wellard*, was broadcast by the BBC. In 1986, Pinter directed Donald Freed's *Circe and Bravo*. In 1987, *The Dumb Waiter*, directed by Robert Altman and starring John Travolta and Tom Conti, was telecast in America, as was *The*

Room, also directed by Altman and featuring Linda Hunt, Annie Lennox, Julian Sands, David Heublen, Abbott Anderson, and Pleasence. Chapter 19 of *The Dwarfs*, the novel begun in 1950, was published in the inaugural issue of *The Pinter Review* that same year, and a second television version of *The Birthday Party*, this one directed by Kenneth Ives, was telecast on BBC-2 with Pinter as Goldberg (the play has also been filmed in French as *L'Anniversaire*, directed by Jean-Michael Ribes). The dramatist was given a Literary Lions Award by the New York Public Library. Chapter 10 from *The Dwarfs* was published in *The Pinter Review*, Vol. 2, in 1988, and Pinter directed the premiere of *Mountain Language*.

Additional film and television credits include his television adaptations of Fred Uhlman's *Reunion*, released in 1989, and Elizabeth Bowen's *Heat of the Day*, directed by Christopher Morahan and televised by the BBC in 1989 and in America in 1990; cinematic adaptations of Margaret Atwood's novel *The Handmaid's Tale*, directed by Volker Schlondorff, and Ian McEwan's *The Comfort of Strangers* were released in 1990; Franz Kafka's *The Trial* was released in 1993. The author wrote a script for Kazu Ishiguro's *Remains of the Day*, but removed his name from the project as filming was to begin. He has also written a screenplay version of Joseph Conrad's *Victory*; although it has not yet been filmed, it was published in 1990.

In 1990, *The Dwarfs* was published and "It is Here," a poem, appeared in the *Times Literary Supplement*. Pinter read Salman Rushdie's "Is Nothing Sacred?" as the Herbert Read Memorial Lecture and "On Superman," a talk by Pinter, was broadcast. He directed Jane Stanton Hitchcock's *Vanilla*. *Party Time* was read at the International Pinter Festival at Ohio State University in 1991 and premiered under Pinter's direction in London. An audio tape of Pinter reciting "Focus on Football Pools" was presented at the Pinter Festival too. As part of the world-wide celebration of Pinter's sixtieth birthday, *Betrayal*, *The Homecoming* (directed by Hall), and *The Caretaker* enjoyed major revivals in 1991. Also in 1991 *The New World Order* was published in the Autumn issue of *Granta* and *The Pinter Review: Annual Essays* (Vol. 5), then performed, with Pinter as director, at the Royal Court Theatre. Among the revivals in 1992 were *No Man's Land* in London (Pinter playing Hirst), *The Birthday Party*

in Glasgow, Scotland, *The Caretaker* in Nottingham, *Betrayal* in Kentucky and Korea, and *The Homecoming* in Columbus, Ohio. In 1993, Pinter directed David Mamet's *Oleanna*, his full-length *Moonlight* premiered in London, his film adaptation of Franz Kafka's *The Trial* was released, and a successful festival of Pinter dramas was mounted in Dublin. His cinematic adaptation of Vladimir Nabokov's *Lolita* was completed in 1994, though problems arose regarding the production of the movie. He also directed a revival of *Landscape* in London in 1994, and he was scheduled to act in a London revival of *The Hothouse* in 1995.

Over the years the playwright has received numerous honorary degrees from American and British universities in recognition of his contributions to the arts.

Literary Analysis

Pinter is such an important figure in contemporary drama that audiences and critics alike tend to approach his work somberly, as though its deep significance can be appreciated only in that mood. Still, in 1971, describing the upcoming premiere of *Old Times*, acknowledged as one of the author's two most important works, director Hall claimed that the play would have the audience rolling in the aisles in laughter. In actuality, some of the playgoers reacted grumpily by walking out of the theater before the conclusion of the first act. As Pinter's playwright friend Gray has observed, "One of the great hurdles that [Pinter] has had to live with is that people, for years, have gone into the theater straight-faced with the piety of the occasion, when actually there is nothing he likes more than to have people laughing" (Raymond, 25).

In fact, from the very beginning of his career the dramatist has filled his works with humor. Indeed, the first three plays (*The Room*, *The Birthday Party*, and *The Dumb Waiter*) have commonly been labeled "comedies of menace" ever since Irving Wardle applied that term to them in the September 1958 issue of *Encore*. That these dramas were labeled comedies of menace because Pinter presents a mood of terror in humorous terms does not diminish the facts that they are funny and were meant to be.

There is, however, a distinction between the uses of humor by literary humorists and the ways that Pinter utilizes humor. Typically, humorists develop their humor through devices such as incongruity and exaggeration. Generally speaking, the humorist's intent may be simply to evoke laughter for the physiological and psychological pleasures that laughter brings, to identify character types, or for the more complex Aristotelian purpose of exposing the foibles of society.

While Pinter certainly employs the same techniques to create humor as do literary humorists (though admittedly with less frequency), his primary goal is not to make people laugh. The exception is his revue sketches, which contain much of the playwright's funniest dialogue. In many ways these delightful short pieces are typical humor in both the devices employed and the author's purpose—to demonstrate the humdrum quality of quotidian life or to reveal character.

The sketch "Last to Go" is a bit of Pinter's humor at its best. The short, quick exchanges, the skewed stichomythia, reflect a lack of communication. Two characters, a barman and an old newspaper seller, talk at rather than to one another, each bouncing words off the wall that is the other, their responses being related though not necessarily relevant to the words of the other as they go through the motions of making conversation. The form is there; it is the meaning that is absent, and it is this dissonance that generates the humor. The situation is a fine example of Henri Bergson's definition of comedy as "something mechanical encrusted on the living":

MAN. You was a bit busier earlier.
BARMAN. Ah.
MAN. Round about ten.
BARMAN. Ten, was it?
MAN. About then. (*Pause.*) I passed by here about then.
BARMAN. Oh yes?
MAN. I noticed you were doing a bit of trade. (*Pause.*)
BARMAN. Yes, trade was very brisk here about ten.
MAN. Yes, I noticed. (*Pause.*) I sold my last one about then. Yes. About nine forty-five.
BARMAN. Sold your last then, did you?
MAN. Yes, my last "Evening News" it was. Went about twenty to ten. (*Pause.*)
BARMAN. "Evening News" was it?
MAN. Yes. (*Pause.*) Sometimes it's the "Star" is last to go.
BARMAN. Ah.
MAN. Or the . . . whatsisname.
BARMAN. "Standard."

MAN. Yes. (*Pause.*) All I had left tonight was the "Evening News." (*Pause.*)
BARMAN. Then that went, did it?
MAN. Yes. (*Pause.*) Like a shot. (*Pause.*)
BARMAN. You didn't have any left, eh?
MAN. No. Not after I sold that one. (*Pause.*)
BARMAN. It was after that you must have come by here then was it?
MAN. Yes, I come by here after that, see, after I packed up.
BARMAN. You didn't stop here though, did you?
MAN. When? [*The Dwarfs and Eight Revue Sketches*, 37]

The men are engaging in phatic dialogue. There is no meaning or any real attempt to exchange information, to communicate anything other than a ritualized recognition of the presence of the other. They are satisfied with the form itself.

Other revue sketches illustrate Pinter's use of language and reversals of social expectations to engender humor. In "Trouble in the Works" employees want to stop making "high speed taper shank spiral flute reamers" and the like and convert the factory to make brandy balls (29–31). Mr. Jakes, the pornographic bookshop owner in "Interview," thinks that all of those who patronize his shop are Communists (42–44).

Among the more common types of humorous devices that Pinter utilizes are an exhibition of the pure banality of everyday life and misunderstandings. While it has strong thematic reverberations later in the drama when Meg approaches her lodger (Stan) in the same manner, the opening sequence of *The Birthday Party* in which she vacuously mothers her husband, Petey, is amusing because of its banality:

MEG. Is that you, Petey?
Pause.
Petey, is that you?
Pause.
Petey?
PETEY. What?
MEG. Is that you?
PETEY. Yes, it's me.
MEG. What? . . . Are you back?
PETEY. Yes.
MEG. I've got your cornflakes ready. . . . Here's your cornflakes. . . . Are they nice?
PETEY. Very nice.
MEG. I thought they'd be nice. [9]

Meg's later misunderstanding of the meaning of the word "succulent" is similarly funny, particularly because it plays off the earlier scene with her husband:

MEG. Was it nice?
STANLEY. What?
MEG. The fried bread.
STANLEY. Succulent.
MEG. You shouldn't say that word.
STANLEY. What word?
MEG. That word you said.
STANLEY. What, succulent—?
MEG. Don't say it!
STANLEY. What's the matter with it?
MEG. You shouldn't say that word to a married woman.
STANLEY. Is that a fact? [17–18]

Most often, though, rather than merely trying to make people laugh, Pinter uses humor as a tool to clarify his themes or to reinforce them through parallelization. Furthermore, at least in his pre-1980s writing, these themes have not been social in the sense of being applicable to a society; instead, they have focused on the nature of individuals and the interrelationships between individuals—which is usually the structure of tragedy. As the playwright's concerns have become more political in character, ironically (given the social nature of politics), his humor has become crueler (see the Sergeant in *Mountain Language* and Nicolas in *One for the Road*) and more directed toward defining the attributes of his characters.

There are two keys to understanding Pinter's use of humor. First, the techniques and devices that he uses to create humor are similar to those that he employs in generating stage dialogue that is considered so realistic sounding that critics attribute the result to his "tape-recorder ear" (repetition, clichés, lack of logical connections, and so on). Second, thematically, humor is a dividing line for the author. When *The Caretaker* premiered in 1960, Leonard Russell wrote to the London *Sunday Times* that he was disturbed because the audience laughed at the play as if it were a farce. To this criticism, Pinter answered, "Certainly I laughed myself while writing 'The Caretaker' but not all the time, not 'indiscriminately.' An element of the absurd is, I think, one of the features of the play, but at the same time I did not intend it to be merely a laughable farce. . . . As far as I'm concerned, 'The Caretaker' is funny, up to a point.

Beyond that point it ceases to be funny, and it was because of that point that I wrote it." An elaboration on this proposition is contained in an interview with Hallam Tennyson in which Pinter explained, "Everything is funny; the greatest earnestness is funny. Even tragedy is funny. And I think what I try to do in my plays is to get to this recognizable reality of the absurdity of what we do and how we behave and how we speak. The point about tragedy is that it is *no longer funny*. It is funny, and then it becomes no longer funny."

In Pinter's first play, *The Room*, the rhythms of the English music hall dialogue along with stichomythic nonlogical progressions reminiscent of S.J. Perelman's Marx Brothers film scripts undercut the realistic sounding speech. Several of the exchanges between Rose and her landlord, Mr. Kidd, illustrate how problems in or avoidance of communication lead to a contrast between surface realism and expected logicalism, the result of which is confusion and a sense of uneasiness on the part of both the characters and the audience:

ROSE. It must get a bit damp downstairs.
MR. KIDD. Not as bad as upstairs.
ROSE. What about downstairs?
MR. KIDD. Eh?
ROSE. What about downstairs?
MR. KIDD. What about it?
ROSE. Must get a bit damp.
MR. KIDD. A Bit. Not as bad as upstairs though.
          . . .
ROSE. What about your sister, Mr. Kidd?
MR. KIDD. What about her?
ROSE. Did she have any babies?
MR. KIDD. Yes, she had a resemblance to my old mum, I think. Taller, of course.
ROSE. When did she die, then, your sister?
MR. KIDD. Yes, that's right, it was after she died that I must have stopped counting . . .
ROSE. What did she die of?
MR. KIDD. Who?
ROSE. Your sister.
Pause.
MR. KIDD. I've made ends meet. [102, 103]

Technically speaking, Mr. Kidd seems to be a few straws short of a bale. Clearly, however, his failure or refusal to communicate, to answer the questions that he is asked, keeps Rose off-guard because she cannot verify anything. This use of humor to raise an underlying horror prepares for the situation that will emerge when Rose is confronted by a strange couple, the Sands, who inform her that her room is for rent. Since she has no reason to believe that her room is to be rented to someone else, her determination of whether the Sands are telling her the truth is of great concern to her, yet we have already seen that there is little likelihood that she will be able to make this determination, no matter what significance it may hold.

The pattern in the Rose/Mr. Kidd verbal exchange parallels the confrontation-with-menace/need-for-verification/need-for-communication/fear-of-exposure/consequent break-down of communication/resultant impossibility of verification and increase in menace that fosters a consequent increase in the need-for-verification cycle that is a thematic construct in much of the writer's work. If questions and answers are not clearly paired, it is difficult or impossible to determine the truth. In *The Dwarfs*, Mark's "I see that butter's going up" is answered by Len's "I'm prepared to believe it, but it doesn't answer my question" (89). The fact that the price of butter is rising may well be true, or as Goldberg says in *The Birthday Party*, "True? Of course it's true. It's more than true. It's a fact" (30). Nonetheless, the importance of the truth is diminished, for the truth may have nothing to do with the question asked. At the same time, the answer given is the only answer that will be forthcoming.

Indeed, in the conversation between Rose and Mr. Kidd, further evidence is provided in a humorous manner to demonstrate that it may be impossible to establish what is true at any level. Rose asks innocently, "How many floors you got in this house?" though why she doesn't know is a mystery in itself. Mr. Kidd compounds the mystery:

> MR. KIDD. Floors. (*He laughs.*) Ah, we had a good few of them in the old days.
> ROSE. How many have you got now?
> MR. KIDD. Well, to tell you the truth, I don't count them now.
> ROSE. Oh.
> MR. KIDD. No, not now.
> ROSE. It must be a bit of a job.

> MR. KIDD. Oh, I used to count them, once. Never got tired of it. I used to keep a tack on everything in this house. I had a lot to keep my eye on, then. I was able for it too. That was when my sister was alive. But I lost track a bit, after she died. She's been dead some time now, my sister. It was a good house then. She was a capable woman. Yes. Fine size of a woman too. . . . I think my mum was a Jewess. Yes, I wouldn't be surprised to learn that she was a Jewess. She didn't have many babies. [102–03]

Apparently, as with the Rollright Stones outside Oxford (which legend holds move about so that they can never be counted accurately), one can never be sure of the number of floors in a house no matter how long one lives there—a constant recounting is necessary. And, if one cannot ever be sure how many floors there are in a house at any specific moment, then how can one be sure of his or her mother's background?

As absurd as this contention may sound, there is still an obvious logic to it. In much of Pinter's canon the events at the end of a play seem far removed from those at the beginning, but a careful analysis shows that there is a step-by-step logical progression throughout. Of course, the logic of that progression may be a kind of lateral thinking instead of the straightforward, linear thinking that the audience is accustomed to. If stones can move about, then certainly floors can too; if one cannot be confident about the number of floors, how confident can one be about the nature of one's parents? So, funny things said in nonhumorous circumstances accentuate the seriousness of what is happening. Coincidentally, humor based on non sequiturs serves to accentuate the prevailing mood of menace that has grown out of the basic situation.

Humor is frequently utilized to provoke laughter, to provide relief, or to emphasize a contrast, and Pinter employs a number of different techniques to create his humor. For instance, interchanges between Len and Mark in *The Dwarfs* diffuse tension, are filled with exaggeration, repetition, non sequiturs, and Yiddish phrasing.

Yiddish phrasing is apparent in many of the author's works, as in an exchange in *The Dwarfs*:

LEN. What's this, a suit? Where's your
    carnation?
MARK. What do you think of it?
LEN. It's not a schmutta.
MARK. It's got a zip at the hips.
LEN. A zip at the hips? What for?
MARK. Instead of a buckle. It's neat.
LEN. Neat? I should say it's neat.

    . . .

MARK. What do you think of the cloth?
LEN. The cloth? (*He examines it, gasps
    and whistles through his teeth. At a
    great pace.*) What a piece of cloth.
    What a piece of cloth. What a piece
    of cloth. What a piece of *cloth.*
MARK. You like the cloth?
LEN. WHAT A PIECE OF CLOTH! [88]

In *Jewish Wry*, Sarah Blacher Cohen distinguishes between the Hebrew and Yiddish languages, especially as they are used in humorous
discourse. Hebrew, she claims, is used for serious matters, such as the study of the Talmud.
Yiddish is the language of everyday usage and
thus the language in which Jewish humor is
likely to appear. Moreover, nineteenth-century
Jews considered themselves the "butt of a cruel
joke, they found that God had singled them out
to be a light unto the nations, but had given
them a benighted existence. Powerful in inter-
preting the vast complexities of sacred texts,
they were powerless in their dealing with brain-
less peasants . . . they felt isolated from the
world at large. To cope with the anxiety produced by these incongruities, they created a
humor in which laughter and trembling were
inextricably mingled. . . . Theirs was a cerebral
comedy of errors which showed the limitations
of strained thinkers—the circularity of their
reasoning, their faulty premises and absurd
proofs" (2). Although not much of Pinter's humor fits the pattern that Cohen describes, most
of his *plays* fit the paradigm.

    The famous interrogation scene in *The
Birthday Party* is an example of many of the
elements described by Cohen:

GOLDBERG. Where was your wife?
    . . .
STANLEY (*turning, crouched*). What
    wife?
GOLDBERG. What have you done with
    your wife?
MCCANN. He's killed his wife?
    . . .

GOLDBERG. Why did you never get
    married?
    . . .
GOLDBERG. Do you recognise an exter-
    nal force, responsible for you, suf-
    fering for you?
STANLEY. It's late.
    . . .
GOLDBERG. Is the number 846 pos-
    sible or necessary?
STANLEY. Neither.
GOLDBERG. Wrong! Is the number 846
    possible or necessary?
STANLEY. Both.
GOLDBERG. Wrong! It's necessary but
    not possible. (52–53)

A refusal to take anything for granted, even
in the most basic theological discussion, is evident in *The Dwarfs*:

LEN. Do you believe in God?
MARK. What?
LEN. Do you believe in God?
MARK. Who?
LEN. God.
MARK. God?
LEN. Do you believe in God?
MARK. Do I believe in God?
LEN. Yes.
MARK. Would you say that again?
    [102–03]

The opposite of refusing to take anything
for granted is literalism, and Pinter uses this
device frequently. For example, in *Moonlight*
Andy and Bel engage in the act of taking a cliché
literally:

ANDY. . . . It's enough to make the cat
    laugh. Do we have a cat?
BEL. We do.
ANDY. Is it laughing?
BEL. Fit to bust. [2]

Repartee is present in the dialogue between
Goldberg and Lulu in *The Birthday Party*[1]:

LULU. You used me for a night. A pass-
    ing fancy.
GOLDBERG. Who used who?
LULU. You made use of me by
    cunning when my defences were
    down.
GOLDBERG. Who took them down?

LULU. That's what you did. You quenched your ugly thirst. You took advantage of me when I was overwrought. I wouldn't do those things again, not even for a Sultan!

GOLDBERG. One night doesn't make a harem.

LULU. You taught me things a girl shouldn't know before she's been married at least three times!

GOLDBERG. Now you're a jump ahead. What are you complaining about?

LULU. You didn't appreciate me for myself. You took all those liberties only to satisfy your appetite.

GOLDBERG. Now you're giving me indigestion. [84]

Bizarre premises or situations—the unexpected—are also a source of humor for Pinter, as in the casual conversation between the husband, Richard, and wife, Sarah, in *The Lover* about her lover's anticipated visit while Richard is away at work,[2] or the act 1 scenes in *The Homecoming* when Lenny finds a strange woman (Ruth) in his front room in the middle of the night but neither she nor he comments upon the situation for some minutes. Similarly, in act 2 of *The Homecoming* the spectacle of Ruth rolling about on the floor in a passionate embrace with Lenny while Teddy, her husband/Lenny's brother, watches unconcernedly is hilarious. But, Richard and Sarah in *The Lover* know that Richard is casual because it is he who will be returning as the lover—a situation that reflects the problems that beset their marriage. As for Lenny and Ruth ignoring the unusual situation in which they find themselves, their psychological needs overshadow their sense of decorum, and Teddy can ignore Ruth's apparently aberrant behavior because she does not fulfill his psychological needs, just as she can place herself in such a position because of the barrenness of her relationship with him.

In much of Pinter's drama the humor hearkens back to the psychological basis of the drama: the characters have reached a stage of desperation where they are perfectly willing to accept anything as normal, any action by another character no matter how absurd that action might seem, on the chance that it will lead to a relationship that will satisfy their emotional needs. *The Homecoming* is filled with examples of this type of character and the resultant humor, as is *The Collection*. In the latter play, for

instance, there is Harry's gloriously understated initial reaction to seeing James throw a knife at Bill, whose hand is cut by the blade: "It's his own fault for not ducking" (76). This reaction is overturned by what follows: "I must have told him dozens of times, you know, that if someone throws a knife at you the silliest thing you can do is to catch it." Naturally, the audience realizes that Bill was not trying to catch the knife, and nobody believes that Harry had literally advised his roommate "dozens of times" about how to behave in this sort of situation. The immediate intent is to create a sense of relief that no one was hurt (to release the tension à la Shakespeare's gatekeeper in *Macbeth*) and to generate a contrast with the serious confrontation that has been taking place. The "strained expectation," as Immanuel Kant would put it, is dissolved and the result is laughter. Harry's words are designed to have another effect, too, though. He is jealous of the possible attraction that Bill may feel toward James, and he wants to make Bill appear foolish in case James is likewise attracted, a motive that is evident in the "slum boy" speech that soon follows.

Examples of reversal are seen throughout *The Homecoming*. At one point Sam describes MacGregor to Max: "He was a lousy stinking rotten loudmouth. A bastard uncouth sodding runt. Mind you, he was a good friend of yours" (18). Elsewhere, talking about his deceased wife, Jessie, Max declares: "Mind you, she wasn't such a bad woman. Even though it made me sick just to look at her rotten stinking face" (9). When Lenny, his son, complains, "Plug it, will you, you stupid sod, I'm trying to read the paper," Max responds, "Listen! I'll chop your spine off, you talk to me like that! . . . Talking to your lousy filthy father like that!" These discourses are funny because they are the complete opposite of the kind of dialogue that one would expect between family members or in describing a dead spouse/mother. More important, the attitudes that are displayed relate directly to the meaning of the play.[3]

In summary, Pinter's humor contains many of the normal elements of stage humor and is mostly verbal in character, containing little slapstick (with a few notable exceptions, as in the pass-the-bag sequence in *The Caretaker*). In addition to the misunderstandings, non sequiturs, noncommunications, Yiddish phrasing, witty wordplay, and reversal elaborated upon above, there are puns and jokes—and all are included for the common reasons of characterization, contrast, relief, plain humorous effect, and so forth. Whatever the device that Pinter employs, however, the most important aspect of humor in his work is the one that grows out of the meaning of a play or the concepts that underlie it, and this has been true from *The Room* right through *Moonlight*.

Summary

Harold Pinter is the most important and influential English-language dramatist of the second half of the twentieth century. Some critics claim that he is the most important and influential playwright of the twentieth century, period, an assessment based on the themes that Pinter explores in his plays, his style, and his influence on other playwrights. His *The Birthday Party, The Caretaker, The Homecoming*, and *Old Times* have been accorded the status of modern classics.

Throughout Pinter's career there has been a steady thematic evolution together with a concurrent and continual stylistic development in his writing. The thematic movement from exposure of menace naturally led him to an investigation into the source of menace, which in turn stimulated his interest in the interconnections of memory and time and the nature of reality. There are clear organic connections between the thematic periods in his writing. Simultaneously, he has changed his style to better express his new themes; form and content are intricately, efficiently, and effectively wedded. Whatever other components of his style have been emphasized, humor has always been an important element in his writing.

Pinter's major contributions to modern drama lie in the areas of language (realistic dialogue) and exposition (the presentation of characters and their motivations as they would be exhibited in real life). The significance of his themes, the insights into human nature that he provides, and the combination of emotional impact and intellectual depth in his works have made Pinter one of the most important playwrights in the history of English drama.

Notes

1. Unfortunately, in the revised edition Pinter deleted some of the humor of this confrontation, just as he dropped the "butter's going up" line in a revision of *The Dwarfs*. No explanation for these changes has ever been given, but it seems that the author felt that the humor in the first case and the clarity of the statement in the second provided the audience with too much humor for the sake of humor (or, in the case of *The Dwarfs,* because it delivered too much overt information).

2. RICHARD (*amiably*). Is your lover coming today?
   SARAH. Mmnn.
   RICHARD. What time?
   SARAH. Three.
   RICHARD. Will you be going out . . . or staying in?
   SARAH. Oh . . . I think we'll stay in.
   RICHARD. I thought you wanted to go to that exhibition. [5] . . .
   RICHARD. Your lover came, did he?
   SARAH. Mmnn. Oh yes.
   RICHARD. Did you show him the hollyhocks? (7)

3. See my *Butter's Going Up* (Durham: Duke University Press, 1977), pp. 136–56, for a full explanation of this connection.

Selected Bibliography

Archival Sources

In 1990, the Harold Pinter Society established the Harold Pinter Archives. These are still very much in the initial stage, but information on the holdings is available from The Harold Pinter Society, Archivist Steven H. Gale, Kentucky State University, Frankfort, Kentucky, 40601. In 1993, Pinter gave sixty-four boxes of materials to the British Library in London.

Primary Sources

Plays
The Birthday Party. London: Encore, 1959; New York: Grove Press, 1967.
The Birthday Party: A Play in Three Acts. London: Methuen, 1960.
The Birthday Party and Other Plays. London: Methuen, 1960. Includes *The Room* and *The Dumb Waiter*.
The Caretaker. London: Methuen, 1960; New York: Grove Press, 1964.
A Slight Ache. Tomorrow (Oxford), No. 4 (1960).
A Slight Ache and Other Plays. London: Methuen, 1961. Includes *A Night Out* and *The Dwarfs*.
The Birthday Party and The Room. New York: Grove Press, 1961.

The Caretaker and The Dumb Waiter: Two Plays. New York: Grove Press, 1961.

Three Plays: A Slight Ache, The Collection, The Dwarfs. New York: Grove Press, 1962.

The Collection and The Lover. London: Methuen, 1963.

The Homecoming. London: Methuen, 1965; 2nd ed., London: Methuen, and New York: Grove Press, 1966.

The Lover and Other Plays. New York: Grove Press, 1967. Includes *Tea Party* and *The Basement*.

The Lover, Tea Party, The Basement. New York: Grove Press, 1967.

Tea Party and Other Plays. London: Methuen, 1967. Includes *The Basement* and *Night School*.

A Night Out, Night School, Revue Sketches: Early Plays by Harold Pinter. New York: Grove Press, 1968.

Three Plays: Tea Party, The Basement, and The Lover. New York: Grove Press, 1968.

Landscape. London: Emanuel Wax for Pendragon, 1968.

Landscape and Silence. London: Methuen, 1969. Also includes *Night*.

Monologue. London: Covent Garden Press, 1973.

No Man's Land. London: Methuen, and New York: Grove Press, 1975.

Old Times. London: Methuen, and New York: Grove Press (Black Cat), 1971.

Other Places: Three Plays. London: Methuen, 1982; New York: Grove Press, 1983. Includes *A Kind of Alaska, Victoria Station*, and *Family Voices*.

Mountain Language. London: Faber & Faber and New York: Grove Press, 1988.

Anthologies

Plays: One. London: Eyre Methuen, 1976. Published in the United States as *Complete Works: One*. New York: Grove Press, 1977; rpt. 1981.

Plays: Two. London: Eyre Methuen, 1976. Published in the United States as *Complete Works: Two*. New York: Grove Press, 1977; rpt. 1981.

Plays: Three. London: Eyre Methuen, 1976. Published in the United States as *Complete Works: Three*. New York: Grove Press, 1978; rpt. 1981.

Plays: Four. London: Eyre Methuen, 1976.

Published in the United States as *Complete Works: Four*. New York: Grove Press, 1978; rpt. 1981.

Essays and Articles on Drama and Theater

"Beckett." In *Beckett at Sixty: A Festschrift*. Ed. John Calder. London: Calder and Boyars, 1967, p. 86.

"Harold Pinter Replies." *New Theatre Magazine*, 11, No. 2 (January 1961): 8–10.

"The Knight Has Been Unruly: Memories of Sir Donald Wolfit." *The Listener*, 79 (April 18, 1968): 501.

Mac. London: Emanuel Wax for Pendragon, 1968. Rpt. *Harper's Bazaar*, 102 (November 1968): 234–35; *Good Talk 2: An Anthology from BBC Radio*, ed. Derwent May, 1969; New York: Grove Press, 1977; Pinter, *Complete Works: Three*, pp. 9–18.

"Pinter on Beckett." *New Theatre Magazine*, 11, No. 3 (May-June 1971): 3.

"Pinter on Pinter." *Cinebill*, 1, 2 (October 1973): 7.

"Two People in a Room: Playwriting." *New Yorker*, 43 (February 25, 1967): 34–36.

"Writing for Myself." *Twentieth Century*, 168 (February 1961): 172–75.

"Writing for the Theatre." *Evergreen Review*, 8 (August–September 1964): 80–82; rpt. Popkin, *The New British Drama*, pp. 575–80; Goetsch, *English Dramatic Theories IV: Twentieth Century*, pp. 118–24; Pinter, *Complete Works: One*, pp. 9–16.

Secondary Sources

Almansi, Guido, and Simon Henderson. *Harold Pinter*. Contemporary Writers. London: Methuen, 1983. An overview.

Baker, William, and Stephen E. Tabachnick. *Harold Pinter*. Writers and Critics series. Edinburgh: Oliver and Boyd, and New York: Barnes & Noble, 1973. An overview, with attention to Jewish elements.

Barnes, Clive. "The Theatre: Pinter's Birthday Party." *New York Times* (October 4, 1967): 40. Review.

———. "Stage: Caught in the Sway of a Sea-Changed Pinter." *New York Times* (October 18, 1971): Sec. C, p. 8. Review.

———. "Stage: Pinter's Small Talk of Reality." *New York Times* (August 3, 1971): 43. Review.

Bensky, Lawrence M. "Harold Pinter: An

Interview." *Paris Review*, 10, 20 (Fall 1966): 12–37.

Bloom, Harold, ed. and introd. *Harold Pinter*. New York: Chelsea House, 1987. An anthology of previously published essays.

Bold, Alan, ed. and introd. *Harold Pinter: You Never Heard Such Silence*. London: Vision Press, 1984; Totowa, NJ: Barnes & Noble, 1985. A collection of original essays by leading Pinter scholars.

Bordewijk, Cobi, and J.M. Knotter. *Pinter Appeal: A Comparative Study of Responses to The Homecoming*. Leiden: Quick Service, 1988. A reporting of audience responses in England and the Netherlands.

Boulton, James T. "Harold Pinter: *The Caretaker* and Other Plays." *Modern Drama*, 6, 2 (September 1963): 131–40. Early overview.

Braunmuller, A.R. "Pinter's *Silence*: Experience without Character." In *Harold Pinter: Critical Approaches*. Ed. Steven H. Gale. Madison, NJ: Fairleigh Dickinson University Press, 1986, pp. 118–28.

Brown, John Russell. *Theatre Language: A Study of Arden, Osborne, Pinter and Wesker*. London: Penguin Books, 1971; New York: Taplinger, 1972.

———. "Mr. Pinter's Shakespeare." *Critical Quarterly*, 5, 3 (Autumn 1963): 251–65. Discusses Pinter's techniques.

Burkman, Katherine H. *The Dramatic World of Harold Pinter: Its Basis in Ritual*. Columbus: Ohio State University Press, 1971.

———, ed. *Pinter at Sixty*. Bloomington: Indiana University Press, 1993. A collection of essays by major Pinter scholars.

Cave, Richard. *New British Drama in Performance on the London Stage: 1970 to 1985*. Gerrards Cross: Smythe, 1987; New York: St. Martin's Press, 1988, pp. 1–55.

Cima, Gay Gibson. "Acting on the Cutting Edge: Pinter and the Syntax of Cinema." In *Critical Essays on Harold Pinter*. Ed. Steven H. Gale. Boston: G.K. Hall, 1990, pp. 244–58.

Diamond, Elin. "The Parody Plays [*The Dumb Waiter*]." In *Critical Essays on Harold Pinter*. Ed. Steven H. Gale. Boston: G.K. Hall, 1990, pp. 47–65.

———. *Pinter's Comic Play*. Lewisburg, PA: Bucknell University Press, 1985. Examines Pinter's comic techniques.

Dukore, Bernard F. *Where Laughter Stops: Pinter's Tragicomedy*. Columbia: University of Missouri Press, 1976. The plays are analyzed in terms of modern tragicomic structure.

Esslin, Martin. "Evaluation." In *Critical Essays on Harold Pinter*. Ed. Steven H. Gale. Boston: G.K. Hall, 1990, pp. 298–304.

———. "Harold Pinter's Work for Radio." In *Harold Pinter: Critical Approaches*. Ed. Steven H. Gale. Madison, NJ: Fairleigh Dickinson University Press, 1986, pp. 47–64.

———. *The Peopled Wound: The Work of Harold Pinter*. New York: Doubleday/ Anchor, 1970; rev. as *Pinter: A Study of His Plays*. London: Eyre Methuen, 1973; *Pinter: The Playwright*. Portsmouth, NH: Heinemann, 1984. A major study by an internationally renowned critic of modern drama.

Feldstein, Elayne Phyliss. "From Novel to Film: The Impact of Harold Pinter on Robert Maugham's *The Servant*." In *Critical Essays on Harold Pinter*. Ed. Steven H. Gale. Boston: G.K. Hall, 1990, pp. 175–83.

Fuegi, John. "The Uncertainty Principle and Pinter's Modern Drama." In *Harold Pinter: Critical Approaches*. Ed. Steven H. Gale. Madison, NJ: Fairleigh Dickinson University Press, 1986, pp. 202–09.

Gabbard, Lucina Paquet. *The Dream Structure of Pinter's Plays: A Psychoanalytic Approach*. Rutherford, NJ: Fairleigh Dickinson University Press, 1976.

Gale, Steven H. "Breakers of Illusion: George in Edward Albee's *Who's Afraid of Virginia Woolf?* and Richard in Harold Pinter's *The Lover*." *Vision*, 1, 1 (Fall 1979): 70–77.

———. *Butter's Going Up: A Critical Analysis of Harold Pinter's Work*. Durham, NC: Duke University Press, 1977. A study of Pinter's themes and stylistics.

———. "Character and Motivation in Harold Pinter's *The Homecoming*." *The Journal of Evolutionary Psychology*, 8, 3–4 (August 1987): 278–88.

———, ed. *Critical Essays on Harold Pinter*.

P

Boston: G.K. Hall, 1990. A collection of essays by Pinter scholars, both reprints and originals.

———. "Deadly Mind Games: Harold Pinter's *Old Times*." In *Critical Essays on Harold Pinter*. Ed. Steven H. Gale. Boston: G.K. Hall, 1990, pp. 211–28.

———. "Harold Pinter." In *Encyclopedia of World Literature in the Twentieth Century*. New York: Frederick Ungar, 1983. 2nd ed. Vol. 3, pp. 533–38.

———. "Harold Pinter." In *The International Dictionary of the Theatre: Volume 2, Playwrights*. Ed. Mark Hawkins-Dady. London: St. James, 1992.

———, ed. *Harold Pinter: Critical Approaches*. Madison, NJ: Fairleigh Dickinson University Press, 1986. Original essays by Pinter scholars.

———. "Harold Pinter's Film Version of *The Servant*; Adapting Robin Maugham's Novel for the Screen." *The Pinter Review: Annual Essays 1990*. Ed. Francis Gillen and Steven H. Gale. Tampa: University of Tampa, 1991, pp. 4–20.

———. *Harold Pinter's The Homecoming and Other Works*. New York: Simon and Schuster's Monarch Notes, 1971.

———. "Harold Pinter's *No Man's Land*: Life at a Standstill." *The Jewish Quarterly*, 24, 4 (Winter 1976/77): 13–18, 20.

———. "McCann's Political and Religious Allusions in Harold Pinter's *The Birthday Party*." *Notes on Contemporary Literature*, 7, 3 (May 1977): 5–6.

———. "Nature Half Created, Half Perceived: Time and Reality in Harold Pinter's Later Plays." *The Journal of Evolutionary Psychology*, 5, 3–4 (August 1984): 196–204.

———. "Observations on Two Productions of Harold Pinter's *Old Times*." *The Pinter Review*, 1, 1 (1987): 40–43.

———, and Francis Gillen, eds. *The Pinter Review: Annual Essays 1990*. Tampa: University of Tampa Press, 1991.

———, and Francis Gillen, eds. *The Pinter Review: Annual Essays 1991*. Tampa: University of Tampa Press, 1992.

———, and Francis Gillen, eds. *The Pinter Review: Annual Essays 1992–1993*. Tampa: University of Tampa Press, 1994.

———, and Francis Gillen, eds. *The Pinter Review: Annual Essays, 1994*. Tampa: University of Tampa Press, 1995.

———. "The Significance of Orson Welles in Harold Pinter's *Old Times*." *Notes on Contemporary Literature*, 13, 12 (March 1983): 11–12.

———. "The Use of a Cinematic Device in Harold Pinter's *Old Times*." *Notes on Contemporary Literature*, 10, 1 (January 1980): 11.

———. "A Woman's Place: Changing Perceptions of the Female Role—Individualism and the Community in Harold Pinter's Film of *The Pumpkin Eater*." In Ronald Dotterer and Tony Whall, eds., *Film, Individualism, and Community*. Selinsgrove, PA: Susquehanna University Press, 1994.

Ganz, Arthur, ed. *Pinter: A Collection of Critical Essays*. Englewood Cliffs, NJ: Prentice-Hall, 1972. A valuable early collection which includes pieces by actors, director Peter Hall, scenic designer John Barry, and critics.

Gascoigne, Bamber. "Love in the Afternoon." London *Observer* (September 22, 1963): 26.

Giantvalley, Scott. "Toying with *The Dwarfs*: The Textual Problems with Pinter's 'Corrections.'" In *Harold Pinter: Critical Approaches*. Ed. Steven H. Gale. Madison, NJ: Fairleigh Dickinson University Press, 1986, pp. 72–82.

Gibbs, Patrick. "People Shut in Private Worlds: Symbolic Plays." *Daily Telegraph* (London, March 9, 1970): 14.

Gill, Brendan. "The Cry." *New Yorker*, 47 (November 27, 1971): 89. Review of *Old Times*.

Gillen, Francis. "'All These Bits and Pieces': Fragmentation and Choice in Pinter's Plays." *Modern Drama*, 17, 4 (December 1974): 477–87.

———. "Harold Pinter's *The Birthday Party*: Menace Reconsidered." In *Harold Pinter: Critical Approaches*. Ed. Steven H. Gale. Madison, NJ: Fairleigh Dickinson University Press, 1986, pp. 38–47.

———. "'Nowhere to Go': Society and the Individual in Harold Pinter's *The Hothouse*." In *Critical Essays on Harold Pinter*. Ed. Steven H. Gale. Boston: G.K. Hall, 1990, pp. 164–75.

Gilliatt, Penelope. "Achievement from a Tight-Rope." *Observer* (London, June 6, 1965): 25. Review of *The Homecoming*.

Gilman, Richard. *Common and Uncommon Masks*. New York: Random House, 1971, pp. 93–113.

———. "Mortal Combat." *Newsweek*, 69 (January 16, 1967): 93. Review of *The Homecoming*.

Goldstone, Herbert. "Not so Puzzling Pinter: *The Homecoming*." *Theatre Annual*, 25 (1969): 20–27.

Gordon, Lois, ed. *Harold Pinter: A Casebook*. New York: Garland, 1990. Essays by Pinter scholars.

Gottfried, Martin. "*The Birthday Party*." *Women's Wear Daily*, 115 (October 4, 1967): 44. Review.

Gussow, Mel. "A Conversation (Pause) with Harold Pinter." *New York Times Magazine* (December 5, 1971): 42–43, 126–29, 131–36.

Hall, Stuart. "Home Sweet Home." *Encore*, 12 (July/August 1965): 30–34. Review of *The Homecoming*.

Hewes, Henry. "Odd Husband Out." *Saturday Review*, 54 (December 4, 1971): 20, 22. Review of *Old Times*.

———. "Pinter's Hilarious Depth Charge." *Saturday Review*, 50 (January 21, 1967): 61. Review of *The Homecoming*.

Hinchliffe, Arnold P. *Harold Pinter*. New York: Twayne, 1967. Twayne's English Authors Series. Rev. ed., New York: G.K. Hall, 1981. First full-length study of Pinter's work. Good insights.

Hobson, Harold. "Larger Than Life at the Festival." *The Sunday Times* (London, December 31, 1957). First review of a Pinter play—*The Room*.

———. "The Screw Turns Again." *The Sunday Times* (London, May 25, 1958): 11. Review of the first run of *The Birthday Party*.

Hollis, James R. *Harold Pinter: The Poetics of Silence*. Crosscurrents/Modern Critiques Series. Carbondale: Southern Illinois University Press, 1970. Hollis concentrates on Pinter's use of language.

Hudgins, Christopher. "*The Basement*: Harold Pinter on BBC-TV." In *Critical Essays on Harold Pinter*. Ed. Steven H. Gale. Boston: G.K. Hall, 1990, pp. 89–101.

———. "Intended Audience Response, *The Homecoming*, and the 'Ironic Mode of Identification.'" In *Harold Pinter: Critical Approaches*. Ed. Steven H. Gale.

Madison, NJ: Fairleigh Dickinson University Press, 1986, pp. 102–18.

Hughes, Catherine. "Pinter and 'Pinteresque.'" *America*, 135 (December 11, 1976): 424. Review of *No Man's Land*.

Jiji, Vera M. "Pinter's Four Dimensional House: *The Homecoming*." In *Critical Essays on Harold Pinter*. Ed. Steven H. Gale. Boston: G.K. Hall, 1990, pp. 101–11.

Keown, Eric. "At the Play." *Punch*, 30 (September 30, 1959): 252–53. Review of the review sketches.

Kerr, Walter. *Harold Pinter*. Columbia Essays on Modern Writers, No. 27. New York: Columbia University Press, 1967; London, 1967. Short analysis of Pinter's works which "function according to existential principle."

Klein, Joanne. *Making Pictures: The Pinter Screenplays*. Columbus: Ohio State University Press, 1985. Study of Pinter's cinematic adaptations of other writers' works.

Knowles, Ronald. "Harold Pinter, Citizen." In *The Pinter Review: Annual Essays, 1989*. Ed. Francis Gillen and Steven H. Gale. Tampa: University of Tampa, 1989, pp. 24–34. Pinter's later political impulses are examined.

———. "The Primacy of Performance in Pinter's Plays." In *Critical Essays on Harold Pinter*. Ed. Steven H. Gale. Boston: G.K. Hall, 1990, pp. 219–20. Focuses on the plays as performed.

Kroll, Jack. "The Puzzle of Pinter." *Newsweek*, 88 (November 29, 1976): 74–78, 81. Wide-ranging review of *No Man's Land*.

Lahr, John, ed. *A Casebook on Harold Pinter's The Homecoming*. New York: Grove Press, 1971. Interesting, important commentary by those involved in the play's original production.

Lambert, J.W. "*The Caretaker*." *Sunday Times* (London, May 1, 1960): 25. Review.

Marcus, Frank. "A Couple of Half-Pinters." *Sunday Telegraph* (London, July 6, 1969): 14. Review of *Landscape* and *Silence*.

———. "Pinter: The Pause That Refreshes." *New York Times* (July 12, 1969): Sec. D, p. 8. The use of language and non-language.

P

Marowitz, Charles. "Theatre Abroad." *Village Voice* (September 1, 1960). Revealing interview with Pinter regarding *The Caretaker*.

Morrison, Kristin. *Canters & Chronicles: The Use of Narrative in the Plays of Samuel Beckett & Harold Pinter*. Chicago: University of Chicago Press, 1986.

Muller, Robert. "Hate Yourself Though You May, You'll Enjoy These Plays." *Daily Mail* (London, January 19, 1961): 3. Review of *A Slight Ache*.

Quigley, Austin. *The Pinter Problem*. Princeton, NJ: Princeton University Press, 1975. Excellent study of Pinter's dramatic language.

Raymond, Gerard. "Q and A with Simon Gray." *Theater Week,* October 12–18, 1992, pp. 21–25.

Sahai, Surendra. *Harold Pinter: A Critical Evaluation*. New York: Longwood, 1981. Overview.

Sakellaridou, Elizabeth. *Pinter's Female Portraits: A Study of Female Characters in the Plays of Harold Pinter*. Basingstoke and London: Macmillan and Totowa, NJ: Barnes & Noble, 1988.

Scott, Michael, ed. and introd. *Harold Pinter: The Birthday Party, The Caretaker, The Homecoming: A Casebook*. London: Macmillan, 1986.

Shulman, Milton. "Pinter in His Best Hypnotic Mood." *Evening Standard* (London, June 19, 1962): 10. Review of *The Collection*.

Smith, Leslie. "Pinter the Player." In *Critical Essays on Harold Pinter*. Ed. Steven H. Gale. Boston: G.K. Hall, 1990, pp. 230–44. The impact of Pinter's acting career on his stage plays is considered.

Sykes, Alrene. *Harold Pinter*. St. Lucia: University of Queensland Press; New York: Humanities Press, 1970. Good examination of Pinter's theatrical techniques.

Taylor, John Russell. *Anger and After: A Guide to New British Drama*. London: Methuen, 1962. Rev. 1969. Published as *The Angry Theatre* in America; New York: Hill and Wang, 1963. Rev. 1969. Outstanding early introduction to Pinter's writing for the stage.

Thompson, David T. *Pinter: The Player's Playwright*. New York: Schocken Books, 1985. Fine detailing of the effect of Pinter's acting career on his writing.

Trussler, Simon. *The Plays of Harold Pinter, An Assessment*. London: Gollancz, 1973.

Tynan, Kenneth. "A Verbal Wizard in the Suburbs." *Observer* (London, June 5, 1960): 16. Review of *The Caretaker*.

Wardle, Irving. "The Birthday Party." *Encore*, 5 (July/August 1958): 39–40. Review.

———. "Pinter Theatrical Twins in Pools of Solitude." *The Times* (London, July 4, 1969): 7. Review of *Landscape* and *Silence*.

Weales, Gerald. "The Stage: Odd Man Out." *Commonweal*, 95 (December 17, 1971): 278. Review of *Old Times*.

Wellwarth, George. *The Theater of Protest and Paradox*. New York: New York University Press, 1964. Revised 1971. Discusses Pinter's "Comedy of Allusiveness."

Biographies

Prentice, Penelope A. *Harold Pinter: Life, Work, and Criticism*. Fredericton, N.B.: York Press, 1991.

Bibliographies

Gale, Steven H. *Harold Pinter: An Annotated Bibliography*. Boston: G.K. Hall, 1978.

Steven H. Gale

Planche, James Robinson

Born: London, February 27, 1796
Education: Private tutorial and Mr. Farrer's boarding school, Chelsea
Marriage: Elizabeth St. George, April 26, 1821; two children
Died: London, May 30, 1880

Biography

James Robinson Planche was born on February 27, 1796 in the Piccadilly district of London, the son of Jacques Planche, a watchmaker, and his wife Catherine Emily. The elder Planche and his wife were first cousins and descendants of French Huguenot refugees. The young Planche's early education was supervised by his mother, who brought him up speaking fluent French. Following his mother's death in 1804, Planche attended a boarding school run by a Reverend Mr. Farrer in Chelsea and studied geometry and perspective with a French landscape painter, Monsieur de Court. At fourteen—the customary age for the son of a tradesman to begin an apprenticeship—Planche was articled to a bookseller.

Planche's literary and dramatic interests first became apparent during his school years when he and his roommates wrote and performed their own theatricals. He continued his involvement with drama during his apprenticeship, acting in amateur productions at several private theaters. His broader literary interests are evident in his participation in the Mnemosynean Society, where he gave readings of his own verse. Planche wrote his first dramatic piece in early 1818, a burlesque called *Amoroso, King of Little Britain*. Described by its author as a "Serio-Comick, Bombastick, Operatick Interlude," this work was intended for amateur production by a theater company in Greenwich. The one-act piece was seen in manuscript, however, by a popular comedic actor, John Pritt Harley, who arranged for it to be staged at Drury Lane. The piece was well received and was given seventeen performances as part of the play-bill through the 1818 season. Drury Lane was one of two theaters in London managed under a royal "patent" dating back to the reopening of the theaters with the Restoration of Charles II, and Planche suddenly found himself acquainted with actors at the very center of the London theatrical community. Encouraged by this success, he turned to playwriting as a career.

On April 26, 1821, Planche married Elizabeth St. George, a moderately successful dramatic author in her own right, with whom he would have two children. During this period, he also traveled frequently to Paris, where he was impressed by developments in French theater. The dramatist's early works were produced, for the most part, at the so-called "minor" theaters outside the City of London proper, such as Sadler's Wells, the Adelphi, and the Lyceum. These plays were short mock operas known as burlettas and melodramas adapted from or heavily influenced by what he observed in Paris. His most notable early melodrama was *The Vampire*, or *The Bride of the Isles*, a seminal English horror story introducing the vampire Lord Ruthven, produced in August 1820.

From 1822 to 1828, Planche worked as the stock-author for the theater company managed by Charles Kemble at Covent Garden. His most notable accomplishment during these years, however, was not as a dramatist, but in costume design. In 1823, at Planche's suggestion, Kemble mounted a production of William Shakespeare's *King John* in historically accurate costume. This was in defiance of the usual practice of dressing all of Shakespeare's plays in either conventional fashions or what could be described, at best, as fancifully picturesque costumes. The

production was a critical as well as a commercial success, and similar efforts were mounted in subsequent seasons. This "antiquarian" movement popularized historically accurate and realistic sets and costumes and sowed the seeds of the revolution in stage practice that occurred by mid-century.

In 1831, Planche joined forces with the actress-manager Madame Vestris in an association that would last until the end of her career in 1855. Planche's first production with Madame Vestris, *Olympic Revels*, established the pattern for his playwriting and costume and set design during this period. The play was a burlesque based on classical themes, or "extravaganza" as Planche termed it, and combined mildly satiric musical comedy with sumptuous staging. For the next twenty years, his further efforts along these lines became the major influence in the stage developments that would eventually lead to the light operas of Sir William Schwenck Gilbert and Sir Arthur Sullivan. According to Planche in his memoirs, *Recollections and Reflections*, the success of *Olympic Revels* and subsequent extravaganzas was attributable to "the novelty imparted to it by the elegance and accuracy of the costume . . . [and] the effect of persons picturesquely attired speaking absurd doggrel."

The research necessary for historically accurate productions led Planche to become a serious scholar and write extensively on historical costume, armor, and antiquities. In 1829, he was elected to the Society of Antiquaries and in 1843 he was prominent in the founding of the British Archaeological Association. He also became interested in genealogy and heraldry and was appointed to the College of Arms in 1845. Scholarly interests and public duties increasingly dominated his life in the 1850s and 1860s. His dramatic output rapidly dwindled to an occasional Christmas pantomime or extravaganza, and in the last decade of his life he quit the theater entirely. By the time of his death in London on May 30, 1880, Planche was remembered more for his accomplishments as a scholar and herald than his work as a major figure in the theater for more than three decades.

Literary Analysis

Planche's dramatic career spanned a significant transitional period in English theater. When his first play was produced in 1818, the major influences were an increasingly moribund "classical" aesthetic in acting and staging rooted in

Restoration and Eighteenth-century theater practice and the growing popularity of "melodrama" imported from the Paris stage. The author's melodramas, like *The Vampire*, or the *Bride of the Isles*, are interesting and significant for his adaptation of French melodrama to the needs of English stock-companies and the expectations of English audiences. It is for his developments in the form of the "extravaganza," however, that he deserves an enduring place in theater history.

Planche's extravaganzas are an important (and often ignored) transitional form between the burlettas of the eighteenth century, notably John Gay's *The Beggar's Opera* (1728), and the comic operas of the late nineteenth century, such as Gilbert and Sullivan's *HMS Pinafore* (1878). Planche's first dramatic effort, *Amoroso, King of Little Britain*, anticipates later developments by the playwright with its combination of verse and song in a burlesque of the tragedy and opera in the contemporary theatrical repertory. For example, the Shakespearean roots (vide *Hamlet*) of the climactic "death" scene are quite apparent:

Enter Roastanda.

Roastanda. Ah! Coquentinda slain!—Die tyrant die! [stabs the King] Who falls the next?
King. You, sir, as well as I. [Stabs the Cook, and dies.]
Roastanda. I'm pepper'd—Nature fades upon my sight, I go, I toddle, so mighty sir, good night [dies.]

Enter Blusterbus.

Ah! art thou slain, Roastanda? lie thou there?
The bravest cook that ever cas'd a hare!
But what can comfort me, all lonely left,
Of sovereign, sweetheart, friends and all bereft!
I may as well die too. [The King sneezes]
Eh! what's that?
Sure 'twas the King! Oh, ho, I smell a rat;
I'll ask a question first before I go,
Pray is your majesty defunct or no?

Air.

King. I don't much think that I'm dead:
    Pray, ma'am are you? [to the Queen]

Queen. I feel a little mended.
Mollidusta. So do I too.
Roastanda. I wasn't cooked completely,
    But in a precious stew.
Blusterbus. Then if none of you intend to
    die, I'm d——d if I do.

Planche wrote a number of fairly conventional burlettas—even mocking his own melodrama *The Vampire* in *Giovanni the Vampire!!! or How Shall We Get Rid of Him?*—until 1825, when he began to introduce elements from French theater practice. He readily admitted the influence: "my visits to Paris made me acquainted with two classes of drama of which I was utterly ignorant—the 'Feerie Folie' and the 'Revue.'" These developments set Planche's work apart from the parody and low comedy of the burletta and led him to emphasize the distinction by calling his efforts "extravaganzas."

Although Planche includes early efforts like *Success, or A Hit if You Like It* (1825) in the 1879 edition of his extravaganzas, the form did not really take a recognizable shape of its own until his association with Madame Vestris in the 1830s. The extravaganzas based on classical stories show elements of the mild satire and plain comedy that mark them as clear antecedents of the light opera of the 1870s and 1880s. A song from *The Golden Fleece* (1845) serves to illustrate:

Air—MEDEA—
You Wanton son of Venus,
My heart in twain you've rent;
Against no other maiden,
Could your wicked bow be bent?
It may seem very bold, but
I love young Jason so;
If he were to pop the question, I
Don't think I could say, "No."
If you wool gathering go, love,
My wits the wool shall gather—
In one boat we will row, love,
In spite of wind and weather;
And if to Davy Jones, love,
We hand in hand should go,
We'll sleep together in the old
Boy's locker down below.

Planche's extravaganzas were arguably the high point of English musical theater in the period from 1830 through 1860. His prominence is probably most telling in that his writing was the standard by which the work of others was judged. Indeed, when Gilbert wrote *Dulcamara, or the Little Duck and the Great Quack* in 1866, a burlesque of Gaetano Donizetti's opera *L'Elisir d'Amore*, he was pleased to have it favorably compared to the work of Planche.

Summary

James Robinson Planche played an important part in the development of English musical comedy theater in the mid-nineteenth century. His burlesque "extravaganzas" included an "antiquarian" approach to costumes and sets and a French influence combined with mildly satirical musical comedy. This format formed the bridge between burlettas and the light opera typified by Gilbert and Sullivan later in the century.

The retirement of Madame Vestris in 1855 and Planche's gradual withdrawal from active involvement marked the beginning of a period of relative decline for musical comedy and English theater in general. The form of the "extravaganza" became moribund when left in the hands of Planche's lesser imitators and costuming and set design settled into doctrinaire adherence to "antiquarian" principles. While Planche had raised theatrical burlesque to the level of high art with his extravaganzas and instigated a revolution in costume and set design, by the time of his death in 1880 the impact on English theatrical practices of his associations with Kemble and Madame Vestris had been largely forgotten. In the re-visioning of English theatrical history that occurred in the first decades of the twentieth century, Planche's melodramas and extravaganzas dropped from the critical horizon along many other casualties of a changing dramatic aesthetic.

Selected Bibliography
Primary Sources
Amoroso, King of Little Britain: A Serio-Comick Bombastic Operatick Interlude in One Act. London: Richard White, 1818.

Giovanni the Vampire!!! or, How Shall We Get Rid of Him? London: John Lowndes, 1821.

The Extravaganzas of J.R. Planche, Esq., 1825–1871. Ed. T.F. Dillon Croker and Stephen Tucker. 5 vols. London: Samuel French, 1879.

Recollections and Reflections by James Robinson Planche; a Professional Auto-biography. New and rev. ed. London: S. Low, Marston, 1901.

Plays by James Robinson Planche. Ed. Donald Roy. Cambridge: Cambridge University Press, 1986. Good modern text of one melodrama, one farce, and five extravaganzas with preface and a complete list of Planche's plays.

Secondary Sources

Articles and Prefaces in Books
Fletcher, Kathy. "Aristophanes on the Victorian Stage: J.R. Planche's Adaption of The Birds." *Theatre Studies*, 26, 7 (1979–1980): 89–98.

———. "Planche, Vestris, and the Transvestite Role: Sexuality and Gender in Victorian Popular Theatre." *Nineteenth Century Theatre*, 15, 1 (Summer 1987): 9–33.

Granville-Barker, Harley. "Exit Planche—Enter Gilbert." In *The Eighteen-Sixties*. Ed. John Drinkwater. Cambridge: At the University Press, 1932, pp. 102–48. Granville-Barker discusses the form of the extravaganza as developed by Planche and the reason for the relative decline of the form in the 1860s preceding the rise in popularity of light opera in the 1870s.

MacMillan, Dougald. "Planche's Early Classical Burlesques." *Studies in Philology*, 25 (1928): 34–45.

———. "Planche's Fairy Extravaganzas." *Studies in Philology*, 28 (1931): 524–32.

Peter C. Hall

Pope, Alexander

Born: London, May 21, 1688
Education: Mostly self-educated
Died: Twickenham, May 30, 1744

Biography

Alexander Pope was born in London on May 21, 1688, to Alexander Pope, a wealthy wholesale linen merchant, and Edith Turner Pope, his second wife. Because of regulations against Catholics, Pope's family left London and lived at Binfield in Windsor Forest. Since schools were not usually open to Catholics, except for short stints at Catholic schools at Twyford and Hyde Park Corner, his education came privately from priests and from his independent reading, primarily, as was the custom of the day, of the Greek and Roman classics, though he also became thoroughly familiar with such earlier English writers as William Shakespeare, John Milton, and John Dryden, the latter becoming the principal influence upon his own work. During this period, he contracted tuberculosis. The disease left him deformed (he had a humpback and grew to only four feet, six inches in height) and frail for the rest of his life. Pope never married.

His early poems (some of which, he later claimed, were written when he was twelve) led to his becoming known to important writers of the day, such as William Wycherley and Joseph Addison and Richard Steele of the *Spectator* papers and other essays; but, as Pope's satires make clear, some to whom he became known became his enemies, including, later in his life, Addison. Pope's first published work was his *Pastorals* (one for each of the four seasons), written, as almost all of his work was, in the popular poetic form of the day, the heroic couplet (rhymed couplets in iambic pentameter), a form of which he is still regarded as the outstanding master. His work includes many lines which became, and have remained, familiar, such as:

> True wit is nature to advantage dressed,
> What oft was thought but ne'er so well
>   expressed. (*Essay on Criticism*,
>   2.97–98)
> Nay, fly to altars; there they'll talk you
>   dead,
> For fools rush in where angels fear to
>   tread. (*ibid.*, 55–56)
> A wit's a feather and a chief a rod;
> An honest man's the noblest work of
>   God. (*Essay on Man*, 247–48)

Indeed, he has more quotations cited in *Bartlett's Familiar Quotations* than any other writer except for Shakespeare.

Pope's later work includes many poems which are still considered among the major poems in English literature. These include: *An Essay on Criticism* (1711), which reflects the standard critical views in the eighteenth century; *Eloisa to Abelard* (1717), a dramatic monologue by Eloisa, based on the lives of two historical figures who had been lovers but repented and retreated into their monastery and nunnery; translations of Homer's *Iliad* (1715–1720) and *Odyssey* (1725–1726); *An Epistle to Dr. Ar-*buthnot (1735); and the *Satires* (*Imitations of Horace*, 1733–1738), based on Horace's satires, with the satirical points transferred from ancient Rome to contemporary England.

The poet spent much of his time in London, visiting friends, and he had a country home on the Thames in Twickenham (complete with an underground "grotto" lined with shells, glass, and semiprecious stones), where many of his friends, including Jonathan Swift, came to visit. He died in Twickenham on May 30, 1744, and was buried in the church there.

Literary Analysis

Of Pope's major works, the two with comic aspects were *The Rape of the Lock* (first published in 1712 and increased from two cantos to five in 1714, with Clarissa's long speech added in the edition of 1717) and *The Dunciad* (first published anonymously in three books in 1728, in an enlarged edition in 1729, with an additional book, *The New Dunciad*, in 1742, and the complete work in four books in 1743).

The Rape of the Lock was based on an actual rift between two upper-class families, caused by the son of one family cutting off a lock of hair from the daughter of the other. The poem is written in the format of a genre popular in the eighteenth century, the mock epic—that is, a satire using many characteristics of the epic in deliberately diminished style and content. This includes, for example, the diminution of supernatural creatures from gods to the tiny and powerless sylphs; the description of a petticoat instead of a shield; the theft of a lock of hair instead of the "theft" of Helen; and the epic battle becoming a card game and therefore lacking any serious injury or death.

In a mock epic and hence humorous style, the poem includes a major characteristic of the epic as the opening statement of the subject:

> What dire offence from am'rous causes
>   springs,
> What mighty contests rise from trivial
>   things,
> I sing. (1.1–3)

It also includes other characteristics such as the epic question:

> Say, what strange motive, Goddess,
>   could compel
> A well-bred *Lord* t'assault a gentle *Belle*?

Oh say what stranger cause, yet unexplored,
Cou'd make a gentle *Belle* reject a *Lord*?
(1.7–10)

There is a sacrifice to the gods as well:

the Baron . . . to *Love* an altar built
Of twelve vast French Romances, neatly
gilt. (2.37–38)

The altar includes other "sacrificial" items—
three garters, one glove, and three sighs. Also
present is the ancient pattern of granting half a
prayer which is useless without the other half:

The Pow'rs gave ear and granted half his
Pray'r,
The rest, the winds dispers'd in empty
Air. (2.45–46)

In the end, in another ancient pattern, the lock
of hair becomes a constellation:

A sudden Star, it shot through liquid Air,
And drew behind a radiant *Trail of Hair.*
(5.127–28)

One of the prominent aspects of the poem
is its satirical view of women. For instance,
women, when they die, retain their characteristics (1.51–56) and become creatures which
match them in terms of one of the four classical elements: the termagants like fire, the "soft"
and "yielding" like water, the prudish like earth,
the flirtatious like air. The flirtatious are protected by sylphs as young women, until, after
being courted by many suitors, they yield and
hence lose that protection.

The poem is full of humorous lines in which
Pope makes fun of the life of the upper classes,
as in "And sleepless lovers, just at twelve,
awake" (1.16) and especially lines which provide a satirical view of women: "Yet graceful
ease and sweetness void of pride / Might hide
her faults, if Belles had faults / to hide" (2.15–
16). Characteristic, too, are lines which provide
a humorous anticlimax:

Whether the Nymph shall break Diana's
law,
Or some frail China jar receive a flaw;
Or stain her honour, or her new brocade;
Forget her pray'rs, or miss a masquer-
ade;

Or lose her heart, or necklace, at a ball;
Or whether Heav'n has doom'd that
Shock must fall. (2.105–10)
. . .
Here, thou, great ANNA! whom three
realms obey
Dost sometimes counsel take—and
sometimes tea
Sooner let earth, air, sea, to Chaos fall,
Men, monkeys, lap-dogs, parrots, perish
all! (4.119–20)

The poem opens with its heroine, Belinda,
still asleep. She is being kept so by Ariel, her
guardian sylph. Ariel does not want her to face
what the day will bring and gives her a dream
of a youth whispering in her ear. The youth tells
her of the spirits who protect her, spirits who
were women before they died. However, he
does warn her that this protection will last only
as long as she rejects men. Then she is wakened
by her dog, Shock, and, seeing a love letter,
wholly forgets her dream. Since the young lady,
in a sense, worships herself as she dresses, the
dressing table, with its "*Cosmetic* Pow'rs"
(1.124), is viewed as a mock-altar.

In canto 2, Belinda goes down the River
Thames to Hampton Court, the meeting place
of the upper classes and a home of Queen Anne.
Like the oracle at Delphi, Ariel foresees but does
not reveal what she regards as a dire occurrence.
The Baron admires and intends to steal two
beautiful locks of Belinda's hair as a keepsake
because he loves her. The key portion of her
beauty is described:

This Nymph, to the Destruction of Mankind,
Nourish'd two locks which graceful
hung
behind. (2.19–20)
. . .
He saw, he wish'd, and to the prize
aspir'd. (2.30)

This is a parody of Caesar's "I came, I saw,
I conquered." The Baron makes sacrifices at
the altar of Love to help him in attaining his
goal. Again in ancient fashion, the gods grant
him only half his desire: to gain the prize, but
only very briefly. The sylphs are threatened
with mock punishment compared to ancient
Hades: "be stopt in vials or transfix'd with
pins" (2.126), or bear a mock resemblance to
the ancient punishment of Ixion in Hades, or,

anticlimactically, "In fumes of burning chocolate shall glow" (2.135). The sylphs who protect Belinda are told by their chief, Ariel, that it is their particular duty to "tend the Fair" (2.91), and that the fairest of the fair (Belinda) faces a disaster, though Ariel does not know what—whether she will lose her virginity or break a vase, commit a dishonorable act, or stain a dress, or a variety of other possibilities, including the death of her lapdog.

In canto 3 the young women have arrived at Hampton Court to gossip. As the sylphs await anxiously what they know is going to happen, the aristocrats engage in a mock-epic battle—a game of cards. Belinda becomes involved in the game, first losing to the Baron and then defeating him. She is overtriumphant at the win, and is guilty of *hubris*. The audience knows, therefore, that as in Greek tragedy in turn she will in some sense lose. The players have tea—or coffee or liquor—and one of the jealous young ladies, Clarissa, gives the Baron her scissors to cut off the lock. Ariel looks into Belinda's mind and, seeing that she is in love, can no longer protect her. The Baron cuts off the lock:

> The meeting points the sacred hair dissever
> From the fair Head for ever and for ever! (3.153–54)

Belinda screams in horror, and in another anticlimax,

> Not louder shrieks to pitying Heav'n are cast,
> When Husbands, or when Lapdogs, breathe their last. (3.157–58)

The Baron in turn experiences *hubris*:

> Let Wreaths of Triumph now my Temples twine,
> (The Victor cry'd) the glorious Prize is mine! (3.161–62)

In canto 4, with Belinda still in agony over her loss, another supernatural creature, Umbriel, goes down to the underworld and the Cave of Spleen, a sort of Hades, where Spleen has transformed the splenetic into various lifeless shapes such as a teapot and a jar. Umbriel requests that Spleen make Belinda experience anger instead of grief. Spleen gives him a bag of emotions. Umbriel takes them to Belinda and breaks the bag over her head as she lies dejected in the arms of a friend, Thalestris. Belinda then experiences outrage, and Thalestris urges her on and goes to her beau, Sir Plume, and orders him to demand the lock from the Baron. Unused to demanding, Sir Plume does, in a comical way, make the demand, but the Baron swears that he will keep the lock no matter what. The jar having been broken over her head, Belinda becomes angry at the Baron, who is not moved, although, as canto 5 begins, everyone else is affected except Thalestris, who thus speaks out against the other women and their attitudes and way of life—ignoring the future when they will no longer be young, ignoring the possibility of disease and other ills, ignoring the possibility that good humor might produce better results than outrage. But, the others are unaffected, and the women go to battle against the men and are winning, when, rather oddly, Jove weighs the case in his scales and the men win, through unusual wiles such as throwing snuff in a man's face. However, when Belinda cries out, "Restore the Lock," no one can find it. The muse and the poets, though, see it shoot up into the air and become a star which the world will praise. Belinda is told to stop grieving and recognize that the star means that her name will live forever.

There would be widespread agreement—and has been through the centuries—that Pope's poem is the most successful mock epic in English literature, revealing everything about the upper classes of the day that one would expect to see revealed through the use of a highly effective story told in a style almost ideally suited to the material and the theme.

The Dunciad is a satire on Pope's and his period's most hated and feared phenomenon, dullness or boredom. Boredom, indeed, was a state the prospect of which in the poet's day actually frightened people.

The fact that the *Dunciad* is a mock epic is immediately obvious, both from the title which relates it to Homer's *Iliad*—it is an Iliad of dunces—and from its opening line (in the 1728 octavo edition), "Books and the man I sing," which is based on the opening of Virgil's *Aeneid*, "Arms and the man I sing," a literary rather than a martial narrative and an appropriate beginning, since the poem deals primarily with books and authors, meaning primarily bad books and authors. The focus turns immediately, therefore, to the bane of good writers and critics and, in a sense, the center of the poem. Dullness is a goddess in the poem, "Daughter of Chaos and Eternal Night" (1.10), an immortal creature, since the human capacity for that quality will never die. Pope then addresses his friend Swift—not addressed by name but by words that almost any educated Englishman would recognize: Dean, followed by "Drapier, Bickerstaff, or Gulliver," three others taken from Swift's works. And, he amplifies his point by pointing out that Swift could be serious like Miguel de Cervantes or funny like François Rabelais, and that he could point out in suitable style the grievances of his country, Ireland, under the rule of England, which is in the process of "hatching a new Saturnian age of Lead" (1.28), rather than a golden age. He then turns to an area of London, Rag Fair, where "in one bed two shiv-ring sisters lye" (1.30), Poverty and Poetry, and where works by bad writers are published by bad publishers—and also where the goddess Dullness resides, rather oddly surrounded by "Four guardian Virtues" (1.44), Fortitude, Temperance, Prudence, and Poetic Justice. As we soon learn, dullness includes "new-born nonsense" (1.48): ineffective and inappropriate similes and metaphors, inappropriate mixtures of comedy and tragedy, and of epic and farce. Soon Pope provides what he regards as actual examples, with real names, regarding "pensive poets" who "painful vigils keep," "Sleepless themselves to give their readers sleep" (1.81–82).

The principle example of this type of poet is, in this edition, Lewis Theobald ("Tibbald"), and, in a later edition, Colley Cibber, both minor writers of the period. One can escape Dullness by turning to the great writers of Greece and Rome, ignored in the world of Dullness except by a very few. Tibbald sacrifices bad books to Dullness and in the process mentions other examples of bad writing such as puns, which were hated in Pope's day, and the Gothic—that is, the elaborateness and, from their point of view, useless detail of Gothic architecture and of similar patterning in poetry. Oddly, Pope also surrounds his goddess with the same four traditional and genuine virtues: Fortitude, Temperance, Prudence, and Poetic Justice.

The goddess is awakened by Tibbald's sacrifice and displays her works (that is, works by dull writers), such as those who confuse verse and prose and those who ignore the virtues of the great ancient writers and recent great ones in France. The goddess sprinkles opium on Tibbald's head, sets her monster of a bird on his head, and calls him her son—a king who will lead her other sons to a land flowing not with milk and honey but with puns and other sorts of bad writing.

Book 2 begins with Tibbald seated on a throne-like seat in a place where the Queen of England proclaims games like the ancient Olympics, where the bad writers now come to compete and win the prize: another bad writer—More—possibly the actual James Moore. One of the bad writers challenges the others. Curl accepts the challenge and ends by falling in the filth of his own wickedness. But, a goddess rescues him, inspiring him by the odor of his own filth, and he wins the race and the prize. The prize, however, turns out to be Nothing; and the Nothing's poems and other papers fly back to the good writers, two of them (Edward Young and Swift) being still well known today, and the third (Abel Evans) being scarcely known at all.

Dullness decks out three booksellers to look like three good writers, William Congreve, Addison, and Matthew Prior, and the bad writers try unsuccessfully to capture them. The goddess tries to comfort Curl by transforming the bad writers into the good: Prior, Swift, Sir Samuel Garth, and Addison. A variety of events occur involving more bad writers, ending with the goddess Sleep having her effect and bringing each one dreams suitable to his foolish wishes. Curl in his imagination descends to Elysium and sees another bad writer, Settle, who greets him as his son and tells him that all past nonsense will come to center on him. Sleep shows him the whole world, including England, which, having long escaped her, is now back in her hands—in her hands because in England the good writers, such as Francis Bacon, John Locke, and Isaac Newton, are gone and the bad writers and playwrights have taken over, a land of anarchy where even philosophy and science are helpless. Hence, with all light gone, there comes sickness of brain, of art and science, of wit and logic and rhetoric, which are replaced by sophistry, false views of morality, and chaos.

In England crowds flock around Dullness, and more crowds pushed by the first crowds, yielding more and more to her power: the poets, the blockheads, courtiers, patriots, and fops. Dullness orders that the genuine authors be torn to bits by bad critics. A specter—the ghost of an actual schoolmaster—arises and speaks, saying that teachers teach words, not ideas, that Reason tells the teacher to take the easier path, that poets deal with words as teachers do, and so do others such as legislators and judges. He calls others, such as logicians, to join him, and says that critics like himself turn verse into prose and make great writers like Horace and John Milton dull. He tells Dullness that wisdom can be as dull as folly and can only puzzle by its explanations, and he gives a variety of examples. More crowds flock in, and one speaks to Dullness in worshipful words saying that Aeneas was an exception but that through the ages, all over Europe, she is honored, and that the use of ancient languages only increases the dullness. Another—again a real person but named otherwise—asks Dullness to let him go on cheating, and he gets into an argument with another worshiper. Dullness honors them both and the words of similar worshipers, including Shakespeare scholars, botanists, and the like. She blesses them all and tells them to continue to be proud, selfish, and dull, and to end by making all of England a Dunciad. She yawns and all of England falls asleep, including fancy (that is, imagination), wit, and all of the arts, as well as truth, philosophy, physics, metaphysics, mathematics, religion, morality. And, in the final line, Universal Darkness buries All.

Summary

Alexander Pope was one of the major poets of English literature and is regarded by many as the outstanding master of the heroic couplet. In *The Rape of the Lock*, perhaps the most successful mock epic in English literature, he makes fun of women and of the upper-class life of his time. Another successful mock epic, *The Dunciad*, satirizes dullness.

Pope's prose writings illuminate his poetry and also his personal life; most of his prose works were published anonymously and never acknowledged by the poet, who wished to avoid personal attack and to protect his poetry from biased judgment.

Selected Bibliography

Primary Sources
An Essay on Criticism. London: Printed for W. Lewis and sold by W. Taylor, T. Osborn, and J. Graves, 1711.
The Rape of the Lock. An Heroi-Comical Poem. In Five Cantos. London: Printed for Bernard Lintot, 1714; rev. ed. 1718.
Trans., *The Iliad of Homer, Translated by Mr. Pope*. 6 vols. London: Printed by W. Bowyer for Bernard Lintot, 1715–1720.
The Works of Mr. Alexander Pope. London: Printed by W. Bowyer for Bernard Lintot, 1717; enlarged ed., Dublin: Printed by and for George Grierson, 1727.
Trans., *The Odyssey of Homer*. 5 vols. London: Printed for Bernard Lintot, 1725–1726.
The Dunciad. An Heroic Poem. In Three Books. London: Printed for A. Dodd, 1728.
An Essay on Man, Being the First Book of Ethic Epistles. To Henry St. John, L. Bolingbroke. Epistles I-IV. London: Printed by John Wright for Lawton Gilliver, 1734; Philadelphia: Printed by William Bradford, 1747.
The First Epistle of The Second Book of Horace, Imitated. London: Printed for T. Cooper, 1737.
The Second Epistle of The Second Book of Horace, Imitated. London: Printed for R. Dodsley, 1737.
The Sixth Epistle of The First Book of Horace, Imitated. London: Printed for Lawton Gilliver, 1738.
The First Epistle of The First Book of Horace Imitated. London: Printed for R. Dodsley, 1738.
An Epistle From Mr. Pope, To Dr. Arbuthnot. London: Printed for Lawton Gilliver, 1735.
The Works of Mr. Alexander Pope, Volume II. London: Printed for Lawton Gilliver, 1735.
Letters of Mr. Alexander Pope, and Several of his Friends. London: Printed by J. Wright for J. Knapton, Lawton Gilliver, J. Brindley, and R. Dodsley, 1737.
The New Dunciad: As it was Found in the Year 1741. London: Printed for T. Cooper, 1742.
The Dunciad, in Four Books. Printed according to the complete Copy found in the Year 1742. London: Printed for M. Cooper, 1743.

Editions
The Prose Works of Alexander Pope. 2 vols. Hamden, CT: Archon Books, 1986. Vol. 1. Ed. Norman Ault. Vol. 2, Ed. Rosemary Cowler.
Memoirs of the Extraordinary Life, Works,

and Discoveries of Martinus Scriblerus. With Jonathan Swift, John Arbuthnot, John Gay, Thomas Parnell, and Robert Harley, Earl of Oxford. Ed. Charles Kerby-Miller. New Haven: Yale University Press, 1950.

Literary Criticism of Alexander Pope. Ed. Bertrand A. Goldgar. Lincoln: University of Nebraska Press, 1965.

Selected Prose of Alexander Pope. Ed. Paul Hammond. Cambridge: Cambridge University Press, 1987.

Letters

The Correspondence of Alexander Pope. Ed. George Sherburn. 5 vols. Oxford: Clarendon, 1956.

Secondary Sources

Bibliographies

Griffith, Reginald Harvey. *Alexander Pope: A Bibliography.* Austin: University of Texas Press, 1922, 1927.

Guerinot, J.V. *Pamphlet Attacks on Alexander Pope: 1711–1744. A Descriptive Bibliography.* London: Methuen, 1969.

Biographies

Johnson, Samuel. *Lives of the English Poets.* Ed. George Birkbeck Hill. Oxford: Clarendon, 1905. Vol. 3.

Mack, Maynard. *Alexander Pope: A Life.* New Haven: Yale University Press, 1985.

Ruffhead, Owen. *The Life of Alexander Pope.* London: Printed for C. Bathurst, 1769.

Sherburn, George. *The Early Career of Alexander Pope.* Oxford: Clarendon, 1934.

Books and Articles

Jackson, Wallace, and R. Paul Yoder, eds. *Pope's Poetry.* New York: Modern Language Association, 1994. Approaches to Teaching World Literature series.

Mack, Maynard, ed. *Essential Articles for the Study of Alexander Pope.* Hamden, CT: Shoe String, 1964.

Rogers, Robert W. *The Major Satires of Alexander Pope.* Folcroft, PA: Folcroft, 1955.

Sitter, John F. *The Poetry of Pope's Dunciad.* Minneapolis: University of Minnesota Press, 1971.

Tillotson, Geoffrey. *On the Poetry of Pope.* 2nd ed. London: Oxford University Press, 1950.

Tomarken, Edward. "Alexander Pope." *Dictionary of Literary Biography.* Vol. 101. *British Prose Writers, 1660–1800.* Ed. Donald T. Siebert. Detroit: Gale, 1991, pp. 262–77.

Williams, Aubrey L. "Alexander Pope." *Dictionary of Literary Biography.* Vol. 95. *Eighteenth-Century British Poets.* Ed. John Sitter. Detroit: Gale, 1990, pp. 169–210.

———. *Pope's Dunciad.* Hamden, CT: Shoe String, 1968. Rpt. of 1955 edition.

Jacob Adler

Potter, Stephen Meredith

Born: Balham, London, February 1, 1900
Education: Westminster Boarding School, 1914; Merton College, Oxford University, B.A., 1922
Marriage: Mary Attenborough, July 7, 1927; divorced 1955; Heather Lyon, March 20, 1955; three children
Died: London, December 2, 1969

Biography

Stephen Meredith Potter, author and satirist, created the theory of gamesmanship or "The Art of Winning Games Without Actually Cheating" and is acknowledged by H.W. Fowler's *Modern English Usage* as creating "the conceit of making facetious formations by treating manship as the suffix."

The son of Frank Collard Potter, a chartered accountant, and Elizabeth (Reynolds), Potter was born in Balham, London, on February 1, 1900, and experienced an uneventful and comfortable childhood. Potter arrived at Westminster Boarding School in 1914, joined the army in 1918, where he graduated top of his company, and in 1919 summarily received a commission in the Coldstream Guards. In 1922, he graduated from Merton College, Oxford, taking a second in English language and literature.

The humorist's early twenties were punctuated by a number of long walks, which took him into the countryside for months, and by various odd jobs. One job, undoubtedly inspired by George Bernard Shaw's *Pygmalion*, found him running an ad in the paper—"Cockney accents cured." It was at this time that he met Henry Arthur Jones and through his own devices was soon serving the playwright as personal secretary and companion.

In 1926, Potter took a full-time position as lecturer at Birkbeck College, London, and was able to support both his writing and subsequently the artistic pursuits of his new wife, Mary Attenborough, whom he married on July 7, 1927. His first novel, *The Young Man* (1929), was followed a year later with a critical work on D.H. Lawrence. There then came three works on the poet Samuel Taylor Coleridge: *Coleridge* (1933), *Minnow Among Tritons* (1934), and *Coleridge and S.T.C.* (1935).

Socially and professionally, 1937 was a big year for Potter. This was the year that he took a job with the British Broadcasting Company (BBC) as a writer-producer in the Features Department, employment that he would hold for ten years and then on and off for the rest of his life. It was also the year that he published *The Muse in Chains: A Study in Education*, a work that satirically attacks the English education system. But perhaps most important to him, 1937 was the year that he was admitted to the Savile Club and his golf game improved.

It appeared as if Potter would henceforth be absorbed in the intellectual and critical pursuits of the academic world while doing regular and irregular pieces for the BBC. However, World War II found him reviewing books and plays for the local London papers to augment his salary. In order to make ends meet he wrote a book on the odd scraps of paper available to him concerning a joke that he had often shared between friends. The joke was transformed into *Gamesmanship*, or "The Art of Winning Games Without Actually Cheating," published in 1947. The "-manship" idea propelled Potter to a certain distinction and was successful enough that he would later expand on the concept and write *Some Notes on Lifemanship* (1950), *One-Upmanship* (1952), *Supermanship* (1958), and *Golf Gamesmanship* (1968).

After *Gamesmanship* he did stints from 1949 to 1951 as editor on both *Leader* and *London Magazine*. Later decades saw the divorce from his first wife, in 1955, the same year that he married Heather Lyon (on March 20); extensive tours of America, during which he lectured on and advertised his "-manship" theories; and a developing sickness, accompanied with a limp, that he would often incorporate in his gamesmanship tactics—his opponents never knew whether to take him seriously or not.

Apart from small articles on other variations of the "-manship" theme, Potter also published *Sense of Humour* (1954), a critical work that deals with the differing forms of English humor through history; *Potter on America* (1956), a satirical look at America; *Steps to Immaturity* (1959), an autobiography concerning his childhood and education; and a number of children's stories. He died in London on December 2, 1969.

Literary Analysis

"Let your knowing itself be an action" is perhaps the key ingredient to the theory and practice of gamesmanship. Through an integral knowledge of the weaknesses of an opponent, of the home court, or through the development of actions or idiosyncrasies that so debilitate an antagonist, gamesmanship may be used subtly to defeat an individual, on or off the court, without a conscious understanding by that person of how he or she has been defeated. This premise, described by Potter as "the moral equivalent to assault and battery," is a psychological tactic that he later incorporated to address almost all facets of life. Strategies range the spectrum from very humorous and outlandish to more subtle and devious ploys that he presents in a wry, textbooklike fashion. It is this manual-like presentation, with extensive footnotes and diagrams, which imbues much of his theory with its satirical, witty edge.

Although gamesmanship and its variations —one-upmanship and lifemanship—may be espoused as a doctrine or general philosophical process, Potter outlines many instances in which certain gambits may successfully be employed. His most often quoted example, and one that he credits with the statement, "the curtain was lifted, and I began to see," took place in a tennis match in which he and his partner, Dr. Cyril Joad, found themselves at a gross disadvantage. Dr. Joad, who figures prominently in the *Gamesmanship* book, apparently disarmed his two younger, more talented opponents by asking if his own return service had landed in or out (although it had clearly, to all concerned, landed out). A conversation ensued in which the younger men offered to play the point again; Joad refused and replied, "I only want you to say clearly, if you will, whether the ball was in or out." Potter follows the scenario with the comment, "there is nothing more putting off to young university players than a slight suggestion that their etiquette or sportsmanship is in question. How well we know this fact, yet how often we forget to make use of it." The two younger men, out of stride and off their game, proceeded to lose the match that they should have won. With the use of precise timing and apparent candor, an individual, as is the case with Joad, may cunningly place the suggestion of doubt into his or her opponent's mind that will somehow, if only faintly, throw that opponent off his game.

The theory of gamesmanship is very diverse. It can be subtle, as the previous example illustrates, yet it also may take on outrageous proportions. Another instance concerning Dr. Joad, discomfiting Potter himself, occurred when the former invented the ruse of taking off his clothes during a friendly game of golf. Undressing, Joad took a dip in a nearby waterhole while Potter watched two foursomes play through. Disturbed and confounded, Potter lost the match. One of Potter's favorite jokes was whistling the same fragment of classical music over and over again between his opponent's golf shots—always whistling the same note off-pitch. In still another ploy Potter asked a friend for a favor at the third hole but did not reveal his request until the sixteenth. Various other techniques included wearing mis-matching clothes to distract opponents, faking a minor injury or ailment, and delaying or rushing a match or game.

Potter's gamesmanship theory is the product of his love of sport, especially golf, coupled with a competitive love of winning. However, the theory was also derivative of a radio program that he wrote with Joyce Grenfell for the BBC. The first of the twenty-nine "How" programs aired in 1943, four years before *Gamesmanship* was published. These programs dealt satirically with everyday life, from "How to listen to radio" to "How to throw a party" and, very timely in 1947, "How to be good at games." A direct connection is apparent in the author's definition of his gamesmanship theory, "how to gain the advantage over one's opponents without their realizing it."

Potter's employment with BBC radio was very distinguished. Along with his war documentaries he was also well known for both the "Professional Portraits" and "New Judgments" series. Still, as he noted, "nobody took much notice of these programs till I started working with my old friend Joyce Grenfell (the actress) on a series called 'How.'" The "How" series lasted roughly ten years and while one of its programs is credited with initiating the Third Programme in September 1946, the whole series, along with Potter, is acknowledged as having introduced sophisticated humor to radio. These programs were also very beneficial to Potter himself, enabling him to enlarge the concept of gamesmanship into the wider forms of one-upmanship and lifemanship.

A sequel to *Gamesmanship*, *Some Notes on Lifemanship*, was preceded by a series of lifemanship lectures given by Potter for the BBC. Not as successful or widely acclaimed as his first book concerning the "-manship" theme, *Gamesmanship* sold 70,000 copies in twenty years of publication and it was treated kindly by critics. Simply stated, lifemanship is a variation of gamesmanship "extended to include the simple problems of everyday life." Various tactics include how to make an expert look a fool, how to make people feel awkward, the art of conversation, various woomanship ploys, and a plethora of other stratagems used to cause "the eternal opponent . . . [to] feel that something has gone wrong, however slightly." For instance, when the lifeman is confronted with the worldly views of a "far-flung traveler or international expert, he can always devastatingly reply, 'Yes, but only in the South.'"

Evident is the fact that "-manship" theory had taken hold and almost any instance could be manipulated and applied to its broad, all-encompassing confines. After *Gamesmanship*, Potter developed a loyal following of admirers in both England and America. Even if the humorist had wanted to, it is unlikely that he could have escaped the chains which he had so cleverly crafted for himself. He wrote *Supermanship* and *Golf Gamesmanship* in the same vein as the others, approaching each from only slightly differing perspectives. *One-Upmanship* held only variations of the "-manship" principle. Typical are two ploys. The first, concerning Doctorship, was addressed to physicians who treated patients as if they were "as ignorant of all anatomical knowledge as a child of four." The simple procedure is for the patient to casually glance at the doctor's credentials which hang on the wall and then ask, "I am, I suppose, right in calling you Doctor?" The other is addressed to the winesman, who when in a restaurant might "look at the wine list before the waiter comes . . . then, when the waiter comes, say to him 'Look, you've got a Chateau-Neon '45 somewhere secreted about the place, I know. Can you let us have a

P

bottle?' (You know he's got it because you have read it off the wine list, cheapest but one.) When the waiter leaves you can say, 'They keep a little cache for favored customers.'" Very shrewd, but impressive.

School for Scoundrels, an extremely amusing film based on the one-upmanship series and directed by Robert Hammer, was released in 1960. Starring Alastair Sim, Ian Carmichael, Terry-Thomas, Janette Scott, and Dennis Price, it was a tribute to Potter's concept (the plot is based on a school devoted to teaching the methods of achieving success through one-upmanship) and a reflection of the popularity of the series.

Potter wrote and lectured extensively on his "-manship" theory until his death. With *Gamesmanship*, the first of the series, he received numerous accolades for coining and elaborating his comic ideas. Yet, after the first book was succeeded by a second, a third, and so on, critics and the general public began to tire of what was no longer a novelty. Often bordering on financial difficulty, Potter most likely wrote the succeeding books to save himself from dire economic straits. Largely unemployed after the publication of *Gamesmanship*, the "-manship" theory and its variations were almost exclusively his source of income. Or, perhaps it was that Potter was trapped; a success after *Gamesmanship*, he found that he had no other choice or resources. Endeared to many as the founder of such humorous ploys, he used the one basic theme over and over again because he was expected to. Nonetheless, many critics and individuals believe that the joke went on too long. Although each book was cleverly written and satirically charming, footnotes and diagrams sometimes spilled over into tedium and the differing vehicles used to express the new "-manship" concepts became trivial. All written in the same spirit, it was simple to absorb the principles of gamesmanship, lifemanship, one-upmanship, supermanship, and golf gamesmanship in one sitting, and only so many examples could illustrate the point. Potter, comfortable with his "-manship" theory, milked the principle for all that it was worth. And, of course, for the reader who reads only one or two of the volumes, there is certainly no sense of satiety.

The theory of gamesmanship and its variations applies to serious sportsmen and intellectuals, who would be most susceptible to its charms. Its tactics might consciously be espoused by "gentlemen" such as Potter himself, or by serious competitors who are willing to do anything short of cheating in order to win, or by club members or individuals who in a jocular manner might make it known that they are trying to pull the wool over their opponent's eyes. In any case, the presentation and style are very assiduous, one might say pseudo-high-brow, and enable the reader to project the author's concept onto a more abstract and variegated level.

Unconsciously, the theory of gamesmanship may have existed from the dawn of time, yet it was Potter who grasped and elaborated on it in such a way as to leave no doubt that it became his own insightful invention. His humor is at times both deadpan and outrageous and often is implemented best when no more than two people are present— encyclopediamanship and readermanship would be good examples, although better appreciated when approached from the former perspective.

Summary

Stephen Potter is best known for his gamesmanship theory, a cunning, psychological tactic used to best a competitor, on or off the field. His basic "-manship" principle was later incorporated to include many everyday events; the progression and elaboration due to his love of sport, basic monetary needs, and in part from the "How" programs that he wrote and produced for BBC radio. Critics were kind to his later variations of the "-manship" themes, although some eventually tired of the joke. He wrote and lectured on his most popular idea and its off-shoots until his death.

Selected Bibliography
Primary Sources
Three-Upmanship: Gamesmanship, or The Art of Winning Games Without Actually Cheating, Some Notes on Lifemanship, One-Upmanship. San Francisco: Holt, Rinehart and Winston, 1966.
The Complete Upmanship: Gamesmanship, or the Art of Winning Games Without Actually Cheating, Some Notes on Lifemanship, One-Upmanship, Supermanship. San Francisco: Holt, Rinehart, and Winston, 1970.
Sense of Humour. Darby, PA: Arden, 1954.

Secondary Sources

Anderson, Dillon. "Elegant Corruption of Sportsmanship." *Saturday Review of Literature* (January 8, 1949): 21. A review of Potter's first book, *Gamesmanship*, the article is for the most part praiseworthy. It does mention that the jokes and footnotes become tedious, but acquiesces with the fact that when it comes to humor, Potter knows "the difference between corn and caviar."

Breit, Harvey. "Talk With Stephen Potter." *New York Times Book Review* (May 20, 1951): 23. A personal interview with Potter, the conversation ranges from Potter's books to his creation of the idea of gamesmanship to the favorable American reception of his theory. The article also relates Potter's close encounter with a ghost, and overall praises the author as one of "the funniest men writing in the English language today."

Grenfell, Joyce. "Stephen Potter." *Dictionary of National Biography, 1961–1970.* London: Oxford Press, 1983, pp. 853–55. Written by Potter's fellow creator of the "How" series for BBC radio, the article favorably credits Potter's contribution to that medium. Mostly, it is a history of the humorist's life.

Jenkins, Alan. *Stephen Potter: Inventor of Gamesmanship.* London: Weidenfeld and Nicholson, n.d. The book documents the humorist's life from his childhood to his death and covers the vast array of "-manship" theories on which Potter chose to elaborate.

Kunitz, Stanley J. "Stephen Potter." In *Twentieth Century Authors.* New York: Wilson, 1963, p. 786. A note, submitted by Potter himself, offers insight into his influences and perspectives on family life and relates Potter's point of view on what exactly he has contributed to the world of literature.

Lardner, Rex. "Eighteen Holes of Dirty Golf." *Book World* (January 15, 1969): 42. In this review of Potter's final book, *Golf Gamesmanship*, the author credits Potter with injecting new life into an old theory. Golf, Potter's favorite sport, provides him with "the richest and most varied of gamesmanship's many fields."

Jason Shaw

Prior, Matthew

Born: *Westminster, London, July 21 or 23, 1664*
Education: *Westminster School, London, 1672–1675; 1676–1683; St. John's College, Cambridge University, B.A., 1687*
Died: *Wimpole Hall, Cambridgeshire, September 18, 1721*

Biography

Matthew Prior, one of the outstanding British humorists in two strikingly different genres—the Hudibrastic and *vers de société*—was born in Westminster, London, on July 21 or 23, 1664. He was the fifth of six children of Elizabeth and George Prior, Dorset natives. George, a joiner (carpenter), had migrated to London, following his two brothers who had become tavern-keepers there. The couple's only child to survive infancy, Matthew showed precocity in language and literature and at the age of eight was sent by his parents to nearby Westminster School, then still ruled with a strong hand by Dr. Richard Busby and boasting among its graduates Ben Jonson, Abraham Cowley, John Locke, Christopher Wren, and John Dryden. Three years later, Prior's studies at Westminster School were abruptly interrupted by the death of his father. He was put to work keeping accounts and waiting bar in his uncle Arthur Prior's Rhenish Tavern on Channel Row. A year later Charles Sackville, sixth Earl of Dorset, discovered the twelve-year-old Prior behind his uncle's bar reading Horace. In repeated visits to the bar, the Earl, a notable patron of artists such as Dryden, William Congreve, Thomas Shadwell, Nathaniel Lee, Thomas Otway, and George Etherege, often asked Prior to construe Horace or Ovid or to translate them extemporaneously into English verse. The latter was an exercise which Busby had stressed at Westminster, and the young Prior performed it so ably that Lord Dorset offered to pay his tuition to return to Westminster School, if his uncle would provide his clothing and other necessities. Under those conditions Prior returned to Westminster School where he became a King's Scholar in 1681. A King's Scholar, named because of his unusual facility in classical languages, did not have to pay tuition or room and board and received an allowance for clothes and for certain festive expenses, as well as ceremonial and practical rights and privileges. Prior held this appointment until he graduated from Westminster School two years later.

Upon his graduation Prior applied for and received one of the five new scholarships set up by the Duchess of Somerset at St. John's College, Cambridge. He enrolled there on April 3, 1683. As had been true his last two years at Westminster School, he was exempted by his scholarship from paying all tuition and received an allowance for living expenses, a bedroom shared with four other young men, and a private study. During his four years at St. John's, Prior pursued studies heavy in logic and divinity. He was later to write that it was "a College where prose was more in fashion than Verse," yet there are extant over thirty Latin poems and a dozen English ones (chiefly pastoral or Pindaric) which he wrote during his college years. On February 9, 1687, he was graduated from Cambridge University with a bachelor of arts degree, eleventh in the *Orde Senioritatis* for that year.

After his graduation from St. John's, Prior returned to London where he achieved his first notable literary-satiric success when he collaborated with his old school friend Charles Montague in writing the prose-verse *The Hind and the Panther Transvers'd*, a burlesque of Dryden's recent *The Hind and the Panther*. Prior's and Montague's piece was an immediate and resounding success, bringing literary renown to both authors.

On April 3, 1688, Prior was entered as a Keyton Fellow at St. John's College, having become a member of the Southwell Minster Choir in order to qualify for the appointment. He moved into the Fellows' quarters of the college in April 1688. Eventually, he was assigned one of the two medical fellowships; it was because of this definition of his duties that he spoke at Cambridge from 1706 to 1710 as Linacre Lecturer on Galen. By about the middle of 1688, Prior had accepted a position as tutor to the sons of the Earl of Exeter, at Burleigh, a post which he held until at least August 1689. In 1688, he also wrote for the college one of his earliest serious pieces which was to remain one of his personal favorites until the end of his life: "On Exodus iii.14," an irregular ode. He continued to write Latin pieces, and he experimented with various forms of humorous verse: a broadside, "The Orange"; two mock-heroics on Fleetwood Shepherd; two familiar verse epistles; and a Hudibrastic travel poem ("Journey to Copt-Hall"), also to Shepherd.

During the years since his college graduation, Prior had been hoping for and seeking a political appointment. It came by November 21, 1690, when he went to The Hague to serve Lord Dursley as secretary. He stayed at The Hague for the next seven years. The Hague was an important city during the War of the League of Augsburg (the Palatinate War), which had already been going on for almost two years when Prior went there and continued until almost the end of his stay. At The Hague, Prior began the diplomatic pattern which would mark most of his political life. Partly because of his low birth, he performed important diplomatic chores for which titled superiors received most of the acclaim—and most of the money. It was Prior's duty in The Hague to report to Daniel Finch, Earl of Nottingham and senior secretary of state, sending him newspapers dealing with England, newsletters from various allied towns, details of battles and of local diplomatic maneuvering—together with Prior's own comments on all of these.

By 1690, Prior had established the first of the three relationships with women which filled his mature life, though he never married. Jane Ansley, a widow, became his housekeeper and mistress in 1690 and served him in both capacities for the next sixteen years, first at The Hague, later in London and Paris.

In June 1695, Edward, Lord Villiers, later Earl of Jersey, was appointed His Majesty's Plenipotentiary at The Hague. Villiers recommended strongly that Prior remain at The Hague; William granted the request and doubled Prior's salary. Over his seven years there, Prior produced a substantial amount of laureate verse, panegyrics upon William III and upon English military victories. On March 16, 1693, William appointed Prior a Gentleman of the King's Bedchamber, and Queen Mary gave him a pension of one hundred pounds per year. His most important poems of the Dutch period, however, were not his panegyrics but the melancholy "To the Honourable Charles Montague, Esq." and the wittily autobiographical "Written in the Year 1696" ("The Secretary"), showing for the first time Prior's full powers as a writer of colloquial light verse. By 1692, his poems had begun to be praised and printed by the two most important publishers in England, Jacob Tonson and Peter Motteux.

The War of the League of Augsburg was drawing to its end by 1696. On May 9, 1697, the first meeting of the Congress of Ryswick was held, and eventually the Treaty of Ryswick was drawn up, ending the war. Now Secretary of the Embassy, Prior checked the French and Latin versions of the treaty, then carried to London the official message that the treaty had been signed by England, Holland, Spain, and France.

These last years at The Hague brought two other significant developments in Prior's life. On May 17, 1697, he was named chief secretary to the Lords Justices of Ireland. More important to the subsequent publication of his poems, he met Adrian Drift at the Congress of Ryswick. Drift, who had been taken there in the service of Lord Villiers, was to become Prior's amanuensis and his friend, transcribing his manuscripts during his lifetime and preserving them after Prior died.

Prior returned briefly to England, but on December 11, 1697, his appointment was announced as secretary to the reopened British Embassy in Paris where he worked again under William Bentinck, first Earl of Portland. Prior stayed in Paris for nineteen months, serving first under Portland, then under the Earl of Jersey. He found his initial stay in France culturally rewarding but financially impoverishing. On March 23, 1698, he was elected a fellow of the Royal Society. On August 27, 1699, he left Paris, going first to Holland, then returning from there to London with Lord Villiers and William III. He was to remain based in London for the next twelve years, serving first William III and then Queen Anne as a roving ambassador. On June 28, 1700, Prior was appointed a commissioner of the Board of Trade and Plantations, filling the vacancy created when John Locke resigned because of ill health. Prior was himself recurrently ill during this London period.

The uneasy peace established by the Treaty of Ryswick lasted only four years; in 1701, the War of the Spanish Succession broke out, lasting another twelve years and pitting England, Holland, and Austria against France and Spain. Prior participated in the diplomatic intrigues of this war mainly from his London base. He managed, nevertheless, to perform a number of important political functions. From February to June, 1701, he served as a Member of Parliament from East Grinstead in Sussex, a pocketborough appointment made by the Earl of Dorset. But although Dorset was a Whig and Prior had belonged to the Whig Kit-Cats Club, he found himself moving politically further and further to the right, favoring a strengthened king and a limited parliament. In the key vote of his four months in Parliament, Prior joined the Tories in censuring the Partition Treaty, though he had played a role in drawing it up. Prior's days in Parliament and as a Whig were effectively ended by this vote.

In 1700, he purchased a home on the west side of Duke Street with its back overlooking St. James's Park. Although the purchase price and the accompanying maintenance charges increased his perennial financial difficulties, "Matt's Palace" was a source of delight to him and became his chief place of residence for the last two decades of his life.

Sometime between 1706 and 1708, Ansley was replaced in Prior's affections by Anne Durham, who would serve him as his second mistress for about a decade, until about 1718.

The crucial years of 1706 to 1708 produced other notable changes in Prior's fortunes beyond the change of mistresses. In politics, on April 22, 1707, he lost his position as member of the Board of Trade and Plantations. In literature, in 1707, Edmund Curll had published a pirated edition of Prior's *Poems on Several Occasions*; Prior worked throughout 1708 to put together an authorized version, bringing it out in 1709 under the same title. The edition was reprinted in 1711, 1713, and 1717. His authorized collection divided his poems into four categories: "Public Panegyrics, Amorous Odes, Serious Reflections, or idle Tales." During this twelve-year period (1699–1711), he had composed a number of new poems in each of these four categories, though the public panegyrics dropped off sharply after the death of William III in a hunting accident in 1702 and Queen Anne's succession to the throne. The best of the eighteen "Amorous Odes" which the poet composed during the period is probably "The Merchant, to secure his treasure." He also wrote during this time three "idle Tales": "To a Young Gentleman in Love. A Tale," "The Ladle," and "Paulo Purganti and His Wife: An Honest, but a Simple Pair." Among the "Serious Reflections" are two poems which were to attract the attention of later, more famous poets than Prior: "Adriani Morientis ad Animam Suam. Imitated" spurred Alexander Pope, a generation younger than Prior, to write two competing poems; over a century later "Written in the Beginning of Mezeray's History of France" led the aged Sir Walter Scott to recite the twenty-four lines by memory, weeping and applying them to himself.

Finally, some of Prior's most famous longer poems from the period do not fit neatly into his four categories. For example, *Henry and Emma* might be considered an "Amorous Ode," but it is long even for an ode (almost 800 lines) and is not so much a lyric as it is an amalgam of narrative and dialogue. *Solomon*, 2,600 lines long, has too much narrative (and too much length) to be called a "Serious Reflection." Two of his wittiest and wisest poems of this period— "An English Padlock" and "Jinny the Just"— are idle tales that are, by turns, both "amorous" and "serious."

Not all of the author's literary ventures in this period were poetic; he made some incursions into Tory journalism as well, efforts related to the most important personal development of this period: his friendship with Jonathan Swift, closely chronicled in Swift's *Journal to Stella*. The *Journal* records thirteen occasions on which Prior dined with Swift, often with the other members of the Tory Brothers Club but sometimes with just two or three of them, between October 15, 1710, and November 18, 1712. Prior gave Swift a fine Plautus—and, most critics think, taught Swift much of what he knew about the writing of light verse. The two friends walked together in St. James's Park, Prior to make himself fat, Swift to make himself thin. They exchanged puns; both men wrote for the Tory *Examiner*; anonymous works by either man might be attributed by the reading public to the other. A Whig newspaper called Prior and Swift "the two Sosias," a reference to the confusion in Plautus's *Amphitryon* between Mercury and the slave.

By 1711, Europe had grown weary of the War of the Spanish Succession, by then a decade old, and Prior was asked to play a large share in the secret negotiations which were to end it. In June 1711, Robert Harley, now Earl of Oxford and Lord Treasurer, asked him to serve as the English negotiator in London and in France, with Abbe Francois Gaultier and Jean Baptiste Colbert, Marquis de Torcy, acting for France. Peace negotiations continued through August and September, often at Prior's Duke Street house. The preliminary documents were signed on October 8, 1711, becoming the basis of the final Treaty of Utrecht. His role in these negotiations was so significant that the Whigs derisively called the final treaty "Matt's Peace." On April 11, 1713, the Treaty of Utrecht was signed between England, Holland, Portugal, Prussia,

Savoy, and France, ending the War of the Spanish Succession for these nations.

On January 25, 1712, Prior was named Commissioner of Customs, an important post, though he complained to Swift that it was killing his creative impulses for he now dreamed of nothing but "Cockets, & Dockets and Drawbacks, and other Jargon words of the Custom house." More to his liking, in September 1712, he was appointed minister plenipotentiary to France and served as acting ambassador in Paris, from August 1713 to August 1714. Then Queen Anne, the last of the Stuart rulers, died; George I and the Hanoverians succeeded her, and the Tories fell from power, Prior along with the others. Anyone who had taken an active role in drawing up the Treaty of Utrecht, which was unpopular with the Whigs, was imperiled. First Prior was removed from his post of commissioner of customs. Then, in January 1715, John Dalrymple, Earl of Stair, came to serve as ambassador to France and relieve Prior of his duties there. By late March 1715, the Whig ministry had grudgingly paid off Prior's ambassadorial debts in France, chiefly so that he could be called home for questioning. The House of Commons set up a secret committee to investigate corruption and treason in the previous ministry, particularly as related to the Treaty of Utrecht. On June 9, 1715, Prior and Thomas Harley were put under house arrest; a week later Prior was summoned to testify before the committee. By his evasive testimony Prior saved both the Duke of Shrewsbury and the Earl of Oxford from the charge of treason, but the committee was enraged that he would not implicate either man, even to save himself. They punished him by continuing to confine him to the house of the sergeant-at-arms of the House of Commons until June 26, 1716.

Although one piece produced by Prior during this hazardous period is heatedly political ("The Viceroy. A Ballad"), two of his most successfully witty poems are surprisingly free of political coloration: "Daphne and Apollo" and *Alma: or, The Progress of the Mind*. The latter belongs to that painfully extensive English subgenre—the prison production—written "to relieve the tedious hours of my imprisonment."

Although he was released from house arrest by the proroguing of Parliament and could return to his Duke Street home, Prior's problems were by no means at an end. He was growing increasingly deaf; his diplomatic career was irrevocably ended; he was short of funds and had no immediate way to raise more. To help him from his financial distress, Lords Allen Bathurst and Edward Harley conceived the plan of bringing out an enlarged *Poems on Several Occasions* as a subscription edition, a method of publication becoming increasingly important in the eighteenth century as an alternative to the patronage system. In the subscription method of publication, the writer solicited funds in advance from subscribers who then had their names printed in the published volume and made a second payment when it was actually printed and delivered—a sort of publisher's advance from a broad reading public. Bathurst, Harley, and Prior, along with Pope, John Gay, John Arbuthnot, and Erasmus Lewis met in January 1717 to plan the subscription edition, and wrote to Swift in Ireland asking for (and receiving) his help there. Tonson, experienced in subscription publishing, brought out the edition; Pope, fresh from his success with the subscription edition of his *Iliad* translation, proved a valuable adviser. The edition contains all of the poems of the Prior's 1709 *Poems on Several Occasions*, rearranged and supplemented by a number of poems which he had written since that time—notably *Solomon* and *Alma*. The large, handsome folio appeared in mid-March 1719: 500 pages long, a foot across and a yard tall, with a list of 1,445 persons who had subscribed for 1,786 books, paying a guinea in advance and another upon delivery. The volume made the writer's fortune with a profit of upwards of 4,000 guineas; he was financially very comfortable for the rest of his life. Furthermore, the publication of the volume demonstrated an important point in publishing history: that a gifted writer could support himself by dealing directly with his reading public without the benefit of a single titled and powerful patron. Dryden and Pope had preceded Prior in making money from subscription editions, but theirs had been translations or modernizations. (An *Iliad* subscriber was patronizing Homer as much as Pope.) Prior made his fortune from works directly "creative."

By about 1715 or 1716, he moved on to the third and last of the mistresses who occupied his mature life—Elizabeth Cox, wife of John Cox, a tavern-keeper in Long Acre. A number of Prior's love lyrics dating from this period were attempts to reassure Durham ("Cloe") that he was remaining faithful to her despite his growing attraction to Cox ("Lisetta"). The poems are charmingly convincing but were bad predictors: by 1718 Cox had supplanted Durham as his mistress.

Prior's new wealth enabled him to fill his Duke Street house with treasures: paintings, prints, drawings, sculpture, books, coins, medals, jewels, trinkets, and antique bronzes. His proudest purchase was made early in 1720, an Essex country estate, Down Hall, which he and Edward Harley bought together with the agreement that Prior would have the use of the estate through his lifetime (after his death it would become Harley's). The estate enlivened and animated Prior's last two years, providing the occasion for his "Down-Hall; A Ballad."

During those last two years, he produced three poems of significance other than "Down-Hall": "The Conversation. A Tale," "The Turtle and the Sparrow," and the fragmentary (but almost 300-line) "Predestination, A Poem," the first two being comic poems while the third emphatically is not.

In August 1721, Prior went as a guest to Wimpole Hall, the Cambridgeshire estate of the Harleys. Through his adult life Prior had been subject to recurrent bouts of cholera morbus and of pleurisy. On September 11, he fell ill once again of cholera morbus; a week later (September 18), he died. Four days afterwards, his body was carried to the Jerusalem Chamber of Westminster Abbey where it lay in state for three days. His elaborate funeral was held there on September 25. James Gibbs, who had drawn up the plans for Prior's new country house at Down Hall, now had no reason to build it. Instead, he designed and executed Prior's monument for the Poets' Corner of Westminster Abbey. Prior died a very wealthy man because of his poetic prowess, not his diplomatic feats. The most impressive monument in the Poets' Corner is his, ruefully described by him as "this last piece of human vanity."

Literary Analysis

Much of Prior's literary production was not humorous; his literary reputation in the eighteenth century depended as much on serious pieces such as *Solomon* or *Henry and Emma* as it did on his lighter pieces. Much of his laureate verse and many of his songs have no comic element. By the nineteenth century, however, he was known almost solely as a writer of light verse, and many of these lighter poems are comic in their intent.

Perhaps the most remarkable trait of Prior's humorous writings is their astonishing range. He is unexcelled in English poetry in two forms of comic verse which call for strikingly different talents: the Hudibrastic and *vers de société*. Beyond these two forms of comic poetry, he produced a number of other humorous types: prose dialogues of the dead, epigrams, comic eroticism, satires, burlesques, fabliau-like tales. His lifetime career was diplomatic, not literary, yet there is hardly a form of comic writing which he did not attempt effectively.

His contemporaries did not know Prior as a *prose* humorist, because the *Dialogues of the Dead* were not printed until 1907. (However, Pope had seen them in manuscript at Harley's estate in 1723 and had later praised them to Joseph Spence: "There are, also, four dialogues in prose, between persons of characters very strongly opposed to one another, which I thought very good.") Prior had projected at least ten of these dialogues; he completed four. The tradition of the dialogue of the dead was a classical one, dating back to Lucian in the second century A.D.; in Prior's own lifetime dialogues of the dead had been most effectively created in France, by Bernard le Bovier de Fontenelle (1683) and François de Salignac de la Mothe Fenelon (1712). Prior follows in the traditions of these three Continental predecessors rather than of his English forerunners.

His approach is similar in all four dialogues. He selects two conflicting figures whose values and lifestyles are strikingly divergent and pits one against the other. Although he has a favorite in each pair, neither man is a clear victor in the debate, because each has been successful only in terms which he values and his opponent despises. Thus, Prior pits Charles V, the Holy Roman Emperor and King of Spain who values fame of military victories, against Nicolas Kleynaerts, a sixteenth-century priest-philologist who prizes peace and scholarship and the life of the mind. John Locke is played off against Michel de Montaigne, Locke being systematic, methodical, intent on knowing oneself, Montaigne being unsystematic, unmethodical, imitative of nature by being irregular and copious, convinced that man, self-deceived, can never know himself. The third and most serious of the debates has as its antagonists Sir Thomas More, beheaded for his faith and his conscience when he was fifty-three, and the Vicar of Bray, More's appointee to a country parish who held his post by changing his faith three times, when the monarch changed, and who died in his bed at eighty. More died for his duty, following his

conscience, even though he knew that a man's conscience might mislead him. The Vicar of Bray saw his duty as teaching his parishioners what Parliament and his monarch told him to teach them. He never missed church, was civil to his parishioners, gave to the poor, held his tongue, and preserved his parish and his life. The final dialogue is between Oliver Cromwell and his mad porter, who argues with Cromwell that they were equal in the land of the living as they are now equal in the land of the dead. The porter (who went mad on the day that Cromwell executed Charles I) was happier ruling his imaginary kingdom in Bedlam than Cromwell was ruling his real kingdom of England. In these four dialogues the author achieves much of his comic effect by permitting disparate value systems to collide in a world which is itself chaotic, mad, and disorderly. The dialogues function effectively through the same use of language which marks the best of the writer's comic poems—colloquial, plain, persuasive.

These same talents mark a literary production of Prior's that would seem formally quite different from the prose dialogues: the epigram. Brief, versified, these epigrams are terse, polished versions of the same comic value conflicts seen in the prose dialogues. Ten of his epigrams are direct translations from the Latin or Greek; more than ten are based on less familiar French sources. Most of them, however, are original with Prior. They strike out at folly, hypocrisy, ingratitude, or vanity, in belles, professions, patrons, spouses, knaves, and fools. Although the poet is generally praised for his excellence in octosyllabics, his epigrams often function best in heroic couplets, on observations predictive of T.S. Eliot's Sweeney:

> WHAT trifling coil do we poor mortals
> keep;
> Wake, eat, and drink, evacuate, and
> sleep.

Or, reminiscent of Pope's Belinda:

> Her time with equal prudence Celia
> shares,
> First writes her billet doux then says her
> prayers.
> Her Mass and Toylet, Vespres and the
> Play;
> Thus God and Astorath divide the
> day. . . .

Prior's epigrams, like all epigrams, assume an audience agreed on social norms and hence capable of responding to a single quick thrust of wit, without authorial commentary.

Despite Dr. Samuel Johnson's rather surprising defense of the non-sexuality of Prior's poetry ("There is nothing in Prior that will excite to lewdness. If Lord Hailes thinks there is, he must be more combustible than other people . . . No, Sir, Prior is a lady's book."), a good deal of the comic effect of some of Prior's poems is anatomical. If not sexually explicit, these poems derive their humor from a surer related source, being sexually implicit. Some of his funniest tales and briefer amorous accounts depend for their final witty turn upon our knowledge of human (particularly female) anatomy, as in the ending ring-dream in *Hans Carvel* or of Cupid's final search of Cloe in "The Dove."

Hans, fearing that his wife is unfaithful, is told in a drunken dream by Satan that, if he will put on this magic ring, his wife will never betray him. But, shoving his finger into the ring beyond his joint, he finds instead that he has thrust it into his sleepless wife:

'Tis done.—What's done, You drunken
    Bear?
You've thrust your Finger G-d knows
    where.

Rather similarly, when Venus's favorite dove is lost, Cupid accuses Cloe of having stolen it and conducts a search at one in the morning, first of Cloe's house, then of her person, insisting that she has hidden the dove in her breast but soon forcing his hand lower:

O, whither do those Fingers rove,
Cries CLOE, treacherous Urchin,
    whither?
O VENUS! I shall find thy DOVE,
Says He; for sure I touch his Feather.

Many of his comic effects may not be precisely pornographic, but assuredly they are gender specific.

Prior also wrote personal satires in the narrow non-technical sense, comic treatments of specific individuals. His four early verse-epistle satires on friends and acquaintances would fall into this category, as would three youthful formal satires on his literary peers: "A Satyr on the Modern Translators," "Satyr on the Poets. In Imitation of the Seventh Satyr of

Juvenal," and *The Hind and the Panther Transvers'd*. "Satyr on the Poets," a project of the writer's college days, is an attack on Dryden and on other authors whose work was included in the miscellanies that Dryden edited. "A Satyr on the Modern Translators," written shortly after Prior's college graduation, is in part an attack on Dryden and on the Duke of Buckinghamshire but is more a rueful statement that England is no country for poets—it permits them to starve, whether they write well or ill. Like these other two poems, *The Hind and the Panther Transvers'd* is an attack on Dryden, but a much more successful one, and one that established the young Prior's literary reputation. In a mixture of verse and prose, Prior and co-author Montague ridicule Dryden's *The Hind and the Panther*, printed just two months earlier, by diminishing Dryden's beasts to two Horatian mice and by letting a vain, tedious, and fatuous Bayes quote lines from his own poem (with key terms occasionally altered for the worse). Meanwhile, Johnson and Smith approach the elegant beast-epic with a sturdy, plodding, common-sense logic that deflates its loftiness.

These seven personal satires shade off into a similar literary approach in which Prior excelled: the burlesque. A burlesque ridicules by exploiting an imaginative distance between subject and style, one lofty, the other debased. *The Hind and the Panther Transvers'd* might well be considered a burlesque of Dryden's serious *The Hind and the Panther*. Prior uses his poem to show that the Drydenic poem does not create the seriousness which it demands, either for the things it is saying or for the way in which it phrases them. Likewise, Prior's *Alma: or, the Progress of the Mind* (to be discussed as a Hudibrastic) operates as a burlesque, making fun of all philosophical system-building by couching this one in verse language generally reserved for comic topics.

Satires *may* be burlesques as well; *all* Hudibrastics are a sub-category of burlesque, mocking a subject that others have taken seriously but which the author finds ludicrous and describes in unsuitably low language, hence preserving the disparity between content and style which marks the burlesque. Two of Prior's funniest burlesques are found where we would be least likely to look for them—among his patriotic verse. In "An English Ballad, On the Taking of Namur by the King of Great Britain, 1695," he mocks Nicolas Boileau-Despreaux's "Ode Sur la Prise de Namur, Par les Armes du

Roy, L'Annee 1692," written to celebrate the earlier French victory at Namur. Now, three years later, it is the English who have won at Namur. Prior prints Boileau-Despreaux's French poem on the left of the page, his own on the right, parodying and mocking Boileau-Despreaux's pretentious claims and diction stanza by stanza. When Boileau-Despreaux calls himself an audaciously soaring Pindaric eagle, Prior retorts that Boileau-Despreaux is closer to being a handsomely rewarded vulture.

Nine years later and in a different war, Prior sees Marlborough lead the Allies to victory at Blenheim and writes "A Letter to Monsieur Boileau Despreaux: Occasion'd by the Victory at Blenheim, 1704." In the four years between the two wars, Prior has become Boileau-Despreaux's friend in Paris and can no longer simply burlesque him, though he plainly sees his French opposite number directed by a "Senile Muse." At this point, though, Prior is more inclined to see Boileau-Despreaux and himself as two parallel human beings and poets on opposite sides of the battle lines ("old Friend, old Foe") but facing the same poetic problems. In a sense the poem shows Prior, at forty, declining to write further panegyric verse.

His "Idle Tales" were a category to which he came rather late. The metrical tale was a popular literary form in the eighteenth century. Prior tended to designate as a tale any fairly longish (fifty lines or more) narrative poem, colloquial in language and realistic (if unflattering) in its suggested motivations. By this loose definition he wrote fourteen tales, all of them late in his poetic career. Two of these tales are, or purport to be, heavily autobiographical: "The Conversation. A Tale" and "Down-Hall; A Ballad." Five others show him doing one of those tasks that he performs best—domesticating classical myths: "Cupid and Ganymede," "The Dove," "Mercury and Cupid," "Protogenes and Apelles," "Daphne and Apollo"—all take familiar Greek or Latin materials and retell them in modern terms which demythologize them by making them folksy, available, and contemporary. Closely related to burlesque, these five mythical domesticatings simultaneously mock both the classical materials and the modern society which has no use for them.

This technique has never been more adroitly practiced than in "Daphne and Apollo," a hundred-line poem ostensibly based upon the first book of Ovid's *Metamorphoses*. Pope read the poem in manuscript and (remembering it as twice as long as it really was) later praised it to Spence as having "pleased me as much as anything of his I ever read." In this poem, Apollo courts Daphne by offering her all the attributes which distinguish him in classical myth. This includes his rule over Claros Isle and Tenedos, his ability to forecast the future, his beautiful locks, his healing arts, his poetry, his skill at archery. She rejects all of these gifts as useless in her own English eighteenth-century society. Instead, she demands that he court her by visiting her father evenings, reading the newspaper with him and giving him the latest political news from the Continent, and by bringing her gifts from his diurnal globe-circling journeys. Finally, he is to marry her, legally and properly, and as long as she lives is not to follow his father Jove's bad example of philandering.

Another of these "Idle Tales," one which Horace Walpole named among his favorite Prior poems, "The Turtle and the Sparrow," contrasts two irreconcilable attitudes toward love, courtship, and marriage, rather a poetic version of the debates between those holding opposing values found in *The Dialogues of the Dead*. The turtle-dove has lost her mate, Columbo, and grieves for him in the loft "BION-style" of the classical elegy. The sparrow is much more cheerful, recounts his numerous marriages and admits that the deaths of his spouses brought a welcome end to these commitments. A widower, he plans to marry again when his year of mourning is over.

Three of the "Idle Tales" are wryly witty considerations of more serious topics. "The Thief and the Cordelier, A Ballad" is yet another dialogue pitting two diametrically opposed points of view against each other, the thief's extreme reluctance to be hanged and the priest's hypocritically easy lecture on the folly of fearing death or trying to escape it. "An English Padlock" raises the question of how a contemporary English husband can be sure that his wife will be faithful, concluding that he must send her out to see the world, trusting that she will finally choose for herself to be faithful to him. In "Truth and Falshood. A Tale" the poet tells how Falsehood steals Truth's garments and disguises herself to travel through the world, behaving like a hypocritical Augustan belle.

When Prior's tales were mentioned in his own time, the ones that sprang immediately to mind were his "merry tales": "Hans Carvel," "The Ladle," and "Paulo Purganti and His Wife: An Honest, but a Simple Pair." All three are colloquial, bawdy, lively narratives of un-happy and incompatible marriages and their ensuing sexual disasters. In the eighteenth century, Thomas Tickell noted that these three bawdy tales and "The Turtle and the Sparrow" were Chaucerian in tone and flavor. In Prior's own time, they went far toward making his reputation. In later and more decorous times, they almost destroyed it. (Oliver Goldsmith in 1767 brought out an anthology for young people which included "Hans Carvel" and "The Ladle"; the Monthly Review attacked his selections, specifically "Hans Carvel," and the anthology failed.) By the end of the eighteenth century, these "idle Tales," once so popular, were condemned as disreputable and corrupting. The nineteenth century had little taste for fabliaux.

In two very different forms of humorous verse, however, the Hudibrastic and vers de société—Prior's literary reputation has never dimmed. He is generally thought to have done as much with each of these forms as it is possible to do—yet they call for markedly different skills and approaches, representing two extremes of humorous writing.

The Hudibrastic draws its name from Samuel Butler's three-part poem Hudibras (1662–1678), a mock-romance which ridiculed the Puritans (Presbyterians and Independents), and is endlessly erudite, endlessly digressive, couched in octosyllabic doggerel with deliberately clumsy rhymes. Prior captured the Hudibrastic so effectively in Alma: or, The Progress of the Mind that the eighteenth century came to think of the Hudibrastic in terms of Prior rather than Butler.

Prior wrote Alma: or, The Progress of the Mind in three weeks, to while away the tedium (and the anxiety) while he was being held under house arrest. At first he apparently did not think highly of it, calling it "a loose and hasty scribble, to relieve the tedious hours of my imprisonment, while in the messenger's hand." Later Pope, Bathurst, and Harley praised the poem, and Prior came to take it more seriously himself and revised it extensively.

Both in style and in content Alma was unusually well suited to Prior's own bent. Its comic octosyllabic couplets, with far-fetched and perilous rhymes and absurdly colloquial tone, suited his own liking for an art which mocked art. His approach to his subject—an attack on philosophical systems—demonstrates a continuation of his conviction (expressed in his serious poems as well) that all such systems were ultimately foolish. (It was a philosophical position shared by his friend Swift, whom Prior taught a great deal about the writing of these roughly comic octosyllables.) The Oxonian and Cantabrigian natural philosophers in Prior's time were disputing as to the seat of the mind. The Oxonians, still following Aristotle, argued that the mind or soul was everywhere throughout the body; the Cantabrigians, converted to Descartes, held that the mind was solely in the brain. In his dialogue with Richard Shelton in Alma, Prior proposes a compromise theory: that the mind moves upward through the body throughout life, from its dwelling in the feet of the child to its final residence in the head of the old man. The philosophical cut of the poem is deeper than this mock-system, however. The term alma would usually be translated soul, not mind; the poem questions implicitly whether the soul exists at all and, if it does, how it relates to the body. It raises these questions, though, in the rollicking semi-doggerel of the Hudibrastic which belies their seriousness. Alma burlesques and ridicules; it intermixes epigrams with apparently uncontrolled rambling; its couplets rhyme outrageously, often doubly or triply. Prior seems perpetually in danger of completely losing control of his medium (which appears much too willful for him to check or direct). Yet, all of this metrical ineptitude is patently a pretense. In Alma, Prior had produced the greatest single Hudibrastic in English.

The other category of humorous verse in which Prior excelled lies in many senses at the opposite pole from the Hudibrastic—vers de société, in which he had few equals and no superiors. Prior's vers de société drew upon his master Horace and upon Cavalier poets such as Ben Jonson, Thomas Carew, John Suckling, and John Wilmot, Earl of Rochester. Prior in turn taught its skills to later practitioners: to William Cowper in eighteenth-century England and Allan Ramsay in eighteenth-century Scotland; to William Makepeace Thackeray and W.M. Praed and Frederick Locker-Lampson and William Johnson Cory in nineteenth-century England, Thomas Moore in nineteenth-century Ireland, Oliver Wendell Holmes in nineteenth-century America. The most frequently anthologized of Prior's poems in the twentieth century and those which have attracted most critical attention have been his vers de société: "An Ode" ("The Merchant, to secure his Treasure," analyzed by Mark Van Doren), "To a Child of Quality of Five Years Old" (explicated by Maynard Mack), "A Letter to the Honorable Lady Mrs. Margaret Candish Harley" (studied by James Sutherland).

Again, it is most striking that Prior's highly successful society verse would seem to call for talents opposed to those which produce the Hudibrastic, for *vers de société* must be polished, sophisticated, graceful, refined, playful, and easy. The subject is itself light and narrow and limited; the poet seems absolutely comfortable with his medium, absolutely in effortless control of it.

The answer may be that the Hudibrastic and *vers de société* are not opposed forms, though perhaps no poet but Prior has ever excelled in both. In both forms the poet is practicing the art which conceals art—under the pretense of perilous ineptitude in the Hudibrastic, under the pretense of relaxed ease in *vers de société*. In both forms his language is colloquial and disarmingly informal and conversational. In both forms the content is more serious and more universal than it at first appears.

It is illuminating to look at the difference between the humorous technique that Prior uses to write Hudibrastics and those that he uses to write *vers de société* on similar subjects. There is, for example, the world of children. In the Hudibrastic *Alma*, he describes rollickingly the activities of exuberant children:

> Now mark, Dear RICHARD, from the
>   Age
> That Children tread this Worldly Stage,
> Broom-staff or Poaker they bestride,
> And round the Parlor love to ride;
> 'Till thoughtful Father's pious Care
> Provides his Brood, next *Smithfield* Fair,
> With Supplemental Hobby-Horses:
> And happy be their Infant Courses!
> Hence for some Years they ne'er stand
>   still:
> Their Legs, You see, direct their Will.
> From opening Morn 'till setting Sun,
> A-round the Fields and Woods They run:
> They frisk, and dance, and leap, and
>   play;
> Nor heed, what FRIEND or SNAPE can
>   say.

These Hudibrastic children are a Brood, apparently either males or hoydens, and lower-middle class (with a Parlor but parents who take them to Smithfield Fair for entertainment and buy them stick horses there). They play by running about, indoors and outdoors. Their activities are boisterous and are described in a jocund vocabulary, slangily colloquial. (A "snape" is dialect slang for someone who rebukes the child.) This section of *Alma* is about a world of children that operates by its own rules, not the rules of the world of adults.

One of Prior's most famous pieces of *vers de société* is on the same topic—a child's world operating by laws not the same as those in the world of adults—but it is a very different world from the Hudibrastic one. Instead, it is graceful, polished, delicate. "To a Child of Quality of Five Years Old, the Author suppos'd Forty" is about a single child, a five-year-old girl, "of quality," who orders all of the grown males about her to write her love letters, though she cannot yet read. The poet complies, and she makes beds for her silk-worms from his love letters and rolls up her doll's hair in them:

> Nor Quality, nor Reputation,
> Forbid me yet my Flame to tell,
> Dear Five Years old befriends my Pas-
>   sion,
> And I may Write 'till she can Spell.
> For while she makes her Silk-worms
>   Beds
> With all the tender things I swear,
> Whilst all the House my Passion reads,
> In Papers round her Baby's Hair.
> She may receive and own my Flame,
> For tho' the strictest *Prudes* shou'd know
>   it,
> She'll pass for a most virtuous Dame,
> And I for an unhappy Poet.

In both poems, the world of childhood moves in ways disparate from those of maturity, but the *vers de société* world is much more elegant and sedate and ladylike, a world of social polish (silkworms and curlers) and courtliness and decorum—and the possibility of scandal. In the boys' world of *Alma*, things move much more turbulently—in vocabulary and rhymes and in sports and games. Yet Miss Mary and the boys in *Alma* are equally distant from the adult world that will later, inevitably, sweep them into it. Into these passages in both poems Prior has sounded the faint note so distinctively his—a nostalgia, almost a melancholy, in the face of mutability, of the inevitable passing of time. Yet, he has sounded the note on two very dissimilar instruments. He was one of the few poets in England who could play the same tune equally well on both, employing either the boisterousness of the Hudibrastic or the delicate grace of society verse.

Summary

Although he was the son of a London carpenter and nephew to two London tavern-keepers, Matthew Prior was educated in one of the finest preparatory schools in Britain and one of its outstanding colleges. He rose to be both the most important diplomat of his era (the Treaty of Utrecht was popularly known as "Matt's Peace") and the most important poet writing in England between the death of Dryden (1700) and the poetic maturity of Pope (1712). The subscription edition of Prior's *Poems on Several Occasions* made him a fortune; more important, it established unequivocally that a poet of sufficient talent (and business acumen) could support himself handsomely by his writings, appealing directly to the reading public without dependence upon a solitary titled patron.

Prior wrote well in an impressive array of genres: prose dialogues of the dead, serious philosophical poems, laureate verse, burlesques, fabliaux, epigrams, satires, comic eroticism. His range of talents was such that he has never been excelled in two very different forms of humorous verse: the Hudibrastic and *vers de société*. Each of these last two forms called, in divergent ways, for him to do the things that he did best: to select a significant subject, pretend to take it lightly, and treat it with a casual colloquialism, in memorably quotable lines. The Hudibrastic appears to be rough and tentative and constantly imperiled; *vers de société* appears to be smooth and certain and absolutely safe. He taught his skill in one or both of these forms to his contemporaries (Swift, Cowper, Ramsay) and to nineteenth-century practitioners of light verse on both sides of the Irish Sea and of the Atlantic (More, Thackeray, Praed, Locker-Lampson, Corey, Holmes).

Selected Bibliography
Primary Sources

Manuscript Collections
See Smith, Margaret M., and Alexander Lindsay. "Matthew Prior: 1664–1721." *Index of English Literary Manuscripts*. Vol. 3, 1700–1800, part 3. London: Mansell, 1992, pp. 79–166.
British Library (London, England). The best English repository of Prior materials.
Library of the Marquis of Bath (Longleat, Warminster, Wiltshire, England). Contains many of Prior's poems, often in rough first draft, recopied by Prior himself in fair copy, or by his amanuensis Adrian Drift, with notes by Alexander Pope indicating his plans for a projected edition of Prior's works which he was never permitted to publish.
Welbeck Abbey (Library of the Duke of Portland, Worksop, Nottinghamshire, England). Vols. xi, xvii, and xviii contain a few Prior manuscripts.
Miami University (King Library, Walter Havighurst Special Collections, Oxford, Ohio, U.S.A. 45056). The only significant Prior collection in America, mostly in Drift's hand, and adding information on the Drift family.

Standard Edition
Wright, H. Bunker, and Monroe K. Spears, eds. *The Literary Works of Matthew Prior*. 2 vols. Oxford: Clarendon, 1959, 1971. The definitive edition. Many biographical and textual details about Prior appeared first in the voluminous notes to this edition and are much more easily accessible through the additional index to the second edition. Includes a bibliography, 1, xxxvii–xxxix.

Letters
Archives of Affaires Etrangeres (Paris) preserve a number of Prior's unpublished letters in French concerning his diplomatic negotiations.
Historical Manuscripts Commission. *Calendar of the Manuscripts of the Marquis of Bath Preserved at Longleat, Wiltshire*. Vol. 3, *Prior Papers*. Hereford: Anthony Brothers, 1908. The most important single source of Prior materials.
Sutton, H. Manners, ed. *The Lexington Papers: or, Some Account of The Courts of London and Vienna; at the Conclusion of the Seventeenth Century, Extracted from the Official and Private Correspondence of Robert Sutton, Lord Lexington, British Minister at Vienna, 1694–1698*. London: John Murray, 1851. Letters from Prior to Lord Lexington or to Lord

P

and Lady Lexington, November 9, 1694, until the Treaty of Ryswick in 1697.

Williams, Harold, ed. *The Correspondence of Jonathan Swift*. 5 vols. Oxford: Clarendon, 1963–65. Letters from Swift to Prior, from Prior to Swift, and from Swift to others about Prior.

Secondary Sources

Books

Bickley, Francis. *The Life of Matthew Prior*. London: Sir Isaac Pitman & Sons, 1914. The first full-length biography of Prior, with more interest in his diplomatic career than in detailed analysis of his literary significance.

Eves, Charles Kenneth. *Matthew Prior: Poet and Diplomatist*. Columbia University Studies in Language and Comparative Literature, no. 144. New York: Columbia University Press, 1939. The best single biographical study of Prior and one of the best critical studies of his literary achievement. Includes a bibliography, pp. 411–21.

Ketton-Cremer, R[obert] W[yndham]. *Matthew Prior*. Cambridge: Cambridge University Press, 1957. "He continued to be read, imitated and admired all through his century and far beyond it."

Legg, L.G. Wickham. *Matthew Prior: A Study of His Public Career and Correspondence*. Cambridge: Cambridge University Press, 1921. Focuses upon Prior's biography and his diplomatic career; mainly concerned with the poems insofar as they afford autobiographical details.

Rippy, Frances Mayhew. *Matthew Prior*. Twayne's English Authors Series #418. Boston: G.K. Hall, 1986. A study of Prior's laureate verse, his shorter poems, *Henry and Emma*, *Solomon*, *Alma*, and his prose and dramas. Includes a bibliography, pp. 154–61.

Articles, Monographs, and Chapters in Books

Barrett, Wilfred Phillips. "Matthew Prior's *Alma*." *Modern Language Review*, 27 (October 1932): 454–58. Prior shows remarkably close familiarity with Montaigne, whose second book of essays provided the main conceit for *Alma* and who influenced Prior in every part of his works.

Bassil, Veronica. "The Faces of Griselda: Chaucer, Prior, and Richardson." *Texas Studies in Literature and Language*, 26 (Summer 1984): 157–82. Bassil sees Prior's *Henry and Emma* as facilitating the "movement from the piety and militarism of the Nut Brown Maid to sadomasochistic pornography, from joyful reunion to epic solitude, from the compactness of the dramatic ballad to the infinite details of melodrama."

Bett, Henry. *The Hymns of Methodism*. 3rd ed. London: Epworth Press, 1945. Bett finds sixteen echoes of Prior in the Wesleys' hymns and argues that Prior taught them "Something of the freedom of their versification as well."

Blackmur, R.P. "Homo Ludens." *Kenyon Review*, 21 (Autumn 1959): 662–68. Blackmur begins with high praise of the Wright-Spears edition of Prior, goes on to praise Prior as well, both for his metrical variety (octosyllabics and anapaests) and for being "homo ludens," with a playfulness almost unknown in our own time.

Bond, Richmond P. *English Burlesque Poetry, 1700–1750*. Harvard Studies in English, no. 6. Cambridge, MA: Harvard University Press, 1932. Bond looks repeatedly at Prior's *Alma*, as burlesque and as Hudibrastic.

Colvile, K.N. "Dialogues of the Dead." *Quarterly Review*, 267 (1936): 308–20. Colvile dislikes Prior's dialogue between Cromwell and his mad porter but thinks his other three dialogues "among the very best of their kind ever written in any tongue."

Dobree, Bonamy. *English Literature in the Early Eighteenth Century, 1700–1740*. Oxford: Clarendon, 1959. Dobree considers Prior "a singularly attractive person . . . approaching life with a gaiety tempered by an uneasy feeling of something being missed," "the master artificer of the occasional poem."

Dobson, Austin. "Matthew Prior." *New Princeton Review*, 6 (November 1888): 281–311. Reprint in Austin Dobson, *Eighteenth Century Vignettes*. Ser. 3. London: Humphrey Milford, Oxford University Press, 1896, pp. 223–69. Dobson dislikes Prior's longer pieces except *Alma* but admires his *vers de société* and pronounces him second to none in the art of Hudibrastic or octosyllabic verse.

Doughty, Oswald. "Matthew Prior (1664–1721)." *English Lyric in the Age of Reason*. London: Daniel O'Connor, 1922, pp. 46–56. Doughty finds traces of Restoration in Prior.

Ewing, Majl. "Musical Settings of Prior's Lyrics in the 18th Century." *English Literary History*, 10 (June 1943): 159–71. Ewing documents Prior's "long continued popularity as a lyric poet": fifty-three lyrics set to music, in addition to three ballads and two longer poems.

Fairchild, Hoxie Neale. *Religious Trends in English Poetry. Vol. I: 1700–1740. Protestantism and the Cult of Sentiment*. New York: Columbia University Press, 1939. Fairchild analyzes Prior's poetry in terms of his family background, of Epicureanism, of Lucretius's atomism, of Calvinism, of Hobbes's determinism, of Newtonianism. Treats *Solomon* as an expression of Prior's skepticism.

Goad, Caroline. *Horace in the English Literature of the Eighteenth Century*. Yale Studies in English, no. 58. New Haven: Yale University Press, 1918. In one chapter, "Matthew Prior, 1664–1721," pp. 90–116, Goad examines the influence of Horace upon Prior's poetry and prose and points out similarities and differences between the two authors.

Higby, John. "Ideas and Art in Prior's *Dialogues of the Dead. Enlightenment Essays*, 5 (Summer 1974): 62–69. Higby interprets the fourth dialogue as summing up the other three and the total work as deserving more attention.

Johnson, James William. *The Formation of English Neo-Classical Thought*. Princeton: Princeton University Press, 1967. Johnson considers Prior "a literary and political link between Dryden and his successors," "pervasively affected by his study of Greek."

Johnson, Samuel. "Life of Prior." *Lives of the English Poets*. London: Printed by J. Nichols for C. Bathurst, 1779–1781. Vol. VI, pp. 1–63. Although essentially unfriendly to Prior, disapproving of his private life and of most of his longer poems, Johnson still concedes to him wisdom as a statesman and elegance as a poet.

Keener, Frederick M. *English Dialogues of the Dead: A Critical History, Anthology, and a Check List*. New York: Columbia University Press, 1973. Reprints in full "A Dialogue between the Vicar of Bray, and Sir Thomas More," "perhaps the subtlest of Prior's four dialogues of the dead," "the best dialogues of the dead ever written by an Englishman."

Loveridge, Mark. "Liberty in *Tristram Shandy*." *Laurence Sterne: Riddles and Mysteries*. London, Totowa, NJ: Vision, Barnes & Noble, 1984, pp. 126–41. "Prior came as readily to Sterne's mind as did the other Augustans, and there are very many similarities, both general and incidental, between Prior's poems," especially *Alma*, and Sterne's *Tristram Shandy*.

Mack, Maynard. "Matthew Prior: et multa prior arte." *Sewanee Review*, 68 (Winter 1960): 165–76. Initially a review of the new Wright-Spears edition of Prior, which turns into a tough modern estimate of Prior's strengths and weaknesses.

Meier, T.K. "Prior's Adaptation of 'The Nutbrown Maid.'" *Moderna Språk* (Stockholm), 68 (1974): 331–36. Meier finds "gentle irony and amused worldliness" in Prior's treatment of the "Christian, mythological, classical and heroic traditions" in *Henry and Emma*.

Morton, Richard. "Matthew Prior's *Dialogues of the Dead*." *Ball State University Forum*, 8 (Summer 1967): 427–41. "From the traditional forms of the dialogue *des morts* Prior absorbs what is meaningful, and he adds insight of his own."

Nelson, Nicolas H. "Dramatic Texture and Philosophical Debate in Prior's *Dialogues of the Dead*." *Studies in English Literature, 1500–1900*, 28, 3 (Summer 1988): 427–41. Nelson finds Prior's chief predecessors in Lucian, Fontenelle, and Fenelon, with whom he compares favorably.

Richards, Edward Ames. *Hudibras in the Burlesque Tradition*. New York: Octagon Books, 1972. Originally Columbia University Press, 1937. Richards offers a six-page section on Prior and Hudibrastics.

Rippy, Frances Mayhew. "Matthew Prior." In *Dictionary of Literary Biography. Vol.*

95. *Eighteenth-Century British Poets*, first ser. Detroit: Gale Research, 1990, pp. 210–39. Rippy finds Prior important in his own time for two accomplishments: helping to keep Restoration metrical variety alive alongside the polished Augustan heroic couplets, and for showing, through the tremendous financial success of his 1718 *Poems on Several Occasions*, that the subscription method of publishing could effectively supplant support from one titled patron.

———. "Matthew Prior as the Last Renaissance Man." *Studies in Medieval, Renaissance, American Literature: A Festschrift*. Fort Worth: Texas Christian University Press, 1971, pp. 120–31, 203. "Though Prior appears in a number of ways to be a Renaissance man, he is always a Renaissance man with a difference. His classicism repeatedly jests at the striking of heroic poses in an unheroic and domesticated middle-class world."

Rogal, Samuel J. *John and Charles Wesley*. Twayne's English Authors Series, no. 368. Boston: Twayne, 1983. In one six-page discussion, Rogal considers John Wesley's *Thoughts on the Character and Writings of Mr. Prior* to have been used more as an excuse to castigate Pope than to quarrel with Johnson.

Roscoe, E.S. "Matthew Prior—Diplomatist and Poet." *Edinburgh Review*, 218 (July 1913): 151–62. Roscoe finds Prior "more remarkable as a man of affairs than as a poet" and "The last of the panegyric poets" and believes that Prior's letters may in time become "the most enduring and most important of his writings."

Rower, Ronald Eugene. "Pastoral Wars: Matthew Prior's Poems to Cloe." *Ball State University Forum*, 19 (Spring 1978): 39–49. "The Cloe poems are impressive examples of Prior's talent for depicting with warmth and understanding the intimate, somewhat childish, but central concerns of ordinary people."

Saintsbury, George. *A History of English Prosody from the Twelfth Century to Present Day*. Vol. 2. London: Macmillan, 1908. Pages 423–35 contain the best single analysis of Prior's often inventive prosody.

———. *The Peace of the Augustans: A Survey of Eighteenth Century Literature as a Place of Rest and Refreshment*. London: G. Bell and Sons, 1916. An original, thoughtful, sympathetic treatment of Prior. "No one, except Thackeray, has ever entered more thoroughly into the spirit of *Ecclesiastes*."

Shepherd, T.B. "John Wesley and Matthew Prior." *London Quarterly and Holborn Review*, 162 (July 1937): 368–73. Cites Prior's influence on both John and Charles Wesley.

Spears, Monroe K. "Matthew Prior's Attitude toward Natural Science." *Publications of the Modern Language Association of America*, 63 (June 1948): 485–507. Spears interprets Prior as "a harbinger of future dissatisfactions," the first imaginative writer to perceive the new science as materialistic and deterministic and to protest against its meaning in human terms.

———. "Matthew Prior's Religion." *Philological Quarterly*, 27 (April 1948): 159–80. The relation between religion and politics as shown in Prior's attitude toward Dissenters and toward Roman Catholics. Finds that Prior most nearly fits the classification of Anglican Fideist, but is a Fideist manque.

———. "The Meaning of Matthew Prior's *Alma*." *English Literary History*, 13 (December 1946): 266–90. A detailed analysis of *Alma* as a carefully planned, significant, and characteristic application of Pyrrhonism to contemporary thought.

———. "Some Ethical Aspects of Matthew Prior's Poetry." *Studies in Philology*, 45 (October 1948): 606–29. Spears treats Prior as a resolute pessimist in ethics, convinced of man's depravity and that the passions triumph over reason, yet unsure that they should.

Spence, Joseph. *Anecdotes, Observations, and Characters of Books and Men, Collected from the Conversation of Mr. Pope and Other Eminent Persons of His Time*. Ed. Samuel Weller Singer. London: W.H. Carpenter, 1820. Almost all of Pope's literary criticism of Prior is contained in these anecdotes, as are Pope's personal, disapproving, gossipy comments on Prior's private life.

Sutherland, James. *A Preface to Eighteenth*

Century Poetry. Oxford: Clarendon, 1948. Close analysis of "Letter to the Honorable Lady Mrs. Margaret Candish Harley" and of Henry and Emma.

Swift, Jonathan. Journal to Stella. Ed. Harold Williams. 2 vols. Oxford: Clarendon, 1948. Swift writes to Esther Johnson and Rebecca Dingley of his friendship with Prior, reporting Prior's personal and political activities from London, October 15, 1710, to November 18, 1712.

Thackeray, William Makepeace. "The English Humorists of the Eighteenth Century: A Series of Lectures. Lecture the Fourth: Prior, Gay, and Pope." The Complete Works. Standard Library Ed. New York: Harper and Brothers, 1854. Prior is found to be "a world-philosopher of no small genius, good-nature, and acumen." His lyrics are "among the easiest, the richest, the most charmingly humorous of English lyrical poems."

Thayer, Harvey Waterman. "Matthew Prior, His Relation to English Vers de Société." Sewanee Review, 10 (April 1902): 181–98. Thayer sets up standards for vers de société, compares and contrasts Prior's light verse with that of Herrick, Carew, Landor, and Praed, and concludes that Prior's most clearly attains this ideal.

Trent, William P. "Thackeray's Verse." Longfellow and Other Essays. New York: Thomas Y. Crowell, 1910, pp. 173–84. Trent places Thackeray with Prior and with Hood (on the latter's comic side) rather than with Herrick or Campbell as a writer of light verse.

Voltaire, François Marie Arouet de. "Sur Mr. Pope et quelques autres poetes fameux." Lettres sur les Anglais, lettre 22, Oeuvres completes de Voltaire, Vol. 24. Melanges Historiques, Vol. 1. Paris: Antoine-Augustin Renouart, 1819, pp. 125–38. Voltaire finds Prior amiable and very agreeable, Alma the most natural account up to the present of the mind/soul, but Solomon tedious.

Warton, Joseph. An Essay on the Writings and Genius of Pope. 2 vols. London: M. Cooper, 1756. Prior (because of Alma) is grouped with those authors who "showed profound knowledge of man . . . treated life and manners in an unrivalled fashion . . . Montaigne, Rochefoucauld, Pascal, Bacon, Hobbes,

Hume, Richardson, Fielding."

Wesley, John. The Journal of the Rev. John Wesley, A.M. Ed. Nehemiah Curnock. Vols. 3–6. London: Epworth Press, 1914, 1938. Wesley quotes frequently from Prior, more often than from any other poet of the eighteenth century or from any other poet of any age except Milton.

Williams, Arthur S. "Making 'Intrest and freedom agree': Matthew Prior and the Ethics of Funeral Elegy." Studies in English Literature, 1500–1900 (Summer 1989): 431–45. Williams considers Prior's "To the King, an Ode on His Majesty's Arrival in Holland, 1695" and his much later "Turtle and the Sparrow" as two different revelations of Prior's dealings with elegiac verse.

Wright, H. Bunker. "William Jackson on Prior's Use of Montaigne." Modern Language Review, 31 (April 1936): 203–05. William Jackson of Exeter in 1798 first pointed out Prior's indebtedness to Montaigne for the central ideas of Alma and of The Thief and the Cordelier.

———, and P.J. Croft. "Matthew Prior's Last Manuscript: 'Predestination.'" The British Library Journal, 11 (Autumn 1985): 99–112. Corrections of previous readings of "Predestination," based on a Prior holograph among the Harleian Manuscripts in the British Library.

Frances Mayhew Rippy

Pritchett, V[ictor] S[awdon]

Born: Ipswich, December 16, 1900
Education: Alleyn's School, Dulwich, London, 1914–1916
Marriage: first wife (name unknown), 1924; divorced 1936; Dorothy Rudge Roberts, October 2, 1936; two children

Biography

V.S. Pritchett's boyhood is encapsulated in what is perhaps the best of all of his books, A Cab at the Door (1968), the title referring to the frequent moves necessitated by his father's uncertain business career. Thus, the fact that he was born in Ipswich on December 16, 1900, was due to a shortlived attempt by his father, Walter Sawdon Pritchett, to leave London and start up in that town as a stationer. Pritchett's early boyhood was partly spent in his father's native county of Yorkshire, where he stayed with his paternal grandmother, Mary Helen Pritchett, née Sawdon, from whom both he and his father gained their second given name. The boy moved between the country life of the small and remote town of Sedburgh and the noise and grittiness of a succession of south London suburbs, between the kindliness but dourness of the Yorkshire people, with their intense cleanliness and respectability, and the slatternliness and gaiety of urban life. A third contrasting element was a return for a year's stay in Ipswich, where his mother's sister now lived, among "the lazy and forgotten country of slow-talking Suffolk people who had been stunned by the east wind" (*A Cab at the Door*, 92).

Eventually, when he was eleven, the family settled in Dulwich, and Pritchett finally started regular schooling at the Rosendale Road elementary school. By extreme good luck, he had as a teacher a Mr. Bartlett who had been allowed to teach by the new "Dalton" or tutorial system. The children were split into groups, encouraged to write and paint, and introduced to the latest literature in Ford Madox Ford's *English Review*—an experience that fixed Pritchett's determination to become a writer. In 1914, he went on to Alleyn's School, where, though he did badly in most subjects, good teaching in French and German opened his eyes to the existence of other countries and other cultures.

Meanwhile, in partnership with a strong-minded woman colleague (who appears as "Mrs. Truslove" in Pritchett's novel, *Mr. Beluncle*), his father had embarked on his own firm of "art needlework manufacturers." Although Beatrice, née Martin, his flirtatious and emotional mother, swinging between extremes of emotion, comes across vividly in his autobiographical works, it is his father who was the dominating figure and who became his "obsessive subject" (*Midnight Oil*, 244). Right up until his final bankruptcy in 1936, Walter Sawdon Pritchett remained the eternal optimist in business while in religion this optimism manifested itself in an adherence to Christian Science, later explained by his son as deriving from "some bewilderment at the fact that other people existed, independently of himself" (*Midnight Oil*, 203). The children (there were two younger brothers and a sister) were perpetually bullied and opposed by their father out of his "wish to be in command of everything they did" (*Midnight Oil*, 105).

Because of this wish, Walter Pritchett was hostile to all his eldest son's literary aspirations and insisted on removing him from school at the age of fifteen and putting him into the leather trade. For four years Pritchett worked in a firm near the London docks, a quaint though sturdy survival from the Victorian age, which gave him ample opportunity for noting all of the oddities of office personnel and their daily routine. But, he was desperate to escape from the endless quarrels of his parents and the claustrophobia of family life—of which he was to make rich use in his later writing. Finally, "the strain of the last few years, the stunned boredom and torn emotions" (*A Cab at the Door*, 234) brought on illness which ended his employment. With back-pay and a bounty from the firm totaling £20, he left home for Paris for a month until his money ran out, his parents thought, but as he knew, for ever.

It is at this point that his second autobiographical novel, *Midnight Oil* (1971), begins, though, as the author remarks at its opening, he had in this volume a more difficult task than he had had in its predecessor: "To write about one's childhood is comparatively simple. One's life has a natural defining frame. But after the age of twenty, the frame is uncertain, change is hard to pin down . . . Also, the professional writer who spends his time becoming other people and places, real or imaginary, finds he has written his life away and has become almost nothing. The true autobiography of this egotist is exposed in all its intimate foliage in his work. But, there is a period when a writer has not yet become one, or just having become one, is struggling to form his talent, and it is from this period that I have selected most of the scenes and people in this book" (9–10).

Pritchett arrived in Paris in the early spring of 1921 at the age of twenty. After three weeks of trying to get work through Christian Science connections (by which time his initial £20 was used up), he found a job as a clerk in a photographer's studio. Meanwhile, he was beginning to get articles placed in the *Christian Science Monitor* and was later sent as the journal's foreign correspondent first to Ireland in February 1923 and then to Spain in January 1924—assignments that had the effect of precipitating his marriage to a woman journalist whom he had met during the months in Dublin. The Spanish landscape had a wholesome effect upon him after his Christian Science upbringing: "The earth did not fade into the transcendental . . . There was nothing of the 'deeply interfused'; there was something that could be known and which it was necessary to know. There was a sense of the immediate and finite, so much more satisfying than the infinite, which really starved me; a sense of the physical not of the spiritual. I felt I was human" (*Midnight Oil*, 138).

Eventually, after a brief unhappy period in Boston and a second posting to Dublin, he was sacked as the *Monitor*'s foreign correspondent, and he returned to live in London. Determined to abandon journalism for literary work, he wrote regular reviews for the left-wing weekly, the *New Statesman*. His final link with the *Monitor*, from which he was at this point receiving £5 a week as review editor, was severed in the mid-1930s on the publication of his short story, "The Saint," in which a seventeen-year-old boy loses his faith when watching a visiting evangelist fall into the water through losing control of a punt-pole, thus disproving the theory of mind over matter.

He had by now separated from his wife (there had been no children to the marriage, and the divorce was made absolute in 1936). At a political meeting on Guy Fawkes' Day, November 5, 1934, in an incident which forms the basis of "The Marvellous Girl," he met and immediately fell in love with Dorothy Roberts, who was to become his second wife on October 2, 1936.

Seeing that war was inevitable after the Munich agreement of 1938, the couple moved out of London to an isolated Georgian farmhouse in the Lambourn valley, eight miles from Newbury, for which he paid £1 a week. A daughter had been born in 1937, to be followed by a son just after the war broke out. During the war, the author was active on what was known as the "home front," as chairman of the Parish Council and as an air-raid warden in London, but afterward he commented: "I am not sure that to be so drowned in the mass was good for the act of writing, for the kind of humanity required of artists is not the same thing as the united public humanness we felt as citizens" (*Midnight Oil*, 228).

Since 1945, Pritchett has produced a novel and seven collections of short stories, and he has been repeatedly honored by the British Government: he was made Commander of the British Empire in 1968, knighted in 1975, made Companion of Literature in 1988, and became Companion of Honor in 1993. It is significant, however, that his second volume of autobiography, though written when he was seventy, should end with the deaths of his parents (who both

lived into their eighties), for it was above all the ferocious family battles of his youth, caused by his father's domineering nature, that were the formative experiences of his life.

Literary Analysis

Pritchett's literary output is largely contained in the two massive collections of his short stories (*The Complete Collected Stories*, 1990) and critical essays (*The Complete Essays*, 1991), of which the latter consist chiefly of the leading review-articles that he wrote each week for the *New Statesman*. The subject-matter of these was established during the Second World War when, "since few new books were published," the editors "decided that the article must deal with a re-reading of the classics" (*Midnight Oil*, 228). The commission was extraordinarily well suited to Pritchett, and the resulting essays, 203 in all, demonstrate both the breadth of his reading and his ability to respond with equal sympathy and judgment to an extraordinarily wide range of literature: most of the major English authors, as well as the classics of America, France, Germany, and Russia.

His observations are both authoritative and persuasive, as, for instance, in his comment that "When she wrote of the peasants . . . and squires of Warwickshire, George Eliot was writing out of childhood, from that part of her life which never betrayed her or any of the Victorians" (*The Complete Essays*, 214–15). Elsewhere he says, "Out of the mess which Twain made of his life, amid the awful pile of tripe which he wrote, there does rise one book which has the serenity of a thing of genius: *Huckleberry Finn* takes the breath away" (*The Complete Essays*, 136). A final example of Pritchett's insight is seen in his statement that "What is it that attracts us to the Russian novelists of the nineteenth century? The aristocratic culture made more vivid by its twilight? The feeling, so readily understood by the English, for ennui? No. The real attraction of that censored literature is its freedom—the freedom from our kind of didacticism and our plots" (*The Complete Essays*, 319). At the same time, he is precisely *not* a literary critic, but rather a last surviving example of the breed of self-educated men of letters who flourished in the nineteenth century. Pritchett is very conscious that today "his profession is not only precarious, but seems to be vanishing" (*Midnight Oil*, 252).

It is on his short stories that the writer's reputation chiefly rests. He himself has de-

P

clared, "I have rarely been interested in what are called 'characters' i.e. eccentrics; reviewers are mistaken in saying that I am. They misread me. I am interested in the revelations of a nature and (rather in Ibsen's fashion), of exposing the illusions or received ideas by which they live or protect their dignity" (*Midnight Oil*, 214). The positivism betrayed in the terms "illusions or received ideas" means that there is a lack of any implied external framework to the stories, and this is perhaps the reason why Pritchett was less successful in the novel-form, which is particularly hard to manage without some such framework.

Thus, the apparent eccentricity of behavior that he depicts is, in fact, the effect of extreme realism operating outside conventional patterns, whether of aesthetics or of belief. Everything is viewed in a clear, disabused light, as if in reaction to the willed optimism of his father and the emotional storms that its imposition had caused in the family. Though Pritchett's characters are minutely observed and their actions described with conviction, the reader is often baffled in accounting for their motivation.

It is, of course, in the stories such as "The Saint," scattered throughout the collected works and inspired by reminiscences of his father, that this sense of disorientation is felt least. In "The Collection" he portrays the father bullying his wife and three sons over Sunday lunch after he has had the glory of taking the collection at the chapel. "The Chestnut Tree" begins with the protagonist and his father kneeling in prayer together on a railway train, as his father takes him at the age of fifteen to start work in an old-fashioned leather firm in London. "The Fly in the Ointment" describes a young man calling on his newly bankrupt father at the works which have been stripped bare by the liquidators: "He was ashamed to think how they all dreaded having this gregarious, optimistic, extravagant, uncontrollable, disingenuous old man on their hands." In "The Lion's Den" a man calls on his aging parents during the bombing in the Second World War; the mother is terrified by the constant threat of death, while the father has an absolute and irrational faith in their survival, shown in his secretly cramming his own bedroom, the lion's den, with valuables. "Just a Little More" shows the old man, now widowed, paying a visit to the son and his wife and terrifying them by his daydreams of buying an expensive house in a seaside town.

In the rest of the stories, however, the reader has to be adroit in gauging the parameters of each new starting-point and will find that the work has to be done afresh on each occasion. Indeed, some stories are consciously humorous, like the duo, "The Chain-Smoker" and "The Last Throw" ("Chatty slipped into Karvo's room like a well-dressed fever," 806), but more frequently the humor arises from the sheer oddity of the human behavior observed. "The Snag," for example, opens with a paragraph of general statements that in the work of other writers would be designed to appeal to the shared experience and judgment of narrator and reader. In this case, though, they are so unexpected as to disrupt any such relationship: "The marriages of middle age, the mad impromptus of reason, are the satisfying ones. By that time our obsessions have accumulated and asserted their rights, and we find peace in the peculiarities of others. I am thinking of Mrs. Barclay and myself. Our difficulty was the common one of turning a love affair into a marriage." The two characters run off together, but then come across an old friend of the narrator's, one of those people whose "role in life was to be the oldest friend of everyone, the man who crops up in one's life on and off for twenty years and always at the unguarded moments" (*The Complete Collected Stories*, 522). In the end it is the woman and the friend who are married.

"The Satisfactory" deals with the relationship between an antique-shop owner and his faded female assistant whose hold over her employer consists in the fact that she times her arrival at the local restaurant so that, having completed his own lunch on the modest scale permitted by food-rationing in the Britain of the Second World War, she can surreptitiously pass her own meal across the table to him. Eventually, he rewards her by satisfying her sexual hunger. However, the story ends with the ominous sentence: "But now, of course, French cooking has come back" (*The Complete Collected Stories*, 380).

The claustrophobic state of England during World War II also provides the background for what Pritchett has described as his favorite story, "When My Girl Comes Home." The setting is Hincham Street in south London, "less a street than an interval, a disheartened connection" (*The Complete Collected Stories*, 444), and the story deals with the impact upon the street's inhabitants—all cautious people with limited horizons—of the delayed post-war return of Hilda, not from the sufferings of a Japanese prison camp as they have all assumed, but as a Japanese war widow (the delay having been caused by American Army interrogation) with twelve cases of luggage that she has been given by a rich American, Mr. Faulkner, on her journey home. She is now hoping—apparently in vain—to be taken off to France by yet another American, Mr. Gloster, an author who has promised to write her life story. Compared with the others, who have suffered the grinding deprivations of the war years, Hilda is curiously untouched by events: her face, comments the narrator, "was the face of someone to whom nothing had happened; or perhaps so much had happened to her that each event wiped out what had happened before. I was disturbed by something in her—the lack of history, I think. We were worm-eaten by it" (*The Complete Collected Stories*, 450).

The impact of this seemingly invulnerable woman on the various members of the family group is carefully individualized, from the matriarch (after a knock at the door, which turns out to be from two journalists who are anxious to interview and photograph Hilda, "Old Mrs. Draper made one of her fundamental utterances again, one of her growls from the belly of the history of human indignation. 'We are,' she said, 'in the middle of our teas. Constance, go and see and tell them'" [*The Complete Collected Stories*, 447–48]) to the young woman from the north of England who has married into this London family ("She was a nimble, tarry-haired woman, impatient of fancies, excitements, and disasters. She liked things flat and factual. While the family gaped at Hilda's clothes and luggage, young Mrs. Draper had reckoned up the cost of them. She was not avaricious or mean, but she knew that money is money. You know that if you have done without" [*The Complete Collected Stories*, 458]). Their mode of speech to each other is oblique and laconic, made more tortuous by the preoccupations of speaker and addressee: "Once Mrs. Fulmino went purple and said to her husband (who told me, he always told me such things) that she believed Constance had lately started sleeping with Bill Williams. That was because Constance had once said to her: 'Bill and I are individuals.' Mrs. Fulmino had a row with Iris after this and stopped me seeing her for a month" (*The Complete Collected Stories*, 464).

It is in such an atmosphere of groping incomprehension that Hilda forms an improbable liaison with the same Bill Williams (despite his having suffered as a Japanese prisoner-of-war), only to find that he and his criminal associates have stolen all the contents of her famous luggage, whereupon she leaves London as an apparently ruined woman, but six months later sends back a photograph of herself sitting in an unidentifiable park between *both* the wealthy Americans. The story ends with the terse paragraph: "But Mr. Gloster's book came out. Oh yes. It wasn't about Japan or India or anything like that. It was about us" (*The Complete Collected Stories*, 491).

Summary

V.S. Pritchett's humor arises not from any conscious effort to see the funny side of life or from any desire to set out to make his readers laugh, but rather as a side-effect of the precise depiction of a disoriented age in which no general assumptions about human behavior are possible, and where actions and attitudes, because unpredictable, are inscrutable, when not actually alarming. As he commented in his introduction to the *Oxford Book of Short Stories* (1981): "Readers used to speak of 'losing' themselves in a novel or a story: the contemporary addict turns to the short story to find himself. In a restless century which has lost its old assurances and in which our lives are fragmented, the nervous side-glance has replaced the steady confronting gaze" (xiii).

Selected Bibliography

Primary Sources

The Complete Collected Stories. New York: Random House, 1991. Comprised of *You Make Your Own Life* (1938), *It May Never Happen* (1945), *When My Girl Comes Home* (1961), *The Key to My Heart* (1963), *Blind Love* (1969), *The Camberwell Beauty* (1974), *On the Edge of the Cliff* (1980), and *A Careless Widow* (1989). Despite the title, this volume does not include the first published collection, *The Spanish Virgin and Other Stories* (1930).

The Complete Essays. London: Chatto & Windus, 1991. Comprised of *In My Good Books* (1942), *The Living Novel* (1946), *Books in General* (1953), *The Working Novelist* (1965), *The Myth Makers* (1979), *The Tale Bearers* (1980), *A Man of Letters* (1985), and *Lasting Impressions* (1990).

Lasting Impressions; Essays 1961–1987.

New York: Random House, 1990.

Mr. Beluncle. London: Chatto & Windus, and New York: Harcourt, 1951.

A Cab at the Door. London: Chatto & Windus, and New York: Random House, 1968.

Midnight Oil. London: Chatto & Windus, and New York: Random House, 1971.

The Oxford Book of Short Stories, Chosen by V.S. Pritchett. New York: Oxford University Press, 1981.

At Home and Abroad. London: Chatto & Windus, 1990.

Secondary Sources

Alvarez, A. "The Self-Education of V.S. Pritchett (Part Two)." *Saturday Review*, 55 (May 6, 1972): 19. Review of *Midnight Oil*.

Baldwin, Dean. *V.S. Pritchett.* Boston: Twayne, 1987. Criticism and interpretation of Pritchett's work.

Guppy, S., and A. Weller. "The Art of Fiction CXXII: V.S. Pritchett (interview)." *Paris Review*, 32 (1990): 183–207.

Hughes, Douglass A. "V.S. Pritchett: An Interview." *Studies in Short Fiction*, 13 (1976): 423–32.

Peden, William. "V.S. Pritchett." In *The English Short Story, 1880–1945: A Critical History*. Ed. Joseph M. Flora. Boston: Twayne, 1985, pp. 143–51. Overview.

Riley, Carolyn. "V.S. Pritchett." *Contemporary Authors*. Ed. Cynthia R. Fadool. Detroit: Gale Research, 1990. Vol. 61–64, p. 434. Brief overview.

Stinson, John J. *V.S. Pritchett: A Study of the Short Fiction.* New York: Twayne/Macmillan, 1992.

"A Special V.S. Pritchett Issue." *Journal of the Short Story in English*, 6 (Spring 1986).

"V.S. Pritchett." *Contemporary Literary Criticism*. Ed. Carolyn Riley and Phyllis Mendelson. Vol. 5. Detroit: Gale Research, 1976, pp. 351–53.

"V.S. Pritchett." *Contemporary Literary Criticism*. Ed. Dedria Bryfonski. Vol. 13. Detroit: Gale Research, 1980, pp. 465–69.

"V.S. Pritchett." *Contemporary Literary Criticism*. Ed. Sharon Gunton and Laurie Harris. Vol. 15. Detroit: Gale Research, 1980, pp. 440–44.

"V.S. Pritchett." *Contemporary Literary Criticism*. Ed. Daniel Marowski. Vol. 41. Detroit: Gale Research, 1987, pp. 327–36.

"V.S. Pritchett." *Current Biography Yearbook*. Ed. Charles Moritz. New York: H.W. Wilson, 1974, pp. 327–30.

David Jago

Pym, Barbara

Born: Oswestry, Shropshire, England, June 2, 1913

Education: Local schools; Liverpool College, Huyton, 1925–1931; St. Hilda's College, Oxford University, 1931–1934, B.A.

Died: Oxford, Oxfordshire, January 11, 1980

Biography

The daughter of Frederic Crampton Pym, a well-to-do solicitor, and Irena Spenser Thomas Pym, Barbara Mary Crampton Pym was born in the Shropshire town of Oswestry, near the Welsh border, on June 2, 1913. The family name Crampton appears in the title of her novel *Crampton Hodnet*, where that name figures as an imaginary parish in a curate's alibi to cover up his brief disappearance with a woman of *his* parish. A younger sister, Hilary, with whom she would remain close and at various times share a dwelling, was born in 1916. Pym first attended local schools—the Bellan House and Queen's Park—and at twelve was sent away to a boarding school: Liverpool College, Huyton. She remained at this Anglican prep school from 1925 to 1931. In 1929, Pym, who from an early age had indicated a desire to write, filled a notebook with a story about a group of fatuous, pretentious, bohemian youths, "Young Men in Fancy Dress." One of the characters in this piece of raw juvenilia is a particularly bumptious and ignorant American cousin (Americans are not commonly dealt with in her numerous novels and short stories). Pym attended St. Hilda's College, Oxford, between 1931 and 1934, receiving a B.A. with second-class honors in English language and literature.

From early adulthood on Pym was caught up in a number of passionate love affairs which are discussed candidly in her "Autobiography in Diaries & Letters," edited by her literary executor Hazel Holt and her sister Hilary, under the title *A Very Private Eye* (1984). These romantic involvements, which seem to have meant a great deal to her, all ended in shattered hopes and left a painful trail of frustrated yearning. Yet, she remained on good terms with her sometime lovers, keeping contact through the mails despite their far removal, their being married, and the unlikelihood that there would be any further involvement.

For the next several years Pym lived either at home in Oswestry, or in Oxford, although she made a number of trips to Europe, visiting Germany in 1934, 1935, and 1937. She also began writing serious fiction during the decade of the 1930s. Having to register for war service in 1941, she accepted a position with the Postal and Telegraph Censorship Board, located in Bristol, and in 1943 joined the Women's Royal Naval Service (WRNS). Before long she was promoted to Third Officer and again found herself taking up censorship duties. A year before World War II ended she was posted to Naples. After her demobilization in 1945, she went back to Oswestry to attend to her mother, who was dying.

In 1946, Pym took a low-paying editorial-assistant job in London with a charitable organization, the International African Institute, which had been founded twenty years earlier to promote research on the languages and cultures of Africa. Though she lacked a personal interest in Africa, she fulfilled her duties quite effectively, becoming assistant editor on the Institute's journal, *Africa*, on a series of cultural studies, and on Institute monographs. She would remain with the Institute until 1974, when poor health obliged her to retire. A considerable source of interest to her in connection with her work there was the staff of anthropologists connected with the Institute: fascinating not only as *men*, but also as quirky, temperamental individuals who made excellent subjects for study themselves for a closely observant fiction writer who might happen to be working at the same institution.

Pym's major occupational concern—writing for publication—was realized during the period from 1950 to 1961 when six of her novels were published. A major shock in terms of her writing career came in 1963 when a seventh novel (like the others, a minor-key, social-comedy drama) was rejected by her publisher and she could find no other publishing house willing to accept it in view of the changed literary fashions and its consequent unsuitability for a popular audience. Still, she continued to write stories and novels over the following decade and a half in the face of the publishers' stony indifference to her mannered fictions, most of

which were about village (or small-town) life or life in a particular area of London. This period was triply discouraging for her: from a social standpoint, "no fond return of love" and no suitable attachments (to adapt two of her titles); from an artistic and commercial standpoint, no market for her wares; and from a health standpoint, serious disorders—cancer necessitating a mastectomy, and several strokes.

A turn in her fortunes (in one area at least) came in 1977 when her literary achievement was recognized in the *Times Literary Supplement* by her being included in a list of the twentieth century's most underrated writers (she had been nominated by Lord David Cecil and Philip Larkin). Renewed literary success followed in short order. Her books were now welcomed by the publishers, and the following of readers who had remained faithful during the period of her initial popularity was now considerably increased. In 1979, she was elected a Fellow of The Royal Society of Literature. That same year Pym developed terminal cancer, but she was able to complete another novel just before her death, which occurred in Oxford, on January 11, 1980. She was buried in the Oxford suburb of Finstock. A number of her shorter and longer fictions were published posthumously, thanks to the editorial efforts of her literary executor Holt, who had been her assistant at the International African Institute.

Literary Analysis

Pym's literary studies at Oxford seem to have exerted a strong influence on her sizable output of fiction. Literary allusions, particularly to the English poets, figure significantly in her novels, highlighting in certain instances one of her major themes: the never-ending search for Mr. Right (*chercher l'homme*) and the associated pangs of lovelonging. For example, the title of her first-published novel, *Some Tame Gazelle* (1950), comes from a poem of Thomas Haynes Bayly, a song writer and dramatist ("Some tame gazelle, or some gentle dove: / Something to love, oh, something to love!"). *Less Than Angels* (1955) has a significant epigraph from Alexander Pope, which includes the lines "What would this Man? Now upward will he soar, / And little less than Angel would be more: / Etc." *A Glass of Blessings* (1958) also has an epigraph, this one from George Herbert: "When God first made man, / Having a glasse of blessings standing by; / Etc." *The Sweet Dove Died* (1978) opens with a particularly poignant epigraph from John Keats: "I had a dove, and the sweet dove died; / And I have thought it died of grieving; / O, what could it grieve for? its feet were tied / With a simple thread of my own hand's weaving." Finally, *Civil to Strangers*, Pym's second novel, written in 1936 and published in 1987, utilizes as title and epigraph words from a couplet taken from John Pomfret: "Her Conduct Regular, her Mirth Refin'd, / Civil to Strangers, to her Neighbours kind." In addition, Holt points out in her edition of this novel and a number of short pieces by Pym, the quotations that open the individual chapters of the novel are all from James Thomson's "The Seasons."

Many writers have been cited as having influenced Pym's style, which is spare, tellingly direct, ironic, and strong on cross-purpose dialogue. Most frequently mentioned in this connection are Jane Austen, Charlotte Brontë, Aldous Huxley, and George Eliot, although other names have been invoked as well: Elizabeth Gaskell, Anthony Trollope, Elizabeth von Arnim (author of *Elizabeth and Her German Garden*), Stevie Smith, Ivy Compton-Burnett, John Betjeman, and Ronald Firbank. For subject matter Pym focuses on parochial life in the country or in London or Oxford, with droll churchmen, self-contained spinsters, academics and anthropologists ("Africanists" especially), office personnel, effete unmasculine floaters, and women "wanting love in that heaven they're dreaming of."

Pym has justifiably been taken as a miniaturist, and in fact a great deal of her writing is about a sharply delineated, tight little enclave in which social relations, church matters, and the problem of coping with loneliness are the salient features. It has been noted that larger issues—those having to do with politics, philosophy and theology, economics, and the like, for instance—are not dealt with by her narrators, who instead show a keen awareness of matters of domestic concern such as cooking, cats as household pets, furniture and antiques, and female attire. Her longstanding attachment to the Anglican Church is the source of one of her major ideals, referred to a number of times in her books, the "excellent women": those who do good works, serve the Church (which in fact could not do without them), and (ironically for Pym) remain spinsters. But, underlying her novels runs a still, deep current of comic humor, casting her fiction plots in a different light from that in which they would otherwise shine.

Not surprisingly, when Pym's novels began to be accepted for publication (once she revised *Some Tame Gazelle* to the satisfaction of her first publisher, Jonathan Cape), she gained sufficient confidence to keep writing what really mattered to her. Cape brought out within a ten-year period *Some Tame Gazelle, Excellent Women* (1952), *Jane and Prudence* (1953), *Less Than Angels* (1955), *A Glass of Blessings* (1958), and *No Fond Return of Love* (1961). During her life after her rehabilitation in the publishing world, Macmillan issued *Quartet in Autumn* (1977) and *The Sweet Dove Died* (1978), then posthumously published *A Few Green Leaves* (1980) and *An Unsuitable Attachment* (1982). Hazel Holt, who had revised *An Unsuitable Attachment* for publication, prepared from Pym's unpublished manuscripts a number of other novels and stories which would subsequently appear in print: the three novels *Crampton Hodnet* (1985), *An Academic Question* (1986), and *Civil to Strangers* (1987)—the last, serving as the title piece for a collection of stories (at least one of which had already been published) and a radio talk, "Finding a Voice," that Pym recorded for the BBC in 1978. A remarkably revealing and skillfully edited collection of her letters and diary entries, *A Very Private Eye* (in which her sister Hilary shared the editorial honors with Holt) appeared four years after Pym's death.

In the radio talk referred to above, Pym made a number of significant points which provide vital clues to what her literary efforts over the decades were all about. First, working in the International African Institute, she learned that it was necessary to develop a detached attitude toward people and toward life in general, and that the investigative "field-work" of the anthropologist could find a parallel in the "field-work" of the novelist. Second, from her personal experience she had knowledge of certain "worlds": those of the church and parish, the village, and (perhaps to a lesser extent) academe. Third, in writing *Quartet in Autumn* (in which she writes about four office workers, two men and two women; the women retire and one dies of cancer), she was mainly concerned with comedy and with irony. Fourth, she tried to write what pleased and amused *her*, hoping that others (scant though their numbers might be) would also be pleased. Fifth, it was her practice to keep notebooks in which she wrote down plot elements, appealing quotations, bits of overheard conversations, and the like—the recording of all of which frequently afforded her more pleasure than the creative writing itself. Sixth, considerable effort as well as the trial-and-error process were required to handle the difficult task of finding the right starting-point of a story.

Commentators on comic elements in Pym's work have noted her fondness for depicting incongruities in behavior or situation, ludicrous misunderstandings, and other instances of the absurd in everyday life. Charles Burkhart, for example, in *The Pleasure of Miss Pym* finds a delightful range of comic ingredients in her characters. Among these qualities, seen in her novels dealing with anthropology, are prejudice, ignorance, and misprision (literally, "mistaking"). Burkhart finds these markers, among others, more generally in her writings: irrelevance, inconsequence, incongruity, and enlargement (i.e., taking the trivial quite literally and building on it).

An example of irrelevance is found in *A Glass of Blessings* when Wilmet Forsyth, the narrator, has attended the Ash Wednesday lunchtime service and is chatting with Mr. Bason, who handles domestic operations at the clergy house. When Bason reaches into his pocket and takes out a piece of paper, she notices that it contains something resembling "a list, written in purple ink in a large bold hand. For one wild moment [she thinks that] it must be a Lenten laundry list—the purple ink, of course, representing the liturgical color." But, it turns out to be almost "as good—a list of menus" for the clergy house in the Lenten season, prepared by Mr. Bason. Elsewhere, Leonora Eyre, the elegant, old-fashioned, egocentric protagonist in *The Sweet Dove Died*, is awakened during the night by a sharp cry. She huddles in fright under her bedcovers, then becomes aware that it is only a cat next door. Unable to go back to sleep, she feels that there is "nothing for it but to go down and make tea, a drink she did not much like because of the comfort it was said to bring to those whom she normally despised."

An example of inconsequence occurs in *Jane and Prudence*. In the course of an Oxford reunion, Jessie Morrow, companion to the wealthy Miss Doggett, accidentally upsets a cup of tea on the lilac cotton dress of the youngish, self-conscious spinster Prudence Bates. Miss Doggett expresses the fear that a mark may be left on the dress: "'It seems to be leaving a mark already,' said Jessie in an unsuitably detached

tone for one who had been responsible for the disaster; 'rather in the shape of Italy. I wonder if that can have any significance?'" In *Crampton Hodnet*, Margaret Cleveland, the wife of an Oxford lecturer, is invited to pay a morning visit by Olive Fremantle, whose husband is a Master of one of the colleges. Dr. Fremantle comes in unexpectedly, and his timorous wife flutteringly and apologetically says that she had not known that he would return so soon. He responds pleasantly that he assumes he does not need anyone's permission to enter his own house, laughingly says that he is Master of this college and what he does not know is not knowledge, and shortly after asks his wife if she had offered Mrs. Cleveland anything to eat. Mrs. Cleveland, ready to take her leave, answers that she never eats anything in mid-morning because it would spoil one's lunch. Dr. Fremantle, repeating her remark about this mid-morning refreshment spoiling lunch, gleefully rubs "his hands, laughing at some private joke."

Incongruity is found in *Some Tame Gazelle*. Bishop Grote, having returned from the foreign mission field in the African country of Mbawawa is giving a slide lecture on that country, telling the audience that the climate there is temperate and the soil is very fertile: "'When I say temperate,' went on the Bishop, 'I dare say many of you might find it rather hot.' He paused and tapped his pointer vigorously on the floor." Another instance of comic incongruity appears in connection with a church jumble (rummage) sale in *A Few Green Leaves*. Emma Howick, a spinster and "very average anthropologist," is embarrassed at having brought such pitiful discards, including "one's old underwear, even though clean." She fears that no one will care to purchase the items. Her friend Daphne Dagnall, sister of and housekeeper for the village rector, agrees: "The village women have such marvellous things now. They wouldn't look at cast-offs—it's we who buy them." Then, thinking that she should say the right thing, Daphne remarks that "it's all to the good," and that there is not as much poverty as there was before. Finally, Marcia Ivory, one of the four drab characters who have been working in a drab office in *Quartet in Autumn*, lies terminally ill. The hospital nurse brings her a good-wishes-and-hopes-for-speedy-recovery card from Marcia's three former office associates (whom the nurse has no knowledge of). Cheerily, she tells Marcia that the card is signed

Letty, Norman, and Edwin: "In the nurse's mind Letty and Norman were a married couple with a little boy called Edwin, rather an unusual name, that, as uncommon as the pinky-mauve chrysanthemums."

Enlargement is found in *Excellent Women*, which features a young spinster named Mildred Lathbury, the daughter of a clergyman, who holds a very minor position in an institution devoted to the assistance of distressed gentle-women. She gives her impressions of the Wednesday lunchtime service at St. Ermin's church in the posh Belgravia section of London. The badly-bombed church (i.e., from World War II) had only one usable aisle, which made it seem more crowded than it really was: "This gave us a feeling of intimacy with each other and separateness from the rest of the world, so that I always thought of us as being rather like the early Christians, surrounded not by lions, admittedly, but by all the traffic and bustle of a weekday lunch-hour." In *No Fond Return of Love,* Monica Beltane, a lecturer at London University, makes the acquaintance of a young innocent, Laurel, who has recently arrived in London. Laurel is mightily impressed to hear that Monica is a lecturer in botany. Monica's mother, Mrs. Beltane, chimes in, echoing Laurel's appreciative response of *how interesting!* "'Yes, it is interesting to see how the same thing has come out in our family,' said Mrs. Beltane. 'My husband was a great gardener and had a gift for water divining . . . Monica has this passion for botany—the scientific side, you see—while Paul is very artistic and loves flowers for their own sake. And Felix is very fond of nature too, aren't you, darling?' She looked down at the poodle, who had lapsed into silence on his little cushion."

Two closely related features seem to stand out in Pym's handling of humorous scenes, which on occasion suggest the insider suddenly turning into an outlander when talking to another insider, on home territory. These are: (1) impetuous associations of ideas and situations and (2) the unreliability of the familiar as a convenient source of security.

In *Civil to Strangers,* Cassandra Marsh-Gibbon (whose husband Adam is not only "a gentleman of means" but a very minor writer) is talking with a Mrs. Wilmot, who is of the opinion that a writer has to be extremely sensitive to Nature, and then adds questioningly, wasn't Wordsworth that way? Cassandra replies she is sure that Wordsworth *was.* This matter is distasteful to her because Adam always quotes Wordsworth to her when he is in a bad mood, so Cassandra constantly associates Wordsworth with their domestic quarrels.

In *An Academic Question* the unreliability of the familiar is evidenced in a scene in which the university librarian, Dr. Cranton, is ruminating to an academic wife, Caroline Grimstone (the narrator), and another staff employee on the subject of the retirement of a member of the academic community: "'A great deal of fuss is being made about what is a perfectly natural event. Retirement is as natural as childbirth,' he declared, surprisingly, I thought, for the two processes seemed to have little in common. I wondered if he had mentioned childbirth to embarrass us or to make us feel at home, since we were both mothers and had three children between us." Similarly, *Crampton Hodnet* owes its title and central anecdote to a flimsy alibi of a new curate, who in an attempt to explain why he missed the evensong service (he had been dallying with a lady parishioner in the countryside) says that a vicar in another parish had asked him to take evensong there. When asked for the name of the parish, he improvises: "Crampton Hodnet." This makes his own companion in deceit wonder whether such a place exists and causes his interrogator to admire the name and speculate that she has not even been there. Holt considers this novel to be funnier than any of the writer's later works.

The essential good humor effect of Pym's fictions (allowing for the occasional discouragements of her female protagonists) is enhanced by certain oddly-named characters, whose appellations suggest the richness of English literary history. Wilmet Forsyth is a well-situated if discontentedly idle housewife in London in *A Glass of Blessings.* As she and her friend Rowena Talbot are sitting under hair driers and chatting in the beauty shop run by Monsieur Jacques, an Englishman with a Midlands accent, she wonders out loud why it is impossible to read a serious book there: do the haircut and shampoo somehow shrivel the brain? Elsewhere, Miss Doggett, a formidable old dowager-type who fancies herself born to command (she is one of Pym's characters who appear in several novels), is gossiping—in *Jane and Prudence*—about a local philanderer. The pace of the conversation is almost too fast for her, and she comments that men are said to want only one thing; then, even her own remark seems to puzzle her in this too-heady discussion: it is as though she forgot what that one thing was. One of the most outrageously funny clergymen in Pym's spacious gallery is the High-Church Father, Julian Malory, who lives with his sister Winifred in *Excellent Women.* In one glorious scene he is painting a wall in the vicarage and step by step making a terrible botch of the whole business. Finally, he expresses regret at not being any good in practical matters and adds his entrenched belief that well-done manual labor must be very satisfying; after all, Malory points out, he has delivered enough sermons about it.

In *An Unsuitable Attachment,* Daisy Pettigrew, who lives with her veterinarian brother Edwin, is thought by certain of his clients to resemble some animal or other, depending on her particular mood: now a marmalade cat, at another time a sheep dog. In *The Sweet Dove Died,* the narrator remarks on the universally accepted truth that owners of pets come to look like their animals. The narrator in *A Few Green Leaves* describes the village general practitioner's "surgery" (office), which was particularly busy on Mondays. The reason is that a number of the patients had not attended church the day before, and they were atoning for that now by going to a place where they could receive comfort, aside from the fact that a few might even worship there too.

There is a scene in *Less Than Angels,* set in two adjoining residential gardens, in which a mixed group of dotty characters—some of them being anthropologists or others connected with the field—are described functionally and metaphorically. Tom Mallow, a budding anthropologist, is introduced to the neighbor, Alaric Lydgate, a retiree from the Colonial Service in Africa. Alaric and Tom, on either side of the hedge dividing the two properties, quickly become "like suspicious animals, eyeing each other doubtfully." They do not want to work together on the African cultural data that Alaric has collected, though they were introduced for that purpose. Father Gemini, a missionary and linguist who is heavily overdressed in musty black garments, throws off two layers of them in the manner of a strip-tease performer. Catherine Oliphant, a writer and Tom's lover, is attracted by the tall, rugged Alaric with his grim, rough-hewn face, and sees in him one of the huge Easter Island statues reduced to the level of a vulnerable, imposed-upon, poor old man. *Some Tame Gazelle* is chock-full of Pym's typical comic types—aging, crotchety spinsters, pretentious pedants, and a gallery of prim cler-

ics. It also contains a plethora of eminent ecclesiastical and literary names: Plowman, Bede, Hoccleve, Donne, Akenside, Gray, Young, Bayly, etc. In this love-and-poetry-drenched romance, one of the males who are *hors de combat* either through preference or because of unfavorable circumstances is Dr. Nicholas Parnell, head of the university library. Belinda Bede, one of the spinster sisters featured in the storyline, scrutinizes Dr. Parnell and concludes that he does not look like the sort of individual a person would wish to marry. Later Parnell, mulling over the rejection of his younger associate Nathaniel Mold by Belinda's sister Harriet, feels pity because of the turndown; notwithstanding his conviction that being married is doubtless "very tiresome," he is certain that marriage is "an interesting state." Parnell also believes that it was Archdeacon Henry Noccleve's good fortune to have won a good woman's love, at the same time considering himself practically as lucky because he himself had not.

Present indications are that Pym's readership will continue to grow and that her subtle, often elusive, sense of humor will be increasingly appreciated for the fascinating diversity of its targets and its powerful ability to transform the commonplace into a rich comic landscape.

Summary

Barbara Pym's low-key manner and penetrating descriptions of amusing social interactions and her characters' psychological responses have belatedly won her a sizable audience. Her geographical setting is within a narrow parochial or neighborhood framework—a village, a town such as Oxford, or even London itself. By her unusual association of ideas and situations, the "far out" quality of her characters' thoughts and images, and her superimposing of the fantastic on the commonplace, the prolific writer of over a dozen novels and a number of short fictions has gained a secure place among the exponents of late-twentieth-century British humor.

Selected Bibliography
Primary Sources

Novels and Fiction Collections
Some Tame Gazelle. London: Jonathan Cape, 1950; New York: Dutton, 1983.
Excellent Women. London: Jonathan Cape, 1952; New York: Dutton, 1978.

Jane and Prudence. London: Jonathan Cape, 1953; New York: Dutton, 1981.

Less Than Angels. London: Jonathan Cape, 1955; New York: Vanguard, 1957.

A Glass of Blessings. London: Jonathan Cape, 1958; New York: Dutton, 1980.

No Fond Return of Love. London: Jonathan Cape, 1961; New York: Dutton, 1982.

Quartet in Autumn. London: Macmillan, 1977; New York: Dutton, 1978.

The Sweet Dove Died. London: Macmillan, 1978; New York: Dutton, 1979.

A Few Green Leaves. London: Macmillan, 1980; New York: Dutton, 1980.

An Unsuitable Attachment. London: Macmillan, 1982; New York: Dutton, 1982.

Crampton Hodnet. London: Macmillan, 1985; New York: Dutton, 1985.

Civil to Strangers and Other Writings. Ed. Hazel Holt. New York: Dutton, 1987.

Autobiography

A Very Private Eye: An Autobiography in Diaries & Letters. Ed. Hazel Holt and Hilary Pym. London: Macmillan, 1984; New York: Dutton, 1984.

Secondary Sources

Biographies

Holt, Hazel. *A Lot to Ask: A Life of Barbara Pym.* New York: Dutton, 1991. An incisive study by Pym's literary executor.

Wyatt-Brown, Anne M. *Barbara Pym: A Critical Biography.* Columbia: University of Missouri Press, 1992.

Books

Burkhart, Charles. *The Pleasure of Miss Pym.* Austin: University of Texas Press, 1987. A brief but stimulating examination of the elements of humor in Pym's fictions.

Cotsall, Michael. *Barbara Pym.* Basingstoke, Hants and London: Macmillan, 1989. A concise survey of Pym's literary works, with emphasis on her novels.

Liddell, Robert. *A Mind at Ease: Barbara Pym and Her Novels.* London: Robert Owen, 1989. A personal friend's critical, rather than scholarly, examination of Pym's novels that she had prepared or submitted for publication.

Long, Emmet. *Barbara Pym.* New York: Ungar, 1986. An excellent overview of Pym's life, career, and major works. Good secondary bibliography of Pym's novels.

Nardin, Jane. *Barbara Pym.* Boston: Twayne, 1985. A sketchy review of Pym's life and career.

Snow, Lotus. *One Little Room An Everywhere: Barbara Pym's Novels.* Orono, ME: Puckerbrush Press, 1987. A brief examination of and commentary on Pym's longer works. No index.

Weld, Annette. *Barbara Pym and The Novel of Manners.* New York: St. Martin's Press, 1992. An interesting, well-informed study of Pym's literary career.

Articles and Chapters in Books

Binding, Paul. "Barbara Pym." In *Dictionary of Literary Biography, British Novelists Since 1960. Vol. 14. Part Two: H-Z.* Ed. Jay L. Halio. Detroit: Gale Research, Bruccoli Clark Layman, 1983, pp. 604–07. Brief overview of Pym's life and literary career.

Cooley, Mason. "Barbara Pym." In *Dictionary of Literary Biography Yearbook: 1987.* Ed. J.M. Brook. Detroit: Gale Research, Bruccoli Clark Layman, 1988, pp. 275–83. Updated version of Pym's life and literary career.

Dobie, Ann B. "The World of Barbara Pym: Novelist As Anthropologist." *Arizona Quarterly,* 44 (Spring 1988): 5–18. Dobie makes the point that "Pym's characters mirror her own penchant for observation and record." As a novelist she "worked as an anthropologist taking her own society as her field of observation."

Stetz, Margaret Diane. "*Quartet in Autumn*: New Light on Barbara Pym as a Modernist." *Arizona Quarterly,* 41 (Winter, 1985): 24–37. Stetz illustrates two modernist tendencies in Pym's fictions (exemplified in *Quartet in Autumn*): the association of ideas in a character's mind and the unifying effect of repetition of verbal expressions and imagery in different sequences of the story.

Samuel I. Bellman

R

Ralegh, Walter

*Born: Hayes Barton near Budleigh Salerton
    Bay, South Devon, ca. 1552*
*Education: Oriel College, Oxford University,
    1568–1569*
*Marriage: Elizabeth Throckmorton, 1592;
    three children*
Died: London, October 29, 1618

Biography

Walter Ralegh, the son of Walter and Catherine
Ralegh, was born at Hayes Barton near Bud-
leigh Salerton Bay, South Devon, around 1552.
He entered Oriel College, Oxford, in 1568 but
left in 1569 to serve among the English volun-
teers who fought the French Huguenots. In
February 1575, Ralegh became a resident of
Middle Temple, where he studied law.

Ralegh was a Renaissance John-do-all,
who had great managerial, military, philosophical, and creative talents. These qualities, along
with his good looks, ready wit, and Sir Francis
Walsingham's patronage won Queen Elizabeth's
favor, which began to grow after 1581. In 1578,
Ralegh had joined his half-brother Sir Humphrey Gilbert as a captain in a privateering expedition against the Spanish. In 1580, he took
an active part in suppressing the Irish rebellions.
Three years later, in 1583, he accompanied the
Duke of Anjou to Flanders, and he received the
grant of Durham House, Strand. Many highly
remunerative patents followed, including those
for licensing vintners and exporting woolen
cloth. In 1584, Ralegh took up the project of
colonizing Virginia and harassing Spanish
trade. He became Warden of Stannaries in 1589
and there showed his skills as an administrator
in regulating mining and smelting. In 1586,
granted 40,000 acres of Irish land, he colonized

this tract with English settlers, potatoes, and
tobacco.

Fifteen ninety-two marked a turning point
in Ralegh's fortunes. Having learned that he had
seduced one of her maids of honor, Elizabeth
Throckmorton, and perhaps that he already had
married her, Queen Elizabeth forced Ralegh to
return from an expedition against the Spanish
and placed him and his bride in the Tower of
London. Upon their release, he and his wife withdrew from court to his estate at Sherborne, Dor-
setshire. The couple eventually had three sons.

In 1595, in a bid to regain public popularity and the Queen's favor, Ralegh mounted an
expedition to Guiana in South America. The
publication of the beautifully written if fantastic account of that voyage only increased a perception of Ralegh as greedy and arrogant.
However, when he was wounded in the English
capture of Cádiz in 1596 he returned to partial
favor, and in 1600 he obtained the governorship
of Jersey and was elected to Parliament for
Penzance. In 1601, he helped suppress Lord
Essex's rebellion and officiated at his execution.

When James I, a friend of Essex's, came to
the throne in 1603, Ralegh's fall was fierce and
precipitate. Within months of James's accession,
Ralegh was expelled from various properties
and positions, deprived of monopolies, accused
of conspiracy, and, after a nasty trial, committed to the Tower, where he passed the next thirteen years of his life, from 1603 to 1616.

Ralegh had always been known as a poet
and a free-thinker, even at times being accused
of atheism. His poetry, which had circulated
widely in manuscript, had been published in
such places as *The Phoenix Nest* (1593) and the
very influential *English Helicon* (1600). He
also had undertaken the patronage of Edmund

Spenser, whose prefatory epistle to the *Faerie Queene* lauds Ralegh as knighthood's mirror. A man of vast practical enterprise and omnivorous learning, in prison Ralegh turned his attention to chemical experiments to create elixirs and to writing, in particular the voluminous *History of the World* (1614).

In 1617, taking advantage of King James's need for money, Ralegh offered to return to Guiana, the mythical El Dorado, to bring back gold. Unfortunately, during the trip up the Orinoco, Ralegh's right-hand man, Lawrence Keymis, engaged the Spanish in a battle in which Sir Walter's elder son perished. This terrible event prompted Keymis to take his own life. A weary and ill Ralegh returned home to face the now revived charges that had first committed him to the Tower. After fifteen years of James's rule, Ralegh was beginning to be viewed as a hero again, the last Elizabethan, the relic of a glorious age. Perceived, therefore, as a potential political danger to the king, he was executed on October 29, 1618.

During the period of the Commonwealth, partly owing to the writing of his son Carew, the legend of Ralegh, along with Francis Drake, was fashioned. He was represented as the ideal English hero, a position that he has occupied since.

Literary Analysis

As a man of his age, a most ingenious, stylish, and practical Jack-of-all-trades, Ralegh, the explorer, chemist, soldier, courtier, administrator, politician, and historian, dabbled in all genres of writing. Humor is a central feature of his poetry and of his sensibility generally. Although a dreamer, Ralegh also presented himself as a realist, and his realism became a test of the ideals and poetics of the age in which he lived. His remark that if one follows the heels of truth too closely one will get his teeth kicked in serves as a model for his wit, a wit in which manners and the intellectual fashions of the day encounter stern and pragmatic realities, producing humor and a point-of-view that may be called "skeptical."

Like the works of so many of his age, Ralegh's writings circulated in manuscript among his powerful friends and reached print only sporadically. His earliest known work appears to be his commendatory verses on George Gascoigne's satirical *Stele Glasse* (1576). Ralegh's poem not only supports the unflattering likenesses drawn in Gascoigne's humorous mirror but suggests a similarly aggressive satirical stance on Ralegh's part: "Sweet were the sauce would please each kind of taste, / The life likewise were pure that never swerved; / For spiteful tongues in cankered stomachs placed, / Deem worst of things which best (percase) deserved."

His best known poem and piece of wit, "The Nymph's Reply to the Shepherd" collected in *England's Helicon*, appears to have been written in collaboration with his friend Christopher Marlowe, whose very verse Ralegh's parodies. Though a far gentler piece than the commendatory verses on Gascoigne, the poem arises from the same impulse to use humor to lift the veil from social pretense and from the self-serving deceits practiced in polite society. In Marlowe's beautiful pastoral lyric, "The Passionate Shepherd to his Love," the youth entices his beloved with an exaggeration of the sensual beauties of the surroundings:

> The shepherds swains shall dance and
> sing
> For thy delight each May-morning.
> If these delights thy mind may move,
> Come live with me and be my love.

Ralegh uses the voice and view of a pragmatic shepherdess, like Miguel de Cervantes's Marcela in *Don Quixote* or Ben Jonson's querulous shepherd in "And must I sing?" The shepherdess parodies the images of Marlowe's courtly shepherd in order to examine and reject his frothy promises and his double entendre (the shepherd's May-morning "dance" suggests sex):

> If all the world and love were young,
> And truth in every shepherd's tongue,
> These pretty pleasures might me move
> To live with thee and be thy love.

The tone is reminiscent of and more delightful than Sir Thomas Wyatt in expressing a disillusionment with the poetic promises of love, and the mirroring of Marlowe's images makes the poem lovely in itself. Still, Ralegh's skepticism underlies even this performance. The poetic doubling in the two poems, presenting an idealistic view mated with a realistic one, has had many imitators since, including John Milton in his "L'Allegro" and "Il Penseroso."

In "On the Life on Man," Ralegh shows how fundamental comedy is to his view of life. In that poem he paints a humorous view of the womb as the tiring room "[w]here we are dressed for this short Comedy." But, he goes on to point out: "Only we die in earnest. That's no jest," suggesting that the comedy of life lacks that which makes theatrical comedy funny, the promise of rebirth, growth, marriage, a world of happy endings. For Ralegh, then, what is comic is deadly serious, just as what is deadly serious is comic.

This playful equivocation on the comic and serious is plain in his humorous caution "To His Son" in which he warns about the trouble when wood, weed, and wag meet—that is, when gallows, rope, and merry rogue are joined. In much of his other verse, such as "The Lie" and "A Secret Murder," the humor is dark and bitter, bordering on invective: "A secret murder hath been done of late, / Unkindness found to be the bloody knife, / And she that did the deed a dame of state, / Fair, gracious, wise, as any beareth life."

Yet, like many others of his age, Ralegh also links "wantonness and wit." His humor is often sly with double meanings, hints, and misdirections, as in "Those eyes which set my fancy on a fire," wherein the poet praises the beloved's eyes, hair, and wit—but especially her hands. This odd list of parts, their praise, and respective merits suggests Ralegh's smirk, scandalous and droll, beneath the surface of his stylish verse. A similar odd and comic, yet sensuous, sensibility informs "Nature that washed her hands in milk" when he speaks of his mistress's "violet breath and lips of jelly." The humor of this poem is connected with gaiety and growth. In this poem, too, however, the realities of age and disillusionment bring dying and death, which is "no jest," and thus the humor here becomes invective.

Ralegh probably wrote much more than we ascribe to him now and probably much that we ascribe to him now is not his at all. So, for instance, "The Lie," an elegant satire on court life, may not be his. In his time there were many candidates for its authorship. The nature of manuscript circulation and the imprecision of the Elizabethan anthology make ascription difficult. Undoubtedly, though, contemporary readers recognized elements in "The Lie" that they thought characteristic of Ralegh's sensibility, style, and humor. These included a penchant for "conceit," the surprising metaphor, and a realism that gives rise to melancholy, partakes heavily of disillusionment, and leads to a skeptical stance, particularly in those poems that either declare a satirical intent or dip into the satirical. Through the lens of Ralegh's poetry and sensibility, one can gain insight into the undercurrent of wit throughout English renaissance verse from Wyatt through Jonson. From Ralegh's sensibilities and others like his were to grow much of seventeenth-century literature, ideas, and wit.

Summary

Sir Walter Ralegh viewed life as a comedy with a tragic ending. This view flowed from his own combination of expansive optimism or idealism and disillusioned realism, exemplified in his best known verse, "The Nymph's Reply to the Shepherd." In his works this combination most often creates a dark humor that can move in a single poem from embracing mirth to rasping satire. Ralegh, who was viewed as the embodiment of the Elizabethan character, was himself an inquisitive idealist and sensualist in whose humor there flowed deep undercurrents of skepticism, melancholy, and even cynicism. His sensibility was important in the fashioning of the Elizabethan ideal of wit and worldliness and in setting the tone for those skeptical and worldly wits who followed in the seventeenth century.

Selected Bibliography

Primary Sources
Selected Prose and Poetry. Ed. Agnes Mary Latham. London: University of London, Athlone Press, 1965.

Secondary Sources

Biographies/Intellectual History
Greenblatt, Stephen Jay. *Sir Walter Ralegh: the Renaissance Man and his Roles*. New Haven: Yale University Press, 1973. An intellectual and social biography concentrating on court relations.
Oakeshott, Walter Fraser. *The Queen and the Poet*. London: Faber & Faber, 1960.
Strathmann, Ernest Albert. *Sir Walter Ralegh: A Study in Elizabethan Skepticism*. New York: Columbia University Press, 1951; New York: Octagon Books, 1973. The "wit" of Ralegh is described and given an account in intellectual history.

Literary Background and Criticism
Bradbrook, M.C. *The School of Night: A Study in the Literary Relationships of Sir*

Walter Ralegh. New York: Russell & Russell, 1965. Account of Ralegh's poetry in the context of those poets with whom he was associated. For specifics on his verse see pp. 75–101.

Clark, Eleanor Grace. *Ralegh and Marlowe: A Study in Elizabethan Fustian*. New York: Russell & Russell, 1965. This work places Ralegh in his literary milieu. "The Ralegh Legend" gives a good account of Ralegh's "tart" verse.

Cousins, A.D. "The Coming of Mannerism: The Later Ralegh and the Early Donne." *English Literary Renaissance*, 9, 1 (Spring 1979): 86–107. An account of the language and wit in Ralegh's writing and its influence on early metaphysical style.

Drummond, C.Q. "Style in Ralegh's Short Poems." *South Central Review*, 3, 1 (Spring 1986): 23–36. A brief account of the subtleties of Ralegh's wry point of view.

May, Steven W. *Sir Walter Raleigh*. Boston: Twayne, 1989. A useful overview of Ralegh's literary art.

David Rosen

Rattigan, Terence Mervyn

Born: Kensington, London, June 10, 1911
Education: Mr. W. Hornbye's school, Sandroyd, 1920; Harrow, 1925–1930; Trinity College, Oxford University, 1930–1933; summer language schools in France and Germany, 1933–1935
Died: Bermuda, November 30, 1977

Biography

Born in middle-class Kensington on June 10, 1911, to career diplomat William Frank (C.M.G.) and Vera Houston Rattigan, Terence Rattigan developed a love for the theater in his early days at Harrow, where he discovered John Galsworthy, Anton Chekhov, and George Bernard Shaw. He dreamed of becoming "the famous playwrite and author, T.M. Rattigan,"[1] and even wrote a play about Cesar Borgia.

Rattigan entered Mr. W. Hornbye's school in Sandroyd in 1920. He attended Harrow on a scholarship (1925–1930), and then read history at Trinity College, Oxford University (1930–1933). At Oxford he served as drama critic for the undergraduate paper, the *Cherwell*, and acted in a one-line walk-on role in *Romeo and Juliet* (with Edith Evans and Peggy Ashcroft, directed by John Gielgud). He used undergraduate life as the subject for his early plays, one of which, *French Without Tears*, became a record-breaking success in London and on the Continent. During the summers of 1933 through 1935, he also attended language schools (crammers) in France and Germany.

Rattigan wrote about the life that he knew, a life with deep roots in English tradition (both of his grandfathers were barristers) and with parental expectations that he would follow in his father's diplomatic footsteps. Given this background, Harrow and Oxford were natural choices for his education, although Rattigan's college was Trinity rather than Magdalen. Eager to write, he persuaded his father that moving to London to do so was more important than finishing his studies at Oxford. He wrote six plays, one of which (*French Without Tears*)was a spectacular success in London and on the Continent. When World War II broke out he entered the Royal Air Force (1939) where he served six years, returning after the war to prove to the critics that he was not just a "lucky fluke" or the "one-play Rattigan"[2] whom they had referred to in their reviews of *French Without Tears*. He continued to write play after successful play, about schoolboys and schoolmasters (*The Browning Version*), the injustices of hallowed English institutions (*The Winslow Boy*), servicemen (*Flare Path, While the Sun Shines*), diplomats (*The Sleeping Prince*), and historical figures (*Ross, Adventure Story*, about Lawrence of Arabia and Alexander the Great).

His successes teamed him with Noel Coward as the two most popular playwrights of the 1940s and 1950s. But, behind the glamour of success lurked a pain that emerged in his later dramas in the flawed figures whose outward achievements were broken through by personal or societal failures. Thus, a failed schoolmaster, a barrister's wife, the lonely inhabitants of a proper boarding house, national heroes, middle-aged women, and so forth, complement the comical, farcical, and sunny characters of his early plays. Even the schoolboys, about whom Rattigan wrote throughout his career, became partial victims, at least, of repressive and hypocritical societal attitudes (*Man and Boy, Cause Celebre*). As a homosexual, the playwright felt these injustices and was compelled to dramatize them obliquely, even disguising some of his male characters as women.

Rattigan increasingly developed themes such as the effects of emotional repression (*le vice anglais*), the inequalities of most relationships, father-son relationships, and societal hypocrisies—all couched delicately in the tradition of the well-made play. In 1956, his *Separate Tables,* a twin bill, was in its second year of a successful run, the same year that John Osborne's *Look Back in Anger,* emotions exploding, burst on the English stage. Rattigan, keenly feeling his relegation by the critics to the category of old-fashioned playwright, said that from now on a dramatist would be measured by how unlike Rattigan he was. He spent much of the 1960s in a self-imposed exile mostly writing films such as *The Yellow Rolls Royce* (1965) and *Goodbye Mr. Chips* (1968). He died of bone cancer at his Bermuda home on November 30, 1977.

Literary Analysis

Rattigan is a traditionalist in his use of comedic devices such as a plot built on misunderstandings and misadventures, confusion caused by the misuse of language, suspense and climax created by timely exits and entrances, and mixups of identity—all of these creating a topsy-turvy world that is eventually returned to normalcy. As he matures, Rattigan loosens his use of conventional strategies and creates character-centered comedies with a quietly Chekhovian irony replacing the emphasis on plot.

First Episode (1934, written with Philip Heimann), Rattigan's first professionally produced play, is a rites-of-passage comedy about carefree undergraduate Oxford life with scenes of drinking, gambling, weekend romances, and cricket. Built on undergraduate jokes which turn serious, the comedy is about male friendships that are restored after a temporary interruption by a visiting actress who forms an obsessive attachment to one of the youths. Even in a comedy whose plot consists of undergraduate antics, a Chekhovian irony is present in the tension that exists between the spoken and the unspoken and between outer details and inner feelings. The tension expresses itself in Rattigan's mastery of dialogue, as in the lines of one friend to another describing the actress who has come between them: "Her eyes are too close together . . . Her mouth too small, and I don't like her voice." "Did you have a good rehearsal?"[3] The sub-texts of his dialogues are a stylistic hallmark of Rattigan's serious comedy.

Follow My Leader (banned in 1938 and produced in 1940, written with Anthony Maurice) is a Chaplinesque farce about Adolf Hitler, who is portrayed as a dummy plumber who rises as a result of an intra-party rivalry. Although dismissed as a piece of good fun, the production was lauded for its standard farce scenes such as the "sight of the poor lumpen-Hitler before the microphone, yelling the ferocious harangues that a lounging secretary dictates to him sentence by sentence" making "an amusing picture that the authors exploit to the fullest possible extent."[4] This auto-characterization technique is found in the masters of farce, such as William Shakespeare, Moliere, and Nikolai Gogol.

French Without Tears (1936), Rattigan's first spectacularly successful play, is described by the author as built "totally on a Chekhovian pattern—very short scenes, no single star roles, a lot of duologues."[5] Drawn from the playwright's experiences in French summer "crammers," the play is Chekhovian with its slight plot and Shavian in the witty dialogue of students who fumble in their attempts to learn French. As in *First Episode,* the carefree male students find their idyllic life interrupted by the appearance of Diana, a seductress and sister of one of the students. Charming several of the students, she plays cat-and-mouse games with them. She represents the recurrent *femme fatale* who, in Rattigan's comedies, manages to keep her composure throughout no matter the potentially embarrassing entanglements that she creates. A comedy on a small scale, its dialogue-based humor steadily entertains from its opening to its closing lines. The play established Rattigan as a dramatist whose main interest, even in farce, is character, with plot subservient to character. With Kay Hammond, Jessica Tandy, Roland Culver, and Rex Harrison, the comedy ran for 1,039 performances in London and was produced in Sweden, Holland, Austria, Hungary, Germany, and even New Zealand.

Rattigan's trilogy of World War II plays, *Flare Path* (1942), *While the Sun Shines* (1943), and *Love in Idleness* (1944), reflects the diverse modes of which he was capable, the first of the three plays being a serious domestic drama, the second a farce, and the third a romance whose long-running American version, *O Mistress Mine,* became legend, with the famous husband-wife duo, Alfred Lunt and Lynn Fontanne, playing the leads.

Like *French Without Tears, While the Sun Shines* broke box-office records. More complex, however, in its use of the conventions of traditional farce, the plot is built around exaggeratedly improbable events, well-timed exits and entrances, the usual series of misunderstandings that end in hilarity, and in the eventual restoration of order. Setting the play in chambers at the Albany, where he lived, Rattigan brings together an intoxicated Irish-American serviceman, a French officer, and, of course, one Lord Harpenden—an English sailor on leave to marry Elizabeth, a member of the Women's Air Force. In one of the funniest scenes, the rapidly accelerated misunderstandings are catalyzed by the three men rolling dice for the first chance to speak to Elizabeth on the phone and then concluded at the end by the American and Frenchman rolling dice for the honor of being best man at the wedding. Like *French Without Tears*, much of the laughter in both plot and dialogue stems from the language misunderstandings. There are the usual themes of close male relationships and of the two kinds of women—one physically attractive and the other sensible, strongwilled, and virtuous. There is, again, the Shaw-like dialogue as seen in the exchange between Harpenden and the left-winger Colbert:

> *Harpenden:* All right. I'm a doomed
> class, but that's no reason I
> shouldn't marry the girl I love, is it?
> *Colbert:* Certainly it is, when that girl is
> Elizabeth. At all costs she must be
> saved from sharing your doom.
> *Harpenden:* Left wing, eh?
> *Colbert:* Socialist.
> *Harpenden:* Well, I read the *New States-man* myself.
> *Colbert:* That will not save you from
> extinction.

Rattigan's last pure farce, *Harlequinade* (1948), is one half of a twin bill, of which *The Browning Version*, regarded by many as Rattigan's best play, is the other half. Again, drawn from his experience at Oxford, *Harlequinade* is about a theatrical company on the road with *Romeo and Juliet*. Again, there are the loose plot, the seemingly shifting focus, and the absence of one dominant character. The usual staging problems of a road performance are complicated by reality which intrudes from the outside world in the form of an unexpected appearance of a local woman whose baby is the consequence of a liaison with one of the actors in his earlier appearance in the town. Into the complications of misunderstandings and misad-

ventures, Rattigan farcically weaves in the line from his own one-line role as a halberdier in *Romeo and Juliet* at Oxford: "Faith, we may put up our pipes and begone." Just as the possible bigamy charges against the actor and the staging problems are resolved, the play concludes with the manager running onstage to announce to the audience, "Take those lights out! It's seven-thirty. There's an audience in front. Look!"

The entanglements of art with life and of illusion with reality reflect Rattigan's main thrust in his plays: honesty about life as revealed in the characters, and honesty in his craft as he steers that craft "adroitly between the nets of artifice and the shallows of sentimentality" (Barber).

In *Who is Sylvia?* (1950), Rattigan blends fantasy with comedy in an approach described by one critic as "humorous invention at its freshest."[6] A diplomat, Lord Binfield, Mark to his friends, has tried for three decades to find his ideal woman, that ideal represented by a sculpture of Sylvia in his Knightsbridge flat. Joined in his rakish life by Oscar, a comic double in the tradition of *miles gloriosus* (a convention of Roman comedy), Mark was "happily able at every stage . . . to run across some fresh . . . approximation to the ideal."[7] Each of the three acts is concerned with a different "Sylvia" in yet another romantic episode of a given decade. Now, however, disillusionment has set in, underscored by the revelation that his wife has known of his affairs. Further (in Rattigan's deliberate use of comic anti-climax), she has suggested to Mark that the first Sylvia, seventeen at the time and now sixty-three, be invited to dinner. Dedicated to his father "with love, with gratitude, and in apology," *Who is Sylvia?* is Rattigan's way of coming to terms with his deep, lifelong ambivalence in his own attitude toward his rakish father. Among the many autobiographical details there is even the son who has chosen the stage over diplomacy as a career.

One remaining romantic comedy, *The Sleeping Prince* (1953), draws on his father's diplomatic background. A Cinderella story in the central-eastern European tradition, the play is about a young Carpathian regent who arrives for the coronation of King George V in 1911 (the year that Vera Rattigan was unable to attend the coronation because of the birth of Terence). Typically, there are misunderstandings created by language difficulties that lead to farcical situations. Once more there is a *femme fatale*, Mary Morgan, an American actress played by Vivien Leigh on the stage and by Marilyn Monroe in the film, with Laurence Olivier in the lead in both versions. Here Mary is both the seductress and the independently practical woman, and as such she precipitates one of the most farcical moments in the play when she is given the same gifts (for services rendered) by three different members of the visiting royal family. Capping the comedy, there is again the use of a strikingly effective line at the end, one used comically throughout by the young regent in response to every new situation: "himmel heilige bimbaum!"

The Sleeping Prince marks the end of the impressive array of Rattigan's comedies and farces. From here on his plays are concerned with the pain resulting from the failures of highly sensitive characters who find themselves trapped in the insensitivity of the social system. The comedy becomes ironic in plays such as *In Praise of Love* (1973), in which playing games, joking, and civilized wit are the means by which a husband and wife handle the pain of her impending death from cancer. The irony turns to bitterness in *Man and Boy* (1964), about Gregor Antonescu, a fictionalized account of the noted confidence-man, Ivar Kreuger.

Summary
A successful dramatist whose plays chronicle the varying moods of the decades in the middle of the twentieth century, Terence Rattigan has reflected those moods in sunny comedies, outright farces, romantic comedies, problem plays, and finally the ironic, sometimes grimly satiric, dramas—all drawn mostly from English upper-middle-class life as he knew it. Adapting the conventions of the well-made play to his own sensitive, oblique style, he wrote dramas of character rather than of plot. Even in the farces such as *French Without Tears*, *While the Sun Shines*, and *Harlequinade*, the characters are sensitive and vibrant, avoiding the flatness of the formulaic farce. In his self-styled "serious comedy," he combines Shavian wit with Chekhovian sub-textual suggestivity. Above all, he keeps intact the inner reality of the character, whether that reality agrees or conflicts with outer reality.

Together with Coward, he enjoyed a reputation as a successful dramatist during what has been referred to as the twilight period between the era of Oscar Wilde, Shaw, and Sean O'Casey and that of Samuel Beckett, Osborne, Harold Pinter, Tom Stoppard, and the plethora of experimental dramatists whose plays dominated critical attention in the decades following 1956.

Notes
1. Terence Rattigan, *Collected Plays* (London: Hamish Hamilton, 1953), II: viii.
2. *Ibid.*, I: xiv.
3. Rattigan, *First Episode*, typescript, p. 51.
4. *Times* (London, January 17, 1940): 6, col. d.
5. Sheridan Morley, "Terence Rattigan at 65," *Times* (London, May 9, 1977): n.p.
6. *New York Times* (October 25, 1950): 47, col. 7.
7. *Times* (London, October 25, 1950): 6, col. e.

Selected Bibliography
Primary Sources

Plays
Collected Plays. London: Hamish Hamilton. Vols. I and II, 1953; Vol. II, 1964; Vol. IV, 1978. Individual plays are published by Hamish Hamilton, London, unless otherwise indicated.
Adventure Story. 1950.
After the Dance. 1939.
The Browning Version. In *Three Modern Plays*. London: Methuen, 1958.
Cause Celebre. 1978.
The Deep Blue Sea. 1952.
Flare Path. 1942.
French Without Tears. 1937.
In Praise of Love. 1973.
Love in Idleness. 1945.
Man and Boy. 1964.
Playbill: The Browning Version and Harlequinade. 1949.
Ross. 1960.
Separate Tables. 1955.
The Sleeping Prince. 1954.
Variation on a Theme. 1958.
While the Sun Shines. 1944.
Who is Sylvia? 1951.
The Winslow Boy. 1946.

Articles
"Concerning the Play of Ideas." *New Statesman and Nation* (March 4, 1950): n.p.
"Drama without Tears." *Times* (London, October 1937): n.p.

R

"Marilyn, Sir Laurence and I." *Daily Express* (London, June 25, 1957): n.p.

"What Audiences Want to See." *Times* (London, August 27, 1964): 11.

Interviews

Barber, John. "Rattigan's Return." *Daily Telegraph* (London, July 30, 1973): n.p.

Hayman, Ronald. "Life for Father." *Times* (London, September 19, 1970): n.p.

Matthews, Geoffrey. "The Winsome Boy of Sixty." *Evening News* (London, June 10, 1971): n.p.

Morley, Sheridan. "Terence Rattigan at 65." *Times* (London, May 9, 1977): n.p.

Oakes, Philip. "Grace Before Going." *Sunday Times* (London, December 4, 1977): 35.

Simon, John. "Rattigan Talks to John Simon." *Theatre Arts*, 46 (April 1963): 23–24, 73.

Secondary Sources

Books

Darlow, Michael, and Gillian Hodson. *Terence Rattigan: The Man and His Work*. London: Quartet, 1979. A valuable biographical study linking Rattigan's plays with his life.

Hill, Holly. *A Critical Analysis of the Plays of Terence Rattigan*. Unpublished doctoral dissertation: City University of New York, 1977. An encyclopedic source of information by a writer who had personal access to his papers during his life.

Rusinko, Susan. *Terence Rattigan*. Boston: Twayne, 1983. An analysis of Rattigan's themes and style, with a chronology.

Young, B.A. *The Rattigan Version*. New York: Atheneum, 1988. A highly personalized account of Rattigan's plays and life, with an appendix of London and New York openings.

Books containing Extended Discussions of Rattigan's Plays

Beaton, Cecil. *Memoirs of the 40's*. New York: McGraw-Hill, 1970.

Elsom, John. *Post-War British Theatre*. Ed. J.J. Gindin. Berkeley: University of California Press, 1962; Westport, CT: Greenwood, and London: Routledge & Kegan Paul, 1976.

Hayman, Ronald. *British Theatre Since 1955, A Reassessment*. Oxford: Oxford University Press, 1979.

Hinchliffe, Arnold P. *British Theatre, 1950–1970*. Totowa, NJ: Rowman & Littlefield, 1974.

Taylor, John Russell. *The Rise and Fall of the Well Made Play*. New York: Hill and Wang, 1967.

Articles

Barber, John. Obituary. *Daily Telegraph* (London, December 1, 1977): n.p.

Curtis, Anthony. "Professional Man and Boy." *Plays and Players* (February 1978): 21–23.

Hobson, Harold. "The Playwright Who Always Hid His Pain." *Sunday Times* (London, December 4, 1977): n.p.

Oakes, Philip. "Grace Before Going." *Sunday Times* (London, December 4, 1977): 35.

Shaw, George Bernard. "The Play of Ideas." *New Statesman and Nation* (May 6, 1950): 426–27.

Smith, Kay Nolte. "Terence Rattigan." *Objectivist* (March 1971): 9–15.

Spurling, Hilary. "Boos from the Stalls." *Observer* (London, 15, 1979): n.p.

Worsley, T.C. "The Expense of Spirit." *New Statesman and Nation* (March 15, 1952): 301.

———. "Rattigan and His Critics." *London Magazine* (September 1964): 60–72.

Susan Rusinko

Russell, Bertrand Arthur

Born: Trelleck, Wales, May 18, 1872

Education: Trinity College, Cambridge University, 1890–1894

Marriage: Alys Pearsall Smith, December 13, 1894; divorced September 21, 1921; Dora Black, September 27, 1921; two children; divorced 1935; Patricia (Peter) Spence, January 18, 1936; one child; divorced 1952; Edith Finch, December 15, 1952

Died: Plas Penrhyn, near Penrhyndeudraeth, Wales, February 2, 1970

Biography

One of the most celebrated philosophers, mathematicians, and political writers of this century, Bertrand Russell came from an old and distinguished aristocratic background. His grandfather, Lord John Russell, was twice prime minister; his parents, Viscount and Viscountess

John Amberly, were both prominent freethinkers who advocated the emancipation of women and birth control; his informal godfather was the philosopher John Stuart Mill. Born in Trelleck, Wales, on May 18, 1872, Russell was orphaned when he was three years old. He and his older brother Frank were raised by their paternal grandmother under stern puritanical rule, despite their parents' wishes that they were to be brought up as agnostics. He was educated by governesses and tutors at Pembroke Lodge until he entered Trinity College, Cambridge, in 1890. On December 13, 1894, he married Philadelphian Alys Pearsall Smith, the sister of Logan Pearsall Smith.

Russell graduated from and was a Fellow (1895–1901) and later a Lecturer (1910–16) at Trinity, where he published his most important works in philosophy and mathematics, including the three volume *Principia Mathematica* (1910–1913) which he coauthored with his friend Alfred North Whitehead. Opposed to England's involvement in World War I, he became passionately concerned with social issues as an active member of the No Conscription Fellowship. He launched a barrage of fiery polemics protesting the war and finally inspired public resentment when he authored a pamphlet attacking the government's treatment of conscientious objectors. The uncompromising idealism and combative temperament that seemed to burgeon at the time are evident in *Mysticism and Logic* (1917). He writes, "Better the world should perish than I, or any other human being, should believe a lie . . . that is the religion of thought, in whose scorching flames the dross of the world is being burnt away" (241).

Eventually he was dismissed from Trinity College, attacked by former associates, fined by the government, and finally in 1918 imprisoned for six months for a pacifist article. While in prison he wrote *Introduction to Mathematical Philosophy*. Outlawed by society, Russell held no academic position again until the 1930s, but he was involved in independent literary, educational, and political pursuits. During the 1920s, he also started writing his popular introductions such as *The A.B.C. of Atoms* (1923) and *The A.B.C. of Relativity* (1925). He also published, among other works, *The Analysis of Matter* (1927) and *Skeptical Essays* (1928) during this period. He and Alys were divorced in 1921.

From 1927 to 1932, Russell and his second wife, Dora Black, whom he had married on September 27, 1921, and with whom he had two children, John Conrad and Katherine Jane, founded and managed the experimental Beacon School for young children which influenced the founding of similar schools in Britain and America. The couple divorced in 1935. Russell then married Patricia (Peter) Helen Spence, a research assistant who had helped him with *Freedom and Organization, 1819–1914* (1937) and *The Amberly Papers* (1937), on January 18, 1936. The couple had one child, Conrad Sebastian Robert. He began teaching in the United States in 1938, first at the University of Chicago and later at the University of California, Los Angeles. In 1940, an offer for a position at the City College of New York was withdrawn because his iconoclastic moral and social philosophies were perceived to be immoral. Though during World War II he abated his pacifism, after the war he renewed his peace stance and took an active role in renouncing atomic weapons. The popular *A History of Western Philosophy* was published in 1945. Russell was awarded the British Order of Merit in 1949 and the Nobel Prize in Literature in 1950. In 1952, he divorced again and married American Edith Finch on December 15, 1952. His first collection of short stories, entitled *Satan in the Suburbs*, appeared in 1953 when he was eighty-one years old.

In his autobiography Russell wrote, "Three passions, simple but overwhelmingly strong, have governed my life: the longing for love, the search for knowledge, and unbearable pity for the suffering of mankind" (3). And, indeed, even toward the end of his long life, internationally acclaimed as an important twentieth-century thinker, his passionate and uncompromising commitments made him more notorious than ever. When Russell was eighty-nine, he and his wife were sentenced to prison (two months reduced to two weeks) for their nuclear disarmament activities. When he was over ninety years old, he founded the Committee of One Hundred in England, an influential group which campaigned, through acts of nonviolent civil disobedience, to halt the proliferation of nuclear weapons. And, just two days before his death, he issued a public statement condemning Israeli air raids on Egypt. For most of his ninety-eight years, then, Russell was a center of controversy.

A complex and forceful personality, an iconoclastic and unyielding social reformer, and an irreverent intellectual gadfly, Russell played a role in his time that compares, in many ways, with François Voltaire's during the Enlightenment. He died at Plas Penrhyn, Penrhyndeudraeth, North Wales, on February 2, 1970.

Literary Analysis

Russell authored over sixty books and more than 2,000 papers and articles. About half of his writings address various social and political ills and how they should be solved, while another third of his writings are technical works on mathematics, philosophy, and logic. Of the latter group, the three-volume *Principia Mathematica* is a classic of logical positivism and widely accepted as his most original and influential work. A number of his books, such as *The A.B.C. of Relativity* and *A History of Western Philosophy*, examine philosophic and scientific problems in a popularizing vein. Other volumes, generally written later in his life, express his unorthodox views on war, politics, sociology, education, and religion, and on such domestic matters as sexual relations and marriage. Later works such as *Common Sense and Nuclear Warfare* (1959), *Has Man a Future?* (1962), and *Unarmed Victory* (1963) show a lifelong pacifist's concern with the threat of nuclear annihilation. Because his thought evolved from a Platonic idealism to a thoroughgoing realism over his long career, almost any generalizations about Russell's views must be accompanied with reservations.

A mathematical logician with a passion for clarity, Russell placed great value on reason and became bitter at its abuse. His quest for complete precision and clarity in both mathematics and human relations was frustrated, however, and though he remained adamantly optimistic, he became a confirmed skeptic and self-described ethical relativist. In this, as in other aspects of his thinking, there is a similarity to the ideas of David Hume and other eighteenth-century rationalists.

Most frequently, Russell's outlook and career are compared to Voltaire's, and not since Voltaire has there been a philosopher with such an enormous popular audience. For Russell, as for Voltaire, cant and hypocrisy were intolerable, and like the views of the French philosopher, Russell's "heretical" opinions and unorthodox ideas were a source of irritation to several generations of moralists and religious conservatives. Russell's prose is also frequently compared to Voltaire's in that philosophical discussions inevitably appear in most of his non-philosophical writings. As authors, both share a graceful writing style and a sophisticated and delightful sense of humor, sometimes biting but more often gentle. And, like Voltaire's, Russell's humor derives its effects from absurd hyperbole, unexpected movements in thought, comical juxtapositions, and calculated irreverence.

The following excerpt from his collection of essays *The Conquest of Happiness* (1930) is but one illustration among many of his penchant for understated humor and his capacity for amused self-effacement:

> At the age of five, I reflected that, if I should live to be seventy, I have only endured, so far, a fourteenth part of my whole life, and I felt the long-spread-out boredom ahead of me to be almost unendurable. In adolescence, I hated life and was continually on the verge of suicide, from which, however, I was restrained by the desire to know more mathematics. (117)

Though few if any of Russell's works were written solely for comic effect, his books and volumes of essays are sprinkled with examples of whimsicality and with pithy statements that expose and comment on what he perceives to be intolerable incongruities. Elsewhere in *The Conquest of Happiness*, for example, he attacks the notion of "sin." From infancy, Russell notes, the sinner is taught that "swearing is wicked; drinking is wicked; ordinary business shrewdness is wicked; above all, sex is wicked." These prohibitions are followed by his wry comment: "He does not, of course, abstain from any of these pleasures" (19). In *Sceptical Essays*, he uses hyperbole to quip that "there is no country where people tolerate the truth about themselves; at ordinary times the truth is only thought ill-mannered, but in wartime, it is thought criminal" (1935 ed., 14). In *Fact and Fiction* (1962), parody is used to spoof the maxims of François de La Rochefoucauld with well-known gems like these: "The purpose of morals is to enable people to inflict suffering without compunction"; and "Liberty is the right to do what *I* like; license, the right to do what *you* like" (205). And, in "Cranks" Russell says, "I have long been accustomed to being regarded as a crank, and I do not much mind this except when those who so regard me are also cranks, for then they are apt to assume that

I must of course agree with their particular nostrum" (177).

Fact and Fiction also includes "The Theologian's Dream," a typical example from Russell's relatively small corpus of fiction. Structurally, the tale is a modification of the classic comic device of placing plausible characters in improbable situations—in this case, dreams—to illustrate their follies and obsessions. He often used the dream structure as a vehicle for his other fictional satires. In this instance, the device is used to genially ridicule mankind's sense of self-importance. In the dream, a theologian dies and goes to heaven where the janitor he questions has never heard of "man." The heavenly librarian who is consulted is also baffled. Only after years of research by 5,000 galactic sub-librarians is it determined that in galaxy XQ321,726 there is an insignificant star called "Sun" around which spin even smaller bodies. "After minute investigation," reports a sub-librarian, "I discovered that some, at least, of these planets have parasites, and I think that this thing which has been making the inquiries must be one of them" (215).

The bulk of Russell's fiction is found in two little-known collections of short stories. The first, *Satan in the Suburbs,* includes five pieces written in a traditional style with conventional plots reminiscent of Max Beerbohm's parodies. All five stories are comic and revolve around themes treating the nature of evil. The second volume, *Nightmares of Eminent Persons* (1953), is a group of thirteen amusing fables which attack a number of the author's *bêtes noires.*

In the introduction to *Nightmares of Eminent Persons,* Russell writes that the nightmares serve as "Signposts to Sanity": "Every isolated passion is, in isolation, insane; sanity may be defined as a synthesis of insanities." In this collection, the dream device is used for the first time, and censorship, psychiatry, existentialism, politics, and the mechanical world of the future become targets for Russell's wit. The subjects of these nightmares include, in part, President Dwight D. Eisenhower's vision of Senator Joseph McCarthy on friendly terms with the Russians, a metaphysician's visit to Hell, an existentialist who finally convinces himself that he exists, Stalin's sentence to live among Quakers, and the apocalyptic vision of Dean Acheson, President Harry Truman's Secretary of State. While his fiction was criticized for its rather pedestrian formulation and uninspired imagery, Russell was undaunted. In *Autobiography, Vol.*

III (1969), he notes that editors and readers were simply reluctant to accept him as an author of fiction because in his long career he had never written it. In his own defense, he explains that his stories were the best release he had yet discovered for expressing hitherto unexpressed feelings (30). And, with typical good humor, he goes on to convey his sadness that the nightmares were never choreographed as ballets.

Though the technique of telling absurd stories to communicate serious ideas has proven effective, the subjects of Russell's fiction are so tightly wedded to the events of his time that they seem dated. However, in these fast-moving and amusing tales, as in many of his essays, Russell efficiently satirizes many of the inconsistencies and inequities of life.

Summary

Though most of his work was not intended to be humorous, Bertrand Russell's cultivated prose frequently reveals his lighthearted exuberance in addition to his universally recognized intellectual power. And, it is his droll nature and talent for sparkling witticisms that have, in part, helped make him one of the most widely read philosophers of the twentieth century. In his voluminous writings, scattered within his carefully crafted essays, and found in his short stories, there are many examples of his perceptive use of humor. His amusing aphorisms are still quoted. And, through satire, sometimes playful and other times merciless, he successfully attacks cruelty, violence, and prejudice. It is clear that throughout his long life as a philosopher, reformer, and leader, Russell recognized the immense power of laughter and employed it as a weapon in the ongoing war against intolerance and stupidity.

Selected Bibliography

Primary Sources

Though not mentioned above, some of Russell's most delightful occasional pieces are also found in *In Praise of Idleness* (1935) and in *Unpopular Essays* (1950).

Co-authored with Alfred North Whitehead. *Principia Mathematica.* Cambridge: Cambridge University Press, 1910–1913.

Mysticism and Logic, and Other Essays. London: Allen & Unwin, 1917.

Introduction to Mathematical Philosophy.

London: Allen & Unwin, 1918.

The A.B.C. of Atoms. London: Allen & Unwin, 1923.

The A.B.C. of Relativity. New York: Harper, 1925.

The Analysis of Matter. New York: Harcourt and Brace, 1927.

Sceptical Essays. London: Allen & Unwin, 1928; Unwin Paperbacks, 1935.

The Conquest of Happiness. New York: The Book League of America, 1930.

A History of Western Philosophy. New York: Random House, 1945.

Common Sense and Nuclear Warfare. Chicago: Northwestern University Press, 1959.

Fact and Fiction. New York: Simon and Schuster, 1962. Includes a section of Russell's fiction.

Has Man a Future? New York: Simon and Schuster, 1962.

The Autobiography of Bertrand Russell. 3 vols. Vol. 1. London: Allen & Unwin, and Boston: Little, Brown, 1967. Vol. 2. London: Allen & Unwin, and Boston: Little, Brown, 1968. Vol. 3. London: Allen & Unwin, and New York: Simon & Schuster, 1969.

Fiction

Nightmares of Eminent Persons. New York: Simon and Schuster, 1953.

Satan in the Suburbs. New York: Simon and Schuster, 1953.

Secondary Sources

Clark, Ronald. *The Life of Bertrand Russell.* New York: Knopf, 1976. The first major, full-scale biography.

Green, Jonathan. *The Cynic's Lexicon.* New York: St. Martin's Press, 1984. Includes fifteen of Russell's epigrams.

Organ, Troy. "The Humor of Bertrand Russell." *The Humanist,* 46 (November and December, 1986): 24–32. Organ briefly describes Russell's techniques for humor in his non-fiction. Includes examples taken from a variety of sources.

Temple, Ruth, and Martin Tucker, eds. *A Library of Literary Criticism: Modern British Literature.* Vol. III. New York: Frederic Unger, 1981, pp. 56–59. Excerpts from selected Russell criticism.

Alan Pratt

Russell, Willy

Born: Whiston, England, August 23, 1947

Education: St. Katherine's College of Education, Liverpool, 1970–1973, Certificate of Education

Marriage: Ann Seagroatt, 1969; three children

Biography

Willy (William Martin) Russell was born in Whiston, Liverpool on August 23, 1947, to William and Margery Russell. Neither parent had extensive formal education. William Russell was one of three children in a rather poor family. His mother died when he was six months old, and his father remarried a widow with four children of her own three months later. His father was a socialist and had some notoriety as a socialist pamphleteer. William left school at fourteen and went into the mines. He then worked for an insurance company and married Margery. As a child, Margery suffered from meningitis and tuberculosis along with other ailments that kept her away from school and made her feel alienated not only from her classmates but from the academic routine as well. In 1947, Willy was born. After the insurance company, William worked in a factory. Ultimately, William and Margery bought and ran a fish-and-chips shop. Willy has one sister, seventeen years his junior.

Willy Russell grew up in Liverpool. Given his background and date of birth, he was undoubtedly influenced not only by the locale but also the Mersey Beat—that new rock-and-roll that the Beatles made famous—and was one with the generation which that music evokes. He went to the Cavern as often as possible. As was the case with his parents, school was not for him. He failed the eleven-plus examination, which placed him in Secondary Modern school—the apprenticeship track for trades—rather than Prescott Grammar School, which quite likely would have led to the university and the professions. As his father before him, Willy left school early, at fifteen, although he did have one "O" level pass in English.

At his mother's suggestion, Russell trained as a ladies' hairdresser and worked at that profession from 1963 to 1969, ultimately coming to manage his own shop. At the same time the Mersey Beat was still there, folk music was part of the culture, and Russell began his first ventures in the entertainment world as songwriter, composer, and performer with his group, the

Kirkby Town 3. In his spare time between customers, he wrote. He was also broadening his reading. Eventually, he knew that hair styling was not for him. To this point Russell's life was not much different from those of his characters: he worked, and yet he wanted something more.

What he wanted was an education. Part of his zeal for education came from Annie Seagroatt (who would become his wife in 1969) and her family, part from the seven-year-old boy who had been an avid reader and writer at junior school. Ann was a university student in education, and when Russell visited her on campus, a new world opened to him. Heretofore he had assumed a university to be but another extension of the Edwardian-style schools in which he had suffered as a boy. Now he discovered a new world—one of tutorials where people called others by their first names, of academic freedom, of debates, of freedom in general. At age twenty, in order to pursue his education, Russell left hair styling, became a temporary stock boy, then moved on to the more lucrative but far more dangerous job of cleaning girders. He remained at this job only long enough to save enough money to pay for his education. He spent a year in night school to prepare for "O" levels, and in 1970 he matriculated in the teacher-training program at St. Katherine's College of Education, Liverpool. He received his Certificate of Education there in 1973. While Russell continued his education, and education is a primary focus in much of his work, he continued playwriting.

A second major influence on his work derives from this time period as well. He saw John McGrath's *Unruly Elements* at the Everyman Theatre in Liverpool and found in McGrath's work the combination of comedy and social commentary that has come to be the hallmark of his own work. On completing his studies, Russell taught for one year (1973–1974) at Toxteth, yet he is candid about his short-lived teaching career. In a 1991 interview, he said, "I don't think I really wanted to be a teacher. What I wanted to be was a student, you know. I didn't ever want to go and teach, but I suppose I told myself that if I taught it was the least worst way of having to do a job because it gave me about thirteen weeks holiday a year in which I could do then what I needed to do which was write. Even though I have very strong and passionate views about education, I didn't want to sacrifice the great need in my life, which was writing, to education. I sometimes feel selfish about

that because I think I was a good teacher and that if one had a number of lives at one's disposal I think one of them I would dedicate to being a teacher in the fullest sense of the word. But I'm too selfish in this one, in regard to my writing, to give up my real sort of thing in order to go and teach." Although he gave up teaching as a profession, occasionally he does teach, and his offices prepare educational packets for school use.

Russell wrote his first noticed works in 1971/1972. *Blind Scouse*—a bill composed of three short plays—was staged at the Edinburgh Festival in 1972. Writing for theater, television, radio, and the screen (he is also a poet and songwriter/composer), Russell has been continuously productive. He has nine stage plays, a number of television and radio plays, and four screenplays to his credit. His first work to gain widespread success came during that one teaching year at Toxteth: *John, Paul, George, Ringo . . . and Bert* (1974), which Russell calls "the Beatles play," opened in early June at the Everyman Theater to smashing success and won "Best Musical" when it transferred to London's West End. In 1975, Russell received an Arts Council grant and during that year wrote *Breezeblock Park,* which also opened at the Everyman. *One for the Road* appeared in 1976, *Stags and Hens* in 1978, *Educating Rita* in 1980, *Blood Brothers* in 1982, *Our Day Out* (originally a television play for the BBC in 1976 and later adapted for stage) in 1983, and *Shirley Valentine* in 1986.

Although Russell abandoned teaching as a formal career, he served as a Fellow in Creative Writing at Manchester Polytechnic from 1977 to 1978. He is an Honorary Director of the Liverpool Playhouse. He received an honorary M.A. from the Open University, a feature in *Educating Rita,* in 1983. Willy and Annie Russell are co-directors of W.R. Limited, the company that oversees his enterprises, in Liverpool, the city that remains his home. Willy and Annie have three children.

Literary Analysis

Russell is a gifted writer of dramatic comedy. He is a master of dialogue, language, and character. His situations—rubbing two sets of class values together and exposing the foibles of each—create hilarious repartee. Whether it is Rita (*Educating Rita*) innocently deflating the pedantry of the academic world by responding to her tutor's essay topic of how to stage Henrik

Ibsen's *Peer Gynt* with "do it on the radio," or Shirley (*Shirley Valentine*) feeding her husband's minced beef to a neighbor's vegetarian bloodhound because "if God had wanted to create it as a vegetarian dog he wouldn't have created it as a bloodhound would he? He would have made it as a grapejuice hound," or Betty (*Breezeblock Park*) not recognizing the phallic vibrator she unwraps as a joke Christmas gift for what it is, missing completely the double entendre when told it is "an electric organ" and then accepting it as a drinks mixer which she proudly displays on the television set, the effect is the same; the plays make us laugh.

One comic technique that appears in almost all of Russell's plays is the error in communication pun. It occurs partly out of character and partly from dialogue that works at two levels. In *John, Paul, George, Ringo . . . and Bert,* for example, the British ambassador to the United States announces to his wife that they are having an obligatory reception for the now-famous Beatles. She replies, "The who?" The ambassador says, "No, the Beatles." While she is asking a question of fact, he "hears" that she thinks the reception is for The Who, another popular rock-and-roll band. Obviously, her character is unfamiliar with either group. Similarly, in *One for the Road,* Jane, lecturing her friend Pauline about the importance of satisfactory sex for a happy marriage, worries about Pauline's "problem" and asks, "Premature is he? Premature? Far more common than you think." Pauline, responding at another level of dialogue, replies, "No Jane. Dennis was carried for the full nine months." Later, as Pauline tries to stop Jane from delivering a karate blow to a bureau, Jane asks, "Pauline, don't you understand what it is you're protecting?" The "it" to Jane is pornography that she assumes is hidden in the bureau; to Pauline, however, "it" is "a genuine Queen Anne bureau."

Russell's plays question class values, and the comedy derives from conflicts that arise within a given sector of society as well as from the juxtaposition of characters from two divergent social sectors. In both *Educating Rita* and *Shirley Valentine* he explores serious subjects: class distinctions in relationship to cultural norms.

Rita, a married twenty-two-year-old hairdresser, sees education as a means of advancement, and Russell exploits her naive character as she studies with Frank. When she discovers a copy of E.M. Forster's *Howards End,* she observes that it "sounds filthy," and when Frank asks if she knows Yeats, she replies from her culture, "The wine lodge?" Russell never mocks Rita in these cultural encounters, although he does mock her in the play. After some months of "educating," Rita becomes a pretentious know-it-all. She has gone from being someone who wanted to know "the difference between Jane Austen an' Tracy Austin" to being an affected snob. The playwright is never uneven in his treatment, though. The supercilious Frank balks at the idea of seeing an amateur production of Oscar Wilde's *The Importance of Being Earnest,* which prompts Rita to observe, "O, y' an awful snob." By the end of the play both characters have become "educated," and the work closes with verbal comedy and a sight gag. Employing sexual innuendo, Russell has Rita state, "I never thought there was anythin' I could give you. But there is." She seats Frank in a chair, but instead of the implied sex, Russell has her pick up a pair of scissors and announce, "I'm gonna take ten years off of you," a perfect reward for one who she called "a geriatric hippie" in act 1, scene 1. A well-received film version of the play, directed by Lewis Gilbert and starring Michael Caine and Julie Walters (in her film debut reprising her stage role), was released in 1983.

Shirley Valentine wonders where her life has gone. Her children are grown; her husband Joe is more concerned about having his chips and egg on Tuesday and steak on Thursday than with the fact that Shirley spends a good deal of her time drinking wine and talking to her kitchen wall. She had wanted to be a courier or airline hostess and speaks of her envy of a classmate whom she thought pursued the latter career. Ironically, she discovers that the classmate is in reality "a high class hooker." When the opportunity arises for her to go to Greece, Shirley worries that people will think "it's for the sex" and does not plan to go. After a fight with Joe she decides to make the trip, and she responds to her daughter's observation that "it's disgustin'" by playing on the stereotype: "Yes, that's right, Millandra—I'm going to Greece for the sex; sex for breakfast, sex for dinner, sex for tea an' sex for supper." Once in Greece, Shirley pokes fun at her fellow British travelers. Unlike Shirley, the Walshes find "Greece too Greek for them" and proceed to put it down in comparison to everything and anything British. Shirley comically deflates this snobbishness by pointing out that the "fresh fish" which they are dining on is squid—which sends them packing. She finds comedy in herself as well. When she has her sexual encounter with Costas, she is far from innocent. She knows that he is feeding her a line about her stretch marks being beautiful, "But the thing about him . . . when he gave y' a load of guff—*he* believed it." As in *Educating Rita* and Russell's other works, this play offers the opportunity of escape from a stereotyped or mundane existence, and while much of the comedy arises from taking or talking about taking that chance, Russell seldom shows the ultimate consequences. The potential for change is what is important. Directed by Gilbert, the cinematic adaptation released in 1989 starred Tom Conti and Pauline Collins (in a reprise of her stage role).

Other Russell plays treat class values more satirically. In *Breezeblock Park* sisters Betty and Reeny constantly one-up each other. A living room suite that cost Betty £220 constantly rises in price; when Reeny announces that her new suite is falling apart, Betty points out that "It never does any good gettin' things on the cheap" and by implication leaves Reeny to believe that Betty has paid more. In *Stags and Hens,* Russell satirizes cultural dictates. Linda at her "hen party" refuses "to drink a proper tart's drink" like Babychams, much to the chagrin of her mates and the disgust of her fiancé's friends. She really does not want to go through with her wedding and into the life that she sees awaiting her. When a former boyfriend who has gone to London and become a success turns up as a band member performing at the club, she accepts his offer to leave with him—no commitments—just a ride out of where she is. Again, Russell gives us no certainty that she will realize anything better.

One for the Road satirizes one-upmanship and pretentiousness. It presents Dennis who, having turned forty, takes his revenge on his meaningless and routine life in the estate by decapitating concrete garden gnomes, spray-painting graffiti on common walls, and refusing to participate in the myriad organizations of the estate. He mocks his wife Pauline and their best friends Roger and Jane for calling a simple cottage pie "Hachis au parmentier" and observes that "Before I met Jane I thought lasagne was a Swedish actress, I thought Jane Fonda was a cheese dip, I thought Prunella Scales was a skin disease." His desire to escape—to hit the road as he had done in his youth—is thwarted by Pauline and Roger and Jane as they decide to join him. Their plans to fix up an old bus dissolve into a re-creation of their current lives. When Dennis manages to slip away, the three others momentarily believe that he has really managed to escape, but then he reappears. As with Hickey and the barflies who cannot realize their pipedreams in Eugene O'Neill's *The Iceman Cometh,* something stops him and maybe he will try next year. The play ends with Dennis in front of the television drinking a beer and the indication is that he will never take the chance.

Our Day Out is a musical that follows the euphemistically named "Progress Class" on a day's outing to an amusement park. The trip affords the children a momentary escape from the dreary lives that they live and what we know will be the even drearier lives that they, clearly earmarked as drop-outs, will face after they leave school. The children transform before us; even the "Bored Girls" (whose response to everything is "borin'") eventually enjoy the day. The comedy comes from the children and their clashes with the bus driver, the cafe owners, and Briggs. The bus driver will not allow the children on the bus until they have been checked for "Chocolate and lemonade. We don't allow it. I've seen it on other coaches madam; fifty-two vomitin' kids." Mrs. Kay, the teacher, appeals to his prejudice, and he ends up buying the children sweets for the bus trip, even though his initial surmise was correct; the children are well supplied with goodies. The cafe owner/servers display equal skepticism and cynicism about the children. When the coach approaches one potential stop, the savvy owners spring to action and replace the "Coaches Welcome" sign with one that reads "Absolutely no Coaches." The "new management" at the next stop allows the children in only after marking everything up: "Always soak the passin' trade. Y' never see them again so it don't matter." The children outcheat them, stealing more than they pay for.

Briggs is more formidable. He initially wants to halt the trip, then goes on the outing to keep things under control. Again it is character that provides the comedy. While his statement on how to enjoy an outing—"we sit in our seats . . . We talk quietly"—suggests anything but fun, it is appropriate to his humorless character. When Briggs admonishes a thirteen-year-old for smoking, the boy acknowledges that although his mother does not punish him his father "belts" him. Briggs asks if this is because the boy smokes; the lad replies with simple truth but comic understatement, "Sir, no sir, because I won't give him one," by which Briggs is nonplussed. In the course of the play, Briggs appears to change when one of the children defies him and forces him to recognize that he really hates them, has no hope for them. Carol, the child, almost falls from the cliffs, but Briggs rescues her. Instead of packing them all back home as he had intended, he insists that they go to the fair, an elevating moment. Even Briggs appears transformed, riding rides, wearing funny hats. On the return trip, Briggs offers to develop a roll of film recording the day in the school lab—something that prior to the "day out" he would have seen as using government facilities for personal use. Once back at the school, however, Russell has Briggs discover the film in his pocket and take it out of its canister. As with Dennis in *One for the Road,* change is too much for Briggs. He contemplates the film for a moment and then exposes it.

Blood Brothers, another musical, is a study of social class differences. A twelve-year hit in London's West End, it opened in New York in 1993 and received four Tony nominations. In it Mrs. Johnstone, the British equivalent of a welfare mother, gives one of her twins to an infertile upper-middle-class couple for whom she works as a cleaning woman, but not without extracting the promise that she can continue to work and thereby see her son daily. Mrs. Lyons, the foster mother, grows paranoid in Mrs. Johnstone's daily presence, fires her, and, playing on her superstitions, warns her that the twins will die if they should ever meet; the boys do meet, become playmates, and eventually and ironically become "blood brothers." Comedy comes from cultural difference. Boasting to Eddie, the twin given away, about the amusing things that they do and say when a policeman asks their names and what they are doing, Mickey and his friend Linda tell him they say, "Adolf Hitler" and "waitin' for the ninety-two bus." Eddie takes them at their word. Stopped by a policeman, Eddie gives these replies as Mickey and Linda stare in horror. Irony occurs as the policeman visits each boy's parents. He threatens Mrs. Johnstone with court; he passes off Eddie's prank to the Lyons as nothing but "boys-will-be-boys" goodwill.

Mrs. Lyons becomes more paranoid, ultimately insisting that her family move to the country. The irony of fate decrees the same move for Mrs. Johnstone as well, and the boys and Linda reunite as teens. In a tour de force

scene, Russell contrasts the education which each class receives. In Eddie's public school the headmaster acknowledges that there is "Talk of Oxbridge," even though Eddie gets suspended for refusing to hand over the locket that his birth mother gave him. For Mickey and Linda, however, the teacher shrieks "shut up" to the class, and even the bright child who has the answers is rewarded with "Oh shut up Perkins, y' borin' little turd." Eddie goes to university while Mickey marries Linda, now pregnant by him, and goes into the factory life. Eddie eventually becomes a councilman. Mickey ends up being fired from the factory where Eddie's father is manager. "Living on Hard Times," as one song goes, Mickey is jailed as the result of a botched robbery that his brother Sammy has drawn him into and is put on Valium for his depression. Linda turns to their old mate Eddie for friendship and support. Eddie's "mother" reveals them to Mickey. Mickey, with a gun, threatens Eddie at a council meeting. In a play filled with irony, Russell affords Mickey the ultimate irony. When Mickey asks Mrs. Johnstone, "Why didn't you give me away! I could have been . . . I could have been him!," he fires and kills Eddie as the police fire and kill him.

Summary

While the plays (and film versions of *Educating Rita* and *Shirley Valentine*) are quite funny, Willy Russell asks us to question what we are laughing about. Behind the laughter are larger questions concerning a person's life, his or her individuality, and his or her place in society. Russell appropriately chooses comedy as his medium, for there he can make a clear and potent subversive statement on life in a class society, and he keeps us laughing while he is doing so.

Selected Bibliography

Primary Sources

Breezeblock Park. London: Samuel French, 1978.

Educating Rita, Stags and Hens, and Blood Brothers. London: Methuen, 1988. With introductions both informative and witty by the playwright.

"John, Paul, George, Ringo . . . and Bert." Ts. C., W.R. Limited. Courtesy of the playwright.

Our Day Out. London: Methuen Young Drama, 1988.

Shirley Valentine and One for the Road. London: Methuen, 1989. With introduction both informative and witty by the playwright.

Secondary Sources
Debusscher, Gilbert. "*Educating Rita;* Or an Open University *Pygmalion.*" In *Communiquer et traduire: Hommages a Jean Dierickx/Communicating and Translating: Essays in Honour of Jean Dierickx.* Ed. Gilbert Debusscher and Jean-Pierre Van Noppen. Brussells: Eds. de l'Univ. de Bruxelles, 1985, pp. 303–17. Discussion of Rita's self-discovery and liberation through the educational process.
Gilby, Liz. "The Man from Liverpool." *Plays International,* 6, 1 (August 1990): 14–15. A brief introduction and commentary on the playwright.

Jones, Christopher Nigel. "Populism, the Mainstream Theater, and the Plays of Willy Russell." Dissertation, Ohio State University, 1990. Jones argues the importance of mainstream theater as a vehicle for populism using Russell's theatrical success as a model. Provides a historical and critical analysis of Russell's career. Includes an appendix with a personal interview with the author.
McGrath, John. *A Good Night Out—Popular Theater: Audience, Class and Form.* London: Methuen, 1981. While not a study of Russell or his plays, this study includes a discussion of the nature of popular theater, an important element in Russell's work.
Russell, Willy. Personal interview. June 10, 1991.

Mary Free

R

S

Saki

Born: Akyab, Burma, December 18, 1870
Education: Exmouth; Bedford Grammar
School
Died: Near Beaumont-Hamel, France, No-
vember 14, 1916

Biography

Hector Hugh Munro was born in Akyab, Burma, on December 18, 1870, the third child of Charles Augustus Munro, a Burma police official of Scottish descent, and Mary Frances Munro. At the age of two, Hector and his older brother and sister were put in the care of a pair of maiden aunts near Barnstaple, north Devon, because their father was rarely in England. The children's mother had returned to the safety of England to bear a fourth child and had been frightened to death on a quiet country lane when she was charged by a wild sow.

The aunts imposed a rigorously Victorian regime on their young charges. This included schooling at Exmouth and Bedford Grammar School. Hector escaped, first to a country house near the aunts and then in 1893, at the age of twenty-three, to Burma where a stint as a military policeman was ended after a year by bouts of tropical fever.

In 1896, Munro went up to London and began a literary career. His first published works were political satires à la Lewis Carroll which appeared in the *Westminster Gazette* and collected in book form as *The Westminster Alice* in 1902. In 1900, his serious book *The Rise of the Russian Empire* was published. Simultaneously, the short stories for which he is best remembered had begun to appear in various periodicals. These were collected in *Reginald* (1904) and *Reginald in Russia* (1910).

Munro's experiences in the Balkans, Warsaw, and St. Petersburg as a correspondent for the *Morning Post* provided the background for the latter volume. He went to Paris in 1906 as a correspondent and returned to England in 1908 where he continued to write both political pieces and stories for the *Morning Post* and other papers. A third story anthology, *The Chronicles of Clovis*, appeared in 1911, followed by two novels: *The Unbearable Bassington* (1912) and *When William Came* (1913). One more volume of stories appeared in his lifetime, *Beasts and Super Beasts* (1914). This was followed by two posthumous collections, *The Toys of Peace* (1919) and *The Square Egg* (1924), which also contained three plays and his sister Ethel's biography of her brother.

The restrictive environment in which he grew up made Munro an ardent practical joker specializing in jokes on the stuffily respectable, both in life and in fiction. Thrilled as a child by history, particularly the brutalities of Russian history, he looked to war as a proving ground for higher values and enlisted enthusiastically in World War I, a war that he had foreseen as the ultimate test of England's valor. Refusing a commission, he fought valiantly in the trenches and died from a sniper's bullet on November 14, 1916, near Beaumont-Hamel in France.

Literary Analysis

Munro never married—his closest female companion was his sister Ethel. She jealously guarded her brother's reputation, refusing permission for adaptations of his works and destroying all of his papers except those which she chose to include in her memoir. Though the pseudonym "Saki," taken from the name of the companion addressed in *The Rubáiyát of Omar*

Khayyám, seems to suggest a mythical stance not to be taken too seriously, and though his stories abound in epicene audacities, bizarre twists, hints of the supernatural, flashes of wit, and clever paradoxes, Munro was one of the generation of idealistic and serious-minded young men destroyed by the First World War, and his intensity often shows through the glittering surface of his stories.

Intended for newspaper publication, Saki's short stories rarely exceed 3,000 words in length. As with the sonnet form, the restrictions of the short-short format often call forth a writer's most distilled and focused concentration. "Tobermory," "The Open Window," "Sredni Vashtar," and "The Schwartz-Metterklume Method," the most frequently anthologized of the satirical short stories, are still widely read.

Saki's stories frequently recount pranks that reveal the insularity and stuffiness of Edwardian life, the vindictiveness beneath the surface of the rector's croquet party, the supernatural lurking just beyond the topiary at the polite countryhouse weekend. His continuing heroes are prankish and aristocratic youths with perfect profiles and a disdain for the beastly stuffiness of the bourgeoisie—superbeasts: Clovis, Reginald, and Bertie. Sometimes, however, and inconsistent with his overall misogyny, his protagonist will be a young woman: the inventive Vera of "The Open Window," or Mrs. Gurtleberry's niece in "The Mappined Terraces," for instance.

Comus Bassington of Munro's first novel, *The Unbearable Bassington,* chooses to be the sort of rotter for whom Munro felt a not entirely unmixed disdain, a young man who chooses to become "the Limit as Beasts go," relying on "youth and health and good looks." His adventures bring him into contact with almost everything and everyone that Munro dislikes: gossip mongers, women novelists, voguish foreign painters, and a pretentious popular playwright named "Sherard Blaw." All options closed to him in this seamy world, Comus dies of jungle fever at a forgotten colonial outpost.

Munro's second novel, *When William Came,* predicts the fall of England to Kaiser Wilhelm in a war that anticipates World War I. More a series of satirical sketches than a novel, the book suggests that British society has grown so effete that England would offer no resistance to a conqueror. Only the Boy Scouts resist German suzerainty. Elitist and chauvinistic at heart, Saki expected the worst from Jews, artists, most of the aristocracy, the middle class, and women, but hoped, a bit faintly, for a resurgence of patriotic nationalism. In his sketches of fashionable life under German occupation he dwells not on how changed British society might be but rather on its continuing and comical pettiness and imperturbability in the face of what should be a humiliating disaster.

The humor in Saki's early stories frequently follows the pattern of Oscar Wilde's witticisms—the inversion of pious platitudes. His "Scandal is merely the compassionate allowance which the gay make to the humdrum" owes much to Wilde's "Hypocrisy is the tribute vice pays to virtue." Reginald's remarks on a truthful woman are clearly derived from Wilde's "Decay of Lying": "It is so easy to slip into the habit of telling the truth in little matters. And then it becomes difficult to draw the line at important things, until at last she took to telling the truth about her age." This Wildean apprenticeship equipped Saki with an ear for paradox, oxymoron, understatement, anticlimax, and *le mot juste,* elements of a perfectly honed style that one critic has characterized as "smooth as a shave with a new razor-blade."

If Saki's humor depended solely on the satiric elements, his works would not have survived. His targets—Jews, suffragettes, pacifists, reformers, the poor—no longer seem to merit his demolition. But his humor redeems the satire, and it is the humor of delight. As A.J. Langguth put it, "He reached that degree of proficiency where the humor came less from his jokes than from the precision of each sentence. The reader laughs with delight at the absolute rightness of his language. Wit may be rebellious in its intent but in its perfection of expression it upholds a universal order."

Munro wrote relentlessly, continuing even in the trenches: history, political satire, newspaper articles, novels, plays, and over a hundred short stories. Some of the stories are little more than sketches spun out to express an intriguing idea or to urge a Tory prejudice. In "The Gala Programme," a late story, suffragettes attempting to disrupt the chariot races on the Emperor Superbus's birthday by lowering themselves into the Circus Maximus are thwarted when the Emperor orders wild beasts loosed upon them. Other tales are wry horror stories that suggest an unseen supernatural element intruding on conventional life. The title beasts in "The Wolves of Cernogratz" flock to the edge of the castle's forest to howl at the death of the aged governess, a true Cernogratz, after ignoring deaths in the *arriviste* family that has purchased the estate.

Perhaps Saki's best works are serious analyses drawn from his deepest personal experience. The plot of "Sredni Vashtar" involves a small boy's worship of a ferocious ferret which he hides in the potting shed, out of the way of his overbearing cousin and guardian, Mrs. de Ropp. Conradin prays to the ferret, which he has named Sredni Vashtar, to "do one thing for him." At the end of the story the ferret kills the pertinacious guardian as she snoops in the shed to see what is engaging the boy's attention. The story concludes: "'Whoever will break it to the poor child? I couldn't for the life of me!' exclaimed a shrill voice. And while they debated the matter among themselves, Conradin made himself another piece of toast." The icy irony of that conclusion puts it on the border between humor and horror, a territory pioneered by Saki and more fully explored by later writers such as John Collier, Evelyn Waugh, and Aldous Huxley.

Mrs. de Ropp was drawn to life, according to Munro's sister, from his hated Aunt Augusta. She "would never, in her honestest moments, have confessed to herself that she disliked Conradin, though she might have been dimly aware that thwarting him 'for his own good' was a duty which she did not find particularly irksome." Seeing her enter the shed to search for his ferret/god, Conradin fears that she will soon emerge "with that pursed smile he loathed so well on her face."

Though some of Saki's stories can sustain themselves on the level of satiric attack, others, because of their anti-Semitism, misogyny, militarism, and other Tory prejudices, now fall flat. Whatever the ostensible satiric thrust of the stories, it is on the level of stylistic audacity that Saki achieves that rare form of humor—delight. Writing of a miserly woman in "The Strategist," Saki says that she "adopted a protective, elder-sister attitude towards money in general, irrespective of nationality or denomination. Her energetic intervention had saved many a rouble from dissipating itself in tips in some Moscow hotel, and francs and centimes clung to her instinctively under circumstances which would have driven them headlong from less sympathetic hands." The passage opens with ironic praise of the woman's "protective elder sister attitude" toward money. Pushing such terms of moralistic cant to the extreme, Saki continues, praising her freedom from prejudice. The word-

play on "denomination" which switches the word from its religious to its monetary denotation sets up an opportunity to describe the fate of roubles, francs, and centimes in similarly evangelical terms. He endows these coins with human traits and plays on the idioms of moral uplift that invest the other sense of "denomination." These coins "saved from dissipation" and "clinging instinctively" to the woman's rectitudinous hands decrease in value, tapering off to mere centimes in a diminuendo of petty parsimony as the diction cumulates pietisms. Women and religion were frequent targets of Saki's satire, but neither the hypothetical miser nor Christian charity is really much the worse for Saki's satire, and the reader's pleasure is in the display of playfulness and mental exuberance. Though such a passage might seem the result of careful calculation and revision, a friend observed that Saki wrote quickly and without correction, which may explain how this complex passage retains a sense of great mental energy, playfulness, and spontaneity.

The editor of the *Spectator*, a paper for which Saki often wrote, reflected after his death that Saki might never gain a wide audience: "He had great gifts—wit, mordant irony, and a remarkable command of ludicrous metaphor—but an intermittent vein of freakish inhumanity belied his best nature, and disconcerted the plain person." To many, caviar has an offensively fishy taste and is much too salty. Nevertheless, Langguth suggests that the pious sentimentalities which Saki outraged have vanished and that his individuality and audacity make him a modern writer: "Saki, aloof and condescending to his own times, turns out to be one of us."

It is tempting to reduce Saki's emotional life to an attempt to stand for everything that his aunts hated most and to diagnose his works as fantasies of prankish vengeance on his guardians and their ilk. (Ethel angrily replied to that assertion when Graham Greene made it in a review, insisting that she and Hector had enjoyed a happy if sheltered childhood.) But at his best, Saki relished exposing the follies of Edwardian society in a prose style which retains its power to enliven and delight.

Summary

Political commentator, world traveler, historian, playwright, journalist, and author, H.H. Munro brought a cosmopolitan sophistication to bear on the narrowness of British life. Polished, focused, elegant, and vindictive, the short stories that he wrote under the pseudonym of Saki satirized the myopic smugness of Edwardian England in a style which seems both flippantly playful and perfectly eloquent. Though his most cherished ideals now seem as quaint and misinformed as the notions that he satirized, the genres of short-short fiction which he pioneered opened new territory for later writers, and his best work remains widely appreciated for its perfect craftsmanship and audacious imaginativeness.

Selected Bibliography

Primary Sources
The Rise of the Russian Empire. London: Grant Richards, 1900.
The Westminster Alice. London: *The Westminster Gazette*, 1902.
The Collected Edition. New York: Viking, 1927–1929. Eight volumes including the novels, stories, and plays with introductions by A.A. Milne, Maurice Baring, H.W. Nevinson, Hugh Walpole, Rothay Reynolds, Sir John Squire, Lord Charnwood, and J.A. Spender. *The Square Egg*, 1929, includes Ethel Munro's biography.
The Complete Works of Saki. New York: Dorset, 1988. Introduction by Noel Coward.

Secondary Sources

Books
Gillen, Charles H. *H.H. Munro (Saki)*. New York: Twayne, 1969. A sympathetic critical exploration of Munro's career.
Langguth, A.J. *Saki: A Life of Hector Hugh Munro With Six Stories Never Before Collected*. New York: Simon and Schuster, 1981. A carefully researched biography based on interviews and unpublished papers. Illustrated with photographs and drawings. Langguth frequently draws on passages from the stories in describing Munro's life. This will probably remain the definitive biography.
Otto, Don Henry. *The Development of Method and Meaning in the Fiction of Saki*. Doctoral dissertation, University of Southern California, 1969. Otto traces Saki's sensibility to Oscar Wilde, cynicism, Toryism, Friedrich Nietzsche, and heroic romanticism.
Spears, George J. *The Satire of Saki*. New York: Exposition, 1963. Spears notes satiric elements in stories, plays, novels, and political articles.

Articles
Cheikin, Miriam Quen. "Saki: Practical Jokes as a Clue to Comedy." *English Literature in Transition*, 9 (1980): 121–37. Cheikin argues that Munro produces a comedy of character rather than mere satire.
Drake, Robert. "Saki: Some Problems and a Bibliography." *English Fiction in Transition*, 5, 1 (1962): 6–26. An extensive and analytical bibliography of Saki criticism by one of his most prolific academic critics.
Orel, Harold. "H.H. Munro and the Sense of Failed Community." *Modern British Literature*, 4, 2 (Fall 1979): 87–96. Orel reexamines Saki's novels and points out the limitations of Saki's social vision.
Note: *English Literature in Transition* periodically updates critical references to Munro in its bibliography numbers.

William Donnelly

Scoggin, John

Born: late 1300s
Died: early-late 1400s

Biography

The identity of "Scoggin," the hero of a durable and popular jestbook of the sixteenth and seventeenth centuries, may well be a matter of confusion of identities. In the mid-1500s, a jestbook appeared entitled "Geystes of Skoggon." The earliest extant fragments date from 1565, and the earliest complete copy is from 1626, although probably there were editions as early as 1545. Though the pamphlet itself is anonymous, later editions say that it was compiled by Andrew Boorde, a scholar, a physician, ambassador, and itinerant factotum. "Compiled" is a good word for it: several of Scoggin's jests are thefts from other sources, notably from *Howleglas* and from the jests of John Skelton. As a jestbook hero, Scoggin represents both the humor and the social tensions of his times.

But, who was "Scoggin"? His identity may include those of up to three men: Henry Scogan, John Scoggin, and John Skelton. Henry Scogan or Scoggin (1361?-1407) was a poet and friend of Geoffrey Chaucer and dedicated a verse epistle to him. This Scogan was born in

Norfolk and had a brother, John, and a son, Robert. He attended King Richard II on his ill-advised expedition to Ireland, and he became a tutor to the four sons of King Henry IV. It is possible that some of his poems became mixed up with those of Chaucer. (He may have written the lovely poem "Flee fro the prees and dwelle with soothfastnesse.") Somehow during the Renaissance this learned, literate man became associated with the life of a madcap humorist—possibly through a remark by John Leland about his jocose wit. Ben Jonson, one of the best-read men in Elizabethan England, thought that the "Scogan" of the jests was this Scogan.

The "Scoggin" of the "Geystes," however, is named John. Again, outside of the jestbook bearing his name, there is no evidence that he ever existed. He is said to have been the court fool of Edward IV and to have flourished around 1480. This Scoggin, says his book, graduated with an M.A. from Oxford University. The plague drove him out of Oxford to St. Bartholomew's hospital in 1470. He moved to London, thence to Bury, then obtained the post of fool in the household of Sir William Neville, through whom he became popular at the court of Edward IV. He served Edward as a semi-official court fool until he offended the King and was banished. He left for Paris and was at first well received. Evidently, fools cannot leave well enough alone, though: banished from Paris, Scoggin returned to England, regained favor with Edward and his queen, died, and was buried on the east side of Westminster Abbey under one of the spouts of the leads ("for I have ever loved good drinke all the dayes of my life"). None of this can be corroborated, not even his burial site, which is now occupied by the chapel of Henry VII.

The third name to be reckoned with is that of John Skelton, laureate and court poet for kings Henry VII and Henry VIII. Skelton was the subject of his own jestbook, which appeared at about the same time as the "Geystes," and he and Scogan are often mentioned in the same breath; indeed, the first line of *Merie Tales Made by Master Skelton* tells us that "Skelton was an Englishman born, as Scogan was." Many facts of Skelton's life parallel those of Scoggin's: Oxford educated, career as court wit. For the next two centuries, "jests of Skelton" and "jests of Scoggin," often confused with one another, became proverbial for wit, low humor, and buffoonery.

Literary Analysis

Scoggin's *Jests* begins with what appears to be an improvised epigraph from Scoggin himself. The quatrain, which stands for the irreverence and excremental vision of the whole collection, became famous in its own right:

A Master of Art is not worth a * * * *,
Except he be in Schooles,
A Bachelor of Law is not worth a strawe,
Except he be among fooles.

This verse immediately classes him as a literary fool: a character with overtones of the jester, the minstrel, the satirist, and the sot. Scoggin's jests are a *Schwankenbiographie*, or "jest-biography," a Renaissance genre of popular fiction in which a series of tales is organized around a central character, often with the rough outlines of a birth, career, and death. The prototype, and quite possibly the book that got it all started, was the Till Eulenspiegel stories which came into English as *Howleglas*. Along with Howleglas and Skelton, Scoggin is one of the three great jest-heroes of the sixteenth century in England. These books were part of the rage for "fool" literature that lasted for a century and a half in Europe.

Scoggin is both jester and wandering fool, a person who is so idiotic that he might be a genius. In his way with words, his many-sidedness, he reveals the foolishness hiding in the world's wisdom. One comic technique is to take a turn of phrase, word, or command absolutely literally. In one tale, a group of wise men ask Scoggin to identify the center of the world. His reply is "Here, where I stand. If you will not beleeve me, then do you take a coard and measure it." In one sense, Scoggin has idiotically misunderstood the question. In another sense, however, he is unassailably correct: the center of each individual's world is where he or she stands. The jest also mocks the uselessness of the question and the impossibility of determining the answer (what "coard" would be long enough to measure it? And, any cord stretched around the world would end where it began, thus establishing any given point as a "center").

In another jest, Scoggin is asked, "How many dayes were past since Adams creation till this time?" His answer turns the question into a jest that is both stupid and literally accurate: "Marry quod Scoggin there be but seaven dayes past: for when the weeke is done, beginneth still another seaven dayes, and so foorth to the end of the world." What is interesting about both this jest and the one above is that they were stolen from the jests of *Howleglas*.

When a lawyer advises him to "make an heir," Scoggin goes home to his wife, hops in bed with her, and begins to make an air of a foul sort. When even Scoggin can't stand it any longer, he returns to the lawyer and lambastes him for his foul advice. In this instance, the narrator assures us that "Scogin knew what was spoken and turned it to a jest," but usually the case is not so clear-cut.

Again like Howleglas, Scoggin is a specialist in practical jokes. Sometimes these can take on political overtones. He begins to roast a pig outside the king's gate, and as he does so, he bastes the pig around the buttocks. When asked why, he replies, "I doe as kings and lords and every man else doth: for he that hath enough shall have more, and he that hath nothing shall go without, and this sow needed no basting nor greasing, for she is fat enough, yet shall shee have more than enough." In another joke, again with political overtones, Scoggin gets the king to allow him to say the *Ave Maria* in his ear each day. Powerful people, seeing this, assume that Scoggin has clout at court. The result: they give him "many gifts and rewards of gold and silver."

He is banished from Edward's court because of a hilarious practical joke in which he introduces the queen to Mrs. Scoggin, having informed each woman beforehand that the other was deaf. When he returns to England from France, he gains forgiveness from the king and queen by lying by the highway and pretending to be dead. When the king and queen say, "Now . . . God forgive him, and wee do," Scoggin leaps up and cries, "I do thank both your Graces, and hereafter I will no more displease you: for I see it is more harder to keepe a friend, then to get one." Like Howleglas, Scoggin deceives a wide range of different people: priests, kings, tapsters, doctors, drapers, shoemakers. Like Howleglas, he uses excrement as a tool of humor (as when he takes a powder to be taste-tested by the local apothecary, who discovers that it is made of dog turds); like Skelton, he wages pointless and irreverent battle with the hypocritical clergy.

Summary

Scoggin (with Skelton) is mentioned so often in the sixteenth and seventeenth centuries that we can confidently accept that his jests were read and retold many times. His popularity attests to a cult of the underdog in the Renaissance, an era in which, again and again, we see jesters, fools, and wandering sots getting the best of much better, more powerful men. In this way humor often purchases a momentary sense of role-reversal and power for the powerless; the symbolic victories-through-defeat of Scoggin and his compeers suggest the social tensions of the era.

Selected Bibliography

Primary Source
Scoggin's Jests. Ed. W. Carew Hazlitt. London: Old English Jest Books, 1866. This is an original-spelling edition of the jests of Scoggin, based on the 1626 edition. There is also an informative introduction and notes.

Secondary Sources
Lee, Sidney. "John Scogan." In *Dictionary of National Biography.* Ed. Sir Leslie Stephen and Sidney Lee. 21 vols. Oxford: Oxford University Press, 1960. Vol. 17, pp. 940–41.
Wardroper, John. "Borde and Scoggin." In *Jest upon Jest.* London: Routledge & Kegan Paul, 1970, pp. 198–99. Wardroper discusses the role of Andrew Boorde in compiling and perhaps authoring the tales of Scoggin.
Zall, P.M. *A Nest of Ninnies and Other Jestbooks of the Seventeenth Century.* Lincoln: University of Nebraska Press, 1970. This is a modern-spelling edition of some of the jests of Scoggin, taken from a late-seventeenth-century edition, along with a helpful introduction.

John Timpane

Seaman, Owen

Born: London, September 18, 1861
Education: Mill Hill School, 1873–1878; Shrewsbury School, 1878–1880; Clare College, Cambridge University, 1880–1883; Classical Tripos, First Class, 1883
Died: London, February 2, 1936

Biography

Son of William Mantle Seaman, dealer in women's garments, and his wife Sarah Ann, Owen Seaman was born on September 18, 1861, at 199 Sloane Street, Chelsea, where his father traded. At Mill Hill School (1873–1878), Shrewsbury School (1878–1880), and Clare College, Cambridge (1880–1883), he was a brilliant pupil and a keen cricketer and oarsman. His formal education culminated with the gaining of a First Class in the Cambridge Classical Tripos. During the decade that followed, he taught at two public schools and the Durham College of Science, and also lectured extramurally. He was in the United States in the summer of 1892, having been invited to teach at Chatauqua.

In 1893, his father died. Settling in London, at the family home, Tower House, Putney Hill, with his mother and an unmarried sister, Seaman was called to the Bar in 1897, but never practiced. His verse appeared in various periodicals. His first contribution to *Punch* was printed in 1894; in 1897 he was made a member of the *Punch* Table, and in 1902 he became assistant editor. At the end of that year he traveled to India, together with the novelist Pearl Craigie (John Oliver Hobbes), whom he wooed in vain, to report on the durbar following the coronation of Edward VII.

In 1906, he succeeded Sir Francis Burnand as editor of *Punch*. He was knighted in 1914. His work for *Punch* was particularly appreciated during the First World War; he was widely congratulated for keeping up the morale of the nation through those gray years. Among the staff, Seaman's closest friend was the conservative Raven Hill; the liberal A.A. Milne felt compelled to leave the journal, and throughout the General Strike *Punch*'s stance was militantly right-wing. Seaman gave up the editorship reluctantly in 1932, received a baronetcy in the next New Year Honors List, and on February 2, 1936, after a short, aimless retirement, he died of pneumonia in London, at his flat in Whitehall Court.

Literary Analysis

Lord Rosebery, in a letter in 1895, found that Seaman's verse recalled "the old masters, Frere and Ellis, and Praed and Canning." Seaman himself acknowledged only one master, Charles Stuart Calverley, and Calverley's buoyant spirit and technical tricks (such as the short final line) are conspicuous in his work. Both men were Cambridge classicists.

Seaman was a prolific writer. During his early schoolmastering and college lecturing years, he found time to publish two volumes—*Oedipus the Wreck* and *With Double Pipe* (both in 1888) —and he was responsible for most of *Paulo-*

postprandials (1883). After settling in London in 1893, he had more leisure time, and his contributions to the magazine *Granta,* whose Cambridge editors idolized Calverley for his craftsmanship and youthfulness, were collected in *Horace at Cambridge* (1895). *Tillers of the Sand* appeared in the same year; it satirized Rosebery, and its victim declared himself charmed.

It was "A Ballad of a Bun," published in *The World* on March 13, 1895 which, according to C.L. Hind, "confirmed Owen Seaman's career as a parodist." Hind adds: "This delighted London. Even I smiled." The parody has lost its impact now, since few readers know John Davidson's "Ballad of a Nun." As Seaman often remarked, that is the problem with a fine parody; it dies if the subject dies. Davidson was one of a number of John Lane's poets to be chosen by Seaman as victims—"A precious few, the heirs of utter godlihead, / Who wear the yellow flower of blameless bodlihead!"—but Lane was an astute businessman and instead of showing anger he offered to publish a volume of these parodies. *The Battle of the Bays* came out in December 1896. It was very successful.

There is general agreement that as a parodist, in prose as well as verse, Seaman is inferior to Max Beerbohm. In an unpublished lecture he declared that "only a man's friend, in the sense of one who is closely in touch with his work, has the right to parody him." There must be a "loving intimacy," he claimed, yet there is no "loving intimacy" in his contemptuous handling of the "dribbling decadents." It is because Beerbohm had that "loving intimacy" with the decadents that "Enoch Soames" is a classic. Seaman is at his worst with subjects that bring out the schoolmaster in him (as when Aubrey Beardsley is patronized as "Master Aubrey"), but when his victim is someone whom he finds over-solemn, such as Sir Edwin Arnold, or an irredeemable silly ass, such as Alfred Austin, his exuberance can be delightful:

A-nutting went the nimble chimpanzee;
And what, you ask me, am I driving at?
Wait on; in less than twenty minutes we
Shall come to that.

Seaman consolidated his reputation with *In Cap and Bells* (1900), *Borrowed Plumes* (1902), *A Harvest of Chaff* (1904), and *Salvage* (1908) without advancing into any new territory. There was some dissatisfaction over this lack of development, and over the occasional dullness and pedantry. In 1908, the *Times Literary Supplement* saw him as "a kindly uncle of middle age, ready with a smile at his own weakness, and a good humoured laugh at the follies which his shrewd eye detects in his nephews and nieces." The 1914–1918 conflict drew from him three volumes of war verse. There was no further book until *Interludes of an Editor* (1929), the contents of which were chosen from about 1,000 pieces published in periodicals.

Seaman's reputation was practically eclipsed soon after his death, and even contemporaries were sharply divided on him. Hind found his work "a little hard and metallic"; Milne felt that "the virtues flourished where graces should have been." Still, the anonymous memorial verses printed in *Punch* in 1936 identify him as a worthy successor to Calverley and J.K. Stephen, much loved by:

> . . . A generation gone
> Who grew with books like those, and
>   thought it normal
> A man should be a wag although a don
> And, though informed, informal.

As an editor, Seaman could be pedantic, puritanical, and occasionally vile-tempered, yet P.G. Wodehouse remained grateful for his advice and encouragement; with friends he could rollick uninhibitedly, and he learned, at least in his middle years, to appreciate the pleasures of the flesh. Interestingly, he can still arouse bitter dislike in some quarters. His work and life were overshadowed—and chilled—by a dominant, morbidly religious mother and a certain social insecurity, which he acknowledged at least once, because of his background "in trade." However, his gift survived all of this, and so did his humanity.

Summary
Owen Seaman stands firmly in the lively and elegant tradition of English nineteenth- and early twentieth-century light verse. A devoted editor of *Punch* and a prolific writer, he is often dismissed as ultra-conservative and dull, but when natural exuberance triumphed over his puritanical and snobbish background he produced a good deal of work that is pure delight.

Selected Bibliography
Primary Sources
Co-authored with Horace Monro.
> *Paulopostprandials.* Cambridge: Jones &

Piggott, 1883.
Oedipus the Wreck. Cambridge: Elijah Johnson, 1888.
With Double Pipe. Oxford: Blackwell, 1888.
Horace at Cambridge. London: Innes, 1895.
Tillers of the Sand. London: Smith, Elder, 1895.
The Battle of the Bays. London: John Lane, 1896.
In Cap and Bells. London: John Lane, 1900 (1899).
Borrowed Plumes. London: Constable, 1902.
A Harvest of Chaff. London: Constable, 1904.
Salvage. London: Constable, 1908.
Interludes of an Editor. London: Constable, 1929.

Secondary Sources
Adlard, John. *Owen Seaman: His Life and Work.* London: The 1890's Society, 1977.
———. "A note on Owen Seaman." *Keynotes* (newsletter of the 1890's Society) New Series. Vol. 1, n. 1, June 1985, pp. 4–5.
Graves, C.L. Biographical and critical *Introduction to Owen Seaman: A Selection.* Ed. Raymond Clement Brown and Mary Sanders. London: Methuen, 1937, pp. xv–xxvii.

John Adlard

Secombe, Harry Donald
Born: Swansea, Wales, September 8, 1921
Education: Dynevor School, Swansea, 1933–1937
Marriage: Myra Joan Atherton, February 19, 1948; four children

Biography
Harry Secombe was born on September 8, 1921, into a working-class family in Swansea, South Wales, the second son and third child of Frederick Ernest Secombe, a commercial traveler for a wholesale grocery firm, and Nellie Lane Gladys Davies. Like Dylan Thomas, another Anglo-Welshman, he has retained strong links with his native country. In his autobiography he confesses to being a less than diligent schoolboy at the Dynevor School in Swansea (1933–1937), but one who loved clowning.

Secombe served with the Royal Artillery in North Africa and Italy during World War II, attaining the rank of lance-bombardier. After suffering from exposure in Italy, he withdrew from active soldiering and joined an army concert party. Upon demobilization Secombe took to the variety stage, then in its last stages of popular esteem. He married Myra Joan Atherton on February 19, 1948; the union produced two sons and two daughters.

Having entertained the troops as an amateur at various garrison theaters, Secombe began to define his talent as a comedian first with a 1946 engagement in *Revuedeville*, a revue at London's Windmill Theatre, which was primarily renowned as a home for "girlie" shows during and after the war. This Vivian Van Dam theater just off Piccadilly Circus was known for its slogan "We Never Close," popularly construed by Londoners as "We never clothe"! In 1948, Secombe graduated to general variety, touring the circuit theaters throughout England and Wales, usually as a second-spot comedian. He also began to find occasional spots on radio as a comedian.

Secombe's first humor success was as a member of the group that came together to create *The Goon Show* (originally called *Crazy People*) for BBC Radio, a show that Spike Milligan later claimed with some justice broke the mold of radio comedy. It ran for nine years, from May 28, 1951, to March 1960, and seems to have retained a worldwide band of devotees.

Secombe is still seen on English-language networks worldwide as the presenter of the British series *Highway*. His burgeoning into a respected television personality has taken him well beyond his first claim on students of humor, namely, as an important member of the cast for the influential *Goon Show*. However, his subsequent career as an actor, singer, and entertainment figure has probably stimulated and enhanced his writing of numerous funny articles and books.

For his charitable work with the Army Benevolent Fund he was awarded a Commander of the British Empire (C.B.E.) in 1963. His popular status as a comedian was underlined by his knighthood (1981), an honor previously accorded to only two other British comedians, Harry Lauder and George Robey. Additional honors that have been bestowed on him include appointment as a Fellow of the Royal Society of Arts in 1971 and an honorary doctorate of music from the University of Wales in 1986.

Secombe has regularly appeared at the London Palladium (ten Royal Command performances between 1951 and 1987). His acting career has embraced one appearance in pantomime and several roles in theater—he appeared in *The Four Musketeers*,[1] *The Plumber's Progress*,[2] and in a leading role in the musical *Pickwick*.[3] He also has appeared in at least nine films, including singing the roles of Bjornsen in *Song of Norway* (1970) and Bumble in Carol Reed's *Oliver!* (1968).

Literary Analysis

Two areas of Secombe's humor invite consideration. Chronologically first is the comic performer using the scripts of others, principally Milligan, in *The Goon Show*. More recently his own prose has been a source of humor: a novel, a partial autobiography, and some short stories.

Sundry selections of *Goon Show* scripts have been published, so it is possible to suggest that these radio texts might be regarded as literary texts. However, since the scripts not only are shorn of the radiophonic sound effects that played an important role in the impact of the original broadcasts but also lack the in-theater sense of live audience that performers found to be so stimulating, it is not entirely fair to use them as a substitute for the BBC program. To some degree these "texts" may work for those already familiar with the typical accents and catch-phrases of the various characters and with the show's zany sound effects. Nevertheless, students of humor are advised to use phonodiscs and tapes of BBC broadcasts in conjunction with the published scripts in analyzing the works.

Secombe played the central role of Neddy Seagoon, which was crucial in most episodes, and a variety of smaller parts. As Seagoon, his part usually called for him to undertake a weekly succession of heroic but wild and stupid tasks. In each weekly farrago of absurd situations, Secombe enjoyed the support of a strong cast of comedians, especially the many-voiced contributions of Peter Sellers, whose talent for mimicry gained him later spectacular success in films. Milligan wrote most of the scripts and also took a leading performing part. The other prominent member of the Goon quartet was Michael Bentine, who left after the second series of shows to pursue an independent career as entertainer. Additional regular contributions to the radio half-hours were by musicians Max Geldray (harmonica) and the Ray Ellington Quartet, who also took on occasional voice roles. *The Goon Show* also featured the Wally Stott Orchestra.

While the scripts for the Goons were written by Milligan, suggestions came from the three other primary performers. The element of fantasy and the surreal is marked, although the material in many of the earlier programs leaned toward social satire, often poking fun at English pomposity, class divisions, and stereotypes. The humor often depends on the taking of a bittersweet, post-war view of the remnants of British Empire, most notably India, where Milligan had been born. The sketches were composed of Seagoon narrating his own typically numbskull exploits and eccentric behavior. One thinks of his characteristically eager signing of a contract to move a piano from one room to another for the princely reward of £5—only to discover that it is the Emperor Napoleon's piano which has to be stolen from the Louvre Museum in Paris and then sailed across the Channel ("in the key of C") to England. Then, again, there is Neddy's quixotic quest to Africa in search of the "Great International Christmas Pudding," where his strange lunatic methods nonsensically bring relative success, and the monster "pud" is finally brought to account. Such surreal scripts often have a marked parodic tendency, especially in topical sketches or in the literary titles ("The Scarlet Capsule" or "The Tay Bridge Disaster," for example).

The dialogues of the *Goon Show*, too, were pervaded with a twisted sense of logic that flowered fully in the contemporary theater of the absurd, especially in the English plays of Harold Pinter or N.F. Simpson. Consider the repartee in the exchange: "My name is Neddy Seagoon," to which the reply is "My! What a memory you have!" ("Napoleon's Piano"). Or again, Seagoon, asked by Daisy if he will have a cappuccino, replies: "No, just coffee." Daisy then enquires, "Black or white?" and he responds, "White, with a dash of milk" ("The Flea").

Goon scripts are filled with preposterous exaggeration, whether it was in the overall program scheme, in the sound effects, or in Secombe's maniacal laughter and nonsense exclamations as Seagoon. Secombe's Seagoon is also the ideal vehicle for puns galore, which were often quite unsophisticated. The popular disparaging phrase "a bit of a Neddy!" may well owe something to the popularity of this British radio show. The Goons certainly launched the "dreaded lurgy" (lurgi) into schoolboy vocabulary worldwide, which reminds one of the once-fashionable cult status of "Goonese."

The members of *The Goon Show* made the most of radio as a medium, but the Goons' wild imaginings and frenetic pace could not translate into the newer medium of television, though an anniversary Goon program was broadcast in the early 1970s. Secombe has characterized the humor as that of young men and ex-servicemen. Here was a show, as Milligan remarked, that catered to people of all ages—especially the Ice, Stone, and Dark. The audience for *The Goon Show*'s twenty-six shows per annum for nine years was measured in the millions.

Secombe's prose will probably never achieve the renown of his radio broadcasts with the Goons. As a laughter-maker, he appears to be man of the stage rather than the page. A number of his books are also being published in the large-print format, which may indicate his market niche. The prose reminiscences and stories inevitably hinge on his wartime, theater, or broadcasting experiences. In chapter 19 of *Goon for Lunch* (1975), he gives a lengthy description of a typical broadcast day at the Camden Theatre for *The Goon Show*. In this book, he also makes the claim that the show was aimed at "an anarchy in comedy" (141) and replaced established forms of English comedy. Some of Secombe's stories that are collected in *Goon for Lunch* (1975) and *Goon Abroad* (1982) had been published in the English magazines *Punch* and *Argosy*. The author is especially drawn to anecdotes pertaining to his own career as a variety entertainer; some of them touchingly tell of fears and failures and, refreshingly, many of the stories are told against himself, though their tone is "sunny side up."

Secombe's recent and very readable autobiography, *Arias and Raspberries* (1989), is structured as a series of chronologically arranged stories about different episodes in his life. Typically, these accounts put a cheerful face on embarrassing moments, as in the incident when Secombe played "the world's worst Dame" in pantomime, complete with a Groucho Marx moustache; he never repeated that role. In his novel *Twice Brightly* (1974)—he seldom resists a pun!—Secombe presents a thinly disguised fictional account of a dispirited actor/entertainer on tour at a dreary old theater in a depressing part of the world.

The characteristic trait in Secombe's prose humor is linked to the common nature of his stage persona. His prose does not approach the imaginative zest of Milligan's *Goon Show* scripts. Instead, the humor in *Arias and Raspberries*, for example, is characteristically broad rather than subtle, accepting rather than subversive, and benign rather than abrasive. In the first volume of his autobiography—a second is promised—and in both his fiction and books of theater reminiscences, there is rarely a sally of wit, but Secombe is well able to project an image of the jolly, irrepressible fellow and comes across as an unfailingly lovable personality, much in keeping with his stage portrayals of Humpty Dumpty in pantomine and Pickwick in the musical.

Secombe's ability to charmingly narrate moments in his career that show the writer in a less than flattering light is pronounced and the source of much humor. There is, for example, his account of a breezy visit by Field-Marshal Bernard Montgomery with his troops in the African desert on a day when the young l/ bombardier's boils were at their worst, his spectacles cracked, and mud clung unrelentingly. Secombe's appearance may well have unnerved the commander-in-chief but the future humorist's enthusiastic if polite platitude at the close of his chief's speech probably did far more damage. The writer seems drawn to cheerful recountings of low moments such as a nervous demonstration of his shaving act before impresario Vivian Van Damm, or recalling a moment at the bar of a theater in Leeds prior to his act when beer was spilled down his white front by a man who merely wanted to say that his wife hated the comedian's act. Other such material includes the laconic Barnsley man who alleged that the humorist's act had almost drawn a laugh out of him, and the manager in Bolton, who, unaware of the nature of the comedian's schtick, fired Secombe for shaving on stage on the manager's time!

Summary

Harry Secombe rose from a second-spot comedian in revues to national fame as a member of *The Goon Show*. Subsequently, he recounted many of his humorous adventures in a number of amusing books.

Notes

1. A comedy-musical, *The Four Musketeers* (book by Jon Pertwee, lyrics by Herbert Kretzmer), produced at the Theatre Royal, Drury Lane, London, enjoyed a run of 462 performances from December 5, 1967, to January 18, 1969. It was panned by the critics—and some were venomous. This confection was written for Secombe as a follow-up to his UK success with *Pickwick*. It was a whimsical travesty of Alexandre Dumas's three originals, now joined by Secombe as the fourth musketeer in Paris. The lyrics and music were subpar; cast defections resulted in numerous crises. The whole production lost the Delfont management over £50,000. Only Secombe's presence in the principal role (acting as a sort of countrified D'Artagnan) kept the show going for fourteen months.

2. *The Plumber's Progress*, a comedy by Cecil P. Taylor loosely adapted from the German play *Burger Schippel* by Carl Sternheim, was an English premiere. The caliber of play is a notch or so above the popular entertainments usually associated with Secombe on stage. It opened October 8, 1975, at the Prince of Wales Theatre, London, but had closed by March 1976. Secombe played a proletarian plumber who rose to social respectability by being able to sing.

3. The musical, based on Charles Dickens' stories, *Oliver!* was a custom-built vehicle for Secombe (the book by Wolf Mankowitz was commissioned by impresario Delfont). It opened for a couple of weeks in Manchester (June 3, 1963) before transferring to London's West End stage at the Saville Theatre, where it ran from July 4, 1963, to February 27, 1965, a total of 694 performances. Secombe was in the title role as Samuel Pickwick. Then, sponsored by David Merrick, *Oliver!* headed for the United States with Secombe in the title role, opening in San Francisco for a seven-week season at the Curran Theater, beginning on April 19, 1965. The West Coast success was not repeated on Broadway; opening on October 4, 1965, at the Forty-Sixth Street Theater, the show closed after a mere fifty-six performances on November 20, 1965.

Selected Bibliography

Primary Sources
The Romantic Wales of Harry Secombe in Picture and Song. Norwich: Jarrold, 1973.

Twice Brightly. London: Robson, 1974; New York: St. Martin's Press, 1975.

Goon for Lunch. Walton-on-Thames: M & J Hobbs; London: Joseph, 1975; New York: St. Martin's Press, 1976.

Katy and the Nurgla. Harmondsworth, Middlesex: Puffin, 1978.

Welsh Fargo. London: Robson, 1981.

Goon Abroad. London: Robson, 1982.

Harry Secombe's Highway. London: Robson, 1984; Oxford: Isis, 1984.

The Highway Companion. London: Robson, 1987.

Arias and Raspberries. London: Robson, 1989; Oxford: Isis, 1990; pbk. London: Fontana, 1991.

The Second Highway Companion, with Ronnie Cass. Oxford: Isis, 1990.

Secondary Sources

Briggs, Asa. *The History of Broadcasting in the United Kingdom*. 4 vols. London and New York: Oxford University Press, 1961. Volume 4, *Sound and Vision*, is especially relevant; Briggs singles out the Goons as one element pointing toward the dissolution of immediate post-war attitudes within the country (iv, 18).

Busby, Roy. *British Music Hall—An Illustrated Who's Who from 1850 to the Present Day*. London: Paul Elek, 1976. A useful encyclopedia, though not all inclusive.

Fawkes, Richard. *Fighting for a Laugh*. London: Macdonald and Jane's, 1978. A history of ENSA and other entertainment for the armed forces in World War II.

Fisher, John. *Funny Ways to be a Hero*. London: Frederick Muller, 1973. An appraisal of popular comic heroes over a period of fifty years, from Dan Leno via Tony Hancock and Harry Secombe to Morecombe and Wise.

Mercer, Derrick. *Chronicle of the Twentieth Century*. London: Chronicle Communications, 1988, p. 753.

Milligan, Spike. *The Goon Show Scripts*. London: Woburn, 1972; pbk. London: Sphere, 1973. Selected, detailed radio scripts by Spike Milligan originally presented from October 1954 through January 1956; includes drawings by Peter Sellers, Secombe, and Milligan.

———. *More Goon Show Scripts*, Foreword by HRH the Prince of Wales. London: Woburn, 1973; New York: St. Martin's Press, 1974; pbk. Sphere, 1974. A selection of scripts from shows broadcast between December 1958 and February 1959.

———, comp. *The Book of the Goons*. London: Robson, 1974. More scripts plus ephemera.

Nathan, David. *The Laughtermakers: A Quest for Comedy*. London: Peter Owen, 1971. See chapters two and three: "Secombe is not just a natural performer; he is only natural when he is performing" (60). Nathan notes Secombe's early talent as an impressionist and devotes a chapter or so to the Goons. He stresses the seminal nature of the Goon Show: "It influenced the whole world of humour" (40).

Palmer, Jerry. "Humor in Great Britain." In *National Styles of Humor*, ed. Avner Ziv. Contributions to the Study of Popular Culture, No. 18. New York: Greenwood, 1988, pp. 85–111. An overview, with emphasis on the twentieth century. Palmer finds *The Goon Show* to be "the best remembered show of the post-war period" and praises its remarkable range of "massively implausible character," the set of "nonsensical situations," and its "elaborate sound effects."

Simon, Ernest Darwin Simon, Baron. *BBC from Within*. London: Gollancz, 1953. Useful background on the status of the BBC's variety department at the time of *The Goon Show*'s emergence.

Took, Barry. *Laughter in the Air*. London: Robson/BBC, 1976. An informal history of radio comedy, including all the important shows with script extracts.

Wilmut, Roger. *From Fringe to Flying Circus: Celebrating a Unique Generation of Comedy, 1960–1980*. London: Eyre Methuen, 1980. Wilmut suggests some of the continuing links of Goon comedy with its immediate successors, the burst of satire on stage and screen. He looks back on the Goons as "a radio comedy series . . . unsurpassed for inventiveness, sheer craziness and an explosive use of the medium" (xvii).

———. *The Goon Show Companion: A History and Goonography, with a Personal Memoir by Jimmy Grafton*. London: Robson, 1976; New York: St. Martin's,

1976; pbk. London: Sphere, 1977. A history of *The Goon Show*, with a complete list of all the transmissions.

———. *Kindly Leave the Stage! The Story of Variety, 1919–1960.* London: Methuen, 1985. A lively look at variety theaters, the music halls, cabaret, and so forth in a period that spans the arrival of radio and television. "The *Goon Show* took surrealistic comedy to a height which has never been matched" (213), according to Wilmut, who also concludes that "if the *Goon Show* took radio comedy to its limit, it also almost killed it off—nothing since then has expanded the field any further" (213).

John S. Batts

Shaffer, Peter Levin

Born: Liverpool, England, May 15, 1926
Education: St. Paul's School, 1942–1944;
Trinity College, Cambridge University,
1947–1950, B.A.

Biography

Nothing in Peter Shaffer's parentage suggested a career in the arts. Born in Liverpool on May 15, 1926, Peter, along with his identical twin brother Anthony, grew up in a middle-class Jewish household. Jack Shaffer, a property company director, took his wife Reka and the family to London in 1936. Although they moved around in the London environs frequently during the Second World War, Peter and Anthony managed to attend prestigious St. Paul's School beginning in 1942. Both were accepted by Trinity College at Cambridge University, but service obligations intervened. Because of eyesight problems they did not qualify for military duty and instead served as Bevin Boys, digging coal in the mines of Kent. In 1947, they enrolled at Trinity where together they edited the college paper.

Peter Shaffer came down from Cambridge in 1950 with a specialty in history but without specific career plans. After holding a variety of jobs, in 1951 he traveled to New York City where he worked at a book shop, retail stores, and the New York Public Library. While living and working in New York City, Shaffer took advantage of the rich theater scene and began to nurture thoughts of writing for the stage. When his jobs in commerce offered little satisfaction, he returned to London in 1954 to work at a large music publishing house. Then *The Salt*

Land, his first play script, was selected to be telecast over ITV, thereby initiating his career in the theater. From that moment forward, Shaffer has devoted his efforts to the stage.

Paradoxically, during this same period, Shaffer also earned a reputation as a writer of fiction with the publication of three mystery novels: *The Woman in the Wardrobe* (1951), *How Doth the Little Crocodile?* (1952), and *Withered Murder* (1955). (The latter two were co-authored with his twin Anthony, who later was to earn a Tony for his mystery drama *Sleuth*.) Two other broadcast dramas by Shaffer were aired in 1957, the unpublished radio play *The Prodigal Father* over BBC Radio, and *Balance of Terror* (also unpublished) over BBC Television. Shaffer has written film scripts as well, including an adaptation of William Golding's *Lord of the Flies* with Peter Brook (1963), an Oscar-nominated movie script of *Equus* (1977), and his Oscar-winning movie script for *Amadeus* (1984).

All the same, the live theater remains Shaffer's paramount interest. The high costs of producing plays in New York means that Shaffer usually opens his works first in London, then transfers them to Broadway. A vigorous man, Shaffer continues to write steadily, staging new works every few years. He resides half of each year in New York City and half in London.

Literary Analysis

Shaffer puzzles some critics today because of the diversity of his dramatic styles and thematic interests. That diversity makes him difficult to categorize within tidy literary designations. In certain of his dramas he seems to be a realist probing psychological and social issues. At the same time he emerges as a metaphysical striver who seeks answers to universal questions. He has won numerous awards for such serious dramas as *Five Finger Exercise* (1958), *The Royal Hunt of the Sun* (1964), *Equus* (1973; which received a Tony Award), *Amadeus* (1979; another Tony), and *Yonadab* (1985). Only *The Battle of Shrivings* (1970; rewritten as *Shrivings*, 1973) failed to win an audience.

Shaffer has also shown himself a brilliant, teasing farceur who targets mundane human follies. His sharp and deft comic writings often are overlooked because of his impressive success with serious drama, but he has, indeed, written many fine comedies. Not counting his comic sketch for the American television series *That Was the Week That Was* (1963) and the skit

"The Merry Roosters' Panto" (1963), written as a Christmas piece for director Joan Littlewood's Theatre Workshop, the author has half a dozen successful comedies to his credit: *The Private Ear* and *The Public Eye* (one-act plays performed on the same bill, 1962), *Black Comedy* (one-act piece, 1965), *White Lies* (one-acter, 1967; revised as *The White Liars* in 1968 and as *White Liars* also in 1968), and the Tony nominated *Lettice & Lovage* (1990; originally called *Lettice and Lovage* in two slightly different earlier versions from 1987 and 1988). In 1989, Shaffer wrote an extended one-act radio comedy entitled *Whom Do I Have the Honour of Addressing?* which suggests that he has not yet played out the comic vein in his genius.

Although each of Shaffer's serious dramas contains some brilliantly witty dialogue, until recently his comic bent was best represented in the one-act plays that he wrote during the 1960s. All four of those works deal with romantic love, ranging in style and tone from outrageous farce to thoughtful comedy. *The Private Ear* and *The Public Eye* first opened as a double bill in London; their New York premiere came a year later. Both pieces are framed in the conventions of modern realism, with straightforward dialogue which reflects naturalistic psychology and with single interior sets. *The Private Ear* is the more traditional of the two, centering on a young man's first encounter with the logistics of romantic courtship. The plot is simple, comprised of the naive lad's attempt to prepare a dinner date with a girl whom he wishes to impress. Bob is a clumsy young bachelor living in modern-day London who meets Doreen at a symphonic concert and decides to invite her to his flat for dinner. He recognizes his lack of experience with the fairer sex and turns to his playboy friend Ted for advice and help. Not unexpectedly, the smooth but insensitive friend wins the heart of the girl, and this three-person comedy concludes with a frustrated Bob discovering how difficult romantic relationships can be.

One key to the effectiveness of Shaffer's one-acter is the clarity of his characterizations. He makes important distinctions between the young men from the outset. Bob is depicted as nervous, forgetful, and exceedingly gauche, while Ted emerges as older, more suave and experienced, and more cynical. To Ted, Doreen merely represents an opportunity for quick sex for Bob, whom he browbeats, insisting, "You know what you're going to do this evening? I mean, you know what I'm expecting you to do, don't you?" But to Bob, Doreen is an idealized, pure creature—particularly since they met at a symphonic concert. He just wants a friendship with her for the time being. His naivete about sexual matters carries over into basic interrelating, and his ineptness with dinner table conversation quickly sabotages his hopes to impress his date favorably. Ted, meanwhile, is in his glory. Through witty though shallow chatter, Ted delights the superficial Doreen. Meanwhile, Bob witnesses the growing attraction between his friends.

Though he does not ordinarily imbibe, this evening Bob drinks himself into sullenness out of utter frustration. He is enraged to find Ted moving in on Doreen, and he angrily sends his colleague away—though not before Ted and Doreen secretly exchange telephone numbers. When Bob and Doreen are finally alone, he is determined to woo her in his own fashion, by playing lush romantic opera music on his record player—the tie-in with the play's title. Surprisingly, Doreen is touched by the passionate love arias he plays from Giacomo Puccini's opera *Madame Butterfly* and Bob attempts to kiss her. When his actions begin to be more earnest, she slaps him and leaves abruptly. Now faced with the truth about his inadequacies in the arena of love, a bitterly unhappy Bob jams the needle of the record player across the disk, destroying the recording just as his hopes for romantic bliss have been ruined.

Shaffer's bittersweet story gains its humor from the comic attributes of the three characters as much as from the eternal laughter inherent in the irrationalities of first love. Comic quips abound, as when Bob expresses fear that Doreen will not show up for the dinner date: "Do you think she's not coming?" Ted sarcastically responds, "Of course she's coming. It's a free dinner, isn't it?" And when Bob asks Doreen which Bach number she wants to hear on the record player ("Which *Brandenburg* would you like? Or maybe you'd prefer the *Goldbergs*? or the *Musical Offering*"?), the musically illiterate girl, "*Who has never heard of any of these*" (Shaffer's stage note), frantically replies, "You choose." Though Shaffer carves out no new terrain in *The Private Ear,* he reveals a firm control of the traditional comic situation and its comic characters who are immersed in a classic romantic conflict.

The Public Eye, match-mate to *The Private Ear,* also employs a three-person cast to treat a love issue, only this time it is a more mature romantic situation. The play's title parodies the term "private eye," and at the center of the plot is the private detective Julian Cristoforou who is hired by the stuffy, middle-aged businessman Charles Sidley to investigate the suspected infidelity of Sidley's young wife Belinda. A thoroughly enchanting one-acter, *The Public Eye* is a comedic version of the centuries-old May-December marital situation. It features sophisticated wit and sustained good humor that grow out of Shaffer's fresh, clearly delineated characters. Of the play's antagonists, Cristoforou is the freest spirit. The dramatist describes him in stage directions as wearing a white trench coat out of whose pockets the eccentric sleuth regularly retrieves packets of raisins and nuts. Very much the unflappable figure, Cristoforou is more concerned with resolving problems than with imposing moral justice.

Sidley's suspicions are wholly false, as Cristoforou proves by detailing Belinda's daily actions and movements. A sparking individualist in the manner of George Bernard Shaw's heroines, Belinda simply has become disillusioned with her husband's stodgy values which control rather than free her spirit. Sidley, a forty-year-old accountant and egoistic prig, thinks himself a Pygmalion whose duty it is to reshape his twenty-two-year-old bride into a socially acceptable image. When he tries to circumscribe her natural, youthful ebullience, Belinda objects. As she complains to Sidley when he insists on socializing alone with his male cronies, "And where were you? In a stuffy old club, surrounded by coughing old men with weak bladders and filthy tempers, scared of women and all mauve with brandy."

Because of her resulting coolness toward him, Sidley believes that she has found someone else. Cristoforou, however, locates the key to the marriage's weakness. He explains to Belinda, "You're Spirit, Belinda, and he's Letter. You've got passion where all he's got is pronouncement . . . Charles Sidley is half dead, and only his wife can save him." Once the true problem is exposed, the couple agrees to try a reconciliation based on trust and respect for each other's values. *The Public Eye* concludes in high spirits with Cristoforou temporarily taking over Sidley's business while the couple heads off on a second honeymoon.

The Public Eye holds up well over time because of its ever-relevant material. Its good-natured humor is counter-balanced with a playful yet plausible dialectic on marriage. Ultimately, though, it is the liveliness of Shaffer's eccentric trio and the cleverness of his dialogue that make the comedy especially effective and enjoyable.

Black Comedy, written in a burst of comic energy in 1965 to meet a short deadline, manifests a quite different style compared to Shaffer's previous comic works. In short, *Black Comedy* is one of the most brilliant one-act farces of our era. It has been enormously popular with critics and general audiences alike and has been lauded for its wit, imaginativeness, and unrelenting laughter. Shaffer relies on several proven comic techniques in this play. Eight very funny, individualized characters become caught up in countless misunderstandings that create hilarious confusions. Razor-sharp pacing is ingeniously imbedded in the play's script, allowing for the characters' near misses and numerous pratfalls. Critical to the play's production is the device of light-dark reversal traceable to Chinese theater—hence the title "black comedy." The process means lighting the stage brilliantly when the plot implies complete darkness in the action, and then total blackout on stage when the story involves a normal, lighted situation. From the audience's perspective, physical humor dominates because they see what the characters assumedly cannot during the blackout periods.

The central situation seems simple enough. As the lengthy one-act play opens, the young artist Brindsley Miller and his fiancée Carol are rearranging the living room of his flat to better display his art work. A renowned art connoisseur, Georg Bamberger, is expected to come soon to look over Brindsley's work. Bamberger's approval of Brindsley's art objects is so crucial to the young artist that in order to create a better first impression he borrows—without asking—the expensive furniture pieces of his gay admirer from next door, Harold Gorringe. Adding to the pressures of the moment is Carol's inadvisable invitation to her stuffed-shirt father, Colonel Melkett, to attend the session with Bamberger and to meet Brindsley for the first time. Brindsley succinctly sums up the moment with prayers muttered under his breath. "Oh, God, let this evening go all right! Let Mr. Bamberger like my sculpture and buy some! Let Carol's monster father like me! And let my neighbor Harold Gorringe never find out that we borrowed his precious furniture behind his back! Amen!" All of this initial exposition, of course, is delivered in complete darkness on stage, though the characters speak as though they are seeing everything.

Brindsley cannot have his wish right away in a comedy, however, and disaster strikes early when a fuse blows, leaving them in total blackness in the middle of shifting Harold's furnishings to Brindsley's apartment, just moments before Bamberger and Colonel Melkett are due to arrive. On stage, because of the light/dark reversal, the lights come up so that the audience sees the set for the first time. From this point until the fuse is replaced at the end of the play, the stage is brightly lit while the characters blindly move about as though in total blackness.

And the blown fuse is certainly not the end of Brindsley's difficulties. His prissy old-maid neighbor, Miss Furnival, out of fear gropes her way to Brindsley's flat in the dark, and she will continue to make a pest of herself throughout the play. Most critical of all, Brindsley's former lover, Clea, slips into his apartment in the "dark" and undertakes a campaign to harass Brindsley once she discovers that his new fiancée (Carol) is present. Harold arrives on the scene during the blackout, as well, to add to the chaotic moment. Brindsley's tasks thus are many: he must placate Clea to avoid her sabotaging his engagement with Carol; he must keep Carol ignorant of his earlier love affair with Clea; he must salve Colonel Melkett's ruffled feathers at the bewildering turn of events; he must keep Miss Furnival calm and quiet; and he must put off Harold's discovery about the borrowed furniture. All this, while still also making plans for Bamberger's arrival. *Black Comedy* is a work of multiple actions, mandating perfect timing on every performer's part to make the show work.

Because sight gags of supposed movements in the "darkened" apartment provoke ongoing laughter, physical actions—often mimed—become crucial. Shaffer provides elaborate stage directions to lead the way for the actors. Brindsley, in particular, must be ever on the move, as indicated in one set of Shaffer's directions: "*The wire of the lamp has followed* BRINDSLEY *round the bottom of the rocking chair. It catches.* BRINDSLEY *tugs it gently. The chair moves. Surprised, the* COLONEL *jerks forward.* BRINDSLEY *tugs it again, much harder. The rocking chair is pulled forward, spilling the* COLONEL *out of it, again onto the floor, and then falling itself on top of him . .* " Brindsley is depicted in ridiculous contortions while attempting the impossible objective of exchanging furniture between adjacent apartments while maintaining lively conversation with a room full of visitors—all in supposed total darkness.

More riotous actions occur in *Black Comedy,* and Brindsley fails to escape detection of his tricks at play's end. But, he does come to realize that Carol is all wrong for him and that Clea is his proper match. The comedy concludes with the eccentric electrician Schuppanzigh replacing the errant fuse, to plunge the real stage into blackness while the characters seemingly again can see. In every way, *Black Comedy* remains a hilarious tour de force filled with outrageous comic situations and even more outrageous comical characters. Although difficult to stage, this work pays back the effort with continuous laughter.

When *Black Comedy* was first being scheduled for a 1967 Broadway production, Shaffer needed another one-act piece to complete the bill. The result was *White Lies.* Compared to *Black Comedy,* however, *White Lies* did not initially earn the audience's enthusiasm, leading Shaffer to re-work the comedy twice, first as *The White Liars* and then as *White Liars*—the last a form that finally satisfied the playwright. Even so, *White Liars* remains the least satisfying of Shaffer's early one-act comedies. The male characters Tom and Frank undergo major transformations from the first to the final version, but even so they fail to touch playgoers as convincing figures. Admittedly, however, the initial concept for this three-person comedy is arresting, and the central figure of Sophie has ample appeal to provide worthwhile dramatic rewards.

Like Shaffer's early detective novels, *White Liars* revolves around finding the answers to a mystery. The sleuth in this case is a fortune teller, the phony Baroness Sophie Lemberg, whose moth-eaten parlor sits on the pier of a desolate seaside resort on England's southern coast. Two young men, rock musicians preparing for a show at the resort, stop by the Baroness's shop, ostensibly to consult with her. Each youth speaks with Sophie separately, and by virtue of their very contradictory narratives, it is clear that each wants the fake clairvoyant to assist him in a personal matter. In a way Sophie thus becomes a detective who must piece together the information that the lads give her and arrive at the "truth."

Frank, the more clean-cut of the two customers, asks to see Sophie first. He soon admits that he has come to her not for a look at the future but for her help in playing an innocent trick on Tom, the other, unkempt boy: "You see, I've—I've got a suggestion. A sort of a—little game. A, well, frankly a . . . look, Baroness, I don't really want my fortune told at all. I've come about something entirely different." His request, at first rejected by the outraged Baroness, eventually is agreed to, thanks to the inducement of an impressive fee. According to Frank, Tom has fallen for Frank's girlfriend, and Frank wants Sophie to frighten off his rival with a threatening "fortune" for Tom if he persists. Frank then offers Sophie sufficient background about Tom to make her pronouncements to the "victim" credible. Frank's inside information about Tom proves totally false, however, once Sophie talks to Tom, trying to steer him away from the girl. Tom had deliberately misinformed his buddy about his background and so realized immediately that a charade was underway. As Tom blurts out to the fortune-teller, "From the moment Frank came in here he handed you a pack of lies. One after another."

At first the fake baroness rejects Tom's disavowal, so caught up is she in Frank's earlier tale. But, eventually, she must face the truth when Frank confesses that his earlier-stated objectives were false. Frank did not want the girl back after breaking off her relationship with Tom; as he tells Sophie, he desired Tom instead: "I wanted him to leave her alone! . . . And to stay with me. In—my—bed." Frank's revelation forces Sophie to judge her own life realistically as well, and the serious comedy ends with the phony baroness calling to the departing Frank, "Take comfort, mister—here's a bit of comfort. It's not only the young who lie, whatever I said, it's not true—the old are worse. They are the biggest liars of them all! He was not a Baron; I am not a Baroness; my mother was not a Romany noblewoman, she was just a gypsy—and not even interesting."

Although a form of love story, *White Liars* treats romance of a quite different sort, given its first production in the mid-1960s. Shaffer displays an uncanny ability to highlight the illusions that his three protagonists perpetrate on one another, while building suspense and filling out interesting, identifiable characters who resist reality. Even if not a complete success, then, *White Liars* still deals comically with intriguing characters caught up in potentially serious philosophical dilemmas.

It was not until twenty years after *White Liars* that Shaffer turned again to comedy. *Lettice & Lovage,* written expressly for British actress Maggie Smith, premiered in London in 1987 where it earned loud and universal acclaim. Again, the playwright focuses on contemporary times and, in this case, London. Furthermore, along with the eternal matters of aesthetic beauty and individual self-discovery, Shaffer's themes concern current issues of historical preservation and aging in an unfriendly society dominated by technology. As were his early one-acters, *Lettice & Lovage* essentially is a three-person comedy, but in format its three full acts make it a full-length play. Moreover, differentiating *Lettice & Lovage* from the earlier comedies is Shaffer's use of two female leads at the play's heart.

Two middle-aged London spinsters of quite dissimilar temperaments are depicted at first colliding and then gradually reconciling in the story. Both lead unexceptional lives in modern-day London. Lettice Douffet, the chief protagonist, is a flamboyant and theatrical woman whose artistic nature leaves her ill-equipped for employment in a technological age. Valuing learning and art above all, Lettice (a nickname for "Laetitia") makes her living at society's outer margins, most recently as a tour guide at historical estates. Hers is a freewheeling lifestyle associated with the Dionysian spirit. (Such characters exist in all of Shaffer's plays.) Lotte Schoen, the Apollonian type, is Lettice's counterpart in *Lettice & Lovage*. Lotte (short for Charlotte) operates according to cool rationality, pragmatism, and absolute adherence to "rule"—not intuition as in Lettice's case. The basis for character conflict is evident early on.

Shaffer frames his plot within three carefully organized acts. The first introduces Lettice in all her eccentric extravagance. Most of act 2 is devoted to defining the character of Lotte. As the women come to know each other better, an alliance forms based on important ideas that they do hold in common. Act 3 leads to a climax when the friendship founders on a misunderstanding. So serious is the rupture that Lettice is threatened with imprisonment for attempted murder and Lotte is humiliated for pursuing her love of history. But once the truth is known, a reconciliation follows to transform the near tragedy into heart-warming comedy.

As is usual with Shaffer, he develops his protagonists clearly and in depth. Lettice is first seen while leading her guided tour group around Fustian House, a fictional estate which she labels "quite simply the *dullest house in England!*" When her tour members show themselves bored to death, Lettice (raised in a theatrical family) begins to improvise on the scripted narrative about Fustian House, adding juicy tidbits of bogus information. Her fanciful embroidering of the facts, however, soon catches the attention of officialdom at the Preservation Trust. Head of Personnel Lotte Schoen accosts Lettice during a tour, ultimately firing her as guide. Lettice's exit interview in Lotte's London office (scene 2) expands on Lettice's background and upbringing. In a brilliantly funny scene of confrontation with Lotte, Lettice defends her improvisation with her mother's unforgettable credo, "Fantasy floods in where fact leaves a vacuum."

Lotte, meanwhile, battles to keep their discussion focused on "facts." Lettice insists instead that one's primary duty is not to propagate dry facts but to inspire the lives of others. Lotte brusquely retorts, "This is nonsense—all of it! They don't matter! . . . None of this matters—your mother—your childhood . . . I am not in the entertainment business—and nor are you. That is all. We are guarding a heritage. Not running a theater." The first act closes with the battle lines clearly drawn between Lettice's idiosyncratic approach to modern life and Lotte's pragmatic stance.

Act 2 gives equal time to developing the character of Lotte. One feature of Lettice's character that earned Lotte's approval and respect was her "spunk," the willingness to speak out on behalf of one's beliefs. Therefore, when Lotte heard of an opening for a tour guide with another firm, she tracked down Lettice in her Earl's Court flat to inform her. It is in this section that Shaffer sets forth the urgency of a historical consciousness. Trained to be an architect, Lotte was strongly influenced by her art book publisher father. The state of late twentieth-century building designs in London consequently appall her. Lotte's sour perspective on contemporary living partly derives from England's loss of aesthetic values. She talks about her father's attitude, one that she has adopted: "He believed anybody born after 1940 has no real idea what visual civilization means—and never can have. 'There used to be such a thing as the Communal Eye,' he'd say. 'It has been put out in our lifetime, Lotte—yours and mine! The disgusting world we live in now could simply not have been built when that eye

was open. The planners would have been torn limb from limb—not given knighthoods.'"

When Lotte narrates how ill she became watching the destruction in London of "elegant facades—street after street," Lettice realizes that she has met a soul mate. They share a profound respect for the glories and beauties of earlier ages—and the displays of "spunk" on the part of noted historical heroes from the past. Act 2 ends with the two women leaving to dine out together, having formed a significant spiritual and intellectual bond.

Their love of heroic displays from the past leads them to meet weekly, to privately re-enact key historical moments when "spunk" was the order of the day—crucial episodes in the lives of such heroes (and heroines) as Joan of Arc, Queen Mary, and the like. When the final act opens, the disarray of Lettice's apartment reveals that something untoward has struck the lives of the women. Lettice is found discussing recent events with Mr. Bardolph, a public solicitor chosen to defend her in some serious legal charge. Their conversation reveals that for many weeks Lettice and Lotte had been privately staging episodes of heroic conduct but that an accident to the head injured Lotte and caused Lettice to be charged with attempted homicide. At first Lotte insists that Lettice keep the historical charades that they played secret, even though Lettice might be jailed for withholding evidence; making public the theatrical games that they played would prove unbearably humiliating to Lotte, and she would lose the high-level managerial post which she holds with the Preservation Trust. However, Lettice's legal plight is so desperate that Lotte reluctantly agrees to expose the truth: Lotte's injury occurred while the women re-created the beheading of King Charles I.

As the embarrassing tale emerges, Lotte tells off Lettice, breaking off their friendship. An ingenious reconciliation is provided at play's end whereby the women reunite forces to undertake a campaign—via guided tours—that would hold up for ridicule the disastrous architectural and social values of contemporary England. Lettice's spirits, utterly destroyed moments before by Lotte's rejection, are revived when their plan of action is decided upon, and she joyously calls the notion "the single most theatrical idea I ever heard." In *Lettice & Lovage,* Shaffer achieves a miraculous fusion of serious thought with dazzlingly comic dialogue and marvelously humorous characters.

("Lovage," incidentally, is a type of parsley that Lettice uses to concoct an alleged Renaissance beverage which she calls quaff—the brew that led the two to become fast friends.) *Lettice & Lovage* received four Tony nominations after its Broadway opening in 1990. A movie version is contemplated.

In 1989, Shaffer wrote a one-character radio comedy script, *Whom Do I Have the Honour of Addressing?*, which was aired over BBC. The author again focuses on a middle-aged woman, Mrs. Angela Sutcliffe, and again sets the story in modern-day London. Shaffer talks of possibly expanding the seventy-minute radio comedy into a full-length stage or television play, but in its present form, *Whom Do I Have . . . ?* features no overt action. Angela is depicted clumsily reciting into a tape recorder. She tells her reasons for committing suicide—which she announces she will do upon finishing her dictation. It is a playful piece, despite the seemingly dire situation, because Angela is as eccentric as Lettice Douffet. During her garrulous "confession," she continually becomes side-tracked. The gist of her life story concerns the handsome Hollywood screen idol Tom Prance who discovered Angela's special abilities (she owns a script-typing firm for movie and television scripts in London) and hired her to run a bogus foundation office in Los Angeles. By the end of the taped statement, which is filled with humorous digressions and chit-chat, it is clear that Angela will not take her life but will continue to lead a buoyant life. The tape proves to be a cathartic outlet, allowing her to carry on in a flawed world.

Summary

Peter Shaffer's impressive and successful comedies confirm that humor is a vital part of his writing arsenal. Though his main reputation in the theater derives from major award-winning serious dramas such as *Five Finger Exercise, The Royal Hunt of the Sun, Equus,* and *Amadeus,* Shaffer has established himself as an extraordinary comic playwright as well. *Black Comedy, The Private Ear, The Public Eye,* and most especially *Lettice & Lovage* have proven successful and popular with wide audiences. Perhaps most revealing about Shaffer's comic talent is the presence of humor in the serious dramas as well as in the comedies. Exceedingly witty dialogue can be found in even profound moments from the grand dramas, as in Pizarro's quips (*Royal Hunt*), Dr. Dysart's sarcastic gibes

(*Equus*), and Salieri's oily comments (*Amadeus*). At the same time, each of Shaffer's comedies contains the core themes also found in the dramas, namely, the collision of the Apollonian side of mankind—that which covets aesthetic perfection and organized orderliness—and the Dionysian facet—that which values intuition, inspiration, and unorganized emotions.

In Shaffer's work, however, comedies and dramas alike focus on the vulnerable weaknesses and surprising strengths to be found in the human will.

Selected Bibliography
Primary Sources
The Private Ear (with *The Public Eye*). London: Hamish Hamilton, 1962; New York: Stein and Day, 1964.
The Public Eye (with *The Private Ear*). London: Hamish Hamilton, 1962; New York: Stein and Day, 1964.
Black Comedy (with *White Lies*). New York: Stein and Day, 1967.
Black Comedy (revised and rewritten). New York: Samuel French, 1968.
White Lies (with *Black Comedy*). New York: Stein and Day, 1967.
White Liars (revised with title change). London: Samuel French, 1968.
The Collected Plays of Peter Shaffer. New York: Harmony Books, 1982.
Lettice and Lovage. London: Andre Deutsch, 1988.
Lettice and Lovage (first revision). London: Andre Deutsch, 1988.
Lettice & Lovage (revised with title alteration). New York: Harper and Row, 1990.

Secondary Sources

Books
Cooke, Virginia, and Malcolm Page, comp. *File on Shaffer.* London: Methuen, 1987. Excerpts of major reviews of plays and of critical commentary by scholars and experts.
Gianakaris, C.J. *Peter Shaffer.* London: Macmillan, and New York: St. Martin's Press, 1991. A comprehensive consideration of Shaffer's work.
———, ed. *Peter Shaffer: A Casebook.* New York: Garland, 1991. A collection of essays on different aspects of Shaffer's writing.

Klein, Dennis A. *Peter Shaffer.* Boston: Twayne, 1979. A concise overview of Shaffer's playwriting.

Plunka, Gene A. *Peter Shaffer: Roles, Rites, and Rituals in the Theater.* Rutherford, NJ: Fairleigh Dickinson University Press, 1988. An in-depth treatment of the themes and conventions that Shaffer uses in his plays.

Taylor, John Russell. *Peter Shaffer.* London: Longman, 1974. Writers and Their Work Series. The earliest look at Shaffer's work, relatively early in the playwright's career.

Articles

Chapman, John. "Peter Shaffer's Surprises." New York *Sunday News* (February 19, 1967): S3. Chapman spotlights the special literary skill in Shaffer's writing, with emphasis on *Black Comedy* and *White Lies.*

Gianakaris, C.J. "A Playwright Looks at Mozart: Peter Shaffer's *Amadeus.*" *Comparative Drama,* 15 (Spring 1981): 37–53. Gianakaris covers Shaffer's comic portrayal of Mozart in *Amadeus.*

———. "*Lettice & Lovage:* Fountainhead of Delight," *TheaterWeek* (April 2, 1990): 22–25. Background and highlights of *Lettice & Lovage.*

Gilliatt, Penelope. "Power-Cut Laughter." In *Unholy Fools, Wits, Comics, Disturbers of Peace: Film and Theater.* New York: Viking Press, 1973. Gilliatt discusses the production of *Black Comedy* at its premiere at the Chichester Festival.

Gow, Gordon. "The Struggle: An Interview with John Dexter." *Plays and Players* (November 1979): 14–16. Dexter's career is discussed, including the director's work on the original production of *Black Comedy.*

Kerr, Walter. "In Black (Comedy) and White (Lies)." *New York Times* (February 26, 1967): Sec. 2, p. 1. Kerr comments on the intellectual versus performance elements in Shaffer's two comedies.

Lewis, Allen. *American Plays and Playwrights of the Contemporary Theatre.* New York: Crown Publishers, 1965. Even though they do not qualify as American in origin, Lewis makes some very positive comments about Shaffer's *The Private Ear* and *The Public Eye.*

Loney, Glenn. "Broadway and Off-Broadway Supplement." *Educational Theatre Journal,* 19 (May 1967): 201. Loney discusses *Black Comedy* as the best comedy of that season in New York.

Prideaux, Tom. "Things That Go Bump in the Dark." *Life* (March 10, 1967): 70A-70D. The author discusses the problems of trying to act as though in total darkness in *Black Comedy.*

Watts, Richard, Jr. "The Versatility of Peter Shaffer." *New York Post* (February 25, 1967): 20. A respected newspaper critic summarizes Shaffer's talents in writing *Black Comedy, White Lies, The Private Ear,* and *The Public Eye.*

Elsom, John. "Peter Shaffer." In *Contemporary Dramatists.* Ed. James Vinson. London: Macmillan, 1982. 3rd ed, pp. 708–11. Elsom covers Shaffer's stage output to that date, including commentary on the comedies.

C.J. Gianakaris

Shakespeare, William

Born: Stratford, England, April 1564
Education: grammar school
Marriage: Anne Hathaway, December (?) 1582; three children
Died: Stratford, April 23, 1616

Biography

The known details of William Shakespeare's life are, on the surface, uniformly dull. The fact that, with two or perhaps three exceptions, more is known about him than about any other playwright of the age has not prevented some from denying that the author of Shakespeare's plays was Shakespeare. The so-called "Oxfordians" or "Baconians"—those who suggest that either the Earl of Oxford or Francis Bacon wrote the plays but, fearing it would look improper for an aristocrat or scholar to work in the theater, passed them off as written by the actor—are embarrassed by Shakespeare's "low" (that is, non-aristocratic) origins or his lack of a university education.

William was born in Stratford in April 1564. The exact date of his birth is not known, though his baptism was recorded on April 26. His mother, Mary Arden, came from a prosperous local family; his father, John, was a maker of gloves and may have traded in farm products. Presumably Shakespeare had the normal grammar-school education of a Stratford youth, one which involved considerable study in Latin. In late 1582, perhaps in December, he married Anne Hathaway, a woman eight years his senior. Six months later their first child, Susanna, was born.

Possibly as early as 1588 or 1589 Shakespeare moved to London, leaving his family behind. Speculation is varied about why he did so. Perhaps it was to escape his father, who, records indicate, had lost his money, and, as a consequence, his position as high bailiff (or mayor) of Stratford. It may be that Shakespeare felt the calling to be an actor and playwright, and only England's major city would provide him an adequate stage.

From 1592 onward there are several records of Shakespeare's life in the big city. In 1592, Robert Greene branded him an "upstart crow, beautified with our feathers," that is, an actor declaiming ("able to bombast") others' lines onstage and writing plays in blank verse which were as good as any then being written. In 1598, he is listed as a "principal comedian," in 1603 as a "principal tragedian," and in 1608 as one of the "men players" in theatrical companies, first with the Chamberlain's Men and then, when the company changed its name in 1603, as a full share-holder of the King's Men. Shakespeare's life in London was, in the best sense of the word, "full." He acted as a member of a repertory troupe, tended to the financial and legal business of his company, and wrote some thirty-seven plays, along with several non-dramatic works. In 1598, Francis Meres links Shakespeare with Plautus and Seneca, the great Roman writers of comedies and tragedies, respectively, and then lists several of Shakespeare's works.

While his visits to Stratford may have been infrequent, Shakespeare continued to function as a member of that community. His twins Hamnet and Judith were born in 1585. In 1597, he purchased New Place, one of Stratford's most impressive houses, with his earnings on the London stage. Retiring from the stage, he spent roughly the last three years of his life in Stratford. In his will, besides providing for his family, he left money, albeit small amounts, to his actor friends. That he left his "second-best" bed to his wife Anne has raised some eyebrows: why not the first-best bed? Was the couple unhappily married? Actually, Shakespeare probably left her the bed on which they slept as a married couple, while the best bed was that reserved for guests. He died on April 23, 1616, and his funeral on April 26 was held in the same church in which he had been christened exactly fifty-two years earlier.

It is important when looking at Shakespeare's life to separate the facts from the fantasies, from those legends and rumors that seem to confirm the image that some would have of the most famous writer of all times. We do not know whether Shakespeare stole deer from the royal forest in his youth, or if he and his lead actor, Richard Burbage, were "ladies men" about London or even if Hamlet reflects Shakespeare's own insecurities and despair. To some degree events of his life and aspects of his personality may be reflected in the plays, since writers tend to draw on personal experience. In this regard, some intriguing motifs appear: the rivalry between brothers (Shakespeare had a brother, Arthur, much younger than himself), the relationship between sons and fathers (how might Shakespeare have felt when, in his youth, he saw his father fall from grace, perhaps because of self-inflicted financial problems?). In a very paternalistic age, it is curious that women in the plays—Titania, Portia, Lady Macbeth—are more than the equal of any man. Of course, we should also remember that in this same age Queen Elizabeth I was on the throne (until her death in 1603).

However, like any great artist Shakespeare surely had keen eyes and ears and the ability to empathize with others. Thus, the material in his works may just as likely mirror the world of those about him as it does the psychological makeup of its author.

Though some have doubted his sincerity (even arguing that while addressing the poem to Shakespeare, he is actually referring to Oxford or Bacon), in his dedicatory poem to the 1623 Folio in which Shakespeare's plays were collected, Ben Jonson speaks of his works as a "monument, without a tomb." Elsewhere, Jonson calls Shakespeare "honest, and of an open and free nature," with "an excellent fantasy, brave notions, and gentle expressions."

Literary Analysis

Shakespeare is not especially given to one-liners, to inserting commonplace jokes or contriving situations so that they are capped with a joke, in the fashion of a lesser or "commercial" playwright. Even when he (apparently) sandwiches a comic scene between more serious matters, the scene in question never stands by itself and is always related, sometimes in very profound ways, to the larger play. The "drunken Porter" speech in *The Tragedy of Macbeth* (1605–1606) is a perfect example, for the Porter's humorous praise and condemnation of liquor—it both arouses sexual desire and impedes performance—is very much related to Lady Macbeth's taunting of her husband when she equates his desire to kill the king with his sexual promises, and then links his inability to perform the twin deeds of assassination and lovemaking. Ariel's neurotically funny reminders to Prospero in *The Tempest* (1611) that he wishes to be free, to become his own man, are at one with Prospero's deeper reluctance to give his daughter the freedom to marry and to free himself of his own deep-seated hatred of his brother.

As much as proponents of classical theater in Shakespeare's day derided his juxtaposition of comedy and tragedy, his mixture of what were assumed to be separate and incompatible styles, the playwright himself felt no shame in having the Fool in *The Tragedy of King Lear* (1605–1606) make the most outrageous and biting jokes about silly old men in the presence of his master, who suffers unspeakable cruelties from his own daughters. If Jessica feels some pain in *The Merchant of Venice* (1596–1597) about leaving her father, that same play also contains a comic scene between Launcelot Gobbo and his father in which the son tricks the old man into believing that he is dead, all the time leaping merrily about the stage, causing his father, who is blind, to stumble and fall in a series of pratfalls that, in our day, would be reminiscent of the theater of the absurd.

Comedy never stands on its own in Shakespeare. Even when the characters seem mere puppets, something less than human and therefore unworthy of much emotional investment on the audience's part, their comic situations never degenerate to farce but rather somehow touch on our own lives. In what may well be Shakespeare's first play, *The Comedy of Errors* (1588–1593), twin brothers and their twin servants, who have not seen each other since birth, are present in the same town on the same day—without knowing it. The comedy here comes when townspeople assume that the "visiting" twin is the twin whom they know; thus, a wife claims her brother-in-law as her husband. Even the servant of one master takes the master of his unknown twin as his own. But, the situation, though extreme—Shakespeare based the play on a Latin model, doubling the number of twins from his source—also speaks to our own need for certainty, for identity. If sometimes we think that our "real" self is at the mercy of the fraudulent opinions of others, then we can see our own human predicament in these seeming puppets caught up in a situation which otherwise defies probability.

The other major quality of Shakespeare's comedy is that it is always humane. To be sure, the dramatist can exercise his razor-sharp instinct for satire or parody, but our reaction to the characters so impaled on his wit is always more complex, never as reductive as it might be in "pure" satire or parody. In *Love's Labor's Lost* (1588–1594), Holofernes, the pedant who is so caught up in the intricacies of grammar and proper usage that he can hardly utter a clear, let alone simple, sentence, does not stand by himself in a play where a major concern is the discrepancy between how we talk and what we really are. In *Twelfth Night* (1599–1600), Malvolio is a parody of the strait-laced, humorless Puritans of Shakespeare's day. A trick is played on him so that he fancies that his mistress is in love with him and thereby he is made to see that he shares the affectation and delight in the flesh with those whom he would ordinarily dismiss as sinners and unlike himself. Similar tricks are played on the two aristocratic lead characters in the same play. Duke Orsino, in his addiction to unrequited love, and the Countess Olivia, in her exorbitant grief over the death of a brother, are as "bad" in their own way as Malvolio is in his.

The character thus satirized never stands alone. Nor does his or her unmasking (or punishment)—the disclosure of a hidden vice or idiosyncrasy—go without providing a parallel comment on the weaknesses of other characters, often the very characters who performed the unmasking. This character holds a mirror up to the audience as well. Can we ever claim immunity, sitting as we do offstage in the security of the playhouse, from what transpires onstage?

Jacques's famous "Ages of Man" speech in *As You Like It* (1599–1600) is a case in point. "All the world's a stage," he proclaims, and then divides a human life into seven smaller stages: the infant "puking in his nurse's arms"; the tardy schoolboy; the lover making ballads to "his mistress's eyebrow"; the soldier seeking reputation that is little more than a "bubble"; the fat country justice who has unduly profited from his high office; the old man looking and acting ridiculous, and at last in his senility resembling nothing so much as a child, "sans teeth, sans eyes, sans taste, sans every thing." Jacques's analysis of a life span seems very much a "set-piece," something that ridiculously catalogues human life that, the audience assumes, cannot be so easily catalogued. It even appears too pat, as if it existed outside the play itself, something, say, that makes a good audition piece for an actor. But, the humor is not so pat; nor is it just (or simply) clever but unrealistic satire. To begin with, Jacques is not a neutral speaker. The speech comes from his own soured character and expresses not so much a freestanding philosophy as it does some very basic emotional needs in Jacques himself. To be more direct, there is no certainty here that Jacques speaks for the author, for Shakespeare. In exposing only himself, Jacques may not be speaking authoritatively about human existence. Nor are any of the categories as reductive as they seem, or even as Jacques may want them to seem. For example, in *The Tragedy of Hamlet* (1600–1601) there is a marvelous scene, often deleted in stage productions, where the title character meets a Captain of Fortinbras's army who complains that the piece of land for which they are going to battle is insignificant, not even worth the effort of plowing the soil. Hamlet, who is bookish and intellectual, the very opposite of the militarist Fortinbras, can nevertheless admire someone like Fortinbras who for the sake of honor would commit 2,000 soldiers to death. By the end of the scene Hamlet pokes fun not at the futility of war but at himself, since he—with greater cause—cannot bring himself to kill Claudius. In this context, then, Jacques's cynical dismissal of a soldier as someone so intent on dying that he would leap into the mouth of a cannon "seeking the bubble reputation," does not, by its own power, make the soldier an object of ridicule. Beyond his conscious intention Jacques may envy the very man whom he mocks.

Indeed, Shakespeare even mocks himself and the high profession of the theater. He parodies his company and the relationship among playwrights, directors, and actors, in the guise of Bottom's inept rustic troupe in *A Midsummer Night's Dream* (1594–1596). In the *Sonnets* (1593–1600), he chides himself, or the person narrating the sonnet, for his infatuation with the unfaithful "dark lady," even punning on the word "will": William, "will" as sexual power, and "will" as the woman's fickle choice. The first victim of the angry mob in *The Tragedy of Julius Caesar* (1599) is a poet, who purely by accident happens to have the same name as the conspirator sought by the Romans who have been aroused to vengeance by Antony's funeral oration.

The reverse is no less true: there is serious matter within the comedy. The trial scene in *The Merchant of Venice* (1596–1597) is often played as comedy, with Shylock the deserving victim. After all, shouldn't we laugh at the exposure and punishment of someone so absurd as to demand a pound of a man's flesh, as Shylock does from Antonio since the merchant has been unable to pay back a loan by the specified time? Even Shylock will not or—what is more likely—cannot give a reason why he prefers a worthless pound of human flesh to double, even triple the amount of money that is his due. Portia, in male disguise as the defense lawyer, at first agrees with Shylock, that the flesh is his; and then, just as he is about to carve his repayment from Antonio's chest, she suddenly invokes a legal qualification: since the deed makes no mention of blood, if Antonio bleeds in the process then the deed is forfeit. Shylock suddenly backtracks. He asks for the money instead; it is denied him—it is the pound of flesh or nothing, he is told. Injury is piled on injury: to save his life, he is forced to give up all of his money and property, and to convert to Christianity. We *ought* to laugh at this scene where the villain—isn't someone who would carve a pound of flesh from a man deserving of the term?—is caught in the act and humiliated, and all of this at the hands of a woman posing as a man. But, since the scene is Shakespeare's, our laughter—at very least of relief, at most of vindication—is qualified, made complex, not pure. This is because elsewhere in the play Shylock, the Jew, has been very much the persecuted victim—they spit on his clothes; they steal his money and his daughter; they insult his religion—of the very people who, mere seconds before, would have been his victim. Who is really on trial here? Who wins? Is the dark humor directed as much at the Christians, the Venetian majority, as it is at Shylock?

Even when the character is so comic, so "wrong" that we laugh at him, even when he or she is set against someone noble, the humor is never fully at the expense of the fool. Nor does the noble character escape unscathed. In *The First Part of Henry IV* (1597), Prince Hal

S

meets Falstaff on the battlefield. Fearful of death, Falstaff begs that play's hero to come to his aid if it be necessary, although the Prince mockingly reminds Falstaff that if he has to stand over (to "bestride") him on the battlefield it will be a difficult task, given Falstaff's bulk. Like a child, Falstaff wishes it were "bedtime" only to be warned by the Prince, as he makes his exit, that as a subject of the king and the child of his creator "thou owest God a death." The moment that Hal leaves, Falstaff, alone onstage and perhaps in direct address to the audience, makes his preposterous argument for cowardice. Why should he pursue the sort of honor of which Hal speaks when, after all, honor cannot heal a wound? Besides, the only people with honor are those who have died, and what use is it to them now? Honor, Falstaff concludes, is a mere word, nothing more substantial than air; and, if you achieve honor, in their jealousy detractors will only be encouraged to take it from you. "Therefore I'll none of it," he reasons. We laugh, of course, at his defensiveness, his rationalizations, his horrendous attempts to convince us, if not himself, that somehow cowardice is a virtue. And, like a coward, Falstaff does all of this behind Hal's back; he does not even have the courage of his own faulty convictions. Yet, in our age of anti-war protests, an age when the establishment has often and justly been called into question, there is a certain logic to what Falstaff says. If he is a coward, he also upholds the principle of survival, of life itself. His counterpart in the play, Hotspur, whose pursuit of honor is so extreme that he leaves a loving wife, preferring contact with his horse to any with her, winds up dead, and disgraced. Each man has what the other lacks. To put it another way, Falstaff values honor too little while Hotspur undervalues life. In Falstaff's humorous defense of cowardice, Shakespeare, then, reverses what he did with Jacques. In *Henry IV,* part 1, the speech, while it unmasks the speaker, likewise unmasks the very notions of honor and authority that are vested in the man who on his recent exit has reminded Falstaff of the proper mission of a loyal subject.

When the character in question is an outright villain and humorous, then the issue of Shakespeare's humor is taken to another level. Richard, the hunchbacked murderer who is even more grotesque within, is the central, indeed the sole source of humor in Shakespeare's early history play, *The Tragedy of Richard III* (1592–1593). At one point he waits for the Lady Anne as she crosses the stage; before her, servants carry the coffin of her husband who has been murdered by none other than Richard himself. As he approaches Anne, she, predictably, scorns him, even as Richard begs her, by the rules of "charity," to be as kind to him as he was unkind to her husband. When she confronts him with the simple fact that he is a murderer, he, wonderfully and comically, converts the injury to a benefit: since her husband, by her own admission, was a "saint," he only did him a favor in murdering the king by releasing his soul back to Heaven. As a saint, he "was fitter for that place than earth." Anne retorts sarcastically that Richard is fit for only one place, Hell. Again, he offers a witty substitute: her bedchamber. Like some character from an Oscar Wilde comedy, Richard always manages to get one leg up on her, matching her scorn with witty rejoinders. It was her beauty, not his ambition or cruelty as she claims, that led him to murder Henry. He murdered her husband to help her to a better husband. Why should she use her lips for scorn when they are much better suited for kissing? Offering her his sword, by which she can wound his "true breast," he gives her two alternatives, the latter laced with sexual innuendo. Either she take up the sword (and kill the murderer of her husband) or "take up" him. Disarmed literally and figuratively by Richard's wit, Anne, suddenly, incredulously, takes him as a lover. That is, within five minutes of stage-time the man who assassinated her husband becomes her promised second husband. On Anne's exit, Richard turns to the audience and asks plaintively, "Was ever woman in this humor wooed?" Then, "Was ever woman in this humor won?" Morally repulsive, Richard endears himself to us because he is a villain not only with a sense of humor but one whose humor is his chief weapon. If Richard comes off the "winner" in this scene, the comedian who seduces the tragic widow, Anne loses in several senses, not the least of which is that in falling prey to Richard she may have revealed, despite her conscious resolve and her fidelity to the memory of her husband, a shallowness, a faulty moral compass which Richard had spied and on which he had capitalized.

Much of the humor in Shakespeare, like that in the scene from *Richard III,* is linked with sex and the problems of men and women in love. It is not that Shakespeare cannot be romantic, but even the moments of romance are never purely romantic. In *A Midsummer*

Night's Dream, for example, Lysander, finding himself alone in the forest with Hermia, proposes, logically, that since they are tired and lost, it would be best if they "rest." All that he seems to mean is that, since it is dark, they should go to sleep. Agreeing, Hermia suggests a practical course: she will sleep here, and Lysander can find a bed over there. Lysander then presents an impassioned romantic argument for their sharing the same sleeping area—since they have "one heart," "one troth," why not a single pillow? His proposal is clearly mixed with some very unromantic, purely sexual desire. Hermia gets his message, and punning on the word "lie" she tells him to "lie further off yet, do not lie so near." Frustrated, Lysander protests that his love is more than physical, that their "two bosoms are interchained with an oath," and therefore he is not lying or being deceptive when suggesting that they lie together. Not willing to take more of his sophistries, Hermia puts her foot down: while she did not mean to imply that he lied, she does insist that he lie further off. Dejected, defeated, and sexually frustrated, Lysander crosses to a far side of the stage, but not before reminding Hermia, rather petulantly, that tonight she will have to lie with "sleep" as her bed-partner rather than an eligible man like himself.

If Lysander's humor is a tool for seduction as unsuccessful as Richard's had been successful, humor can also be the enemy of sex, seemingly (but just seemingly) at odds with it. Deep down, one suspects, love is a serious matter for Petruchio and Kate in *The Taming of the Shrew* (1593–1594), despite the fact that he claims to come to Padua to find a wealthy wife, while she, hating the various suitors proposed by her father, adopts the stance of a shrew, a man-hater. Since he wants a woman only for her money and she hates men, their first meeting becomes a battle of wits wherein the humor is designed to protect one's integrity rather than to woo a mate. However, though Kate tries her best to appear her most shrewish, Petruchio persists in flattering her as pretty and dainty, as mild, and full of virtue, daring her to challenge what is clearly a series of falsehoods, of conscious misapprehensions on his part. When he condescendingly uses the word "move" to refer to his suit to her—"Myself am moved to woo thee for my wife"—she turns the word against him: "remove you hence." Then the humor gets physical. Petruchio tells her to sit on his knee; she calls him an ass if he wishes thus to "bear" the weight of a woman. He counters with, "Women are made to bear and so are you." He calls her a wasp; she advises him to beware of her "sting." He says that he will pluck out her sting; she claims he is not bright enough to find it. When he tells her that the sting is in her tail, she, making a foolish mistake, insists that it is in her tongue and thereby sets him up for a bawdy, comic victory:

> *Petruchio*: Whose tongue?
> *Kate*: Yours, if you talk of tales; and so farewell.
> *Petruchio*: What! with my tongue in your tail?

With such scatalogical humor one would imagine the two as bitter enemies, unlikely candidates for lovers. Yet, this is exactly what they become in the course of the play, not only lovers and husband and wife, but—as the final scene shows, when Kate alone of the three wives respects her husband's wishes—an ideal couple. For the actor and actress playing the two parts, the end of the play must be found here, in this first humorous meeting between these two rivals who in their sarcasm and their biting jests, not to mention the physical bashing that directors put into the scene, seem to hate each other. However, "seem" is the operative word. Somehow the humor rooted in the conflict between the genders cannot exist for itself but must instead be a sign to deeper feelings between Kate and Petruchio. Perhaps their humor is a defense, not so much against the other, but against the self, an effort to deny in the play's own shallow, materialistic, unromantic world—epitomized in the contract that Kate's father makes with Petruchio to get his daughter off his hands—feelings that more properly belong to a romance.

Throughout Shakespeare's career, that same humor continues to serve more than one master. In *Measure for Measure* (1604), Isabella has been propositioned by the deputy Angelo, who has told her that if she has sexual relations with him, he will spare the life of her brother Claudio, who is in prison for the crime of having premarital sex with one Juliet. Isabella, who is about to enter a convent, goes confidently to her brother expecting that, once she tells him of Angelo's wicked offer, the brother, like any good brother, will rather choose death for himself than dishonor for his sister. But, Isabella's own confidence is undercut by the round-about way in which she raises the issue with Claudio, and there is a grim comedy about her argument for the insignificance of death: "The sense of death is most in apprehension. / And the poor beetle that we tread upon. / In corporal sufferance finds a pang as great / As when a giant die." In short, death is death—so what's the big problem? The audience may wince at Isabella's ability to speak so authoritatively about a subject of which she has no experience, and this to a man about to die. Still, once he understands her, Claudio, eager to show himself the loving brother, is glad to die for his sister's honor. For her part, she cheerfully tells him to "be ready . . . for [his] death tomorrow." Suddenly, however, it hits him, and Claudio checks her exit with a simple "Death is a fearful thing." Isabella stops in her tracks, as Claudio launches into a terrified, neurotic description of what death must be like before begging his sister to let him live. She storms out of the prison cell, dismissing her brother as a "beast" and "faithless coward," even as someone who would commit "a kind of incest" by seeking to preserve his own life at the cost of his "sister's shame." The would-be nun, on her exit line, will now "pray a thousand prayers for [her brother's] death." Here, Shakespeare forges a comedy out of potential tragedy, mixing sex and death, darkening the otherwise saintly character of the sister and elevating the otherwise shallow brother to someone who, like Falstaff earlier, values survival over abstract principle. Isabella seems absurd, even cruelly comic to us, disturbingly so in that she selfishly would value her chastity over her brother's life, asking him a favor which she will not allow him to deny her.

Death itself is not immune from comedy. Indeed, death as a comic subject is not even separable from love, for in Shakespeare's day "to die" had a double meaning: to cease to be alive and to have sexual intercourse. The act that ends life was thus, paradoxically, linked with the physical act that begets life. In fact, this linking of seeming opposites, bringing them together in a single word such as "die" was what Shakespeare's age meant by "wit." To be witty was not simply being humorous, but rather having the ability to make connections between two entities that appear to be opposites, or to inhabit different words. In this way Shakespeare's contemporaries, in their conception of wit, anticipated modern theories of comedy which might define humor as a situation where the perceiver has an unnerving sense of discordancy in a union that defies our usual expectation of order or decorum or even logic. In such witty situations our laughter is both an acknowledgment of and a release from our encountering the unexpected that calls into question, makes fun of, and challenges the unexpected or the rational.

Three examples, from the early, middle, and late stages of Shakespeare's career, show this notion of wit and the degree to which humor was a philosophical enterprise in the plays. The dramatist used humor as a way of finding a union, a new relationship between otherwise disparate things, and in that union both questioning and expanding our sense—to put the issue in the most positive light—of what is normal and, therefore, "real."

At the beginning of the twentieth century *A Midsummer Night's Dream* was usually dismissed as a "light" comedy of romantic love, a series of adventures where four young Athenians go into a forest mismatched and, through the operations of a benevolent deity in that forest, come out nicely arranged as couples, all of this to the accompaniment of the rustics who in staging a wretched production parody Shakespeare's own theater. Now, a half-century of productions and scholarly writings have put *A Midsummer Night's Dream* in a different light. It is a comedy and will always be so—after all, isn't a comedy a play that ends happily?

Still, the degree of its comedy now seems deeper, more significant. What appears to be combined in this play through Shakespeare's own wit are the otherwise antithetical worlds of reason and the imagination, of reality and fantasy, of that which is tangible and that which is beyond rational measurement. If the world of tragedy is one where circumstances, either fated or self-inflicted or both, close down on people, comedy, in this light, offers an expansive world—one where change and growth are possible. Accordingly, when the four lovers tell Theseus (the sober, highly rational Duke of Athens) of their adventures in the forest, he dismisses what they saw as nonsense. The amazing fact is that the lovers went into that forest mismatched (two men chasing one woman, with the second woman "unchased") and later emerged perfectly matched: Lysander has his Hermia, Demetrius his Helena. Theseus, who has no sense of humor or wit, also has no sympathies for what he defines as illogical, as fanciful. The fact is that he is not real, for he is only an actor's impersonation. In fact, in modern productions it is common to double the parts of

Theseus and Oberon: that is, Theseus has a supernatural counterpart, Oberon, of which he is blissfully and arrogantly unaware. And, in trying to make a comedy of the play within a play, *Pyramus and Thisbe* (a tragedy if there ever was one), in part by their own bad acting, Bottom and his company also forge a union of what would otherwise be opposites. In the same way in the larger play Shakespeare refashions a potential *Romeo and Juliet* (performed, most likely, in the same year as *A Midsummer Night's Dream*), a tragedy of young love, into a comedy where at the end three couples exit joyfully to consummate their marriages. *A Midsummer Night's Dream* is about a single, larger world, one where mortals and fairies live together, where the rational and the irrational exist in harmony, a world denied consciously by Theseus, but one that is generated by the author's concept of comedy. In joining what seems asunder with his wit, Shakespeare asks us to entertain a larger definition of what is real, and what is "normal."

In *Hamlet,* when Polonius, playing the detective who is sure that he can pluck out the heart of the prince's "mystery," casually and subtly—or so he imagines—engages Hamlet in conversation, we see this same principle operating. In the midst of Polonius's social platitudes, Hamlet brands him as a "fishmonger," that is, a pimp. Polonius is, predictably, thrown by the remark. Then Hamlet throws him again by asking if Polonius is "honest," with its double meaning of being truthful—Polonius, of course, is not being truthful since his motive in engaging the prince in conversation is hardly social—and sexually chaste (or, for a married person, faithful). No sooner has Polonius struggled to get back into a conversation that at the start he imagined would be under his control—he has told Claudius and Gertrude that he will "board" Hamlet—than he is thrown once again by Hamlet's seemingly insane line, "For if the sun breed maggots in a dead dog, being a god kissing carrion." Although the Renaissance theory of spontaneous creation is involved here, Hamlet's lines picture a topsy-turvy world where the intercourse between the sun and a dead dog results in a maggot child. In larger measure, Hamlet imagines an absurd universe where the noble (the sun, the sun god) cohabit with the ignoble (dogs, death), a world of "dark" wit, to play on that wit otherwise so positive in the plays. All of this is unintelligible to Polonius, so Shakespeare gives

him an aside, a breathing space where he can try to figure out what the prince is saying. Once out of the aside, Polonius's question, "What is the matter, my lord?" (that is, what is the subject matter of the book that you are reading) is met with a pun from Hamlet, "Between who?" By the end of the conversation, Polonius, in another aside, tells us that he is going to loose his daughter, Ophelia, on Hamlet to see if she can pry out the secret of his unhappiness. If we take "fishmonger" or pimp in the general sense of someone who uses another's body for his or her own personal gain, then Polonius has stepped into the very role that Hamlet had announced for him and which Polonius himself had angrily denied.

Hamlet's humor in this scene, in the form of puns, insults, and language that defies clarity or common sense, is at one with his ability to see into Polonius's real aim in the conversation, to go even deeper and to uncover an emotional need of this father to keep his daughter chaste (perhaps out of the same sort of Platonic incest that drives Lear to want to keep his Cordelia with him as an obedient daughter rather than as an independent married woman). Beyond this, Hamlet's humor allows him to predict a role that Polonius will shortly enact when he hides behind the arras, watching his daughter Ophelia, on his own instructions, engage Hamlet in conversation, using sexual attraction, or former attraction in Hamlet's case, as the means to finding out the source of Hamlet's madness.

In this same scene Hamlet tells Polonius that the "matter" of the book which he is reading is a satire of old men with "grey beards," watery eyes, and "a plentiful lack of wit, together with most weak hams" (that is, impotent). Surely, Hamlet makes up the material here, for what he "reads" is Polonius himself rather than any book. By his wit, his ability to see that dark reality behind this apparently chance social meeting, Hamlet turns the detective on his head. Hamlet remains a mystery, indeed becomes an even greater mystery to Polonius. It is the detective who is exposed, found guilty of everything from deception to dishonesty to covert incest. We are taught to honor old people, and there is a serious comedy here in the dishonoring of Polonius. Like Hamlet's confidants, we laugh with him at Polonius's expense, doubly so because Polonius cannot perceive that he is the subject of Hamlet's wit. Nevertheless, it is the presence of this humor,

S

however dimly perceived, that troubles Polonius, for in one aside he recognizes that though Hamlet's conversation smacks of "madness," yet there is "method" in it.

In *The Tragedy of Antony and Cleopatra,* a late play (1606 or 1607), this concept of wit is exercised on the ultimate subjects (and extremes) of birth and death. The clown, appropriately, has brought Cleopatra a basket containing two asps, small, highly poisonous snakes that live in the mud on the banks of the Nile. Knowing of Cleopatra's sexual reputation, the Clown makes crude puns on "dying" and "death," implying that the snakes will function as some sort of sexual surrogate for Cleopatra. On Shakespeare's stage a boy actor would play Cleopatra and most likely the two asps would be two pieces of short rope. These asps (this rope) will soon become a magnificent symbol in the scene, the product of Cleopatra's wit, as voiced by the boy actor. With his lewd speculations about Cleopatra's purpose in asking for asps, the Clown, in essence, makes the asps a symbol of degradation, of obscenity. On his exit, however, Cleopatra takes the first asp to her breast and after it has bitten her compares it to a "lover's pinch / Which hurts, and is desired." She places this first asp, its poison spent, back in the basket, and pulls out the second one. As it bites her, Cleopatra's maid-servant, Charmian, cries out, "O eastern star," but Cleopatra quiets her with a curious line, "Peace, peace! / Does thou not see my baby at my breast, / That sucks the nurse asleep?" Cleopatra thus metamorphoses the second asp to a baby feeding at rather than poisoning her. Through her imagination Cleopatra sees herself as a nursing mother rather than as a suicide or the snake's victim. When she gathers the first asp back to her, calling it her "Antony" and now holding both asps at her breast, we have an idyllic picture, the nuclear family—mother, father, and child sleeping at its mother's breast, full of mother's milk. As she dies, Cleopatra's final line is a question for the audience as well as her servant onstage: "What [or why] should I stay?" A possible subtextual reading is: I have everything that I want in life, a husband and our child, and therefore there is nothing more on this earth, in this life, that I require; I might as well die. The comedy, as broadly defined in Shakespeare, is pulling here at the historical tragedy which Shakespeare found in the sources for *Antony and Cleopatra,* one of lovers' suicides, the defeat of love at the hands of politics.

The comedy allows us a much more complicated, conflicted reaction to the scene. Cleopatra's death is, in a way, pleasurable, as comedy itself is.

It is difficult to speak of the "development" of Shakespeare's use of humor over his career for several reasons. First, from the start the principles of playwriting, the conception of the theater, even the thematic concerns already seem in place. Even as the comic mix-ups in *The Comedy of Errors* are not gratuitous, in cruder form in that play Shakespeare also treats the same great issues, the relationship between fathers and children, the search for one's own identity, that blossom so richly in *Hamlet* and *King Lear.*

Second, the range of comedy in Shakespeare's plays is almost always proportionate to the needs of a particular play and, more to the point, the playwright's concerns at any given time in his career. For instance, Mercutio's "Queen Mab" speech in *The Tragedy of Romeo and Juliet,* in which he claims that people fall in love not out of will but because of the nocturnal visits of a mischievous old lady, occupies a central position in that play because the drama is very much about youthful love and the ways in which willful youths unintentionally cause their own deaths. In contrast, *The Tempest* does not give center-stage to its Romeo and Juliet, Ferdinand and Miranda, because at this point in Shakespeare's career romantic love must share the stage with other concerns. This includes what well may be Shakespeare's final self-portrait in Miranda's father, the magician Prospero who rules the magic island named—appropriately—the Globe. The force of the humor in the latter play, therefore, is directed more at the adults than at youthful lovers and, as a consequence, there is no pressing need for the sort of comic business that we get from Mercutio. It should also be noted that even Mercutio's speech is not an insert, or something directed exclusively at the lovers. It well may be that Mercutio unconsciously delivers this harangue against love out of a fear that his boyhood friend, Romeo, is going to abandon him for Juliet, that Romeo is moving from an all-male world that excludes women by debasing them, thinking that love is something just for the "weaker sex," to a fuller heterosexual world where women play a vital role. Hence, the "Queen Mab" speech is as much defensive as it is offensive. Romeo, in fact, punctures Mercutio's resolve when he admonishes him, "Peace! / Thou talk'st of nothing."

Finally, patterns of development when applied to an artist as wide-ranging and complex as Shakespeare may be reductive, too given to our need for order at the expense of flexibility or even the disorder that comedy asks us to entertain. Moreover, such efforts may only reveal the person, the mind suggesting the pattern. This is not to say that humor in Shakespeare does not evolve or change. But, perhaps it is more profitable to see these changes as meeting the needs of a practical, practicing dramatist, or as inseparable from the immediate demands of a given play, or at one with the larger evolution of what have been called his "philosophical patterns."

Bertrand Evans, for example, in his book *Shakespearean Comedy* notes that in the early works the audience always knows as much if not more than any given character, that we sit, in effect, at the right hand of the playwright in our knowledge of what is happening. In *A Midsummer Night's Dream,* for instance, we know that there are two couples in the forest. Theseus assumes that there is only one and this mistake leads to confusion when Lysander wakes up to find Helena rather than Hermia before him. His eyes anointed with a love-producing potion, Lysander, the victim of Oberon's imperfect knowledge, falls for the wrong girl.

In the later comedies there is an increasingly larger gap between the audience's knowledge of the plot at any given moment and that of the playwright. One scene after Portia announces in *The Merchant of Venice* that she and Nerissa will "live as maids and widows" until their husbands' problems with Shylock are resolved, we learn that in reality the women will disguise themselves as men and, far from retreating to a convent, will actively battle Shylock in male disguises at Antonio's trial. That is, at the time of Portia's announcement, we know no more than do Bassanio and Gratiano. Similarly, with *The Winter's Tale* (1610–1611) we, as does the grieving husband Leontes, assume that his wife Hermione has died, when all the time she has been preserved for sixteen years by Paulina in a chapel.

This growing discrepancy between author and audience very much affects how we feel about the worlds of the plays, about how we respond to the humor. Our superior position in *The Comedy of Errors* where we know that both sets of twins are present (although we do not know until the final scene that the mother of the two Antipholi is also present) affords us a sort of Olympian perspective on the comic frustrations and mix-ups experienced by the characters. By the middle comedies that perspective has been challenged; our laughter, as a consequence, deepens as what Aristotle called our "pity" (our emotional removal from the characters since we know more than they do and understand that it is all a play) is overbalanced by "fear" (our identification with the characters, our taking their stage lives as bearing on our own reality).

This change in the audience's response to humor in Shakespeare's plays is reflected in the changes in the comic worlds themselves. The early comedies such as *The Comedy of Errors, The Two Gentlemen of Verona,* and *A Midsummer Night's Dream* are sustained in large measure by plots where the "uncomplicating" of complex events in the final scene leads to a "happy ending." In *Love's Labour's Lost* this uncomplicating is directed at the artificial language by which the characters have substituted affectations ranging from scholarship to celibacy for real emotions. In *The Taming of the Shrew* the resolution comes with the emergence of the deeper, more attractive dimensions of the personalities of the warring lovers, Petruchio and Kate.

In the middle comedies, extending from *The Merchant of Venice* through works like *As You Like It* and *Twelfth Night,* through the so-called dark comedies *The History of Troilus and Cressida, All's Well That Ends Well,* and *Measure for Measure,* plot, character, and language are more firmly rooted in ethical and political concerns, and issues of gender. The word "resolution" itself must be qualified. Cressida is at best "compromised" at the end in her union with Diomedes and there is a savagery in the humor of the clown Thersites that surpasses anything of which, say, Jacques is capable in *As You Like It.* Like Portia, Rosalind in *As You Like It* must intervene to bring about a comic ending, and if in the final, seemingly bucolic scene of *The Merchant of Venice* the lovers unite, if Shylock has been vanquished, still his memory lingers. For some directors, Jessica, his daughter now converted to Christianity, remains a disturbing presence. The resolution in *Measure for Measure* comes from tricks (as does that in *All's Well That Ends Well*) and fortuitous accidents; the happy ending is not just a matter of affectations being stripped away or the benevolent intervention of well-meaning supernaturals or the characters' discovering the very key to happiness that the audience knew was there from the start.

In the final comedies, the "romances," time itself becomes a factor in the resolution. The "green" or "garden" middle-world of plays such as *A Midsummer Night's Dream* where characters escape the confines and potential tragedies of the city, in *Pericles* (1608–1609), *Cymbeline* (1609–1610), and *The Winter's Tale* (1610–1611) are replaced by distant places, reached over time and where the agents for the restoration of happiness and good will are activated. Over time, the "worst returns to laughter," to borrow Edgar's line from *King Lear.* In *The Tempest,* Prospero's account of the past, of his expulsion from his throne and the perfidy of his brother, an account that so bores his daughter Miranda that she falls asleep while her father is talking, places this sad past outside the play proper. What we see is that final stage after years of tragedy where Prospero, like Shakespeare, enforces a happy ending by his art. Here the issue, as in the middle comedies, is not simply the exposure of a foible or the scraping away of some idiosyncrasy but instead the reformation of character itself, Prospero's included. Only when his desire for revenge, his bitterness, and his concomitant sense of superiority are abandoned can he rejoin the human community and in the process laugh at himself.

As the sense of comedy in Shakespeare's comedies deepens to include important human issues (the nature of justice, the treatment of women, the ability of a community to be inclusive rather than exclusive), so too does comedy invade the writer's histories and tragedies. In the former, Richard III, the comic villain, must later share the stage with Falstaff, the comic who mocks the concern with political succession and the rights and responsibilities of a ruler expressed in the histories. That Hal succeeds as the ideal king in *Henry V* (1598–1599) has much to do with his tutelage at the hands of Falstaff. The fat knight's comedy sustains our private self as it associates with others in the cultivation of all that is not serious but life-giving. In his great speech before the battle of Agincourt, Hal knows just what he has given up—a playful, private, irresponsible, joyous self, the half of him that was tutored by Falstaff—even as he knows that this loss is the price that he must pay in order to be king. He has a perspective on himself through the mirror of comedy that Bolingbroke, his father, and the various unhappy kings of the first tetralogy did

not have. This very sense of humor is anticipated in a minor chord in Richard II's own joking with a humorless Bolingbroke when the latter dethrones him.

There is a marvelous scene in *1 Henry IV* where Falstaff plays Hal's father and then the roles are reversed, with Falstaff's playing Hal to Hal's playing his father. For Falstaff it is all good fun, besides being a chance to buff up his tarnished reputation as a coward. For Hal, it is no less fun. Yet, as he observes Falstaff attempt through his acting to fashion himself as something other than he is, as a responsible, wise, old man, Hal uses this humorous situation along with Falstaff's own unintentionally humorous defensive posture to see himself and to determine what he must do. Accordingly, at his coronation at the end of *2 Henry IV* (1597–1598), Hal banishes Falstaff from his presence. The comic character thus absorbed within the psyche of the new king, now expendable, sets the stage for *Henry V,* a history play that, with the English defeat of the French, and Henry's marriage to the French princess is, properly, a comical-history.

When Shakespeare's humor invades the tragedies, when Hamlet himself decides to play the antic, to bring to life in his own person the court clown Yorick, then we know that the divisions between comedy and tragedy have been eased. Far more than merely an emotional release or a way of wounding the shallow or deceptive courtiers of Denmark, humor is Hamlet's defense against the world. Playing the antic—the court jester, besides being a eunuch, was also insane—he separates himself from the world. As Hamlet tells Ophelia, "What should a man do but be merry." The paradox is that the grieving young man who refuses to change out of his funeral clothes, much to the anguish of his mother and step-father, with his puns and jokes is also Shakespeare's most profound and intense comedian. Hamlet models himself after Yorick, whose skull he addresses as "a fellow of infinite jest, of most excellent fancy." Yorick's "gibes," "gambols," and "flashes of merriment" that "were wont to set the table on a roar" are reborn in the prince. Humor is his way of warding off insanity, the condition to which, without humor, he would have fallen prey, given the incest, fratricide, and regicide that stain Claudius's court.

In larger measure, humor in Shakespeare's plays is a way of surviving, the countermovement to tragedy and despair and nihilism. As a humorist, Shakespeare takes the joke and converts it into a way of life, valuing, as he seems to do, homo sapiens (thinking man) no more than homo ludens (playing man).

Summary

William Shakespeare draws from a common bag of comic techniques: exaggeration, reversal, sometimes frustrating and at other times more than meeting audience expectations, one-liners, tall tales, unintended humor, absurdity—the range of comedy from farce to parody to satire. In this sense he is like other humorists. What distinguishes Shakespeare among humorists is the fact that the comedy in his plays is never gratuitous. It is, instead, inseparable from characterization, from the way that the character views (or fails to view) himself or herself, and from the audience's own larger response to the world of the play. Moreover, humor is infused in otherwise serious, even tragic moments, as a counterbalance. Characters with a good sense of humor, especially as it applies to themselves, tend to value survival over principle, or, if they must attend to principles, realize just what "cost factor" is involved in public or political responsibilities. While it is difficult to mark clear stages in the development of Shakespeare's humor, a general pattern does emerge: humor based on plot, language, and character in the early works; humor that is inseparable from the entertainment of serious issues in the middle works; and, in his final dramas, a comic view of life where humor aided by time is the key to a happy resolution. When humor—the elements of comedy—becomes a major factor in Shakespeare's histories and tragedies, then the playwright has expanded the comic perspective on life toward a philosophy.

Selected Bibliography

Primary Sources

Numerous good modern editions exist of Shakespeare's works, both in collections and in individual play formats. Below is a list of the plays and non-dramatic works with the suggested dates of their composition.

The Comedy of Errors. 1588–1593.
Love's Labour's Lost. 1588–1594.
The Second Part of Henry the Sixth. 1590–1591.
The Third Part of Henry the Sixth. 1590–1592.
The First Part of Henry the Sixth. 1591–1592.

Venus and Adonis. 1592.
The Tragedy of Richard the Third. 1592–1593.
The Tragedy of Titus Andronicus. 1592–1594.
The Taming of the Shrew. 1593–1594.
The Rape of Lucrece. 1593–1594.
The Two Gentlemen of Verona. 1593–1595.
Sonnets. 1593–1600.
The Tragedy of Romeo and Juliet. 1594–1596.
The Tragedy of King Richard the Second. 1595.
A Midsummer Night's Dream. 1594–1596.
The Life and Death of King John. 1596–1597.
The Merchant of Venice. 1596–1597.
The First Part of Henry the Fourth. 1597.
The Second Part of Henry the Fourth. 1597–1598.
The Merry Wives of Windsor. 1597–1601.
The Life of Henry the Fifth. 1598–1599.
Much Ado about Nothing. 1598–1600.
The Tragedy of Julius Caesar. 1599.
As You Like It. 1599–1600.
Twelfth Night, or What You Will. 1599–1600.
The Tragedy of Hamlet, Prince of Denmark. 1600–1601.
The Phoenix and the Turtle. 1600–1601.
The History of Troilus and Cressida. 1601–1602.
All's Well That Ends Well. 1602–1604.
The Tragedy of Othello, the Moor of Venice. 1603–1604.
Measure for Measure. 1604.
The Tragedy of King Lear. 1605–1606.
The Tragedy of Macbeth. 1605–1606.
The Life of Timon of Athens. 1605–1608.
The Tragedy of Antony and Cleopatra. 1606–1607.
The Tragedy of Coriolanus. 1607–1609.
Pericles, Prince of Tyre. 1608–1609.
Cymbeline. 1609–1610.
The Winter's Tale. 1610–1611.
The Tempest. 1611.
The Famous History of the Life of Henry the Eighth. 1612–1613.

Editions

The Riverside Shakespeare. Ed. G. Blakemore Evans. Boston: Houghton Mifflin, 1974.
The Complete Signet Classic Shakespeare. Ed. Sylvan Barnet. New York: Harcourt, Brace, Jovanovich, 1963.

S

Secondary Sources

Barber, C.L. *Shakespeare's Festive Comedy: A Study of Dramatic Form and Its Relation to Social Custom.* Princeton: Princeton University Press, 1959.

Berry, Ralph. *Shakespeare's Comedies: Explorations in Form.* Princeton: Princeton University Press, 1972.

Charlton, H.B. *Shakespearian Comedy.* London: Methuen, 1938.

Evans, Bertrand. *Shakespearean Comedy.* Oxford: Clarendon, 1960.

Foakes, R.A. *The Dark Comedies and the Last Plays: From Satire to Celebration.* Charlottesville: University of Virginia Press, 1971.

Frye, Northrup. *A Natural Perspective: The Development of Shakespearean Comedy and Romance.* New York: Columbia University Press, 1965.

Goldsmith, R.H. *Wise Fools in Shakespeare.* East Lansing: Michigan State University Press, 1955.

Hunter, G.K. *William Shakespeare: The Late Comedies.* London: Longmans, Green, 1962.

Hunter, R.G. *Shakespeare and the Comedy of Forgiveness.* New York: Columbia University Press, 1965.

Huston, Dennis. *Shakespeare's Comedies of Play.* New York: Columbia University Press, 1980.

Nevo, Ruth. *Comic Transformations in Shakespeare.* London: Methuen, 1980.

Palmer, John. *Comic Characters in Shakespeare.* London: Macmillan, 1946.

Parrott, T.M. *Shakespearean Comedy.* New York: Russell and Russell, 1946.

Philias, P.G. *Shakespeare's Romantic Comedies.* Chapel Hill: University of North Carolina Press, 1966.

Salingar, Leo. *Shakespeare and the Tradition of Comedy.* London: Cambridge University Press, 1974.

Tillyard, E.M.W. *Shakespeare's Early Comedies.* New York: Barnes & Noble, 1965.

Weiss, T. *The Breadth of Clowns and Kings.* New York: Atheneum, 1971.

Westlund, Joseph. *Shakespeare's Reparative Comedies: A Psychoanalytic View of the Middle Plays.* Chicago: University of Chicago Press, 1984.

Wheeler, Richard. *Shakespeare's Development and the Problem Comedies: Turn and Counter-Turn.* Berkeley and Los Angeles: University of California Press, 1981.

Wilson, John Dover. *The Fortunes of Falstaff.* Cambridge: Cambridge University Press, 1964.

Wilson, John Dover. *Shakespeare's Happy Comedies.* Evanston: Northwestern University Press, 1962.

Note: The books listed above are only a fraction of the enormous amount that has been published on comedy and humor in Shakespeare—and only suggestive at best. *Shakespeare Quarterly* annually provides an annotated bibliography of the past year's publications on the subject.

Sidney Homan

Sharpe, Tom

Born: London, Holloway, March 30, 1928
Education: Bloxham (Bucks.); Lancing College; Pembroke College, Oxford University, M.A., 1951
Marriage: Nancy Anne Looper, August 6, 1969; three children

Biography

Tom (Thomas Ridley) Sharpe has challenged P.G. Wodehouse for excellence and popularity in the United Kingdom (if not sufficiently in the United States). He was born in Holloway, a suburb of London, on March 30, 1928, to George Coverdale Sharpe (a Unitarian minister, aged fifty-eight) and Grace Egerton Sharpe (whose English family had long had connections with South Africa). The Reverend Sharpe was a former socialist and a supporter of National Socialism in Germany, so Tom grew up affected by his father's Nazi sympathies, which caused problems for him at school. As a result, he ran away from Bloxham (Bucks.) and attended Lancing College during World War II. In 1951, he received an M.A. from Pembroke College, Oxford. Meanwhile, the truth about Nazi atrocities in World War II came as a great shock to Tom as did his exposure to race relations in South Africa, where he went to work there after his national service in the Royal Marines (1946–1948).

Satire was an inevitable response to what he experienced in South Africa. Sharpe's first job was for the Department of Non-European Affairs in a black township (now famous as Soweto) outside Johannesburg. He then taught white children in Natal and opened a photographic studio in Pietermaritzburg in 1956. He wrote nine or ten political plays but as soon as one was produced (in London, 1960), he was imprisoned in South Africa and then deported. Sharpe married an American, Nancy Anne Looper, on August 6, 1969. The union produced three daughters. In 1971, he retaliated for his South African imprisonment and deportation with two vehement satires of Afrikaans police-state idiocy. *Riotous Assembly* is set in Piemburg (Pietermaritzburg) and excoriates its police chief (Commandant van Heeren) and other Afrikaans functionaries as well as some resident English (one of whom expects to get away with killing her transvestite Zulu cook with whom she has been having an affair).

The success of *Riotous Assembly* started Sharpe on a career as a professional writer—he had been in the educational trenches at the Cambridgeshire College of Arts and Technology, teaching history, and was to use that dire experience joyfully in his *Wilt* books. He followed up *Riotous Assembly* with *Indecent Exposure* (1973) in which the Afrikaans police and the English expatriots continue outrageous foolishness: "all good, dirty fun" (*Daily Telegraph*) with the police force turned *gay* (aversion therapy misfiring) and all hell breaking loose in "a lusty and delightfully lunatic fantasy," according to the *Evening Sun* reviewer.

Moving from what the *Times Literary Supplement* reviewer called "revealing the criminal idiocies of apartheid" in violent derision and what another critic called "a barely controlled hysteria" of lunatic plots, Sharpe picked a target nearer home. *Porterhouse Blue* (1974) is set in Cambridge. A failed Labor politician becomes the master of the college and introduces new ideas in cafeterias, curriculum change, and condom dispensers. Sharpe uses the ensuing havoc to mock academic politics and British resistance to educational and social reform, so his time at Cambridge as a student was not wasted.

The Oxbridge Establishment having suffered, it was now the turn of what Americans would call the junior colleges. Sharpe's experiences at Cambridgeshire College of Arts and Technology was mined for the story of a minor teacher of liberal arts named Henry Wilt. The hero, teaching, as it were, obstetrics in an intellectual or non-intellectual nunnery, clashes with both colleagues and police in *Wilt* (1976), a book that was even better than its predecessor, *Blott on the Landscape* (1975), because of personal venom. In *Blott*, Sharpe had attacked Lo-

cal Authority bureaucrats and environmental planners, but *Wilt* went for the throat of educational "authorities" and curriculum planners, even sleazier villains.

Then the writer satirized the world of literature and publishers, agents, critics, and even readers in *The Great Pursuit* (1977). The volume includes not only a madcap cut-to-the-chase plot—peopled by literary agent F.A. Frensic (posing as a bestselling author) and the nymphomaniacal wife of a movie mogul—but the pursuit of literary values in a bad way in our ditzy, decadent, and doomed culture.

In *The Throwback* (1978), which American humorist Roy Blount, Jr., hailed as "far more satisfying than Kingsley Amis or any other nasty Brit novelist since Evelyn Waugh," Sharpe sank his serpent's tooth into lawyers et al. The character of Wilt is replaced by a more determined protagonist: Lockhart Flawes, who may be illegitimate but who is going to get his inheritance even if he has to be a bastard about it and sue or slay. At the end of the book Flawes drives the tax collector completely mad. This may reflect the personal desires of a British writer who has stayed at home, made a good living entirely by his pen, and had to bear the slings and arrows of the Inland Revenue yearly since giving up teaching and starting to earn real money by selling a couple of million copies of hardcover and paperback books.

Wilt returned in triumph in *The Wilt Alternative* (1979). Once again educational stupidity and police ineptitude are Sharpe's principal topics. International terrorists take over Wilt's happy home (which includes the wife that he once wanted to murder but now accepts and the quadruplet daughters who are the fruit of the rocky marriage). When the authorities, as they always do in Sharpe farces, screw up, Wilt screws his courage to the sticking place and takes charge.

Left-wing academics, right-wing capitalists, incompetent authorities of all sorts (including traditional British stereotypes of high and low degree) stuff the farce of *Ancestral Vices* (1980), which went through a number of reprintings in hardcover even before paperback publication (1982). This time the British aristocrats, having risen from what Oscar Wilde described as "the purple of commerce," are a major target, Lord Petrefact of Petrefact Consolidated Enterprises especially. "Another bawdy and brutal romp," said Nicholas Shrimpton in the *New Statesman*. To his regular characters such as the silly, the stuffy, and the sexually kinky, this time the novelist adds still another sure-fire British Aunt Sally: the ridiculous American, Professor Walden Yapp of Kloone University who is commissioned by Lord Osprey Petrefact to write a history of the family. High jinks abound with Sharpe in his usual high spirits and high dudgeon.

In 1982, the author created the character of Peregrine Roderick Clyde-Browne, who started life as the perfect baby and grew up to be a pupil who did everything his schoolmaster told him to do. In *Vintage Stuff* (1982), the horrible results are recounted in an hilarious hodgepodge of a plot which is set in an obscure public school that was "founded in the latter half of the nineteenth century by a hopelessly optimistic clergyman to bring Anglo-Catholic fervour to the local farmers' sons." There are many really crazy accounts of public schools, some intentionally funny and some (like the two by Dean Farrar that Rudyard Kipling mocks in *Stalky & Co.*) inadvertently so. *Vintage Stuff* is determinedly uproarious and may be the funniest of all. Peregrine ends up "in a hedge in South Armagh" as a danger to the IRA, the RUC, and more, still, in dogged British fashion, sticking to his guns and mindlessly doing what he is told. This may be both the most British and the most anti-British of all Sharpe's novels.

William Shakespeare had a hard time getting rid of Falstaff; Arthur Conan Doyle a hard time getting rid of Sherlock Holmes. Everyone rejoiced when Wilt appeared on the scene again in *Wilt on High* (1984). In this novel the police as informers on narcotics violations target Wilt, and this time sex means Mrs. Wilt slipping an aphrodisiac into his drink. Farce and decay are apparent all around—and, as is only right, in the end Wilt emerges triumphant. By now the always bitter Sharpe is truly nasty. His writing is still funny but in the minds of critics (probably because their culture, not the Afrikaans, is now bearing the full brunt of Sharpe's sharp eye) he is more savage. The author creates fictional mayhem to reflect the madness in real life. *Wilt on High* is, in fact, extremely funny fiction fueled by profound moral indignation.

Sharpe as a writer, and perhaps as a person, has gone beyond the genial foolishness of Wodehouse and, unlike Sir Pelham, tackles the contemporary world, not some Edwardian construct. In Sharpe's writing there is the political commitment of a George Orwell mixed with the juvenile anarchy of a Richmal Compton. There is also the personal involvement that character-

ized Alexander Pope and the moral outrage that drove Jonathan Swift to despair and denunciation. Sharpe's novels exhibit a move from the kind of rather nasty mood that characterizes the works of Kingsley Amis to the really nasty mood found in the writing of his son, Martin Amis. It is the underlying anger in Sharpe that has caused him to be ranked with cantankerous old Evelyn Waugh and the brilliance with which he transforms it into irresistible laughter which has caused Auberon Waugh to hail Sharpe as the greatest comic novelist writing in Britain today.

Some of Sharpe's canon has been published in the United States and a very few critics here have praised him highly, but basically Sharpe is too English for American tastes, which is why television adaptations of his works (let alone his novels themselves in our less than book-bound society) have not been widely seen here.

In a 1985 interview, Jean W. Ross asked Sharpe painfully and awkwardly, "Is there a lot of literary criticism-type [*sic*] of writing done in England about your work? I didn't find much here." Sharpe explained that his satire of academics and critics made statements not "calculated to make a writer popular with professors and people who earn their living doing what I attack." He also said that Random House, in reprinting some of his novels in a Vintage series, was "afraid Americans would misinterpret the satire" of the anti-South African novels and even, in light of American touchiness about race, consider them anti-black. "If I were black and in America, I'd find that downright insulting," he said. But, despite his marriage to an American woman, Sharpe does not understand the United States' craziness with regard to all matters of race. About most of the rest of American interests he has much to tell us, the bitter pill usually delightfully sugar-coated.

Literary Analysis

To introduce Sharpe's very British humor, it is instructive to consider two related jokes, one American, one British. First, Dorothy Parker is credited with the quip, "If all the sweet young things at the Yale prom were laid end to end, I wouldn't be the least bit surprised." Second, a character at The Drones Club in a Wodehouse short story is discussing Freddie Widgeon's love life:

> "Do you know," said a thoughtful Bean, "I'll bet that if all the girls Freddie

Widgeon has loved and lost were placed end to end—not that I suppose one could do it—they would reach half-way down Piccadilly."

"Further than that," said the Egg. "Some of them were pretty tall."

The American joke is a wisecrack, short, sharp, surprising. The British one relies on characters (an unnamed old Bean and The Egg), a literary allusion from Alfred, Lord Tennyson ("loved and lost"), whimsy, and the caricaturing of chinless-wonder, rather dim members of The Drones Club. In the British version, sexual sniping gives way to more genial satire.

Sharpe likes the wisecrack and shares with American humorists a belief that the police are always oafs and usually corrupt; that snobbery and the high horse and the high hat cry out for leveling; that too much is never enough in low comedy or complexities never enough in farcical plots; that there is no joke like an old joke; and that wrenching dada punchlines—*da-da-DUM*—taken from cliched expressions is fun. "I'm my own worst enemy," for example, traditionally elicits "Not while I'm around." Sharpe displays a similarity with the Marx Brothers, who have influenced the comedy of Samuel Beckett and Sharpe, among others. For example, in one of their films Chico and Harpo are in court. Chico asks the witness, the silent Harpo, what is a big, gray animal with big ears and a long trunk. Angrily, authority (the judge) says, "That's irrelevant!" Triumphantly, Chico crows, "Thatsa *right*!" Sharpe likewise plays with the misunderstandings inherent in words until a tottering structure of chaos is erected, fated to crash, meanwhile suspenseful and fantastic.

But, Sharpe is not American in his vehemence and in going into darker regions than Ben Jonson explored when he decided "to sport with human follies, not with crimes." Sharpe handles touchy topics such as apartheid that in American humor is considered "no laughing matter," and his comedy can be so bitter and vituperative that Piers Brendon can say of it: "The farce is so violent, extravagant and unremitting; it contains such a wealth of bestial ferocity and technicolor perversion that there is a distinctly manic flavour about it."

American humor contains jokes about freeways, mothers-in-law, and other politically correct, "safe" subjects. People have become so touchy that comedians are practically confined to making fun of themselves; the lunge for the joking jugular is "in bad taste" and anything ethnic is likely to arouse angry protest. Sharpe is British, British of the type that is right, knows it, and is intolerant of those who persist in being wrong even after they have been told. They must be dealt with, and (as Gwendolyn puts it in Wilde's *The Importance of Being Earnest*) nastily putting them in their place is more than a moral duty, it is a *pleasure* which is cruel, cathartic, and delicious. The British have a special flair for "ticking one off," and it is thrilling to those who live in the only country of the world in which "Sorry" is a calculated insult.

Moreover, Sharpe likes a fight and he loves to go to extremes. "Shits in shits' clothing" deserve all that they get. In Sharpe's works, as an American might say, they are dumped on. There is no moderation; restraint is unhealthy and could bring on a fatal apoplexy. Some readers see this approach as equivalent to running victims through with a rapier. Some accuse the writer of overkill with a blunt instrument. Affectation (which Joseph Addison said was "the only true source of the ridiculous") receives not disapprobation but dismemberment. Pomposity calls for exploding condoms—"What had Sir Giles done for the future? Nothing . . . He deserved to die." There is a lot of mayhem in Sharpe's truly nasty (and not just in the British idea of "nasty," which usually carries a sexual connotation) chronicles of people getting theirs. When a dying man telephones the Samaritans, in American comedy he might be put on hold. In Sharpe's comedy someone has to one-up him personally: "I can't take personal calls," the man's wife (who works the help line) tells him, "I have to be helping people in trouble."

To add to the distress of the overly sensitive, Sharpe relishes cloacal humor and can never resist the most outrageous sexual joke. Some ladylike critics (of both sexes) fault him not for his bile but for what Anthony Thwaite in the *Observer* called "disgrace notes." Sharpe is in the tradition of British music-hall, stag-party, rugby-song unabashed ("unquotable") loo and genitalia jokes.

Those who bypass Sharpe miss not only the bawdy burlesque but also the highly moral spectacle of the comeuppance visited upon those villains who are exploded, eaten by lions, or otherwise disposed of in colorful and wholly deserved ways. Vengeance is mine, saith the satirist.

Sharpe's humorous techniques naturally derive from his fundamental approach, which is that of the furious farceur who compounds anger and amusement. His inventiveness suits the depiction of a mad, modern world peopled with outrageous characters who are swept up by fast and furious events. He combines startling effects with occasional deadpan humor and loves stark contrasts, careening narrative, and eccentric people caught up in hilarious confusions. His dialogue is deft and more restrained than his characterization, which sometimes is mere caricature (shown in such onomastic choices as Bilger and Symper and Wilt and Blott, of *Blott on the Landscape*) but suits the way-out "doctrinaire shits" (the phrase is from *The Wilt Alternative*) such as fascist pigs, dyed-in-the-wool conservatives, postmodern yahoos, and other villains and ninnies involved in his risible ball-ups.

His swift pace and bold strokes and hilarious dialogue recommend Sharpe to television adaptation. If Britain were still prominent in the field of comic cinema his work would be better known.

The author may be vivacious or vicious by turns, but his literary skill is almost always in evidence. He is unrestrained and occasionally unstable in his plots, which the critics like to compare to houses of cards. Sharpe is, according to Robert Nye in the *Guardian Weekly,* an awkward amateur "when he describes action or seeks to enact thought," but the humorist is hailed even by Nye as a master of comic dialogue, whether he is parodying bureaucratic jargon or educationese or American, making atrocious puns, using "pertinacious verbal energy" and "bilious coarseness" (Thwaite), and sheer satiric genius and abandon. The scholarly consensus is that the attacks on Afrikaaners are more powerful and more palatable than subsequent satires but that with *The Great Pursuit,* even though that book was not as popular as some of his other volumes, Sharpe gave promise of improved work. Since then his writing has grown more gloomy and less funny. Simon Edwards concludes, "the reviewers of Sharpe's novels have missed much of his real importance, tending to see each novel as a joyously anarchic squib and calling Sharpe a remarkable intelligence making welcome use of an accessible popular form. In fact, the works taken together create a far more troubled world, brooding on humankind's tenuous reproduction and survival. Thus the novels are apocalyptic, haunted by recurring motifs of sterility, impotence, and both moral and physical perversion."

Newspaper critics have been more affable, claiming that *Riotous Assembly* is "crackling, spitting, murderously funny" (*Daily Telegraph*), *Indecent Exposure* is "explosively funny, fiendishly inventive" (*Sunday Times*), *Blott on the Landscape* shows "Tom Sharpe is writing what are very possibly the funniest novels in English today" (*Washington Post Book World*), *The Great Pursuit* is "Tom Sharpe's individual blend of robust farce and deeply cutting satire" (*The Listener*), *The Throwback* finds Sharpe "funny, bitter, a danger to his public" (*The Listener*), *Wilt* is "superb farce" (*Tribune*), *Wilt on High* plunges "into the bottomless vulgarity and hysteria of our times" (*Mail on Sunday*), *The Wilt Alternative* is "sublime orgiastic satire" (*The Guardian*), and *Vintage Stuff* is "a roar of derring-do, misunderstandings and catastrophes" (The *Times*). Only Francis King faults the novelist for "not human comedy but inhuman farce . . . too gruesome to be funny" (The *Spectator*). Auberon Waugh strikes the proper balance: "Satirical purists would probably say that [*Riotous Assembly*] is a failure in that it falls between two stools—savage political satire and loathing of man's brutality etc. on the one hand, slapstick on the other. They would be right to say that the book falls between two stools, but wrong to say that it is therefore a failure. It is extremely enjoyable to read and therefore a success. Its imperfections are only relative to its many excellences."

Since his first novel, Sharpe has gotten better and better, and he has moved more securely onto the savage stool. He sits, in fact, high on a throne of royal state among the funniest and fiercest writers of comic fiction now alive.

Though possibly the funniest British novelist writing in the 1970s and 1980s, he has been called an historian of "contemporary literature and culture," like Anthony Powell and Anthony Burgess: "Sharpe's novels, regardless of setting, form a vast and grotesque counterpastoral of contemporary English life as much concerned with myths as realities. He has created a history of England at once both cruel and sentimental, where liberated sexual mores—in which social classes meet in illusory freedoms together with barbarian outsiders disguised in shabby parodies of the conventions—threaten to destroy the contradictory fabric of their inception" (Edwards). Imagine Margaret Thatcher in a rubber fetishist outfit directing a war for The Malvinas, waving a Union Jack borrowed from the last night of the Proms, shouting the battle cry, "Don't Give Up The Sheep!" Think of flags, punks, Labor peers, The Chunnel, Britain becoming a province of a New Europe led by (who else?) the Germans. It is getting more difficult to write satire by the minute.

Sharpe has managed to write satire beautifully even if lately he has been getting (as the Brits say) "too near the bone." The elements of his art are: the love of bawdy; the love of a good, exciting yarn (such as written by Sir Walter Scott and Kipling, who wrote the boys' books that Sharpe loved as a youngster); a keen eye (his hobby is photography) for current lunacies; a British taste for what will "make your flesh creep"; fictive names for caricatures (Slyme, Flint, Skullion) and other Dickensian touches (with some echoes of his favorite Dickens novels, such as *Martin Chuzzlewit*); slapstick and vulgarity in the tradition of the Carry On films and Benny Hill; juvenile capers à la *The Boy's Own Paper, The Magnet, The Gem,* and the *William* books; a conviction that decadence and degeneracy is hilarious; masquerade and other standard devices of comic confusion; lowlife "base mechanicals" and Mummersetshire peasantry for laughs, along with upperclass twits similar to those in Wodehouse and Nancy Mitford; puns and double meanings with singular force, often naughty; verbal felicities and self-indulgences; the triumph of the Little Man with a joy when the worm turns and the high are brought low; a conviction that there is irresistible humor inherent in certain words ("knickers" is one of them) and all scatology (the latter in the style of Swift); formidable women such as Lady Maud Lynchwood in *Blott* and even Eva Wilt, with whom Sharpe confesses he identifies (as he does on other grounds with her husband, Henry) as she "leaps from one theory to another, many of them phony" (Sharpe adds, "I also share her anger when the phoniness becomes too apparent"); an abiding conviction that all foreigners are funny but that Americans are notably weird; what Sharpe terms "the madcap action of the silent movies" which catches up the viewer and liberates him from all pedestrian logic, propelling him into a world of hysterical fantasy; the certain knowledge of how to keep a farce moving at dazzling speed; the serious undercurrents beneath the fun; the telling touch with dialogue, incorporating age-old British elements of light

literary allusion, the verbal equivalents of a "funny walk," and other features done deftly by comic writers who have a piercing insight into contemporary real life and those who make up an imaginary world out of whole cloth and out of all real-time frame; parody of other literature, especially popular literature to which the reader may be secretly addicted (for Sharpe, Dornford Yates); subjects for satire familiar (pomposity, bureaucracy, hypocrisy, all authority) and only occasionally done (but always appreciated, like Academia and its political struggles); politics and the inherent grotesqueries, especially by a writer deeply committed in some respects but on the whole ready to see foolishness wherever it lies, left or right. Finally, there are whimsy and wit and a fierce sense of outrage, without which Sharpe would never have stuck to his writing (two decades passed before he became an instant success), or been so demanding (out of 400,000 words written 80,000 were quarried for *The Great Pursuit*) or so polished (twenty-five versions of the opening chapter of *Indecent Exposure* were done). As a result, he has become, according to *Punch*, "Britain's leading practitioner of black humour."

Summary

Tom Sharpe's novels are riotous assemblies of comic devices. They make people laugh out loud. They also are well adapted to reading out loud, for his humor has a strong verbal element: his ear is as sensitive to the ludicrous as is his eye. That his puns can sometimes be atrocious or certain details silly should not blind anyone to the fact that he is at bottom a savage commentator on foolishness who (like Jonson) "sports with human follies, not with crimes."

Selected Bibliography

Primary Sources

Fiction
Riotous Assembly. New York: Viking Press, 1971; Atlantic, 1987.
Indecent Exposure. London: Secker & Warburg, 1973; Atlantic, 1987.
Porterhouse Blue. New York: Prentice-Hall, 1974.
Blott on the Landscape. London: Secker & Warburg, 1975; Vintage, 1984.
Wilt. London: Secker & Warburg, 1976; Vintage, 1984.
The Great Pursuit. London: Secker &

Warburg, 1977; Harper, 1978; Vintage, 1984.

The Throwback. London: Secker & Warburg, 1978; Vintage, 1984.

The Wilt Alternative. London: Secker & Warburg, 1979; New York: St. Martin's Press, 1980; Vintage, 1984.

Ancestral Vices. London: Secker & Warburg, 1980; Pan, 1982.

Vintage Stuff. London: Secker & Warburg, 1982; Pan, 1983; Vintage, 1984.

Wilt on High. London: Secker & Warburg, 1984; New York: Random House, 1985.

Drama

The South African. Three-act play, premiered Questor's Theatre, Ealing (London), 1961.

Television Drama

She Fell Among Thieves. 1977 BBC-TV adaptation of Dornford Yates's novel.

Blott on the Landscape. Adapted by Malcolm Bradbury for BBC-TV, 1985.

Porterhouse Blue. Adapted by Malcolm Bradbury for ITV, 1987.

Secondary Sources

Ackroyd, Peter. "On the Road." *Spectator,* 234, 7665 (May 24, 1975): 637. Blott is "nifty," "combining predictability and risibility," and "over it all hangs the air of mild prurience which is so necessary in matters of humor."

Ashley, Leonard R.N. "Sharpe Criticism: Onomastics in Tom Sharpe's Satires of South Africa." *Journal of the North Central Name Society* (Winter 1988–1989): 1–12. The names in *Indecent Exposure* and *Riotous Assembly* mix "the chaotic and incongruous, the outlandish and the outrageous" and create a satire of "both implausibility and trenchant comment on reality."

Bragg, Melvin. "[Graham] Greene & [Tom] Sharpe." *Punch,* 274 (March 22, 1978): 505. "Sharpe is one of the funniest contemporary novelists writing in Britain today and *The Throw Back* (sic) sees him in top form, piling jokes on comic inventions with all the skill of a literary illusionist."

Brendon, Piers. "*Riotous Assembly.*" *Books and Bookmen,* 16, 9 (June 1971): 42–44. *Riotous Assembly* is "hilarious farce which is peopled chiefly with vicious, moronic, and grotesque gendarmes who are made to jump through a number of lurid hoops . . . behind the camouflage of uproarious slapstick is a complex allegory of South African life . . . an outstanding *tour de force.*"

Davis, L.J. "A Farce on the Trendy Side." *Washington Post Book World* (March 3, 1985): 5. *Wilt on High* fails "because of three surprisingly commonplace mistakes: a curiously British notion that there is something inherently uproarious about male genitalia, a compulsion to arrange a finale of surpassing hilariousness in the manner of a West End farce, and a by no means exclusively British belief that once you know a foreigner's nationality, you know something useful about him."

Dold, Bernard E. *Two Post-1945 British Novelists . . . .* Roma: Herder, 1985. Sharpe compared and contrasted with Olivia Manning, author of *The Balkan Trilogy* and other realistic novels.

Downing, Angela. "Strategies of Verbal Humor in a Contemporary British Novelist." *Language & Literature,* 8 (1983): 17–32. Sharpe's "zingers" are clever if sometimes outrageous but his comic art is seen best in extended passages as chaos careens along.

Edwards, Simon. "Tom Sharpe." *Dictionary of Literary Biography, Vol. 14: British Novelists Since 1960, Part I: A-G.* Ed. Jay L. Halio. Detroit: Gale Research, 1983, pp. 646–54. "Reviewers were universally enthusiastic about his earlier work, but recently they have begun to take him to task for a lack of generosity toward his characters . . . criticisms that may not be justified."

Hepburn, Neil. "Latin-Americans in Paris." *The Listener,* 95, 2447 (March 4, 1976): 285–86. It is "P.G. Wodehouse to whom Mr. Sharpe has been tediously compared; and he was, I used to think, in real danger of being trapped in that master's empty room, too small to swing his vicious gifts in. Wilt is at least halfway to breaking out of that cozy den into the ferocious satire for which Mr. Sharpe's gifts best fit him."

Hewison, R. "Ancestral Vices." *Times Literary Supplement,* 4050 (1980):

1280. Review.

Hope, Mary. "*Ancestral Vices.*" *Spectator*, 245, 7594–595 (December 20, 1980): 34. "The moral is that the world is a random place, a constant struggle between conflicting and dangerous idiocies . . . savage foolery of each camp: a plague on both your houses."

Keates, Jonathan. "Whelk in the Soup." *Observer* (September 30, 1984): 20. Sharpe exploits "all the most fundamentally English springs of fun . . . lavatories . . . sex in its Chaucerian guises, and policemen . . . bladder trouble . . . well-worn shapes of farce and slapstick."

Kemp, Peter. "Idylls and Hells." *Listener*, 102, 2622 (August 2, 1979): 158–59. "Something more pointed than Sharpe's blunt instruments" is needed in the "old-fashioned English silliness" of *The Wilt Alternative*.

King, Francis. "Wise Cracks." *Spectator*, 240, 7812 (March 25, 1978): 20–21. In *The Throwback* sex is "usually—and unusually—repellant . . . The aggression consists largely of brutal practical jokes."

McCall, Raymond G. "The Comic Novels of Tom Sharpe." *Critique*, 25, 2 (Winter 1984): 57–65. Useful survey.

Nollet, Thomas. "Tom Sharpe and *Porterhouse Blue* . . . ." *Studies in Contemporary Satire*, 15 (1987): 23–29. Brief try at "the techniques of comedy and the satirist's vision"; less analytical than some reviews.

Nye, Robert. "Comic Violence, Violent Comedy." *Guardian Weekly*, 121, 6 (August 5, 1979): 22. "To have created a character of such infinite ridiculousness / as Wilt / is an achievement. His wife and his mother are well observed too . . . Sharpe improves on Wodehouse in the depiction of female comic-cuts."

Reynolds, Stanley. "The Sharpe End." *Punch*, 283, 7407 (November 1, 1982): 743–44. The "admirable but outdated values of Richard Hannay and Bulldog Drummond come up against the modern world" in the "rattling good yarn" that is *Vintage Stuff* and "*The Thirty-Nine Steps* et al. will probably never seem the same again."

Shrimpton, Nicholas. "Cold Feet in Moscow." *New Statesman*, 100, 2590 (November 7, 1980): 30. "Sharpe's satire is astonishingly, at times almost worryingly, even-handed . . . Occasionally he comes close to direct contradiction . . . The truth is that everything is grist to Mr. Sharpe's comic mill and he doesn't believe in thinking too hard about his raw material before he tosses it in."

Sutherland, S. "*Vintage Stuff.*" *Times Literary Supplement*, 4154 (1982): 1243. Insightful review of *Vintage Stuff*.

Treadwell, T. "*Wilt on High.*" *Times Literary Supplement*, 4254 (1984): 1166. Generally favorable review.

Thwaite, Anthony. "Freewheeling Fantasies." *Observer* (March 25, 1973): 36. Sharpe specializes in letting "a semantic misunderstanding grow and accelerate in a shower of *double-entendre* . . . " "Ruthlessness and muddle collide . . . all ends in carnage and chaos."

———. "Capers on the Cam." *Observer* (April 14, 1974): 31. "He is the funniest new writer to have emerged for several years." In *Porterhouse Blue* "the whole mesh turns into a garotte."

Waugh, Auberon. "Lancing Farce." *Spectator*, 226, 7455 (May 15, 1971): 671. "Savage political satire and loathing of man's brutality" are combined in *Riotous Assembly* with "slapstick," so "the book falls between two stools" yet remains "extremely enjoyable to read and therefore a success."

Leonard R.N. Ashley

Shaw, George Bernard

Born: Dublin, Ireland, July 26, 1856
Education: Wesleyan Connexional School, 1865, 1867–1868; Central Model Boys' School, 1869; Dublin English Scientific and Commercial Day School, Dublin, 1869–1871
Marriage: Charlotte Payne-Townshend, June 1, 1898
Died: Ayot St. Lawrence, England, November 1, 1950

Biography

Born July 26, 1856, in Dublin, Bernard Shaw was the only son of George Carr Shaw and Lucinda Elizabeth Shaw. There were two sisters: Elinor Agnes (born 1855) died of tuberculosis at the age of twenty; Lucinda Francis (born 1853) appeared on the stage until stricken by pneumonia and tuberculosis—she died in 1920. Bernard was later to describe himself as a "downstart and the son of a downstart."[1] Both of his parents were of respectable middle-class connections, but the Shaw family was impoverished and George Carr Shaw was an alcoholic.

Bernard's education was, to him, boring and uninspired. Briefly tutored by a governess and a clergyman uncle, he attended the Wesleyan Connexional School for three months in 1865, for another three months in 1867, and for nine months in 1868. He moved from there to the Central Model Boys' School, which he attended from February to September 1869, and, finally, to the Dublin English Scientific and Commercial Day School (1869–1871)[2] without perceptible effect. His real education, he said, came through his reading and instinctive appreciation of such works as the King James Bible, William Shakespeare, John Bunyan, and Charles Dickens; his vast reading also extended to all types of popular writing. He learned music under the influence of his mother, a mezzo-soprano whose talent and private lessons supported the family. (She brought music teacher John Vandaleur Lee into the Shaw household.) He learned art from visits to the National Gallery of Dublin. He saw opera and drama at Dublin's Theatre Royal.

Shaw left school at age fifteen and took a job as a junior clerk in a real estate office. Two years later, in 1873, Vandaleur Lee left Dublin to make his reputation in London. Shaw's mother left soon after, taking Agnes and later sending for Lucy. In 1876, Shaw, shortly after Agnes's death, gave up his position to follow them to London.

At first he accomplished little. Appointed music critic to *The Star,* Vandaleur Lee paid Shaw to write his criticism. To teach himself to write, Shaw tried his hand at fiction, short stories, essays, and much else, completing five novels. The first, *Immaturity,* written in 1879, was not published until the 1930–1938 *Collected Edition of The Works of Bernard Shaw.* The *Irrational Knot* was completed late in 1880; this was not published until 1905 when it appeared in both British and American editions. *Love Among the Artists,* completed in 1882, was serialized in Annie Besant's *Our Corner* in 1888 and separately published in 1900. *Cashel Byron's Profession* was serialized in *To-Day* and separately published in 1886. *An Unsocial Socialist,* serialized in *To-Day* in 1884, was first separately published in 1887. Only as a journalist/reviewer did Shaw find success in these early years. Reading in the British Museum, he attracted the attention of influential drama critic William Archer. (Shaw's reading matter was a French translation of Karl Marx's *Das Kapital* and an orchestral score of Richard Wagner's *Tristan and Isolde.*) Through Archer, he became art critic for *The World* in 1885; he later was to write music criticism for *The Star* and *World,* drama criticism for the *Saturday Review,* and much else.

The criticism remains perceptive and witty; the novels, while not of the quality of those of Dickens, are certainly superior to much that was published in the period. They undoubtedly, however, presented problems to publishers of the time, for characters and events are frequently too sensational for the drawing room readers of George Eliot and William Makepeace Thackeray, while the ideas shaping the action are too complex for the average late nineteenth-century reader of sensational fiction. What these writings reveal above all else, though, are the issues and ideas that later dominate Shaw's writing: evolution, and specifically creative evolution; socialism and its critique of capitalism; feminism and its critique of idealized sexual roles. By the time that he began writing his plays, Shaw was familiar with Charles Darwin and Samuel Butler's critique of Darwin, and his home life had led him to a lifelong refusal of alcohol and an equally felt skepticism concerning Victorian ideals of family life. His readings of Percy Bysshe Shelley's works led him to vegetarianism. In 1882, he heard a talk by Henry George, the American Single Tax advocate, which triggered his interest in economics; that is when he began study of Marx's *Das Kapital.*

Shaw was affiliated with many London societies, but the most important allegiance of these years, and after, was to the Fabian Society, which he joined shortly after its founding in 1884. Advocating gradual social change rather than revolution, the Fabians published tracts, wrote newspaper and magazine articles, spoke on street corners, and circulated boxes of books throughout England. Shaw was heavily involved in these activities, which led to some of his most important non-fiction: *The Quintessence of Ibsenism* (1891), *The Intelligent Woman's Guide to Capitalism and Socialism* (1928), and *Everybody's Political What's What?* (1944). Although his active participation in Fabian affairs decreased in later years, he maintained some measure of contact with the then-powerful organization for more than a half century; the Fabians, among other things, gave birth to the *New Statesman*, the London School of Economics, and more than half of the Labor members of Parliament who were to come to power in 1945.[3]

By the late 1880s, then, Shaw had developed the ideas that were to dominate his writing and had polished his prose style. He had not yet, however, found a forum through which to present those ideas or a vehicle for that style. This came in 1892, when he completed a drama entitled *Widowers' Houses*, begun with Archer in 1885. Based on his studies of Marx and Lloyd George, this was a no-nonsense comedy about land ownership. His prolific and highly successful career as playwright had begun, although this play and the two that followed (*The Philanderer* and *Mrs. Warren's Profession*, both 1893) met with cool receptions—the latter was censored both in England and the United States and did not receive its first public performance in England until 1925.

Popular success came with his increasing sensitivity to audience demands, which caused him to sugarcoat the socialist pill with more acceptable layers of comedy. His first real success was *Arms and the Man* (1894). This play and his other early dramas were published in 1898 as *Plays Pleasant and Unpleasant;* on June 1 of that same year, Shaw married Irish heiress Charlotte Payne-Townshend.

Despite Shaw's later, much publicized affair with actress Stella (Mrs. Patrick) Campbell and his flirtatious correspondence with actress Ellen Terry, marriage provided the writer with the personal tranquility and companionable relationship needful for the prolific creativity that would follow. In 1906, the Shaws moved to Ayot St. Lawrence in Hertfordshire, where they resided for the remainder of their lives except for the trips and cruises that Charlotte Shaw relished. One such trip, in 1933, took Shaw to the United States, where he lectured at the Metropolitan Opera House in New York and visited William Randolph Hearst's castle at San Simeon, California. This later period also included a trip to Russia, during which Shaw met with Josef Stalin; seeing only what he was permitted to see, Shaw came away with a romanticized picture of Russian successes. How much this caused him to shift from his Fabian belief in gradual revolution to a hard-line belief in violent revolution remains a matter of controversy.

By these years, however, his period of greatest creativity was over. His most produc-tive years were between 1893 and 1925; his most successful years began with the decision, in 1903, by Harley Granville-Barker to present a season of uncommercial drama at the Court Theatre in Sloane Square, London. The unexpected success of this season both encouraged the development of serious drama in London and gave Shaw a wide reputation; eleven of his plays were presented, and their performances totaled 701 of the 988 performances staged before the experiment ended in 1907.[4] By then, his dramas had already been produced in the United States, in Germany, in various parts of England and Scotland, and in private theater companies. After that time, the development of talking films was to lead him to a still wider audience. In 1938, for example, Gabriel Pascal's production of the movie version of *Pygmalion* (directed by Anthony Asquith) led to an Academy Award nomination for Shaw's script (which was honored with an Oscar), the picture, and actors Leslie Howard and Wendy Hiller. While no other Oscar nominations were forthcoming during Shaw's lifetime, Pascal's 1941 *Major Barbara* and his 1945 *Caesar and Cleopatra* included distinguished performances by Rex Harrison, Wendy Hiller, Sybil Thorndike, Deborah Kerr, and Emlyn Williams in the former, and Claude Rains and Vivien Leigh in the latter. The most famous of the films, of course, is the Academy Award winning *My Fair Lady* of 1964 which earned an Oscar for adaptors Ian Dalrymple, Cecil Lewis, and W.P. Lipscomb. These, and continual amateur and professional productions of the plays, secured Shaw a lasting reputation.

Although his Nobel Prize for Literature in 1925 marked the end of his most productive period, he continued to write until the end of his life, producing tracts, plays, journalism, and more of his always voluminous correspondence. Charlotte died at Ayot St. Lawrence in 1943. Shaw, having expressed increasing weariness, followed on November 1, 1950, at the age of ninety-four. His ashes were mingled with his wife's and scattered in the garden there; at the announcement of his death, the lights of Broadway were dimmed in a five-minute salute.

Literary Analysis

Shaw's career as dramatist cannot be divided into tidy stages. At the beginning of his career there were the "unpleasant plays." After these, when he had learned to sugarcoat the pill, came the comedies with socialist themes that gradually introduced new mythic and religious dimensions where appropriate. *Heartbreak House,* Shaw's Chekhovian play of disillusionment written in 1913 but held back until the end of World War I, is alone of its type. After it, religious and mythic themes dominate his important drama, but that drama itself tapers off with *St. Joan* (1923); the aging playwright's later production tended to be of shorter works reiterating themes and ideas more strongly presented in earlier times. He was still to produce amusing plays, but there was no significant work after that point.

The *Unpleasant Plays* (*Widowers' Houses, The Philanderer,* and *Mrs. Warren's Profession*) are frequently called "blue-book" plays; the term, derived from the color binding of official Parliamentary reports, has been unflatteringly applied to plays in which social and political proselytizing dominates theatrical values. Shaw's publication of these plays under the title *Unpleasant Plays* expressed his awareness of their lecture-platform quality. All of them concern the "disillusioning of a central figure with current ideals."[5] In *Widowers' Houses,* for instance, Shaw forced both characters and audience to share the guilt for slum-landlordism; in *The Philanderer,* he revealed the odd sexual compacts made between men and women; and in *Mrs. Warren's Profession,* he forced a realization of the economic basis of prostitution. Yet, despite the too frequent lecture-platform tone, in these plays Shaw developed many of the comic techniques that he used to better effect in his later plays.

Basic to these techniques are his reversal of stock stage stereotyping and his reversal of stock male/female lines and gestures. If the "dark, volcanic stereotype" of woman[6] was the villainess of contemporary melodrama, she would be the heroine of such plays as *Widowers' Houses,* and she would be allowed to strike her servant and pursue her male without sacrificing her role as female lead. Through such reversals, audiences expecting dramatic heroines and heroes were instead confronted, to comic effect, by real people who are a mixture of qualities. The brooding dramatics of the vamp/siren create comedy when she is cast in the role of ingenue.

The same is true of her dialogue. Almost certainly, Shaw's early familiarity with Darwin's *Origin of Species,* as ridiculed by Butler, gave him the notion of attacking the stage stereotype of manly man and womanly woman. Darwin's statement that "females are most excited by, or prefer pairing with, the more ornamented males, or those which are the best songsters, or play the best antics"[7] places the sexual choice squarely with the female, whatever conclusions traditionalists might prefer. Not surprisingly, then, the conventional Dr. Harry Trench in *Widowers' Houses* and the philandering Leonard Charteris of *The Philanderer* find themselves comically frustrated when, instead of being the manipulators, they are systematically manipulated by seemingly modest, cliché-spouting heroines. The supposedly shy but actually aggressive female remains a stock Shavian character as late as Ann Whitefield in *Man and Superman* (1901), although by that point her manipulation is motivated by the life force and her clichés merely the result of the social proprieties to which she must give lip service while stalking her chosen mate. She generally is a figure in a play primarily about something else, although in *Candida* (1894) she holds the stage in her own right, and the action of the play arises from the stereotypes that her husband and lover attempt to impose on her.

As Shaw's craftsmanship evolves, these reversals become more and more complex. In their more sophisticated form, they become a reversal of social class. In *Pygmalion* (1913), for example, Shaw turns the social classes upside down. Eliza Doolittle, of course, is the Cockney flower girl (Galatea) who is transformed into a lady by Henry Higgins, as Shaw, the socialist puppet/master behind the scenes, shows that the virtues of the upper classes are not the product of natural superiority but rather the simple results of good food, healthy living, decent clothes, and training in the right ways to move and speak. In a central scene of the play, Eliza slips and uses the British expletive "bloody likely"[8]; hearing this, the sister of the play's young juvenile lead, Freddy Eynsford-Hill, becomes convinced that she is hearing the latest fast set slang. She uses the expression, and, as Eliza rises above her class, the "lady" sinks beneath hers. Similarly, in *Major Barbara,* several of the characters in the Salvation Army shelter in which the second act occurs might be played by the aristocratic characters of the first act. The helpless Jenny Hill of the shelter, struck by Bill Walker and ordered about by Barbara, might well be Sarah Undershaft, Barbara's sister, without the protection of wealth and power, while the unctiousness of Snobby Price and the platitudes of Peter Shirley in the shelter are comically contrasted with similar attitudes that sounded considerably more impressive in the grand Undershaft library in the first act. Much the same set of contrasts underlies the "Don Juan in Hell" scene from *Man and Superman,* in which Ann Whitefield returns as Dona Ana, John Tanner as Don Juan, Mendoza the bandit as the devil, and Roebuck Ramsden, who in life is fossilized in liberal political platitudes, as the Statue. The parallels and contrasts in all of the scenes and the comedy that results are emphasized by Shaw's tendency to write for soprano, contralto, tenor or baritone, and bass voices, producing a musicality that helps hold the seemingly disparate scenes together and point to the resemblances.

Even in his earliest plays, too, the dramatist created comedy by exaggeration of stage gesture. Fond of the staginess of the stage, the author's earliest theatrical experiences showed him actresses and actors of the grand manner, but early on he was aware that these grand gestures carried one step too far were the material of high comedy. In *Widowers' Houses,* Blanche, the heroine, stalks her prey/future husband in the last scene much as a cat stalks a bug, while in *Mrs. Warren's Profession* the second act curtain mocks every melodramatic reconciliation scene and, probably, every second-rate painting of Madonna and child that Shaw winced at in the Dublin gallery and in his days of art criticism. In that act, Mrs. Warren has just convinced her daughter Vivie, and the audience, that her early decision to become a prostitute was her only rational decision, given the economic realities of the time for women. (What Vivie does not know is that Mrs. Warren remains a brothel madam even though the days of her poverty are long past.) Coarsened by her life and accustomed to getting her own way with young girls, Mrs. Warren captivates her daughter with her story, and then, content with her performance, embraces "her daughter protectingly," and "instinctively" looks "up to heaven for divine guidance."[9] In *Arms and the Man,* Raina's exaggerated veneration of the portrait of her warrior suitor produces much the same effect. Such stagey gestures carried to the point of comedy occur throughout the later writing, as when, in *Man and Superman,* Ann wraps her feather boa around the future husband upon whom she is ready to pounce.

Shaw's verbal humor is more difficult to analyze, and most critics have avoided trying. Most typically, it comes from the presence of a naive, Candide-like figure who voices a common sense point of view while all those about the character attempt to swamp him or her in the social or political or religious platitudes of the culture. The contrast creates comedy as when in *Mrs. Warren's Profession* pimp Sir George Crofts and artist Praed attempt to force Vivie into their conventional notion of the feminine, while she, ignoring them completely, retorts with the common sense of a young woman preparing to earn a living for herself; that same contrast, much later, creates the comedy in *Heartbreak House* when young Ellie Dunn, another female Candide, finds herself speaking simple truths of the heart among worldly and occasionally drunken sophisticates, and it creates the comic elements in *St. Joan* (1923) in which Joan's simple home truths are unintelligible to the play's idealists who, in reality, are enmeshed in the irrational political and religious clichés of their age.

If Shaw's devices for creating comedy did not undergo much change with the passage of time, the nature of that comedy did. The *Unpleasant Plays* take place on small sets with limited casts, costumes, and visual effects; the dialogue is everything. But, like a preacher who finds himself with no congregation, the author found that these plays would preach social doctrine only to those already converted; the rest would not attend.

His earliest successes came when he expanded the scope of his drama to widen its appeal to the eye and emotions as well as to the head. In *Arms and the Man,* he set his anti-war play in the Balkans, his stage set a mishmash of the gewgaws and whatnots of natives misguidedly attempting to imitate bourgeoisie Englishmen and women instead of being the magnificent creatures that they are when they forget their Anglo-Saxon attitudes. The comic contrast in the play is between Bluntschli, the Swiss mercenary and experienced fighting man who is more interested in survival than heroics, and the macho posturings of Sergius, Raina's suitor, who, as a would-be Britisher, mistakes heroic posturing and disastrous cavalry charges for warfare. Raina, too, is contrasted with her earthy servant Louka. The former mistakes romantic posturings for love and almost marries the wrong man; Louka, with the practicality born of poverty, arranges her own marriage to her own satisfaction and economic enrichment.

In *The Devil's Disciple,* Shaw used U.S. history to similar effect. This was among his early efforts to define the nature of true political and social leadership. As he did in *Arms and the Man*, in *The Devil's Disciple* (1896), the dramatist makes full use of devices to appeal to the eye and ear, some of them stock melodramatic devices of his day. There is a reading of a will, a friendless orphan, and a gallows scene with a last-minute deliverance. Shaw savages both of the military men in the play, the historical General Burgoyne who would execute the hero merely for the sake of expedience and the militaristic and macho Sergeant Swindon. In a typical Shaw reversal, the figure who represents the devil, the outcast Dick Dudgeon, turns out to be the man of a higher god than the American Puritans know, while the preacher of the play, Anthony Anderson, turns out to be an effective secular leader, an organizer of men.

While that use of history created a witty and popular comedy, Shaw's later use gave his drama still more depth, as is apparent in *Caesar and Cleopatra* (1898). The audience, expecting a sensual heroine, instead meets a barbaric kitten; Shaw's Cleopatra is still a child and represents a child's ruthless use of power for selfish ends. She is opposed to Caesar, the first of Shaw's supermen, whose ideas of morality and virtue transcend those of his time and place and who tranquilly follows them, even as they lead to his death. While Sphinx and murder appeal to eye and ear, the play is essentially about true and false leadership as they existed in Caesar's time and Shaw's own. As in his later plays, Shaw assumed that some attitudes and human limitations are timeless; many of the characters, such as Caesar's secretary Britannus, speak in the jargon of cultural chauvinism. (T.S. Eliot, in *Murder in the Cathedral*, may have borrowed from Shaw when he made the knights, murderers of Becket, speak in twentieth-century political oratory when they attempt to justify their carnage.[10]) At about the same time, in *Captain Brassbound's Conversion* (1899), Shaw used space, not time, to add those elements of stagecraft that had been missing from his earliest plays. This play takes place in Morocco, which permits exotic scenery and costuming, and has the melodramatic elements of kidnapping, a Navy rescue party, and a man seeking vengeance against someone whom he blames for defrauding him and his mother of their rightful inheritance. Again, Shaw exaggerated these melodramatic elements to the point of comedy, allowing the matter-of-fact heroine, Lady Cicely, to underscore their comic qualities by deflating their pretensions with her common sense.

By the turn of the century Shaw was less concerned with history and exoticism than with myth, and his use of myth and legend adds a new dimension to the now richly textured drama. *Man and Superman* is the first play of this type. In part, it is a play of true and false marriages. Violet, her hat trimmed with a dead bird, stalks a husband for purely practical and financial reasons; it is the kind of marriage that socialists such as Shaw regarded as legalized prostitution. At the same time, the play's heroine, Ann, pursues her husband because she is possessed by a procreative urge stronger than herself. She is in the hands of the life force, an evolutionary force urging the best of men and women to mate and procreate for the good of the human race. As is pointed out in the "Don Juan in Hell" scene, humankind, by the turn of the century, has progressed only in its ability to create instruments of destruction and ways of wasting life. Humans, Shaw maintains, are capable of transcending this nihilistic tendency; in his thinking here, the playwright borrows from Thomas Carlyle and Butler's critique of Darwin and is on a parallel course with popular French philosopher Henri Bergson. The result is a comedy accessible on many levels—as a romantic comedy, a parody of romantic melodrama with brigands and chases across Spain, an intellectual comedy, a drama of ideas, and even farce.

This texture, Shakespearean in its appeal to multiple audiences, is even more deftly woven in *Major Barbara* and *Pygmalion*. In the former, the Greek myth of Dionysus as interpreted by Euripides underlies the play; the religion of millionaire Andrew Undershaft, associated in the play both with Mephistopheles and Dionysus, comes, as did that of Dionysus, to revive a dead world, in this case the world of Lady Britomart's liberal platitudes and the Salvation Army's economic bankruptcy. At the end of the second act, Shaw used the musical instruments of the Salvation Army, placed in the hands of Undershaft and the newly converted Euripides (Barbara's suitor Adolphus Cusins) to create a vividly Bacchaean procession. As the procession leaves the shelter, Barbara utters Christ's heartbreaking cry of desolation: "My God: why hast thou forsaken me?"[11] For the intellectually sophisticated, the symbolic replacement of old gods by new is evident; for the more general audience, the comedy of the characters in the shelter and of the diabolic Undershaft and the excitement of the procession is sufficient to carry the scene.

Only in *Pygmalion* did Shaw's technique fail him. There, he used the myth of Pygmalion and Galatea not only to question generally accepted assumptions concerning social caste but also to question truisms about men and women embodied in the myth from which he borrowed. His questioning of caste succeeds; nowhere is the author more effective in sugarcoating the socialist pill than in his convincing the audience to accept the meteoric social ascent of Eliza and her garbageman father. But, he was less successful in his handling of sexual roles. Basically, as his epilogue evidences, he questioned whether a fully developed Galatea would want Pygmalion. He did not intend for his Galatea to do so. She is her creator's equal. Unfortunately, in writing the play, Shaw erred. In offering Freddy Eynsford-Hill as an alternative suitor, Shaw gave Eliza a choice between a bully and too great a weakling. Audiences, actors, and directors alike insisted on knowing what happened to Eliza and preferred that she marry the bully.

In other of the plays, only enough is borrowed from myth to save the work from becoming another blue book play. *The Doctor's Dilemma* (1906) threatens to become pure debate, although a witty one, among physicians who, entirely ignorant of ethical matters, proceed to kill the right man for the wrong reason. The play is given depth by the introduction of the victim's wife, Jennifer Dudebat, who brings with her echoes of Queen Guinevere. As usual, Shaw combats sexual stereotyping; it is not Jennifer who brings about her husband's death but an ignorant physician's romanticization of what is merely a flesh and blood woman. Similarly, in *John Bull's Other Island* what might be an ordinary debate about Ireland is redeemed by the saintly and mystic presence of defrocked Father Peter Keegan, unfrocked because he gave absolution to a black man (a Hindu). His mythic quality is the mysticism of a William Blake, but his simplicity also gives him the Candide-like practical vision that comically contrasts with the other characters' more worldly pretensions.

That mystic vision is continued, more bitterly, in *Heartbreak House*, but this play is singularly unlike anything else Shaw wrote in its bitterness and despair. The product of his disillusionment at the carnage of World War I, *Heartbreak House* creates its own mythology. The house itself is shaped like a ship—it is the ship of state. In it meet the sophisticated classes, preoccupied either with personal relationships and love affairs or with horses and the outdoors, playing their petty games as the ship of state disintegrates around them. The captain of the ship is Captain Shotover, a drunken prophet frequently portrayed by an actor made up to look like Shaw himself; he is the prophet without a country, the preacher without a congregation, helpless to prevent the ruin that he sees ahead. In the final act, the characters talk about their heartbreak as the bombing raids begin. Shaw associated this play both with Anton Chekhov's *Cherry Orchard* and William Shakespeare's *King Lear,* but while these influences are obvious, it is pure Shaw in its insistence that man, as a political animal, is a disaster.

More and more, Shaw became convinced that the answer to human self-destruction lay in creative evolution. In the last of his great plays, *Saint Joan* and *Back to Methuselah* (1920), myth and legend no longer add texture to realistic elements. Instead, they dominate. *St. Joan,* the writer's masterpiece, is best read in conjunction with an earlier play, *Androcles and the Lion* (1912), for an understanding of Shaw's critique of Christianity, although such a critique is not necessary for the pure enjoyment of the play. When the two works are read together, the evolutionary position of Joan is clear. Just as earlier Cleopatra is a leader for the childhood of the world and Caesar for its maturity, so Joan is an evolutionary figure pointing onward toward the future leadership needed for human survival. Joan is both of her time and of eternity; there is a sense in which this is Shaw's Christ play. That there is comedy in this play about Joan's martyrdom is Shaw's artistic achievement, and that comedy comes, as before, from Joan's clear, peasant common sense pitted against the more sophisticated, and less intelligent, banalities of church and state. There are no villains in this play; Joan's martyrdom is simply, like Christ's, a necessary evolutionary step, and one character, a foreshadower of Martin Luther, is so maddened by the smell of her burning flesh that, it is suggested, in his reaction lies the birth of the Reformation.

Back to Methuselah (1920) is a cycle of five plays recounting the history of humankind from the Creation to 30,000 years beyond the date of the play. As in a medieval cycle of plays, in this cycle Shaw explains the evolution of man from creation and the introduction of death into the Garden of Eden, through man's realization that he must live longer if he is to progress rather than cause his own extinction, and the result of that great evolutionary discovery. The devices that create comedy are as before; warmth and humor are also added by Lilith, the first mother, whose voice ends the play.

After this, Shaw's work weakened. The most amusing of the last plays is the 1939 *In Good King Charles's Golden Days*. If much of his late drama is heavy-handed and doctrinaire, this short play summons up his capacity for wit, with its dialogue among Charles II, George Fox (who founded the Quakers), Sir Isaac Newton, Charles's queen (Catherine of Braganza), and several of Charles's mistresses (including Nell Gwynn, Barbara Villiers, and Louise de Keroualle). Like *Caesar and Cleopatra* and *St. Joan,* this play is less concerned with history's accuracy than with its meaning.

Summary

As a writer of comedies, George Bernard Shaw is the most important figure of the late nineteenth- and early twentieth-century theater. His was a rare ability to appeal to political liberals and radicals, seekers after intelligent entertainment, and, especially in the twentieth century, a popular audience. In the lengthy span of his career, he incorporated into his canon an unusual virtuosity in the invention of comic and witty drama, from his introduction of comedy into the Ibsenian problem play in his early works to the blending of comedy with symbolic and even surrealistic elements in his later ones. In all, Shaw maintained an unerring eye for what is comic in life and in art.

Notes

1. Stanley Weintraub, ed., *Shaw: Autobiography, 1856–1898* (New York: Weybright, 1969), p. 11.
2. Michael Holroyd, *The Search for Love.* Vol. 1 of *Bernard Shaw* (New York: Random House, 1988), pp. 33–36.
3. Norman and Jeanne MacKenzie, *The Fabians* (New York: Simon, 1977), p. 409.
4. Dan H. Laurence, *Bernard Shaw: Collected Letters, 1898–1910* (New York: Dodd, 1972), p. 390.
5. Martin Meisel, *Shaw and the Nineteenth-Century Theater* (Princeton: Princeton University Press, 1968), p. 128.
6. *Ibid.*, p. 25.
7. Charles Darwin, *The Origin of Species by Means of Natural Selection . . . and The Descent of Man* (New York: Modern Library, n.d.), p. 573.
8. Bernard Shaw, *Pygmalion, The Bodley Head Bernard Shaw* (London: Bodley Head, 1972), Vol. 4, p. 730.
9. Shaw, *Mrs. Warren's Profession, The Bodley Head Bernard Shaw* (London: Bodley Head, 1970), Vol. 1, p. 316.
10. T.S. Eliot, "Poetry and Drama," Selected Prose of T.S. Eliot, ed. Frank Kermode (New York: Harcourt, 1975), p. 141.
11. *Shaw, Major Barbara, The Bodley Head Bernard Shaw* (London: Bodley Head, 1971), Vol. 3, p. 136.

Selected Bibliography

Primary Sources
Bernard Shaw: Agitations, Letters to the Press 1876–1950. Ed. Dan H. Laurence and James Rambeau. New York: Unger, 1985.
Bernard Shaw and Mrs. Patrick Campbell: Their Correspondence. Ed. Alan Dent. London: Gollancz, and New York: Knopf, 1952.
Bernard Shaw: Collected Letters, 1874–1898. Ed. Dan H. Laurence. New York: Dodd, and London: Reinhardt, 1965.
Bernard Shaw: Collected Letters, 1898–1910. Ed. Dan H. Laurence. New York: Dodd, and London: Reinhardt, 1972.
Bernard Shaw: Collected Letters, 1911–1925. Ed. Dan H. Laurence. New York: Viking Press, 1985.
Bernard Shaw: Collected Letters, 1926–1950. Ed. Dan H. Laurence. New York: Viking Press, 1988.
Bernard Shaw: The Diaries, 1885–1897. Ed. Stanley Weintraub. 2 vols. University Park: Pennsylvania State University Press, 1986.
Bernard Shaw on Language. Ed. Abraham Tauber. New York: Philosophical Library, 1963.
Bernard Shaw on the London Art Scene, 1885–1950. Ed. Stanley Weintraub. University Park: Pennsylvania State University Press, 1989.
Bernard Shaw: Practical Politics, Twentieth-Century Views on Politics and Economics. Ed. Lloyd J. Hubenka. Lincoln: University of Nebraska Press, 1976.
Bernard Shaw's Nondramatic Literary Criticism. Ed. Stanley Weintraub. Lincoln:

University of Nebraska Press, 1972.

The Bodley Head Bernard Shaw: Collected Plays with Their Prefaces. 7 vols. London: Bodley Head, 1970–1974.

Collected Music Criticism of Bernard Shaw. 4 vols. New York: Vienna House, 1974.

The Collected Screenplays of Bernard Shaw. Ed. Bernard K. Dukore. London: Prior, 1980.

Ellen Terry and Bernard Shaw: A Correspondence. Ed. Christopher St. John. New York: Putnam, 1932.

Platform and Pulpit. Ed. Dan H. Laurence. New York: Hill, 1961.

The Religious Speeches of Bernard Shaw. Ed. Warren Sylvester Smith. University Park: Pennsylvania State University Press, 1963.

The Road to Equality: Ten Unpublished Lectures and Essays, 1884–1918. Ed. Louis Crompton. Boston: Beacon, 1971.

Shaw and Ibsen. Ed. J.L. Wisenthal. Toronto: University of Toronto Press, 1979.

Shaw: Autobiography, 1856–1898. Ed. Stanley Weintraub. New York: Weybright, 1969.

Shaw: Autobiography, 1898–1950, The Playwright Years. Ed. Stanley Weintraub. New York: Weybright, 1970.

Shaw On Religion. Ed. Warren Sylvester Smith. London: Constable, 1968.

Shaw on the Theatre. Ed. E.J. West. New York: Hill, 1958.

Shaw's Music. Ed. Dan H. Laurence. 3 vols. London: Bodley Head, 1981.

The Works of Bernard Shaw: Standard Edition. 37 vols. London: Constable, 1931–1951.

Secondary Sources

Bibliographies

Laurence, Dan H. *Bernard Shaw: A Bibliography.* 2 vols. Oxford: Clarendon, 1983. Most important single listing of works by Shaw; limited list of works about him.

Shaw: The Annual of Bernard Shaw Studies. 11 vols. University Park: Pennsylvania State University Press, 1981–1991. Annual "Continuing Checklist of Shaviana," the best source for works about Shaw; in 1981, this annual supplanted the *Shaw Review* (formerly *Shaw Bulletin*) where the checklist had appeared since 1951.

Biographies

Ervine, St. John. *Bernard Shaw: His Life, Work and Friends.* London: Constable, and New York: William Morrow, 1956. Extremely detailed account of Shaw, his activities and acquaintances by someone who knew most of the figures involved.

Henderson, Archibald. *Bernard Shaw: Playboy and Prophet.* New York: Appleton, 1932. Most readable of three studies by Shaw's authorized biographer.

———. *George Bernard Shaw: His Life and Works.* London: Hurst, and Cincinnati: Stewart, 1911. Useful for background and most productive years.

———. *George Bernard Shaw: Man of the Century.* New York: Appleton, 1956. Final volume representing fifty years of study; Henderson's mass of largely undigested facts useful to beginning student since he does not shape his data to prove a critical or biographical theory.

Hill, Eldon C. *George Bernard Shaw.* Boston: Twayne, 1978. Twayne's English Authors Series no. 236. Sound starting place for the beginning student of Shaw; contains basic facts of life, critical appraisal of major works, bibliography.

Holroyd, Michael. *Bernard Shaw. Vol. 1. 1856–1898, The Search for Love.* London: Chatto, and New York: Random House, 1988. Valuable for discovery of new facts, but psychobiography does not do justice to Shaw as an artist or to his art.

———. *Bernard Shaw. Vol. 2. 1898–1918, The Pursuit of Power.* London: Chatto, 1988; New York: Random House, 1989. Must be consulted for the new information it contains, but the view of art as a product of neurosis proves inadequate as a way to understand Shaw in his most productive period.

———. *Bernard Shaw. Vol. 3. 1918–1951, The Lure of Fantasy.* London: Chatto, and New York: Random House, 1991. Despite psychoanalytical approach and absence of sources, a valuable source for information on Shaw's later years, ignored by most scholars.

———. *Bernard Shaw. Vol. 4. 1950–1991, The Last Laugh.* London: Chatto, 1992; New York: Random House, 1993. Ninety pages of text deal with estate and later editions and performances; also reprints text of Charlotte and Bernard Shaw's wills, list of films made from Shaw's plays, notes and index to all four volumes.

Minney, R.J. *Recollections of George Bernard Shaw.* Englewood Cliffs: Prentice, 1969. Recollections of Shaw by contemporaries including H.G. Wells, Rex Harrison, and Bertrand Russell.

Books

Adams, Elsie B. *Bernard Shaw and the Aesthetes.* Columbus: Ohio State University Press, 1971. Scholarly study of Shaw's thought in relationship to such contemporaries as Oscar Wilde and Walter Pater.

Bentley, Eric. *Bernard Shaw.* New York: New Directions, 1957. Revision of 1947 study of Shaw as dramatist that was highly regarded by Shaw himself.

Boxhill, Roger. *Shaw and the Doctors.* New York: Basic, 1969. Provides background for *The Doctor's Dilemma* and remarkable overview of medical knowledge at time the play was written.

Carpenter, Charles A. *Bernard Shaw and the Art of Destroying Ideals: The Early Plays.* Madison: University of Wisconsin Press, 1969. Carpenter analyzes target of Shaw's social criticism in early plays.

Chesterton, G.K. *George Bernard Shaw.* New York: Lane, 1909. Sensitive study of Shaw as man and thinker by a writer who was also Shaw's friend and his opponent in public debate; with Hill, above, a good starting place for a beginning student.

Crompton, Louis. *Shaw The Dramatist.* Lincoln: University of Nebraska Press, 1969. Scholarly study of historical, social, and philosophical background of the major plays.

Evans, T.F., ed. *Shaw and Politics.* Vol. 11. *Shaw: The Annual of Bernard Shaw Studies.* University Park: Pennsylvania State University Press, 1991. Valuable collection of essays illumine Shaw's thought; especially valuable for study of Shaw's political thought in later years.

Irvine, William. *The Universe of G.B.S.* New York: McGraw-Hill, 1949. Irvine studies Shaw's social and political writings as they illumine his drama.

Kaufman, R.J., ed. *G.B. Shaw: A Collection of Critical Essays.* Twentieth-Century Views Series. Englewood Cliffs: Prentice, 1965. Includes essays by Eric Bentley, Bertolt Brecht, Louis Crompton, G. Wilson Knight, and others.

Kaye, Julian B. *Bernard Shaw and the Nineteenth-Century Tradition.* Norman: University of Oklahoma Press, 1955. Kaye relates Shaw's drama to that of other playwrights of his time including Ibsen and French writers of well-made plays.

Kronenberger, Louis, ed. *George Bernard Shaw: A Critical Survey.* New York: World, 1953. Reprinted essays by Max Beerbohm, W.H. Auden, G.K. Chesterton, Thomas Mann, and others.

Langer, Lawrence. *G.B.S. and the Lunatic.* New York: Atheneum, 1963. Account of Shaw's long relationship with the New York Theatre Guild, which staged twenty-five Shaw plays including several world premieres.

MacKenzie, Norman, and Jeanne MacKenzie. *The Fabians.* New York: Simon, 1977. Most readable account of Fabians despite rather unsympathetic treatment of Shaw.

Mander, Raymond, and Joe Mitchenson. *Theatrical Companion to Shaw: A Pictorial Record of the First Performances of the Plays of Bernard Shaw.* New York: Pitman, 1955. Contains photos, cast lists, descriptions, several brief essays.

Meisel, Martin. *Shaw and the Nineteenth-Century Theater.* Princeton: Princeton University Press, 1963. Meisel shows how theatrical conventions of Shaw's day influenced his craftsmanship; relates Shaw to the popular theater of his age.

Weintraub, Rodelle, ed. *Fabian Feminist: Bernard Shaw and Woman.* University Park: Pennsylvania State University Press, 1977. Contains scholarly essays about Shaw's feminism, the influences upon his thought, and his feminist characters as well as five relevant essays by Shaw.

Weintraub, Stanley. *Journey to Heartbreak: The Crucible Years of Bernard Shaw, 1914–1918.* New York: Weybright, 1971. Weintraub studies Shaw's despairing reaction to the carnage of World War I and Shaw's *Heartbreak House* but also provides an excellent general introduction to that period.

Wilson, Colin. *Bernard Shaw: A Reassess-*

ment. New York: Atheneum, 1969. An admiring assessment by a highly original thinker from outside the academic establishment.

Wisenthal, J.L. *Shaw's Sense of History.* Oxford: Clarendon, 1988. Wisenthal provides context for Shaw's ideas in Victorian historical thought, especially focusing on opposing camps of Thomas Carlyle and T.B. Macaulay.

Articles

Holland, Michael. "Shaw's Short Fiction: A Path to Drama." In *Shaw Offstage: The Nondramatic Writings,* Vol. 9, *Shaw: The Annual of Bernard Shaw Studies.* Ed. Fred D. Crawford. University Park: Pennsylvania State University Press, 1989, pp. 113–29. Holland explores generally neglected area of Shaw's writing.

Smith, Warren Sylvester. "The Adventures of Shaw, The Nun, and The Black Girl." *Shaw and Religion,* Vol. 1, *Shaw: The Annual of Bernard Shaw Studies.* Ed. Charles A. Berst. University Park: Pennsylvania State University Press, 1981, pp. 205–22. Shaw's critique of Christianity in *Adventures of The Black Girl in Her Search For God,* one of Shaw's retellings of the Candide story as religious allegory, comes under scrutiny by Dame Laurentia McLachlan, Benedictine sister, later Abbess of Stanbrook Abbey and longtime Shaw correspondent.

Weintraub, Stanley. "The Embryo Playwright in Bernard Shaw's Early Novels." *University of Texas Studies in Literature and Language,* 1 (1959): 327–55. The best study of Shaw's full-length fiction.

Betty Richardson

Shenstone, William

Born: The Leasowes, Halesowen, near Birmingham, November 18, 1714
Education: Sara Lloyd's "dame school"; Halesowen Grammar School; Solihull Academy; Pembroke College, Oxford University, 1732–1736
Died: The Leasowes, February 11, 1763

Biography

The son of Thomas Shenstone, a gentleman farmer of the Leasowes, and Ann Penn, of the Penn family from Harborough, William was born at the Leasowes, Halesowen, near Birmingham on November 18, 1714, the older of two children. His brother Joseph Shenstone (1722–1751) became a lawyer, though he never practiced. He lived with William until his death.

Shenstone was an early and avid reader. His first school was the "dame school" of Sara Lloyd, who became the subject of his most famous poem, "The Schoolmistress." He attended the Halesowen grammar school and then was tutored by a Mr. Crupton at the Solihull Academy. There he and Richard Jago met and remained friends for the remainder of their lives. In May 1732, Shenstone was admitted to Pembroke College, Oxford, where he stayed until 1736. He took no degree even though his name remained on the lists until 1742. By the accounts in his letters, the years at Oxford were the happiest in his life. Besides Jago, Shenstone met Richard Graves and Anthony Whistler. These men, along with Henrietta Knight, were the chief recipients of his letters after 1736.

When Shenstone came of age in 1735, he inherited the Leasowes from his father (who had died in 1724) and 300 pounds annually from his mother (who had died in 1732). Exactly when he determined to change his beloved Leasowes from a working farm into an ornamented one (the *ferme ornee*) is not known. Its improvements began in 1736, but it was only after he took up permanent residence at the Leasowes in 1745 that he began his work with care.

From 1745 until his death in 1763, Shenstone was a perfect example of an educated country gentleman. His work at the Leasowes brought him fame. Robert Dodsley, the London publisher and bookseller, became dependent upon Shenstone as editor for his anthology of English poetry and for his *Fables* (1761).[1] Thomas Percy in the preface to *Reliques of Ancient English Poetry* acknowledged that Shenstone was, in effect, a co-editor.[2] Shenstone practiced all of the arts from harpsichord playing and singing to painting and writing. He collected snuff boxes and enjoyed entertaining. He became the acknowledged arbiter of taste to the Warwickshire coterie. Shenstone died at the Leasowes on February 11, 1763, while he was preparing his own miscellany and an edition of his work.

During his lifetime, Shenstone published *Poems Upon Various Occasions* (1737), *The Judgment of Hercules* (1741), and *The School-*

mistress (1742). After 1742, his work was represented in the final three volumes of Dodsley's anthology. *Shenstone's Miscellany* was known in manuscript but remained unpublished until 1952. Robert Dodsley published the first collected edition of poetry and prose in 1764. James Dodsley added a third volume of letters in 1769. Before 1800, Shenstone's work had gone through eighteen separate printings.

Literary Analysis

As a poet, Shenstone experimented with various stanza forms, varying moods, and a large number of subjects. His *Poems Upon Various Occasions* written while he was in college are short, clever, public lyrics imitating Samuel Butler, Jonathan Swift, and Alexander Pope. As Shenstone matured as a poet, he tended to write personal and melancholy poetry. His most famous poem, "The Schoolmistress," went through two entire revisions and best shows how Shenstone changed: the first version (1737) was a 105-line imitation of "Spencer's stile"; the final version (1748) was expanded to 315 lines and changed from an imitation of Edmund Spenser's "ludicrous" style to an appreciation of Spenser's "peculiar tenderness of sentiment."

If a large number of Shenstone's lyrics fail to please late twentieth-century readers, it may be that we fail to read them correctly. Underlying all that Shenstone wrote was his neo-classical belief in teaching by pleasing. He also had simplicity as a goal for his poetic expression. He experimented with varying stanza forms while writing odes, elegies, and songs, never finding one that he especially liked.

The poet knew Greek and Latin, but his humorous poetry is not merely an imitation of the classical writers. Had it been so, then he might have had better success as a writer. His imitations were done in the manner of popular English imitators like Edmund Waller, Pope, and Matthew Prior. Thus, one cannot read Shenstone's humorous poetry without hearing echoes of the English poets who immediately preceded him. Another problem is that his basic nature was not humorous. Even though he acknowledged an indebtedness to Swift, Shenstone was not consistently satiric in his humor. His humorous poems are more like William Goldsmith's prose couched in neo-classical poetic style.

In spite of the problems outlined above, Shenstone's humorous poems deserve to be read. In "A Simile," a booby squire's life is likened to bear-baiting. It is reminiscent of Butler's *Hudibras*, and "A Simile" was written in octosyllabic couplets and doggerel verse known as "Hudibrastics." In satirizing inflated epitaphs, Shenstone wrote a mock "Inscription" about a self-important squire who died from embarrassment after he passed wind in public. Any coarseness of subject is made funny by the inflated language or by control of the stanza, as in "Hint from VOITURE":

> Let SOL his annual journey run
> And when the radiant task is done,
> Confess, thro' all the globe 'twould pose him,
> To match the charms CELIA shows him.
> And shou'd he boast he once had seen
> As just a form, as bright a mien,
> Yet must it still for ever pose him,
> To match—what CELIA never shows him.

As Shenstone was able to make "low" subjects acceptable by polished language, he was also able to use burlesque quite effectively in his "Colemira, A Culinary ECLOGUE." The humor is directed at the ignorance of the stable hand and kitchen wench who imitate their betters. Damon, the stable hand, sings to Colemira:

> Ah! How it does my drooping heart rejoice,
> When in the hall I hear thy mellow voice!
> How wou'd that voice exceed the village-bell
> Wou'dst thou but sing, "I like thee passing well!"

In "The Beau to the Virtuoso," Shenstone's Beau, the speaker and stock figure for ridicule, at least has more sense than the virtuoso whose life is dedicated to propagating flies and moths:

> And speak with some respect of beaux,
> Nor more as triflers treat 'em;
> 'Tis better learn to save ones' cloathes,
> Than cherish moths that eat 'em.

The poem "The Rape of the Trap" is as close as any Shenstone wrote to the Augustan definition of satire as a hodgepodge. The poem mocks the state of learning and politics. In mock heroic fashion, a rat, with comic inevitability, drags away the elaborate trap set for it.

By the end of the poem's sixteen stanzas, the need for good scholars, effective politicians, and a workable mousetrap have been made equal.

As he grew older, Shenstone became increasingly personal in his poetry. He took delight in describing his particular landscaping activities in pastoral terms. His lyrics and letters delineate how important his friends—not mere acquaintances or visiting tourists—were for his personal happiness. The tone and style of his writing after 1745 are in marked contrast to his earlier and humorous poetry.

Summary
In subject and technique, William Shenstone's humorous poetry lacks Pope's consistently brilliant wit and Swift's undying savagery. However, Shenstone does treat a large variety of subjects with humor and his comic verses are a humorous and tasteful vision of folly and hypocrisy in social man.

Notes
1. Raymond D. Havens, "Changing Taste in the Eighteenth Century: A Study of Dryden's and Dodsley's Miscellanies." *Publications of the Modern Language Association of America,* 44 (1929): 501–36.
2. Irving Churchill, "William Shenstone's Share in the Preparation of Percy's Reliques." *Publications of the Modern Language Association of America,* 51 (1936): 960–74.

Selected Bibliography
Primary Sources
Letters of William Shenstone. Ed. Duncan Mallam. Minneapolis: University of Minnesota Press, 1939. Incomplete.
The Letters of William Shenstone. Ed. Marjorie Williams. Oxford: Basil Blackwell, 1939. Incomplete.
Shenstone's Miscellany: 1759–1763. Ed. Ian A. Gorden. Oxford: Clarendon, 1952. An important anthology of poetry by Shenstone collected to show his own theory of poetry.
"A Complete Edition of the Poetry of William Shenstone." Richard C. Snyder. Diss., University of Pittsburgh, 1955. The only complete and textually reliable edition of Shenstone's poetry.
The Correspondence of Thomas Percy and William Shenstone. Ed. Cleanth Brooks. Vol. VII of *The Percy Letters.* New Haven: Yale University Press, 1977.

Secondary Sources
Graves, Richard. *Recollections of Some Particulars in the Life of the Late William Shenstone, Esq.* London: James Dodsley, 1788. An impressionistic rather than documentary life, but it is the basis for all biographical writing about Shenstone.
Hazeltine, Alice. *A Study of William Shenstone and His Critics.* Menasha, WI: Collegiate Press, 1918; Folcroft, PA: Folcroft Library Editions, 1973. Although this is appreciative criticism, it came at a time when Shenstone needed to be seen once again as a poet, not merely a gardener who wrote verse.
Pagliaro, Harold. "The Aphorisms of William Shenstone." Ph.D diss., Columbia University, 1961. The only extended study of Shenstone's prose; Pagliaro traces the influences and argues that the prose is better than the poetry.
Prettyman, Virginia. "The Poetic Career of William Shenstone." Ph.D. diss., Yale, 1944. Although it is over fifty years old, this is the best extended discussion of Shenstone's entire body of poetry.
Tillotson, Geoffrey. "William Shenstone." In *Essays in Criticism and Research.* Cambridge: Cambridge University Press, 1942, pp. 105–10. A short but insightful account of Shenstone's various activities.
Williams, Marjorie. *William Shenstone: A Chapter in Eighteenth-Century Taste.* Birmingham: Cornish Brothers, 1935. The fullest and most accurate life and times study of the man, his work, and his friends.

Randall Calhoun

Sheridan, Richard Brinsley
Born: Dublin, October or November 1751
Education: Harrow School, 1762–1768
Marriages: Elizabeth Linley, April 13, 1773; one child; Hester Jane Ogle, April 27, 1795; one child
Died: London, July 7, 1816

Biography
Richard Brinsley Sheridan surpassed the expectations of his playwright mother, Frances Chamberlaine, and his actor-manager-scholar

father, Thomas Sheridan. He was the second son of their marriage, and responsibility for his education was given to others rather than domestic as for their first son and their two daughters. Born and christened in Dublin, on November 4, 1751, just twenty-four years later he had produced what Samuel Johnson called the "two best comedies of his age," shortly thereafter assumed ownership of the most profitable theater of his day, and won a seat in Parliament, which he would hold for three decades. He attended Harrow School between 1762 and 1768. On April 13, 1773, Sheridan married Elizabeth Linley; the couple had one son. She died on June 28, 1792. On April 27, 1795, the author married Hester Jane Ogle, and this union produced his second son. For three of his comedies we know Sheridan as the greatest comic playwright between William Shakespeare and George Bernard Shaw—between, that is, the Renaissance and the early modern period. His bons mots, his oratory, and his very considerable figure on the stage of England's public affairs create the picture of a person who deserved the encomia by which Lord Byron and others sketched him. He died, if not a pauper, in considerable financial straits in London on July 7, 1816.

Literary Analysis
Sheridan's major plays are *The Rivals* (1775), *The School for Scandal* (1777), and *The Critic* (1779). He wrote two other plays of some note: the comic opera called *The Duenna* (1775; with *The Rivals* the work for which Johnson lauded him) and the politically appropriate melodrama called *Pizarro* (1799). He cut a considerable figure in public affairs, particularly for his oratory on the occasion of the trial of Warren Hastings for improprieties in the management of the British East Indies Company and for his quick-witted parliamentary debate: he is recorded as saying, for instance, "The honorable gentleman owes his facts to his imagination and his invention to his commonplacebook." On another occasion, he spoke to the House of Commons a sentence or two in Greek, or at least it appeared so to the cowed members who had not enough ancient languages to contradict him. William Hazlitt wrote that "whatever he touched he adorned with all the ease, grace, and brilliancy of his style . . . He was assuredly a man of first-rate talents," and Byron believed of the Sheridan whom he knew in the 1810s that "Whatever Sheridan has done or chosen to do

has been, par excellence, always the best of its kind."

The Rivals opened on January 17, 1775, and closed on its second night. It was judged to be smutty and ill-cast. Eleven days later it reopened, this time with Lawrence Clinch, portraying Sir Lucius O'Trigger, and Ned Shuter, re-creating his role as Sir Anthony Absolute, but now in control of his lines. To allow an unsuccessful play to take the stage a second time was nearly unprecedented in London, and this action reflects great credit upon Thomas Harris, the Covent Garden Theatre manager, with whom Sheridan would have two other important collaborations. *The Rivals* presents an amusing story of the wooing of Lydia Languish by Captain Jack Absolute, who first presents himself as the penniless Ensign Beverley in order to get her attention. Simultaneously, Lydia receives the addresses of a country bumpkin and an Irish adventurer, but her aunt confuses the issue by becoming an object herself. The imbroglio is worked out at the scene of a putative duel where no one is hurt and the old folks restore order, matching up the appropriate couples and welcoming the outsiders into the new society.

The great strengths of *The Rivals* lie in its creation of comic characters, types as old as dramatic comedy itself (the irascible father, the amorous widow) but in Sheridan's hands strikingly new and original in its verbal brilliancies, and in its management of comic dramatic irony. Mrs. Malaprop's "nice derangement of epitaphs" so ingeniously applied has given the word "malapropism" to our language; in Squire Bob Acres, Sheridan combined all of the humor of the outsider from the country with foppishness; Sir Lucius O'Trigger may be a typical Irish fortune hunter but his good-humored pugnacity makes him memorable among a very large tribe of similar stage types; Lydia's romantic imagination, born of reading popular novels, does not distract from her youthful vivacity. For each of these, as for the father and son, Sheridan devised characteristic dialogue which is remembered not only as an aspect of character but as separable bons mots—Bob's "oaths referential" or Malaprop's description of Jack as "the very pine-apple of politeness." Mixed together in scenes comic because of the varying levels of the characters' knowledge of the real circumstances, with the audience always a participant in the joke rather than a surprised viewer, they reflect a youthful buoyancy not seen on the

British stage since George Farquhar. The handling of the overly delicate lover Faulkand and his suffering fiancée Julia is less sure, however.

Four months later Sheridan gave to Clinch, the actor who had stepped in to portray Sir Lucius after that disastrous initial opening, a farce called *St. Patrick's Day; or, The Scheming Lieutenant*. This occasional piece provided something novel for Clinch's benefit night. (Georgian actors earned as much as half of their annual salaries by performing one night a year on an evening when all profits devolved to them rather than to the theater's manager-owners.) It reminds the careful reader of *The Rivals* in tone, if not substance; clearly a virtuoso piece, it provides the title character with a series of disguises (in which impostures the audience is a trusted confidant) whereby the actor can display his control over a wide variety of comic impersonations. The farce reflects a deft understanding of stage conventions but is apprentice work rather than a masterpiece.

Sheridan's wife Elizabeth was the most noted singer of her day, and Dr. Johnson remarked that their decision to forego her career after their marriage represented a special and appropriate sacrifice. But, Sheridan's relationship with her father and her brother, both named Thomas Linley, allowed him to create his second major hit, *The Duenna,* a comic opera for which the Linleys provided most of the music. Appearing again at Covent Garden on November 21, 1775, just four days after the birth of the Sheridans' son Tom, it featured only two actors who had originated roles in *The Rivals*, John Quick (Acres; Isaac) and Jane Green (Malaprop; Margaret). Not seen much today, *The Duenna* presents a complicated tale of two Spanish families warring about marriages. (The Spanish setting and characters were never-never-land tropes in seventeenth- and eighteenth-century British comedy.) The presence of Isaac, a wealthy converted Jew who is a suitor to one of the young ladies, complicates the situation. Margaret, the Duenna, manages to marry Isaac by trickery. The play is a sweet musical, its songs wonderfully contrived as poetic lyric and perfectly composed; it reflects against Sheridan's deft handling of disguise and dramatic irony, with the audience always in on the jokes; but its undisguised anti-Semitism does not recommend it to audiences today.

Yet on the profits of this play, which appeared more times in its first season than did John Gay's *The Beggar's Opera* (the most frequently produced play on the eighteenth-century stage), Sheridan was able to purchase a controlling share of Drury Lane Theatre from David Garrick, the great actor, whose health was failing. His assumption of the management (through a leveraged buyout that set a pattern of financial obligation that Sheridan's son, Tom, once said had changed the family name to "O'Sheridan") raised the expectations of theater-going London for new and brilliant comedy. Not much happened for two years. Sheridan re-directed many of the plays then appearing on the Drury Lane stage, especially those of his predecessor William Congreve; he produced a new version of *The Rivals* with Drury Lane actors; and he offered a major revision of Sir John Vanbrugh's racy comedy, *The Relapse,* as *A Trip to Scarborough,* though without sowing the ground which he had cleared and plowed. Finally, on May 11, 1777, he produced *The School for Scandal*, the finest comedy of manners in the English language.

The School for Scandal presents the story of Lady and Sir Peter Teazle, a May-and-December coupling, against the backdrop of two other conflicts: Charles Surface's route to rehabilitation, and Joseph Surface's self-exposure as a hypocrite. The characterization of Lady Sneerwell and her friends in the "Scandalous College" gives the play its name and warrants Sheridan's reputation as an author of witty dialogue. Joseph Surface's "sentiments" seem to us as witty as Sir Benjamin Backbite's reflections.

Sir Peter Teazle has married for the first time rather late in life, and his bride is a "country" girl whose head is turned by fashionable London society. Sir Peter's bachelor friend, Sir Oliver Surface, returns to London after a profitable career in India not only to tease his friend for marrying but also to discover which of his nephews, Charles or Joseph, is most appropriate to become his heir. Charles has been leading a dissipated life on his uncle's largesse, but has been mostly a good fellow; Joseph has become a confidant of Lady Sneerwell, a widow whose chief satisfaction lies in wounding the reputations of her "licentiate" of the Scandalous College. Joseph, whose name is an ironic reflection upon the pure Biblical character, speaks "sentiments," scraps of morality which for much of the action have Sir Peter enthralled with his goodness; but in a crucial scene four-fifths of the way through the play, a screen behind which Joseph has been hiding Lady Teazle during an unexpected visit to his apartment by

Sir Peter and Charles falls, and Sir Peter finds that his wife is involved with the seemingly-chaste Joseph and that his low estimation of Charles has been as wrong as his respect for Joseph. The fifth and final act reconciles Sir Peter and Lady Teazle, banishes Joseph, Lady Sneerwell, and the scandalmongers, and rewards sentimental Charles with the hand of the long-suffering Maria, Sir Peter's ward.

There had been nothing so brilliant on the London stage since Congreve's time—a fact for which Sheridan was stuck with the sobriquet "the modern Congreve"—and yet the comedy was not at all Congrevian. The great achievement in the scandal scenes arises from malicious talk about others, in contrast to Congreve's verbal brilliancies about common ideas; and Joseph's sentiments ("to smile at the jest which plants a thorn in another's breast is to become a principal in the mischief," for instance) amuse chiefly because of the disjunction between the speaker and the substance rather than the originality of the idea. When we speak of Sheridan's playwriting wit, we are in fact most often referring to his scandal scenes.

What makes the play work on stage is the comedy of adjustment whereby Sir Peter and Lady Teazle reconcile themselves and the comedy of merit rewarded whereby Charles earns his place as Sir Oliver's heir. Both are sentimental stories, reflective of a faith that in the end well-meaning human beings will work out their temporary difficulties and that, at its base, original sin is amenable to social correction. Not since Henry Fielding's *Tom Jones* had the comedy of merit rewarded been so well clothed, though Sheridan was unable to create the moral seriousness that pervades Fielding's massive novel. Not since William Wycherley's *The Country Wife* had the May-and-December story been so well told, and the Georgian audience much preferred the happy ending that Sheridan provided.

Twenty-eight months later Sheridan produced as an afterpiece (the second offering in the five-hour-long evening of Georgian theater) his short, three-act play called *The Critic.* Without peer as the greatest theatrically self-reflective farce between *The Rehearsal* by George Villiers, duke of Buckingham (1671) and *Rosencrantz and Guildenstern Are Dead* by Tom Stoppard (1967), *The Critic* begins with a mannered scene of Mr. and Mrs. Dangle receiving theatrical visitors and moves to a rehearsal of Mr. Puff's play, "The Spanish Armada,"

wherein we see burlesqued almost every commonplace of bad theater, including credulous audiences. The joining of the manners scene with the rehearsal motif is artificial but works quite well on stage; the object of the satiric attack is far more general than either Buckingham's or Stoppard's efforts and as a result is far more enduring. One needs to know something about John Dryden to appreciate *The Rehearsal,* and one needs to know *Hamlet* to understand *Rosencrantz and Guildenstern Are Dead,* but one only needs to have been to the theater to appreciate *The Critic.*

When *The Critic* was produced in October 1779, Sheridan was just twenty-eight. A year later he was elected to Parliament, wherein he found his life's work, though he always maintained his active participation in Drury Lane, which was to him what landed estates were to his social and political peers. Thirty-three years later, in 1812, he lost his seat, a blow made more painful by the burning of Drury Lane Theatre three years before and the refusal of backers to permit him a place in the continuing management after 1811; on July 7, 1816, he died in London, penniless according to some reports.

Summary

Richard Brinsley Sheridan and his theater made a lot of money from his adaptation of German dramatist August Kotzebue's tragedy, *Pizarro,* in 1799; its application to current political realities in an England which had experienced the American revolution and was undergoing reactions to the events just across the British Channel, made it a hit. But despite promises and abjurations, Sheridan did not write *Affectation* or any of his other projected comedies which he claimed to have in progress; as his friend, the musician and memorialist Michael Kelly recorded, Sheridan was "afraid of the author of *The School for Scandal.*" That fear hardly matters, for he lives in our memory as the author of *The Rivals* and *The School for Scandal,* the two most memorable plays of the late eighteenth century and two of the best examples of what has been called "comedy of manners."

Selected Bibliography

Primary Sources
The Rivals: A Comedy. As it is Acted at the Theatre-Royal in Covent-Garden. London: Printed for John Wilkie, 1775; rev. as *The Rivals, A Comedy. As it is Acted*

at the Theatre-Royal in Covent Garden. Written by Richard Brinsley Sheridan, Esq. The Third Edition Corrected. London: Printed for John Wilkie, 1776.

Songs Duets, Trios, &c. in The Duenna; or, The Double Elopement. As Performed at the Theatre-Royal in Covent-Garden. London: Printed for John Wilkie, 1775.

Verses To the Memory of Garrick. Spoken as A Monody, at the Theatre-Royal in Drury-Lane. London: T. Evans, John Wilkie, E. & C. Dilly, A. Portal, and J. Almon, 1779.

The School for Scandal. A Comedy. Dublin, 1780. [Pirated edition].

The Critic or A Tragedy Rehearsed. A Dramatic Piece in three Acts as it is performed at the Theatre-Royal in Drury-Lane. By Richard Brinsley Sheridan Esq. London: Printed for T. Becket, 1781.

A Trip to Scarborough. A Comedy. As Performed at the Theatre-Royal in Drury-Lane. Altered from Vanbrugh's Relapse; or, Virtue in Danger. By Richard Brinsley Sheridan Esq. London: Printed for G. Wilkie, 1781.

St. Patrick's Day; or, The Scheming Lieutenant. A Comic Opera: As It is Acted at the Theatre-Royal, Smoke-Alley. Dublin: Printed for the booksellers, 1788. [Pirated edition].

The Duenna: A Comic Opera. In Three Acts. As Performed at the Theatre-Royal, Covent-Garden: With Universal Applause. By R.B. Sheridan, Esq. London: Printed for T.N. Longman, 1794.

The Camp. A Musical Entertainment, As Performed at the Theatre-Royal in Drury-Lane. By R.B. Sheridan, Esq. London, 1795. [Pirated edition].

Pizarro; A Tragedy, In Five Acts; As Performed at the Theatre-Royal, Drury-Lane: Taken from the German Drama by Kotzebue; and Adapted to the English Stage by Richard Brinsley Sheridan. London: Printed for James Ridgeway, 1799.

Contemporary editions

The Dramatic Works of Richard Brinsley Sheridan. Ed. Cecil J.L. Price. 2 vols. Oxford: Clarendon, 1973. The standard edition of the drama.

The Letters of Richard Brinsley Sheridan. Ed. Cecil J.L. Price. 3 vols. Oxford:

Clarendon, 1966. The standard edition of the correspondence.

Secondary Sources

Bibliographies

Durant, Jack D. *Richard Brinsley Sheridan: A Reference Guide.* Boston: G.K. Hall, 1981. The standard bibliography of works about Sheridan, by the author of a major critical study.

Critical Studies

Auburn, Mark S. *Sheridan's Comedies: Their Contexts and Achievements.* Lincoln: University of Nebraska Press, 1977. A study of the comedies in light of contemporary theatrical practice and the actors who created the original roles.

Ayling, Stanley. *A Portrait of Sheridan.* London: Constable, 1985. A biographical and critical study.

Davidson, Peter, ed. *Sheridan: Comedies.* London: Macmillan, 1986. A collection of essays about Sheridan's dramatic works.

Dulck, Jean. *Les Comedies de R.B. Sheridan: Etude Litteraire.* Paris: Didier, 1962. A dissertation on Sheridan and his art, notable for its completeness. In French.

Durant, Jack D. *Richard Brinsley Sheridan.* Boston: G.K. Hall, 1975. A brief syncretic biography and critical appreciation.

Loftis, John. *Sheridan and the Drama of Georgian England.* Cambridge, MA: Harvard University Press, 1977. A study of Sheridan's dramatic work in relation to literary and political history.

Moore, Thomas. *Memoirs of the Life of the Right Honorable Richard Brinsley Sheridan.* London: Longman, Hurst, Ress, Orme, Brown & Green, 1825. The first and still standard biography.

Morwood, James. *The Life and Works of Richard Brinsley Sheridan.* Edinburgh: Scottish Academic Press, 1985. A biographical and critical study.

Rae, W. Fraser. *Sheridan, A Biography.* London: Richard Bentley, 1896. A comprehensive but Victorian appreciation.

Sichel, Walter. *Sheridan.* London: Constable, 1909. Another comprehensive biographical and critical study marked by Victorian assumptions.

Mark S. Auburn

Shirley, James

Born: London, September 3, 1596
Education: Merchant Taylors' School, 1608–
1612; St. John's College, Oxford Univer-
sity, 1612; perhaps apprenticed to a
scrivener, Thomas Frith, 1612–1615;
matriculated at St. Catherine's Hall,
Cambridge University, 1615–1617, B.A.
Marriage: Elizabeth Gilmet of St. Albans,
June 1, 1618; five children; Frances
Died: London, October 29, 1666

Biography

James Shirley was born in London on September 3, 1596. Baptized on September 7 in the parish church of St. Mary Woolchurch, he was the eldest son of James Sharlie of London, profession unknown, but probably a middle-class tradesman. Some seventeenth-century gossip avers that Shirley believed himself descended from an important family of either Warwickshire or Sussex, but there is no evidence to confirm this. He received a sound classical education and, after trying two other professions (those of clergyman and schoolmaster), found a measure of fame and economic success as a playwright during the reign of King Charles I. His attendance at the Merchant Taylors' School (1608–1612) suggests a fairly prosperous middle-class background. His first effort to earn a university degree at St. John's College, Oxford, in 1612 was short-lived, but he succeeded in completing his work at St. Catherine's Hall, Cambridge, in 1617, taking a B.A. Ordained as an Anglican clergyman, he married Elizabeth Gilmet on June 1, 1618, and was appointed a curate in a parish in Lincolnshire, where he served until 1620. During this time, his first child, a son, Mathias, was born (1619), and subsequently he and Elizabeth were to have two more sons and two daughters. After Elizabeth's death (at an undetermined time), he married Frances (about whom we know only because she is mentioned in his will and who, like her husband, was to die in 1666).

Shirley left the ranks of the clergy to become a schoolmaster at St. Albans in 1621. His change of professions has been linked to a supposed conversion to Roman Catholicism in the period of 1620 to 1625, according to a widely accepted tradition recorded by Anthony A. Wood. Clearly, the rest of his career was dominated by royalist sympathies and by apparent support for Catholic values (despite the villainy of the Cardinal in his final tragedy). At any rate,

Shirley's later association with the values of the court of Charles I and the internal evidence of his plays provide strong corroboration of the tradition attesting to his conversion. However, he toiled as a country schoolmaster until 1625, when the surprising success of his first play, *Love Tricks,* a comedy, enabled him to win a place as dramatist for the company of Queen Henrietta Maria.

Through the next decade, Shirley enjoyed his greatest fame as the leading voice of Cavalier ideals in the theater, in numerous comedies, tragicomedies, and tragedies, including *The Witty Fair One* (1628), *Love's Cruelty* (1631), and *Hyde Park* (1632). This period of success (during which Shirley was hailed as one of the "sons of Ben," the cavalier followers of Ben Jonson's classicism) featured several amusing social comedies set in contemporary London, culminating with the well-known comedy of manners, *The Lady of Pleasure* in 1636. Also in 1636, the playwright went to Dublin to produce plays for theaters there. In 1637, his *St. Patrick for Ireland,* a historical drama, was performed for John Ogilby's recently constructed Werbergh Street theater. Subsequently, some other plays, including the late comedy, *The Constant Maid,* a sentimental work influenced by Massinger, were performed in Dublin. Still, most of these plays, such as the romantic comedy *The Royal Master* (1638), were soon produced also by companies in England, usually the second Queen's Men. He returned to London in 1640 and continued to write plays until the Puritans' closing of the theaters in 1642. He achieved a major success with his best tragedy, *The Cardinal* (1641).

Shirley may have served with Royalist forces under the Earl of Newcastle in 1644, but he soon returned to London and published his occasional verse in 1646. From 1646 until his death, he supported himself by returning to his profession as a teacher, taking employment in the Whitefriars district of London. He published a grammar text in 1656 and *The Contention of Ajax and Ulysses* in 1659, a masque that contains his best known poem, the dirge beginning with the lines "The glories of our blood and state / Are shadows, not substantial things." This elegiac poem was to keep his name alive in the anthologies. Although the theaters reopened in the Restoration, the aging Shirley lacked the energy to attempt any plays for the new age. He died in London, apparently of natural causes, on October 29, 1666,[1] and he was, therefore, mercifully spared from hearing the gibes of newer playwrights and poets such as John Dryden, who in *MacFlecknoe* (1682), makes Shirley and Thomas Heywood models of dullness.

Literary Analysis

Shirley made his chief contribution to British humor in his comedies. As a dramatist who arrived after the flowering of Elizabethan and Jacobean drama (1580–1625), he was at least moderately familiar not only with Shakespearean romantic comedy but also with Jonsonian satirical and "humors" comedy. Perhaps even more significant, however, was the influence of the sexual conflicts of John Fletcher's comedies and tragicomedies which were somewhat primitive attempts to depict comedies about manners and amorous adventures.

Love Tricks, Shirley's first comedy and theatrical debut, owes debts to both Jonson and Fletcher. In his ridicule of affected social behavior (exaggerated compliments and polite forms of address) the playwright suggests that he was inclined to be a classicist and that he found the Restoration or the age of George Farquhar and Sir John Vanbrugh congenial. Though the eccentric characters and dialect humor (a comic Welshman) in the play owe something to Jonson's "comedy of humors," and perhaps to William Shakespeare (especially such early plays as *Love's Labour's Lost,* with its mockery of affected styles of language), the play lacks Jonson's satirical bite and Shakespeare's lively wordplay and is likely to seem tedious to today's reader.

With *The Witty Fair One,* Shirley moved into the territory of Fletcherian comedy, as it is exemplified in plays like *The Wild Goose Chase* (1621) and *The Woman's Prize, or The Tamer Tamed* (written sometime between 1604 and 1606?), in which a clever but chaste ingenue of the gentry pursues or tames a rebellious young would-be rake of the same class. Unfortunately, though, *The Witty Fair One,* while anthologized by Edmund Gosse in the Mermaid Drama volume devoted to Shirley, lacks much of the charm and wit that would appear in the writer's later comedies. Although in the play he depicts a gentleman rake, Fowler, being pursued and "converted" to chastity by the "witty fair one," Penelope, Fowler is an unappealing hero, and the wily Penelope's efforts to convert him by a series of clever stratagems fail to create much amusement or a convincing resolution of the conflict.

Nevertheless, Shirley's skill at portraying clever heroines produced better results in a number of subsequent comedies set in contemporary London which combine amusing battles between the sexes with witty dialogue and sometimes ingenious intrigue. In his London comedies, Shirley tends to present actions that play around the edge of scandal without crossing the realm of sexual dalliance—with a couple of exceptions. In the first of these, *The Ball* (1632), the charming "merry widow," Lucina, displays urbane poise and moments of wit in her exchanges with her suitor, a gruff and inexperienced Colonel. Curiously enough, however, objections to some of the humor—and perhaps rumors about the practice of presenting elaborate balls—apparently caused Shirley to make changes and the printed version seems rather moralistic. The second of these exceptions is *The Gamester* (1633), a comedy of intrigue in which he develops humor from the ability of a clever heroine to avoid the unwanted advances of her kinswoman's husband. Clever tactics are demonstrated by this clever ingenue, another Penelope, and her lover, the gambler Will Hazard, to ensnare the would-be philanderer, Wilding, in a situation replete with comic embarrassment. They use the familiar Elizabethan comic device of the "bed trick" to humiliate Wilding, arranging a rendezvous between Penelope and Wilding which is kept by Wilding's wife. No doubt this revival of an ancient comic device amused contemporary audiences.

Despite a deft handling of his plots of intrigue, some flashes of wit in the dialogue, and amusing comments on contemporary social fads, neither *The Ball* nor *The Gamester* contains enough liveliness or originality to rise above mediocrity. Both plays are designed to entertain the upper-middle class and courtly audience which had supported the comedies of Fletcher and Philip Massinger, without causing such spectators to change their expectations or question their assumptions.

Shirley's two comic masterpieces, by contrast, are spirited portraits of the London gentry which many readers still find entertaining, though theatrical revivals of them remain rare. *Hyde Park* and *The Lady of Pleasure* have found admirers among readers and critics, though the tones of the two comedies differ considerably. Whereas *Hyde Park* is a cheerful and sometimes romantic comedy, *The Lady of Pleasure* is a more satirical work which is sometimes viewed as forerunner of the more cynical

S

Restoration comedies. But, both plays draw much of their humor from the perennial conflict between the sexes.

The lively *Hyde Park* is constructed around a festive occasion, a wedding celebrated by a holiday in the Park on its opening day, which also happens to be the wedding day of another "merry widow," Mrs. Bonavent. This festive and holiday atmosphere provides the occasion for two swift and energetic duels of wits between two pairs of lovers, Lord Bonvile and Julietta, and Fairfield and Mistress Carol. The conflicts are presented in a humorous tone, with much of the amusement arising from a series of unexpected twists and reversals in the action. Carol, Mistress Bonavent's cousin, is a "scornful" and mocking lady who values her independence and professes disdain for men and marriage: though at first something of a proto-feminist, she is induced to fall in love with Fairfield, Julietta's handsome brother, by a paradoxical stratagem. To begin with, she is persuaded to commit herself (by swearing an oath) to a resolution never to fall in love with Fairfield. Shirley's handling of the Fairfield-Carol romance has received critical praise for the swiftness and dexterity of their exchanges:

> *Fairfield:* Lady, I am come to you.
> *Carol:* It does appear so.
> *Fairfield:* To take my leave.
> *Carol:* 'Tis granted, sir; good-bye. (act 2, scene 4, Methuen edition)

After blithely agreeing to grant Fairfield a parting wish, so long as it is not anything that she excludes beforehand, Carol reveals a playful imagination in describing her favorite and cherished whims:

> You shall not ask me before company
> How old I am, a question most
> untoothsome.
> I know not what to say more: I'll not be
> Bound from Spring-garden and the
> Sparagus.
> I will not have my tongue tied up, when
> I've
> A mind to jeer my suitors, among which
> Your worship shall not doubt to be re-
> membered,
> For I must have my humour, I am sick
> else. (act 2, scene 4, Methuen edi-
> tion)

When Fairfield tricks Carol into swearing never to love Fairfield, she is surprised into the realization that courtship is a game that can be played out with a clever antagonist. Much of the subsequent comedy in this relationship arises from her ability to pursue Fairfield in order to entrap him, while pretending to stick to the letter of her oath never to love him.

Although scholars have frequently compared Carol and Fairfield to William Congreve's much later Mirabell and Millamant in *The Way of the World* (1700), a more apt comparison might be George Bernard Shaw's Ann Whitefield and John Tanner in *Man and Superman* (1903). As in Shaw's Edwardian comedy, normal expectations about courtship are reversed as Carol pursues Fairfield, while he alternately taunts her and tries to play the role of a dominant lover. However, she escapes from her oath to reject his love finally by forging his name to a lame Petrarchan sonnet written by another lover and pretending to take the trite Petrarchan hyperbole seriously. Thus, in a bold move, she agrees to marry him to "save his life," offering in the process an amusing parody of Petrarchan love conventions. When the comic exchange of trick for trick reaches this point, however, Fairfield threatens to call off the game, and the lovers reach a compromise settlement; a marriage in which each will respect the other's intelligence and rights. In this ending, one of the English stage's most amusing comic wars between a pair of lovers is resolved by a negotiated peace and a mood of festivity involving the other pairs of lovers in the play.

A comic spirit pervades Shirley's handling of the secondary plot also, though the resolution of this action takes a more serious tone. In the second courtship plot, Lord Bonvile, an aristocratic roué, pursues the virtuous and charming Julietta under the mistaken impression that she is an expensive "lady of pleasure." Although this courtship provides additional comedy, it culminates in a more sentimental conclusion when Julietta persuades Lord Bonvile to reform, and he, chagrined at his mistaken estimate of Julietta, vows to court her in a more orthodox fashion. Lord Bonvile's comic embarrassment is exceeded by the greater humiliation of Julietta's suitor, Frank Trier, who has encouraged Lord Bonvile's mistaken impression in order to test Julietta's virtue. When Trier's duplicity is revealed, Julietta quite reasonably breaks off the relationship. In this plot, as in the Carol-Fairfield conflict, Shirley develops comedy by revealing the folly of masculine complacency about women.

If the primary plot of *Hyde Park* offers a satirical parody of Petrarchan courtship and the secondary plot verges on farcical misunderstanding, the third and least interesting plot strand resorts to conventional intrigue. This action, involving Mrs. Bonavent, Lacey, her suitor, and her long lost husband in an Enoch Arden situation, is only occasionally interesting, though it supports the general comic theme of a group of lovers lost in a comic labyrinth (a theme developed with less success in another comedy of 1632, *The Changes, or Love in a Maze*).

Shirley's clever characterizations, which range from subtle portraits to caricature, help to make *Hyde Park* a memorable comedy. Carol's rough-hewn comic suitors, Venture and Rider, are insensitive buffoons who sometimes seem to adumbrate Oliver Goldsmith's Tony Lumpkin, and Venture's clownish efforts at wooing and poetry certainly provoke laughter. Exasperated at being the victim of Carol's practical jokes and mockery, Venture bursts into a mood of angry expostulation that amuses everyone but himself:

I could tear her ruff! I would thou wert
A whore, then I'd be revenged, and bring
 the 'prentices
To arraign thee on Shrove Tuesday; a
 pox upon you! (act 2, scene 4)

As this speech demonstrates, part of Shirley's comic skill with language in this play results from his easy command of the London colloquial idiom. At any rate, the clever plotting, amusing characters, and the memorable creation of Carol, Shirley's best trickster heroine, make *Hyde Park* an impressive model of farce and high comedy, blending festivity with light romance and tolerant satire on contemporary manners.

Shirley's other major comic play, *The Lady of Pleasure,* has a more satirical edge. The dramatist develops an ironic contrast between Celestina, a clever but innocent young lady, and Aretina, a foolish wife from the country who seeks to become better acquainted with London's gamier amusements and night life. The name of each heroine contains a literary allusion and a clue to her nature: the bright and virtuous Celestina carries the name of a trickster heroine in Spanish Renaissance literature (in the classic romance usually called *La Celestina*), though her Spanish counterpart is not quite so innocent; by contrast, Aretina's name is an obvious and immediately recognizable reference to Pietro Aretino, Renaissance Italy's sophisticated pornographer.

Aretina's effort to break away from provincial sobriety and her determination to experiment with the latest fashions lead her into a number of amusing follies which are counterpointed by her husband's deliberate abandonment of responsible conduct and plunge into gambling. The husband, Sir Thomas Bornwell, is essentially an honorable man who would prefer a sober life running his country estate; unlike Aretina, who is a portrait of a woman seduced by the latest trends, Sir Thomas chooses reckless conduct in an attempt to shock his wife into restraint.

Their competition in fashionable folly is often hilarious, but Aretina's foolish pursuit of London's "pleasure" does not end because of Bornwell's behavior, but because she is finally shocked by the results of her own conduct. Having disguised herself and entered an ill-advised adultery with the worthless Kickshaw, she is appalled to overhear Kickshaw's unexpected account of her sexual performance. Instead of being able to revel in romantic praise of her beauty, she is stunned by his comparison of her to a demon. The masked Aretina is coarsely described as "the devil":

'Twas a she-devil too, a most insatiate
 abominable devil, with a tail thus
 long. (act 5, scene 1, Mermaid edition)

To add to her discomfort, Kickshaw later describes her as "a hellcat." Aretina's discovery of how her conduct appears to her lover is one of Shirley's harshest comic epiphanies and leads her to a fresh awareness of social responsibility. This comic embarrassment also prompts her to return to her husband in a chastened state.

If Shirley satirizes social aberrations from morality and good sense in Aretina's conduct, he provides a more agreeable model in the charming "merry widow," Lady Celestina Bellamour. In contrast to Aretina's folly, Celestina skillfully uses wit and persuasion to turn her aristocratic suitor from seduction to honorable courtship. Celestina, a merry young widow who values her freedom, is genuinely moral, but less ingenuous than she seems. Her command of clever repartee appears in such casual and apparently artless lines as her comment to one of her feckless suitors:

> How long do you imagine you can love
> sir?
> Is it a Quotidian, or will it hold
> But every other day? (act 1, scene 2)

While in *The Lady of Pleasure* a less innocent London is depicted than was the case in *Hyde Park, The Lady of Pleasure* contains several hilarious scenes, and Aretina's elaborate affair with the obtuse Kickshaw approaches grotesque satire. Though Aretina's illusions lead her and her husband into several comic humiliations, Shirley's social satire is handled with his usual lightness of touch, until Aretina's affair. Yet his treatment of Aretina's adultery and Bornwell's dissipation is clearly satirical, and there is no doubt that, beneath the humor, the author is presenting a firm moral position. Moreover, the presence of such sympathetic and admirable characters as Celestina and Aretina's husband, Sir Thomas, provide support for the moral substance underlying Shirley's humor. Still, this play never seems didactic. To sum up, an effective combination of caricature, elements of farce, biting wit, and satirical realism are blended in *The Lady of Pleasure* to make this comedy the writer's most convincing moral statement.

After *The Lady of Pleasure*, the comic sparkle seemed to wane in Shirley's work, perhaps because the courtly and aristocratic way of life he often depicted was beginning to be imperiled by the winds of social unrest. He tended to turn to a world of romantic comedy or tragicomedy, usually set in a distant Mediterranean world. His final major work of stature was *The Cardinal*, a skillfully crafted tragedy of revenge set in a treacherous world like that depicted in the drama of John Webster and Thomas Middleton. It is hard to avoid the conclusion that Shirley's somber later plays, written during and after his sojourn in Ireland, reflect a sense of the deepening political conflicts that were to produce the English Civil War between Royalists and Puritans.

During the 1630s, Shirley's work was extremely popular with an audience associated with the court of Charles I and his beloved queen Henrietta Maria. There are also some indications that Shirley's plays enjoyed some popularity with whatever remained of the middle-class audience for the London theaters, no doubt in part because his plays contain a clear moral center.

When the theaters were reopened after 1660, his plays were revived, but they failed to regain their former popularity. The plots appeared to be too tame for a generation which preferred George Etherege and William Wycherley, and the play of wit was not sufficiently surprising or coarse enough to please Restoration audiences.

Over the next two centuries, Shirley's reputation improved slowly, after falling to its nadir in Dryden's time. Charles Lamb wrote favorably of him, and by the end of the nineteenth century Gosse was willing to refer to him as a "man of genius." Twentieth-century evaluations remain somewhat equivocal, and even his best works have received only infrequent performances.

Summary

James Shirley was a major dramatist of the Caroline era: he was not only the most prolific playwright of the 1630s but probably the one writer who articulated the ideals of the predominantly Royalist and aristocratic audience. In his later years, he added little to his canon or his reputation. Deprived of his livelihood by the closing of the theaters in 1642, he returned to his original profession of schoolmaster during the Cromwell era.

When the theaters were reopened, his work seemed to have become rather dated, as the new generation of Restoration playwrights quickly noted. Though later eras have found four or five of his best plays interesting and entertaining, it is unlikely that his reputation will ever reach the heights that it attained in Charles I's time. Shirley usually produced well-organized and controlled plays in whatever genre he chose, yet he seldom was able to elevate his work to the high intensity of the great Elizabethan and Jacobean dramatists, since his smooth and lucid verse (which sometimes seems to anticipate the Augustan style) infrequently evinces force and originality.

Aside from a few poems and his best tragedy, *The Cardinal*, Shirley's lasting value depends largely on his genial and urbane humor and the social observation in his comedies about London life. In particular, he was most clever and inventive in portraying virtuous but clever heroines who succeeded by becoming charming tricksters and in describing—with considerable dash and spirit—animated battles of the sexes between men and women of the Caroline gentry.

In his two major comedies, *Hyde Park* and *The Lady of Pleasure*, Shirley demonstrates clever heroines at their best and offers amusing depictions of the tricks and stratagems of courtship. With *Hyde Park* the author manages to impart a romantic and festive spirit to its London setting and the work seems worthy of comparison with the lesser comedies of Shakespeare. By contrast, in *The Lady of Pleasure* the writer maintains a more satirical tone, and the play merits comparison with Jonson's lighter comedies, such as *Epicoene, or The Silent Woman*. Both plays anticipate the comedy of manners of Restoration drama, but Shirley's work neither achieves the hard, witty surfaces of Congreve nor descends to the coarseness of Etherege or Wycherley at their worst.

In addition to his skill at drawing subtle comic portraits of his heroines, Shirley was an able if rather tolerant satirist of fashionable London life. Like Fletcher and Jonson, he successfully developed amusing comic portraits of a variety of comic types, mostly from the gentry. On occasion, too, he combined witty dialogue with skill at handling farcical situations and complicated comic intrigues. Generally speaking, the major characters in the dramatist's best plays—and in particular his heroines—are more attractive and sympathetic than the majority of the major characters in Restoration comedy, with the notable exception of the incomparable Mirabell and Millamant in Congreve's *The Way of the World* and perhaps the exception of Wycherley's Manly in *The Plain Dealer*.

In his comedies, Shirley generally assumes the importance of the hierarchy of conventional Renaissance humanist values, and the rhetoric of his attractive heroines often suggests the value of honor and a stable social order. If his faith in such values seemed boring or banal to Restoration audiences, his deft social satire in *The Lady of Pleasure* remains sharp and frequently acidulous, while graceful courtship comedy in *Hyde Park* can continue to amuse audiences who are aware of the conventions that it mocks. Like Mirabell and Millamant, Fairfield and the sprightly Carol of *Hyde Park* lift the comic interplay of courtship conflict to a level of considerable art.

Notes

1. Some scholars believe that Shirley died as a result of injuries sustained during the Great Fire of London (September 2–6, 1666).

Selected Bibliography

Primary Sources

The Dramatic Works and Poems of James Shirley. Ed. William Gifford and Alexander Dyce. 6 vols. London, 1833; New York: Russell and Russell, 1966. First collected edition of the plays which were published in individual editions in various years ranging from 1629 to 1655. Six plays were published together in 1653.

Plays (The Witty Fair One, The Traitor, Hyde Park, The Lady of Pleasure, The Cardinal, The Triumph of Peace). Ed. Edmund Gosse. London: T.F. Unwin, 1888. Mermaid edition.

Hyde Park. London: Methuen, 1987. A Programme Text with Commentary by Simon Trussler. This text was brought out in connection with a rare revival by the Royal Shakespeare Company at the Swan Theatre, Stratford-upon-Avon, April 7, 1987. It contains some useful critical commentary and notes on the stage history of *Hyde Park*.

Note: Some modern critical editions of individual plays have been published in the Renaissance Drama Series (New York: Garland, 1979 and 1980), and one of *The Traitor*, ed. John Stewart Carter, has appeared in the Regents Renaissance Drama Series (Lincoln: University of Nebraska Press, 1965). Unfortunately these modern editions are almost entirely tragedies and tragicomedies.

Secondary Sources

Books

Bentley, Gerald Eades. *The Jacobean and Caroline Stage*. 7 vols. Oxford: Clarendon, 1941–1968. Indispensable reference book for theater history and plays of the period.

Burner, Sandra K. *James Shirley: A Study of Literary Coteries and Patronage in Seventeenth-Century England*. Lanham, MD: University Press of America, 1988. A study of Shirley in relation to the literary backgrounds of his work.

Butler, Martin. *Theatre and Crisis, 1632–1642*. Cambridge: Cambridge University Press, 1984. The most important recent book on Caroline drama.

Forsyth, Robert Stanley. *The Relations of*

Shirley's Plays to the Elizabethan Drama. New York: Columbia University Press, 1914; New York: Benjamin Blom, 1965. An exhaustive effort to find sources and influences for nearly every one of Shirley's scenes. Some conclusions are dubious.

Lucow, Ben. *James Shirley.* Boston: Twayne, 1981. An important and ground-breaking recent study of Shirley's career.

Nason, Arthur Huntingdon. *James Shirley, Dramatist.* New York: 1915; New York: Benjamin Blom, 1967. First extended biographical and critical study, but now quite dated in its critical assumptions.

Zimmer, Ruth K. *James Shirley: A Reference Guide.* Boston: G.K. Hall, 1980. A helpful, annotated bibliography of Shirley's works and numerous secondary sources.

Articles in Journals

Hoy, Cyrus. "The Shares of Fletcher and His Collaborators in the Beaumont and Fletcher Canon." *Studies in Bibliography,* 8 (1956): 129–46; 9 (1957): 143–62; 11 (1958): 85–106; 12 (1959): 91–116. Hoy tries to establish the extent of Shirley's collaboration with Fletcher, mainly by study of style.

Levin, Richard. "The Triple Plot of *Hyde Park.*" *Modern Language Review,* 62 (1967): 17–27. An interesting article in which Levin shows the varying appeals of the three plots in this adroit comedy. Levin suggests that they are intended to create different types of responses.

McGrath, Juliet. "James Shirley's Uses of Language." *Studies in English Literature 1500–1900,* 6 (1966): 323–39. One of the few attempts to approach Shirley as a poet and stylist, but the point of view is rather negative.

Stadtfeld, Frieder. "'Fortune,' 'providence,' and 'manners' in James Shirley's *Hyde Park.*" *Anglia,* 93 (1975): 111–39. An approach to *Hyde Park* emphasizing Shirley's stylized use of theatrical conventions.

Stafford, Tony J. "Shirley's *Lady of Pleasure:* The Dialectic of Earth and Sky." *Journal of the Rocky Mountain Medieval and Renaissance Association* (January 4, 1983): 125–34.

Wertheim, Albert. "Games and Courtship in James Shirley's *Hyde Park.*" *Anglia,* 90 (1972): 71–91. Wertheim describes the emphasis on games and sports as a key to the battle of the sexes in this courtship comedy.

Edgar L. Chapman

Sidney, Philip

Born: Penshurst Castle in Kent, November 30, 1554
Education: Shrewsbury School, 1563; Christ Church College, Oxford University, 1568
Marriage: Frances Walsingham, September 1583; one child
Died: Netherlands, October 17, 1587

Biography

Philip Sidney was born at Penshurst Castle in Kent on November 30, 1554. His father, Sir Henry Sidney, was the Lord President of the Marches of Wales, three times the Deputy of Ireland, and knighted by King Edward VI. The Sidney family was so politically influential that King Philip II of Spain was Philip Sidney's godfather. His mother, Mary Dudley, was the childhood companion of the future Queen Elizabeth. Philip entered Shrewsbury School in 1563 at the age of nine, where he befriended Fulke Greville, and Christ Church College, Oxford in February 1568 at the age of fourteen. He did not earn a degree.

In 1572, Sidney began a tour of the Continent, beginning in Paris, France, where he assumed a position of confidence in the court of King Charles IV. However, the St. Bartholomew Massacre compelled him to leave France. He continued to travel throughout Europe until 1575 when he returned to England. In 1577, he was made the ambassador to Germany, and he helped to form the Protestant League. Nonetheless, the Queen was not happy with his employment, and upon his return, she refused to give him a commission for eight years.

During this interim, Sidney began work on his literary masterpieces, although none of them were published while he was alive. *The Lady of May* and the *Old Arcadia* were finished in 1580, and *The Defense of Poesie* (considered by many to be his most important work—he states that poetry moves rather than persuades), *Certain Sonnets,* and *Astrophel and Stella* were written between 1580 and 1582. In 1583, he completed the revision of the *Old Arcadia* which was so radically altered from its original form that it came to be known as the *New*

Arcadia. Also during this period of political idleness, Sidney was knighted and married. He wed Frances, the daughter of Sir Francis Walsingham (Queen Elizabeth's Secretary of State), in September 1583 after two years of negotiations. The couple had one daughter.

Finally, in 1585, while Sidney was planning a voyage to the West Indies, Queen Elizabeth selected him to be the Governor of Flushing, and it was on a trip to the Continent that he died in Arnhem on October 17, 1587, as a result of wounds suffered in a battle in which he fought valiantly. He was only thirty-two years old. A list of his friends reads like a who's who of the nobility and literati of the time.

Literary Analysis

The humor of Sidney's work has not been fully appreciated in the past. Many scholars of his poetry and prose have regarded him as uncompromisingly sincere and sentimental, especially in his sonnet sequence *Astrophel and Stella.* Perhaps the maudlin reading of these poems that has become almost universal is a consequence of efforts to see the sequence as autobiographical. The series of poems has been considered a reflection of Sidney's frustrated love for Penelope Devereux, and this has hindered an objective evaluation of the humor in the text. It is difficult to recognize the comedy in a situation when one believes that the sentiments expressed spring from real grief and despair. Still, the biographical reading of the text has been challenged more recently, and this opens up the sequence to interpretations that do not maintain a careful reverence for the poet/speaker's anguish but, instead, recognize the silliness of Astrophel's predicament, the exaggerated sentiment of his complaints, the unflattering absurdity in his descriptions of Stella, and the melodrama of his mock battles with Cupid.

The pose of the unrequited lover is fraught with comedic potential. Astrophel allows himself to become obsessed with a woman who, for most of the sequence, will not spare him even a moment of attention or affection. Nevertheless, he follows Stella, admiring her from afar, complaining of her indifference and his pain, coveting the good fortune of those with whom she is affectionate, stealing kisses while the unsuspecting lady sleeps, and triumphing in his insubstantial and meaningless encroachments upon her chilly virtue. In his desperation and undaunted devotion, Astrophel only succeeds in making himself ridiculous.

In several poems Sidney stresses Astrophel's absurd preoccupation with the woman by making him the object of slapstick humor. In "Sonnet 19," for instance, Astrophel describes his infatuation, but acknowledges that his love is in vain. He says that his "heart strings" are "bent" to string cupid's bow, yet he regrets his passion. He indicates that his writing has only one subject—Stella—even though that theme brings "disgrace" rather than fame. Finally, he portrays himself, in his admiration for Stella, as a man who "Looks to the skies, and in a ditch doth fall." The silliness of this scene is evident; in his self-pitying self-absorption, Astrophel becomes the object of amusement and ridicule. Similarly, in "Sonnet 53," Astrophel reveals his inability to concentrate on "martial sports." While preparing to joust with a clearly unworthy opponent, Astrophel is distracted by the appearance of Stella in a window. He is so shaken by her beauty and blinded by her brightness that he forgets to rule his horse and to defend against his opponent's assault. Fortunately, however, the unskilled rival entirely misses the unwitting Astrophel. In this situation the speaker's foolishness is only surpassed by his adversary's farcical incompetence. Astrophel's boyish enthusiasm and delight over his first stolen kiss falls into this same category of humor. He is so exhilarated by the experience that he does not recognize the sincerity of Stella's anger. In "Sonnet 73," he is amused and further impassioned by her indignation: "Anger invests with such a lovely grace / That anger's self I needs must kiss again." Astrophel's failure to take Stella seriously here is both comic and tragic; his reckless elation is quite humorous, while Stella's rejection of him looms ominously.

The seriousness of the sonnet sequence is further undermined by the poems that suggest Astrophel's intentions are more salacious than is readily apparent. In "Sonnet 15," the speaker reveals his preoccupation with Stella's sexuality when he advises the derivative writers of his age who seek originality in their craft to observe Stella and, thereby, "to nurse at the fullest breasts of fame." The suggestion that contemplating Stella's beauty is equivalent to milking her is irreverent, erotic, and humorous. A similar disregard for propriety appears in the extended conceit of "Sonnet 50" where Sidney reverses male and female reproductive roles, suggesting that Astrophel is made pregnant by Stella's beauty: his children are his poems, all of which bear Stella's image. Unfortunately, because words cannot pay adequate tribute to the lady's beauty, the poet laments that all of his children are born dead. This clever tribute to Stella carries the additional connotation of sexual stimulation. The poet is impregnated just as Stella would be if she submitted to his carnal desires. Perhaps the most glaring and witty example of the speaker's lasciviousness can be seen in "Sonnet 52." Here Astrophel describes a conflict between "Virtue" and "Love," each contending for dominance over Stella. He argues that "Love" possesses her eyes, lips, and other physical attributes, while "Virtue" controls her soul and her inner self. Making a considerable concession, Astrophel concludes that "Virtue" can "have that Stella's self" as long as it reserves her body for "Love" and Astrophel. In this roguish yet humorous admission, the speaker reveals that he is indifferent to Stella's character; he only desires her body. He thereby undercuts the sincerity of his love complaints, indicating that his intentions are superficial and licentious. Finally, in "Sonnet 59," he reveals his jealousy of Stella's lap dog, which enjoys more of the lady's favors than he. The lap dog is traditionally regarded as the guardian of a young lady's virginity. Thus Astrophel also harbors a resentment toward the dog because it, at least symbolically, constitutes an obstacle to the fulfillment of his desires. He initially asks the lady why she grants the dog so many favors since he (Astrophel) demonstrates much greater devotion to her. The dog loves Stella, but not with Astrophel's heated passion; the dog will wait for her instructions, but not for as long as Astrophel has already lingered; the dog barks for her, although Astrophel's songs are much more pleasing; and finally, the dog will fetch an article of her clothing, but Astrophel will bring her his very soul. The speaker cannot understand why Stella will allow a dog to lick her lap and her lips with its foul breath when she will not grant the same permission to a pleasantly scented man. At last, in frustration, he concludes that if she is only willing to reward the service of "witless things," then he will gladly sacrifice his wit since it is an impediment to his desires. The speaker subtly alludes to his clearly carnal intentions when he covets the dog's opportunity to lick its lady's lap and lips.

Some of the most clever and humorous poems in the sequence are those which reveal the silly melodrama of Astrophel's battles with Cupid. The roguish young god of love is portrayed as a reckless boy who is relentless in his persecution of Astrophel. In "Sonnet 8," the explana-

tion for Cupid's presence in Astrophel's heart is quite comic. Astrophel indicates that the love god was born in Greece, but he became unhappy there because the "Turkish hardened heart / Is no fit mark to pierce with his fine pointed dart." Therefore, Cupid flew to England, but finding the weather too harsh, he sought to warm himself in the fires of Stella's eyes. However, when he found that she was as cold as "morning sun on snow," he fled into Astrophel's heart, and there, attempting to build a fire to warm himself, accidentally scorched his wings and "cannot fly away." In this humorous allegory, Astrophel subtly admonishes Stella for her unresponsiveness and also explains the origins of his love: with the beams of her eyes, Stella ignited the flames of love in his heart. In "Sonnet 17," Astrophel reveals that his passion resulted from a dispute between Cupid and his mother Venus. The goddess desired Cupid to shoot Mars with one of love's arrows, so that the war god would fall in love with her. Cupid, however, was frightened of Mars and would not act on the demand. Incensed, his mother broke his bow and arrows, but while Cupid mourned his loss, nature made him two new bows from Stella's eyes. In a fit of boyish excitement, Cupid, delighted with his new weapon and firing arrows randomly, accidentally struck Astrophel, making him enamored of Stella. Similarly, in the silly melodrama of "Sonnet 20," Astrophel descries his death wound and denounces Cupid's treachery. He claims that the love god, hidden in the dark of Stella's eyes, ambushed him and, before he could flee, punctured his heart with an arrow. Perhaps the most humorous of all of the Cupid poems is "Sonnet 49." In an extended conceit, Astrophel complains that Cupid rides him like a horse. He explains that "humble thoughts" are the "reins" controlling him, and his "bit" is reverence. The rider's crop is his "will"; the saddle is fastened by "memory"; and he is spurred by "sharp desire." Still, after his catalog of complaints, Astrophel suggests that he has become so accustomed to Cupid's commands that he now takes delight "in the manage." This image of Astrophel as a compliant horse is clearly intended to evoke the reader's laughter rather than his/her sympathy. Although in each of the preceding poems Astrophel maintains that he is the unwitting victim of love's sadistic caprices, the absurdity of his portrayals only serves to undermine the seriousness of the sentiment.

Ironically, the most subtle form of humor in the sequence can be found in Astrophel's descriptions of Stella. He sometimes abandons praise to employ often uncomplimentary Petrarchan conceits. Of course, the continual references to the beams of Stella's eyes portray her as a farcical caricature rather than a beautiful woman. Perhaps the most startling example of this unflattering flattery can be found in "Sonnet 9," where Astrophel rather unsagaciously chooses to compare Stella's face to the front of a building. The result is uncomplimentary:

> Queen Virtue's court, which some call
> Stella's face,
> Prepared by nature's chiefest furniture,
> Hath his front built of alabaster pure;
> Gold is the covering of that stately place.
> The door by which sometimes comes
> forth her grace,
> Red porphir is, which lock of pearl
> makes sure
> Whose porches rich, which name of
> cheeks endure,
> Marble mixed red and white do interlace.
> The windows now through which his
> heav'nly guest
> Looks over the world. . . .

It is difficult to believe that anyone could think such a portrayal laudatory. Indeed, it seems clear that the main objective of the poem is not to praise Stella but to demonstrate wit in the execution of a clever conceit. In other poems as well, the poet seems less than commendatory. For example, "Sonnet 51" initially appears to compliment Stella's intelligence and her beauty, yet Astrophel's praise for the former attribute is so exaggerated that his sincerity becomes suspect. He may actually be annoyed by Stella's conversation. He unconvincingly maintains that her "grave conceits" are too heavy for him to bear, and he pleads with her to cease her serious discourse because it is inconsistent with her frivolous beauty. Although he could be sincere, he may also be suggesting that she is painfully simpleminded. Not wishing to offend her, he has developed this elaborate excuse to quiet her and thus end his torment. This lack of sensitivity undermines Astrophel's respectability, but it is also quite funny.

Summary
In the past the failure of literary critics to recognize and applaud the humor of Sir Philip Sidney's *Astrophel and Stella* has been the result of over-sentimentalizing the subject matter. The belief that the poems were the product of Sidney's own deep grief made the overly-sensitive scholars tread lightly when examining the works. Although the end of the sequence becomes maudlin and unrelentingly melancholy, this does not subvert the occasionally playful, irreverent, and comic tone of the early sonnets. A more lighthearted reading of the text, one which examines Astrophel's obsessiveness, his overly melodramatic complaints, and his occasional insensitivity proves quite fruitful, revealing that the sequence is a brilliant exercise in poetic wit and creativity, and not necessarily a sober tribute to a genuine historical beauty.

Selected Bibliography
Primary Sources
The Poems of Sir Philip Sidney. Ed. William A. Ringler. Oxford: Clarendon, 1962.
The Prose Works of Sir Philip Sidney. Ed. Albert Feuillerat. 4 vols. Cambridge: Cambridge University Press, 1962.

Secondary Sources

Biographies
Boas, F.S. *Sir Philip Sidney: Representative Elizabethan.* London: Staple Press, 1955. A biography of Sidney.
Greville, Sir Fulke. *The Life of the Renowned Sir Philip Sidney.* Ed. Nowell Smith. Oxford: Clarendon, 1907. A biography written by one of Sidney's contemporaries in 1612.
Howell, Roger. *Sir Philip Sidney: The Shepherd Knight.* Boston: Little, Brown, 1968. A biography that discusses the three categories of Sidney's activities.
Wallace, Malcolm Williams. *The Life of Sir Philip Sidney.* Cambridge: Cambridge University Press, 1915. A biography.
Wilson, Mona. *Sir Philip Sidney.* London: Duckworth, 1931. A biography.

Books and Articles
Banks, Theodore Howard. "'Astrophel and Stella' Reconsidered." *Publications of the Modern Language Association of America,* 50 (1935): 402–12.
Brown, Russell M. "Astrophel and Stella, I." *Explicator,* 32 (1973): Article 21.
Buxton, John. *Sir Philip Sidney and the English Renaissance.* London: Macmillan, 1964. Buxton discusses Sidney's role in

the formation of the English Renaissance.

Castley, J.P. "*Astrophel and Stella*—'High
Sidnaean Love' or Courtly Compliment?" *Melbourne Critical Review,* 5
(1962): 54–65.

Cooper, Sherod M. *The Sonnets of Astrophel
and Stella: A Stylistic Study.* The Hague,
1968.

Donow, Herbert S. *A Concordance to the
Sonnet Sequences of Daniel, Drayton,
Shakespeare, Sidney, Spenser.*
Carbondale: Southern Illinois University
Press, 1969.

Fabry, Frank J. "Sidney's Poetry and Italian
Song-Form." *English Literary Renaissance,* 3 (1973): 232–48.

Fienberg, Nona. "The Emergence of Stella in
Astrophel and Stella." *Studies in English
Literature,* 25 (1985): 5–19. A feminist
analysis of the poems.

Hamilton, A.C. "'The Mine of Time': Time
and Love in Sidney's *Astrophel and
Stella.*" *Mosaic,* 13 (1984): 81–91.

Jones, Ann Rosalind, and Peter Stallybrass.
"The Politics of *Astrophel and Stella.*"
Studies in English Literature, 24 (1984):
53–69.

Kalstone, David. *Sidney's Poetry: Contexts
and Interpretations.* Cambridge, MA:
Harvard University Press, 1965.
Kalstone discusses Petrarchanism in
Astrophel and Stella.

Lanham, Richard. "*Astrophel and Stella:*
Pure and Impure Persuasion." *English
Literary Renaissance,* 2 (1972): 100–15.

Montgomery, Robert L. *Symmetry and Sense:
The Poetry of Sir Philip Sidney.* Austin:
University of Texas Press, 1961. Montgomery discusses the way that Sidney
conforms to the literary traditions of his
age.

Nichols, J.G. *The Poetry of Sir Philip Sidney:
An Interpretation in the Context of his
Life and Times.* Liverpool: Liverpool
University Press, 1974.

Purcell, James Mark. "Sidney's *Astrophel and
Stella* and Greville's *Caelica.*" *Publications of the Modern Language Association of America,* 50 (1935): 413–22.

Robertson, Jean. "Sir Philip Sidney and Lady
Penelope Rich." *RES,* 15 (1964): 296–
97.

Sinfield, Alan. "*Astrophel and Stella.*" *Studies
in English Literature,* 20 (1980): 25–41.

Spencer, Theodore. "The Poetry of Sir Philip
Sidney." *English Literary History,* 12
(1945): 251–78.

Stillinger, Jack C. "The Biographical Problem
of *Astrophel and Stella.*" *Journal of English and Germanic Philology,* 59
(1960): 617–39. The study tries to determine whether Penelope Devereux was
Stella.

Young, Richard B. "English Petrarke: A
Study of Sidney's *Astrophel and Stella.*"
*Three Studies in the Renaissance: Sidney,
Jonson, and Milton.* Yale Studies in English. New Haven: Yale University Press,
1958. Young discusses the conventions
of sonnet writing.

James Keller

Sillitoe, Alan

Born: Nottingham, March 4, 1928
*Education: Nottingham schools through age
    fourteen*
Marriage: Ruth Fainlight, 1959; two children

Biography

Born in Nottingham on March 4, 1928, the
second child of Sylvina and Christopher Sillitoe,
a tannery worker, Alan Sillitoe left school at the
age of fourteen to work in various factories (a
bicycle plant, a plywood mill, and as a capstan-
lathe operator) until becoming an air traffic
control assistant with the Ministry of Aircraft
Production in 1945. He enlisted in the Royal
Air Force in May 1946, was trained as a wire-
less operator, and spent two years on active service in Malaya in that capacity (1946–1948). At
the end of 1949, as the result of his having contracted tuberculosis, he was invalided out of the
service with a 100 percent disability pension.
During the year-long hospitalization that followed, Sillitoe began to read extensively, famil-
iarizing himself with literature and beginning to
write fictionalized accounts of his experiences
in Malaya. For the following six years, he lived
in France and Spain. The earlier portion of his
life has been described in his semi-autobiographical novel *Key to the Door* (1961); the
period from his post-war return to England, his
hospitalization, and his departure for France are
depicted in its sequel, *The Open Door* (1989).

While living in Majorca, he befriended the
poet and novelist Robert Graves, who encouraged him to write about the world of working-
class Nottingham—a milieu that had remained

virtually unexplored in fiction previously. Sillitoe's first stories were published in *The Nottingham Weekly Guardian,* but his reputation was established with the publication of *Saturday Night and Sunday Morning* (1958) and *The Loneliness of the Long-Distance Runner* (1959). The latter was awarded the Hawthornden Prize for Literature, and both works were made into successful and critically acclaimed films, for which he also wrote the screenplays.

Although he remains best known for his first two books, Sillitoe's *oeuvre* is surprisingly diverse. In addition to over twenty novels and collections of short stories, he has published seven volumes of poetry, four plays, a collection of essays, several works of children's literature, and travel writings, including a book on Nottingham for which his son David took the photographs. With such a variety of works, Sillitoe has established himself among the most prolific and versatile writers of his generation.

Literary Analysis

From the moment when, at the beginning of the first chapter of *Saturday Night and Sunday Morning,* young Arthur Seaton tumbles headlong down a flight of stairs at the local pub after having downed seven gins and eleven pints of ale in a drinking contest on a raucous Saturday night, it is clear that both literally and figuratively he is a man of almost larger-than-life capacities. The roisterous twenty-one-year-old factory worker is in fact a violator of all decorum, a despoiler of middle-class proprieties, and a seducer of other men's wives. *Saturday Night and Sunday Morning,* Sillitoe's first published novel, is a riotous but forthright account of Arthur's life, from the shop-floor to the working-class neighborhood and the "cosy world of pubs and noisy tarts" in which each weekend "the effect of a week's graft in the factory was swilled out of [his] system in a burst of goodwill."[1] Yet, beyond the rowdy humor for which the novel is deservedly well-known, there is in Arthur Seaton the prototype of a decidedly *proletarian* hero who, despite his defiance of all traditional (middle-class) norms of "respectability," is in many ways the modern counterpart of earlier comic scapegraces—a character who not only engages in a variety of (mock-)heroic adventures but also, albeit reluctantly, by the novel's end proves himself capable of a certain "redemption" through surprisingly traditional means.

As Arthur Seaton soon learns at his capstan-lathe, the piece-work routine of factory life requires only actions that soon become automatic, in effect reducing him to a mere operative extension of the factory's machinery in exactly the way that Karl Marx described in *Das Kapital.* For Arthur and other such protagonists in the working-class fiction of the 1950s, however, relief is to be found in the pleasures of the body, which provide refuge from the workaday monotony, fragmentation, and dreariness of factory-bound life and a class-ridden world. His rowdy behavior on and off the factory floor asserts the primacy of the body—and thus of life itself—against the demands for automaton-like conformity that the industrial system imposes and requires. In the pub and in the beds of his various girlfriends, Arthur finds—quite unabashedly—the pleasures and satisfactions that make his life worthwhile.

Like all of Sillitoe's subsequent comic protagonists, Arthur exuberantly violates all possible forms of social conventions, "respectability," propriety, and traditional moral concepts. Thus, following his victory in the drinking bout, he vomits—twice—over the newly-pressed suit of a middle-aged pub-goer whose ineffectual response ("Look at this! . . . Oh dear!" [13]) is overshadowed by the militant but equally ineffectual outrage of the woman who is his companion. With her rougher language and marked dialect ("Look what yer've done, yer young bleeder!" [13]), Sillitoe deftly and unmistakably differentiates her class background from the man's more educated, standard English of the middle class. More than likely, she is one of the aforementioned "noisy tarts" entertaining a middle-class, effete, almost Prufrockian client; she is almost certainly not his wife. Such subtle use of dialect for comic effect as well as for class differentiation typifies Sillitoe's style throughout his works, though it has seldom been acknowledged in critical commentary.

From the pub, Arthur goes to the bed of Brenda, the wife of one of his workmates who is on the night shift, and he remains there until the next morning, exiting (after hurriedly enjoying the breakfast that she has cooked for him) out the front door as her husband comes in the back. He becomes similarly intimately involved with Brenda's sister Winnie, before meeting Doreen, with whom he will eventually plan to "settle down" in marriage, something foreseen by the end of the novel but which has not yet taken place when the book ends. Although he is noticeably a kinder, gentler character in the final chapters of the book (the section titled "Sunday Morning"), Arthur resolves that he will always struggle against the stifling forces of conformity and deadening, mind-forged "respectability" to which he is inherently opposed.

Primary among the embodiments of these latter qualities, and Arthur's literal target in an act of revenge during his rowdier days, is Mrs. Bull, his neighborhood's foremost gossip, "a tight-fisted defender of her tribe, queen of the yard because she had lived there for twenty-two years, earning names like 'The News of the World' and 'Loudspeaker'" (23–24). Bellicose and censorious, Mrs. Bull confronts Arthur about his "carryin' on with married women" (90) so that even his brothers hear about his now less-than-secret affairs with Brenda and Winnie. Feeling that "she was ruining his reputation in addition to risking his neck" and committing "an unforgivable sin because she happened to be right" (103), Arthur retaliates by sniping at Mrs. Bull with his air-rifle, taking aim from his upstairs window and hitting her across the cheek with its lead pellet as she stands gossiping in her usual post at the corner of the yard. Though Mrs. Bull is not seriously injured, the fact that she is wounded near the eye and thus potentially blinded reduces the incident's humor, making it Arthur's most literally dangerous misdeed and also his most indefensible (in the film version of the novel, she is shot in the rump instead, a more legitimately and harmlessly farcical bit of retaliation). Still, within the book itself the incident establishes that, as one of his brothers realizes, Arthur sometimes "was not a very nice bloke . . . [and] can be a real bastard . . . do[ing] what seem very dirty tricks indeed if you didn't know his motive was revenge" (103). Angered more than injured, the raging Mrs. Bull, accompanied by her cowed husband, confronts Arthur, who even dares to show her the gun, which is then hidden when she returns with the police and all allegations are denied.

Like the title character of Bill Naughton's *Alfie* (1966), Arthur Seaton at times expresses a forthrightly chauvinistic attitude toward women, a blithe condescension which, combined with his sexual opportunism, would increasingly be recognized in subsequent decades as offensively exploitative. Paradoxically, however, Arthur's *appreciation* of women and his recognition of their unfulfilled romantic needs also sets him apart from and enables him to triumph over the stolid majority of husbands, whose neglectfulness and workaday passionlessness he deplores. Accordingly, Arthur's advances are *welcomed* by the women with whom he maintains his clandestine sexual relationships, which are not only willingly entered into but actively enjoyed by both partners. Whether Arthur's triumphs are to be considered amoral or immoral, they are furtively won, precariously enjoyed, and literally dangerous when they are discovered or disclosed. His relationship with Brenda is further complicated by her inadvertent pregnancy which (counseled by Arthur's Aunt Ada) she attempts to terminate during an afternoon of extremely hot baths endured while drinking large quantities of gin.

Although a severe beating arranged by Brenda's husband brings Arthur to his personal nadir and abruptly ends not only his days of carousing with Winnie and Brenda but also the twelve-chapter "Saturday Night" portion of the book, his final "fling" with them and (separately) with his soon-to-be-fiancée Doreen at the Goose Fair shows him at his raucous, rowdy, mock-heroic best. He is, in fact, the modern counterpart of the traditional epic hero, making his archetypal hell-descent during his disruptive ride on the Ghost Train, braving "the mock-death whose horrors had been written on the facade outside" (140) and literally doing battle with "the luminous bones of a hanging skeleton dangled before them, a sight that filled the tunnel with echoing screams" (141). During the fray, he terrifies the passengers in another car on the ride (a man named Alf and his indignant female companion, possibly the same couple that he outraged in the pub in the first chapter of the novel) and eventually becomes entangled in the black cloth attached to the skeleton before being "buried . . . six feet under in a sackcloth coffin" and causing even greater pandemonium when he yells "Fire!" (141). He manages to escape not only the ersatz clutches of Death and the fire of Hell but also the "spanner-wielding mechanic" who chases him for disrupting the ride (142); like the heroes of old, he returns triumphantly "into the open air, into flashing lights and music, swirling roundabouts and the thud-thud-thud of engines" of the world (142). Though he is fresh from his symbol-laden victory over Death and enjoys taking "a kiss from each woman where the crowd was thickest and when one had her back turned," he soon undergoes a more *literal* near-encounter with death when he is beaten senseless by the "swaddies" that Brenda's husband has hired.

As suggested by the book's title, Arthur undergoes a traditional but wholly secular process of conversion in the latter portion of the novel. After his separate literal and symbolic confrontations with death, he is no longer the swaggering roisterer that once he was; finally rousing himself from the "half-sleep in which he lay buried for three days" (155), he quite symbolically "rises again" as a transformed man, "redeemed" if not transfigured by the love of Doreen. The four chapters of part 2 of the novel— appropriately labeled "Sunday Morning"—depict the process of Arthur's gradual conversion and the effects of his wholly secular "redemption." He will indeed, as he intuits, "pay for [her love] with his [former] life" (159), forsaking his wild and rakish ways for the comfort, security, stability, and responsibilities of his impending marriage (the standard ending of all traditional comedy)—his first mature, non-illicit, and genuinely loving relationship.

Nevertheless, as Sillitoe makes clear, Arthur's conversion is a gradual process that does not, and will never, wholly overcome the vital "life" inside him. Rather than being extinguished in his new relationship, Arthur's "life" and vitality will be redirected in ways that are less overtly disruptive or "anti-social," though they are—typically, as throughout Sillitoe's works—fundamentally anti-authoritarian. With all of its picaresque and mock-epic adventures, *Saturday Night and Sunday Morning* is fundamentally a working-class "comic epic in prose" whose hero, like his counterparts in works composed centuries ago, undergoes a process of conversion and is "tamed" through the power of steadfast love. As such, the novel recapitulates the pattern established in such literary forebears as Henry Fielding's *Tom Jones* and *Joseph Andrews*.

While Arthur Seaton is in many ways a twentieth-century counterpart of earlier comic and heroic literary figures, he is also—most importantly—a distinctly *working-class* protagonist, giving voice to views and values that have seldom been accorded serious and sustained consideration in fiction heretofore. Although he is in many ways an embodiment of Youth, he is a specifically *proletarian* youth who does not share many of the standards and presumptions of the more middle-class ethos or ideology inherent in earlier fictions. In stark contrast to Alfred Doolittle, Andy Capp, Alf Garnett, and countless others, Arthur towers over his parents and his bosses at work— even though, symbolically, "his tall frame was slightly round shouldered from stooping day in and day out at the lathe" (58). The "thinking" and "cunning" that are his main defense against his adversaries (all of society's agents of life-stifling conformity, propriety, and bourgeois convention) are precisely those qualities that (as Marx pointed out) the modern industrial worker is presumed not to need. Nevertheless, Sillitoe has repeatedly insisted that his characters should not be considered as prototypical proletarians. As he remarked in an interview in the *Daily Worker* in 1961, "Those who see Arthur Seaton as a symbol of the working man and not as an individual are mistaken. I wrote about him as a person, and not as a typical man who works at a lathe. I try to see every person as an individual and not as a class symbol, which is the only way I can work as a writer."[2]

Arthur's final affirmation that his is ultimately a *good* life is central to an understanding of both his character and the ideology of secret subversions that recurs throughout the author's comic fiction. For all of the character's vaunted rebelliousness and his exuberant defiance of bourgeois social conventions, he recognizes that the life which he enjoys is far more comfortable than that of even his parents' generation. "Though no strong reason for belligerence existed as in the bad days talked about, it persisted for more subtle reasons that could hardly be understood but [were] nevertheless felt" as a part of the ethos in his working-class milieu (53); thus, though Arthur contends that he would willingly blow up the factory with dynamite if given the opportunity (and handed the plunger by somebody else), he also remarks that it's "not that I've got owt against 'em, but that's just how I feel now and again. Me, I couldn't care less" (34).

In adapting his novel for the screen in 1960, Sillitoe made few changes in the character of Arthur, despite several significant changes in the plot. In the role of the protagonist, Albert Finney (in his first major screen role) conveyed both the roguishness and the vitality that make him an attractive diversion for Brenda (Rachel Roberts) and a suitable match, as well as a formidable challenge, for Doreen (Shirley Anne Field). Under the direction of Karel Reisz, the film emphasizes the dreariness of working-class life in industrial Nottingham, against the background of which Arthur's antics seem an appropriate, even necessary, assertion of vitality and life. Nonetheless, the plot and action have been subdued in a number of ways. The relationship with Winnie has been eliminated (as, in fact, has her entire character), and Doreen is introduced far earlier than in the novel. Brenda is counseled about the abortion by Aunt Ada (in a conversation that is unheard by the audience), but the attempt fails; the method is briefly described but is unshown. Subsequently, Brenda considers having the abortion performed illegally for a fee of forty pounds, but she decides against it and resolves to have the child. Mrs. Bull is shot in the hip instead of in the face. Arthur's vomiting in the pub is not shown (he spills beer on the woman instead), though the drinking bout and his tumble down the stairs are retained. The book's scenes involving Arthur's military stint have been eliminated, and the visit to the Goose Fair, while still suitably raucous, is no longer the symbolic confrontation with Death that appears in the novel. Despite the excision of many of the incidents which presumably would have most offended audiences of the early 1960s, the film was rated X (no one under the age of sixteen admitted) by the British Board of Film Censors, banned by some local authorities in Great Britain, and condemned as "immoral" by the Catholic National League of Decency in the United States.

Like Arthur, Smith, the narrator and protagonist of Sillitoe's novella *The Loneliness of the Long-Distance Runner*, is an exuberant rebel whose vitality is juxtaposed against the society's conventional proprieties and values as he relies on "cunning" and secret subversions to resist the standards and expectations that others constantly seek to impose. From the opening sentence of the story, the relationship between "them" and "me" (later, "us," including the other boys) is readily apparent, as is "their" power and "their" ability to define their young charges' lives: "As soon as I got to borstal, *they* made *me* a long-distance runner" (emphasis mine).[3] Significantly, Smith is given no say in the matter; without being consulted in even a perfunctory way, he is told what he will be and given a training regimen that will, they confidently expect, "win *them* the Borstal Blue Ribbon Prize Cup for Long Distance Cross Country Running (All England)" (11; emphasis mine). His decision that he will deliberately lose the race, disclosed to the reader in the early pages of the story, is motivated primarily by his desire to assert fundamentally *human* freedoms:

not to be dehumanized, not to suborn himself, not to conform, not to comply.

Smith's "us-them" duality is further characterized as the fundamental opposition of "Out-laws" like himself and "In-laws" (9) like the governor of the borstal and all other ostensibly "respectable" and law-abiding citizens. Though he recognizes that such people "have the whip-hand [race horse metaphor] over blokes like me, and I'm almost dead sure it'll always be like that" (13), he defies and derides them with characteristically vigorous comic invective that provides most of the work's humor: "Them bastards over us aren't as daft as they most of the time look . . . . They're cunning, and I'm cunning. If only 'them' and 'us' had the same ideas we'd get on like a house on fire, but they don't see eye to eye with us and we don't see eye to eye with them . . . all the pig-faced snotty-nosed dukes and ladies—who can't add two and two together and would mess themselves like loonies if they didn't have slavies to beck-and-call" (7).

Although the protagonist thus posits himself against the entire respectable In-law world, his foremost adversary is the governor of the Borstal, the nameless embodiment of all authority figures who exercise institutionalized control. Like Arthur, Smith assumes that "it's war between me and them," though he also asserts that "it's a good life . . . if you don't give in to coppers and Borstal bosses and the rest of them bastard In-laws" (11). As does Arthur, he, too, relishes the "fun and fire" (12) to be gotten out of life and is not seriously interested in social or political issues, noting that "government wars aren't my wars; they've naught to do with me, because my own war's all that I'll ever be bothered about" (15).

Whereas the screen adaptation of *Saturday Night and Sunday Morning* excluded a number of key characters and episodes that appear in the novel, the film of *The Loneliness of the Long-Distance Runner* (1962) contains a number of added scenes. Directed by Tony Richardson from Sillitoe's own screenplay, the film necessarily shifts from the subjectivity of the book's first-person narrative to a more objective, external view; yet, apart from an initial voice-over accompanying the opening credits, the film relies on the frequent use of flashbacks to build Smith's character and to reveal his thought processes, the various influences on which are recapitulated in a final montage as he deliberately loses the race. Tom Courtenay's portrayal of

Smith is an appropriately alienated anti-hero, although his adversaries—particularly the governor and the policeman—are far less authoritarian than in the book; in the role of the governor, Michael Redgrave seems much more benign than Smith's subjective description in the novella makes him appear, and the policeman lacks the Hitler-like mustache that is attributed to him in the prose version.

In the film, however, Smith gains not only a first name (Colin) but also a girlfriend (Audrey), whom he meets while "joyriding" with Mike in a stolen car which they return without being apprehended. The train outing to the coastal town of Skegness is an idyllic interlude, a time of erotic play and personal self-assessment, an all-too-temporary release from the monotony and problems of Nottingham life. Scenes of the family shopping spree are satirically punctuated with animated white starbursts that parody advertising techniques of the day. The television also purveys middle-class (rather than working-class) values through its homologizing "mass" culture; Colin and Mike enjoy mocking an unctuous political speech in which English youths are said to be "uninfected by the disease of continental existentialism" which Smith himself in fact (unknowingly) embodies.

Despite Courtenay's bravura performance, and although the film version makes Smith's complex motivation amply clear, to many audience members (particularly those who are unfamiliar with the novella) he may seem far less sympathetic than the subjectivity of the book's first-person narrative allows him to be. This is particularly the case when the governor, as portrayed by Redgrave, is not caricatured as harshly as in the novel and therefore seems to provide a comfortably conventional, seemingly unoppressive and unobjectionable, obviously middle-class alternative to the values that Smith represents. Yet, finally, it is the articulation of those values that is Sillitoe's foremost achievement in the work. Like Brendan Behan's autobiographical *Borstal Boy* (1958), *The Loneliness of the Long-Distance Runner* introduced readers to the realities of borstal life as seen through the eyes of a teenaged protagonist who, despite the anti-social acts of which he was convicted, proves himself to be an exuberant, irrepressible, and defiant anti-hero, expounding—in a surprisingly comic work—values that remain irreconcilable with those of the prevailing culture but nonetheless are important for all that.

As a novelist from a working-class background who gained prominence during the 1950s by writing about iconoclastic and outspoken working-class protagonists, Sillitoe was quickly identified in the popular press as one of the generation of "Angry Young Men" who transformed post-war fiction and drama with their forthright, vigorous, and unabashedly "vulgar" style that combined rowdy humor and occasionally harsh satiric animus against "respectable" society and its middle-class mores. In spite of such a characterization, Sillitoe insists that any such similarities between his works and those of Kingsley Amis, John Wain, John Braine, John Osborne, and Keith Waterhouse were entirely coincidental; living abroad at the time, he was unaware of the writing of those with whom he was categorized as part of a "movement" that existed, as he rightly insists, only in the minds of the reviewers of that time.

Many of Sillitoe's subsequent novels are interrelated, even though some were published decades apart. Thus, for example, Brian Seaton, the semi-autobiographical protagonist of *Key to the Door* and *The Open Door*, is the older brother of Arthur Seaton; the first novel to have been written in what is now termed the "Seaton trilogy" is actually the third in the chronology of the plots. The novels of the "William Posters Trilogy," however, were published in chronological order—*The Death of William Posters* (1965), *A Tree on Fire* (1967), and *The Flame of Life* (1974), though unrelated works also appeared in the interim. Other noteworthy novels include the allegorical fable *The General* (1960), the dystopian fantasy *Travels in Nihilon* (1971), and domestic "character studies," including *The Widower's Son* (1976), *The Storyteller* (1979), and *Her Victory* (1982). While many of these works cannot be classified as primarily comic, virtually all of them include typically raucous (and sometimes anarchic) comic scenes, as well as occasional wit and inventiveness. Thus, for example, the title character of the "William Posters trilogy" (whose major themes include then-topical revolutionary politics, the artistic avant-garde, and spiritual enlightenment) is a non-existent folk-hero, the imaginary alter-ego of the novels' protagonist, Frank Dawley, who fantasizes about a modern-day Robin Hood, a perennially unapprehended outlaw whose name he derives from the ubiquitous urban warnings that "Bill Posters Will Be Prosecuted."

Among Sillitoe's later novels, however, *A Start in Life* (1970) and its sequel *Life Goes On*

(1985) provide the best examples of the type of picaresque, raucous comedy for which his earliest books (and many of his short stories) established his reputation—although the later works are significantly more complex and more intricately plotted, featuring a much larger cast of characters than their better-known predecessors. The main character, Michael Cullen, is a self-described, "real no-good, genuine twenty-two-carat bastard in every sense of the word."[4] He is Sillitoe's most traditionally picaresque working-class rogue-hero since Arthur Seaton, and, like Smith in *The Loneliness of the Long-Distance Runner,* he is a first-person narrator and a self-styled outlaw who relies on cunning to succeed in life. In these novels, Sillitoe's plot is more carefully constructed, though, and their humor reveals an increasingly sophisticated satirical animus, wielded not only against contemporary English society but also (particularly in *Life Goes On*) against the literary and cultural scenes in contemporary London as well.

Growing up in working-class Nottingham, Michael left school to take a briefly-held factory job before deciding to pursue another line of work—though in part he does so to escape being promoted to an office-job that would necessitate an engagement to his then-girlfriend Claudine. His adolescence is "absorbed in what [he] called the three -ings: reading, working, and fucking, all of which I did to the best of my time and ability," as he resolves "to go on getting more out of life, and learning more from it" (26). With such goals in mind, he launches a varied career that takes him from being a real-estate agent to a participant in an international crime syndicate. At this time he is a gold-smuggler as well as the chosen chauffeur, cohort, and would-be son-in-law of the head of the crime syndicate—who is also a "respectable" businessman who eventually earns a place in the House of Lords. Throughout all of his comic adventures, Michael maintains a resilient devil-may-care attitude that is well suited to his role as a modern-day picaresque hero: "I didn't mind what happened to me, as long as there was no possibility that I could have made things any better. Because of that I learned early to have no vain regrets, and never to recall the lost chances that, had I taken them, might have made life easier for me" (28–29).

Essentially a genial and cunning if amoral opportunist, Michael Cullen is always primarily concerned with "getting on," in both meanings of the phrase: moving from one position (whether job or romantic liaison) to the next and gaining more prosperity. In these ways, he is quite different from either Arthur or Smith, and he is the first Sillitoe protagonist who needs to slip back into his "homeliest Radford accent" when among his factory-working friends, who are not fooled by such "patronizing bonhomie, this twisted attempt to put things back as they were" (29). They realize intuitively that he has (through "cunning" and "association") moved from one class into another, *at least ostensibly*; he is the only one of the novelist's protagonists to do so, and, like his employer's ostensible respectability, the change is more an illusion than a reality.

At the end of *A Start in Life,* as at the end of many traditional picaresque novels, the bastard-hero learns the true identity of his father—he is Gilbert Blaskin, a womanizing novelist who had abandoned Michael's mother; Michael is thus a "bastard's bastard," though he hopes to arrange a marriage between his parents. The epilogue of *A Start in Life* also contains a very traditional closure, with a number of marriages and a seemingly final account of all of the major (and many minor) characters. Their story is resumed in *Life Goes On,* which begins ten years after the end of *A Start in Life* when Michael is thirty-five. Although he refers to himself in the book's "preamble" as "King Bastard the First," Michael finds that he is no longer quite "the bone-idle, happy-go-lucky, feckless, come-what-may, jaunty, fuck-you-jack, how's-your-father, let's-have-a-lovely-strike sort of person which [he] had been . . . and with which this country at any rate will always be overrun and no doubt affectionately remembered, at least according to the newspapers."[5] Leaving behind this former self (a characterization which could equally well fit Arthur), Michael hopes to become a person "with flair, improvisation, creative ability, hard work, love of money, flexibility, lack of panic in a tricky situation, luck (of course), a refusal to regard long hours as anathema and imaginative attention to detail when drawing up a plan or programme" (116). Such were, of course, the quintessential virtues of the 1980s, particularly in Thatcherite Britain—making Michael Cullen clearly the prototypical bastard of his times if not, indeed, a bastard for all seasons.

One of these novels' relatively minor characters, known as Almanack Jack, succinctly defines Sillitoe's understanding of the nature of comedy as he offers his personal credo: "It's always better to act. Never stifle what you feel to be a fundamental impulse. If it causes chaos, so much the better, because maybe the right sort of order and happiness will arise from it. It can never come out of anything else, and that's a fact, my friend" (130). Not only is this claim the *de facto* creed of virtually every picaresque hero, and certainly all of Sillitoe's, but it embodies in many ways the *essential* "matter of comedy" itself which runs from ancient times to the modern day: the unstifled, chaos-causing (often sexual) "fundamental impulse" typically subverts all social conventions, ersatz "respectability," propriety, and "decency," exactly as Arthur Seaton had done in his heyday. The eventual triumph of this "impulse" over all of the nay-saying, life-denying forces by which it has been opposed enables "the right sort of order and happiness" to be achieved—through sexual consummation, life-generation, species-preservation, and renewal. Uniquely, throughout the broad range of his writings, with characteristic vigor and exuberant inventiveness, Sillitoe has celebrated this "triumph of life," giving inimitable voice to characters whose working-class origins and attitudes are neither belittled nor betrayed. That achievement is his foremost contribution to modern comedy.

Summary
Alan Sillitoe's rowdy and roisterous comic protagonists are in many ways the modern-day working-class counterparts of such traditional picaresque heroes as Tom Jones and Joseph Andrews. Described in a vernacular that is as vigorous and robust as the characters themselves, their ribald adventures and misadventures are the age-old matter of comedy robustly transposed into a modern working-class setting. However "immoral" they may be by conventional (and, especially, middle-class) standards, Sillitoe's protagonists engage in series of amoral, rakish, erotic, and even anarchic escapades that affirm (like all traditional comedy) the life-force of fertility and the vitality of the body against the stifling forces of conformity and the deadening, mind-forged "respectability"—a form of "domestication" to which they are inherently opposed.

Notes
1. Alan Sillitoe, *Saturday Night and Sunday Morning* (New York: NAL-Signet, 1958), pp. 33, 7. All subsequent references cite this edition and have been inserted parenthetically into the text.
2. Sillitoe, "Arthur Seaton is not just a 'Symbol,'" *The Daily Worker* (January 28, 1961): 2.
3. Sillitoe, *The Loneliness of the Long-Distance Runner* (New York: NAL-Signet, 1959), p. 7. All subsequent references cite this edition and have been inserted parenthetically into the text.
4. Sillitoe, *A Start in Life* (1970; London: Grafton Books, 1986), p. 71. All subsequent references cite this edition and have been inserted parenthetically into the text.
5. Sillitoe, *Life Goes On* (1985; London: Grafton Books, 1987), pp. 5, 116. All subsequent references cite this edition and have been inserted parenthetically into the text.

Selected Bibliography
Primary Sources

Novels
Saturday Night and Sunday Morning. London: W.H. Allen, 1958; New York: Knopf, 1959.
The General. London: W.H. Allen, 1960; New York: Knopf, 1962.
Key to the Door. London: W.H. Allen, 1961; New York: Knopf, 1962.
The Death of William Posters. London: W.H. Allen, and New York: Knopf, 1965.
A Tree on Fire. London: Macmillan, 1967; New York: Doubleday, 1968.
A Start in Life. London: W.H. Allen, 1970; New York: Charles Scribner's Sons, 1971.
Travels in Nihilon. London: W.H. Allen, 1971; rpt. New York: Charles Scribner's Sons, 1972.
Raw Material. London: W.H. Allen, 1972; New York: Charles Scribner's Sons, 1973. Revised and augmented eds., Pan Books, 1974; Star Books, 1978; W.H. Allen, 1979.
The Flame of Life. London: W.H. Allen, 1974.
The Widower's Son. London: W.H. Allen, 1976; New York: Harper and Row, 1977.
The Storyteller. London: W.H. Allen, and New York: Simon and Schuster, 1979.
Her Victory. London: Granada, and New York: Franklin Watts, 1982.

The Lost Flying Boat. London: Granada, and New York: Little, Brown, 1983.

Life Goes On. London: Granada, 1985.

Out of the Whirlpool. London: Hutchinson, 1987.

The Open Door. London: Grafton, 1989.

Last Loves. London: Grafton, 1990.

Leonard's War: a love story. London: Harper Collins, 1991.

Snowstop. London: Harper Collins, 1993.

Short Stories

The Loneliness of the Long-Distance Runner. London: W.H. Allen, 1959; New York: Knopf, 1960.

The Ragman's Daughter. London: W.H. Allen, 1963; New York: Knopf, 1964.

Guzman Go Home. London: Macmillan, 1968; New York: Doubleday, 1969.

Men, Women and Children. London: W.H. Allen, 1973; New York: Charles Scribner's Sons, 1974.

Down to the Bone. Exeter: Arnold-Wheaton, 1976.

The Second Chance and Other Stories. London: Jonathan Cape, 1981.

Down From the Hill. London: Granada, 1984.

Poetry (excluding private press limited editions)

The Rats and Other Poems. London: W.H. Allen, 1960.

A Falling Out of Love and Other Poems. London: W.H. Allen, 1964.

Love in the Environs of Veronezh and Other Poems. London: Macmillan, 1968; New York: Doubleday, 1969.

Storm: New Poems by Alan Sillitoe. London: W.H. Allen, 1974.

Snow on the North Side of Lucifer. London: W.H. Allen, 1979.

Sun Before Departure: Poems 1974–1982. London: Granada, 1984.

Tides and Stone Walls. London: Grafton Books, 1986.

Plays

All Citizens are Soldiers: Fuente Ovejuna. Trans. and adapted from the Spanish of Lope de Vega by Ruth Fainlight and Alan Sillitoe. London: Macmillan, and Chester Springs, PA: Dufour, 1970.

Three Plays: The Slot-Machine, The Interview, Pit Strike. London: W.H. Allen, 1978.

Essays

Mountains and Caverns: Selected Essays. London: W.H. Allen, 1975.

Non-Fiction and Travel Writings

Road to Volgograd. London: W.H. Allen, and New York: Knopf, 1964.

The Saxon Shore Way from Gravesend to Rye. London: Hutchinson, 1983.

Alan Sillitoe's Nottinghamshire. London: Grafton Books, 1987. With photographs by David Sillitoe.

Autobiographical essay (uncollected)

"Alan Sillitoe." *Contemporary Authors Autobiography Series.* Ed. Adele Sarkissian. Detroit: Gale Research, 1985. Vol. 2, pp. 371–89.

Screenplays (unpublished)

Saturday Night and Sunday Morning. Continental, 1960.

The Loneliness of the Long-Distance Runner. Continental, 1962.

The Ragman's Daughter. Penelope, 1972.

Juvenile Fiction

The City Adventures of Marmelade Jim. London: Macmillan, 1967.

Big John and the Stars. London: Robson Books, 1977.

The Incredible Fencing Fleas. London: Robson Books, 1978.

Marmalade Jim at the Farm. London: Robson Books, 1980.

Marmalade Jim and the Fox. London: Robson Books, 1984.

Collections

A Sillitoe Selection: Eight Short Stories. London: Longmans, 1968.

Every Day of the Week: An Alan Sillitoe Reader. London: W.H. Allen, 1987. Works selected by the author.

Secondary Sources

Bibliographies

Gerard, David. *Alan Sillitoe: A Bibliography.* London: Mansell, 1988.

Books

Atherton, Stanley S. *Alan Sillitoe: A Critical Assessment.* London: W.H. Allen, 1979. Analysis of Sillitoe's works through *The*

Widower's Son, focusing on "social and political background, biographical material, the author's views on the nature and function of literary art, the place of a working-class frame of reference in the tradition of the English novel, and independent sociological evidence to provide an assessment of Sillitoe's early work."

Hitchcock, Peter. *Working Class Fiction in Theory and Practice: A Reading of Alan Sillitoe.* Ann Arbor: UMI Research Press, 1989. Emphasizing only Sillitoe's early work, this is "an attempt to analyze and explicate the cultural forces at work in the production and reception of a literature that challenges and to some extent undermines predominant notions of the literary . . . [Sillitoe's] works . . . throw into stark relief the theoretical and sociopolitical problem involved in assessing what we may call the counter-literary . . . [i.e.,] working-class writing."

Penner, Allen R. *Alan Sillitoe.* New York: Twayne, 1972. Useful overview of Sillitoe's works through *A Tree on Fire,* emphasizing Sillitoe's developing "sense of identity" through his identification with both the working class and revolutionary causes.

Vaverka, Ronald D. *Commitment as Art: A Marxist Critique of a Selection of Alan Sillitoe's Political Fictions.* Uppsala: University of Uppsala Press, 1978. Vaverka considers Sillitoe's writing as a "struggle against economic and political repression" and discusses his "commitment to the creation of art that captures the political realities of his day."

Articles and Chapters in Books

Craig, David. "The Roots of Sillitoe's Fiction." In *The British Working Class Novel in the Twentieth Century.* Ed. Jeremy Hawthorn. London: Edward Arnold, 1984. Stratford-upon-Avon Studies 2, pp. 95–110.

Gindin, James. "Alan Sillitoe's Jungle." *Texas Studies in Language and Literature,* 4, 1 (1962): 35–48. Rpt. in *Postwar British Fiction,* Berkeley: University of California Press, 1962, pp. 14–33. Discussing characters in Sillitoe's first three books, Gindin considers them "energetic, forceful, and irrational," noting their "jeers and catcalls at any social organization or anything smacking of noble purpose or ideal" and the "'I'm all right, Jack' attitude [that] permeates a good deal of Sillitoe's fiction."

Gray, Nigel. "Life is What You Make It." *The Silent Majority: A Study of the Working Class in Post-War British Fiction.* New York: Barnes & Noble/Harper and Row, 1973, pp. 101–32. Although Gray acknowledges Sillitoe's use of humor and his incisive description of factory workers' lives in *Saturday Night and Sunday Morning,* he contends that "Sillitoe is too much taken with the working class-hero cult" and "has gone in for cheapness here . . . . [He is] too ready to get laughs from the audience at the expense of people who ought to be understood."

Halperin, John. "Interview with Alan Sillitoe." *Modern Fiction Studies,* 25 (Summer 1979): 175–89. Sillitoe's most extensive interview, including frank assessments of his literary influences, forebears, and many contemporary writers.

Hutchings, William. "Proletarian Byronism: Alan Sillitoe and the Romantic Tradition." In *The Twentieth Century Novel and English Romanticism.* Ed. Alan Chavkin. AMS Studies in Literature 21. New York: AMS Press, 1993, pp. 83–112. Hutchings traces Sillitoe's acknowledgments of the English romantic poets and the presence of their ideas in his early fiction, paying particular attention to *Saturday Night and Sunday Morning, The Loneliness of the Long-Distance Runner,* and the William Posters trilogy.

Meckier, Jerome. "Looking Back at Anger." *Dalhousie Review* (Spring 1972): 47–58. Meckier contends that the "persistently comic, occasionally satiric tone" of *Saturday Night and Sunday Morning* "suggests that Sillitoe sees Arthur as a character who never achieves complete self-discovery . . . basically a sincere but comic-book villain whose exploits pose no threat to 'the bastards' who run the factory where he works and the country at large."

Osgerby, J.R. "Alan Sillitoe's *Saturday Night and Sunday Morning.*" In *Renaissance and Modern Essays Presented to Vivian de Sola Pinto in Celebration of his Seventieth Birthday.* Ed. G.R. Hibbard. London: Routledge & Kegan Paul, 1966, pp. 215–30. Arthur's life in part 1 of the novel is discussed as "a cycle of violent rebellion and imposed conformity, each breeding the other," in a world of savage "jungle justice rewarding jungle behavior." At the annual Goose Fair, he is a Lord of Misrule who is both symbolically and literally (violently) dethroned, and "Saturday night's anarchistic revolt brings Sunday morning's lifeless conformity" in part 2.

Roskies, D.M. "'I'd Rather Be Like I Am': Character, Style and Language of Class in Alan Sillitoe's Narratives." *Neophilologus*, 65 (1981): 308. Detailed stylistic analysis of Sillitoe's "characteristic signature" in fiction as well as his "maverick" —and "eccentric"—achievement.

Rothschild, Janice. "The Growth of a Writer: An Interview with Alan Sillitoe." *Southern Humanities Review*, 20, 2 (Spring 1986): 127–40. Rothschild focuses primarily on biographical aspects of Sillitoe's fiction, with detailed commentary on his later works.

Staples, Hugh B. "*Saturday Night and Sunday Morning*: Alan Sillitoe and *The White Goddess*." *Modern Fiction Studies*, 10 (Summer 1964): 171–81. Assessment of *Saturday Night and Sunday Morning* as "a dramatic analysis, on an essentially comic level, of the immemorial rhythms of birth, life and death that Robert Graves maintains is the theme of 'all true poets' from Homer to the present day." The mythological system set forth in Graves's *The White Goddess* is shown to be "the major structuring device" for Sillitoe's first novel.

Wilson, Keith. "Arthur Seaton Twenty Years On: A Reappraisal of Alan Sillitoe's *Saturday Night and Sunday Morning*." *English Studies in Canada* (1981), pp. 414–25. Developing the argument first advanced by Staples (above), Wilson points out that "Sillitoe structures Arthur Seaton's life around a parody of seasonal community ritual"; emphasizing the recurrence of a central metaphor in Sillitoe's novel and Anthony Burgess's *A Clockwork Orange*, he assesses Arthur's sometimes-violent resistance to the "mechanistic world in which the inevita-

bility of the machine governs all human action." Similarities between values expressed at the end of Sillitoe's novel and those in W.B. Yeats's poem "The Fisherman" are also discussed.

William Hutchings

Simple, Peter (joint pseudonym)

Peter Simple is the joint pseudonym of Michael Bernard Wharton and James Colin Ross Welch.

Wharton, Michael [Bernard]

Born: place unknown, April 19, 1913
Education: Bedford Grammar School; Lincoln College, Oxford University
Married: Joan Atkey, 1936, one child; Catherine Mary Derrington, 1952, divorced, 1972, one child; Susan Moller, 1974

Biography

Michael Wharton, the son of Paul Nathan and Bertha Wharton, was born on April 19, 1913. Wharton took his mother's name over the Jewish surname of "Nathan" because, he says, that name did not "suit him." He attended Bedford Grammar School, then turned from privileged education at Lincoln College, Oxford. When World War II broke out, he served in the Royal Artillery and on the General Staff from 1940 to 1946, at which time he met many of the models of his characters and formed many of the views that he would later express in his satire. After leaving the Service, he joined the BBC as producer and scriptwriter of such dramas as *Under the Dome* (1947, typescript in The British Library, unpublished).

After ten years in television (1946–1956), Wharton began to write the humorous *Daily Telegraph* "Peter Simple" columns which have made him one of the most widely-read of recent British humorists and on which his reputation as a writer rests, despite the fact that under his own name he has authored political history (*A Nation's Security*, 1955), a novel (*Sheldrake*, 1958), and an autobiography (*The Missing Will: The Making of "Peter Simple,"* 1984, the only one of his non-Peter Simple books currently in print, 1990).

Wharton married Joan Atkey in 1936 and divorced her in 1947. The union produced a son. In 1952, Wharton married Catherine Mary Derrington, whom he divorced twenty-one years later. His second union produced a daughter. Susan Moller became his third wife in 1974. Wharton lives at Forge Cottage, Naphill Common, High Wycombe, Buckinghamshire, and he has devoted himself to satiric social comment on his neighbors and London types, as well as to walking, gardening, and Celtic studies. Over the years he has collected his popular *Daily Telegraph* columns in a dozen or so anthologies and ignored his early promise as a writer of detective fiction. (As "Simon Crabtree" he published *Forgotten Memories*, 1941, and *Hector Tumbler Investigates*, 1943, dashed off in his spare time in the Service.)

He shares with Colin Welch the credit for the wit and wisdom of the whimsical and acerbic Peter Simple.

Welch, [James] Colin [Ross]

Born: Cambridgeshire, April 23, 1924
Education: Stowe School; Peterhouse College,
*   Cambridge University, B.A. with honors*
Married: Sybil Russell, 1950; two children

Biography

Columnist and critic for the *Spectator* since 1982 and parliamentary correspondent for the *Daily Mail* since 1984, Colin Welch added to his duties as editorial (British: leader) writer and parliamentary sketch writer at the *Daily Telegraph* (1950–1964) his contributions to the creation of "Peter Simple."

The son of James Peter Welch and Irene Margherita Paton Welch of Cambridgeshire, Colin was born on April 23, 1924. He went to Stowe School on a scholarship and after attending Peterhouse College, Cambridge University, where he received a B.A. with honors, he was commissioned in the Royal Warwickshire Regiment in 1942. He served throughout World War II in Northwest Europe and was twice wounded. After the war he worked for the *Glasgow Herald* (1948) and the Colonial Office (1949), and in 1950 he went to the *Daily Telegraph*. In 1950, Welch and Sybil Russell married; they have two children. He served as a department editor at the *Telegraph* (1964–1980), then a columnist (1981–1983). He was editor-in-chief of *Chief Executive* (1980–1982) and has won a British Press Award as a specialist writer (1986). His articles have appeared in the *Spectator*, the *New Statesman*, and elsewhere. He edited Sir Francis Ponsonby's memoirs, *Recollections of Three Reigns* (1951), and with his wife translated for the BBC Johann Nestroy's *Liberty Comes to Krahwinkel* (1954). He contributes to journals and symposia and lives in Aldbourne, Wiltshire. Poland has awarded him the order *Polonia Restituta* (1972) but many Britons would consider his participation in the "Peter Simple" legend to be a greater honor.

Literary Analysis

"Peter Simple" is the pseudonym under which Wharton earned the accolade from the *Spectator*'s Richard West as "both the funniest and wisest writer in England." In the *Daily Telegraph*, Anthony Howard called Wharton "one of the few original British eccentrics left to us—a kind of Evelyn Waugh in aspic." After decades as a humor columnist ("The Way of the World" in the *Daily Telegraph*), after millions of words in print, Peter Simple (with Welch as an early collaborator) is something of a British national treasure, though practically unknown outside his tight little island. This is largely because his brand of satire is a sort of family joke, a "sending up" (as the British say) of the all-too-common man "on the Clapham omnibus" (as the Brits used to say), distinctly British class types, and the passing parade of political, literary, and other local idiocy. Still, satire rooted in the particular can speak of universals, the ludicrous has no nationality, and, while foreigners may miss some of the in-jokes, caricature drawn with a broad brush can be seen even across the Atlantic and deciphered and appreciated in both Britain and America.

In satire, as Dr. Samuel Johnson wrote, "wickedness or folly is censured." In Peter Simple there is ridicule and mockery, raillery and invective, wit and whimsy. He casts a conservative and cold eye on the decline of empire and the debasement of standards. He "has a go at" affectation, pomposity, snobbery, hypocrisy, tastelessness, red-brick universities, left-wingers, journalists who write fluff and readers who write in to journalistic advice-givers, the trendy, the titled, and the proletarian, anything ridiculous that creeps into the news, crawls into the BBC, or swims into his ken by any other means. Simple's columns are, as critic Alvin B. Kernan tells us, all that satire must be: "always crowded, disorderly, grotesque." Wharton is himself "always indignant, dedicated to truth, pessimistic, and caught in a series of unpleasant contradictions" in a world which the satirist sincerely believes is going to Hell in a handcart. His weapons are, first of all, a deep conviction that he is right and other people are wrong; that over-inflated balloons ought to be pricked with the sharp pin of wit; that mockery can serve the purpose of moral improvement as well as entertainment; and that effective change can be wrought by the correct choice of bitter sarcasm, subtle understatement, wild exaggeration, *reductio ad absurdum* (or absurd reduction, cutting down to size), trivializing, playing on unattractive sounds or associations, puns and parody, bold lies and bald statements, bisociation (Arthur Koestler's term for double association) and clever reference, snob appeal and superior attitudes, and farce and fun.

In the 1950s, the *Daily Telegraph* column was first signed "Yorick." That harkened back to both William Shakespeare and Laurence Sterne. The principal personages of the satire soon appeared and they have been joined over the decades by more hilarious creations attributable to Peter Simple, a name selected when other writers began to use "Yorick." The pseudonym "Simple" has a long tradition in British satire, in which "Simple," "Simon Simplex," "Simon Simple" (1808), "Tristram Simple" (1811), and "Peter Simple" (supposed the author of *Newton Foster*, actually Captain Frederick Marryat of *Mr. Midshipman Easy* fame, 1834) are found. Peter Simple is worthy of his genealogy. He is the latest and arguably the greatest of the wise simpletons, a very complex *Simplicius* indeed.

Peter Simple reached many more readers than those who followed him religiously in the *Daily Telegraph*. His fans called for collected columns. The first book of these was published by the *Daily Telegraph* in 1957: *Way of the World, Reprinted from "The Daily Telegraph," October 1955–October 1957*. A second series came more quickly: *Way of the World. Second Series. Reprinted from "The Daily Telegraph," October 1957–October 1958*. These collections reached nine volumes and then a tenth appeared as *The Stretchford Chronicles: 25 Years of Peter Simple* (first published by the *Daily Telegraph* in 1980, then more widely distributed in a "Papermac" edition from a branch of Macmillan, 1981). For those who could not find volumes such as *The Best of Peter Simple* (1963), *Peter Simple in Opposition* (1965), *More of Peter Simple* (1969), *The World of Peter Simple* (1973), and so on, *The Stretchford Chronicles* became an affordable treasury of an author affectionately called The Master (a title

given also, significantly, to such comic geniuses as Noel Coward and Sir P.G. Wodehouse, two other writers who proved that the intelligently insular could become internationally sophisticated).

Simple may well be more crotchety and cantankerous than Coward, but at least he does not deal in a long-dead Edwardian England scene like Wodehouse. In an age in which Martin Amis has succeeded Kingsley Amis, Simple may not be the most mod or the most mad of commentators on Perfidious Albion and its disgruntled, diminished inheritors, but he does attack those evils of the day which his readership wants to see trounced, whether they reside in tacky caravans (mobile homes) or the salons of Hampstead radical intellectuals, the residence of the side-splittingly funny Socialist Royal Family, or the no less crazy corridors of power in Parliament, debased education, debilitated Church, or "in-a-state" State.

In 1597–1598, Joseph Hall wrote in *Virgidemiarum* that the satirist needed a store of slings and arrows:

> The *Satyre* should be like the *Porcupine*
> That shoots sharp quilles out in each
>   angry line.

Today the satirist still needs his zingers and his anger. What he needs most, though, and often discovers is hard to find, are not only definable targets of satire but definite audiences for satire. In his *Daily Telegraph* readers, Simple had a clearly identified audience that would appreciate his barbs and have a clear idea of what targets they would like to see hit. His readers shared his predictable, coherent, conservative ethical and rational norms, his political outlook, his prejudices against everything new and banal from the memoirs of Nazi field marshals (Erich Buber von Nittwitz's *Sleeping Panzer* casts "no more than a pallid, fitful light on the rise and fall of the Third Reich") to pop poets such as Eric Lard. Knowing and sharing the readers' social and political outlooks, Simple can write with assurance and conviction, expecting agreement on what is comic and what is contemptible in the contemporary world. The author knows that he will not be met with an outraged "That isn't funny!" when he writes of the Hampstead leftist Mrs. Dutt-Pauker (who also has country houses: "in Dorset, Beth Garth, another in Wales, Glyn Stalin, and another in the West of Ireland, Lenimmore"), or of Gotheby's auction receiving £2,500 for "Kevin," a "rare plastic gnome by Mulligan," or (after the *New Statesman* said that the monarchy was part of the civil service) a Socialist Queen Gran (like the "Queen Mum," the dowager Queen Elizabeth) and a *naph* (irredeemably bourgeois) royal family with a king belonging to the Monarchial Workers Union, or *Modcomforce* (Moderate Commando Force, with hints of *mod con[veniences]* such as indoor toilets) and General Sir Frederick "Tiger" Nidgett and The Royal Army Tailoring Corps ("The Grey Devils from East Ardley Junction" and "The Lads wi' the Needles and Thread"). Swami Ron S. Battacharya, "the only Indian holy man with a first-class degree in chartered accountancy, who owns a successful chain of yoga betting-shops in the Nerdley area," the Irish, the Welsh, and the Scots as objects of humor, not to mention easy real-life targets such as Michael Foote, Enoch Powell, Lord George Brown, various non-entities who happened to get to be prime minister, various eccentrics who did not (such as Jeremy Thorpe, Anthony—formerly Sir Anthony—Blunt, Tony Benn, formerly Tony Wedgewood Benn, formerly Lord something-or-other, not as Has Benn) also serve as subjects for the humorist's satirical attention.

There are occasional swipes, too, at foreigners, such as "President Ngrafta of Gombola (formerly Gomboland), known as 'The Redeemer,'" and Americans (for whom the name Elihu Jones III seems to Simple to be usual). In addition, "Peter Simple" exhibits a mastery of comic names of people (Doreen Brontë, the unknown sibling of the famous family, who used to dress up as her brother Bramwell to drink at the local pub and who founded the Haworth Girls' Small Bore Rifle Club), places (Suction Road, Wednesbury; Numb Lane Caravan Site, Canby Island; Simplehampton; Bog Lane Secondary Modern School, Stretchford), and things (Ombra Mai-Fu automobile, the Nadirco chain of supermarkets, Mary Lou Ogreburg's Multi-Racial Bread and Marmite People's Dance Theatre Group, and Rentacrowd, which supplies crowds for all occasions, chiefly political, such as the Aldermaston or peace-march type, Trafalgar Square "in various sizes," Kassem Howling Mob No. 2, Lumumba Super-Raving Anti-Colonialist Mob No. 4, etc.).

In the ingenuity and significance of the satirical names with which Simple dots his prose can be seen a great deal of the art and attitude of the writer, some general principles of the art

of satire itself, and some of the difficulties of translating a text (with all of its linguistic subtleties and cultural allusions) from English into American.

A few examples will illustrate Simple's technique and charm, available to all the English-speaking world despite the barriers of contemporary reference and cultural context, language and slanguage in-jokes, and so on. To begin, there are the colorful characters: Stanley and Doris Gloater, living in a decayed caravan in a bleak Midlands housing estate (i.e., a trailer in a project); Edith Grampus of Ilkey, Yorks., and Mostyn Foodbothamm, of Cleckheaton, arguing in letters to the column about the potted palms once seen on the tops of Bradford busses; Doreen Gass, "girl political expert"; Viper & Bugloss, publishers; Jeremy Cardhouse, M.P.; Kay Gristle, harpist of the Stretchford Orchestra, accused of being under the influence of drink "during a four-hour performance of Mahler's Symphony No. 13 ('the Intolerable')" on a tour of Belgium; the Reverend Bruce Nethers, vicar of St. Atilla's and chaplain to the local teenage vandals; Nembutalov, a boring political writer who sent Karl Marx a copy of his 250,000-word pamphlet on *The Roots of Political Inertia* and was rewarded for his pains by being called "a decaying cabbage-stalk of the bourgeoisie"; Sir Frank Tombs, Brass Stair Rod-in-Waiting (a mocking of the official messenger between the two houses of Parliament, Black Rod); Murray Fringeburg, a pop American poet of the 1960s; and Julian Birdbath, the author of *The Disconnected Goalposts*, "the first 'avant-garde' football novel . . . full of alienation, homosexuality, sadism, heroin-addiction and psychosomatic diseases" and featuring Kafka-like characters (Krebs, no forename, and S., N., and V.), displaying (according to *The Observer* reviewer) "the anguished post-Christian world of professional football," Britain's battleground between wars.

There are also the places: Doomchester (from Dorchester), Norbiton (from Surbiton), Sadcake Park (beloved of exhibitionists and other deviates), home of R.D. Viswasswami, "the only naked sadhu [hermit] in this country," employed by the Stretchford Council "to live in a specially-built hermit's cave of artificial stone" as an amenity, with the status of environmental amenity officer (grade three).

Among these cleverly named things are a confectionary called Fry's Turkish Disgust;

Clackmannanshire terriers, "mostly used by Scots landowners to evict tenants" but now recommended "to Glasgow football fans as an additional weapon for their armoury"; the Boggs automotive works, producing the Boggs Yobbo and the Boggs Super-Oaf; Au Petit Coin Anthrophage, "the trendy West End restaurant that specializes in New Guinea dishes"; The British Boring Board of Control (Sir Herbert Trance, Pres.); and "rubbishist" art, the successor to "destructivist" and "aggressivist" art of the period when defacing public property was taken by fools to be graffiti art and the legitimate "terrorist" art of the seething masses.

Simple ranged all the way from raging at, or ragging, crackpot educational and other social engineering schemes for the post-war British utopia to taking down a peg the people who wrote in to newspaper columnists. For instance, in "Is this your surname?," published in 1958, he states:

> If your name is Fruitperson, you probably had an ancestor who held his land under feudal tenure, being obliged to deliver a certain quantity of fruit to the Lord of the Manor annually. The seneschal on announcing the arrival of the fruit would probably say: "Here is the fruitperson." Hence the name.

> The name Musicseller, common in parts of Worcestershire, has no connexion with music. It is probably of Gaelic origin, and means "one who removes the eyes of partially gnawed potatoes."

> If your name is Sadcake, you may be descended from the famous Red Indian tribe who emigrated to Manchester in the 1860s and took up birdcage manufacture in Salford. J.R. Sadcake, who played full-back for Accrington Stanley in the 1892 Cup Final, is probably the best-known scion of this dauntless race. (Next week: McSeedy, Gongworthy and Lemonsodawallah.)

This is very British in nature, demonstrating an interest in genealogy and the R.A.F. (*gongworthy* = deserving of a medal), an anti-Hibernian prejudice, traces of the *Raj* (*wallah* = "fellow," here not a waterboy like Gunga Din but a lemon soda provider), and the superior attitude toward hackwriting in the style of

"Beachcomber," perhaps, and maybe with some of the slyness of "Saki."

Elsewhere a reader writes to *"Genuflex"* (a parody of journalist pseudonyms) to ask how he ought to address his "elder brother Eric, who is in holy orders and who also holds medical and dental degrees," now that he has become both a detective sergeant and inherited a baronetcy. The reply to this reader (Mostyn Sheep-Harris, Loughborough, a real place name that Simple includes among those he thinks silly enough not to need tampering with) is: "'The Rev. Det.-Sgt. Dr. Sir Eric Sheep-Harris, Bt., DD, MD, LDS' is the correct form. Should your brother be appointed a Privy Councillor, join the Navy, Army or Air Force, or make a pilgrimage to Mecca, please write to me again." If you did not know that the pilgrimage to Mecca adds to the titles of Islam, now you do. Whatever you previously thought about the honorifics of Britain, you must now find them faintly foolish, especially when they confuse a man to the point where he does not know how to address his own brother. Pretension has been scourged.

In a parody of the medical-advice column, a doctor named Henbane (a surname that the humorist seems to like to use to denigrate his characters, employing it also for a dimwit detective inspector) writes:

> Quite a number of people have been writing to me for hints on how to cope with the hot weather. Mrs. F.S. of Aston-Garfinkle (Nott.,) is typical. "The other day," she says, "my feet got so overheated that they left charred patches on the grass as I walked along, and partially melted asphalt. Now I face a bill for damage from our local council."

> Her problem is not as uncommon as she may think. Trabb's Foot (or pedal hyperpyrexia, as we medicos call it) is a recognized condition. In the old days it was slow to yield to treatment. Patients usually wore a clumsy type of surgical boot with a compartment containing cold water, which had to be continually renewed as it turned to steam.

> Today a course of injections—borboromycin or one of the newly synthesized amphibogulene group—plus a few days' rest should do the trick.

Another, related foot trouble is Pedal Effloritis (also called Herbaceous Foot or Olwen's Syndrome, after an early Welsh sufferer) . . .

There is a similarity in these pieces to the writing of twentieth-century American humorist S.J. Perelman in the humor derived from the masterful mimicry of jargon (a good ear) combined with the deft use of exotic reference (a compliment to the reader's education). An anti-Welsh thread runs through all of Simple's writing—he finds Welsh names as weird as Irish names—but in this case he proves his knowledge of Welsh myth and calls on the reader's knowledge of the same, along with a familiarity with hack writers' cliches, medical pomposities, the fads for miracle drugs, the associations of *bog*, and the neat leap from the mundane to the impossible "charred patches . . . partially melted asphalt."

Finally, there is a parody of the style of the Old Salt's yarn. The subject is Dag Hammarskjold, the secretary-general of the United Nations before U Thant (the "Burma wallah" here). *Dag* suggested *drag*, though Hammarskjold, often said to be a homosexual (thus the aptness of *queer* here), was never accused of cross-dressing:

> Stannard sucked his pipe ruminatively. "It was a rum joint," he began, "and no mistake—New York East Side, right down on the slums of the river. A gloomy Swede kept it when I knew it— Dag the Drag they called him; a queer chap for the job you might think, but then it was a queer job. A Burma wallah has it now they say . . .

To understand and appreciate this passage, the reader needs to know more than *rum* and *queer* both mean "odd." There must also be some familiarity with history, gossip, a popular fiction style, the United Nations, and Simple's objection to that organization.

Now extremes in Academe (Marxist, deconstructionist, feminist, and curriculum-corrective theories) make Simple's jokes pale. Recent political scandals and idiocy in Britain and abroad challenge satire to be as wild. The *Daily Telegraph*, a conservative paper run by Lord Camrose and Lord Hartwell (his son) for nearly six decades, has gone and with it the world that Anthony Sampson in *Times Literary*

Supplement described as "rigid office hierarchy, something between that of a large country house and an officers' training barracks." Sampson adds: "The mystery about the *Telegraph* to outside observers was how such clever journalists—ranging from Michael Muggeridge to Colin Welch—could produce so dull a paper."

One contributor who was never dull was Simple. His satire will remain, though his vehicle, some of his targets, and maybe even some of his audience (the complacent middle class secure in traditional privileges and inherited ideas) have vanished forever.

Summary

Michael Wharton and Colin Ross's "Peter Simple" was the pseudonym under which a long series of humorous columns, "The Way of the World," were printed in London's conservative newspaper, the *Daily Telegraph*, starting in 1955. Limited though he may be by his political slant and dated though he may be by his close attention to the events of his daily world, Simple deserves to outlast "The House the Berrys Built" (that is, the old *Daily Telegraph*), of which the humorist's columns were a valuable feature, crusading against the Barbarians (as the conservative readership defined them).

"And what shall become of us, without any barbarians?" asked the Greek poet Constantine Cavafy. "Those people were a kind of solution." Certainly by offering satiric targets for Simple's writing, they contributed to the amusement of nations and to our permanent store of humorous literature. Criticism of Simple is scant, but there is enough salt in his work; it will be preserved.

Selected Bibliography

Primary Sources

Way of the World, Reprinted from "The Daily Telegraph," October 1955–October 1957. London: *Daily Telegraph*, 1957.

Way of the World. Second Series. Reprinted from "The Daily Telegraph," October 1957–October 1958. London: *Daily Telegraph*, 1958.

Way of the World. The Best of Peter Simple. Selected Extracts from the "Way of the World" Column in The Daily Telegraph. London: Johnson, 1963.

Peter Simple in Opposition. Extracts from the "Way of the World" Column in The Daily Telegraph. London: Johnson, 1965.

More of Peter Simple. Extracts from the "Way

of the World" Column in *The Daily Telegraph*. London: Macmillan, 1969.

The World of Peter Simple. Extracts from the "Way of the World" Column in The Daily Telegraph, 1969–1971. London: Johnson, 1971.

The World of Peter Simple. Extracts from the "Way of the World" Column in The Daily Telegraph, 1971–1973. London: Johnson, 1973.

A Choice of Peter Simple, 1973–1975. London: *Daily Telegraph*, 1975.

Peter Simple's "Way of the World," 1975–1977. London: *Daily Telegraph*, 1978.

The Stretchford Chronicles: 25 Years of Peter Simple. London: *Daily Telegraph*, 1980. London and Basingstoke: Macmillan, 1981.

Michael Wharton. *A Dubious Codicil: An Autobiography.* London: Chatto & Windus, 1991. Confessional autobiography of a "state registered melancholic" who amused others, a man of Jewish extraction who changed his surname from "Nathan" because it "did not suit" him and yet railed about "alien people" spoiling English "homogeneity," a charming grump and delightful fogey.

Secondary Sources

Ashley, Leonard R.N. "'Simple' Satire: The Onomastics of the Satirical *Genre* Illustrated by the Works of Michael Wharton in 'Peter Simple''s *Way of the World* Columns in the *Daily Telegraph*." *Literary Onomastic Studies*, 10 (1983): 211–59. Extensive study of names in satire with the emphasis on "Peter Simple."

Howard, Anthony. "To the Simpleham Manor born . . . " *Daily Telegraph* (November 2, 1984): 20. A fellow journalist's appreciation of Peter Simple.

Sampson, Anthony. "The Rewards of Dullness" (reviews of Duff Hart-Davis's *The House the Berrys Built* and Nicholas Garland's *Not Many Dead: Journal of a Year in Fleet Street*). *Times Literary Supplement* (April 13–19, 1990): 389. The history of the *Daily Telegraph* and of a successor, *The Independent*, in two books under review; Peter Simple's world of Fleet Street.

Wheen, Francis. "Not Simple but Honest." *Times Literary Supplement* (January 25, 1991): 28. Review of *A Dubious Codicil*.

Leonard R.N. Ashley

Simpson, N[orman] F[rederick]

Born: London, January 29, 1919
Education: Emmanuel School, London, 1930–1937; Birkbeck College, London, 1950–1954
Marriage: Joyce Bartlett, 1944; one child

Biography

N.F. Simpson came to the theater later in life than did his younger contemporaries among the new post-World War II dramatists. He was born to George Frederick (a glassblower at a lamp factory in Hammersmith, London) and Elizabeth Rossiter Simpson in London on January 29, 1919. He attended Emmanuel School from 1930 to 1937. After working in a bank for a few years, he served with the Royal Artillery from 1941 to 1943 and with the Army Intelligence Corps in Italy and the Middle East from 1943 to 1946. He married Joyce Bartlett in 1944, and in 1948 their daughter was born. Upon demobilization he entered Birkbeck College of the University of London (1950–1954) where he took an honors degree in English. Until 1963, when he decided to devote full time to writing, he taught "A level" English to adults at the City of Westminster College in London.

With important dramatists such as John Osborne, Ann Jellicoe, and John Arden, Simpson found a home for his plays in the experimental Royal Court Theatre. In 1956, the year in which the English stage revolution began, *A Resounding Tinkle* shared third prize in the *Observer* playwriting competition with Jellicoe's *The Sport of My Mad Mother* and John Beynon's *The Shifting Heart. One Way Pendulum* (1959), his most popular play (which one critic maintained should be revived annually) was awarded second prize in the 1962 Britannica Awards for Playwrights. *One To Another*, published in 1960, includes plays by Simpson, John Mortimer, and Harold Pinter—all three recognized as among the most promising of the new dramatists. Some of his television plays (*Three Resounding Tinkles*, 1966, and *Four Tall Tinkles*, 1967), as their titles suggest, are drawn from *A Resounding Tinkle*, his first full-length play. His novel, *Harry Bleachbaker* (1976), is based on his 1972 play, *Was He Anyone?*

By the time Simpson became literary manager at the Royal Court Theatre (1976–1978), he had written more than a dozen stage and television plays, won several awards, and earned a reputation as a satirist in the absurd tradition of the Rumanian-born French dramatist, Eugene Ionesco. Like that of a number of his younger contemporaries who were a part of the heady years of the two waves of the English stage revolution, Simpson's writing for the stage diminished, perhaps even ceased. He lives in Bedford, outside of London where, although he has been absent from the stage since the 1970s, he continues to write.

Literary Analysis

If Ionesco dramatized the plight of humans reduced to objects and animals such as an empty chair and rhinoceroses, Simpson took objects such as talking weight machines and energized them with a life of their own in his creation of a lunatic fantasy world. He populated his stage with characters obsessed with fantasies which they attempt to carry out by the same rules that govern the conventional and logical world. Those rules include the reasoning process conducted in a vacuum or in a totally impossible context. Frequently, minor or unintended ends take over as the raison d'être for major actions. For example, one character prepares huge amounts of food and then pays a neighbor to carry off the leftovers. Another eats constantly so that eating will become a habit and not a distracting weight on his mind, and still another reasons that if speaking weight machines (common in England) can speak one's weight, 500 of them should be able to join in singing the "Hallelujah Chorus" from George Frideric Handel's *Messiah*. His stage nonsense, Simpson has explained, is intended as a corrective for the lunatic nonsense that is modern life.

The playwright's humorous devices are those of Ionesco's distinctive version of the theater of the absurd. The essence of their style is the paradox, the non-sequitur, and other perversions of the logical process. To this end, Simpson's characters, like Ionesco's, behave mechanically and speak in clichés without regard to context. Simpson goes beyond Ionesco, however, in substituting active fantasies for the dysfunctional, empty, and mechanical lives of his characters. His plays are wildly alive even though the life resides in the objectification of their fantasies, not in the characters.

A view of his techniques may begin with the telling titles of the plays, matched by equally telling names of his characters—a traditional farce technique. The titles themselves are paradoxes (e.g., *A Resounding Tinkle* and *One Way Pendulum*), and the characters are unabashedly named (e.g., Mr. and Mrs. Paradock). In *The Hole*, the characters are the Visionary, Endo, Cerebro, and Soma, the latter three suggesting the fragmented approaches of their attempts to understand the meaning of a simple street excavation.

Puns and clichés—the stock-in-trade of absurdist drama—are given new dimensions as art joins suburbia as the target of Simpson's satire. He imposes a gaggle of theatrical figures on a suburban household in his full-length version of *A Resounding Tinkle*. The crew includes comedians, cleaners, a technician, an author, and critics.

Simpson's plentiful verbal puns are enhanced, sometimes taken over, by visual puns like the elephant and snake in *A Resounding Tinkle* and the hole in his play by that title. His most outlandish collection of visual images, however, is that in *One Way Pendulum*, the erection of the Old Bailey courtroom in a living room, for example, and the singing of the "Hallelujah Chorus" by speaking weight machines, and one female's obsession with the length of her arms.

Yet another technique is the use of confusing and changing identities, like that of the Paradocks' son who turns out to be a female.

Simpson's three major stage plays, all of which premiered in the early years of his dramatic career, demonstrate ingenious approaches to the absurdity of the modern world. These plays have not been superseded in quality or popularity by his subsequent dramas. In the first, *A Resounding Tinkle*, he defies the very idea of a dramatic construct by the absence of any linkage or progression in plot or characters. In the second, *The Hole*, he writes a philosophical fable in the style of Samuel Beckett, satirizing man's intellectual attempts to understand life. In the third, *One Way Pendulum*, Simpson is at his most hilarious in the demonstration of the *idée fixe*, a theory made famous by Henri Bergson, a French theoretician who propounded the theory of habit as the source of all humor.

In *A Resounding Tinkle*, in the absence of any identifiable plot structure non-sequiturs dominate what action there is. There is no reason, for instance, that a loose group of theater figures should arrive at the suburban home of Mr. and Mrs. Paradock. Individual members of both the family and the visitors exist in isolation from each other, each compulsively acting out his/her fixed habits of behavior and speech. Simpson himself has said that "from time to

S

time parts of the play may seem to become detached from the main body. No attempt should be made to nudge these back into position . . . [as they] will eventually drop off and are quite harmless."[1] The play has been described by critics as an anti-play, a term Ionesco uses as a subtitle for *The Bald Soprano*.

Unsurprisingly then, two unrelated series of events comprise the plot of *A Resounding Tinkle*. There is, first of all, the problem of a large elephant which the Paradocks' small house will not accommodate. The problem exists for no other purpose than as a framework for Simpson's satirical thrusts at suburbia, the obsessive greed of one neighbor to outdo another, in particular. Eventually they solve the problem by exchanging the elephant for a neighbor's snake.

When the play opens, Mr. and Mrs. Paradock (Bro and Middie) are arguing, among other things, about a visitor wearing an old coat who asks Bro to form a new government. Bro thinks that the man may be his Uncle Ted up to one of his usual pranks. Bro's concern is not about the absurdity of the request but rather about the difficulty of forming a government at six o'clock in the evening. Similarly avoiding the normal response to so abnormal a request, Middie's problem is with the identity of the man. As a solution to her enigma, she suggests giving him her husband's overcoat: "It's too small for you except when you're in one of your pint-sized moods. But if he'd tried it on I could have seen in a glance he wasn't a man of your build. I might after a time have been able to narrow it down to Uncle Ted. As it is I don't know what to think."[2] Both husband and wife ignore the major premise for a minor point, one of a chain of such illogicalities in the play.

In an incident reminiscent of Ionesco's *The Bald Soprano* (1948), Middie, in the middle of a game of patience, twice calls out a "Come in" to a doorbell ringer and finally goes to the door only to find nobody there. She concludes: "I made sure that somebody was at the door" (57). Ionesco's maid, responding three times to a bell, finds no one there and concludes that the function of the bell is to announce that no visitor has arrived.

In a scene involving the visit of their daughter who turns out to be their son, there is another deflection of an important issue from its realistic context:

Mr. Paradock: Where is Don?

Mrs. Paradock: Gone where you can't harm her anymore with your bitter words.
Mr. Paradock: I think I'll have a turn in the garden.
Mrs. Paradock: We haven't got a garden. You know that as well as I do.
Mr. Paradock: I understood it's in the deeds.
Mrs. Paradock: Is it?
Mr. Paradock: I wouldn't have bought the house otherwise.
Mrs. Paradock: House? This is a bungalow.
Mr. Paradock: I wouldn't have bought it without looking pretty closely at the deeds to see if there was any mention of a garden. (64)

The garden squabble is followed by still another in which Middie gives a fresh twist to a cliché. She envies "the man in the street who's never learned to drink for himself." She berates the average man who seems "quite content to let the rest of us do all his drinking for him" (65).

The second series of actions—they can hardly be seen as a plot or subplot—is introduced arbitrarily by Middie, who decides that she must leave the room as the producer wants it for a meeting. There is no motivation for her departure or his arrival except Middie's statement. Two comedians who had earlier entered for no discernible reason had taken on the mission of explaining humor in a nonsensical list of figures of speech. Now the author arrives to taunt the members of the audience with their reliance on critics as purveyors of jargon-ridden explanations of meanings. Without critics, "the coastguards of the mind," he insists, authors would be "hard put to it to arrive anywhere at all" (66).

Critics then take their turn in providing the audience with their judgments:

Salt: I protest!
Pepper: I deplore!
Mustard: I condemn! (43)

Then, reversing themselves, respectively, one hails, another salutes, a third predicts, and a fourth acclaims.

Academic jargon comes in for Simpson's biting satire as one critic mentions Bertolt Brecht's *Verfrumdungseffekt*. Another sees no

Brecht at all in the play, and still another sees the Brechtian technique carried on beyond Brecht. Pepper summarizes the play as "The Comedy of Errors rewritten by Lewis Carroll to provide a part for Godot or somebody" (71).

Simpson concludes his play with a repetition of scene 1 and with the author's congratulations to the audience for taking insult after insult in such good spirit.

Shortened to include only the characters involved in the Paradocks' dilemma of the elephant, A Resounding Tinkle enjoyed a more successful production at the Royal Court Theatre the next year with its companion piece, The Hole, the first of Simpson's many one-act plays and skits. Together, the two short plays represent contrasts in the dramatist's style, the satire of the earlier farce primarily verbal with that of The Hole being intellectual as well.

If the elephant and the snake in A Resounding Tinkle are metaphors for Simpson's satire of suburban greed and aridity, the hole in his second play is his metaphor for man's logical attempt to understand the world around him and, failing to do so, making a religion from the detritus of the process. The writer exploits one of the most common and singular of English habits: the queue (or waiting line). The main character, a Visionary, peers into a hole, awaiting the unveiling of a stained glass window of a cathedral which he insists he sees in the hole. While he watches, a line of curious onlookers assembles. Claiming his now-diminished aim is his wish to be the nucleus of the queue, he reveals that once he had aspired to having "a queue stretching away from me in every direction known to the compass . . . like the spikes from a prison railing." The consummation of his hopes and ambitions at that time would have been "to be first in an infinity of queues."3

However, his main function in the play is to sit and wait as the group of curious onlookers grows and takes over the dialogue of the drama. Three men—Endo, Soma, and Cerebro —obviously representing biological fragments of the human body, do most of the conjecturing about what is in the hole. At first they see what appears to be the shadows of two people playing dominoes in boxing gloves, then a golfer, a fish, a prisoner, a ritual murder, and so on, working themselves into a near frenzy until the worker emerges from the hole. Joining the conversation are two wives, Mrs. Ecto and Mrs. Meso, who keep up a continuous complaining about the problems of their husbands, one of whom prides himself on being non-conformist, the other who is terrified of being different. The women's mindless chatter interlocks with the men's speculations about the meaning of the hole, a hostility toward the Visionary growing underneath their comments.

When the men engage in eating pickled onions speared with a fork, Cerebro speculates on what would have happened had the fork become a knife, and Endo responds with "That sort of thing couldn't happen here, old Man" (41). It is then that both men see a blood-stained knife, a ritual murder, a human sacrifice in the hole. The leap in logic marks a turn in the play, several pages of stichomythic dialogue creating a Pinter-like sense of menace:

> Endo: We've no time to lose.
> Cerebro: We stayed too long talking.
> Endo: We're late on the scene.
> Cerebro: We took the wrong turning.
> . . .
>
> Soma: Look up voodoo.
> Endo: Send for dictionaries.
> Cerebro: They're atavistic. (43)

Their fears take on the forms of Asian hordes, the Mau-Mau, or the Ku Klux Klan, and in their fervor the men march in all directions.

When the workman with his tools emerges from the hole, Cerebro disdainfully pronounces the hole to be nothing more than a place for an electric junction box with cables and then proceeds to speculate on the one cable which "enters the junction-box from the only side on which we are unable to see it enter—from underneath." The other two men and the women seem shocked by the discovery. Soma questions the word "junction box." "Does it mean anything? Or is it just a new name for something we've been looking at all along" (49). They extend increasingly ludicrous meanings to a box and cables, their comments gradually taking on a menacing tone directed at the Visionary and climaxing in Mrs. Meso's conclusion that the Visionary should be put away.

The final monologue in the play is Soma's as he declares the junction-box to be "electricity made manifest." He concludes:

> For each time we draw near to the cavity
> and together peer down into the depths,
> we are not only giving expression by that

S

act to the unquenchable curiosity that is in us, but we are at the same time reaffirming the truth of the eternal and inscrutable paradox—that it is upon this cavity that we build our faith. (54)

Martin Esslin sees Cerebro (playing Karl Marx to Soma's Josef Stalin) consoling himself with the "potentialities of power and mass emotion" (221). *The Hole* is a metaphor for man's leap from his limited knowledge of life to the creation of a religion from that knowledge. The logical process by which Simpson's characters deduce their religion is as empty as the thoughts of the characters in *A Resounding Tinkle*. Only the Visionary remains unchanging as he continues watching, optimistic that in a short time he will be rewarded with his vision. In a jumble of words and logic, he distorts lines from William Wordsworth's "Ode on the Intimations of Immortality": "whose quote or rather misquote many-coloured glass will God willing in all probability stain the white radiance of eternity" (55).

The new electromagnetic holiday, to be known as Generating Sunday, is a satiric contrast with the idealism of Wordsworth, whether on the part of the Visionary who can look into a hole in the earth for something to appear or on that of the curious Soma and friends who, with a newly acquired confidence, decree a new faith which raises technology to the level of a religion.

The language of *The Hole* shares with *A Resounding Tinkle* what could be called the dialogue of the dead; for all of their pretense to logic, the characters succeed only in defying logic. Neither common nor rational sense informs their empty speech and their bankrupt thinking. Simpson's torrents of nonsense, as critics have described his plays, are either hilarious or boringly repetitious, depending on whether one can work one's way through the nonsense. The absurdist humor contains a latent cruelty found in the ordinary routines of small town life such as that in Agatha Christie's Miss Marple mysteries or in the more devastatingly serious treatment of Friederich Deurenmatt's village life in *The Visit*. Simpson's updating of this menacing potential in *The Hole* links him with Pinter and David Rudkin—playwrights who deal with menaces lurking beneath ordinary behaviors.

Simpson's funniest play is *One Way Pendulum*, its paradoxical title an apt description of the movement of each person's life as it swings only in one direction. The first of the farce's two acts depicts the hilariously magnificent obsessions of a not-so-ordinary family who proceed with their lives as though they are as ordinary as the next family. In the second act, most of the obsessions converge in a trial conducted in a replica of the Old Bailey courtroom in the Groomkirbys' home. The nuclear family consists of Arthur and Mabel Groomkirby and their son and daughter, Kirby and Sylvia. A wheelchair-bound Aunt Mildred joins the ménage.

Leading the preposterous goings-on is Kirby, who reasons that machines can be trained to sing the "Hallelujah Chorus." Kirby's additional obsessions include his habit of eating only when called by a Pavlovian bell and his wearing of black. After all, as his mother informs the Court at her son's Old Bailey trial, "even his baby things were all black . . . black shawl and rompers . . . even down to his bib . . . and his sheets and pillow-cases."[4]

His father, who earns his living taking care of parking meters, remains in front of a meter until the time has run out. In addition, he gathers do-it-yourself books on law and carpentry and is building the courtroom replica. Meanwhile, Mrs. Groomkirby keeps herself busy preparing meals, always laying an abundant table in expectation of providing leftovers for a neighbor (Mrs. Gantry) who may or may not arrive on a given day. Finally, there is Sylvia Groomkirby, who complains about her grotesque appearance, the result of the length of her arms which, although normal to others, to her are too short to reach her knees without her bending. Adding superfluously to the family oddities, Aunt Mildred devotes her time to her passion for travel and transports of all sorts, her current project an obsessive attempt to locate a tricycle.

One Way Pendulum is different from Simpson's two previous plays in its plot unity, the act 1 lunatic goings-on actually converging in the second act. The point of convergence takes the form of Kirby's trial. The not-so-secret device by which Simpson manages the trial is Kirby's love of wearing black, the funeral being the raison d'être for his habit, and murders, the rationale for the funerals. The particular crime, newly revealed, is Kirby's murder of forty-three persons by means of a blow on the head, each death having been preceded by a joke to make the victim laugh.

The outcome of the trial is determined by an even more ludicrous situation in Kirby's plan to transport his weight machines to Alaska in the hope of luring huge numbers of people to their death, their weight causing a further tilting of the earth's axis with disastrous consequences for all. Thus, his defense counsel argues, he hopes to provide for himself "a self-perpetuating pretext for wearing black" (85). The judge, however, declares Kirby innocent on other grounds, that "in sentencing a man for one crime, we may be putting him beyond the reach of the law in respect of those other crimes of which he might otherwise have become guilty" (92).

Simpson's devastating satire is both visually simple and logically complex as he twists and perverts logic to the straining point in his satire of two of England's most revered institutions, family and justice. The simplicity of his satire is represented in Harold Hobson's example of the author's humor: if an elephant walked through his front door, Mr. Simpson would not be surprised in the least at asking "it to stay to tea."[5] The complexity is recognized by Kenneth Tynan, who sees Simpson's nonsense as "pure farce, wild and liberated, on a level accessible to anyone who has ever enjoyed the radio Goons (Peter Sellers and Spike Milligan, especially) or treasured the memory of W.C. Fields."[6]

Of all of Simpson's plays, One Way Pendulum with its memorably visual plot complementing the verbal nonsense remains his most popular. Like that of his other plays, the plot, with its random swings from one absurd action to another, is impossible to follow except as a series of disconnected actions, each of which has its own built-in logic with no connection to another action except for a similarity in the twists and turns of the logical process. Any piece of action, dialogue, or monologue is whole unto itself, intended in its outrageousness as a corrective of the nonsense of modern life. For one viewer the effect may be repetition and for another it may be an intellectually stimulating satire on contemporary life. The range of satiric targets is wide, from the mundane do-it-yourself habits of suburban existence to the moral-philosophical nature of contemporary life.

Two other full-length plays, The Cresta Run (1965) and Was He Anyone? (1972) complete the list of Simpson's major stage writing, the former a confusingly fantastic story of es-

pionage and counterespionage and the latter about national charitable institutions and their elaborate methods of helping those in distress. In Was He Anyone? the person needing help is a man who has been treading water in the Mediterranean Sea for twenty-seven months. His predicament is only being prolonged by the endless bureaucratic arguments about his rescue among the vying charitable institutions. Seen by some as Simpson's change into a more direct social commentary, the drama seems a prophecy of the aid programs of the 1980s by various musical groups.

The greater number of Simpson's pieces have been short plays or skits for revues on stage or television. Illustrative of these and indicative of his habit of self-cannibalizing are the titles of seven television plays Three Resounding Tinkles and Four Resounding Tinkles.

Critical reactions to Simpson's work have generally fallen somewhere between that of George Wellwarth, who sees Simpson's plays as "perfect examples of the drama of protest and paradox that sprang directly out of Jarry's Ubu Roi"[7]—although more directly influenced by Ionesco—and that of John Russell Taylor, to whom Simpson's dramas look "very parochial and unresourceful"[8] when compared with those of Ionesco. Wellwarth describes Simpson's peculiar comic form as one of pataphysics: "the perversion of logic—the impossible carried out in accordance with the laws by which the possible exists" (212), whereas Taylor's basis for dismissal of Simpson's seriousness is the use of the "gag (frequently derived from some sort of pun or double-entendre) as the basic dramatic unit" (72). Taylor, then, as does Esslin, calls attention to Simpson's use of gags which "reduce themselves to various forms of the same obsessive doodling" (73) so that the charm is lost as the law of diminishing returns eventually sets in. Esslin sees Simpson as a serious satirist whose humor is rooted in the Bergsonian theory of habit and social convention as the "great deadeners of the inauthentic society."[9]

Alan Brien describes Simpson's prose as "hardly ever deviating into sense" and his style as "a palimpsest of non-sequiturs, a double acrostic of crossword clues . . . provoking head laughs as well as belly laughs . . . the Swiftian conjuring trick performed in the manner of Feydeau."[10] Hobson sees the humor as being based in the fact that the incongruous and bizarre are accepted as perfectly ordinary and normal. Thus, "obsessional delusions of ordinary men and women: Old Baileys, gorillas, weighing machines, holocausts of Jews, massacres—they are all forms of madness, of the same madness. We are all mad. But if we are all mad, then Mr. Simpson is mad, too." The flip side of the seriousness, Hobson continues, is the uproariousness of a "succession of first rate funny stories."

In his review of the double bill of *A Resounding Tinkle* and *The Hole*, Simpson's most effusive supporter among the critics, Tynan, pronounced the playwright to be "the most gifted comic writer the English stage has discovered since the war" (219–20). On the strength of *One Way Pendulum*, he suspected "Mr. Simpson to be the possessor of the subtlest mind ever devoted by an Englishman to the writing of farce" (14).

Summary

If Pinter is the most Beckettian of English dramatists in the stage events since 1955, N.F. Simpson remains the most Ionesco-like. Ionesco's characters are post-World War II conformists who have been conditioned into people who cannot think because they can no longer feel. Metamorphosed from humans to objects, they act from habit, habits in which Simpson's plays make them victims of fantasy and objects of farce.

Simpson has cut short his early promise as a major dramatist, retiring from the stage after fewer than a half-dozen full-length plays and only three plays by which he is remembered: *A Resounding Tinkle*, *The Hole*, and *One Way Pendulum*. Sooner than many of the new dramatists—such as Peter Nichols who has stopped writing for the stage or Pinter and Stoppard whose stage writing diminished noticeably in the 1980s—Simpson's current reputation is reflected in the slight attention paid him by critics and scholars. In *Modern British Drama: 1890–1990* (1992), Christopher Innes makes only two cursory references to Simpson, and in the latest *Oxford Companion to the Theatre* (1992), Phyllis Hartnoll and Peter Found, in even briefer reference, merely mention him under the rubric "Theatre of the Absurd." Yet, the images from Simpson's three major farces are indelibly imprinted on the consciousness of the theater world as a hilarious indictment of the nonsense of contemporary life, and he remains the Ionesco-like conscience of England, evoking, as one critic has said, both head and belly laughs.

Notes

1. John Russell Taylor, *Anger and After* (London: Methuen, rev. ed., 1983), p. 69.
2. N.F. Simpson, *A Resounding Tinkle* (London: Faber & Faber, 1968), p. 14. After the first quotation from a play, pages of subsequent references occur in the text.
3. Simpson, *The Hole and Other Plays and Sketches* (London: Faber & Faber, 1964), p. 12.
4. Simpson, *One Way Pendulum* (London: Faber & Faber, 1960), p. 88.
5. Harold Hobson, *Sunday Times* (December 27, 1959). Rpt. in *Plays In Review: 1956–1980*, ed. Gareth and Barbara Lloyd Evans (London: Batsford Academic and Educational London, 1985), p. 91.
6. Kenneth Tynan, *A View of the English Stage* (Frogmore, St. Albans: Granada, 1976), p. 219.
7. George Wellwarth, *The Theater of Protest and Paradox* (New York: New York University Press, 1964), p. 220.
8. Taylor, p. 67.
9. Martin Esslin, *The Theatre of the Absurd* (Garden City, NY: Doubleday, 1961), p. 224.
10. Alan Brien, *Spectator* (January 1, 1960). Rpt. in *Plays In Review: 1956–1980*, ed. Gareth and Barbara Lloyd Evans (London: Batsford Academic and Educational London, 1985), p. 92.

Selected Bibliography

Primary Sources

Plays

The Cresta Run. London: Faber & Faber, and New York: Grove Press, 1966.
The Form. London and New York: Samuel French, 1961.
The Hole and Other Plays and Sketches. London: Faber & Faber, 1964. Includes *The Hole, A Resounding Tinkle, The Form, Gladly Otherwise, Oh, One Blast and Have Done.*
One Way Pendulum. London: Faber & Faber, 1960; New York: Grove Press, 1961.
A Resounding Tinkle. London: Faber & Faber, and New York and London: French, 1968.
Some Tall Tinkles. London: Faber & Faber,

1968. Includes *We're Due in Eastbourne in Ten Minutes*, *The Best I Can Do By Way of a Gate-Leg Table Is a Hundredweight of Coal*, and *At Least It's a Precaution Against Fire*.

Was He Anyone? London: Faber & Faber, 1973.

Novels

Harry Bleachbaker: A Novel. London: Harrap, 1976; rpt. as *Man Overboard: A Testimonial to the High Art of Incompetence*, New York: William Morrow, 1976.

Secondary Sources

Brien, Alan. *Spectator* (January 1, 1960). Rpt. in *Plays in Review: 1956–1980*. Ed. Gareth Evans and Barbara Lloyd Evans. London: Batsford Academic and Educational London, 1985.

Esslin, Martin. *The Theatre of the Absurd*. Garden City, NY: Doubleday, 1961, pp. 217–24. Esslin sees Simpson's absurdity as a weapon of social criticism more powerful than the satire of the social realists.

Hobson, Harold. *Sunday Times* (December 27, 1959). Rpt. in *Plays In Review: 1956–1980*. Ed. Gareth Evans and Barbara Lloyd Evans. London: Batsford Academic and Educational London, 1985.

Lumley, Frederick. *New Trends in Twentieth-Century Drama*. Oxford: Oxford University Press, 1972, pp. 305–08. Lumley emphasizes Simpson's love of logic as the "key to his dramatic method" (300).

Marowitz, Charles, Tom Milne, and Owen Hale, eds. *New Theatre Voices of the Fifties and Sixties*. London: Methuen, 1981, pp. 89–91. First published in 1965 by Methuen. A contrast-comparison of Simpson and Pinter as writers of the comedy of menace.

Rusinko, Susan. *British Drama, 1950 to the Present: A Critical History*. Boston: Twayne, 1989, pp. 82–87. Rusinko places Simpson with Joe Orton and David Rudkin as fantasists—absurd, farcical, and primal, respectively.

Taylor, John Russell. *Anger and After*. rev. ed. London: Methuen, 1983, pp. 66–73. Published in America as *The Angry Theatre*; New York: Hill and Wang, rev. ed.

1969. Analysis of Simpson's work as "all written in pretty well the same style" (66), his one principle being the non-sequitur.

Tynan, Kenneth. *Right and Left*. New York: Atheneum, 1968.

———. *A View of the English Stage*. Frogmore, St. Albans: Granada, 1976, pp. 219–20. First published in Great Britain by Davis-Poynter, 1975. Tynan reviews *A Resounding Tinkle* and *The Hole* as the work of a dazzling new playwright and England's most gifted comic writer.

Wellwarth, George. *The Theater of Protest and Paradox*. New York: New York University Press, 1964, pp. 212–20. Wellwarth views Simpson as literary heir of Alfred Jarry. Both are pataphysicians who create a parallel fictional reality as context for existing social reality.

Worth, Katherine. "Avant Garde at the Royal Court Theatre: John Arden and N.F. Simpson." In *Experimental Drama*. Ed. W.A. Armstrong. London: Bell, 1963, pp. 204–23.

Zimmerman, C.D. "N.F. Simpson." In *Dictionary of Literary Biography*. Ed. Stanley Weintraub. Detroit: Bruccoli-Clark, Gale Research, 1982. Vol. 13:2, pp. 474–81. Remains a major short survey of Simpson's canon.

Susan Rusinko

Sitwell, Edith

Born: Scarborough, Yorkshire, September 7, 1887
Education: Self-educated
Died: London, December 9, 1964

Biography

Edith Sitwell was born in Scarborough, Yorkshire on September 7, 1887. Hers was a prominent family whose name (Cytewel? Citwell? Sitewell?) could be traced back to the early Middle Ages. Among the Sitwell progenitors were kings of France and the English Plantagenets. During the Elizabethan period, in collateral lines, were Francis Bacon and William Shakespeare's patron Henry Wriothelesey. The Sitwells were truly an imperial, influential family. But on the debit side, there were just as many eccentrics as great movers among them. Sir George Sitwell, Edith's father, serves as a good example. A proper sort of fellow, Sir George would appear in white tie and tails at dinner time regardless of where he might be. One day he decided to beautify his estate by having blue Chinese characters painted on his white cows. Possibly his chief claim to fame, or so he believed, was that he captured a spirit at the British National Association of Spiritualists. Today, however, Sir George is remembered less for his idiosyncratic behavior and his spirit chasing—though he would have been reluctant to admit it—than for having been Edith's father. For Sir George, writing was at best only an incidental accomplishment, hardly something to which an individual might devote energy, time, and talent. One day, in fact, he warned Edith about a cousin's friend who killed himself after writing a novel. And when he first heard of Edith's success with poetry, he lamented that she had made a great mistake by not going in for lawn tennis.

The self-educated Edith published her first book of verse, *The Mother and Other Poems,* in 1915. Three years later she published *Clowns' Houses,* followed in 1920 by *The Wooden Pegasus.* It was not until 1923 with her public recitation of *Facade* at London's Aeolian Hall that she became a celebrity, a poet to be reckoned with. Over the next forty years of her life she produced over fifty volumes of poetry, fiction, and literary criticism; and she contributed over 300 essays, articles, and assorted pieces to a multitude of books and periodicals. Among her most important and ambitious poems are *Bucolic Comedies* (1923), *The Sleeping Beauty* (1924), *Elegy on Dead Fashion* (1926), *Gold Coast Customs* (1929), *Street Songs* (1942), *The Song of the Cold* (1945), *Canticle of the Rose* (1949), *Gardeners and Astronomers* (1953), and *The Outcasts* (1962). Chief among her prose works are *I Live Under a Black Sun* (1937), a novel loosely based upon the life of Jonathan Swift; *Fanfare for Elizabeth* (1946), a biography of the monarch; *The Queens and the Hive* (1962), a biography of Elizabeth of England and Mary of Scotland; and *Taken Care Of* (1965), her posthumously published autobiography.

All of Sitwell's books received their share of bouquets and brickbats. Lytton Strachey, for one, had little love for her personally. In his own vituperative fashion, he once described her nose as "longer than an ant-eater's" and her poetry as "absurd stuff." F.R. Leavis dismissed Edith as belonging "more to the history of publicity than poetry." Malcolm Muggeridge was of the opinion that she was one of "the major bores of the age." Geoffrey Grigson even attacked her after her death. Not one for eulogy, he assailed her "sneering malice, megalomania, arrogance and . . . considerable stupidity"; and in a final bit of overkill he concluded that in everything she wrote she was "an amateur, a poseur of Art."

Much of the adverse criticism leveled against Sitwell was hyperbolic and *ad femina.* But, as Evelyn Waugh, one of her admirers, once remarked: "She took the dullness out of literature." All sorts of honors were conferred upon her. In 1947, Leeds University bestowed an honorary doctorate upon her. In 1949, the American Institute of Arts and Letters named her an Honorary Associate; and in the same year Durham University conferred another honorary doctorate upon her. Oxford University did the same in 1951. In 1954, she was named a Dame Commander of the Order of the British Empire. Poet Edith, after being Doctor Edith, was now Dame Edith. A few years before, when she visited Hollywood, famous personalities lined up to meet her; among them were Charlie Chaplin, Greta Garbo, and Marilyn Monroe. At a literary party given for her in New York she received obeisance from Horace Greeley, Gore Vidal, Tennessee Williams, Marianne Moore, Randall Jarrell, Delmore Schwartz, and other famous literati.

The greatest tribute to her and her work occurred on October 9, 1962, at a Celebration Concert at London's Royal Festival Hall. "Never before," she quipped, "had anyone attended their own Memorial Service." The concert provided a triumphal climax to Sitwell's lifelong dedication to literature. Present at her apotheosis were many of her closest friends and admirers: Sir Kenneth Clark, Sir Charles Snow, Cyril Connolly, Harold Acton, and Steven Spender. A high proportion of those who packed the auditorium were young enthusiasts who knew her only from her works.

To lead things off, Sitwell read several of her recent poems. The *pièce de résistance* was a recitation of the twenty-one poems from *Facade* delivered by Irene Worth and Sebastian Shaw to the Chamber Orchestra. The audience, as one of Edith's friends remembered the night, "seemed absolutely determined to give her a tremendous ovation," and all during the performance responded "to every turn of wit, every fantastic image and rhyme, with a low growl of laughter and delight." Those in the audience could not have been more appreciative of *Facade*, which, over a span of forty years, had achieved the status of a classic. At the end of the performance, after wildly applauding the readers, the instrumentalists, and Sir William Walton, the 3,000 members of the audience in Royal Festival Hall turned as one to the box in which Sitwell was sitting and thunderously clapped and cheered for almost five minutes. Overcome, the author waved and wept.

Sitwell died in London on December 9, 1964.

Literary Analysis

When Sitwell died, hundreds of newspapers throughout the world carried the sad news. The *New York Times*, for one, gave a good indication of her importance in modern literature by featuring her obituary on its front page and continuing for approximately eight more columns, complete with photographs, on another page. Most of the important things that could have been said about her were included, except for the opinion that if John Masefield (who died in 1967) had predeceased her, she might have been declared his successor as England's Poet Laureate. Those who may prefer to argue against such a contention could claim that she would not have been the recipient of such a distinction because (1) she was too eccentric; (2) she was a woman, and no woman had ever been Poet Laureate of England; and (3) she was a convert to the Roman Catholic Church. Each of the three negative reasons for possibly not granting her the laureateship makes her an even more interesting individual to read about; and, on the positive side, there is, of course, the brilliance and wit of her poetry.

A woman of keen wit, Sitwell was once asked why she preferred to dress all in black. "I'm in mourning to the entire world," she replied. She could be deadly serious about her dress and yet flippant in her everyday life—which often carried over into her works. Scattered liberally throughout the hundreds of poems, works of fiction, biography, autobiography, and social history that she wrote is a great deal of humor, burlesque, ridicule, and satire.

If pressed to explain the juxtaposition of the serious and the flippant in her poetry, she might answer that she was fascinated by the endless, minute triviality of life. In "Aubade," for example, she depicts the sad stupidity of a servant girl on a country farm rising from bed day after day and coming down to light a morning fire:

> Jane, Jane
> Tall as a crane,
> The morning light creaks down again;
> Comb your cockscomb-ragged hair,
> Jane, Jane come down the stair.
> Each dull wooden stalactite
> Of rain creaks, hardened by the light.
> Sounding like an overtone
> From some lonely world unknown.
> But the creaking empty light
> Will never harden into sight.
> Will never penetrate your brain
> With overtones of blunt rain.

The dawn creaks about Jane in the third line because, as Sitwell once explained, early light does not run smoothly: "it falls in hard cubes, squares, and triangles, which again, give one the impression of a creaking sound, because of the association with wood." The image, though clearly visible, she prefers to render as audile, in keeping with Arthur Rimbaud's "derangement of senses" with which she was familiar from a close reading of his poetry. As an audile image, "creaks" anticipates the sound of stairs in line five as Jane descends, as well as the sound in line six made by branches of trees that are straining in the wind and rain. And, once more there is a "creaking empty light" in the tenth line:

> The light would show (if it could harden)
> Eternities of kitchen garden,
> Cockscomb flowers that none will pluck,
> And wooden flowers that 'gin to cluck.
> In the kitchen you must light
> Flames as staring, red and white,
> As carrots or turnips, shining
> Where the cold dawn light lies whining.
> Cockscomb hair on the cold wind
> Hangs limp, turns the milk's weak
>   mind . . .
> Jane, Jane
> Tall as a crane,
> The morning light creaks down again!

Facing daily chores of weeding in the garden, Jane feels that the flowers there cluck and mock her. The flowers "cluck," apparently, because they are cockscombs. The flames of fire remind her of the carrots and turnips she has to clean, cut, and cook. Her spirits hang limp as "the milk's weak mind." The concluding triplet echoes the first three lines and emphasizes the endless, boring days of a servant girl.

The intellectual play that Sitwell experimented with in "Aubade" can be found throughout her *Clowns' Houses*, *The Wooden Pegasus*, and *Bucolic Comedies*; but, she surpassed herself in her public recitation of *Facade*. Friends were enthusiastic both before and after her performance. They approved of most of the poems, and they especially enjoyed the music that William Walton had written for their accompaniment.

The work came into being chiefly because of technical experimentations with prosody that Sitwell was conducting at the time. She decided to write poems with assorted rhythms, including those of the waltz, the fox trot, the polka, the mazurka, the tango, the passodoble, and country and sailor dances. In addition, she wanted to explore the effects that various impressions have upon the senses and to what extent she could capture notational images. The title of the work she took from a snide remark she overheard. Speaking about Sitwell, someone complained: "Very clever, no doubt—but what is she but a facade." Sitwell's choice of title was also meant to imply that though something at first glance may appear to have only surface meaning, humor and wit, closer inspection and reflection may reveal far more.

Everything at the first public performance provoked controversy. To begin with, Sitwell sat with her back to the audience, barely visible behind a transparent curtain adorned with a rather crudely painted moonface. The purported purpose of the curtain and the author's sitting backward was to allow the audience to concentrate chiefly upon the auditory qualities of the poems. The moonface was in keeping with the dreamlike world of apes, ducks, grotesque lords and ladies, clowns, peasants, and servant girls that she has written about. To magnify her voice above Walton's music Edith used an instrument called a Sengerphone, named for its inventor, George Senger, a Swiss opera singer, who first used his device to approximate the voice of a dragon. Out of the Sengerphone, which was made of compressed grasses meant to retain the purity of magnified tonal quality, came Sitwell's words, half recited, half chanted—such baffling words as "The sound of the onycha / When the phoca has the pica / In the palace of the Queen Chinee!" The words

brought a bit of polite applause from certain members of the audience, friends of Sitwell's no doubt, but the general reaction was hostile. Noel Coward, for one, walked out. Most of the audience stayed, mainly out of curiosity, wondering what they might hear next. After the performance, some of those who had endured the entire recitation became so threatening that she was cautioned to remain on stage behind the curtain. Someone whispered to her that one old lady was waiting to thrash her with an umbrella.

Many complained that what they had heard was gibberish. Had they listened more attentively they might have discovered—in addition to a great deal of humor and gaiety— subtle criticisms of modern life, innuendoes of despair, decay, and death. In the press, Sitwell was attacked as an ostentatious fool, an eccentric avant-garde iconoclast, and worse. Yet, in her defense it must be pointed out that when she was writing *Facade* she had come to believe that a change in the direction, imagery, and rhythms of poetry had become necessary, owing, as she put it, "to the rhythmical flaccidity, the verbal deadness, the dull and expected patterns of contemporary verse." She sought for effects that speed had on equivalent syllables. Using one trisyllabic word, she discovered, had greater rapidity than three monosyllabic words. The use of two rhymes placed immediately together at the end of each two lines, furthermore, would be like "leaps in the air." In "Fox Trot," for example, she wrote: "Sally, Mary, Mattie what's the matter, why cry? / The huntsman and the reynard-coloured sun and I sigh."

Perhaps one of the chief reasons that *Facade* was so often misunderstood was that Sitwell had experimented too freely with abstract patterns. Then, too, the apparent vacuity of some of the poems made them suspect. They seemed butterflies; but, even butterflies, the poet retorted, can adorn the world and delight the beholder. Among her "butterflies" is "Hornpipe," a jaunty piece set to nautical music:

Sailors come
To the drum
Out of Babylon;
Hobby horses
Foam, the dumb
Sky rhinoceros-glum
Watched the courses of the breakers'
    rocking horses and with Glaucis,

Lady Venus on the settee of the horseless
    sea . . .
And the borealic iceberg; floating on
    they see
New-arisen Madam Venus for whose
    sake from far
Came the fat and zebra'd emperor from
    Zanzibar
Where like golden bouquets lay far Asia,
    Africa, Cathay,
All laid before that shady lady by the
    fibroid Shah . . .
Queen Victoria sitting upon the rocking-
    horse
Of a wave said . . . "This minx of course
Is as sharpe as any lynx and blacker-
    deeper than the drinks and quite as
Hot as any hottentot, without remorse!
For the minx,"
Said she,
"And the drinks
You can see
Are hot as any hottentot and not good
    for me!"

"Trio for Two Cats" has more than an
amusing title; its fast rhythm creates an eerie
mood accentuated with castanets. "I Like to Do
Beside the Seaside" is set to a tango rhythm.
"Scotch Rhapsody" begins with "Do not take
a bath in Jordon, Gordon," and a heavy drum
beat sounds throughout. "Polka" has clever
running rhymes like "Robinson Crusoe rues so"
and "The poxy, doxy dear." "Popular Song" is
a joyful and carefree lyric about "Lily O'Grady
/ Silly and Shady, / Longing to be / A lazy lady."

In "The Drum," the verse conveys a sense
of menace, of deepening darkness, through the
use of subtle dissonances. The opening lines
establish the mood:

In his tall senatorial
Black and manorial
House where decoy-duck
Dust doth clack—
Clatter and quack
To a shadow black.

The words "black," "duck," "clatter," and
"quack," with their hard consonants and dead
vowels, Sitwell explained, are "dry as dust, and
the deadness of dust is conveyed thus, as also
by the dulled dissonance of the *a's*, of the *u* in
'duck' followed by the crumbling assonance of
'dust.'" A duck's quacking, she obligingly

added, was for her the driest of sounds: "it has
a peculiar deadness."

All through "The Drum," Walton's music
provided the proper beat and rolls, brilliantly
emphasizing Edith's narrative. Unfortunately,
critics who set out to tar Edith also besmirched
Walton with the same brush; one went so far as
to carp that the music "had been collected from
the works of the most eccentric of the ultra-
moderns." Ernest Newman, one of the more
perceptive contemporary musicologists, felt
otherwise. He complimented Walton for his
contribution to *Facade* and labeled the composer "a humorous musical talent of the first
order." In truth, Walton's music did not disturb
those at the first public performance; Sitwell's
rushing delivery and prosodic pyrotechnics did.

The audience had been forewarned that
they might not be able to catch every word; but
this many forgot. Newman did not. He claimed
that some of the poems were actually improved
by not being able to catch every word. The
important thing, he suggested, was that the
poems did not have to be read as ordinary verse
but required sledge-hammer emphasis on certain words. "The music, the words, the mega-
phone and the piquant phrasing of the lines . . .
were as much of each other's bone and flesh as
the words and the music are of one in *Tristan*
or *Pelleas*," he insisted. Newman's words
pleased the writer, of course, but she still
thought it necessary to rebut statements of detractors by supplying long, instructive analyses
of individual poems.

Sitwell's long and profuse explanations of
the aural techniques and technicalities contribute little to the average person's enjoyment of
the humorous quality of many of the poems in
Facade. One of her close friends, the photographer Cecil Beaton, for one, once admitted that
her explanations were wasted on him. He just
loved to hear the writer recite her lines, for as
he put it, "Edith could make any rubbish sound
like poetry."

Exactly what Beaton may have meant by
his remark is open to question, but there is no
debate that in *Facade* Sitwell revealed her gift
for endless word spinning. Much of the humor
in her various poems arises from the incongruity of crystal fantasy and human folly. Her dry
wit may not be everyone's cup of tea; still, there
is no denying that her cleverness, when perceived, is distinct, if not always delicate. Much
of the fun is consequent upon a reader's reactions to her adroit choice of words set to vari-

S

ous musical patterns. To fully appreciate her humor demands an understanding of the prosodic pyrotechnics that she employed. And like most humor, Sitwell's witty displays require recognition on the part of the reader, not prolonged explanations of why something should be funny. Her brilliant entanglements of language, it is true, can be a stumbling affair for some, while a true delight for others.

Those less than enthusiastic about *Facade* may have a right to maintain that the work had a measure of success mainly because of Sitwell's personality and showmanship. To rebut such adverse judgments was undoubtedly the reason that she emphasized the technical aspects and musical cadences of her verse. But, the question remained in the minds of many: was she a great poet or merely a talented charlatan? Over the next forty years of her life—in volume after volume of verse—she attempted to prove that she was a gifted author, a great poet worthy to reign in England's literary pantheon.

The trajectory of her career varied from decade to decade. In the 1920s, she was in the vanguard of artistic experimentation. In the 1930s, the pendulum swung the other way and a more socially concerned generation tended to think of her as irrelevant if not outmoded. However, during the period of World War II, Sitwell found her widest audience, principally because of her war poems. In the 1950s, she reveled in being lionized on two continents. She became the toast of New York and even conquered Hollywood. At the height of her fame, she suffered a debilitation of health that brought on her death in the 1960s. To state that she was somewhat forgotten during the 1970s in no way diminishes her accomplishments, for Sitwell never wrote for the multitude, the platitudinous, being more concerned with reaching an elite, cultivated readership. Though there has been little scholarly interest in her work in the 1980s and into the 1990s, most of her best works are still in print and presumably are being read.

Summary

Any evaluation of Edith Sitwell has to take into account that as a writer she was widely admired and narrowly detested. Still, she could never be ignored. Virtually all that she wrote has had an impact on modern poetry; yet, she has had few imitators. An identifiable school never grew up around her. Her uniqueness simply could not be duplicated.

Sitwell always wanted to be read, of course, but what was even more important to her was that so many of her fellow poets, among them W.B. Yeats and T.S. Eliot, Dylan Thomas and Stephen Spender, spoke of her as one of the most creative artists of the century. Today admirers of her work rank the poems of her mature years higher than the verbal legerdemain of her earlier experimental periods. That she was a master technician, an adroit inventor of rhythms and of rhymes to mark them percussively, is obvious to anyone familiar with *Facade*—the work that first brought her notoriety and still draws an abundant number of readers to her other works. Her *Collected Poems* still finds a substantial audience, though individual readers may not be as enthusiastic as was Cyril Connolly, who wrote: "When we come to compare the collected poems of Dame Edith Sitwell with those of Yeats or Eliot or . . . Auden it will be found that hers have the purest poetical content of them all."

Connolly is entitled to this judgment, but what Sitwell's reputation may be a decade or a century from now is difficult to forecast. The odds are that she will not be forgotten, that she is not destined for the oblivion which she often wished on her enemies. Similar to the Sitwell family's own revenant, who for hundreds of years has been reputed to visit his living relatives to bestow an occasional kiss while they sleep, Sitwell's poetry is destined to haunt the history of English literature for generations to come.

Selected Bibliography
Primary Sources

Poetry
The Mother and Other Poems. Oxford: Blackwell, 1915.
Clowns' Houses. Oxford: Blackwell, 1918.
Facade. London: Favil, 1922.
Bucolic Comedies. London: Duckworth, 1923.
The Sleeping Beauty. London: Duckworth, 1924.
Elegy on Dead Fashion. London: Duckworth, 1926.
Gold Coast Customs. London: Duckworth, 1929.
Street Songs. London: Macmillan, 1942.
Green Songs and Other Poems. London: Macmillan, 1944.
The Song of the Cold. London: Macmillan, 1945.

Canticle of the Rose. London: Macmillan, 1949.

Gardeners and Astronomers. London: Macmillan, 1953.

Collected Poems. London: Macmillan, 1954.

The Outcasts. London: Macmillan, 1962. Enlarged as *Music and Ceremonies.* New York: Vanguard, 1963.

Fiction

I Live Under a Black Sun. London: Gollancz, 1937.

Biographies

Alexander Pope. London: Faber & Faber, 1930.

Victoria of England. London: Faber & Faber, 1936.

Fanfare for Elizabeth. London: Macmillan, 1946.

The Queens and the Hive. London: Macmillan, 1962.

Autobiographies

Taken Care Of. London: Hutchinson, 1965.

Literary Criticism

Pleasures of Poetry. London: Duckworth, 1932.

Aspects of Modern Poetry. London: Duckworth, 1934.

Secondary Sources

Bowra, C.M. *Edith Sitwell.* Monaco: Lyrebird, 1947. A brief study of her principal poems.

Brophy, James. *Edith Sitwell: The Symbolist Order.* Carbondale: University of Illinois Press, 1968. Discussion of Edith's place in the symbolist tradition.

Cevasco, G.A. *The Sitwells: Edith, Osbert and Sacheverell.* A bio-critical study that focuses on the literary accomplishments of Edith and her two brothers.

Elborn, Geoffrey. *Edith Sitwell.* New York: Doubleday, 1981. A biography in which Elborn considers Edith's complexities, personal and creative.

Glendinning, Victoria. *Edith Sitwell: A Unicorn among Lions.* New York: Knopf, 1981. A biography of Sitwell as a contemporary woman and gifted poet.

Mills, Ralph J. *Edith Sitwell: A Critical Essay.* Grand Rapids, MI: Eerdmans, 1966. A succinct study in Eerdman's *Contemporary Writers in Christian Perspective Series.*

Pearson, John. *Facades: Edith, Osbert and Sacheverell Sitwell.* London: Macmillan, 1978. A comprehensive biography of the Sitwells in which the trio is portrayed as aesthetes, eccentrics, celebrities.

Salters, Elizabeth. *The Last Years of a Rebel: A Memoir of Edith Sitwell.* Boston: Houghton Mifflin, 1967. A personal account of Sitwell's last years by a woman who was her secretary and confidante.

G.A. Cevasco

Skelton, John

Born: Possibly Northumberland or Yorkshire, ca. 1460

Education: Studied at Oxford and Cambridge Universities; M.A. Cambridge, 1484; Laureate degree at Oxford ca. 1488; University of Louvain, Laureate, 1492; Cambridge University, Laureate, 1493; admitted to Holy Orders, 1498

Marriage: Common-law wife; one child

Died: London, June 21, 1529

Biography

John Skelton is important as a leading humanist of the early Renaissance; as a translator, playwright, and poet; and as the hero of one of the most popular jestbooks in the sixteenth century. He is the first great poet of the English Renaissance and one of its great humorists. He created a new verse form, "Skeltonics," which, influential on and off for five centuries, has been practiced by some of the modern period's most prominent poets, including Gerard Manley Hopkins, Robert Graves, and W.H. Auden.

Skelton's family may have originated in Yorkshire or Northumberland; though some scholars believe that he was born in London, Skelton's vocabulary suggests that he was born around 1460 in one of the northern counties. His mother's name may have been Johanna or Joan—little else is known about his childhood. He demonstrates in his writing an extensive knowledge of Latin, French, Italian, and Scots, with some knowledge of Greek, and extensive knowledge of music and musical instruments. He probably studied for a time at Oxford before switching to Cambridge and graduating with an M.A. from there in 1484. He must have continued studying and teaching, because he achieved a degree of "laureate" at Oxford around 1488. He was to style himself "Skelton Laureat" ever after.

A word is in order about this famous honor. "Laureate" was not the same as "Poet Laureate," though Skelton acted later as though it were. "Laureate" was the name of a postgraduate degree available at both universities to any comer who could pass an examination in Latin and deliver a public lecture, usually on Cicero. It demonstrated world-class mastery of Latin language and literature—a skill highly prized in the England of the late fifteenth century. Being created laureate usually indicated the scholar's intention to pursue scholarship, teaching, or a high position in the national bureaucracy.

Skelton was after all three. From early in his career, he set out to become an internationally famous intellect and poet. The same year that he was laureated at Oxford, Skelton started his service to King Henry VII who had only recently assumed the throne after defeating Richard III at Bosworth Field. Skelton became the court poet: his habit was white and green and bore the picture of Calliope, the muse of poetry, embroidered in gold. The writer traveled with the king to France in 1490; while there, he challenged and gained the laureate at the University of Louvain (1492). He continued to write, translating Latin authors such as Cicero and Diodorus Siculus. In 1490, William Caxton praised Skelton as already an accomplished translator. In 1493, Cambridge became the third university to confirm him laureate—the only laureate that Cambridge has ever granted.

Skelton wrote poems for state occasions and composed and staged court entertainments. His most important post, however, was as tutor to King Henry's two sons, Arthur and Henry (the latter eventually became Henry VIII). In 1498, Skelton took Holy Orders, and during this time he wrote the first known poem in "Skeltonic" meter, "Upon a Dead Man's Head."

But 1498 was the height of his bureaucratic career; within a few years, Skelton had left the Court. Though the exact reasons are not known, some of his poems from the period are distinctly anti-court. *The Bowge of Court*, a satiric poem aimed at the hypocrisy of court life, was printed in 1499, and it may have angered more than a few court hypocrites. In 1502, Prince Arthur died, and the household of Prince Henry, who was now heir to the throne, was revamped.

Skelton seems to have been a casualty of these changes, for by 1504, he was living as a parson in a small parish in the town of Diss, Norfolk. There he stayed in relative obscurity for seven years—seven of the best years for his poetry, for he wrote some of the most famous of his Skeltonics during this time. He became well-known as a madcap parson, waging war with friars, monks, bishops, and even his parishioners. Biographers and jestbooks alike report that he kept a mistress who bore him a child. During these years, the traditions grew that later became the jestbook bearing his name.

In 1509, Henry VII died, and his son became Henry VIII. Skelton began sending poems and translations to Henry as gifts; they bore praise, advice, reminders of Skelton's past service. Henry evidently paid attention. Though technically still the parson of Diss, Skelton was soon back at court—in 1513, he was officially recognized as *orator regius*, the court poet and rhetorician. There followed some of Skelton's most ambitious works, including his only extant drama, *Magnificence* (1516).

These years saw the rise of Cardinal Wolsey, a former acquaintance of Skelton's from his university days. Wolsey was quickly becoming one of the most powerful and corrupt people in the court of Henry VIII. Skelton began to write impassioned warnings to Henry about Wolsey; these included *Magnificence*, *Speak, Parrot* (1521), *Colin Clout* (1522), and *Why Come Ye Not to Court?* (1523). Evidently, the author thus earned Wolsey's hatred. There is a tradition that Wolsey had Skelton imprisoned (perhaps at the Tower) and that on being freed from prison Skelton took sanctuary at Westminster, where he lived for the rest of his life. It is true that Westminster was Skelton's last home. Whether because he had genuinely reconciled with Wolsey or because Wolsey had become too powerful to oppose, Skelton's tone changes in 1523 to one of commendation and obsequiousness.

At some point the writer apparently acquired a common-law wife, and the couple had one child. Skelton died in London on June 21, 1529.

Literary Analysis

Skelton's poetry was idiosyncratic, inventive, and inimitable. Although he wrote in many verse forms, languages, and genres, he has always been best known for his Skeltonics. These are two- or three-beat lines, written in plain, direct, not to say vulgar English; the poet keeps rhyming on the same sound for as long as he can think of rhymes. The effect is uncannily like watching someone make up a rhyme on the spot. It is this impression of improvisation—our sense that we are watching a witty, trenchant mind spew forth ideas right in front of us—that makes Skeltonics so forceful and so much fun, as for example, in the first eight lines of *Colin Clout*:

> What can it avayle
> To dryve forth a snayle,
> Or to make a sayle
> Of a herynges tayle?
> To ryme or to rayle,
> To wryte or indyte
> Other for delyte
> Or elles for despyte?

There is much to smile at here: the two metaphors for the "trivial" occupation of writing; the five straight rhymes on "-ayle," giving way without warning to three straight rhymes on "-yte," and the very audacity of such a beginning. Such poetry has both a form and an anarchic, willful voice. As Auden and others have pointed out, the two-beat line is very close to the natural rhythm of spoken English. This, too, gives it the air of improvisation and a breathlessly inventive pace.

Many critics are uneasy with such poetry, which has attracted words such as "primitive" and "crude." That granted, Skelton's poetry is nevertheless capable of a surprising range in subject, effect, and emotion. He characteristically mixes the sacred and profane, sobriety and mirth. He maintains an element of fun even when writing of serious matters, and even in his lowest humor there is something serious and worth remembering. His first Skeltonic, "Upon a Dead Man's Head," contemplates the grisly evidence of his mortality:

> Oure days be datyd
> To be checkmatyd,
> With drawttys of deth
> Stoppyng oure breth;
> Oure eyen synkyng,
> Oure bodys stynkyng,
> Oure gummys grynnyng,
> Oure soulys brynnyng.

There is as much to grin at as there is to be afraid of.

In the poem "To Maystres Margaret Hussey," the poet's Skeltonics become sweet and almost delicate:

> Mirry Margaret,
> As mydsomer flowre,
> Jentill as fawcoun
> Or hawke of the towre,
> With solace and gladnes,
> Moche mirthe and no madnes,
> All good and no badnes,
> So joyously,
> So maydenly,
> So womanly
> Her demeaning.

Skelton wrote in many other meters (notably the Chaucerian iambic line), as well, and he also wrote excellent "macaronic" verse (poetry composed in more than one language at once). His two most characteristic modes were satire and low humor. He was especially sharp when he had something or someone to insult; accordingly, he became an adept at "flyting," or ritualized insult-matches, a few of which exist as poems. His satire combined his zest for invective with his moral sense. *Colin Clout* is full of scorn and outrage at the corruption of the Church:

> Farewell benygnyte,
> Farewell symplycyte,
> Farewell humylyte,
> Farewell good charyte.

In the poem, a country bumpkin visits the Court and is shocked at what he finds there. The following lines have often been quoted as Skelton's own description of his poetry. They also suggest how closely Skelton identifies with Colin:

> And yf ye stande in doute
> Who brought this ryme aboute,
> My name is Collyn Cloute.
> I purpose to shake oute
> All my connynge bagge,
> Lyke a clerkely hagge.
> For though my ryme be ragged,
> Tattered and jagged,
> Rudely rayne-beaten,
> Rusty and moth-eaten,
> Yf ye take well therwith,
> It hath in it some pyth.
> For, as farre as I can se,
> It is wronge with eche degre.

Very much like a minstrel come to perform, Colin promises to empty the bag of his brain and to examine all of society, which he does with vituperative vigor.

In *The Tunning of Elinor Rumming*, his most famous poem, Skeltonics furnish gross, repellent descriptions of ugly bodies. Frowzy women from the dregs of society make a mock pilgrimage to the Running Horse, evidently an actual tavern in Leatherhead, Surrey, run by a woman named Alianora Romyng:

> Some wenches come unlased,
> Some huswyves come unbrased,
> With theyr naked pappes,
> That flyppes and flappes,
> It wygges and wagges
> Lyke tawny saffron bagges—
> A sorte of foul drabbes
> All scurby with scabbes.

In a mock religious rite, the women give offerings and drink a mock communion. But, beyond the religious humor, which is undoubtedly there, is the sheer disgusting vitality of the bodily descriptions. Of one Maude Ruggy it is said that:

> She was ugly hypped,
> And ugly thycke-lypped,
> Lyke an onion syded,
> Lyke tan ledder hyded . . .
> Ones hed wold have aked
> To se her naked.

This sort of ambivalent, gross, affirmative humor has come to be associated with the Renaissance, and *Elinor Rumming* belongs with anything by François Rabelais, Friedrich Dedekind, William Shakespeare, Ben Jonson, or Miguel de Cervantes.

Skelton holds an important place in the history of the English language. He wrote at a time when English was rapidly undergoing some decisive changes, and he happens to be one of the first poets to become well-known to his contemporaries through the printing press. (He wrote the first known published English ballad, "Ballade of the Scottyshe King.") Being much published, much read, and much imitated, the poet was influential in establishing the London or Middlesex dialect of English as the dominant branch of English. He was also an innovator in vocabulary. About 1,500 English words have their first printed use in his work.

Skelton has a final important role in the history of English humor: that of the hero of a collection of fifteen humorous tales about his life. Where the jests came from, who collected them, or how they came to be published is unknown. Our first complete copy of the *Merie Tales, Newly Imprinted, Made by Master Skelton Poet Laureate* dates from 1567. There were probably much earlier editions. Evidence suggests that the tales arose and were written down while Skelton was still living—possibly by the poet himself (after all, the title says the tales were "made by" Skelton). Our first extant mention of a collection named "the jestes of Skelton" actually occurs in an inventory of the possessions of Thomas Cromwell in 1534— only five years after Skelton's death. Furthermore, one tale in particular (about two capons named Alpha and Omega) even appeared during Skelton's lifetime, being printed in 1525 in *A Hundred Merry Tales*, the first fully native English jestbook.

There is no way to determine how much of the tales are true. They are faithful to his biography, mentioning Oxford, Diss, Skelton's personal war with monks, friars, and Cardinal Wolsey. The stories concentrate mainly upon Skelton's life as parson at Diss; none concern his life at court. Thus, they focus on traditions corroborated in other accounts of the writer's life: his irascibility, his penchant for practical jokes, his common-law wife, his son, and his ready wit.

In perhaps the most famous tale, Skelton, having learned that his parishioners have complained to the bishop of his mistress and their son, delivers a sermon in church in which he calls for the baby:

> And he, shewynge his childe naked to all the parishe, sayde, Howe say you, neibours all? is not this child as fayre as is the best of all yours? It hathe nose, eyes, handes, and feete, as well as any of your: it is not lyke a pygge, nor a calfe, nor like no foule nor no monstruous beast . . . I say, as I said before . . . you be, and have be, & wyll and shall be knaves, to complayne of me wythout a cause resonable.

In another tale, when the Bishop of Norwich calls him on the carpet, the Skelton character brings two capons with him, which the Bishop assumes are presents. Skelton informs him that his capons have names: "this capon is named Alpha, this is the fyrst capon that I dyd ever geve to you; and this capon is named Omega, and this is the last capon that ever I will give you; & so fare you well."

However mad-cap he may have been as a person, his ability as a writer was recognized by Desiderius Erasmus, the most important figure in the northern Renaissance. Skelton, Erasmus claimed in a visit to England in 1499, was the "incomparable light and glory of English letters."

Summary

John Skelton is notoriously hard to classify. Is he late Medieval or early Renaissance? He mixes styles, languages, tones, and genres with a merry, insolent versatility—but then, insouciance is what made him famous. Though not a humanist to the extent that Erasmus and Sir Thomas More were, Skelton nevertheless was part of the humanist movement in his own idiosyncratic way. He represented many old attitudes. For example, even though Greek scholarship was sweeping Renaissance Europe, Skelton favored Latin and appears to have had little if any Greek. As did More, Skelton vehemently resisted the Lutheran reformation. Yet, in his broad range, from vulgar invective to the language of court to the learned translation, in his insistence on the importance of poetry in the state, and in his sheer originating energy, Skelton may be the figure that, more than any other, takes us from the Middle Ages to the Renaissance.

Selected Bibliography

Primary Sources
Works. London: Thomas Marshe, 1568.
Poems. Ed. Robert S. Kinsman. Oxford: Clarendon, 1969. This collection does not include all the poems, but it does give the best ones, along with a helpful introduction, notes, and glossary.
A Hundred Merry Tales and Other English Jestbooks of the Fifteenth and Sixteenth Centuries. Ed. P.M. Zall. Lincoln: University of Nebraska Press, 1963. This contains a modern-spelling edition of *Merry Tales Made by Master Skelton*, with a short introduction and a few notes.

Secondary Sources

Biographies
Lee, Sidney. "John Skelton." In *The Dictionary of National Biography*. Ed. Sir Leslie Stephen and Sidney Lee. 21 vols. Oxford: Oxford University Press, 1960. Vol. 18, pp. 327–32.
Pollet, Maurice. *John Skelton, Poet of Tudor England*. Trans. John Warrington. London: J.M. Dent, 1971. This exhaustive biography gives us much more than the facts of Skelton's life; it tries to set those facts in their historical context. Any reader wanting to understand Skelton the man and poet should read this book.

Books
Carpenter, Nan Cooke. *John Skelton*. New York: Twayne, 1967. A fine introduction for both new and inexperienced readers, with a chronology of the known facts of Skelton's life and a survey of the works and the critical heritage.
Fish, Stanley. *John Skelton's Poetry*. New Haven: Yale University Press, 1965. The distinguished literary critic began his career with this dissertation on Skelton, which remains one of the best-considered critical studies of him. Fish sees Skelton as a poet trying to reconcile the medieval expectations of poetry with a growing awareness of the corruptions of the Court. Excellent discussions of *The Bowge of Court*, *The Tunning of Elinor Rumming*, *Speak, Parrot*, and *Philip Sparrowe*.
Gordon, Ian A. *John Skelton, Poet Laureate*. Oxford: Oxford University Press, 1943. A good discussion of the poet's work, especially as a prominent member of the writing community in the Tudor court.
Green, P. *John Skelton*, 1960.
Heiserman, A.R. *Skelton and Satire*, 1962.

Articles
Sharratt, Bernard. "John Skelton: Finding a Voice—Notes after Bakhtin." In *Medieval Literature: Criticism, Ideology, History*. Ed. David Aers. Brighton, Sussex: Harvester, 1986, pp. 192–222. Sharratt uses the theories of the eminent linguist and thinker Mikhail Bakhtin to shed light on Skelton and his poetic practice.

John Timpane

Smith, Sydney

Born: Woodford, Essex, June 3, 1771
Education: Winchester School; New College, Oxford University; B.A., 1792; M.A., 1794
Marriage: Catherine Amelia Pybus, July 2, 1800; five children
Died: London, February 22, 1845

Biography

Sydney Smith was born in Woodford, Essex, on June 3, 1771, the second of five children of Robert and Maria Olier Smith. Robert Smith devoted a long career to working his way up through the middle class by speculating with varying success in securities and real estate. He was capable of exerting considerable charm with business associates and social acquaintances. His behavior toward his family, however, was consistently querulous, irascible, and miserly. The four boys were educated at public schools, their intellectual gifts earning them support from the schools' foundations. Since they were close in age, born only a year apart, the two oldest each looked after a younger brother at school. Sydney was responsible for Courtenay at Winchester, and Robert Percy (nicknamed Bobus) looked after Cecil at Eton. Through his friendship with the Chairman of the East India Company, Robert sent Cecil and Courtenay to India immediately upon their completion of public school to pursue careers in the colonial service. Maria, the youngest Smith child, remained unmarried and at home. After the death of their mother in 1802, she was the main link and peacemaker between her father and her brothers. Until his death in 1827, Robert continued to quarrel with his sons. He interfered in their careers and marriages, and refused financial assistance to Sydney, who was struggling to support a family on a small income.

Bobus and Sydney were allowed to continue their education, each having secured a scholarship. Sydney, at New College, Oxford, won a fellowship in 1791 and thenceforth received no allowance from his father. He also wanted to study the law, but his father would not allow that to his second son. He received a B.A. in 1792 and an M.A. in 1794. When Sydney refused to follow his younger brothers to India, his father told him, "You may be a college tutor or a parson." Unhappy with the narrow focus of the classical curriculum, Sydney chose a clerical career. He was ordained a Dea-con of the Church of England in 1794 and entered holy orders as a priest two years later.

Smith inherited some of his father's irritability; but tempered by his mother's warmth and his own good humor, he turned that irritability into a keen sense of injustice. Aware of his many difficulties in making his own way in the world, he was always the champion of the poor and dispossessed throughout a long career as a clergyman and essayist. His slow advancement in the Church and his more rapid recognition in literary circles were always dependent on the patronage of others. Although he was a recipient all of his life of favors from a circle of politically active aristocrats, he was able to maintain complete independence of mind and spirit. He suffered throughout life from periodic depression which was reinforced by frequent professional and financial disappointments. He was saved from a melancholic disposition by his sense of humor and recognition of the ridiculousness of much human behavior, his own included. Determined to make the best of everything and everyone, he became the foremost wit and humorist of his day, in and out of print.

Smith's connection to the Whig aristocracy began in 1797 when he married his brother Bobus to Caroline Vernon, a relative of Richard Henry Fox, third Baron of Holland. Lord Holland was active in Parliament. His uncle, Charles James Fox, led the Whig coalition government called the "Ministry of All the Talents" which governed in 1806 and 1807. Throughout the remainder of the reigns of King George III and King George IV, from the American Revolution until the Reform period of the 1830s, the government of Britain was solidly Tory, united behind a strong monarchy and the absolute political domination of the Church of England. The Whigs remained in opposition and pursued policies of Parliamentary supremacy, religious toleration, free trade, and Parliamentary reform.

Elizabeth, Lady Holland, had shocked society by leaving her first husband to elope with Lord Holland. Holland House in Kensington, just west of London, was a center of Whig politics and social brilliance. Though most women of the aristocracy refused to visit, Lord and Lady Holland gathered a circle of the most intelligent, influential, and witty men of their day. As one of their proteges, Smith soon was introduced to Whig society. Among his most important friends were Lord Grey, who became Prime Minister in 1831 at the head of a reform-minded Whig government, and Lord Carlisle, whose family seat at Castle Howard was near Smith's Yorkshire parish. Had Smith been a layman, he would certainly have been put into the House of Commons by one of his wealthy patrons. As a clergyman, however, he could only hope for their influence in gaining him a decent clerical living. Most English parishes provided small incomes, and advancement to the more affluent livings or to Cathedral posts required the patronage of bishops or cabinet ministers.

Smith's introduction to literary circles began in Edinburgh. His first religious post, as Curate of Netheravon from 1794 to 1796, led to his being hired by the local squire, Michael Hicks Beach, to tutor his eldest son and prepare him for the university. When the war with France made travel to the Continent impossible, Smith and his student took up residence in Edinburgh. The University of Edinburgh was the center of the new and exciting disciplines of moral philosophy and political economy (now called psychology and economics). The Scottish "Common Sense" school of philosophy was attempting to apply the scientific method to understanding human and social behavior, following in the footsteps of David Hume and Adam Smith. Sydney Smith attended lectures and became acquainted with the leading lights of the University, Dugald Stewart, John Playfair, Adam Walker, and others. He also joined a circle of young attorneys, particularly Francis Jeffrey, Francis Horner, and Henry Brougham, all of whom shared his liberal politics and love of literature.

On June 2, 1800, Smith married Catherine Amelia Pybus, the daughter of a retired banker. As a married man, he could no longer draw the small income associated with his fellowship at New College, Oxford. Catherine brought some money into the marriage, but Smith insisted on reserving this for her use. He supported his family (the Smiths had five children) by tutoring two Hicks Beach sons, as well as a few other young men. He also did some occasional preaching in Charlotte Chapel, the only Anglican place of worship in Edinburgh, and he published *Six Sermons* in 1800.

In 1802, Smith proposed to Jeffrey, Horner, and a few other Edinburgh friends that they publish a literary review. The *Edinburgh Review* became a powerful literary voice of its day. Contributors included most of the Edinburgh liberal attorneys and university profes-

sors. Walter Scott was a regular contributor until 1809, when he decided that the *Edinburgh* was too Whig for his political tastes and he helped establish the *Quarterly Review* in competition.

Smith made financial arrangements with Archibald Constable to publish the review in Edinburgh and T.N. Longman to publish the journal in London; he edited the first issue. Jeffrey took over as editor with the second issue and remained in that post until 1829.

In 1802, the same year as the founding of the *Edinburgh Review*, Sydney and Catherine's first child was born, a daughter whom they named Saba. A son, Noel, was born the following year; a sickly child, he died in infancy. With a growing family and no chance of regular clerical employment in Presbyterian Scotland, Smith resolved to move to London, hoping for more lucrative opportunities. Catherine's mother had recently died and left her daughter some valuable jewelry which was sold to enable the Smiths to set up housekeeping in the capital.

From 1802 to 1806, Smith supported his family primarily by his writing for the *Edinburgh Review*, supplemented by occasional preaching at various London chapels and by two popular series of lectures on moral philosophy at the Royal Institution, later published by his widow as *Elementary Sketches of Moral Philosophy* (1850). In 1806, during the brief Whig ministry, Lord Holland prevailed upon Lord Chancellor Thomas Erskine to appoint Smith Rector of Foston, a small town in Yorkshire. Smith served his parish through a curate and continued to reside in London.

In March 1807, the Ministry of All the Talents left office when it refused to obey the command of George III to abandon its pursuit of Catholic emancipation. A series of four pamphlets, called *Letters on the Subject of the Catholics, to My Brother Abraham, Who Lives in the County*, were published between the summer of 1807 and early 1808, under the pseudonym Peter Plymley. Smith's authorship was an open secret. The pamphlets attacked the prevailing Tory policy of sustaining outdated legislation which placed a variety of civil restrictions on Catholics. The *Peter Plymley Letters* were immensely popular, running through sixteen editions in the first two years and being republished five more times over the next thirty.

In 1807, a new Archbishop of York decided to enforce the regulations on clerical residence. With Smith's political allies out of office,

S

and with a fiercely anti-Catholic Bench of Bishops, he was unable to exchange his Foston living for one closer to London. In 1809, the Smiths were required to move to a remote and unsophisticated corner of Yorkshire, in his words "twelve miles from a lemon." He published two volumes of *Sermons* to help finance the move. Two more children had been born during their London residency, Douglas in 1805 and Emily in 1807. The youngest Smith child, Windham, was born in 1813.

For almost twenty years, Smith lived the life of a country parson. Foston had not had a resident rector for 150 years. The rectory was a ruined cottage and the 300 acres of farmland attached to the living had been rented out at a very low rate and allowed to run down. For five years, the Smiths lived in a rented house in the nearby village of Heslington, while Smith busied himself with parish duties as, in his words, "village parson, village doctor, village comforter, village magistrate, and Edinburgh Reviewer." He rented out a major portion of the land to a local farmer and farmed the rest himself through tenants. He introduced agricultural improvements and designed and built a new rectory in Foston into which the family moved in 1814.

Although rural life was not his preference, Smith made do with good humor and good will. He maintained social and political connections with his Edinburgh and London friends through a stream of correspondence and an annual visit of a month or two to London, as his financial means and parochial duties allowed. He entertained many of these friends when they were traveling between London and Edinburgh. He also made local connections, most importantly with the family of Lord Carlisle.

Smith continued to write for the *Edinburgh Review* throughout his residency in Foston. He also remained politically active, primarily espousing the cause of Catholic emancipation whenever possible. His financial situation improved in 1823 when Lord Carlisle's daughter-in-law, Lady Georgiana Morpeth, secured him the additional parish living of Londesborough to hold until her son was ordained in 1832.

In 1827, Whigs returned to political office in a coalition cabinet under George Canning, finally bringing Smith some clerical preferment. In January 1828, he was appointed a Prebendary of Bristol Cathedral and given an additional small living in Halberton. The following

year, he was also allowed to exchange the living of Foston for that of Combe Florey near Taunton in Somersetshire. After two decades of rural exile he was finally established in the south of England with financial security. In 1831, Lord Grey, Prime Minister of a new Whig government, appointed Smith Canon Residentiary of St. Paul's Cathedral. This was the highest position that he reached in the Church of England.

Smith resented the fact that after his long years of loyalty Whig patrons such as Lord Grey, Lord Holland, and Lord Melbourne did not nominate him for a Bishopric when they finally had it in their power to do so. While he protested in his letters that he would probably have refused on account of his age, he made it clear that he should have at least been offered the position. In fact, his vigorous activity at St. Paul's over the next decade demonstrated that he still had the health, as well as the administrative ability, to have served well as a Bishop. But, although Catholic emancipation had been finally legislated in 1829, his long and unpopular stand had made him an anathema to the Anglican clergy. His reputation as a wit and humorist in print and in society also militated against his appointment to high clerical office. Although Lord Melbourne later said that the greatest regret of his career was not having made Smith a Bishop, it is obvious that to have done so would have been an unacceptable political embarrassment.

Smith spent his final years in dividing his time between London and Combe Florey, delighted that the railroad now allowed him to move easily between the two. Thinking that anonymous publication was inappropriate for a Church dignitary (and no longer needing the income) he had stopped writing for the *Edinburgh Review* when appointed to Bristol Cathedral. He continued to publish under his own name: occasional sermons, particularly on religious toleration; a few pamphlets on political questions such as the secret ballot; and, most importantly, the *Letters to Archdeacon Singleton*, a series of pamphlets published from 1837 to 1839, criticizing some of his old Whig friends and the Bishops for the ways in which they were going about reforming the Church of England.

Both of Smith's daughters married well, and Saba published a *Memoir* of her father in 1855 as Lady Holland (not to be confused with Elizabeth, Lady Holland, of Holland House). Smith was less fortunate in his sons.

The author's social life flourished during this last period, when his reputation for witty table-talk and his residence in London made him a highly prized dinner guest. He died in London on February 22, 1845.

Literary Analysis

Smith's most important contribution to English letters was the establishment of the *Edinburgh Review*, which introduced a totally new kind of periodical literature. Previous journals were largely of three types: personal commentary on society and the passing scene, like Joseph Addison and Richard Steele's *Spectator* or Samuel Johnson's *Rambler*; partisan political journals; and literary reviews published by booksellers to puff their own publications or attack those of rivals. Smith's plan was to remain independent of party hacks or of booksellers by paying contributors well. The purpose was to persuade well-educated men to write anonymously for the journal, and thus to offer unbiased criticism on works and topics of general interest—from a liberal Whig point of view, of course. The *Edinburgh* offered lengthy and generally learned essays by authors who not only criticized current books and pamphlets but also discussed in great depth the literary, political, social, philosophical, or scientific topics involved. It rapidly became the national intellectual journal of issues and ideas. The *Edinburgh* led the way for such followers as the *Quarterly Review* and *Westminster Review* in England and the *North American Review* and *Atlantic* in the United States.

Between 1802 and 1828, Smith contributed about a hundred articles to the *Edinburgh*. Sixty-five were republished during his lifetime in his collected works; twenty-five others are clearly attributable to him on the basis of his own correspondence or the testimony of his contemporaries; and twelve others are of unclear or disputed authorship, but probably are his. Naturally, as a clergyman he wrote most frequently on topics related to the church. He did not address theological questions but wrote on contemporary moral issues, church governance, and, most importantly, religious toleration.

By the late eighteenth century, laws barring non-Anglicans from holding public office or high military rank came under frequent attack by those with more liberal opinions. Parliament annually passed resolutions allowing Protestant dissenters to serve, but regulations barring Catholics from their full civil liberties were strongly defended by the Church of England and the king. In several sermons, Smith preached on the purely moral obligation of religious toleration. "Charity towards those who dissent from us on religious opinions is always a proper subject for the pulpit," he said. "If such discussions militate against the views of any particular party, the fault is not in him who is thus erroneously said to introduce politics into the Church, but in those who have really brought the Church into politics." In several *Edinburgh Review* articles, and much more fully in the *Peter Plymley Letters*, Smith argues the political side of the question: England cannot afford a permanently disaffected substantial minority within its own country and overwhelming majority in Ireland. In the best of times, alienating this segment of the population is a loss to the nation; with Napoleon threatening invasion and publicly inviting the Irish to join him in overthrowing the British crown, such a policy is suicidal. With irony reminiscent of Swift, Smith suggests that the Church of England should sustain its self-esteem by persecuting some smaller and weaker minority than the Catholics: "Why torture a bull-dog when you can get a frog or a rabbit? I am sure my proposal will meet with the most universal approbation. Do not be apprehensive of any opposition from [Cabinet] ministers. If it is a case of hatred, we are sure that one man will defend it by the Gospel: if it abridges human freedom, we know that another will find precedents for it in the Revolution." In addition to attacking, often in personal terms, the self-serving politicians who had inflamed public prejudices to win elections, Smith offers rational bases for extending civil liberties to Catholics. The Church of England and the House of Hanover are firmly established and no longer need to rely on restrictive legislation reflective of the persecutions common under Bloody Mary and Queen Elizabeth. He attacks the notion that Catholics' oaths are not to be trusted by pointing out that Catholics are actually kept out of office by their own refusal to take oaths of office swearing fidelity to the Church of England. These and similar arguments are echoed in many sermons and articles from 1806 through 1829, when Catholic emancipation finally was passed by Parliament.

Despite Smith's pleas for civil equality, he had little respect for the Catholic religion itself and often ridiculed "the thumbs and offals of

S

departed saints" and "the enormous wax candles, and superstitious mummeries, and painted jackets of the Catholic priests." Once introduced by Daniel O'Connell to a Catholic group as "the ancient and amusing defender of our faith," Smith laughingly interrupted, "Of your *cause*, if you please; *not* of your faith." Smith showed a similar attitude towards Protestant dissenters, particularly the various Evangelical sects, all of which he lumped together under the title of "Methodists." In several articles dealing with Methodism, Smith derides the religious enthusiasm, sense of personal salvation, extreme moralism, and exaggerated rhetoric common to the Evangelical sects. At the same time, he attacks various efforts to curb the civil rights of dissenters by extension of the Test and Corporation Acts which demanded Anglican communion of public officials or by suggestions that all Protestant marriages be conducted according to the Anglican rites: "Cupid cares not for creeds; the same passion which fills the parsonage house with chubby children, beats in the breast of the Baptist,—animates the Arminian,—melts the Unitarian maid,—and stirs up the moody Methodist to declare himself the victim of human love."

Behind Smith's passion for religious toleration as well as his lack of sympathy for both Catholicism and Evangelical Protestantism is his own brand of Christianity, very strong on practical morality and very light on mystical theology. In London and other cities, his sermons usually dealt with issues of social justice; in his country parish, he was more likely to preach the virtues of sobriety, honesty, and family. He rarely preached or wrote on theological topics and therefore could not sympathize with those who were ready to persecute their fellow humans over a difference in religious faith. By the same token, he was suspicious of the emphasis which Catholicism placed on ritual and ceremony and the reliance which Evangelicalism placed on personal and emotional revelation.

Smith saw the Church of England which he served as a branch of national government, responsible for the education and welfare of the people as well as their spiritual and physical health. As a country parson, he studied and practiced rudimentary medicine, established schools, served as a local magistrate, and encouraged advanced agricultural practices as well as baptizing, marrying, burying, and preaching to his parishioners. Many of his

Edinburgh Review articles are on topics of social justice, and he considered them an extension of his religious duties. He wrote about education, supporting the development of universal practical schools and attacking the classical curriculum which encouraged the study of Latin and Greek and little else. He deplored the employment of children as chimney sweeps, dooming them to hard and miserable lives cut short by premature cancer. As a local magistrate and through his close acquaintance with many attorneys, he became aware of and attacked various injustices in the criminal law. He was particularly opposed to the Game Laws which reserved to landowners the right to shoot game and made its sale illegal. Justified as encouraging the aristocracy to spend time on their country estates, the Game Laws also encouraged poor men to become poachers, selling game on the black market. "For every ten pheasants which fluttered in the wood," Smith said, "one English pheasant was rotting in gaol." He believed that imprisonment should be for punishment, not for rehabilitation. He argued for prisons which subjected inmates to tedious labor and simple diets, while being clean and wholesome. At the same time, he believed that the law must be scrupulous in defending the rights of the accused and in apportioning punishment. He was most eloquent in attacking the current laws which allowed representation by counsel for misdemeanors and for treason while denying it for the common felonies, including burglary and theft, which were capital offenses at that time. The reason for this disparity, the writer argued, was that most felonies were committed by the poor: "Gentlemen are rarely hung. If they were so, there would be petitions without end for counsel . . . Let two gentlemen on the Ministerial side of the House (we only ask for two) commit some crimes which will make their execution a matter of painful necessity. Let them feel, and report to the House, all the injustice and inconvenience of having neither a copy of the indictment, nor a list of witnesses, nor counsel to defend them."

Smith's view of the Church of England as a branch of the civil service was very appropriate for his time. As the careers of Smith and his brothers illustrate, a talented man could rise in social class through the Church, the law, or the colonial service. The tasks of the Church of England far exceeded its resources and resulted in a very unequal distribution of wealth. Thousands of clergy served in small parishes on insufficient incomes in hopes of the recognition or patronage which would secure them the more lucrative livings of urban parishes or appointments to cathedrals or universities. Patronage, the authority to appoint clergymen to livings, was treated as a form of property. Aristocratic landowners appointed the rectors of the villages on their estates. If a bishop died with a vacant parish in his diocese, his heirs could sell that appointment. The success of Anthony Trollope's *Barsetshire* novels illustrates the wide interest of Victorian England in Church governance.

One of Smith's first articles in the *Edinburgh Review* attacked the proposed Clergy Residence Act which would have barred clergymen from holding more than one living. He argued that the Church was like a lottery in which many invested their efforts and education in hopes of winning one of the great prizes. Years later, in the *Letters to Archdeacon Singleton*, the writer repeated this argument in describing the rise of a baker's son from working class to aristocracy:

> Young Crumpet is sent to school—takes to his books—spends the best years of his life, as all eminent Englishmen do, in making Latin verses—knows that the *crum* in crum-pet is long, and the *pet* short—goes to the University—gets a prize for an Essay on the Dispersion of the Jews—takes orders—becomes a Bishop's chaplain—has a young nobleman for his pupil—publishes an useless classic, and a serious call to the unconverted—and then goes through the Elysian transitions of Prebendary, Dean, Prelate and the long train of purple, profit, and power.

The *Letters to Archdeacon Singleton* were written in response to the proposals of the Ecclesiastical Commission, a body of Whig laymen and bishops appointed during the reform period to address the problems of Church governance. Among their proposed reforms was a plan to strip the cathedrals of considerable wealth and patronage in order to raise the income of clergy to be appointed by the bishops. In defense of his own St. Paul's Cathedral, and following his lifelong maxim "that a Bishop must always be in the wrong," Smith went on the attack. He poked fun, sometimes gentle and sometimes cutting, at the Commissioners (particularly the bishops) as they went about redistributing Cathedral property but preserving their own Episcopal income and patronage.

Predicting that the property of the bishops would also eventually come under attack, Smith described the future scene: "The Commission was separated in an instant; London clenched his fist; Canterbury was hurried out by his chaplain, and put into a warm bed; a solemn vacancy spread itself over the face of Gloucester; Lincoln was taken out in strong hysterics." Although the Cathedrals eventually prevailed in many points, Smith recognized that his wittiness prevented his being taken seriously. When Bishop Blomfield of London called him "my facetious friend" in a speech, Smith replied with a letter to *The Times* in which he wrote, "I hasten with gratitude in this letter to denominate you my solemn friend; but you and I must not run into commonplace errors; you must not think me necessarily foolish because I am facetious, nor will I consider you necessarily wise because you are grave."

The author's affinity for clerical metaphor cropped up in other writings as well. Thirty of his *Edinburgh Review* articles dealt with books of travel, and he enjoyed exercising his sense of humor in describing the exotic fauna of distant places:

> The campanero may be heard three miles!—this single little bird being more powerful than the belfry of a cathedral, ringing for a new dean,—just appointed on account of shabby politics, small understanding, and good family!

> The sloth, in its wild state, spends its life in trees . . . he lives not *upon* the branches but under them. He moves suspended, rests suspended, sleeps suspended, and passes his life in suspense—like a young clergyman distantly related to a bishop.

In many of his travel book reviews, Smith describes primitive peoples; he is fascinated by their customs, laws, crafts, and religions. He does not exhibit any of the enthusiasms of the Romantic movement for the "noble savage," but instead always makes his reader aware of the civilized advantages of Europe.

A similar mixed attitude marks his articles about the United States. He wrote three articles on America for the *Edinburgh Review* (in 1818,

1820, and 1824), each reviewing a number of recent books about travels in the United States. Most nineteenth-century British books on America were highly critical, pointing out all of the crudities and inconveniences of a new and raw country. In all three articles, Smith's approach is typical of that taken by the *Edinburgh Review*, if not by other British publications, on American topics. He admires the progressiveness of American government and society. As a liberal Whig, he saw in America the tangible expression of many of the political causes which he espoused for Britain: religious toleration, freedom of speech and press, social equality, direct government at the local and national levels, accessible courts, free enterprise, and widespread public education. The one exception he notes is slavery, "an atrocious crime . . . which makes liberty itself distrusted, and the boast of it disgusting." At the same time he points out that America is a new country, just emerging from the wilderness, without the cultural refinements and civilized comforts of older and more sophisticated Europe. Americans, he says, should be satisfied with their considerable accomplishments in government with industry and not be overly sensitive about their lack of cultural accomplishments:

> America seems, on the whole, to be a country possessing vast advantages, and little inconveniences: they have a cheap government, and bad roads; they pay no tithes, and have stage coaches without springs. They have no poor laws and no monopolies—but their inns are inconvenient and travellers are teased with questions. They have no collections in the fine arts; but they have no Lord Chancellor, and they can go to law without absolute ruin. They cannot make Latin verses, but they expend immense sums in the education of the poor. In all this the balance is prodigiously in their favour.

In his second article on America, Smith wrote his most memorable passage on American pretensions to artistic and intellectual culture:

> In the four quarters of the globe, who reads an American book? or goes to an American play? or looks at an American picture or statue? What does the world yet owe to American physicians or surgeons? What new substances have their chemists discovered? or what old ones have they analysed? What new constellations have been discovered by the telescopes of Americans? What have they done in the mathematics?

Smith's questions were not prompted by prejudice against America or ignorance of its culture. In 1820, American art and science were, indeed, in their infancy, and very few people in Europe read American books. At worst, his timing was bad. Within a year after his comments, Washington Irving's *Sketch Book*, James Fenimore Cooper's *The Spy*, and William Cullen Bryant's *Poems* were beginning to gain international recognition for American literature. Smith's relationships with individual Americans were excellent, and he frequently entertained visiting Americans, including scholars such as George Ticknor and politicians like Edward Everett and Daniel Webster, whom Smith compared to "a steam-engine in trousers."

Smith's final word on America came in 1843 when a general recession caused several American states to default on the payment of dividends from bonds that they had issued for the construction of roads, canals, and railroads. Pennsylvania attempted to repudiate its debts altogether. Smith sold his Pennsylvania bonds at a financial loss. He wrote a petition to Congress and two letters in the public press, then republished all three pieces as a pamphlet, *Letters on American Debts*. The writer's main point was that financial irresponsibility would hurt America's reputation and example of liberal government precisely among the very Britishers most likely to admire the United States, those who had invested their money in American bonds. He said it, however, in his usual style: "Figure to yourself a Pennsylvanian receiving foreigners in his own country, walking over the public works with them, and showing them Larcenous Lake, Swindling Swamp, Crafty Canal, and Rogues' Railway, and other dishonest works." Although many of his American readers acknowledged the justice of his attack and sent him letters of support and gifts, these remarks were not calculated to win Smith friends in the United States. Eventually, the furor caused by his *Letters on American Debts* died down, even in Philadelphia. Still, American literary history has never forgiven his low opinion of American culture. Throughout the nineteenth century whenever a new memoir or collection of his works appeared, American periodicals would attack Smith as the enemy of American literature. In our own day, very few American literary students have read him. Those who know his name know only his mocking question, "Who reads an American book?"

Smith never pretended to be a literary or aesthetic critic. He left that department of the *Edinburgh Review* to Jeffrey. He did write reviews of four novels and one play, apparently because they raised moral issues which he could discuss. He enjoyed contemporary fiction, particularly that of Scott and Dickens, and commented frequently in his letters on their depiction of character. Both authors were personal friends, especially Dickens who named one of his children for Sydney Smith. Both writers certainly share a talent for satirizing the arrogance of the old Tory aristocracy and the rigidity of the new Whig bureaucracy alike.

Smith's reputation as the leading wit of his day rested more on his conversation and his letters than on his published writings. The current edition of *Bartlett's Familiar Quotations* contains twenty-six quotations from Smith, all but one taken from correspondence or table-talk. The only citation from his writings is from *Elementary Sketches of Moral Philosophy* in which he illustrated mismatches between people's personalities and their roles in life by inventing the metaphor of square pegs in round holes. Some of his wittiest remarks were gathered from his conversations. Lady Cork was "so moved by a charity sermon that she begged me to lend her a guinea for her contribution. I did so. She never repaid me, and spent it on herself." The Prince of Wales's oriental pavilion at the sea looked as if "St. Paul's had come to Brighton and pupped." Thomas Babington Macaulay's conversation was much improved by "brilliant flashes of silence."

Smith's writings are characterized less by wit than by humor, the ability to take a whimsical view of human frailty. In the *Letters to Archdeacon Singleton*, he captures the breezy confidence with which the Whig reformers applied their Utilitarian theories to real social problems:

> There is not a better man in England than Lord John Russell; but his worst failure is that he is utterly ignorant of all moral fear; there is nothing he would not undertake. I believe he would perform the operation for the stone—build St. Peter's—or assume (with or without ten minutes' notice) the command of the Channel Fleet; and no one would discover by his manner that the patient had died—the Church tumbled down—and the Channel Fleet been knocked to atoms.

The description is telling yet so good-natured that it did not affect Smith's warm friendship with Russell. It is no wonder that Lord Dudley, whose eccentricities and absentmindedness often made him the butt of cruel jokes, once said, "You have been laughing at me constantly, Sydney, for the last seven years, yet in all that time you never said a single thing to me that I wished unsaid."

Summary

Sydney Smith's reputation as a wit rests mainly on his conversations and correspondence. During the early and late years of his career, he resided in London and was a popular dinner guest of the Whig aristocracy. His humor is exhibited in his published writings, the most important of which are his articles for the *Edinburgh Review*, in which he discussed a variety of social and ecclesiastical topics from a liberal point of view, and the *Peter Plymley Letters*, in which he argued for the removal of various laws abridging the civil rights of Catholics. These positions did not assist him in his advancement as a priest in the Church of England during a period of strong political reaction. He spent the middle two decades of his career as a country parson, preaching practical morality and tending to the needs of his parishioners. His most important legacies are the founding of the *Edinburgh Review* and a personal brand of political liberalism based in good humor rather than in dogma. Strongly committed to social justice and rational argument, he was distrustful of all sweeping theories that did not make room for the accidents of life and the ludicrousness of most human behavior.

Selected Bibliography

Primary Sources

Miscellaneous Sermons. Philadelphia: Carey and Hart, 1846.

The Works of the Rev. Sydney Smith. London: Longman, Orne, Brown, and Longmans, 1939; 4th ed., London: Longmans, and Philadelphia: Carey and

Hart, 1848.

Elementary Sketches of Moral Philosophy. London: Longman, Brown, Green, and Longmans, 1850.

The Letters of Sydney Smith. Ed. Nowell C. Smith. 2 vols. Oxford: Clarendon, 1953.

The Selected Writings of Sydney Smith. Ed. W.H. Auden. New York: Farrar, Straus, and Cudahy, 1956.

For a list of Smith's uncollected *Edinburgh Review* articles, see below: Sheldon Halpern, *Sydney Smith*, pp. 158–59.

Secondary Sources

Books

Bell, Alan. *Sydney Smith: A Biography.* Oxford: Clarendon, 1980. This is the most recent biography and relies heavily on collected and uncollected correspondence by and to Smith to provide previously unknown details about his family and social life. The author is preparing an expanded edition of Smith's letters.

Bullett, Gerald. *Sydney Smith: A Biography and a Selection.* London: Michael Joseph, 1951. Now outdated by Auden's selections and Bell's biography.

Burdett, Osbert. *The Rev. Smith, Sydney.* London: Chapman & Hall, 1934. Still the fullest discussion of Smith's contributions to moral philosophy.

Chevrillon, A. *Sydney Smith et la Renaissance des Idees liberales en Angleterre au XIX siecle.* Paris: Hachette, 1894. A French summary of Smith's political ideas. In French.

Clive, John L. *Scotch Reviewers: The Edinburgh Review 1802–1815.* Cambridge, MA: Harvard University Press, 1957. A valuable account and analysis of the early days of the *Edinburgh Review.*

Halpern, Sheldon. *Sydney Smith.* New York: Twayne, 1966. The only American biography, Halpern emphasizes Smith's literary career and contributions.

Holland, Lady [Saba]. *A Memoir of the Rev. Sydney Smith.* London: Longman, Brown, Green, and Longmans, and New York: Harper, 1855. The first biography, by Smith's daughter, is still the most intimate portrait of his family and social life. The second volume, a collection of letters, is outdated.

Pearson, Hesketh. *The Smith of Smiths.* London: Hamilton, and New York: Harper, 1934. A popular biography, emphasizing social and political life.

Reid, Stuart J. *A Sketch of the Life and Times of the Rev. Sydney Smith.* New York: Harper, 1885. Placing Smith in the mainstream of nineteenth-century clerical and political liberalism, Reid includes many contemporary memoirs and testimonials.

Russell, George W.E. *Sydney Smith.* London: Macmillan, 1905. In the English Men of Letters series, informative rather than analytical.

Articles and Chapters in Books

Anonymous. "Sydney Smith as a Minister of Religion." *Biblical Repertory and Princeton Review*, 38 (1856): 418–43. A review of Lady Holland's *Memoir*, this is an extreme example of American anti-Smith feeling.

Epstein, Joseph. "The Mere Common Sense of Sydney Smith." *The New Criterion*, 8 (November 1989): 9–20. A highly appreciative and articulate summary of Smith's humor and practical liberalism.

Houghton, [Richard Monckton Milnes] Lord. "The Rev. Sydney Smith." In *Monographs: Personal and Social.* London: John Murray, and New York: Holt and Williams, 1873. The best of several such accounts by contemporaries.

K[ingsley], C[harles]. "Sydney Smith." *Fraser's Magazine*, 52 (1855): 84–91. An appreciation by one liberal writer and Anglican clergyman of another.

Dissertations

Pickering, Samuel F., Jr. "Sydney Smith: A Whig Divine, a Study of His Early Writings, 1800–1814." Ph.D. dissertation, Princeton University, 1971.

Sheldon Halpern

Smollett, Tobias George

Born: Dalquhurn, Dumbarton, Scotland, March 1721

Education: Dumbarton Grammar School, ca. 1727–ca. 1732; Glasgow University (?) mid-1730s; surgical apprentice, 1736–1739

Marriage: Anne Lassells, ca. 1744; one child

Died: Leghorn, Italy, September 17, 1771

Biography

Born on the estate of Dalquhurn, near Bonhill, Dumbarton, Scotland, Tobias George Smollett was baptized in the parish church of Cardross, Dumbartonshire, on March 19, 1721. His father, Archibald Smollett, had married Barbara Cunningham without parental consent; consequently, when Archibald died shortly after the birth of the future novelist, Sir James Smollett, Archibald's father, refused to provide the family financial assistance, which had to come from the author's cousin, also named James Smollett. Like so much else of Smollett's early life, these incidents would appear in *The Adventures of Roderick Random* (1748), the stingy grandfather modeled on Smollett's own, the generous cousin transformed into the nautical Tom Bowling.

In 1727 or 1728, Smollett entered Dumbarton Grammar School, a much better institution than that which his character attends. Smollett made great progress in the classics and was to display his knowledge of Greek and Latin throughout his writings. He may have attended Glasgow University in the mid-1730s; he definitely worked in the Glasgow dispensary, and in April 1736, he began what was supposed to be a five-year apprenticeship to two noted Glasgow surgeons, William Stirling and John Gordon (the latter possibly the prototype of Potion in *Roderick Random*).

Perhaps because of ill-health, perhaps fired by literary ambition, Smollett did not serve out his five years. He had written a blank-verse tragedy, *The Regicide* (1749), about the murder of King James I at Perth in 1439, and with this work he set off for London in 1739. His struggles to get the piece produced—it never was—form the subject of chapters sixty-one through sixty-three of *Roderick Random*, and its failure to reach the stage prompted Smollett to satirize various leading theatrical figures of the day, including the managers John Rich and David Garrick, in several of his works.

Unable to earn a living as a playwright, Smollett returned to medicine. On March 10, 1740, he secured a license as a surgeon's second mate, and the next month he joined the *HMS Chichester*, an eighty-gun ship that participated in the disastrous campaign against Cartagena (1741). Smollett's activities between September 1741 and May 1744 are uncertain, but he probably married Anne Lassells, a Jamaican heiress, during this period. By 1744, he was back in London attempting to establish a medical practice. In that year or the next he published a

song; in 1746, he responded to the Duke of Cumberland's barbarous treatment of the Jacobite rebels by writing *The Tears of Scotland*, which he followed with two other poems, *Advice* (1746) and its sequel *Reproof* (1747). Much of 1747 he devoted to his first novel, his most successful literary effort, which appeared in January 1748. That same year he published a translation of Alain-Rene LeSage's *Gil Blas*, which had served as a model for *Roderick Random*.

Still trying to balance medicine and literature, in 1750 he purchased a medical degree from Marischal College, Aberdeen, and visited Paris, probably to gather material for his second novel, *The Adventures of Peregrine Pickle* (1751). Over the next few years he wrote for *The Monthly Review* and produced another novel (*The Adventures of Ferdinand Count Fathom*, 1753) as well as a pamphlet urging sea-bathing and attacking what he regarded as the unsanitary conditions at Bath (*An Essay on the External Use of Water*, 1752); he was also editing William Smellie's work on obstetrics.

By 1755, when he published a translation of Miguel de Cervantes's *Don Quixote* and issued proposals for *The Critical Review*, he had apparently decided that he was more likely to survive by his pen than by his pills. Over the next seven years he edited three journals, wrote a fourth novel and a four-volume history of England, began a *Continuation* of that work, and provided annotations to the early volumes of *The Works of . . . Voltaire* (1761–1769). Such industry, which generated over half a million words, taxed his constitution. Compounding the strain was the collapse on February 12, 1763, of the *Briton*, a periodical that Smollett began in 1762 to counteract anti-Scottish sentiment in England and to defend the Earl of Bute and his ministry. Still more grievous was the loss of his only child, fifteen-year-old Elizabeth, on April 3, 1763.

Physically and mentally exhausted, Smollett left England very much in the mood of the persona in *Travels through France and Italy* (1766) who feels "traduced by malice, persecuted by faction, abandoned by false patrons, and overwhelmed by the sense of a domestic calamity, which it was not in the power of fortune to repair."[1] Two years later he was back in England, recovered in spirit though not in health. He may have begun working on *The Expedition of Humphry Clinker* (1771) as early as 1765. In 1766, his *Travels* appeared, followed three years later by the satiric *The History and Adventures of an Atom* (1769). The novelist returned to Italy in 1763, where he completed his masterpiece, *Humphry Clinker*, and lived just long enough to see its publication on June 15, 1771. Three months later, on September 17, 1771, Smollett was dead; on September 19, 1771, he was buried in the English cemetery at Leghorn.

Literary Analysis

In *The Adventures of Sir Launcelot Greaves* (1762), the eponymous hero declares that he has donned the armor of his ancestors because he intends "to act as a coadjutor to the law, and even to remedy evils which the law cannot reach; to detect fraud and treason, abase insolence, mortify pride, discourage slander, disgrace immodesty, and stigmatize ingratitude."[2] In that novel, and later in *Humphry Clinker*, Smollett praises Alexander Pope and Swift, whom he took as his literary models. Although Smollett's reputation rests on his novels, and even though he long hoped to earn his living as a dramatist, his first important publications were the verse satires *Advice* and *Reproof*, modeled on the Horatian imitations of the recently deceased Pope. These works reveal themes and techniques that will resurface in Smollett's fiction over the next two and a half decades.

The intent of these poems, Smollett writes in *Advice*, is to "fix the brand of infamy on vice" (1.130). Like Pope before him, though with less subtlety, he lampoons a series of individuals—the Duke of Newcastle, the Duke of Grafton, and the Earls of Granville and Bath—and attacks various vices, including homosexuality and sycophancy. He recognizes that in contemporary society "'Tis infamous . . . to be poor" (1.2), but he refuses to succeed by exploiting the "weakness, vice, and folly" (1.210) with which the world abounds.

Similarly, in *Reproof,* he proclaims his devotion to truth and condemns a society in which:

> Corruption, roll'd in a triumphant car,
> Displays his burnish't front and glitt'ring star;
> Unknown alike to honour and remorse.
> Behold the leering belle, caress'd by all,
> Adorn each private feast and public ball,
> Where peers attentive listen and adore,
> And not one matron shuns the titled
>   whore. (2.135–136, 138–142)

In the England of 1747, "Each low pursuit, and slighter folly bred / Within the selfish heart and hollow head, / Thrives uncontroul'd and blossoms o'er the land" (2.147–149). As in *Advice*, he does not hesitate to name those guilty of such failings; among the specific targets of the poem are theater manager Rich, various financiers and writers, and general Henry Hawley, and the quack Thomas Thompson.

Attacks on individuals as exemplars of vice and folly, a dim view of the world in general and of England in particular, and a desire to reform evil characterize Smollett's fiction as well as his poetry. As Smollett writes in the preface to *Roderick Random*, he seeks "to animate the reader against the sordid and vicious disposition of the world" (*Roderick Random*, xlv). Specifically linking the novel to satire, he observes that the most effective way to change individuals and society is by introducing instruction "in the course of an interesting story, which brings every incident home to life" (xliii). This connection with satire is made clear, too, by the epigraph on the title page, "Et genus et virtus, nisi cum re, vilia alga est" (Both birth and merit, if lacking money, are worth less than seaweed), drawn from Horace and again expressing the view of *Advice* that in the England of Smollett's day poverty is the greatest crime.

A similar moral purpose of exposing and chastising evil informs Smollett's other novels. In *Ferdinand Count Fathom* he seeks "to subject folly to ridicule, and . . . vice to indignation," to brand iniquity with reproach and shame" (*Ferdinand Count Fathom*, 4). The letter of Jonathan Dustwich to Henry Davis that opens *Humphry Clinker*, while highly fanciful, speaks of the book's intention to inform and edify.

To reveal the follies and vices of English society, in *Roderick Random* Smollett portrays the adventures of a naive Scottish youth struggling against "the selfishness, envy, malice, and base indifference of mankind" (*Roderick Random*, xlv). Because Random is poor, his schoolmaster ignores him, his relatives abuse him. He quickly discovers the truth of the advice that the moneylender gives Ferdinand Count Fathom: "Without money there was no respect, honour, or convenience to be acquired in life; that wealth amply supplied the want of wit, merit and pedigree, . . . and that the world never failed to worship the flood of affluence" (*Ferdinand Count Fathom*, 225). A cabman purposely splashes Random with mud; a servant thinks himself a great wit for directing Random to the River Thames instead of to the address that the youth requests. Wounded and captured by a press gang, Random asks a fellow prisoner to take the handkerchief from his (Random's) pocket to make a bandage; instead, the fellow steals it to sell for a dram of gin. Aboard the ship *Thunder* the first surgeon's mate insists on eating dinner before attending to a patient; meanwhile, the sick man dies. To please Captain Oakum, Dr. Mackshane declares that sick people are healthy. They are then assigned tasks that kill them. Shipwrecked and beaten on the coast of Sussex, Random finds no one to shelter him except an old woman whom everyone else regards as a witch.

Even *Humphry Clinker*, that most genial of Smollett's novels, reveals a world replete with selfishness and ignorance. Tabitha Bramble cannot believe that her brother would give away twenty pounds to a needy widow. She assumes that the money must be payment for sex, and she thinks of all the finery which money could buy her. The servants at Bath conspire to defraud their masters, who in turn squander money they don't have in order to impress other pretenders to wealth. Baynard's wife would rather ruin her husband than sacrifice one of her whims.

In Smollett's universe, seeming benevolence most often masks baser emotions. After Roger Potion, Random's distant relation, evicts the youth because he can no longer pay his keep, Launcelot Crab takes Random home with him. Crab's apparent generosity is prompted by his hatred for Potion and his need for an assistant. Later, Crab urges Random to seek his fortune in London and lends him ten guineas. Again, though, Crab has an ulterior motive. Crab's maid, who is also his mistress, is pregnant; once Random has left town, she can blame the absent Random. In London, Random and his friend Strap are stopped by a person who attempts to return half a crown to them. When they deny that the money is theirs, he offers to split the money with them three ways. This "prodigy of integrity" (*Roderick Random*, 69) proves to be a "coin-dropper" who cheats the two Scotsmen of all of their money. While serving in the French army Random loses a duel, and an Irishman, professing regard for his countryman, offers to instruct the young man so that he can succeed in a rematch. Later Random discovers that the Irishman's "true motive was no other than a jealousy he entertained of a correspondence between the Frenchman and his wife,

which he did not think proper to resent in person" (248). The governess of Sir John Sparkle's daughter refuses all bribes from the heiress's would-be suitors, but Smollett questions whether the woman does so because of honesty, envy of her charge, or greed so excessive that no offer has yet been sufficient to tempt her.

This cynicism informs the later novels as well. Fathom's mother kills and despoils those wounded in battle. She spares an Englishman not out of compassion but because she "foresaw greater advantage to herself in attempting to preserve his life, than she could possibly reap from" dispatching him (*Ferdinand Count Fathom*, 12). When Fathom appears sympathetic to the plight of Don Diego de Zelos, he is trying to win the Spaniard's trust and so rob him of his jewels. In *Humphry Clinker*, Tabitha's compassion for the apparently crippled Micklewhimmen is prompted by her matrimonial designs upon him.

"Homo homini lupus" (Man is a wolf to man), Plautus observed, and Smollett's novels share that view. As Paul-Gabriel Bouce states, "Smollett introduces his readers to a world swarming with rogues, crooks, thieves, prostitutes and highwaymen" (300). Though praised for his realism, and though he draws on life, including his own experiences, the novels are not so much realistic as surrealistic: evil is exaggerated for satiric ends.

Nightmarish scenes darken the novelist's fictional world still more. For example, there is the picture of Random, stripped and wounded, seeking shelter at night in Sussex and not finding any. Another example is found in the sick bay aboard the *Thunder*, where there are "about fifty miserable distempered wretches, suspended in rows, so huddled one upon another, that not more than fourteen inches of space was allotted for each with his bed and bedding; and deprived of the light of the day, as well as of fresh air; breathing nothing but a noisome atmosphere of the morbid steams exhaling from their own excrements and diseased bodies, devoured with vermin hatched in the filth that surrounded them" (*Roderick Random*, 149). And, there is the battle in which Random, shackled to the ship's deck, is blinded by the brains of a sailor whose head has been shot off. In a particularly harrowing episode that anticipates the Gothic novel, Fathom, seeking refuge from a storm, takes a room in a lonely cottage. After his hostess locks him in for the night, he finds the still-warm body of a

S

murdered man. Fathom runs to the window to escape but finds this exit guarded with iron bars. He saves himself only by placing the body in bed and hiding himself under some straw, for at midnight two killers enter the room and stab the corpse, thinking that it is Fathom. Having dispatched their guest, they do not bother to relock the door, thereby allowing him to escape.

Yet, Smollett's novels are more comic than dark. One reason is that they are ruled by a benign providence. Whenever Random most needs assistance, it appears, whether in the timely appearance of Tom Bowling, the devoted Strap, Random's resurrected (and rich) father, or his beloved Narcissa, who rightly observes at the end of the book that his sudden good fortune "seemed to have been brought about by the immediate direction of providence" (*Roderick Random*, 425)—at least by the direction of an author who would not let his hero end his life in misery. In such a world the good triumph and the evil are punished. Too sensitive to tolerate Captain Oakum's treatment, Thomson jumps overboard. But, he does not drown; rescued by another ship, he prospers in Jamaica. Miss Williams, though she suffers because of various false lovers, finds a true husband in Strap. On the other hand, the evil Mackshane ends in jail, the selfish Crab dies, one of Random's haughty cousins marries an ensign who impoverishes her, and another marries a former footman after bearing him a child.

In *Ferdinand Count Fathom,* the supposedly dead Monimia returns to life, and the virtuous Don Diego discovers that he is not a murderer after all. Despite his great charm, Fathom cannot seduce the truly virtuous, and at the end of the novel even he repents and is rewarded with a devoted wife and a country retreat. *Humphry Clinker* concludes with three marriages, and the death of Baynard's wasteful wife allows him to recoup his fortune. As Winifred Jenkins, now Loyd, writes in the final letter of the work, "Providence hath bin pleased to make great halteration in the pasture of our affairs" (*Humphry Clinker*, 352). The heading of the last chapter of *Peregrine Pickle* could serve for the conclusion of all of the novels, since in each the hero "makes himself ample Amends for all the Mortifications of his Life."

Smollett thus fuses sentimentalism with satire. While most of the characters in the novels are malicious, enough benevolent figures appear to thwart them. Strap, Hauser Trunnion (*Peregrine Pickle*), Renaldo (*Ferdinand Count Fathom*), Launcelot Greaves (*Sir Launcelot Greaves*), Matt Bramble and Humphry Clinker (*Humphry Clinker*) are models of virtue. Their presence does not negate the proposition that the world is a wicked place, but in Smollett's novels, unlike Pope's *Dunciad*, universal darkness does not bury all.

Further tempering the satire is the behavior of Smollett's heroes. Even while Random's experiences justify Strap's assertion that "surely the devil had set up his throne in London" (*Roderick Random*, 73), Random's naivete is such that readers cannot always sympathize with him. One is more likely to smile with a sense of superiority at his being gulled by the coin-dropper or Lord Straddle than to rage at the iniquity of these people. Peregrine Pickle, too, is overly eager to lend his money and foolishly falls prey "to the unsuspecting integrity of his own heart" (*Peregrine Pickle*, 612). Matt Bramble's strictures against Bristol Hot Well, Bath, and London are more funny than bitter because they are qualified by favorable accounts of these places in the letters of Lydia and Jery. Also, Bramble's temper varies with his health, so his comments reflect more about him than about the conditions that he purports to describe.

Conversely, just as the innocence of Random and Pickle elicits smiles of indulgence rather than frowns of indignation toward their antagonists, so many of Smollett's villains appear more ludicrous than evil. His novels attracted the talents of Rowlandson and George Cruikshank because, like them, he is a caricaturist. He describes Launcelot Crab as "about five foot high, and ten round the belly; his face was capacious as a full moon, and much of the complexion of a mulberry; his nose resembling a powder-horn, was swelled to an enormous size, and studded all over with carbuncles; and his little grey eyes reflected the rays in such an oblique manner, that while he looked a person full in the face, one would have imagined he was admiring the buckle of his shoe" (*Roderick Random*, 26). Captain Weazel sounds like a giant but proves so small "that on the whole, he appeared like a spider or grasshopper erect,—and was almost a *vox & preterea nihil*" (voice and nothing else; *Roderick Random*, 50). Such villains are hard to take seriously. Even Fathom, whom Smollett claims to find so evil that at one point he regrets writing about him, often gets himself into laughable predicaments, as when he carries on an intrigue with both a mother and daughter or when he attempts to fleece Sir Stentor, ostensibly an English booby, who proves the more accomplished cheat of the pair.

Smollett is a keen observer of incongruities, which serve as targets for satire, yet the descriptions are comical. In *Humphry Clinker,* the bookseller Henry Davis relies on two critics for theological works. One is a ship's carpenter, the other even less suitable—he has fled town "to avoid a prosecution for blasphemy" (*Humphry Clinker,* 3). His sudden departure is the more disappointing to Davis because this expert on theology had been writing a religious work himself. In both *Roderick Random* and *Humphry Clinker,* Scotsmen teach English pronunciation. Jery finds a Grub Street author engaged in producing a book on practical agriculture, undeterred by his inability to distinguish rice from corn or his aversion to the countryside. Random's traveling companion in France is a monk who "loved good eating and drinking better than his rosary, and paid more adoration to a pretty girl than to the Virgin Mary" (*Roderick Random,* 240). Like Henry Fielding, Smollett recognized the humor arising from unexpected behavior, and both authors attacked affectation by laughing at it.

As Smollett's descriptions suggest the caricatures of William Hogarth, so many incidents in the novel indicate a keen dramatic sense. On the way to London, Random and Strap spend the night at an inn with four others, Captain and Mrs. Weazel, Jenny, and Isaac Rapine. In a sequence that Dickens would refine in his *The Posthumous Papers of the Pickwick Club,* Strap mistakes Captain Weazel's room for his own and gets into bed with the soldier's wife. The captain, who has gone to use a chamberpot, returns and feels a man's head in bed. He concludes that he has mistaken Jenny's bed for his own and that she is entertaining someone. Angered, he throws the full chamberpot at the couple—Smollett, perhaps because of his medical training, indulged in much excremental humor. The bedmates jump up; the captain begins strangling Strap, while Mrs. Weazel belabors her husband's head with a shoe to punish him for dousing her. At the same time Jenny, who in fact has been sleeping with Isaac, yells, "Rape! Murder! Rape! . . . O! you vile, abominable old villain, . . . would you rob me of my virtue?" (*Roderick Random,* 52). Dickens would also borrow the election scene in chapter 9 of *Sir Launcelot Greaves.* To cite but one of this novel's comical incidents, Vanderpelft concludes his speech by declaring the principles that he maintains: "This . . . is the solid basis and foundation upon which I stand." At that moment the barrel on which he is standing collapses, Vanderpelft disappears, and the fox-hunting supporters of Valentine Quickset shout, "Stole away! stole away!" (*Sir Launcelot Greaves,* 75).

Finally, there is the exuberance of Smollett's language which manifests itself in various ways. Smollett loved malapropisms at least as much as he did chamberpots. In *Roderick Random,* a soldier sings a tune that begins, "Would you taste the noontide Air? / To yon fragrant Bower repair." The soldier, however, sings, "Would task the Moon-ty'd hair, / To yon flagrant beau repair" (*Roderick Random,* 325). Jackson in that novel is much taken by a letter from "Clayrender," who opens her epistle, "Dire creatur, As you are the animable hopjack of my contempleshons" and speaks of "old whorie time" (*Roderick Random,* 81). Frequently, such errors contain a deep truth beneath the comic illiteracy. Jackson, a cheat, is dire, and time often is a whore, flattering one with fair promises that it then betrays.

In its malapropisms as in many other regards, *Humphry Clinker* is Smollett's masterpiece. The letters of Tabitha Bramble and Winifred Jenkins are replete with hilarious solecisms, many of them with sexual or scatalogical implications. Tabitha is so angered by Dr. Lewis that she swears never to write to him again "though he beshits me on his bended knees" (*Humphry Clinker,* 156). Win Jenkins urges Mary Jones to "pray without seizing for grease to prepare you for the operation of this wonderful instrument [Humphry Clinker], which, I hope, will be exorcised this winter upon you." Later, Tabitha expresses a similar wish that Clinker may "have the power given to penetrate and instill his goodness, even into your most inward parts"; meanwhile, she wants Roger to "search into, and make a general clearance of the slit holes which the maids have in secret" (275). Win claims to be discreet, but "if I was given to tail-baring, I have my own secrets to discover" (220). These women provide only about one-fifth of the letters but, like the seasonings in a stew, they greatly heighten the flavor of the product.

Jargon creates laughter too. A lawyer speaks of the Battle of Dettingen in legal terms: "Although the English had drawn themselves into a premunire at first, the French managed their cause so lamely in the course of the dispute, that they would have been utterly nonsuited, had they not obtained a noli-prosequi" (*Roderick Random*, 325). The humor works on multiple levels. The terminology seems inappropriate, yet it reminds one that the judicial system can be as adversarial—and as deadly—as warfare. Further, the statement suggests that the English behaved as if they were in a courtroom, not on a battlefield, for if the English had acted aggressively and pursued the routed French, the retreating army would have been captured and stripped of its weapons, France of its defenses. Smollett also uses legalese to create double entendres. When a lieutenant and a supposed prude go off together, the lawyer remarks, "I suppose the lady knows him to be an able conveyancer, and wants him to make a settlement intail" (*Roderick Random*, 332). Another attorney offers a similar comment as he illustrates a legal concept by declaring, "I seize Dolly *in tail*" (*Sir Launcelot Greaves*, 5).

Smollett introduced the sailor to English fiction, and he genuinely admired common seamen for their bravery and generosity. Commodore Hauser Trunnion (*Peregrine Pickle*) is as much a compliment to human nature as Laurence Sterne's Uncle Toby, who is modeled on Smollett's character. Still, these sailors are literally out of their element on land; Trunnion rides a horse as if he were navigating a ship, tacking in a stiff wind. Nothing so clearly reveals their failure to fit into landlubber society as their speech. When Tom Bowling confronts Random's cousin, he warns the insolent young man, "Look 'ee, you lubberly son of a w—e, if you come athwart me, 'ware your gingerbreadwork. I'll be foul of your quarter, d—n me" (*Roderick Random*, 9). Every one of Smollett's novels offers at least a glimpse of similar figures.

Other characters also reveal verbal eccentricities. Morgan (like Fluellen in William Shakespeare's *Henry V*) combines a Welsh accent with a love of iteration: "I will impeach, and accuse, and indict him for a roppery," he asserts (*Roderick Random*, 178). Narcissa's aunt, a learned lady not entirely in touch with reality, asks Random, "Whether didst thou come on shore on the back of a whale or a dolphin?" (218). Gamaliel Pickle's curious proposal to Sally Appleby indicates his commercial background: "Understanding you have a parcel of heart, warranted sound, to be disposed of, shall be willing to treat for said commodity, on reasonable terms" (*Peregrine Pickle*, 14).

Smollett learned many of these comic devices from the stage. His seamen are descendants of William Congreve's Ben (*Love for Love*, 1695); his eccentrics owe their characteristic names and much of their behavior to Ben Jonson's comedy of humors. Alan Dugald McKillop notes, for example, that Sir Cadwallader Crabtree in *Peregrine Pickle* is "the malcontent and misanthrope of post-1600 English comedy, and the sequence in which he sets up as a necromancer and derides and gulls those who expose themselves by consulting him is thoroughly Jonsonian" (161). Strap's attire resembles that of Scrub in George Farquhar's *The Beaux' Stratagem* (1707). Smollett's novels have been accused of lacking careful plotting, of consisting rather of a series of scenes which often could be omitted or rearranged without affecting the story. The charge is valid, but the author conceived of the novel as "a large diffused picture, comprehending the characters of life, disposed in different groups, and exhibited in various attitudes" (*Ferdinand Count Fathom*, 2). A major influence on this view of the novel is the picaresque tradition exemplified by such works as *Gil Blas* and *Don Quixote*, both of which Smollett translated, but the very language of the description also indicates his debt to drama. This connection becomes even clearer as Smollett continues his dedication. Justifying his choice of a villain as protagonist in *Ferdinand Count Fathom*, he maintains, "In the Drama . . . we are as well pleased to see the wicked schemes of a Richard blasted, and the perfidy of a Maskwell exposed, as to behold a Bevil happy, and an Edward victorious" (3). Fathom smacks of the stage villainy of Shakespeare's Richard III and Congreve's Maskwell in *The Double Dealer* (1694).

Summary

Tobias Smollett drew on French and Spanish romance, drama, and satire to produce five lively novels. As Sir Walter Scott observed, "There is so much of life, action, and bustle, in every group he has painted; so much force and individuality of character."[3] Other writers, in turn, learned from him—Sterne, Frederick Marryat, Dickens, James Joyce (who found in Smollett the kind of wordplay that characterizes *Ulysses* and *Finnegan's Wake*), John Barth (*The Sot-Weed Factor*, 1961, could easily have been written by Smollett). Long overshadowed by Samuel Richardson, Fielding, and Sterne, Smollett deserves to be recognized as their equal. If *Tom Jones* provides a history of the eighteenth century, *Humphry Clinker* does, too. If Fielding and Sterne have fused humor and satire in prose fiction, so has Smollett. As is written on his monument, erected by his generous cousin, James Smollett of Bonhill, on the banks of the Levern, "If fertility of genius and an unequaled talent in delineating the characters of humanity have ever attracted your admiration, pause a while on the memory of TOBIAS SMOLLETT, M.D."

Notes

1. Tobias Smollett, *Travels through France and Italy*, ed. Frank Felsenstein (Oxford: Oxford University Press, 1979), p. 2.
2. Smollett, *The Life and Adventures of Sir Launcelot Greaves*, ed. David Evans (London: Oxford University Press, 1973), p. 14. All references in the text are to Smollett's novels as issued by Oxford University Press.
3. Quoted in K.G. Simpson, "Tobias Smollett: The Scot as English Novelist," in *Smollett: Author of the First Distinction*, ed. Alan Bold (Totowa: Barnes & Noble, 1982), p. 65.

Selected Bibliography
Primary Sources

Novels

The Adventures of Roderick Random. London: J. Osborn, 1748; New York: Oxford University Press, 1981.
The Adventures of Peregrine Pickle. London: D. Wilson, 1751; New York: Oxford University Press, 1983.
The Adventures of Ferdinand Count Fathom. London: W. Johnston, 1753.
The Adventures of Sir Launcelot Greaves. London: J. Coote, 1762.
The History and Adventures of an Atom. London: J. Almon, 1769.
The Expedition of Humphry Clinker. London: W. Johnston & B. Collins, 1771; New York: Oxford University Press, 1984.

Poetry

Advice: A Satire. London: M. Cooper, 1746.
Reproof: A Satire. The Sequel to Advice. London: W. Owen & M. Cooper, 1747.

Non-Fiction

An Essay on the External Use of Water. London: M. Cooper, 1752.
A Complete History of England. London: James Rivington and James Fletcher, 1, 1757–1758.
Continuation of the Complete History of England. London: R. Baldwin, 1760–1765.
Travels through France and Italy. London: R. Baldwin, 1766; New York: Oxford University Press, 1981.

Translations

The Adventures of Gil Blas of Santillane. London: J. Osborn, 1749.
The History and Adventures of the Renowned Don Quixote. London: A. Millar, 1755.

Secondary Sources

Bibliographies

Spector, Robert D. *Tobias Smollett: A Reference Guide.* Boston: G.K. Hall, 1980.
Wagoner, Mary. *Tobias Smollett: A Checklist of Editions of His Works and an Annotated Secondary Bibliography.* New York: Garland, 1984.

Biographies

Knapp, Lewis M. *Tobias Smollett: Doctor of Men and Manners.* Princeton: Princeton University Press, 1949. The standard biography.

Books

Bold, Alan, ed. *Smollett: Author of the First Distinction.* Totowa: Barnes & Noble, 1982. Part 1 contains four essays on "Smollett in General"; Part 2 offers five essays, one on each of the major novels.
Bouce, Paul-Gabriel. *The Novels of Tobias Smollett.* Trans. Antonia White. London: Longman, 1976. Excellent critical study of the fiction; includes good short biography (ch. 1).
Giddings, Robert. *The Tradition of Smollett.* London: Methuen, 1967. Giddings discusses Smollett's use of the picaresque tradition and notes his influence on writers of the eighteenth through the twentieth centuries.
Goldberg, M.A. *Smollett and the Scottish School.* Albuquerque: University of New Mexico Press, 1957. Goldberg relates Smollett's satiric intentions in the novel to the Scottish Common-Sense School of philosophy.
Martz, Louis L. *The Later Career of Tobias*

Smollett. New Haven: Yale University Press, 1942. Martz relates *Travels, Atom,* and *Humphry Clinker* to Smollett's journalistic work.

Rousseau, George S. *Tobias Smollett: Essays of Two Decades.* Edinburgh: T. & T. Clark, 1982. A collection of fifteen previously published pieces surveying such matters as Smollett's letters and his role in the medical controversies of his day. Denies that Smollett's novels are picaresques.

————, and Paul-Gabriel Bouce, eds. *Bicentennial Essays Presented to Lewis M. Knapp.* New York: Oxford University Press, 1971. A collection of ten essays on Smollett's writings, mainly on the novels.

Spector, Robert Donald. *Tobias George Smollett.* Boston: Twayne, 1989. Good general introduction, with a chapter devoted to each of the five major novels. Includes a useful bibliography.

Articles

McKillop, Alan Dugald. "Tobias Smollett." In *The Early Masters of English Fiction.* Lawrence: University of Kansas Press, 1956, pp. 147–81. A good survey of the novels, noting their relationship to Smollett's life and the literary tradition he inherited. Also discusses Smollett's contribution to the development of English prose fiction.

Piper, William B. "The Large Diffused Picture of Life in Smollett's Early Novels." *Studies in Philology,* 60 (January, 1963): 45–56. A discussion of characterization in Smollett's first three novels.

Stevick, Philip. "Stylistic Energy in the Early Smollett." *Studies in Philology,* 64 (October, 1967): 712–19. Hyperbolic style, even more than character or incident, enlivens *Roderick Random, Peregrine Pickle,* and *Ferdinand Count Fathom.*

Joseph Rosenblum

Somerville and Ross

Edith Somerville and Violet Martin (Ross) published together as Somerville and Ross.

Somerville, Edith Anna Oenone

Born: Corfu, Greece, May 2, 1858
Education: Alexandra College, Dublin; South Kensington School of Art, 1870; Dusseldorf School of Art, 1881–1882; studios of Colarossi and Delecluse in Paris, 1884–1885; Royal Westminster School of Art, London
Died: Drishane, Castle Townshend, Ireland, October 8, 1949

Biography

Edith Anna Oenone Somerville was born in Corfu, Greece, on May 2, 1858, the first daughter and eldest of six surviving children to Lieutenant Colonel Thomas Henry Somerville and Adelaide Eliza Coghill. Most of her life was spent at Drishane, Castle Townshend, Ireland, the ancestral family home. Her greatest childhood pleasures were dogs, horses, art, and music. She was educated at Alexandra College in Dublin and the South Kensington School of Art (1870). As she recounts in *Irish Memories* (1917), she defied contemporary convention by studying art and music first in Dusseldorf (at the Dusseldorf School of Art, from 1881 to 1882) and later in Paris in the studios of Colarossi and Delecluse (1884–1885). Her narration about the campaign to study in Paris reveals her sense of humor while simultaneously pointing out the strictures applied to young unmarried women at that time: "'Paris!' They all said this at the tops of their voices. . . . They said that Paris was the Scarlet woman embodied; they also said, 'The IDEA of letting a GIRL go to PARIS!' This they said incessantly in capital letters, and in 'capital letters' (they were renowned for writing 'capital letters'), and my mother was frightened. So a compromise was effected, and I went to Paris with a bodyguard, consisting of my mother, my eldest brother, a female cousin, and . . . another girl."[1]

Somerville served as the organist and choir director of Castlehaven Church for seventy-five years. She managed the family estate from 1898, when her father died, until 1943, when she was eighty-four years of age. Among her innovations was the importation of the first herd of Friesian cows into Ireland. She bought and sold horses in America and in England, and added to the family income by exhibiting and selling her paintings. An avid rider, she was the first woman named Master of Foxhunting in West Carbery, a position that she held from 1903 to 1908 and 1912 to 1919.

Somerville was a charter member of the Irish Academy of Letters, which was formed in 1932. That same year Trinity College, Dublin, awarded her an honorary Litt. D. degree. The Irish Academy recognized the excellence of the works of Somerville and Ross in 1941 when it bestowed the Gregory Gold Medal on them. Somerville chaired the bicentennial celebration of the death of Jonathan Swift, which was held at the University of Cork in 1945. To commemorate her ninetieth birthday, the BBC aired a special program dedicated to the achievements of Somerville and Ross. She died on October 8, 1949, at Drishane and was buried in the Castlehaven Churchyard next to her friend, cousin, and collaborator, Violet Martin.

Martin, Violet Florence

Born: Ross, County Galway, Ireland, June 11, 1862
Education: Alexandra College, Dublin
Died: Cork, Ireland, December 21, 1915

Biography

Violet Florence Martin, the daughter of James Martin and Anna Selina Fox, was born June 11, 1862, in Ross, Connemara, Ireland. She was the eleventh daughter and youngest child in a family of fourteen (James Martin was married twice and had four daughters by his first wife, who died in childbirth). As the youngest child (and a girl), Violet was "a dear little child, but quite unnoticed in the nursery" (*Irish Memories*, 97). She was a precocious child, learning to read at an early age and excelling at the piano. She received her early education at home, a curriculum which included French and Greek. When her father died in 1872, the family moved to Dublin. It was there that Martin attended Sunday school and rubbed elbows with many elements of Irish society. These experiences with people culturally different from her were later used in her writings with Somerville. Like Somerville, she attended Alexandra College.

Martin's writing career began with articles in *Argosy* (1887) and *The World* (1888). It was from money made by selling such articles that she and her mother were able to return to Ross in 1888. Somerville says that while Mrs. Martin first broached the subject of moving back to the estate, "it was Martin who saved Ross" (*Irish Memories*, 154). Letters written to Somerville at this time reveal the amount of work necessary to restore the house to habitability (*Irish Memories*, 158–65). They illustrate Martin's descriptive capacity and her ability to see humor in trying situations: "An experience of last week was going to see a party of sisters who are tenants, and work their farm themselves. In the twinkling of an eye I was sitting 'back in the room,' with the sisterhood exhausting themselves in praise of my unparalleled beauty, and with a large glass of potheen before me, which I knew had got to be taken somehow" (*Irish Memories*, 163).

Martin loved riding as much as Somerville did, even though she was extremely myopic. In 1898, she sustained a fall while hunting and needed several years to recuperate from a serious back injury, although she resumed writing within a short time. Ultimately, she recovered to the extent that she was finally able to ride again. Her last illness was an inoperable brain tumor. She died on December 21, 1915, in Cork.

Literary Analysis

Somerville and Martin (whom Somerville always called "Martin Ross") were distant cousins through their mothers, both of whom were descended from Charles Kendal Bushe, Lord Chief Justice of Ireland. They did not meet, however, until January 17, 1886. Somerville grudgingly received the news that she would be expected to entertain her cousin when the Martin family came to Castle Townshend for a visit. At the time she was engaged in freelance writing and illustrating for the *Graphic*. Nevertheless, as Somerville said, the meeting proved to be "the hinge of my life, the place where my fate, and hers, turned over, and new and unforseen things began to happen to us" (*Irish Memories*, 122).

The collaboration of Somerville and Ross resulted first in the unexpectedly successful *An Irish Cousin* (1889), and *Naboth's Vineyard* (1891). They then toured Ireland, France, Wales, and Denmark, accumulating material for a series of travelogues commissioned by periodicals. *Through Connemara in a Governess Cart* (1893) is a collection of articles which first appeared in *The Ladies' Pictorial* and in which the humor that became a Somerville and Ross trademark is already evident: "'I'd be ashamed to show such weather to a Connemara pig,' I replied. Now Connemara is a sore subject with my second cousin, who lives within sight of its mountains, and, as is usually the case, has never explored the glories of her native country . . . She generally changes the conversation on these occasions; but this time she looked me steadily in the face and said, 'Well, let's go to Connemara!' I was so surprised that I inadvertently pressed the indiarubber ball of the whistle on which my hand was resting and its despairing wail filled the silence like a note of horror. 'Let's get an ass and an ass-car!' said my cousin, relapsing in her excitement into her native idiom."[2] Thus begins the saga of the trip through Connemara, fraught with adventures with stubborn horses and mules, aggressive beggar women (reputedly cousins of Ross), and "mad dogs." Interspersed with the narration is dialogue in Irish dialect as interpreted by the authors: "'A betther never shtud in Galway!' said another voice. 'She's better able to kill anny horse on the road'" (27). Somerville and Ross kept a notebook in which they collected specimens of dialect or amusing statements which they later used in their writings, often without alteration. Their written renderings of Irish dialect are considered among the finest attempted. One suspects that the maid "whose painful habit it was to whisper 'Do ye choose cherry or clarry?'" was based on recollections of actual maidservants whose command of English was entertaining even if less than perfect.[3]

While The Real Charlotte (1894), a novel about the conflict between good and evil, was considered by readers and critics alike to be their masterpiece (it was published in The World's Classics while Somerville was alive, an honor only similarly bestowed upon George Bernard Shaw), today Somerville and Ross are noted chiefly for three collections of short stories set in contemporary Ireland. Their chief protagonist is Major Sinclair Yeates, an Irish Royal Magistrate. Yeates, an Irishman himself, describes with droll humor the people, animals, and events with which he comes into contact in his official capacity as royal magistrate and leader (by virtue of his position) of the local social set. Mr. Florence Knox, affectionately called Flurry, Yeates's wife Philippa, and Maria, the family retriever, are only a few of the engaging characters found in Some Experiences of an Irish R.M. (1899), Further Experiences of an Irish R.M. (1908), and In Mr. Knox's Country (1915). The popularity of Some Experiences of an Irish R.M. can scarcely be overestimated. The book went through five reprintings in 1900 alone and three more in 1901. It is the only Somerville and Ross volume never to have been out of print. Somerville received letters from soldiers serving in World War I who told her that they listened to recitations from these stories while crouching in the trenches.

Yeates's first-person accounts spare no one, particularly himself. Although Yeates considered himself Irish and is thoroughly a gentleman, he is no match for the locals who delight in discomfiting him with their antics. Concerning his early days in Skebawn while waiting for his house to be readied, for example, he comments: "My most immediate concern, as anyone who has spent nine weeks at Mrs. Raverty's hotel will readily believe, was to leave it at the earliest opportunity; but in those nine weeks I had learned, amongst other painful things, a little, a very little, of the methods of the artisan in the west of Ireland. Finding a house had been easy enough. I had had my choice of several, each with some hundreds of acres of shooting, thoroughly poached, and a considerable portion of the roof intact. I had selected one; the one that had the largest extent of roof in proportion to the shooting, and had been assured by my landlord that in a fortnight or so it would be fit for occupation" (7). That the promise was not kept is the basis for a good share of the story, as Yeates routinely nails boards over rat holes, endures unbearable smells, and is plagued by the "ghost" of Great-Uncle McCarthy.

Hunting forms an important part of the gentry's entertainment and Yeates, an avid hunter, enters into the sport happily. The disasters that he encounters on his outings are related with tongue-in-cheek aplomb. For example, he calls attention to the required "trappings" of hunting when he relates the outcome of a duck hunting expedition: "I had left Mrs. Brickley's house a well-equipped sportsman, creditably escorted by Peter Cadogan and the widower. I returned to it a muddy and dripping outcast, attended by two little girls, two goats, and her own eight ducks whom my hand had widowed" (344). His relationships with the "locals" provide further examples of merriment and simultaneously show how Somerville and Ross combined elements of the unexpected to create humorous conclusions for their stories. In "Trinket's Colt," Flurry Knox, the resident horse trader par excellence, offers Yeates a colt which his grandmother, the venerable Mrs. Knox, has given to him as a birthday present. The only hitch is that Mrs. Knox refuses to relinquish the colt, forcing Flurry to steal him: "The trouble began later, and was due, as trouble often is, to the beguilements of a short cut. Against the maturer judgement of Slipper, Flurry insisted on following a route that he assured us he knew as well as his own pocket, and the consequence was that in about five minutes I found myself standing on top of a bank hanging on to a rope, on the other end of which the colt dangled and danced, while Flurry, with the other rope, lay prone in the ditch" (69–70). The climax of this story occurs when Major Yeates finds the colt buried up to its neck in sand and covered with furze bushes to hide it from the justifiably irate Mrs. Knox. Mrs. Knox's dog then finds Yeates himself crouching in a ditch, also hiding from her. The ensuing tussle as Yeates tries to quiet the dog draws the irascible grandmother away from her argument with Flurry to investigate. When she sees the buried colt, the truth dawns upon her, but instead of suffering the heart attack that the ever-gentlemanly Major fears, she breaks into peals of laughter and hands over the colt, avowing she will have nothing to do with receiving "stolen goods." The final twist occurs when Mrs. Knox admits to Flurry: "Upon my conscience, Tony, I'd give a guinea to have thought of it myself" (75).

The character of Philippa Yeates provides more humorous opportunities for Somerville and Ross. Although a stranger to Ireland and the ways of the Irish when she becomes Yeates's bride, she soon becomes intrigued with her new environment and the oddities of her neighbors. Says Yeates: "Philippa, however, proved adorably callous to these and similar shortcomings. She regarded Shreelane and its floundering, foundering menage of incapables in the light of a gigantic picnic in a foreign land; she held long conversations with Mrs. Cadogan, in order, as she informed me, to acquire the language; without any ulterior domestic intention she engaged kitchen-maids because of the beauty of their eyes, and housemaids because they had such delightfully picturesque old mothers" (111). The development of her personality over the course of the short stories as she becomes the mother of two preserves its humorous aspects, as is illustrated by her ecstatic welcome of the chimney-sweep Cantillon in "Harrington's" (468). Philippa summarily evicts her houseguests so that the sweep, whom she treats with great dignity and respect, can do his work in peace: "'My poor friends,' she continued, 'this means a cold luncheon for you and a still colder reception for me from Mrs. Cadogan [the housekeeper], but if I let Cantillon escape me now, I may never see him again—which is unthinkable" (469). The exaggerated courtesy accorded the chimney-sweep humorously points out his importance in nineteenth-century Ireland where fireplaces provided the chief means of heat and cooking.

Philippa's reception of Cantillon must have been duplicated many times over with similar fervor throughout the countryside.

Philippa's delight in foxhunting belies her knowledge of the reason for the chase. In "Philippa's Foxhunt," she mistakenly believes that Mrs. Knox sends the urchin Johnny into the culvert to save a cub's life after the hunting dog has trapped it. While many contemporary readers may not find the ending amusing, the events leading up to it provide ample humor, particularly as the Major, who related the story, is unable to provide an accurate description on account of Philippa's confusion of the actual sequence of events. As Philippa runs to obtain help to extract the now-trapped boy, she encounters a troop of local clergy, one of whom is Mrs. Knox's "sworn enemy," out for a hike. Her garbled tale makes them believe that Mrs. Knox herself is drowning and precipitates a headlong cross-country chase with Philippa in the lead. When Yeates himself appears on the scene, having witnessed Philippa apparently being pursued by the ministers, he finds Mrs. Knox and her enemy each pulling on a leg of poor Johnny who is still stuck in the culvert while they simultaneously are carrying on a spirited argument.

Philippa's untroubled personality is a foil to the perennially serious Yeates. This is clearly evidenced in "A Horse! A Horse!": "Any fair-minded person will admit that I had cause to be excessively angry with Philippa. That a grown woman, the mother of two children, should mistake the bellow of a bullock for the note of a horn was bad enough; but that when, having caused a serious accident by not knowing her right hand from her left, and having by further insanities driven one valuable horse adrift into the country, probably broken the back of another, laid the seeds of heart disease in her husband from shock and over-exertion, and of rheumatic fever in herself; when, I repeat, after all these outrages, she should sit in a soaking heap by the roadside, laughing like a maniac, I feel that the sympathy of the public will not be withheld from me" (371–72). Yeates's exasperation and his desire to maintain decorum at all costs is opposed by Philippa's unrestrained reaction to the day's bizarre chain of events. His fears are soon discovered to be unfounded, and the whole episode ends happily as Philippa, still convulsed with laughter, is helped to a waiting automobile and taken home while her husband is left to contemplate the outcome bemusedly.

The humor of Somerville and Ross extends to the thoroughly recognizable personalities and behaviors that they attribute to the horses and dogs which they include in their stories. By far the most memorable is Maria, the Yeates' retriever, whose character was taken from a real dog having the same name. Maria features in "The House of Fahy," one of the most incongruous and therefore one of the most hilarious of all of the stories, in which are successfully combined a shipwreck, an insane asylum, and an aggressive cockatoo.[4]

Anyone who has lived for any length of time with a pet will readily identify with Yeates's description of his dog: "Nothing could shake the conviction of Maria that she was by nature and by practice a house dog. Every one of Shreelane's many doors had, at one time or another, slammed upon her expulsion, and each one of them had seen her stealthy, irrepressible return to the sphere that she felt herself so eminently qualified to qualify . . . She knew to a nicety which of the doors could be burst open by assault, at which it was necessary to whine sycophantically; and the clinical thermometer alone could furnish a parallel for her perception of mood in those in authority" (184).

In this instance, Maria has been left behind as Sinclair and Philippa board a yacht for what will be a very eventful weekend. Maria decides to join the party and thus swims to the ship where she is brought aboard by her sympathetic mistress despite the loud but futile protestations of her master. Thus, as Yeates intones, "the element of fatality had already begun to work" (188). Almost everyone onboard, including Maria, instantly becomes seasick. Philippa and a female companion soon discover that the bed linens are filthy, and they set about cleaning everything. The next "element of fatality" occurs when the yacht runs aground in the dark and threatens to sink, forcing the whole party, including Maria, to abandon ship and look for shelter. They locate a house which is soon identified as the local insane asylum. One of the inmates, Mrs. Buck, owns a nasty cockatoo which attacks the unwilling guests, causing them to flee in terror to another room.

The next morning Maria, who has temporarily disappeared, is found holding the bird's corpse between her front paws, thereby contributing again to Yeates's prophecy of "fatality." Yeates and a companion, both exhausted after spending a restless night and overtly aghast at what Maria has done (though secretly very happy about the bird's demise), decide to conceal the evidence by burying the bird in the garden before making their escape back to the ship which has been raised off the sandbar. They convince themselves that they have committed the perfect crime which they vow never to reveal to the ladies. They have not, however, reckoned with Maria. Their crime and their plan are summarily and humorously revealed in the tale's final sentence as the last "element of fatality" is introduced: "At this time juncture Maria overtook us with the cockatoo in her mouth" (201).

Sir Patrick Coghill, describing Somerville and Ross, remembered his famous aunt and cousin in this way: "Both had a blazing sense of humour, the golden gift of sympathetic conversation and cast-iron memories."[5] They used these talents liberally to laugh at themselves and their families in their work. Somerville says, for example, that when she and Ross were unable to pay a doctor's bill in full, the doctor suggested they "toss for it." "'Done!' called Martin feebly, from within. The doctor and I tossed, double or quits, sudden death. I won. And there came a faint cock-crow from the inner chamber" (*Irish Memories*, 296–97). Their efforts at canvassing for political candidates were so successful that they received the nickname of "Irish locusts" from a local Radical group.

Describing her mother's "common sense," Somerville says that the problem of what to give an elderly servant for Christmas was solved when her mother suggested, "Give her a nice shroud: There's nothing in the world she'd like as well as that" (*Irish Memories*, 89)! On the subject of aunts, she writes, "When I consider their attitude towards the other sex, and specially with reference to husbands and brothers, and sons—(less severely in the case of sons)—(I have known a woman who, when asked the foolish question which she loved best, her husband or her son, replied unhesitatingly, 'Me son of course! Why wouldn't I love me own son better than a strange man!')—their point of view was as entirely illogical as it was practical. Not at all did they dispute the Biblical pronouncements as to the superiority of the male sex, nor challenge men's Divinely allotted Supremacy. Yet they were serenely aware that in all the basic facts of life, illness, servants, children, their decisions overruled all others, standing firm, unshaken by masculine objections, and quite uninfluenced by the views expressed in the Old

Testament."[6] On herself and her incessant quest for models for her drawings, Somerville remarks, "Of another series dealing with the adventures of a student of the violin in Paris, I find in my diary the moving entry, 'Crucified Martin head downwards, as the fiddle girl, practising, with her music on the floor. Compelled H . . . . to pose as a Paris tram horse, in white stockings, with a chowrie for a tail'" (*Irish Memories*, 123). Ross's diary entry about the acceptance of *An Irish Cousin* clearly shows her sense of humor: "All comment is inadequate. Wrote a dizzy letter of acceptance to Bentley, and went to church, twice, in a glorified trance" (*Irish Memories*, 136).

Somerville and Ross were ardent supporters of women's suffrage and were members of the Women's Council of the Conservative and Unionist Women's Franchise Association. Both held executive positions in the Munster Women's Franchise League: Somerville was elected president, and Ross was vice president. Ross was a strong unionist, and opposed Home Rule for Ireland—*Irish Memories* contains an exchange of letters between her and Stephen Gwynn on this subject (314–23). Her death preceded Irish independence. Somerville supported dominion status for Ireland because of her desire for peace, and she ultimately reconciled herself to the new political order in her country.

A commonly asked question was how the two women created their texts. Somerville's invariable response was that the effort was conversational: "One or other—not infrequently both simultaneously,—would state a proposition. This would be argued, combated perhaps, approved or modified; it would then be written down by the (wholly fortuitous) holder of the pen, would be scratched out, scribbled in again."[7] Because their handwriting was so similar, in later years even Somerville could not determine who had written particular passages in their notebooks. Furthermore, it is not readily possible to detect within the texts two separate minds at work. The only way to undertake an analysis is to examine articles known to be written by Ross alone. According to Somerville, Ross had a flawless sense of style, a "more knife-edged slice of sarcasm," and greater poetic feeling than she did. To herself, based on her artistic training, Somerville ascribed the descriptive passages and the movement of the action. Somerville alleged that she continued to collaborate with Ross after her cousin's death in

1915, and she insisted that both names appear on the title page of many subsequent novels.

Somerville and Ross were active during the early days of the Irish Literary Revival but for reasons known only to themselves, they remained distanced from it, perhaps by mere geography or perhaps by conscious design. A request for a play, made by Lady Augusta Gregory, a cousin of Ross's, was politely but firmly refused.

Summary

Though their literary output was prodigious, the reputation of Edith Somerville and Martin Ross remains firmly fixed on the many adventures of Sinclair Yeates, Irish R.M., and his zany friends, relatives, and associates. These vignettes of contemporary Irish life provide a realistic but thoroughly humorous view of a culture in transition.

Notes

1. E. OE. Somerville and Martin Ross, *Irish Memories* (New York: Longmans, Green, 1918), pp. 110–11.
2. Somerville and Ross, *Through Connemara in a Governess Cart* (London: W.H. Allen, 1893), pp. 2–3.
3. All citations for the "Irish R.M." stories will be taken from Somerville and Ross, *The Irish R.M.* (New York: Penguin Books, 1984). This is the first collection of all three works into one volume. See page 111.
4. This tale, retitled "Maria," is the lead story in *Maria, and Some Other Dogs* (London: Methuen, 1949).
5. Sir Patrick Coghill, "Somerville and Ross," *Hermathena*, 79 (1952), p. 56.
6. Somerville and Ross, *Happy Days!* (Toronto: Longmans, Green, 1946), p. 37.
7. Maurice Collis, *Somerville and Ross: A Biography* (London: Faber & Faber, 1968), p. 45.

Selected Bibliography
Primary Sources
  This listing represents only the major works of Somerville and Ross.

Novels and Collections of Short Stories
An Irish Cousin. London: R. Bentley, 1889; London: Longmans, Green, 1903. Somerville used the pseudonym of

Geilles Herring in the 1889 first edition and Viva Graham in the second edition.

Naboth's Vineyard. London: Spencer Blackett, 1891.

The Real Charlotte. London: Ward and Downey, 1894.

The Silver Fox. London: Lawrence and Bullen, 1898.

Some Experiences of an Irish R.M. London: Longmans, Green, 1899.

A Patrick Day's Hunt. London: Constable, 1902.

Slipper's ABC of Foxhunting. London: Longmans, Green, 1903.

All on the Irish Shore. London: Longmans, Green, 1903.

Some Irish Yesterdays. London: Longmans, Green, 1906.

Further Experiences of an Irish R.M. London: Longmans, Green, 1908.

Dan Russel the Fox. London: Methuen, 1911.

The Story of the Discontented Little Elephant. London: Longmans, Green, 1912.

In Mr. Knox's Country. London: Longmans, Green, 1915.

Mount Music. London: Longmans, Green, 1919.

The Big House of Inver. London: Heinemann, 1925.

The Smile and the Tear. London: Methuen, 1933.

The Sweet Cry of Hounds. London: Methuen, 1936.

Sarah's Youth. London: Longmans, Green, 1938.

Notions in Garrison. London: Methuen, 1941.

The Irish R.M. New York: Penguin Books, 1984.

Autobiographical and Biographical Books, Essays, and Articles

Irish Memories. London: Longmans, Green, 1917; New York: Longmans, Green, 1918.

Stray-Aways. London: Longmans, Green, 1920.

Wheel-Tracks. London: Longmans, Green, 1923.

An Incorruptible Irishman. London: Ivor Nicholson and Watson, 1932.

"Two of a Trade." *Irish Writing*, 1 (1946): 79–85.

Happy Days! London: Longmans, Green, 1946.

Maria, and Some Other Dogs. London: Methuen, 1949.

Miscellaneous

Through Connemara in a Governess Cart. London: W.H. Allen, 1893.

In the Vine Country. London: W.H. Allen, 1893.

Beggars on Horseback. London: Blackwood, 1895.

Published under Somerville's name alone

An Enthusiast. London: Longmans, Green, 1921.

Secondary Sources

Books

Collis, Maurice. *Somerville and Ross: A Biography.* London: Faber & Faber, 1968. Generally balanced account of the lives of the two authors.

Cronin, John. *Somerville and Ross.* Lewisburg, PA: Bucknell University Press, 1972. Bio-critical text, with emphasis on criticism. Especially interesting is Cronin's analysis of the works done by Somerville after Ross's death. Contains useful bibliography.

Cummins, Geraldine. *Dr. E. OE. Somerville: A Biography.* London: Andrew Dakers, 1952. Cummins was a friend of Somerville in later life. Her sentimental biography treats of, among others, their mutual interest in spiritualism. Contains Robert Vaughan's listing of the first editions of Somerville and Ross.

O'Brien, Conor Cruise. *Writers and Politics.* London: Chatto & Windus, 1965. Considers Somerville and Ross in light of the changing political situation in Ireland.

Powell, Violet. *The Irish Cousins.* London: Heinemann, 1970. Insightful but rambling biography. Contains summaries of major works.

Robinson, Hilary. *Somerville and Ross: A Critical Appreciation.* Dublin: Gill and MacMillan, 1980. Important for its extensive bibliography of works by and about Somerville and Ross.

Articles

Coghill, Sir Patrick. "Somerville and Ross." *Hermathena*, 79 (1952): 47–60. Biographical, critical article originally presented as an address in 1951. Coghill was nephew of Somerville and cousin of Ross.

Cronin, John. "Dominant Themes in the Novels of Somerville and Ross." In *Somerville and Ross: A Symposium.* Belfast: The Queen's University, 1969, pp. 8–19. Cronin explores the novels which reflect Anglo-Irish Ascendancy as portrayed by Somerville and Ross.

Lyons, F.S.L. "The Twilight of the Big House." *Ariel,* 1 (July 1970): 110–22. Biographical, critical article. Lyons considers how the two women composed their texts.

MacCarthy, B.G. "E. OE. Somerville and Martin Ross." *Studies* (1945): 183–94. MacCarthy discusses lesser-known novels by Somerville and Ross.

McMahon, Sean. "John Bull's Other Ireland: A Consideration of *The Real Charlotte* by Somerville and Ross." *Eire/Ireland,* 3, 4 (1968): 119–35. In-depth critical article on "their best work together."

Mitchell, Hilary. "Somerville and Ross: Amateur to Professional." In *Somerville and Ross: A Symposium.* Belfast: The Queen's University, 1969, pp. 20–37. Mitchell employs letters and diaries to consider "to what extent being women and being Anglo-Irish influenced the development of Somerville and Ross as writers."

Power, Ann. "The Big House of Somerville and Ross." *The Dubliner,* 3 (1964): 43–53. Another examination of novels reflecting the Anglo-Irish Ascendancy. Power discusses and compares novels written after death of Ross.

Natalie Joy Woodall

Southey, Robert

Born: Bristol, August 12, 1774
Education: Westminster School, April 1788–April 1792; Balliol College, Oxford University, November 1792–July 1794
Marriage: Edith Fricker, November 14, 1795, eight children; Caroline Bowles, June 5, 1839
Died: Keswick, March 21, 1843

Biography

Robert Southey was born in Bristol on August 12, 1774. The son of a linen-draper, he was entrusted, from age two to six, to a tyrannical maiden aunt. After attending schools at Bristol and Corston he entered Westminster, a leading public school, in 1788 but he was expelled in 1792 for writing a pamphlet in which corporal punishment was stigmatized as inspired by the Devil. Admitted to Balliol College, Oxford University, in November 1792, he became friendly with Samuel Taylor Coleridge in June 1794 and planned with him a utopian scheme of emigration to America that came to nothing.

On November 14, 1795, the very day of his secret marriage to Edith Fricker (the sister of Coleridge's wife), he left for Portugal alone in order to visit an uncle of his, the Reverend Herbert Hill, chaplain to the British Factory at Lisbon. Two stays in the Iberian Peninsula (December 1795–April 1796 and May 1800 to June 1801) were to turn Southey into an authority on Spanish and Portuguese literature and history. In September 1803, he settled in the Lake District, at Greta Hall, Keswick, which remained his home till his last day. There he led a secluded life remarkable for unremitting literary activities (he received an honorary D.C.L. from Oxford on June 14, 1820). His being appointed poet laureate in 1813 was hailed by the radicals as evidence of his ideological apostasy; indeed, by 1810, the former enthusiastic supporter of the French Revolution had become a staunch conservative vilified as a "turncoat" by his political enemies. The publication in 1821 of *A Vision of Judgement,* a ridiculous poem in praise of George III, led to a severe quarrel with Lord Byron. A warm advocate of public order and a leading contributor to the *Quarterly Review,* he resented social inequality but strongly opposed Catholic emancipation and parliamentary reform.

The loss in 1816 of nine-year-old Herbert, his favorite of his eight children, was a terrible blow from which he never recovered. Following the death of his wife in 1837, on June 5, 1839, he married Caroline Bowles, a woman of letters with whom he had long been corresponding. Shortly afterward his mind and memory failed, and the insanity that spoiled the last four years of his life can almost certainly be diagnosed as Alzheimer's disease. The author died in Keswick on March 21, 1843.

Literary Analysis

The bulk of Southey's literary output is astounding. The poetical works readily fall into three categories: the early poems, the long narrative poems, and the laureate verse. Of the latter very little need be said. *The Poet's Pilgrimage to Waterloo* (1816) and *A Vision of*

Judgement, which gave rise to Byron's devastatingly parodic *The Vision of Judgment* (1822), are dull poems that deserve only sarcasm. A striking sample of political invective, "Ode Written during the Negotiations with Buonaparte, in January, 1814" is the only laureate ode worth preserving from oblivion.

Southey's early poems were influenced mostly by the French Revolution. He expressed his revolutionary views as early as 1794 in his *Botany Bay Eclogues,* (in which he depicted convicts as victims of an oppressive State), as well as in two crude radical "dramas," *The Fall of Robespierre* (1794) and *Wat Tyler* (1817). The humanitarianism of "The Pauper's Funeral," "The Soldier's Wife," "The Widow," "The Soldier's Funeral," and "The Battle of Blenheim" (*Poems*, 1795, 1797) should also be related to his early revolutionary ideals. His would-be epic *Joan of Arc* (1796), whose eponymous heroine Coleridge dubbed "a Tom Paine in petticoats," boils down to a provocative political manifesto in which the medieval background is but an excuse for extolling the 1789 French ideal of liberty, equality, and fraternity. *English Eclogues* (composed between 1797 and 1803) offers a realistic picture of country life not unlike that in William Wordsworth's *Lyrical Ballads*.

Southey's long narrative poems, in which exoticism is artificially coupled with Christian preoccupations, are seldom read today. The hero of *Thalaba* (1801), which is set in Arabia, is a young, brave Muslim whose long quest ends in the destruction of the Domdaniel cavern under the sea. In *Madoc* (1805) the poet deals with the adventures of a twelfth-century Welsh prince bent on fighting the Aztecs in the New World. To the oriental imagery of earth, heaven, and hell in *The Curse of Kehama* (1810), a poem based on Hindu mythology, the modern reader will invariably prefer the less outlandish Spanish setting of *Roderick, the Last of the Goths* (1814), in which the guilty protagonist, a man "more sinned against than sinning," is incomparably closer to us than immaculate characters such as Ladurlad and Thalaba. And yet, *Thalaba* and *The Curse of Kehama* greatly appealed to Percy Bysshe Shelley and proved seminal poems whose influence is traceable in *Queen Mab, Alastor,* and even *Prometheus Unbound*. The author of *Joan of Arc, Botany Bay Eclogues,* and *English Eclogues* actively participated in the regeneration of poetry, paving the way for greater poets than himself. His contemporaries regarded him as a zealous champion of the new spirit permeating late eighteenth-century poetry. Characteristically, Southey, and not Wordsworth or Coleridge, was hailed by *The Anti-Jacobin* as the leader of "the New School of Poetry."

The most vital part of Southey's verse is *Metrical Tales, and Other Poems* (1805). Ballads such as "Donica," "Jaspar," "Rudiger," "Lord William," "Roprecht the Robber," and "Mary, the Maid of the Inn," in which the threefold influence of Thomas Percy's *Reliques* (1765), Gothic fiction, and German Romantic poetry is easily traceable, testify to a vigorous handling of the supernatural, the terrifying, and the gruesome. In "The Inchcape Rock" (a masterpiece of comic invention according to many critics), "The Old Woman of Berkeley," and "God's Judgement on a Wicked Bishop," the terrifying vein is inseparable from a simple moral lesson: villains are always punished in this or another world. Sir Ralph, the pirate of "The Inchcape Rock," is unintentionally the cause of his own death as his ship smashes against a submerged reef previously signaled by a bell that he himself had maliciously removed one year earlier: the grim humor of the poem lies in the fact that, like Lord William, Sir Ralph meets the same end as the one that he has inflicted upon his unfortunate victims.

Southey's producing a burlesque parody of "The Woman of Berkeley" called "The Surgeon's Warning" shows evidence of his desire to integrate humor into his ballads. "St. Michael's Chair" is about the accidental death of Rebecca, a cantankerous shrew who gets killed, to her husband's complete satisfaction, for wanting to be a domineering wife. In "The King of the Crocodiles," Southey depicts a domestic quarrel between Mr. and Mrs. Crocodile in which the representative of the stronger sex is rapidly defeated. In "King Charlemain" the writer shows the illustrious emperor under a spell that makes him fall in love with an octogenarian bishop to whom he makes indecent proposals. In "The March to Moscow" (composed in 1813), the poet's verve is directed against Napoleon, irreverently called "The Emperor Nap"; fun is mainly derived from the systematic use of swear words like "Morbleu," "Sacrebleu," and "Ventrebleu," and from the accumulation of Russian names ending in *-itch*, *-off*, or *-offsky*. The Devil is often a laughingstock in Southey's ballads. In "A True Ballad of St. Antidius, the Pope, and the Devil," the writer comically depicts the joy of the Devil on hearing that the Pope has committed a deadly sin:

> He wagg'd his ears, he twisted his tail,
> He knew not for joy what to do,
> In his hoofs and his horns, in his heels
>   and his corns,
> It tickled him all through.

"The Pious Painter" presents Beelzebub in a ridiculous light as he complains of the unflattering portrait that has been made of him.

When Southey derides the Devil in *Ballads and Metrical Tales*, he removes the terrifying aspects of a creature that probably frightened him even though he would not acknowledge his fear. Humor thus appears as one of the means that he used to escape the hold of the supernatural. Mocking one's own anxiety is the surest way of controlling it. When Southey ridicules Napoleon in "The March to Moscow," for instance, he actually silences his unavowed fear of the French tyrant, whose image is reflected in the raja (an embodiment of evil) of *The Curse of Kehama*. The author of an article in the *Edinburgh Review* in January 1839 judiciously pointed out that Southey's most interesting ballads are those in which the poet opts for a humorous or half-serious tone and plays with the supernatural: "We have often suspected, when perusing these *pia hilaria* . . . that the superstitions that he ridicules have a strong and inexplicable hold on his understanding. . . . Dealers in burlesque ghost stories are generally those who have a lurking credulity about apparitions." Indeed, the humor that is used by the poet of *Ballads and Metrical Tales* to neutralize the supernatural looks very much like a self-defense device.

Southey's vigorous, direct, pellucid prose, utterly devoid of mannerism, is the very opposite of Samuel Johnson's Latinized style. "My rule of writing," Southey said, "whether for prose or verse, is the same, and may very shortly be stated. It is, to express myself, 1st, as perspicuously as possible; 2nd, as concisely as possible; 3rd, as impressively as possible." This statement is echoed by Coleridge's assertion that "in the very best of styles, as Southey's, you read page after page, understanding the author perfectly, without once taking notice of the medium of communication:—it is as if he had been speaking to you all the while." A more versatile and prolific prose writer than Southey can hardly be found in the whole of English literature. His prose writings include committed essays, history books, biographies, travel journals, editorial labors, translations, an unclassifiable work with autobiographical overtones entitled *The Doctor, etc.*, and—last but not least—an exceptionally voluminous correspondence.

Essays, Moral and Political (1832) represents only an infinitesimal portion of the numerous review articles that he wrote for the *Monthly Magazine*, the *Critical Review*, the *Annual Review*, and the *Quarterly Review*. *Letters from England* (1807), supposedly written by a young Spaniard spending one and a half years in Britain, arose from a sincere love of the Iberian Peninsula combined with a genuine interest in the social and political problems with which England was confronted in the days of the Industrial Revolution. The manufacturing system, poverty, education, the condition of women, and Catholic emancipation are discussed at some length in *Sir Thomas More: or, Colloquies on the Progress and Prospects of Society* (1829).

The laureate was undoubtedly even more successful as a biographer than as a historian. Prolixity, overemphasis of details, and a damaging lack of synthetic views mar both his bulky *History of Brazil* (1810–1819) and his *History of the Peninsular War* (1823–1832). Interesting and well-documented as the *Life of Wesley* (1820) is, it cannot vie in popularity with the *Life of Nelson* (1813), a neatly arranged little book with an epic quality that proved largely instrumental in making the hero of Trafalgar a legendary figure whose halo has never faded since.

In his travel journals (*Letters Written during a Short Residence in Spain and Portugal* [1797], *Journals of a Residence in Portugal 1800–1801 and a Visit to France 1838*, *Journal of a Tour in the Netherlands in the Autumn of 1815*, and *Journal of a Tour in Scotland in 1819*), Southey proves an attentive and often humorous observer of men and manners.

Eccentricity is the dominant note of *The Doctor, etc.*, the first two volumes of which were first published anonymously (1834). According to Edgar Allan Poe, "The wit and humour of the 'Doctor' have seldom been equalled." "A lengthy and elaborate jest" in Walter Bagehot's opinion, *The Doctor* similarly appealed to George Saintsbury, who regarded it as "one of the most delightful books in English," as well as to Edmund Blunden, who unhesitatingly asserted that "if any one of Southey's many books could freshen his presence among the authors of England, it is *The Doctor*." This highly disconcerting book is a hybrid work with hardly any plot. The story of Dr. Daniel Dove of Doncaster forms only a slender thread. The bulk of the work consists of endless digressions upon innumerable authors. "I see in the work," Southey aptly remarked, "a little of Rabelais, but not much; more of Tristram Shandy, somewhat of Burton, and perhaps more of Montaigne; but methinks the *quintum quid* predominates." That the *quintum quid* is Southey himself cannot be doubted. As M.H. Fitzgerald rightly pointed out, "Southey delights us, in *The Doctor*, with his displays of curious learning, his brave and cheerful outlook upon life, his meditative wisdom; now and again with some quaint stroke of humour which hits the mark; while such passages as the story of the Three Bears, the memoir of the Cats of Greta Hall, or the accounts of Joseph Glover's statues, make our hearts warm towards 'one whose spirit, grave with a man's wisdom, was pure as the spirit of a little child.'" The blue gothic letters of the enigmatic dedication "To the Bhow Begum Kedora Niabarma" in chapter II.A.I., the intriguing symbol of chapter IV.A.I. and of the title-page, the three successive question and exclamation marks of chapter VI.A.I., the descending pagination of the seven chapters before the ante-preface and the preface, and the "initial chapter" distinct from chapter I, are all clownish tricks reminiscent of Laurence Sterne's fancifulness in *Tristram Shandy*. Just as Southey piles up quotation upon quotation, he relishes handling and parading words. Reading *The Doctor,* one often feels as if the handling of so many words—English, foreign, or coined—made him giddy. He coins substantives (*potamology, felisofy, kittenhood*), adjectives (*unipsefying, farraginous, bablative*), and verbs (*to crabgrade, to impossibilitate*). He has a penchant for such barbarous terms as *agathokakological, Prothesis, Epenthesis, Antiptosis, Ischnotesism,* and *Plateasm.* He takes pleasure in actually juggling with words as in the following sentence: "Secondly, the flea which came upon my paper was a real flea, a flea of flea-flesh and blood, partly flea-blood and partly mine, which the same flea had flea-feloniously appropriated to himself by his own

process of flea-botomy. That which appeared upon St. Dominic's book was the Devil in disguise." Such verbal pirouettings are typical of Southey's humor in *The Doctor*, a book in which the boundaries of language seem to have been pushed further and further, with the words taking on a magic virtue independent of their meaning. Certainly, "Aballiboozobanganorribo" is the utmost limit reached by a language the function of which is less to mean than to be. *The Doctor*, therefore, appears as an unusual work in which the author, deliberately parodying himself, displays the kind of supreme detachment that is a hallmark of humor. *The Doctor* is not so much the story of Dr. Daniel Dove of Doncaster as it is the story of a Lake man of letters looking at himself writing a story.

Summary

"Take my word for it, Sir," Edgeworth once said to Robert Southey, "the bent of your genius is for comedy." A very emotional man, Southey, hailed as "the Chief Bard of the Lakes" by many of his contemporaries, insisted on methodically repressing the sensibility and unconscious anxiety that formed the deeper aspect of his personality. His rejection of heartfelt lyricism should be related to a characteristic process of censorship in which the deeper self was overcome by the superego. It was in such a process that Southey's quaint humor had its origins. The author of the long narrative poems *Madoc*, *Thalaba*, and *The Curse of Kehama* never actually integrated the substance of his dreams (which he wrote down in his "dream-book") into his poetry. A Lake man of letters rather than Lake poet, Southey stood halfway between rationalism and Romanticism, participating in both, possessed by neither. Even so, his influence in the development of English Romanticism was far greater than is commonly admitted.

Selected Bibliography

Primary Sources

Verse
The Poetical Works of Robert Southey, Collected by Himself. 10 vols. London: Longman, 1837–1838. Reprinted in one volume, 1845, 1850, 1863, 1873.
Poems of Robert Southey. Ed. M.H. Fitzgerald. Oxford University Press, 1909. Contains *Thalaba, The Curse of*

Kehama, Roderick, Madoc, A Tale of Paraguay, and Selected Minor Poems. Ed. M.H. Fitzgerald. London: Oxford University Press, 1909.

A Choice of Robert Southey's Verse. Ed. G. Grigson. London: Faber and Faber, 1970.

Prose
Letters from England: By Don Manuel Alvarez Espriella. Translated from the Spanish. Ed. J. Simmons. 1807. London: Cresset Press, 1951.

History of Brazil. 1810–1819.

The Life of Nelson. London: Murray, 1813; ed. G. Callender, 1922; ed. E.R.H. Harvey, 1953.

The Life of Wesley; and the Rise and Progress of Methodism. 1820. Ed. M.H. Fitzgerald, 1925.

History of the Peninsular War. London: Murray, 1823–1832.

Sir Thomas More: or, Colloquies on the Progress and Prospects of Society. 1829.

The Doctor, etc. 1834–1847. Ed. (abridged) M.H. Fitzgerald. London: G. Bell and Sons, 1930.

Journal of a Tour in the Netherlands in the Autumn of 1815. Ed. W.R. Nicoll. London, 1903.

Select Prose of Robert Southey. Ed. J. Zeitlin. New York: Macmillan, 1916.

Journal of a Tour in Scotland in 1819. Ed. C.H. Herford. London, 1929.

Journals of a Residence in Portugal 1800–1801 and a Visit to France 1838. Ed. A. Cabral. Oxford: Clarendon, 1960.

Works Edited or Translated by Southey
The Works of Thomas Chatterton. In collaboration with J. Cottle. London, 1803.

Amadis of Gaul. London, 1803.

Palmerin of England. London, 1807.

Chronicle of the Cid. London, 1808.

The Pilgrim's Progress. With a Life of John Bunyan. London, 1830.

The Works of William Cowper. With a Life of the Author. London: Baldwin and Cradock, 1835–1837.

Letters
The Life and Correspondence of Robert Southey. Ed. C.C. Southey. 6 vols. London, 1849–1850.

Selections from the Letters of Robert Southey. Ed. J.W. Warter. 4 vols. London, 1856.

The Correspondence of Robert Southey with Caroline Bowles. To which are added: Correspondence with Shelley, and Southey's Dreams. Ed. E. Dowden. Dublin: Hodges, Figgis, 1881.

Letters of Robert Southey: A Selection. Ed. M.H. Fitzgerald. Oxford, 1912. World's Classics.

New Letters of Robert Southey. Ed. K. Curry. 2 vols. New York: Columbia University Press, 1965.

Secondary Sources

Biographies
Simmons, J. *Southey.* London: Collins, 1945. The standard biography.

Books
Bernhardt-Kabisch, E. *Robert Southey.* Boston: Twayne, 1977. A fair though not entirely reliable survey of Southey's verse and prose.

Carnell, G. *Robert Southey and His Age. The Development of a Conservative Mind.* Oxford: Clarendon, 1960. Essential for a full understanding of Southey's political thought.

Curry, K. *Southey.* London and Boston: Routledge & Kegan Paul, 1975. A neat, well-documented presentation of Southey's poems and prose works.

Haller, W. *The Early Life of Robert Southey.* New York: Columbia University Press, 1917. A sound critical analysis of Southey's early poetry, notably *Joan of Arc, Thalaba,* and minor poems as ballads.

Madden, L., ed. *Robert Southey. The Critical Heritage.* London and Boston: Routledge & Kegan Paul, 1972. A useful compilation of reviews of Southey's literary productions.

Raimond, J. *Robert Southey. L'homme et son temps. L'oeuvre. Le rôle.* Paris: Didier, 1968. A detailed study, at once analytic and synthetic, of all aspects of Southey's enormous literary output, including a definition of Southey's significance to his own generation.

Robert Southey. British Council pamphlet. London: Longmans, Green, 1964; 1971.

A short but pithy introduction to Southey's life and writings.

Articles
Anonymous. "Robert Southey: A Problem of Romanticism Poet Who Lost His Way." *Times Literary Supplement* (March 20, 1943): 142.
Curry, K. "Southey." In *The English Romantic Poets and Essayists. A Review of Research and Criticism.* Ed. C.W. and L.H. Houtchens. New York: Modern Language Association of America, 1957, pp. 158–87. By far the best bibliography of Southey.
———. "The Library of Robert Southey." *Tennessee Studies in Literature*, special number (1961): 77–86.
Elwin, M. "Robert Southey." *Quarterly Review*, 281 (1943): 187–201.
Jacobus, M. "Southey's Debt to *Lyrical Ballads*, 1798." *Review of English Studies*, NS, 22 (February 1971): 20–36.
Lounsbury, T.R. "Southey as Poet and Historian." *Yale Review*, NS, 4 (January 1915): 330–51.
Raimond, Jean. "Humour et romantisme: le cas de Robert Southey." Université de Clermont, Centre du romantisme anglais, Seminaire March 8–9, 1974.
"Southey's Early Writings and the Revolution." *The Yearbook of English Studies*, 19 (1989): 181–96.
"Wordsworth, the *Lyrical Ballads*, and Southey's Early Poetry." *Annales de l'Université Jean Moulin* (Lyon 3), 1978-2 (April 1979): 69–80.
Wright, H.G. "Three Aspects of Southey." *Review of English Studies*, 9 (1933): 37–46.

Jean Raimond

Spark, Muriel Sarah

Born: *Morningside, Edinburgh, Scotland, February 1, 1918*
Education: *James Gillespie's High School, Edinburgh; Heriot Watt College, Edinburgh*
Marriage: *Sydney Oswald Spark, 1937; dissolved 1938; one child*

Biography
The daughter of a Scottish Jewish father, Bernard, and an English mother, Sarah Elizabeth Maud Camberg, Muriel Sarah Camberg was born at the family home in Bruntsfield Place, Edinburgh on February 1, 1918, nine months before the end of World War I. She received both primary and secondary education at James Gillespie's High School where the school endowment scheme "allowed for parents like my own, of high aspirations and slender means, to pay moderate fees in return for educational services far beyond what they were paying for" (Spark, *Curriculum Vitae*). Her experiences at Gillespie's, where she was designated the "school poet," underpin her most famous novel, *The Prime of Miss Jean Brodie*. After commercial studies at Heriot Watt College, Muriel Camberg taught at a small private day school, the Hill School in Edinburgh, in return for free tuition in shorthand and typing, and worked in the office of a department store.

In 1937, Muriel became engaged to Sydney Oswald Spark, a man thirteen years her senior who was about to take up a teaching post in Southern Rhodesia, where the couple was married and where Muriel gave birth to a boy. As World War II began, she decided that her marriage was over due to her husband's mental instability. Leaving her son in the care of Dominican nuns, Muriel Spark risked the hazardous trip back to Britain and arrived there in March 1944, finding work in London with the Foreign Office. This work involved the dissemination of "black" propaganda or disinformation, such truth-mangling later becoming a strong concern in Spark's fiction.

In 1947, Spark became editor of the *Poetry Review*, the organ of the Poetry Society, after working as a researcher and writer on the *Argentor*, the quarterly of the National Jeweller's Association. Her editorship of the *Poetry Review* lasted two years in which time she made some very vocal antagonists within the Poetry Society. This eventually led to her dismissal. Throughout the 1950s, Spark produced literary criticism and critical editions of nineteenth-century English writers, including William Wordsworth, Mary Shelley, and Emily Brontë, sometimes in collaboration with Derek Stanford. Stanford, Spark claims, later produced grossly distorted memoirs of her life.

Spark enjoyed her first literary success in 1951 when her short story "The Seraph and the Zambesi" won the *Observer* newspaper Christmas story competition. Having been influenced by her strong interest in John Henry Newman, she became a Roman Catholic in 1954, but she claimed that "the Roman Catholic faith corresponded to what I had always felt and known and believed; there was no blinding revelation in my case" (*Curriculum Vitae*). Contracted to write a novel, Spark received financial support from Graham Greene and set about writing while living in Carmelite convents. In 1957, *The Comforters* was published and was admired by Evelyn Waugh.

Spark's career as a novelist was assured with the publication of her highly successful *Memento Mori* (1959) and *The Prime of Miss Jean Brodie* (1961). In 1965, she went to live in the United States and published *The Mandelbaum Gate*, a novel exploring Judaism and Catholicism which won the James Tait Black Memorial Prize. Two years later she was awarded the Order of the British Empire and took up residence in Rome. Her most experimental period began with the publication of *The Driver's Seat* (1970), which was followed by three more novels displaying an often harsh Post-Modern playfulness.

Since the mid-1970s, Spark has turned to a less complex mode of fiction, a more realistic mode than is evident in either her earliest novels or her Roman Nouveau period. Most recently Spark has published her nineteenth novel, *Symposium* (1990), and *Curriculum Vitae* (1992), the first volume of her autobiography.

Literary Analysis

Spark's humor emanates from her religious and aesthetic beliefs. As a Roman Catholic, she frequently qualifies reality in her fiction with *contemptus mundi* devices; as something of a Formalist and Post-Modernist, she often subverts realism by devices of authorial intrusion. Very often the end result of such maneuvers is a rather cruel black comedy as the combination of her religious and aesthetic tendencies locate Spark as something of a "cosmic joker." We see this most sharply in her short-story writing (which a number of critics have taken to be her strongest genre) where she is often at her most playful. In "The Portobello Road," for instance, she energizes a cliché by writing about a woman named Needle who is found murdered in a haystack. The seemingly gratuitous mocking of such a horrific event, however, has to be seen in relation to Spark's religious beliefs. The physical world is to be disregarded in its collision with the more essential reality of Grace and the spirit, as the comment of Needle's friend shows: "Kathleen, speaking from that Catholic point of view which takes some getting used to, said, 'She was at Confession only the day before she died—wasn't she lucky.'"

Spark again makes an almost facile joke in "The Black Madonna" when a childless couple is, after many years of fruitlessness, granted a child after praying to a black Madonna icon. The white, middle-class couple is shocked, though, to find that their child is black (as the result of a "throwback") and their discomfiture is further compounded by the fact that at the time of the child's conception they had been providing lodging for two young black men. The story confronts the couple's social and racial snobbery and reveals an uncomfortable, sardonic God.

On the larger scale of the novel, Spark's trickery is all the more shocking and her black humor perhaps reaches its apotheosis in *Not to Disturb* (1971) where her treatment of her characters might be labeled "casual" (as opposed to causal) when she metes out fate with a warm (relishing) humor but with a cold eye:

> Meanwhile the lightning, which strikes the clump of elms so that the two friends huddled there are killed instantly without pain, zig-zags across the lawns, illuminating the lily-pond and the sunken rose garden like a self-stricken flash photographer, and like a zip-fastener ripped from its garment by a sexual maniac, it is flung slapdash across Lake Leman and back to skim the roof-tops of the house, leaving intact, however, the well-insulated telephone wires which Lister, on the telephone to Geneva, has rather feared might break down.

The fatalities here are reduced by grammatical subordination and by run-away metaphorizing and this oblivion-rendering compound denudes the deaths of any gravity or human dignity. As is so often the case with Spark, the result is an ostentatious foregrounding of style. This passage demonstrates an analogy between the novelist and God which Spark often makes use of.

From her earliest novels the mundane human world is intruded upon by God or the demonic—often these forces are not easily distinguishable—and a comedy is made of the self-centered lives of humanity. In *Memento Mori*, the author narrates the fears of a group of geriatrics who are terrorized by a man on the telephone reminding them that they "must die."

The gruesomeness of this situation lies ultimately not in the seeming threats but in the fact that the caller is God attempting to make the old people aware that they are sinners. The novel is both funny and macabre in a mode that recalls the Medieval period, and in the end it becomes a kind of *danse macabre* as one of the geriatrics considers the mortal fate of his contemporaries:

> Lettie Colston, he recited to himself,
> comminuted fractures of the skull;
> Godfrey Colston, hypostatic pneumonia;
> Charmain Colston, uraemia; Jean Taylor,
> carcinoma of the cervix; Ronald
> Sidebottome, carcinoma of the bronchus;
> Guy Leet, arteriosclerosis; Henry
> Mortimer, coronary thrombosis . . .

In *The Ballad of Peckham Rye* (1960), the manipulator is not God (or Spark herself) but a very physical character within the novel, Dougal Douglas, who, with his hunchback and "horns" (or cysts) might be diabolical. Dougal is a cruel manipulator, interfering and creating patterns with the lives of others. As assistant personnel manager in a factory, Dougal interferes with the personal lives of employees, most spectacularly when he counsels the factory manager and leads him to such a pitch of emotional confusion that he murders his mistress. Dougal's other activities include "ghosting" the autobiography of the retired actress Maria Cheeseman and grafting onto it untruths such as a story of a Scottish soldier in wartime London up whose kilt Maria thrusts her hand. Dougal has taken this story from his landlady in fact and this is typical of the economy (always an important word for Spark) which informs his method of conflating experiences and persons to highlight hilariously the drabness and folly of so many lives. In Dougal we see something of Spark's view of how she functions as a novelist. She tells us that after leaving Peckham, Dougal becomes a literary artist: "Thereafter, for economy's sake, he gathered together the scrap ends of his profligate experience . . . and turned them into a lot of cock-eyed books."

Jean Brodie, in *The Prime of Miss Jean Brodie*, is also a fabulist. In this novel, Spark takes for her setting 1930s Edinburgh and Marcia Blane's school, modeled on James Gillespie's. Brodie attempts to mold the lives of her pupils according to her own unconventional principles, which include a belief in the transcendence of art and allegiance to the ideas of Italian Fascism. The teacher is complexly drawn: she is attractive in her love of art and as a woman; at the same time her strenuous attempts to shape the destinies of her chosen pupils is compared to the Calvinist conception of God. She is both comically eccentric and romantically dangerous. Brodie beguiles men as well as the girls in her charge and, as her personal intrigues proceed, two of her pupils naively write a story about her which shows Spark's talent, demonstrated throughout her *oeuvre*, for the comedy of observation of age and social groupings. The girls' fictionalizing includes writing a letter to her lover, the music master, rejecting his proposal of marriage, and ending, "Allow me, in conclusion, to congratulate you warmly upon your sexual intercourse, as well as your singing." Ronald Neame directed a popular film version of the novel in 1969. Adapted by Joy Presson Allen, the movie starred Maggie Smith in an Oscar-winning portray of Brodie.

In her most experimental period in the early 1970s, Spark takes the method often found in her short stories of elaborating on a cliché toward comical and theological effects. In *Not to Disturb*, the stock props of the gothic novel (and its derivative the horror film), the sinister house, the butler, the imbecile in the attic, aristocratic intrigue, and lightning are all to be found. The stage-managing butler, Lister, "waits in the wings" as an eternal triangle between Baron and Baroness Klopstock, and their secretary, Victor Passerat, is bloodily resolved in the library. Lister and the other servants plan to sell the film rights to the tragedy which has yet to happen but which Lister knows to be inevitable, as the predictable, decadent lives of the Klopstocks have brought things to this pass. A bizarre, nightmarish, fictive world is constructed by Spark as events happen in accordance with the inevitability of the form which reflects then, the redundant and morally empty lives of the Klopstocks and their secretary. In this novel Spark presents the reader with a view of the hell of predestination.

The Abbess of Crewe (1974) is a satire on the Watergate scandal as nun and self-justified aesthete, Alexandra, contrives the electronic surveillance of her convent in her bid to be "elected" Abbess. Again, a cliché is pressed into service as furor surrounds a missing thimble, stolen by two Jesuit novices as part of a campaign against Alexandra's "rival" for the abbacy. Alexandra is exuberantly immoral, or creative, in her control of the convent, highlighting again the theme of human self-importance and the corruption which follows from this. Alexandra demonstrates this "cock-eyed" creativity as she immolates her nuns by feeding them pet food, robs their dowries to buy jewels for the convent's icons, and recites classic English poetry during the formal hours of prayer.

Alexandra, like Dougal and Jean, is an attractive and entertaining character in her wrong-doing and points to the paradoxical nature of the creative process for Spark. Creativity involves a willful ordering of events and the assumption of a somewhat god-like perspective for one's own ends. If many of the author's characters demonstrate this iniquitous tendency, it is something that she herself as novelist might be charged with. She recognizes this and the exhausting negativity of satire in her prefacing of her novel with lines from W.B. Yeats's "Nineteen Hundred and Nineteen": "Come let us mock at the great / . . . Mock mockers after that / . . . for we / Traffic in mockery" [My deletions].

It is perhaps no surprise, then, that after *The Abbess of Crewe* Spark turns from her formalistic and fabulistic experiences to a more realistic mode of fiction. Sparkian verbal trickery and black comedy remain, but there is less attempt to introduce agents of theological verity into her realistic settings as Spark satirizes the literary London that she knew in the 1950s in *Loitering With Intent* (1981) and *A Far Cry from Kensington* (1988), explores the problem of human suffering in *The Only Problem* (1984), and the criminal manipulation of middle-class society and manners in *Symposium* (1990).

Summary

Muriel Spark's technique involves a light (some critics have claimed a frivolous) treatment of the world owing to her Newman-inspired belief that the natural world is "the outward manifestation of realities greater than itself." This belief licenses and in turn is illuminated by her dark humor which shows a shocking disregard for human activity. As an analogy to the divine economy, the novel is used by Spark to confound the aspirations of character and this is conveyed to the reader by her treatment of her characters, both in the workings of plot and in blatant authorial intrusions, and the stylistics involved in these procedures.

S

Selected Bibliography
Primary Sources
The Go-Away Bird and Other Stories. London: Macmillan, 1958; Philadelphia: J.B. Lippincott, 1960.
Memento Mori. London: Macmillan, and Philadelphia: J.B. Lippincott, 1959.
The Ballad of Peckham Rye. London: Macmillan, and Philadelphia: J.B. Lippincott, 1960.
The Prime of Miss Jean Brodie. London: Macmillan, 1961; J.B. Lippincott, 1962.
The Mandelbaum Gate. London: Macmillan, and New York: Knopf, 1965.
Collected Stories 1. London: Macmillan, 1967; New York: Knopf, 1968.
The Driver's Seat. London: Macmillan, and New York: Knopf, 1970.
Not to Disturb. London: Macmillan, and New York: Knopf, 1971.
The Abbess of Crewe. London: Macmillan, and New York: Viking Press, 1974.
Loitering With Intent. London: Bodley Head, and New York: Coward, McCann, and Geoghegan, 1981.
The Only Problem. New York: Putnam, 1984.
A Far Cry from Kensington. Boston: Houghton Mifflin, 1988.
Symposium. London: Constable, 1990.
Curriculum Vitae. London: Constable, 1992.

Secondary Sources
Bold, Alan, ed. *Muriel Spark: An Odd Capacity for Vision.* London and Totowa, NJ: Vision and Barnes & Noble, 1984. A collection of essays by different hands dealing with Spark's handling of the supernatural, religion, fictional form (especially in relation to characterization), and Spark as critic, poet, and short story writer, and in her relation to Scotland.
Kemp, Peter. *Muriel Spark.* London: Paul Elek, 1974. The best extended analysis of Spark's formal mechanics.
Massie, Allan. *Muriel Spark.* Edinburgh: Ramsay Head Press, 1979. A good general introduction to Spark that is particularly illuminating on Spark and Calvinism.
Whittaker, Ruth. *The Faith and Fiction of Muriel Spark.* London: Macmillan,

1982. A work that is excellent on some of the tensions and paradoxes inherent in Spark's art.

Gerard Carruthers

Steele, Richard

Born: Dublin, Ireland, early March 1672 (baptized March 12)
Education: Charterhouse School, 1684–1689; Christ Church College, Oxford University, 1690–1694
Marriages: Margaret (Ford) Stretch, April 1705; Mary Scurlock, September 9, 1707; four children; one natural child with Elizabeth Tonson
Died: Camarthen, Wales, September 1, 1729

Biography

Richard Steele was born in early March of 1672 in Dublin, and baptized on March 12, 1672, at St. Bridget's Church in the same city. Steele's father, also Richard Steele, was a successful attorney; he had a country house at Monkstown and once served as sub-sheriff of Tipperary. Steele's mother, about whom little is known, was Elinor Symes, née Sheyles. Both of Steele's parents died while he was quite young, and he passed into the care of an uncle, Henry Gascoigne, who was private secretary to James Butler, first Duke of Ormonde. Through his connection with Ormonde, young Steele had access to social and educational opportunities. In November of 1684, he entered the Charterhouse School (of which the Duke was governor). Joseph Addison would enter Charterhouse two years later, and there begin his celebrated friendship with Steele. In late 1689, Steele elected to attend Oxford, Addison having preceded him there, and on March 13, 1690 Steele matriculated at Christ Church College (Addison had opted for Magdalen College). On August 27, 1691, Steele was appointed a "postmaster," or fellowship student, in Merton College; Addison held a "demy," or fellowship, in Magdalen.

While Addison was drawing attention to himself as a student of the classics, Steele's educational progress appears to have been more haphazard. In 1694, he left Merton without taking a degree and entered the army as a cadet, or gentleman volunteer, in the Second Troop of Life Guards, commanded by the second Duke of Ormonde. As he began his military life, he also began his literary career when in December 1694 "The Procession," a poem occasioned by the funeral of Queen Mary, was published. The poem was dedicated to John, Lord Cutts, Colonel of the Second or Coldstream regiment of Foot Guards. Steele worked as Cutts's confidential agent and secretary in 1696 and 1697, and this position apparently helped him to advance in rank. In 1700, Steele fought a duel in Hyde Park with a Captain Kelly, whom he wounded dangerously but not mortally. This event had an enduring effect upon Steele. In both his drama and his non-fiction prose, he repeatedly would argue against the custom of duelling. Furthermore, his desire to elevate the moral tenor of his own life, stimulated by the duel, resulted in his tract *The Christian Hero*, published by Jacob Tonson in 1701. In this work Steele proposed a new model for heroism, a model distinct from traditional aristocratic notions of military and sexual prowess.

In the late 1600s and early 1700s, Steele, with his military posting at Landguards gun emplacements near London, was very much a man about town—besides his duel with Kelly, he also fathered a natural child with Elizabeth Tonson, the sister of the man who later became the author's publisher, Jacob Tonson the younger. Steele provided for this daughter, Miss Ousley, and eventually saw her marry a Welsh gentleman. But in this case, as in the duel, he felt remorse for his behavior. Following *The Christian Hero*, he began to write for the stage. In a series of plays, he attempted to reform the theater, moving away from the libertinism and cynicism of the comedies of the Restoration period. His first play, *The Funeral; or Grief a-la-Mode*, premiered at Drury Lane Theatre late in 1701. Colley Cibber and John Wilks took major roles in the play, which was followed in December 1703 by *The Lying Lover; or, the Ladies Friendship* and in April 1705 by *The Tender Husband; or, the Accomplished Fools*, the latter with a "Prologue" written by Addison, who had just returned from a four-year Grand Tour, sent partly at public expense by Charles Montagu (later Lord Halifax) and John Lord Somers, both of whom assumed that Addison's literary gifts would later be of political value.

Although Steele garnered some income from his plays and from his appointment in February 1702 as Captain in Lord Lucas's regiment, he spent the first decade of the eighteenth century in financial need, seeking, as did other men about town, government sinecures and/or an advantageous marriage. His finances were particularly desperate after he lost money sometime in the late 1690s in an alchemical quest after the philosopher's stone. Shortly after the production of *The Tender Husband*, in April 1705 he married Margaret Stretch (née Ford), a widow with estates in Barbados. In August 1706, he was appointed gentleman waiter to Prince George, a position that brought him £100 yearly. In December 1706, the first Mrs. Steele died, and the author began a complicated series of transactions related to divesting himself of her estates. In the spring of 1707, he was appointed Gazetteer, that is, given responsibility for compiling the official government digest of news, foreign and domestic. On September 9, 1707, Steele married Mary Scurlock, daughter and heiress of Jonathan Scurlock, a prosperous Welshman. The second Mrs. Steele would preserve all of her husband's letters to her (some 400); they give a fascinating portrait of Steele's ever-busy, sometimes wayward life and of his times. The couple had four children.

Despite a salary of £300 per year as Gazetteer, Steele was perpetually in debt, and his letters to "Dear Prue" record his financial difficulties. Following the birth of his daughter Elizabeth in March 1709 (Addison and Edward Wortley Montagu were her godfathers), on April 12, 1709, Steele published the first number of the *Tatler*. The goal of the paper was a large readership, and Steele, anticipating one of the devices of modern mass marketing, offered the opening numbers *gratis* in the hope (soon justified) that he could attract an audience. The *Tatler* benefited from Steele's experiences as Gazetteer, as well as the access which that position gave him to news and notices. Like the *Gazette*, the *Tatler* reprinted news items, but it also included an essay, frequently a humorous comment upon contemporary manners and mores. Addison's first contribution to the paper came in Number 18, but the paper remained largely Steele's; 188 of the 271 numbers were written by him.

In January 1710, Steele received another lucrative government appointment: Commissioner of Stamps at £300 per year. By year's end, however, he found himself a victim of political upheaval that, in the short term, led him to prison and near ruin, but in the long term resulted in something like well being. In the early years of the eighteenth century, Great Britain fought the War of the Spanish Succession, a war to decide whether the vacant Spanish throne would be held by a grandson of Louis XIV, a Bourbon, or by an Austrian prince. Given the power of France and fears of Franco-Spanish unification, the English joined an alliance with the Dutch—a Protestant coalition—to fight Roman Catholic France. In 1704, at Blenheim, English and allied troops under the command of John Churchill, soon to be Duke of Marlborough, routed the French, the greatest English victory on the continent since the 100 Years War. In following years, Marlborough "won" less convincing, more costly battles at Oudenarde and Malplaquet. These victories did not weaken the hold of the Bourbon prince, to be known as King Phillip V, on the Spanish throne, and the cost of the war began to be a divisive political issue, particularly since taxes on land had to be increased to pay for Marlborough's army. At the time of the *Tatler*, then, British society was dividing between landed men and moneyed men, between those who saw their taxes rise because of the war and those who profited from the commercial opportunities that the war brought, particularly through the system of credit that the government invented to fund its debt. Added to this economic division were controversies about the role and the prerogatives of the Anglican Church, especially the continuation of the sacramental test for government employees and officeholders and the nature of provisions for occasional conformity. The slogan "The Church in danger" dominated electoral politics in 1709 and 1710, as politicians tried to link the economic discontentment of the landed men to a broader sense that all English traditions (including the Church) were at risk in this new, war-based, and debt-driven economy. The great slogan for those who supported Marlborough and the war effort was, "No peace without Spain."

In August 1710, Queen Anne replaced Sidney Godolphin, Marlborough's brother-in-law and political agent, as First Lord of the Treasury with Robert Harley, who ascended to the peerage as the Earl of Oxford. Harley formed a government with Henry St. John, Viscount Bolingbroke, a leading espouser of the cause of the landed men. The goal of the Oxford ministry was to negotiate an end to the war and, as a means to that end, the ministry employed propagandists—most notable among them Jonathan Swift—to discredit Marlborough and the Dutch. The political situation was complicated by the uncertain health of Queen Anne (none of whose five children would survive her), the presence in France of a Roman Catholic Pretender to the English throne, and the obscurity of the Elector of Hanover, the German prince to whom the throne by the Act of Settlement (1701) would descend upon the death of Anne. In the years 1710 to 1714, Steele would be the most visible and most impassioned defender of Marlborough and of the Protestant Succession—a Succession that he repeatedly would accuse the Oxford ministry of threatening. In October 1710, his pro-war views cost him the Gazetteership, but (Swift claimed with his help) Steele held on to his other sinecures. Steele responded to this financial loss by starting the *Spectator*, the first number of which appeared on March 1, 1711. From its beginning this paper was a joint venture with Addison, who also had lost state offices. Published daily, the paper ran for five hundred fifty-five numbers and achieved unprecedented popularity. Even a Stamp Tax on printed matter, passed in August 1712, could not dint the *Spectator*'s circulation, which, in some estimates, reached ten thousand copies per week.

The *Spectator* opened by claiming for itself "an exact neutrality" in political matters. But by 1712, Steele wished to assume a larger and more overt political role. The *Spectator* concluded its run on December 6, 1712, and in March 1713, Steele began to publish the *Guardian*, which he would follow in October 1713 with the *Englishman*. Both of these papers devoted themselves to "guarding" the traditional "English" liberties that, Steele claimed, the Oxford ministry was sacrificing in its treaty negotiations with France, and then in the Peace of Utrecht which in 1713 ended hostilities. In August 1713, Steele was elected member of Parliament for Stockbridge only to be expelled from that body and prosecuted for publishing seditious libels in March of the next year. A pamphlet of Steele's, *The Crisis*, published on January 19, 1714, was the main source of the charges brought against him.

With the death of Queen Anne on August 1, 1714, and the arrival in England of George I on September 18 following, Steele's political fortunes took a great and positive turn. Bolingbroke had discredited his followers and associates by fleeing to France to join the court of the Pretender, James III (thus seeming to vindicate all of the charges of Jacobitism that Steele had made against the Oxford ministry), and it was time for the defenders of the Protestant Succession, usually grouped under the label "Whigs," to prosper. While Addison was appointed to a series of positions in the Department of State, Steele was quickly appointed justice of the peace and deputy lieutenant for Middlesex, surveyor of the royal stables at Hampton Court, and then made a patent-holder for the Royal Theatre at Drury Lane. This patent—the right to produce plays—was worth roughly £1,000 per year. On February 2, 1715, Steele was returned to Parliament for Boroughbridge, Yorkshire; later that year he was knighted.

In the years after his political resurrection, Steele, for all of his increased income, still lived beyond his means and still pursued a remarkable range of projects. In June 1716, he was named one of thirteen commissioners to adjudicate claims upon and pursue the distribution of estates forfeited in Scotland by those who had joined the Jacobite rebellion in 1715; his stipend was £1,000 per year. In June 1718, he took out a patent for a "fish pool," a well boat in which he planned to bring live salmon from Ireland to London. He wrote pamphlets publicizing the scheme and (because he needed capital to build a prototype) announcing the incorporation of a company to pursue it. Still a member of Parliament, he became involved in a dispute over a bill to limit the sovereign's power to create new peers (a strategy that Oxford and Bolingbroke had used in 1713 to win approval of the Peace of Utrecht). Steele wrote against the bill, Addison for it, and their disagreement was not mended before Addison's death on June 17, 1719, only six months after Steele's wife, "Dear Prue" in the letters, had died.

Also, almost from the beginning of his appointment as patentee at Drury Lane, Steele had been involved in disputes with Cibber and Wilkes, the other managers, about both expenses and repertoire. In part to make his case against the other managers, Steele published a periodical, the *Theatre*, during four months in early 1720. The paper outlined his standards for comedy, even as it commented upon specific actors and plays. In individual numbers of the *Theatre*, Steele alluded to a play upon which he was working, a play that he had started perhaps during his early days on the London stage but put aside during the political struggles of 1709–1719. Throughout the early 1720s, Steele, like contemporary movie distributors, tried to build an audience for this play, which, debuting in November 1722 as *The Conscious Lovers*, became the model for "sentimental" comedy, a comedy focusing upon good feelings and tears of joy rather than seeking harsh laughter directed at the foibles of social and intellectual inferiors.

While its characterization perhaps seems wooden and its plot improbable by post-modern standards, *The Conscious Lovers* was a "hit" in its own day. Steele received a gift of 500 guineas from King George I (to whom the play was dedicated), and with the profits from the staging (in which he shared both as author and as patentee) and the published version, Steele derived enough income to work out a settlement with his creditors. As part of that settlement, he retired to Camarthen, Wales, in 1724, away from the temptations to spend beyond his means with which London always presented him. He died in Camarthen on September 1, 1729.

Literary Analysis

Steele contributed to the development of British humor in two important ways: one generic; one thematic. With Addison, he shares the distinction of popularizing the periodical essay—the short essay written to instruct (to improve the morals and manners of) the reader, but to do so in an appealing, congenial way. As Addison and Steele sought to build a large public for their work, they avoided the harsh, biting satire of Swift. While the three men maintained close literary and personal relationships during the early years of the eighteenth century (Steele takes the name of his persona in the *Tatler*, Isaac Bickerstaff, from Swift's *Bickerstaff Papers*), the War of the Spanish Succession divided them first politically and then literarily and socially. Addison and Steele satirize groups rather than individuals, and in their satire seek always to be temperate, even gentle in effect. Their single most famous creation, Sir Roger de Coverley, typifies their humor. Sir Roger is a landed man, a Tory, the political opposite of his creators. While his failings are described—falling asleep at church services after requiring all of the other members of the congregation to remain awake; making speeches about legal matters that he does not understand—Sir Roger also is lauded and even loved for his good nature. He is portrayed as simultaneously superannuated and admirable.

Critics long have debated the question of the respective contributions of Addison and Steele to the *Tatler* and the *Spectator*, the topic

being a particularly important one for nineteenth-century men of letters. Thomas Babington Macaulay praised Addison for bringing "suavity and moderation" to the stormy literary life of the early eighteenth century. As part of his celebration of Addison, Macaulay denigrated Steele, claiming: "His writings have been well compared to those light wines which, though deficient in body and flavor, are yet a pleasant drink if not kept too long, or carried too far" (Macaulay, 106). Steele found his defenders, however, principal among them Leigh Hunt and John Forster, the former of whom wrote:

> Addison's stories are of a more fanciful sort, and more elegant in the style; some of them are charming; but they are pieces of writing—these [stories by Steele] are relations. They have all the warmth as well as brevity of unpremeditated accounts, given as occasion called them forth. Steele, indeed, may be said to have always talked, rather than written; and hence the beauties as well as the defects of his style, which is apt to be carelessly colloquial. (*A Book for a Corner*, 40)

In his biography of Addison, William John Courthope follows Macaulay's line, although much more temperately, even as he solves the problem of whether to credit achievements to Addison or to Steele by describing Steele as an impetuous pioneer who opened areas that Addison then properly cultivated. In a typical passage, Courthope writes, "As usual, Addison improves the opportunity which Steele affords him" (158). In his biography of Steele, Austin Dobson advocates his subject's cause but more temperately than Hunt did. He sharply dissents from William Makepeace Thackeray's description of Steele in his "Lectures on the English Humorists of the Eighteenth Century," arguing that Thackeray, while "Doing justice to Steele's generosity, kindliness, amiability . . . leaves upon us the impression that he was weaker, frailer, more fallible than the evidence warrants." Dobson goes on to argue that Steele's "virtues redeemed his frailties," that Steele's humor is "so cheerful and good-natured, so frank and manly that one is often tempted to echo the declaration of Leigh Hunt—'I prefer open-hearted Steele with all his faults to Addison with all his essays'" (217, 225). Dobson and Courthope typify the other nineteenth-century critics in the high place that they accord Addison and Steele for their inventing the periodical essay. But these nineteenth-century critics do differ in their standards—suavity versus sentimentality—for humor.

Besides pioneering the periodical essay, Steele, both in his plays and in his criticism of the drama, redefined comedy. Despite being something of a rake as a young man, beginning with *The Christian Hero*, Steele assumed a visible and ongoing role in the movement for stage reform in England. He set himself against the cynicism and ribaldry of Restoration comedy. He made it one of his goals to write comedy in which diction was pure (none of the salacious double entendre of the famous "china scene" in William Wycherley's *The Country Wife*). He also offered protagonists who were selfless, trustworthy, and chaste (none of the predatory sexuality typified by Wycherley's Harry Horner). In his "Preface" to *The Conscious Lovers*, the author expresses directly his wish to overturn the tradition of Restoration comedy, a literary loyalty that corresponds with his Whiggish, anti-Stuart political loyalties. As both Shirley Strum Kenny and John Loftis point out, however, the "Preface" to *The Conscious Lovers* only culminates trends that were visible in Steele's early comedies (in which rakish diction and behavior were assigned to minor or to unsuccessful characters), in his *Spectator* No. 65 (a sharp criticism of the morality of George Etherege's *The Man of Mode*), and in his papers for the *Theatre*. Steele, then, provided what one might call a new theme for English stage comedy, the triumph of good feeling, the celebration of sentiment—all of this over against the emphasis in Restoration comedy upon base motives and duplicitous means to realizing them. In Restoration comedy laughter finds its origin in a Hobbesian "sudden glory," an assertion of superiority. In Steele, laughter is less a goal than are virtuous tears, tears that bespeak compassion and sympathy rather than superiority.

Even in his early plays, Steele goes outside the norms of Restoration comedy, as he makes acts of generosity and trust part of his resolutions. In *The Tender Husband*, Biddy Tipkin and Captain Clerimont overcome deceptions, some self-imposed, to pursue their romance. While Biddy, early in the play, is laughable in her affectations, she finally is rewarded for her virtues; she never becomes the butt of satire. In the play's last lines, both Clerimont Senior and Pounce return to their victims money that they have won by cunning, and the company adjourns to a dinner and dance. Captain Clerimont summarizes the play in a final address to the audience:

> You've seen th' extreams of the
>   Domestick Life,
> A Son too much confin'd—too free a
>   Wife;
> By generous bonds you either shou'd
>   restrain,
> And only on their Inclinations gain.
>   (Kenny, 272)

His emphasis upon "generous bonds" adumbrates the lush sentimentality of *The Conscious Lovers*, the "laudable . . . Love . . . born of Virtue!" that the latter play's characters share and which makes them "burn to embrace" each other (Kenny, 377).

In *The Conscious Lovers*, Steele also celebrates social change, emphasizing the rise to economic and political power of the great merchant, Mr. Sealand. While Sealand, at play's end, is revealed to be of gentlemanly blood, the play, as it varies John Hobbes's definition of laughter, also challenges the elitist politics of the Restoration court of Charles II, the king for whom Hobbes wrote. Sealand is Steele's fulfillment of the prediction made by Addison in the *Spectator* No. 108—a paper in which Will Wimble is introduced as a younger son of an aristocratic family who can find no social role suitable to his many gifts. Will wanders through Sir Roger's neighborhood doing good deeds, catching large fish, knitting stockings, but he has no social function, and Addison concludes the paper with a point that cannot be "too much inculcated": Will was "perfectly well turned" for "Trade and Commerce," would his parents have allowed him to pursue gainful employment. Sealand vindicates Addison's call for social toleration, even as he plays a major role in Steele's new model for comedy.

While Steele directly challenges Restoration standards for comedy, he also indirectly challenges Aristotle's classical definition of comedy as a genre in which we witness the laughable foibles and failures of our social inferiors. Steele treats seriously his merchant and middle-class characters rather than subjecting them to the scornful diminution that they suffer in the plays of Menander or Plautus. Always an innovator, Steele, in his "sentimental" comedy, works outside the Aristotelian principle of separation of styles. He accords serious treatment to characters of humble social origin, reserving comic treatment only for those servants, such as Tom in *The Conscious Lovers*, who would ape their social superiors because they mistakenly assume that their superiors are their betters.

Early in *The Conscious Lovers* (act 1, scene 1), Steele exploits the possibilities for humor created by Tom's pretensions. In a dialogue with his uncle and fellow servant Humphrey, Tom claims: "Why now, Sir, the Lacquies are the Men of Pleasure of the Age; the Top-Gamesters; and many a lac'd Coat about Town have had their Education in our Party-colour'd Regiment. We are false Lovers; have a Taste of Musick, Poetry, Billet-deux, Dress, Politicks, ruin Damsels, and when we are weary of this lewd Town, and have a mind to take up, whip into our Masters Wigs and Linens, and marry Fortunes" (Kenny, 312). Humphrey's reply to all this coxcombery is a pithy "Hey-Day!" for as Tom redacts all the great motifs of Restoration comedy and uses the diction of the rake, the incongruities are both laughable and socially significant. Tom, as he strings together objects for "taste of" but then breaks the parallel structure with "ruin Damsels," reveals his own inaptitude for rakishness, even as he suggests that the social categories of the Restoration period have become blurred. Servants like Tom at least can envision a change in their clothes opening the chance for them to marry a "Fortune." Tom's version of rakishness is both laughably off the mark, yet remarkably (at least in his gestures and his words) close to the original. Thus, Steele, a Whig in politics, practices a literary version of toleration and republicanism, mixing the serious and the comic, the sublime and the common.

As Calhoun Winton, Steele's most recent biographer, has insightfully shown:

> He [Steele] was the benevolent man in theory and in practice, but the friendly face he showed the world overlay a tough and resilient character, as his contemporaries realized. No one could have accomplished what Sir Richard Steele accomplished without extraordinary resources of persistence and determination. As much as any man of his times, perhaps, he owed his success not to family connections or to inherited wealth or even good luck, but to himself. He bought his independence, and he paid for it. (*Sir Richard Steele, M.P.*, 240)

Summary

Richard Steele's was a remarkably busy life. His work as a playwright, essayist, and critic always was sandwiched between numerous other activities—be they as noble as making speeches in Parliament or as ignoble as fending off debt collectors. A full appreciation of his "business" makes his achievements as a humorist even more impressive. Not only did he pioneer a new genre for humor—the periodical essay—he also redirected the course of English stage comedy and changed that course in a very basic and profound way. As his letters to "Dear Prue" attest, Steele was gone from home so often, not only because he was an immensely sociable man, but also because he had to hustle in London's literary and political scene, ever alert for opportunities for patronage, for money-making. As a result, he was remarkably sensitive to his audience, to changes in the theater-going and the reading publics in the early eighteenth century. The box office failure of William Congreve's brilliant *The Way of the World* had shown Steele (and others) that audiences wanted humor different from that which the formulae of Restoration comedy offered. Steele's gentle and genteel humor was a response to that new audience, but the humor, for all of its toleration and good nature, was pursued amidst demonstrably difficult circumstances.

As a matter of fact, Steele always sought a large audience for his humor. He needed for the *Spectator* to succeed, to replace the income that he lost when the gazetteership was taken from him. In touch with changes in British society, with the rise of commerce and of what today is called the middle class, he moved energetically to find new types of and new themes for humor so that he might appeal to men and women who were only just entering the literary world. In his career, as there was a shift from a literary world dominated by great patrons to a literary world dominated by entrepreneurial booksellers, so too was there a shift from the elitist, stylized, and cynical humor of the Restoration to the more tolerant, more (as Hunt points out) conversational humor of sentimental comedy.

Perhaps Steele's greatest achievement is his use of humor to mediate social change and thus to avoid social conflict. In Sir Roger de Coverley, readers can witness the transformation of a rakish youth into a good natured old man, readers can move with toleration but also with decisiveness from the world of the Stuart kings to the world of the Hanoverians. In his humor, Steele achieved political mediations that he was not always capable of in his life. In the pages of the *Tatler* and the *Spectator*, at least some readers found a model for accommodation between the landed men and the moneyed men, between tradition and innovation, between the aristocracy and the bourgeoisie—accommodation of the sort that British society as a whole would move toward in the years after Steele's death.

Selected Bibliography

Primary Sources

The Funeral. London: Jacob Tonson, 1701.

The Christian Hero. Ed. Rae Blanchard. London: Jacob Tonson, 1701; Oxford: Oxford University Press, 1932.

The Lying Lover. London: Bernard Lintot, 1704.

The Tender Husband. London: Jacob Tonson, 1705.

Correspondence. Ed. Rae Blanchard. Oxford: Clarendon, 1941.

The Ladies Library. London: Jacob Tonson, 1714.

The Englishman. Ed. Rae Blanchard. London: Samuel Buckley, 1714; Oxford: Clarendon, 1955.

The Guardian. Ed. John Calhoun Stephens. London: Jacob Tonson, 1714; Lexington: University Press of Kentucky, 1982.

The Political Writings of Sir Richard Steele. London: Owen Lloyd and J. Brown, 1715.

The Conscious Lovers. London: Jacob Tonson, 1723.

Poetical Miscellanies. London: Jacob Tonson, 1727.

Periodical Journalism 1714–16. Ed. Rae Blanchard. Oxford: Clarendon, 1959.

The Plays of Richard Steele. Ed. Shirley Strum Kenny. Oxford: Clarendon, 1971.

The Theatre, 1720. Ed. John Loftis. Oxford: Clarendon, 1962.

Tracts and Pamphlets by Richard Steele. Ed. Rae Blanchard. Baltimore: The Johns Hopkins University Press, 1944.

With Joseph Addison

Spectator. Ed. Donald F. Bond. 5 vols. London: Samuel Buckley and Jacob Tonson, 1712–1713; Oxford: Clarendon, 1965.

Tatler. Ed. Donald F. Bond. 3 vols. London: J. Morphew, 1711; Oxford: Clarendon, 1987.

Secondary Sources

Books

Aitken, George A. *The Life of Richard Steele.* 2 vols. Boston and New York: Houghton Mifflin, 1899. The standard nineteenth-century biography of Steele and an eloquent defense of his good nature.

Bond, Richmond P. *The Tatler: The Making of a Literary Journal.* Cambridge, MA: Harvard University Press, 1971. Bond describes the newspapers that preceded Steele, his work on the *Gazette*, and the circumstances of his publishing the *Tatler*.

Courthope, William John. *Addison.* New York and London: Harper, 1901. English Men of Letters Series. Courthope sets the Addison-Steele contrast in favor of Addison, but notes Steele's special gift for describing domestic scenes, for sentiment.

Dobson, Austin. *Richard Steele.* London: Longmans Green, 1888. English Worthies Series. Dobson summarizes the nineteenth-century praise of Steele and reviews earlier criticism.

Goldgar, Bertrand A. *The Curse of Party: Swift's Relations with Addison and Steele.* Lincoln: University of Nebraska Press, 1961. Goldgar summarizes the impact of the War of the Spanish Succession upon literary life in Queen Anne's England, particularly the conflict into which the war brought Swift and Steele.

Hunt, Leigh. *A Book for a Corner.* New York: Putnam, 1852. An appreciation of Steele for his sentimentality and informality.

Loftis, John. *Comedy and Society from Congreve to Fielding.* Stanford, CA: Stanford University Press, 1959. Loftis summarizes the movement for theater reform in late seventeenth- and early eighteenth-century England and Steele's place in that movement.

Macaulay, Thomas Babington. *Essays on Milton and Addison.* Ed. Thomas Marc Parrott. New York and London: Globe School Book Company, 1901. The values that motivate Macaulay's harsh treatment of Steele are described.

McCrea, Brian. *Addison and Steele Are Dead: The English Department, Its Canon, and the Professionalization of Literary Criticism*. Newark: University of Delaware Press, 1990. A summary of the responses of nineteenth- and twentieth-century critics to Addison and Steele and describes how Addison and Steele's pursuit of a large audience distinguished them from Swift.

Winton, Calhoun. *Captain Steele: The Early Career of Sir Richard Steele*. Baltimore: The Johns Hopkins University Press, 1964. Winton helpfully summarizes Steele's education, his military career, and his early efforts as a dramatist.

———. *Sir Richard Steele, M.P.: The Later Career*. Baltimore and London: The Johns Hopkins University Press, 1970. The critic describes how Steele combined literary and political careers; also gives a fine account of the genesis of *The Conscious Lovers*.

Articles and Chapters in Books

Dobree, Bonamy. "The First Victorian." In *Essays in Biography 1680–1726*. London: Oxford University Press, 1925, pp. 197–345. An argument that Addison and Steele helped to shape British manners, that their public role was important.

Forster, John. "Sir Richard Steele." *The London Quarterly Review*, 96 (1855): 263–93. The most influential defense of Steele from the charges of weakness and sloppiness brought against him by Macaulay.

Kenny, Shirley Strum. "Richard Steele and the Pattern of Genteel Comedy." *Modern Philology*, 70 (1971): 22–37. Kenny analyzes the persistence with which Steele sets himself against the comedies of the Restoration and his designing *The Conscious Lovers* as a model for new comedy.

Loftis, John. "The Blenheim Papers and Steele's Journalism 1715–1718." *Publications of the Modern Language Association of America*, 66 (1951): 197–210. Loftis shows how Steele used his active social life as a basis for his essays by studying a memorandum book of Steele's in the Blenheim papers.

McCrea, Brian. "The Great War and Mid-Eighteenth-Century Memory." In *Henry Fielding and the Politics of Mid-Eighteenth-Century England*. Athens: University of Georgia Press, 1981, pp. 26–49. McCrea summarizes the impact of the War of the Spanish Succession upon eighteenth-century writers, particularly Swift.

Milic, Louis T. "The Reputation of Richard Steele: What Happened." *Eighteenth-Century Life*, 1 (1975): 81–87. Milic traces the neglect of Steele after World War II.

Thackeray, W.M. *The English Humorists of the Eighteenth Century: A Series of Lectures*. New York: Harper and Brothers, 1853, pp. 71–129. Thackeray helpfully summarizes the nineteenth-century critical consensus concerning Addison's "suavity" and Steele's "sentimentality."

Brian McCrea

Sterne, Laurence

Born: Clonmel, Ireland, November 14, 1713
Education: Hipperholme School, Halifax, England, 1724–1733; Jesus College, Cambridge University, 1733–1737, B.A., 1737; M.A., 1740
Marriage: Elizabeth Lumley, March 30, 1741; one surviving child
Died: London, March 18, 1768

Biography

Laurence Sterne was born in Clonmel, Ireland, on November 14, 1713. A gentleman born, like Jonathan Swift, he took holy orders in the Church of England and remained a priest his entire adult life. His great grandfather, Dr. Richard Sterne (d. 1683), had been an Archbishop of York and a Master of Jesus College, Cambridge University—which Sterne would later attend on a Sterne family scholarship. Sterne's uncle, Jaques (d. 1759), to whom he would later owe church preferments, was the Archdeacon of Cleveland and Precentor of York.[1] But, Sterne's father, Roger (d. 1731), was a low-ranking army officer (an ensign); and his mother, Agnes (d. 1759), was the daughter, in Sterne's facetious description, of a "noted sutler" (that is, someone who supplied the army with supplies, but who was generally regarded as not much more than a camp follower).[2] No doubt the first ten years or more of Sterne's life were full of hardship. The family was uprooted by the repeated transfers of Roger's regiment (the 34th Regiment of Foot) and the family was to lose, in the process, at least four of its infant-members, every one, according to Sterne's *Memoirs*, "of a fine delicate frame, not made to last long." However, his army experiences were later to reward him with material for two characters for his novel, *The Life and Opinions of Tristram Shandy, Gentleman*: Uncle Toby, an army captain, and Corporal Trim. In *A Sentimental Journey*, Sterne calls Uncle Toby the "dearest of my flock and friends" (Stout, 170).

At Hipperholme School and at Cambridge, Sterne studied the classics (a subject that he was to love all of his life), French (which would later serve him well on his trips abroad), and logic, rhetoric, and theology. He perhaps first discovered the writings of John Locke at Cambridge, a possible influence on representations of time, or "succession," in *Tristram*. Much of his satire against pedantry in that novel, particularly with the character of Walter Shandy and the tale of Slawkenbergius, came as a result of his study in logic and metaphysics. An acquaintance with the works of François Rabelais, another major influence on Sterne's masterpiece, was probably made at Cambridge through a friend there, John Hall (later Hall-Stevenson). It is likely that the character of Eugenius in both *Tristram* and the later *A Sentimental Journey* was based in part on Hall-Stevenson. Sterne was often a guest at Hall-Stevenson's Skelton Castle (on the Yorkshire coast) where he was a sometime member of the Demoniacs, a sort of men's club and where, he said, he and Hall-Stevenson would drive their "chariots" along the beach "with one wheel in the sea." At the time Sterne was Vicar of Sutton and, in plurality, of Stillington.

On March 30, 1741, Sterne married Elizabeth Lumley, the daughter of the Reverend Robert Lumley. The couple had one surviving daughter. Sterne's lasting reputation as a comic writer started with the first two volumes of *Tristram Shandy*, which were published in 1760, though he was already a published author. Local political squabbles in the early 1740s had led to the publication of letters in the *York Courant* and the *York Gazetteer* and what has been called his first "book," *Query upon Query* (1741). His last purely political work, *Hamlet*, was published in the *York Journal* in 1747. One of his very few known poems, *The Unknown World*, was published in the *Gentleman's Magazine* (a London newspaper) in July 1743. *World*, ponderous in subject and tone, anticipates, in its odd typographical features,

the eccentric structure and punctuation of *Tristram*. The immediate predecessors of Sterne's masterpiece were a *Fragment in the Manner of Rabelais* and *A Political Romance* (later called *The History of a Good Warm Watch-Coat*, 1759). *Fragment*, which was apparently never completed, is partly a satire on sermon writing, in the character of Homenas, and partly a "Pope-like parody of Longinus's *Peri Hupsous* (*On the Sublime*)" (New, DLB, 475). *Political Romance*, a satire on Francis Topham, a Yorkshire attorney, was said to have accomplished the successful ridicule of Topham's greed and social pretensions. "I have hung up Dr. Topham," Sterne wrote to his wife much later (December 28, 1761), "in a ridiculous light." The work was printed in several hundred copies but none, apparently, was offered for sale, and Sterne was later to destroy all but six copies.

Tristram Shandy was published, in five installments (or nine volumes), from 1760 (or possibly, 1759) to 1767. With the exception of volumes 1 and 2, first printed and advertised at York (December 1759?), all of the volumes were printed and sold in London, the first four by the well-known Dodsley Brothers and the rest by T. Becket and P.A. De Hondt. Sterne had arranged, by various subterfuges, to get the endorsement of David Garrick (the actor) for the first volumes of the novel, and they were quickly sold out. Something of the reason for its early popularity can be judged from a February 1760 review in the *London Magazine*: "Oh rare Tristram Shandy!—Thou very sensible—humorous—pathetick—humane—unaccountable!—what shall we call thee?—Rabelais, Cervantes, What?" A second edition, with a dedication to the Prime Minister, William Pitt, and an engraving by Ravenet, after a drawing by William Hogarth, soon followed. It has been said that Sterne's profits from the sale of the first two volumes approximated £30,000 in today's money (Cash, 2, 10). In addition, in his early days he made the acquaintance of such notables as Lord Chesterfield, the Duke of York (Edward Augustus), and Lord Bathurst, a friend of Alexander Pope and Swift. On the first of April 1760, Sterne wrote to a friend, Catherine Fourmantel, that "I have 14 engagements to dine now in my books, with the first nobility." One of this nobility was Lord Fauconberg, who presented Sterne with the parish living at Coxwold, a more lucrative position than those which he then possessed at Sutton-on-the-Forest and Stillington.

After his success with *Tristram*, Sterne made two trips to the Continent. One, from early 1762 to the spring of 1764, was to France and the second, from October 1765 to June (?) 1766, was to France and Italy. From these travels came his second major work, *A Sentimental Journey through France and Italy By Mr. Yorick*, published on February 27, 1768, by Becket and De Hondt. It, like *Tristram*, was a success, the first edition selling out within a month. *Journey* was in part a satire on the travel books of the times (especially that of Tobias Smollett's *Travels through France and Italy*, 1766). His hero is Yorick, a Sterne persona from both the *Sermons* and *Tristram*. Although Sterne has Yorick refer to time spent in Italy, the author only describes travel that occurs, and ends, in France, for Sterne was by now a very sick man and apparently did not have the energy to conduct Yorick and the reader into Italy. "I have torn my whole frame into pieces by my feelings" (as expressed in the *Journey*), he wrote to an unidentified Earl on November 28, 1767. The book appeared in late February 1768 and a second edition in March, several days after the author's death.

The Journal to Eliza, discovered in 1851 and first published by the well-known Sterne scholar Wilbur Cross, is an account of the writer's emotional involvement in 1767 with Elizabeth Draper, the young wife of an East India Company official. It reveals, according to Cross, "the pathological state of the emotions . . . whence sprang the *Sentimental Journey*, during the composition of which Sterne was fast dying of consumption" (434). However, there is no real consensus on its place in the Sterne canon—especially its relationship, in subject and tone, to the *Journey*. If Eliza, the woman, can be seen as Sterne's muse in writing the *Journal*, then she may have also played that role in his composition of the *Journey*. Both, in effect, are representations of emotions strained to the limits, what the age would sometimes call the "pathetic."[3]

Sermons of Mr. Yorick, volumes 1 and 2, were published in May 1760 and volumes 3 and 4 in January of 1765. The final volumes, 5 through 7, were published on June 3, 1769, by Lydia de Medalle (Sterne's daughter). For these last two volumes the title had been changed to *Sermons by the Late Rev. Mr. Sterne*. A second edition came out later in the same year.

One night at Cambridge (1736?), after bleeding the "bed full," Sterne learned that he had pulmonary tuberculosis, or "tisick." The disease, which eventually killed him, often left him without a voice, unable to deliver his sermons. The illness gave Sterne the look of "a bale of cadaverous goods consigned to Pluto" and an intense appreciation for the fragile hold that he had on health and life. Preserving what little health they have and giving death the slip are major concerns of both the hero of *Tristram* and of *A Sentimental Journey*. "DEATH himself knocked at my door," Tristram says, "had I not better, Eugenius, fly for my life? . . . Then my heaven! I will lead him a dance he little thinks of" (7.1). The bad state of the writer's health is a recurring theme in *The Journal to Eliza* as well: "April 16. And got up so ill, I could not go to Mrs. James as I had promised her"; "April 24. So ill, I could not write a word all this morning." Sterne dosed himself with tar-water and took James's Powder; he was bled by surgeons and given mercury in the belief (possibly a false one) that he was suffering from syphilis. He died in London on March 18, 1768.

Soon after burial, Sterne's body was stolen by grave robbers (who were usually medical students) and taken to Cambridge for dissection, apparently by Dr. Charles Collignon and his students. Someone in attendance, however, recognized the body as being that of Sterne, the famous author, and Collignon had Sterne's body returned to his grave at London (Paddington) for re-burial. In 1969, Sterne's bones were again re-buried at Coxwold where he had been the parson.

Literary Analysis

For the general public, Sterne's reputation as a writer depends largely on *Tristram Shandy* and *A Sentimental Journey* (the *Sermons*, *Political Romance*, and *Journal to Eliza*, although they help to illuminate Sterne's techniques and intentions, are mostly of interest to scholars). *Tristram* and *Journey* are now recognized as masterpieces of comedy and irony; both have influenced twentieth-century writers and critics[4] and both, as representative of Sterne's stated intentions, are highly personal and idiosyncratic: "For in writing what I have set about, I shall confine myself neither to Horace's rules, nor to any man's rules that ever lived" (*Tristram*, 1.4); "I am well aware, at the same time, as both my travels and observations [in *Journey*] will be altogether of a different cast from any of my forerunners" ("The Desobligeant," Stout, 82).

The "different cast" is particularly applicable to the personae, Tristram and Yorick, of the works. The two, in a sense, are early examples of the anti-hero, victims of chance in their life but at the same time aware of how difficult it is to tell a story or clearly represent a fact. As Tristram says, "I declare I have been at it [the story of his life] these six weeks, making all the speed I possibly could—and am not yet born" (*Tristram*, 1.14). This persistent self-indulgence in a problem or, more generally, in the problems of living and writing about one's own life, travels, and opinions, will remain an essential feature of Sterne's work to the end of his writing career.

There are substantial differences between *Tristram* and *Journey,* and the books were received differently by the public. *Journey*, it seems fair to say, was initially more popular in France, Germany, and Italy than in England. And, in the following century, its author became something of a cult figure, especially in Germany. Heinrich Heine said of him that "He was the darling of the pale, tragic goddess. Once in an access (sic) of fierce tenderness, she kissed his young heart with such power, passion, and madness, that his heart began to bleed and suddenly understood all the sorrows of this world, and was filled with infinite compassion."[5] At the same time, *Journey* and *Tristram* also share, and represent, several of the author's salient concerns. First, they are satires on contemporary forms of writing or, more generally, conventional ways of telling a story. In *Tristram*, Sterne is satirizing not only the plot of the novel (and storytelling) but also qualities traditionally given the hero. The Aristotelian definition of narration, beginning to middle to end, is one of his targets. Tristram's story of the mid-wife, for example, is interrupted by that of Yorick; a sentence of Uncle Toby, "I think, says he" (1.21), is stopped, and not allowed to finish until some thirty pages further on (2.6); essential parts of sentences, especially subjects and predicates, are given long separations by dashes, parentheses, or asterisks. In fact, punctuation serves not to establish order and succession as in traditional written narrative but rather fragmentation and disruption. For example, "My mother, you must know—but I have fifty things more necessary to let you know first—I have a hundred difficulties which I have promised to clear up" (3.38). The same kind of fragmentation, although in diminished intensity, also occurs in *Journey*: "Now shall I triumph over this *maitre*

d'hotel, cried I—and what then?—Then I shall let him see I know he is a dirty fellow.—And what then?—What then!—I was too near myself to say it was for the sake of others.—" ("The Case of Conscience. Paris," Stout, 242).[6]

In *Journey*, Sterne's general satire is against travel writing, especially the kind that is represented as being completely trustworthy and replete with the facts about persons, places, and weather. He is following the satiric pattern set by Swift in parts of *Gulliver's Travels*. But, particular targets are his contemporary novelist and travel-writer, Smollett ("Smelfungus" in the narrative) and (perhaps) one R. Baldwin. Sterne's classification of travelers in *Journey* partially may be a parody of a similar classification offered by Dean Tucker, another travel-writer.[7] *Journey*, though, according to Sterne's stated aims, was to be more than a travel book. On November 12, 1767, he wrote to his friend Mrs. James that the "design in it [*Journey*] was to teach us to love the world and our fellow creatures better than we do—so it runs most upon those gentler passions and affections, which aid so much to it." Short scenes between Yorick, Father Lorenzo, La Fleur, and the Fille de Chambre are intended to exemplify such "design." Yorick is attracted to all of them and he is very particular about the emotions which they stir in him: "My heart smote me the moment he shut the door" ("The Monk. Calais." Stout, 75), and "I was mortified with the loss of her hand" ("The Remise Door. Calais." Stout, 96–97). Yorick likes to touch people, take them by the hand and even, in the case of the Fille de Chambre, record changes in his blood pressure: "the pulsations of the arteries along my fingers pressing across hers, told her what was passing within me" (Stout, 97).

Yorick's desires, usually addressed to the other sex, sometimes expand to embrace the need for wholeness, for what would later be called by another writer the "Oversoul." His address to "Dear sensibility . . . the great—great SENSORIUM of the world" is an example ("The Bourbonnois." Stout, 278). With such desires comes the fear of being alone, "an atom," robbed of human contact. As Melvyn New suggests, in an important commentary on the relationship between the *Sermons* and Sterne's fiction, the need expressed in *Journey* for human contact is part of mainstream eighteenth-century Anglicanism—particularly, in its focus on benevolence.[8] Certainly, *Journey* can often be read as a statement of Sterne's faith, of

"God's continuing hand in human affairs" (New, *DLB*, 496). It also is the kind of statement, especially in those places where Yorick mixes spiritual with sexual love, that often discomforts believers in the twentieth century.[9] Of course, "there is nothing unmixt in this world" ("The Passport. Versailles." Stout, 228).

Benevolence, and the humor which often accompanies it, is also evident in *Tristram*, Uncle Toby's release of the fly from the room being a good example: "Go . . . why should I hurt thee?—This world surely is wide enough to hold both thee and me" (2.12). But here, the family is the source of the benevolence, not a traveler's temporary contact with strangers. Tristram (the son and narrator), Walter (the father), Uncle Toby, Trim (Toby's servant), Susannah and Obadiah (family servants) obviously love each other and work together for the survival of the Shandy family. (The birth of Tristram may mean not only that the family will survive biologically [for its own time?] but also historically in the written record [but see Lamb, 141, "blocked patrilinearity"].) Still, their will goes often in different directions and at cross-purposes. This is often due, as in the example of Walter and his wife, to an inability to agree on basic issues about Tristram: who should assist at his birth, his name and education or what kind of pants he should wear—or even at what age he should be allowed to wear them. The main source of their cross-purposing, though, lies in what Tristram variously calls the "original character throughout" (1.21), "contrariety of humours" (1.21), or, more often, each character's "Hobby-Horse" (1.23–24). The best examples of this, and the source of much of the fun of the work, are the respective "hobby horses" of Walter and Uncle Toby. Walter is a "philosopher" who likes to describe, analyze, and manufacture "hypotheses." Toby is modest, quiet, and likes to think, and talk, about military matters, especially fortifications. But, neither wants to listen to what the other says on his favorite subject—despite the fact that they attend closely to what the other has to say about family affairs. The problem of not listening, or listening and not understanding, also afflicts the narrator and his alleged reader. For example, in Tristram's attempt to explain to a female reader a cause of Toby's modesty: "He got it, Madam, by a blow.—A blow!—Yes, Madam, it was owing to a blow from a stone, broke off by a ball from the parapet of a horn-work at the siege of Namur, which struck full upon my uncle Toby's groin.—Which way could that effect it?" (1.21). Not understanding the sexual significance of the "blow" will also be a problem later for the Widow Wadman in her pursuit of Uncle Toby (9.20, 26).

All men, says Aristotle, "need, by nature, to know" (*Metaphysics*, 980 a, 22), but men acquire different kinds of information, a major distinction for Aristotle being either certain, "apodeistic," knowledge (*Posterior Analytics*, 72 b, 18–33; 73 a, 15–35), or "opinions" (*dogmata*)—"We opine what we do not quite know," and one can opine about everything, the "eternal" as well as the "impossible" (*Nicomachean Ethics*, 1111 b, 30–35; 1112 a, 8). Sterne, who knew Aristotle and Aristotelian ideas well, takes these distinctions as a theme for *Tristram*. For Tristram, writing his opinions as well as his life, makes his reader know not only about the Shandy Family at large but also about maps and fortifications (2.3), noses (3.31–41), whiskers (5.1), and Socrates's children (5.15). Such opinion-giving often becomes a parody of the question of who knows what and why (and where and when he knows it). The Widow Wadman, for example, wants to know "where" Toby was wounded; he sends for a map, shows her where the siege of Namur took place, and invites her to put her hand on it (9.26–27); Tristram's mother, in the midst of sexual intercourse with Walter, wants to know if he has, as is his weekly custom, wound up the clock (1.1); Tristram, playing with the reader's what happens next question, tells him in one place that the reader will never be able to guess (1.25), in another that Walter's propagation of children is "not worth talking about" (2.13), and in another that the reader, if he wishes, might "skip" some of the book (1.4). Walter's exercise with questions (what Tristram calls the "auxiliaries") on the subject of a white bear (5.42–43) clearly directs the parody to an opinion-acquisition procedure: "If I should never see a white bear, what then? . . . —Is the white bear worth seeing?—Is there no sin in it?—Is it better than a BLACK ONE?" (5.43). Significantly, these questions, which end the chapter, are never answered—nor, presumably, should they be.[10]

What much of this points to is a comedy dependent on the failure, fatigue, or misuse of *procedural* knowledge. (Knowledge which differs from *declarative* knowledge as "how" does from "what.") Procedural failure is, first of all, writing failure: "Lay down the book, and I will allow you half a day to give a probable guess at the grounds of this procedure" (1.10). Running parallel with it are sexual failure, Tristram, Toby and the Shandy bull, rhetorical fatigue and failure, Walter's arguments with Mrs. Shandy (6.39), and "artifactual" collapse, the collapse of Toby's bridge (3.24), the fall of the window sash (5.17), and the disintegration of Toby's scarlet breeches and gold-laced hat (8.35; 9.2). Obadiah's tying knots in Dr. Slop's green bag (3.7), Trim's fabricating mortars from boots (3.22), and the coach-painter's work on Walter's coach (4.25) are examples of the misuse (or, perhaps, the overuse) of procedural knowledge. Each example of such knowledge makes intelligible certain idiosyncrasies of the characters, as for instance, Dr. Slop's violence, Walter's familial propriety, and the unreflective master-servant relationship of Walter and Obadiah. In the execution of such procedures lies a parody of traditional discussions of cause and effect—or, perhaps, traditional, and contemporary, attempts to explain cause and effect (cf. 8.14),[11] for what consistent explanations can one have of it if boots become mortars, bowling greens battlefields, or lead window weights cannons?

As Alan B. Howes shows, Sterne has had many commentators, detractors, and supporters. He has been praised by Virginia Woolf, Samuel Taylor Coleridge, and Milan Kundera and dismissed (or condemned) by Johnson, Oliver Goldsmith, and William Makepeace Thackeray. It is not always easy to evaluate his position in eighteenth-century literature as a whole or his influence on modern literature. Sterne's pioneering work in "metacommentary," as New points out (*DLB*, 472), has certainly interested modern writers. Yet, many of the topics of *Tristram*, such as those drawn from contemporary medicine, law, and rhetoric, are now either obsolete, rejected as false, or forgotten.[12] Prominent among those rejected is the humors doctrine (ultimately derived from the Greek Physiologists and Aristotle) used extensively by Sterne in *Journey* and *Tristram* to describe behavior or distinguish characters.[13]

Sterne's use of language, especially in *Tristram*, continues to fascinate scholars and inspire writers. He is possibly the first novelist to see, and fully exploit for the purposes of comedy, the "language" of the body, handedness, posture and bodily stances, sitting, standing, leaning, pointing, and the like. Handedness, the use and misuse of the right and left hands, is espe-cially evident. The affair of Walter, his wig, and his handkerchief is one such example: "'What prodigious armies you had in Flanders!—Brother Toby,' replied my father, taking his wig from off his head with his right hand, and with his left pulling out a striped India handkerchief from his right coat pocket, in order to rub his head . . . As my father's India handkerchief was in his right pocket, he should by no means have suffered his right hand to have got engaged" (3.2; cf. 9.1). A key word here is "should," an authorial comment that informs the reader that what he is about to witness is not only Walter's cross-handedness but also a picture of how handedness and intentions ought to work together. This is/should contrast, along with the usual interruptions, not only allows Sterne to prolong the scene for three chapters (two through five) but also to parody the mind-body theories of the seventeenth century—specifically that of René Descartes: "A man's body and his mind, with the utmost reverence to both . . . are exactly like a jerkin, and a jerkin's lining,—rumple the one—you rumple the other" (3.4; cf. 9.13).

It is in his development of the "self-conscious" text, the use of kinship relations, and the representation of synchronic events, however, that Sterne is most innovative. Many eighteenth-century texts (*Gulliver's Travels* and *Tom Jones*, for example), insofar as they contain sentences that take themselves, the reader, or the author as referent, are "self-conscious." In *Tristram*, self-consciousness is not so much an effect of self-reference as the original problem. How is writing achieved and sustained? How does one keep the reader aware that *this* is writing, not simply a record of the Shandy family, the life of Tristram, and the like? Sterne's main answer is to emphasize writing as process, struggle, and failure. Tristram begins a chapter with "—But to return to my mother," then addresses the reader on the subject of Uncle Toby (5.12); he leaves chapters 18 and 19 of volume 9 blank, then returns after chapter 25 to write them; and, he finally gets around to writing, in chapter 20 of volume 3, his Preface. Nevertheless, his main problem is with time, his own approaching mortality, and the infinite nature of his subject: "In short, there is no end of it," that is, subjects to write on, he declared when he noted that he had been writing for six weeks . . . and was not born yet (1.14; cf. 2.8, 7.1, 9.8). Correlative with Tristram's struggle to write and get everything in are his attempts to explain the structure of his work. "My work is digressive, and it is progressive too,—and at the same time" (1.22; cf. 6.40, 8.1, 9.4).

Every eighteenth-century novel has a family or two as part of the subject. The Western and Allworthy families of *Tom Jones* and the Harlowe family of *Clarissa* are examples. Matters such as marriage, parental control, the education of children, and so forth become important parts of the narration. With the proliferation of kinship relations in *Tristram* ("endless genealogies," 1.14), and what Sterne does with each relation, a new kind of fiction appeared. The opening chapters of volume 1 of the book are characteristic: from the first scene between Tristram's father and mother the focus shifts first to the Homunculus (1.2), then to Uncle Toby (1.3), then to Walter (1.4); in chapter 10 the focus moves to Yorick, the local parson, to his family background (1.11), and then to his illness and death (1.12). Concern is expressed about Tristram's great Aunt Dinah (1.21), Tristram's brother Bobby (5.2), and Trim's brother, Tom (2.17, 4.4, 9.4). Tristram's great-grandfather and great-grandmother are given a scene in which to discuss noses (3.33). We learn that Tristram's genealogy goes back to "King Henry VIII's time" (3.33). Familial topics include the neglect of husbands during childbirth (4.12), a possible illegitimacy in the family (4.25), and the ingratitude of children (9.18).[14] Almost a whole chapter is given to a discussion of a family heirloom, the jackboots of Sir Roger Shandy, Toby's great-grandfather—boots which Trim has made into two mortarpieces (3.22).

The shifting from one generation to another, and from one family member to another, has not pleased all readers. Horace Walpole, for example, wrote to a friend that the "whole narrative" in *Tristram* was "always going backwards" and that he expected the next volumes to "reach backwards to his [Sterne's] great-grandfather."[15] Modern readers see in this structure a clever, and successful, strategy for the comic writer. It gives *Tristram*, for one thing, great time-depth and with that an opportunity for Sterne to move between generations and among the members of one generation, and to poke fun at such common matters as the family arms and familial pride (4.25), marital disagreements (1.15), and the naming of children (1.19, 4.18). Such matters, since they are part of the literary families of the age, take on the nature of universal topics—something that

Sterne may have recognized when he wrote to his publisher, Robert Dodsley, that "all locality is taken out of the book, the satire [made] general" (October 1759?).

One might also hazard the opinion that in the kinship relation Sterne discovered one important, and successful, means of "going on"—to the next episode, the next chapter, or volume. It is not only the kinship relations that a character possesses at a certain time and place that afford an author matter but also the relations that he or she *potentially* possesses. A son in chapter 1, for example, may become (or be made) a husband in chapter 2 or 3, a father in 4 or 5, an uncle in 6 or 7, and a grandfather also in 6 or 7. Sterne does not take Tristram this far, but the sequence he does follow in expanding the web of Tristram's kin is a natural one. From being a son in chapters 1 and 2 of volume 1 he goes to being a nephew (Uncle Toby) in chapter 3 and a great grandnephew (great Aunt Dinah) in chapter 21. In chapter 31 of volume 3, he becomes a great grandson and learns that he has had a brother, Bobby, now dead. Each new kinship relation for Tristram means a new member of the Shandy family and for the novelist a new opportunity to define, exemplify, and expand Shandyism. This seems to be heard, for example, in Tristram's mother raising the possibility of Mrs. Wadman having children by Toby (9.11). The new kinship relation also is a way for the novelist to develop, by the addition of attributes, the character of a known relation. Walter's reaction to the history of Tristram's great aunt, Dinah, and to the death of Bobby are examples. Perhaps with the Shandy family Sterne created the family he himself did not have.

With *Journey*, the emphasis on kinship, or the lack of it, becomes a way of creating sympathy for a character. Widowhood, for example, comes in for special notice (Stout, 94), as do the feelings aroused by viewing the mutual support within a family (Stout, 212–14, "The Sword. Rennes."). As Stout points out, the sympathy commonly evoked by the condition of widows is a frequent theme in Sterne's sermons (94. 33.34n).

Sterne is also an innovator in what can be called the comedy of synchronic events; that is, the representation of simultaneous events occurring in different places. Sometimes, for this, parallel sentence structure appears in the narrative: "When . . . my uncle Toby sat down before the mistress [Widow Wadman],—corporal Trim

S

incontinently took ground before the maid [Mrs. Bridget]" (3.24). More often the representation features domestic arrangements. So, we have Tristram's description of simultaneous goings-on in different parts of the Shandy house. Discussions between Walter and Toby in the parlor, for example, are described along with goings-on upstairs (2.6); outside the parlor door with Tristram's mother (5.5), or in the kitchen with Obadiah and Susannah (5.7). And, Tristram often represents himself as being *there* with the reader, sharing the same emotion, enacting the same role, or anticipating the same event. He gives encouragement to the reader when he thinks he (she?) is getting bored (5.41); he credits the reader for thrusting him "almost into the middle of" the story (8.7), and he promises the reader that they will discuss the topic of the married man after supper (9.22).

Such representations require a deft handling of tense, aspect, and modality. Events begun and interrupted are aspectual representations; events distinguished by their temporal context, Toby's past military life, his affair with Mrs. Wadman, or the long history of the Shandy family are consequences of tense. Tristram's wish list, both as a person and an author, features modal forms such as "could," "should," and "had," as in these lines from the opening scene of *Tristram*: "I wish either my father or mother . . . had minded . . . had they duly consider'd how . . . Had they duly weighed and considered all this" (1.1; cf. the *Journey*), "had she remained close . . . I should have" ("In the Street. Calais." Stout, 107). At other times modals like "could" and "would" express Tristram's desire to write a chapter upon sleep or button-holes (4.15).

In the end infinite matter defeats the constraints that sentence Tristram to finite representations. He cannot write fast enough to catch up (1.14); he loses writing time in the necessity of fleeing from death (7.1–3). He knows that while writing is linear, one sentence after another, his life and opinions are everywhere, recursive and non-linear, "running parallel," both in the parlor and the kitchen (5.6). One cannot complete the task, but one still goes on trying. In a letter to Dr. John Eustace (February 9, 1768), Sterne identifies a similar paradox as the problem of the comic writer. Nobody can learn the skill, "'tis the gift of God," yet nobody knows that he does not have the skill until he tries his hand at it—and has proof that he is what he is trying to be by the approval of a sympathetic reader, "a true feeler [who] brings half the entertainment along with him."

If a summarizing term for Sterne's work as an author exists, then it would have to be "difference." Not a difference, for his time, in ideological notions about gender, religion, or law, nor one in the particular role that a writer has in society or in his reasons for writing, but a difference in exploiting the representational capacities of language. He is, for one thing, more sensitive than his contemporaries to polysemy—the capacity of language to represent more than one thing, or idea, with one term. In *Tristram*, "place," in both its singular and plural forms, probably has more polysemous force than any other word. There are many examples in both *Tristram* and *Journey*: "purse," a container for money/female genitals (Stout, 188. 31–37n, 236. 59–68n), "bridge," part of the body/part of a military fortification (*Tristram* 3.23), or "auxiliary," part of speech/a military unit (4.42, 5.42–43). Without polysemy his work would lose much of its humor—especially that effected by punning and innuendo. Some of his major characters, especially Walter and Toby, would also lose a basis for their contrasting personalities. With terms having polysemous values in the sister arts, "sketch," "design," "paint," and the like, Sterne is able to link his work as a writer to that of a painter like Hogarth (see, e.g., 2.5, 17; 3.12; 4.15).

Sterne also differs from his contemporaries in his common use of what can be called, after C.S. Peirce, "thirdness" (*On Signs and the Categories*). This is the tendency of the mind, through language, to structure memory and experience by the "third" thing, the thing between two other things, the third word of a predicate, the third person in a scene, and so on. Some of this may be, as New suggests, a formula borrowed from Rabelais (*Tristram*, 3.239.228.5); most examples are uniquely Sterne's: the representation of conscience as "neither Protestant nor Catholic" (*Tristram* 1.16), the "transition" between attitudes (4.6), or the introduction of a third person to move the action or complete a scene in the *Journey* (see, e.g., Stout, 107–108 introduction of "A little French *debonaire* captain"; 121–23, introduction of La Fleur; cf., the "three several roads" as both fictive plot and factual crossroads, 3.23). Thirdness is especially important for Sterne in writing the "self-conscious" text because consciousness minimally involves the third thing, that which "knows" the existence of the I-subject (the first thing) and the it-object (the second thing). With *Tristram*, this works out to be the knowledge that Tristram has of himself as author, the reader as a particular person, as "Jenny," "madam," etc., and the text itself as a specific *kind* of artifact, as, for example, "this cyclopaedia of the arts and sciences" (2.17).

Such consciousness is not as evident in *Journey*, but it does make its appearance (like the third actor in a scene?) wherever Yorick is at pains to distinguish himself from other travel-writers, especially Smollett (e.g., Stout, 78–86; 114–20; 75–9). And, insofar as consciousness is uncertain—either about its object of knowledge or its linguistic representation of the object—thirdness for Sterne may become the nexus of additional uncertainties raised in the mind of the reader of either *Tristram* or the *Journey* (cf. Lamb, 137, "Tristram's private sublime").

Summary

One can give many reasons for Laurence Sterne's achievement as a humorist. One might mention, for example, his sense of play, the self-referential nature of his fiction, or his mixing of what might be called the sacred and the secular. However, one can always *feel*, without perhaps fully knowing them, the force and presence of the reasons by listening closely to his words and experiencing what they represent—as, for example, in Tristram's words on why he wrote the story of his father's theory of names: "—'tis wrote, an' please your worships, against the spleen; in order, by a more convulsive elevation and depression of the diaphragm, and the successations of the intercostal and abdominal muscles in laughter, to drive the *gall* and other *bitter juices* from the gall bladder, liver and sweet-bread of his majesty's subjects, with all the inimicitious passions which belong to them, down into their duodenums" (4.22).

Notes

1. Jaques and Laurence later became enemies. See Lewis P. Curtis, *Letters of Laurence Sterne* (Oxford: Clarendon, 1935), pp. 4, 427–28.
2. Sterne, according to Curtis, may have falsified his mother's background because of her later demands on him. Her real father was, according to Curtis, the "youngest child of Capt. Christopher Nuttal, son of Laurence Nuttal, Esq . . . . the head of an ancient family, after whom the infant Laurence was probably named" (5). But, see Arthur H. Cash, *Laurence Sterne* (London: Methuen, 1975), vol. 1, p. 1, 2 n.
3. See Ian Jack, ed., *Laurence Sterne: A Sentimental Journey through France and Italy by Mr. Yorick* (Oxford and New York: Oxford University Press, 1988), pp. 130–33.
4. See Alan B. Howes, *Sterne, the Critical Heritage* (London: Routledge & Kegan Paul, 1974), pp. 26–33. Cf. Milan Kundera, *The Art of the Novel*, trans. Linda Asher (New York: Grove Press, 1987), pp. 160–61: "Of all that period's novels, it is Sterne's *Tristram Shandy* I love best . . . Every novel . . . offers some answer to the question: What is human existence, and wherein does its poetry lie . . . for [Sterne] the poetry lies not in the action but in the interruption of the action."
5. Quoted by D.W. Jefferson, "Laurence Sterne." In *British Writers*, ed. Ian Scott-Kilvert (New York: Charles Scribner's Sons, 1980), vol. 3, pp. 124–35.
6. *Journey* may have been responsible, during the 1760s, in giving the meaning of "tender feelings" to the word "sentimental." Previously, its core meaning had been "thought" or "reflection." Sterne seemed to have used the word ("sentimental repasts") in its new meaning first in a letter to Elizabeth Lumley in 1739 or 1740. Curtis, pp. 11, 13.
7. See Jack, pp. ix–xiii.
8. Melvyn New, *Laurence Sterne as Satirist* (Gainesville: University Press of Florida, 1969), pp. 31–49.
9. See, e.g., Yorick's reference to Bevoriskius and the sparrows and his encounter with Madame de V***. Gardner D. Stout, ed., *A Sentimental Journey Through France and Italy By Mr. Yorick* (Berkeley and Los Angeles: University of California Press, 1967), pp. 228–29 ("The Passport. Versailles."), pp. 264–65 (Paris).
10. Cf. Sterne's general motto, from Epictetus, for *Tristram*. "It is not things that disturb men, but opinions [dogmata] about things."
11. E.g., Aristotle, *Metaphysics*, 983 a 24–

S

985 b 21; Thomas Reid, *Essays on the Active Powers of the Human Mind*, Essay #4.

12. See D.W. Jefferson. *"Tristram Shandy* and the Tradition of Learned Wit." *Essays in Criticism*, 1 (1951): 225–48.

13. See, e.g., 1.12 ("cholerick reader") and 4.22 (*Tristram* written against the "spleen").

14. Cf. vol. 3, p. 39. Importance of the Shandy family to Sterne to "shift the scene."

15. Quoted Howes, *Critical Heritage*, p. 55.

Selected Bibliography

Primary Sources

Letters of Laurence Sterne. Ed. Lewis P. Curtis. Oxford: Clarendon, 1935. The most complete collection of Sterne's letters.

A Sentimental Journey Through France and Italy by Mr. Yorick. Ed. Gardner D. Stout. Berkeley and Los Angeles: University of California Press, 1967. The authoritative text for the *Journey.* Contains, in addition to the text itself, an Introduction, Note on the Text, Appendices A-E, and twelve Illustrations. The Introduction is a very full discussion of the historical background of the work and the notes to the text relate specific passages to Sterne's reading and his other works—especially his *Sermons.*

Laurence Sterne: A Sentimental Journey through France and Italy By Mr. Yorick. Ed. Ian Jack. Oxford and New York: Oxford University Press, 1988. Contains *The Journal to Eliza* and *A Political Romance.*

The Florida Edition of the Works of Laurence Sterne. Ed. Melvyn New. Vols. 1 and 2, *The Text of Tristram Shandy,* Melvyn and Joan New, eds. Gainesville: University Press of Florida, 1978. Vol. 3, *The Notes to Tristram Shandy,* Melvyn New, Richard A. Davies, and W.G. Day, eds. Gainesville: University Press of Florida, 1984. The authoritative edition of *Tristram Shandy.*

Secondary Sources

Bibliographies

The Scriblerian. Bi-annual bibliography of criticism on Sterne.

The Shandean. Ed. Peter J. de Voogd. An annual journal on Sterne. The Laurence Sterne Trust, Shandy Hall, Coxwold, York, United Kingdom.

Books and Chapters in Books

Brooks, Douglas. *Number and Pattern in the Eighteenth-Century Novel.* London: Routledge & Kegan Paul, 1973. Chapter 7 is on *Tristram.* Brooks discusses the possible significance of numbers and number-pattern in *Tristram.* At times, however, the argument seems strained; e.g., that circumcision is "traditionally associated with the number 8" (p. 173).

Cash, Arthur H. *Laurence Sterne.* 2 vols. *The Early and Middle Years; The Later Years.* London: Methuen, 1975; 1986. The latest, and most definitive, biography of Sterne. Contains letters not collected by Curtis.

———. *Sterne's Comedy of Moral Sentiments: The Ethical Dimensions of the Journey.* Pittsburgh: Duquesne University Press, 1966. A thorough discussion of the relationship of the *Sermons* to *A Sentimental Journey.*

———, and John M. Stedmond, eds. *The Winged Skull. Papers from the Laurence Sterne Bicentenary Conference.* Kent, OH: Kent State University Press, 1971. Contains important essays on Sterne's social milieu; the meaning, and structure, of *Tristram Shandy,* and Sterne's influence in the modern world.

Cross, Wilbur L. *The Life and Times of Laurence Sterne.* New York: Macmillan, 1909. An early, and still useful, biography of Sterne.

Erickson, Robert A. *Mother Midnight: Birth, Sex, and Fate in Eighteenth-Century Fiction.* New York: AMS Press, 1986, pp. 195–242. Erickson examines the possibility of a feminine influence, "matrix," in *Tristram.*

Fluchere, Henri. *Laurence Sterne: From Tristram to Yorick.* Trans. Barbara Bray. London: Oxford University Press, 1965. Detailed discussion of themes, structure, style, and characterization of *Tristram Shandy.*

Graves, Patricia. "A Computer-Generated Concordance to Sterne's Tristram Shandy." 4 vols. Ph.D. diss., Emory University, 1974.

Howes, Alan B., ed. *Sterne, the Critical Heritage*. London: Routledge & Kegan Paul, 1974. Quotations from original sources of (mostly) contemporary comments, opinions, and the like about Sterne.

———. *Yorick and the Critics. Sterne's Reputation in England, 1760–1868*. New Haven: Yale University Press, 1958. The most complete account of Sterne's reputation as a writer and man in the 100 years following his death.

Lamb, Jonathan. *Sterne's Fiction and the Double Principle*. Cambridge: Cambridge University Press, 1989. Lamb discusses Sterne's use of the uncertainty often holding between word-referent-meaning. Finds analogs of the double principle in David Hume, Joseph Addison, and John Dryden.

New, Melvyn. *Laurence Sterne as Satirist: A Reading of "Tristram Shandy."* Gainesville: University Press of Florida, 1969. The most complete discussion of Sterne's relationship to mainstream Anglicanism and the role it plays in *Tristram Shandy*.

———. "Laurence Sterne." *Dictionary of Literary Biography*, 39. *British Novelists, 1660–1800*. Ed. Martin C. Battestin. Vol. 2, pp. 471–99. Perhaps the best single short introduction to Sterne. Gives indispensable information about Sterne's life, the relationship between his faith and his fiction and clues to the structure of his novels, especially *Tristram Shandy*.

———, ed. *Sterne's Tristram Shandy*. New York: Modern Language Association, 1989. Approaches to Teaching World Literature series. The best available guide to teaching the novel. Contains a very full bibliography of recent writings on the novel and classroom approaches used by leading Sterne scholars.

———, ed. *Approaches to Teaching Sterne's Tristram Shandy*. New York: Modern Language Association, 1989. The best available guide to teaching the novel. Contains a very full bibliography of recent writings on the novel and classroom approaches used by leading Sterne scholars.

Pasta, Betty B., and David J. Pasta. *A Short Concordance to Sentimental Journey*. 2 vols. Champaign–Urbana: University of Illinois, 1974. Available through the Computer Science Department.

Scott-Kilvert, ed. "Laurence Sterne." *British Writers*. New York: Charles Scribner's Sons, 1980.

Gene Washington

Stoppard, Tom

Born: Zlinn (now Gottwaldau), Czechoslovakia, July 3, 1937

Education: Attended the American school, Darjeeling, India 1942–1946; Dolphin School, Nottinghamshire and Pocklington School, Yorkshire 1946–1954

Marriage: Jose Ingle, 1966; divorced 1972; two children; Miriam Moore-Robinson, 1972; two children

Biography

Born on July 3, 1937, in Zlinn, Czechoslovakia, to Eugene and Martha Straussler, Tomas Straussler was two when his father, a company doctor for Bata (now Svit), an international shoe company, was transferred to Singapore on the eve of Adolf Hitler's invasion of Czechoslovakia. Then on the eve of the Japanese invasion of Singapore, Mrs. Straussler and her two sons were evacuated to Darjeeling, India, where she managed a Bata shoe shop. With his older brother, Tom attended a multinational American school. After the death of her husband during the Japanese invasion, Mrs. Straussler married a British officer, Major Kenneth Stoppard, who moved his family to England when the war ended.

Working in the machine tool industry, Major Stoppard was transferred a number of times, with the family finally arriving in Bristol where Tom at seventeen, bored by Greek and Latin classics, William Shakespeare, Charles Dickens, and so forth, found employment as a reporter with the *Western Daily Press*. He then wrote for the *Evening World*, during which time his interest in the theater developed. When he moved to London in 1962, he reviewed plays for *Scene* magazine, writing under the pseudonym of William Boot (a character appearing in a number of Stoppard's plays), a name taken from Evelyn Waugh's novel, *Scoop*. As a prelude to his major plays, such as *Rosencrantz and Guildenstern Are Dead*, *Jumpers*, *Travesties*, and *The Real Thing*, Stoppard wrote some short stories, one novel, and many short pieces for radio and television. His first play produced on stage in 1966 at the Aldwych Theatre in London was an adaptation of a Polish play, Slawomir Mrozek's *Tango*. His first original stage play, *Rosencrantz and Guildenstern Are Dead*, which premiered at the 1966 Edinburgh Festival, opened in 1967 at London's Old Vic.

In 1966, Stoppard married Jose Ingle, a nurse, and two sons—Oliver and Barnaby—were born of this marriage. After his divorce from Jose in 1972, Stoppard married Dr. Miriam Moore-Robinson, the medical director for Syntex Pharmaceuticals. An articulate television personality well known for her discussions of women's issues (and the author of two books on health hints for women), she is the mother of Stoppard's two younger sons—William and Edmund. The Stoppards reside in Iver Heath just outside London, and Stoppard and Harold Pinter have played on the same cricket side on occasion.

Literary Analysis

Writing during a time when the second of two waves of post-World War II drama was inundating the English stage, Stoppard avoided the socio-political ferment that was the subject of the new plays which then were being encouraged, especially at the Royal Court and many small fringe theaters. Without the social or political commitment of most of his contemporaries (such as John Osborne, Arnold Wesker, John Arden, Edward Bond, Trevor Griffiths, David Hare, Howard Brenton, Pam Gems, and Caryl Churchill), Stoppard, like Pinter, regarded the theatrical event primary in and of itself, not as a forum for causes or political commitments. Both of these master dramatists created styles with which each became immediately identifiable. However, in the mid-1970s, Stoppard became actively involved in human rights movements, including Charter 77 and Amnesty International. He met with dissident Czechoslovakian playwrights Vaclav Havel and Pavel Kohout, and a number of his plays at this time reflect that involvement: *Every Good Boy Deserves Favor* (1977), *Night and Day* (1978), *Professional Foul* (1977, a television play), and *Dogg's Hamlet, Cahoot's Macbeth* (1979).

The dramatist received honorary degrees from the universities of Leeds and Sussex in 1980. In addition to his radio, television, and stage plays, he has written many film scripts, and in 1990 he was awarded first place at the Venice Film Festival for *Rosencrantz and Guildenstern Are Dead*, the cinematic version released twenty-three years after the play's debut on the London stage.

With the success of *Rosencrantz and Guildenstern Are Dead*, which catapulted him into international fame, Stoppard joined the ranks of dramatists such as Oscar Wilde and George Bernard Shaw, all writers of a high comedy of ideas. Although a debate of ideas is at the center of Stoppard's high comedy, the ideas are frequently overshadowed by: (1) the dazzling wit and vivid imagery of the playwright's language; (2) the daringly plagiaristic usage of other writers' plots and characters; and (3) the incongruous situations that stem from a disjointedness between the characters and their times.

The first of these elements, discussed only briefly here, is the witty dialogue in his plays. Taking the form of debates between conflicting desires within a character or between conflicting artists or philosophers, Stoppard's dialogue winds through labyrinthine paths. The author indulges in unresolved contradictions; in metaphors of skyrocketing brilliance; in repetitions and puns (one of the latter being the "cognomen syndrome," a playing around with names); and in literary, historical, and popular allusions. At times the debates disappear into a linguistic intoxication. There is seldom any conclusion to the debate of ideas, but, rather, there is an emotional, moral, or intellectual release of them. One feels, for example, the tension and anxieties in the stichomythic questioning of their existence by Rosencrantz and Guildenstern, the disintegration of traditional absolutes by the moral relativists in *Jumpers*, and the conflicting attitudes about art represented by Tristan Tzara, James Joyce, and Vladimir Lenin in *Travesties*.

A second component of Stoppardian style, as extravagant as his use of language, is the daring reinvention of other writers' characters and plots or of real-life characters and situations. For example, not only is *Rosencrantz and Guildenstern Are Dead* a perverse borrowing directly from Shakespeare, but its two Shakespearean protagonists, Ros and Guil, are stylistic re-creations of Samuel Beckett's Gogo and Didi of *Waiting for Godot*. In *Travesties*, characters and scenes from Wilde's *The Importance of Being Earnest* and a famous scene from Joyce's *Ulysses* are but two borrowings from which Stoppard creates a new work of art. This re-creation of art from art or from the shards of history is, in fact, a theory which Joyce, a character in that play, debates with two other revolutionaries, Lenin and dadaist Tzara.

In addition to borrowing from literature and history, Stoppard freely borrows from contemporary life. In *Jumpers,* he deliberately confuses his character, George Moore, with the real-life philosopher, G.E. Moore. Another character is patterned after the Wyckham Professor of Logic at Oxford University and an acquaintance of Stoppard. Even George's wife Dotty is drawn from a real-life popular songstress. Other borrowings or influences are contained in *Night and Day* (1979), from Waugh's novel, *Scoop,* referred to earlier as the source of Stoppard's early pseudonym, William Boot. In *The Real Inspector Hound* (1968), Stoppard brilliantly parodies Agatha Christie. In *Neutral Ground* (1968), he reaches back to the Greeks to re-create the myth of Philoctetes in modern terms. He even goes so far as to reinvent himself, as in his reworking a radio play, *Artist Descending a Staircase* (1972, the title a borrowing from Marcel Duchamp's famous painting) into the full-length stage play, *Travesties.* About other writers, critics speak of influences. With Stoppard, influence takes on the imagery of injections of insulin (his own term).

A third characteristic of Stoppard's high comedy is the premise of the disjointedness between man and his times. Out of touch with the modern world, his characters find themselves in conflict with modern values. As a result, they attempt to create a context in which they can function. Some succeed and others do not. Nowhere is this situation more vividly demonstrated than in Stoppard's only novel, *Lord Malquist and Mr. Moon* (1966). Malquist is a "boot" character who survives by virtue of insisting on style. Moon, hired by Malquist to record his (Malquist's) statements, is himself interested in writing a history of the world and is constantly plagued by his inability to understand the world and history, and, indeed, even the vagaries of his own personal life, a life that includes a nymphomaniacal wife named Jane. As events swirl around them, Malquist and Moon ride through the congested streets of modern London in Malquist's eighteenth-century carriage (a malquist) on the day of the funeral of England's last man-of-action hero (presumably, Winston Churchill). As they ride, Malquist dictates his pronouncements to Moon, a James Boswell to Malquist's Samuel Johnson. At the end a bomb carried by Moon explodes accidentally, and he is killed, but Malquist, a boot character, survives. Moon is the dreamer, who, in his anguished attempt to understand his context, disappears into it. From this boot-moon premise derives the basic situations of Stoppard's plays and a long series of boot and moon characters as well.

Absurdities grow incrementally from the basic incongruity of a malquist among motor cars. Among the most hilarious characters are the two American cowboys—Jasper Jones (a punning of Jasper Johns) and Long John Slaughter, who vie for the favors of "Fertility" Jane (Moon's wife), as they have nicknamed her. There is also a black-Irish-Catholic named O'Hara and a Risen Christ whose donkey carries a dead body. All join or interrupt the funeral procession. The jokes grow with each episode in this amalgam of absurdities caused by the disjointedness of characters and context. Malquist, who survives by creating his style, is a forerunner of a character, James Joyce, who, in the later *Travesties,* creates his own style and who, like Stoppard himself, is known primarily as a stylist in linguistic experiments.

Illustrating the disjunction between character and context, Stoppard's two most famous characters in *Rosencrantz and Guildenstern Are Dead*—arguably Shakespeare's most insignificant named characters—are given significance simply by the role that Stoppard assigns them. Knowing only that one morning someone had summoned them from Wittenburg to Elsinore, they attempt to understand why they are there and, indeed, who they are. To this end, they play what seems an interminable game of coin-tossing, speculating all the while on the mathematical probabilities of the coin coming up heads or tails. The coin game leads into philosophical speculations on the reason for their being in Elsinore. When the strolling players arrive, the questions broaden into Pirandellian considerations of role-playing as reality. Then, on their journey to England, they debate matters of choice, destiny, and death. Taking the Player's advice to act out their roles, rather than being the mere spectators they are in Shakespeare's play, Guil in earnest stabs the Player (though with the Player's retractable knife, a parallel to his earlier winning of a coin game by deception), thus demonstrating the Player's contention that role-playing is reality. As spectators who turn actors by opting to choose the role that fate has assigned them, Rosencrantz and Guildenstern play their game with fate, but on their own terms, emerging with some identity and dignity. In support of his theory, the Player earlier had said that he is never out of his costume.

Like Beckett's, much of Stoppard's dialogue consists of minimalist, stichomythic lines, nagging and unanswered questions, repetition, contradictions, puns, and verbal games, games that begin with the coin tossing at the opening of the play.

The second of Stoppard's four major dramas, *Jumpers* (which premiered in 1972) continues the theme of disjointedness and the stylistic traditions of *Rosencrantz and Guildenstern Are Dead*. The ideas in this play, however, are reinforced with farcical and melodramatic images and events that create a colorful circus ambience. This time the debate (between traditional moralists and modern relativists) takes the form of a lecture competition for a university chair in moral philosophy. While one candidate, George Moore, rehearses his lecture, his wife, Dotty, throws a party in celebration of a political victory. Also on this night, a moon landing is being televised. The entertainment for the party consists of pyramid-building by a team of yellow-clad jumpers (gymnasts) and of songs by Dotty, who is a popular singer. During the party a shot is fired, killing George's rival, Duncan McFee. Detectives arrive to take charge, only to cover up the murder.

Against the background of these events, George obliviously continues his lecture rehearsal. Using a bow and arrow to demonstrate a theoretical point from the philosopher, Zeno, he later discovers that he has accidentally impaled a pet hare, Thumper. As he steps down from his discovery, he crunches to death his pet tortoise, Pat. He is devastated. Dotty is similarly traumatized by the lunanauts' demythologizing of her romantic moon associations. She finds it difficult to sing her moon songs. In the guise of a therapist, Sir Archibald Jumper (Archie), a logical positivist, arrives and jumps into bed with her.

In the surrealistic coda to the play, George fantasizes the lecture competition with McFee's replacement, Archbishop Clegthorpe, a philosophical gymnast of the persuasion shared by McFee and Archie. As at the beginning, a shot is heard, and Clegthorpe, like McFee earlier, is knocked from the pyramid of jumpers. Attempting to be a "boot" character, George becomes a "moon." In his disintegration, he confusingly calls as witnesses certain philosophers—all of them dead—Zeno Evil, St. Thomas Augustine, and Jesus Moore, as well as the late Herr Thumper.

Spectacles, manic action, and long fantasy monologue by George and Dotty constitute the style of *Jumpers*, in contrast with the low-keyed, Beckettian rhythms of *Rosencrantz and Guildenstern Are Dead*. A combination of university debating hall, gymnasium, music hall, and courtroom, Stoppard's high comedy of ideas is a fusion of the "merely physical" and the "metaphysical" (Dotty's words). Disjointed from their times, Dotty and George attempt to create their contexts and farcically disintegrate into moon characters.

In this play, although the plot is Stoppard's, the characters are drawn from real life. George Moore has been given the same name as the author of *Principia Ethica*. Sir Archibald Jumper is patterned after Sir Alfred Ayer, a logical positivist from Oxford. At one point, George even considers writing a book entitled *Language, Truth and God*, a parody of Ayer's *Language, Truth and Logic*. Dorothy Moore is a popular English singer.

The third of Stoppard's major stage plays, *Travesties* (which premiered in 1974), represents his creative plagiarism and his linguistic wizardry at their best. Going beyond the earlier plays, he uses James Joyce as his *raisonneur* in the play and then borrows from Wilde two characters, Gwendolyn and Cecily, adapting one into a librarian and the other into a secretary to Joyce. He further adapts several key episodes from *The Importance of Being Earnest*: the famous misplacing of a bag in a railway station and a mistaken identity complication caused by the "bunburying" of Algernon. And, from Joyce's *Ulysses*, Stoppard parodies the equally famous Ithaca scene.

As the basis for his plot and setting, the author takes liberties with history. He exploits the possibility that three revolutionaries in politics, literature, and art—Lenin, Joyce, and Tzara—who were residing in Zurich during the turbulent end of the World War I era, may have met in the Zurich library. History and fiction are merged in the person of a narrator, Henry Carr, whose erratic memories of the events are acted out as he recalls them. Carr, a real-life minor British consular figure, was stationed in Zurich after having been wounded in the war. While in Zurich, he had played Algernon in a production of Wilde's play which was directed by Joyce. In a petty episode, Carr sued Joyce for reimbursement for a suit that he had purchased for his role. Joyce countersued for both the money and slander. In a scene reminiscent of the surrealistic coda in *Jumpers* in which George gets some revenge in a dream courtroom scene, Carr dreams that he had Joyce "in the witness box . . . and I flung at him—'and what did you do in the Great War?'"[1] The reference is to Joyce's neutrality in World War I.

The choice of a minor character with memory problems as the central intelligence through which the events of that time are filtered allows Stoppard free play with his literary jokes on a scale not present in either *Rosencrantz and Guildenstern Are Dead* or *Jumpers*. These jokes, by means of which he trivializes momentous revolutionary events and the historical characters of the time, are played out in a brilliance of language unequaled in his other plays. T.E. Kalem comments on the "tinderbox of a play with wit, paradox, parody, and, yes, ideas. It is exhilaratingly, diabolically clever. The bloodline of Wilde and Shaw is not extinct while Stoppard lives."[2] Joycean scholar Richard Ellmann notes the "laundered obscenities" which "convey some sense of the flagrant high spirits of this admirable play."[3]

The debates on art, carried on by the three main characters (Lenin, Tzara, and Joyce) are conducted in sharply contrasting styles of discourse. There is the stodgy, heavy, didactic prose of Lenin who insists that art exists as an instrument for social change. In his free-wheeling style, Tzara argues, frequently in nonsense language, that art, like history, is pure chance and that chance is even the design of art. Art must smash existing forms, he claims, and in demonstration of his theory he cuts up a sonnet into its words, letting them fall where they will. In his richly allusive language, Joyce holds that the artist is the magician "put among men to gratify—capriciously—their urge for immortality." Art consists of the broken pots of history, "enriched, by a tale of heroes . . . above all, of Ulysses, the wanderer, the most human, the most complete of all heroes—husband, father, son, lover, farmer, soldier, pacifist, politician, inventor, and adventurer . . . yes by God there's a corpse that will dance for some time yet and leave the world precisely as he finds it" (62, 63). As a spokesman for a Philistine view of art, Carr asserts that the artist's duty is "to beautify existence" rather than to "jeer and howl and belch at the delusion that infinite generations of real effects can be inferred from the gross expression of apparent cause" (60).

Stoppard's linguistic exuberance is illustrated in parodies such as that involving Tzara who, when wooing Gwen, feigns admiration for her employer and, indeed, indulges in linguisms that are clearly Joycean:

> For your masterpiece
> I have great expectorations
> (Gwen's squeak, "Oh!")
> For you I would eructate a monument.
> (Oh!)
> art for art's sake—I defecate (48).

Joyce replies with a parody of an old ballad:

> Who is the meek philosopher who
>   doesn't care a damn
> About the yellow peril or the problem of
>   Siam
> and disbelieves that British Tar is water
>   from life's fount
> And will not gulp the gospel of the German on the mount (50).

Another of Stoppard's language tricks is a play on foreign words spelled phonetically in English, as in a conversation between Lenin and Nadya: "Da-da. Idiom damoi" (20). (Yes, yes, we are going home.) The punning on dada creates a double entendre.

There is also a parody of Wildean rhythms in the conversations of Cecily and Gwendolyn:

> *Gwen:* A gross deception has been practiced upon us. My poor wounded Cecily!
> *Cecily:* My sweet wronged Gwendolyn! (94)

Still another Stoppardian joke is the occasional use of the "cognomen syndrome"—a confusion of names. Carr, having received favorable reviews for his role as Algernon, peevishly refers to Joyce's having given him a "tip" of ten francs for the performance and resorts to name-calling: Irish lout, Deirdre, Bridget, Joyce, Sponger.

The three revolutionaries have, like Lord Malquist, strongly defined their own contexts in a world of rapidly changing events. In so doing, they are boot characters, and they are also subject to travesties by others. Yet it is Carr, the insignificant moon character, to whom Stoppard fittingly gives the final scene. Reminiscing with his wife (both now old), he num-

S

bers the lessons that he has learned—a masterpiece of empty statement: "Firstly, you're a revolutionary or you're not, and if you're not you might as well be an artist as anything else. Secondly, if you can't be an artist, you might as well be a revolutionary . . . I forget the third thing" (99).

In an ironic twist, as though to confound fiction, real life impinged unexpectedly on the play shortly after its opening in London. Stoppard received a letter from Mrs. Noel Carr, Carr's second wife, who, fascinated with the reviews of the play, provided him with details of her husband's life, including his death in St. Mary Abbots Hospital, Kensington, in 1962.

Michael Billington's review of *Travesties* is one of the many extravagant judgments of the work: "A dazzling pyrotechnical feat that combines Wildean pastiche, political history, artistic debate, spoof-reminiscence, and song-and-dance in marvelously judicious proportion. It radiates sheer intellectual *joie de vivre*. Exuberant and freewheeling."[4] Stoppard's own term for the debate of ideas, linguistic richness, and action-packed plots of his dramas is "ambushes for the audience."[5]

A debate on the purpose and nature of art in *Travesties* is also the basis of Stoppard's fourth major full-length play, *The Real Thing*. The debate, however, exists in a personalized situation. Having been criticized for creating characters who lacked emotional and realistic credibility, Stoppard chooses for his main characters: a playwright, Henry, whose personal life is complicated by an actress, Annie, who becomes his second wife; a wife, Charlotte, from whom he separates in the course of the play; a precocious daughter, Debbie; and an actor-friend, Max. Henry's problem is that his personal relationships suffer as a result of the time and attention that his writing occupies. The plot centers on Annie's finding professional and personal satisfactions in her acting and fellow-actors when her life with Henry provides few such satisfactions. Annie's complaints are reinforced by both Debbie and Charlotte.

As with the more traditionally realistic character development, the action of *The Real Thing* is plotted fairly conventionally with Stoppard's own version of the standard play-within-a-play technique. But even here, Stoppard has an ambush for his audience. In the first scene, in what appears to be a typical marriage triangle, Charlotte returns home from a supposed business trip to Switzerland. Her husband, an architect named Henry, suspects the real nature of the trip. Not until the next scene is there any hint that this opening scene is only a play (titled *A House of Cards*) by an author named Henry and that the roles of the architect, Henry, and his wife, Charlotte, are being played by Max and by Henry's wife, Charlotte. So begin Stoppard's ambushes, in his deliberate confusion of names—the cognomen syndrome. Slowly, the names sort themselves out, and it becomes obvious that the marital difficulties of the architect and his wife of the play-within-a-play are to be played out in the real-life triangle of Henry, Charlotte, and Annie. Brief scenes from other dramas also serve as metaphors for Henry's marital dilemma, as for example, in scenes from August Strindberg's *Miss Julie* and John Ford's *'Tis A Pity She's A Whore*, plays in which Annie performs. Her love scenes on-stage with an actor named Billy reflect a passion lacking in her relationship with Henry.

When Annie's dedication to liberal causes converges with her acquaintance with a liberal playwright, Brodie, tensions between her and Henry grow. In a climactic scene, Brodie's coarseness loses the day for him, and she returns to Henry. Meanwhile, Henry has realized the importance of Annie's need for fulfillment of both her passion and profession, having been educated not only by Annie, but also by Debbie and Charlotte whose accusations in several witty scenes mirror Annie's frustrations. The play is a constant refraction of life by art, at times one fusing with the other indistinguishably. Debbie insists that Henry cannot write about love until he is educated in love. This education includes his recognition that exclusive rights to a woman are not love but colonization. Even with Henry's education by the three women, his reconciliation with Annie at the end suggests her continuing insistence on the satisfying of her needs.

Although the debates between Henry and the women are primarily about traditional and modern views of love, they are also about two kinds of art, one represented in Henry's insistence on style and the other in Brodie's overriding emphasis on socio-political causes. The difference between the two is a variation of that between Joyce and Lenin in *Travesties*. Henry, the familiar boot character, survives as a writer, whereas Brodie, a moon character, disappears into the causes that he espouses. Like George's demonstration of his moral philosophy with the aid of a bow and arrow and like Tzara and

Joyce demonstrating their art theories with cut-up sonnets and magicians' hats, Henry Boot uses a cricket bat to illustrate his art. As he holds the bat, he comments on its being so cunningly put together that, if hit right, the ball will travel 200 yards in four seconds. His contempt for Brodie's loutish style is obvious.

The Real Thing can be seen as Stoppard's reply to those critics who accused him of not writing about emotionally credible, realistic characters. It is a modern, witty play about love, and it is, as well, a reaffirmation of the theory of art and the artist put forth in *Travesties* without the farcical linguistic and literary parodies or the imaginative dramatic reinventions of *Rosencrantz and Guildenstern Are Dead*, *Jumpers*, or *Travesties*.

Three additional full-length plays deserve some mention. The first, *Enter a Free Man* (1968), was optioned in 1960 by H.M. Tennent under the title *A Walk on the Water*, and also produced on BBC Radio under that title. The play is interesting as an early work and as an English imitation of Arthur Miller's *Death of a Salesman*. Instead of a salesman, however, a failed would-be-inventor is a comic version of Willy Loman. Another play, *Night and Day* (1978), about journalists caught in the midst of an African revolution, contains echoes of Waugh's novel, *Scoop*. *Hapgood* (1988), a spy thriller à la John Le Carre, turns out to be another debate-of-ideas comedy. Its dizzying confusion of identities turns into a semi-scientific discourse in physics, on the subject of light particles that may simultaneously pass through two holes. The physics debate is conducted primarily by Kerner, a Russian spy who sees the particle world as the dream world of the intelligence officer. The particle world becomes a metaphor for the nature of identity (a subject in *Rosencrantz and Guildenstern Are Dead*) and the randomness of truth. Confusions multiply right to the end of the play so that more than any of his other plays, *Hapgood* illustrates Stoppard's self-styled dramaturgy as ambushes for the audience.

Another group of plays is that which was referred to earlier as the work of his politically conscious period. Sensational in its use of the eighty-piece London Symphony Orchestra, *Every Good Boy Deserves Favor* was first produced at the Royal Festival Hall in 1977. A comic-serious confusion of identities by two characters named Ivanov, one a political prisoner and the other a mental patient in an east-ern European prison, provides the writer with an opportunity to indulge in linguistic fantasies equal to those in his major plays. *Professional Foul* (1977), a television play that uses soccer terms as a metaphor for repressive measures, is about Westerners attending a linguistic conference in Prague. *Dogg's Hamlet, Cahoot's Macbeth* (1979) begins with a schoolboy production of *Hamlet* utilizing the code language of the English public school and broadens into the code language supplied to Pavel Kohout's Czechoslovakian players as they attempt a private, truncated performance of *Macbeth* in the playwright's living room. The freewheeling nonsense language dominates plot and the almost non-existent character development.

Most serious and least linguistically flamboyant, perhaps, of all of Stoppard's dramas is *Squaring the Circle* (1984), a television play utilizing, as in *Jumpers*, real-life characters. These include Leonid Brezhnev, Edward Gierek, Wojciech Jaruzelski, Lech Walesa, and others. Again a narrator (as in *Travesties*) is used, and again there are the usual tricks of language and plot, as Stoppard dramatizes the early stages of the Polish Solidarity movement. Although the play has a documentary flavor, it contains comic ironies that doubled as a result of a cinematic war between the English director and the American producers. This war resulted in two different television productions, and the play earned for Stoppard, at least by one reviewer, the title of England's most brilliant right-wing writer.

Too numerous to mention here are many short stage, radio, and television plays and the many radio scripts, among the most famous of which are, perhaps, *The Real Inspector Hound* (1968), *After Magritte* (1970), and *Dirty Linen and New-Found-Land* (1976), the latter Stoppard's fantasy tribute to America's bicentennial.

Summary

For his literate, literary, and sparklingly inventive stage language, his daring borrowing of plots and characters from other writers, and his high comedies of ideas debated by characters—boots and moons—Tom Stoppard has distinguished himself as one of two (the other being Pinter) major English linguistic stylists whose drama swept the English stage in the second half of the twentieth century. Liberal critic Kenneth Tynan describes Stoppard as a playwright more English than the English: "It is essential to remember that Stoppard is an emigre . . . You have to be foreign to write English with that kind of hypnotized brilliance . . . Stoppard loves all forms of wordplay, especially puns, and frequently describes himself as a 'bounced Czech' . . . Nowadays, he is *plus anglais que les anglais*—a phrase that would please him, as a student of linguistic caprice, since it implies that his English can best be defined in French."[6]

Notes

1. Tom Stoppard, *Travesties* (London: Faber & Faber, 1975), p. 65. Subsequent documentations appear in the text.
2. T.E. Kalem, "Dance of Words," *Time* (November 10, 1975): n.p.
3. Richard Ellmann, "The Zealots of Zurich," *Times Literary Supplement* (July 12, 1974): 744.
4. Michael Billington, quoted on the jacket of *Travesties* (London and New York, 1975).
5. Stoppard, "Ambushes for the Audience: Towards a High Comedy of Ideas," *Theatre Quarterly* (May-July 1974): 3–17.
6. Kenneth Tynan, "Withdrawing with Style from the Chaos," in *Show People: Profiles in Entertainment* (New York: Simon and Schuster, 1979), p. 64.

Selected Bibliography

Primary Sources

Plays
Unless otherwise noted, the works of Tom Stoppard are published by Faber & Faber of London and Grove Press of New York.
"Life, Times: Fragments," "Reunion," and "The Story" (short stories). In *Introduction 2: Stories by New Writers*. London, 1964.
Lord Malquist and Mr. Moon. London: Anthony Blond, 1966.
Rosencrantz and Guildenstern Are Dead. London and New York, 1967.
Tango (adaptation of Slawomir Mrozek's play, trans. Nicholas Bethell). London: Jonathan Cape, 1968.
Undiscovered Country (English version of Arthur Schnitzler's *Das Weite Land*). London: Jonathan Cape, 1968.
Enter a Free Man. London, 1968; New York, 1972.
After Magritte. London, 1971.
Jumpers. New York, 1972.

Travesties. London and New York, 1975.
Dirty Linen and *New-Found-Land*. London and New York, 1976.
Albert's Bridge and other Plays. New York, 1977. Includes *If You're Glad, I'll be Frank*, *Artist Descending a Staircase*, *Where Are They Now?* and *A Separate Peace*.
Dogg's Hamlet, Cahoot's Macbeth. London: Inter-Action Imprint, 1977.
Every Good Boy Deserves Favor and *Professional Foul*. London, 1977; New York, 1978.
Dogg's Our Pet. In *Ten of the Best British Short Plays*, ed. Ed Berman. London: Inter-Action Imprint, 1979.
Night and Day. London and New York, 1979.
On the Razzle (adaptation of Johann Nestroy's *Einen Jux Will Er Sich Machen*). London, 1981.
The Real Thing. London, 1982.
The Dog It Was That Died and Other Plays. London, 1983. Includes *The Dissolution of Dominic Boot*, *"M" Is for Moon among Other Things*, *Another Moon Called Earth*, *Neutral Ground*.
Squaring the Circle. London, 1984; New York, 1985.
Rough Crossing. London, 1985.
Dalliance and *Undiscovered Country*. London, 1986.
Hapgood. London, 1988.
Arcadia. London, 1993.

Articles
"Something to Declare." *Sunday Times* (London, February 25, 1968): 47.
"Playwrights and Professors." *Times Literary Supplement* (London, October 13, 1973): 1219.
"Ambushes for the Audience: Towards a High Comedy of Ideas." Editorial interview. *Theatre Quarterly*, 4 (May-July 1974): 3–17.
"Prague: The Story of the Chartists." *New York Review of Books* (August 4, 1977): 11–15.

Secondary Sources

Books
Bigsby, C.W.E. *Tom Stoppard*. Writers and Their Work Series. London: Longman, 1976; rev. 1979. Bigsby introduces Stoppard in one long, incisive, eminently

readable essay.

Billington, Michael. *Stoppard, the Playwright*. London: Methuen, 1987.

Brassell, Tim. *Tom Stoppard: An Assessment*. New York: St. Martin's Press, 1985. Comparative analysis of Stoppard in the context of other dramatists; contains interesting items such as the original ending of *Rosencrantz and Guildenstern Are Dead*.

Bratt, David. *Tom Stoppard: A Reference Guide*. Boston: Twayne, 1982.

Cahn, Victor L. *Beyond Absurdity: The Plays of Tom Stoppard*. Rutherford, NJ: Fairleigh Dickinson Press, 1979. Cahn looks at Stoppard through existentialist/absurdist lenses.

Corballis, Richard. *Stoppard: The Mystery and the Clockwork*. London: Methuen, 1985.

Dean, Joan Fitzpatrick. *Tom Stoppard: Comedy as a Moral Matrix*. Columbia: University of Missouri, 1981. Dean traces Stoppard's development from non-commitment to commitment (to causes); does not include an index, bibliography, or chapter titles.

Gabbard, Lucina Paquet. *The Stoppard Plays*. Troy, NY: Whitston, 1982.

Hayman, Ronald. *Tom Stoppard*. London: Heinemann, 1977. This volume remains a basic study of Stoppard's plays up to the late 1970s, with two valuable interviews with Stoppard in 1974 and 1976.

Hunter, Jim. *Tom Stoppard's Plays*. New York: Grove Press, 1982. Hunter analyzes central themes of Stoppard's plays and contains a valuable forty-four-page study guide for each play up to 1980.

Jenkins, Anthony. *The Theatre of Tom Stoppard*. Cambridge: Cambridge University Press, 1987. Jenkins integrates his own acting and directing experience in a lively, impressionistic view of Stoppard's plays as events and roles, with emphasis on the worlds that each play creates; no index or bibliography.

Londre, Felicia. *Tom Stoppard*. New York: Ungar, 1981. Londre focuses on the linguistic richness of Stoppard's style, with valuable identifications of allusions in the plays.

Page, Malcolm, comp. *File on Stoppard*. London and New York: Methuen, 1986. A handy collection of review excerpts and some factual Stoppardiana.

Rusinko, Susan. *Tom Stoppard*. Boston: Twayne, 1986. Rusinko traces the boot/moon characters through Stoppard's opus; devotes a chapter to each major play; includes chapters on minor stage plays, his novel, and sub-genres such as radio, television, adaptations, and political dramas.

Sammells, Neil. *Tom Stoppard: The Artist as Critic*. New York: St. Martin's Press, 1988. Sammells argues questionably that in "abandoning aesthetics of engagement he [Stoppard] promotes a conservative message by adapting topics he had previously condemned . . . in the service of a political thesis which is at best self-contradictory and banal and, at worst, cynical and dishonest" (142).

Whitaker, Thomas. *Tom Stoppard*. New York: Grove Press, 1983. Whitaker treats Stoppard as stylist who "knows what it means to write 'a trivial play for serious people'"; interweaves critics' reactions with his analyses.

Articles
Ellmann, Richard. "The Zealots of Zurich." *Times Literary Supplement* (London, July 12, 1974): 744.

Gordon, Giles. "Tom Stoppard." *Transatlantic Review* 29 (Summer 1968). Reprinted in *Behind the Scenes*, ed. Joseph McCrindle, pp. 77–87. London: Pitman, 1971. Interview.

Nightingale, Benedict. "Have Pinter and Stoppard Turned to Naturalism?" *New York Times* (December 3, 1978): D4.

———. "Stoppard Gets Emotional." *New York Times* (December 5, 1982): H5.

Tynan, Kenneth. "Withdrawing with Style from the Chaos." *New Yorker* (December 19, 1977): 44–111. Revised and reprinted in *Show People: Profiles in Entertainment*, 44–123. New York: Simon and Schuster, 1979. Profile.

Susan Rusinko

Strachey, [Giles] Lytton

Born: Stowey House, Clapham Common, London, March 1, 1880

Education: Parkstone, 1889–1893; Abbotsholme, 1893–1894; Leamington College, 1894–1897; Liverpool University Col-

lege, 1897–1899; *Trinity College, Cambridge University, 1899–1905*
Died: Ham Spray House, Hungerford, Berkshire, January 21, 1932

Biography

On March 1, 1880, at Stowey House in Clapham Common in London, Giles Lytton Strachey was born into a large and prominent family with Anglo-Indian ties. The eleventh of thirteen children, his name, in true Victorian fashion, proclaimed his family's pride in its lineage and connections; he was named after a sixteenth-century ancestor (whose travel account provided William Shakespeare with background for *The Tempest)* and his godfather, the first Earl of Lytton, liberal Viceroy of India, son of the novelist Edward Bulwer-Lytton, and himself a poet under the name of "Owen Meredith."

Strachey's family comprised a more than usually comprehensive index of the concerns and professions of educated and socially aware high Victorians, and this fully equipped him to attack them later where they were most vulnerable. For at least the two centuries before his birth, his family had helped build and support the British empire. His father, Lieutenant-General Sir Richard Strachey, was the very model of an energetic and practical-minded colonial administrator. Strachey's mother, Jane Maria Grant, came from a more aristocratic Anglo-Indian family. She was a formidable woman, especially in the domestic circle, but she could be surprisingly unconventional, as when she corresponded for many years with the ostracized George Eliot. A voracious reader, she passed on her love of French literature to her son Lytton.

As a family, the Stracheys were eccentrically speculative, intellectually advanced, and incessantly talkative. A great deal of Lytton's later social repute rested on his witty conversation; the seeds of his skill were sown at 69 Lancaster Gate, the house to which this large, chattering family moved in 1884. His essay on the house is reprinted with other autobiographical pieces in *Lytton Strachey by Himself* (1971). Many of Strachey's brothers and sisters went on to notable careers. Dorothy married the painter Simon Bussy, wrote the autobiographical novel *Olivia* (1949), and was Andre Gide's English translator; Philippa was quite active in the women's suffrage movement; and his younger brother James was the noted disciple and translator of Sigmund Freud.

After a varied and generally unhappy education at a bizarre combination of minor public schools (Parkstone, 1889–1893; Abbotsholme, 1893–1894; Leamington College, 1894–1897; Liverpool University College, 1897–1899), in 1899 Strachey found himself at Trinity College, Cambridge. His academic career at Cambridge was spotty: although he won the prestigious Chancellor's Medal for his poem "Ely: An Ode" in 1902, he received a disappointing double second on the History Tripos. Socially and intellectually, however, his true life began at Cambridge. Attracted by the aggressively subjective moral philosophy of G.E. Moore, he met the greatest friends and profoundest influences of his life, including the male nucleus of what was later to be called the Bloomsbury group: Leonard Woolf, Thoby Stephen (the brother of Virginia Woolf and Vanessa Bell), Clive Bell (the group would later include notably E.M. Forster, Roger Frye, and sisters Virginia and Vanessa), and the slightly younger John Maynard Keynes. Strachey found his niche when he was elected to the Cambridge Conversazione Society, better known as the Apostles, an august, secret, and indeed practically mythic society. Once established as an Apostle, Strachey immersed himself in the Society's lore. He not only read many papers to members on such topics as "Does Absence Make the Heart Grow Fonder?" and "Was Diotima Right?" but he also threw himself into the Society's political center—especially trying to get younger and attractive members elected. Some of his papers for the Apostles have been reprinted with other previously unpublished material in *The Really Interesting Question and Other Papers* (1972).

Strachey trained as an historian and began work on his doctoral thesis, an encyclopedic dissertation on his colonial ancestor, Warren Hastings, which unfortunately did not impress his examiners. After Trinity twice refused him for a fellowship, Strachey's hopes for becoming a don were dashed. With the encouragement of his cousin St. Loe Strachey, then editor of the *Spectator*, he began to make a living as a journalist in London in 1907. He wrote some drama reviews, signing himself "Ignotus," along with many book reviews.

In London, Strachey was at the center of the now exhaustively studied Bloomsbury group. This collection of writers, artists, and thinkers was an informal bundle of friends rather than a school, but they did share distinctive characteristics—disdain for Victorians and Victorianism, sexual experimentation, and a desire to *epater les bourgeois*. Strachey's intellectual, social, and love life centered on this set, particularly in his relationship with his cousin, Duncan Grant. So intermingled were their relations that at one point the homosexual Strachey proposed to Virginia Stephen (later Woolf) by whom, to his relief, he was rejected. For the last fifteen years of his life he lived at Ham Spray House in Hungerford, Berkshire, with the artist Dora Carrington and her husband, Ralph Partridge.

As an invalid, Strachey was exempt for military service in the Great War, but in 1916 after the passage of the two Military Service Acts making conscription compulsory, Strachey applied for exemption on grounds of health and conscience. When asked by the military tribunal what he would do if he saw a German soldier attempting to rape his sister, Strachey famously replied, with fully intended ambiguity, "I should try and come between them."

He spent the remainder of the war finishing a group of iconoclastic portraits of representative Victorian figures: "an ecclesiastic [Cardinal Manning], an educational authority [Thomas Arnold], a woman of action [Florence Nightingale], and a man of adventure [General Gordon]."[1] Published at the end of the war in 1918, *Eminent Victorians* instantly became a great critical and commercial success; from then on Strachey was both well-to-do and well-known. His initial popular success was followed by *Queen Victoria* (1921) and *Elizabeth and Essex* (1928). As an historian, he was always more appreciated by amateurs than professionals, but his stylistic talents were much in demand from both. To his sly delight, he was chosen to give the annual lecture at Cambridge in memory of that arch-Victorian, Leslie Stephen. Much of Strachey's most wittily elegant work lies in his many essays, collected in *Books and Characters* (1922), *Portraits in Miniature* (1931), and *Characters and Commentaries* (1933). His final historical project was a scholarly edition of the Greville family papers, completed only after his death. Michael Holroyd and Paul Levy, Strachey's joint literary executors through the Strachey Trust, have brought renewed interest to his works and have been responsible for the publication of much material, such as the lightly pornographic *Ermyntrude and Esmeralda* (1969, with illustrations by Erte), that had only circulated privately.

Strachey had always been sickly, but from 1930 on he was never really well. He died at Ham Spray House on January 21, 1932, from what was posthumously discovered to be stomach cancer. Witty to the end, Strachey's last words, to his sister Pippa, were, "If this is death, I don't think much of it." Carrington committed suicide soon afterward, on March 11, 1932.

Literary Analysis

The historian and biographer Strachey is now best known as an ironic stylist, a champion of witty *éclaircissement* such as "We do not reflect that it is perhaps as difficult to write a good life as to live one." The highly polished surface of his writing, however, has frequently fooled critics into judging his works to be merely superficial. Strachey regarded history-writing as a partisan enterprise, and, as *Eminent Victorians* demonstrated, he was not afraid to take sides. Although his biographical works are all grounded in research, he expanded the traditional scope of the genre by using techniques more usually thought of as fictional, as in the famous stream-of-consciousness final paragraph from *Queen Victoria* and the imaginative characterizations of *Elizabeth and Essex*, praised by Freud for their psychological insight.

His literary sensibility claims descent from the eighteenth century, particularly in France, when reason and wit were admired virtues. As a writer, Strachey primarily modeled himself after French rather than English authors. At the beginning of *Eminent Victorians*, he took as his motto François Voltaire's aphorism, *Je n'impose rien; je ne propose rien; j'expose* (I impose nothing; I propose nothing; I expose). For Strachey, the spicy subtlety of meaning in "expose" is fully intended; in his most stringent works, exposure becomes exposé. From Voltaire he took his tone of satirical mockery, from Marie Henri Stendhal his interest in psychological manners.

Strachey was at pains to separate his writing from what he thought of as the accreted hypocrisies of the Victorians. He was, nonetheless, fascinated by them. In his 1914 "A Victorian Critic," a review of a book on Matthew Arnold, Strachey wrote:

To the cold and youthful observer there is a strange fascination about the Age of Victoria. It has the odd attractiveness of something which is at once very near and very far off; it is like one of those queer fishes that one sees behind glass at an aquarium, before whose grotesque proportions and sombre menacing agilities one hardly knows whether to laugh or to shudder; when once it has caught one's eye, one cannot tear oneself away.[2]

For Strachey, a distinctly cold and youthful observer, chilliness did not necessarily imply detachment. Even more than most of the members of the Bloomsbury group, Strachey loathed the Victorians. The age he thought blind ("everything was discovered and nothing known") and the people inept ("the beds were full of bugs and disasters"). In his first famous book he set out to display their dirty linen.

In the autumn of 1912, Strachey had written to Lady Ottoline Morrell: "I am . . . beginning a new experiment in the way of a short condensed biography of Cardinal Manning—written from a slightly cynical standpoint." His original plan was a group of balanced portraits including some figures whom he admired—Charles Darwin, John Stuart Mill, and Thomas Carlyle. The outbreak of war in 1914, however, apparently caused him to abandon this idea in favor of a more polemical exposure of Victorian repression and hypocrisy. Certainly at this time his feelings for Victorians were crystallizing into the disaffected detachment that proved symptomatic of the age.

Eminent Victorians caused a great stir when it appeared on May 9, 1918. A few people were shocked—notably Mrs. Humphry Ward, the granddaughter of Thomas Arnold, Strachey's second victim. Many more readers representing a broad range of concerns were amused, including Herbert Henry Asquith, who had just stepped down as Prime Minister, and Bertrand Russell, imprisoned as a conscientious objector ("It caused me to laugh so loud that the officer came to my cell, saying I must remember that prison is a place of punishment").

One reason for the volume's popularity was its timeliness at the end of the war. The author's cynicism toward his eminent Victorians had struck a sympathetic chord in an audience fresh from the horrors begun, so they thought, on account of Victorian imperialism and continued on account of Victorian pigheadedness and bungling. Although Strachey was not the first to speak out against Victorian stuffiness, hypocrisy, and religious peculiarity (Edmund Gosse's 1907 *Father and Son* set a noteworthy precedent), his ironic malice struck a new note. He makes no attempt to play fair, be impartial, or give equal time to all sides of a question. As a judge, he is quite frank in allowing all decisions to be irreverent, arbitrary, and final.

The preface to *Eminent Victorians* has been called the biographer's manifesto. Rejecting the prolix and hagiographic biographical tradition that began with James Boswell and continued in Victorian two-volume encomia, Strachey also set up new standards of judgment; people were no longer to be judged by works or by faith, but rather on every word that marked them as unaesthetic and humorless. He specializes in insidious comparisons. About one particularly pious Victorian, he speculates, "The sort of ardour which impels more normal youths to haunt Music Halls and fall in love with actresses took the form, in Froude's case, of a romantic devotion to the deity and an intense interest in the state of his own soul" ("Cardinal Manning").

Typically, much of Strachey's debunking humor resides in metaphors that mention the unmentionable; the more serious and august the institution, the more extreme his tropes. For example, at the end of the Oxford Movement, "[t]he University breathed such a sigh of relief as usually follows the difficult expulsion of a hard piece of matter from a living organism" ("Cardinal Manning"). In his essay on Thomas Arnold, headmaster of Rugby, Strachey comments that "[t]he public schools of those days were still virgin forests, untouched by the hand of reform" ("Thomas Arnold"). Undoubtedly the sexual, and homosexual, teasing that runs throughout *Eminent Victorians* and, to a lesser extent, *Queen Victoria* satisfies schoolboy sniggerers, but Strachey aims not merely at the easy target of Victorian sexual repression but also at the whole comic underside of Victorianism. Thus, he is a master of comic elevation and deflation; in the portrait of Florence Nightingale, for whose struggles he had some sympathy, the technique is double-edged: "So she dreamed and wondered, and, taking out her diary, she poured into it the agitations of her soul. And then the bell rang, and it was time to go and dress for dinner" ("Florence Nightingale").

The cold-hearted iconoclasm of *Eminent Victorians* and the essays that preceded it became muted in his later works. The writer retains many of the same techniques—posing loaded questions, quoting droll diary entries, recreating inner monologues—but in *Queen*

Victoria his subject is treated with light comedy and sympathetic humor. His few sarcastic barbs are saved for the Teutonic Albert and the faithful servant John Brown: "[A]nd yet—such is the world!—there were those who actually treated the relations between their sovereign and her servant as a theme for ribald jests."[3]

Of his major works, *Elizabeth and Essex* is the most ambitious but the most dated, yet like all of Strachey's works, it bears the hallmarks of elegance and readability. *Eminent Victorians* and *Queen Victoria*, his most wholly successful works, are frequently reprinted in popular edition; his literary and biographical essays have been recollected and reissued.

Summary

Lytton Strachey's reputation now lies less in his work as an historian than in his witty and ironic portraits of a bygone age. He is particularly remembered for his place within the Bloomsbury group and for his first success, *Eminent Victorians*.

Notes

1. *Eminent Victorians* (London: Chatto & Windus, 1918), p. viii.
2. Reprinted in *Literary Essays* (London: Chatto & Windus, 1948).
3. *Queen Victoria* (London: Chatto & Windus, 1921), p. 274.

Selected Bibliography

Primary Sources
Landmarks in French Literature. London: Williams and Norgate, and New York: Henry Holt, 1912.
Eminent Victorians. London: Chatto & Windus, and New York: Putnam's, 1918.
Queen Victoria. London: Chatto & Windus, and New York: Harcourt, 1921.
Books and Characters French and English. London: Chatto & Windus, and New York: Harcourt, 1922.
Pope (The Leslie Stephen Lecture). Cambridge: Cambridge University Press, and New York: Harcourt, 1925.
Elizabeth and Essex. London: Chatto & Windus, and New York: Harcourt, 1928.
Portraits in Miniature and Other Essays. London: Chatto & Windus, and New York: Harcourt, 1931.
Characters and Commentaries. London: Chatto & Windus, and New York: Harcourt, 1933.
The Greville Memoirs. Ed. with Roger Fulford. (Joint editors: Ralph and Frances Partridge). 8 vols. London: Macmillan, 1937–1938.
Literary Essays. London: Chatto & Windus, 1948; New York: Harcourt, 1949.
Biographical Essays. London: Chatto & Windus, and New York: Harcourt, 1948.
Spectatorial Essays. Preface by James Strachey. London: Chatto & Windus, 1964; New York: Harcourt, 1965.
Ermyntrude and Esmeralda: An Entertainment. (1913) Intro. by Michael Holroyd, illustrations by Erte. London: Anthony Blond, and New York: Stein & Day, 1969.
Lytton Strachey by Himself. Ed. and intro. by Michael Holroyd. London: Heinemann, and New York: Holt, 1971.
The Really Interesting Question and Other Papers. Ed. with intro. and commentary by Paul Levy. London: Weidenfeld, 1972; New York: Coward, 1973.
The Shorter Strachey. Selected and intro. by Michael Holroyd and Paul Levy. Oxford: Oxford University Press, 1980.

Secondary Sources

Bibliographies
Edmonds, Michael. *Lytton Strachey, A Bibliography.* New York: Garland, 1981. Although not complete for secondary sources, the single most thorough source; includes locations of manuscript material.
Kallich, Martin. "Lytton Strachey: An Annotated Bibliography of Writings About Him." *English Literature in Transition,* 5 (1962): 1–77.

Books
Beerbohm, Max. *Lytton Strachey.* New York: Knopf, 1943. Originally delivered as a Rede lecture at Cambridge, an impressionistic view of Strachey's techniques by a fellow ironic stylist.
Ferns, John. *Lytton Strachey.* Boston: Twayne, 1988. Part of the Twayne's English Authors Series, this is a very useful and well-written basic presentation of Strachey's life and work.
Hoberman, Ruth Sarah. *Modernizing Lives: Experiments in English Biography, 1918–1939.* Carbondale: Southern Illinois Uni-

versity Press, 1987. A revision of "Biography in England Between the Wars: Modernist Literary Strategies." Ph.D. diss., Columbia University, 1984. Hoberman places Strachey's narrative self-consciousness in a line of modernist innovations in biography.

Holroyd, Michael. *Lytton Strachey: A Critical Biography*. 2 vols. New York: Holt, 1967, 1968. The standard biography, this two-volume work comprehensively considers Strachey's life and work but can prove intimidatingly detailed to the beginning student.

Johnstone, J.K. *The Bloomsbury Group: A Study of E.M. Forster, Lytton Strachey, Virginia Woolf and Their Circle*. New York: Farrar, Straus, 1978. Two chapters explicitly on Strachey's values and writings within the context of the Bloomsbury group and the guiding intellectual lights G.E. Moore and Roger Fry.

Merle, Gabriel. *Lytton Strachey (1880–1932): Biographie et Critique d'un Critique et Biographe*. 2 vols. Paris: Librairie Honore Champion, 1980. An extremely valuable long study from a continental perspective, with detailed chronology and bibliography.

Articles and Chapters in Books

Altick, Richard. *Lives and Letters: A History of Literary Biography in England and America*. New York: Knopf, 1965. In chapter 9 Altick provides a systematic and clear-headed approach to Strachey's effect on biography-writing.

Kallich, Martin. *The Psychological Milieu of Lytton Strachey*. New York: Bookman, 1961. A reductive reading of Strachey, it nonetheless offers some insights into early psychobiography.

Spurr, Barry. "Camp Mandarin: The Prose Style of Lytton Strachey." *English Literature in Transition (1880–1920)*, 33, 1 (1990): 31–45. An intelligent reassessment of Strachey's ironic style and his homosexuality.

Dissertations

Simson, G.K. "Lytton Strachey's Use of His Sources in *Eminent Victorians*." Ph.D. dissertation. University of Minnesota, 1963. An excellent study.

Alexandra Mullen

Suckling, John

Born: Whitton, Twickenham, Middlesex, February 1609
Education: Entered Trinity College, Cambridge University, July 3, 1623; admitted to Gray's Inn, February 23, 1627
Died: Paris, May or June 1642

Biography

John Suckling was born into a distinguished Norfolk family at Whitton, in the parish of Twickenham, Middlesex, in February of 1609. His father, Sir John Suckling, was a member of the Privy Council and Comptroller of the King's Household; his mother, Martha Cranfield, who died when Suckling was four, was the sister of Lionel Cranfield, a powerful favorite of James I and Earl of Middlesex. Thus, in his early years Suckling was immersed in London life and the splendors of the Jacobean court.

According to contemporary accounts, Suckling possessed a good ear for music and was a precocious learner, speaking Latin at five and writing it at nine. Popularly reputed as a scholar, he went up to Trinity College, Cambridge, on July 3, 1623, but entered Gray's Inn on February 23, 1627, without having taken his degree. In 1627, Suckling's father died, leaving an immense fortune to his eighteen-year-old son.

In 1628, Suckling traveled through Italy and France, returning to be knighted by Charles I on September 19, 1630. In 1631, he joined the army of Gustavus Adolphus and during the Thirty Years War fought anti-Imperial forces at Breitenfeld and participated in the siege of Leipzig.

Handsome, rich, and generous, on his return to England in the spring of 1632 Suckling took up an extravagant mode of living, made possible by his immense wealth. As a result, he became an emblem of the dissipated cavalier, a reputation that would dog him till his last unhappy days. He became notorious as a gamester, wine bibber, tobacco sipper, wit, and womanizer. He loved cards (John Aubrey supposed that he had invented cribbage), bowling, and versifying, and was intimate with other poets linked to court causes. These included Thomas Carew and Sir William Davenant.

In 1635, however, Suckling apparently gave up city life and resettled in his estates near London. Perhaps he was responding to a 1635 proclamation of the Star Chamber against absentee landlords, but rumor gave another reason: in the autumn of 1634, Sir John Digby had so soundly cudgeled Suckling in a love dispute that humiliation forced Suckling to abandon the carefree life of the city for his rural retreat and the philosophical country salon of Lord Falkland. Much of Suckling's writing was produced during this period.

In November 1638, Suckling purchased the position of Gentleman of the Privy Chamber Extraordinary. In 1639, as civil war slowly began to simmer, he rallied to the king's aid against the Scottish episcopacy, at his own great expense raising and outfitting one hundred knights to follow Charles I in the First Bishops' War. The outfittings were so lavish and the expedition so disastrous that once again Suckling found himself the butt of roundhead ridicule. Yet he gained more royal favor through his actions, and in February 1640 he was made captain of carbineers for the Second Bishops' War in which, however, he saw no action.

In April 1640, Suckling was elected to the Short Parliament for Bramber, Sussex. When in 1641 his part was exposed in the First Army Plot, a conspiracy to use the army to control Parliament and prevent the execution of Thomas Wentworth, Earl of Strafford, Suckling fled to France. A series of new roundhead satires, like "Newes from Sir John Sucklin" (1641) and "The Sucklington Faction, or Suckling's Roaring Boyes" (1641), followed him abroad, burlesquing his flair for clothes, his gambling, and his reputation for repartee.

Little is known about his end. It is supposed that faced with the loss of his estates, the possible distresses of poverty, and the humiliation of defeat, Suckling took his life in Paris, probably by poison, between late 1641 and June 1642.

Literary Analysis

Suckling is a minor literary figure, yet an important innovator in the development of "wit." To the Parliamentary party he epitomized decadent affectation in taste and style. Although he devoted his art to exposing court affectations, such as Neoplatonism, Petrarchanism, and Euphuism, his attempt to root out older courtly fashions gave rise to a new style typified by freedom from convention and an easy grace, as he suggests in his satire "Sessions of the Poets" (1637): "A Laureats Muse should be easie and free" (1.38). In formulating this easy style, Suckling looks back to the idea of *Sprezzatura*, the Renaissance Italian writer Baldassare Castiglione's ideal of accomplishing the difficult with the appearance of an innate gracefulness.

The easy grace and freedom of this style was itself a new affectation, one that became the model for the heroes of the Restoration comedies, with their paradoxical mixtures of bawdiness and polish, their interesting poses of disinterestedness, and their never-ending stream of easy-flowing witticisms. During the Restoration, Suckling's dramas and reputation were revived, and as late as the last quarter of the eighteenth century Richard Brinsley Sheridan found Suckling's plays a powerful influence on the comedy of manners, satirical drama aimed at social affectation and inhabited by characters of gentility, verbal wit, and licentiousness.

Weighed in themselves, then, Suckling's works may appear slight and eclectic. Still, Suckling's "wit," in its dizzying multiplicity, shaped a new and powerful entity, a gentlemanly persona that combined highly mannered ease, artificial grace, and melodic smoothness, with licentious, profane, and withal coolly urbane realism bordering on cynicism. His poem "Out upon it!" exemplifies such a combination:

> Out upon it! I have lov'd
> Three whole days together;
> And am like to love three more,
> If it prove fair weather.

In "Out upon it!" the speaker's pique in the opening exclamation is laced with a tone of world-weariness. The cool, mannered stance of dispassionate sophistication from which the character surveys the situation seems at once seductively coy and affectedly nonchalant. The speaker winks aside to his friends as he addresses the woman.

One finds a similar pose in "Why so pale and wan, fond lover?" The first lines describe the familiar sonnet-tradition pallor affected by Petrarchan lovers, while the smooth rhythm and soft sounds suggest sympathy for the lover's condition: "Why so pale and wan, fond lover? / Prithee, why so pale?" But the next lines turn to mockery, revealing an altogether different attitude: "Will, when looking well can't move her, / Looking ill prevail? / Prithee, why so pale?" By poem's end, the singer unleashes the full force of derision:

> Quit, quit, for shame; this will not move,
> This cannot take her.
> If of her self she will not love,
> Nothing can make her:
> The devil take her!

The poem combines a high degree of the natural and the artificial. The diction is simple and unstrained, yet the rhythms and sounds are highly wrought and melodic. This is, after all, a song. Similarly, the singer imposes a realistic view to deride the literary idealism of the lover, yet the stance of the singer seems itself affected. The nuances of the singer's position fluctuate in a lively manner from sympathy to mock sympathy to derision. The liveliness of these changes marks another important attribute of the poet's style. Not only does his humor flow from the creation of a paradoxical, quick-witted, cynical superiority, but the wittiness is always shifting, always lively. It is a liveliness parodied by the Restoration playwright William Congreve in his witless witty-would-be, Witwoud, but exemplified in his major characters such as Mirabell and Millamant, whose wit combines easy grace and realism.

This mannered attitude, typical of much of Suckling's work, evolved from the urbane wit of Ben Jonson, exemplified by his city comedies. Suckling undoubtedly owes his cynicism and plain speech to Jonson. Nevertheless, Suckling, who was part of Jonson's circle, disapproved of the master's pretentious classicism, which he lampoons in "The Sessions of the Poets," in the unfinished play *The Sad One* (ca. 1633), and in *The Goblins* (1638). He also parodies Jonson's style in several verses, such as "Upon the first sight of my Lady Seimor," a parody of "A Song to a Lute." Other influences on his style were William Shakespeare's comedies, which he identified with natural easiness, and John Donne's rakish verses, from which he borrowed the everyday image used in surprising and unusual ways and the dramatic persona.

Donne's influence can be seen clearly in Suckling's extension and distortion of images and metaphors, as in "Farewell to Love," with its grotesque *momento mori* of the beloved, or "'Tis now, since I sat down," with its clever use of the siege/lovemaking metaphor. In each case, the humor created by the unusual images appears as the witty improvisations of a smooth and urbane persona. In fact, Suckling's stance of the polished, witty, urbane gentleman precludes the roughness often associated with Donne. Suckling's one attempt at invective, the satirical art of the cursing, in "Detraction Execrated," fails, sliding from thundering "Thou vermin slander . . . !" to harmless "[n]o briny tear hath furrow'd her smooth cheek."

The author's single most imitated work is his satire "The Sessions of the Poets," which caricatures contemporary poets as they vie for Apollo's laurel. This work served as the model for many other poetic tournaments, such as "The Trial of the Poets for the Bays," in which John Wilmot, second Earl of Rochester, mocks John Dryden, Thomas Otway, George Etherege, and Aphra Behn; John Sheffields's "The Election of a Laureat," in which the writer lightly teases Alexander Pope, Colley Cibber, Thomas D'Urfey, and Congreve; James Henry Leigh Hunt's "The Feast of the Poets," concerning his romantic contemporaries; Robert Buchanan's "The Sessions of the Poets," poking fun at Robert Browning, Matthew Arnold, Algernon Swinburne, and himself. In Suckling's own *poetomachia* (battle of the poets) between such literary notables as Jonson, Carew, Davenant, Edmund Waller, Thomas May, and George Sandys, an alderman walks off with the wreath because "[t]he best sign / Of good store of wit was to have good store of coin." Suckling's satire exhibits a characteristic aristocratic disdain of vulgar judgment. In fact, the poet's chummy mockery of his friends conveys a sense of a group that is distinguished from the vulgar by a wittiness that includes mild raillery, thorough learning, and graceful manner. Above all, the group seems to appreciate irony, an appreciation that some in the early eighteenth century said separated the civilized from the uncivilized.

Suckling's "Letters" demonstrate a similar kind of coterie humor. Constructed for the most part like essays, the letters addressed to familiar companions provide a means for Suckling to display a fashionable gentlemanly wit. The letters demonstrate an enjoyment of clever variations on a theme. "A letter to a friend to dissuade him from marrying a widow," probably written to the poet Carew, abounds in the cliquish jocularity of the rib-elbowing friend: "Life is sometimes a long journey. To be tied to ride upon one beast still, and that half tied to thy hand too! Think upon that, Tom." At other times epigrammatic wit emerges, as in "A Dissuasion from Love," written to Jack Bond, where, after mentioning all of the cures for love, Suckling comes to the final cure—marriage: "Marrying . . . would certainly cure it; but that is a kind of live pigeons laid to the soles of the feet, a last remedy, and (to say truth) worse than the disease."

At times Suckling puts on the guise of a bumpkin in order to amuse his friends. When he does, his rustic is no aristocratic pastor re-creating the golden age for personal pleasure; instead he resembles a knowing and cynical cavalier. Suckling's rustics puncture pretentious court fictions, creating only that degree of realism and earthiness that will encourage companionable laughter among aristocratic friends. This is clear in his much imitated "A Ballade. Upon a Wedding." Written on the marriage of John, Lord Lovelace and Lady Anne Wentworth, "A Ballade. Upon a Wedding" exhibits Suckling's use of the rustic perspective in the poem's most famous lines:

Her feet beneath her petticoat
Like little mice, stole in and out,
As if they feared the light.

The vivid image of the dainty feet in their delicate movement offers light, humorous criticism of the bride's mincing steps. At the same time, the use of mice, a symbol of sexual activity, offers a more ribald possibility. The lines, then, are simultaneously delicate, sensual, ribald, bestial, sophisticated, and laugh-provoking. The effects arise by a witty juxtaposition of the "low" and the urbane, a wit that seems to point to the cleverness of the poem's maker rather than away from him.

A similar rustic point-of-view turned on the more polished members of society becomes a successful vehicle for comedy in "A Pedlar of Small-Wares," in which the peddler sells appropriate trinkets to several great ladies, or "A Barber," who is puffed up with his importance, because he keeps a "state" (raised chair) like the king and because "who comes to me / Whos'e'er he is, he must uncover'd be," that is, must remove his cap, as before a king. In these poems the satire is more pointed and the mockery seems to anticipate Jonathan Swift's "Description of a City Shower" (1710). In the very clever "Love, Reason, Hate," the personified emotions and attitudes surrounding the relationships of men and women enjoy a rural game of barley-break, a kind of tag played by couples.

At this lower end of the social scale Suckling's comedy is usually very effective. And he excels at bawdy, a type of sexually innuendoed low comedy affected by gentlemen. In fact, he composed some of the funniest, bawdiest, most outrageous pieces of the period. For instance, "If When Don Cupid's dart" includes the unlikely comparison of love and flatulence: "It pains a man when 'tis kept close, / And others doth offend when 'tis let loose." Others, like "The Deformed Mistress," "His Dream," "Upon T.C. Having the Pox," and "A Candle," show that Suckling delighted in grotesque and obscene humor.

The writer's plays, which were influenced by Shakespeare's and which, despite their seeming lack of dramatic energy, influenced the next generation, show a mixture of style and wit familiar from Suckling's letters and verses. *The Goblins*, his most thoroughly comic play, exploits the sentimental and heroic aspects of Shakespearean romance, combining pieces of *The Tempest*, *As You Like It*, and *A Midsummer Night's Dream*. In *The Goblins*, Suckling again uses the device of urbane characters masking as bumpkins. Here he turns Shakespeare's greenwood government of forest faeries into Robin Hood-like nobles masquerading as devils in order to extract a satirical justice from their victims who think that the band's dark cavern headquarters is hell. This comic vehicle allows for social and literary criticisms. But, what appears a view of the world from the bottom is really a view of the *nouveau riche* by hereditary aristocrats. For instance, one character, a "foolish utensil of the state . . . brought forth to make a show" is sentenced like this: "Get baths of Sulphur quick, and flaming oils, this crime is new, and will deserve it. He has inverted all rule of State, confounded policy . . . . Let him be boiled in scalding lead a while to inure and prepare him for the other" (3.1).

Satirical punishment, however, is only one small detail in the play's variegated fabric. *The Goblins* seems to have been planned primarily to allow the stitching together of many humorous patches, from fine verbal wit and topical commentaries to burlesque and buffoonery. The whole is a confusing series of improbable and interlocking stories of lost brothers, virtuous maidens, and court intrigues. The humor is catch-as-catch-can, inserted at any possible and often improbable point. As Orsabrin, the Prince's brother, flees headlong for his life, he nevertheless pauses to complain: "This house is full of Thresholds, and Trap-doors, / I have been i'th Cellar, where the Maids lie too, / I laid my hand groping for my way / Upon one of them, and she began to squeak" (2.3). Imprisoned and awaiting death, Orsabrin burlesques Hamlet's "To be or not to be" meditation: "To die! yea what's that? / For yet I never thought on't seriously; / It may be 'tis—hum—It may be 'tis not too—" (3.3.1–3). The general playful tone of the play, not the specifics of plot, captured the imagination of Restoration playwrights. They emulated *The Goblins'* liveliness, its breakneck action, complicated scheming, gay songs, and witty characters.

Of his other plays, only *Aglaura* (1637–1638), a lavish court entertainment, qualifies as comedy. *Aglaura* is a much darker and more ornamental telling of a story similar to *The Goblins*, of court intrigue, brothers, mistresses, lovers, and virtuous men and women. Written at first as a tragedy of misunderstandings, *Aglaura* gained an alternate fifth act to make it a comedy of errors. Despite the ambiguities of the play, Suckling clearly triumphs in the creation of Orsames, a character fashioned after the witty, melancholic Jacques from Shakespeare's *As You Like It*. A cynic and realist, in his speeches Orsames anatomizes the courtly conventions of the day, particularly the resurgence of platonic love at court (2.2). Orsames's wit can be rough, as in his comments on his fall from a horse: "Well when I hunt next, . . . may I fall into a saw-pit, and not be taken up, but with suspicion of having been private, with mine own beast there. Now I better consider on't too, Gentlemen, 'tis but the same thing we do at Court" (1.4.17–21). Yet Orsames can also fashion smooth witty phrases, as when he describes Cupid's food as "Hearts newly slain / Serv'd up entire, and stuck with little arrows, / instead of Cloves" (1.5). Orsames is best known for his anti-platonic "Why so pale and wan fond Lover?" the humor of which was intensified because an on-stage song denoted off-stage sexual conversation (4.2). Throughout the play, witty and elegant conversation more than any other trait distinguishes the nobility of the characters.

In both *Aglaura* and *The Goblins*, Suckling manages to create the language of witty gentlemen, a language that mixes natural easy grace and quickness with cynicism and almost scurrilous realism. The wit of his creations is ready and rash, like that of an amusing drinking companion, the dashing gentlemanly dog-about-town, playing dress-up ruffian or bumpkin, being bawdy and sly, languorous and quixotic, throwing off an occasional epigram. In addition, Suckling's images are fresh and contemporary, drawn from metropolitan and upper-class customs and foibles, heavy in allusions to the activities of the gentlemanly class: hunting, dueling, and hawking. In all, he originates what Pope termed "the *à la mode* style," a wit that is fashionable, flexible and ephemeral.

Summary

Sir John Suckling's works are minor and modest, yet they have major importance. Suckling succeeded in separating gentlemanly fashion from the affected styles of Petrarchanism, Neoplatonism, and Euphuism. Following in part an urbane and sometimes scurrilous "cavalier" line of wit, he created a gentlemanly persona of lively, free, and graceful wittiness—commenting cynically on the pretentious fashion, pretending to be rustic, indulging in bawdy, framing epigrams. This facile and supple wit became the model for many well-bred characters of Restoration and eighteenth-century poetry, fiction, and drama. Of his individual works, "A Ballade. Upon a Wedding" is his most famous and polished piece. "The Sessions of the Poets," a poem about poets vying to become laureate, has found emulators in nearly every age, and "Why so pale and wan, fond lover?" is still widely anthologized.

Selected Bibliography

Primary Sources
The Works of Sir John Suckling. Ed. Thomas Clayton and Lester A. Beaurline. 2 vols. Oxford: Clarendon, 1971. Vol. 1: The non-dramatic works, ed. and intro. with commentary by Thomas Clayton; vol. 2: The plays, ed. and intro. with commentary by Lester A. Beaurline.
Sir John Suckling's Poems and Letters from Manuscript. Ed. Herbert Berry. London: Humanities Department of the University of Western Ontario, 1960.

Secondary Sources
Parker, Michael P. "'All are not born (Sir) to the Bay': 'Jack' Suckling, 'Tom' Carew and the Making of a Poet." *English Literary Renaissance*, 12, 3 (Autumn 1982): 341–68. Parker compares the two "Cavalier" poets' use of love, sex, society, and wit.
Squier, Charles L. *Sir John Suckling*. Boston: Twayne, 1978. The best overview of life and works with attention to individual works. Includes a bibliography.

David Rosen

Swift, Jonathan

Born: Dublin, Ireland, November 30, 1667

Education: Kilkenny School, Kilkenny, Ireland, 1673–1681; Trinity College, Dublin, 1682–1686, B.A., speciali gratia; Hart Hall, Oxford University, M.A., 1692

Marriage: Possibly to Esther Johnson in 1716

Died: Dublin, October 19, 1745

Biography

Jonathan Swift was born in Dublin, Ireland, on November 30, 1667, seven months after the death of his father, Jonathan, and just in time, he told Laetitia Pilkington, "to save his mother's credit." Two years later, his misfortunes continuing, he was kidnapped by his nurse (known only as the "Woman from Whitehaven") to Whitehaven, Cumberland, where he remained for three years.

After attending Kilkenny School (1673–1681), Swift matriculated at Trinity College in Dublin in 1682. He received his B.A., *speciali gratia* (with special favor), in 1686. Without a father's support, he had to depend on the charity of an uncle, Godwin, a successful lawyer, for his education. In *A Fragment of Autobiography*, Swift was later to characterize this support, uncharitably, as the "ill treatment of his nearest relations" and the direct cause of his poor performance in Trinity College.

Uncle Godwin's friendship with two of Ireland's leading Anglo-Irish families, the Ormondes and the Temples, was later to provide Swift with influential friends in London. Sir William Temple (1628–1699) was especially important to Swift during his early adulthood. He was made a member of Temple's household at Sheen and then Moor Park (in Surrey) for three periods, from 1689 to 1690, from 1691 to 1694, and again from 1696 to 1699. It was during his Moor Park days that Swift began his writing career (poems, political pamphlets and, perhaps, his first great satire—*A Tale of a Tub*, which was first published in 1704) and where he made his first acquaintance with Stella, his pseudonym for Esther Johnson. Whether or not they were eventually married (if they were, it was probably in 1716) still remains, and perhaps always will, an open question. Marriages with two other women who were attracted to Swift, Jane Waring (Varina) and Hester Vanhomrigh (Vanessa) were delayed, and finally dropped, presumably because of what he describes in an early letter as "a thousand household thoughts, which always drive matrimony out of my mind" (February 11, 1692).

In 1692, Swift received an M.A. from Hart Hall, Oxford, by "incorporation," having spent only a few days at the university to obtain the degree. In 1694, he took holy orders in the Church of Ireland (a branch of the Church of England). The earliest of his publications, *Ode to the Athenian Society*, appeared in 1692 and Swift was given, successively, a prebend (Kilroot in Ulster, 1695) and made Vicar of Laracor, Ireland (1700). He became chaplain to Lord Berkeley the following year. Swift's sometimes used title, "doctor," comes from the honorary Doctor of Divinity degree which he received from Trinity College in February of 1702. During this period, Swift made friends with John Gay, Alexander Pope, and other writers, and they formed the Scriblerus Club. *Memoirs of the Extraordinary Life, Works, and Discoveries of Martinus Scriblerus*, first published in an edition of Pope's works in 1741 was, in all likelihood, a joint work of the club. In 1713, Swift was made Dean of St. Patrick's Cathedral in Dublin. This position, in spite of his desire to be a bishop in England, was to be the highest rank that he would reach in the church.

From 1707 to 1714, he was, off and on, in London, first seeking to have the government remit revenues to the Church of Ireland and later as a major spokesman for the Harley (Tory) Administration. He made other literary friends, including Joseph Addison and Matthew Prior, and his writings from this period include *The Bickerstaff Papers*, *An Argument Against Abolishing Christianity* (1708), *Journal to Stella* (1710–1711), and *The Conduct of the Allies* (1711). He also continued to publish poems and to write for the *Examiner* (1710–1713), the chief Tory newspaper. Swift's only other returns to England, first to publish *Gulliver's Travels* and then to visit Pope and his circle of friends, were in 1726 and 1727. The most notable publications in the last decade of his life include *A Modest Proposal* (1729), *Verses of the Death of Dr. Swift* (1731), *Directions to Servants* (1738), and *Polite Conversation* (1738). Three of his twelve surviving sermons (one of which is of doubtful authenticity) were published in 1744 by Dodsley, the London bookseller. The so-called "scatalogical" poems, *The Lady's Dressing Room* (1730), *Strephon and Chloe*, *Cassinus and Peter*, and *A Beautiful Young Nymph going to Bed* (1731), date from the early part of this period. *Miscellanies in Prose and Verse*, a joint work with Pope, appeared between 1727 and 1732.

In 1742, a lunacy commission found Swift insane and relieved him of his clerical duties. He died in Dublin on October 19, 1745, and was buried, alongside Stella, in St. Patrick's Cathedral.

Literary Analysis

Swift's writing career lasted some forty years and the existing canon is, consequently, very large—in the standard editions, *Correspondence* (5 volumes), *Prose Writings* (14 volumes), *Poems* (3 volumes), and *Journal to Stella* (2 volumes). His *Account Books*, in which he recorded his daily expenses, have also been published in one volume. In subject, tone, and form, Swift's writings are extremely diverse. In *The Bickerstaff Papers*, for example, the subject is astrology and the form, in part, epistolary; *Advice to Grub-Street Verse Writers*, a poem, is mock-advice, a form popular in the early eighteenth century. *A Meditation upon a Broomstick* is a parody of a popular form of religious meditation. *A Modest Proposal*, perhaps his most famous satire, anticipates in some ways the absurdist irony of Franz Kafka and Samuel Beckett. Swift was a master at both light and serious allegory, as shown in *The Battle of the Books*, *Gulliver's Travels*, and *A Tale of a Tub*. But, he was also fond of puns, riddles, and whimsical verse—what he liked to call "bagatelles."

Thus, while it is perhaps too much to say, as Henry Craik does (*The Life of Jonathan Swift*, 1881), that "From first to last, with all his changes of mood, Swift's authorship is a thing of accident, pursued with no certain aim," it is certainly true that many of his works were prompted by a specific occasion. This is especially true of his poems.

On the whole, Swift's writings can be said to show three salient concerns: with reason, or the lack of it; with politics; and with language and style. "Reason," and its variations, "reasonableness," "rational," and the like, occur often in Swift's works, both prose and poetry. Nevertheless, reason is not something that he ever completely defines. In a famous letter to Pope (September 29, 1725), he states his belief that humans, by nature, are not rational; they only have the "potential" (*rationis capax*) for rationality. In *Cadenus and Vanessa* (1713) friendship, at least for the principal male figure, is defined as a "constant, rational delight"

(1.781), and in "On the Trinity," a sermon, the "right rules of reason" are set up as the norm of human conduct. Still, it is obvious, especially from the evidence of the satires, that it is the absence of reason which most engages his attention. Unreason, he says more than once, corrupts politics and manners; it allows the "passions" to rule—especially in women. And, with the Yahoos he reaches perhaps his most graphic dramatization of unreason and its consequences.

In particular, the triadic Yahoo:Gulliver: Houyhnhnm of Gulliver's last voyage is important in the problem of defining Swiftian reason. At first everything seems straightforward: both the Yahoos and Houyhnhnms exemplify states of being. They had arrived at what they were to become before Gulliver's arrival. Now, with Gulliver, a creature *rationis capax* is introduced—one in a state of becoming, neither rational, Houyhnhnm-like, nor irrational, Yahoo-like. Gulliver's lodging, between the house of the Master Houyhnhnm and his stable of Yahoos, his clothes, and one of his names, "gentle Yahoo," seem to indicate a half-this, half-that status. The opposing Yahoo:Houyhnhnm states, moreover, seem the complete deprivation of the "substance" of the other. By means of having been exposed to the orderly life of the Houyhnhnms, the reader "knows" the wild disorder of the Yahoos; by Houyhnhnm control of biological urges, a similar *lack* of control by the Yahoos; by the monogamy of the Houyhnhnms, the sexual promiscuity of the Yahoos—and so on. The argument, if it can be called that, is similar to that of knowing a false witness; that is, by contraries, "a faithful witness: like everything else is "known by his contrary" ("On False Witness," a sermon).

However, if the Houyhnhnms occupy a perfect state of reason, why do they want to remedy conditions every four years when one of their Grand Assemblies meets? Why, in particular, every four years do they want to "debate" about the extermination of the Yahoos? The Houyhnhnms, moreover, are cognitive and linguistically inconsistent. Gulliver says that they have no concept of the human act of lying; no means, that is, of expressing *negation*, what is when it is known *not* to be or what is *not* when it is known to exist.[1] Yet, Gulliver says that they use the negative in their definition of not lying, "said the thing which was not." Also, in their knowledge of their own personal death they seem to express knowledge of the nonexistent, a thing not yet present. Perhaps Swift's intention in all of this is to redefine reading as an act of *rationis capax.* Or, it may be that Swift's purpose is to exemplify, by paradoxical reduction, the indefinableness of human reason.

A second major interest of Swift's is in politics and public life. He is especially concerned with the tension between public and private life; how, in particular, public life and identity are necessary for individual happiness but how the selfish interests of the individual can lead to the ruin of the public and the unhappiness of many as well. This was, he thinks, a constant in human nature from early times: "The people of Athens impeached Pericles for misapplying the public revenues to his own private use" (*Discourse of the Contests and Dissensions . . . in Athens and Rome* [1701]). In the *Discourse,* the tension between things of the public and personal selfishness is made intelligible by an analogy between modern England and ancient Athens and Rome. Just as the ancient world lost its freedom through political squabbling motivated by personal willfulness, so he predicts, will be the modern result of the party strife between the Whigs and Tories. (This theme will appear again in book 1 of *Gulliver's Travels* in the episode of the Big-endians and in "On False Witness," a sermon.)

Political squabbling, and its harmful effect on political freedom, is again the theme of the later *Remarks on the Barrier Treaty* (1712) and *Public Spirit of the Whigs* (1714). Swift's quarrel with the Whigs, as it would be for the rest of his life with individuals and parties holding similar views, springs from a mixture of economic, religious, and political fears. In the Whiggish tendency toward freedom of expression, he sees the danger of anarchy and disorder. In their encouragement of a stock market economy, he discerns a loss in power of the agricultural interest and power based on the ownership of land. The writer argues that the making of laws should be solely in the hands of landowners: "Law in a free county is, or ought to be, the determination of the majority of those who have property in land" (*Thoughts on Various Subjects,* 1727). The standing of the established church is threatened, he concludes, by too much Whiggish tolerance of Catholics and Dissenters, groups like the Presbyterians and Quakers. Such groups, as his satire against religious fanatics in *A Tale of a Tub* and *Mechanical Operation of the Spirit* shows, tend to reduce religion to dogmatism and "enthusiasm."

On its most general level, Swift's fear of the Whigs and what they stand for becomes transformed, on the one hand, into fear of the stronger party against the weaker one and, on the other, fear for the loss of public identity. The presence of the strong against the weak motivates his opposition in *The Drapier Letters* (1724–1725) to a scheme of Prime Minister Robert Walpole's to introduce new coinage into Ireland. (It was the *Letters,* more than any other of his writings, that was to make Swift into the leading Irish patriot of his time.) Loss of political identity, and its effect on the individual, finally, is a major theme of *Gulliver's Travels.* Everywhere Gulliver is alienated from power. This is evidenced by the fact that nowhere in the narrative is the protagonist's proper name, "Lemuel Gulliver," used. Instead, he is addressed by temporary titles such as "Man-Mountain" and "Relplum Scalcath" or with the pronouns "you," "he," and "it." The sailors who accompany Gulliver on his voyages are similarly denied a political identity, as are the ordinary citizens of Lilliput and Lord Munodi, a character from Gulliver's third voyage. In the decade and a half after his return to Ireland, during which he wrote the *Travels,* Swift often expressed similar sentiments about his own personal situation: "I am in an obscure scene, where you know neither thing nor person . . . the scene and the times have depressed me wonderfully" (August 10, 1716), he says, and "[I am in] so obscure a corner, quite thrown out of the present world, and within a few steps of the next" (December 1, 1731).

In the background of Swift's concern with the absence of identity is the larger issue of political authority. Where does the ruler get his authority to rule? Under what conditions can he be deprived of the right to rule? In general, two answers were possible in the author's time. One, coming from the theory of the divine-right of kings, held that authority was vested in the king by God, and he could not be held accountable by his subjects. Moreover, to resist the king was to rebel against God. The other, one that grew popular after the restoration of Charles II in 1660 and relied on the writings of political theorists such as George Lawson and John Locke, maintained that communities had the right to resist the ruler or to dissolve the government and form a new one, if he became a tyrant. In *The History of the Four Last Years of Queen Anne's Reign* (written in 1713; published in 1758), Swift declares that the divine-right theory is "an absurd notion." He claims that no ruler has the right to use that bogus principle or any other like it in order to exempt himself from the laws of the country or to deny "fundamental" liberty to his subjects. Swift would later use (in the *Drapier Letters*) a similar argument against accepting Wood's coinage in Ireland. The king does not have the right to force it; to do so is to violate his "prerogative," rights given him by the laws of England. None of the rulers of the *Travels* openly espouses the divine-right doctrine. Yet all, with the exception of the King of Brobdingnag, seem to practice it. Neither the subjects of the Emperor of Lilliput nor those of the King of Luggnagg, for example, have any apparent freedom, nor any functional political identity.

Scholars Charles Firth and A.E. Case have argued for a detailed political allegory in the *Travels*. They contend, among other things, that Flimnap, the Lilliputian treasurer, represents Walpole, that the Emperor stands for George I, and that Gulliver's impeachment by the Lilliputians represents a similar act against Oxford and Bolingbroke by Walpole. Other scholars, Phillip Harth and F.P. Lock, for example, see the satire of the work directed more against political corruption in Europe and as forming a "series of observations on the imperfections, the follies, and the vices of man" (Harth).[2] It can be argued that the satire is directed also at the emergence of a new public world, one legitimized by expediency, "present private advantage," and the quick fix (in Swift's view), and instead of religion, the rule of law or "regard for public good" ("Doing Good: A Sermon").

In modern terminology such a public world is "secular," or perhaps, "secularized." In a weak form it involves matters such as the disestablishment of a national church, the watering down of legal equity, or the development of a stock market. Its citizenry reads newspapers instead of sermons, novels instead of the classics. They go around in mobs, like the Yahoos, and involve themselves in get-rich schemes like the South Sea Stock Company (one in which Swift and many of his friends lost money). In its strong form, a "community of obedience" within the old public is replaced by "a community of will," the public good by private interest. One is presented with something like the public (political) world of the *Travels*.

Nowhere, significantly, is there any sign of religious activity or faith (although, at least in Gulliver's first voyage, plenty of superstition and fear), nor is there any functional religious edifice. (The Lilliputian temple which houses Gulliver temporarily is "polluted" and abandoned.) Indeed, Gulliver is himself moved, and victimized too, by secular concerns, the need to "get a job," support his family, or "do" various parts of the world like a tourist: "My insatiable desire of seeing foreign countries would suffer me to continue no longer [in England]" (book 1, chapter 8). At times, moreover, his knowledge is thoroughly secular and procedural, involved with the "how" of things rather than with their intrinsic quality or ethical worth. Making a comb from the King of Brobdingnag's whiskers (book 2, chapter 6), a silver cup from the callouses of a maid of honor's toe (book 2, chapter 8), or clothes out of the skins of rabbits (book 4, chapter 10) are examples.

Gulliver's combs and cups bring to mind a society cluttered with things, things not only made, bought, and sold but also owned and stored, or, in the case of the Yahoos, fought over. Swift's ideal is another kind, though, one resembling that which he sketches in the *Sermons*. Instead of the concern for things, one is concerned with the care of others. Instead of procedural knowledge for its own end, or consumer products, there is the execution of such knowledge for the "good" of the "public." Of such a world in the *Travels* only a few citizens remain, Pedro de Mendez (book 4), the King of Brobdingnag and, perhaps, Lord Munodi (book 3).

It is, moreover, the duty of the historian, Swift notes, to give a truthful "representation" of the ideal public, "neither [mixing] panegyric or satire with an history intended to inform posterity, as well as to instruct those of the present age." Nor, Swift continues, should the historian emphasize the local at the expense of the national or the general at the expense of the particular. He should not write solely for a London audience but also for "gentlemen at a distance," and he should record not only the "word and gesture" of the personages in his history but also their motives and "character." Extracting the general basis of character from the written record, public documents, letters, proceedings, and the like, should always be the main purpose and writing strategy of the historian (*The History of the Four Last Years of Queen Anne's Reign*; cf. *Gulliver's Travels*, book 3, chapter 8 [the writing of "modern history"]).

Style, Swift's third major concern, is part of his interest in language as a whole and in what he perceives as conditions necessary for the writer to do his work. Gulliver, we remember, is not only a traveler but also a writer, the author of *Travels into Several Remote Nations of the World*. Furthermore, a major theme of *A Tale of a Tub* is modern literature and the written text. Even the modern projector of *A Modest Proposal* is conscious of his own efforts to have his "intentions" known by means of the written word: "I have too long digressed; and therefore shall return to my subject . . . But this, and many other [details], I omit, being studious of brevity." This awareness of language, what makes it function as a means of communication or threatens this function, was an early concern of Swift's. In 1712, afraid that the "corruptions" entering the language would prevent authors from having a "chance for immortality," he proposed that an academy along the "example of the French" be set up to "ascertain" and "fix" linguistic rules (*A Proposal for Correcting, Improving and Ascertaining the English Tongue*). Swift and Robert Harley, the Prime Minister, apparently went as far as drawing up a list of proposed members for the academy—presumably, as Swift notes in the *Proposal*, persons chosen "without regard to quality, party, or profession."

Several of his minor humorous pieces, notably *Hints Towards an Essay on Conversation* (1710), *A Modest Defence of Punning* (1716), and *Polite Conversation* (1738), also take language corruption as their subject and for the same general reason: the need to preserve linguistic intelligibility between speaker and listener or writer and reader. In at least two book reviews, one of Anthony Collins's *Discourse of Free-Thinking* (1713) and one of the Bishop of Sarum's *A Preface . . . Introduction of the Church of England* (1713), it is as much their language, or "stile," as their politics or religion that fires Swift's criticism. Burnet, especially, catches Swift's scorn: having "that peculiar manner of expressing himself which the poverty of our language forces me to call [his] stile." Correct standards of language also apply to the surface appearance and placement of lines in letters. Lines that run aslant the page, odd forms of punctuation, or words run together are usually noted critically in answering letters to correspondents. Swift's major quarrel on this head is with the handwriting of his female friends; this is obviously something that was on his mind when he has Gulliver describe the writing of the Lilliputians as "very peculiar; being neither from the left to the right, like the Europeans; nor from the right to the left, like the Arabians . . . but aslant from one corner of the paper to the other, like ladies in England."

The concerns just discussed were shared, in part, by many of Swift's contemporary satirists—especially Gay and Pope. But, certain of Swift's writing techniques, plus the intensity in which he drives them on, set him apart from them. Three of these, the use of a persona (or "mask"), the world-upside-down theme (*mundus inversus*), and making the figurative or metaphoric, literal, are particularly noteworthy.

In most cases the persona is Swift's main satirical device and the source of most of the humor of the piece. This is especially true of his two most famous personae (speakers or the "I"), Gulliver and the Modest Proposer. Also, while most of the personae have much in common (they are generally dogmatic, proud, and argumentative), they do distinguish themselves by profession or interest. The persona of *A Tale of a Tub* is a Grub-Street Hack and bookseller whose main interest is in promoting modern letters. He questions whether ancient literature exists and professes to be a servant of all "modern forms" and, consequently, the author of "momentous truths." In *A Modest Proposal*, the persona characterizes himself as a "projector" (usually a pejorative term in the eighteenth century), one whose main "intention" is to "provide" for the poor children of Ireland and their parents and to bring some pleasure to English landlords. We learn, in the course of his outlining his scheme, that he has been married for some time (his youngest child is "past nine" and his wife past childbearing), that he got his scheme from a "very knowing American," and that he is fond of numeric operations—adding, subtracting, and the like. What escapes him, of course, are the moral and legal consequences of his proposal. Nowhere, significantly, do the terms "murder" or "cannibalism" appear in his narrative.

Personae like the Grub-Street Hack and the Modest Proposer (one could also include the Footman of *Directions to Servants* and the astrologer of *The Bickerstaff Papers*) are somewhat simple in construction. Their motives, although expressed with demonic intensity, rise from essentially prosaic emotions, the need to pontificate, to force an opinion, and so forth. Gulliver, a persona-character of many years making, is far more complex. Like the Modest Proposer, he is married with children; like the Grub-Street Hack, he follows a profession (he is a surgeon); and he is not given overmuch to reflection on the effects of his words and actions. But unlike them, Gulliver's nature changes from one voyage to the other. During the voyage to Lilliput, he is gentle, obliging to his hosts, and somewhat naive; in Brobdingnag, he is nervous, impatient, and at times shrill. In Laputa, where he has very little interaction with the natives, he becomes much like a modern tourist, looking, wandering from place to place, and puzzling over local ways. And, with his fourth and final voyage to Houyhnhnmland, he turns misanthropic—a condition not predictable from the character-persona established in any previous voyage. No doubt, the complexity of Gulliver's character is at least partially responsible for the popularity of the work. Indeed, imitations of the character, collected under the title of *Gulliveriana*, began appearing immediately after the publication of the work (1726), and several film versions of *Gulliver* were made in the twentieth century, clear evidence of the importance and staying power of the book.

The Preacher says that he has seen servants riding horses while their masters walk (Ecclesiastes 10:7); Herodotus notes that in Egypt men stay at home cooking and keeping house while women go out buying and selling, and men squat to urinate while women stand (*Histories*, 2:35). These are examples of the world-upside-down theme (*mundus inversus*). The theme had special appeal for Swift, sometimes because of its comic effect, as in *A Meditation upon a Broomstick* or *Directions to Servants*. *Inversus* also had its serious purpose for him, though, especially in representing the experiences of Gulliver. In Lilliput, his protagonist is confronted by size-inversion (he is twelve times larger than the natives), an inversion which is then re-inverted in Brobdingnag; in Houyhnhnmland, where the horses are rulers, the inversion is in the "ordinary" man:master, horse:servant relationship. Even within the social hierarchy of the Houyhnhnms, inversion of the traditional color hierarchy is the case. Instead of white, as is traditional in Western culture, the equine color black is the "best" color: "among the Houyhnhnms, the white, the sorrel, and the iron-grey were not so exactly shaped as the bay, the dapple-grey and the black; nor born with equal talents of mind or a

capacity to improve them; and therefore continued always in the condition of servants." Perhaps such color-categorization and its social effects alludes to Swift's later description in the *Travels* of Spain's subjugation of the black natives of South America.

Obviously such inversion, in the reader's perception, has much the same effect as irony. Both achieve their ends by negation, by a reversal of the expected, by the appearance of the unexpected. Gulliver wins a suit in the Court of Chancery, he tells the King of Brobdingnag, that "almost ruined" him in the process; the Modest Proposer's scheme to solve the Irish problem would end in the elimination of Ireland's population; the Grub-Street Hack's advocacy of modern letters, which he admits do not exist, ultimately becomes an advocacy of writing on non-existing subjects: "I am now trying an experiment very frequent among modern authors; which is, to write upon nothing; when the subject is utterly exhausted, to let the pen still move on." Where the resemblance between inversion and irony seems to end, however, is in the constraints that the latter puts on visual representations, in pictures, sketches, and the like. Irony, being more cognitive than visual, needs the visual depictions of topsy-turvyism to ground it in the material world of size, color, and shape. In part this might explain why Swift's use of the theme tends to predominate in those parts of the *Travels* where he suppresses the irony, as in the episode of the flying island in the third voyage. The minimal use of cause and effect to explain Gulliver's actions would seem to be another example of such suppression.

Finally, one often finds in Swift, for purposes of his satire, the representation of an idea, or expression, as a thing. Syntactically, this often means the listing, after the manner of François Rabelais, of adjectives or nouns: "the historical account I gave him [the King of Brobdingnag] of our affairs during the last century . . . was only an heap of conspiracies, rebellions, murders, massacres, revolutions, banishments; the very worst effects that avarice, faction, hypocrisy, perfidiousness, cruelty, rage, madness, hatred, envy, lust, malice and ambition could produce."

But, reification of the idea also means its embodiment in a specific form and substance. In *The Mechanical Operation of the Spirit*, for example, religious enthusiasm becomes a bodily disease, a "tentiginous humor"; in *The Battle of the Books*, the ill-will and bad temper of the moderns is depicted as a bitter, discolored substance—the "spleen" or "gall." Perhaps the best-known example of this idea-into-thing appears in the Academy of Lagado episode of *Gulliver's Travels* where things have been substituted for words. Instead of speaking and referring to the conversational subject, speakers display the subject-thing itself. This means that the length of a conversation is fixed by the quantity of portable things—no more things to show, no more subjects to discuss, no more language. Additionally, nothing can be qualified since nothing can function as the predicate of a thing, only of another word. In this Swift is partly satirizing the language reformers, mostly of the seventeenth century, who wanted to simplify the language by having one word stand for one thing.

He is also calling into question the need for language to exist—and his own warrant as a writer. In his collections of bons mots, *Thoughts on Various Subjects* (1706, 1727), Swift traces the sources of similar paradoxes to time, memory, and vanity: "No preacher is listened to, but time; which gives us the same train and turn of thought, that elder people have tried in vain to put into our heads before" (1706). Men, moreover, not only have bad but also selective memories. And, there is a correlation between the kind of memory which they have and their age, gender, and social standing. Whenever young men want something they only "remember" its good side, yet when they have it, they recall only its bad side. The memories of old men are abstracted and "view best at a distance" (1727). Unfortunately, old people are harder to please than young ones because they remember better times. Young people, conversely, think that present times are better—because their pasts, being short, do not offer them material enough for temporal comparisons: "When I was young, I thought all the world as well as myself was wholly taken up in discoursing upon the last new play" (1727). All people, but most of all women, have a "reluctance and unwillingness to be forgotten" (1727) and need to have grave inscriptions, yet the "smallest accident intervening" (1706) can upset all intentions, memories, and histories, personal and collective. Where Swift thinks that human expectations correlate with vanity, experience with indifference, and accomplishment with failure, one seems to hear the voice of the Old Testament prophets, especially that of Ecclesiastes. Yet, the voice of the *Thoughts*,

unlike the preacher's, finds that the paradox of things lies in their causes, not their effects. Moreover, Swift likes to express the causes with a parody of three-term logic which he had studied at Trinity College: "No man will take counsel, but every man will take money; therefore money is better than counsel" (1727). Swift uses a similar logical form in a representation of memory loss in the Struldbrugs (*Gulliver's Travels*, book 3, chapter 10).

Finally, his skill in ending an argument in a paradox will later find, for different reasons, a disciple in Laurence Sterne, author of *The Life and Opinions of Tristram Shandy*.

Summary

Of all of the writers of eighteenth-century England, Jonathan Swift must be counted among the most popular and influential. More scholarly articles and books appear on him during the course of a year than any other writer of the period (with the possible exception of Samuel Johnson). There is now a scholarly journal devoted exclusively to Swift, *Swift Studies* (Munster, West Germany), and Swift's name is also mentioned more often in *Encyclopedia of American Humorists* (Garland, 1988) than is that of any of his contemporaries—more, in fact, than any other English humorist-satirist.

Interestingly, Swift also has a place in popular culture. "Yahoo," as a term of reproach, is known to practically everyone, for example, and varieties of the Yahoo figure appear in American folklore. Elsewhere, as befits his madcap style of humor, the Australian comic, actor, director, and writer, Greg Pead, has taken the name, "Yahoo Serious." John F. Sena notes, furthermore, that place-names, and the title of *Gulliver's Travels* itself, appear as the names of contemporary travel agencies, motels, and on billboards in the United States, Canada, and England.[3] And, as about everyone knows, mock-proposals for some outrageous act, often one involving eating, are commonly imitations of *A Modest Proposal*.

Swift's influence is still being felt, in part because of his choice of subject which, at least in the case of *Gulliver's Travels*, *Verses on the Death of Dr. Swift*, and *A Modest Proposal*, is an examination of lasting human concerns. Just as important is his use of language. His words are simple, used in "a wise thrift and economy, as he used his money" (Thackeray, vol. 26, 159–60). He does not, as many of his contemporaries (William Temple in particular) did, use a Latin expression where one, or none, will serve. *A Letter to a Young Gentleman* (1719), which contains his definition of a "true" style as "proper words in proper places," is perhaps his most complete statement of the principles that ruled his own use of language, principles that he would urge on any who speak or write for either a specific or general audience. Not everyone, certainly, admires the simplicity of Swift's language, but it does seem fair to say that everyone with an average capacity for reading understands his meaning, and the comic expression of that meaning has resulted in his lasting influence.

Notes

1. This is the so-called correspondence theory of truth. See John H. Reichert, "Plato, Swift and the Houyhnhnms," *Philological Quarterly*, 47 (1968): 179–92.
2. A.E. Case, *Four Essays on Gulliver's Travels* (Princeton: Princeton University Press, 1945); Charles Firth, "The Political Significance of *Gulliver's Travels*," *Proceedings of the British Academy*, 9 (1919–1920): 237–59; F.P. Lock, *The Politics of Gulliver's Travels* (Oxford: Clarendon, 1980); Phillip Harth, "The Problem of Political Allegory in *Gulliver's Travels*," *Modern Philology*, 73 (1976): 540–47.
3. John F. Sena, "Teaching *Gulliver's Travels*." In *Approaches to Teaching Swift's Gulliver's Travels*. Ed. Edward J. Rielly (New York: Modern Language Association, 1988), pp. 44–51.

Selected Bibliography

Primary Sources
The Prose Writings of Jonathan Swift. Ed. Herbert Davis. 14 vols. Oxford: Basil Blackwell, 1939–1968.
The Account Books of Jonathan Swift. Ed. Paul V. Thompson and Dorothy Jay Thompson. Newark: University of Delaware Press; London: Scolar Press, 1984.
The Correspondence of Jonathan Swift. Ed. Harold Williams. 5 vols. Oxford: Oxford University Press, 1963–1965.
The Poems of Jonathan Swift. Ed. Harold Williams. 3 vols. Oxford: Oxford University Press, 1958.
Journal to Stella. Ed. Harold Williams. 2 vols. Oxford: Basil Blackwell, 1948.

Secondary Sources

Biographies
Ehrenpreis, Irvin. *Swift, the Man, His Works, and the Age*. 3 vols. Cambridge: Harvard University Press, 1962–1983. The most complete biography of Swift by, arguably, the best Swift scholar of the twentieth century.
Nokes, David. *Jonathan Swift, A Hypocrite Reversed*. Oxford: Oxford University Press, 1985. Perhaps the best single volume biography of Swift now available. Focuses on Swift's reserve, secrecy, and self-deprecation.

Bibliographies
Landa, Louis, and J.E. Tobin. *Jonathan Swift: A List of Critical Studies Published from 1895 to 1945*. New York: Cosmopolitan Science and Art Service, 1945.
Rodino, Richard. *Swift Studies 1965–1980: An Annotated Bibliography*. New York: Garland, 1984.
Stathis, J.J. *A Bibliography of Swift Studies, 1945–1965*. Nashville: Vanderbilt University Press, 1967.
Teerink, H. *Bibliography of the Writings of Jonathan Swift*. Ed. Arthur Scouten. 2nd ed. Philadelphia: University of Pennsylvania Press, 1963.
Vieth, David. *Swift's Poetry, 1900–1980: An Annotated Bibliography*. New York: Garland, 1982.

Books
Elias, A.C. *Swift at Moor Park*. Philadelphia: University of Pennsylvania Press, 1982. A discussion of Swift's work and life with William Temple (1689–1690, 1691–1694, 1696–1699). Temple's "world view" and its influence on Swift are stressed.
Landa, Louis. *Swift and the Church of Ireland*. Oxford: Oxford University Press, 1954. Landa discusses Swift's position in the Church of Ireland, the Church's institutional organization, its problems as a minority church in Ireland, and Swift's support of the Church.
Quintana, Ricardo. *The Mind and Art of Jonathan Swift*. Oxford: Oxford University Press, 1936. Still the best discussion of Swift's "governing ideas."
Rielly, Edward J., ed. *Swift's Gulliver's Trav-*

els. New York: Modern Language Association, 1988. Approaches to Teaching World Literature series. The best single guide to how to teach Swift's masterpiece to modern university students.

Thackeray, William Makepeace. *The Works of Thackeray*. 32 vols. New York: Charles Scribner's Sons, 1904.

Welcher, Jeanne K, and George E. Bush Jr., eds. *Gulliveriana*. Vols. 1–6. Delmar: Scholars' Facsimiles and Reprints, 1970–1976. Vols. 7–8, Jeanne K. Welcher, ed. Delmar: Scholars' Facsimiles and Reprints, 1986–1988. Imitations, parodies, and the like of *Gulliver's Travels*— mostly from the eighteenth century. There are also annotated critiques of writings on Swift in the scholarly journals *Restoration* and *The Scriblerian*, and unannotated ones in *Swift Studies*.

Gene Washington

Symons, Arthur William

Born: Milford Haven, Wales, February 28, 1865

Education: Formal education ended at W.J. Jeffery's High Street Classical and Mathematical School, Bideford, Devon, in 1882

Marriage: Rhoda Bowser, January 19, 1901

Died: Island Cottage, Wittersham, Kent, January 22, 1945

Biography

The son of the Reverend Mark Symons, a Wesleyan minister, and Lydia Pascoe Symons, Arthur Symons was born in the port of Milford Haven, Wales, approximately eight miles from Haverfordwest, on February 28, 1865. In 1880, a new teacher, Charles Churchill Osborne, whom Symons used as a mentor for several years, became a particularly strong source of encouragement for Symons's literary and scholarly pursuits. Symons's formal education ended at W.J. Jeffery's High Street Classical and Mathematical School in Bideford, Devon, in 1882. Eventually, in that same year, at the age of seventeen, he informed his parents that he would no longer attend church because it held no interest for him and that he would rather starve than go into business; instead, he began to pursue a literary career, perceiving art as an insulating defense against the vulgar, provincial world.

The young Symons became a regular correspondent of Browning Society co-founder Frederick J. Furnivall who, along with Osborne, J. Dykes Campbell (of the Browning Society), and Dr. Richard Garnett (of the British Museum), helped foster Symons's budding career. As early as December 1882, Symons began publishing scholarly studies on Robert Browning, William Shakespeare, and others, and within a few years he had, despite the lack of a university education, established himself as a respected critic, winning the encouragement and endorsement of such leading figures as Browning, John Addington Symonds, Havelock Ellis, George Meredith, and Walter Pater. In September 1889, Symons made his first trip to Paris (in the company of Ellis), an "unforgettable" eight-day visit that "truly enchanted" him and reinforced in him his Baudelairean ties with bohemian life and his allegiance to the Decadent "Religion of Art."

In August 1890, Symons had met Katherine Willard, his first love, with whom over the next five years he formed a deepening relationship but who ultimately rejected him as a suitable mate, probably because of her inability to accept his "decadent" lifestyle, his restlessness, and his insatiable hunger for experience. On January 5, 1891, Symons moved into rooms at 2 Fountain Court in the Temple area of London which would be his home and base of operations for the next ten years, the most significant period in his career. He hosted numerous famous artists and writers at Fountain Court, including Paul Verlaine during the French poet's much-cited visit to England in November 1892. Indeed, he regularly sublet part of his quarters (the two rooms overlooking Essex Street) to Ellis, who became a major force in cultural studies, and William Butler Yeats, certainly one of the greatest poets of his time. It was during this period that Symons made the acquaintance of virtually everyone who was anyone in literary and artistic circles in late nineteenth-century England and France, and in the process he became a major spokesperson for the cultural avant-garde.

He had a reputation as a womanizer, at least by Victorian standards; yet as an unusually sensitive and receptive but rather submissive personality, he often placed himself in a position of dependency on strong but emotionally volatile women. In late 1893, he became deeply involved with a ballet dancer whom he met at the Empire Theatre and whom we know only as "Lydia."

This torrid relationship was to become his "grand passion." Although the affair actually lasted only some two and a half years (ending, with the exception of one additional series of trysts, in early 1896, when the dancer wed an elderly suitor), it became an obsession for the remainder of the writer's life and shaped much of the focus of, and ideas in, his art.

In the latter part of 1895, Symons helped found a new literary journal, *The Savoy* (often cited as the era's best such magazine), which first appeared in January 1896 with Symons as its literary editor. In the late 1890s, he traveled extensively, mostly (in addition to his customary jaunts to France) in Italy and Spain, writing much impressionistic travel literature and deepening his interest in the French Symbolist Movement.

Shortly after Symons's father died in May 1898, Symons made the acquaintance of an aspiring actress and his future wife, Rhoda Bowser, the daughter of a wealthy Newcastle businessman. Conditioned by his Wesleyan upbringing, Symons tended to see his life as largely an evasion of conventional responsibility and Rhoda as a source of grounding for him. Rhoda resisted him because she correctly perceived that they were both emotionally self-absorbed, her tastes were too extravagant for the struggling writer, and in any case he needed "absolute mental & physical freedom." However, eventually they set up a comfortable fourth-floor flat in Maida Vale, London, and subsequently married on January 19, 1901, Symons being dressed as usual all in black, which had become virtually a "signature" for him. As predicted, despite a rather frugal lifestyle aided by a mutual desire not to have children, they soon found it difficult to live on his earnings as a writer.

In 1900, Symons became the drama critic for the London *Star* at a salary of £4 per week (initially signing his reviews "Silhouette," an allusion to, among other things, his successful second volume of poems). In early 1902, he became the drama and music critic for the *Academy*. Yet, despite his almost Herculean productivity—he averaged over sixty-five articles, reviews, poems, stories, or other works every year between 1892 and 1908—and fairly regular employment as a reviewing journalist (a job for which he had increasing distaste), Symons was under constant financial pressure and found it difficult to maintain even his very modest standard of living. Beginning in the summer of 1901, he experienced increasing pressure and depression, certainly over his increased financial needs but perhaps also over the relatively insignificant benefits that he felt he was getting from his self-sacrifice at the altar of Art.

In 1903, he met painter Augustus John, an event that Symons once said was one of the most important in his life inasmuch as John proved to be a steadfast friend during the most difficult period of Symons's later life. In 1904, the author began a friendship with Irish-American lawyer John Quinn, who represented James Joyce in the defense of *Ulysses* and who would also give crucial aid to Symons after his breakdown in 1908. In 1906, the Symonses decided to buy a late-seventeenth-century timbered cottage in Wittersham, Kent, a purchase that while it provided a restful, country retreat also placed an even greater financial burden on him, which he sought to meet by taking on still more literary projects and hoping to complete them at an even more frenetic pace. To reduce expenses in London, the Symonses moved from their spacious Maida Vale flat to a small house in St. John's Woods, but Arthur continued to be constantly worried about money. On Christmas Day, 1907, Symons was stunned by the sudden death of his dog Api, a "surrogate child" to which he was profoundly attached and which had momentarily made him feel "normal, human, like other people."

The Symonses were in Italy in September and October 1908, having "rashly" accepted an invitation (which they doubted they could afford) to stay in a palace on the Grand Canal in Venice. While Venice was one of Symons's favorite cities, he also associated it with the themes of sex, decadence, and death which so often disturbed him. In late September 1908, he had a psychotic breakdown, what he described as a "thunderbolt from hell," suddenly leaving Rhoda to go to Bologna, then Ferrara, wandering about, running in panic, falling into deep ditches and ponds, emerging covered with mud, and ending up manacled hand and foot in a dungeon in Castello Vecchio. Eventually transferred to Dr. A. Watson Griffin's institution in Crowborough, England, Symons was "certified" incurably insane and committed to Brooke House, in Upper Clapton Road, East London. In light of these circumstances, Edmund Gosse obtained a Royal Literary Fund grant for Symons in 1909 and ultimately a Civil List Pension in 1913.

Although Symons's doctors held out no hope of recovery and predicted death within eighteen months, he miraculously improved and returned to a relatively normal life by the middle of 1910. He resumed his literary career, attempting to restore his former brilliance. However, although he continued to be quite productive through the late 1920s, his thinking seemed somehow muted and he was never able to rise to his previous level of lucidity or acuity, and he intermittently manifested varying degrees of incoherence.

After her husband's recovery, Rhoda pursued a rather anemic acting career, appearing in some dozen or more plays from 1912 to the mid-1920s, but, partly due to her lack of success, she generally fell prey to increasingly frequent cycles of depression and self-reproach. Symons continued to keep company with the literary world, spending much time with Joseph Conrad and Maud Gonne, among others, and even trying to relive the period of his previous glory through nightly carouses in London or sentimental sojourns to Paris in 1920 and 1924–1925. For the most part, however, especially after the mid-1920s, Symons remained at Island Cottage in Wittersham, except for visits to the quiet Clifton Hill home that Rhoda had rented in London.

In 1926, hastened perhaps by the death of her brother-in-law and subsequent suicide of her sister, Rhoda's physical and psychological health began to worsen significantly, and a housekeeper, Mrs. Bessie Seymour, was retained to look after Symons. Rhoda underwent treatment for an unnamed illness (probably the beginnings of leukemia) in 1930 and she tended to spend more and more time in London as her health worsened. In November 1935, she fell on the stairs of their London home, inducing a heart attack, and her doctor eventually sent her to rest at a seaside resort in Sussex where she died in November 1936.

Symons's handwriting and eyesight deteriorated progressively after 1930, as did his general mental condition. His later years, under servants' care arranged by Mrs. Seymour through Rhoda's will, were passed in quiet contentment. He died on January 22, 1945, at his Island Cottage home in Wittersham, Kent, having seven years earlier bequeathed to Bessie Seymour all of his property, including the copyrights of his work.

Literary Analysis

Symons, who often wrote prose of breathtaking beauty, was considered by many to be "the best critic of his generation."[1] That Symons was judged to be a critic of such high quality was particularly noteworthy, since he was also one of the most prolific writers of his time. He depended solely on his writing for his livelihood (albeit a very meager one), and, writing with great speed, he produced—not including many unpublished works—an astonishing total of some sixty books, seventy-five editions, and 1,300 articles, reviews, and notes over his career, the most significant portion of which were written during the especially frenetic period between 1883 and his breakdown in 1908.

Symons's lifelong interest in establishing his ancestral origins, his image of himself as a Celtic outsider, his continuing interest in the lore of wandering gypsies, and his persistent fear of death (and associated obsession with experiencing life intensely before it was snuffed out) may have derived in part from his early sense of rootlessness, as a result of his father's frequent clerical reassignments. Because ministers at the time were routinely assigned to circuits for no more than three years, the Symons family moved frequently during his youth—from Wales to Guernsey, Channel Islands in 1866; to Alnwick, Northumberland in 1868; to St. Ives, Cornwall in 1871; to Tavistock, Devon in 1873; to Tiverton, Devon in 1876; to Bideford, Devon in 1879; and to Yeovil, Somerset in 1882. As an adult, the author liked to claim that the wandering life was "the best of all lives for an artist."

Although Symons grew up in the country, even his early youth was characterized by a love of art rather than any interest in nature, prefiguring his view that the city was the proper subject and symbol of modern life. As a young teenager, he wrote poems influenced by eminent Victorians Robert Browning and A.C. Swinburne and indulged his Romantic tastes by reading works by Charlotte Brontë, John Webster, Thomas Carlyle, William Makepeace Thackeray, and Dante Gabriel Rossetti. He published *An Introduction to the Study of Browning*, his first book of criticism, in 1886 (at age twenty-one), and *Days and Nights*, his first book of poetry, in 1889. Symons modeled his early verse, very often psychological studies in the form of dramatic monologues, after Browning, and he modeled his prose style after Pater, whose famous *The Renaissance* (1873), Symons claimed, "opened a new world to me, or, rather, gave me the key or secret of the world in which I was living."[2] Symons's aesthetic principles also derived from Browning and Pater, emphasizing the need to isolate and reveal the human soul in strikingly significant dramatic moments.

Like many of the artists of the Victorian Decadence, Symons's views on the artistic life were unusually closely linked with the force of personality, his many personal friendships with illustrious figures having given him a strong sense of purpose. His second visit to Paris between mid-March and mid-June 1890—during which he met his idols Verlaine and Stéphane Mallarmé, established contacts with numerous important French writers and artists, and thoroughly investigated the more exotic haunts of the city—was perhaps the most important experience of Symons's youthful career. It was the beginning of his important role as a cultural mediator between French and English authors and as the expert on French Decadence/Symbolism. It was also an important step forward in his own efforts, like Verlaine's, to fuse out of disorder and disturbance some "final harmony" in both art and life. Not surprisingly, he was one of the first members of the famous Rhymers' Club of the early 1890s, although he soon became a less-than-faithful attender of the meetings. Reflecting the views of the Decadence and in reaction against nineteenth-century scientific materialism and Benthamite utilitarianism, Symons envisioned artists as the necessary new priests of the imagination, disciples who treated art as "a kind of religion, with all the duties and responsibilities of the sacred ritual" (*Collected Works*, vol. 8, p. 104). In his famous article "The Decadent Movement in Literature," which originally appeared in November 1893, he speaks of the Decadent's quest for *la vérité vraie* ("the very essence of truth") to "flash upon you . . . the soul—the finer sense of things unseen, the deeper meaning of things evident" in an effort to achieve "the ideal of Decadence": "To fix the last fine shade, the quintessence of things; to fix it fleetingly; to be a disembodied voice, and yet the voice of a human soul" (*Dramatis Personae*, 99, 106). The article confirmed Symons's place as the spokesperson for an exotic new Decadent literature that presented an odd conflation of the spiritual and the carnal, two forces which seemed constantly at war within the author himself.

Personally, Symons saw life in terms of extremes—to be authentic, it needed to be "hell or heaven"—and in his art and criticism as well, he gave particular value and importance to passion, intensity. During the 1890s, Symons became not only a renowned critic of the arts, but a noted "Decadent," a devotee of London's risqué music-halls, especially the famous Alhambra and Empire theatres, and the frequent companion of numerous "immoral" actresses and dancers. He readily confessed that sex had been for him "my chief obsession," and he considered it "a centre of Life and of Death" and "also the centre of Creation. Without the possession of women, how can one create?" (*Memoirs*, 138). Traveling in Spain in the spring of 1891, Symons's attraction to music-halls and to dance in particular as metaphors for art and the Decadent desire to fuse life and art strengthened. Yeats called him "a scholar in music-halls,"[3] a reference to Symons' progressive obsession with *femmes fatales* and his fascination with dance as an emblem for the isolated, perverse, self-absorbed, narcissistic artist. Particularly in his "impressionistic" books of poetry, *Silhouettes* (1892) and *London Nights* (1895), he developed themes—drawing on the works of such figures as Charles Baudelaire—about the superiority of artifice, the world as the embodiment of desire, the possibilities of sin as a vehicle of transcendence, and the fact that the fleeting impressions of the urban landscape provoke and reflect the inner world of the spectator. The notoriously sensational debut in April 1894 of *The Yellow Book*, one of the most famous literary journals of the age, was due in no small part to the inclusion of Symons's poem "Stella Maris," whose title evoked the Virgin Mary but whose content involved a random liaison with a prostitute, what Symons called a "Juliet of the night."

Symons developed a personal myth of himself as having "no interest in what is proper, regular, conventionally virtuous," but being "attracted by everything that is unusual, Bohemian, eccentric" (*Selected Letters*, 79). He held the belief that strangeness is an essential characteristic of beauty and that the quality of strangeness is connected to the essential individuality of the work of art. Standard modes of perception are to be avoided, since true art is the embodiment of new insights surprising the reader/viewer. At times Symons even tends to identify abnormality, the grotesque or the perverse, with artistic quality, emphasizing the importance of unconscious impulses in all artistic creation.

He was also revolutionary in applying high-art principles to the previously denigrated art of popular culture. In particular he saw circus and music-hall performers as representing a liberation from puritanism and demonstrating the beauty and strength of the human form. In his essay "The World as Ballet" (1898), he describes dance as an embodiment of both flux and stasis, a living symbol combining animalistic sensory experience together with spiritual transcendence. The piece is a continuation of Symons's attempt to reconcile flesh and spirit through art. He tended to view the world in relation to its corruption, its imperfection, and he saw in art's perfect expression of sin a means of transcending sin, a form of morality itself, "sin transfigured by beauty" (*Collected Works*, vol. 9, p. 99). The natural world was often chaotic and disordered, and the "symbolic corruption" of a self-consciously formed, artificial world could provide a kind of aesthetic transcendence and order unavailable in nature. Indeed, one of the more intriguing elements of his art is the way that he often seeks to distance and aestheticize a fascination with the flesh by means of the ordering forms of art. In *London Nights* (1895), for example, much of the lovemaking is almost clinical rather than erotic. Its intensity is emphasized but often distanced by the transformation of the lover into a reflection (or projection) of the speaker's desire, a living work of art. In such fashion devastating romantic losses may even be transformed into artistic triumph and consolation.

Although Symons often claimed that art had no obligation to morality, that art and morality were separate spheres, much of his own art is distinctly moral (even moralistic) in its premises and themes, among the most prevalent being an implicit respect for the moral will, an unrelenting guilt over forbidden desires, and a fear of eternal damnation. Such themes, and the tendency to split aesthetic pleasure from morality, may have had their seeds in his Wesleyan religious upbringing which assumed a division of flesh and spirit and taught that sex was generally evil, and in his perception of his parents. He apparently viewed his mother as having a "joy of life" and being sensitive and accepting of "every aspect of the world," in severe contrast to his father, an exceptionally conscientious Wesleyan pastor from whom Symons felt somewhat alienated and who was "dryly intellectual and despondent" and reproachful (*Collected Works*, vol. 5, p. 10; vol. 5, p. 14). Perhaps reinforcing Symons's lifelong feelings of transgression, guilt, rejection, and loss was the coincidence, which he readily acknowledged, that Lydia was the name of both his mother and his most "destructive" lover, and the further coincidence that his mother, who showed some symptoms of insanity in her last years and who was concerned and generally disappointed over his bohemian existence, died in March 1896, a short time after the breakup of his affair with the dancer Lydia.

As a result, at least in part, of this affair, women often serve in Symons's work, at least in their roles as *femmes fatales*, as "cruel and relentless" mythic symbols of lust—as vampires or entrapping sirens. This characterization was in line with a general Decadent tendency to play the sacrificial victim as a means of neutralizing one's own implicit guilt. The figure of Salome, for instance, was a lifelong obsession of Symons, a symbol of sterile, narcissistic autonomy and the author's own potential for self-destructive isolation. Certainly, *Amoris Victima* (1897), which was modeled on George Meredith's famous *Modern Love* (1862) and in effect traces the transformation from love to hate in Symons's relationship with Lydia, is a record of the pain of deception and the agonizing memory of a once ecstatic love (or lust) now lost. The poems in the volume reflect a sense of imprisonment and a view of sex as separate from love and essentially cruel and victimizing, even pressing at the limits of human sanity.

Symons was increasingly struck by what he took to be "the universal instinct of cruelty" and his own share in it. As a consequence of this "instinct," he was often preoccupied by themes of punishment. It was perhaps a reflection of the writer's attraction to unconventional and dangerous modes of life, and even some self-flattering prescience of his own eventual breakdown, that he tended throughout his life to associate genius and intense sensitivity with insanity and to dwell on the danger that dreams might loosen one's hold on "external things."

As the literary editor of *The Savoy* in 1895 and 1896, Symons clearly chose material that emphasized his own indebtedness to the earlier Pre-Raphaelites, especially Rossetti (whom he said he would rather have known than any other man in modern times), and most obviously to French Symbolism and the psychological explorations of French-influenced Naturalism—a blending, in effect, of his own bohemian tastes with his father's moralistic Wesleyanism and his mother's aesthetic and mystical responses to nature and religion. While he was always careful to translate French influences into an English context, Symons obviously wished to proselytize for French literature and art in order to undermine British cultural chauvinism. He was eager, for example, to translate for *The Savoy* Verlaine's account of his 1893 lecture visit to London and to extol Verlaine as "the greatest French poet since Baudelaire." More subtly, Symons also used *The Savoy* to attack bourgeois Philistinism in as much as a number of selections focused on the dilemma of the artist's diminished place in the world. Scornful of the commonplace, he conceived of Art as having always to be "an aristocracy," if a necessarily unconventional aristocracy, a salvational force against the unreliable "facts" and leveling triviality of mass journalism and vulgar bourgeois provincialism.

Symons was generally not noted as a humorist; indeed, he was known primarily as the rather solemn, at times ultra-serious spokesperson for the 1890s "Religion of Art." But, he possessed a keen wit and a dry irony, often facetious and self-deprecating, which frequently found their way into his conversation and writing, especially in the 1890s. He especially turned his ironic wit on the moralistic Philistine press and public. Perhaps the most noted examples of such humor occur during his time with *The Savoy*—two prefaces to the second editions of books of poetry and his editorial comments in *The Savoy*.

In "Being a Word on Behalf of Patchouli" (February 1896), his preface to the second edition of *Silhouettes*, Symons wryly makes the case that, after all, art is artifice and so logically should be judged on its quality of craftsmanship rather than merely on the morality of its subject matter. He argues, therefore, that many subjects previously considered frivolous or even immoral are absolutely proper and indeed desirable topics for art. Feigning an inability to comprehend "the hesitations, and compromises, and timorous advances, and shocked retreats, of the Puritan conscience once emancipated and yet afraid of liberty," he begins his short essay by amusingly hoisting an antagonist by his own petard:

> An ingenuous reviewer once described some verses of mine as "unwholesome," because, he said, they had "a faint smell of Patchouli about them." I am a little sorry he chose Patchouli, for that is not a particularly favourite scent with me. If he had only chosen Peau d'Espagne,

> which has a subtle meaning, or Lily of the Valley, with which I have associations! But Patchouli will serve. (*Collected Works*, vol. 1, p. 95)

Going on to defend himself, facetiously, referring to the critical firestorm that *London Nights* provoked, Symons writes:

> I have not, if my recollection serves me, been accused of actual immorality. I am but a fair way along the "primrose path," not yet within singeing distance of the "everlasting bonfire." In other words, I have not yet written "London Nights," which, it appears (I can scarcely realise it, in my innocent abstraction in aesthetical matters), has no very salutary reputation among the blameless moralists of the press. (*Collected Works*, vol. 1, p. 96)

In his "Preface to the Second Edition of *London Nights*" (September 1896), he observes that the original edition "was received by the English press with a singular unanimity of abuse. In some cases the abuse was ignoble: for the most part, it was no more than unintelligent . . . Happening to be in France at the time, I reflected, with scarcely the natural satisfaction of the Englishman, that such a reception of a work of art would have been possible in no country but England" (*Collected Works*, vol. 8, p. 165).

The Victorian satirical journal *Punch* had lampooned the initial number of *The Savoy* for its immoral tone, declaring with much sarcasm: "There is not an article in the volume that one can put down without feeling the better and the purer for it . . . . This book should be on every schoolroom table; every mother should present it to her daughter, for it is bound to have an ennobling and purifying influence" (February 1, 1896, p. 49). Amusingly, in an advertisement in the second number of *The Savoy*, Symons excerpted this section and shamelessly placed it, out of context, at the head of a series of press notices which ostensibly praised the new quarterly (April 1896, p. 203). His brief "Editorial Note" for the second number of *The Savoy* was hardly less perverse:

> I wish to thank the critics of the press for the flattering reception which they have given to No. 1. That reception has been none the less flattering because it has

been for the most part unfavourable . . . . I confess cheerfully that I have learnt much from the newspaper criticisms of the first number of "The Savoy." It is with confidence that I anticipate no less instruction from the criticisms which I shall have the pleasure of reading on the number now issued. (April 1896, p. [5])

Such wry humor was typical of many of the iconoclastic Decadents and even taken to a high art by such figures as Oscar Wilde.

From the mid-1890s, Symons's writing reflected his rich and expanding interests within his Decadent sensibility. He became more and more interested in the French Symbolist Movement, wrote an increasing amount of travel literature that reflected his Symbolist bias, and began writing serious art criticism. What he called his "first serious attempt at art criticism" (letter to Gosse, May 9, 1898, Leeds University Library)—a brilliant article on Aubrey Beardsley shortly after the artist's death—ended up shaping the course of Beardsley studies for the next ninety years and remains one of the best pieces ever written on Beardsley.

Symons spent much time in the mid-1890s with fellow poet Yeats, and Yeats, who had immense respect for Symons's judgment of literature, was instrumental during this period in getting Symons to shift his emphasis from "Decadent" to "Symbolist," which was to culminate in Symons's landmark critical study *The Symbolist Movement in Literature*. In his November 1897 article "A Note on George Meredith" for the *Fortnightly Review*, Symons redefines "Decadence" as primarily stylistic, a "deliberately abnormal" distortion of the organic and unified relationship between language and literary form. While the "decadent spirit," with its withdrawal into dream and its intimation of futility, was fundamental to the anguish felt by most of the Symbolists, he sought to separate Decadence from Symbolism as a way of lending more authority to the latter movement. In October 1898, while revising chapters for his momentous *Symbolist Movement* at a famous Benedictine monastery on Montserrat (the site of the Grail Quest castle in Richard Wagner's *Parsifal*), he experienced a moving spiritual awakening that only reinforced his natural attraction to the mystical movement.

Personally, Symons lived with an almost constant sense of insecurity and disconnectedness, so as a critic, he idealistically sought always for universal "first principles," even if he rarely strayed very far from specific, concrete incidents. His attraction to Impressionism, Decadence, and Symbolism reflected in large part his faith in intense moments through which the poet could snatch an experience of beauty from the jaws of time and decay—the use of dreams, religion, and art as means for escaping the oppression of death. In *The Symbolist Movement*, which finally appeared in bookstores on March 5, 1900 (although he had finished most of it a year and a half earlier), Symons argued that the movement was essentially transcendental or spiritual, "a form of expression . . . for an unseen reality," a "kind of religion, with all the duties and responsibilities of the sacred ritual" (*Collected Works*, vol. 8, pp. 99, 104). Symbolism established "the links which hold the world together, the affirmation of an eternal, minute, intricate, almost invisible life, which runs through the whole universe" (*Collected Works*, vol. 8, p. 193) even as Symons acknowledged that such creative insight was often purchased at the price of madness.

Gosse called Symons's *Symbolist Movement* "the finest product of pure criticism which has been seen in England for years" (letter to Symons, March 7, 1900, Kenneth A. Lohf Collection, Columbia University), and indeed, Symons's treatise soon became widely regarded as virtually a sacred book, profoundly influencing the careers of such notable modern writers as Yeats, Joyce, Ezra Pound, and T.S. Eliot. In fact, the young Joyce sought out the author, and Symons was subsequently responsible for placing Joyce's *Chamber Music* (1907) with a publisher.

Symons's next book, *Images of Good and Evil* (1900), was one of his better volumes of poetry and an advance technically over his previous verse, although it dealt with familiar Symonsian themes—dancing *femmes fatales* as universal destructive forces, an allegorical progression of death which was arguably the ultimate fusion of Body and Soul. Symons typically dwelt on psychological and spiritual crises, particularly the impulse to self-destruction and the inherent danger of surrendering to a stronger will and having the security of one's self obliterated. In the essay on John Keats in his book *The Romantic Movement in English Poetry* (1909), he lamented what a "frightful thing" it is to "shift one's centre" which is the frequent effect of loving a woman (*Romantic Movement in English Poetry*, 300–301). In his play *The Fool of the World* (1906), he depicts Death ironically as a blind jester who, revealing herself as a woman at the end, pleads for pity.

In 1903, Symons published another landmark piece of art criticism, a three-part essay on James McNeill Whistler, shortly after the artist's death in July, in which he once again emphasized the epiphanous Symbolist moment. In *Plays, Acting, and Music* (1903), Symons hoped to begin "the concrete expression of a theory, or system of aesthetics, of all the arts" (*Plays, Acting, and Music,* vii), or for that matter, of life itself as a form of art. Drawing on the Symbolist conception of a basic unity or synesthesia of all the arts, he conceived "the business of the critic" to be to divine the unique language of each art and "to find some approximate means of transposing it into the terms of another language."[4] Like Pater and many of his other fellow artists at the turn of the century, Symons believed that music, as the art form that came closest to achieving a perfect fusion of style and content, was the standard for all art. He continued his Paterian approach to life and art first in a collection of articles and reviews, *Studies in Prose and Verse* (1904), which he introduced by saying that he was "interested only in first principles" and that criticism is not the awarding of prizes but "a valuation of forces . . . indifferent to their direction" (*Studies in Prose and Verse*, v), and then in perhaps his most important book of criticism (next to *The Symbolist Movement*), *Studies in Seven Arts* (1906).

In 1905, Symons published a volume of fictional "character studies," *Spiritual Adventures*, most of which were written years earlier and modeled on Pater's famous *Imaginary Portraits* (1887). Besides the obviously autobiographical "A Prelude to Life," many of the stories in the collection are highly self-reflexive inquiries into Symons's own spiritual concerns, not the least of which is the psychological isolation that often separates the artist from life. "Christian Trevelga," based on a combination of Symons's impressions of Polish pianist Vladimir de Pachmann and his own personality (Frederic Chopin was one of his earliest enthusiasms, and Wagner a continuing one), is an allegory of the perils of a dehumanized aestheticism. Presciently anticipating his own breakdown in 1908, in it Symons describes a progressive mental collapse, the result of a total absorption of the protagonist in his art. "The

Death of Peter Waydelin" represents two sides of Symons: the Decadent devoted to the order of art, and the traditional Romantic devoted to natural harmonies. "Extracts from the Journal of Henry Luxulyan," which concludes with the hero's death in Venice, similarly investigates the fears and isolation of an artistic sensibility, a person who constantly searches for epiphanous symbols of inner beauty. Yet another semi-autobiographical story, "Seaward Lackland," the setting of which was Symons's spiritual home of Carbis Bay, Cornwall, is about a sin-obsessed preacher who blasphemes God as a self-immolating expression of his love. "Esther Kahn," based on Symons's observation of actress Rachel Kahn and a troop of Yiddish actors in Whitechapel in July 1890, deals with painful relationships in both life and art and the ways that art can be used as a means—if a problematical one—of triumphing over the vexations of life. As with much of Symons's work, *Spiritual Adventures* assumes the typically Romantic-Decadent view of art as a force potentially both redemptive and destructive.

In *William Blake* (1907), one of his more important critical studies, Symons interprets this Romantic poet in the transcendentalist tradition of the French Symbolists. He draws parallels between Blake and Friedrich Nietzsche, arguing for the existence of a "vital contradiction of opposites equally true" and the difficulty in coordinating those oppositions (*Collected Works*, vol. 4, p. 111)—a telling continuation of Symons's 1890s sensibility and, perhaps, a portent of his imminent mental collapse.

Many of his publications after his breakdown in 1908 are fascinating, if only for historical and biographical reasons, but rarely does he break new ground thematically or technically. In 1920, he gathered poems written between 1887 and 1919 into the volume *Lesbia and Other Poems*, with numerous *femmes fatales*, vampiric dancers, and phallic serpents invoking the Decadence of the 1890s even more relentlessly than his work of that period. In 1923, he finished the striking *Confessions* (1930), his "dramatic and tragic account" of his mental collapse in Italy and reaffirmation of his long-held belief that the artist is fundamentally abnormal; he also published *Dramatic Personae*, a collection of mostly post-breakdown articles dealing with Victorian and Edwardian figures and issues. Surely his most enduring post-breakdown publication is *From Toulouse-Lautrec to Rodin* (1929) which contains his earlier momentous essays on Beardsley and Whistler, among others. Indeed, most of Symons's post-breakdown work is a thematic recycling (sometimes self-plagiarized, word-for-word repetition) of pre-breakdown themes and works. After 1908, he seemed to take almost no interest in new writers. His world became almost solely the world of the Victorian Decadence and its immediate aftermath, as he turned virtually every human subject into a figure of the 1890s and searched for parallels to his own tortured experience.

It is perhaps an indication of Symons's sense of personal failure that two of his plays, *Outlaws of Life* (1925) and *The Last Day of Don Juan* (1926), satirize characters who are obvious dramatizations of Symons himself—a perverse, death-obsessed poet, who writes highly sensual verse, and a dying, egocentric, Symbolist Don Juan. Still, for all of his doubts and fears about the dangers of undisciplined passion and egocentric aestheticism, Symons never gave up his Romantic faith in "intensity," in the impassioned moment that becomes the means for capturing beauty's truth and an emblem for it.

Symons wrote of himself (quoting Blake), "I was born, 'like a fiend hid in a cloud,' cruel, nervous, excitable, passionate, restless, never quite human, never quite normal" (*Memoirs*, 56). He was constitutionally a shy, guilt-plagued, sometimes melancholic Romantic who sought to accommodate his sharp critical intellect to both a tolerance for experiential complexity and an unusually acute need for moral justice. Fellow poet Maurice Maeterlinck described him as a born fighter for aesthetic ideals—brisk, alert, even disputatious, launching delicately poised sentences with precision—though for all of his intellectual intensity and "obstinate" will, Symons was a fundamentally gentle person, characteristically kind and compassionate, even to those who wronged him. In short, his was a paradoxical, even bifurcated, temperament quite typical of the Victorian 1890s. Most of his wit and humor grows out of and reflects that fundamental irony.

Aestheticism (and certainly Decadence) fell into much disfavor in the early twentieth century, and as a result Symons's reputation declined after 1910. However, even setting aside the key insights his art and criticism have provided us, his place in literary history is secure as a central figure in the Victorian 1890s and as a major stimulus to Modernism.

Summary

As a poet, fiction writer, playwright, critic of all of the arts, theorist of poetry and criticism, scholar, editor, and translator, Arthur Symons championed an "aristocratic" art as a necessary protest against a barbaric civilization indifferent to aesthetic and spiritual values. He was one of the most important "priests" of the Decadent "Religion of Art." An unusually sensitive critic of the arts and a writer of extraordinary prose, he was the embodiment of the aestheticism of the Victorian *fin de siècle* (end of the century) and a stimulus to twentieth-century Modernism, having a particularly significant influence on Yeats, Joyce, Pound, and Eliot.

Notes

1. William Butler Yeats, Letter to Rhoda Symons, October 13, 1908, Columbia University Library.
2. Arthur Symons, "Introduction," *The Renaissance* by Walter Pater (New York: Modern Library, [1919], xv. Reprinted from "Walter Pater," *Monthly Review*, 24 (September 1906): 14–24.
3. Yeats, "The Rhymers' Club," *Letters to the New Island*, ed. Horace Reynolds (Cambridge, MA: Harvard University Press, 1934), p. 144.
4. Symons, "An Art-Critic and Criticism," *Weekly Critical Review*, 1 (April 9, 1903): 2.

Selected Bibliography

Primary Sources

Silhouettes. London: Elkin Mathews & John Lane, 1892; Portland, ME: Thomas B. Mosher, 1909.

"The Decadent Movement in Literature," *Harper's New Monthly Magazine*, 87 (November 1893): 858–67; rpt. in *Dramatis Personae* (Indianapolis, IN: Bobbs-Merrill, 1923), pp. 96–117.

London Nights. London: Leonard C. Smithers, 1895; Boston: John W. Luce, 1923.

Amoris Victima. London: Leonard Smithers, and New York: George H. Richmond, 1897.

The Symbolist Movement in Literature. London: William Heinemann, 1899; New York: Dutton, 1923.

Plays, Acting, and Music. 1903. London: Duckworth, and New York: Dutton, 1909.

Studies in Prose and Verse. London: J.M. Dent, and New York: Dutton, 1904.

Spiritual Adventures. London: Archibald Constable, 1905; New York: Dutton, 1908.

Studies in Seven Arts. London: Archibald Constable, 1906; New York: Dutton, 1925.

William Blake. London: Archibald Constable, and New York: Dutton, 1907.

The Romantic Movement in English Poetry. London: Archibald Constable, 1909. First American edition published in New York by E.P. Dutton, 1909; New York: Phaeton Press, 1969.

The Collected Works of Arthur Symons. 9 vols. London: Martin Secker, 1924; New York: AMS Press, 1973.

From Toulouse-Lautrec to Rodin. London: John Lane, The Bodley Head, [1929]; New York: Alfred H. King, 1930.

Confessions: A Study in Pathology. New York: Fountain Press, 1930.

The Memoirs of Arthur Symons: Life and Art in the 1890s. Ed. Karl Beckson. University Park, PA, and London: Pennsylvania State University Press, 1977.

Arthur Symons: Selected Letters, 1880–1935. Ed. Karl Beckson and John M. Munro. Iowa City: University of Iowa Press, 1989.

Secondary Sources

Biographies

Beckson, Karl. *Arthur Symons: A Life.* Oxford: Clarendon, 1987. Now the standard biography, superseding Lhombreaud.

Lhombreaud, Roger. *Arthur Symons: A Critical Biography.* London: Unicorn Press, 1963.

Bibliographies

Beckson, Karl, and Ian Fletcher, Lawrence W. Markert, and John Stokes, eds. *Arthur Symons: A Bibliography.* Greensboro, NC: ELT Press, 1990.

Books and Articles

Fletcher, Ian. "Explorations and Recoveries— II: Symons, Yeats and Demonic Dance." *London Magazine,* 7 (June 1960): 46– 60. A landmark discussion of Symons's *femme fatale* figure, building on Kermode's study and treating Symons's influence on Yeats and Diaghilev.

Gordon, Jan B. "The Dance Macabre of Arthur Symons." *Victorian Poetry,* 9, 4 (Winter, 1971): 429–43. Very insightful discussion of how Symons's images of the *femme fatale* dancer implicate the solipsistic world of the poet's desire.

Kermode, Frank. *The Romantic Image.* London: Routledge, 1957. Contains one of the first serious treatments and appreciations of Symons's contributions, particularly his use of the image of the dancer.

———. "Poet and Dancer Before Diaghilev." *Partisan Review,* 28 (January-February 1961): 48–75. Amplification of Kermode's previous discussion of Symons in *The Romantic Image.*

Markert, Lawrence W. *Arthur Symons: Critic of the Seven Arts.* Ann Arbor and London: UMI Research Press, 1988. A fine study of Symons's aesthetic theory and critical world view integrating all of the various arts.

Munro, John M. *Arthur Symons.* New York: Twayne, 1969. A useful early introduction to Symons and his work.

Snodgrass, Chris. "Decadent Mythmaking: Arthur Symons on Aubrey Beardsley and Salome." *Victorian Poetry,* 28, 3 & 4 (Autumn/Winter 1990): 61–109. Snodgrass discusses Symons's and Beardsley's respective treatment of the Salome icon and how Symons's landmark 1898 essay on Beardsley and related poetry created a misleading myth of the artist which disguised the significantly differing views of these two famous Decadent figures.

Stokes, John. "Arthur Symons's 'Romantic Movement': Transitional Attitudes and the Victorian Precedent." *English Literature in Transition,* 31, 2 (1988): 133–50. Stokes treats little-discussed, perhaps more "conservative," elements of Symons's Romantic critical assumptions.

Chris Snodgrass

T

Tarlton (or Tarleton), Richard

Born: Condover, Shropshire, ca. 1555
Education: Possibly some grammar school
Marriage: A wife "Kate" is mentioned; ca.
*   1573; at least one child*
Died: Shoreditch, September 5, 1588

Biography

Richard Tarlton was born in Condover, Shropshire about 1555. He may have attended grammar school until around twelve years of age, after which he worked on his father's farm until being apprenticed to a traveling actors' troupe; he may have learned some German, Italian, and French as well as Latin while he traveled abroad; he became proficient in singing, songwriting, dancing, tumbling, and fencing. He married sometime around 1573, possibly to a woman named Kate, and he is known to have fathered at least one son.

Tarlton was the most famous clown of his day. England had lacked a true "clown laureate" since the death of King Henry VIII's beloved Will Sommers in 1560. After joining the select royal acting troupe called the Queen's Men in 1583, Tarlton became a semiofficial court jester and favorite in the court of Elizabeth for five years. He was also a pamphleteer of renown and easily the most popular comic actor of the pre-Shakespearean stage. His wife died before him, and Tarlton himself died on September 5, 1588 in a house of ill repute in Shoreditch, leaving a son behind and a will over which his survivors squabbled in court.

Literary Analysis

Tradition has it that on a swing through Shropshire the acting troupe known as the Lord Leicester's servants found Tarlton tending swine in the fields. The actors sparred with the boy and, amazed at his ready wit, apprenticed him for the stage on the spot. Tarlton was to become renowned for the number and breadth of his talents. In Elizabethan England the meanings of the words "minstrel," "player," and "musician" overlapped: the entertainer thrived best who mastered as many talents as he could. By all accounts, Tarlton was a master among masters. A famous woodcut shows him playing the pipe and tabor together with one leg raised in the dance. This not only underscores his versatility but reminds us of Tarlton's most famous trait: his talent for improvisation.

Contemporary accounts make it clear that a good clown was not only a comedian and a one-man band but also an extemporizer, one who could make up the words to a tune as he danced or tumbled. Tarlton became known for his ability to make up songs and jigs on the spot. When on the road, he would work on the town outskirts on the day of a show, offering to ad-lib on any "theame" that passers-by might assign him. Thus, he earned a few pence for himself and advertised that evening's show. Historian John Stow tells us that "for a wondrous plentifull pleasant extemporall wit, hee was the wonder of his time."

Despite his odd, stocky build, Tarlton was also a true athlete. In 1587, his fencing abilities earned him the title of "master of the fence," the highest degree at the school of the science of defense in London. Such versatile virtuosity characterized his career.

Tarlton played a major role in determining the future of Elizabethan entertainment. In London he often acted at the major private theaters of the rough-and-tumble early days of Elizabethan drama: the Bel Savage, the Theatre, the Bell, the Curtain, and the Bull. In the 1570s, the English stage was just on the brink of the great theater boom that would last until the Revolution. Tarlton, present at its creation, helped establish several features of early secular drama, foremost among these being the "jig" and the "merriment," two forms of short comic interlude that included song, dance, physical humor, and often some form of dramatic plot. Jigs and merriments, which ranged from the satirical to the bawdy, soon became required features of any play. A jig or merriment might be performed by itself or it could be inserted almost anywhere in a longer dramatic piece, regardless of plot or genre. Indeed, accounts of actual performances tell of merry dances just after each show, whether the play had been tragic or comic. Some of the music for Tarlton's jigs still survives.

Dick Tarlton (if this is the same Dick Tarlton; the name was not uncommon) also became a well-known writer of pamphlets, including *Tarltons Toyes* (1576), *Tarltons Tragical Treatise* (1578), and *Tarltons devise upon this unlooked for great snowe* (1579), all of which are lost. His earliest extant piece may be *Tarltons jigge of a horse loade of fooles* (1579), though the authenticity of this jig is doubted by some scholars. His name was so commercially potent that many of these pamphlets may have been by other writers who stole his name.

The tradition concerning his career with Queen Elizabeth I bears some reconsideration. Tarlton was a member of Leicester's Men until 1583, when a select dozen of England's best actors were chosen for the Queen's Men. (His immediate assumption into that prestigious troupe gives some idea of his prominence.) He is supposed to have assumed the role of court jester, relying on the traditional "fool's privilege" to point out Elizabeth's mistakes and foibles without fear of punishment. Some writers contend that Tarlton gained such favor that greater men would use him as a go-between with Elizabeth.

Tradition also holds that he had a great fall. As the story goes, Tarlton, emboldened by success, began to toss politically ill-advised barbs at the powerful men of the court. Pointing at Sir Walter Raleigh, he is supposed to have said, "See, the Knave commands the Queen!" This disturbed Elizabeth, but it was only after Tarlton satirized Leicester that Elizabeth banned her clown from court, after which Tarlton became old and embittered and declined to his grave.

This story probably is more romance than truth. All of the evidence suggests that Tarlton reached his peak during the last five years of his life. There was no trailing off, no gradual decline at all. If he made a mistake somewhere, would it have been one of such colossal and insistent stupidity? (Leicester had been a former patron, was the person who had introduced Tarlton to Queen Elizabeth, and was among the most dangerous and powerful men in England.) Further, the sources for this tale never say that he was banned from court but from Elizabeth's "table," a sign of being out of favor but not of outright banishment. A court record of 1587, only a year before his death, shows that Tarlton was an "ordenary grome off her majestes chamber." A year later, he is still listed as a household player and ordinary groom. If he did fall, then, it must have been precipitous indeed, and death must have been almost immediate. He would not, at any rate, have been very old, in his mid-thirties at most. It is most likely that he died from disease or from want—for an "ordinary groom" received court clothes and tips but no regular stipend. He would not have been the first or the only player to grow lean while under contract to the court. Tarlton also had a reputation for heavy drinking, which may have played a role in his plummet.

Despite all of his fame and all of his accomplishments, Tarlton was never other than a poor man. As a jester at court, he was dependent on the tips that he earned with his jests. This, as ever, was a precarious way to make a living; if a clown stopped being funny, he risked total ruin. To make ends meet, Tarlton evidently operated various taverns in Gracechurch Street, Paternoster Row, and Colchester. It is odd to think that he was running alehouses during the very years that he was clowning at the court of Elizabeth, but such seems to have been the case.

As a performer, Tarlton's great talent lay in his ability to manipulate his voice, his facial expressions, and his actions to delight an audience. It is often written that Tarlton was thus more of a "physical" clown than a "verbal" one, but that can be said only in the mountainous light of William Shakespeare and Ben Jonson. In his own time, Tarlton was popular as the composer of songs and jigs, as a maker of "quick answers" and improvised poems, and as a good hand at one-liners. Quotes from him are scattered throughout public and private discourse for the next two centuries. He is supposed to have made up a rhyme that has made its way into thousands of nurseries:

> The king of France, with forty thousand
> men,
> Went up a hill, and so came downe agen.

He once said that Queen Elizabeth resembled "nothing more fitly than a sculler [a single rower in a small boat], for . . . neither the Queene nor the sculler hath a fellow," a dig at the Queen's vaunted virginity. Tarlton could not have survived in the rough world of Elizabethan foolery without having some way with words.

That way with words was combined with the dance, the jig, the mugging look. If we wish to see Tarlton at work, the jig entitled "The Crow Sits on the Wall," which is quite possibly his, shows the minstrel at his best: the singer satirizes each member of the audience according to class or profession. It is written in a series of minstrel conventions so that the performer can easily ad-lib according to the types of people who happen to be present:

> Please one and please all,
> Be they great, be they small,
> Be they little, be they lowe,
> So pypeth the crowe,
> Sitting upon a wall,
> Please one and please all,
> Please one and please all.
> Be they white, be they black,
> Have they smock on their back,
> Or a kircher on their head,
> Whether they spin silk or thred,
> Whatsoever they them call,
> Please one and please all,
> Please one and please all.

One could improvise all day like this: the ready rhymes are there to fit any group, and the refrain gives the performer time to look about, see who else is there, and fashion a verse for them ahead of time. The same holds true for "A Jigge of a Horse Load of Fools":

> What do you lacke? What do you lacke?
> Ive a horseload of fooles,
> Squeaking, gibbering of everie degree;
> Ime an excellent workeman,
> And there are my tooles:
> Is not this a fine merie familie?

And now, the performer will run down sixteen sorts of "fooles" in his "familie." It is unfortunate that we lack the music for this verse, the better to gauge the timing needed to supply new rhymes as one danced. But this indeed was Tarlton's great fame: contemporaries marveled at his capacity for improvisation, the evident capaciousness of his brain to carry so much wit.

Another extant work widely thought to be by Tarlton is the drama *The Seven Deadly Sins* (ca. 1585). This is a "morality play," an old kind of play dramatizing the conflict of good and evil with personified characters such as Gluttony, Sloth, and so forth. We have only the "plott" of the play; it is designed with a great deal of room for ad-libbing and improvisation. The author evidently roughed out a plot line and worked out the details of the performance with the other actors. This was a common way of putting a play together, and if the players knew one another well and were themselves very talented, the results could be very good—and different from performance to performance.

Some scholars feel that Tarlton also had a hand in *The Famous Victories of Henry the Fifth* (ca. 1583–1586), the model for Shakespeare's *Henry IV* plays and for the character of Falstaff. In light of the energetic and farcical approach to history in *Famous Victories*—and in light of the heavy emphasis on improvisation in the text—there may be some merit in this guess. Tarlton certainly acted in the play: he became famous for doubling as Judge and Derick (the clown part), as well as for his hilarious ad-libs as he switched from role to role.

Above all, Tarlton could make people laugh: "the self-same words, spoken by another, would hardly move a man to smile; which, uttered by him, would force a sad soul to laughter." Court records indicate that Queen Elizabeth had to beg her men "to take the knave away for making her laugh so excessively." Fame and funny looks rendered him instantly recognizable: he had a broad head, flat nose, and squinting eyes, all of which he treated as comic capital. Audiences would burst into laughter at the first sight of him on stage. His dress—red coat, buttoned cap, moneybag and staff—recalled the minstrels of an earlier age and became standard garb for Elizabethan clowns.

Without a doubt, Tarlton greatly influenced the next generation of clowns and writers. In his early teens, the Londoner Ben Jonson would have been able to see Tarlton in his prime in London (later, Jonson would swear that there was no one alive like him). Shakespeare may not have gotten to London until as late as 1587 or 1588, meaning that if he did see or meet Tarlton, it was just before the end. There are, however, at least two direct bridges between Tarlton and Shakespeare. Will Kempe, Shakespeare's first clown, was widely recognized as an heir to the Tarlton tradition of jigs, merriments, and knock-about humor. Furthermore, Tarlton is supposed to have personally apprenticed Robert Armin, who became Shakespeare's specialist in fool roles when Kempe left the Globe Company in 1599. A popular tradition holds that Tarlton was the original for Hamlet's Yorick.

Summary

Richard Tarlton belongs among the handful of the funniest Englishmen of all time; he certainly deserves a place as one of England's most important actors. After his death, a flood of pamphlets bearing his repentance, retractation, ghostly messages, and so forth appeared for the next twenty years. For two centuries afterward, he was remembered in jokes, tales, and the names of alehouses.

Selected Bibliography

Primary Sources
The Seven Deadly Sins. London, ca. 1585.
The Famous Victories of Henry the Fifth. London, ca. 1583–1586.
Tarltons jigge of a horse load of fooles. London, 1579.
"*The Crow Sits on the Wall.*" London, 1585?

Secondary Sources

Biographies
Barber, H.B. *English Actors.* New York: Holt, 1879. Contains an appreciative notice of Tarlton's life and is one of the first books to recognize his historical importance as an actor.
Carlyle, Edward I. "Richard Tarlton." In *The Dictionary of National Biography.* Ed. Sir Leslie Stephen and Sidney Lee. 21 vols. Oxford: Oxford University Press, 1960. Vol. 19, pp. 369–71.
Chambers, E.K. "Richard Tarlton." In *The Elizabethan Stage.* Oxford: Clarendon, 1923. Vol. 2, pp. 342–45. Chambers' entry on Tarlton is still among the best collections of evidence and recorded mentions.
Ingram, William. "Minstrels in Elizabethan London: Who Were They, What Did They Do?" *English Literary Renaissance,* 14 (1): 29–54. Ingram discusses the shifting meaning of the word "minstrel" in Elizabethan English and furnishes the names of many men who evidently made their living as versatile entertainers in the mold of Tarlton.

Books
Baskervill, C.J. *The Elizabethan Jig.* Chicago: University of Chicago Press, 1929. Contains the best available discussion of the "jig" and Tarlton's role in popularizing it. An excellent look at Tarlton's career as entertainer.
Welsford, Enid. *The Fool: His Social and Literary History.* New York: Farrar & Rinehart, 1936. This is the best introduction to the profession of fool in Elizabethan times.

John Timpane

Taylor, John

Born: Gloucester, August 24, 1578
Education: Grammar school in Gloucester and apprenticeship to a Thames waterman
Marriage: May have had two wives, both named Alice
Died: Long Acre, London, December 1653

Biography

John Taylor was born on August 24, 1578[1] in Gloucester, where he attended grammar school. Having been apprenticed in his youth to a London waterman, Taylor served in the Royal Navy, perhaps impressed into service, on the expedition of the Earl of Essex against Cadiz in 1596 (among others on the expedition was the poet John Donne). On a later naval voyage he became stranded in the Azores for a time and nearly starved to death. He told the story of this incident in such a way that it is clear that he was hoarding food. Yet, completely oblivious to the unfortunate imputation, he was rather proud of himself for sharing some food with Sir Henry Withrington when begged to do so.

After sixteen voyages he returned to life on the River Thames, having been lamed during his naval service. He then served for fourteen years as the waterman entitled to extract the levy of wine due the Lieutenant of the Tower of London from wine merchants doing business on the River. Eventually, however, he was dismissed because he refused to purchase the right to continue in the office, as he reports in *Taylors Farewell to the Tower-Bottles* (1622), and he became an independent waterman. Even before this he had realized that hard times beset the river trade because of the rising number of watermen, governmentally fixed fares, and a decline in need after theaters were allowed on both sides of the river. Taylor first came to public prominence when he made an unheeded appeal to the king for relief of the watermen.

He resolved his personal plight by turning to writing full time as a means of support, establishing himself early on as "The Water-Poet." Indeed, a case could be made that he was the first person to earn his living by writing. He is considerably earlier than Aphra Behn, for whom the claim is usually made. Averring to have been called by the Muses, he was accused of pandering to his uneducated public by parading a patina of classical knowledge that was not supported by a genuine familiarity with the ancients. But, he seems to have prepared for his life as a writer by reading voraciously and perhaps by study, informally, at Oxford University, where he took refuge from the plague in 1625.

He certainly made a formal dedication of his life to writing, including the disingenuous claim that he would avoid "profane, obscene, palpable and odious lies, or scandalous libels." He also became a very effective self-promoter. The plan that he developed was to announce from time to time a publicity stunt of the sort nowadays chronicled in *The Guinness Book of World Records*. By issuing a prospectus (or "Taylor's bill") he solicited subscriptions for the book that he promised to write about his experience upon completing the stunt, typically a tour made under peculiar conditions. He earned a good, steady livelihood from his indefatigable writing, keeping his name very effectively before the public with the stunts. On one occasion, he undertook to sail from London to Queensborough, Kent, in a paper boat (reported in *The Praise of Hemp-Seed*, 1620). The excursion came to an abrupt conclusion when the boat was ripped to pieces by souvenir hunters. These trips took him as far afield as central Europe (reported in *Taylor His Travels: From the Citty of London in England, to the Citty of Prague in Bohemia,* 1620), where he dandled the future

Cavalier General Prince Rupert of and by Rhine on his knee, taking away the prince's baby shoes as a souvenir of his own.

Only once did his method fail him. He promised to walk to Scotland and back without any money. When he failed to complete the task, more than half of the subscribers wanted their money back and were not satisfied by a book describing how he had failed to accomplish the task, *Pennyless Pilgrimage*. Still, he turned a profit even on this occasion through the sales of the amusing satire *Kicksey Winsey; or, Lerry cum Twang* (1619), written to excoriate the defaulting subscribers.

Another method of raising money was to write funeral elegies on speculation—for example, for the Duke of Richmond and Lennox (1624), the Earl of Nottingham (1625), the Earl of Holdernesse (1626), and Bishop Lancelot Andrewes (1626). John Moray and Richard Wyan (memorialized, 1620 and 1638) were former patrons whose families could be expected to reward the poet who remembered them. *Great Brittaine All in Blacke* (1612), his elegy for Prince Henry and probably his first publication, on the other hand, was clearly heartfelt, although Taylor must have correctly anticipated a substantial public interest in such a work, as in his elegy on King James (1625).

The poet may have had two wives, both named Alice (their surnames are unknown). He states in *Man Verse,* published in 1644, that his wife has died; his widow, who died in January 1657/1658, was the executrix of his will. There seem to have been no surviving children.

During the Civil War, Taylor naturally took the Royalist side, which was staunchly supported by his lower-class audience. His political poems were so popular that other royalists imitated his work and even appropriated his name. When the Parliamentarians took London in 1642, he retired to Oxford once again, this time to keep a public house. In 1645, having survived the siege of Oxford, which was a royalist stronghold, he returned to London, where he opened another public house (actually in Long Acre or Covent Garden, now administratively part of Westminster), which he called The Crown and then attempted to rename The Mourning Crown when the king was executed in 1649. When prevented from doing this, he used a portrait of himself for the tavern sign, calling the establishment The Poet's Head and, according to John Aubrey, inscribing on it the

T

legend "There's many a head stands for a signe, / Then, gentle reader, why not mine?"

Citing him "for keeping up a correspondence with the enemy," a warrant was issued for Taylor's arrest on August 15, 1649, but it seems not to have been executed, perhaps because he was in failing health. He died at his public house early in December 1653 and was buried on December 5 at St. Martin's-in-the-Fields. His widow, who continued to run the public house, died a few years later.

Literary Analysis

Taylor's reputation has been damaged by the great popularity in his own day of a number of works of his that can most accurately be called reference books (Southey, 35). Among these works are the thumb Bibles—miniature books (less than two inches square) comprising paraphrases of Scripture. Perhaps even more popular was his book *A Briefe Remembrance of All the English Monarchs* (1618). In contrast to this verse history of the English kings, which is actually illustrated with inaccurate portraits of all the kings earlier than Henry VIII, the thumb Bibles are still favorites of collectors.

Such books are clearly hack work, but hack work of a sort that still finds a market today. Indeed, Robert Bruce Dow has suggested that Taylor's low reputation as a writer comes from the tradition of seeing him as a poet when he was in fact a journalist by modern lights. As such, he has importance as a historical figure in popular culture, and outside his reference works his verse has a readability that goes well beyond antiquarian interest. Other reference books include *The Booke of Martyrs* (1616), *An Armado, or Navye of 103 Ships* (1627), *The Carriers Cosmographie* (1637), *The Number and Names of All the Kings of England and Scotland* (1649), and *The Names of the Dukes [etc.] . . . Dead or Living since Elizabeth* (1652).

While sometimes a facile rhymester, Taylor cannot be said to have a subtle ear for meter. Wallace Notestein thinks that the line "Day found him work and night allowed him rest" from Taylor's elegy for Thomas Parr, who had supposedly lived more than 150 years, to be "probably the nearest to poetry of anything Taylor ever wrote" (184). However, this judgment is too harsh. Taylor's narrative poems, many of them autobiographical books of travel and topography (for example, *A Very Merry Wherry-Ferry-Voyage; or, Yorke for my Money*, 1622, and *The Certain Travailes of an Uncer-*

tain Journey, 1654), flow as smoothly as anything in George Wither or Edmund Waller. "The first-born issue of my Worthless wit," Taylor calls another such work, the one with which he began his publishing career, *The Scoller . . . ; or, Gallimawfry of Sonnets, Satyres, and Epigrams* (1612—reissued as *Taylor's Water-Work*, 1614).

In another vein, but both in prose and in verse, Taylor is a practitioner of the character as a genre, a growing popular fad in his day. *A Bawd, a Virtuous Bawd, a Modest Bawd* (1635) is a representative title in mixed prose and verse. *A Common Whore* (1622) and *An Arrant Thief* (1622) are verse characters. Feeding the popular interest in natural wonders were such works as *The Great Eater of Kent* (1630), *The Unnatural Father* (1621—about a contemporary murder sensation)—and *The Olde, Old, Very Olde Man* (1635), his elegy on Thomas Parr.

In a series of pamphlets in an engagingly Dickensian spirit, he pursues another element of popular taste when he laments the prohibition of traditional Christmas celebration under the Protectorate. The pamphlets use a Bunyanesque technique since Christmas appears as a character, a puzzled traveler disappointed by the bleakness until he comes to Devon and Cornwall, where the old values still hold.

Taylor wrote many other works in praise of the old values and the traditional way of life. *Taylors Pastorell* (1624) is his praise of the sheep industry. He also wrote pamphlets in praise of clean linen (1624—although he saw little of it on his travels), beggary (1621), and jails (1623). Despite his feud with the carriers, *The World Runnes on Wheeles* (1623) is in praise of the stage coach. *Taylors Feast* (1638) is a sort of Rabelaisian cookbook. *Jack-a-Lent* (1620) is similar, the descriptions of the dishes often degenerating into shaggy dog stories.

In all of the works discussed so far, Taylor was a poet for the popular taste, which he judged—or mirrored—quite successfully. In *Timber* (1641), Edmund Jonson complained that Taylor was more popular than Spenser: "If it were put to the question of the water-rimer's works against Spencer's, I doubt not that they would find more suffrages; because they most favour common vices, out of a prerogative the vulgar have to lose their judgments and like that which is naught." As the Romantic poet Robert Southey pointed out, Taylor's standard of workmanlike verse is fairly high, certainly as high as that of many minor poets routinely included in anthologies (37–38). He is frequently dismissed as the author of nothing but doggerel verse. However, lapses in this direction seem to be quite calculated. His satires, for example, use ludicrous rhymes to undermine the dignity of their targets. And, his vast reading also gave him a clear control of genre in his satiric writings. For their narrative *exempla*, their biting wit, and their frequent mixture of prose and verse, many of Taylor's works are correctly categorized as Menippean satire (Kirk, 179–82).

His satiric verse is of two sorts. He engaged in a number of "flytings" or pamphlet wars with other writers. In one series of pamphlets, beginning with *Laugh and Be Fat* (1612), he excoriates Thomas Coryate. This is probably an example of professional jealousy since Coryate also made a living from subscription travel books and satires much like Taylor's. In another series of pamphlets he attacks William Fennor. In *A Reply as True as Steele* (1641), he engages the Puritan propagandist Henry Walker, who had responded to Taylor's pamphlet *A Swarme of Sectaries, and Schismatiques* (1641). *Aqua-Musae* (1645) is a "Short Lashing Satire" on Wither with occasional parody of that poet. The parodies are successful, but with the complete eclipse of Wither from public consciousness they can hardly be called telling at this length of time. Of course, the political point to this satire has lost the requisite partisan audience as well. *Taylor's Motto* (1621) and other works also satirize Wither.

Taylor engaged in less personal satire, damning the vices of the age. A series on contemporary fashions includes *Mad Fashions, Od Fashions* (1642), a work quite amusing in its curmudgeonly support of traditional values. One of these fashion books, *Heads of All Fashions* (1642), is done in character genre format. *The Nipping and Snipping of Abuses* (1614) opposes the use of tobacco.

In *A Juniper Lecture; With the Description of All Sorts of Women* (1669), Taylor satirically engages the question of the place of woman in society. In *The Women's Sharp Revenge; or, an Answer to Sir Seldom Sober* (1640), Taylor pretends to be Mary Tattle-well and Joan Hit-him-home, "spinsters," while answering his own *Juniper Lecture* in its attack on scolds. Thus, as Simon Shepherd, the modern editor of this tract, says, "Taylor takes from women their voice," but the pamphlet is still important for suggest-

ing that there was interest in gender roles during the period. The pamphlet does make some telling criticisms of male prerogatives, although the greatest censure is reserved for habitual drunkenness, a staple Taylor theme despite his frequent celebration of the joys of drink in such works as *Drinke and Welcome* (1637).

Explicitly political satires abound in his writing. *A Plea for Prerogative* (1642) and *The Kings Most Excellent Majesties Wellcome to His Owne House* (1647) are royalist polemics. *Rebells Anathematized, and Anatomized* (1645) is a diatribe against Parliamentary newspapers. In *The Fooles of Fate* (1648), an attack on Parliament in mixed prose and verse, the Scots are described memorably as "Inhuman Vipers hatch'd to be / Midwives of our Miserie."

The poet also found time for religious topics, often parodying Puritans for hypocrisy and sabbatarianism. *A Swarme of Sectaries*, a characteristic work in religious controversy, is an attack on the Puritans in couplets reporting case histories in the most scurrilous fashion. In *A Pedlar and a Romish Priest* (1641) he manages to be genial and fairly mild mannered while exposing the foibles of Roman Catholicism in true Protestant fashion. *A Delicate Dainty, Damnable Dialogue, Between the Devil and a Jesuite* (1642) is in a similar vein. On a more specific contemporary topic Taylor wrote in mixed prose and verse *Westminster Fayre, Newly Proclaimed* (1647) to attack the Westminster Assembly, which was then convened for religious reform. In all religious controversy he so reflexively supported the establishment that he even wrote a satire against episcopacy in 1642 when Parliament arrested the bishops for treason: *The Apprentices Advice to the XII Bishops*. Of course, he shortly came to see that Parliament had itself begun an attack on traditional values.

In a different religious mood he wrote devotional works, specifically the verse history of Jerusalem entitled *Taylors Urania* (1615) and the prose *Life and Death of the Virgin Mary* (1620). *Taylors Arithmeticke, from One to Twelve* (1650) might be called a numerological catechism as it considers in turn the theological significance of each of the numbers of the title: "Two Natures the most High, most Blest did beare, / The Godhead great, and Manhood pure and cleare."

And, in his merely playful mood Taylor in essence founded the English tradition of nonsense poetry, giving him his chief claim to a place in the history of British humor. He probably drew on the traditions of the river to do so. *Sir Gregory Nonsense His Newes from No Place* (1622, misdated 1700) is perhaps the first book of nonsense poetry announced as such:

> Thus doe I make a hotch potch messe of *Nonsense*,
> In darke Enigmaes, and strange sense upon sense:
> It is not foolish all, nor is it wise all,
> Nor is it true in all, nor is it lies all.

A dense text of oxymorons ("scalding Ice"), contradictions ("a Crimson Robe, as blacke as Jet"), and incongruities ("aged *Ganymede*"), the work cannot be regarded as a success: numerous classical allusions make the piece impenetrable to children, and there is no substantive satire or social commentary to interest adults.

Similar to *Sir Gregory Nonsense* is *Nonsense upon Sence* (1651), perhaps a little more accessible and yet a little less nonsensical. Expanded and renamed *The Essence, Quintessence, Insense, Innocence, Lye-Sense, and Magnificence of Nonsense upon Sense* (1654), the work is general social satire in which Taylor finds the world too much imbued with nonsense (in the non-literary meaning). He rather cleverly proposes that "For Nonsense [he] will tax all Christendome, / Great Emperours and Kings shall pay [him] some." He will accumulate a "universal Magazine, / For Universities to worke upon." From this store of incendiary material he will "make Poets rich, and Usurers poor." What he labels in the margin the "Deep Philosophy" of the work is no more than wordplay, although with a clear Carollian flair:

> I grant indeed, that whoso may and can,
> Can never may, sith may doth can abey;
> But he that can and will, may will as man,
> But man can will, yet his will cannot may.

Mad Verse, Sad Verse, Glad Verse, and Bad Verse (1644) could equally be called an autobiographical travel book or a Royalist polemic so far as genre is concerned. But, despite a stanza form of the usually slow-moving alexandrine couplet (with numerous triples), the rhyming style throughout is Hudibrastic (with feminine endings used consistently), so the work should perhaps be classified as a conscious nonsense work as well—the title certainly seems to suggest as much. Taylor shows an admirable control of the curious couplet form that he uses and exercises a good deal of charm in selecting his rhymes. For example, ending a line of political commentary with the name "Lord Rochfort," he improvises for the next line: "(Pardon my Rime good Reader I must botch for't)." And, in the autobiographical material, we find couplets such as the following: "'Twas neare the time of Marches Equinoctiall, / I had good meat, and such drink as would fox ye all."

Wit and Mirth (1626) is a jest book compilation, which might be called prose nonsense. The following is typical of the material included:

> There was a Scottish Gentleman that has sore eyes, who was counselled by his Physitians to forbeare drinking of wine; but hee said hee neither could nor would forbeare it, maintaining it for the lesser evill, to shut up the windowes of his body, than to suffer the house to fall downe, through want of repair.

There is a childlike innocence to humor of this sort. Also in the jest book tradition is much of the riddling material in *Epigrammes Written on Purpose to be Read* (1651).

Summary

John Taylor's numerous satires on the religious and political topics of his day are interesting now less for their bite—which is genuine at least for scholars familiar enough with the issues—than as cultural history. Southey expressed the usual verdict when he concluded, "There is nothing in John Taylor which deserves preservation for its intrinsic merit alone; but . . . there is a great deal to illustrate the manners of his age" (86).

On the other hand, some of the works dismissed as doggerel are in fact imaginative and readable mirrors of popular taste. Furthermore, Taylor's general command of verse is substantially better than he has been given credit for; his handling of witty Hudibrastic rhymes is in particular quite facile. His humor apart from such wordplay is, however, perhaps best likened to the low comedy in Shakespeare: the modern reader knows that it was meant to be funny, but the topicality is so obscure and the cultural distinctions so out of fashion that the material is mystifying rather than risible.

As a figure in the history of English humorous writing, Taylor should also be remembered as the first popular journalist to earn his living through writing. His most significant historical importance, however, is as the father of the peculiarly English tradition of nonsense poetry.

Notes
1. Established by the research of Ferdinand Lohmann and Robert Bruce Dow, although most sources give 1580.

Selected Bibliography

Primary Sources

Supposed Caricature of the Droeshout Portrait of Shakespeare [edition of Taylor's probable work *The Watermans Suit, Concerning the Players* (1614?)]. Ed. Basil Brown. New York: privately printed, 1911.

Wit and Mirth. Ed. William Carew Hazlitt. 1626. *Shakespeare Jest Books.* Vol. 3. London: Willis and Sotheran, 1864.

A Dog of War; or, The Travels of Drunkard, the Famous Curre. ca. 1628. Ill., Hester Saintsbury. London: Frederick Etchells and Hugh Macdonald, 1927.

All the Workes. 1630. Menston, Yorkshire: Scolar, 1973.

The Olde, Old, Very Olde Man. Ed. J. Caulfield. 1635. London: Caulfield's Editions of Curious Tracts, 1794.

Newes and Strange Newes. 1638. In *Two Tracts.* Ed. Cyril H. Wilkinson. Oxford: privately printed, 1946.

Under pseudonym Mary Tattle-well and Joan Hit-him-home. *The Women's Sharpe Revenge.* Ed. Simon Shepherd. 1640. *The Women's Sharp Revenge: Five Women's Pamphlets from the Renaissance.* Ed. Simon Shepherd. London: Fourth Estate, 1985.

Tailors Travels from London to the Isle of Wight. Ed. James Orchard Halliwell-Phillipps. 1648. *The Literature of the Sixteenth and Seventeenth Centuries.* London: privately printed, 1851.

Occasional Fac-Simile Reprints of Rare and Curious Tracts of the Sixteenth and Seventeenth Centuries. Ed. Edmund William Ashbee. 2 vols. London: Spenser Society, 1868–1872.

Works of John Taylor the Water Poet Not Included in the Folio Volume of 1550. 5 vols. [numbered 7, 14, 19, 21, and 25].

Manchester: Spenser Society, 1870–1878. New York: Burt Franklin, 1967.

The Old Book Collector's Miscellany; or, A Collection of Readable Reprints of Literary Rarities. Ed. Charles Hindley. 4 vols. London: Reeves and Turner, 1871–1873. The individual volumes have the half-title *Miscellanea Antiqua Anglicana.*

John Taylor's Wandering, to See the Wonders of the West. Ed. Charles Hindley. Newcastle: privately printed, 1967.

Secondary Sources

Aubrey, John. "John Taylor." In *Brief Lives. The World of John Aubrey.* Ed. Richard Barber. London: Folio, 1988, pp. 124–25. Gossipy notes of a seventeenth-century antiquary.

Brown, Huntington. *Rabelais in English Literature.* Cambridge, MA: Harvard University Press, 1933, pp. 31–32, 35, 69, 73, 77–79, 86. Based on Taylor's ignorance of French, Brown proves the existence of the Gargantua myth in England before the translation of Rabelais.

Caldecott, J.B. "John Taylor's Tour of Sussex in 1653." *Sussex Archeological Collections,* 81 (1940): 19–30. Topological.

Capp, Bernard. "John Taylor 'The Water Poet': A Cultural Amphibian in Seventeenth-Century England." *History of European Ideas,* 11 (1989): 537–44. Social criticism.

Freeman, Arthur. "Octavo Nonce Collection of John Taylor." *The Library,* 18 [5th ser.] (1963): 51–57. Addressed to book collectors.

Frost, Everett C. "William Blake's John Taylor." *Notes and Queries,* 26, 224 (1979): 48–49. Blake's citation of Taylor.

Goodwin, Gordon. "John Taylor (1580–1653)." *The Dictionary of National Biography.* Ed. Sir Leslie Stephen. 21 vols. London: Oxford University Press, 1885–1890. Vol. 19, pp. 431–38. Brief, scholarly biography.

Holden, William P. *Anti-Puritan Satire, 1575–1642.* New Haven: Yale University Press, 1954. Holden notes the strong political element in Taylor's Erastianism.

Johnston, William. *A Bibliography of the Thumb Bibles of John Taylor.* Aberdeen: privately printed, 1910. Miniature books described for the book collector.

———. "The Thumb Bibles of John Taylor."

Publications of the Edinburgh Bibliographical Society, 9 (1973): 73–85. Miniature books described for the book collector.

Jordan, Peter Ridgeway. "Allusions in Two Early Seventeenth-Century Plays." *Notes and Queries,* 31, 229 (1984): 31. Allusions to Taylor and the grammarian William Lily in two plays by John Mason.

Kendall, Lyle H. "Taylor's Piracy of *The Pack-Mans Paternoster.*" *Publications of the Bibliographical Society of America,* 57 (1963): 201–10. Taylor caught in the act of plagiarism—or adaptation—of Sir James Sempill in *A Pedlar and a Romish Priest.*

Kendall, Lyle H., Jr. "Two Unrecorded Editions of John Taylor's *Verbum Sempiternum.*" *The Library,* 12 [5th ser.] (1957): 46–48. Bibliographical note.

Kirk, Eugene P. [also known as Bud Korkowski]. *Menippean Satire: An Annotated Catalogue of Texts and Criticism.* New York: Garland, 1980. An extensive annotated descriptive bibliography in which a number of works by Taylor are treated.

Lohmann, Ferdinand. *Taylor the Water-Poet: Sein Leben und seine Werke nach der Folio von 1630.* Dulmen: Sievert, 1911. A study of Taylor's life and of his works up to the 1630 folio; originally a Ph.D. dissertation (Freiberg, 1911).

Notestein, Wallace. *Four Worthies: John Chamberlain, Anne Clifford, John Taylor, Oliver Heywood.* New Haven: Yale University Press, 1957. Popular biography.

Phelps, Wayne H. "John Edwards and the Date of the Lost [play] 'Saturnalia.'" *Notes and Queries,* 26, 224 (1979): 150–52. Bibliographical note on a lost play by Taylor.

Richardson, T.M. "John Taylor's Allusion to Spenser Reconsidered." *Notes and Queries,* 30, 228 (1983): 435–37. Richardson disputes Sousa's citation of an allusion to Spenser in Taylor.

Rushforth, Marjorie. "Two Taylor Manuscripts [*The Causes of the Diseases and Distempers of This Kingdom Founded by Feeling of Her Pulse and Aqua Musae; or, Cacafogo, Cacademon, Capataine George Wither Wrung in the Withers, Being a Short Lashing Satire,*

11 [4th ser.] (1930): 179–92. Bibliographical description.

Sousa, Geraldo U. de. "A 1634 Allusion to Spenser." *Notes and Queries,* 28, 226 (1981): 519. Sousa notes allusion to Spenser by Taylor.

Southey, Robert. *The Lives and Works of the Uneducated Poets.* Ed. J.S. Childers. 1831; London: Humphrey Milford, 1925, pp. 15–88. A biographical study with substantial literary appreciation; Southey argues that Taylor illustrates the manners of his age and that his very poverty turned him into a writer.

Stone, Wilbur Maley. *The Thumb Bible of John Taylor.* Brookline MA: privately printed, 1928. Reprint curiosity for book collectors.

———. "The *Verbum Sempiternum* of John Taylor." *American Collector,* 5 (1927): 46–59. Miniature books described for the book collector.

Tate, William Edward. *An Alphabet of English Inn Signs Based on the Travels and Circular Perambulation of John Taylor the "Water Poet."* Newcastle-upon-Tyne: Frank Graham, 1968. Adaptation of Taylor for the modern reader.

Taylor, E.G.R. "John Taylor the Water-Poet and the Transport Problems of the Early Stuart Period." *Scottish Geographical Magazine,* 49 (1933): 129–38. Taylor is used as source material for discussion of the decline of river traffic and rise of passenger coaches.

Thorp, Willard. "John Taylor, Water Poet." *Texas Review,* 8 (1922): 32–41. A case study of Taylor as a popular or people's poet.

Waage, Frederick O. "John Taylor (1577–1654) and Jacobean Popular Culture." *Journal of Popular Culture,* 7 (1973): 589–601. A case study of Taylor's life and works.

Williams, Sheila. "A Lord Mayor's Show [orchestrated by Taylor]." *Bulletin of the John Rylands Library,* 41 (1959): 501–31. A historical discussion of social customs.

Dissertations

Dow, Robert Bruce. "The Life and Times of John Taylor, the Water-Poet, with a Descriptive Bibliography of His Writings." Ph.D. dissertation, Harvard University,

1933. Abstracted in *Harvard University . . . Summaries of Theses . . . 1931*. Cambridge, MA: Harvard University Press, 1931, pp. 218–23. Dow rehabilitates Taylor's reputation by showing him to have been a journalist in a very modern sense.

Edmund Miller

Thomas, Dylan

Born: Swansea, South Wales, October 27, 1914

Education: Swansea Grammar School, 1925–1931

Marriage: Caitlin Macnamara, July 11, 1937; three children

Died: New York City, November 9, 1953

Biography

Dylan Marlais Thomas was born on October 27, 1914, in Swansea, South Wales, the second child and only son of David John Thomas, the senior English master at Swansea Grammar school. Both of his bilingual parents' ancestors came from the small communities of Carmarthenshire and Cardiganshire in West Wales. Beginning in 1925, he was educated in the same school where his father taught, and on leaving school in 1931, he joined the *South Wales Daily Post* as a reporter. He left the paper toward the end of 1932 to become a professional writer of poetry and short stories, and later of radio broadcasts and film scripts.

In 1934, Thomas moved to London but frequently returned to Swansea and in 1937, following his July 11 marriage to Caitlin Macnamara, by whom he had two sons and a daughter, he settled in Laugharne, a small town on the sea in Carmarthenshire. He spent most of World War II in London but frequently returned to South Wales and finally returned to Laugharne in 1949. During this period, he published several volumes of poetry including *Eighteen Poems* (1934), *Twenty-Five Poems* (1936), *The Map of Love* (1939), *The World I Breathe* (in America, 1939), and *Deaths and Entrances* (1946), which established him as one of the leading poets of his generation, a reputation confirmed by *In Country Sleep* (in America, 1952) and *Collected Poems: 1934–1952* (1952).

Although he was not a conventional believer, Thomas's poems have a profoundly religious quality and explore the nature of life and death, the innocence of childhood, and man's place in the landscape of creation. They were, in Thomas's own words, "written for the love of man in praise of God." In the 1940s, he also gained a reputation as a gifted radio broadcaster, and in addition to writing for radio he worked extensively for the BBC as a reader of poetry (including his own poems) and as an actor. In 1950, he undertook the first of a series of tours of the United States, lecturing and reading his poems. On November 9, 1953, during his fourth tour, Thomas, who was already a sick man, died in New York of alcoholic poisoning after a bout of excessive drinking. He was buried in Laugharne, Dyfed, South Wales.

Literary Analysis

Thomas brought to his humorous works the same commitment and talent for words and imagery that had made him one of Britain's most notable twentieth-century poets and the greatest of Welsh poets writing in English. His willingness to excel in both humorous and serious writing is a standing reproach to those who see the humorous mode as intrinsically inferior to the serious or the tragic. Thomas's first volume of humorous short stories, *Portrait of the Artist as a Young Dog*, appeared in 1940, but he had been writing stories as well as poems since childhood, and his poetry collections *The Map of Love* and *The World I Breathe* contain short stories.

Many of his humorous stories were written to be broadcast and appear in the posthumous collection of his radio writings, *Quite Early One Morning* (1954). The distinctive skills that he acquired as a writer for radio and a broadcaster underpin his comic masterpiece *Under Milk Wood*, which he termed a "play for voices." As such it is ideal for radio, but as W.M.S. Russell has shown, it is also part of an ancient tradition of sound drama that antedates Guglielmo Marconi and goes back to the time of the Roman dramatists such as Seneca who wrote plays for voices rather than for staging. Because it is written for voices and has a central narrator, the drama allows Thomas to make full use of his talent for the comic and indeed serious description which are missing from his film scripts such as *The Doctor and the Devils* (1944; based on a version of the script revised by Ronald Harwood, the film, directed by Freddie Francis and starring Timothy Dalton, Jonathan Pryce, Twiggy, Julian Sands, and Stephen Rea, was released in 1985) and *The Beach of Falesa* (1948). The first part of the play *Under Milk Wood* appeared in *Botteghe Oscure* (1952) under the title *Llareggub*, the name of the little seaside town clustered under Milk Wood where the entire action of the play takes place within a single cycle of twenty-four hours. Llareggub looks like one of the typical Cymric place names of Wales that foreigners find such difficulty in pronouncing but it is in fact the English phrase "Bugger All" spelled backward. This is a literary example of the sly, humorous pleasure that the Welsh take in subtly winding up visitors through comic deception, a quality also brilliantly captured by the English humorous writer Kingsley Amis, who taught English for many years at the University College of Wales in Swansea. *Under Milk Wood* had its first performance at the Poetry Center in New York in October 1953 with the author playing some of the voices—just a month before he died. He continued working on the play until the time of his death and the final version was broadcast on the BBC's *Third Programme* early in 1954. Since then, it has been produced innumerable times on radio, the stage, television, film, and even as a cartoon film, but it remains preeminently a "play for voices." The film (released in 1973) was directed by Andrew Sinclair and starred Richard Burton, Elizabeth Taylor, Peter O'Toole, Glynis Johns, Sian Phillips, and Vivien Merchant. While attracting great publicity, the movie was not considered an adequate adaptation of Thomas's work.

Under Milk Wood was not Thomas's last published humorous writing; after his death a further book of stories, *A Prospect of the Sea* (1955), and his unfinished novel *Adventures in the Skin Trade* (1955), about a young poet's coming to London, were also published. His humorous works, like his poems, enjoy an undiminished popularity and, indeed, have stimulated a hunt for and publication of his juvenilia, occasional pieces, and letters, many of which display his characteristic humor.

Many of Thomas's stories are set in, and much of his humor derives from, the peaceful frontier town of Swansea, where he grew up. Swansea lies on the linguistic boundary between English-speaking Wales and Welsh-speaking Wales and on the economic boundary between industrial Wales and rural Wales. The writer's humor is rooted in a childhood spent in the safe and secure ambiguity of a predominantly English-speaking, industrial town with a Welsh-speaking, rural hinterland where his relatives lived and from which his ancestors came. Thomas spoke no Welsh but in his writing and his mimicry he could move effortlessly between standard English and the various South Wales dialects of English. It is a talent that has delighted the Welsh people who recognize and revel in his comic picture of themselves, but it has annoyed Welsh nationalists, who, quite wrongly, see his comedy as drawing on a crude stage Welshness, something that he himself had decried in his radio broadcast "Wales and the Artist." It is said that he only once expressed an opinion of Welsh Nationalism. He used three words; two of them were "Welsh Nationalism." He is also said to have written, "Land of my fathers, and my fathers can keep it"—"Land of My Fathers" is the English translation of the title of the Welsh national anthem, *Mae hen wlad fy nhadau*. Thomas was confident enough of his own individual talent and secure enough in his Welsh identity not to care whether his humor was politically correct. In consequence, he has angered hundreds and delighted millions.

Thomas's shift into the dialect of South Wales to produce comedy can be well illustrated from the opening narration of the First Voice in *Under Milk Wood*. It starts with his characteristic poetic style full of nouns used as adverbs, and sliding, punning rhymes as he describes the sleeping town of Llareggub:

[Silence]

First Voice (*very softly*)

To begin at the beginning:

It is a spring, moonless night in the small town, starless and bible-black, the cobblestreets silent and the hunched, courters'-and-rabbits' wood limping invisible down to the sloeblack, slow, black, crowblack, fishingboat-bobbing sea. The houses are blind as moles . . .

Now comes the comic use of dialect: "Hush, the babies are sleeping, the farmers, the fishers, the tradesmen and pensioners, cobbler, schoolteacher, postman and publican, the undertaker and the fancy woman, drunkard, dressmaker, preacher, policeman, the webfoot cocklewomen and the tidy wives."

Smuggled into this list of occupations are those antithetical sexual categories "the fancy woman" (with whom someone is carrying on, on the side) and the tidy wives (tidy in the South

Wales dialect means respectable, proper, substantial). The actor playing "First Voice" should savor these words and make them stand out from the list to the delight of those who know and love the dialect. The tidy wives are, of course, also the censorious upholders of local morality and propriety and they later enter the nightmare of "Mister Waldo, rabbitcatcher, barber, herbalist, catdoctor, quack," and denounce him in the shrill rhythms of female South Wales that go into harmony even when speaking of discord:

> *Wife*: Oh, what'll the neighbors say,
>   what'll the neighbors . . .
> *First Neighbor*: Poor Mrs. Waldo
> *Second Neighbor*: What she puts up with
> *First Neighbor*: Never should of married
> *Second Neighbor*: If she didn't had to
> *First Neighbor*: Same as her mother
> *Second Neighbor*: There's a husband for
>   you . . .
> *First Neighbor*: And carrying on
> *Second Neighbor*: With that Mrs. Beattie
>   Morris
> *First Neighbor*: Up in the quarry
> *Second Neighbor*: And seen her baby
> *First Neighbor*: It's got his nose
> *Second Neighbor*: Oh it makes my heart
>   bleed
> *First Neighbor*: What he'll do for drink
> *Second Neighbor*: He sold the pianola
> *First Neighbor*: And her sewing machine
> *Second Neighbor*: Falling in the gutter
> *First Neighbor*: Talking to the lamp post
> *Second Neighbor*: Using language
> *First Neighbor*: Singing in the w
> *Second Neighbor*: Poor Mrs. Waldo.

In his humorous writings, Thomas often uses with varying success the technique of inserting a short, sometimes bizarre, passage that subverts conventional propriety and morality into an apparently mundane account of everyday life. Sometimes this is done by retrospectively revealing his own thoughts as in his story *The Fight*, where the then fourteen-year-old author is having supper at the home of a friend:

> Mrs. Jenkyn said, while everyone except Mr. Bevan was watching Mrs. Bevan moving her knife slowly along the edge of her plate: "I do hope you like cold lamb."

Mrs. Bevan smiled at her, assured, and began to eat. She was grey-haired and grey faced. Perhaps she was grey all over. I tried to undress her, but my mind grew frightened when it came to her short flannel petticoat and navy bloomers to the knees. I couldn't even dare unbutton her tall boots to see how grey her legs were.

Later Thomas uses yet another Welsh comic script, that of playing with deceit for its own sake, and of "winding someone up," particularly a senior or a more powerful and prestigious person:

> [Mr. Jenkyn said] "Now see if he can do this little sum."
>
> He finished his supper and laid out matches on the plate.
>
> "That's an old one, dad," Dan said.
>
> "Oh, I'd like to see it very much," I said in my best voice . . . When I failed to place the matches rightly, Mr. Jenkyn showed me how it was done, and, still not understanding, I thanked him and asked him for another one. It was almost as good being a hypocrite as being a liar; it made you warm and shameful.

Thomas uses the same trick of comic shock, this time through a sudden change of tone in the dialogue, here also marked by demotic emphasis, in his story *Where Tawe Flows* set in the 1930s in Swansea. The author is in session with two collaborators, Mr. Humphries, a schoolteacher, and Mr. Roberts, "a cheerful, disreputable man . . . (who) had once held a high position in a brewery office." They are collectively composing the clearly never to be written "Where Tawe flows . . . a Novel of Provincial Life" but the writers in turn become the characters of Thomas's own retrospective story:

> "Onlooker is a *nom de plume* for Basil Gorse-Williams," said Mr. Humphries. "Did any one know that?"
>
> "*Nom de guerre*. Did you see his article on Ramsay Mac? 'sheep in wolf's clothing.'"

"Know him!" Mr. Roberts said scornfully. "I've been sick on him."

The humor here lies not in the bad jokes of the two "intellectuals" or of the absent Basil Gorse-Williams, who presumably writes for the local paper, the *South Wales Daily Post*, on which Thomas had been a reporter. The wisecrack about the then Prime Minister, Ramsay Macdonald, is not original, though it does add realism, as it is the kind of put-down that would have circulated and been repeated in such a group. Rather, it lies in the coarse intervention of the ex-brewer Mr. Roberts, which enables the author to employ another recognizable Welsh comic script, that of the crude, blunt, matey egalitarian, beer-swilling South Walian. Today such a script is perhaps more commonly associated with Australia and the hard-vomiting characters Barry McKenzie and Dr. Sir Les Patterson created by Barry Humphries, who are forever indulging in a "technicolor yawn" over the clothes of a superior person. In Wales as in Australia a subsequent brazen claim of intimate acquaintanceship with the puked-on is a standard part of the comedy.

Thomas's paradoxical mixing of formal, solemn, pretentious speech with the coarse demotic can, of course, go much further than this, as in the sermon ascribed to his rustic cousin Gwilym, who is studying to be a minister in Thomas's story *The Peaches*. Gwilym's slump from rhythmic ecstatic hwyl to crudity is also a switch from the sincere, if, here at least, awkwardly expressed religious rhetoric of West Wales and of Thomas's own ancestors and kin to a phrase more appropriate to Mr. Roberts's ex-brewery:

I sat on the hay and stared at Gwilym preaching, and heard his voice rise and crack and sink to a whisper and break into singing and Welsh and ring triumphantly and be wild and meek . . . "O God, Thou art everywhere all the time, in the dew of the morning, in the frost of the evening . . . Thou canst see and spy and watch us all the time, in the little black corners, in the big cowboys' prairies, under the blankets when we're snoring fast, . . . Thou canst see all the time. O God, mun, you're like a bloody cat.

Much of Thomas's comedy is an attempt to recapture the last comic idyll of childhood when adults and authority can be mocked because they are safe, secure, permanent, unchanging figures. They are not yet associated with the "yellowing dickybird—watching pictures of the dead" or "The Front," from which many of one's neighbors never came back. Life is funny and for ever. It is to recapture this innocence that Thomas embarks on what John Ackerman aptly called his nostalgic "*recherche du temps Gallois*." This is particularly true of his *Memories of Christmas* which begins:

One Christmas was so much like another, in those years, around the sea-town corner now, and out of all sound except the distant speaking of the voices I sometimes hear a moment before sleep, that I can never remember whether it snowed for six days and six nights when I was twelve or whether it snowed for twelve days and twelve nights when I was six . . . All the Christmasses roll down the hill towards the Welsh-speaking sea, like a snowball growing whiter and bigger and rounder.

Later, with his friends, Thomas went out "school-capped and gloved and mufflered" into the snows of Swansea's hills above the sea to seek that other essential element of childhood, nostalgia-mischief:

We went padding through the streets, leaving huge deep footprints in the snow on the hidden pavements. "I bet people will think there's been hippoes. What would you do if you saw a hippo coming down Terrace Road?"

. . . "What would you do if you saw *two* hippoes . . . ?"

Iron flanked and bellowing he-hippoes clanked and blundered and battered through the scudding snow towards us as we passed by Mr. Daniel's house.

"Let's post Mr. Daniel a snowball through his letterbox."

. . . "Let's write 'Mr. Daniel looks like a spaniel' all over his lawn."

The childhood comedies have a gentle, safe quality (though at times shot through with a reminder of the poet's sense of mortality) that is an appealing reminder to readers of their own idealized childhood or a construction of the childhood that they would like to have had but did not. It is a secure world of extensive family relations and predictable regularity. It is the opposite of the emptiness with which Thomas ends the last Swansea story, "*One Warm Saturday,*" in his collection *Portrait of the Artist as a Young Dog*: "The light of the one weak lamp in a rusty circle fell across the brick-heaps and the broken wood and the dust that had been houses once, where the small and hardly known and never to be forgotten people of the dirty town had lived and loved and died and, always, lost."

Thomas's comedies of childhood are not isolated, unthinking pieces of sentimentality as is so much humor involving children, but they are part of a broader plan in which the structured, timeless world of the child is seen in opposition to the awareness of entropy that afflicts adults and from which the humorous recall of remembered childhood is one temporary means of escape. It is one of the universal themes that runs throughout Thomas's work which give his Welsh-flavored humor an appeal for peoples who have never been to, perhaps never heard of, Wales. He is Wales' national humorist in the same sense that Jaroslav Hašek represents the Czechs, Miguel de Cervantes the Spaniards, or François Rabelais the French; for all that, they each belong to all of us.

Summary
Dylan Thomas, though perhaps best known both in England and America for his poetry, also used his unique talent with words in stories, broadcasts, and his famous play for voices, *Under Milk Wood*, to become the most notable Welsh humorist writing in English. His humor is at one and the same time distinctively Welsh and universal in its appeal; it is secure, cozy, sometimes even sentimental, yet built over a profound and uneasy sense of the mortality and mutability of all things.

Selected Bibliography
Primary Sources

Poetry
Eighteen Poems. London: Sunday Referee and Parton Bookshop, 1934.
Twenty-Five Poems. London: Dent, 1936.
The Map of Love. London: Dent, 1939.
The World I Breathe. New York: 1939.
Deaths and Entrances. London: Dent, 1946.
In Country Sleep and Other Poems. New York: New Directions, 1952.
Collected Poems, 1934–1952. London: Dent, 1952. Republished as *The Collected Poems of Dylan Thomas*. New York: New Directions, 1953.
Poet in the Making. The Notebooks of Dylan Thomas. Ed. Ralph Maud. London: Dent, 1968.
Dylan Thomas: The Poems. Ed. Daniel Jones. London: Dent, 1971.
Dylan Thomas: Collected Poems 1934–53. Ed. Walford Davies and Ralph Maud. London: Dent, 1988.

Prose: Stories, letters, miscellaneous
Portrait of the Artist as a Young Dog. London: Dent, 1940.
A Prospect of the Sea and Other Stories and Prose Writings. Ed. Daniel Jones. London: Dent, 1955.
Adventures in the Skin Trade. London: Putnam, 1955.
Letters to Vernon Walkins. London: Dent and Faber, 1957.
Dylan Thomas: Early Prose Writings. Ed. Walford Davies. London: Dent, 1971.
The Death of the King's Canary. Co-authored with John Davenport. London: Hutchinson, 1976.
The Collected Stories. London: 1983.
Dylan Thomas: The Collected Letters. Ed. Paul Ferris. London: Dent, 1985.

Broadcasts and the Play for Voices
Quite Early One Morning. London: Dent, 1954.
Under Milk Wood. London: Dent, 1954.
Dylan Thomas: The Broadcasts. Ed. Ralph Maud. London: Dent, 1991.

Film Scripts
The Doctor and the Devils. London: Dent, 1953.
The Beach of Falesa. London: Jonathan Cape, 1964.
Twenty Years A-Growing. London: Dent, 1964.
Me and My Bike. London: Triton, 1965.
Rebecca's Daughters. London: Triton, 1965.
The Doctor and the Devils and Other Scripts. New York: New Directions, 1966.
Dylan Thomas' Film Scripts. Ed. John Ackerman. London: Dent [Forthcoming].

Bibliographies

Maud, Ralph. *Dylan Thomas in Print: A Bibliographical History.* Pittsburgh: University of Pittsburgh Press, 1970; London: Dent, 1972; with an Appendix covering 1969–1971 by Walford Davies.

Rolph, J. Alexander. *Dylan Thomas a Bibliography.* London: Dent, 1956.

Secondary Sources

Ackerman, John. *Dylan Thomas: His Life and Work.* London: Oxford University Press, 1964.

———. *Welsh Dylan.* Cardiff: John Jones, 1979.

———. *A Dylan Thomas Companion.* Basingstoke: Macmillan, 1991. Ackerman's work combines biography with analyses of Thomas's poetry, prose, and broadcasts. His work is clear, insightful, invaluable, indeed essential.

Brinnin, John Malcolm. *Dylan Thomas in America.* London: Dent, 1956.

Cleverdon, Douglas. *The Growth of Milk Wood.* London: Dent, 1969. Contains various texts of *Under Milk Wood* and shows how Thomas's most famous humorous work was crafted.

Davies, Christie. "The Comic Welshman in British Literature from Shakespeare to Dylan Thomas." In *Papers of the Dylan Thomas Society of Wales,* ed. Gilbert Bennet. Swansea: Dylan Thomas Society, 1982, pp. 17–35. A comparative study of Thomas's comic perceptions of the Welsh with those of other authors writing about them in a humorous vein.

———. "Ethnic Jokes and Social Change; The Case of the Welsh." *Immigrants and Minorities,* 4, 1 (March 1985): 46–63. A historical study of comic images of the Welsh in jokes and of the way these ethnic scripts are used by humorists.

Davies, Walford. *Dylan Thomas.* Cardiff: University of Wales Press, 1990. A short but succinct and helpful study of Thomas as a "writer of Wales."

Ferris, Paul. *Dylan Thomas.* London: Hodder & Stoughton, 1977. A very thorough biography of Thomas.

Fitzgibbon, Constantine. *The Life of Dylan Thomas.* Boston: Little, Brown, 1965. A sympathetic biography that relates Thomas's life and work in a meaningful way.

Jones, Daniel. *My Friend Dylan Thomas.*

London: Dent, 1977. A readable, entertaining, and at times humorous volume of reminiscences by one of Thomas's closest and most talented friends.

Russell, W.M.S. "Sound Drama Before Marconi." In *Papers of the Radio-Literature Conference* 1977, ed. P. Lewis. Durham Radio Literature Conference, 1978. The leading study of "plays for voices."

Tindall, William York. *A Reader's Guide to Dylan Thomas.* London: Thames and Hudson, 1972.

Christie Davies

Tinniswood, Peter

Born: Liverpool, England, December 21, 1936
Education: University of Manchester, 1954–1957
Marriage: Liz Goulding

Biography

Peter Tinniswood has described himself as a thorough-going Northerner in temperament and outlook. Certainly, his work has been deeply influenced by the speech, customs, and attitudes of the north of England in which he grew up and worked as a young journalist. Born in Liverpool on December 21, 1936, and brought up in Manchester, Tinniswood began his career in journalism working for local newspapers in Sheffield. This early exposure to the broadly similar yet subtly differing cultures of Lancashire and Yorkshire provided him with a complete education in the ways of the north. The natural humor of this region, in both its conscious and unconscious forms, is a rich seam which Tinniswood has exploited brilliantly and to the delight of his many readers.

After attending the University of Manchester (1954–1957), Tinniswood began his career as a journalist in 1958. He continued to work on newspapers in Sheffield, Liverpool, and Cardiff until, in the 1970s, success as a novelist and radio playwright enabled him to become a full-time freelance writer. Since turning to writing full-time, he has established himself as one of the finest of all British humorists, with a large and loyal following. His lasting commitment to radio as a medium—to the formats of both the radio play and serial comedy—has helped to make him known to an even wider audience. British radio has long been an outlet for some of the country's richest comic writing. Tinniswood's prolific yet consistently excellent output for radio contributes significantly to the maintenance of a high standard of humorous work in sound broadcasting.

Tinniswood married Liz Goulding and is unwilling to give any further information regarding his personal life.

Literary Analysis

Tinniswood's first published work was for the BBC satirical television series of the early 1960s, *That Was The Week That Was*. His breakthrough as a writer, however, came with the publication of the novel, *A Touch of Daniel*, in 1969. This book, which won the Best First Novel of the Year Award, is one of the most accomplished works of comic fiction since World War II. It takes the familiar material of working-class life in the north of England and stamps it with the striking originality of the author's imagination.

In *A Touch of Daniel*, Tinniswood created the Brandon family, whose fortunes are followed in three subsequent novels, *I Didn't Know You Cared* (1973), *Except You're a Bird* (1974), and *Call It A Canary* (1985). The core of the family are Mr. and Mrs. Lesley Brandon, their son, Carter, and Mrs. Brandon's brother, Mort. In the relationships between these characters, Tinniswood imitates, to brilliant comic effect, the way of life and speech of the North of England. His ability to go beyond mere comedy of manners, to create a kind of humorous magic realism *avant la lettre* is best exemplified by the figure of Daniel, the eponymous hero of his first novel. Daniel is the improbable offspring of Uncle Mort and the equally elderly Auntie Lil. Widowed and taken into the bosom of the Brandon family, Mort and Lil produce a baby whose influence on the household, and on the silent, long-suffering Carter in particular, is spectacular, for Daniel has powers—curative ones to transform the geriatric back to health and strength and talismanic ones which make him the alter ego of the taciturn but reflective Carter. Daniel dies of pneumonia, part of a surge of black comedy which marks the ending of *A Touch of Daniel*, but his spirit and voice live on inside Carter's head, accompanying the young man through the three Brandon family novels which follow.

Interspersed among the Brandon novels in the writer's early fiction are a number of comic works in which the elements of the grotesque and the fanciful are given freer rein. In these books, particularly *The Stirk of Stirk* (1974) and *Shemerelda* (1981), Tinniswood's gift for observing the ludicrous in the everyday is subordinated to a darkly tinged lyrical fantasy. The best of them, *The Stirk of Stirk*, confirmed the author's unerring gift for taking an established formula and deftly twisting it to achieve a sense of the bizarre. The book is a cod version of the Robin Hood legend with the fearless outlaw of popular legend transformed into a mincing, camp figure of fun and overshadowed by the *bona fide* hero, the Stirk. *The Stirk of Stirk*, though parodic in Tinniswood's handling of myth and romance, is a concentrated expression of the lyrical and dramatic elements which are present throughout Tinniswood's canon. Indeed, it is precisely the playing off of a lyrical impulse against the farcical, vulgar, and bathetic elements of the everyday which gives his writing its richness and individuality. Most humor is based on the exploitation of incongruity; Tinniswood's does so in a way which locates desire and yearning squarely in the midst of the laughably commonplace.

His strength as a writer comes from just this depth to his comic vision. In the Brandon novels, the narrative focus is provided by the experience of the character of Carter, in whom all manner of contradictions are met but not resolved. The working-class hero (or anti-hero) is a stock figure of post-war British fiction and the hallmarks of the character's condition are, typically, entrapment in social class and the attendant struggle to articulate an identity. Treated in a serious vein, this theme is manifest in the angst-ridden characters of David Storey and the rebellious roisterers of Alan Sillitoe; handled tragicomically, it is evidenced in Keith Waterhouse's fantasist, Billy Liar. Carter Brandon, nine-tenths of his silent, day-dreaming being concealed beneath the surface of a routine existence, embodies the dividedness of a certain kind of male working-class experience in a way that is no less convincing for being rendered in humorous form. Arthur Hugh Clough's great nineteenth-century poem *Dipsychus* is an example of what could be achieved by using comedy as a medium for dramatizing the dialogue between ego and super-ego. Carter is a more robust and decidedly less genteel Dipsychus in prose—and the ironical, ever-present voice of Daniel, conscience one minute and tempter the next, is a blunt, vulgar, northern version of Clough's Spirit.

The Brandon family novels are undoubtedly Tinniswood's major achievement in comic prose. Though they hold a particular and obvious appeal for English readers familiar with the life of the industrial North, their comic genius is a universal one. Tinniswood's humor, vital and robust though it is, also has a dark edge. This is generated by a sense of the tension between boredom and desire, between the comfort blanket of routine and the yearning for escape and excitement. Brandon menfolk are torn between women as temptresses, fearful yet desirable, and women as domestic jailers, resented yet deeply needed. The war between the sexes is acted out according to grim rules of engagement; Carter's sardonic alter ego, the baby Daniel, chirpily spells out for him the choice between a life of indefatigable home improvement and the dangers and delights of sexual adventure. In the final Brandon novel, *Call it a Canary*, these tensions explode at last, sending Carter hurtling down the slope of self-destructive debauch. The bitter note of this last full-scale novel has much to do with Tinniswood marking the decline not just of his hero but of the older, industrial North and its way of life. The satirical element in Tinniswood's writing has consistently been directed at the materialism of modern cultures, even as his most passionate affirmation has always been of the natural environment. In *Call it a Canary*, all of the author's complex feelings about the North and about his own adroit skirting of nostalgia in writing about the Northern way of life reach a climax in a novel where the humor is grim rather than uproarious.

Tinniswood's style is unmistakable. The two essential characteristics are a richly idiomatic comic dialogue and a descriptive technique which exploits to the full short phrases and sentences. "Short sentences, Tinny," the author recalls being told by the chief reporter of the Sheffield *Star*. Tinniswood has turned that sound journalistic advice to good account in his imaginative writings. The short sentences of his prose function like springs, coiled and then released to give forward momentum. They generate expectancy as well as mirroring the bluntness of the northern speech patterns that his Brandon books rely on for their comic essence.

Nowhere are these features of Tinniswood's writing better displayed than in the two sequels to the Brandon family novels, *Uncle Mort's North Country* (1986) and *Uncle Mort's South Country* (1989). In these volumes the writer turns Carter and his Uncle Mort into a pair of picaresque heroes, taking them on a series of excursions across the north and south of England respectively. Carter's Volkswagen Beetle is the vehicle, in every sense, from which his Uncle Mort's hilariously scathing commentary on modern life in general and the alien south in particular is delivered. Without question, Mort is one of the great comic creations of modern English writing. His mind is a ragbag of folk memories and lovingly nurtured prejudices, and from his unstoppable mouth flows a kind of comic version of the North's collective unconscious. The dour Northerner, candid to the point of rudeness, is a stock figure in English popular culture; Mort is the super-charged, free-associating version of that type raised to mythic proportions. His enthusiasms are passionate and his vulgarity and abusiveness so highly developed that they all but amount to a kind of refinement. In Mort's bouts of comic nostalgia and acerbic commentary on contemporary England, the novelist's own quirky eye for the flotsam and jetsam of popular consciousness is at its keenest.

Tinniswood's ability to do what many great comic writers do, to marry the eccentric with the typical, is not limited to the theme of the Northern working class. His imagination, like the author himself, has migrated southward in recent years, in the process creating several comic types that approach the great Uncle Mort in rude vitality. Tinniswood has a number of passions which permeate his books. One is ornithology and another is sport. The outlet for the latter has been the cricketing reminiscences of yet another memorable raconteur, the Brigadier. Love of cricket transcends social class in England to a greater degree than do most activities. But, by the same token, each class has its own clearly defined attitude toward "the summer game." For the Brigadier, the great past of English cricket is like a lost imperial possession, a world bathed in the glow of lingering summer sunsets but very imperfectly remembered. To splendid effect, Tinniswood uses the Brigadier's failing memory as a device for comic conflation; the names of famous cricketers, past and present, slide in and out of those of film stars, crowned heads of Europe, politicians. In his rambling reminiscences, the game is turned into a whimsical portmanteau metaphor for modern England, with hybrid versions of the twentieth century's cultural icons created on every page. Heroes of empire undergo hilariously painful changes of name and sex to be turned into strange creatures, half-beefy opening batsmen, half-goddesses of the silver screen. For readers who delight in sheer wordplay, Tinniswood's Brigadier books, beginning with *Tales from a Long Room* (1981) through *Tales from Witney Scrotum* (1987) are an endless source of pleasure. Indeed, the Brigadier's anecdotal ramblings may well, like "the summer game" itself, go on for some time yet when the author decides to open the next innings.

Tinniswood has enjoyed a long and successful career as a writer of plays and comic serials for radio. His sheer virtuosity with language fits him admirably for his medium. It is out of his writing for radio that much of the author's recent published work has come, notably *Hayballs* (1989) and *Winston* (1991). In the Rabelaisian figure of Winston, Tinniswood has created a kind of lustful, low-life version of the Admirable Chrichton, amorous companion and counselor to the middle-class Nancy, who finds in his embraces consolation from her vexatious, eccentric family. Winston, part bucolic, hedonistic poacher of traditional popular imagining, part social security scrounger of contemporary political mythology, is a character for our times and a fitting addition to the comic gallery of Tinniswood's work.

As BBC serials, *Winston* and *Hayballs* proved enormously popular and enhanced Tinniswood's established reputation as a writer for radio. His attachment to the stage and radio stems largely from the particular pride and pleasure that he takes in working with actors. That they, and directors, clearly reciprocate is evidenced by the long list of distinguished British character actors who have performed his work. Judi Dench, Maurice Denham, Denholm Elliot, and Robin Bailey are among the many household names of the British theater who have taken parts written by Tinniswood. The author has also enjoyed a fruitful collaboration with one of the most successful of all British stage directors, Alan Ayckbourn; his stage plays *You Should See Us Now* (1982), *At the End of the Day* (1983), and *The Village Fete* (1991) have all been directed by Ayckbourn. More recently, Tinniswood's adaptation of Eduardo de Fillipo's play, *Napoli Milonaria*, was staged at the National Theatre under the direction of Richard Eyre and starring Sir Ian McKellen. Whether Tinniswood's intense involvement with stage and radio has displaced fiction as his principal activity, or whether it simply opens up a second front in his career as a writer remains to be seen. The many admirers of his comic prose are bound to hope that it is the latter.

Summary

Sheer comic energy and the ability to create the idiosyncratic out of the everyday: these have been the hallmarks of Peter Tinniswood's work and the keys to his sustained success as a writer. No contemporary writer has a sharper eye for the details of English life in all of its forms, or a greater gift for the creation of distinctive comic character. Some writers of humorous prose rely on nuance, some on broad farce; few are able to blend the two in a way which creates a highly effective blend of situation comedy and sophisticated allusiveness. Tinniswood's ability to do just that singles him out from more run-of-the-mill comic writers and continues to assure him of wide readership across the social and intellectual spectrum.

Selected Bibliography

Primary Sources
A Touch of Daniel. London: Hodder & Stoughton, 1969.
Mog. London: Hodder & Stoughton, 1970.
I Didn't Know You Cared. London: Hodder & Stoughton, 1973.
Except You're a Bird. London: Hodder & Stoughton, 1974.
The Stirk of Stirk. London: Macmillan, 1974.
Shemerelda. London: Hodder & Stoughton, 1981.
Tales from a Long Room. London: Arrow Books, 1981.
More Tales from a Long Room. London: Arrow Books, 1982.
Collected Tales from a Long Room. London: Hutchinson, 1982.
The Brigadier Down Under. London: Macmillan, 1983.
The Home Front. London: Severn House, 1983.
The Brigadier in Season. London: Macmillan, 1984.
Call it a Canary. London: Macmillan, 1985.
The Brigadier's Tour. London: Pan Books, 1985.
The Brigadier's Brief Lives. London: Pan Books, 1985.
Uncle Mort's North Country. London: Pavilion Books, 1986.
Tales from Witney Scrotum. London: Pavilion Books, 1987.
Uncle Mort's South Country. London: Arrow

Books, 1989.

Hayballs. London: Arrow Books, 1989.

Winston. London: Arrow Books, 1991.

Glyn Turton

Tolkien, J[ohn] R[onald] R[euel]

Born: Bloomfontein, South Africa, January 3, 1892

Education: Exeter College, Oxford University, B.A., 1915; M.A., 1919

Marriage: Edith Mary Bratt, March 22, 1916; four children

Died: Bournemouth, England, September 2, 1973

Biography

John Ronald Reuel Tolkien was born in Bloomfontein, South Africa on January 3, 1892, the son of Arthur Reuel Tolkien and Mabel Saffield Tolkien. The family moved to England when Tolkien was three years old. He was educated first in Birmingham, then at Exeter College, Oxford University from which he received a B.A. in 1915 and an M.A. in 1919. In the meantime, he married Edith Mary Bratt on March 22, 1916; the couple had four children. During the 1930s, Tolkien formed a literary society at Oxford. It was named "The Inklings" and included such notable authors as Charles Williams and C.S. Lewis. The function of this society was to read aloud whatever the various authors were writing at the time, and the men exchanged opinions and ideas. It was during this period that *The Hobbit* (1937) was being written.

In 1938, Tolkien won the *New York Herald Tribune* Children's Book Award. He taught at Leeds University and at Oxford University, where he was Merton Professor of English from 1945 to 1959. In 1957, he became a Fellow of the Royal Society of Literature and also won the International Fantasy Award. In 1966, he won the Benson Medal, and in 1972, he became a Commander in the Order of the British Empire. Tolkien also was awarded honorary doctoral degrees from both University College in Dublin (D.Litt., 1954) and the University of Liege in France (Ph.D., 1954).

Tolkien was an excellent linguist and philologist, and served as an Oxford don and the Rawlinson and Bosworth Professor of Anglo-Saxon for nearly fifty years. He was one of the leading philologists of his day and in many ways continued the tradition of the Brothers Grimm.

The fairy-tale stories that he wrote were an extension of his life as a philologist in that these stories were said to have been found as a document entitled "The Red Book of Westmarch." His mythological story and his writing style are also derivative of his scholarly methods, as ancient and archetypal patterns of events and characterizations can be traced to Greek, Germanic, Celtic, and Old and Middle English roots. Tolkien's story has the length and the trappings of a narrative, and a number of his characters are archetypal. According to Robert Giddings:

> Reading *The Lord of the Rings* can give the illusion of handling great literature—yet it is easy, compared, say, with effort required to accomplish a reading of Henry James, George Eliot, Joseph Conrad or even D.H. Lawrence. *The Lord of the Rings* is like climbing Mount Olympus by escalator. (8)

Well over 3,000,000 copies of *The Lord of the Rings* trilogy (in at least nine languages) had been sold within the first twenty-five years after its publication. Tolkien originally created the hobbit characters to entertain his small children. It was a Tolkien holiday tradition that each Christmas the children would receive a letter from Father Christmas recounting the year's adventures of Bilbo and his friends. This was verified by Father Christmas' dirty footprint on the floor by the fireplace, where he had left the letter. According to Mary Salu and Robert T. Farrell, these letters were the origin of *The Hobbit* (34). In the foreword to the Ballantine edition of the trilogy, Tolkien indicated that another motivation in writing his fairy stories was "primarily linguistic in inspiration" (Kolich, 523).

Tolkien considered himself to be a hobbit:

> I like gardens, trees, unmechanized farm lands. I smoke a pipe and like good, plain food—unrefrigerated—but I detest French cooking. I like—and even dare to wear in these dull days—ornamental waistcoats. I'm fond of mushrooms out of a field, have a very simple sense of humor (which even my most appreciative critics find tiresome). I go to bed late, and get up late, when possible. (Grotta, 10)

Tolkien laughed more than most men, and he often amused himself by making up jokes and stories, but his mind outraced his social skills, for whenever he told a joke or a story, he would invariably muff the punch line, or forget to come to the punch line at all, or swallow it in a mumble, or laugh heartily in the middle of the story (Grotta, 12). An English journalist once described the novelist as a cross between Bilbo and Gandalf (Grotta, 10).

Tolkien died of a chest infection caused by a bleeding gastric ulcer at Bournemouth on September 2, 1973.

Literary Analysis

Tolkien would not normally be classified as a comic or humorous writer. Nevertheless, there are many qualities that make his writing appropriate to this volume. His writing tends to be whimsical, satiric, ironic, parodic, and incongruous. It is both awesome and awful. His fantasies are fantastic, and his fables are fabulous. And his characters are genuinely funny in both their looks and their demeanor. In an essay entitled "On Fairy-Stories," Tolkien explains something of his literary intentions: "The peculiar quality of the 'joy' in successful fantasy can . . . be explained as a sudden glimpse of the underlying reality or truth" (Kolich, 522).

In *Farmer Giles of Ham*, the author's humor very much reflects his training as a linguist. Here Tolkien frequently plays the Latin against the Anglo Saxon as the story develops. When he first introduces the farmer, Tolkien says, "In full his name was Aegidius Ahenobarbus Julius Agricola de Hammo; for people were richly endowed with names in those days." He later adds, however, that "in the vulgar form: he was Farmer Giles of Ham" (*Farmer Giles*, 125). The dragon in this story was given a Latin name, "Chrysophylax Dives," and even Farmer Giles's sword was called "Caudimordax." This was "the famous sword that in popular romances is more vulgarly called Tailbiter" (*Farmer Giles*, 147).

Tolkien liked to play with Latin terminology. Farmer Giles's king was named "Augustus Bonifacius rex et basileus" (*Farmer Giles*, 161). After Farmer Giles had conquered the dragon, he was given the title of "Giles, Dominus de Domito Serpente, which is in the vulgar Lord of the Tame Worm" (183). At the end of the story, Giles became the King of his Little Kingdom of Ham: "He was crowned in Ham in the name of Aegidius Draconarius; but he was more often known as Old Giles Worming" (*Farmer Giles*, 184). The final word of this story

is "Finis," but of course Tolkien must translate this word for his readers as "The End" (*Farmer Giles*, 187).

Farmer Giles's sword was humorous in that it would not stay sheathed if there was a dragon within five miles. The parson tried, for example, to sheath the sword with the following results: "He picked the sword up carefully and tried to put it back in the sheath; but it would not go so much as a foot in, and it jumped clean out again, as soon as he took his hand off the hilt" (*Farmer Giles*, 146).

In order to become a proper knight, Farmer Giles had to obtain some armor: "The blacksmith shook his head. He was a slow, gloomy man, vulgarly known as Sunny Sam, though his proper name was Fabricius Cunctator. He never whistled at his work, unless some disaster (such as frost in May) had duly occurred after he had foretold it. Since he was daily foretelling disasters of every kind, few happened that he had not foretold" (*Farmer Giles*, 149). The armor which the blacksmith prepared for Farmer Giles was rather strange, and in it, Farmer Giles cut a humorous figure: "They had stitched on the rings so that they overlapped, each hanging loose over the one below, and jingle they certainly did. The cloak did something to stop the noise of them, but Giles cut a queer figure in his gear. They did not tell him so. They girded the belt round his waist with difficulty, and they hung the scabbard upon it; but he had to carry the sword, for it would no longer stay sheathed" (*Farmer Giles*, 152).

When Farmer Giles met the Dragon, the language of the Dragon was not what would be expected of a dragon. The Dragon said, "Excuse my asking, but were you looking for me, by any chance?" The Dragon later said, "Those are your holiday clothes, I suppose, A new fashion, perhaps?" Farmer Giles's felt hat had fallen off and his grey cloak had slipped open; but he brazened it out (*Farmer Giles*, 154).

As a scholar specializing in Medieval British and European literature, Tolkien was intimately acquainted with a number of imaginary worlds, notably the "Middangeard" (Middle-earth) of *Beowulf*, "The Volsunga Saga," and the "Eddas." At one time, Tolkien lamented to a friend that the English had few myths of their own, and said that he might make one himself. Readers who have tried to construct maps of Tolkien's world have used many devices to help them with the relative distances:

Many mileages had to be estimated, based on our Primary World. How many miles per hour could be sustained for more than a day—by a Man on foot (with an Elf and a Dwarf)? Armored cavalry on horseback? Halflings on short rations? Ponies on mountain paths? . . . with adjustments for change of travel speed (e.g., being chased by wolves). (Fonstad, xiii)

The writer also had a sincere and passionate love for languages, especially Welsh, Old English, Greek, and Finnish. By his own admission he invented several languages when he was about eight or nine, but he subsequently destroyed them (Grotta, 22). There is an archaic tone in Tolkien's writing, a tone that is partly scriptural, and partly the tale of a chronicler. This gives the impression that the author's world is "God-willed, long matured by human experience and the lessons of history" (Giddings, 9). Furthermore, he sees a close affinity between creativity and Christianity. "Man, he said, had a natural desire to create because he was himself a created being 'made in the image and likeness of a Maker'" (Duriez, 9).

Tolkien creates fairy stories about witches, trolls, giants, dragons, halflings, elves, fays, dwarfs, hobbits, and men. His world is ordered by the sun, the moon, the seas, and the sky, and the earth, and all the things that are in it, trees and birds, water and stone, wine and bread, and ourselves, mortal humans (Kocher, 1). These stories may not be about the real world in the sense that they are about Europe or Africa, or about shortages of natural resources, or the threat of nuclear disaster. But, they *are* about the real world in that they are about good and evil, and sorrow, and pain, and injustice, and sometimes about heroism and joy. Thus, Crabbe suggests that Tolkien's stories are not so much about reality as they are about truth (2).

Tolkien's "fairy stories" were varied in characterization and action, detailed in description, and expansive in philosophy. The writer was constantly revising, correcting, and amending manuscripts in the interest of verisimilitude. August M. Kolich suggests that "not since Milton has any Englishman worked so successfully at creating a secondary world" (521). Tolkien's Middle-earth is a sideshow of strangely humorous characters including hobbits, elves, dwarfs, orcs, and the men of Westernesse. Although his writing covers the full ten thousand years of

Middle-earth history, he concentrates on the Third Age, the age which sets the stage for Man, who is to come in the Fourth Age.

This Third Age is about three millennia in length and is treated chronologically in five books: 1) *The Hobbit*; 2) *The Fellowship of the Ring*; 3) *The Two Towers*; 4) *The Return of the King*; and 5) *The Silmarillion*, with the middle three novels commonly being referred to as "The Trilogy."

The Hobbit (1937) establishes the battle between the forces of evil, led by Sauron, and the forces of good, led by Gandalf the wizard. During the Elder days, Sauron tricked the Elf smiths at Eregion into making seventeen rings of power. Seven were to be for dwarfs; nine were to be for men; and then there was made "One Ring," the ring with the most power because it controlled all of the other rings. But this One Ring was very seductive and very dangerous, because its power could be misused, and in fact tended to corrupt whoever was wearing it. So Gandalf wanted the ring to be worn by someone who was not easily corruptible, and the least corruptible race on earth were the hobbits.

Hobbits are what Robley Evans calls "improbable heroes." They are "improbable" because they are unadventurous, small, peaceful, and devoted to such creature comforts as two dinners when they can get them. The faces of Tolkien's hobbits were good-natured rather than beautiful. They had broad bright eyes, and red cheeks, and their mouths were especially shaped for laughter, eating, and drinking. "And laugh they did, and eat, and drink, often and heartily, being fond of simple jests at all times, and of six meals a day (when they could get them). They were hospitable and delighted in parties, and in presents, which they gave away freely and eagerly accepted" (Grotta, 10).

Nevertheless, these hobbits have a large share in carrying on the adventures of Tolkien's novels because they are capable of great fortitude and endurance. Their inner, or hobbit-strength is related to their "commitment to a greater vision of life than oneself" (Evans, 15). In *Mother Night*, Kurt Vonnegut wrote, "We are what we pretend to be, so we must be careful about what we pretend to be." In applying this statement to Tolkien, we would say that we all have the obligation to attain our full "hobbithood" (Evans, 14).

Hobbits resemble both an English countryman and a rabbit. They love peace and quiet and good tilled earth. Their lives are well ordered, and the pastoral countryside is their favorite place to be. They are skillful with such tools as forge-bellows, watermills, or handlooms, but they dislike anything more complicated than that. They have a strong sense of tradition, and are totally unobtrusive. The hobbit Bilbo Baggins is small, frail, and under four feet tall. He loves the comfort of his own hole and has no sense of adventure. A hobbit, especially Bilbo, would not abuse the power of the One Ring. Bilbo's transformation, his growing up, is the main point of *The Hobbit*. Gandalf knows that hobbits, although they tend to be quite domestic and unassuming, are capable of incredible feats.

Bilbo is a hero, though a reluctant one, and whenever he is provoked to action, he responds in a pragmatic, steadfast, and effective way. As Thorin says to Bilbo, "There is more in you of good than you know . . . Some courage and some wisdom, blended in measure. If more of us valued food and cheer and song above hoarded gold, it would be a merrier world" (Kolich, 525).

The humor of *The Hobbit* can be seen as Bilbo confronts various other characters. When he first encounters the wizard Gandalf, for example, he describes him as being quite old and a bit decrepit looking, with an extremely long white beard and immense black boots. He addresses the wizard with "Good morning," and Gandalf looks back at him through extremely bushy white eyebrows and asks, "What do you mean? . . . Do you wish me a good morning, or mean that it is a good morning whether I want it or not; or that you feel good this morning, or that it is a morning to be good on?" (*Hobbit*, 13).

When Bilbo confronts the evil dragon Smaug, he addresses the dragon thus, "O Smaug, the chiefest and Greatest of Calamities," and Smaug commends Bilbo on "nice manners for a thief and a liar." What follows is an example of slippery talk. Bilbo dances around the subject of his true identity by calling himself a number of power-titles, such as "he that walks unseen, ringbearer, luckwearer, clue-finder. . . . " This, according to Bilbo, is "the way to talk to dragons" (*Hobbit*, 190).

The Lord of the Rings is a journey and a quest. According to the lyrics of one of the songs of Middle-earth:

The Road goes ever on and on
Down from the door where it began.

Now far ahead the Road has gone,
And I must follow, if I can . . .

As Bilbo says to Frodo, "It's a dangerous business . . . going out of your door" (Duriez, 13). When Sam asks "Don't adventures ever have an end?" he is able after a moment's reflection to answer his own question, "I suppose not. Someone else always has to carry on the story" (Evans, 14).

Tolkien confesses that *The Lord of the Rings* began as an exercise in "linguistic esthetics." At first he had no intention of writing *The Lord of the Rings*, but Stanley Unwin, Tolkien's publisher, wanted another book about the Hobbit. The author responded that "Mr. Baggins began as a comic tale among conventional Grimm's fairy-tale dwarves, and got drawn into the edge of it—so that even Sauron the terrible peeped over the edge. And what more can hobbits do?" (Helms, *Silmarils*, ix–x). *The Lord of the Rings* was, therefore, an afterthought, an accident of the success of *The Hobbit*. Once committed to the task of writing *The Lord of the Rings*, however, Tolkien decided to write a "really long story that would hold the attention of readers, amuse them, delight them, and at times maybe excite them or move them" (Helms, *Silmarils*, xiii).

The Lord of the Rings trilogy is not designed for people who cannot come to grips with an author who would go to elaborate lengths to create an entire history, geography, literature, and language as a background for his work of fiction. Ironically, though, it is precisely these features of *The Lord of the Rings* which readers find most appealing (Duriez, 8). Tolkien's readers and his characters are worlds apart. Nevertheless, readers can identify with the characters' feelings, and share their dreams and fears: "Heart in mouth, we follow Frodo and Sam on their struggle through the ash-pits of Mordor towards Mount Doom." Colin Duriez continues, "The presiding virtue of Tolkien's tales is hope. Always, even in the longest and darkest night of Middle-earth, there glimmers a light—however small and flickering—of humanity, compassion and courage" (Duriez, 9–10). These are features which would help to define *The Lord of the Rings* not as a tragedy, but as a comedy, since the literary world would acknowledge that a "comedy" may be mostly serious or even grim, but in which the story moves from ironic chaos to a renewal of human hope and spirit.

Tolkien follows Horace's statement that "the aim of the poet is to inform and to delight; he will succeed at the former only insofar as he succeeds at the latter" (Flieger, viii). Verlyn Flieger believes that the novelist puts us in touch with the supernatural by opening our eyes to wonder. Tolkien gives us a glimpse into the universe of beauty and meaning and purpose, but then Flieger goes on to say, "Whether there really is such a universe is less important than the undeniable truth that we need one badly" (Flieger, viii).

In *The Fellowship of the Ring*, Bilbo passes the one ring, the ring of invisibility, on to his nephew, Frodo. In *The Two Towers* (1955), all of the hobbits are separated as they all have to perform their individual tasks of glory. Sauron's flaw is that he fails to understand the mind of his opponent; he cannot understand how it would be possible for someone having the power of the One Ring to want to destroy it rather than to use this power to enhance his own glory. At the end of *The Return of the King*, Frodo does finally succeed in throwing the ring into the fires of Mount Doom. This ending of the Lord of the Rings trilogy is what Tolkien calls a "Eucatastrophe," or a "good catastrophe." The hobbits, dwarfs, elves, and wizards all sail off into "the Uttermost West."

In *The Return of the King* (1956), Sauron's demonic rule has been total and relentless, and the Mere of Dead Faces has become a surrealistic and horrible battlefield where the faces of the fallen soldiers are mirrored in the swamp water.

According to Flieger, the *Silmarillion* (1977) was written before, during, and after both *The Hobbit* and *The Lord of the Rings*. It subsumed *The Hobbit*, engulfed *The Lord of the Rings,* and turned the *Hobbit* sequel into an extension of the broader mythology. Though it took fifty years for Tolkien to write the book, he never finished it, and it was not published during his lifetime (x). Flieger notes that this body of myth, legend, folktale, and song imitated the primary mythologies of the world by later being collated, edited, and published in bits and pieces (xii). According to Flieger, "the governing principles of Tolkien's world are explicit in *The Silmarillion*, implicit in *The Lord of the Rings*. Without the one, the other could not exist" (xiii).

Ironically, although *The Silmarillion* is the most significant of Tolkien's works, it would have no audience at all had it not been for *The Lord of the Rings*. It is damped by biblical language and by a narrative that is "constructed along the lines of the Old Testament." In *Time* magazine, it was said that Tolkien's prose here sounds like "a parody of Edgar Rice Burroughs in the style of *The Book of Revelation*." *The New York Review of Books* reviewer predicted that many more people would purchase the book than would read it all the way through (Flieger, xiv). In *Splintered Light,* Flieger discusses *The Silmarillion*. Flieger's title is based on the fact that "myth and language create one another," and he agrees with Owen Barfield that "the polarities of light and dark, perceived through and expressed in language, define one another and develop Tolkien's world" (xx).

According to Neil Isaacs and Rose Zimbardo, *The Lord of the Rings* is filled with "narrative power, droll charm, intricate playfulness, and physical and psychological detail. All this is substantially absent from the solemnly sacred text of *The Silmarillion*" (7). A major paradox of *The Silmarillion* is that "those who are most eagerly drawn to the book as a major object of their cultic attention will most easily be put off by its remoteness from *The Lord of the Rings*" (Isaacs and Zimbardo, 6).

Tolkien wrote *The Silmarillion* because he was enchanted by words. In Rivendell, Frodo hears a song sung in the Sindarin language about Elbereth Star-Kindler. Frodo is enraptured by "the elvish craft" of the song: "The beauty of the melodies and the interwoven words in the Elven-tongue . . . hold him in a spell . . . Almost it seemed that the words took shape, and visions of far lands and bright things that he had never yet imagined opened out before him" (Helms, *Silmarils*, xii).

The book which is most closely associated with Tolkien's personal and professional life is *The Red Book of Westmarch*, published as *The Adventures of Tom Bombadil and Other Verses from the Red Book* in 1962, six years after publication of *The Return of the King*. According to Helms, this is a parody of the Welsh version of *The Red Book of Hergest*, edited by William F. Skene, and is a parody not only of the earlier book but also of the poor research methods of its editor. To enhance the parody, Tolkien presents *The Red Book of Westmarch* as a found document, a red, leather-bound volume containing a large number of verses. It contains "an exquisite parody of a scholarly introduction to a long-lost manuscript" (Helms, "Gleanings," 126). Taking a mock scholarly stance, Tolkien theorizes about the authorship, the sources, and the linguistic relationships of the manuscript in what Helms describes as "one of the best jokes in recent literary history" (126). The preface parodies the methods of textual and philological scholarship, and many of the poems are parodies of scholarly themes common during the writer's life. "With loving humor, he gently deflates some of the more puffy parts of two things dear to him, his hobbit creations and his profession of literary and philological scholarship" (126).

The verses of *The Red Book of Westmarch* are humorous doggerel in nature: "The hobbits of the Shire scribbled into the Red Book margins poems about elves, gold-lust, journeys to an unknown land, and passage into the west" (Helms, "Gleanings," 132). Since they were not adventurers, much of their understanding of these things was inaccurate or inadequate, as much of the humor of the poems lies in the readers' recognition of the limitations of the poets' grasp of the subjects they wrote about.

By attributing the poems to hobbits, Tolkien was able to use self-parody as a way of passing off his bad poetry. But another level of parody is that Tolkien also takes the stance of amused critic and as such is able to explain exactly why the poems are so bad—because hobbits were "fond of strange words, and of rhyming and metrical tricks" (128), which they evidently regarded as poetic virtues. Tolkien's statement that the verses were "mere imitations of Elvish practices" adds still another level to the irony of his criticism of the hobbit verses, which are actually his own verses in disguise. Readers can join Tolkien in chuckling at himself while criticizing the less-than-keen poetic minds of the supposed poets.

Although written in doggerel form, the poetry is skillfully contrived and presents excellent comic morals like "never kick a stone troll's behind, for you'll break your foot"—the moral of "The Stone Troll" (Helms, "Gleanings," 134). Hobbits enjoyed writing comic "circle" poems, and "Errantry" is an example. Such circle poems return to their own beginnings, and therefore they may be recited continuously until the hearers finally revolt. In his preface, Tolkien compares the comic circularity of the poems to the comic circularity of the Hobbits themselves.

In *The War of the Ring*, Christopher Tolkien discusses the origins of the "Errantry" poem. In Jacobite England there was a song

attacking William of Orange as usurper of the English crown of his father-in-law, James II. This poem was entitled, "D'ye ken the rhyme to porringer," and read as follows:

> What is the rhyme for porringer?
> What is the rhyme for porringer?
> The king he had a daughter fair
> And gave the Prince of Orange her.

This poem may have become entrenched in Tolkien's mind because of its metrics and because of its wordplays, for his poem also contains the unlikely word "porringer" (which is an alteration of the ME *potinger*, a shallow cup or bowl with a handle), which is linked with the word "orange":

> There was a merry passenger,
> A messenger, an errander;
> he took a tiny porringer
> and oranges for provender. (Christopher
>   Tolkien, xi)

Charles Williams was a member of Tolkien's "Inkling" group that read poems to each other, and Williams was writing his "Taliessin" poems during this time. One of the features of Williams's verse was his trick of rhyming the middle or final word of a line with the middle word of the next line. In parody fashion, Tolkien used this same poetic trick in much of the hobbit poetry. In "Errantry," this poetic device was "embellished to the point of caricature" (Helms, 138). Tolkien also parodied linguistic scholarship in a discussion of the sources and meanings of "Hey Diddle Diddle." One possible source is ancient Greek, but Tolkien also suggests five other possible sources. According to the best evidence, however, Tolkien concludes that Bilbo Baggins wrote it. He goes on to explain why the cat and the cow and the little dog, and the dish and the spoon are all behaving so strangely. He suggests that there is a merry old inn beneath an old grey hill in Middle-earth where they brew a very powerful beer. And the location of this inn is very close to the location of where the *Red Book of Westmarch* was found. Finally, the expression "hey diddle diddle" is explained as "Bilbo's onomatopoeic representation of the fiddle's squawk" (Helms, 141). The author does not stop here, however, and he suggests that Bilbo is not the original source, for in fact he received much of his inspiration from an even earlier source—Gondor, providing an excellent satiric exposé on the way in which literary scholarship is conducted, and the nature of its evidence and conclusions.

In view of Tolkien's parodies, it is ironic how many scholars have tried to trace the words in his works back to legitimate sources. In an article entitled "Tolkien's Elvish," Thomas Donahue points out that various scholars have traced "alcar," "amhar," "anar," "certa," and "cor" to Kenyon words meaning "glory," "world," "sun," "rune," and "circle" respectively; it is interesting to note in this regard that Tolkien invented a language of his own and named it "Qenyun." Different scholars have traced these same words to Welsh words meaning "reindeer," "greensward," "uncultivated," "cart," and "dwarf" respectively. And these scholars, unlike Tolkien, were making no attempt to be humorous, and were in fact generally unaware of each other's work. Donahue points to Tolkien's scholarly humor as he suggests that Tolkien "just knew that some day someone would spend a real nerd of an afternoon with Celtic and Quenya dictionaries, proving *nothing*" (64). Donahue goes on to suggest that chasing these words back and forth through *The Lord of the Rings* is "like wading waist deep in a wet and soggy marsh. In fact there is such a marsh in the story, a bog certain to more hobbits down waist-deep. The name of the marsh is 'Wetwang'" (64).

Summary

J.R.R. Tolkien shows us time and time again that there are no easy solutions, no dreams or hopes that are not also fraught with the possibilities of nightmarish defeats. Aragorn, the first human ruler of the Fourth Age of Middle-earth, says to his friends, "Ours is but a small matter in the great deeds of this time" (Kolich, 530).

As a linguist, Donahue suggests that many of Tolkien's Elvish sounds are lateral, bilabial, alveolar, or labiodental. From this evidence, Donahue contends that we can conclude absolutely nothing. Tolkien was merely trying to haunt us with the phonemic inventory of Elvish; he wanted the reader to suspect that there was significance when in fact there was none. In writing his Elvish language, Tolkien took on an attitude that was droll, arch, wry, and puckish, an attitude which Donahue finally describes as "elfin." This is consistent with Tolkien's answer to the question of what the most beautiful phrase in the English language was: he re-

sponded, "cellar door." His interest in words has had an effect on the English language, for we can now mutter the word "Orc" at any uncouth behavior, or exclaim "Mordor in our midst" at any instance of ugliness in modern life (Duriez, 11).

Selected Bibliography
Primary Sources

Novels
The Hobbit; or, There and Back Again. London: Allen & Unwin, 1937; Boston: Houghton Mifflin, 1938.
Farmer Giles of Ham. London: Allen & Unwin, 1949; Boston: Houghton Mifflin, 1950.
The Fellowship of the Ring. London: Allen & Unwin, and Boston: Houghton Mifflin, 1954; rev. ed. London: Allen & Unwin, 1966; Boston: Houghton Mifflin, 1967.
The Two Towers. London: Allen & Unwin, and Boston: Houghton Mifflin, 1955; rev. ed. London: Allen & Unwin, 1966; Boston: Houghton Mifflin, 1967.
The Return of the King. London: Allen & Unwin, and Boston: Houghton Mifflin, 1956; rev. ed. London: Allen & Unwin, 1966; Boston: Houghton Mifflin, 1967.
The Adventures of Tom Bombadil and Other Verses from the Red Book. London: Allen & Unwin, 1962.
Tree and Leaf. London: Allen & Unwin, 1964.
The Tolkien Reader. New York: Ballantine, 1966.
Smith of Wooton Major. London: Allen & Unwin, 1967; Boston: Houghton Mifflin, 1967.
The Father Christmas Letters. London: Allen & Unwin, and Boston: Houghton Mifflin, 1976.
The Silmarillion. London: Allen & Unwin, and Boston: Houghton Mifflin, 1977.

Essays
"The Monsters and The Critics" and Other Essays. Boston: Allen & Unwin, 1983.
Salu, Mary, and Robert T. Farrell, eds. *J.R.R. Tolkien, Scholar and Story Teller: Essays in Memorium.* Ithaca, NY: Cornell University Press, 1979.

Letters
The Letters of J.R.R. Tolkien. Ed. Humphrey

Carpenter. Boston: Houghton Mifflin, 1981. These letters provide for important insights on the thoughts and feelings of Tolkien, the man.

Songs
Songs for the Philologists. London: Privately Printed, 1936.
The Road Goes Ever On. Boston: Houghton Mifflin, 1967.

Anthologies
Sir Gawain and the Green Knight. Ed. J.R.R. Tolkien, and E.V. Gordon. Oxford: Clarendon, 1925.
Ancrene Wisse. Ed. J.R.R. Tolkien. London: Oxford University Press, 1962.

Scholarly Books
A Middle English Vocabulary. London: Oxford University Press, 1922.
Beowulf: The Monsters and the Critics. London: Oxford University Press, 1937.
Chaucer as a Philologist. London: Oxford University Press, 1943.
The Return of the Shadow: The History of the Lord of the Rings. London: Unwin Human, 1988.

Secondary Sources

Bibliographies
Kolich, August M. "J.R.R. Tolkien." British Novelists, 1930–1959. Ed. Bernard Oldsey. Detroit, MI: Gale, 1983.
West, Richard C. Tolkien Criticism: An Annotated Checklist. Kent, OH: Kent State University Press, 1970.

Biographies
Carpenter, Humphrey. Tolkien: A Biography. Boston: Houghton Mifflin, 1977. Tolkien did not approve of biography; it is ironic, therefore, that late in life he seems to have made preparation for his biography by annotating a number of old letters and adding explanatory notes on some of his papers.
Grotta, Daniel. The Biography of J.R.R. Tolkien: Architect of Middle-earth. Philadelphia: Running Press, 1976. Tolkien was a large man, but in every other way, he seems to have been a hobbit.
Kolich, August M. "J.R.R. Tolkien." British

Novelists, 1930–1959. Ed. Bernard Oldsey. Detroit, MI: Gale, 1983. Kolich suggests that Tolkien's Middle-earth develops three types of "Archetypes."

Books
Beard, Henry N., and Douglas C. Kenney. Bored of the Rings: A Parody of J.R.R. Tolkien's The Lord of the Rings. New York: New American Library, 1969. Tolkien not only wrote parodies; he inspired them as well. The tone of this book can be ascertained from the following quote, "Now it is a curious fact that Dildo never told this story explaining that he had gotten the Ring from a pig's nose or a gumball machine—he couldn't remember which . . . "
Crabbe, Katharyn F. J.R.R. Tolkien. New York: F. Ungar, 1981. Crabbe notes that Tolkien's three major works look at the same characters, places, and events of the quest from three different perspectives.
Duriez, Colin. The Tolkien and Middle-earth Handbook. Tumbridge Wells, England: Monarch, 1979. This book is written in a dictionary format.
Evans, Robley. J.R.R. Tolkien. New York: Warner Paperback Library, 1972. Part of a series entitled "Writers for the Seventies."
Flieger, Verlyn. Splintered Light: Logos and Language in Tolkien's World. Grand Rapids, MI: Eerdmans, 1983. As a linguist, Tolkien was fascinated with words; he therefore uses words to conjure up power, variety, and magic.
Fonstad, Karen Wynn. The Atlas of Middle-earth. Boston: Houghton Mifflin, 1981. Tolkien warned his readers not to ask to see the bones boiled to make the soup. Fonstad notes that the more Tolkien's world differs from the real world the more difficult it becomes to keep it credible. She compares Tolkien's subjective map to those of medieval cartographers.
Giddings, Robert, ed. J.R.R. Tolkien, This Far Land. London: Vision Press, 1984; Totowa, NJ: Barnes & Noble, 1983. This book contains articles dealing with the problems and difficulties encountered in The Lord of the Rings and suggests that for all of these problems there are ultimately answers.

Giddings, Robert, and Elizabeth Holland. *J.R.R. Tolkien: The Shores of Middle-earth*. New York: Aletheia, 1981. This book is about the construction, mythology, and deep thematic structure of *The Lord of the Rings*. The tone is light.

Harvey, David. *The Song of Middle-Earth: J.R.R. Tolkien's Themes, Symbols and Myths*. Boston: Allen & Unwin, 1985. Harvey examines Tolkien's writings not as derivation, but as mythology. His organization is therefore thematic.

Helms, Randel. *Tolkien and the Silmarils*. Boston: Houghton Mifflin, 1981. *The Silmarillion* was basically linguistic in its inspiration, as it was to provide the necessary background for the "history" of the Elvish tongues.

Isaacs, Neil D., and Rose A. Zimbardo, eds. *Tolkien and the Critics: Essays on J.R.R. Tolkien's The Lord of the Rings*. Notre Dame, IN: University of Notre Dame Press, 1968. Isaacs and Zimbardo are convinced that in general enormous popularity can act as a deterrent to critical activity and in fact made The Lord of the Rings "eminently suitable for faddism and fannism, cultism and clubbism" (1).

———, eds. *Tolkien: New Critical Perspectives*. Lexington: University Press of Kentucky, 1981. Like the Isaacs and Zimbardo 1968 anthology, this volume is a continuation of the editors' attempt to distinguish between those efforts produced by and for Tolkien fans and those which have value for serious students (or readers) of literature.

Johnson, Judith Anne. *J.R.R. Tolkien: Six Decades of Criticism*. Westport, CT: Greenwood Press, 1986. Here there is no attempt to differentiate popular from scholarly criticism or to distinguish between reviews, review articles, articles, and essays.

Kocher, Paul H. *Master of Middle-earth: The Fiction of J.R.R. Tolkien*. Boston: Houghton Mifflin, 1972. Secondary worlds of the imagination should be internally consistent, and be filled with strangeness and wonder arising from their freedom from being dominated by observable fact. But, they should also be grounded in the primary world, because in order for an audience to feel sympathy and interest for persons or things, they must recognize a good deal of themselves and the world of their everyday experiences.

Lobdell, Jared, ed. *A Tolkien Compass*. La Salle, IL: Open Court, 1975. Lobdell's book sticks very closely to Tolkien's text and is designed "to show that within the world of the Tolkien fans there is scholarship, high seriousness, and good writing" (3).

Mathews, Richard. *Lightning from a Clear Sky: Tolkien, The Trilogy, and The Silmarillion*. San Bernardino, CA: Borgo Press, 1978. C.S. Lewis described Tolkien's "illumination" of the vision of millions of readers as "lightning from a clear sky." Mathews considers this to be an apt metaphor.

Miesel, Sandra. *Myth, Symbol, and Religion in The Lord of the Rings*. New York: T.K. Graphics, 1973. Miesel suggests that the secondary world of *The Lord of the Rings* is self-consistent and that it offers recovery, escape, and consolation to people in the primary world.

Nitzche, Jane C. *Tolkien's Art: A Mythology for England*. London: Macmillan, 1979. Tolkien considered himself not to be an inventor of story so much as a discoverer of legend. His legend ranges from the large and cosmogonic to the level of a romantic fairy story.

Noel, Ruth S. *The Mythology of Middle-earth*. Boston: Houghton Mifflin, 1977. Noel defines the functions of myths and indicates that mythologies have evolved in virtually all cultures because in all cultures humans face the same challenges, ask the same questions, and live in awe of the same natural forces.

O'Neill, Timothy R. *The Individual Hobbit: Jung, Tolkien and the Archetypes of Middle-earth*. Boston: Houghton Mifflin, 1979. O'Neill believes that Jung and Tolkien both draw their waters from the same enchanted well. Both Jung and Tolkien are concerned with "the transforming archetypes of Self-realization and the personifying archetypes of the various characters in the psyche" (xiii).

Petty, Anne C. *One Ring to Bind Them All: Tolkien's Mythology*. University: University of Alabama Press, 1979. Petty's book is based on Joseph Campbell's delineation of the four basic aspects of myth.

Purtill, Richard L. *J.R.R. Tolkien: Myth, Morality, and Religion.* San Francisco: Harper and Row, 1984. Purtill feels qualified to write about Tolkien's attitudes toward myth, morality, and religion because he, like Tolkien, is a university professor, has written fantasy, lived in England, is a Catholic, and is familiar with the Church of England.

Ready, William. *The Tolkien Circle.* Chicago: Henry Regnery, 1966. Ready states that Tolkien wields language easily, using riddles, evocations, incantations, songs, rhymes, poetry, brave talk, and slippery talk (43).

———. *The Tolkien Relation: A Personal Inquiry.* Chicago, IL: Henry Regnery, 1966. Ready agrees with Herbert Merritt that Tolkien is a man of "lore." For Ready, this word implies that Tolkien is a man of "counsel and learning, scholarship, erudition, guile and more—the marks of a wizard" (3).

———. *Understanding Tolkien and The Lord of the Rings.* New York: Warner Paperbacks, 1969. Ready believes that Tolkien's stories were made to provide a world for the languages rather than the reverse.

Rogers, Deborah Webster, and Ivor A. Rogers. *J.R.R. Tolkien.* Boston: Twayne, 1980. Rogers and Rogers declare that the main thing wrong with Tolkien criticism would be to consider the criticism more important than the works which inspired it.

Salu, Mary, and Robert T. Farrell, eds. *J.R.R. Tolkien, Scholar and Storyteller: Essays in Memoriam.* Ithaca, NY: Cornell University Press, 1979. This festschrift is a tribute to Tolkien by his students and colleagues. Part 1 is an introduction to the man himself; in part 2 Tolkien's major interests—Old Norse, Old English, and Middle English—are discussed; and in part 3 his popular writings, especially *The Lord of the Rings,* are discussed.

Simpson, Catharine. *J.R.R. Tolkien.* Columbia Essays of Modern Writers, No. 41. New York: Columbia University Press, 1969. Tolkien often treats words not as reference, but as things in and of themselves. He implies that specific languages and sounds radiate specific moralities.

Strachey, Barbara. *Journeys of Frodo: An Atlas of J.R.R. Tolkien's The Lord of the Rings.* New York: Ballantine, 1981. This atlas contains five maps and the Frontispiece, drawn to different scales.

Tolkien, Christopher. *The War of the Ring: The History of the Lord of the Rings, Part Three.* London: Unwin Hyman, 1990. J.R.R. Tolkien proposed two books to be added to his trilogy: book 4, *The Ring Goes East,* and book 5, *The War of the Ring.*

Tyler, J.E.A. *The New Tolkien Companion.* New York: St. Martin's Press, 1979. Tyler notes that *The Lord of the Rings* is chiefly a "translated historical narrative from the pen of Frodo Baggins (heir of that Hobbit who had written the earlier, smaller section), with some amendments by contemporary sources and additions by later hands" (viii).

West, Richard C., ed. *Tolkien Criticism: An Annotated Checklist.* Rev. ed. Kent, OH: Kent State University Press, 1981. West attributes the enormous interest in Tolkien's fiction to stem in part from its being so multifaceted as to make it enjoyable to almost any age or degree of literary sophistication.

Wilson, Colin. *Tree by Tolkien.* London: Covent Garden Press, 1973; Santa Barbara, CA: Capra, 1974. Wilson compares the world created by Tolkien with the world created by Wagner in the Ring cycle. Considers *The Lord of the Rings* to be "a children's book which has somehow got out of hand."

Articles

Donahue, Thomas S. "Tolkien's Elvish." *WHIMSY,* 1 (1983): 64–65. Donahue suggests that Tolkien was having fun with future scholars whom he knew would seriously try to trace the words in his works back to legitimate sources.

Helms, Randel. "Last Gleanings from the Red Book: Scholarly Parody in The Adventures of Tom Bombadil." In *Tolkien's World.* Boston: Houghton Mifflin, 1974, pp. 126–47. Helms claims that Tolkien's *The Red Book of Westmarch* is a parody not only of *The Red Book of Hergest* but of the poor research methods of its editor.

Don L.F. Nilsen

Townsend, Sue

Born: Leicester, April 2, 1946
Education: South Wigston Girls High School,
 Leicestershire
Marriage: Keith Townsend; three children;
 Colin Broadway; one child

Biography

Sue Townsend was born in Leicester on April 2, 1946. The daughter of Grace and John Ball, both bus conductors, Townsend was educated at South Wigston Girls High School. Although she left school two weeks before turning fifteen, she has read avidly from the age of eight, finding particular inspiration from the Russian "greats," P.G. Wodehouse, John Updike, and various diarists. By working at a series of jobs, ranging from a dress shop worker to a hot dog seller to a trained community worker, she gathered information for use in her writing. Her careful observations of society's victims, who have included, at times, herself and her family, allow her to write about social problems with sensitivity and understanding as well as humor.

Townsend was a "secret scribbler" for about fifteen years before her first play was produced in 1979. She felt compelled to hide her work partly because of society's attitude that women should do housework, not write. For Townsend, writing comes first, and the housework gets "sandwiched in" somehow.[1]

Beginning her career as a playwright, Townsend joined the writers' group at the Phoenix Arts Centre in Leicester in 1978. Her play *Womberang* won a Thames Television bursary in 1980, allowing her to become writer-in-residence at the Phoenix for a year. During this time, she wrote play after play, learning her craft through constant practice. In the past decade, many of her plays have been produced in London's West End.

Townsend is best known for creating Adrian Mole, an adolescent diarist whose trials include acne, his parents' infidelities, and his unrecognized attempts to become an intellectual. The books about this youngster, now translated into twenty-three languages, have sold more than five million copies in Britain alone, where they are enjoyed by young and old alike. The American edition, unfortunately marketed for young adults, has been less successful. Aside from the radio play and novels, Adrian has been the subject of a stage play with music, a television series, and commercial products such as computer games and diaries.[2] The

author allows her creation to endorse only products that encourage writing.

A full-time writer since 1982, Townsend has contributed to periodicals, including the *Times* (London) and the *New Statesman*, and had a regular column in *Woman's Realm* from 1983 to 1985. She recently completed the film script called *A Mole in Moscow* for Thames Television and is currently writing a screenplay adaptation of her novel *Rebuilding Coventry*. She also adapted her novel *The Queen and I* (a number 1 best-seller), in which a Republican government dispatches the royal family to a council estate in the Midlands, for production in the fall of 1994 at the Royal Court Theatre. The newest Adrian Mole book, *Adrian Mole, the Wilderness Years*, was published in 1993. In it, a twenty-six-year-old Mole will study the newt population for the Department of the Environment.[3] Amusingly, as a marketing gimmick, the Mandrin paperback edition of this volume included, a card for a game, "The Great Mole Hunt," which readers could play to win "1000s of PRIZES!"

Townsend, who has three grown children by her first marriage to Keith Townsend, now lives in Leicester with her husband Colin Broadway and their daughter.

Literary Analysis

Adrian Mole, Townsend's most popular character, has been compared to such famous adolescents as Huck Finn and Holden Caulfield.[4] To create Adrian, Townsend poured the experiences from her own youth and from her job at a youth club onto paper. The books capture a spirit of adolescence common to both sexes.

Adrian is an earnest, well-meaning boy, beset by a steady stream of threats to his existence which range from the family dog's erratic and repellent behavior to his parents' infidelities and illegitimate children. His diary entries, with their sudden shifts of focus and voice, exaggerate the barely contained chaos of his life. As problems pile up, Adrian reacts to them all with equal intensity; in fact, much of the humor stems from his inability to sort the trivial from the essential and his failure to see anything funny in his situation.

In the first entry of the *Secret Diary*, published in 1982, Adrian attempts to impose order on his life. He lists eight New Year's resolutions, including: "help the blind across the road," "stop squeezing my spots," and "be kind to the dog."[5] But, events soon rush out of control, and by March he complains: "So the worst has happened, my skin has gone to pot and my parents are splitting up."[6]

An incurable worrier, Adrian braces himself for the worst, but life constantly surprises him. Often his worries prove irrelevant: his acne, for example, troubles no one but himself. However, it takes him months to recognize that "kind" Mr. Lucas next door is his mother's lover. Adrian's innocent misreading of what, to the reader, are obvious situations endears him to us.

Although Adrian overreacts to some of his problems, others stem from real social conditions beyond his control. The book is a vivid satire of Margaret Thatcher's England, encompassing joblessness (for Adrian's father), cutbacks in social programs (no more school lunches), and inadequate care for the elderly (the neglected Bert Baxter). The innocent and conscientious Adrian takes responsibility for himself, his parents, and even Bert.

On the whole, *Secret Diary* has a light tone, which continues into parts of the sequel, *The Growing Pains of Adrian Mole*, written in 1984. For example, in the second book Adrian can't read the *Guardian*'s editorial on the Falklands War because the paper is "not in its usual place in the dog's basket."[7] On the whole, though, this book has a darker tone. By re-reading his early diary entries, Adrian recognizes the innocence he has lost. He now has a cynical view of adults who "break all their own rules."[8] Near the end of the book, he labels himself "an existential nihilist,"[9] and even tries homelessness for a week.

Still, hope does not vanish from Adrian's life. His love for his girl friend Pandora, shown as both ridiculous and touching throughout the diary, remains intact. And, perhaps most importantly, Adrian keeps writing. Thanks to his diary, he has a start at writing, a start at understanding his life, and perhaps one day, he will start to laugh.

In the Adrian Mole books Townsend considers problems such as poverty, homelessness, and joblessness that threaten the security and dignity of the characters. In her plays she often takes one such problem and explores it in detail. For example, in *Groping for Words*, first produced in 1983, an ill-assorted group of individuals struggles to deal with the problem of illiteracy. Irony pervades the play from the opening scene, which places a literacy class in a kindergarten setting: the tiny chairs and tables mock the adult students, reminding them that they are misfits.

The irony deepens as the students face the barriers to literacy imposed by society. According to one man, who loses his job and despairs of finding another, "They don't want us to read! There ain't room for all of us is there?"[10] Doubly ironic, it is this man who provides the play with a sense of hope when he finally seeks help for his illiteracy. Without knowing if he will ever learn to read, or if reading will in fact improve his life, he acknowledges that the effort is worthwhile.

In the 1982 play *Bazaar & Rummage*, the characters struggle with a different handicap: agoraphobia. Three women leave their homes for the first time in years for the absurd purpose of holding a rummage sale. Through a patchwork of comic situations, the characters gradually uncover their frailties, fears, and hopes. As in the Mole books, the serious and trivial are juxtaposed for comic effect as the characters struggle for balance between extremes. For instance, one woman cries both because of "how wicked the world is" and because her vacuum cleaner has broken down.[11]

As Townsend says in her introduction, the caregivers of these women have a "sometimes parasitic stranglehold" on their charges,[12] keeping them in an unbalanced state. For instance, the excessive caregiving of one woman's husband insures that she need never leave the house. More sinister is the social worker who uses the women to fill her own empty life; if they get well, she will suffer. At the end of the play the women form a tentative community independent of their care-givers. Like the characters in *Groping for Words*, they may never overcome their handicap, but their struggle together will be worthwhile. According to the author, "agoraphobia is only an outward symptom of other deeper problems."[13] At stake is the way that women are controlled by those close to them.

The theme of control also appears in Townsend's favorite play, *The Great Celestial Cow*, written in 1984. On one level, the play examines the culture-shock experienced by Sita, an East Indian woman uprooted from her rural homeland to live in Leicester. But, Sita adapts well enough to English languages and customs; her main struggle is with the restrictions imposed by her own male-dominated society.

At first, the older women in Sita's family side with the men. In the end, though, they join forces: together, in a dream-like sequence that shows women auctioned like cattle, these women defeat the auctioneer, a symbol of male oppression.

In Townsend's novel *Rebuilding Coventry*, published in 1988, the title character also escapes from a caregiver (her husband) when she takes to the streets of London after accidentally killing a neighbor with an Action Man doll. Coventry leaves her husband and children (the "dreary" people) for a series of picaresque adventures in London. In these adventures the novelist satirizes the way that Prime Minister Thatcher's policies have isolated and hardened people at all levels of society. All who meet Coventry quickly label and dismiss her as worthless, until she meets another homeless woman who works to improve both of their lives. Although the book has an improbable resolution, it reaffirms the idea of people working together to bring about change.

Much of the writer's humor comes from the struggles of her characters to rise above the mundane annoyances that clutter their lives. For example, in *The Secret Diary*, Adrian finds himself becoming an intellectual from "all the worry" (15). Spurred on by writing his first poem ("it only took me two minutes," 16), he works to keep his brain active with "improving" books. His choices form an ironic counterpoint to the dreary reality of his life: he reads *The Female Eunuch* while his mother flirts with feminism and with Mr. Lucas; he tries *Hard Times* after the electricity is cut off. Such comic incongruity underlines the tawdriness of his life while poking gentle fun at his attempts to take himself too seriously.

We find more incongruity in the recurring theme of the naif, the character who plunges into unfamiliar surroundings without the appropriate knowledge or equipment. For example, Sita arrives in Leicester with no knowledge of English, Coventry flees to London without her purse, and Adrian tries homelessness with the dubious help of the family dog. Even when Adrian is ready to return home, he has trouble bringing his adventure to a halt: "I have asked three policemen the time, but none of them have spotted me as a runaway. It's obvious that my description hasn't been circulated."[14] Ultimately, the awkwardness of Sita, Coventry, and Adrian in their new surroundings reflects their inability to find their place in their regular lives.

While the author is always quick to uncover the incongruities in her characters' lives, she saves her sharpest satire for the social conditions of contemporary Britain. For example, in *Rebuilding Coventry,* she exposes the wretched conditions of the homeless along with the heartlessness of those with the power to bring about change. When Coventry looks for shelter in London, she discovers Cardboard City, a collection of dwellings "constructed on the DIY principle from the detritus of other people's lives."[15] Ironically, Dodo, with whom Coventry shares a shelter, expresses nostalgia for the mental hospital that she was forced to leave: "You could be as mad as you liked . . . And it was warm and safe."[16] Later, when Coventry and Dodo join a Cabinet Minister at a dinner party, snatches of dialogue reveal the upper-crust stand on social issues: "You can say what you like about Hitler, but he knew . . . how to *prioritize*."[17] We also meet a representative of the police force, the boorish Detective Inspector Sly, who never offers comfort to the grieving: "in his experience it only started them off again."[18]

Although Townsend exaggerates her situations and characters for comic effect, she remains remarkably true to the reality of her own experience. In 1989, she set down some of this experience in a group of essays, *Mr. Bevan's Dream*, for the CounterBlasts series (books that tackle critical social issues). Here, for example, we meet a headmaster, a supposed "care-giver" who demonstrates his collection of canes while complaining that "most of the children in his school were mongrels."[19] In these essays we see the grim reality that Townsend transforms with her comic vision.

Summary

Sue Townsend, most famous for creating the character of Adrian Mole, has produced plays, novels, and articles since the late 1970s. She finds humor, notably irony and satire, her best tool for making "sense of the world."[20] A serious social purpose underlies all of her writing as she strives to uncover problems often ignored by society. With her comic touch, she gives dignity to her characters and shows that even the most unpromising lives have the "possibility of change."[21]

Notes

1. Helga McCue, ed., "Townsend, Sue." In *Something About the Author*, vol. 55 (Detroit: Gale, 1988), p. 160.
2. Elizabeth Thomas and Jean W. Ross.

"Townsend, Sue," *Contemporary Authors*, New Rev. Ser., vol. 127 (Detroit: Gale, 1989), p. 459.

3. The material on Townsend's current work comes from a March 1993 publicity release obtained from her secretary, Kate Boldry.
4. Thomas and Ross, p. 457.
5. *The Secret Diary of Adrian Mole Aged 13–3/4.* (London: Methuen, 1982), p. 11.
6. *Ibid.,* p. 46.
7. *The Growing Pains of Adrian Mole.* (London: Methuen, 1984), p. 154.
8. *Ibid.,* p. 76.
9. *Ibid.,* p. 167.
10. *Bazaar & Rummage, Groping for Words, and Womberang.* (London: Methuen, 1990), p. 137.
11. *Ibid.,* p. 37.
12. Introduction, *Bazaar & Rummage*, p. vii.
13. *Ibid.,* p. vii.
14. *Growing Pains*, p. 184.
15. *Rebuilding Coventry,* p. 92.
16. *Ibid.,* p. 93.
17. *Ibid.,* pp. 112–13.
18. *Ibid.,* p. 38.
19. "Mr. Bevan's Dream," *CounterBlasts 9* (London: Chatto, 1989), p. 31.
20. *Commire,* p. 160.
21. Thomas and Ross, p. 459.

Selected Bibliography
Primary Sources

Plays
In the Club and Up the Spout. Produced 1979.
Womberang. Produced 1979.
The Ghost of Daniel Lambert. Produced 1981.
Dayroom. Produced 1981.
Captain Christmas and the Evil Adults. Produced 1982.
Bazaar & Rummage. Produced 1982.
Groping for Words. Produced 1983. Rev. as *Are You Sitting Comfortably?* (produced 1986).
Clients. Produced 1983.
Bazaar & Rummage, Groping for Words, and Womberang. London: Methuen, 1984.
The Great Celestial Cow. London: Methuen, 1984.
Ear, Nose, and Throat. Produced 1988.
Ten Tiny Fingers, Nine Tiny Toes. Produced 1989.
The Queen and I. Produced 1994.

Novels
The Secret Diary of Adrian Mole Aged 13–3/4. London: Methuen, 1982; New York: Avon, 1984.
The Growing Pains of Adrian Mole. London: Methuen, 1984.
The Adrian Mole Diaries. London: Methuen, 1985; New York: Grove Press, 1986.
Rebuilding Coventry: A Tale of Two Cities. London: Methuen and New York: Grove Press, 1988.
True Confessions of Adrian Albert Mole, Margaret Hilda Roberts and Susan Lilian Townsend. London: Methuen, 1989.
Adrian Mole from Minor to Major. London: Methuen, 1991.
The Queen and I. London: Methuen, 1992.
Adrian Mole: The Wilderness Year. London: Methuen, 1993; London: Mandarin, 1994.

Radio Plays
The Diary of Nigel Mole Aged 13–3/4. Produced 1982.
The Growing Pains of Adrian Mole. Produced 1984.
The Great Celestial Cow. Produced 1985.
Flowers. Produced 1990.
A Ladder in the Stocking. Produced 1991.
The Ashes. Produced 1992.
The Queen and I. Produced 1992.

Television Plays
Revolting Women (contributor), 1981.
Bazaar & Rummage, 1984.
The Secret Diary of Adrian Mole series, 1985.
The Growing Pains of Adrian Mole, 1987.
The Refuge series, with Carole Hayman, 1987.
Think of England (contributor), 1991.

Essays
Mr. Bevan's Dream: Why Britain Needs a Welfare State. CounterBlasts 9. London: Chatto, 1989.

Secondary Sources
Carlson, Susan. "Townsend, Sue." *Contemporary Dramatists.* Ed. D.L. Kirkpatrick.

4th ed. Chicago: St. James, 1988, pp. 524–26. According to Carlson, Townsend's "feminism and class consciousness have led her to write committed plays about neglected groups."

McCue, Helga, ed. "Townsend, Sue." *Something About the Author*. Vol. 55. Detroit: Gale, 1989, pp. 158–62. Townsend describes how and why she became a writer.

Thomas, Elizabeth, and Jean W. Ross. "Townsend, Sue." *Contemporary Authors*. New Rev. Ser. Vol. 127. Ed. Susan M. Trosky. Detroit: Gale, 1989, pp. 456–60. A summary of Townsend's career plus a lengthy interview.

Deborah Wills

Travers, Ben

Born: Hendon, London, December 12, 1886
Education: Abbey School, Beckenham Surrey, and Charterhouse, Surrey
Marriage: Violet Mouncey, 1916; one child
Died: London, December 18, 1980

Biography

Ben Travers was born to working-class parents, Walter Francis and Margaret Burgess Travers, in Hendon, London on December 12, 1886. It was intended that he would run their family wholesale grocery business, but instead he grew to be an institution in the British theater. Travers attended the Abbey School, Beckenham Surrey, and Charterhouse, also in Surrey. He was not an excellent student, though, and in 1904 he left Charterhouse to join his family's business. However, Travers proved unskilled in business, too, and he was soon sent to the Singapore office in Malacca. While there, he began to study the plays of Arthur Wing Pinero and to develop his own style of playwriting.

Travers finally left the wholesale grocery business in 1911 and became apprenticed to John Lane at the Bodley Head publishing company. Before his apprenticeship was interrupted in 1914, Travers took part in nearly every step of the publishing process and met many celebrated literary figures. In 1914, Travers joined the Royal Naval Air Service, and during World War I he rose to the rank of major and met two lifelong friends, Violet Mouncey, whom he married in 1916, and Laurence Irving.

After the war, Travers settled with his wife and daughter in Burnham and devoted his time to writing. He revised and re-revised his plays, and he claimed to have thrown away more than 80 percent of his work. On the advice of Irving's mother, actress Dorothea Baird, Travers decided to try writing humor, and he created *The Dippers*, which he hoped would be produced by actor-manager Charles Hawtrey. Afraid that no leading actor or director would accept the farce, however, Travers rewrote it as a novel, and in 1920 it was published by Lane, who would publish all of Travers's novels. In 1921, Baird sent *The Dippers* to Golding Bright, the leading play agent in London, and ultimately the script was accepted by Hawtrey. Finally, in 1922, the play opened with Cyril Maude playing the lead. It ran for 173 performances.

Travers's second novel, *A Cuckoo in the Nest*, was published in 1922 and received good reviews, but Travers did not become an eminent author until the novel was adapted into a farce and produced by Tom Walls at the Aldwych Theatre in 1925. *A Cuckoo in the Nest* was very successful and was the first of a long series of plays written by Travers for the Aldwych company, which included the famous farcical actors Walls, Ralph Lynn, Mary Brough, Robertson Hare, Winifred Shotter, and Alfred Drayton. Known as the Aldwych Farces, *A Cuckoo in the Nest*, *Rookery Nook* (1926), *Thark* (1927), *Plunder* (1928), *A Cup of Kindness* (1929), *A Night Like This* (1930), *Turkey Time* (1931), *Dirty Work* (1932), and *A Bit of a Test* (1933) ran for a total of nearly 2,700 performances. This success inspired Travers to rewrite most of the farces as screenplays during the late 1930s. Directed by Walls, the films were popular, and many were adapted for television in the early 1970s.

Although his early success with the Aldwych Farces was not to be repeated, the author continued to write farces throughout the 1930s and 1940s. In 1936, Travers's *Chastity, My Brother* was staged at the Embassy Theatre in London and *O Mistress Mine* opened at the St. James's Theatre, London. His next notable success was not until 1938, when *Banana Ridge* was mounted at the Strand Theatre, also in London. The play was written for the increasingly popular pair of actors, Hare and Drayton, and Laurence Irving designed the especially elaborate sets and costumes. No one could be found to play a bit character who spoke the Malayan language, so Travers acted the part, never missing one of *Banana Ridge*'s 400 performances.

Travers continued to write for Drayton and Hare, and in 1939, *Spotted Dick* opened at the Strand Theatre. World War II, during which Travers rejoined the Royal Air Force, caused a short intermission in the running of the play, but when the war ended, *Spotted Dick* was performed again and ran for a total of 110 performances.

After the war, Travers wrote *Outrageous Fortune* (1947) as a farcical commentary on the nuisances of rationing. The play was popular, but it was the last play that he wrote for some time. His wife's death in 1951 induced a seventeen-year period of silence during which *Wild Horses* (1952) was the only Travers farce professionally produced.

Occasional revivals and amateur performances of the Aldwych Farces throughout this time period provided the playwright with a moderate income, and he traveled extensively. Finally, in 1968, *Corker's End* was performed at the Yvonne Arnaud Theatre, Guilford, and his last play *The Bed Before Yesterday* (1975), opened shortly after Travers's eighty-ninth birthday and was very well received.

Before his death in London on December 18, 1980, Travers received much recognition for his work, and many of his plays were revived and republished during the late 1970s. The *Evening Standard* (London) presented Travers with a special award for his services to the theater, and during Queen Elizabeth's birthday honors he was appointed Commander of the British Empire, both in 1976. In addition, a theater bearing Travers's name was constructed in Charterhouse. Though his farces are now outdated because the targets of his humor no longer exist, many of the plays have been reproduced as period pieces and are still pleasing audiences.

Literary Analysis

Farce has traditionally been ignored and considered illegitimate by drama critics, but Travers's farces constituted some of the most popular theater of the early twentieth century. This is partly due to the dramatist's treatment of current issues and the resultant relevance of his farces to the audiences of the 1920s and 1930s. This, however, does not account for the success of revivals of his plays in recent years.

Travers was greatly influenced by the man generally considered England's foremost farceur, Arthur Wing Pinero. About his late-nineteenth- and early twentieth-century predecessor

Travers wrote, "I discovered for myself the real secret of Pinero's mastery and success, the observance, in every line and every episode, of the value of climax." Travers went beyond his exemplar, though. In effect, he developed a formula for writing farce that has been the model for all subsequent British farce such as Joe Orton's *What the Butler Saw* and *Loot*, Alan Ayckbourn's *Bedroom Farce* and *The Norman Conquests*, and Tom Stoppard's *Dirty Linen*. His methods were effective enough that he was able to successfully create numerous farces with little variation in form, but without boring repetition.

Travers wrote as a product of early twentieth-century Britain and for the audiences of that society. It was during the time between the world wars that the farce which Travers developed was most needed and most appreciated. Farce has typically come to the foreground of theater production when the social structures of a society are threatened with breaking down; Travers's plays, although first of all entertaining, were also commentaries on the social traditions and problems of the 1920s and 1930s.

Because his plays are set in a distinct period, they have not enjoyed the success in performance in recent years that they did when they were originally mounted. The reason for this is that a large portion of the humor is character driven, and the characters were then recognized as familiar stereotypes either tenaciously clinging to the strict social standards or villainously straying from them. Unfortunately, to modern audiences they seem to be highly exaggerated caricatures. In fact, much of the humor in the author's plays is achieved by his too-accurate portrayal of reality.

The personalities that Travers created for the stage are the foundations of each of his plays, all of which followed, with some variation, the formulas that he adapted from foreign farce and which he further developed. The dramatist explained that the characters in his plays "are recognizable types of human beings. The funniness must be in the situations and circumstances . . . and these are only funny because the characters are so recognizably human" (*Vale of Laughter*, 92–93).

In the creation of characters, especially for the well-loved Aldwych Farces, Travers's first obligation was to satisfy the stipulations of the acting troupe that would perform his plays. His two lead actors, Walls and Lynn, each had to receive the same number of laughs whenever they shared a scene. Walls unvaryingly played the deceiving ladies' man, and Lynn the asinine simpleton. After their triumphant work in *Rookery Nook* with Hare playing "the intimidated little male relative," Travers explained that the farces then "generally had to contain a situation in which [Hare] stood between an inexorable Walls and a more plausible but no less ruinous Lynn, to be fleeced of his fair repute, of his cash, of his trousers" (*Vale of Laughter,* 124).

In Travers's plays, these three male characters generally work together, helping one another to untangle their circumstantial problems. The situations are always complicated by the extraordinary beauty of a pristinely innocent girl, as in *Rookery Nook* when Rhoda appears at the end of the play, dispelling all preconceived assumptions, which are forgotten because she is so virginal. There are, nevertheless, characters whose reputations are not so commendable. Travers's plays normally include an unbelievably ugly and meddling woman such as *Plunder*'s Mrs. Leverett, whose clothes could be sold "to a man who makes circus tents!" (20). Amusing insults of this nature abound in the farces, as evidenced later in the same play by the following exchange:

> JOAN. . . . My grandfather married you?
> MRS. HEWLETT. . . . He did.
> JOAN. He must have been mad.
> D'ARCY. He must have been blind.

Finally, there are always the menacing men who try to ruin everything for the lead characters. Among them are some especially clichéd foreign types such as Putz, the domineering German father in *Rookery Nook*.

Because the characters were so stereotypical and because the social hierarchy of the time was so important, the abnormal social placement of the characters provided much of the humor. For example, in *Plunder*, no one is where he or she belongs. The housekeeper has become the mistress of the house while the dead master's daughter has been turned out with nowhere to go, and the respected members of high society have grown rich by practicing thievery.

These characters did not seem outrageous to Travers's audiences, but they were contrived enough to prevent the audiences from relating directly to them and feeling any sort of personal shame or blame. Travers's characters allowed the viewers to laugh at themselves, especially when the characters were given outrageous and punning names such as D'Arcy Tuck, Cherry Buck, Clive Popkiss, and Poppy Dickey.

Travers also made use of irony in many of his plays. Although the characters may not have been laughing, the audience was sure to find quite amusing the contrast of their understanding of the truth and the characters' misunderstandings and attempts to discover the truth. In *Thark*, Benbow and Ronny dance around the truth at Benbow's expense:

> BENBOW. I've had some very awkward—news, my boy. Your aunt's coming back home to-night.
> RONNY. What? And Kitty?
> BENBOW. No. Just your aunt—that's enough, ain't it?
> RONNY. I say, why is auntie coming home? Has she heard something about you?
> BENBOW. Wat d'yer mean? There is nothing to hear about me.
> RONNY. I know. That's why I asked in that surprised way.
> BENBOW. There's nothing to hear, I tell you. . . .
> RONNY. I know—that's just what I say. And very glad I am of it.
> BENBOW. Glad of what?
> RONNY. Glad that she heard nothing—because she can't have, because there's nothing to hear. . . .
> BENBOW. I can think of nothing that could have brought her home.
> RONNY. Well, naturally, *I* can think of nothing. . . . But now auntie's coming home, Kitty will be left all alone in Bath.
> BENBOW. That's all right, she's old enough to look after herself. . . .
> RONNY. I know, and that's just when girls begin to get looked after. You know, uncle, Bath's a very dangerous place. . . . Full of Beaux—you know—Beau Somethings.
> BENBOW. Not now. Only old people with gout.
> RONNY. Oh, I see, bow legs.
> BENBOW. . . . They only go there to drink water.
> RONNY. . . . Oh, really? I'm surprised you've heard of the place.

The puns are characteristic as well.

The only one of Travers's farces that is a mystery to the audience as much as to the characters is *Plunder,* in which the vital fact which provides the solution to all the problems of the play is kept a secret until the last scene. However, even in this play, as in most Travers farces, the audience often knows that there is someone behind a door (or someone *else* behind a door) while the characters' actions are completely incongruent with that fact.

The typical setting for a Travers farce is perfectly suited for this kind of ironic play and farcical humor. Nearly every scene in the writer's plays is set in the two-level interior of a home. At the top of the stairs there are normally at least two bedroom doors that allow for games of sexual hide-and-seek, while the several doors that exit into other rooms off the main area provide quiet passageways and niches where a character can see without being seen. The layout is useful in providing for the kind of quick entrances and exits, one door closing just as another opens, that are common ingredients in stage farce. And, as Travers recalls in *Vale of Laughter,* this kind of humor was responsible for one of the best moments in *Thark,* the haunted-room sequence in which the "incident of Tom and Ralph as joint occupants of a small doublebed [*sic*] produced a longer and louder sequence than any other scene between the two in the history of Aldwych farce" (172–73).

As Christopher Innes points out, the hectic pacing reflects one of farce's basic themes, "man as helpless victim of circumstances" (260). Innes goes on to claim that the absurd improbability of the on-stage actions similarly mirrors the "incongruity between the obvious innocence of his protagonists, and their unambiguously compromising situations" (263).

The physical aspect of acting as exemplified in the characters' bodily movements is important in performances of Travers's works as well. For example, Putz of *Rookery Nook* characteristically makes a quirky bob whenever he is excited; the audience can hardly help but be amused.

Physical antics such as this are necessary because much of the plot of many of Travers's farces is very simple. In the creation of his farce, he adopted Pinero's formula, which Travers explained as, "Act 2—the sympathetic and guileless hero is landed into the thick of some grievous dilemma or adversity. Act 1—he gets into it. Act 3—he gets out of it." Thus, the body of the plays is composed simply of the characters dealing with a situation and finding themselves in compromising positions.

Ironically, for most of Travers's career (until the Licensing Act of 1737 was abolished in 1968) all drama was strictly regulated by censorship laws. Political topics, sexual subjects, and profane language were disallowed, and his plays sometimes seem to be a series of things that don't happen. In *Rookery Nook,* for instance, the momentum of the play is based on the attempt to convince everyone that nothing happened between Rhoda and Gerald; indeed, nothing did happen between Rhoda and Gerald. Except for *The Bed Before Yesterday,* no man and woman in Travers's farces share a bed, and usually such an action is not even suggested.

The author wisely took advantage of the censorship stipulations, and he drew humor out of the fact that things weren't said and didn't happen. However, when censorship was abolished in the 1970s, Travers was no longer afraid to discuss sexuality and use profanity. Consequently, he wrote *The Bed Before Yesterday,* which documents a woman's overdue discovery of the joys of sex and includes a lying whore and an immoral, drunken, swearing young man. Travers explained, "I think I really started to write the play for my own enjoyment and self-satisfaction—to prove to myself—if to no one else, that I could exploit this new found freedom."

The Bed Before Yesterday was a wonderful success for Travers and, had he been a younger man, it might have marked a turning point in his career. However, Travers died less than five years later and was unable to completely explore the censor-free world. Nevertheless, he is remembered as a great British farceur who held captive theater audiences of two decades.

Summary

In the 1920s and 1930s, Ben Travers raised the form of stage farce to its high point in the British theater. His refinement of the format and his creation of recognizable characters placed in contemporarily significant situations made his plays among the most popular produced during the period.

Selected Bibliography

Primary Sources

Plays
The Dippers, April 10, 1922, Court Theatre,

Liverpool.

The Three Graces, January 26, 1924, Empire Theatre, London.

A Cuckoo in the Nest, July 13, 1925, Court Theatre, Liverpool. London: Bickers, 1938.

Rookery Nook, June 21, 1926, King's Theatre, Southsea. London: Bickers, and London and New York: French, 1930.

Thark, June 27, 1927, King's Theatre, Southsea.

Plunder, June 18, 1928, King's Theatre, Southsea.

Mischief, July 9, 1928, King's Theatre, Southsea.

A Cup of Kindness, April 29, 1929, King's Theatre, Southsea.

A Night Like This, February 18, 1930, Aldwych Theatre, London.

Turkey Time, May 26, 1931, Aldwych Theatre, London.

Dirty Work, March 7, 1932, Aldwych Theatre, London.

A Bit of a Test, January 30, 1933, Aldwych Theatre, London.

Chastity, My Brother, May 18, 1936, Embassy Theatre, London.

O Mistress Mine, December 3, 1936, St. James's Theatre, London; revised as *Nun's Veiling*, 1953, London.

Banana Ridge, April 27, 1938, Strand Theatre, London.

Spotted Dick, August 23, 1939, Strand Theatre, London.

She Follows Me About, October 15, 1943, Garrick Theatre, London.

Outrageous Fortune, November 13, 1947, Winter Garden Theatre, London.

Runaway Victory, 1949, London.

Wild Horses, November 6, 1952, Aldwych Theatre, London.

Corker's End, October 22, 1968, Yvonne Arnaud Theatre, Guilford.

The Bed Before Yesterday, December 9, 1975, Lyric Theatre, London.

Fiction

The Dippers. New York and London: John Lane, 1920.

A Cuckoo in the Nest. London: John Lane, 1922; Garden City: Doubleday, Page, 1925.

Rookery Nook. London: John Lane, 1923; Garden City: Doubleday, Page, 1925.

Mischief. London: John Lane, and Garden City: Doubleday, Page, 1925.

Thark. London: French, 1927.

The Collection Today. London: John Lane, 1929.

Plunder. London: Bickers, 1931.

The Dippers, Together with Game and Rubber and The Dunkum Jane. London: John Lane, 1932.

Hyde Side Up. London: John Lane, 1933.

A Cup of Kindness. London: Bickers, 1934.

Turkey Time. London: Bickers, 1934.

Banana Ridge. London: Bickers, 1939.

She Follows Me About. London: French, 1945.

Outrageous Fortune. London and New York: French, 1948.

Wild Horses. London: French, 1953.

Nun's Veiling. London: French, 1956.

Vale of Laughter. London: Bles, 1957.

The Bed Before Yesterday. London and New York: French, 1976.

Five Plays. London: Allen, 1977. Includes *A Cuckoo in the Nest, Rookery Nook, Thark, Plunder,* and *The Bed Before Yesterday.*

Mischief. New York: Harper & Row, 1978. Includes *Mischief, Rookery Nook,* and *A Cuckoo in the Nest.*

A-Sitting on a Gate. London: Allen, 1978.

Screenplays

Rookery Nook. Herbert Wilcox/Gaumont-British, 1930.

Chance of a Night Time. Gaumont-British, 1931.

Thark. Gaumont-British, 1932.

A Night Like This. Gaumont-British, 1932.

Just My Luck. Gaumont-British, 1933.

A Cuckoo in the Nest. Gaumont-British, 1933.

Turkey Time. Gaumont-British, 1934.

Lady in Danger. Gaumont-British, 1934.

A Cup of Kindness. Gaumont-British, 1934.

Dirty Work. Gaumont-British, 1934.

Fighting Stock. Gaumont-British, 1935.

Stormy Weather. Gainsborough/Gaumont-British, 1935.

Foreign Affairs. Republic Pictures/Gaumont-British, 1935.

Pot Luck. Gainsborough/Gaumont-British, 1936.

Dishonour Bright. Capitol-Cecil/General Film, 1936.

For Valour. Capitol/General Film, 1937.

Second Best Bed. Capitol/General Film, 1938.

Old Iron. Tom Walls/British Lion, 1938.

Miscellaneous

Editor. *The Leacock Book*. London: John Lane, 1930.

Editor. *Pretty Pictures, Being a Selection of the Best American Pictorial Humour*. London: John Lane, 1932.

Secondary Sources

Barker, Felix. "Rookery Nook." *Plays and Players*, 398 (November 1986): 16–17. A production review of a revival of what may be Travers's most popular work.

Garebian, Keith. "A Cuckoo in the Nest."

Hendrickx, Johan Remi. *Ben Travers and the English Farce Tradition. Dissertation Abstracts International*, 42, 1 (July 1981): 226A.

Innes, Christopher. *Modern British Drama, 1890–1990*. Cambridge and New York: Cambridge University Press, 1992, pp. 260–67. Innes examines Travers's work ("society as farce") in his chapter "The Comic Mirror—Tradition and Innovation." A good overview of the plays and techniques.

Richards, Horace. "Being Funny Is No Joke! Says Ben Travers in an Interview with Horace Richards." *Theatre World*, 30 (December 1938): 248.

Shorter, Eric. "Ben Travers." *Drama*, 119 (Winter 1975): 22–26.

Small, Barbara J. "Ben Travers." In *Dictionary of Literary Biography: Modern British Dramatists, 1900–1945*. 2 vols. Ed. Stanley Weintraub. Detroit: Gale Research, 1982. The dramas are considered in the context of Travers's life.

Smith, Leslie. "Ben Travers and the Aldwych Farces." *Modern Drama*, 27 (September 1984): 429–48. Smith examines the importance of actors and acting in the presentation of Travers's farces.

Trewin, J.C. "Rare Ben Travers." *Plays and Players*, 23 (February 1976): 12–18.

Shannon Gale

Trollope, Anthony

Born: London, April 24, 1815
Education: Harrow (1823–1827); Winchester (1827–1830)
Marriage: Rose Heseltine, June 11, 1844; two children
Died: London, December 6, 1882

Biography

Anthony Trollope was born in London on April 24, 1815, the fourth child of Thomas Anthony Trollope, an unsuccessful "gentleman farmer," and Frances Trollope, who became a prolific novelist to save the family. Because of the family's financial difficulties, Trollope attended three different schools, including Harrow (1823–1827) and Winchester (1827–1836), in five years. His *Autobiography* records a childhood of perpetual floggings; he was "always in disgrace." Furthermore, he said, "My boyhood was, I think, as unhappy as that of a young gentleman could well be" because of the humiliations brought about by poverty.[1]

Trollope began in those early years a systematic form of escape—creating stories that went on for months at a time with himself as the hero. The humiliations increased as shopkeepers no longer extended Anthony credit; nor did he have the money to give the servants their expected quarterly tip. His feelings of shame culminated when he was forced to leave Winchester because his fees had not been paid. Financial problems effectively limited his formal education; while both of his brothers attended university, Trollope could not continue his education because he failed to earn a scholarship to attend either Cambridge or Oxford. The family fled to Belgium in 1834 to escape their creditors despite the financial success of his mother's first book, *Domestic Manners of the Americans*. While in Belgium, his sister Emily, his brother Henry, and his father all began dying of consumption. "They were all dying," recalled Anthony, "except my mother, who would sit up night after night nursing the dying ones and writing novels all the while,—so that there might be a decent roof for them to die under" (*Autobiography*, chapter 2). Fiction, for both Trollopes, represented escape and financial survival. No wonder, that some fifty years later, Anthony meticulously recorded every pound earned by writing.

In 1834, Trollope left for London and a job as a Junior Clerk in the General Post Office. He was nineteen. He was never to see Emily, Henry, or his father again. His first seven years with the post office were little different from his life at school, for he "was always in trouble" (chapter 3). In 1840, life altered significantly; Trollope left London for a job as a surveyor's clerk in the Central Post Office in Ireland, leaving behind twenty-six "years of suffering, disgrace, and inward remorse" (chapter 4).

He seems to have found himself in Ireland. His job offered him more responsibility; he married Rose Heseltine on June 11, 1844 (the couple had two sons); he discovered what would become his lifelong love of hunting; and he wrote his first novel, *The Macdermots of Ballycloran*, in 1847. He produced novels with astonishing regularity while he worked for the post office. His fiction eventually became so profitable that Trollope was able to quit his job in 1867. In those twenty years before he left the post office, he produced nineteen novels, four travel books, helped create the *Fortnightly Review*, and contributed regularly to the *Pall Mall Gazette*. In 1868, freed from the responsibilities of his job and while writing of Phineas Finn's political career, Trollope stood as a Liberal candidate for parliament from Beverly. The experience of losing a dirty campaign became the subject of his novel *Ralph the Heir*. All told, Trollope wrote forty-seven novels and sixteen other books, including travel books on North America, the West Indies, and Australia. His later books, including his satiric look at English morals, *The Way We Live Now*, were not as well received as his earlier work. In the last years of his life, he worked at his *Autobiography*. He suffered a stroke in November 1882 and died in London on December 6 of that year.

Literary Analysis

Trollope's reputation has undergone volatile shifts since his lifetime. He is currently receiving tremendous scholarly and biographical attention. This appreciation of his work brings his literary reputation full circle. Although he was not without his critics during his lifetime, Trollope was one of the most popular writers of the period. While his popularity did decline in his last years, it was the publication of his *Autobiography* that initiated a critical backlash against his work that lasted well into the twentieth century. In his memoir, he methodically listed the sum earned from each of his books, a total of nearly £70,000. He noted that he made no claim to "literary excellence . . . But I do lay claim to whatever merit should be accorded to me for persevering diligence in my profession" (chapter 20). That workman-like attitude, seen also in his narrator's asides in the novels, greatly damaged his posthumous reputation. As Henry James saw it, the revelations in the *Autobiography* only confirmed what was evident in the novels themselves: Trollope took pleasure in refusing to see himself as an artist. James com-

plained that Trollope "took a suicidal satisfaction in reminding the reader that the story he was telling was only, after all, a make-believe."[2] Critics since James have often concurred, finding Trollope "anti-literary" and inartistic.[3] The content as well as the form of his novels has received critical comment. The novelist has been charged with pandering to the assumptions of his age—assumptions so antithetical to our own.[4] One is reminded that, incomprehensible as it now seems, Dickens was once seen as pandering to Victorian culture. No longer is Trollope dismissed as an apologist for the Victorian patriarchy; recent critics have persuasively demonstrated that Trollope is anything but a conventional spokesman for Victorian earnestness.[5]

Contemporary literary theory has reversed the Jamesian critical trend, finding in Trollope a playful, rhetorical stance that is anything but "anti-literary." As the twentieth century nears its end, Trollope's artistry has never been considered so carefully by academicians, and readers continue to find pleasure within the pages of a Trollope novel. His current popularity with readers can be measured by the host of biographies of Trollope written since 1988: C.P. Snow, R.H. Super, Richard Mullen, and, most recently, N. John Hall and Victoria Glendinning have provided us with massive versions of the writer's life. Proof of his popularity can be seen also in Pickering and Chatto's decision to produce for the first time a complete edition of his forty-eight novels. By the year 2000, all of Trollope's novels will be available for the first time since his death. He continues to be read today because, like other Victorians still read for pleasure, he did not draw a line between entertainment and art. The vitality of the nineteenth-century novelists is a direct result of their commitment to entertain us.

Trollope uses humor for subversive purposes. The narrator's wit reveals the juxtaposition between appearance and reality and deflates the pretensions of Victorian life. Thus, comedy provides readers with a clarity of vision, an intelligent and sympathetic perspective on human and cultural failings. In *Trollope and Comic Pleasure*, Christopher Herbert has written the most informed and persuasive book examining how Trollope's comedy subverts the assumptions of his age. Herbert questions the generally held critical assumption that comedy's end is ultimately serious, tracing "comedy's mischievous gift for arousing anxiety" in

Trollope's fiction. As contemporary reviews and the twentieth-century critics who share James's objections demonstrate, Trollope *does* arouse anxiety. It is no wonder, since, as Herbert sees it, the "frivolous and impudent character" of comedy was "so obviously antagonistic to the Victorian's cult of earnestness." Trollope's fiction, Herbert argues, has "two separate strata": the realism for which Trollope is so famous and a "submerged stratum with its . . . elaborate deployment of the comic mode." It is in this latter stratum that the author takes "seditious liberties" with his culture and his readers.[6]

Humor becomes a way of seeing what is wrong in the world, of undercutting Victorian values. It abounds in Trollope's prodigious body of work. It is primarily located in two areas: the rhetorical humor rests largely in the narrator's control of everything in the novel; the structural humor resides in his characters and their explicit, sometimes outrageous, comic scenes. The rhetorical humor is the subtler, of course, but it exerts considerable influence. One of the real pleasures to be found in reading nineteenth-century English fiction comes in the reader's relation with the narrator. Jane Austen and William Makepeace Thackeray, whom Trollope admired, give the reader the illusion of spending time with a wise companion, valued above all things for their wit and intelligence. Trollope, more than any other writer given the length of time that one can "spend" with him if one chooses to read all of his work, becomes a trusted guide to the follies and tragedies of life. The narrator's voice, so biting, yet so often bemused, so remarkably tolerant, finds humor in the very fabric of life. Trollope never descends to what he called "that worst of all diseases,— a low idea of humanity" (*The Eustace Diamonds*, chapter 28). The insight essential to his humor in both *The Chronicles of Barsetshire* and *The Palliser Novels* is that good is never purely good. Nor are those characters who excel at making life uncomfortable for others— Mr. Slope, the Proudies, or Adolphus Crosbie— ever purely bad. Thus, not only his passionate schemers but the best of men and women of his novels are the object of his rhetorical humor.

His fiction is rarely purely comic. In the later works especially, the structural humor is often lodged in several of the subplots which humorously reflect the more sobering main plot. For instance, the main plot of *The Last Chronicle of Barset*, with its focus on clerical madness and monomania seems headed for tragedy, yet Trollope locates humor in the subplot of amorous intrigue in London.

The humor in *The Chronicles of Barsetshire* changes over the course of the six novels. Nowhere is the satire as sharp or the mock-heroic apparatus as extended as in *The Warden*. Trollope had not yet found his voice—or his audience, it seems. The book earned just over £20 in two years, which later prompted Trollope later to note with characteristic self-deprecation, "Indeed, as regarded remuneration for the time, stone breaking would have done better" (*Autobiography*, chapter 5).

The tone of *The Warden* is harsher and less subtle than it is elsewhere in *The Chronicles of Barsetshire*. The mock-epic perspective dominates. Trollope burlesques the obsession with reform by employing a grand rhetorical style in this novel. The discrepancy between the misguided reformers and the narrator's elevated language signals Trollope's disapproval. The ludicrously overstated language calls attention to the reverence with which people accept the pronouncements of the London reform newspaper, the *Jupiter*: "Who has not heard of Mount Olympus,—that high abode of all the powers of type, that favoured seat of the great goddess Pica, that wondrous habitation of gods and devils, from whence, with ceaseless hum of steam and never-ending flow of Castilian ink, issue forth eighty thousand nightly edicts for the governance of a subject nation?" (chapter 14).

While the tone is never so sharp as in this first novel, throughout the entire series Trollope focuses on cultural change as the subject of his humor. He presents a series of juxtapositions in this first novel which will dominate the second, *Barchester Towers*: between the past and the present; the quiet traditions of Barchester and the rush of London; the formal rituals of Septimus Harding's High Church versus the religious enthusiasm of Mrs. Proudie's Low Church. In this novel, Trollope tells the tale of a good man, Septimus Harding, who comes to question the justice of his professional position, living on a very secure income as Warden of Hiram's Hospital, a charity. In doing so, the novelist celebrates tradition and the old guard, despite their real flaws, and mounts a scathing humorous attack on the young and the agents of reform.

The reformers who seek to change Barchester do considerable harm in this novel: the twelve old bedesmen of Hiram's Hospital are worse off once Harding vacates his post.

Trollope succeeds in making his point that good and evil are never comfortably distinct from one another by making the agents for reform blind to the good they destroy. But, he does so with humor. He attacks John Bold (the hero of the romance plot who wins Eleanor Harding as his bride) as a reformer who undermines society itself. Trollope relies upon understatement to establish his point: in Bold's attempt to right all wrongs, he had "so worried three consecutive mayors, that it became somewhat difficult to find a fourth" (chapter 2). When Trollope turns beyond the purviews of Barchester itself, his rhetorical humor becomes more scathing, but his point is the same: zealous reform undermines society. The *Jupiter* finds that "Parliament is always wrong." On the other hand, "It is a fact amazing to ordinary mortals that the *Jupiter* is never wrong" (chapter 14). In a famous passage, when the narrator turns to Thomas Carlyle, cast as "Dr. Anticant," he identifies the central problem with all reformers: "No man ever resolved more bravely than he to accept as good nothing that was evil; to banish from him as evil nothing that was good. 'Tis a pity that he should have recognized the fact, that in this world no good is unalloyed, and that there is but little evil that has not in it some seed of what is goodly" (chapter 15). Trollope's recognition of this fact allows him to view his characters as never purely "good" or "bad" and often wondrously funny.

Trollope's Barchester is no utopia. It is a place where ambition and passion thrive, but they do so beneath the surface of a sedate Cathedral city. The author finds humor in the discrepancy between what ought to be in the life of a Cathedral community and what, in fact, it is. In his humorous handling of the all-too-human "vices," he acknowledges the need for reform in the world—and the church. His clerics reveal what is wrong with much of Victorian England: an earnest, moral exterior masks a self-centered worldliness. Archdeacon Grantly, whose excitability and profound confidence in his own position makes him one of Trollope's most humorous "good" characters, opens the second novel in the series, *Barchester Towers*, in a scene presenting the "unalloyed" nature of goodness. Grantly is caught between his own vain ambition to become bishop and his love for his dying father, the present bishop. Kneeling at the father's death-bed, the archdeacon contemplates his fate. If his father dies before the prime minister is out of office—an event that is sure to happen at any moment—he will become bishop. Grantly is not really bad; the "proud, wishful, worldly man" could not wish to hasten his father's inevitable death, though hastening it by a matter of hours would further his own episcopal career (chapter 1). Trollope manages to balance the poignance of the elder man's death with the archdeacon's humorous scramble to get the news of the vacancy to the outgoing prime minister. But, it is too late; a new ministry has made a Dr. Proudie the Bishop of Barchester. On that appointment rests much of the subsequent humor of this book.

The two characters who dominate the two worlds in conflict, Archdeacon Grantly and Mrs. Proudie, are both passionate defenders of their own flank of the Church. They are both blustery people, confident in the sanctity of their own position, who leap to the heights of passion at the very mention of the other side. These egoists are so alike that all that Trollope has to do is bring them together and the situation becomes comic. Mrs. Proudie provides her husband much distress and gives the reader pleasure in direct proportion.

The humor resides in both Mrs. Proudie's handling of the bishop and the narrator's handling of the "bishopess." The narrator relies upon reversal; he repeatedly leads his readers in one direction, only to twist his meaning with a final qualification. A seasoned Trollope reader waits for and then relishes the twist, the inevitable "but": "Dr. Proudie may well be said to have been a fortunate man, for he was not born to wealth, and he is now bishop of Barchester; but nevertheless he has his cares . . . he has a wife." Sometimes the final twist concisely sums up what all of the evidence suggests: "It is not my intention to breathe a word against the character of Mrs. Proudie, but still I cannot think that with all her virtues she adds much to her husband's happiness. The truth is that in matters domestic she rules supreme over her titular lord . . . and stretches her power over all his movements, and will not even abstain from things spiritual. In fact, the bishop is henpecked" (chapter 3). The comic punch comes from the simplicity of the last sentence. Likewise, the narrator makes clear his dislike of the slippery Mr. Slope from his first introduction. Readers quickly learn to enjoy the careful build-up toward the final damning phrase: Mr. Slope's "face is nearly of the same color as his hair, though perhaps a little redder: it is not unlike beef, beef, however one would say, of a bad quality." Even when he seems to compliment, the writer twists the praise for his own humorous ends. After cataloguing the flaws of Slope's physiognomy, Trollope sets us up for a reversal: "His nose, however, is his redeeming feature: it is pronounced, straight, and well-formed; though I myself should have liked it better did it not possess a somewhat spongy, porous appearance, as though it had been cleverly formed out of a red coloured cork" (chapter 4).

The humor in this novel is broader than it will be elsewhere in the series. A consideration of Trollope's technique and structure in one scene demonstrates its forceful presence. The novelist brings many of the humorous characters together for the first time when the new bishop and his wife hold a reception at the palace. From that encounter springs much of the novel's plot—where clerical ambitions collide with the misunderstandings which complicate romance. As the plot progresses, we see Trollope exploring the comic possibilities and moral ramifications of excessive ambition.

Central to this scene, if not to the novel as a whole, is La Signora Madeline Vesy Neroni, a beautiful, bewitching woman who, like other strong characters in the novel, comes from outside the comfortable world of Barchester to disrupt the peace. Trollope describes her as a witty woman who possesses the "fire of passion." Cruelty replaces love and combines with her courage, her desire to master, and her "wish for mischief" to create comic chaos. Her beauty is made more tantalizing by a self-induced paralysis. Injured while riding, she chooses never to walk again rather than reveal her physical imperfection. Before the party begins, the bishop, enjoined not to sit upon the sofa as it is to be kept for a lady, jumps from it. He meekly asks if it is for a "particular" lady, and his wife refuses to explain. "She has got no legs, papa," his daughter announces (chapter 10). Madeline is brought into Mrs. Proudie's drawing-room upon a sofa and the men in the room flock to her. Thus, Madeline is both the object of some of the novel's humor and the orchestrator of the final comic undoing of Mr. Slope. As James R. Kincaid observes, Madeline uses "a kind of Freudian humour to transform her pain into clever parody and continual witty victories."[7] Her pain provides her with the energy to unmask Slope's hypocritical ambition.

The sofa serves as the focal point for the evening's disasters. Madeline's ne'er-do-well brother Bertie strains the bishop's powers of conversation as they stand by his sister, who is draped provocatively upon the sofa. The bishop confides to Bertie "with considerable dignity" that his responsibility is very great. Bertie responds: "'Is it?' said Bertie, opening wide his wonderful blue eyes. 'Well; I never was afraid of responsibility. I once had thoughts of being a bishop, myself.' 'Had thoughts of being a bishop?'" returns the incredulous Dr. Proudie (chapter 10). By the end of the evening, Dr. Proudie and the hypocritical Mr. Slope will be entranced by what they see as the angelic Madeline Neroni. We are repeatedly given the temptress and the priests together; Mr. Slope's attraction to Madeline, while he simultaneously woos the rich widow Bold, allows Trollope to explore the disjunction between appearance and reality in the cathedral city. Slope's attraction to Madeline alienates him from his great supporter, the bishop's wife. Once Mr. Slope begins to act independently of Mrs. Proudie, much of the novel's humor—and a great deal of the episcopal characters' discomfort—depends upon the power conflict as husband, wife, and Mr. Slope all fight to run the diocese.

In a moment of physical comedy characteristic of the sub-plots throughout Trollope's work, Madeline's sofa is shoved across the room accidentally; as it gathers momentum it takes part of Mrs. Proudie's train with it: "Gathers were heard to go, stitches to crack, plaits to fly open, flounces were seen to fall and breadths to expose themselves." Bertie, on his knees, begs forgiveness, promising to seek the help of the fairies, as he attempts to free Mrs. Proudie's dress. The already furious Mrs. Proudie takes the allusion to the fairies as "direct mockery": "'Unhand it, sir!' said Mrs. Proudie." The narrator's understated comment follows immediately: "From what scrap of dramatic poetry she had extracted the word cannot be said" (chapter 11). Madeline laughs and the two women become enemies. Thus, the charming Bertie deflates the pretentious earnestness of the palace as his sister instigates and enjoys mischief.

Madeline's power is confirmed and the joke about her legs reintroduced when the central characters swarm around her sofa at the *fête champêtre* at Ullathorne Manor. She has only to look derisively at the Countess De Courcy to defeat her: "The Countess De Courcy, in spite of her thirty centuries and De Courcy castle, and the fact that Lord De Courcy was grand master of the ponies to the

Prince of Wales had not a chance with her." Moments later Mrs. Proudie and the Countess exchange their opinions, ending with a characteristic twist:

"She's an abominable woman, at any rate," said Mrs. Proudie.

"Insufferable," said the countess.

"She made her way into the palace once, before I knew anything about her; and I cannot tell you how dreadfully indecent her conduct was."

"Was it?" said the delighted countess.

"Insufferable," said the prelatess.

"But why does she lie on a sofa?" asked Lady De Courcy.

"She has only one leg," replied Mrs. Proudie.

"Only one leg!" said Lady De Courcy, who felt to a certain degree dissatisfied that the signora was thus incapacitated. "Was she born so?"

"Oh, no," said Mrs. Proudie,—and her ladyship felt somewhat recomforted by the assurance,—"she had two. But that Signor Neroni beat her, I believe, till she was obliged to have one amputated. At any rate, she entirely lost the use of it."

"Unfortunate creature!" said the countess, who herself knew something of matrimonial trials. (chapter 37)

Madeline and Mrs. Proudie are the two strongest women in the novel. One asserts her power through her beauty while the other asserts authority by renouncing her femininity.

The rich humor of the novel lies in the role reversal in the Proudie household. "In truth, Mrs. Proudie was all but invincible; had she married Petruchio, it may be doubted whether that arch wife-tamer would have been able to keep her legs out of those garments which are presumed by men to be peculiarly unfitted for feminine use" (chapter 33). The discretion of the Victorian conventions does not permit Trollope the freedom to use the word "trou-

sers." Elsewhere, Trollope is less decorous; Mrs. Proudie has all but become a man. The hen-pecked bishop, no Petruchio he, is no match for his wife. At one point, having enjoyed a temporary triumph over his wife's authority, he retires to their bedroom. The seemly narrator leaves us at the bedroom door. Victorian conventions once again increase the humor because we are left to witness only the results of the marital battle. Mrs. Proudie's victory has marked the bishop physically: he is unmanned; he is "attenuated," "one might almost say emaciated"; he has "aged materially" (chapter 32).

If the forces of reform, the John Bolds and *Jupiters*, seem to win the battle in *The Warden*, much of the humor of *Barchester Towers* rests upon their failure to transform the magnificent cathedral and its clerics to the new evangelical mood. Mr. Slope is routed. His amorous and professional aspirations are both undone, at least locally. It is the one thing that Mrs. Proudie and Madeline Neroni come to agree upon: that Slope must be destroyed. Mrs. Proudie is so outraged by his flirtations with Madeline and his attempt to exert his own power against hers that she battles him for control of her husband. Indeed, "Mrs. Proudie was the Medea of Barchester; she had no idea of not eating Mr. Slope . . . she would pick him to the very last bone" (chapter 33). And, it is not just in the "spiritual" skirmish for power that Slope fails; Madeline punishes him for daring to desire both the demure but rich Eleanor Harding and herself. While the cathedral city is not unduly influenced by the Evangelical fervor emanating from the palace, Mrs. Proudie retains power over her husband and so the comic conflict continues throughout the six-volume series. Still, the problems raised in this novel are resolved: Barchester withstands the attack from without.

Later in the series, Trollope's humorous appreciation of human failings continues, but his confidence that past values can withstand the present pressures fades. In *The Small House at Allington*, as in *Barchester Towers*, he presents a closed, conservative, comfortable world where the traditional values of duty, firmness, and constancy are articulated by the old bachelors Lord De Guest and Squire Dale. As always with Trollope, though, the "good is not unalloyed." Christopher Dale had remained "obstinately" true to his unrequited love. He is "a constant, upright and by no means insincere man . . . thin and meagre in his mental attributes." Despite his failings, he is "worthy of regard in that he had realized a path of duty and did endeavour to walk therein" (chapter 1). For Trollope, that is high praise indeed. In this essentially conservative humorist's work, the values of the aristocrats are the conscience of the country.

This comfortable world is disrupted by the appearance of Adolphus Crosbie from London who woos and wins one of Trollope's most interesting heroines, Lily Dale. The author's satiric view of Crosbie comically diminishes him with the characteristic twist. He has pretensions to be a "swell": "He had set himself down before the gates of the city of fashion, and had taken them by storm; or, perhaps, to speak with more propriety, he had picked the locks and let himself in." Trollope deflates Crosbie's pretensions further: " . . . even great men acknowledged the acquaintance of Adolphus Crosbie, and he was to be seen in the drawing rooms, or at any rate on the staircases, of Cabinet Ministers" (chapter 2). When Crosbie comes to regret his love for Lily, he extricates himself from his engagement so that he may marry for money. As Lily continues to be faithful to this faithless man, the novelist questions whether such traditional fidelity is a virtue.

Trollope clearly presents Crosbie as an agent for the values of a new world. Squire Dale cannot understand how it is possible that a man can jilt his fiancee: "It makes me feel that the world is changed, and that it is no longer worth a man's while to live in it" (chapter 27). Dale cannot fathom that Crosbie should go unpunished. What the Squire does not know is that the man *is* punished. Much of the novel's humor centers on the price that Crosbie pays for his infidelity. The man stuck on the staircases of the powerful gains access to their drawing room by marrying money but in doing so he comes to pay a terrible price. Trollope presents Crosbie's wooing of Lady Alexandrina De Courcy, while he is still engaged to Lily, as a battle: "the lady was fighting her battle with much courage, and also with some skill" (chapter 23). The lady wins the battle and Crosbie must pay the price: "in this world all valuable commodities have their price; and when men such as Crosbie aspire to obtain for themselves an alliance with noble families, they must pay the market price for the article which they produce." The narrator's tone and his humorous handling of Crosbie makes readers enjoy watching Crosbie suffer. There is justice in this world, although it is not the justice that the Squire expects. Unlike

"villains" in the earlier novels, Crosbie himself acknowledges that he made a terrible mistake. If Crosbie is punished, however, so is Lily. The main plot asks this question: is she punishing herself? Quite clearly, the answer seems to be "yes." Far from accepting his culture's ideal of womanhood, Trollope explores the degree to which the culture pushes women into destructive molds.

While the love story has the most somber implications of anything yet seen in this series, in the various subplots, which reflect the major theme of constancy in love, elements of broad farce are used to examine the consequences of inconstant love. Johnny Eames, who loves Lily, is too much of a "hobbledehoy" to be a real hero and temporarily gets caught in the snares of the wily Amelia Roper, the daughter of his London boardinghouse landlady. Like Crosbie, Amelia hopes to improve her status through marriage. Pressured by her, Johnny makes the mistake of writing of his love for Amelia with the "perfidious pencil [that was] near to his hand." Amelia's utter ignorance of worldly ways suggests that Johnny may well escape. Her only concern is "whether such a promise, in order that it might be used as legal evidence, should not have been written in ink." Trollope, who often views love as war, paints the comedy of the London boardinghouse scenes with a broad brush. He casts the vying feminine wiles of Amelia and Mrs. Lupex, a married woman with a notoriously loose reputation, as a naval battle. Mrs. Lupex, the adulteress, has "more matured power, a habit of fighting which had given her infinite skill, a courage which deadened her to the feeling of all wounds while the heat of the battle should last . . . But then Amelia carried the greater guns, and was able to pour in heavier metal than her enemy could use" (chapter 11).

In a world in which Johnny struggles to become a man as he tries to win the girl, he does manage a certain amount of heroism of the old-fashioned sort. In one of Trollope's funniest scenes, Johnny rescues Earl De Guest, who has a red handkerchief in his pocket, from an attacking bull. Trollope undercuts Johnny's heroism by focusing his attention on the bewildered bull. When Johnny jumps into the fray, Trollope writes of the bull, "When the animal saw with what unfairness he was treated, and that the number of his foes was doubled, while no assistance had lent itself on his side, he stood for a while, disgusted by the injustice of humanity."

The bull charges, first toward Johnny and then the Earl, "with that weak vacillation which is as disgraceful in a bull as in a general." Bested by the two men, the bull "looked wistfully at his last retreating enemy," who finds safety on the other side of a ditch. The bemused bull becomes, for a moment, a representative of Johnny and his hopeless love. The narrator muses, "How many of us are like the bull, turning away conquered by opposition which should be as nothing to us, and breaking our feet, and worse still, our hearts, against rocks of adamant" (chapter 21).

Johnny's penchant for amorous dallyings with dangerous women continues in the final novel in the series, *The Last Chronicle of Barset*, in which he meets a far more skillful enemy than Amelia or the bull. While the main plot is the series' darkest, focusing as it does on the question of whether the poor cleric Mr. Crawley stole money, Johnny becomes involved in the fast world of those new to London and considerable wealth. Trollope provides us with a comedy of manners wherein "the game of love-making" is life's greatest pleasure. There is, of course, a caveat: the game is fun for the players, "providing [they] can be quite sure that there shall be no heart in the matter. Any touch of heart not only destroys the pleasure of the game, but makes the player awkward and incapable and robs him of skill" (chapter 26). Johnny is almost trapped by this amoral world of surface glitter when he meets a more sophisticated foe than Amelia. Madalina Demolines is a cunning actress, interested in catching Johnny as a husband. She is so cunning that in a final farcical scene he must avail himself of a policeman's assistance to escape unscathed.

One joy in reading Trollope's novels is the ongoing relationship with characters over time. In bringing the series to a close, Trollope gathers together the major characters from the early novels with those from *Small House*: the lives of Lily, Crosbie, and Johnny become intertwined with those of Mr. Harding, his daughter Eleanor, Archdeacon Grantly, and the Proudies. In two parallel confrontation scenes concerning Mr. Crawley's fate, Mrs. Proudie twice meets her match. Readers have been waiting for this since *Barchester Towers* and the humor and the pleasure is all the greater for that several-thousand-page wait. Mrs. Proudie, in a "dress of awful stillness and terrible dimensions," displays the "awful face of the warrior, always ready for combat." She carries "her ar-

mor all complete, a prayer-book, a bible, and a book of hymns" (chapter 17). Despite the allegations made about him, Mr. Crawley reveals great dignity when discussing his future with the bishop. He steadfastly refuses to acknowledge Mrs. Proudie's presence or answer her questions. Mrs. Proudie fumes; he recognizes the bishop's misery and smiles. The narrator sputters Mrs. Proudie's frustrations: she "had never before encountered a clergyman so contumacious, so indecent, so unrevered,—so upsetting." Thus, the "half-convicted thief" is victorious (chapter 18). Later, Mrs. Proudie faces "a foe as wary as herself" in the form of Dr. Tempest, the spokesman for Crawley. Dr. Tempest remains patient and principled. Mrs. Proudie's famous temper ignites; Dr. Proudie writhes in powerless agony. Readers cheer Dr. Tempest on.

Trollope's ability to combine comedy with pathos is never clearer than in his resolution of the Proudie story. Just as readers glory in her defeat, they find that both Dr. Proudie and his wife have grown in complexity from the stock characters of hen-pecked husband and dominating wife. The writer explores the poignant feelings of the broken bishop whose life has been made miserable by his own weakness but whose elevated position in the world is due to his wife's strength. At the height of her victory against her husband, Mrs. Proudie loses, for "she had loved him dearly, and she loved him still . . . At the bottom of her heart she knew that she had been a bad wife. And yet she had meant to be a pattern wife! She had meant to be a good Christian; but she had so exercised her Christianity that not a soul in the world loved her" (chapter 66). The chapter concludes with a twist that adds further poignancy and complexity to this couple.

Trollope ends this novel and his series by observing that "to me Barset has been a real country, and its city a real city, and the spires and towers have been before my eyes, and the voices of the people are known to my ears, and the pavement of the city ways are familiar to my footsteps" (chapter 84). It is because the country, city, and its people become real to readers as well that his great popularity continues more than a century after his death.

Much of this series' humor can be found in the love plots where mistaken alliances and a lack of communication complicate the lives of young lovers. In *Doctor Thorne* and *The Last Chronicle*, as with the centuries-old stage tradition, parental objection (and, in a Victorian variation on the theme, the young lady's principles) impedes the course of true love. Critics disagree about Trollope's attitude toward his heroines—with good reason. Clearly he is ambivalent. While observing that John Bold was not "good enough" for his wife, Trollope writes of Eleanor, "Hers was one of those feminine hearts which cling to a husband not with idolatry, for worship can admit of no defect in its idol, but with the perfect tenacity of ivy." The passage continues, calling to mind the conclusion to Thackeray's *Vanity Fair*: "As the parasite plant will follow even the defects of the trunk which it embraces, so did Eleanor cling to and love the very faults of her husband" (chapter 2). So, too, will Lily cling to and love the very faults of Crosbie. The power of these gentle, tenacious girls do not harm others as their more active counterparts, the comic ones (Amelia, Madalina, Madeline Vesy Neroni, and Mrs. Proudie) do. If Herbert is right that comedy's principle characteristic is its ability to produce anxiety, and Trollope's novels suggest that he is, then Trollope chose the perfect approach to consider the power that women wield. Dr. Proudie is only an example *in extremis*; men, it often seems, do not have a chance against women in the diocese of Barchester.

In the political world of the Palliser novels things are different. Alice Vavasor, the heroine in *Can You Forgive Her?*, like Lily as well as Emily Warton in *The Prime Minister*, "had been mistaken in her first love" (chapter 3). Having made that mistake, Alice doubts herself worthy of her second lover. "Can you forgive her?" Trollope asks; the question throughout the novel is "can she forgive herself?"

It is the other sort of heroine, the strong (and sometimes purely self-interested) woman, who most interests Trollope in the Palliser novels. It is not Lucy Morris, the "good" heroine of *The Eustace Diamonds*, who dominates that novel but rather Lizzy Eustace, pretty, rich, clever, and bad. As a Peer of the realm contemplates marriage with this engaging woman, Trollope, with his characteristic twist, observes that Sir Florian "knew nothing about her . . . for aught he knew she might be afflicted by every vice to which a woman can be subject. In truth, she was afflicted by so many, that the addition of all the others could hardly have made her worse than she was. She had never sacrificed her beauty to a lover,—she had never sacrificed anything to anybody,—nor did she drink. It would be difficult, perhaps, to say

anything else in her favour" (chapter 9). She is, in fact, a liar and a cheat who all but steals the disputed diamonds of the title. Her selfishness and her naivety about the world of law lead her into a deepening fix from which she tries to extricate herself.

The novelist explicitly sets up Lucy and Lizzie as "opposite in their characters as two poles," one good, one bad. Most characters are not so fixed, so consistent. Frank Greystock, like Johnny Eames, because his goodness is unalloyed, is torn between the two poles: "There are human beings who, though of necessity single in body, are dual in character:—in whose breasts not only is evil always fighting against good,—but to whom evil is sometimes horribly, hideously evil, but is sometimes also not hideous at all." They will not suffer from the "vulgar" vices, "but ambition, luxury, self-indulgence, pride, and covetousness will get hold of them, and in various moods will be to them virtues in lieu of vices. Such a man was Frank Greystock" (chapter 18). For Trollope, the vices of ambition, luxury, self-indulgence, and pride are the source of humor. The pressures of Victorian culture push all of those self-interests under ground so that surface "virtues" are juxtaposed against the reality of grasping ambition.

The Eustace Diamonds was not originally intended to be part of the series. Still, those novels that were have a full complement of independent women. In the two Phineas books alone we are brought to appreciate the spirited Lady Laura, the witty Violet Effingham, Madame Max, and Glencora Palliser for their strengths. A strong woman's story will not always proceed with humor and end in love and happiness, as Lady Laura's story proves, but through the strength and independence of these women Trollope continually questions the cultural restrictions placed upon the gender. One of the most respectable dowagers considers Violet's independent nature and frantically calls upon higher powers: "Why had not the law, or the executors or the Lord Chancellor, or some power levied for the protection of the proprieties, made Violet absolutely subject to her guardian till she should be subject to a husband?" (*Phineas Finn*, chapter 45). Clearly, it is those who seek to levy power to protect proprieties that Trollope satirizes.

Perhaps the most interesting woman in the *Palliser* series is Marie (Madame Max) Goesler, a woman of great wealth, beauty, and intelligence. Madame Max has been called by one critic "the most perfect gentleman in Trollope's novels."[8] She is far removed from the manly Mrs. Proudie; Madame Max's adventuresome spirit, her integrity, and her respect for herself do not make her the object of Trollope's wit but rather an eloquent advocate for an appreciation of life. She has considerable power. Injured by the old Duke of Omnium's snub, Madame Max does what no one has done: she refuses him what he wants. First, she teaches him to want her by initiating a flirtation, and then she refuses his eventual proposal of marriage. While Finn, the man who will become her husband, looks to her for friendship and elsewhere for love, Madame Max breaks the convention of courtship by proposing to him herself. In each of the novels that includes a character learning to make a proper choice in a spouse, be it Alice Vavasor or Finn, Trollope reworks the tradition of stage comedy to his own ends. As in *Can You Forgive Her?*, the broad humor in the subplot serves to reflect the main subject of choosing a proper spouse.

Trollope tells the story of Lady Glencora Palliser (later Duchess of Omnium) in the six Palliser novels, *Small House at Allington*, and *Miss Mackenzie*. In the ongoing account of first her passionate attachment to Burgo Fitzgerald and her subsequent prudent marriage to Plantagenet Palliser, Trollope depicts a marriage very different from that of the Proudies. Nevertheless, the issues of power and love are intertwined here too. There is less comedy in the Palliser's relations than we find in the Proudies, as the novelist charts the struggle of a strong woman, sometimes tempted to rush "headlong to the devil . . . tempted to rebel" (*Can You Forgive Her?* chapter 68). At times her story seems headed for disaster and far away from humor. However, Lady Glencora is a fighter and she wins a number of battles with her wit—and her claws. "You must hold your ground," she advises Alice, "and show your claws,—and make [the old cat] know that if she spits, you can scratch . . . She'll find I'm of the genus, but of the tiger kind, if she persecutes me" (chapter 43).

By the time that the Duke becomes prime minister, Glencora, committed to her husband and his political career, balances her frustrations against her ability to see humor in any situation. In *The Prime Minister*, Glencora is irritated with Plantagenet for not attending the lavishly successful parties that she has thrown to support his coalition government. She approaches the problem with humor: "I feel myself to be a Lady Macbeth, prepared for the murder of any Duncan or any Daubeny who may stand in my lord's way. In the meantime, like Lady Macbeth herself, we must attend to the banqueting. Her lord appeared and misbehaved himself; my lord won't show himself at all,—which I think is worse" (chapter 11). Her tone is not unlike that of the narrator, who observes of a politician who dislikes the political coalition, "He had so accustomed himself to wield the constitutional cat-of-nine-tails, that heaven will hardly be happy [for] him unless he be allowed to flog the cherubim," and of a popular budget, "Budgets, like babies, are always little loves when first born. But as their infancy passes away, they also become subject to many stripes. The details are less pleasing than was the whole in the hands of the nurse" (chapter 12). Ultimately, it is in the narrator's witty and often ironic exploration of this series' political world that one finds subtle, on-going humor.

Summary

Anthony Trollope is a master of finding humor in the social, religious, political, and personal transformations of mid-nineteenth-century England. His work stands as an eloquent attack on the moral idealizing so central to Victorian middle-class culture. Humor is present in the narrator's perspective on human failings; the characteristic tone of detached, bemused tolerance invites us to embrace characters for their flaws as well as their virtues. While plot lines are not consistently humorous, even in the later novels, his humor is contained in the subplots which reflect the main plot.

That humor is manifest in a wide range of styles. Trollope adapts the traditional patterns of stage comedy in his romance plots in which lovers are mismatched and misguided. In his examination of the clashes between the old world and the new and between the aristocracy and middle-class climbers, his work follows the tradition of satiric comedy of manners. His subplots often contain elements of broad farce. Woven throughout these distinctly different humorous strategies and even through the most somber of the main plots, it is the subtle humor found in the narrator's voice which provides us with a rich appreciation of how funny human beings really are.

Notes

1. Anthony Trollope, *An Autobiography* (London: Blackwood, 1882), chapter 1.

Subsequent references to this text and to the fiction of Anthony Trollope appear in parenthetical notes.

2. Henry James, "Anthony Trollope," in *Essays on Literature, English and American Writers* (New York: 1984), p. 1343.

3. Walter M. Kendrick, *Novel Machine: The Theory and Fiction of Anthony Trollope* (Baltimore: Johns Hopkins University Press, 1980), p. 84. While Kendrick finds Trollope "anti-literary," Robyn Warhol finds both that Dickens and Trollope point "subtly and explicitly—to the literary nature of their texts." Robyn R. Warhol, *Gendered Interventions: Narrative Discourse in the Victorian Novel* (New Brunswick, NJ: Rutgers University Press, 1989), p. 134.

4. See Michael Sadlier's *Trollope: A Commentary* (New York: Farrar, Straus, 1949), Mario Praz's *The Hero in Eclipse in Victorian Fiction,* ed. Angus Davidson (London: Oxford University Press, 1956), and Carolyn Heilbrun, who in *Toward A Recognition of Androgyny* (New York: Knopf, 1973), p. 57, finds that Trollope "accepts without question his culture's view of women."

5. See Rebecca West, *The Court and the Castle* (New Haven: Yale University Press, 1957), who was the first to call Trollope a feminist; Richard Barickman, Susan MacDonald, Myra Stark, *Corrupt Relations* (New York: Columbia University Press, 1982); Rajiva Wijesinha, *The Androgynous Trollope: Attitudes to Women Amongst Early Victorian Novelists* (Washington, D.C.: University Press of America, 1982); Christopher Herbert, *Trollope and Comic Pleasure* (Chicago: University of Chicago Press, 1987), Deborah Denenholz Morse, *Women in Trollope's Palliser Novels* (Ann Arbor, MI: UMI Research Press, 1987).

6. Herbert, pp. 4–11.

7. James R. Kincaid, "Introduction," *Barchester Towers* (Oxford: Oxford University Press, 1980), p. xviii.

8. Shirley Robin Letwin, *The Gentlemen in Trollope: Individuality and Moral Conduct* (Cambridge, MA: Harvard University Press, 1982), p. 74.

Selected Bibliography

Primary Sources
The Chronicles of Barsetshire (in order of publication within the series)
The Warden. London: Longman, Brown, Green and Longmans, 1855.
Barchester Towers. London: Longman, Brown, Green, Longmans and Roberts, 1857.
Doctor Thorne. London: Chapman & Hall, 1858.
Framley Parsonage. London: Smith, Elder, 1861.
The Small House at Allington. London: Smith, Elder, 1864.
The Last Chronicle of Barset. London: Smith, Elder, 1867.
The Palliser Novels (in order of original publication within the series):
Can You Forgive Her? London: Chapman & Hall, 1864.
Phineas Finn. London: 1869.
The Eustace Diamonds. London: Chapman & Hall, 1873.
Phineas Redux. London: Chapman & Hall, 1874.
The Prime Minister. London: Chapman & Hall, 1876.
The Duke's Children. London: Chapman & Hall, 1880.
An Autobiography. London: Blackwood, 1882.

Secondary Sources
Barickman, Richard, Susan MacDonald, and Myra Stark. *Corrupt Relations: Dickens, Thackeray, Trollope, Collins and the Victorian Sexual System.* New York: Columbia University Press, 1982. The authors find all four writers to be "feminists" (161) and to be "radical and even revolutionary" (viii). They focus on their recognition that Victorian sexual mores "were inflicting massive, radical damage" on individual men and women (vii). The authors argue that Trollope's criticism of Victorian sex roles is found in the analogic structure of the multiple plots.
Glendinning, Victoria. *Anthony Trollope.* New York: Knopf, 1993.
Hall, N. John. *Trollope: A Biography.* Oxford: Clarendon Press, and New York: Oxford University Press, 1991.
Heilbrun, Carolyn. *Toward A Recognition of Androgyny.* New York: Knopf, 1973. This now classic feminist consideration of androgyny finds that Trollope "accepts without question his culture's view of women" (57).
Herbert, Christopher. *Trollope and Comic Pleasure.* Chicago: University of Chicago Press, 1987. Herbert analyzes how Trol-

lope's comedy subverts the assumptions of his age. For Herbert, the last line of *Twelfth Night,* Feste's direction to the audience, "We'll strive to please you every day," provides a significant insight into the purpose of comedy which he describes as "comedy's nearly all-absorbing concentration on the production of pleasure." Herbert questions the generally held critical assumption that comedy's end is serious: "These persistent, always futile attempts to force the dangerous genie of comic hilarity into a bottle of grave respectability all bear witness to comedy's mischevious gift for arousing anxiety" (11).

James, Henry. *Essays on Literature, English and American Writers.* New York: 1984, pp. 1326–1354. A collection of James's essays which includes his assessment of Trollope, which was first published in the *Century Magazine,* July 1883 and reprinted in *Partial Portraits,* 1888.

Kendrick, Walter M. *Novel Machine: The Theory and Fiction of Anthony Trollope.* Baltimore: Johns Hopkins University Press, 1980. Kendrick examines the *Autobiography* as presenting a theory of realistic fiction which shows it to be "a design for reading as much as for writing" (62). He gives close atttention to *He Knew He Was Right,* with an eye to Trollope's rhetoric of realism.

Kincaid, James R. "Introduction," *Barchester Towers.* Oxford: Oxford University Press, 1980.

Letwin, Shirley Robin. *The Gentleman in Trollope: Individuality and Moral Conduct.* Cambridge, MA: Harvard University Press, 1982. Focusing on the "Oddity," "Condition," and "Conduct" of the Victorian gentleman by examining Trollope's fiction, Letwin argues that this morality offers us a coherent understanding of what it meant to be human in nineteenth-century England.

Morse, Deborah Denenholz. *Women in Trollope's Palliser Novels.* Ann Arbor, MI: UMI Research Press, 1987. Provides a more in-depth discussion of the duality in Trollope than *Corrupt Relations.* The novelist's ambivalent attitudes toward the Victorian cultural ideals are explored in terms of Trollope's impulse to disrupt the narrative, the differences between narrative intent and plot resolution, and between character and commentary. Morse finds Trollope's more "elastic" than other writers of the period and sees his intent as subversive (6).

Mullen, Richard, ed. *Anthony Trollope: A Victorian in His World.* London: Duckworth, 1990.

Praz, Mario. *The Hero in Eclipse in Victorian Fiction.* Ed. Angus Davidson. London: Oxford University Press, 1956. In a far-ranging discussion of heroism, Praz's comments about Trollope follow Sadlier's lead in seeing him an apologist for his culture.

Sadlier, Michael. *Trollope: A Commentary.* New York: Farrar, Straus, 1949. Sadlier's assertion that Trollope was the "voice of an epoch" epitomized the early view of Trollope.

Snow, C.P. *Trollope: His Life and Art.* New York: Charles Scribner's Sons, 1975. Rpt. as *Trollope.* New York: New Amsterdam Books, 1991.

Super, R.H., ed. *The Fixed Period: A Novel by Trollope.* Ann Arbor: University of Michigan Press, 1990.

Warhol, Robyn R. *Gendered Interventions: Narrative Discourse in the Victorian Novel.* New Brunswick, NJ: Rutgers University Press, 1989. Combining both feminist theory and narratology, Warhol explores the engaging strategies of direct address adopted by women writers and the distancing strategies employed by male writers. Her discussion of Trollope explores *Can You Forgive Her?,* which, despite its engaging title, seeks to distance readers. This novel and Dickens's *Bleak House* are examples of men's narrator's "who cross gender" (134–39).

West, Rebecca. *The Court and the Castle.* New Haven: Yale University Press, 1957. West finds Trollope a "greater" writer than William Makepeace Thackeray in certain respects (133). Trollope fits into the theme of her book because she finds that Trollope viewed "the world as a necessary court crowded with courtiers" (161).

Wijesinha, Rajiva. *The Androgynous Trollope: Attitudes to Women Amongst Early Victorian Novelists.* Washington, D.C.: University Press of America, 1982.

Marnie Jones

U

Ustinov, Peter

Born: London, April 16, 1921
Education: Westminster School, London,
*   1934–1937; London Theatre Studio,*
*   1937–1939*
Marriages: Isolde Denham, 1940; one child;
*   Suzanne Cloutier, 1954; three children;*
*   Helene du Lau d'Allemans, June 17, 1972*

Biography

"I see myself as a commentator on what I see, and whatever form that takes depends on inspiration."[1] With that observation, Peter Ustinov, who has often been described as a Renaissance man, succinctly sums up his diverse talents as a humorist, actor, producer, director, cartoonist, critic, and raconteur as well as an author of stage plays, screenplays, articles, novels, and short stories. Though he does not subscribe to conventional notions about such subjects as nationality, religion, and politics, Ustinov is nonetheless a moralist. His global vision and mastery of numerous avenues of expression, along with his urbane intelligence and satiric bent, have enabled him to fashion a vital body of work, the best of which joins a fantastic fairy tale quality with a hard core of common sense and a shrewd perception of the problems of life today, especially in their international rather than provincial dimensions. Ustinov draws upon that Russian literary tradition, unrooted in a classical context, which blends inextricably comedy and tragedy. His best plays, for example, have a strong tension between the two, revealing him as a master of the light touch, even when dealing with the most serious issues.

The son of Iona and Nadia Benois Ustinov, Peter Alexander Ustinov was born on April 16, 1921, in London, soon after his parents arrived in England. His father, descended from a liberal Lutheran family which had left Russia in 1868, was a celebrated journalist known professionally as "Klop." His mother, an artist, was born in Russia of an architect father, Louis Benois. Ustinov had numerous relatives who were concerned with both diplomacy and the arts. Consequently, he grew up in a cosmopolitan family, unusually alert to European cultural climate.

Even as a child, Ustinov was a brilliant mimic. His extraordinary vocal range and the mobility of his facial features aided him in his impersonations of people ranging from his parents' friends and guests to his schoolmasters. At sixteen, following an undistinguished academic career at Westminster School in London (1934–1937), Ustinov studied acting under Michel Saint-Denis at the London Theatre Studio, where he also experimented with playwriting (1937–1939). In 1939, Ustinov joined the Players Theatre Club, delighting audiences with his sketches and inventions of larger-than-life characters such as Madame Liselotte Beethoven-Finck, a Wagnerian prima donna. His legendary versatility soon manifested itself. In 1940, he directed Valentin Petrovich Katayev's *Squaring the Circle* at the Arts Theatre and completed his first play, *House of Regrets*. The same year, he also married Isolde Denham; they would have one daughter, Tamara.

In 1942, Ustinov was inducted into the army, which he hated, though he did find himself fascinated by the eccentricities of military life. Service in the Royal Sussex Regiment, where he acted for a time as David Niven's batman, was followed by a stint with the Royal Army Ordnance Corps. Following its lavish praise by the *Sunday Times*' influential reviewer

James Agate, Ustinov's *House of Regrets* was presented in 1942 at the Arts Theatre, with sets by his mother. His second play, *Blow Your Own Trumpet*, opened in 1943, the same year that he was transferred to a unit making propaganda films. In 1944, Ustinov's play, *The Banbury Nose*, was a considerable success in London. By war's end, he had earned an enviable reputation as a promising dramatist and a brilliant actor.

In 1946, Ustinov played Petrovitch in Rodney Ackland's adaptation of *Crime and Punishment*. Two years later, he appeared in his own adaptation of Ingmar Bergman's *Hets* (*Frenzy*). After directing and playing Sergeant Dohda in Eric Lindlater's *Love in Albania* in 1949, Ustinov embarked on a successful film career, being seen in the theater after that time mainly in his own dramas. His 1948 play *The Indifferent Shepherd* was moderately successful, but his *The Love of Four Colonels* (1951) was his first real hit as a dramatist. The latter won a New York Drama Critics' Award as best foreign play. Yet, the same year found Ustinov's more serious play, *The Moment of Truth*, pleasing neither critics nor the public. Following his divorce from Isolde Denham Ustinov in 1950, he married the actress Suzanne Cloutier in 1954; they would have three children—Pavla, Igor, and Andrea.

In 1956, *Romanoff and Juliet*, a romantic comedy, was another major success for Ustinov, winning the *Evening Standard* Drama Award in 1957 for the best new play. It was subsequently filmed (with a screenplay by Ustinov) and provided the basis for the 1973 musical *R Loves J*. Subsequent Ustinov entertainments such as *Photo Finish* (1962), *Halfway up the Tree* (1967), *Who's Who in Hell* (1974), *Overheard* (1981), and *Beethoven's Tenth* (1982) have tended to confirm his reputation as a dramatist who can write effective and very funny individual scenes, but lacks the singlemindedness and self-discipline to create a wholly satisfactory play.

As a screen actor, Ustinov made his debut in the British picture *Hello Fame* in 1941. He wrote and acted in Carol Reed's film *The Way Ahead* (1944) and wrote, produced, and directed *School for Secrets* (1946), about the development of radar. In 1947, he made his first film as a civilian, *Vice Versa*, which he wrote and directed. It was the last motion picture with which he was involved without appearing as an actor. Since he was making a considerable impact in London as a stage actor, it was difficult for him to avoid the blandishments of movie producers. Among the many films that he appeared in are *Quo Vadis* (1951), *The Egyptian* (1954), *We're No Angels* (1955), *The Sundowners* (1960), *Romanoff and Juliet, Lady L.* (1965), *The Comedians* (1967), *Logan's Run, Death on the Nile* (1978), *Ashanti* (1979), and *The Great Muppet Caper* (1981). In films, Ustinov has performed mostly as a supporting player, though more often than not he has been the actor who made the greatest impression. Invariably, he rises above his material. Two of his roles brought him an Academy Award for the Best Supporting Actor—*Spartacus* (1960) and *Topkapi* (1964). In 1962, Ustinov wrote (with Robert Rossen and DeWitt Bodeen), acted in, and directed the critically acclaimed film version of Herman Melville's *Billy Budd*.

During his long and versatile career, Ustinov has published two novels, *The Loser* and *Krumnagel*, two volumes of short stories, *Add a Dash of Pity* (1959) and *The Frontiers of the Sea*, two memoirs, *Dear Me* and *My Russia*, and a book of photographs, *Ustinov's Diplomats* (1961). *The Wit of Peter Ustinov* was compiled by Dick Richards and published in 1969. Like his plays, the writer's novels and short stories have been praised for their sometimes brilliant set pieces, their portrayal of national characters, and the enlightened and liberal views they embody, but criticized for superficial characterization and lack of narrative momentum.

In 1962, Ustinov produced three operas in London's Covent Garden (a triple bill: *L'Heure Espagnole* by Maurice Ravel, *Gianni Schicchi* by Emillio Puccini, and *Erwartung* by Arnold Schoenberg), and in 1973, he produced and designed the Edinburgh Festival's version of Wolfgang Amadeus Mozart's *Don Giovanni*. In the meantime, he and Suzanne Cloutier Ustinov divorced (1971), and he married Helene du Lau d'Allemans on June 17, 1972.

In collaboration with actor-dramatist Peter Jones, Ustinov wrote and performed in the popular BBC radio series *In All Directions*, in which he held a slightly distorted but amusing and understanding mirror to contemporary civilization. In addition to writing such television plays as *Ustinov Ad Lib* (1959) and *Imaginary Friends* (1982), he made a reputation for himself as a superb conversationalist on television. He has won the Emmy Award three times for his television work. He received the Benjamin Franklin Award of The Royal Society of Arts in 1957. He held the rectorship of Dundee University from 1968 to 1973, was appointed Commander of the British Empire in 1976, and was knighted in 1995. Presently, Ustinov lives in France.

Literary Analysis

"It's impossible," writes Tony Thomas, "to think of Ustinov as anything other than a funny man."[2] In terms of what it means to be funny, Ustinov once offered the following brief definitions:

> A *sense of humour*: Difficult to define in case you light on its mystery and destroy its innocence. But I would say that it's a readiness to see the funny side extant in everything.
>
> A *sense of the ridiculous*: Thinking of the unfunny side of a situation first and then realizing its funny side immediately afterward.
>
> A *sense of comedy*: To contrast a situation with its unfunny side.
>
> A *sense of the satirical*: To recognize all the above and then bring it home swiftly to a third party.[3]

In Britain, Ustinov is considered by many to be the country's unlicensed and unpaid court jester. Often judging him to be more of an entertainer than an artist, critics have proclaimed that his strongest creative trait is his civilized, mischievous wit. Yet throughout his career, Ustinov has based his work on the premise that the serious and humorous sides of life are tightly intertwined:

> . . . I have always been interested in the comic side of things tragic and in the melancholy [side] of things ribald. Life could not exist without its imperfections, just as the human body could not survive without germs. And to the writer, the imperfections of existence are life-blood.[4]

In the introducton to his *Five Plays,* he observed:

> Sometimes at a place like the Royal Automobile Club, you get four generals who've just played squash, and the generals' clothes and hats are hung up and they're absolutely purple in the face, with a line around their necks and the·

rest of them as white as a sheet—and they're looking into the distance and clearing their throats and discussing things as though they are dressed. It's these moments in life that I think indicative of the follies and pretensions of human beings. Yet I'm inspired by the effort of man to get away from his nakedness and build something solid and reliable and worthy, even if it means abandoning such ridiculous rituals as battleships and their firing salutes to each other.[5]

Ustinov asserts:

> Comedy is just another way of being serious, the only way I know of being serious. The extremes of life are very close to each other. I can be easily moved, but I find that in my case humour is a stabilizing influence, because it can easily be turned to irony. There are many things I feel strongly about, but when I express myself on them they turn out as ironical rather than flat dramatic statements.[6]

The fact that he is more appreciated by many for the lighter side of his talent than for the serious may be the most ironic thing about him. He seems to realize this and does not appear bothered by it.

The fusion of cultural influences in Ustinov's background contributed to his liberal-minded and often very satiric approach to politics and cross-cultural attitudes. In many of his plays he explores some political or cultural characteristic contrasted with its polar opposite. His first produced play, *House of Regrets* (1942), examines an exiled White Russian community living in genteel poverty in wartime London amidst dreams of Tsarist restoration. The elder generation tries desperately to prevent the past from crumbling completely, while the younger generation sees the simulated grandeur of the elders as the decaying facade that it actually is. With its brilliant comic characterizations, *House of Regrets* reveals early Ustinov's sympathetic identification with eccentrics. His depiction of the old general and admiral plotting their coup to re-enter Russia also demonstrates his early interest in the humbug of the military.

The writer's gift for the fantastic is seen in *The Banbury Nose,* in which he traces a great military family, the Hume-Banburys, through three generations—all of whom share the family's distinctive physical characteristic, the Banbury nose—in reverse order. The older family members are first seen as tradition ridden, bitter in failure, and harassed by the rebellious younger generation. As the play moves backward in time, however, the elder generation is also depicted as once having confronted the future with hope and zeal. A technical tour de force, *The Banbury Nose* may well be Ustinov's most original and completely effective play.

After such plays as *The Tragedy of Good Intentions* (1945), a chronicle about the crusades, and *The Indifferent Shepherd*, a study of a clergyman's crisis of conscience, Ustinov scored his first major comedy success with *The Love of Four Colonels*. Conceived as a wicked fairy tale set in a European state, the play is a satire on national characteristics—including notions of love and the ideal woman as well as militarism—when the four colonels reveal their hopes and ideals as they awaken to Sleeping Beauty's love. Though some critics found *The Love of Four Colonels* to be somewhat superficial in its observation of national characteristics, it enjoyed a very long run in London and a respectable one in New York. *The Moment of Truth* is Ustinov's interpretation of the tragedy of Marshall Petain. Though more serious in intent than *The Love of Four Colonels*, this play also demonstrates his use of political ridicule as a senile marshall is plucked from retirement and used as a figurehead by a government tottering on the edge of defeat in a civil war.

In his 1953 play, *No Sign of the Dove*, Ustinov experimentally reworked the Noah legend. An elderly Matthew constructs an ark in the crowded confines of an attic in a mansion which is about to be flooded. The first act is a biting satire of the Bloomsbury literary circle; the second is a bedroom farce. With his self-made weapons of destruction, man is faced with obliteration in the third act. Only in the child Hope, with whom Matthew sails away, can mankind find survival and the possibility of beginning again. A promising opening section and a good cast did not prevent *No Sign of the Dove* from quickly becoming a resounding public and critical failure.

In *Romanoff and Juliet*, Ustinov takes a tongue-in-cheek swipe at diplomatic pomposity and political hypocrisy. He lightly and amusingly adapts the Romeo and Juliet story to the Cold War rivalry between the Russian and American embassies in Ruritania. A Russian boy and an American girl fall in love while their parents serve as diplomats in the smallest country in Europe. The author's polyglot ancestry ensures that he will mock both sides, maintaining an allegiance only to all of humanity. Successful detente between the two sides is reached after an extremely funny scene in which the doddering and forgetful archbishop marries the young lovers. Beneath the play's fairy tales and Ruritanian trappings, Ustinov reveals a humanist understanding of contemporary international problems, one which is free from either the right-wing or left-wing suppositions of power-politics.

Produced the same year, Ustinov's *The Empty Chair* (1956) was overshadowed by the success of *Romanoff and Juliet*, which ran for 379 performances in London followed by 389 in New York. *The Empty Chair* is an allegorical commentary on the French Revolution and revolution in general. Key characters are Danton and Robespierre, and the chair of the title becomes empty as one man of power after another falls victim to the guillotine. The irony and wit which characterize the talk of the play's protagonists is made all the more barbed by the realization that a revolution cannot bear the cost of humor.

A number of Ustinov's plays of the 1960s to some extent involved a fuller exploration of earlier ideas and themes. An autobiographical play, *Photo Finish*, recalls *The Banbury Nose* with its flashback time sequences as well as an old and famous writer who confronts his younger selves. Ustinov's *Halfway up the Tree* proved to be a long-running success, while the same year's *The Unknown Soldier and His Wife* revealed in its scope and assurance a playwright at the height of his powers. The latter work is an indictment of war as it follows the fortunes of a soldier who sets forth from his home and wife in successive historical periods ranging from ancient Rome to modern times. What might have been a little more than a series of amusing sketches is forged by the writer into a complex, multilayered play which rates with his best work.

Ustinov's *Who's Who in Hell* is set in an anteroom in hell where the ultimate destinations of the Russian premier and the American president—like that of all new arrivals—will be decided. The promise of sharp political humor is undercut by, among other things, rather stale jokes. *Overheard* is a comedy about an English diplomat and his wife which displays wit and psychological insight. In *Beethoven's Tenth*, a psychic causes the composer, now speaking perfect English, to materialize in the home of a London music critic. Following this promising opening of what might have been a buoyant comedy of ideas, the play falters, never regaining its initial comic energy.

Though Ustinov does not consider film his primary medium, he is best known to the largest number of people through motion pictures. As a filmmaker, he was put on the map with his *School for Secrets*, a spirited and witty motion picture. Suspense and humor merge as a group of select British scientists are moved to a small town during World War II to concentrate on their radar project. The following year Ustinov wrote and directed *Vice Versa*, his first film as a civilian. Pure Ustinov, it is highly stylized, whimsical, and somewhat surrealistic. The script is peppered with sly digs and witty asides as he takes on Victorian England and gives a sound drubbing to the law, the military, the public school system, and female opportunism. In 1949, Ustinov co-directed (with Michael Anderson) *Private Angelo*, basing his screenplay on the novel by Eric Linklater. It is the picaresque story of an amiable chump caught in the War, drifting from one embarrassment to another.

In 1961, Ustinov directed and adapted for the screen his successful play, *Romanoff and Juliet*, a satiric lampooning of national characteristics. Perhaps in an effort to make the material more palatable for a much wider audience, he diluted some of the play's barbed satire. Full of Ustinovian wryness, the film version of *Romanoff and Juliet* is carried along by a droll and whimsical kind of humor.

In 1965, Ustinov directed and provided the screenplay for *Lady L*. The plot as a whole lumbers and creaks, but the writer's humorous and offbeat touches shine through. Fun is poked at the pretensions of European aristocracy. Truly comic highlights include an attempted assassination and chaos in a concert hall. *Hot Millions* (1968) was in the tradition of the witty Alec Guinness comedies of the mid-1950s. Ira Wallach developed the script; Ustinov reshaped and added to it after he was signed for the film. The story of a likable larcenist pitted against a machine, *Hot Millions* is an English comedy whose humor originates from character. Sharp in observation, it takes sly, satiric gibes at British mores.

In 1972, Ustinov directed *Hammersmith Is Out*, with a screenplay by Stanford Whitmore. The story of the rise and fall of a redneck Texan and a satire of the American lust for money and power, it is both too elaborate and not quite witty enough to be particularly convincing as a contemporary morality play. *Memed My Hawk* (1983), directed by Ustinov with his screenplay based on the book by Yashar Kemal, is a thin comedy set in an exotic clime; the general effect is farce.

Throughout his career, Ustinov has accomplished the rare feat of performing in plays and films of his own authorship, usually to popular and critical acclaim. Reflecting on his multifaceted career, he has observed that acting is intrinsically easy and much safer than writing and directing. Yet those who do not credit comedians with acting ability tend to underrate Ustinov, who is indeed a highly amusing and entertaining man, as an actor. Others proclaim playing comedy to be perhaps the most difficult type of acting; they find his humor as a very effective device through which he communicates with his audience.

When the film *Quo Vadis* was released, Ustinov, whose portrayal of Nero was clever if a bit overblown, became a movie star, though a reluctant one. Suddenly, millions of people who had never heard of Ustinov as a stage actor or playwright found him to be a most enjoyable film actor. Though he did not receive the Academy Award for which he was nominated for his role in *Quo Vadis*, he did receive an "Oscar" for best supporting actor twice, for his roles in *Spartacus* and *Topkapi*.

Ustinov's humorous touch can be found in the fiction that he has managed to write during his busy career as a one-man entertainment conglomerate. In his first collection of short stories, *Add a Dash of Pity*, Ustinov's bent is satire; his chief medium is a wryly witty irony. If a single theme runs through these stories, it is the author's affection for the eccentric and unadapting. He writes with a crisp malice and apparent enjoyment. His wit is astringent, and he reveals his dramatist's eye for the high and low comedy of the pretentious. Though the stories in this collection are uneven and rather old-fashioned in construction, they show that he possesses the rarest of a satirist's gifts—that of using mockery to express compassion.

In 1961, Ustinov published his first novel, *The Loser*. The protagonist is a young German named Hans Winterschild, a product of the Nazi generation. Late in World War II, Hans is transferred to Italy, where German discipline and character are beginning to crumble. He wantonly massacres a Tuscan village, then falls helplessly in love with a Florentine prostitute. The war is over before either can save the other. Hans sheds his uniform and makes his way to the village that he destroyed. There, he is hired as an extra by an American film company making a gaudy movie about the town's martyrdom. Through his compounding of small ironies, the author produces a thought-provoking portrait of man's tragic aspects. The writer's talents at burlesque and satire work effectively in a number of scenes, especially in the movie-making sequence. The glimpses into the Nazi underground of post-war Italy and the travesty of the movie company's re-creation of the battle scenes are both frightening and funny. For the scene in which the Germans destroy the village, Olympic Pictures "had rebuilt an intact village in wood and plaster not a hundred yards from San Rocco, having realized, rather late in the day, that it is extremely difficult to show a village being destroyed by false Germans after the job has already been effectively done by real Germans."[7]

Ustinov is also able to do one of the things that he does best: hold up national types to clever, cynical scrutiny. Portraying Hans in love, Ustinov writes:

> . . . in his effort to grapple with the pressing problems of the heart, [he] was falling into the trap, peculiar to the German spirit, of trying to experience all sensations at once. He wished to be cruel and tender, victorious and humble, right and openminded. The human brain will not respond logically to such a crushing emotional load, and so being unselected, is a kind of folly.[8]

In Ustinov's own spirited and essentially theatrical way, *The Loser* is a tour de force.

Ustinov's second collection of short stories, *The Frontiers of the Sea*, was published in 1966. The tales in this volume are international in setting. Several of them have the quality of simplicity in the turns of thought and expression of the Italian official, the Spanish fisherman, and several others. In "Dreams of Papua," Ustinov suggests that all the problems of the East and West could be solved if the heads of state, who are harmless human beings at heart, could get together over some neat hobby such as stamp collecting.

In 1971, Ustinov's second novel, *Krumnagel*—a satire on contrasting British and American ways of life, death, and legality—was published. Krumnagel, the police chief of a midwestern American city, is awarded a trip around the world with his wife. He never gets any further than England, where, during a drunken brawl in a pub, he pulls his pistol and kills a man. Though he is tried, found guilty, and sent to prison, British officials conspire to let him escape, thus removing a source of great embarrassment. Krumnagel's adventures allow Ustinov to satirize British justice, experimental prisons, American lovemaking, hard-hat types, street corner Buddhists, and forensic psychiatry—among other topics. The humor is bitter, and there are some shrewd comments on national traits. When Krumnagel receives an offer for his serialized memoirs, Jeremy Sabak, a notorious criminal whose own memoirs were being published, gives him advice about serial rights in other countries:

> Italy's very hot on success stories in crime, and you can make a mint in lire if you box clever. This may not mean much in the open market, but you can live in comfort in Sicily for years, bribes and Mafia protection included, if you happen to be lying low for any reason. Germany's good, too, but they're bigger on crimes with a political or sexual edge—if you can work fur-clad Amazons with high boots and a whip into the story, so much the better, and if she was Goering's mistress on the side, you got it made. Holland, Belgium, small markets admitted, but millionaires make their fortunes counting pennies—after a while, the big stuff comes by itself. America? There's too much competition, and then they find it cheaper to make the stories up. They get sued less.[9]

Ustinov is preeminently the dramatist; consequently, *Krumnagel* is a collection of memorable and frequently humorous confrontations.

With bemused satire, the author continues to comment on the insanity of the world that surrounds him in the two novellas in *The Disinformer* (1989). In the title story, the author contrasts Europe and the Middle East as he portrays one man's outrage and amusement at the foibles of politicians, policemen, the media, and, ultimately, himself. In "A Nose by Any Other Name," Ustinov skillfully and amusingly depicts the gap between Old World traditions and the seemingly infinite possibilities of America.

In *The Old Man and Mr. Smith: A Fable* (1991), God (The Old Man) and Satan (Mr. Smith), long archenemies, engage in a joint fact-finding mission on earth. As irrepressible as ever, Ustinov ranges from the White House to a New York porno palace and from Tiananmen Square to Red Square with the immortals offering insights into the contemporary world. The result is provocative, witty, and often hilarious.

In his 1977 autobiography, *Dear Me*, Ustinov relates with intelligence and much wit his career as a gifted actor, author, director, and raconteur. There are, as one might expect, many very amusing and entertaining anecdotes. Even the most important vicissitudes in his life are blunted with an irrepressible jokiness. The writing is vivid and at times epigrammatic. In the end, his wit bears witness to his seriousness. Ustinov's *My Russia* (1983), a long essay on the history of Russia from the Tartars to Brezhnev, shows his romantic affection for his roots.

Finally, there is Ustinov the great talker and raconteur. He amuses and amazes with his seemingly inexhaustible store of knowledge of people, places, and things. A multilingual mimic, he seems able to reproduce a variety of speaking or singing voices, any accent, and many mechanical and musical sounds.

Audiences large and small find him a man to listen to and be amused by.

Summary

A one-man creative industry, Peter Ustinov has turned his witty and urbane intelligence to numerous facets of public entertainment. His tangled national and ethnic background has provided him with much material for comic thoughts. Also, he maintains that comedy and tragedy have been driven from their "ivory towers" by "the extraordinarily graphic quality of current events diffused by the news media, and the growing public sense of skepticism about the nature and possibilities of government." As a consequence, he holds, "This is the time of the tragic farce, the comic drama, of the paradox, of the dramatized doubt."[10] In such a world, Ustinov the serious clown has repeatedly reminded his audience of civilization's myriad follies.

U

Notes

1. Quoted in Tony Tanner, *Ustinov in Focus* (London: A. Zwemmer, 1971), p. 11.
2. *Ibid.*, p. 11.
3. Quoted in Dick Richards (comp.), *The Wit of Peter Ustinov* (London: Leslie Frewin, 1969), pp. 120–121.
4. Quoted in James Vinson (ed.), *Contemporary Dramatists* (London: St. James Press, 1977), p. 801.
5. Peter Ustinov, "Introduction," *Five Plays* (London: Heinemann, and Boston: Little, Brown, 1965), p. 9.
6. Quoted in Tanner, *Ustinov in Focus*, p. 11.
7. Peter Ustinov, *The Loser* (London: The Book Club, 1962), p. 165.
8. *Ibid.*, p. 94.
9. Peter Ustinov, *Krumnagel* (Boston: Little, Brown, 1971), p. 185.
10. Quoted in Vinson (ed.), *Contemporary Dramatists*, p. 801.

Selected Bibliography

Primary Sources

Plays
The Bishop of Limpopoland. Sketch. Produced London, 1939.
Sketches in *Swinging the Gate.* Produced London, 1940.
Sketches in *Diversion* and *Diversion 2.* Produced London 1940, 1941.
Fishing for Shadows. Adaptation of a play by Jean Sarment. Also director; produced London, 1940.
House of Regrets. Produced London, 1942. London: Jonathan Cape, 1943.
Beyond. Produced London, 1943. London: English Theatre Guild, 1944; also in *Five Plays.* London: Heinemann, 1965.
Blow Your Own Trumpet. Produced Liverpool and London, 1943. In *Plays About People.* London: Jonathan Cape, 1950.
The Banbury Nose. Produced London, 1944. London: Jonathan Cape, 1945.
The Tragedy of Good Intentions. Produced Liverpool, 1945. In *Plays About People.* London: Jonathan Cape, 1950.
The Man Behind the Statue. Produced Manchester, 1946.
The Indifferent Shepherd. Produced London, 1948. In *Plays About People.* London: Jonathan Cape, 1950.
Frenzy. Adaptation of a play by Ingmar Bergman. Produced London, 1948.

The Man in the Raincoat. Also director; produced Edinburgh, 1949.

The Love of Four Colonels. Also director; produced Birmingham and London, 1951; New York, 1953. London: English Theatre Guild, 1951; New York: Dramatists Play Service, 1953. Also in *Five Plays*. London: Heinemann, and Boston: Little, Brown, 1965.

The Moment of Truth. Produced Nottingham and London, 1951. London: English Theatre Guild, 1953. Also in *Five Plays*. London: Heinemann, and Boston: Little, Brown, 1965.

High Balcony. Produced London, 1952.

No Sign of the Dove. Also director; produced Leeds and London, 1953. In *Five Plays*. London: Heinemann, and Boston: Little, Brown, 1965.

The Empty Chair. Produced Bristol, 1956.

Romanoff and Juliet. Produced Manchester and London, 1956; New York, 1957. London: English Theatre Guild, 1957; New York: Random House, 1958. Also in *Five Plays*. London: Heinemann, and Boston: Little, Brown, 1965. Revised as *R Loves J*, music by Alexander Faris and lyrics by Julian More. Produced Chichester, 1973.

Paris Not So Gay. Produced Oxford, 1958.

Photo Finish. Also director; produced Dublin and London, 1962; New York, 1963. London: Heinemann, 1962; Boston: Little, Brown, 1963.

The Life in My Hands. Produced Nottingham, 1964.

The Unknown Soldier and His Wife. Also director; produced Chichester, 1967, London, 1973; New York, 1967. New York: Random House, 1967; London: Heinemann, 1968.

Halfway up the Tree. Produced on tour, Germany, 1967; also director; produced New York, 1967; London, 1967. New York: Random House, 1968; London: English Theatre Guild, 1970.

Who's Who in Hell. Produced New York, 1974.

Overheard. Produced Brighton, 1981; London, 1981.

Beethoven's Tenth. Produced Paris, 1982; Birmingham, 1983; London, 1983; Los Angeles, 1983; New York, 1984.

Screenplays

The New Lot (documentary), 1943.

The Way Ahead, with Eric Ambler, 1944.

The True Glory (documentary), with others, 1944.

Carnival, with others, 1946.

School for Secrets, 1946.

Vice Versa, 1947.

Private Angelo, 1949.

School for Scoundrels, with others, 1960.

Romanoff and Juliet, 1961.

Billy Budd, with Robert Rossen and DeWitt Bodeen, 1962.

Lady L., 1965.

Hot Millions, with Ira Wallach, 1968.

Memed My Hawk, 1983.

Ustinov as an Actor: Plays

Waffles in *The Wood Demon* by Chekhov, Shere, Surrey, 1938; in *The Bishop of Limpopoland*, London, 1939; Aylesbury Repertory Company: in *French Without Tears* by Terence Rattigan, *Pygmalion* by G.B. Shaw, *White Cargo* by Leon Gordon, *Rookery Nook* by Ben Travers, and *Laburnum Grove* by J.B. Priestley, 1939; Reverend Alroy Whittingstall in *First Night* by Reginald Denham, Richmond, Surrey, 1940; *Swinging the Gate* (revue), London, 1940; M. Lescure in *Fishing for Shadows*, London, 1940; *Hermoine Gingold Revue*, London, 1940; *Diversion* and *Diversion 2* (revues), London, 1940, 1941; Petrovitch in *Crime and Punishment* by Rodney Ackland, London, 1946; Caligula in *Frenzy*, London, 1948; Sergeant Dohda in *Love in Albania* by Eric Linklater, London, 1949; Carabosse in *The Love of Four Colonels*, London, 1951; The General in *Romanoff and Juliet*, London, 1956, New York, 1957; Sam Old in *Photo Finish*, London, 1962, New York, 1963; Archbishop in *The Unknown Soldier and His Wife*, Chichester, 1968, London, 1973; Boris Vassilevitch Krivelov in *Who's Who in Hell*, New York, 1974; title role in *King Lear*, Stratford, Ontario, 1979, 1980; Stage Manager in *The Marriage*, Milan, 1981, Edinburgh, 1982; Ludwig in *Beethoven's Tenth*, Paris, 1982, Birmingham, London, and Los Angeles, 1983, New York, 1984.

Ustinov as an Actor: Films

Hello Fame, 1941; *Mein Kampf, My Crimes*, 1941; *The Goose Steps Out*, 1942; *Let the People Sing*, 1942; *One of Our Aircraft Is Missing*, 1942; *The New Lot*, 1943; *The Way Ahead*, 1944; *The True Glory*, 1944; *School for Secrets (The Secret Flight)*, 1946; *Vice Versa*, 1947; *Private Angelo*, 1949; *Odette*, 1950; *Quo Vadis*, 1951; *Hotel Sahara*, 1951; *The Magic Box*, 1951; *Beau Brummell*, 1954; *The Egyptian*, 1954; *Le Plaisir (House of Pleasure)* (narrator), 1954; *We're No Angels*, 1955; *Lola Montes (Lola Montez, The Sins of Lola Montes)*, 1955; *I girovaghi (The Wanderers)*, 1956; *Un angel paso sobre Brooklyn (An Angel over Brooklyn, The Man Who Wagged His Tail)*, 1957; *Les Espions (The Spies)*, 1957; *The Adventures of Mr. Wonderful*, 1959; *Spartacus*, 1960; *The Sundowners*, 1960; *Romanoff and Juliet*, 1961; *Billy Budd*, 1962; *La donna del mondo (Women of the World)* (narrator), 1963; *The Peaches* (narrator), 1964; *Topkapi*, 1964; *John Goldfarb, Please Come Home*, 1964; *Lady L.*, 1965; *The Comedians*, 1967; *Blackbeard's Ghost*, 1967; *Hot Millions*, 1968; *Viva Max!*, 1969; *Hammersmith Is Out*, 1972; *Big Truck and Sister Clare*, 1973; *Treasure of Matecumbe*, 1976; *One of Our Dinosaurs Is Missing*, 1976; *Logan's Run*, 1976; *Robin Hood* (voice in animated film), 1976; *Un Taxi mauve (The Purple Taxi)*, 1977; *The Last Remake of Beau Geste*, 1978; *The Mouse and His Child* (narrator), 1978; *Doppio delitto (Double Murders)*, 1978; *Death on the Nile*, 1978; *Tarka the Otter* (narrator), 1978; *Winds of Change* (narrator), 1978; *Ashanti*, 1979; *Charlie Chan and the Curse of the Dragon Queen*, 1981; *The Great Muppet Caper*, 1981; *Grendel, Grendel, Grendel* (voice in animated film), 1981; *Evil under the Sun*, 1982; *Memed, My Hawk*, 1984; *Appointment with Death*, 1988.

Ustinov as an Actor: Television
The Life of Dr. Johnson, 1957; *Barefoot in Athens*, 1966; *In All Directions* series; *A Storm in Summer*, 1970 (USA); *Lord North*, 1972; *The Mighty Continent* (narrator), 1974; *A Quiet War*, 1976 (USA); *The Thief of Bagdad*, 1978; *Jesus of Nazareth*, 1979; *Einstein's Universe* (narrator), 1979; *Imaginary Friends* (5 roles), 1982; *The Well-Tempered Bach*,

1984; *13 at Dinner*, 1985; *Dead Man's Folly*, 1986; *Peter Ustinov's Russia*, 1986 (Canada); *World Challenge*, 1986 (Canada); *Murder in Three Acts*, 1986; *Peter Ustinov in China*, 1987; *Around the World in 80 Days*, 1988–1989; *Secret Identity of Jack the Ripper*, 1989.

Novels
The Loser. London: Heinemann, and Boston: Little, Brown, 1961.
Krumnagel. London: Heinemann, and Boston: Little, Brown, 1971.
The Disinformer: Two Novellas. Boston: Little, Brown, 1989.
The Old Man and Mr. Smith: A Fable. New York: Arcade, 1991.

Short Stories
Add a Dash of Pity. London: Heinemann, and Boston: Little, Brown, 1959.
The Frontiers of the Sea. London: Heinemann, and Boston: Little, Brown, 1966.

Miscellaneous
Ustinov's Diplomats: A Book of Photographs. New York: Geis, 1961.
We Were Only Human (caricatures). London: Heinemann, and Boston: Little, Brown, 1961.
The Wit of Peter Ustinov, compiled by Dick Richards. London: Leslie Frewin, 1969.
Rectorial Address Delivered in the University 3rd November 1972. Dundee: Dundee University Press, 1972.
Dear Me (autobiography). London: Heinemann, and Boston: Little, Brown, 1977.
Happiness (lecture). Birmingham: University of Birmingham, 1980.
My Russia. London: Macmillan, and Boston: Little, Brown, 1983.
Ustinov in Russia. London: O'Mara, 1987; New York: Summit, 1988.
Ustinov Still at Large. Amherst, NY: Prometheus Books, 1995. Collected columns from *The European*.

Secondary Sources
Tanner, Tony. *Ustinov in Focus*. London: A. Zwemmer, 1971. Though Tanner focuses on Ustinov's film work, this book contains a good deal of biographical material as well as commentary on Ustinov's comedic sense. There is an excellent

U

chapter on "Ustinov and the Second World War." Individual discussions of Ustinov's films range from *Vice Versa* (1947) to *Viva Max!* (1969).

Ustinov, Nadia Benois. *Klop and the Ustinov Family*. London: Sidgwick and Jackson, 1973. A study by Ustinov's mother, Nadia Ustinov, of her husband and the Ustinov family. Contains a good bit of material on Peter. In the book's "Foreword," Peter recalls his father.

Willans, Geoffrey. *Peter Ustinov*. London: Peter Owen, 1957. A useful biographical account, but now very dated.

Williamson, Audrey. *Contemporary Theatre, 1953–1956*. London: Salisbury Square, 1956, pp. 26, 47–48, 160–161, 182.

———, and Charles Landstone. *The Bristol Old Vic: The First Ten Years*. London: J. Garnet Miller, 1957, pp. 37, 106–107, 138, 148–149, 170–171. The two works by Williamson contain accounts of the production of such Ustinov plays as *The Love of Four Colonels*, *The Empty Chair*, and *No Sign of the Dove*.

L. Moody Simms, Jr.

Vajda, Albert

Born: Budapest, Hungary, September 9,
  1917
Education: Budapest Grammar School
Marriage: Lucy Vajda
Death: Sarasota, Florida, April 10, 1991

Biography

Albert Vajda was born on September 9, 1917, in Budapest, Hungary, where he attended the Budapest Grammar School. A tall *and* large man with heavy glasses, bear-like in appearance, he "wore his humour lightly."

After World War II, Vajda was a journalist on the staff of *Fuggetlen Magyarorszag* (Independent Hungary) from 1945 to 1956. Following the military defeat of the Hungarian Revolution, he escaped to Britain, settled in London, and became a British subject in 1963. Vajda had been a well-known humorist in Budapest, a master of the humorous short story. He had also written amusing satirical sketches for the stage.

In London ("I am already on my second life without having given up the first one," he used to say), he continued writing in Hungarian to exile audiences, and he learned to write in English for the British and the English-speaking public. His wife Lucy was a great help to him, and their guests delighted in her excellent cooking. In the 1960s, he was a contributor to Radio Free Europe (RFE), Munich. In 1970, he became an editor on the staff of RFE and moved to Munich. Soon Vajda became one of the stars of the radio station, a kind of humorous disc jockey, and continued to enjoy popularity until his retirement to Florida in 1983. He died in Sarasota on April 10, 1991, while writing his autobiography.

Literary Analysis

The Hungarian Vajda was essentially a brilliant super-compère who learned his one-man shows by heart without a lapse or a fault. He had a velvety baritone voice and a superb memory. This latter characteristic stood him in good stead when, from the late 1950s onward, he was steadily losing his sight. *Journey round my i* (1962) is his epic story of repeated operations and how to cope with oncoming blindness. The journey, after many vicissitudes (not unlike those of the Duke of York to whom he was once presented), finished with a happy ending: *Lend me an eye* (1974) concludes with his getting back the sight of one eye. Vajda wore his affliction with fortitude and made fun of his own helplessness and disability. "When you chop up a big bad thing, like blindness into smaller ones, things will not get worse, they will get better," he used to say.

Before anything else, and after everything else was said, the figure of Vajda should be imagined on a half lit stage. As his eyesight was always bad, bad lighting never bothered, perhaps even inspired him. "I know you by your voice," he used to say, and we knew him by his baritone that mimicked, cajoled, and excused "everybody's foolishness" including "his own." In "Vajda country" everything was possible: people could grow an extra ear, or a limb, could fly or crawl fast, speak with the speed of a machine gun, or be numb and dumb, not because of the author's flight of fancy but because surreal exaggeration highlighted a truth (or part of *the* truth) that he wished to convey.

Some of Vajda's works such as *Jung bleiben—ober wie* (1970) were translated into German, and he received praise for *The East-*

ern Triangle, his last work in English, which was published in 1986.

Vajda was essentially an autobiographical writer who wrote about themes taken out of his experiences. But, some of his stories go into the land of satire without his personal appearance in them, and they are not the worse for it. In "One step forward, two all over the place," he managed to combine biting anticommunism with slapstick humor. In *How to be a Communist* (1960) and *Madsummer Night Dream* (1971), he provided witty vademecums for an ideology which died the same year that he did. He had helped to undermine a relentless ideology by ridiculing it tirelessly.

Summary

Albert Vajda's importance is attested to by the fact that he could "foresee" events before they happened. The fall of communism and the futile pursuit of textualism are but two examples. His career is that of a heroic fighter who detested heroism and pomposity. He started off as a young humorous journalist in Hungary and was "graduated" as a British humorist who gave one-man shows and was honored by Royal invitations, and ended up as the "resident" humorist of Radio Free Europe in Munchen. His legacy of books brings him to life-size: he was a bear-like man, over six feet, and as gentle as a babe.

Selected Bibliography

Primary Sources
How to be a Communist. London, 1960.
Journey round my i. London: Hutchinson, 1962.
Jung bleiben—ober wie. Bertelsman, 1970.
Madsummer Night Dream. Toronto: Eler, 1971.
Lend me an eye. Toronto: Eler, 1974.
Egy lepes elore. London: Panorama Books, 1979.
The Eastern Triangle. Toronto: Canadian Stage, 1986.

Thomas Kabdebo

Wakefield Master

Born: Goodybower (?), ca. 1300
Education: Secular (?)
Marriage: Unknown; improbable
Died: 1350 (?)

Biography

Little is known about the life of the medieval secular dramatist referred to as the Wakefield Master. He is best known as a writer with extraordinary dramatic skills, evidenced by the most renowned work attributed to him, the *Secundo Pastorum* or *Second Shepherds' Play* (ca. 1385). The Wakefield Master has also been acknowledged as the author of all or parts of several other plays found in the Townley or Wakefield Cycle of mystery plays, including *Abel*, *Noah*, and *Herod*, which have been dated around the first half of the sixteenth century. From the content of the plays attributed to the Wakefield Master, it can be assumed that he was a medieval scholar or cleric who was devoted to or had a passion for writing treatises of religious abstraction in dramatic form. The outlandish farce of *The Second Shepherds' Play* heightens this belief; only an author with a great sense of the exegetic would be able to transcribe the sanctity of the Nativity into the dual levels of *The Second Shepherds' Play* and to incorporate the bawdy humor of the three shepherds into a parallel of the Magi.

While the identity and dates of the Wakefield Master are unknown, the Townley Hall manuscript, which includes the plays of the Wakefield Master, has been dated ca. 1500. The works included are written mainly in a dialect common to the Wakefield, England area, and there are frequent references to places located around Wakefield. It is likely that the author of these plays was male, for women were customarily excluded from the composition of and participation in such works. Further, the author's apparent grasp of the Scriptures and understanding of his audience's religious convictions brings about the hypothesis that the Wakefield Master was a cleric. Thus, it is unlikely that he was ever married.

Literary Analysis

During the Middle Ages, the English miracle or mystery plays were works devoted to illustrating a saint's life or a scriptural subject. These plays were rarely performed as individual works; rather, groups of plays were combined into "cycles" and performed during a particular holiday period (i.e., Corpus Christi Day). Most of the extant works of this genre are found in four major cycles with each cycle being named for the locality where it was performed: Chester, York, Wakefield, and Lincoln. Scholars maintain that the trade guilds were responsible for dramatizing scripture which related to their particular talent: the carpenters portrayed the Great Flood; the bakers, the Last Supper; the Shepherds, the Gift of the Magi.

The Wakefield Master's genius is evident in the ways in which his dramas differ from the traditional composition and performance of the other cycle plays. He wrote sophisticated plays as a display of his unique literary gifts, which seems to be an exception to the tradition of guildmen composing and performing the plays. While the Wakefield Master appears to have had his hand in the composition of several works in the Townley cycle, including *The First Shepherds' Play*, *Herod*, *Noah*, and *The Buffeting*, his best-known work is *The Second Shepherds' Play*. This text is the thirteenth play in the Townley cycle and is marked by its high humor and a dramatization of exploited workers, wives, and husbands. David Bevington (383) notes, "The story of Mak the sheep stealer and his wife Gill is remarkably successful burlesque of the Nativity." This juxtaposition of common secular problems and religious farce makes the play as fascinating to modern readers as it was to its contemporary audience.

Like the other works attributed to the Wakefield Master, *The Second Shepherds' Play* employs alliteration and is written in nine-line stanza, rhyming *aaaabcccb*. The initial four lines of each stanza also rhyme at midline. It seems to be a later version of *The First Shepherds' Play*, for both works depend upon farce to illustrate and dramatize the plight of a fallen world which must be saved by Christ's arrival. The shepherds drink, grumble, and bemoan their fates until the angel appears and leads them to the Savior's manger. However, *The Second Shepherds' Play* contains considerably more humor than its contemporaries, and the dramatist also employs a tighter structure reflective of the Holy Trinity (such as three shepherds and three gifts), thereby far surpassing its predecessors stylistically.

The Second Shepherds' Play is actually the unification of two distinct episodes. At first the play is a comic farce concerning Mak's haphazard effort to steal a sheep from three neighboring shepherds, Coll, Gib, and Daw. Initially, Mak's scheme is successful, but his thievery is finally discovered. The three shepherds see through his plot and swear vengeance against the wily thief; they then renounce their punishment of Mak and simply toss the thief roughly in a blanket before returning to their fields to sleep. Although blanket-tossing can result in serious injuries, this act demonstrates man's ability to forgive and exemplifies the love needed for acceptance of the miracle of Christ as God's son.

The second, shorter part of *The Second Shepherds' Play* parallels the first, but the comedy abates and the true Nativity is treated in a serious manner. The shepherds are awakened by an angel and transported to Bethlehem, where they view the Christ child.

The rationale behind the two-leveled plot is clear: spirituality and forgiveness will be rewarded. It has been suggested that the play in this form appeals to the masses of common folk as well as to the highly educated and clearly demonstrates the allegoric principles mandated by the miracle plays. The parallels between the two scenes illustrate the Wakefield Master's brilliance in unifying the farce of the first part

of the play with the serious drama of the second. When the shepherds visit Mak's home with presents for the dubious newborn, they are anticipating the arrival of the Magi at baby Jesus's manger. Mak's comic actions following the discovery of his crime work as double entendres concerning the sheep/child which clearly denote Christ as the lamb of God and the glory of his birth. The fraud of the first part, which ends with the ceremonial triumph of charity over hatred, provides a suitable transition into the play's second part and helps the dramatic mood shift from the ordinary trials of the lives of the poor to the intimacy and peace of the Nativity.

The Wakefield Master's characterization of the wily Mak and his contemporaries make *The Second Shepherds' Play* a wonderful work. Each of Mak's victims has a distinct character which differentiates him from the others. The first shepherd laments the plight of the common man and his suppression by the landed gentry. The second is a henpecked rogue who warns the audience of the woes of marriage. The third shepherd constantly grumbles and berates his lazy master. Too, these shepherds are given distinct characterization in the Nativity scene when they present the child with three gifts: a ball, cherries, and a bird.

Still, it is the character of Mak who displays comic characterizations which make him a classic figure in humorous literature. He reacts hyperbolically when confronted by the shepherds, and the double entendres of his speeches are matchless, as exemplified when Mak is accused of theft by the shepherds and he proclaims his innocence: he points to the cradle which contains the sheep and announces that he will eat the contents of the cradle if he is guilty. Here, the farce of the blasphemic Mak is actually symbolic allegory. It is obvious that Mak indeed plans to make a lovely meal of the purloined lamb; on a higher level, this idea relates directly to the eating of Christ's flesh or the communion sacrament as the pathway to salvation. The significance of the play is heightened when one realizes that *The Second Shepherds' Play* may actually be the first comedic farce of religious content in English literature. It is certainly the oldest extant example of the genre.

The Wakefield Master's *Second Shepherds' Play* is also important as a precursor to later English dramatic conventions. The anachronism and free movement of the shepherds from the English countryside to the Christ's manger in the Holy Land precludes the Renaissance playwrights' movements of their characters from alien to English soil within the same play. Additionally, the comic subplot with which the Wakefield Master begins *The Second Shepherds' Play* foreshadows those found in the works of Christopher Marlowe, William Shakespeare, and other Elizabethan playwrights.

While noted critics such as Hardin Craig believe that the Wakefield Master's *The Second Shepherds' Play*, with its emphasis on farce, distorts readers' images of the mystery play, it is still clear that the play's artistic comedy and unity have made it a timely masterpiece. More importantly, in *The Second Shepherds' Play* the Wakefield Master gave the literary world one of its first tastes of farcical comedy, one which is as delightful to audiences today as it was to the English masses centuries ago.

Summary

Little personal background is actually known about the Wakefield Master; however, *The Second Shepherds' Play*, generally agreed to be his best work and perhaps England's earliest literary farce, acts as a precursor to the literature of the Renaissance. The comedic interaction between the shepherds in the initial part of the play gives way to the solemnity and peacefulness of the Nativity. In this short piece, the Wakefield Master demonstrates his writing genius; he composed the play in the difficult nine-line stanzaic form (aaaabcccb) with middle rhyme in the first four lines. The work is also important because of the author's highly individualized characters, especially the protagonist Mak. It is Mak's comedic encounters with the shepherds, his theft of their lamb, and his use of double entendres, coupled with the shepherds' gifts to the baby sheep, which establish the first part of the play's brilliant parallel to the gifts of the Magi. It is only after the shepherds' forgiveness of the villain that they prove themselves worthy of finding the Christ child and thus their own salvation. Clearly, the Wakefield Master's reputation as one of the first great comedic writers in English literature is well-deserved. Further, this fine dramatist had the ability to retain the spirituality and mysticism of the Nativity—even while he developed one of the first British farces.

Selected Bibliography

Primary Sources

The Second Shepherds' Play from Townley Hall in Lancashire, now in the Hunting-ton Library, San Marino, California.

Medieval Drama. Ed. David Bevington. Boston: Houghton Mifflin, 1975.

Specimens of Pre-Shakespearean Drama. Ed. J.M. Manly. Boston, 1901.

The Townley Plays. Early English Text Society. Ed. G. England and A.W. Pollard. London: Kegan Paul, Trench, Trubner, 1897.

Secondary Sources

Carpenter, Nan Cook. "Music in the *Secundo Pastorum*." *Speculum*, 26 (1951): 696–700. Carpenter examines the relationship between musical elements and structural technique in the *Secundo Pastorum*. Carpenter finds that musical overtones mark the play into symmetrical divisions and heighten the characterizations of the shepherds. The three shepherds are seen as "good" because of their musical abilities and Mak as "bad" because he is tone deaf.

Craig, Hardin. "York-Wakefield Plays" in *English Religious Drama of the Middle Ages*. 1955. Oxford: Oxford University Press, 1967, pp. 199–238. A seminal chapter in which Craig introduces and thoroughly examines the relation of the texts and the structures of the plays of these two cycles. While not devoted to the Wakefield Master, this work provides a key analysis of the history and production of these two collections.

Manly, W.M. "Shepherds and Prophets: Religious Unity in the Townley *Secundo Pastorum*." *Publications of the Modern Language Association of America*, 78 (1963): 151–55.

Ross, Lawrence J. "Symbol and Structure in the *Secundo Pastorum*. *Comparative Drama*, I (1967–1968): 122–43. Ross discusses the wide implications of the problems of unity in the play and the difficulties of modern readings which impose ideals upon the text. Suggests that the play is representative of the modes available to and, therefore, demonstrably used by the Wakefield Master.

Watt, Homer A. "The Dramatic Unity of the 'Secunda Pastorum.'" In *Essays in Honor of Carlton Brown*. New York, 1940, pp. 158–66. Watt notes that the Wakefield Master succeeds in subduing the tradition of structure to fulfill his dramatic needs. In this way, the author is able to relate the comic interlude of the work with the dramatic representation of the biblical shepherd story. Thus, this usurpation of structure allows a merging of the two stories, a technique which stands up under strict structural analysis.

Robert T. Lambdin

Waller, Edmund

Born: Colehill, Hertfortshire (now Buckinghamshire), March 3, 1606
Education: Eton College, King's College, Cambridge University, ca. 1619
Marriage: Anne Banks, July 5, 1631; two children; Mary Bresse, ca. 1644; thirteen children
Died: Hall Barn (near Beaconsfield, Buckinghamshire), October 21, 1687

Biography
Edmund Waller was a member of an old gentry family. Born at Colehill, Hertfortshire (now Buckinghamshire as a result of border changes) on March 3, 1606, he was a distant relation of Oliver Cromwell and a cousin of the John Hampden who later became famous in the Ship Money Case and a member of the same family as the Parliamentary general Sir William Waller and the regicide Sir Hardress Waller. His father died when Edmund was only about ten. After indifferent schooling at High Wycombe, he matriculated at King's College, Cambridge when he was just into his teens.

He seems not to have taken a degree, but since he went into Parliament while still in his teens, this is understandable. Waller went on to become a career parliamentarian and sat in Parliament over the course of fifty years during one of the most turbulent periods in English history. When notice is first taken of him in Parliament, he is among the advocates of religious reform, although he was already, as he was to remain throughout his long public life, a voice for toleration and moderation.

During the eleven-year gap between the Short Parliament (1629) and the Long Parliament (1640), Waller showed his initial interest in literary matters when he became a member of a coterie called the Club which was founded by Lucius Cary, Viscount Falkland, at Great Tew. In this company he tried his hand at verse for the first time. During this same period, he eloped with a recently orphaned heiress. Anne Banks, whom he married on July 5, 1631, gave Waller a son and a daughter in rapid succession but died in 1635 giving birth to the second child. In the late 1630s, Waller courted Lady Dorothy Sidney, the great-niece of Sir Philip Sidney. Although her parents saw to it that she married a wealthy nobleman, she is celebrated in Waller's poetry as Sacharissa. His most accomplished lyric poems date from this period. Sometime after Parliament reconvened, perhaps in 1642 or 1644, Mary Bresse (or Bracey) became his second wife in a marriage that produced thirteen children.

In the early 1640s, Waller was busy in Parliament as a voice of moderation during this troubled time of a nation on the brink of civil war. His moderation, however, was out of tune with the times and as early as 1641 he was censured for remarks which the radical leader John Pym perversely interpreted as impugning his loyalty and patriotism when Waller was, in fact, speaking against a motion of Pym's which suggested that Parliament had the right to rule without the king.

Issues came to a head for Waller in 1644 with what is known historically as "Waller's Plot." This "plot" was a device by which the moderates tried to reconcile the majority of Parliamentarians to King Charles I. Unfortunately, the premature discovery of the plan was manipulated by Pym in such a way that definitively polarized the House of Commons and led to the final breach with the king. Waller himself escaped being executed with his fellow conspirators only by virtue of his immunity as a member of the House. By dint of legal maneuvers, craven confession, and informing on his associates, he was able to delay his trial even after he was disenabled from sitting in the House. Eventually he was fined a huge amount and exiled.

Having sold his estates to pay the fine, Waller was able to live for a time only by selling pieces of his wife's jewelry. He made a grand tour in the company of the diarist John Evelyn and seems to have employed the philosopher Thomas Hobbes as a tutor to his son. Pardoned in 1651, he returned to England the following year. The assurances that Oliver Cromwell provided for his safety are the occasion of his greatest political poem, "A Panegyric on My Lord Protector."

Waller's personal charm had probably helped to ingratiate him with Cromwell. Perhaps his charm also explains the ease with which he found favor at Court with the Restoration of Charles II. When his panegyric "To the King, Upon His Majesty's Happy Return" was thought by that monarch to fall short of the standard set by the panegyric on Cromwell, Waller had the wit to reply, "Sir, we poets never succeed so well in writing truth as in fiction." Other Restoration occasional poems are more successful, particularly "Instruction to a Painter," which celebrates a naval victory of the Duke of York (later James II).

Sitting in the reconvened Long Parliament, Waller was again active as a voice of moderation against extremism—Royalist extremism this time—and he spoke forcefully in favor of religious toleration. His conduct in the House continued to be characterized by charm and wit. According to Gilbert Burnet, Bishop of Salisbury, he was "the delight of the House: And even at eighty he said the liveliest things." He was, however, also considered "a vain and empty, tho' a witty man." As a writer, Waller could not have had a higher reputation, and his easy facility in verse became the model for the new age. Still, the poetry of this period of his life is probably his weakest. *The Divine Poems*, his only attempt to write devotional poetry, is particularly disappointing.

Having survived into his eighties by devoting himself to beauty (as one friend put it), he died at Hall Barn (near Beaconsfield, Buckinghamshire) on October 21, 1687 on the eve of the Glorious Revolution that was about to change the country yet again.

Literary Analysis

Waller was venerated by Restoration and Augustan poets as the master of their style. John Dryden's valuation is typical. In a preface that he provided for William Walsh's *Dialogue Concerning Women*, Dryden remarks of Waller that "unless he had written, none of us could write." Aphra Behn went even further, claiming that Waller taught poets "how to Love, and how to Write." Earlier poets, however, including Ben Jonson and all the Sons of Ben, had used heroic couplets as effectively. The explanation for the contemporary preeminence of Waller is perhaps found in just those qualities that now make him seem so clearly minor in comparison to Jonson or Alexander Pope, Robert Herrick, and Andrew Marvell.

Waller's heroic couplets tend to have a special clarity of form. Indeed, he was praised shortly after his death by Francis Atterbury specifically for avoiding enjambment and for making sound coincide with sense. That is to say, his verse is not simply end-stopped (each line a rhetorical and grammatical unit); it is also the case that his rhyme words characteristically emphasize just the ideas most important to the sense. In effect, Waller changes the heroic couplet from the medium for continuous narrative that it is in Geoffrey Chaucer's writing into a stanza form, a way of making a single complete point. This is exactly how the heroic couplet comes to be used by Dryden and Pope. It is perhaps the very simplicity of Waller's intellectual content that made his development of the form of the heroic couplet possible (although following a direction taken by Sir John Beaumont, George Sandys, and Edward Fairfax). This simplicity of Waller's also made his development of the couplet into a particularly attractive alternative to the intellectual intricacies of the Metaphysical Poets for his contemporaries.

If Waller is read at all nowadays, it is as the author of love lyrics. The Sacharissa poems have no special character differentiating them from the bulk of his other love lyrics which have, as a rule, nothing particularized to say about the ladies celebrated to enable those ladies to live beyond the page. Actually, the virtues of Waller's love poems, like those of his politics, lie precisely in their freedom from intensity and particularity. This may be seen most easily in a comparison with John Donne. Donne's love lyrics unfold as miniature dramas, intensely immediate, idiosyncratic, and personal. Through an artful reworking of traditional images and themes, Donne conveys moments of enormously complex dramatic specificity. By contrast, Waller's talent may be said to lie in his ability to evoke, with a kind of tactful and delicate clarity, the typical, the characteristically human in love. Donne's carefully disarranged metrics and perturbed imagery create the illusion of authentic experience. Waller's nonchalant perfection, on the other hand, suggests that he has survived the pangs of disprized love unscathed and is able to focus on its universal features. His finest effects tend to grow out of moments of anxiety, hesitancy, regret, resignation, and renunciation rather than anguish, aggression, or possessive desire.

Thus, for example, Waller is able to give new energy to the near-exhausted trope of the poet promising his mistress immortality in verse. Though he laments his failure to win love through poetry ("with numbers he the flying nymph pursues"), Waller ironically triumphs—by winning fame as a poet. As he says in "The Story of Phoebus and Daphne, Applied":

Yet what he sung . . .
Though unsuccessful, was not sung in
    vain;
All, but the nymph that should redress
    his wrong,
Attend his passion, and approve his
    song.
Like Phoebus thus, acquiring unsought
    praise.
He catched at love, and filled his arms
    with bays.

This passage also illustrates the point that Waller's use of mythological allusions is merely decorative, a criticism made by Samuel Johnson. Another weakness of Waller's is his tendency to be stronger at the beginning of a poem than at the end. He often follows an interesting opening couplet with a fairly mechanical working out of an idea. Both the strength and the weakness of Waller as a lyric poet are summed up by the fact that many of his lyrics were set to music in his own day by Henry Lawes and others. As Waller himself said of Lawes, "Verse makes heroic virtue live, / But you can life to verses give." Composers can make indifferent verse sing, but the complex ideas of the best poetry are too delicately counterpointed to be contained by the strait jacket of the regular musical line of a song lyric. As a lyric poet, Waller was a lyricist.

Unlike his love poetry which, in common with most other love poetry of the period, may have been written with a purely literary motive, Waller's political poetry, as his biography attests, was motivated by personal concerns. Although he is remembered in infamy as an informer and a turncoat, in fact he sacrificed his fortune and very nearly his life in the pursuit of his political principles. Unfortunately for his reputation, however, these principles cannot be associated with an unswerving loyalty to one or another of the competing factions. Unlike many of his contemporaries, Waller adhered to neither person nor party, maintaining instead a passionate commitment to the politics of moderation and stability throughout his life. For this reason he was always prepared to celebrate any person who promised to unite or subdue factions or who claimed the mantle of legitimacy. The irony is that while Waller's love poems—

ostensibly directed to the practical aim of winning the love of a mistress—now seem studied and cool, his political poems—ostensibly directed to the disinterested recognition and praise of virtue—carry with them an appealing air of hopefulness.

Waller's only truly original venture was a poem of praise which inadvertently established a vogue that flourished for several years. To commemorate the 1665 naval victory of the Duke of York (later King James II) over the Dutch fleet, Waller composed "Instructions to a Painter, for the drawing of the Posture and Progress of his Majesty's Forces at Sea, under the Command of his Highness-Royal: together with the Battle and Victory obtained over the Dutch, June 3, 1665." The poem uses the familiar notion *ut pictura poesis* ("as with a picture, so with a poem") to provide a vivid, "painterly" image of battle scenes, to praise the conduct of the English in battle, and to laud the King for having equipped the navy ("His club, Alcides, Phoebus has his bow, / Jove has his thunder, and your navy you"). The poem argues as well the superiority of words to paint in conveying the confusion of battle: "though you draw arm'd heroes as they sit, / The task in battle does the Muses fit."

"Instructions to a Painter" develops both a narrative and a conceptual force that Waller's shorter productions do not prepare readers to expect. Though replete with familiar fulsome praise ("There York appears; so prodigal is he / Of royal blood, as ancient as the sea! / Which down to him, so many ages told, / Has through the veins of mighty monarchs roll'd!"), the exaggerations do not cause the modern reader to cringe since they are at least appropriate to, if not fully justified by, the epic tone of the entire production. Though the verse throughout exhibits Waller's characteristic balance, flow, and ease, there are some final local effects. In the lines "Where burning ships the banish'd Sun supply, / And no light shines, but that by which men die," the disturbing thought, which makes the lines memorable, is nonetheless perfectly in keeping with the poem's governing image.

The poem, as such poems do, celebrates the victor's military prowess and preparedness and suggests that victory itself was connected with the intrinsic virtue of the British. This particular victory was, however, the prelude to a period of military reverses and other natural disasters. These cried out for a treatment as ironically heroic as Waller's had been sincerely heroic. There thus appeared a series of "Second," "Third," "Further," and "Final" advices or instructions to a painter.

These poems were immensely popular and a few of them—particularly the two generally attributed to Marvell—have earned an important place in the history of English satire. Waller's poem thus became notorious (the characterization is Douglas Bush's) as the progenitor of a race of parodies. Just as the idea of the "Instructions to a Painter" provided almost inexhaustible material for parody, the mythical apparatus with which Waller tried to elevate the tone of the poem proved equally serviceable to poets who wished to diminish the tone of theirs. Thus, Waller's "Instructions" not only inaugurated a genre but also provided a powerful impetus toward the development of mock-heroic verse in the half-century after his death. It might be argued that Waller's single most enduring contribution to the development of English literary humor was, in fact, the writing of this serious poem.

It is not easy to speak of Waller as a consciously humorous writer. His attempt to be a humorous poet is most explicit in his epigrams, but the humor there is rather thin by the standards of the age and seems quite forced and unconvincing by modern standards. He never rouses laughter—he rarely even raises a smile—and his wit does not express itself in the forceful distillation of thought that would permit the reader to find humor in detached lines of verse or even in complete short poems. In Waller, instead of distinct comical effects, there is a complacent attitude of urbanity, of civilized enjoyment of the world and of life. The overall impression that the modern reader takes from Waller is, strictly speaking, comedic rather than comic: one of reconciliation, harmony, and smoothness. Waller's poetry breathes out a spirit of acceptance of all of the vicissitudes of life—the expression of love accepted or spurned, the pleasures of wealth or the shifts necessitated by poverty, the joy of receiving the king's favor or the taint of political disgrace. In his verse, as in his life, Waller's talent was for happiness, for praise, for finding the good.

Summary

Edmund Waller is one of the Cavalier Poets or the Sons of Ben. Easy versification made these poets popular in their own day, and in fact Waller was in some ways the chief poet of his age. While the Metaphysical poet Francis Quarles

sold more volumes, Waller's work was received with a critical esteem never accorded to Quarles. And, Waller did sell well—better than John Milton, Donne, George Herbert, or Jonson, his predecessor in the same style. Late in the eighteenth century, critical assessment of the previous century clarified and matured so that Milton was finally recognized as the great poet of the age and Waller's star faded, never to shine again. Since Waller's wit is more rhetorical and less conceited than the wit of the Metaphysical Poets, his poetry still remains pleasant, easy reading.

Although his days of regard as a major poet are over, Waller as a humorist should also be remembered for the wit with which he conducted his long public life. His wit is indeed perhaps less at home in verse than in prose—as in his Parliamentary speeches. Since these speeches are topical, they are, however, now even less read than the poems.

As a wit, Waller is likely to be cited today neither for his poetry nor for his prose but for remarks he made in conversation. Like Oscar Wilde, he might well have said of himself, "I put all my genius into my life; I put only my talent into my works." Many instances of witty retorts of his are recorded over the whole course of his long career. When in her old age Sacharissa, for example, asked when he would again write "beautiful verses" for her, he said "When, Madam, your Ladyship is as young and as handsome again."

Selected Bibliography

Primary Sources

Mr. Wallers Speech in Parliament, at a Conference of Both Houses in the Painted Chamber. 6 July 1641. London: Abel Roper, 1641.

A Speech Made by Master Waller Esquire, in the Honourable House of Commons, Concerning Episcopacie, Whether It Should Be Committed or Rejected. [London], 1641.

A Worthy Speech Made in the House of Commons This Present Parliament, 1641. London: John Nicholson, 1641.

Mr. Wallers Speech in the House of Commons, on Tuesday the Fourth of July, 1643. London: G. Dexter, 1643.

With Sidney Godolphin. *The Passion of Dido for Aeneas.* London, 1658.

Act 1 of *Pompey the Great.* In Edmund Waller and others. *Pompey the Great.*

Translated out of French by Certain Persons of Honour. London: H. Herringman, 1664.

The Poems of Edmund Waller. Ed. G. Thorn-Drury. 1893. London and New York: Routledge and Dutton, [1905].

"On the Marriage of Sir John Denham." In *A Little Ark: Containing Sundry Pieces of Seventeenth-Century Verse*. Ed. G. Thorn-Drury. London: Dobell, 1921.

Secondary Sources

Allison, Alexander Ward. *Toward an Augustan Poetic: Edmund Waller's "Reform" of English Poetry*. Lexington: University of Kentucky Press, 1962. Allison treats Waller's influence on the development of eighteenth-century verse.

Bateson, F.W. "A Word for Waller." *English Poetry: A Critical Introduction*. London: Longmans, 1950, pp. 165–74. An appreciation of Waller's historical importance and lament for his diminished reputation.

Buxton, John. *A Tradition of Poetry*. New York: St. Martin's Press, 1967, pp. 87–101. Buxton studies poetry as part of courtly tradition.

Chambers, A[lexander] B. *Andrew Marvell and Edmund Waller: Seventeenth-Century Praise and Restoration Satire*. University Park: Pennsylvania State University Press, 1991. Chambers argues that Waller should be given more credit than he has for influencing the forms and themes of Marvell's poetry and that Marvell should be seen as more like Waller.

Chernaik, Warren L. *The Poetry of Limitation: A Study of Edmund Waller*. New Haven: Yale University Press, 1968. Chernaik argues that for his eighteenth-century emulators Waller represented particularly the ideal of beauty or sweetness that they were attempting to combine with a second ideal of strength or clarity of wit; originally a Ph.D. dissertation, Yale University, 1962.

Chew, Beverly. "The First Edition of Waller's Poems." *The Bibliographer*, 1 (1902): 296–303. Bibliographical comparison of the four editions of 1645.

Emperor, John B. "The Catullian Influence in English Lyric Poetry, Circa 1600–1650." *University of Missouri Studies*, 3, 3 (1928): 1–133. Emperor sees Catullus as an important influence on the love poetry of the Sons of Ben.

Erskine-Hill, H.H. "Edmund Waller and Samuel Butler: Two Poetic Debts to Hall's *Occasional Meditations*." *Notes and Queries*, 12, [210] (1965): 133–34. The influence of Joseph Hall on Waller is examined.

Gilbert, Jack G[lenn]. *Edmund Waller*. Boston: Twayne, 1979. Readable general survey of the life and works.

Gosse, Edmund. *From Shakespeare to Pope*. 1885. Rpt. New York: Franklin, 1968. Full treatment of historical background.

Haller, William. "Two Early Allusions to Milton's *Areopagitica*." *Huntington Library Quarterly*, 12 (1949): 207–12. An allusion to Milton in a pamphlet attacking Waller for *A Panagyrick on My Lord Protector* is cited.

Hayman, John. "An Image of the Sultan in Waller's 'Of Love' and 'A Very Heroical Epistle in Answer to Ephelia.'" *Notes and Queries*, 15 [213] (1968): 380–81. Hayman attributes the authorship of a disputed poem to John Wilmot, Earl of Rochester, on the basis of its characteristically Rochesterian imitation of Waller.

Hillyer, Richard. "Better Read Than Dead: Waller's 'Of English Verses.'" *Studies in English Literary Culture, 1660–1700*, 14 (1990): 33–43. A note on Waller as literary theorist.

Holtgen, Karl Joseph. "Why Was Man Created in the Evening? On Waller's 'An Apologie for Having Loved Before.'" *Modern Language Review*, 69 (1974): 23–28. Explication.

Johnson, Samuel. "Waller." *Lives of the English Poets*. Ed. G.B. Hill. Oxford: Clarendon, 1905. Vol. 1, pp. 249–300. Biography in which Johnson offers judicious praise of Waller as originator of the line of eighteenth-century poetry.

Judkins, David C. "Recent Studies in the Cavalier Poets: Thomas Carew, Richard Lovelace, John Suckling, and Edmund Waller." *English Literary Renaissance*, 7 (1977): 243–58. Review of recent criticism and annotated bibliography.

Korshin, Paul J. "The Evolution of Neoclassic Poetics: Cleveland, Denham, and Waller as Poetic Theorists." *Eighteenth-Century Studies*, 2 (1968): 102–37. Korshin argues that the contribution of Waller to eighteenth-century poetics is eloquence.

Leavis, F.R. *Revaluation: Tradition and Development in English Poetry*. 1936. Rpt. New York: Stewart, 1947. Influential modern reiteration of the long-standing dismissal of Waller as trivial.

Lloyd, Claude. "Waller as a Member of the Royal Society." *Publications of the Modern Language Association of America*, 43 (1928): 162–65. Biographical note.

Miner, Earl. *The Cavalier Mode from Jonson to Cotton*. Princeton: Princeton University Press, 1971. Includes a number of sensitive readings of Waller.

Nevo, Ruth. *The Dial of Virtue: A Study of Poems on Affairs of State in the Seventeenth Century*. Princeton: Princeton University Press, 1963. Waller is placed in the tradition of political writing.

O Hehir, Brendan. "The Early Acquaintance of Denham and Waller." *Notes and Queries*, 13, [211] (1966): 19–23. Biographical note.

Plank, Jeffrey. "Augustan Conversion of Pastoral: Waller, Denham, and Etherege's *The Man of Mode*." *Essays in Literature*, 12 (1985): 189–99. Etherege adapted Waller's pastoral mode.

Richmond, H.M. "The Fate of Edmund Waller." *South Atlantic Quarterly*, 60 (1961): 230–38. Striking explications find unexpected depth in the poet.

———. *The School of Love: The Evolution of the Stuart Love Lyric*. Princeton: Princeton University Press, 1964. Richmond shows that Waller was influential in the development of Continental neoclassicism.

Riske, Ella T. "The Date and Occasion of Waller's *Panegyric to My Lord Protector*." *Publications of the Modern Language Association of America*, 43 (1928): 1201–02. Riske places the poem in its historical setting.

Rivers, Isabel. *The Poetry of Conservatism, 1600–1745: A Study of Poets and Public Affairs from Johnson to Pope*. Cambridge: Rivers, 1973. Rivers credits major formative influence to Waller.

Skelton, Robin. "The Cavalier Poets." *British Authors Edited Under the Auspices of the British Council*. Ed. Ian Scott-Kilvert. New York: Charles Scribner's Sons, 1979, pp. 221–39. Brief introductory survey.

Summers, Joseph H. *The Heirs of Donne and Jonson*. Oxford: Oxford University Press, 1970, pp. 49–50, 132, 171–72. Summers makes several references to Waller's underrated status.

Thorn-Drury, George. "Waller, Edmund (1606–1687)." In *The Dictionary of National Biography*. Ed. Sir Leslie Stephen. 21 vols. London: Oxford University Press, 1885–1890, pp. 580–84. A brief scholarly biography with bibliography of original works.

Wallerstein, Ruth D. "The Development of the Rhetoric and Metre of the Heroic Couplet, Especially in 1625–1645." *Publications of the Modern Language Association of America*, 50 (1935): 166–209. The importance of Waller in this development is noted.

Wedgwood, C[ecily] V[ictoria]. *Poetry and Politics Under the Stuarts*. Cambridge: Cambridge University Press, 1960. Wedgwood studies the problems of poets in the political climate of Stuart England.

Wikelund, P[hilip] R. "Edmund Waller's Fitt of Versifying: Deductions from a Holograph Fragment, Folger MS. X. d. 309." *Philological Quarterly*, 49 (1970): 70n, 74n. Wikelund describes Waller's method of composition.

———. "Thus I Passe My Time in This Place: An Unpublished Letter of Thomas Hobbes." *English Language Notes*, 6 (1969): 263–68. Personal letter to Waller.

Williamson, George. *The Proper Wit of Poetry*. London: University of Chicago Press, 1961. Williamson notes the importance of Waller in the development of eighteenth-century verse satire.

Martin Beller and Edmund Miller

Waterhouse, Keith Spencer

Born: Hunslet, Leeds, West Yorkshire, February 6, 1929

Education: Osmondthorpe Council School, Leeds

Marriage: Joan Foster, October 21, 1951; three children; Stella Bingham, 1984

Biography

Prolific writer Keith Waterhouse is a Northerner with a background in the working class and experience in a variety of employments before he found his niche as a writer. He was born in Hunslet, Leeds, in West Yorkshire on February 6, 1929, the son of Ernest and Elsie Edith Waterhouse. His father sold fruit. The fifth child in the family, Keith attended the Osmondthorpe Council School, an ordinary state-run school, until he was fifteen, when he left and spent a year at Leeds College of Commerce learning typing. He then began a succession of jobs including undertaker's assistant, newsboy, rent collector, clerk, and others. At eighteen he entered the Royal Air Force.

When he had finished his national service he began work as a newspaperman, a profession in which he has been ever since. From an assignment as reporter on the Yorkshire *Evening Post* in his home town, he moved on to London where he became a feature writer for the *Daily Mirror*. Waterhouse's life up to this point included many features which appear in his fiction from *There Is A Happy Land* and *Billy Liar* to *Office Life* and *In the Mood*: working-class life in Yorkshire, longings for the metropolis, the undertaker's shop, work as a rent collector and clerk.

Since October 21, 1951, when he married Joan Foster (with whom he had three children), he has lived in London and made his living as a writer. Though he left full-time journalism in 1958, he has always contributed to newspapers and, later, magazines: he began a regular association with *Punch* in 1966, became a columnist on the *Daily Mirror* in 1970, and continued there until he moved his column to the *Daily Mail* in 1986. The Waterhouses divorced in 1968. Sixteen years later (1984), he married Stella Bingham; the marriage was dissolved in 1989. The writer won "Columnist of the Year" awards in 1970, 1973, and 1978 and a special Quarter Century Award from Granada Television in 1982.

In 1956, during a newspaper strike, Waterhouse wrote his first novel, *There is a Happy Land*. Its publication the next year led to his leaving full-time newspaper employment, and he has since published ten more novels. His main work, though, at least as measured by volume, is scriptwriting for the stage, films, television, and radio. Waterhouse knew Willis Hall, his eventual collaborator, from childhood in Leeds; in 1951, Waterhouse had written a radio play, *The Town That Wouldn't Vote*, and Hall had written television and radio plays as well as stage plays which had appeared in the provinces. In 1960, they first collaborated on a play,

dramatizing Waterhouse's popular novel *Billy Liar*, and they have since co-written a score of plays, as well as movies and television shows.

In addition to these activities, Waterhouse has found time to write, also in collaboration with Hall, television scripts for a children's show, *Worzel Gummidge*; a serious book on newspaper style; a history of the Cafe Royal; and lighthearted books on *The Theory and Practice of Lunch* and *The Theory and Practice of Travel*.

Literary Analysis

Waterhouse's very versatility—and perhaps his extraordinary productivity—have undoubtedly worked against an adequate appreciation of his talents. He is a first-class novelist, a humorous and insightful columnist of real importance, and a playwright who, though probably not in the class of Tom Stoppard or Alan Ayckbourn, is nevertheless worthy of more admiration than he seems to receive. Another reason for his lack of widespread appreciation may be exactly because he is thought of as a humorist, and in the theater his work has tended more and more toward classic farce; but, though comedy is rare enough to need no defense, his range is very wide and some of his novels are darkly moving as well as funny. Judith Thompson sums him up as "a man of exceptionally varied talents; his wit, intelligence, and capacity to entertain are fired by an acute and compassionate observation of society and human behavior, a modest humanitarianism which cares deeply that people should have access to beauty—and to laughter" (538).

He is most purely a humorist in his newspaper and magazine columns, which have been collected and published as *The Passing of the Third-Floor Buck* (1974), *Mondays, Thursdays* (1976), *Rhubarb, Rhubarb* (1979), *Fanny Peculiar* (1983), and *Waterhouse at Large* (1985). Unlike many columnists for humorous magazines, Waterhouse does not create a comic persona, he seldom invents extravagant fictions, and he does not rely either on outrageous vilification of his targets or the tired comedy of funny names. Instead, he writes as himself, in a clear and forceful style, pointing out the ridiculous sides of things. A good many of his columns are autobiographical, about his youth in Yorkshire, with a nostalgic commentary on how much things have changed. Others seem more adversarial, and we are able to discover (what also appears fairly clearly in his novels) his opposition to sociologists and jargon, bureaucracy, and especially local governments. *Fanny Peculiar* contains a running series making fun of the "Clogthorpe Council" and its maladministration. Waterhouse is also an accomplished parodist, and he has a deep interest in language, its joys and deformations, which enlivens his columns.

Before turning to his plays and novels, some other productions which elude easy categorization should be noted. *The Theory and Practice of Lunch* (1986) and *The Theory and Practice of Travel* (1989) are serio-comic how-to books. Both subjects are obviously close to the author's heart. His *Who's Who* entry gives "lunch" as his only recreation. And, *The Theory and Practice of Travel* makes clear how very much traveling he has done ("travel" to Waterhouse means leaving England). In this book he combines lighthearted observations, discussion of the writer's voyages, and useful advice. Though it includes "Twenty-five reasons for staying put," the later chapter on "Twenty-five reasons for going abroad" is clearly more heartfelt. There are sections on maps, on making complaints, on arranging a dirty weekend, on traveling with children—all illustrated with cartoons and Victorian drawings.

Also illustrated with at least mock-Victorian drawings are his *Mrs. Pooter's Diary* and *The Collected Letters of a Nobody, Including Mr. Pooter's Advice to His Son.* Charles Pooter is the title character of the 1892 *The Diary of a Nobody* by George and Weedon Grossmith. Pooter is a wonderful comic character, a mixture of the unassuming and the falsely self-confident; much of the humor of his diary comes from its revelation of an absolutely ordinary man, perhaps extraordinary only in the number of minor humiliations that he endures. Waterhouse not only had the idea but the ability to create the diary (heretofore unsuspected) of Mr. Pooter's long-suffering wife Carrie. He has done a good job of recapturing the late Victorian atmosphere, and reading Carrie's diary with Charles's in mind (they are accurately synchronized) provides another view of many of the events first revealed in the 1892 volume. This book is parasitic, relying on *The Diary of a Nobody* for its full component of enjoyment, but it succeeds within that limitation.

In 1986, Waterhouse returned to the Pooters, publishing *The Collected Letters of a Nobody.* There is a long mock-scholarly apparatus here, explaining how these letters came to survive, and they are annotated with speculations about which of them were sent, why some might be missing, and so on. Waterhouse has invented a process called the Ee-zee-kopi to explain how Pooter was able to keep copies of his letters (a realistic stroke, this; his self-satisfaction was such that he would have saved his correspondence). The letters themselves are of only moderate interest, most of them about Lupin, the Pooters' disappointing son. Waterhouse is limited, here, by the conditions of the *Diary;* as Charles and Carrie are always together, and in fact Lupin moves in with them as well, there is little excuse for letters between the Pooter family, and letters to outsiders *about* the Pooter family are a poor substitute. This book is less successful than *Mrs. Pooter's Diary,* and perhaps the author has finished with the Pooters.

Waterhouse's plays written with Hall move, generally, from what is sometimes called "council-house drama" about the lives of the urban poor in Northern England to bright and glittering farces about the marital and extra-marital complications of the middle class in London and the Home Counties. Their first play was *Billy Liar,* a dramatization of Waterhouse's novel about a dreamer and fantasist whose lies are exposed, along with his cowardice about challenging the big world that he claims to be fitted for, in one day. Billy Fisher is a bright lad who resents the narrow limits of his family, his work in an undertaker's office, and the poky northern city in which he lives. He also resents the limits of human claims on his attention: he is engaged to two girls while really being most interested in a third. This deception, along with cheating of his employers which he believes he has gotten away with, is exposed. Billy's fantasy world is funny, but the play shows it as destructive.

Billy Liar has proven very popular for Waterhouse; not only has he written another novel about the same character, *Billy Liar on the Moon,* but he and Hall adapted it for the movies in 1963 (the excellent film version was directed by John Schlesinger and starred Tom Courtenay and Julie Christie) and as a series for London Weekend Television in 1973–1974.

Billy Liar is set in Stadhoughton, a city based on the Yorkshire in which Waterhouse was reared. Billy is lower-middle-class; his father has a car repair shop. But, several other Waterhouse and Hall plays focus on the life of those a notch or two below the Fishers. These include *Celebration: A Double Bill* (1961), *All*

Things Bright and Beautiful (1963), and *Come Laughing Home* (1966). *Celebration* features a large family in two settings; in the first act they are preparing for a wedding, with a lot of incidental bickering about the cost, who is not helping out enough with the decorating, who should be invited, who should not be invited but is, and so on. The scene is where the reception will be held, in a room above a pub. Act 2 has roughly the same cast drinking in a sitting room following the funeral of Uncle Arthur; their routine is upset by the arrival of May, who lived with Uncle Arthur, and thus is not respectable. The humor in this play is largely in the unconscious pretensions of the characters and their finely drawn social and moral distinctions, as well as some funny remarks by a feeble-minded niece.

All Things Bright and Beautiful is a play that is funny in almost all of its parts while being sad overall. In it the dramatist portrays a northern, working-class family called the Hesseltines who live in substandard housing and are hoping to be relocated to a nice new council house. It becomes clear that, with the possible exception of the daughter Deanna and the son Rory (who is heard singing but never appears), they are hopeless scroungers and thieves. The action, such as it is, is catalyzed by the news that their whole street is being relocated: the Hesseltines begin to dream of a better life, nicer friends for Rory, a garden, and so on. The other main event is the discovery of a beautiful carved eagle lectern from an abandoned church. It is stolen, of course, but the Hesseltines see it as special and have plans to make it a feature of the garden in their new house. When they learn that they will be getting an eighth-floor flat instead, their aspirations subside and we are back where we began.

Come Laughing Home is a study of the frustrated life of Vera, a girl whose eminently respectable family has moved up from the slums to a new estate. Her father devotes his time to building model galleons, and her fiancé is the same sort though a bit duller. Vera has become pregnant by a boy from the slums, a nearly bestial reminder of the life they have left behind. As in *All Things Bright and Beautiful*, we see her aspire to something higher than her environment would seem able to provide, then watch as she is forced to settle for less.

These Yorkshire plays all address themselves to the theme of stunted lives; though filled with incidental humor (*Billy Liar* is by far the funniest), they have a predominantly somber tone.

In *England, Our England* the authors broaden their scope while reducing their depth. This is a revue, with music by Dudley Moore, made up of sketches and songs. It touches on the lives of people from all classes, with no strongly felt political position other than a bit of a critique of the complacency of the Conservative government.

With plays like *Say Who You Are*, *Whoops-a-Daisy*, *Children's Day*, and *Who's Who*, Waterhouse and Hall turn to a lighter kind of theater. *Whoops-a-Daisy* perhaps has the most important theme: personality change. We begin with a very tight-laced family, the Wormalds: James, Lily, and Marigold. A crude couple from Rugby, Ken and Thelma Smedley, move in next door; the Wormalds fear the working-class, Northern ways of their neighbors, and they are initially offended by their slang and their obtuse inability to see how the Wormalds shrink from them. The Smedleys are finally so unself-consciously coarse, so *vital* in some way, that they begin to warp James and Lily Wormald to them, even changing the way that they talk. Soon everyone is saying "whoops-a-daisy" (Ken's catch-phrase), and James, previously so prissy, refers to his daughter as "sitting there like a tart in a trance." The effect on Marigold is different and more troubling. Irving Wardle's complaint that in this play "a cheap and nasty method is being used to demolish a cheap and nasty target," assumes that the target is suburban, middle-class complacency. It is more than that.

A number of the collaborators' other plays are characterized by intricate structure and contrived situations, rapid action, and a basis in the complications of adultery. *Who's Who* is set in a hotel in Brighton where Bernard White and Timothy Black have come for a dirty weekend with their lovers. The lover in each case is Helen Brown. In acts 1 and 2, each man's wife arrives—both played by the same actress. There is much mistaken identity, confusion, deception, and the second act repeats the first, with complications. *Say Who You Are* is a frenetic, but finally somewhat predictable, farce about two interlocked couples and their adulteries. The set includes a lift and a stairway, permitting characters to just miss each other going up or coming down; there is much mistaken identity and a good deal of old-fashioned battle-of-the-sexes.

Children's Day is the best of the farces, focusing again on two couples and occurring during a children's party. The plot is extraordinarily complex, involving not just the marital complications of the characters but also a lost rabbit, children attacking each other, and one of the children repeatedly removing his clothes. The party is offstage, and an uproar is heard whenever the door is opened.

Waterhouse and Hall began as adaptors, making a play out of the novel of *Billy Liar*, and they have adapted other works for the stage as well, including *Saturday, Sunday, Monday* (1974) and *Filumena* (1977), adapted from dramas written by Italian playwright Eduardo de Filippo in 1959 and 1946; *The Card*, adapted from a 1911 Arnold Bennett novel; and a stage play, *Worzel Gummidge* (1981), adapted from the television adventures of this cartoon character, also created by Waterhouse and Hall. On his own Waterhouse has written *Mr. and Mrs. Nobody* (1986), based on the Pooters, and *Jeffrey Bernard is Unwell* (1989), adapted from the column "Low Life" written by Jeffrey Bernard for the *Spectator*.

The Waterhouse/Hall playwriting team has been characterized as "that dual chameleon Waterhouse 'n' Hall" and more unkindly as "a factory" (Gellert, 936; Bowen, 4). Given his extraordinary productivity in other areas, Waterhouse's eleven novels in thirty-five years almost qualifies as a writer's block. Yet, it is as a novelist that Waterhouse has produced his best work.

His first novel, *There Is a Happy Land* (1957) is not comic. It is, instead, a subtle, touching study of childhood set in the Yorkshire of Waterhouse's childhood, probably around 1940; the unnamed narrator is a boy about ten years old. He has problems with his friends; for part of the novel he is ostracized by the other boys for no good reason. He also makes friends with a girl, who becomes involved in a sexual relationship with another boy (only dimly understood by the narrator) and is eventually killed. There is a character called Uncle Mad, an eccentric who may be a child molester. The strengths of this novel are its evocation of the time and place, a very sensitive grasp of childhood, and an accomplished use of the child narrator.

The next novel, *Billy Liar* (1959) is still the book by which Waterhouse is best known. Appearing soon after John Wain's *Hurry On Down* and Kingsley Amis's *Lucky Jim*, this novel led some commentators to place Waterhouse in the Angry Young Men school. It is in some ways a study of provincial dissatisfaction. Billy is a young man in whom reality and fantasy are sharply at odds. He lives with a family which is the quintessence of ordinariness; his work at the undertakers' is mundane and meaningless, so he compensates by a rich fantasy life and by dishonesty. He has imagined a job for himself in London, writing jokes for a radio comedian. He amuses himself and his mate by inventing a Yorkshire dialect ("ah'm just about thraiped"), and he readily invents phantom sisters for himself, broken legs for his mother, and so on as an escape from reality.

As John Updike wrote in his review, "this pungent, shapely and instructive novel begins, and for the first half continues, comically," although he goes on to object to the problems caused in the second half by realism and the demands of the plot (4). Billy is an original character whose fantasy life is funny throughout. Though chronic lying is not admirable and his coldness toward his family and his fiancées is a dislikable trait, still, overall, Billy is an attractive character, and we can pity him as his rather pathetic pretenses are exposed, while still seeing the justness of the exposure.

Billy Liar illustrates nicely the kinds of comic techniques and practices which feature in Waterhouse's best books. As we would expect from his plays, and particularly the complex farcical ones, he invents clever and convoluted plots. Billy, for instance, is more or less engaged to three girls, all of them meant to be unknown to the others. He possesses one engagement ring which by desperate maneuvers, and plenty of lying, he keeps whisking around from one girl to another. Like his lies about his promising career writing for the radio in London, this is cheerful and becomes more and more funny as he moves closer and closer to the edge of discovery, over which he eventually falls.

There is also a rich verbal humor, which may be Waterhouse's greatest strength as a comic writer. He is an accomplished mimic. Particularly in his later novels he chooses narrators who are not only very different from him but often in some catastrophic mental state. In Billy he has created an intelligent mimic in his own right, whose sarcastic attitude toward his home Stadhoughton often takes the form of comic playacting:

Stadhoughton was littered with objects for our derision. We would make Fascist speeches from the steps of the rates office, and we had been in trouble more than once for doing our Tommy Atkins routine under the war memorial in Town Square . . .

The memorial vase to Josiah Olroyd in Shadrack's window always triggered off the trouble at t' mill routine, a kind of serial with Arthur taking the part of Olroyd and I the wayward son.

As we begun to walk down St. Botolph's Passage, Arthur struck up: "Ther's allus been an Olroyd at Olroyd's mill, and ther allus will be. Now you come 'ere with your college ways and you want none of it!"

"But father! We must all live our lives according to our lights—" I began in the high-pitched university voice.

"Don't gi' me any o' yon fancy talk!" said Arthur, reflecting with suspicious accuracy the tone of the old man at breakfast. "You broke your mother's heart, lad. Do you know that?"

"Father! The men! They're coming up the drive!"

We turned into Market Street swinging our arms from side to side like men on a lynching spree. (41)

In fact, this imaginary scenario bears a close relationship to Billy's life—his longing to leave Stadhoughton—though the high-voiced university son has actually done something about it. The protagonist's funniest bits are often his most self-revealing as well.

In 1975, Waterhouse wrote a sequel, *Billy Liar on the Moon*, which follows the same pattern as the original. Billy is now a local government employee in a town called Shepford, somewhat closer to London than he was; we can deduce that he now lives somewhere near Birmingham. He is married and is cheating on his wife with a woman named Helen. Typically, he is cheating on his job, too, doing as little work as possible while scheming to get a promotion, spending time in pubs or with Helen when he should be at work. Billy is a liar of the ordinary sort, telling his wife fantastic tales to cover up for his visits with Helen. He is also, as

in the previous novel, the creator of a rich fantasy life. In *Billy Liar*, he dreamed a lot about an imaginary place called Ambrosia; here he dreams about America, including a fantasy American friend named Oscar who gives him advice on the high life and how to manage his extramarital affairs.

Billy's lying gets him into trouble. One of the funniest consequences comes from his impromptu claim, made one night while standing around in the stairwell looking for Helen, that his set of golf clubs has been stolen. Though the clubs never existed, an officious neighbor reports the theft, and through the rest of the book he is trying to fend off an investigating policeman, seeking to buy some clubs so he can claim that his have turned up, and trying to get Helen to steal a set from a member of the Council in an escalating comedy of frustration.

In *Billy Liar on the Moon*, Waterhouse shows Billy creating and just barely sustaining a house of cards. In the end, most of it collapses. A job that he wanted goes to someone else; Helen's husband discovers their affair; his wife proves to be pregnant. When fantasy and reality are forced to coexist, reality—despite being dull and unromantic—wins.

Alan Hollinghurst has summarized Waterhouse's career as a novelist: "In Keith Waterhouse's succession of funny and original novels since *Billy Liar* in 1960 he has compacted two kinds of comedy: a relentlessly observant ridicule of the world, and a private systematization of things carried out by the characters to protect themselves from their uncharitable and ridiculous circumstances" (18). Billy's fantasizing and lying are a fairly recognizable kind of systemization of things. In *Jubb*, the novel that Waterhouse published in 1963, the focus is transferred from the ridiculousness of life to the strategies, now much more peculiar, of a stranger protagonist. There are funny things here, and a fairly effective satire on New Towns and local government (Jubb is a rent collector for Chapel Langtry, a new town), but our primary interest is in the progressively unraveling personality of the narrator and protagonist. Mr. Jubb, we come to learn, is a misfit and outcast. A quondam "youth leader" at the community center, he has no followers. His time is devoted to following women on buses, peeping through windows, and dreaming of social accomplishments which are clearly far beyond his abilities. His wife has left him, and he keeps getting into trouble. Even a fascist group will not have him as a supporter. As Billy Fisher lives in fantasies of Ambrosia or America, C.L. Jubb dreams of the Reeperbahn in Hamburg.

In disturbing flashbacks we learn of Jubb's unhappy childhood, during which he may well have killed his parents and aunt. At the end of the book he is headed for Hamburg, but it seems more likely that he is going to kill himself. One reviewer wrote that "squalid and pathetic Jubb may be, but Mr. Waterhouse has somehow managed to make him a gloriously comic character . . . a man not only psychopathic, but also a repulsive bore, who nevertheless emerges as profoundly sane and even, in his own odd way, quite jolly" ("Heading," 730). This is undoubtedly overstating the case; but it is true that, despite Mr. Jubb's quite horrible qualities, and fate, the novel remains funny. It is a genuine tragicomedy, a brilliant book.

Waterhouse's other novels may be divided between those in which the serious matter predominates over the comedy and those which are primarily comic. In the first group are *The Bucket Shop*, *Maggie Muggins*, *Thinks*, and *Our Song*. These are all studies of odd people, people who don't fit in.

In *The Bucket Shop*, the main character is William, a failed antique-shop proprietor who is desperate to be fashionable. Everything that William does is for effect: he nicknames his wife Poodle, hoping that she will become interesting; he is continually cheated by sharper people who take advantage of his pretended savoir-faire. He would like to play some part in the world of show business, but this comes to no more than investing and losing a great deal of money in a play and carrying on an affair (which also involves investing and losing money) with a girl who once made a cat food commercial. William has another mistress, though they almost never make love because of his fear of discovery. One suspects that he likes *having a mistress* more than he likes sex. As in many of his novels, in this one Waterhouse details the coming apart of a life, as William's marriage, both affairs, his business, and even his daughter's character suffer as a result of his flaws.

Maggie Muggins is the funny but terrible story of a day in the life of a drunken, sexually indiscriminate Londoner, a girl who moves from one squalid room to another in the sleazier parts of the city. On the single day of the novel, Maggie is making her "mail round"— that is, going around to all of the places she has lived to pick up her letters, as she is deeply se-

cretive and never leaves a forwarding address. Each stop on the mail round uncovers a bit of her history, and much of the novel is retrospective. Moreover, she finds at each of her mail drops a card from her friend Sean, a homosexual hustler who, we gradually realize, is the only person whom she loves. We also learn a bit about Maggie's child, whom she is giving up for adoption, and her troubles with various social service agencies.

The plot is both thin and somewhat predictable, and the ending is a bit forced, but Maggie is a fascinating character, and the atmosphere of Earl's Court and the other venues for Maggie's life is very well captured. The novelist has provided Maggie with a vigorous, slangy way of talking, as evidenced in her disquisition on the difference between "punters"—that is, ordinary people—and "faces"—people like her and Sean, marginal sorts who live by their wits. Maggie is clearly a girl of the streets and her story is heartbreaking in some ways, but it is also funny and energetic, and *Maggie Muggins* is a fine novel.

Our Song is another predominantly sad account of life in London, this time among the well-paid dwellers in the world of advertising. The narrator, Roger, is writing a letter to his former mistress, Angela, and the letter is the book. It is a story of obsessive love pitted against reason, like *Of Human Bondage*, with Roger giving up everything for a woman who is dishonest, rude, exasperating, unreliable, and shifty; she may be a prostitute, although she will seldom go to bed with her supposed "lover." There is some good satire about the advertising business but this is not a funny book. Rather, it is a powerful study of obsession.

Perhaps the starkest of Waterhouse's novels is *Thinks*. Like *Billy Liar* and *Maggie Muggins*, this is another day-in-the-life, the life of a certain Edgar Samuel Bapty, a nonentity. During this day, Bapty goes up from a town on the south coast, where he has an unimportant job in local radio, to London for an interview with a cable television firm. He also calls on his doctor in London and on one of his ex-wives. Throughout the day he drinks almost incessantly.

This book has a chatty, engaging narrator who explains to the reader the unusual convention of the novel; we are privy to all of Bapty's thoughts, except when he is in private with another person, but we cannot hear his words. The immediately striking fact about his thoughts is how vicious they are. He is in a rage against everybody and everything. As far as we can tell, though, he is "in reality" very deferential to everybody. So, his rage is purely internal. We are also privy to his uncertainties, as when he drafts statements and has to edit them to remove all of the detectable lies. The main point is the enormous and dangerous disparity between his inner and outer lives. Toward the end the convention of the novel is violated. Likewise, Bapty lets his inner and outer worlds coalesce, by actually saying to his ex-wife what he was thinking about her ("you pigging, poxing cowbag"). Bapty is an unlikeable protagonist, though finally more pitiable than anything else; the novel is another striking study of drunkenness and failure.

Waterhouse's more purely comic novels (in addition to the two about Billy Liar) are *Office Life*, *In the Mood*, and *Bimbo*. In *Office Life*, he imagines a vast company, British Albion, which employs an army of white-collar workers, all of whom are losers. The narrator, Clement Gryce, is a committed clerk who has sometimes quit previous jobs to avoid promotion. Here he soon begins to notice odd things: the telephones never ring; nobody knows what business British Albion is in; and *nobody does any work*. Gryce joins a group of conspirators dedicated to digging out the secret of British Albion and finally discovers that it is a shell company set up to provide artificial employment for unemployables. The explanation is that if the populace were to suspect how bad the economy of England actually is there would be universal despair.

This is a whimsical approach to a serious problem—England's economic woes—and naming the company British Albion seems to be an invitation to the readers to see it as symbolic of a country going nowhere. But, the main strength of this book is in its picture of office routine. Gryce's co-workers, like Gryce himself, are marginal, pointless people who have evolved a repertoire of behaviors to lend significance to their lives. There is some good satire about how people behave in offices: the jokes they make, the way they laugh, who brings in candy, how many times they go to the bathroom. And, life in this company which does nothing is only a slight exaggeration of life in any office—the minor thefts of office supplies, coming in late and leaving early, and so forth. The employees all have their self-respect; they know that they are not doing any work, but they think that others are doing even less. The novel provides an alternative to this drone-like existence (not a very realistic one), but that seems less important than the brilliant satire on office life.

In the Mood, published between *Maggie Muggins* and *Thinks*, is in marked contrast to those two novels of drunkenness, suicide, and the failure of love. It is a nostalgic look at adolescence, the flavor of which is indicated by the beginning:

> I lived in a different country once. Nothing there was the same as now. All that happened then, if it happened here, would be strange and fresh.
>
> Everything was sharper. Cigarette smoke had a pungency it has since lost. Even stale beer smelled full-bodied and good. Girls' breasts were whiter. Like alabaster, we said, though none of us knew what alabaster was in that long-ago place. The air was as crisp as apples, and all the sad songs were sweeter, then.
>
> Youth was our visa to this country. (5)

The narrator is Raymond Watmough, a seventeen-year-old living in Grippenshaw, Yorkshire, a place which, like Billy's Stadhoughton, seems another avatar of Waterhouse's Leeds. Paul Schlueter has referred to "Waterhouse's consistent antipathy toward his northern roots" (565). This novel proves how poorly Schlueter has understood Waterhouse. Raymond and his friends Douglas Beckett and Terry Liversedge, newly graduated from the Grippenshaw College of Commerce, are not only ready for the real world (jobs as clerks in banks, travel agencies, and other small-scale white collar work) but are determined to begin seducing girls. *In the Mood* has two real plots. One centers on the 1951 Festival of Britain and a scheme by the three boys to arrange a bus trip to London. The other is a sort of competition between them to be the first to sleep with a girl. There is a great deal of period detail here, much funny material about their clothes, about the odd folkways which govern people's behavior at dances and movies, and about the formalities of going out together and breaking up. Their conversation about girls is funny, partly because it is so obsessive and yet so unrealistic. They regularly take note, when first seeing a female, of how her clothes would be removed—"Miss Cohen, the shorthand teacher, walked down the assembly hall on her way to one of the form-rooms. Something rustled as she passed, probably a starched petticoat under the flared cotton dress that could be unzipped to the navel and then slid gently over her hips" (170)—and they theorize endlessly about which types of girls are most eager for "it"; nurses and handicapped girls, in particular, they think.

The most striking feature of *In the Mood* is its sunny tone. Though it has a bittersweet ending—Raymond winds up on the bus to London with a last-minute substitute, whom, we gather, he goes on to marry—this is a cheerful novel. It is about adolescence, and it carries a feeling that becoming adult (in the language of Raymond, a dodo or a fossil) is a terrible remove from the country of youth.

In *In the Mood,* Waterhouse worked with a narrator of his own age, regional and educational background, and class. In *Bimbo,* he tries something completely different: a young, uneducated girl's account of her rise and fall as a Page Three pinup queen. The results are not very successful. This book is presented as an autobiography by Debra Chase, written as a corrective to a sensational ghostwritten story in a tabloid paper. The beginning gives some of the flavor: "Now it can be told. The biggest majority of the Debra Chase by Herself series in the *Sunday Shocker* which I am sposed to of written was a load of rubbish, a virago of lies from start to finish" (7).

The story itself is not very interesting, and very likely its commonplace quality is part of Waterhouse's point. Debra is an ordinary girl—perhaps below the ordinary in intelligence, certainly in education—who becomes involved in beauty contests and fashion modeling and finally in posing naked for a national newspaper. There is some satire on the world of night clubs and swinging photographers and "bonking baronets," the world referred to in tabloid headlines generally, but most of the humor is derived from Debra's style, which is naive and filled with malapropisms. The chapters have titles like "I Grow Boobs" and "The Commencal of My Career." Waterhouse has never been short of good *ideas* for novels, and this is another good one, but it does not amount to very much. There is undoubtedly something touching about the lives of Page Three girls, but Waterhouse has not found it, and the humor is of a routine, mechanical quality.

Summary
It is hard to summarize an accomplishment as big and diverse as that of Keith Waterhouse. He is a productive, inventive, clever writer, whose success as a humorous columnist would be worthy of note even if it were not for his work as a novelist and playwright. In his plays with Willis Hall, he brings out the comedy in pathetic life and the pathos in comic life. His is a drama of frustration: sexual frustration in his more recent farces, frustration of ambition in the council house dramas. In his novels, Waterhouse has focused on the gap between aspiration and reality and on the mechanisms that lonely people use to give their lives meaning. Apparently he can write almost any sort of book, and in all of them, in some measure, he blends wit and humor with sympathy and an unsentimental tenderness.

Selected Bibliography
Primary Sources

Novels
There Is a Happy Land. London: Michael Joseph, 1957.
Billy Liar. London: Michael Joseph, 1959; New York: Norton, 1960.
Jubb. London: Michael Joseph, 1963; New York: Putnam, 1964.
The Bucket Shop. London: Michael Joseph, 1968; rpt. as Everything Must Go. New York: Putnam, 1969.
Billy Liar on the Moon. London: Michael Joseph, 1975; New York: Putnam, 1976.
Office Life. London: Michael Joseph, 1978.
Maggie Muggins, or, Spring in Earl's Court. London: Michael Joseph, 1981.
In the Mood. London: Michael Joseph, 1983.
Thinks. London: Michael Joseph, 1984.
Our Song. London: Hodder & Stoughton, 1988.
Bimbo. London: Hodder & Stoughton, 1990.

Plays with Willis Hall
Billy Liar. London: Michael Joseph, and New York: Norton, 1960.
Celebration. London: Michael Joseph, 1961.
All Things Bright and Beautiful. London: Michael Joseph, 1963.
The Sponge Room and Squat Betty. London: Evans, 1963.
England, Our England. London: Evans, 1964.
Come Laughing Home. London: Evans, 1966.
Say Who You Are. London: Evans, 1966;

published as *Help Stamp Out Marriage!*
London and New York: French, 1974.

Who's Who. London and New York: French,
1974.

Children's Day. London and New York:
French, 1975.

Whoops-a-Daisy. London: Evans, 1978.

Miscellaneous

The Passing of the Third-Floor Buck. London: Michael Joseph, 1974.

Mondays, Thursdays. London: Michael Joseph, 1976.

Rhubarb, Rhubarb, and Other Noises. London: Michael Joseph, 1979.

Fanny Peculiar. London: Michael Joseph, 1983.

Mrs. Pooter's Diary. London: Michael Joseph, 1983.

Waterhouse at Large. London: Michael Joseph, 1985.

The Collected Letters of a Nobody. London: Michael Joseph, 1986.

The Theory and Practice of Lunch. London: Michael Joseph, 1986.

The Theory and Practice of Travel. London: Hodder & Stoughton, 1989.

Secondary Sources

Algren, Nelson. "The Ginger Man Who Couldn't." *The Nation*, 198 (April 16, 1964): 351–52. Review of *Jubb*.

Bowen, John. Review of *Everything Must Go*. *New York Times Book Review* (January 26, 1969): 4, 34. An unsympathetic review of Waterhouse's fourth novel which traces its flaws to the collaboration with Willis Hall.

Cassill, R.V. "A 'Herbert' Who Wished to Be a 'Lion.'" *New York Times Book Review* (April 5, 1964): 46. Review of *Jubb*.

Churchill, Thomas. "Waterhouse, Storey, and Fowles: *Which Way Out of the Room?*" *Critique*, 10 (1968): 72–87. Churchill compares *Billy Liar* and *Jubb* to *This Sporting Life*, *The Magus*, and *The Collector*.

DeVitis, A. "Life as an Antique Shop." *Saturday Review*, 52 (March 1, 1969): 50. Review of *Everything Must Go* (i.e., *The Bucket Shop*).

Gellert, Roger. "Love and Sponges." *New Statesman*, 64 (December 28, 1962): 936. Review of Waterhouse and Hall's *The Sponge Room* and *Squat Betty*.

Gindin, James. *Postwar British Fiction: New Accents and Attitudes*. Berkeley: University of California Press, 1962, pp. 108–14. Contains a fairly brief account of Waterhouse.

Gray, Nigel. *The Silent Majority: A Study of the Working Class in Post-War British Fiction*. London: Vision, 1963. An oddly hysterical book which has an original look at *Billy Liar*.

"Heading For a Fall." *The Times Literary Supplement*, 3213 (September 27, 1963): 730. Review of *Jubb*.

Hollinghurst, Alan. "Ways of Escape." *New Statesman*, 101 (June 12, 1981): 18. Review of *Maggie Muggins*.

Lowrey, Burling. "Neurotic in a Community of Madmen." *Saturday Review*, 47 (April 4, 1964): 39. Review of *Jubb*.

Malcolm, Donald. "Steps Going Down." *The New Yorker*, 40 (November 7, 1964): 234–38. Long, thoughtful review of *Jubb*.

Marowski, Daniel G., and Roger Matuz, eds. *Contemporary Literary Criticism*. Detroit: Gale, 1988. Vol. 47, pp. 414–24. Good collection of critical comment, much of it from British sources, on Waterhouse's books up through *The Collected Letters of a Nobody*.

"Mirror Image." *Harper's*, 228 (March 1964): 120–21. Review of *Jubb*.

Richardson, Maurice. "New Novels." *New Statesman*, 5, 58 (September 12, 1959): 328. Review of *Billy Liar*.

Saal, Hubert. "There Will Always Be an English Novel." *Saturday Review*, 43 (February 27, 1960): 22–23, 31–32. Saal focuses on *Billy Liar*, along with novels by John Goldthorpe, Raymond Postgate, Dave Wallis, and John Bowen.

Schlueter, Paul. "Keith Waterhouse." In *Dictionary of Literary Biography*, *British Novelists, 1930–1959: Part Two: M–Z*. Vol. 15. Ed. Bernard Oldsey. Detroit: Gale, 1983. A good combination of biography and summary criticism, though Schlueter does not seem to like Waterhouse's novels much.

Thompson, Judith. "Keith Waterhouse." In *Dictionary of Literary Biography*, *British Dramatists Since World War II: Part Two: M–Z*. Vol. 13. Ed. Stanley Weintraub. Detroit: Gale, 1982. Some of the same information as in Schlueter, but from a more sympathetic commentator.

Updike, John. "Nightmares and Daymares." *New York Times Book Review* (January 3, 1960): 4, 22. Review of *Billy Liar* by another then little-known novelist.

Wardle, Irving. "'Whoops-a-Daisy,' Play on Suburbia, Is Given in London." *New York Times* (December 15, 1968): 61. Very mixed review.

Merritt Moseley

Waugh, Auberon Alexander

Born: Dulverton, Somerset, November 17, 1939

Education: Downside School 1952–1956; attended Christ Church College, Oxford University, 1959–1960

Marriage: Teresa Onslow, July 1, 1961; four children

Biography

The eldest son of novelist Evelyn Waugh and Laura Herbert, Auberon Waugh has followed his father's example: he is the author of five novels, some of them reminiscent in tone and attitude of his father's works; he lives in Combe Florey House, the imposing seventeenth-century manor bought by Evelyn; and he speaks for hierarchical values and traditional Roman Catholicism. In other respects he is very different. Despite his novels, his most important work is in journalism. And, while the senior Waugh was in some respects a self-creation (if not an unconscious self-parody), Auberon has adopted a similar strategy, creating an "Auberon Waugh" which is his face before the world, but much more deliberately, and with some self-mockery along with the self-importance of his father's persona.

Born in Dulverton, Somerset on November 17, 1939, Auberon was educated at Downside School, a Roman Catholic public school (1952–1956), after which he entered the Royal Horse Guards. During his service in Cyprus, where there were hostilities between Greeks and Turks, he accidentally machine-gunned himself: he noticed that the gun in his armored car was not working, and, "Seizing hold of the end with quiet efficiency, I was wiggling it up and down when I noticed it had started firing. Six bullets later I was alarmed to observe that it was firing through my chest, and got out of the way pretty sharpish" (*In the Lion's Den*, 77). He lost a finger, one lung, and his spleen, and was disabled

out of the army. He subsequently entered Christ Church College, Oxford (one of the most prestigious of the colleges; his matriculation at the institution was much envied by his father), in 1959 but left after a year because of failure in his preliminary examinations. He then turned to journalism.

He has been a busy and versatile journalist ever since. His first job was as an editorial writer on the *Daily Telegraph* of London (1960–1963), and he has been a columnist for the *Catholic Herald* (1963–1964) and a political commentator for the *Spectator* (1967–1970). He has written columns for the *Spectator* (1976 to the present), the *New Statesman* (1973–1975), the *News of the World* (1969–1970), the *Sun* (1969–1970), the *Times* (1970), and the *Sunday Telegraph* (1982 to the present). For the *Spectator* (1970–1973), the *Evening Standard* (1973–1980), the *Daily Mail* (1981–1986), and the *Independent* (1986 to the present), he has served as the chief fiction reviewer. He has been the Wine Correspondent for various publications, including the *Spectator*, and has written a medical column for *British Medicine*. In addition, he has contributed articles and reviews to *Esquire*, the *New York Times*, *Le Monde*, and other publications.

Two more journalistic positions are of even more importance. From 1970 to 1986 Waugh wrote for *Private Eye*, the satirical and investigative fortnightly magazine. He had been dismissed as a political columnist for the *Spectator*, allegedly because his "abusive political column had been a source of growing discomfort to a paper which was (in those days) of fairly orthodox Conservative views" (Marnham, 115). He was named the "political correspondent" of *Private Eye*, but his column was "a unique mixture of jokes, abuse and accurate political gossip" (Marnham, 115). In 1972, he became the *Eye's* "diarist," continuing that same mixture in the form of a daily account of his thoughts, reflections on the news, and pretended activities. "Auberon Waugh's Diary" continued until he left the journal in 1986.

At that time he became editor of the *Literary Review*. Owned and underwritten by Naim Attalah, the proprietor of Quartet Books, this is a lively journal of literary opinion which carries many reviews every month, a few columns including an editor's page by Waugh, and a "real poetry contest," soliciting entries each month on a set topic and requiring that the poetry rhyme, scan, and make sense.

During this thirty-year journalistic career, Waugh has also written five novels, including one (*The Foxglove Saga*) written while he recuperated from his injuries in Cyprus. He has not published a novel since 1972, declaring that he would not write another until the British enacted a Public Lending Rights act designed to permit authors to profit from their books lent out by libraries. He has also written a number of non-fiction books. One of these is on Biafra, a subject of some importance to the author: Waugh was passionately opposed to his government's support of the Nigerian government during the Biafran civil war. Biafra is an important subject in his last novel, *A Bed of Flowers,* and he gave one of his sons the middle name Biafra. In addition he wrote *The Last Word: An Eyewitness Account of the Trial of Jeremy Thorpe* (the leader of the Liberal Party who was tried for soliciting the murder of a male model with whom he had had a homosexual relationship), and he has written a book on wine and, with his wife, Teresa Onslow (whom he married on July 1, 1961 and with whom he has had four children), a book on entertaining.

In his late fifties, Waugh continues with remarkable energy and visibility. According to his *Who's Who* entry, his hobby is gossip, and this devotion, added to his strong opinions and full life, helped to make his memoirs, *Will This Do?* (published in 1991), controversial and interesting reading.

Literary Analysis
Though he had begun his career as a columnist, it was as a novelist that Waugh first received public attention, especially in the United States where his journalism did not appear and where the Waugh family name ensured a reading. His five novels span the years between 1960 and 1972; their critical reception has been mixed, and perhaps the relative lack of success of *A Bed of Flowers*, which has never found an American publisher, helped him to decide against writing more novels. All of his novels provide amusement; all contain satire on all sorts of pretensions and, even more insistently, on the major trends of the twentieth century. When that critique of modernity becomes too strenuous, when Waugh's right-wing premises drive the fiction too purely, the humor thins out and the novels become sour.

The first book, published in 1960, is very much a juvenile production, written while he was a teenager and concentrating on life among the privileged in a Catholic boys' school and the larger world into which the boys later move. *The Foxglove Saga* is a study of one Martin Foxglove, a charming and unscrupulous young man from a "good family," and his oddly chosen companion, Kenneth Stoat, who is ugly and unappealing. Since we follow Martin and Kenneth through the Catholic school, the army, and a nursing home, it is probable that the novel is a fantasia on Waugh's Downside, the Guards, and the recovery from his wounds in Cyprus.

The generally good reviews of this novel praised the author's wit, quite rightly. The volume abounds in the sort of affectless treatment of horrible things which produces laughter. For instance, it begins with a group of monks discussing the imminent death of one of their number, and their worldliness—they are most interested in who will get his typewriter and special mattress—is delightfully comic. This deadpan presentation of outrageous material is a characteristic of Evelyn Waugh's novels, as well, and critics chided Auberon for his similarity to his father. Similarities between Martin Foxglove and Sebastian Flyte were noted. That Evelyn published a revised edition of *Brideshead Revisited* in the same year as *The Foxglove Saga*, and through the same publisher, undoubtedly encouraged comparisons.

Auberon's second novel, *Path of Dalliance* (1963), did nothing to discourage the comparison. The setting in this book moves on from school to university, where the focus is on a young man named Jamey Sligger who (like Waugh) is sent down after a year at Oxford. The author has apparently called this an autobiographical novel (Grumman, 746), though again it clearly takes the materials of his life and inflates them for comic effect. Somewhat like Stoat and Foxglove, Jamey is the less privileged and somewhat marginalized friend of a boy named Frazer-Robinson, who is always treated well because his family is rich. Both have come from a cranky old Catholic school called Cleeve. The plot is frenetic and loose; Jamey and Frazer-Robinson become involved in university politics, and in sponsoring a show by a fraudulent artist from London. A girl with whom they are friendly dies, and Jamey is sent down from Oxford for no very good reason. He goes to live with his mother, a comic eccentric; meanwhile his brother, who has been in prison, brings home a fellow inmate to stay with them and Mrs. Sligger falls in love with the former convict. She is a parody of unthinking liberalism. Jamey eventually goes into journalism in London.

In the background is an odd conspiratorial story about a priest at Cleeve named Rapey Rawley (but nicknamed Creepy Crawley) who corresponds with a network of Cleeve boys, all of whom spy on each other and give him information which he uses in unsavory ways. Part of the flavor of the book—its rather sophomoric humor in some ways—may be found in Creepy Crawley's name, the group name of the Rapists used for his acolytes, and the name of one character, Mrs. Droppings.

This novel, like *The Foxglove Saga*, has very much the flavor not of *Brideshead Revisited*—that has too many serious themes—but of Evelyn Waugh's much earlier novel *Decline and Fall*, which also includes the cold and completely unjust dismissal of the protagonist from Oxford as a move in a game of unquestioned privilege.

Auberon's third novel, *Who Are the Violets Now?* (1965), is his poorest, intermittently funny but incoherent and finally rather unpleasant. In it a man named Arthur Friendship works for *Woman's Dream* magazine and spends his evenings working for Education for Peace. He is a foolish idealist and events mock him. The leader of Education for Peace turns out to be a Nazi who is eventually kidnapped and taken to Israel for trial. Arthur loves Elizabeth Pedal, who falls in love with a crudely caricatured American black activist and poet named Thomas Gray. Arthur heroically goes into a burning room to save a baby but accidentally saves no more than a bundle of laundry while being completely disfigured himself, and when, on the strength of a promotion to writing the Pet's Corner column, he sets out to propose to Liz Pedal, he is killed. Among these awful events Waugh has included plentiful satire on women's magazines, the peace movement, attitudes toward black people, and black people themselves, at least those of the more flamboyant kind.

In 1968, Waugh published *Consider the Lilies*, which is easily his best book. It is narrated by a modern Anglican clergyman named Nicholas Trumpeter. Niocholas is completely without scruples, having gone into the ministry as the easiest way to make a living. In the eventful plot, he considers killing his wife, though this becomes unnecessary; he has an affair with the daughter of his patron (a funny millionaire named Mr. Boissaens) while fending off Mr.

Boissaens's predatory young wife; and he becomes involved in lots of little activities like raising funds for a dance hall for Old Age Pensioners and an innocent witchcraft party. The village is a hotbed of gossip and narrow-mindedness. The clergy are all misfits and eccentrics: one member of the chapter thinks that he is Christ, another is exclusively interested in pets, another refuses to hold services, even on Easter.

Trumpeter spends most of his time in his study watching television or reading Erle Stanley Gardner while complaining of his work load. His sermons are on subjects such as the dangers of inflammable nightgowns, until he finally develops an obsession with the belief that the world is suffering from an anal obsession.

There is rich satire on the Church here. Waugh frequently inveighs against the gibbering trendiness of modern religious leaders—usually the Catholics, though the Anglicans come in for their share as well—and in this novel he seems determined to demonstrate how completely empty modern Christianity has become.

In *A Bed of Flowers; Or As You Like It* (1972), Waugh seems to have been trying to do something about the appearance of looseness or extemporaneity which his earlier novels create. This book is mapped onto *As You Like It*, as the subtitle suggests, with characters named Oliver and Orlando, Rosalind and Celia, and so on. The plot concerns a sort of hippie retreat into Somerset, and plot turns like Orlando's taking bad acid and becoming unable to discern that Rosalind is a girl—thus updating Shakespeare's transvestite theme—sustain the parallel. Rather surprisingly, for Waugh, the hippies are the sympathetic characters, the representatives of wealth, status, and power the bad people. There is a good deal about religion, as usual, and a good deal of mysticism (partly due to the proximity of Glastonbury), and the fact that the hippies find the Holy Grail at one point, but bury it again.

This novel is more concerned with the larger world than his others. It begins on the night of Harold Wilson's election as prime minister, in 1966, and ends with the election of Edward Heath in 1970. It is also intensely concerned with the war in Biafra, that is the attempt of Eastern Nigeria to achieve its independence which was followed by a war of attrition (supported by the Wilson government) in which several million people were killed. All of the people at Williams Farm, the hippie enclave, are sympathetic to the

Biafrans; the establishment, for purely venal and wicked reasons, opposes them.

Waugh's particular qualities of forceful writing, wit, and perhaps cruelty also inform his activities as a book reviewer. Peter Hebblethwaite names his chief qualities as "a brusque common sense, a savage irony, and a disregard for the niceties of *lit. crit.* that have made him enemies" (534). Waugh is famous for reviewing an author's picture on the dust jacket, commenting, for instance, that he looks like an ape, or seems to be dying of syphilis. He writes with absolute conviction. He never hedges. These qualities, according to J.A. Sutherland, have made Waugh "the most influential reviewer of novels in Britain" (98). Sutherland goes on to quote Waugh as explaining that "the key quality in reviewing is not judiciousness or erudition or good taste, least of all is it moderation. It is liveliness of response" (99). This approach also explains the vitality of the *Literary Review* under Waugh's editorship.

In his personal columns, Waugh voices his convictions in a lively style as well. He describes his "own small gift" for "making the comment, at any given time, which people least wish to hear" (*Will This Do?* pp. 214–215). He often takes stands against what he perceives as sentimental or "wet" liberalism. He is scathing, for instance, on the subject of the nation's protectiveness toward old people; he questions special provisions for the handicapped; he has no use for the working class. He also assumes some positions purely for amusement, it seems, including his campaign against the campaign against drunken driving, his defense of massage parlors, and his claim that Canadian seal pups represent a threat to modern civilization because women are breeding with them and producing inferior children. His most frequent complaint is about the low quality of modern Britons—he writes that "the British national character is something nobody discusses unless to tell lies" (*In the Lion's Den*, 135)—and the fact that most social trends encourage and reinforce mediocrity rather than correcting it. About education, for instance, he says:

> What a good idea it would be if British teachers, instead of filling their pupils' heads with a lot of boring, out-dated rubbish about contraception, abortion, and how to masturbate, could teach each generation an entirely different language. Only those who wish to promote strife

for their own sinister purposes can seriously pretend that there is anything to be gained at this stage of our nation's history by the generations talking to each other. (*Country Topics*, 26)

Despite the conservative tendency of his thinking, Waugh's column was dropped at one point by the conservative *Spectator* and at another appeared in the left-wing *New Statesman*. He has vilified Mrs. Thatcher and her predecessor Heath as much as the Labor politicians who are their conventional adversaries.

Though Waugh certainly represents an original voice in the British social, literary, and political landscapes, his novels and columns are well within the formal traditions of modern British writing. His original invention, his great contribution, is the mock diary. Though diary literature has, of course, existed for a very long time, what Waugh brought to his diary in *Private Eye* was not only an unfettered freedom of commentary but a willingness to invent even his own supposed activities. He writes often, for instance, of his friends in the royal family—the advice that he has given to Prince Charles on a marriage partner, for example; he gives full accounts of trips (to Japan, Libya, Uruguay) which he never made; he invents books, opinions, events, nicknames. A typical entry reads in its entirety:

> (Tuesday 29th January 1975): Spend all morning outside County Hall singing hymns with some fine people from the Salvation Army and a nondescript collection of religious maniacs protesting about film censorship.
>
> I have no strong feelings either way about dirty films and don't really know what I am doing here, but there is nothing else to do in the morning in this ghastly city where nobody seems to get up before lunchtime. If only they would have community singing on the Circle Line it might keep some of us away from the massage parlours. (*Four Crowded Years*)

Through it all his tone is an odd mixture of urbanity and savagery. Calling a famous newspaper proprietor an "Elephant Man lookalike" is an example, as is the parenthetical identification of a woman as "the moustachioed hellcat." Claiming that he had called for Winston

Churchill to be hanged at the end of World War II (Waugh, who was born in 1939, often writes as if he is much much older), he explains that "Churchill's unsuitability for peace time conditions had been shown well enough by his persecution of P.G. Wodehouse, and this gesture would have spared Englishmen who wanted to hero-worship the old brute from the sad spectacle of his senile degeneration" (Wednesday, January 5, 1974). Writing of an election for an office in the National Union of Journalists, Waugh comments only on the "hideous faces" of the candidates: "One looks more like a pig than a human being, one like a drunken stoat; one tries hard to look like Jesus blowing bubbles, another is an obvious murderer of small children" (*The Diaries*, 26).

As for his friendships with the great, Waugh writes for June 14, 1980:

Today is Arthur Askey's [a working class comedian] 80th birthday. What a grand little chap he is, to be sure. I send him a collection of old cigarette cards, two bottles of stout and a monkey skin with a message of congratulations and thanks that he has not decided to come and spend his retirement in the West Country, like many great-hearted little old people from the North.

For the Queen Mother's 80th birthday later this year we are sending her a parcel of Good Boys, the doggie sweets to which she has apparently taken a fancy. They are much healthier than Kit-e-Kat, which can be bad for the breath. (*The Diaries*, 102)

And, as an example of sheer invention (the people really exist), there is this meditation in which Waugh pretends to be thinking of changing his name to Bruce:

In my own case I expect I was influenced by my admiration for Colonel "Bruce" Page, who was born Vernon Catterpox in a treehouse near Geelong, New South Wales. But I have always been discouraged by the example of Bruce Forsyth (born Sebastian Jonibagger in an outside lavatory near Barking). (*The Diaries*, 118)

Other recurrent features of the diaries include denunciations of the working class, the invention of nicknames (for instance, for Harold Evans, editor of the *Sunday Times*, first called "the Dame" after Edith Evans, and eventually "Dame Twankypoo Fancyshanks," 53), and the creation of amusing rumors. Waugh claims that Prince Andrew has never learned to speak, that Princess Anne's son has four legs, that Lord Mountbatten is a homosexual Communist spy, that Lord Snowdon is a half-Jewish Welsh dwarf, that Marshal Tito was a woman: "My late Father claimed to have seen her once during the war breast-feeding a seal pup on the Island of Vis. 'There's nowt so queer as folks,' he remarked in his broad Lancashire accent" (*The Diaries*, 98).

Presumably some people were wounded by their treatment in the diaries, and Waugh has been sued for libel more than once (once, successfully, by a woman of whom he claimed that "she had gone to bed with half the members of the Cabinet but no impropriety occurred" [Koenig, 92]). He is a man of strong likes and dislikes, and despite the suavity of his style, he is far more willing to outrage than most writers. He seems to lack a level of inhibition which prevents other writers from writing, even if they might occasionally or momentarily think it, that English children, workers, and old and handicapped people are spoiled, that they enjoy being rich, that they would like to own some Filipino servants. He writes on one occasion that "My whole life, as this Diary shows, is a lie. All the characters in it are invented, none bears any resemblance to anyone living or dead" (*The Diaries*, 165). Of course, in one sense that is false—Edward Heath and Margaret Thatcher do exist—in another it is quite true: by putting them through the transformation of diarizing, Waugh has made comic, fictional characters of real people, not the least of whom is himself.

Summary

Auberon Waugh has created an original niche for himself in recent British writing as the journalist who is more unfettered than any other, who fights the class war from the middle-class side using the weapons of satire and cool, outrageous wit. He uses these weapons in a vivid and, more impressively, prolific journalism—personal columns and book reviews most notably—which has made him a major force in contemporary British letters. As a novelist, he is less original, though to be comparable to Evelyn Waugh is no mean feat; his best fiction, *Consider the Lilies*, is a fine comic novel by any standards. His most important creation is "Auberon Waugh's Diary," which both released his best work and added a new kind of writing to the literary landscape.

Waugh has been highly visible in the literary scene for thirty years, but he was precocious, he is still a fairly young man, and he may be expected to add his portion of amusing and tart commentary, in a variety of forms, for years to come.

Selected Bibliography

Primary Sources

The Foxglove Saga. London: Chapman & Hall, 1960; New York: Simon and Schuster, 1961.

Path of Dalliance. London: Chapman & Hall, 1963; New York: Simon and Schuster, 1964.

Who Are the Violets Now? London: Chapman & Hall, 1965; New York: Simon and Schuster, 1966.

Consider the Lilies. London: Michael Joseph, 1968; Boston: Little, Brown, 1969.

A Bed of Flowers; Or As You Like It. London: Michael Joseph, 1972.

Country Topics. London: Michael Joseph, 1974.

Four Crowded Years: The Diaries of Auberon Waugh, 1972–76. London: Andre Deutsch, 1976.

In the Lion's Den. London: Michael Joseph, 1978.

The Last Word: An Eyewitness Account of the Thorpe Trial. London: Michael Joseph, and Boston: Little, Brown, 1980.

The Diaries of Auberon Waugh: A Turbulent Decade, 1976–1985. London: Andre Deutsch, 1985.

Another Voice: An Alternative Anatomy of Britain. London: Sidgwick & Jackson, 1986; published as *Brideshead Benighted*. Boston: Little, Brown, 1986.

Will This Do?: Memoirs. London: Century, 1991.

Secondary Sources

Davenport, Guy. "Tales of Transformation." *National Review*, 21 (February 11, 1969): 130–32. Review of *Consider the Lilies*.

Dennis, Nigel. "Morality as Monster." *New York Times Book Review* (July 27, 1961): 5. Review of *The Foxglove Saga*.

Grumman, Joan, and Anne Kowalewski.

"Auberon Waugh." In *Dictionary of Literary Biography. Vol. 14: British Novelists Since 1960: Part Two: M–Z*. Ed. Jay L. Halio. Detroit: Gale, 1983. An analysis of Waugh's writing in a biographical context.

Hebblethwaite, Peter. "Son of Waugh." *America*, 126 (May 20, 1972): 534–36. An introductory article on Waugh, on the occasion of the publication of *A Bed of Flowers*, relating the reception of that novel to his own sharp reviewing.

Hicks, Granville. "Literary Horizons." *Saturday Review*, 52 (January 4, 1969): 93. Review of *Consider the Lilies*.

Koenig, Rhoda. "A Handful of Mud: Auberon Waugh's War on Manners." *Harper's*, 261 (December, 1980): 86–92. Generally approving article on Waugh's ideas, manners, and place in the English literary scene.

Littler, Frank. "Poor Arthur in a Stew." *New York Times Book Review* (May 29, 1966): 22. Negative review of *Who Are the Violets Now?*

Marnham, Patrick. *The Private Eye Story: The First 21 Years*. London: Andre Deutsch, 1982. Interesting account of *Private Eye* and of Waugh's activities and impact there.

Moon, Eric. "Mr. Friendship Finds Peace." *Saturday Review*, 49 (May 28, 1966): 33. Review of *Who Are the Violets Now?*

Painter-Downes, Mollie. "And Be the Stoat Under It." *The New Yorker*, 37 (September 2, 1961): 75–77. Review of *The Foxglove Saga*.

Pippett, Aileen. "The Sweet and Savage Touch." *Saturday Review*, 44 (August 5, 1961): 12. Review of *The Foxglove Saga*, which also includes a biographical sketch of Waugh with some quotations based on an interview.

Sutherland, J.A. *Fiction and the Fiction Industry*. London: The Athlone Press, 1978, pp. 98–102. Good account of Waugh's role and importance as a fiction reviewer.

Tracy, Honor. "Chips Off the Old Block." *The New Republic*, 145 (August 7, 1961): 23–24. Review of *The Foxglove Saga*.

Wilson, A.N. *Penfriends from Porlock*. London: Hamish Hamilton, 1988. Wilson's chapter on satire (pp. 254–266) in contemporary journalism sheds some light on *Private Eye* and on Waugh.

Weeks, Edward. "The Light Touch." *The Atlantic Monthly*, 208 (September 1961): 98. Review of *The Foxglove Saga*.

Merritt Moseley

Waugh, Evelyn Arthur St. John

Born: Hampstead, London, October 28, 1903
Education: Heath Mount, 1910–1917; Lancing, 1917–1921; Herford College, Oxford University, 1922–1924
Marriage: Evelyn Gardner, June 27, 1927; divorced 1930 (annulled by the Catholic Church 1936); married Laura Herbert, April 17, 1937; six children
Died: Combe Florey, April 10, 1966

Biography

Evelyn Waugh was born at 11 Hillfield Road, Hampstead, London on October 28, 1903, the son of Arthur, a publisher, and Catherine Waugh. In 1907, his family moved to North End Road, Hampstead, and from 1910 to 1917 he attended Heath Mount preparatory school as a Day-Boy. He was sent in 1917 not to Sherborne, the public (in American terms, private) school attended by his father and by his brother Alec, but to Lancing, a school of High Church orientation. He attended Lancing from 1917 to 1921 and won a scholarship to Herford College, Oxford. During his time at Oxford (1922–1924) he devoted himself more to social than to academic pursuits.

Waugh had always wanted to be a writer, and at the age of eleven became interested in Anglo-Catholicism, constructing a small shrine in his bedroom before which he burnt incense. At Heath Mount he became the editor of his school magazine, the *Cynic*, and at the age of thirteen he wrote a three-canto poem entitled *The World to Come*, an apocalyptic vision of war and death that was privately printed by a friend of his father.

At Lancing, Waugh contributed to the *Lancing College Magazine*, of which he subsequently became the editor, was president of the debating society, helped found the Dilettanti Society, and was founder of the Corpse Club.

At Oxford he debated at the Oxford Union, contributed cartoons to *Isis*, tutored in history, and became a member of various clubs, including the Hypocrites. He published stories

in students' magazines, but because he spent little time at his studies he barely managed to pass his examinations, and at the end of the term he left Oxford. With Terence Greenidge he produced a movie, *The Scarlet Woman—An Ecclesiastical Drama*, featuring Elsa Lanchester and Waugh's writer brother Alec.

In 1925, Waugh worked as a schoolmaster at Arnold House in Wales. He also wrote the early chapters of a novel to be called *The Temple at Thatch*, which his friend, Harold Acton, read without enthusiasm, and which Waugh subsequently burned. He was also depressed by his teaching post and by his failure to get another job with Scott Moncrieff (the translator of Marcel Proust's *Remembrance of Things Past*), all of which led to an attempted suicide.

This attempt, or at least Waugh's later account of it in his autobiographical *A Little Learning* (1964), shows him in the guise of one of his own characters. After leaving his clothes with a slip of paper containing a quote from Euripides, he began to swim out to sea. "I swam slowly out," he writes, "but long before I reached the point of no return, the Shropshire Lad was disturbed by a smart on the shoulder. I had run into a jellyfish. A few more strokes, a second more painful sting. The placid waters were full of the creatures."

Thoughts of death were interrupted by absurdity, which the later Waugh could observe with ironic detachment, and he swam back to shore: "As earnest of my intent I had brought no towel. With some difficulty I dressed and tore into small pieces my pretentious tag, leaving them to the sea, moved on that bleak shore by tides stronger than any known to Euripides, to perform its lustral office." The absurd, pompous language is appropriate to the anticlimax of the scene.

Waugh was a schoolmaster at Aston Clinton, Buckinghamshire, in 1926, and in Notting Hill, London, in 1927. Also in 1927, he was employed for three weeks on the *Daily Express* and was a gossip columnist on the *Weekly Dispatch*. On June 27 of that year he married Evelyn Gardner, the daughter of Lord Barghclere. Their identical first names led their friends to refer to them as He-Evelyn and She-Evelyn. In 1928, Waugh's first book, a biography, *Rosetti, His Life and Works*, was published, followed by *Decline and Fall*, his first novel, which received some very favorable reviews. J.B. Priestley commented that "Mr. Waugh has done something very difficult to do, he has created a really comic character." The novel was, in fact, a broad farce that established Waugh as a humorous writer of great skill, though the novel did not make as much money as the author had hoped.

In 1929, the Waughs went on a Mediterranean cruise, a trip that served as the basis for *Labels*, a highly personal travel book. She-Evelyn was ill with a near-fatal bout of pneumonia throughout much of this trip. During this year, Waugh wrote articles on the younger generation for the *Evening Standard* and the *Spectator*. In July, while Waugh was at work on the novel *Vile Bodies*, his wife left him for John Heygate. The two Evelyns were divorced in 1930 (the marriage was annulled by the Catholic Church in 1936).

Also in 1930, *Vile Bodies* and *Labels* were published. *Vile Bodies* was a literary and social success, though Priestley "found it a sad disappointment, lacking the shape and quality of *Decline and Fall*." Priestley was looking for humor and found satire.

In September, after instruction from Father Martin D'Arcy, Waugh was received into the Roman Catholic Church. He traveled to Abyssinia as a correspondent for *The Times* to report on the coronation of Haile Selassie as emperor, and traveled in east and central Africa, before returning to England in 1931. This trip became the basis of *Remote People*, which was published in November, and *Black Mischief*, which was published the following year. Waugh continued to be involved in journalism and made short visits to France, Italy, and Spain. His arduous journey through the back country of British Guiana and Brazil was recorded in *Ninety-Two Days* and served as the basis of the South American section of *A Handful of Dust*. He returned to England in May 1933, and in the late summer he went on a Mediterranean cruise in the course of which he met Laura Herbert, whom he would later marry.

In 1934, Waugh spent the winter in Morocco. *Ninety-Two Days, The Account of a Tropical Journey through British Guiana and Part of Brazil* was published, and Waugh completed the stories later published with "Mr. Loveday's Little Outing." In July and August he took a trip to Spitzbergen.

In 1935, he returned to Africa to report on the Italian-Abyssinian war for the *Daily Mail*. This experience provided the material for *Waugh in Abyssinia* (1936) and the satirical novel *Scoop, A Novel About Journalists* (1938). A quite different kind of book, *Edmund Campion: Jesuit and Martyr*, was published in this year. In June 1936, *Mr. Lovejoy's Little Outing and Other Sad Stories* was published, and the annulment of his marriage to Evelyn Gardner was confirmed in July, making it possible for Waugh to marry again with the blessing of the Church.

On April 17, 1937, Waugh was married to Laura Herbert, a granddaughter of The Earl of Carnarvon (and a distant relative of Evelyn Gardner), and the couple settled at Piers Court, Stinchcombe, Gloucestershire, in September. They would eventually have six children, among them Auberon (born in 1939), a humorist in his own right. Waugh reviewed books for *Night and Day* and became a director of Chapman and Hall, the publishing company in which his father had been senior editor. In 1938, Waugh made a trip to Hungary. Having been commissioned to write a book exposing the anti-Catholic socialist government of General Cardenas, he visited Mexico as well. The resulting book, *Robbery Under Law, The Mexican Object Lesson*, was published in 1939.

With the beginning of World War II he tried to enter the army, though he was overage, and in December was commissioned in the Royal Marines. In 1940, he participated in the unsuccessful Dakar expedition and later transferred to the Commandos. In 1941, he went to Egypt with No. 8 Commando Forces to take part in the battle for Crete against the German invasion that involved massive use of paratroops. He was finally evacuated to Egypt with the remnants of his unit. Like many other participants, he was becoming increasingly disillusioned about the war. He returned to England and to the Royal Marines in September.

Waugh was transferred to a staff position in the Royal Horse Guards and spent 1942 in the United Kingdom on routine duties. *Put Out More Flags* was published in March, and *Work Suspended*, two chapters of an unfinished novel, was published in December. In June 1943, when Waugh was undergoing a dispiriting period of inactivity, his father died. After a dispute with Lord Lovat in July, Waugh resigned from the Commandos and in October he joined the Special Air Service Regiment. He entered parachute training in December but was injured in a jump accident. On leave because of his disability, he spent the time from January to June of 1944 working on *Brideshead Revisited*.

In July, he accompanied Randolph Churchill to Yugoslavia as part of the 37th British Military Mission to the partisans and was stationed at Topusko. In December, he became Liaison Officer in Dubrovnik.

In 1945, he was demobilized, and he returned to Piers Court. He wrote a report on religious toleration in Yugoslavia, and in May *Brideshead Revisited: The Sacred and Profane Memories of Captain Charles Ryder* was published. This book was a widely popular success, especially in America, and considerably increased his audience. Indeed, in the United States it was a Book-of-the-Month Club selection.

When the Going Was Good, material from earlier travel accounts, was published in 1946. That spring he attended the Nuremberg trials, and in June he went to an international conference in Madrid which became the basis for *Scott-King's Modern Europe*. From January to March 1947, he was in Hollywood to discuss possible film treatment of *Brideshead Revisited*, but the negotiations failed because he could not agree to changes that the filmmakers wanted. While he was in America, he became fascinated by the strange folkways of the Americans, especially the funeral customs represented by Forest Lawn Cemetery in Los Angeles, to which he made frequent visits. He also received an honorary degree from Loyola College in Baltimore.

In 1948, *The Loved One: An Anglo-American Tragedy* was published in *Horizon*. The word "tragedy" here is one of the author's wilder flights of irony; *The Loved One* is perhaps the zaniest piece of humor to come from Waugh since his first novel and quite unlike the more religiously oriented work that he had been writing. This was the period too of his growing friendship with Ronald Knox, and he made a lecture tour of Catholic universities in the United States.

At this time the author was also at work on *Helena*, which was published in October 1950. He was disappointed by the reception of *Helena*, a historical novel about the supposed discoverer of Christ's cross. In 1951, Waugh traveled in the Near East for *Life* magazine and wrote articles that were collected in 1952 as *The Holy Places*. At this time he was also at work on *Men at Arms*, the first volume of what was to be his war trilogy.

The next year, he traveled to Sicily with Acton. *Men at Arms* was published and won the James Tait Black Memorial Prize. Waugh spent Christmas in Goa and then returned to England. *Love Among the Ruins: A Romance of the Near Future* was published. He was interviewed for the BBC radio programme, "Frankly Speaking," an experience that features prominently in *The Ordeal of Gilbert Pinfold* (1957). This book had its origin in a voyage to Ceylon in early 1954 when Waugh suffered from hallucinations. On Waugh's return to England a psychiatrist friend suggested that he might write about his ordeal as a kind of therapy. In the highly autobiographical *Ordeal*, he portrays a world in which it is not clear which experiences are hallucinations and which are "real." In 1954, however, he was at work on *Officers and Gentlemen*, the second volume of his war trilogy, and *Tactical Exercises*, a volume of short stories, was published.

Waugh wintered in Jamaica in 1955, as the guest of Ian and Ann Fleming, and *Officers and Gentlemen* was published. In 1956, he moved to Combe Florey, near Taunton, Somerset. The following year his friend Knox died. Waugh began research for his biography of Knox, and he worked on the life of Knox through 1958, even traveling to Rhodesia to collect material.

In 1959, he was in Africa again, with a commission from the *Sunday Times* for travel articles. This journey was the basis of *A Tourist in Africa*, published the next year. In October, *The Life of the Right Reverend Ronald Knox* was published, and at the beginning of 1960 Waugh traveled in Europe and wrote a series of articles on contemporary customs and travel, "Passport into Spring," for the *Daily Mail*. In addition, he was at work on *Unconditional Surrender* (1961), the final volume of his war trilogy. He made another trip to British Guiana, financed by the *Sunday Times*, and returned to England in 1962. In 1963, *Basil Seal Rides Again, or The Rake's Regress* was published after being serialized in the *Sunday Telegraph*.

In 1964, *A Little Learning, The First Volume of an Autobiography* was published. Was his calling it a "first volume" an instance of his bitter irony? It was, in any case, his last book. In 1965, *Sword of Honour*, the one volume recension of his war trilogy, was published. Waugh died at Combe Florey, near Taunton, Somerset, on Easter Sunday, April 10, 1966, after attending mass.

Literary Analysis

Opinions vary widely concerning Waugh's talent as a humorist, satirist, writer of comedy,

Catholic writer, and a progressively misanthropic pessimist. He was all of these and more, though in his later volumes his humor appears more and more as incidental touches in works that were predominantly of a more serious nature. His war trilogy is about a very serious matter indeed, but even death and defecation and the decay of corpses can be the subjects of humor.

In his first novel, *Decline and Fall*, manic humor predominates. Priestley wrote in *English Humour* in 1976 that the novel "still holds up very well indeed, revealing all over again a new and original humorist with a very cool, impudent, deadpan manner, together with some excellent prose." In the 1930s, according to Priestley, Waugh went off in another direction. His writing did, in fact, become progressively more serious, and although many of his works, even the most serious, did contain humorous incidents and scenes, a serious, sometimes satirical, tone dominated most of the time. It is only in the short novel *The Loved One* that Waugh returns to the humorous lunacy that dominates *Decline and Fall*.

Humor depends upon the absurdly incongruous event or person that amuses the observer. Things are not what they seem, though the humorist, unlike the satirist, does not make moral judgments about them. In *Decline and Fall* much depends upon plays on words, on the suggestiveness of names, on the discrepancy between what things appear to be and what they are underneath. The relationship between the narrator and the matter under narration is essential to a humorous perspective. In Waugh's first published novel the deadpan narration combines with dialogue that parodies then current fashionable speech and is essential to the effect. Even the title of the novel lends itself to the absurdity of the events. The title's allusion to Edward Gibbon's *The History of the Decline and Fall of the Roman Empire* links the seriousness of Gibbon's subject to the triviality of the lives of the novel's characters: if degeneracy can do it, the British Empire is certainly headed for a fall.

Paul Pennyfeather, the innocent protagonist, is a Candide-type character who never really learns from experience. He learns facts, but he never makes the kinds of judgments about them that lead to moral interpretations and right actions. Unlike Jonathan Swift or François Voltaire, Waugh seems to accept the world as it is, merely showing its incongruities without judging them. In his later works, the writer becomes more judgmental and is less prone to show the humor in the situations in which his characters find themselves. He becomes more the satirist and the moralist. But the young novelist still sees the amusing side of the matter.

At the beginning of *Decline and Fall*, Paul, a divinity student, is the victim of a prank by drunken members of the Bollinger Club who strip off his trousers on the college green and get him expelled from Scone College for indecent exposure. The name of the college, by the way, suggests a Scottish Calvinism which is one of the butts of Waugh's humor. Paul's guardian swindles him out of his inheritance, and in order to make a living Paul turns to schoolteaching. He is hired by Augustus Fagan, the headmaster of Llanaba Castle, a school in Wales whose medieval architecture is as fake as its inhabitants which include Fagan's ugly daughters, Flossie and Dingy, Captain Grimes (who is always "in the soup"), Prendergast (a "Modern Churchman" who is afflicted by "Doubts"), and Philbrick (the butler who later reappears in his true form as a con man).

Things come to a head on the occasion of a school fete when drunken "Prendy" shoots little Lord Tangent in the heel at the start of one of the races. At the same time there is an exchange of insults between the Clutterbucks, the mother of Tangent and one of the horsy set, with language to match. Much of the humor is sophomoric, which is a large part of its charm— if it were more sophisticated it would be considerably less funny. The humor is also based on social class and racial prejudices that would be less acceptable today.

Lady Margot Beste-Chetwynde, whose name is intended to suggest gassy cattle, appears with her American lover, Sebastian "Chokey" Cholmondley. One of the jokes here is that Waugh assumes that Americans will mispronounce the name "Cholmondley" (English pronunciation: Chumley), and he makes Cholmondley not only black but also a jazz musician—two of Waugh's many *bêtes noirs*. Chokey shows his feelings in a speech that is a parody of Shylock's "do we not bleed" speech in William Shakespeare's *The Merchant of Venice*, one of Waugh's many farcical paraphrases of well-known speeches.

Margot hires Paul to tutor her son, Peter Pastmaster. Paul arrives at her estate to discover that the avenue of old trees leads not to a historically important Tudor mansion, which has been razed, but to a Bauhaus building of glass and chromium built from a design influenced by Professor Silenius, who understands that both the contemporary architectural problem and the problem of all art is "the elimination of the human element from the consideration of form." Paul arrives during a party attended by social climbers, politicians, homosexuals, and others of the smart new set. He is seduced by Margot's beauty, unaware that she is a drug addict, a nymphomaniac, and the owner of a prostitution business called the "Latin American Entertainment Company." She employs the innocent Paul to ship girls to South America, but he is arrested for engaging in the white slave trade. At his trial he is upbraided for dragging down "to his own pitiable depths of depravity a lady of beauty, rank and stainless reputation." Margot, of course, is not implicated.

The prison to which Paul is sent is run by a sociologist who is convinced that crime can be cured by aesthetic expression. He proves a mad religious zealot whose visions tell him to "kill and spare not" with the carpenter's tools that he uses in an attempt to saw off the head of the prison chaplain—who turns out to be Prendergast, still trying to find himself.

While in prison, Paul is provided by Margot with books, sherry, clothes, and oysters. He is mysteriously released from jail and sent to a nursing home, run by Fagan, for the removal of his appendix—which had been removed years earlier. A doctor there certifies that Paul died on the operating table. Wearing a moustache as a disguise, Paul returns to Scone College to take up his theological studies once more.

The logic of the story is equivalent to that of a story by Waugh's friend P.G. Wodehouse or a film by the Marx Brothers. There is much in the story that is the material of satire, but it is presented with a light touch and a zaniness that leads the reader not to moral judgments but to laughter.

In all of Waugh's work, including even some of the most serious, light humorous touches occur. Sex, authority, religion, suffering, death: all fall within the realm of humor. An especially fertile area is the misunderstanding of language or the misunderstanding by one person of the utterances of another. An example of this occurs in *Vile Bodies*. A visitor to Doubting Hall is told by a cigar-smoking bishop that, along with other Wesleyans, Colonel Blount is being shot. "I dare say you'd like to come round to the front and see the fun," he informs the astonished listener. Furthermore, "there's been some damn bad management. Why, yesterday, they kept Miss LaTouche waiting the whole afternoon, and then the light was so bad when they did shoot her that they made a complete mess of her—we had the machine out and ran over all the bits carefully last night after dinner—you never saw such rotten little scraps—quite unrecognizable half of them. We didn't dare show them to her husband." It is only later that the hearer learns that the bishop is talking about shooting a film.

This is humor based on the misapprehension of language, but Waugh can present literal death in as light a fashion. In *Scoop*, he refers to the nineteenth-century Europeans who came to Ishmaelia "as missionaries, ambassadors, tradesmen, prospectors, natural scientists. None returned. They were eaten, every one of them; some raw, others stewed and seasoned—according to local usage and the calendar (for the better sort of Ishmaelites have been Christian for many centuries and will not publicly eat human flesh, uncooked, in Lent, without special and costly dispensation from their bishop)." There is a verbal parallel here to Francis Bacon's discussion of books in "Of Studies," in which some books are to be tasted, some swallowed whole, and some chewed and digested, as well as an evocation of Swift's "A Modest Proposal."

The Loved One is a comedy of death and dying in which there is embedded a satire on American burial customs and attitudes toward death, a love story that stresses the silliness and banality of the characters' emotional involvements, and some very funny scenes and wordplay. It was instigated by Waugh's fascination with Forest Lawn Cemetery, the novel's "Whispering Glades." He is concerned about the immature refusal of Americans to recognize death and instead play games with euphemisms. "Even the names given to their various sections—Eventide, Babyland, Graceland, Inspiration Slope, Slumberland, Sweet Memories," he wrote in *Life* magazine in 1947, "are none of them suggestive of the graveyard." For Waugh, Forest Lawn has evaded not only questions of death, but any religious meaning; death has become part of show business.

The central character is a young English poet in Hollywood, Dennis Barlow, who quit his job in a movie studio for a job in a pet mortuary, the Happier Hunting Ground (which parallels Whispering Glades, the human facility). His experiences, like those of Paul Penny-feather or any of the other young innocents in Waugh's novels, are of one horror after another, but because of his innocence he never really experiences the horror, and the reader sees the humor inherent in even the most shocking situations. When Sir Francis Hinsley, a publicity agent and former scriptwriter, commits suicide after being fired (real tragedy is never far from humor in Waugh), Dennis handles his funeral arrangements at Whispering Glades. There he meets Aimee Thanatagenos (a combining in her name of French and Greek words which add up to love of death). She is an assistant cosmetician with a "glint of lunacy" in her green eyes. She is in love with Mr. Joyboy, the head mortician whose glamorous position in the mortuary is contrasted with his dreary private life, dominated by his "Mom" and a parrot. Aimee is torn between Mr. Joyboy and Dennis, who has been giving her poems plagiarized from John Keats and Edgar Allan Poe. She consults a "Guru Brahmin" whose real name is Mr. Slump, an alcoholic who tells her to jump out a window. Being very literal minded, she commits suicide in Mr. Joyboy's embalming room by giving herself a lethal injection of embalming fluid. Mr. Joyboy discovers her body and begs Dennis to help him save his reputation. Dennis cremates Aimee at the Happier Hunting Ground and blackmails Mr. Joyboy into giving him money to return to England. At the pet cemetery, Dennis treats the whole affair in a routine manner, as if a favorite pet has died, and leaves in the files the notice that on every anniversary of Aimee's death, a card will be sent to Mr. Joyboy reading "Your little Aimee is wagging her tail in Heaven tonight."

The plot can give no sense of the humor of the story without examples of the way in which it is told. Burial customs of humans are parodied in the burial customs of pets, which Waugh presents as identical. When Dennis consults with a client about the funeral arrangements of a Sealyham terrier, Dennis speaks in a professionally lugubrious tone:

And the religious rites? We have a pastor who is always pleased to assist . . .

Mr. Barlow, we're neither of us what you might call very church-going people, but I think on an occasion like this Mrs. Heinkel would want all the comfort you can offer. Our Grade A service includes

several unique features. At the moment of committal, a white dove, symbolizing the deceased's soul, is liberated over the crematorium.

Ironically, references to the embalming of humans by Mr. Joyboy, and their presentation in "slumber rooms" looking more alive than they ever did, omits any references to religion, a matter of considerable concern to Waugh. Ultimately, humor to him is a very serious matter. For this reason, some critics see his novels more as works of satire than of humor, and even the most nonsensical touches reflect a grim view of the world. "Waugh's temperament is not sunny," one critic has said, "nor are his books—even the funniest of them." A hilarious movie version of *The Loved One*, directed by Tony Richardson and featuring an all-star cast (Robert Morse, Jonathan Winters, Rod Steiger, Dana Andrews, Anjanette Comer, Milton Berle, James Coburn, John Gielgud, Tab Hunter, Margaret Leighton, Liberace, Roddy McDowell, Robert Morley, Lionel Stander), was released in 1965. Scripted by Terry Southern and Christopher Isherwood, the film was advertised as the picture with something to offend everyone.

Summary

Called the most brilliant satirical novelist and one of the masters of prose of his time, Evelyn Waugh, the son of a publisher, intended to be a writer from an early age, and from an early age he had strong conservative religious beliefs. These beliefs, together with his sense of the absurdity of the world around him and his love of the play of language, are important elements in his writings. He published works of biography, fiction, and travel, as well as essays on a variety of topics. In religion he was a High Church traditionalist who converted to Roman Catholicism in his late twenties after separation from his first wife. During the 1930s, he wrote a great deal of social satire, but especially during World War II his work became more and more explicitly religious. Humor is an important element in all of his writing, including much of his serious writing, but even his funniest work had its grim aspect. From his first novel, *Decline and Fall,* in which he dealt humorously with corruption of schools, prison, and society in general, to *The Loved One*, in which he dealt with death and the decay of funeral customs and religious attitudes, in his comic novels he made witty comments on essentially serious subjects.

Selected Bibliography
Primary Sources

Novels

Decline and Fall: An Illustrated Novelette. London: Chapman and Hall, 1928.

Vile Bodies. London: Chapman and Hall, 1930.

Black Mischief. London: Chapman and Hall, 1932.

A Handful of Dust. London: Chapman and Hall, 1934.

Scoop: A Novel About Journalists. London: Chapman and Hall, 1938.

Put Out More Flags. London: Chapman and Hall, 1942.

Brideshead Revisited: The Sacred and Profane Memories of Captain Charles Ryder. London: Chapman and Hall, 1945.

The Loved One. London: Chapman and Hall, 1948.

Helena. London: Chapman and Hall, 1950.

Men at Arms. London: Chapman and Hall, 1952.

Officers and Gentlemen. London: Chapman and Hall, 1955.

The Ordeal of Gilbert Pinfold. London: Chapman and Hall, 1957.

Unconditional Surrender. London: Chapman and Hall, 1961.

Sword of Honour. London: Chapman and Hall, 1965.

Travel Volumes

Labels: A Mediterranean Journal. London: Duckworth, 1930.

Remote People. London: Duckworth, 1931.

Ninety-Two Days: An Account of a Tropical Journey through British Guiana and Part of Brazil. London: Duckworth, 1934.

Waugh in Abbyssinia. London: Longman, Green, 1936.

When the Going Was Good. London: Duckworth, 1946.

A Tourist in Africa. London, Chapman and Hall, 1960.

Collections

A Little Order. Ed. Donat Gallagher. Boston: Little, Brown, 1977. A collection of Evelyn Waugh's journalism.

The Essays, Articles and Reviews of Evelyn Waugh. Ed. Donat Gallagher. London: Methuen, 1983.

Personal Documents

A Little Learning (Autobiography). London: Chapman and Hall, 1964.

The Diaries of Evelyn Waugh. Ed. Michael Davie. London: Weidenfeld and Nicholson, 1976.

The Letters of Evelyn Waugh. Ed. Mark Amory. London, Weidenfeld and Nicholson, 1980.

Secondary Sources

Acton, Harold. *Evelyn Waugh.* London: Methuen, 1948.

Carens, James F. *The Satiric Art of Evelyn Waugh.* Seattle: University of Washington Press, 1966.

Crabbe, Catheryn W. *Evelyn Waugh.* New York: Continuum, 1988.

Lane, Calvin W. *Evelyn Waugh.* Boston: Twayne, 1981.

Littlewood, Ian. *The Writings of Evelyn Waugh.* Oxford: Basil Blackwell, 1983.

Lodge, David. *Evelyn Waugh.* New York and London: Columbia University Press, 1971. Columbia Essays on Modern Writers, No. 58.

Stannard, Martin. *Evelyn Waugh: The Early Years, 1903–1939.* New York: W.W. Norton, 1986.

———. *Evelyn Waugh: The Later Years 1939–1966.* New York: W.W. Norton, 1992.

Donald R. Swanson

Wells, H[erbert] G[eorge]

Born: Bromley, Kent, September 21, 1866

Education: Normal School of Science, South Kensington; London University, B.S., 1890; D.S.

Marriage: Isabell Mary Wells, October 31, 1891; divorced, 1895; Amy Catherine Robbins, 1895; two children; one child with Rebecca West

Died: London, August 13, 1946

Biography

Herbert George Wells was born in Bromley on September 21, 1866. At that time the area was still a separate community from London but within Wells's lifetime would virtually become a suburb of the great city. His parents, Joseph and Sarah, maintained a modest lifestyle on the tenuous margin between the lower-middle class and the working poor. Joseph Wells ran a small shop that stocked kitchenware and sporting goods. He was far more interested in his career as a semiprofessional player in county cricket than in selling teapots, and the business suffered accordingly. Sarah Wells worked as a housekeeper to supplement the family income. An important formative experience for young "Bertie" Wells was an introduction to reading fiction that fired his imagination: while recuperating from a broken leg he was kept entertained by books and periodicals supplied by his father from the local library. Wells's parents, however, had only a limited vision for their son's future. Instead of encouraging his intellectual abilities, they enrolled him at age eight in a commercial academy that specialized in training shop clerks.

In 1880, Wells began the first of his trade apprenticeships, his mother having secured a position as a draper's assistant for him. The young man was unhappy and unsuccessful in the clothing business and was next apprenticed to a pharmacist who marketed his own patent medicines. This apprenticeship was slightly more to Wells's liking, especially since his employer encouraged him to take a course in basic Latin at the local grammar school. In later years, the writer would draw heavily upon his apprenticeship experiences in some of his novels, especially *The Wheels of Chance, Kipps, Tono-Bungay,* and *The History of Mr. Polly.*

Wells was generally unhappy as an apprentice and with the help and encouragement of his Latin tutor he prepared for government-sponsored exams intended to find students capable of university studies. In spite of his mother's objections and her arranging of yet another draper's apprenticeship, Wells persisted and eventually won a scholarship to the Normal School of Science in South Kensington in 1884. Higher education would eventually become the launching pad for his career as a writer. In 1890, he earned a bachelor of science degree from London University, and while subsequently working as a lecturer and tutor, compiled enough material for a book, *Textbook of Biology,* which was published in 1893.

In the meantime, Wells married his cousin, Isabell Mary Wells, on October 31, 1891. When he suffered a serious hemorrhage, he abandoned his dull job and marriage and ran off with one of his students, Amy Catherine Robbins. Wells divorced his first wife in 1895 and married Robbins on October 27 of the same year. The couple had two children. The author's search for a soul mate is occasionally reflected in his writing (as in *The Sea Lady,* 1902). Indeed, by 1914 he had entered into a firey love affair with the young English writer Rebecca West, one result of which was the birth of his third child.

By 1894 Wells was regularly publishing essays and fiction. A significant portion of his writing during the middle of the decade was in the "New Humor" vein established by Jerome K. Jerome and other young journalists in the late 1880s. Although Wells never considered himself to be a humorist, he found the ready market for these essays useful in establishing himself as a professional writer. In 1895, Wells published three novels—including the scientific romance, *The Time Machine*, that would make him famous—and was well and truly established as a writer. *The Time Machine* was followed in 1898 by *The War of the Worlds,* later made vivid for modern audiences by the Orson Welles radio broadcast (film versions of *The Time Machine* appeared in 1960 and 1978, and of *The War of the Worlds* in 1953).

The next forty years of his life and career were extraordinarily varied and prolific. In the years prior to World War I, Wells became a major figure in the development of the modern novel, publishing four enduring works, *Kipps* (1905), *Tono-Bungay* (1908), *Anne Veronica* (1909), and *The History of Mr. Polly* (1910). After World War I, however, he was less engaged as a writer of imaginative fictions than as a polemicist for various causes, among them sexual freedom and the world state. He sought to establish himself as an influential educator and as a sage for modern times, propounding his thesis that humankind must adapt its political, educational, and social institutions to the enormous changes in material conditions brought about by advances in technology or disappear from the face of the earth. Arguably, the most significant products of Wells's thought in this period are the novel *The Shape of Things to Come* (1933) and his script for the film version directed by William Cameron Menzies, *Things to Come* (1936). The film version has become a classic cinematic expression of the spirit of modernism and remains a very accessible example of Wells's belief in the beneficence of technology and the necessity of the emergence of a world state to secure the future of humanity.

Although he produced an enormous body of journalistic writing and fiction in the 1920s and 1930s in which he propagandized for his causes, this writing is for the most part of lesser literary quality and intrinsic merit than his achievements in the scientific romances and novels of the late-Victorian and Edwardian periods. Wells died in London on August 13, 1946. He had been born in the year that saw the invention of dynamite, and, in the course of a life and career in which he continuously observed and commented on the impact of technology on society, lived to see the beginning of the nuclear age.

Literary Analysis

Most of Wells's humorous writing dates from the early period when he began to establish his career as an author. The humorous essays published in the *Pall Mall Gazette* were his response to the ready market for such essays during the vogue of the "New Humor" of the 1880s and 1890s. Accordingly, he wrote essays depicting the quirks, annoyances, and vagaries of lower-middle-class London life in a manner similar to that of Jerome. Perhaps typical of Wells's essays are "The Art of Staying at the Seaside," a breezy and facetious examination of the drawbacks of a holiday at the shore; "The Shopman," dealing with the exasperating ways of shop clerks; and "Of Blades and Bladery," instructing the would-be man-about-town in wearing his hat at the properly rakish angle, tying a cravat in the correctly careless way, and in using the latest slang for ordering drinks at a bar. Although thirty-nine of Wells's humorous essays were collected and published as *Certain Personal Matters* in 1897, the usefulness of such work to his career had already passed and he abandoned the genre of the New Humor essay for the novel and the scientific romance.

The humor in Wells's early short fiction often is rooted in the disparity in perception between members of different social classes. A typical example may be found in "The Jilting of Jane," where a maid is explaining to her mistress the nature of her attachment to a young man:

> "He is second porter at Maynards, the draper's," said Jane, "and gets eighteen shillings a week—nearly a pound a week, m'm; and when the head porter leaves he will be head porter. His relatives are quite superior people, m'm. Not labouring people at all. His father was a greengrosher [*sic*], m'm, and had a tumour, and was bankrupt twice. And one of his sisters is in a Home for the Dying. It will be a very good match for me, m'm," said Jane, "me being an orphan girl."
>
> "Then you are engaged to him?" asked my wife.
>
> "Not engaged, ma'am; but he is saving money to buy a ring."

The passage also reflects the mixture of humor and genuine pathos with which Wells depicts lower-class life in his later writing.

The influence of the New Humor is apparent in his early novel writing. *The Wonderful Visit* (1895) was undoubtedly intended by the author to be a wide-ranging satire on the human condition. The story involves an angel's appearance in a small English village and his ensuing stay with the local vicar. The most memorable parts of the novel, however, are the charm and humor of the angel's confrontations with the ordinary occurrences in everyday village life. In 1902, Wells used the same satiric device in a slightly different guise in *The Sea Lady*, this time having a mermaid observe and comment on the social and sexual mores of Edwardian England.

Wells's only completely comic novel was published in 1896, in the midst of a tremendous vogue for bicycling which occurred during the late 1880s and 1890s. *The Wheels of Chance* clearly shows the tremendous influence of Jerome's *Three Men in a Boat* (1889) on the form of the comic novel during this period. In addition to being a minor comic classic, *The Wheels of Chance* is significant because it is Wells's first attempt to deal with themes that would dominate his major novels in the next decade. The main character, Mr. Hoopdriver, is the first of Wells's lower-middle-class protagonists who feel the insufficiencies of their mundane lives. Hoopdriver hopes at least temporarily to escape the constraints of his life as a draper's assistant with an extended bicycle tour. A novice rider, Hoopdriver takes a tumble with an experienced woman cyclist in gray bloomers who comes to his aid. Since bloomers were invariably associated with women holding "advanced" ideas, Hoopdriver speculates that "Probably she was one of these here New Women. He had a persuasion the cult had been maligned. Anyhow she was a Lady . . . His mind came round and dwelt some time on her visible self. Rational dress didn't look a bit unwomanly" (*The Wheels of Chance*, 39).

Jessie Milton is the first of Wells's New Woman characters, and her credentials as a nascent feminist are clearly outlined. At seventeen she is trying to escape the influence of her stepmother, a woman who after writing an anti-marital novel titled "A Soul Untrammeled" married into a life of potted respectability in Surbiton. Jessie tells Hoopdriver, "I want to lead a Free Life and Own myself. I can't go back. I want to obtain a position as a journalist" (198). She has read Olive Schreiner's *The Story of an African Farm* and the short stories of "George Egerton" (Mary Chavelita Dunne). Having escaped the oppressive conventionality of Surbiton, she "knew that the thing to do was to have a flat and go to the British Museum and write leading articles for the daily papers" (252). The rest of the plot involves Hoopdriver's aspirations to knight-errantry and visions of the New Woman as damsel-in-distress as he attempts to help Jessie escape the clutches of her mother and an unwanted fiancé.

Although the period in which Wells worked as a humorist ends with the publication of *The Wheels of Chance*, the comic influence may be seen in his major Edwardian novels. The label of "Dickensian" is often applied to *Love and Mr. Lewisham, Kipps, Tono-Bungay,* and *The History of Mr. Polly*, because of the novelist's ability to include moments of genuine humor and pathos in novels about a character's sense of dislocation and the need for adjustment in lower-middle-class life. The description of the protagonist's educational experience in *The History of Mr. Polly* is perhaps representative of the humor found in Wells's novels written during the Edwardian period:

> Mr. Polly went into the National School at six and left the private school at fourteen, and by that time his mind was in much the same state that you would be in, dear reader, if you were operated upon for appendicitis by a well-meaning, boldly enterprising, but rather overworked and under-paid butcher boy, who was superseded towards the climax of the operation by a left-handed clerk of high principles but intemperate habits,— that is to say it was in a thorough mess. The nice little curiosities and willingnesses of a child were in a jumbled and thwarted condition, hacked

and cut about—the operators had left so to speak, all of their sponges and ligatures in the mangled confusion—and Mr. Polly had lost much of his natural confidence, so far as figures and sciences and languages and the possibilities of learning things were concerned.

While the Edwardian novels share some of the same thematic concerns present in *The Wheels of Chance* and occasionally some of the humor, in the great middle phase of his career Wells was writing serious, realistic fiction outside the comic vein that he had exploited in the early 1890s.

Summary

H.G. Wells's monumental career as novelist, journalist, and polemicist overwhelms his brief period of writing as a humorist. Indeed, he was perhaps never truly a humorist. Instead, his "New Humor" essays published in the early 1890s are the work of an aspiring writer trying to make a name for himself and earn his living by publishing in an easily accessible market. His one comic novel, *The Wheels of Chance*, still has the quaint charm of a good period piece. The novel's strengths and enduring qualities are not found in the humor of the story, however, so much as in the fact that in *The Wheels of Chance* Wells was finally beginning to find his subject matter.

Selected Bibliography

Primary Sources
The Time Machine: An Invention. London: Heinemann, 1895.
The Wonderful Visit. London: Dent, 1895.
The Wheels of Chance. London: Dent, 1896.
Certain Personal Matters. London: Lawrence & Bullen, 1897.
Love and Mr. Lewisham. London and New York: Harper, 1900.
The Sea Lady. London: Methuen, 1902.
Kipps: The Story of a Simple Soul. London: Macmillan, 1905.
Tono-Bungay. New York: Duffield, 1908.
Anne Veronica: A Modern Love Story. London: Unwin, 1909.
The History of Mr. Polly. London, Edinburgh, Dublin, New York, Leipzig, and Paris: Nelson, 1910.
Bealby: A Holiday. London: Methuen, and New York: Macmillan, 1915.
Works of H.G. Wells. New York: Charles Scribner's Sons, 1924.

The Shape of Things to Come. Toronto: Macmillan, 1939.

Screenplays
Things to Come. 1936. Although he did not write the screenplays except for *The Time Machine* and *The War of the Worlds*, other filmed versions of Wells's novels include *The Island of Dr. Moreau* (1977; as *Island of Lost Souls*, 1932); *The Invisible Man* (1933 and 1975); *Things to Come* (1936); *The Man Who Could Work Miracles* (1935); *Kipps* (1941); and *The History of Mr. Polly* (1949).

Secondary Sources
Batchelor, John. *H.G. Wells*. Cambridge: Cambridge University Press, 1985. An excellent survey of Wells's literary career.
Bergonzi, Bernard. *The Early H.G. Wells*. Manchester: Manchester University Press, 1961. A solid survey of Wells's writings through the early scientific romances. Particularly useful for placing Wells against the background of the 1890s—a decade dominated by writers associated with the aesthetic and decadent movements.
Costa, Richard Hauer. *H.G. Wells*. rev. ed. Boston: Twayne, 1985. A useful, but basic, assessment of Wells's life and career.
Hammond, J.R. *H.G. Wells and the Modern Novel*. New York: St. Martin's Press, 1988. An interesting assessment of Wells's novels in and as part of the early modernist period of literature.
Murray, Brian. *H.G. Wells*. New York: Continuum, 1990. A basic biography and literary assessment.
West, Anthony. *H.G. Wells: Aspects of a Life*. New York: Random House, 1984. A provoking commentary on Wells's life, written by his illegitimate son by Rebecca West.

Peter C. Hall

Wilde, Oscar

Born: Dublin, Ireland, October 16, 1854
Education: Portora Royal School, Inniskillen; Trinity College, Dublin; Magdalen College, Oxford University, first in Mods, first in Greats, B.A., 1878
Marriage: Constance Lloyd, May 29, 1884; two children
Died: Paris, November 30, 1900

Biography

Oscar Fingal O'Flahertie Wills Wilde was born in Dublin, Ireland, on October 16, 1854. His mother, (Jane) Speranza Francesca Wilde, was a writer of patriotic poems and articles; his father, William Robert Wilde, was a physician—an eye and ear specialist and author of pioneering textbooks in this field—and Surgeon Oculist to the Queen in Ireland. This pair provided a cosmopolitan upbringing for Wilde, who eventually developed into an excellent classicist. He studied classics, first at Trinity College under the tutelage of John Mahaffy, with whom he traveled in Italy (1875) and Greece (1877), and second at Magdalen College, Oxford, where he entered as Demy in October 1874. At Oxford, Wilde received first in Mods and first in Greats, earning his B.A. degree in November 1878. His two mentors at Oxford were Walter Pater and John Ruskin. Following in Ruskin's footsteps, Wilde won the Newdigate Prize in poetry with "Ravenna" (1878).

His first book, *Poems* (1881), decried as derivative, received not only poor reviews but also the dubious distinction of having been solicited and then rejected by the Oxford Union Library. Nevertheless, this collection fostered Wilde's reputation as an aesthete, as did also his flamboyant dress, epigrams, and public worship of such theatrical notables as Lily Langtry. During 1882, Wilde toured the United States and Canada in the role of an aesthete in order ostensibly to lecture on art and pre-Raphaelitism but actually to acquaint Americans with the Aesthetic Movement, the satiric butt of William Schwenck Gilbert and Arthur Sullivan's operetta *Patience*. In America, too, Wilde's first play, *Vera, or the Nihilists*, received its premiere run.

After his return to England, Wilde married Constance Lloyd (May 29, 1884), supporting this marriage by editing the women's journal *Women's World*. A mildly innovative editor, Wilde encouraged broad intellectual and artistic interests for women through the articles that he solicited and through the reviews that he wrote for this journal. Before giving up the editorship in 1889, he published his first collection of fairy tales, *The Happy Prince* (1888).

This collection heralded a rapid succession of increasingly important works, beginning with *The Picture of Dorian Gray*, a novel published first in *Lippincott's* magazine in 1890 (appearing in the same issue as Arthur Conan Doyle's "The Sign of Four") and then in book form the following year. *Intentions*, a collection of critical dialogues and essays, including "The Decay of Lying," which offered the famous maxim that "life imitates art," was published in 1891. That same year saw the publication of Wilde's second collection of fairy tales, *A House of Pomegranates*, a collection of short stories, *Lord Arthur Savile's Crime*, which contained the still-popular "The Canterville Ghost," and the completion of *Salome*, a play originally written in French.

The next year, 1892, his first comedy, *Lady Windermere's Fan*, was produced to immediate and great success. *Salome*, the title role to be played by Sarah Bernhardt, was denied any possible theatrical success when it was banned from production due to a law forbidding the depiction on the stage of biblical characters. *Salome* appeared in book form with illustrations by Aubrey Beardsley in 1893.

Wilde followed the success of his first comedy with the three comedies which contribute so much to his continuing fame: *A Woman of No Importance* (1893), *An Ideal Husband* (1895), and *The Importance of Being Earnest* (1895). While this last play was still in production to great acclaim, Wilde instituted a libel suit against the Marquess of Queensberry, father of Wilde's intimate friend Alfred Douglas. Queensberry had left a card at Wilde's club describing Wilde as a "sodomist." At the conclusion of the ensuing trial, Queensberry was acquitted of libel while Wilde was arrested for "acts of gross indecency with other male persons." After two trials, in 1895 Wilde was found guilty and sentenced to two years hard labor in prison.

In jail in Pentonville, Wandsworth, and Reading, Wilde endured the rigors of a harsh penal code which enforced silence and solitary confinement. While in prison, he was declared bankrupt, was divorced from his wife, and lost custody of his two sons; also, he wrote the self-justifying letter to Douglas now known as *De Profundis* (1897).

After his release from prison, Wilde wrote *The Ballad of Reading Gaol*, a poem that he published under his prison identification number C33, a generic identity which accorded well with the work's theme of universal sin and guilt. Living under the pseudonym Sebastian Melmoth (after the martyred saint and after his famous relative Maturin, the author of *Melmoth the Wanderer*), Wilde led a peripatetic life before dying in Paris on November 30, 1900.

In 1995, a stained glass window bearing his name was dedicated in the Poet's Corner of Westminster Abbey.

Literary Analysis

> Cecily. Do you suggest, Miss Fairfax, that I entrapped Ernest into an engagement? How dare you? This is no time for wearing the shallow mask of manners. When I see a spade I call it a spade.
> Gwendolen. (*Satirically.*) I am glad to say that I have never seen a spade. It is obvious that our social spheres have been widely different.[1]

It would be rather difficult to call this particular spade of an exchange in *The Importance of Being Earnest* a spade. Wilde labels Gwendolen's response in the stage direction as satire (the only instance of his actually so doing) but it is an unusual type of satire. Instead of an attack on the individual or his/her actions, the attack is on the individual's style. The author's humorous satire deflects painlessly from the individual to his/her style because Wilde's concern is with art, less with the essential person—with "that dreadful universal thing called human nature" ("The Decay of Lying," 15)—than with the individual's style which expresses a unique personality; therefore, this seeming deflection is actually point-blank accuracy in its satiric aim.

Satire can be formal, or direct, as in the works of Horace and Juvenal, or it can be informal, or indirect, in which case, as Northrop Frye elaborates in his essay "On the Nature of Satire," the word satire designates "a tone or quality of art which we may find in any form: in a play by Shaw, a novel by Sinclair Lewis, or a cartoon by Low."[2] The characteristics of satire, in the latter case, are humor and an attempt to criticize a subject. Many forms of humor, such as burlesque, parody, irony, and wit, are available to satire while the common subject for satiric criticism is human vice or folly.

Several critics, assessing Wilde's humorous satire, either characterize it as a "satire of manners" or deny its existence altogether. Edouard Roditi writes: "In spite of the polished brilliance of its paradoxical dialogue and the sure pace of its surprising action, *The Importance of Being Earnest* . . . never transcends, as a work of art, the incomplete or the trivial. Its tone is that of satire, but of a satire which, for lack of a moral point of view, has lost its sting and has degenerated into the almost approving banter of P.G. Wodehouse. Satire . . . must be founded on more than a dandy's mere tastes and opinions; from some sounder moral philosophy, it must derive necessary bitterness without which the satirist remains ineffectual while the manners of his comedies, not yet structurally integrated, seem superimposed as mere ornament on an arbitrary plot of farce."[3] Wilde's humorous satire, though, operates from a sound aesthetic philosophy, "the philosophy of the superficial" (*A Woman of No Importance*, 110). With this philosophy, the superficiality of style becomes serious while seriousness becomes a sin. It is, however, this very philosophy which gives his satire its unique, nonbitter quality.

Wilde's humorous satire is of the indirect mode, nestled complacently within melodramas of fallen women and, worse, fallen men and Gothic tales of moral immorality and dutiful murder. The playwright uses every device available to humor from wit to symbol. This formidable battery of attack is brought to bear on a special type of vice and folly: that which is inimical to art and, since Wilde equates the two in his essay "The Soul of Man Under Socialism," individualism (304). The integrity of his satire rests in its combination of method and concern: both are artistic. His satire is, in short, a unique type of satire which I will call, for want of a better term, aesthetic satire.

Through this aesthetic satire Wilde promotes his concept of individualism. He paradoxically makes virtue a vice and desanctifies society's accepted standards, eliminating society's mediating role; consequently, the individual is left free to develop and to adhere to his or her own standards. According to Wilde, in individualism the necessity is propounded for people to realize their passions for complete self-expression and for a perfect harmony of conscience and instinct.

Such self-realization will prevent man's injustice to man which, in Wilde's opinion, proceeds from society's denial of the individual: "All modes of government are wrong. They are unscientific because they seek to alter the natural environment of men; they are immoral because, by interfering with the individual, they produce the most aggressive forms of egotism" ("The Soul of Man Under Socialism," 294). Furthermore, Wilde asserts, "Selfishness is not living as one wishes to live; it is asking others

to live as one wishes to live. And unselfishness is letting other people's lives alone, not interfering with them" ("The Soul of Man Under Socialism," 328). Self-realization will also prevent man's injustice to himself: "But the bravest man amongst us is afraid of himself. The mutilation of the savage has its tragic survival in the self-denial that mars our lives. We are punished for our refusals. Every impulse that we strive to strangle broods in the mind and poisons us . . . the only way to get rid of a temptation is to yield to it" (*The Picture of Dorian Gray*, 22).

Roditi's criticism of Wilde's stingless and therefore ineffectual satire quite simply overlooks its basis in this concept of individualism. Individualism merges with art, says Wilde: "Art is Individualism, and Individualism is a disturbing force. Therein lies its immense value. For what it seeks to disturb is monotony of type, slavery of custom, tyranny of habit, and the reduction of man to the level of a machine" ("The Soul of Man Under Socialism," 304). Here, then, are the explicit deviations from Wilde's norm that he satirizes. His intent is to criticize conventions which stultify the individual, to allow the individual to be untrammeled in his/her attempt to bring art to his/her life.

Wilde's norm, because it is artistic, lends his satire its stingless, infinitely good-humored quality. The aesthetic critic—or satirist—contemplates life, a life that has for its aim not doing but being. Because he does not act, he avoids pain, for it is doing and acting which promulgate pain: "The sure way of knowing nothing about life is to try to make oneself useful . . . That the desire to do good to others produces a plentiful crop of prigs is the least of the evils of which it is the cause" ("The Critic as Artist," 184). Wilde's aesthetic satire has for its norm art and individualism and for its purpose the bringing of art and beauty into the individual's life; its philosophy is aesthetic. It is based on a philosophy of the superficial, on manners, style, and poses rather than on morality and truth. It frees the individual from custom, habit, and the standard conception of virtuous behavior, for the individual is virtuous when he/she is true to him/herself.

The one unifying feature which Wilde's satire shares with that of other satirists is its humor, its comicality. Wilde uses contrasts and incongruities within generalizations, generalizations which the author raises in order to highlight individual differences, and in his humor asserts the validity of the subjective impression. His tone is amoral, flippant, skeptical, exaggerated; the structure of his writing is staccato and abrupt. Its intent is to transvalue society's materialistic and nonindividualistic values: "The heavy, cumbrous, blind, mechanical forces of society . . . [which do] not recognize the dynamic force . . . in a man or a movement" (*De Profundis*, 492). Wilde's humor therefore depends largely on paradox which is the essence of transvaluation.

In discussing the forms of Wilde's humor, most critics consider only his epigrams and paradoxes; indeed, Robert Jordan argues that his epigrammatic paradoxes are his sole instruments of serious satire.[4] These critics fail, however, to perceive the wide extent of his forms of humor, forms which include, besides epigrams and paradoxes, situational humor, repartee, parody, and even symbol. Underlying and lending coherence to each of these forms is the author's philosophy of art and individualism.

Wilde is, of course, famous or infamous for his epigrams. Among his more famous are: "The first duty in life is to be as artificial as possible. What the second duty is no one has as yet discovered" (*An Ideal Husband*, 27); "Pleasure is the only thing one should live for. Nothing ages like happiness" (*An Ideal Husband*, 27); "No crime is vulgar, but all vulgarity is crime. Vulgarity is the conduct of others" (*An Ideal Husband*, 138). Critics often consider the dandies in Wilde's plays to be mouthpieces for the dramatist himself; the one characteristic that they share with Wilde is their finesse in the use of epigrams. Lord Henry Wotton speaks almost consistently in epigrams throughout *The Picture of Dorian Gray*. "So sorry I am late, Dorian," he apologizes. "I went to look after a piece of old brocade in Wardour Street, and had to bargain for hours for it. Nowadays people know the price of everything and the value of nothing" (55). Lord Illingworth's only saving grace is his epigrammatic style of conversation: "the only difference between the saint and the sinner is that every saint has a past, and every sinner has a future" (*A Woman of No Importance*, 119).

The content of these epigrams makes them apparently contentless, superficial; but, they consistently express Wilde's philosophy of the superficial in their definition of self as style. Their style is appropriate to their content, for epigrammatism forces regularity and control upon the disordered state of language and serves as a self-consciously artistic mode of speech.

Wilde glories in paradox. Again, the style and content often coalesce, for he uses paradox most effectively to alter an old cliché. "The platitudinous phrases embodying some conventional sentiment or morality or social behavior are taken," Jordan writes. "One or two words (preferably toward the end) are altered, and the whole thing is blown sky-high" (101). Thus, not only does Wilde satirize the over-crusted, fossilized, and fossilizing sentiment, but he also satirizes the style in which people express these sentiments. Some examples are: "Work is the curse of the drinking classes"; "Don't be led astray into the paths of virtue"; "He hasn't a single redeeming vice."[5] More incisively, Wilde gives this paradoxical description of a widow's grief at the loss of her husband: "Her capacity for family affection is extraordinary. When her third husband died, her hair turned quite gold from grief" (*The Picture of Dorian Gray*, 214). While inverting the cliché, and the fossilizing effect of its conventional sentiment upon the individual, Wilde not only negates it but also creates an inversion that sounds as true as the original cliché. Because the cliché exists as a record of some accepted attitude toward its subject, Wilde satirizes the illusions and hypocrisies of those who use it: "In modern life nothing produces such an effect as a good platitude. It makes the whole world kin" (*An Ideal Husband*, 41). He, in effect, exposes the superficiality of these sentiments and releases individuals from their limits and restraints.

In addition to his epigrams and paradoxes, Wilde presents situational humor which usually entails a running joke with characters commenting upon another absent or rarely seen character such as Mrs. Daubeney in *A Woman of No Importance*, Agatha in *Lady Windermere's Fan*, and Lord Bracknell in *The Importance of Being Earnest*. These characters ideally represent their society: Mrs. Daubeney is the English stoic who, despite being blind, deaf, and bedridden, is "so very cheerful" (129); effusive Agatha's "clever talk" consists solely of "Yes, mama" (31); and Lord Bracknell stays docilely at home, for "the home seems to be the proper sphere for the man" (117). These characters represent a society which complacently accepts stereotypic and superficial behavior without truly understanding the philosophy of the superficial, a philosophy which promotes Wilde's concept of individualism. These characters are unindividual because they do not choose a self-expressive style or superficiality but instead conform to conventions and consequently suppress their individuality.

Wilde also uses parody. As Richard Foster points out, the writer parodies literary clichés in *The Importance of Being Earnest* through his artistic method of exaggeration. Jack Worthing represents the lover surmounting insuperable odds to marry his beloved. His parents, however, prove peculiarly insuperable barriers since they are a handbag and a parcel. His foe is the dragon Lady Bracknell—or is she a Gorgon? "I don't know what a Gorgon is like" (50). Algernon represents the reformed rake. His reformation, though, arises from sheer stupefaction at the sweet, innocent, young Cecily's paradoxical acceptance of his evil past: "I hope you have not been leading a double life, pretending to be wicked and being really good all the time. That would be hypocrisy" (77). Once more the basis of Wilde's satire is aesthetic: it criticizes the public which perpetuates and accepts these literary clichés. Since Wilde believes art to be "the most intense form of Individualism" ("The Soul of Man Under Socialism," 300), the public's demand for popular art encroaches on the individual. So, he satirizes the mediocre tastes of a public which, as he writes in "The Soul of Man Under Socialism," wants art "to please their want of taste . . . to tell them what they have been told before, to show them what they ought to be tired of seeing" (301).

Since much of Wilde's work is dramatic, it offers ample opportunity for repartee, both short and extended. Lord Illingworth excuses himself to Mrs. Allonby: "I'll be back in a moment. People's mothers always bore me to death. All women become like their mothers. That is their tragedy." Mrs. Allonby caps this with, "No man does. That is his" (85). An extended example is:

> Lady Hunstanton. I think on the whole that the secret of life is to take things very, very easily.
> Mrs. Allonby. The secret of life is never to have an emotion that is unbecoming.
> Lady Stutfield. The secret of life is to appreciate the pleasure of being terribly, terribly deceived.
> Kelvil. The secret of life is to resist temptation, Lady Stutfield.
> Lord Illingworth. There is no secret of life. Life's aim, if it has one, is simply to be always looking for temptation. (125–26)

At the conclusion to *The English Renaissance in Art*, Wilde offers a corrective for Lord Illingworth: "We spend our days, each one of us, in looking for the secret of life. Well, the secret of life is in art" (277).

Finally, Wilde creates a unique humorous symbol in his "Bunburyism." Otto Reinert defines the term thusly: "Bunburyism is most simply defined as a means of escape from convention" (15). Bunburyism is the artistic mask from behind which a person may express his/her true self. While indicating in his article Wilde's satire of conventions which lead to hypocritical behavior, Reinert fails to place the basis of this criticism in Wilde's concept of individualism: "Bunburyism" is the individual's response to "Victorianism."

Wilde fuses these several humorous devices into the single intention of his aesthetic satire: to criticize the customs and habits of the age which are inimical to individualism. In his introduction to *The Picture of Dorian Gray and Other Writings by Oscar Wilde*, Richard Ellmann observes that Wilde "anatomiz[es][6] conventional moral standards," that he "cut[s] across accepted ideas: [In *Earnest*] the themes are the same [as in his other works] . . . All the Victorian virtues, including virtue itself, are paraded then fusilladed" (xvi). Ellmann identifies targets such as earnestness, sincerity, and the Church. Although he acknowledges Wilde's transvaluation of such values, Ellmann does not locate the philosophical bases for these transvaluations in Wilde's individualism.

Focusing on objective codes and conventions, Wilde's individualism transvalues their values. As noted above, his criteria for art and individualism paradoxically reverse the conventional conception of vice and folly; virtue becomes a vice: "Nowadays, with our modern mania for morality, everyone has to pose as a paragon of purity, incorruptibility, and all the other seven deadly virtues—and what is the result? You all go over like ninepins—one after the other" (*An Ideal Husband*, 46). Wilde attests to the "sincerity" of this criticism in his letter of November 28, 1897, to Leonard Smithers in which he writes:

> I never came across anyone in whom the moral sense was dominant who was not heartless, cruel, vindictive, log-stupid, and entirely lacking in the smallest sense of humanity.

Moral people, as they are termed, are simple beasts. I would sooner have fifty unnatural vices than one unnatural virtue. It is unnatural virtue that makes the world, for those who suffer, such a premature Hell.[7]

Wilde's concept of art and individualism carries the immorality of morality and duty to its "logical" conclusion in *Lord Arthur Savile's Crime* in which the hero is told by a chiromantist that he is destined to commit murder. Lord Arthur, at first understandably perturbed, ultimately manages to reconcile himself to his duty: "Many men in his position would have preferred the primrose path of dalliance to the steep heights of duty; but Lord Arthur was too conscientious to set pleasure above principle" (178). He attempts to poison his second cousin, Lady Clementina, and to blow up his uncle, the Dean of Chichester. He achieves the supreme feat by tipping the chiromantist, Mr. Podgers, into the Thames—after which, he lives happily-ever-after. In *The Importance of Being Earnest*, Dr. Chasuble's true Christian charity appears in his gentle reproach of Miss Prism's rather harsh acceptance of Wicked Jack's death by a severe chill as divine justice: "Charity, dear Miss Prism, charity! None of us are perfect. I myself am peculiarly susceptible to draughts" (87).

Noninterference is charity to the individual. Indeed, as Lord Henry says, "All influence is immoral . . . Because to influence a person is to give him one's own soul" (*The Picture of Dorian Gray*, 158). And, he speaks more truthfully than he realizes, for his influence upon Dorian Gray proves disastrous. In Wilde's opinion, all reform derives from selfishness: "None of us can stand other people having the same faults as ourselves. I quite sympathize with the rage of the English democracy against what they call the vices of the upper orders. The masses feel that drunkenness, stupidity, and immorality should be their own special preserves" (*The Picture of Dorian Gray*, 149). An aesthetic individual finds sympathy with pain and suffering "morbid" (*The Picture of Dorian Gray*, 184) because it sympathizes with life's decay and destruction; sympathy with success evinces true "health" and growth. Such aesthetic sympathy diffuses joy while philanthropy perpetuates pain, for, as Wilde writes in a sentence in which paradox may blunt the edge of his criticism, "Philanthropic people lose all sense of humanity" (*The Picture of Dorian Gray*, 178).

The slavery of custom sanctifies the Victorian family, and Wilde exposes the superficial, because nonindividual, qualities of the age's respect for family. Lady Berwick, with true maternal heroism, throws her daughter Agatha into the arms of the first suitable suitor: "Of course, we should be very sorry to lose her, but I think that a mother who doesn't part with a daughter every season has no real affection" (*Lady Windermere's Fan*, 31). As the patriarchal figure gains preeminence from his place in his home, his proper sphere is necessarily domestic: "And certainly once a man begins to neglect his domestic duties he becomes painfully effeminate" (*The Importance of Being Earnest*, 117). Relatives, indeed, are so superficial that they have lost all sense of their noblest contribution to family life, their deaths: "Relations are simply a tedious pack of people who haven't got the remotest notion how to live, nor the smallest instinct about when to die" (*The Importance of Being Earnest*, 50).

Marriage is inimical to the individual: "The people who love only once in their lives are really the shallow people. What they call their fidelity, I call either the lethargy of custom or their lack of imagination" (*The Picture of Dorian Gray*, 199). The moment that marriage stultifies the individual by becoming a habit, it becomes a degenerative force. When Lord Windermere declines a game of cards, Lord Dumby sighs, "Good Heavens! How marriage ruins a man! It's as demoralising as cigarettes, and far more expensive" (*Lady Windermere's Fan*, 128–29). Algernon in *The Importance of Being Earnest* is similarly, and for the same reasons, scandalized to learn that the best champagne is rarely served in married households. And when marriage is thought of as a virtue in itself, it becomes positively indecent:

> Mary Farquer . . . always flirts with her own husband across the dinner table. That is not very pleasant. Indeed, it is not even decent . . . And that sort of thing is enormously on the increase. The amount of women who flirt with their own husband is perfectly scandalous. It looks so bad. It is simply washing one's clean linen in public (21).

Eric Bentley, in discussing *The Importance of Being Earnest*, feels that it is sufficient to indicate the "serious" intention of Wilde's criticism when he says that Wilde criticizes marriage as an institution which promotes hypocritical behavior (176). Like Reinert in his discussion of "Bunburyism," Bentley fails to indicate that to Wilde every type of conformity is hypocrisy because one's virtues are not one's own. One behaves in a superficial manner by accepting the accepted customs of the age without considering one's individual desires. Virtue, like truth, is a personal matter.

Lady Bracknell represents a superficial because conformative society, an institution which values stupidity in husbands and profiles in wives. Cecily Cardew's "really solid qualities" (*The Importance of Being Earnest*, 161) are her thirty-thousand pounds in the Funds, and Algernon's ostentatious eligibility rests on the fact that "he has nothing but he looks everything" (165). Lord Illingworth, too, exposes society, or the English aristocracy, as mere fiction: "You should read the Peerage . . . It is the best thing in fiction the English have ever done" (*A Woman of No Importance*, 115).

In Wilde's canon the educational code spreads ignorance and conformity by ignoring the individual. For example, "The thoroughly well-informed man—that is the modern ideal. And the mind of the thoroughly well-informed man is a dreadful thing. It is like a bric-a-brac shop, all monsters and dust, with everything priced above its value" (*The Picture of Dorian Gray*, 14). The only reason to tolerate education is that "in England, at any rate, [it] produces no effect whatsoever" (*The Importance of Being Earnest*, 41)—possibly because such education only reinforces British superficiality.

In addition, the code of the Church is conventional and superficial because its leaders "really have nothing to say" ("The Soul of Man Under Socialism," 322), and, like the House of Commons, they say it, as Dr. Chasuble proves in his discussion of his next sermon:

> You would no doubt wish me to make some slight allusion to this tragic domestic affliction next Sunday . . . My sermon on the meaning of the manna in the wilderness can be adapted to almost any occasion, joyful, or . . . distressing . . . I have preached it at harvest celebrations, christenings, confirmations, on days of humiliation and festal days. (*The Importance of Being Earnest*, 88)

That superficiality without the philosophy of the superficial which promotes aesthetic individualism is folly and vice (vice because it stultifies the individual); this is the concept that lies behind Wilde's critical treatment of earnestness and sincerity. Lord Illingworth declares that "One should never take sides in anything . . . Taking sides is the beginning of sincerity, and earnestness follows shortly afterwards, and the human being becomes a bore" (*A Woman of No Importance*, 21). In *The Importance of Being Earnest*, Jack finds the most compromising position of his life to be having to speak the truth to a nice, sweet, refined girl like Gwendolen. Art rather than truth is beauty, and art involves lying: Gwendolen brings her diary on the train "in order to have something sensational to read" (*The Importance of Being Earnest*, 123). Miss Prism punctures Cecily's expectations for her three-volume novel with the sententious description: "The good ended happily, and the bad unhappily. That is what fiction means" (*The Importance of Being Earnest*, 71). Algernon tells Cecily that he lied about his identity in order to meet her. When Gwendolen asks Cecily if she believes him, Cecily replies, "I don't. But that does not affect the wonderful beauty of his answer." Gwendolen agrees: "True. In matters of grave importance, style, not sincerity is the vital thing" (*The Importance of Being Earnest*, 149–50).

Wilde calls Lord Goring of *An Ideal Husband* the "first well-dressed philosopher in the history of thought" (137), and Goring's conversation with his valet, an expansive auditor, espouses perfectly Wilde's own philosophy of the superficial.

> Lord Goring. Got my second buttonhole for me, Phipps?
> Phipps. Yes, my lord.
> Lord Goring. Rather distinguished thing, Phipps. I am the only person of the smallest importance at present who wears a buttonhole.
> Phipps. Yes, my lord. I have observed that.
> Goring. You see, Phipps, fashion is what other people wear.
> Phipps. Yes, my lord.
> Goring. Just as vulgarity is simply the conduct of other people.
> Phipps. Yes, my lord.
> Lord Goring. And falsehoods the truths of other people.
> Phipps. Yes, my lord.
> Goring. Other people are quite dreadful. The only possible society is oneself.

Phipps. Yes, my lord.
Goring. To love oneself is the beginning
of a lifelong romance.
Phipps. Yes, my lord. (137–39)

Wilde further opposes his individualism to seriousness: "Seriousness is the world's original sin. If the cavemen had known how to laugh, history would have been different" (*The Picture of Dorian Gray*, 185). Life should be treated trivially because it is "far too important a thing ever to talk seriously about it" (*Lady Windermere's Fan*, 20). Buttonholes, then, are a matter of grave concern—because they express an individual's style—as are good cooks: "I regard Henry as infamous, absolutely infamous. But I am bound to state . . . that he is excellent company, and he has one of the best cooks in London, and after a good dinner one can forgive anybody, even one's own relations" (*A Woman of No Importance*, 75).

And, "Bunburyism," the art of enjoying oneself—and it is an art since its basis is lying—is quite a serious matter, indeed. "Serious Bunburyist! Good heavens!" Jack huffs. Algernon replies serenely, "Well, one must be serious about something if one wants any amusement out of life. I happen to be serious about Bunburying. What on earth you are serious about I haven't got the remotest idea. About everything, I should fancy. You have such an absolutely trivial nature" (*The Importance of Being Earnest*, 136).

Critics often note that Wilde's paradoxes tend to be absolutely true. In his essay "The Decay of Lying," Wilde hopes for the day when art will supersede truth. On that day, a true revolution will occur, and:

Romance will return to the land . . .
Champing his gilded oats, the Hippogriff
will stand in our stalls and over our
heads will float the Blue Bird singing of
beautiful and impossible things, of things
that are lovely and that never happen. Of
things that are not and that should be.
("The Decay of Lying," 54)

Wilde's satire, which consistently promotes art and individualism, is aesthetic because its philosophy is based on the belief that art is the greatest truth. Further, it criticizes the conventions, customs, and habits which trammel the individual, which prohibit him/her from bringing art to his/her life:

Man has sought to live intensely, fully, perfectly. When he can do so without exercising restraint on others, or suffering it ever, and his activities are all pleasurable to him, he will be saner, healthier, more civilised, more *himself* . . . The new Individualism . . . will be perfect harmony. ("The Soul of Man Under Socialism," 334)

Wilde's aesthetic satire, then, attempts to allow people to realize in their lives what is not and what should be: a new Individualism.

Summary

Considered one of England's greatest wits, Oscar Wilde is renowned especially for the socially insightful and philosophically powerful epigrams and paradoxes which can be found in his conversation, essays, short stories, novel, and comedies. These comedies, beginning with *Lady Windermere's Fan* and culminating with his classic *The Importance of Being Earnest*, revived Victorian British theater. They directly link Wilde with William Shakespeare, William Congreve, Richard Sheridan, and George Bernard Shaw. Wilde's method of combining aesthetic/philosophic content with humor also influenced the comedic aspects of such writers as James Joyce, Virginia Woolf, E.M. Forster, Rebecca West, Barbara Pym, and Anita Brookner.

Notes

1. Oscar Wilde, *The Collected Works of Oscar Wilde*, ed. Robert Ross (New York: Methuen, 1908), vol. 2, p. 124. All subsequent quotes of Wilde's work taken from this edition.
2. Northrop Frye, "On the Nature of Satire," *The University of Toronto Quarterly*, 14 (October 1944), p. 75.
3. Edouard Roditi, *Oscar Wilde* (Norfolk: New Directions, 1947), pp. 138–89.
4. Robert J. Jordan, "Satire and Fantasy in Wilde's *The Importance of Being Earnest*," *Ariel*, 1, 3 (1970): 103.
5. Hesketh Pearson, *Oscar Wilde: His Life and Wit* (New York: Harper and Brothers, 1946), p. 101.
6. Richard Ellmann, "Introduction," *The Picture of Dorian Gray and Other Writings by Oscar Wilde* (New York: Bantam, 1982), p. xv.
7. *The Letters of Oscar Wilde*, ed. Rupert Hart-Davis (New York: Harcourt, Brace and World, 1962), p. 686.

Selected Bibliography

Primary Sources

The Collected Works of Oscar Wilde. Ed. Robert Ross. 14 vols. New York: Methuen, 1908.

The Letters of Oscar Wilde. Ed. Rupert Hart-Davis. New York: Harcourt, Brace and World, 1962.

Bibliographies

Mickail, E.H. *Oscar Wilde: An Annotated Bibliography of Criticism.* Totowa, NJ: Rowman & Littlefield, 1978. This bibliography is the starting point for any study of Wilde.

Biographies

Ellmann, Richard. *Oscar Wilde.* New York: Knopf, 1988. The definitive biography on Wilde; an outstanding study.

Pearson, Hesketh. *Oscar Wilde: His Life and Wit.* New York: Harper and Brothers, 1946. A useful and interesting examination for those interested in pursuing Wilde's humor.

Secondary Sources

Articles and Chapters in Books

Bentley, Eric. *The Playwright as Thinker.* New York: Reynal and Hitchcock, 1946. Some very intelligent observations on Wilde's plays.

Foster, Richard. "Wilde as Parodist: A Second Look at *The Importance of Being Earnest.*" *College English*, 18 (1956): 19–25. A structuralist approach.

Frye, Northrop. *Anatomy of Criticism: Four Essays.* Princeton: Princeton University Press, 1971, pp. 227–39. A classic.

Henkle, Roger B. *Comedy and Culture: England 1820–1900.* Princeton, NJ: Princeton University Press, 1980. Henkle contextualizes Wilde's comedies well.

Henderson, Archibald. *European Dramatists.* Cincinnati: Stewart and Kidd, 1913. An early serious study of Wilde's dramatic comedies.

Jordan, Robert J. "Satire and Fantasy in Wilde's *The Importance of Being Earnest.*" *Ariel*, 1, 3 (1970): 101–09. Reprinted in *Modern Critical Interpretations: Oscar Wilde's* The Importance of Being Earnest, edited by Harold Bloom. New York: Chelsea House Publishers, 1988. Jordan suggests that Wilde's play is a fantasy in which ideals are realized; it is not a social satire or farce, he contends.

Reinert, Otto. "Satiric Strategy in *The Importance of Being Earnest.*" *College English*, 18 (1956): 14–18. Wilde's satiric targets are identified.

Roditi, Edward. *Oscar Wilde.* Norfolk: New Directions, 1947. Reissued in a revised, enlarged edition as New Directions Paperbook. New York: New Directions Pub. Corp., 1986. Roditi denies that Wilde's comedies were written with any seriousness of intent.

Toliver, Harold E. "Wilde and the Importance of 'Sincere and Studied Triviality.'" *Modern Drama*, 5 (1962–1963): 389–99. An intelligent response to Roditi's contentions.

Bonnie J. Robinson

Willans, [Herbert] Geoffrey

Born: February 4, 1911
Education: Blundell's, Tiverton, Devon
Marriage: Pamela Wyndham Gibbs, 1940
Died: London, August 6, 1958

Biography

Nigel Molesworth, the Curse of St. Custard's, has long enjoyed a large following among "conoisuers of prose and luvers of literature hem-hem."[1] Less well known is Nigel's creator, Geoffrey Willans, who, besides creating Molesworth, wrote many comic novels and pieces popular during his brief lifetime.

Born on February 4, 1911, Willans was educated at Blundell's School (endowed in 1604). The customs of schoolboys, the eccentric behavior of masters, and the architectural idiosyncrasies of the old school provided valuable background material for his depiction of St. Custard's (Blundell's appears briefly in the Molesworth canon as Grunts, also in Devonshire, to which Molesworth will go instead of Eton after leaving St. Custard's). Willans was himself a schoolmaster for a short time, which helped fill out his exposure to the mores of the English public school system. From his books, it is clear that he concurred with Evelyn Waugh's assessment of the moral and intellectual caliber of most schoolmasters: "I expect you'll be becoming a schoolmaster, sir. That's what most of the gentlemen does, sir, that gets sent down for indecent behaviour."[2] Molesworth finds masters, no matter what their social background, the chief drawback of school:

> Thin ones fat ones little ones tall ones some with cranky cars other with posh ties, some you can rag and others who strike mortal fear into our tiny harts it is cruelty to expose us to such monsters. Everywhere a boy goes at skool there is liable to be a master chiz chiz seeking you out with his fierce burning eyes.[3]

Willans had always liked messing about in boats, and, early in the Second World War, he received a commission as a Sub-Lieutenant in the Royal Naval Volunteer Reserve, serving first on the corvette HMS *Peony*, one of the Flower Class corvettes whose names frequently "lent [themselves] to some ribaldry."[4] Life in the Navy reminded Willans of life at school: "There was the great big toady ('I bet you know the Thames Estuary like the back of your hand, sir'), the keen types, the man who tried to catch the teacher out and, of course, the class dunce."[5] On the *Peony* (and her sister minesweeper, the HMS *Salvia*), Willans spent the beginning of the war in the Atlantic and was in the Mediterranean during the Greek campaign. In 1940, he married Pamela Gibbs. The following year, he moved to the aircraft carrier HMS *Formidable*, which was sent to the United States for repairs. After a largely enjoyable and alcoholic stay, he returned to England. Two of his books—the war memoir *One Eye on the Clock* (1943) and the humorous *Admiral on Horseback* (1954)—draw on his wartime experiences.

Despite having a busy war, Willans was surprisingly prolific; his writing appeared in *Punch* frequently. Most of his humorous pieces were topical—as exemplified by the small serial on an officer's training program entitled "Signals Celibates" (1942)—and short essays based on wartime subjects. It was at this time that the first Molesworth episodes appeared. Between 1939 and 1942, pages from Molesworth's hilariously misspelt diary revealed the horrors of "skool" evacuees, grandmothers, and his brother Molesworth 2's rendition of "Fairy Bells" on the school piano.

In 1953, Willans met his ideal collaborator in the artist Ronald Searle. Searle had already made a name for himself with his drawings of the fearsome denizens of the girls' school St. Trinian's. In 1952, Searle and "Timothy Shy," a pseudonym of the satirist D.B. Wyndham Lewis (not to be confused with the novelist Percy), had had an immediate success with *The Terror of St. Trinian's*. The first Molesworth book, *Down With Skool!* (1953), was an even greater hit. After it appeared in the fall 1953 *Booklist*, it sold almost 55,000 copies before Christmas. Under the pen of Searle, Molesworth, his brother Molesworth 2, Peason (his "grate frend who hav a face like a squished tomato"), Basil Fotherington-Thomas ("hullo clouds hullo sky"), and the rest of the cast at St. Custard's took on their now familiar barmy countenances. The other Molesworth books were equally popular. According to Searle, Willans was "delighted to learn that schoolmasters, far from feeling publicly disrobed, were in fact giving away his books as end-of-term prizes."[6] Searle and Willans continued their partnership in *The Dog's Ear Book* (1958), a humorous catalogue of "doggy types," both two- and four-footed.

In addition to the Molesworth volumes, Willans wrote many other books, ranging from the humorous sketches of *My Uncle Harry* (1957) to the biographical portrait of the actor and playwright *Peter Ustinov* (1957), from the comic guide to air travel and travelers in *Fasten Your Lapstraps!* (1955) to the fictional account of the people who make and fly aircraft in *The Whistling Arrow* (1957). In *The Wit of Winston Churchill* (1956), a birthday celebration, Willans and Charles Roetter selected and annotated Churchill's parliamentary repartee. Much of Willans's work first appeared in magazines such as *Punch*, *Blackwood's Edinburgh Magazine*, *Lilliput*, and *Young Elizabethans* before being anthologized in book form. His books, especially the Molesworth ones, were well received on both sides of the Atlantic, garnering good notices in such varied publications as the *Times Literary Supplement*, *Time*, and the *New Yorker*.

After the war, Willans had sought a career in journalism and worked for a time with the BBC European Service. With the growing success of his books, he left the BBC in 1957 in order to write full time. Willans died suddenly in London on August 6, 1958, from a heart attack.

Literary Analysis

Willans's admiration for the young Peter Ustinov reveals what he strove for in his own humor: highbrow high jinks, verbal twist, hypertrophied stereotypes, and parodic invention that is at once irreverent and unthreatening. Willans has a keen eye for characteristic failings of both people and institutions. Much of his humor derives from his characters' penchant for generalizations. An English naval man, for example, voices the stereotypical Englishman's disdain for the French: "Just what you would expect from a navy which [keeps] chickens on board their ships."[7] Behind his mockery, the author frequently shows real affection for the types behind the stereotypes. Two of his books in particular—*My Uncle Harry* and *Admiral on Horseback*—are each in their way case-studies of "dying species which, unless protected like wildfowl, will soon be extinct."[8]

Uncle Harry, Willans's representative British Clubman, at first seems to be nothing more than a hidebound if unintentionally amusing late Edwardian buck whose arrogant unconcern in a post-Edwardian world both damns and saves him. As Uncle Harry's narrator-nephew remarks, "It is said that the hall-mark of a gentleman is that he is only rude intentionally. One never knew with Uncle Harry whether he was rude intentionally or not, but he was certainly rude to nearly everybody."[9] Willans is delighted to poke fun at some of Uncle Harry's more preposterous habits, but he stops short of condescension for him and his ilk: "Those same glazed eyes may yet have seen their fellows, the cream and stuffing of the nation, dying beside them in the mud of Flanders" (12).

In *Admiral on Horseback*, Rear-Admiral Sir Strangways Foxe-Forsyth, whose only indulgence is "an oil-painting of HMS *Nelson* at sea in bad weather" (13), first appears equally typical. Many of Foxe-Forsyth's adventures are conventionally humorous, as when, in Paris, he inadvertently buys tickets for *Phedre* instead of for the *Folies Bergeres*. But, as his NATO encounters with the American Admiral Burnett J. Kzecky show, the very qualities that Foxe-Forsyth admires in Robert Southey's *Life of Nelson* that make Nelson appear risible also work to his real advantage. Foxe-Forsyth and Kzecky together demonstrate that behind American notions of stock Englishmen and British notions of stock Americans lie complementary strengths. It is finally their shared senses of honor and humor that hold the promise of fraternal victory in the Cold War.

In these works Willans prods the establishment, but his attitude is sympathetic and the world that he caricatures remains a familiar if not altogether cozy one. The Molesworth books, however, prove to be a more incisive commentary on both English society and human frailty. St. Custard's seems to be founded to support the view that "any skool is a bit of a shambles" and that life, consequently, will not be noticeably different. Willans, through the voice of Molesworth, can never resist irreverence toward the clichéd sermonizing of those in authority. As the ever-wary Molesworth sardonically notes, "Skool according to headmaster's pi-jaw is like Life chiz if that is the case wot is the use of going on?"[10]

Molesworth particularly loathes the particularly English game of cricket: "Give me a thumbscrew or slo fire every time." The notion that cricket, for example, is good training for life had become a hackneyed sentiment of late Muscular Christianity. One offshoot of the resurgence of preparatory and public schools for boys in the nineteenth century was the English schoolboy story which presented a group of "typical" English public school boys. Thomas Hughes's *Tom Brown's Schooldays* (1857), the earliest and most influential example (based on Rugby School under Thomas Arnold), firmly establishes the conventions of loyalty to school, love of sport, and honor among right-minded boys. Later versions, such as the stories that appeared in *The Magnet* well into the middle of the twentieth century, perpetuated the pattern. In the figure of Nigel Molesworth, Willans challenges this tradition; St. Custard's is reminiscent of Charles Dickens's Dotheboys Hall rather than Hughes's Rugby.

Certain aspects of the Molesworth antiheroic character had appeared before. Frank Richard's Greyfriars School (where headmaster Quelch is a less terrifying colleague of St. Custard's Grimes) housed the plump, obtuse, and greedy Billy Bunter, whose farcical "dodges" resemble Nigel's "wizard wheezes." The victoriously imaginative adventures of Richmal Crompton's William resemble Nigel's more far-fetched (but less successful) daydreams and fantasies. Both Richard and Crompton, however, wrote for children. By writing primarily for adults, Willans was able to draw on his own taste for Aldous Huxley and Evelyn Waugh, ensuring that irony rather than sentiment or whimsy is the governing humor.

The Molesworth of the books is a more fully developed and canny character than the Molesworth who first appeared in *Punch*, largely because Willans recast Molesworth's voice from the unwittingly comic one of the diaries to a more knowingly sardonic one. As an observer of the world around him, Molesworth possesses a healthy skepticism and, when the world is too much with him, escapism. Alas, as he realizes even at his young age, no world can be entirely satisfactory; even outer space will most certainly prove disappointing; on the moon, for instance, "you can jump three times as high as you can on earth but so can everyone else so there is not much fun in it."[11]

Molesworth expends most of his intellectual energy devising ways to avoid lessons, but he has clearly mastered the forms of school life. Some of his parodies of academic conventions are positively inspired:

> Proposition: Masters are swankpots.
> Proof: Wise boys like me use Flatery
>   with masters from time to time . . .
>   [D]uring a bit of parsing or drawing
>   a map of Spane you can just look up
>   and sa.
> "Did you hav a tomy gun during the war
>   sir?"
> "Get on with your map molesworth
>   one."
> "No but did you sir really?"
> "As a mater of fact i did molesworth."
> "gosh sir did you shoot many germans
>   sir."
> "Get on with your map, boy."
> "No sir but did you?"
> "Altho it hav nothing to do with the lesson i got 9 thousand with one burst once . . . etc." Q.E.D.[12]

Molesworth, constitutionally unable to respect masters, takes great pleasure in exposing the sordid truth: the prizes for school sports have just come back from the pawn-broker's, masters drink gin and torture boys with knuckle-dusters, the headmaster spends his holiday in "spane, the s. of france, then on for a couple of weeks to the italian riviera. This term, of course, the fees will be higher to meet the mounting costs."[13]

A child of the 1950s, the Molesworth of the books is concerned with the modern world: television, "atomms," space ships, and intergalactic journeys. Obviously resentful of the time that he must spend with the traditional studies of the British prep school, he fantasizes about elaborate gags to avoid hateful lessons in "lat," "french," "geog," "hist," "algy," "geom," or "botany." His fertile brain designs such inge-

nious labor-saving devices as the Molesworth Self-Educator, the Molesworth Self-Adjusting Thank-You Letter, and the Molesworth-Peason Lines Machine, doubtless for those times when he is caught daydreaming plots against masters.

Although less lethal than their female counterparts of St. Trinian's, the schoolboy inhabitants of St. Custard's are unprepossessing: "swots, bulies, cissies, milksops greedy gust and oiks." The books contain all-too-convincing reminders of prep-school impedimenta: school songs and the school dog, school food ("the piece of cod which passeth understanding"), canes, carbolic, and bungies. Much of the humor of the Molesworth books is grounded in the routine and slang of British preparatory and public schools where Kennedy's Shorter Latin Primer has been called Shortbread Easting Primer from time immemorial. Molesworth claims to be an unabashed Philistine, rebelliously declaring that subjects such as poetry have little place in the atomic age:

> Occasionally english masters chide me
> for this point of view o molesworth one
> you must learn the value of spiritual
> things until i spray them with 200
> rounds from my backterial gun. i then
> plant the british flag in the masters
> inkwell and declare a whole holiday for
> the skool. boo to shakespeare.[14]

Despite his claims, Molesworth's fantastic daydream and wizard wheezes frequently raid the English literary past and can prove just as killing as his "backterial gun." Consider such assaults on the familiar school curriculum as Molesworth's recitations of Alfred, Lord Tennyson's "Charge of the Light Brigade" ("Har fleag har fleag har fleag onward / Into the er rode the 100") or of Macbeth's "Tomorrow and tomorrow" soliloquy:

> Tomowandtomowandtomow
> Creeps in this um um
> Out!
> Out!
> brief candle
> Yes i kno sir half a mo sir
> Yes
> fie
> O fie
> Um um tis an unweeded syllable an un—
> No!
> Tomowandtomowandtomow ect . . . .

Molesworth's suspicious belligerence is particularly directed at grownups and masters ("Beware of addults, whether parent or beaks").[15] After all, what happens to the "snekes" and "bulies" when they grow up? Grimes the headmaster and Sigismund Arbuthnot, the mad maths master, are particular menaces, but masters in general are despairingly anatomized: "English master hav long hair red ties and weeds like wordsworth throw them into exstatsies"; "If you wake up for long enuff you find that everything in lat. hapned a long time ago. latin masters therefore are always old and bent with age"; "Acording to ancient tradition no fr. master can keep order." Adult hypocrisy and self-aggrandizement are transparent to Molesworth's beady eyes; for equally suspicious but less perceptive readers, he helpfully provides cribs to their "reel thorts." Adult vagaries do not seem to promise much for life outside St. Custard's: "Grown ups are wot `is left when skool is finished."[16]

Whether "goril of 3B" or Young Elizabethan, Molesworth displays, as Searle remarks, "behind his misspelt observations of life all the wiles of a diplomat in foreign affairs." The Molesworth books have been cherished and chortled at for more than fifty years. Although they have largely escaped academic and critical notice, nonetheless they have inspired popular and even literary interest. Sue Townsend's Adrian Mole, for example, although slightly older and slightly lower on the social scale, is clearly indebted to the figure of Molesworth. Simon Brett has added to the Molesworth *oeuvre* with *Molesworth Rites Again* (1983) (dedicated to Willans's memory) and *How To Stay Topp* (1987) which bring devotees up to date on Molesworth and his St. Custard's coterie.

Summary

Geoffrey Willans's humorous writings possess a period charm and tend to be gently ironic rather than satirical. In the schoolboy Nigel Molesworth, however, Willans created a memorable modern sceptic whose highly developed capacity for puncturing the absurd and embellishing the mundane makes him a classic comic figure.

Notes

1. *Whizz for Atomms* (London: Max Parrish, 1956), "Prefface."
2. Evelyn Waugh, *Decline and Fall* (Boston: Little, Brown, 1928), p. 8.
3. *Whizz for Atomms*, p. 57.
4. Peter Elliott, *Allied Escort Ships of World War II: A Complete Survey* (London: Macdonald and Jane's, 1977), p. 171.
5. *One Eye on the Clock* (London: Macmillan, 1943), p. 15.
6. Willans obituary in the *Times* (London, August 9, 1958): 8e.
7. *Admiral on Horseback* (London: M. Joseph, 1954), p. 50.
8. *My Uncle Harry* (London: Parrish, 1957), p. 12.
9. *Ibid.*, p. 17.
10. *How To Be Topp* (London: Max Parrish, 1954), p. 63.
11. *Ibid.*, p. 33.
12. *Down With Skool!* (London: Max Parrish, 1953), p. 28.
13. *Back in the Jug Agane* (London: Max Parrish, 1959), p. 9.
14. *Down with Skool!*, pp. 37–38.
15. *Back in the Jug Agane*, p. 44.
16. *How To Be Topp*, p. 94.

Selected Bibliography
Primary Sources
Shallow Dive. London: Rich & Cowan, 1934.
Romantic Manner. London: Rich & Cowan, 1936.
One Eye on the Clock. London: Macmillan, 1943.
Down With Skool! London: Max Parrish, 1953.
Admiral on Horseback. London: M. Joseph, 1954; New York: Vanguard, 1955.
Crisis Cottage. London: M. Joseph, 1956.
The Whistling Arrow. London: Hutchinson, 1957.
My Uncle Harry. London: Parrish, 1957.
Peter Ustinov. London: Peter Owen, 1957.

With David Mathias
Fasten Your Lapstraps!: A Guide for All Those Who Wing the World in Super-Comfort and Super-Luxury in Super-Aeroplanes. London: Max Parrish, 1955.

With Charles Roetter
The Wit of Winston Churchill. London: Max Parrish, 1956.

With Ronald Searle
Down With Skool! A Guide to School Life for Tiny Pupils and Their Parents. London: Max Parrish, 1953.

*How To Be Topp: A Guide to Sukcess for
Tiny Pupils, Including All There Is to
Know about Space*. London: Max
Parrish, 1954.
*Whizz for Atomms: A Guide to Survival in
the 20th Century for Fellow Pupils,
Their Doting Maters, Pompous Paters
and Any Others Who Are Interested*.
London: Max Parrish, 1956; published
in the United States as *Molesworth's
Guide to the Atommic Age*. New York:
Vanguard, 1957.
*The Dog's Ear Book, with Four Lugubrious
Verses*. London: Max Parrish, 1958;
New York: Crowell, 1960.
Back in the Jug Agane. London: Max Parrish,
1959. Published in the United States as
Molesworth Back in the Jug Agane. New
York: Vanguard, 1960.
The Compleet Molesworth. London: Max
Parrish, 1959; reissued with Forewords
by Tim Rice and Ronald Searle, London:
Pavilion 1985.

Secondary Sources

Articles

Rice, Tim. "Foreword" in *The Compleet
Molesworth*. London: Pavilion, 1985.
Pithy overview by well-known fan.
Searle, Ronald. "Molesworth ography" in
The Compleet Molesworth. London:
Pavilion, 1985. A warm chronicle by
Willans's chief collaborator.
Sisk, John P. "Molesworth Rides Again."
Commonweal, 63 (November 4, 1955):
123–24. The most perceptive contempo-
rary review, placing Willans within the
British satirical tradition.

Alexandra Mullen

Wilson, Sandy

*Born: Sale, Cheshire, England, May 19, 1920
Education: Elstree Preparatory School; Har-
row; Oriel College, Oxford Unversity,
B.A.*

Biography

Sandy (presumably a nickname for Alexander,
but he has never been known by the more formal name) Wilson was born in England on May
19, 1920, the son of George Walter Wilson and
his wife Caroline Elsie (Humphrey) Wilson.
After Elstree Preparatory School, he went to
Harrow (the distinguished English public
school) and on to Oriel College at Oxford,
where he obtained a bachelor's degree in English literature. Wilson's early life made an
important impression on him and he devotes
about a third of his 1975 autobiography to it.

Though elegantly and expensively educated, he insisted during his army service that
he was not officer material and after the army
he entered the Old Vic School in London to
begin his career in the theater.

Wilson had a natural inclination toward
the theater's bright lights and as early as 1948
he was contributing material to revues such as
Oranges and Lemons and *Slings and Arrows*,
frothy entertainments that offered a market for
songs and skits by clever and independent
talents. In 1950, he wrote lyrics for *Caprice*, a
touring revue, and in 1951 and 1952 he
contributed material to the popular revues at
The Watergate in London. By the time *See You
Again* was produced at The Watergate in 1952,
it was clear that he had a light and popular
touch and that what he needed was a framework on which to hang his ideas.

The framework turned out to be a parody
of the musicals of the Roaring Twenties. Underneath the arches of Charing Cross Station was
The Players Theatre, the inheritor of the Victorian music-hall tradition. For an enthusiastic
membership of old-time theater buffs, The Players re-created music hall and vaudeville. It was
at The Players that Wilson produced his great
hit, *The Boy Friend*, in 1953. The play was
transferred to Wyndham's Theatre in mid-Janu-
ary 1954 and enjoyed a West End run of 2,084
performances with Anne Rogers (who had
starred at The Players) and the formidable Joan
Sterndale Bennett (a Players' standby who never
failed to convulse audiences with her prim self-
confidence as chaos struck the scenery and all
around her). In September of 1954, Julie
Andrews made her Broadway debut in *The
Boy Friend* at The Royale in New York. At age
twenty-nine, Wilson was an international celebrity of the musical theater. His autobiography,
I Could Be Happy, its title a line from a song in
The Boy Friend, is essentially the story of how
he reached the top with *The Boy Friend* and
what happened to it and to him in the process.

He followed up with more musicals, none
of them equaling the success of *The Boy Friend*.
The Buccaneer opened at The Apollo in London's West End on February 22, 1956 with the
irrepressibly camp Kenneth Williams as a pre-

cocious schoolboy whose rich and doting mother buys him a boy's paper so that he can save it from becoming a mere American comic book. *The Buccaneer* ran for 203 performances, barely. On October 2, 1957, a better but even less popular musical of Wilson's opened at The Lyric Hammersmith: *Valmouth*, a musical version of Ronald Firbank's fey novel, directed by Wilson's familiar collaborator Vida Hope (with Harry Naughton) and starring Beatrice Reading (later replaced by Cleo Laine) and the incomparable Fenella Fielding. *Valmouth* transferred to the West End, going to The Seville the next January, where it ran 186 performances. In New York, *Valmouth* was caviar to the general: at the York, Off-Broadway, it opened on October 6, 1960 and "closed like an umbrella" soon after, though some people treasured the London cast recording and the *Valmouth* LP has become a collector's item.

Meanwhile, Wilson was doing pretty well on the London stage. With high-powered colleagues such as Harold Pinter and Peter Cooke, he contributed to the revue *Pieces of Eight* at The Apollo (430 performances, beginning September 23, 1959), starring Williams and Fielding. It was easier to write funny lines for character actors whose delivery one could "hear" as one penned them.

The Boy Friend did very well on foreign stages (it was revived in London in 1966 at The Comedy Theatre, and ran in New York with Sandy Duncan and Judy Carne for fifteen weeks in 1970) as well as being made into a film (1971) by Ken Russell and starring Twiggy, Christopher Gable, a campy Max Adrian, terrifically tapping Tommy Tune, Moyra Fraser, and Barbara Wilson. Russell's idea was to script the film to be the story of a provincial company putting on *The Boy Friend* for a big film director who throws everything into a tizzy by being "out front." *The Boy Friend* cultists (who by this time had seen the show in various cities— and languages) thought that the Russell treatment was too Busby-Berkeley-on-acid, not as charming as Hope's triumph with the tiny stage of The Players' Club or as smashing as Andrews's bringing the audience to their feet at The Royale in New York.

In 1964, Wilson staged a sequel to *The Boy Friend*. In *Divorce Me, Darling,* the characters are moved forward from the 1920s to the 1930s and the plot is ridiculous: wives go away on vacation to escape their husbands, who wind up in the same place, and we take it from there.

Starring at The Players' under Steven Vinaver's direction, *Divorce Me, Darling* moved to The Globe, but the West End run was only seventy performances, better than the Off-Broadway revival of *The Boy Friend's* embarrassing seventeen performances but still disappointing for so tuneful a show.

In 1971, Wilson adapted a novel by John Collier, *His Monkey Wife*, which opened in December to no great critical acclaim. The same year saw the playwright himself in a one-man show at The Hampstead Theatre Club (*Sandy Wilson Thanks the Ladies*, which was revived by Lindsay Kemp at The Edinburgh Festival in 1972).

Wilson also wrote music for television series such as *The World of Wooster* (1965–1966) and theater anthologies such as *As Dorothy Parker Once Said* (The Fortune Theatre, London, 1969), a collection of slight short stories (*The Poodle from Rome*, 1962), his autobiography *I Could Be Happy,* and lighthearted books such as *This Is Sylvia?* (1954), *Who's Who for Beginners* (1957), *Ivor* (1975, about Ivor Novello), *Caught in the Act* (1976), and *The Roaring Twenties* (1979). He also wrote *The Clapham Wonder* (1978). He wrote songs for female impersonator Danny La Rue's version of Brandon Thomas's classic *Charley's Aunt* on BBC-TV in 1969 and a Christmas pantomime, *Alladin,* presented at The Lyric, Hammersmith in December 1979.

Now the Bright Young Thing of the 1950s is in his seventies and lives quietly in Southwell Gardens, London SW 7. A new generation, hearing songs from *The Boy Friend* occasionally, thinks that they were written in the 1920s.

Literary Analysis

Wilson does not make it into Margaret Drabble's supposedly standard *Oxford Companion to English Literature*, though scholars such as Edmund Wilson, John Dover Wilson, and F.P. Wilson do, Sir Angus Wilson and Colin Wilson of *The Outsider* and the occult do, and so do sixteenth-century Thomas Wilson (*The Arte of Rhetorique*), seventeenth-century John Wilson, and nineteenth-century John Wilson. Although he is missing from many other reference books, too, he is of some importance as a composer and lyricist, a creator of popular musicals, a satirist, an author of clever and campy books (some with illustrations by himself), and of a life-in-the-theater but not personally revealing autobiography. With *The Boy*

Friend, Wilson brought pleasure to millions and infected many people too young to recall the 1920s with a nostalgia for that raucous and rather romantic Jazz Age.

Wilson's comic techniques are largely those of camp and nostalgic parody in general. His best-known work, of course, is *The Boy Friend,* and that is a loving if somewhat camp "send up" (as the British say) of the lightweight and stereotypical musical comedies and the witty revues that were so popular on the London stage (and sometimes in America) between the world wars. The book and the music are to be regarded more as a tribute to the charm of frivolous musicals, with ingenues and chorines and tapdancing and plot clichés, than as a ripoff of them. In London, The Players' Club re-created the British music hall of Edwardian times but occasionally staged pseudo-Victorian pantomimes and remembrances of early twentieth-century vaudeville. It was for The Players' Club that Wilson wrote the first version of *The Boy Friend* and the play was staged there with a certain tongue-in-cheek quality. That was such a success that the show went to the West End, to America, to the movies, and the rest is history.

Wilson's satire is always more sweet than saucy, his wit genial, his verbal dexterity from a time when Noel Coward and Cole Porter and their ilk put scintillating and slightly wry cleverness into popular lyrics. It looks old-fashioned today, perhaps unsuited to the wider and duller audiences of today's splashy musicals, though its satiric thrust and deft touches still survive in such New York traditions.

His career began in earnest (but genially and joyfully) on April 14, 1953 when the tacky curtain, painted with a portrait of Queen Victoria, went up at The Players' Theatre on his comic valentine to the musicals of the 1920s. Vida Hope staged it and the cast included Larry Drew, Malcolm Goddard, and Anne Rogers. Players' Club runs have always been short, and *The Boy Friend* moved to the suburban Embassy Theatre, then to the West End. Americans Feuer and Martin later booked it for Broadway. In the liner notes to the Broadway original cast RCA record, Bill Zeitung wrote:

> *The Boy Friend* is much more than a mere parody of the twenties. It is a pastiche, a group of crowded scenes acted with enormous vitality by a young company, in which the twenties are torn apart in much the same stylized, old-fashioned manner with which they were originally put together. The play is, really, a huge musical joke—one which visibly and audibly takes the older theater-goer back to his salad days and reminds the younger that the world was not always filled with bebop and brass-lunged baritones.

. . . Like all such musicals it must have a vibrant title tune; there is the inevitable dance number (*Won't You Charleston with Me?*; the love ballad (*I Could Be Happy with You*); the production number (*Sur le playe*); the song of longing (*A Room in Bloomsbury*); and the humorous ditty (*It's Never Too Late to Fall in Love*).

The Boy Friend's book is not nearly as silly as many of those from the musical theater of the 1920s (when even Wodehouse and Guy Bolton perpetrated some *doozies*), and the lyrics are brilliant, totally "of the period," though, of course, involving some "marriages" (modern carpentry). Coward or Porter would not have blushed to have written *The Boy Friend,* nor would they have been unhappy at having had such an enormous hit.

The old LP preserves the saccharine sweetness of the voice of Andrews and the rowdy rasp of Dilys Lay, the hi-jinks of the "you may run up against a rajah" beach number (which the record label gets wrong as *Sur la place*). However, it cannot quite capture the delicious moments of Ruth Altman in a Fransoise Rose part as the headmistress of an exclusive girls' finishing school on The Riviera or the show-stopping number of the old roue (Geoffrey Hibbert, "a fiddle that's old is more in tune") and the flapper (Lay, "yes, you're *rather* old"). The dialogue that makes old American musicals so painful now is spoofed in this British send-up ("I am Pierrot. You are Pierrette. Surely *we* cannot be *strangers*") and is "a hoot." Even high-school revivals of it are triumphant.

The Boy Friend is one of the best musical hits of the century, never a dull moment from the overture (by "The Bearcats") to the boys-get-girls grand finale.

Firbank died in the year (1926) in which *The Boy Friend* is supposed to take place. Wilson made Firbank's novel *Valmouth* (1919, set in a spa ruled by the exotic, erotic black masseuse, Mrs. Yajnavalkya) into a musical which is superior in some ways to *The Boy Friend* but which never received its full share of acclaim. "I expected it to have a minority appeal," said Wilson when *Valmouth* was described as decadent and depraved by the critical press. But, he expected the same thing of *The Boy Friend*, many have pointed out.

In the Edwardian seaside resort of Valmouth, elderly Roman Catholic ladies try to recapture their youth, some of it wild. (Post-centenarian Mrs. Hurstpierpoint, who now mortifies the flesh, was briefly and very long ago a royal mistress.) Some are man-crazy: Lady Parvula de Panzoust in one show-stopper sings of *Only a Passing Phase* but she has her eye on a shepherd and would like to "spank the white walls of his cottage." There's a priest who is unfrocked for having christened a dog, but some society ladies do think of dogs as children, and a screaming scarlet cardinal, a shepherd without a flock, who cannot be trusted around *chic* (*The Cathedral of Clemenza*). Fire from Heaven destroys the decadent. A few primitives survive to go off to peace in the South Seas. The *Daily Express* denounced *Valmouth* as "a world of perfumed immorality," yet granted that the whole fantastic farrago was done with "a sort of contemptuous confidence which is a sign of the highest possible style."

Those who stayed away from the show (or will not listen to the faint hint of its charm captured on the LP record from Pye, 1959) miss some memorable moments: Fielding, Betty Hardy, Barbara Couper in the nostalgic *All the Girls Were Pretty*; Geoffrey Dunn as the worldly Prince of The Church; *I Will Miss You*, the black masseuse and the crotchety crone who is well over one hundred; *Big Best Shoes* with Mrs. Yaj again; *Just Once More* with Fielding, even the exotic *Where the Trees Are Green with Parrots*.

Maybe the admonition in such comedies as *No Sex, Please—We're British* (which, I think, are more pornographic than anything in the grotesque world of *Valmouth*) should have been heeded. *Valmouth* is reminiscent of the Scarlet Sin, the Green Carnation, the *Yellow Book*, and other colorful symbols of British vice. It is also full of fun, fantasy, and social irresponsibility as well as satire on religiosity (not religion) and promiscuity (not sex). These are women who have been both chaste and caught ("chaste for several days / But it was only a passing phase") women whose motto has been "No harm in trying." Maybe a prelate who says when he

stays at The Ritz in New York that he is "given the bridal suite" is shocking to some, but in this musical he is funny. *Valmouth* is not "indubitably divine," but it deserves to be better known than it is.

Also worth more attention is the sequel to *The Boy Friend*, the farcical *Divorce Me, Darling* which B.A. Young reported to the *New York Times* included a large cast that managed to "bubble away satisfactorily" and that Wilson's rush of scenes, just an excuse for lively numbers, was "fast and witty." *Divorce Me, Darling* has some exceptionally clever songs and a stunning parody of Porter that surpasses the Alice Ghostley bit in *New Faces* (*The Boston Beguine* in which "even the palms seemed to be potted"). In *Divorce Me, Darling*, Young writes, the parody of Porter was "funnier than anything the maestro ever did because it reproduces his strength and his weakness with equal candor."

His Monkey Wife, based on the Collier novel, is workmanlike, and that is all. Some of the scattered revue material still has a lot of bubbles in it for champagne open so long. It is to be hoped that some day portions of it may be collected in a musical equivalent of Donald Oliver's *The Greatest Revue Sketches*. In the first half of this century a considerable amount of light musical comic material was presented in revues by Andre Charlot and others. This aspect of British comedy, involving writers as famous as Coward and not so famous, such as Wilson, needs to be recovered and reexamined. Much of it was evanescent, some too trivial, some too topical, and now obscure, forgotten. Still, much of it was first-rate.

Remember, Saki's Clovis Sangrail told a princess that his mother had taught him "the difference between good and evil—but I've forgotten." We cannot remember everything, but in forgetting the wit and wisdom of some revue songs and sketches we lose out on a minor but significant, surely occasionally hilarious, aspect of British humor. Revue is a nearly dead but once typical *genre*, one to which Wilson contributed a share.

It is unfortunate, really, that slight collections of short stories, such as Wilson's *The Poodle from Rome* (reviewed in *Times Literary Supplement,* the *New Statesman,* the London *Times Weekly Review,* but unheard of in America then, and elsewhere since), are noted for posterity, while musicals (unless on phonograph records or on film) perish when the last curtain falls and revue materials are enjoyed, discarded, gone.

Most people who know anything of Wilson's work probably saw the Russell film of *The Boy Friend* with Twiggy (Leslie Hornsby). The *Variety* critic ("Whit") thought of Wilson's musical as "a beautiful vehicle" for this "clever young performer" with her "unspoiled charm" in a film that is "virtually a one-woman show" and "box office fare which will no doubt enjoy wide word-of-mouth bally." There was not much praise for the memorable music, the scintillating lyrics—just a mention of the overall "flair" and the "studiously arch plot."

In fact, the Russell film was too hectic and confused, and word-of-mouth, if not the critics, soon dashed cold water on its hopes. Twiggy's "unspoiled charm" did not work nearly so well on screen as Andrews's hard-edged virginity did on the stage.

It is for *The Boy Friend* that Wilson will be remembered whenever the twentieth-century musical theater is discussed. *The Economist* review of his autobiography compared Wilson to Wodehouse and concluded that "His touch is light, but the underlying technique is so assured that his work generates a compulsive, beguiling momentum."

Summary

One great hit, some other works of lesser fame if not altogether lesser quality—these are the legacy of Sandy Wilson. His work shows both literary and musical talent (if of a derivative sort) and is always executed with verve and polish. It was not always easy for him to make his way in the theater—his autobiography makes that abundantly clear, even when he avoids telling us about his personal relationships and intimate thoughts—but he persisted over more than two decades. *The Boy Friend*, which started out (like *Hair* and some other hits) in a small theater, went on to international fame. Alistair Cooke said that, despite it being the *succes fou* of London, anyone "ought to have his head examined" who would attempt to take so British a triumph elsewhere. (Wilson retaliated by describing Cooke, who has spent most of his life in America reporting back to the British, as an "ex-patriot.")

One cannot dwell on the academic critics' or theater historians' estimates of Wilson's work. They ignore him, as much as one can ignore a single-megahit talent (such as the authors of *Lightnin'*, *Abie's Irish Rose*, *Harvey*, and *Once*

Upon a Mattress). The only way to get an idea of the critical reception of Wilson is to read the theater and film reviews. The only way to appreciate Wilson fully is to skim his sometimes flimsy books and enjoy the fun without becoming too serious—and to see one of his musicals or at least listen to the score on a record. He is a master of his minor art, his lyrics are deft and "funny in themselves" (*New York Times*), and, very often, deserve what he would call "Alpha plus" as a grade.

Selected Bibliography
Primary Sources

Plays

Oranges and Lemons. 1948. Revue material.

Slings and Arrows. 1948. Revue material.

Caprice. 1950. Contributed lyrics to the musical.

See You Again. 1952. One of the Watergate revues to which Wilson contributed material.

The Boy Friend. 1953. New musical of the Twenties. Revived, Edinburgh Festival, 1967; Old Vic, 1984.

The Buccaneer. 1953. Musical at The Watergate, London. At The Apollo, London, 1956 (203 performances); also at The Saville, 1959; New York, 1960; Chichester, 1982.

Pieces of Eight. 1959. Revue at The Apollo Theatre, London. Contributed material.

Call It Love. 1960. Musical at Wyndham's Theatre. Songs.

Prince What Shall I Do. 1961. Illustrated, with Rhoda Levine.

The Poodle from Rome. 1962. Collection of short stories.

Divorce Me, Darling. 1964, Players' Theatre; 1965, Globe Theatre. Musical sequel to *The Boy Friend*.

The World of Wooster. 1965–1966. Music for television series drawn from the fiction of P.G. Wodehouse.

As Dorothy Parker Once Said. 1969. Revue, Fortune Theatre. Music for a revue.

Charley's Aunt. 1969. Songs for Danny La Rue in a television version of Brandon Thomas's classic farce.

His Monkey Wife. 1971. Stage adaptation of the John Collier novel of the same name.

Sandy Wilson Thanks the Ladies. 1971. One-man show at Hampstead Theatre Club. Revived for the Edinburgh Festival by

Lindsay Kemp, 1972.

Who's Who for Beginners. 1971. Satire, with photographs by Jon Rose.

I Could Be Happy. 1975. Autobiography.

Ivor. 1975. Concerning matinee idol Ivor Novello.

Caught in the Act. 1976. Satire.

The Clapham Wonder. 1978. Comedy at Cambridge.

The Roaring Twenties. 1979. The Jazz Age remembered.

Alladin. 1979. Pantomime at The Lyric, Hammersmith.

Recordings

The Boy Friend. 1955. RCA Victor LOC-1018. Broadway cast.

Valmouth. 1959. Pye Group (London) NPL 18029. London cast.

Secondary Sources

Reviews

The Boy Friend:

America, 92 (October 30, 1954): 138.

America, 122 (May 9, 1960): 54–55.

Catholic World, 180 (December 1956): 226.

Commonweal, 61 (October 29, 1954): 93.

Dance Magazine, 32 (May 1958): 17.

Dance Magazine, 44 (January 1970): 84.

Life, 37 (October 25, 1954): 113–14.

Mademoiselle, 40 (November 1954): 142.

Nation, 179 (October 16, 1954): 349.

Nation, 210 (May 11, 1970): 574.

New Republic, 131 (November 1, 1954): 23.

New York Theatre Critics' Reviews (1954): 299+.

New York Theatre Critics' Reviews (1970): 277.

New York Times (September 20, 1954): II: 1.

Time, 79 (June 1, 1962): 83.

The Boy Friend (Ken Russell film of the musical):

Commonweal, 95 (January 7, 1971): 326.

Newsweek, 78 (December 27, 1971): 61–62.

Time, 98 (December 20, 1971): 82–83.

Variety, 22 (December 1971).

I Could Be Happy:

Economist, 255 (May 10, 1975): 128.

Library Journal, 100 (September 15, 1975): 1649. Helen Guy.

Times Literary Supplement (May 9, 1975): 503. E.S. Turner.

The Poodle from Rome:

New Statesman (October 26, 1972): 586.

Neal Ascherson.

Times (London) *Weekly Review* (November 9, 1962): 861.

Times Literary Supplement (November 1, 1962): 13.

Ivor:

Lingua (January 8, 1976): 28. S. Trotter.

Times Literary Supplement, 3849 (December 19, 1975): 1506.

Divorce Me, Darling:

Young, B.A. Special report to *New York Times,* 29 (February 2, 1965): 6.

Leonard R.N. Ashley

Wodehouse, P[elham] G[renville]

Born: Guildford, Surrey, England, October 15, 1881

Education: Dulwich College, 1894–1900

Marriage: Ethel Rowley, September 30, 1914; one step-child

Died: Long Island, New York, February 14, 1975

Biography

The son of Henry Ernest Wodehouse, a civil servant and judge, and his wife Eleanor Deane, Pelham Grenville Wodehouse was born in Guildford, Surrey, England on October 15, 1881. From 1894 to 1900, he attended Dulwich College, where he was on the cricket team. He worked as a bank clerk in England from 1901 to 1903, and then he turned to writing full time. Under various pseudonyms Wodehouse wrote the "By the Way" column for the *London Globe* from 1903 to 1909. He was the drama critic for *Vanity Fair* from 1915 to 1919 and also wrote for the *Strand.* On September 30, 1914, Wodehouse married Ethel Rowley.

In 1929, the author made his first trip to Hollywood. It was at this time that he began collaborating with composers such as Guy Bolton and Jerome Kern. The Wodehouses happened to be in France in 1940 when the Pétain government fell. He was interned by the Germans and was imprisoned for under a year. During that time, he made what have come to be known as the "Berlin Broadcasts." While Wodehouse made the broadcasts in innocence, actually hoping to reassure his friends in England that he was alive and well, since the broadcasts were made with the permission of the occupying German government, they were interpreted as being treasonous by many people in England and Wodehouse received very hostile publicity for his act. He did not return to England after 1938.

At the end of World War II, the Wodehouses moved to Southampton, Long Island, New York. Ironically, the creator of Bertie Wooster and his servant Jeeves (two stereotypical Englishmen) achieved his greatest success in America, the place that he chose to spend the rest of his life. Plum, as he was known to all and sundry, was knighted on the New Year's Lists of 1975 and died of a heart attack on Long Island on February 14 of that year. A measure of both the author's popularity and the high regard with which his work is held, was evidenced in the early 1990s by the *Masterpiece Theatre* telecast of *Jeeves and Wooster,* a series based on his writing.

Literary Analysis

P.G. Wodehouse has long been regarded as one of Britain's foremost humorists. He began his writing career while still employed in a bank, creating short stories for boys' magazines such as *Captain*. These are most often referred to as the "school stories" because they describe events taking place in such places as St. Austin's School. Wodehouse drew extensively on his experiences at Dulwich College for his subject matter. Many of Wodehouse's early readers were exposed to his work through these stories from the first phase of his career.

The second phase of the writer's career may be said to start with the book *Mike* in which the character of Psmith is introduced. Psmith soon became quite popular and reappeared in *Psmith, Journalist* and *Psmith in the City*. Other than Psmith, the characters for which Wodehouse is probably best known are his team of Bertie and Jeeves, the permanent fixture at the Angler's Rest Pub, Mr. Mulliner and the patriarch of Emsworth Castle, Lord Emsworth. Bertie is a young man about town and Jeeves is his faithful valet. The reader is left to wonder if Bertie would survive many days on his own, if it were not for Jeeves, for Jeeves has control over everything from aunts to zoo animals and anything in between. The pairing works so well because of the contrast presented between the two characters. Bertie is rather casual in his manner, while Jeeves is decidedly stuffy. Bertie is likely to consider lavender spats an appropriate article of dress; Jeeves would rather die than have them in the house. Bertie is constantly getting into difficult situations and Jeeves is constantly extricating him from them.

The Bertie and Jeeves combination can be said to be the prototype for all of Wodehouse's major characters. They are loveable, somewhat eccentric, and prone to stumbling unawares into complex situations. This is not to say that Wodehouse's characters are carbon copies of each other, though, for within each character there are individual quirks which make that character unique.

In all of his works, Wodehouse deals with a very select group within British society—the upper class. These are the people who attend places like Dulwich College and who have the leisure to do what they want when they want to do it. This is part of the attraction of Wodehouse. The reader is introduced to a group of people with whom he or she might not normally be familiar. After all, what is more fun than spying on people one wishes one knew?

All of Wodehouse's characters inhabit an ideal English world and are permanently encased in the years between the two world wars. Theirs is a world of spats, morning coats, tea time, valets, and unending social engagements, a world that may be contrasted with Evelyn Waugh's treatment of the same time in *Brideshead Revisited*. While Waugh's writings are often funny, in, for example, *Put Out More Flags,* his humor is frequently based on sarcasm and cynicism, forcing the reader to confront the more serious matters at hand. Wodehouse, however, uses a more gentle form of humor. He is funny, but the reader must be aware that more complex issues can lurk beneath the patina of humor.

Wodehouse often uses a matter-of-fact tone which misleads the reader into thinking that the events outlined are quite trivial. Beneath this trivial exterior, though, the writer is dealing with many serious issues. For example, when he deals with the monetary problems of the landed gentry in "The Fiery Wooing of Mordred," the reader may believe that when the Sprockett-Sprocketts attempt to burn down their ancestral home in an effort to avoid the high taxes, this is an unimportant event in the life of an English country family. The effect of this technique is to amuse readers while at the same time confronting them with important social issues.

Thus, in "The Fiery Wooing of Mordred," Wodehouse takes a moment to reflect upon the plight of both the poet and the landed gentry. The plight of Mordred is funny; that of the Sprockett-Sprocketts is rather tragic. This is one of several instances in which the author focuses on the landed gentry and their problems because they remain landed. In each case, he shows the gentry ready to go to any extreme simply to be rid of the ancestral digs which are eating up all of their income. The Sprockett-Sprocketts are facing the plight of many of the landed gentry in England—they are simply too poor to keep up the ancestral residence. They are even willing to resort to illegal means to collect the insurance money and be able to move to London. What the family wants is for the whole place to burn. Hence, the entrance of Mordred, who had managed to set a wastebasket full of paper on fire while waiting for the same dentist as Annabelle Sprockett-Sprockett. Hence also the presence at the ancestral place of other young swains, aptly supplied with cigarettes and over-flowing ashtrays. Mordred does manage to set a wastebasket on fire; the other swains, however, are a coordinated bunch and manage, alas, to put it out.

This entire tale, told with Wodehousian matter-of-factness, is very funny, and the author keeps the undertone from becoming an overtone, which would make the story ponderous, by creating light and slightly fluffy characters and by providing an abundance of verbal humor.

There are also problems associated with the status and hierarchy within the Anglican church—conflicts between the ranks of the curates, vicars, and the bishops as all vie for position and power in one way or another. These rivalries are presented in terms of ridiculous events which take place and the situations which the characters get themselves into.

In his stories about the clergy, Wodehouse has done his best to parody the picture that most people have of this profession, yet he parodies clergymen in typical ways. Clerics are pale, vicars are loud, and bishops are fat and jolly. Wodehouse may have derived the characteristics of his clergymen from various contemporary depictions, such as William S. Gilbert and Arthur Sullivan's "The Sorcerer" and Anthony Trollope's Barchester novels, both of which would have been relatively familiar to his audience.

Wodehouse exploits the hierarchy present in the Anglican church by abusing all offices with equal zeal. He begins with the pale, young curates and moves upward through the ranks, raking vicars and bishops over the coals. Making fun of a person in a position of authority in the social frame is always more successful than picking on the average person. People seem to have a secret desire to see those in authority humbled to a certain extent. Wodehouse takes full advantage of this very human trait when he chooses to exhibit the faults of characters taken from the hierarchy of the church.

Within the clerical system, he uses the ordering of the offices as a source of humor. He pits the lowest members of the hierarchy, the clerics, against those next in line, the vicars. The vicars, those caught in the middle, are in turn pitted against the bishops, those at the top of the clerical ladder. There is some danger in this approach because the calling to the priesthood has always been seen as a sacred one. Thus, even the most lowly of the profession are accorded a degree of respect because they are considered to be spiritually superior to the *hoi poloi*. But, for that reason, they serve all the better as targets for ridicule.

In the Mr. Mulliner stories, the reader meets two pale young curates, Augustine and Anselm. Both are waiting for the chance to prove themselves in the clerical world. Augustine gets his break when he rescues a bishop from a dog, and Anselm gets his when he preaches a singularly inspiring Evensong sermon on Brotherly Love. Considering how foolish each of these characters in fact is, the reader might ask two questions: why are these curates endearing, and why are they given a chance at all? First, Augustine and Anselm endear themselves to the reader because they are the underdogs among the clerical caste. They are automatically at the bottom of any clerical scale. Both must fight their prospective fathers-in-law in order to gain enough money and enough respect to marry. Augustine gains respect and money by becoming the secretary to the bishop. Anselm gains the same by preaching a sermon on Brotherly Love and inspiring his future father-in-law to buy a stamp collection for 10,000 pounds. Neither is ever really discouraged. There are some bleak moments, as when Augustine is unable to ask his vicar for his daughter's hand and when Anselm believes that the stamp collection is worthless, but the two clerics do not give up. Neither does the reader, who keeps cheering them from the wings because they are daring to attempt to move up.

Of course, not only clergymen, but all professionals, must play roles. Wodehouse uses writers to show how these roles sometimes contradict the person's original personality, with humorous consequences. He points out that people are often thrust into socially imposed roles with which they may or may not be comfortable.

Furthermore, the author shows just how the roles are set up in society. He also demonstrates that many times the profession shapes the personality of the person. In other words, when a person enters a given profession, his personality adapts in order to conform to societal and professional expectations. In the hierarchical systems, Wodehouse also shows the reader the nature of structure and how it can be broken down. All hierarchies have their fatal flaws, and Wodehouse illustrates how these flaws work within the system itself and gradually wear away the established structure.

The most basic structure in human life, however, is neither the hierarchy nor the profession; it is the family. For Wodehouse, family and family-like relationships are a rich source of material, humorous on the surface, serious underneath. In the stories there is often some confusion as to what part each member of the family has to play. In addition, the majority of family-like units are not biological, and the roles that people play in these situations are quite different from those played in the traditional nuclear family. There are even instances when the biological familial roles conflict with other professional and hierarchical relations.

Encompassing all of these issues is the question of loyalty. Characters are constantly being asked to reevaluate their loyalties on a religious, professional, and/or familial level. Divided loyalties may also intrude on the normal activities associated with the church, job, and family. In Wodehouse's work, the very real loyalty conflicts are trivialized on the surface in one way or another. The reader is constantly being asked to look beneath the mask of humor in order to confront the serious issues beneath it. The result is a kind of story that makes the reader both laugh at the silly situation and examine his own loyalties.

Despite all of this laughter and breaking down of structures, there is acceptance. Wodehouse believes that no matter how much of a buffoon a person might be, he or she should be accepted for his or her redeeming qualities. The author is pointing out to the reader that no matter who people are or how they act, they are still human in one way or another and should be accepted for their inner qualities, not for the office that they hold.

While showing the humanity in all of his characters, Wodehouse also shows the reader that all of the characters are in some sense the reader himself. Every reader is able to pick out characteristics that he has exhibited at some time or another. These are not always flattering appraisals of humanity, and the blow is softened somewhat by the tone of triviality present in all of the descriptions and situations. Because of this trivializing tone the reader accepts both the characters and the situations in which they find themselves since the personality traits, even the undesirable ones, are presented humorously.

All of this softening of the scathing situations is compounded by the fact that all of the traits of the characters are highly exaggerated for humorous effect. Every detail of every personality is made larger than life so that not a single fault is missed by the reader. Paradoxically, this makes for easier acceptance because the reader cannot believe that any real person could be this bad or this stupid. He can now believe that he could be a little like the character.

In addition to exaggerating the characters, Wodehouse exaggerates the situations in which they find themselves. The situations are so improbable that the reader knows that he would never be caught in such a ludicrous situation—he will never be caught attempting to burn down his own house. He can believe that he might set a wastebasket on fire, and in this way jointly sympathize with Mordred and digest the lesson which Wodehouse is trying to teach him.

All of these characteristics contribute to the irony in the stories. There are two diametrically opposed forces in Wodehouse: the trivial and the exaggerated. The trivial tone is used to present even the most ludicrous events and make them seem natural and banal. At the same time, there is exaggeration of events and people's characteristics. The power of the stories is derived from the paradoxical tension which exists between the humorous surface events and the serious issues beneath them.

Throughout his long career, Wodehouse was, first and foremost, a craftsman of the language. He is known for his incredible ability to construct a sentence which is both straightforward and humorous. For example, at the beginning of *The Code of the Woosters* (1938), Bertie is trying to recover from an evening of drinking. He calls upon Jeeves for one of his never-failing hangover cures: "I loosed it down the hatch and, after undergoing the passing discomfort, unavoidable when you drink Jeeves's patent morning revivers, of having the top of the skull fly up to the ceiling and the eyes shoot out of their sockets and rebound from the opposite wall like racquet balls, felt better." The wording is relatively concise and conveys a very accurate description of the situation. This is true for all of Wodehouse. While his early works are somewhat less polished, even they are not the typical early works of a writer, and Wodehouse simply went from rather good to quite polished over the years.

Summary

P.G. Wodehouse is probably best represented by his works involving Bertie and Jeeves, Lord Emsworth, Mr. Mulliner, and Psmith. In his canon, Wodehouse displays his talent as a craftsman of the English language as he amuses his readers in his treatment of the British upper class in an idyllic world between the two world wars.

Selected Bibliography

Primary Sources

The Pothunters. London: Adam & Charles Black, and New York: Macmillan, 1902.

A Prefect's Uncle. London: Adam & Charles Black, and New York: Macmillan, 1903.

Tales of St. Austin's. London: Adam & Charles Black, 1903.

The Gold Bat. London: Adam & Charles Black, 1904; New York: Macmillan, 1923.

William Tell Told Again. London: Adam & Charles Black, and New York: Macmillan, 1904.

The Head of Kay's. London: Adam & Charles Black, 1905; New York: Macmillan, 1922.

Love Among the Chickens. London: George Newnes, 1906; as *Love Among the Chickens: A Story of the Haps and Mishaps on an English Chicken Farm,* New York: The Circle Publishing Company, 1909; rev. ed. London: Herbert Jenkins, 1921.

The White Feather. London: Adam & Charles Black, 1907; New York: Macmillan, 1922.

Not George Washington. London: Cassell, 1907.

The Globe By the Way Book: A Literary Quick-Lunch for People Who Have Only Got Five Minutes to Spare. With Herbert Westbrook. London: "The Globe," 1908.

The Swoop! or How Clarence Saved England: A Tale of the Great Invasion. London: Alston Rivers, 1909.

Mike: A Public School Story. London: Adam & Charles Black, 1909; New York: Macmillan, 1910; London: Adam & Charles Black, 1935; rpt. as *Enter Psmith* (chapters 30–59 of *Mike* with a few changes), New York: Macmillan, 1935; as *Mike at Wrykyn* (chapters 1–29 of *Mike* with a few changes), London: Herbert Jenkins, 1953.

The Intrusion of Jimmy. New York: W.J. Watt, 1910; as *A Gentleman of Leisure,* London: Alston Rivers, 1910.

Psmith in the City: A Sequel to "Mike." London: Adam & Charles Black, and New York: Macmillan, 1910.

The Prince and Betty. New York: W.J. Watt, and London: Mills & Boon, 1912.

Psmith Journalist. London: Adam & Charles Black, and New York: Macmillan, 1915.

The Little Nugget. London: Methuen, 1913; New York: W.J. Watt, 1914.

The Man Upstairs and Other Stories. London: Methuen, 1914.

Something New. New York: D. Appleton, 1915; rpt. as *Something Fresh,* London: Methuen, 1915.

Uneasy Money. New York: D. Appleton, 1916; London: Methuen, 1917.

Picadilly Jim. New York: Dodd, Mead, 1917; London: Herbert Jenkins, 1918.

The Man with Two Left Feet. London: Methuen, 1917; New York: A.L. Burt Company by arrangement with Doubleday, Doran, 1933.

My Man Jeeves. London: George Newnes, 1919.

Their Mutual Child. New York: Boni and Liveright, 1919.

The Coming of Bill. London: Herbert Jenkins, 1920.

A Damsel in Distress. New York: George H. Doran, 1919; London: Herbert Jenkins, 1919.

The Little Warrior. New York: George H. Doran, 1920; rpt. as *Jill the Reckless,* London: Herbert Jenkins, 1921.

Indiscretions of Archie. London: Herbert Jenkins, 1921; New York: George H. Doran, 1921.

The Clicking of Cuthbert. London: Herbert

Jenkins, 1922; rpt. as *Golf Without Tears*, New York: George H. Doran, 1924.

Three Men and A Maid. New York: George H. Doran, 1922; rpt. as *The Girl on the Boat*, London: Herbert Jenkins, 1922.

The Adventures of Sally. London: Herbert Jenkins, 1922; rpt. as *Mostly Sally*, New York: George H. Doran, 1923.

The Inimitable Jeeves. London: Herbert Jenkins, 1923; rpt. as *Jeeves*, New York: George H. Doran, 1923.

Leave It to Psmith. London: Herbert Jenkins, 1924; New York: George H. Doran, 1924.

Bill the Conqueror: His Invasion of England in the Springtime. London: Methuen, 1924; New York: George H. Doran, 1924.

He Rather Enjoyed It, New York: George H. Doran, 1923; rpt. as *Ukridge*. London: Herbert Jenkins, 1924.

Carry On, Jeeves! London: Herbert Jenkins, 1925; New York: George H. Doran, 1927.

The Small Bachelor. London: Methuen, 1927; New York: George H. Doran, 1927.

Meet Mr. Mulliner. London: Herbert Jenkins, 1927; Garden City, NY: Doubleday, Doran, 1928.

Money for Nothing. London: Herbert Jenkins, and Garden City, NY: Doubleday, Doran, 1928.

Mr. Mulliner Speaking. London: Herbert Jenkins, 1929; Garden City, NY: Doubleday, Doran, 1930.

Very Good, Jeeves. Garden City, NY: Doubleday, Doran, and London: Herbert Jenkins, 1930.

Big Money. Garden City, NY: Doubleday, Doran, and London: Herbert Jenkins, 1931.

If I Were You. Garden City, NY: Doubleday, Doran, and London: Herbert Jenkins, 1931.

Louder and Funnier. London: Faber & Faber, 1932.

Hot Water. London: Herbert Jenkins, and Garden City, NY: Doubleday, Doran, 1932.

Mulliner Nights. London: Herbert Jenkins, and Garden City, NY: Doubleday, Doran, 1933.

The Great Sermon Handicap. London: Hodder & Stoughton, 1933.

Heavy Weather. Boston: Little, Brown, and London: Herbert Jenkins, 1933.

Thank You, Jeeves! London: Herbert Jenkins, and Boston: Little, Brown, 1934.

The Luck of the Bodkins. London: Herbert Jenkins, 1935; Boston: Little, Brown, 1936.

Young Men in Spats. London: Herbert Jenkins, and Garden City, NY: Doubleday, Doran, 1936; not included in the American edition: "Tried in the Furnace," "Trouble Down at Tudsleigh"; not included in the English edition: "There's Always Golf!," "The Letter of the Law," "Farewell to Legs."

Laughing Gas. London: Herbert Jenkins, and Garden City, NY: Doubleday, Doran, 1936.

Lord Emsworth and Others. London: Herbert Jenkins, 1937; "There's Always Golf!," "The Letter of the Law," and "Farewell to Legs" from the American edition of *Young Men in Spats* are included in this volume.

The Crime Wave at Blandings. Garden City, NY: Doubleday, Doran, 1937.

Summer Moonshine. Garden City, NY: Doubleday, Doran, 1937; London: Herbert Jenkins, 1938.

The Code of the Woosters. Garden City, NY: Doubleday, Doran, and London: Herbert Jenkins, 1938.

Uncle Fred in the Springtime. Garden City, NY: Doubleday, Doran, and London: Herbert Jenkins, 1939.

Eggs, Beans, and Crumpets. London: Herbert Jenkins, and Garden City, NY: Doubleday, Doran, 1940.

Quick Service. London: Herbert Jenkins, and Garden City, NY: Doubleday, Doran, 1940.

Money in the Bank. Garden City, NY: Doubleday, Doran, 1942; London: Herbert Jenkins, 1946.

Joy in the Morning. Garden City, NY: Doubleday, 1946; London: Herbert Jenkins, 1947.

Full Moon. London: Herbert Jenkins, 1947.

Spring Fever. Garden City, NY: Doubleday, and London: Herbert Jenkins, 1948.

Uncle Dynamite. London: Herbert Jenkins, and New York: Didier, 1948.

The Mating Season. London: Herbert Jenkins, and New York: Didier, 1949.

Nothing Serious. London: Herbert Jenkins,

1950; Garden City, NY: Doubleday, 1951.

The Old Reliable. London: Herbert Jenkins, and Garden City, NY: Doubleday, 1951.

Pigs Have Wings. Garden City, NY: Doubleday, and London: Herbert Jenkins, 1952.

French Leave. London: Herbert Jenkins, 1956; New York: Simon and Schuster, 1959.

Cocktail Time. London: Herbert Jenkins, and New York: Simon and Schuster, 1958.

A Few Quick Ones. New York: Simon and Schuster, and London: Herbert Jenkins, 1959.

The Ice in the Bedroom. New York: Simon and Schuster, and London: Herbert Jenkins, 1961.

Service with a Smile. New York: Simon and Schuster, 1961; London: Herbert Jenkins, 1962.

Stiff Upper Lip, Jeeves. New York: Simon and Schuster, and London: Herbert Jenkins, 1963.

Plum Pie. London: Herbert Jenkins, 1966; New York: Simon and Schuster, 1967.

Do Butlers Burgle Banks? New York: Simon and Schuster, and London: Herbert Jenkins, 1968.

The Girl in Blue. London: Barrie & Jenkins, 1970; New York: Simon and Schuster, 1971.

Bachelors Anonymous. London: Barrie & Jenkins, 1973; New York: Simon and Schuster, 1974.

Sunset at Blandings. London: Chatto & Windus, 1977; New York: Simon and Schuster, 1978. Sixteen of the twenty chapters of this book were completed when Wodehouse died. Richard Usborne edited the incomplete manuscript and added notes and appendices.

Omnibus Volumes

Jeeves Omnibus. Herbert Jenkins, 1931. Reissued by Herbert Jenkins in 1967 as *The World of Jeeves* and by Manor Books, New York, 1974.

Nothing but Wodehouse. Garden City, NY: Doubleday, Doran and Company, 1932, 1946.

P.G. Wodehouse (Methuen's Library of Humour). London: Methuen, 1934.

A Century of Humour. Ed. P.G. Wodehouse. London: Hutchinson, 1938.

Mulliner Omnibus. London: Herbert Jenkins, 1935.

The Week-End Wodehouse. New York: Doubleday, Doran, 1939.

Wodehouse on Golf. New York: Doubleday, Doran, 1940.

The Best of Wodehouse. New York: Pocket Books, 1949.

The Best of Modern Humor. New York: Medill Mcbride, 1951.

The Week-End Book of Humor. New York: Ives Washburn, 1952.

Selected Stories. New York: The Modern Library, 1958.

The Most of P.G. Wodehouse. New York: Simon and Schuster, 1960.

A Carnival of Modern Humor. New York: Delacorte Press, 1967; London: Herbert Jenkins, 1968.

The Golf Omnibus. London: Barrie & Jenkins, 1973.

The World of Psmith. London: Barrie & Jenkins, 1974.

The World of Ukridge. London: Barrie & Jenkins, 1975.

The World of Blandings. London: Barrie & Jenkins, 1976.

Jeeves, Jeeves, Jeeves. New York: Avon, 1976.

The Uncollected Wodehouse. New York: Seabury Press, 1976.

Vintage Wodehouse. Ed. Richard Usborne. London: Barrie & Jenkins, 1978.

The Swoop! and Other Stories. Ed. David A. Jasen. New York: Seabury Press, 1979.

The Eighteen-Caret Kid and Other Stories. Ed. David A. Jasen. New York: Continuum, 1980.

Wodehouse on Wodehouse. London: Hutchinson, 1980; New York: Heinemann, 1983.

Yours, Plum: The Letters of P.G. Wodehouse. Ed. Francis Donaldson. New York: Heinemann, 1990. A selection of the letters Wodehouse sent to his daughter, Leonora, and his closest friends. Many of these letters are published here for the first time.

Plays

Adaptations

Hearts and Diamonds: A New Light Opera. London: Keith Prowse, 1926. Adapted from *The Orlov* by Ernst Marischka and Bruno Granichstaedten, English adaptation by P.G. Wodehouse and Laurie Wylie.

The Play's the Thing. New York: Brentano's, 1927.

Good Morning Bill: A Three-Act Comedy. London: Methuen, 1928. *Candle-Light: A Comedy in Three Acts.* By Siegfried Geyer. Adapted by P.G. Wodehouse. London and New York: Samuel French, 1934.

The Three Musketeers: A Romantic Musical Play. Book by Wm. Anthony McGuire. Lyrics by P.G. Wodehouse and Clifford Grey. Music by Rudolf Friml. London and New York: Harms, 1937.

Uncle Fred Flits By. Dramatized by Perry Clark (pseudonym of Christopher Sergel). Chicago: Dramatic, 1949. Dramatization of the story by the same name.

Don't Listen, Ladies: A Comedy in Three Acts. By Stephen Powys and Guy Bolton. From The French of Sacha Guitry. London: Samuel French, 1952. Stephen Powys had been used as a pseudonym by either Guy or Virginia Bolton for *Wise To-Morrow* (1937). For this production, Powys was Wodehouse.

Too Much Springtime. Dramatized by Marjorie Duhan. Chicago: Dramatic, 1955. Dramatization of *The Mating Season.*

Oh Clarence!: A Comedy. By John Chapman. Adapted from "Blandings Castle" and other Lord Emsworth stories. London: English Theatre Guild, 1969.

Collaborations

Baa, Baa, Black Sheep: A Farcical Comedy in Three Acts. With Ian Hay. London and New York: Samuel French, 1930.

A Damsel in Distress: A Comedy of Youth, Love, and Adventure in Three Acts. With Ian Hay. New York and London: Samuel French, 1930.

Leave It to Psmith: A Comedy of Youth, Love, and Misadventure in Three Acts. With Ian Hay. London and New York: Samuel French, 1932.

Anything Goes: A Musical Comedy. With Guy Bolton. Music and lyrics by Cole Porter. London and New York: Samuel French, 1936.

Come On, Jeeves: A Farcical Comedy in Three Acts. With Guy Bolton. London: Evans Brothers, 1960.

Radio Scripts

"Berlin Broadcasts." *Encounter*, 3, nos. 4–5 (October-November 1954): 17–24, 39–47. Text of the broadcasts Wodehouse made during World War II.

Articles

"How I Write My Books." In *P.G. Wodehouse: A Centenary Celebration 1881–1981.* Ed. James H. Heinemann and Donald R. Bensen. New York: Oxford University Press, 1981, pp. 3–4. Short article on Wodehouse's writing process.

Semiautobiographical Works

Bring On the Girls! The Improbable Story of Our Life in Musical Comedy, with Pictures to Prove It. With Guy Bolton. New York: Simon and Schuster, 1953; London: Herbert Jenkins, 1954.

Performing Flea: A Self-Portrait in Letters. London: Herbert Jenkins, 1953.

Author! Author! New York: Simon and Schuster, 1962.

America, I Like You. New York: Simon and Schuster, 1956.

Secondary Sources

Bibliographies

Jasen, David A. *A Bibliography and Reader's Guide to the First Editions of P.G. Wodehouse.* Hamden, CT: Archon Books, 1970. Bibliography of first editions published through 1969 with a brief description of characters appearing in each novel. Also includes a list of some magazine stories and songs in musicals and movies.

McIlvaine, Eileen, Louise S. Sherby, and James H. Heinemann, eds. *P.G. Wodehouse: A Comprehensive Bibliography and Checklist.* New York: Heinemann, 1990.

Whitt, J.F. *The Strand Magazine, 1891–1950: A Selective Checklist Listing All Material Relating to Arthur Conan Doyle, All Stories by P.G. Wodehouse, and a Selection of Other Contributions, Mainly by Writers of Detective, Mystery or Fantasy Fiction.* London: J.G. Whitt, 1979. Chronological listing of Wodehouse articles, including the names of illustrators.

Biographies

Connolly, Joseph. *P.G. Wodehouse: An Illustrated Biography with Complete Bibliog-*

raphy and Collector's Guide. London: Orbis, 1979. Connolly concentrates on the English editions and includes descriptions of the dust jackets.

Donaldson, Francis. *P.G. Wodehouse: A Biography*. New York: Knopf, 1982. Donaldson, a close friend of the Wodehouses, produced this biography.

French, R.B.D. *P.G. Wodehouse*. London: Oliver and Boyd, 1966. Issued in New York by Barnes & Noble. Biography.

Jasen, David A. *P.G. Wodehouse: A Portrait of a Master*. First edition: New York: Mason and Lipscomb, 1974; London: Garnstone Press, 1975. Rev. ed. New York: Continuum, 1981. Also issued in paperback by Continuum. Biography of Wodehouse which he was allowed to read before it was published.

Books

Cazalet-Keir, Thelma, ed. *Homage to Wodehouse*. London: Barrie & Jenkins, 1973.

Davis, Lee. *Bolton and Wodehouse and Kern*. New York: Heinemann, 1991. A detailed study of the collaboration of Guy Bolton, Jerome Kern, and Wodehouse in which Davis provides information on their work on the musical stage.

Edwards, Owen Dudley. *P.G. Wodehouse: A Critical and Historical Essay*. London: Martin Brian and O'Keefe, 1977.

Gould, Charles E., Jr. *The Toad at Harrow: P.G. Wodehouse in Perspective*. New York: Heinemann, 1990. Monograph which discusses the importance of Wodehouse to the canon of humorous English literature.

———. *What's in Wodehouse? Or Jeeves Has Gone A-Shrimping and The Fat Pig Has Grown Even Stouter*. New York: Heinemann, 1989. A collection of quizzes designed to test the reader's knowledge of all of Wodehouse.

Hall, Robert A., Jr. *The Comic Style of P.G. Wodehouse*. Hamden, CT: Archon Books, 1974. An analysis of Wodehouse's writing style.

Jaggard, Geoffrey. *Blandings and the Blest and the Blue Blood: A Companion to the Blandings Castle Saga of P.G. Wodehouse, LL.D. with a Complete Wodehouse Peerage, Baronetage & Knighthood, Embodying a Bulk of But-* *lers: Caledonia Stern and Wile: Royalty, Vintage and Modern: Who's Who in the Nobility and Gentry: Taverns in the Town: A Genealogical Tree of the Threepwood Family of Shropshire: Together with All That High-Mettled and Exalted Brouhaha, Tan-Tantara, Tzing-Boom!* London: Macdonald, 1968. A guide to the Blandings Castle stories; in dictionary format.

Jasen, David A. *The Theater of P.G. Wodehouse*. London: B.T. Batsford, 1979. A compilation of performances and cast lists for theater productions featuring Wodehouse's work.

———. *Wooster's World: A Companion to the Wooster-Jeeves Cycle of P.G. Wodehouse, LL.D., containing a Modicum of Honey from the Drones and Reviewing a Surging Sea of Aunts: Brief Instances: Collectors' Corner: A Pleasing Diversity of Dumbchummery: Racing Intelligence: The Stately Homes of England Together with All That Stimulating Brouhaha the Laughing Love God Has Hiccoughs with Some Consideration of What the Well-Dressed Young Man Is Not Wearing and a Useful Now We Know Department*. London: Macdonald, 1967. Also issued as a Coronet paperback. A collection of characters, items, and instances which are featured in the works which deal with Bertie Wooster; in dictionary format.

Murphy, N.T.P. *In Search of Blandings*. Topsford, MA: Salem House, 1986. A study of the possible location of Blandings.

Sproat, Iain. *Wodehouse at War*. New York: Ticknor & Fields, 1981. Sproat discusses the Berlin broadcasts.

Usborne, Richard. *After Hours with P.G. Wodehouse*. New York: Heinemann, 1991. A variety of articles and talks on Wodehouse.

———. *Dr. Sir Pelham Wodehouse—Old Boy: The Text of an Address Given by Richard Usborne at the Opening of the P.G. Wodehouse Corner in the Library of Dulwich College, October 15, 1977*. London: Heinemann, 1978; New York: Heinemann, 1990.

———. *The Penguin Wodehouse Companion*. New York: Penguin Books, 1989. The standard companion to Wodehouse, listing people, places, etc.

———, William Douglas Home, Malcolm Muggeridge, and Angus MacIntyre. *Three Talks and a Few Words at a Festive Occasion in 1982.* New York: Heinemann, 1990.

———. *Wodehouse at Work to the End.* Rev. ed. London: Barrie & Jenkins, 1976. Also issued by Penguin Books, 1978. First edition: *Wodehouse at Work: A Study of the Books and Characters of P.G. Wodehouse across Nearly Sixty Years.* London: Herbert Jenkins, 1961. A discussion of the major Wodehouse characters.

Voorhees, Richard J. *P.G. Wodehouse.* New York: Twayne, 1966. Contains a short biographical section and chapters on the various types of works that Wodehouse published.

Wind, Herbert Warren. *The World of P.G. Wodehouse.* New York: Washington: Praeger, 1972. Most of the contents appeared as "Chap with a good Story to Tell" in *The New Yorker*, May 16, 1971.

Articles and Chapters in Books

Belloc, Hilaire. "Homage to Wodehouse." *John O'London's Weekly*, 43 (August 30, 1940): 1–2. Belloc discusses why he believes Wodehouse is the best writer of his time.

Benson, Donald R. "Exclusive Interview with P.G. Wodehouse: Two Comic Works." *Writer's Digest*, 51 (October 1971): 22–24, 43. Ninetieth-birthday interview.

Bowen, Barbara C. "Rabelais and P.G. Wodehouse: Two Comic Works." *Esprit Createur*, 16 (Winter 1976): 63–77. Similarities between Rabelais and Wodehouse are examined.

Cannadine, David. "Another 'Last Victorian' P.G. Wodehouse and His World." *South Atlantic Quarterly*, 77 (Autumn 1978): 470–90. Wodehouse's work placed in historical context. The influence of Victorian society is considered.

Clarke, Gerald. "Checking with P.G. Wodehouse: Notes in Passing on a Life *Still* in Progress." *Esquire*, 81 (May 1974): 98–99, 202, 204, 208, 210–11. General interview.

Edwards, Thomas R. "P.G. Wodehouse." *Raritan: A Quarterly Review*, 7, 4 (Spring 1988): 86–107. Edwards examines social order and convention in Wodehouse's works.

Flannery, Henry W. *Assignment to Berlin.* London: Michael Joseph, 1942, pp. 117–18, 244–51.

Falligan, Edward L. "P.G. Wodehouse: Master of Farce." *Sewanee Review*, 93, 4 (Fall 1985): 609–17. A discussion of Wodehouse's use of farce.

Green, Benny. "The Truth Behind the Fiction." *Spectator*, 234, 7653 (March 1, 1975): 234–35. An argument that Wodehouse's England is at least partially factual. He is compared with Max Beerbohm.

Hall, Robert. "The Persecution of P.G. Wodehouse." *Journal of Historical Review*, 7 (1986): 345–51. Hall discusses the Berlin broadcasts.

———. "The Transferred Epithet in P.G. Wodehouse." *Linguistic Inquiry*, 4 (1973): 92–94. An analysis of Wodehouse's use of the transferred epithet.

Hayward, John. "P.G. Wodehouse and the Edwardians." *Spectator*, 155, 5602 (November 8, 1935): 771. Edwardian elements in Wodehouse are discussed.

———. "P.G. Wodehouse." *Saturday Book*, 1941–1942, 1 (1941): 372–89. Hayward presents justification for serious study of Wodehouse.

Kingsmill, Hugh. "P.G. Wodehouse." In *The Progress of a Biographer*. London: Methuen, 1949, pp. 139–42. A discussion of why Wodehouse's humor has endured. In addition, information on the Berlin broadcasts.

MacDermott, Kathy. "Light Humor and the Dark Underside of Wish Fulfillment: Conservative Anti-Realism." *Studies in Popular Culture*, 10, 2 (1987): 37–53. A discussion of Wodehouse as an anti-realist novelist.

Medcalf, Stephen. "The Innocence of P.G. Wodehouse." In *The Modern English Novel: The Reader, the Writer, and the Work*. Ed. Gabriel Josipovici. New York: Barnes & Noble, 1976, pp. 186–205. An analysis of Wodehouse's use of language. The author draws comparisons with Chaucer, among others.

Mikes, George. "P.G. Wodehouse." In *Eight Humorists*. London: Allan Wingate, 1954, pp. 153–75. Mikes examines why

Wodehouse is funny.

Muggeridge, Malcolm. "The Wodehouse Affair." In *Tread Softly for You Tread on My Jokes*. London: Collins, 1966, pp. 83–93. Also issued in paperback by Collins, Fontana, 1968. Further discussion of Wodehouse's experience during World War II.

———. "The Wodehouse Affair." *New Statesman*, 62, 1586 (August 4, 1961): 150, 152. A discussion of the Berlin broadcasts.

Olney, Clarke. "Wodehouse and the Poets." *Georgia Review*, 16 (Winter 1962): 392–99. Literary allusions in Wodehouse.

Robinson, Robert. "Of Aunts and Drones: P.G. Wodehouse Talks to Robert Robinson." *Listener*, 92 (October 17, 1974): 496. Brief interview with Wodehouse.

"Seaside Home of Famous Humorist: Villa at Touquet." *Arts and Decoration*, 50 (August 1939): 16–18. A look at the villa and lifestyle of the Wodehouses.

Sheed, Wilfrid. "P.G. Wodehouse: Leave It to Psmith." In *The Good Word and Other Words*. New York: Dutton, 1978; London: Sidgwick and Jackson, 1979, pp. 215–22.

Stephenson, William. "The Wodehouse World of Hollywood." *Literature/Film Quarterly*, 6 (1978): 190–203.

Stevenson, Lionel. "The Antecedents of P.G. Wodehouse." *Arizona Quarterly*, 5 (Autumn 1949): 226–34. Literary precedents for plot devices in Wodehouse are detailed.

Sykes, John. "The German for P.G. Wodehouse." *The Incorporated Linguist*, 24, 1 (Winter 1985): 55–58. A brief discussion of the difficulties of translating Wodehouse into German.

"Talk of the Town." *The New Yorker*, 47 (October 30, 1971): 40–41. Wodehouse's ninetieth-birthday party.

Thompson, Anthony Hugh. "The P.G. Wodehouse Affair." In *Censorship in Public Libraries in the United Kingdom During the Twentieth Century*. Epping, Essex: Bowker, 1975, pp. 34–55. An examination of the Berlin Broadcasts in relation to censorship.

Usborne, Richard. "My Blandings Castle." *Blackwood's Edinburgh Magazine*, 312 (November 1972): 385–401. Usborne's reminiscences of a summer that he spent as a tutor for a titled family. He draws many comparisons to Wodehouse characters in similar circumstances.

———. "P.G. Wodehouse's Family of Fiends." *Blackwood's Edinburgh Magazine*, 316 (July 1974): 47–58. A look at Wodehouse's use of fiendish children in his writing.

Voorhees, Richard J. "The Jolly Old World of P.G. Wodehouse." *South Atlantic Quarterly*, 61 (Spring 1962): 213–22. A discussion of themes and attitudes in Wodehouse.

———. "Wodehouse at the Top of His Form." *University of Windsor Review*, 16, 1 (Fall-Winter 1981): 13–25. A general discussion of Wodehouse's characters and plots.

Wallace, Malcolm T. "The Wodehouse World I: Classical Echoes." *Cithara*, 12 (1973): 41–57. A look at the classical elements of epic timelessness, development of cycles and stock characters in Wodehouse.

Watkins, Alan. "The Young Wodehouse." *New Statesman*, 74 (December 1, 1972): 834. Praise for the early works of Wodehouse.

Wodehouse, Leonora. "P.G. Wodehouse at Home." *Strand*, 77 (January 1929): 20–25. A look at the life of Wodehouse.

———. "What His Daughter Thinks of P.G. Wodehouse." *American Magazine* (October 1931): 77, 78, 122. A "Behind the scenes" look at Wodehouse from the point of view of his step-daughter, Leonora.

Victoria E. McLure

Wycherley, William

Born: Clive, Shropshire, May 28, 1641
Education: Queen's College, Oxford University, 1660; Inner Temple
Marriage: The Countess of Drogheda, 1679; Elizabeth Jackson, 1715
Died: London, January 1, 1716

Biography

William Wycherley was born, the first of six children, to Daniel and Bethia Shrimpton Wycherley; his father was high steward to the Marquess of Winchester and, much later, a barrister. The son of a family comfortably well off,

William was born, possibly on May 28, 1641, and raised in Clive, Shropshire, near Shrewsbury. When he was fifteen, his father sent him to France for four years (1655–1659) for an education because of the civil strife at home. Associating in the circle of the Duchess of Montausier, Wycherley converted for a time to Catholicism and became a well-mannered sophisticate. In 1660, he returned home and studied at Queens College, Oxford, although he never took a degree. Briefly thereafter, he entered the Inner Temple to study law. In 1664, he served abroad with the English fleet.

All of Wycherley's dramatic success occurred during the years 1671 to 1679. His first play, *Love in a Wood* (1671?), earned him the favor of the Duchess of Cleveland, King Charles's mistress, and Wycherley entered the circle of the Court and of the Court Wits. His other plays rapidly followed, *The Gentleman Dancing-Master* (1672?), *The Country Wife* (1675), and *The Plain Dealer* (1676). His fame was rapid, sensational, and evanescent— dramatist William Congreve, commenting on Wycherley's satirical attacks on their times, called him one appointed to "lash this crying age." For most of his life, however, he was destined to be wracked by monetary troubles.

He lost the favor of the king in 1679, when he secretly wed a wealthy widow, the Countess of Drogheda, daughter of the Earl of Radnor. Upon her sudden death two years later, Wycherley became destitute as a result of a legal battle over his wife's contested will and was jailed for debt for seven years. The playwright finally was pensioned by King James II in 1686. The remainder of his life he spent in seclusion at Clive, writing rather indifferent verse. In 1704, he formed an enduring friendship with the young Alexander Pope. In December 1715, eleven days before his demise, he contracted, under duress, a deathbed marriage with a young girl, Elizabeth Jackson. After receiving the last rites of the Roman Catholic church (to which he apparently reverted after his rescue from prison), Wycherley died on January 1, 1716.

Literary Analysis

Together with Sir George Etherege, Wycherley was one of the major comic dramatists in the early Restoration (1660–1680). Throughout the Civil War, kings and cavaliers had been forced into exile in France, and Puritan sects had outlawed plays at home as species of lewd-ness. With the king's Restoration to the throne, the Cavaliers sought to make up for lost time and to wreak vengeance upon the extremist Protestant sects. The theaters were reopened, and so-called Restoration Comedy was flauntingly profligate and lubricious. This courtly or Cavalier comedy was supposedly a "comedy of manners," concerned with the appropriate and debonair behavior of courtiers. According to the "code" of conduct formulated in these dramas, there was a suitable mean of poised mannerly behavior, and upon either side of that mean were the attendant flaws of defect and excess. On the defective side was any coarseness or ignorance; the typical emblems of such folly were country bumpkins and middle-class London merchants and dissenters (the citizens or "Cits," as they were derogatorily termed), who were presented as being devoid of manners, polish, class, and style. The figures of excess at the opposite extreme were the would-be-wits, awkwardly aspiring town gallants, and fops—those who tried too hard to be humorous, gentlemanly, and *à la mode*; their strainings destroyed the easy smoothness and grace of an artful behavior that only succeeded when it appeared artless, casual, and blasé.

The "mean" was intended to serve as the ideal. Aristocratic men or women who fit this model, usually the protagonists in such plays, were relaxed and stylish, flippant, libertine, and witty, fraught with self-confidence. They engaged in sexual affairs, and utilized ploys and disguises to effect their ends, but they did so with a poised and lazy assurance that distinguished their manners from the gross ineptitudes of those sparks who merely aped wit and fashion and intrigue. And, whereas the coarse didappers and would-wits usually failed in their undertakings, the refined wits succeeded, often concluding the drama with a "perfect" marriage.

Comedy was achieved by heavy doses of special social effects: drawing-room gossip and intrigue, lovers' deceits and assignations, gulls who could not comprehend the machinations or the jests, and a brace of pert and scandalous lovers chiefly devoted to rendezvous, repartee, and seduction. Small wonder that such stuff managed to shock or insult the newly emergent middle class and the Protestant devout. The dramas seemed to be composed essentially to salve courtly insiders and as a means of "getting even" for the recent civil wars that had ousted the courtiers from the country.

In addition, there were internal problems concerning such plays. The ceaseless attentiveness to fashion and promiscuity seemed to make virtues of poise, affectation, haberdashery, and fornication. After all, the line between a true wit and his foppish imitator was preciously thin: both idolized the glib tongue, social disguises, amorous trysts, and sexual conquests. From a certain point of view, all of the characters could be comprehended as being likeminded and superficial.

It was precisely in this light that Wycherley came to view them. His first two plays (*Love in a Wood* and *The Gentleman Dancing-Master*) were filled with wits and fops and their several ploys and complications. A wit might often pause to denigrate an age devoted to tinseled exteriors and hollow fashions and vacuous forms—hardly recognizing that he himself was a principal exemplar of such shallowness and superficiality.

Increasingly, Wycherley directly confronted this satiric truth. He adopted some of the critical themes of Moliere, but his tone was often more closely akin to shrill Elizabethan satirists like John Marston or Joseph Hall, although he also incorporated some of the succinct tartness of Duc François de La Rochefoucauld. His comedy is etched in overdoses of vitriol. The characters are all prosaic in the extreme, speaking with crassness and acerbity. The earlier plays had featured addle-pated English fops who affected to be French or Spanish in breeding, speech, and dress (e.g., Monsieur de Paris and Don Diego in *The Gentleman Dancing-Master*), but in the later plays, the coarse "humor" characters in the tradition of Ben Jonson are devised with a tincture of acid. For instance, Widow Blackacre in *The Plain Dealer* (the best of this type) is litigious in the extreme, forging a cruel business out of claims, writs, briefs, subpoenas, and lawsuits; at last she herself is cruelly cheated of jointure and estate. Manly caustically observes to Freeman in *The Plain Dealer* that everyone is an ingrate: "Those you have obliged most most certainly avoid you, when you can oblige 'em no longer . . . ; friends, like mistresses, are avoided for obligations past" (5.2). Another character type, Jack Pinchwife, the jealous husband of Margery in *The Country Wife*, although himself a rakehell, is monomaniacally overprotective, locking up his wife and keeping her a close prisoner—even threatening savagely to stab out her eyes with a penknife. In Wycherley's hands, cartoon figures grow distorted, lunatic, and Goyesque, the creations of questionable humor on the verge of brutality and the grotesque.

In *The Country Wife* (1675), Harcourt cynically observes that "Most men are the contraries to that they would seem. Your bully, you see, is a coward with a long sword; the little humbly fawning physician . . . is he that destroys men." To which Horner concurs: "Ay, your arrantest cheat is your trustee, your jealous man the greatest cuckold, your church-man the greatest atheist" (1.1). They appear to be casual and disinterested in the fact that they dwell in a world of blackguards.

Indeed, Horner (1675) is a protagonist quite overtly flawed. He completely yields to a compulsion to philandery; he aspires no less than to have sexual relations with any and every woman whom he can lay his hands upon. He feigns impotency from too much sexual activity and from consequent disease; his aim is to mislead husbands into lowering their guard so that he may have a free hand with their wives. He succeeds magnificently. All of the women, especially the wives, while overtly and loudly protesting their decency and love of virtue, covertly flock to him in cadres for sexual gratification. The exposure of feminine imposture and hypocrisy is palpable in the extreme. Wycherley's most famous scene occurs in *The Country Wife* and concerns the episode of the "china"; Horner's sexual attractions and prowess are concealed behind the screen of his reputedly possessing an enviable and eminently desirable collection of chinaware; women flock from all over London to ogle, to handle, and to be possessed of a "piece" of it. There follows, behind closed doors, a heated flurry of business and trade that resembles a Wall Street stampede.

But, if Horner wishes to expose the age for its lust, adultery, and abandon, surely he emerges triumphantly as Exhibit A for that which he is trying to expose. Moreover, the "country wife," Margery, a supposedly foolish innocent from the boondocks who cannot don masks or assume disguises and openly publishes her love for Horner, is no mere doltish lout. Instead, the raw freshness of her candor and the forthright directness of her natural emotions are a healthy antidote to City stealth and Cavalier Deceit. Wycherley manages to satirize Horner the Satirist as well as the entire Restoration comic mode. Although his drama was adjudged rude and pornographic in the nineteenth century (Thomas Babington Macauley compared him to a skunk), many a recent critic has justifiably come to rank this drama as the playwright's highest satiricomic achievement.

Nonetheless, *The Plain Dealer*, Wycherley's last play, is also potently satiric. Captain Manly, the unusual protagonist, is a sea-captain, an outsider to cosmopolitan fashion. For once, the chief actor has become overtly akin to the country bumpkin. He savagely berates the depraved age—one given over entirely to sexual betrayals, patent cheating, litigation, and crass materialism. As a result, the era extols civility without true friendship and sexual congress without love. Manly rails and rails at such a licentious world; he literally becomes a species of Moliere's Misanthrope. But he, too, is ultimately exposed for his shallowness and folly; the one friend whom he has chosen and the one mistress whom he adores are precisely the two worst individuals in an admittedly tawdry and defective society. At one stroke, almost everyone is exposed as coarse, graceless, and nearly witless in an age presumably dedicated to suave savoir-faire. Thus, as criticism in our present century has increasingly come to recognize, Wycherley was not only a master of the Restoration comic mode, he was also the master of a savage assault upon that very mode. What his wit coyly presented, his satire managed to explode.

Summary

William Wycherley's most important works are his four plays, and his major dramatic skills are chiefly satiric. Comedy for the playwright has to be acrimonious and overdone. Even witty stage business and double entendres are flagrant and radical.

Wycherley is a master of hyperbole; his finest characters are all gross and excessive: holier-than-thou gossips and fleering scandal-mongers, doltish fops fantastically attempting to replicate French or Spanish manners, flirtatious jilts and money-grubbing panders, empty-headed beaux and fortune-hunters, pretended friends and lovers, and outright blackmailers and usurers. And, at the center of his poignant portrayals of the late seventeenth century which was just upon the verge of entering the modern world are corrosive depictions of faltering and fallen heroes and heroines: slanderous jades and sex-pots, gruff and surly misanthropes, and avowed whoremasters on the loose. Wycherley's drama is rough and coruscating indeed, pushing comedy into the realm of biting satire, and exposing all of Restoration society—the new acquisitive middle class as well as the debauched chevaliers—with the acid of his pen. It is not for nothing that he was known in his theatrical heyday as "brawny" or "manly" Wycherley.

Selected Bibliography

Primary Sources

Miscellany Poems: As Satyrs, Epistles, Love-Verses, Songs, Sonnets, &c. London: Printed for C. Prome, J. Taylor, and B. Tooke, 1704.

The Works of the Ingenious Mr. William Wycherley, Collected into One Volume. London: Printed for Richard Wellington, 1713. Contains the four plays.

The Posthumous Works of William Wycherley, Esq.; in Prose and Verse. Ed. Lewis Theobald. London: Printed for A. Bettesworth, 1728.

The Posthumous Works of William Wycherley, Esq.; in Prose and Verse. Ed. Alexander Pope. London: Printed for J. Roberts, 1729. Vol. 2.

The Complete Works of William Wycherley. Ed. Montague Summers. 4 vols. [1924] New York: Russell and Russell, 1964.

The Plays of William Wycherley. Ed. Arthur Friedman. Oxford: Clarendon, 1979. Includes extensive notes.

The Plays of William Wycherley. Ed. Peter Holand. Cambridge: Cambridge University Press, 1981. Includes brief introductions and textual notes.

Secondary Sources

Biographies

Connely, Willard. *Brawny Wycherley: First Master in English Modern Comedy [1930].* Port Washington, NY, and London: Kennikat Press, 1969. The first important modern biography, mostly popular.

McCarthy, B. Eugene. *William Wycherley: A Biography.* Athens, OH: Ohio University Press, 1979. The best-researched biography; authoritative.

Bibliographies

McCarthy, B. Eugene. *William Wycherley: A Reference Guide.* Boston: G.K. Hall, 1985. Important annotated bibliography, covering material from 1669 to 1982.

Critical Studies

Chadwick, W.R. *The Four Plays of William Wycherley: A Study in the Development of a Dramatist.* The Hague: Mouton, 1975. Chadwick studies Wycherley's dramatic growth; includes close readings of *The Country Wife* and *The Plain Dealer.*

Markley, Robert. *Two-edg'd Weapons: Style and Ideology in the Comedies of Etherege, Wycherley and Congreve.* Oxford: Clarendon, 1988. A specialized language study, utilizing Bakhtin's theories. Markley argues that Wycherley's language and usage undermine popular ideology and the accepted conventions of wit.

Rogers, Katherine M. *William Wycherley.* New York: Twayne, 1972. A short, convenient study, covering Wycherley's life and works.

Thompson, James. *Language in Wycherley's Plays.* University: University of Alabama Press, 1984. Thompson argues that Wycherley's language reveals that the author favors morality and correctness.

Zimbardo, Rose A. *Wycherley's Drama, A Link in the Development of English Satire.* New Haven: Yale University Press, 1965. A major study, the first to focus upon Wycherley as a satirist.

John R. Clark

Contributors

Melinda J. Adams

Professor Adams received a Ph.D. from Ball State University, where she has been teaching composition since 1980. A selection of W.H. Auden's revised/repudiated poems was the subject of her dissertation.

John Adlard

Professor Adlard received an M.A. and a B.Litt. from the University of Oxford (Merton College). He taught at the University of Novi Sad in Yugoslavia, the Catholic University of Lublin and the University of Lodz, both in Poland, the University of Jyvaskyla in Finland, the University of Groningen in Holland, and the University of St. Ignatius in Belgium, as well as a variety of institutions in London and elsewhere. Professor Adlard authored *Stenbock, Yeats and the Nineties* (1969), *The Debt to Pleasure* (1974), *Owen Seaman* (1977), *The Timid, Bending Venus* (1992), and a volume of poetry, *The Lichfield Elegies* (1992).

Jacob Adler

Professor Adler received a Ph.D. from Harvard University. He retired as professor of English at Purdue University in 1989. He arrived at Purdue in 1969 as head of the English department, a position he held for twelve years. Previously he had taught for twenty years at the University of Kentucky and had been department chair for five. Professor Adler's special areas are eighteenth-century English literature and modern drama, but he has actually published in almost all periods of English and American literature, a total of some seventy publications, including two books: *The Reach of Art: A Study in the Prosody of Pope* and *Lillian Hellman*.

Jonathan Alexander

Professor Alexander received a Ph.D. in comparative literature from Louisiana State University, where she has taught English rhetoric, composition, and literature. His primary academic interest is in nineteenth- and early twentieth-century literature, and he has published articles on Christina Rossetti, Gerard Manley Hopkins, and C.S. Lewis, and essays on literary theory. Professor Alexander has lectured widely on modern fiction and on Pre-Raphaelite art and poetics. He is at work on a book about Walt Whitman's poetry.

Brooke Allen

Brooke Allen received a B.A. in French and linguistics from the University of Virginia, an M.A. in English from the Université de Paris, Sorbonne, an M.A. from Columbia University Teachers' College, and a Ph.D. from Columbia University in 1993 with a dissertation on Evelyn Waugh. She has taught at the American College in Paris, the Université de Paris-Sorbonne, and Columbia University. Professor Allen's criticism has been published in the *New Criterion*, the *New York Times Book Review*, the *European*, and the *Wall Street Journal*, and she has published scholarly articles in *Twentieth Century Literature*, the *Dickens Quarterly, Nineteenth-*

Century Prose, and *University of Mississippi Studies in English.* She has written for the theater and for television, wrote the text for *The Sleeping Beauty,* a new children's book published in association with the 1991 New York City Ballet production, and is working on *Laura Gilpin: A Divided Life.*

Leonard R.N. Ashley

Professor Ashley received a Ph.D. from Princeton University and is professor of English at Brooklyn College of the CUNY. He has published extensively in many fields from literary biography (*Colley Cibber* and *George Peele*) and criticism (*Authorship and Evidence in Renaissance Drama* and *History of the Short Story*) to anthologies (*Elizabethan Popular Culture* and *Nineteenth-Century British Drama*), textbooks (*Mirrors for Man* and *Other People's Lives*), and books on the occult (*The Wonderful World of Superstition, Prophecy, and Luck* and *The Wonderful World of Magic and Witchcraft*), onomastics (*What's in a Name?*), and military history (*The Air Defence of North America* for NORAD, collaboration on *A Military History of Modern China*). Professor Ashley has published about 100 scholarly articles and has contributed to many reference books, including *History of the Theatre, Reader's Encyclopedia of World Drama, Cyclopedia of Short Fiction, Great Writers of the English Language, Reference Guide to American Literature, British Women Writers, Modern American Drama: The Female Canon, Dictionary of American Fictional Characters,* and *Omni Gazetteer of the United States of America.* He has been president of national organizations such as the American Name Society and the American Society of Geolinguistics and serves on the Place Name Commission of the United States.

Joel Athey

Professor Athey received a B.A. in mathematics from Kansas State University and a Ph.D. in English from the University of Texas. He is associate professor of English at California State University, Northridge, where he has taught since 1989. He also taught at Oklahoma State University. Professor Athey is the author of three entries in the *Encyclopedia of Victorian Britain* (Garland).

Mark S. Auburn

Professor Auburn received a B.A. in English and B.S. in mathematics from the University of Akron and a Ph.D. in English from the University of Chicago. He is senior vice president and provost and professor of English at the University of Akron. He has taught and been an administrator at the Ohio State University, Arkansas State University, the University of Arkansas system, and Indiana University–Purdue University at Fort Wayne. His books include *Sheridan's Comedies, Drama through Performance,* and *Marriage à la Mode.*

Sarah Barnhill

Sarah Barnhill received a B.A. and an M.A. from Clemson University, an M.F.A. from Warren Wilson College, and a Ph.D. from the University of South Carolina. She owns and runs her own trading/communications business in Brevard, North Carolina.

John S. Batts

Professor Batts received a B.A. from the University of Wales, a Dip. Ed. from the University of London, an M.A. from Carleton University, Ottawa, and a Ph.D. from the University of Ottawa, where he is associate professor. He has also taught at K.C.S., Wimbledon, and the University of Hull (England). He was for several years book-review editor of *Thalia: Studies in Literary Humor.* He recently served a term on the Executive Board of the International Society for Studies in Humor. A contributor to *Humor: International Journal of Humor Research* and *Thalia,* Professor Batts has delivered numerous conference papers on Victorian and modern British literary humor. He has received awards from the British Council, Canada Council, and SSHRC. He is the author of *British Manuscript Diaries of the Nineteenth Century* and of articles on Victorian literary, cultural, and sporting milieu, diaries, and literary humor. His current reserach is on Canadian diaries, Victorian literature, and humor.

Marya Bednerik

Professor Bednerik received a B.A. from Bennington College, an M.A. from Bowling Green State University, and a Ph.D. from the University of Iowa. She is a stage director and professor of theater at Kent State University. Professor Bednerik has taught playwriting at the University of Massachusetts, served as director of theater at the University of Oregon, and chaired the theater Division at Emerson College. She has directed new plays at the Piccolo Spoleto Festival and the Circle Repertory Lab in New York. Her recent writing includes "Some Particular Pursuits: The Double Fiction of Simon Gray" in *Simon Gray: A Casebook*. She is at work on a book entitled *Simon Gray: Playwright at Play*.

Martin Beller

Professor Beller received a Ph.D. from Ohio State University with a dissertation on Shakespeare's eighteenth-century editors. He is assistant professor of English at the C.W. Post Campus of Long Island University. After having been a major development officer for the Brooklyn Museum, Long Island University, the New Orleans Symphony, and other institutions, he has recently returned to teaching. Professor Beller has made presentations at conferences on such topics as "Fathers and Daughters in Shakespeare," "Getting the Lore Back to the Folk," "Taking a Hard Line on the Humanities," "The Humanities and Aging," and "The Brooklyn Bridge and the Artists."

Samuel Bellman

Professor Bellman received a B.A. from the University of Texas, an M.A. from Wayne University, and a Ph.D. from Ohio State University. He is professor of English at California State Polytechnic University, Pomona, and is the author of the Twayne United States Authors Series biographies of Marjorie Kinnan Rawlings and Constance M. Rourke. Professor Bellman's biographical and bibliographical essays have appeared in literary sourcebooks, as have his critical essays on individual fictional works. His poems, book reviews, and assorted essays have also been published widely. He presented a paper on Barbara Pym, "Order in Disorder: Humor in the Novels of Barbara Pym," at the Eighth International Conference on Humor, which was held at the University of Sheffield in South Yorkshire, England, in 1990.

Bruce Bennett

Professor Bennett received an A.B., an A.M., and a Ph.D. from Harvard University. He is professor of English and director of creative writing at Wells College in Aurora, New York. He taught at Oberlin College from 1967 to 1970. He is author of three volumes of poems, *Straw into Gold*, *I Never Danced With Mary Beth*, and *Taking Off: Poems, Parodies, Palimpsests*, as well as several poetry chapbooks. He reviewed *The Gavin Ewart Show* and *The Young Pobble's Guide to His Toes* for the *New York Times Book Review*. He also edited a chapbook of Ewart's poems, *Poems from Putney*, published in 1990.

Lee Bliss

Professor Bliss earned a B.A. from Stanford University and a Ph.D. in English literature from the University of California, Berkeley. She is professor of English at the University of California, Santa Barbara, where she has taught since 1975. She has taught at a number of other schools as well. Scholarly journals have published her critical essays on plays by Shakespeare, Chapman, Webster, Fletcher, and Beaumont; her studies of Renaissance tragicomedy have appeared in *Comedy from Shakespeare to Sheridan* (edited by A.R. Braunmuller and J.C. Bulman) and in *The Cambridge Companion to English Renaissance Drama*. Professor Bliss is also the author of *The World's Perspective: John Webster and the Jacobean Drama* and *Francis Beaumont*.

Peggy Broder

Professor Broder received a B.A. from the University of Michigan and an M.A. and Ph.D. from Western Reserve University. She is associate professor of English and director of composition at Cleveland State University. She teaches courses in Irish literature and has contributed reviews and articles on this subject to *Eire-Ireland*, *Raft*, *Canadian Journal of Irish Studies*, *American Committee for Irish Studies Newsletter*, *Iowa English Bulletin*, and *Concerning Poetry*.

Ross Brummer

Professor Brummer received a B.A. and an M.A. from Brooklyn College, and he has been a teacher for thirty-six years on both high school and college levels. He is currently on the faculty of St. John's University, New York. He has also taught at The College of Staten Island and Queensborough Community College. He has written for several encyclopedias, including *The Eighteen Nineties: An Encyclopedia of British Literature, Art and Culture* and *Reference Guide to English Literature*. His writing credits also include an assortment of poetry, general articles, and educational writing.

Alizon Jayne Brunning

Professor Brunning received a degree in English with linguistics at Lancashire Polytechnic, where she is now a lecturer in English literature. Professor Brunning is currently working on a Ph.D. on misrule in Jacobean drama.

Randall Calhoun

Professor Calhoun received a B.A. and an M.A. from Western Illinois University and a Ph.D. from Ball State University with a dissertation on "William Shenstone's Aesthetic Theory and Poetry." He is the author of *Dorothy Parker: A Bio-Bibliography*. He is preparing a complete edition of Parker's poetry and prose.

Gerard C. Carruthers

Professor Carruthers received a B.A. in English Studies from the University of Strathclyde (first class honors, winner of the Meston Prize) and an M.Phil. from the University of Glasgow. He is a lecturer in Scottish Literature at the University of Glasgow and the University of Strathclyde and is working on his Ph.D. thesis for the University of Glasgow. Professor Carruthers has also lectured at Clydebank College, Anniesland College, Langside College, James Watt College, and Reid Kerr College. He was a contributor to *Post-War Literatures in English: A Lexicon of Contemporary Authors* and has reviewed for the periodical *Books in Scotland*.

G.A. Cevasco

Professor Cevasco received a B.A. from St. John's University (New York), an M.A. from Columbia University, an honorary D.Litt. from the University of London, and F.R.S.A. He is associate professor of English at St. John's University. Professor Cevasco's latest book is *The 1890s: An Encyclopedia of British Literature, Art, and Culture*. Among his other books and monographs are such works as *Three Decadent Poets: Ernest Dowson, John Gray and Lionel Johnson; The Sitwells: Edith, Osbert and Sacheverell; John Gray, J. K. Huysmans: A Reference Guide; New Words for You; The Population Problem; Oscar Wilde;* and *Salvador Dali*. In addition to his books, Professor Cevasco has written dozens of articles, essays, and over 350 reviews that have appeared in some fifty scholarly journals, magazines, and newspapers; most have been in American sources, but he has also been published in Canada, England, France, Italy, Taiwan, and the Philippines. He serves on the Editorial Boards of *English Literature in Transition* and *Mississippi Studies in English*.

Edgar L. Chapman

Professor Chapman received a B.A. from William Jewell College and an M.A. and a Ph.D. from Brown University. He has been a professor of English at Bradley University since 1963 and has published a monograph on Philip José Farmer along with numerous articles and reviews in journals, anthologies, and reference books, including *Texas Studies in Literature and Language, Heritage of the Great Plains, Illinois Writers Review, Science Fiction Studies, Christianity and Literature,* and *Seventeenth Century News*.

John R. Clark

The late professor Clark received a B.A. from Pennsylvania State University, an M.A. from Columbia University, and a Ph.D. from the University of Michigan. He was professor of English at the University of South Florida. From 1973 to 1995 he also taught English at Alfred University,

Muhlenberg College, CUNY–City College of New York, Fordham University, and New York University. He was the author of *Form and Frenzy in Swift's 'Tale of a Tub,' Satire—that blasted Art*, *Senecan Tragedy*, *Seneca: A Critical Bibliography, 1900–1980*, and *The Modern Satiric Grotesque*.

John Cloy

Professor Cloy received a B.S. and an M.L.S. from the University of Southern Mississippi and an M.A. in English from Mississippi State University. He is currently bibliographer for the humanities at Williams Library at the University of Mississippi and has also worked as a reference librarian at Mississippi State University. Prior publications include "Richard Graves: An Annotated Bibliography of Secondary Sources" (*Bulletin of Bibliography*) and "Two Altered Endings—Dickens and Bulwer-Lytton" (*University of Mississippi Studies in English*).

Nancy Cohen

Nancy Cohen received a B.A. from Yale University and an M.A. and a C.Phil. from the University of California, Los Angeles, where she is completing work on a Ph.D. in English. Her major interests are twentieth-century British and American poetry.

Robert Cooperman

Robert Cooperman is a Ph.D candidate in English at Ohio State University. He received his B.A. and M.A. from Queens College of the City University of New York. He has taught at Adelphi University as well as Ohio State University. He is the author of *Clifford Odets: An Annotated Bibliography, 1935–1989,* along with articles on Eugene O'Neill, Lanford Wilson, Marsha Norman, and David Henry Hwang.

Kevin L. Cope

Professor Cope received a B.A. from Pitzer College and an M.A. and a Ph.D. from Harvard University. He is associate professor of English and comparative literature at Louisiana State University, Baton Rouge, visiting fellow of Wolfson College, Oxford, and Salvatori fellow of the Heritage Foundation, Washington, D.C. The author of *Criteria of Certainty: Truth and Judgment in the English Enlightenment*, he is editing *Enlightening Allegory: Theory, Contexts, and Practice of Allegory in the Late Seventeenth and Eighteenth Centuries* and *Compendious Conversations: The Method of Dialogue in the Early Enlightenment*. Professor Cope has authored numerous essays on eighteenth-century subjects, from Samuel Johnson's prayers to oenological poetry, and has penned countless reviews and commentaries on both Augustaniana and academic policy. He is presently at work on a book on maxims, lawgiving, and institutional foundations of genre in the early modern period.

Denise Cuthbert

Professor Cuthbert is a graduate of the Universities of Queensland and Sydney and is a lecturer in English at Monash University, Melbourne, where she teaches courses on seventeenth-century literature and drama. She has published reviews and articles on seventeenth-century subjects and is working on a book on Andrew Marvell's political writing under Oliver Cromwell.

Curtis Dahl

Professor Dahl received a B.A., an M.A., and a Ph.D. from Yale University. He is the Samuel Valentine Cole professor of English Literature, Emeritus at Wheaton College. He also taught at the University of Tennessee, Southern Illinois University, University of Washington, and Brown University. Professor Dahl is the author of *Robert Montgomery Bird* and editor of *There She Blows: A Narrative of a Whaling Voyage*. He has published articles in a large number of journals and was a Carnegie fellow at Harvard from 1954 to 1955, a Guggenheim fellow from 1957 to 1958, and a Fulbright professor at the University of Oslo from 1965 to 1966.

Christie Davies

Professor Davies received an M.A. degree in economics (first class honors) and a Ph.D. in social and political sciences from the University of Cambridge. He is currently professor of sociology at the University of Reading in Great Britain. He has previously taught at the University of Leeds and the University of Adelaide and has been a visiting lecturer in Bulgaria, Hungary, India, Poland, and the United States. His most recent book is *Ethnic Humor Around the World: A Comparative Analysis*, and he has also published numerous academic articles about humor. His humorous work has appeared in *Cambrensis*, *Chronicles*, the *Daily Telegraph*, *Le Devoir* (Montreal), *Huronia* (Ontario), the *Irish Independent* (Dublin), the *National Review* (New York), the *Times* (London), the *Wall Street Journal*, and the *Western Mail* (Cardiff).

William Donnelly

Professor Donnelly received a Ph.D. from the University of Wisconsin. He is currently associate professor of literature and communications at Grove City College in Pennsylvania.

Margaret J. Downes

Professor Downes received a B.A. from LeMoyne College, an M.A. in literature from Southern Illinois University, and a Ph.D. in humanities from Florida State University. She is associate professor and chair of the department of literature and language at the University of North Carolina—Asheville. Her scholarly and teaching interests are medieval literature, William Blake, and the history of human culture. Her articles have been published in many journals, including the *Asheville Reader*, *Colby Quarterly*, *Midwest Quarterly*, *Perspectives*, *Oral English*, and *Journal of the Illinois Speech & Theatre Association*.

James E. Evans

Professor Evans received a B.A. from the University of North Carolina at Chapel Hill and an M.A. and Ph.D. from the University of Pennsylvania. He is a professor of English and head of the department at the University of North Carolina at Greensboro. Professor Evans is the author of *Comedy: An Annotated Bibliography of Theory and Criticism* and the coauthor of *A Guide to Prose Fiction in the Tatler and the Spectator*. His numerous essays on eighteenth-century comic literature have been published in many journals, including *Comparative Literature Studies*.

Robert C. Evans

Professor Evans received a B.A. from the University of Pittsburgh and a Ph.D. from Princeton University. He is associate professor of English at Auburn University at Montgomery. He is the author of *Ben Jonson and the Poetics of Patronage* and articles published in *English Literary Renaissance*, *Philological Quarterly*, *Texas Studies in Literature and Language*, *English Language Notes*, *Renaissance and Reformation*, *Renaissance Papers*, *Comparative Drama*, *John Donne Journal*, and other journals and collections.

Benjamin F. Fisher IV

Professor Fisher received a B.A. from Ursinus College and an M.A. and a Ph.D. from Duke University. He is professor of English at the University of Mississippi, where he specializes in teaching American writers of the nineteenth century, the Victorian era, and Gothic and detective fiction. The author or editor of six books on Edgar Allan Poe, Gothicism, and detective fiction and of one hundred articles and notes, Professor Fisher serves on the editorial boards of *Poe Studies*, *English Literature in Transition*, *Studies in American Humor*, and *Victorian Poetry*. He is past president of the Poe Studies Association, the American Humor Studies Association, and the Frank Norris Society, and the American vice president of the Housman Society.

John Frayne

Professor Frayne received a B.A. from Fordham University and an M.A. and a Ph.D. from Columbia University. He is professor of English and comparative literature at the University of Illinois at Urbana–Champaign, where he teaches twentieth-century British literature with special emphasis on Anglo-Irish literature. He has edited, with Colton Johnson, two volumes of the *Uncollected Prose by W.B. Yeats*, and he has published articles on the opera librettos of W.H. Auden and Chester Kallman. His pamphlet on Sean O'Casey appeared in the Columbia Essays on Modern Writers series. He regularly broadcasts programs on opera for WILL-FM, the Broadcasting Service of the University of Illinois. His music criticism appears in the *Champaign-Urbana News-Gazette*.

Mary Free

Professor Free received a B.A. from Louisiana State University, an M.A. from Northeast Louisiana University, and a Ph.D. from the University of Georgia. She is associate professor and associate chair of the English department at Florida International University—North Miami Campus. She has also taught at the University of Georgia. Professor Free's publications and papers deal with Shakespeare, Renaissance, and contemporary drama. She contributed chapters to *Acting Funny*, *Legacy of Thespis: Drama Past and Present*, *Renaissance Papers 1983*, and *Occasional Papers in Women's Studies*. Her article "Shakespeare's Comedic Heroines: Proto-Feminists or Conformers to Patriarchy?" appeared in *Shakespeare Bulletin*.

Rebekah N. Galbreath

Professor Galbreath received a B.A. from the University of Wisconsin—Stevens Point and an M.A. from Miami University in Oxford, Ohio. She is an English instructor at the University of North Alabama. Her master's thesis, *The Unexplored Mayhew*, focuses on Mayhew's farce and juvenile biographies. She has also taught at Widener University.

Shannon Gale

Shannon Gale is an independent scholar.

Steven H. Gale

Professor Gale received a B.A. from Duke University, an M.A. from the University of California at Los Angeles, and a Ph.D. from the University of Southern California. He is the Endowed Chair of Humanities at Kentucky State University. He has taught a wide range of subjects at the University of Southern California, the University of California at Los Angeles, the University of Puerto Rico, the University of Liberia (as a Fulbright professor), the University of Florida, and Missouri Southern State College (where he served as department head and director of the honors program). Author of over 100 articles on a diversity of topics, he has published three books on S.J. Perelman, five volumes on Harold Pinter, the *Encyclopedia of American Humorists* (a companion volume to *Encyclopedia of British Humorists*), a composition textbook, and *West African Folk Tales*. His volume *Liberian Folktales* is forthcoming, and he is working on a volume on Pinter's films. He is president of the Harold Pinter Society, coeditor of the annual book series *The Pinter Review*, editor of the *Harold Pinter Society Newsletter*, and general editor of Garland's "Studies in Humor" series.

Helen Gazeley

Helen Gazeley received a B.A. (honors) in history from Southampton University and a diploma in the history of fine and decorative art from the Study Centre, London. An assistant and researcher for Burlington Gallery, London, she is a historian with an interest in the literature and art of the early twentieth century. Her publications include articles on Cecil Aldin in *Journal of the Print World* and *Fun, the Magazine of the Cartoon Art Trust*.

C.J. Gianakaris

C.J. Gianakaris received a B.A. and an M.A. from the University of Michigan and a Ph.D. from the University of Wisconsin. Professor of English and Theater at Western Michigan University, Professor Gianakaris helped found the international, interdisciplinary quarterly *Comparative Drama*. He has published widely in journals such as *Modern Drama*, *Theatre Journal*, *Comparative Drama*, *TheaterWeek*, *Opera News*, *Renaissance Quarterly*, *Shakespeare Studies*, and *Huntington Library Quarterly*. In addition to a dozen essays and reviews concerning Peter Shaffer, he has published two books on the British playwright.

Kyle Grimes

Professor Grimes received a Ph.D. in English from the University of Illinois at Urbana–Champaign.

He is assistant professor of English at the University of Alabama at Birmingham. He has published works on British Romanticism and on contemporary American poetry.

Anthony R. Haigh

Professor Haigh was born and educated in England, where he received a certificate from the Rose Bradford College (Professional Acting School) and an M.A. from the University of Lancaster. His early career was as an actor. He moved to America in 1980 and received his Ph.D. from Michigan State University. He has taught at Michigan State University, Ferris State University, and Colorado State University (Fort Lewis Campus). Haigh is currently chair of the Drama Program at Centre College in Danville, Kentucky, and he is president of the Kentucky Theatre Association. His research interests include contemporary British theater, educational drama, and Jacobean theater, and he is active in the professional theater as an actor and director.

Peter C. Hall

Professor Hall received a B.A. from the University of Cincinnati and an M.A. and a Ph.D. from Miami University (Ohio), where he is assistant professor of English. He has also taught at Ohio Northern University, Indiana University East, and Miami University at Hamilton. Professor Hall has previously published essays on science fiction and film and the influence of Pre-Raphaelite painting on the staging of late Victorian and Edwardian plays. He is currently working on a book-length study of Jerome K. Jerome's plays and the theater of the 1890s and the Edwardian period.

Sheldon Halpern

Professor Halpern received a B.A. from City College of New York and an M.A. and a Ph.D. from Columbia University. He is currently dean of enrollment at Caldwell College. He has taught English at Indiana University—South Bend and Bowling Green State University, and as a visiting professor at Tel Aviv University and Hebrew University, specializing in the Romantic movement. Professor Halpern has also served as an administrator at Trenton State College. His dissertation was published as *Sydney Smith* in the Twayne English Authors series. He has published several articles on Wordsworth, Keats, and popular culture, as well as articles on academic administration and college admissions and recruitment.

Michael Hayes

Professor Hayes received a B.A. in English from the University of London, an M.A. in linguistics from the University of Lancaster, and a Ph.D. from the University of London. He is senior lecturer in English and linguistics at the University of Central Lancashire. Professor Hayes has also taught at Poulton-Le-Fylde College of Education. He has published an article on Isaac D'Israeli's study diaries in *Northwest Journal of Historical Studies* and has contributed to *American Crime Fiction*, *Twentieth-Century Crime Fiction*, and *The British Critical Tradition*.

Sidney Homan

Sidney Homan received a B.A. from Princeton University and an M.A. and a Ph.D. from Harvard University. He is professor of English and theater at the University of Florida, and visiting professor at Jilin University in the People's Republic of China. Several times an award-winning teacher, Professor Homan is the author of seven books on Shakespeare and on modern playwrights, including a prize-winning study of Samuel Beckett that emerged from a tour of Florida's ten state prisons with a production of *Waiting for Godot*. He is a member of the Editorial Board of *Shakespearean Criticism*. An actor and director in commercial, university, and experimental theater, he has directed works as varied as *The Comedy of Errors*, Bogosian's *Talk Radio*, Brecht's *Galileo*, and a production of *The Merry Wives of Windsor* in China. More recently, he has done television films of Harold Pinter's *Old Times* and Beckett's five works for that medium. Professor Homan is a member of the National Artistic Board of the Orlando Shakespeare Festival. In the future, he will direct an opera based on Christopher Fry's *The Lady's Not for Burning*.

Craig Howes

Professor Howes received an Honors B.A. in English from Victoria College in the University of

Toronto and an M.A. and a Ph.D. in English from Princeton University. He is a professor in the department of English at the University of Hawaii at Manoa. Professor Howes has published essays on nineteenth-century British and American literature, on children's literature, on critical theory, and on biography. He is the author of *Voices of the Vietnam POWs: Witnesses to Their Fight*.

William Hutchings
William Hutchings received a B.A. from Transylvania University and an M.A. and a Ph.D. from the University of Kentucky. He is professor of English at the University of Alabama at Birmingham. He has also taught at the University of Kentucky. Professor Hutchings has published *The Plays of David Storey: A Thematic Study*, and he is the editor of *David Storey: A Casebook*, a volume of the Garland Contemporary Dramatists series. Professor Hutchings is currently completing a book on Alan Sillitoe.

Maura Ives
Professor Ives received a B.A. from Bethany College and an M.A. and a Ph.D. from the University of Virginia with a dissertation titled *George Meredith's Publications in the New Quarterly Magazine: A Critical Edition*. She is an assistant professor of English at Texas A & M University.

David M. Jago
Professor Jago received an M.A. from Jesus College, Cambridge, and a Ph.D. from the University of Leicester. He is senior lecturer in English studies at the University of Strathclyde in Glasgow (Scotland), where he has lectured since 1965. A contributor to *Abstracts of English Studies* for many years, Professor Jago has published on Hilaire Belloc, G.K. Chesterton, and the Edwardians, as well as on Shakespeare. His articles have been published in *College English*, *Antigonish Review*, *Renascence*, and *Shakespeare Quarterly*. He contributed three entries to *The Eighteen Nineties: An Encyclopaedia of British Literature, Art & Culture* (Garland, 1992).

Vera Jiji
Professor Jiji received a B.A. degree from Queens College and an M.A. and a Ph.D. from New York University. Now professor emeritus, she taught at Brooklyn College, CUNY, where she specialized in drama and in literature and psychoanalysis. She has published articles on modern dramatists such as Pinter and O'Neill and produced videotapes of *Uncle Tom's Cabin* and *One-third of a Nation* as part of the series, Multimedia Studies in American Drama.

Marnie Jones
Professor Jones received a B.A. from Gettysburg College and an M.A. and a Ph.D. from Northwestern University. She is associate professor of English and director of the honors program at the University of North Florida. She has written essays on Elizabeth Gaskell, Henry James, Virginia Woolf, and the art of biography in the *American Scholar*, *Biography*, and the *New Criterion*. She is at work on a biography of "Golden Rule" Jones, a turn-of-the-century progressive reformer.

Jean E. Jost
Professor Jost received a B.A. from Nazareth College of Rochester (New York) and an M.A. and a Ph.D. from the University of Cincinnati. She is associate professor of English at Bradley University. Previously she has taught at Millikin University and Virginia Commonwealth University. She has published *Ten Middle English Arthurian Romances: A Reference Guide*, and *Chaucer's Humor: The Playful Pilgrimage to Canterbury and Beyond* and is working on *"Trouthe is the hyeste thying...": Behests and their Breaking in Chaucer's Canterbury Tales*. Professor Jost contributed to *The Rusted Hauberk: Studies in the Decline of the Feudal Ideal*, *Proceedings of International Courtly Literature Society Meeting for 1989, Salerno*, *Medieval Perspectives*, and *South Eastern Medieval Association Conference Proceedings for 1986*. Her articles have been published in *Tristania*, *Arthurian Interpretations*, and *CEA Critic*.

Thomas Kabdebo

Thomas Kabdebo received a Ph.D. from the University of Manchester. He is currently the librarian at St. Patrick's College, National University of Ireland. He has lectured at the University of Manchester, Ohio State University, University of Wales (Cardiff), University College London, University College Dublin, the Hungarian National Library, and the University of Buffalo. He has served as librarian at the University of Wales, University College London, University of Guyana, City of London Polytechnic, and the University of Manchester. His publications include *Diplomatic in Exile, Hungary, Arthur Griffith's Sources, Blackwell's Mission,* and *The Dictionary of Dictionaries.* He has also edited and translated numerous literary texts.

James R. Keller

Professor Keller received an M.A. and a Ph.D. from the University of South Florida, with a specialization in Renaissance drama. He is currently professor of English at St. Petersburg Junior College. He has also taught at the University of South Florida and Hillsborough Community College.

Richard Kelly

Richard Kelly received a B.A. from the City College of New York and an M.A. and a Ph.D. from Duke University. He is the Lindsay Young Professor of English at the University of Tennessee, Knoxville. Professor Kelly is the author of several books, including *Douglas Jerrold, George du Maurier, Graham Greene, Daphne du Maurier, V. S. Naipaul, Lewis Carroll,* and *The Andy Griffith Show.* He has also edited *The Best of Mr. Punch: The Humorous Writings of Douglas Jerrold* and *Great Drawings and Illustrations from Punch.* He is currently completing a book on the short fiction of Graham Greene and is beginning a study of the Carolina watermen.

Laura Cooner Lambdin

Professor Lambdin received an M.A. and Ph.D. from the University of South Florida. She is professor of English at Francis Marion University. Professor Lambdin has had several articles concerning Victorian and Middle English literature published, and with Professor Robert Lambdin she is editing a reference book on Chaucer's pilgrims.

Robert T. Lambdin

Robert Thomas Lambdin received his Ph.D. from the University of South Florida, specializing in medieval English literature. He is professor of English at the University of South Carolina, and he has also taught at the University of South Florida. With Professor Laura Lambdin, he is editing a reference book on Chaucer's pilgrims.

Ken Lawless

Ken Lawless was an Andrew Mellon fellow and earned an M.A. and an A.B.D. at the University of Pittsburgh. He taught at Michigan State University, City College of New York, and Baruch College. His articles have appeared in the *Antioch Review, Sports Illustrated,* and *People's Almanac 2.* As a humorist, he has written over a dozen titles for major trade paperback publishers (*Cat's Revenge, The Bumpee Gardening Catalog, Who's the Next President? Bluff Your Way in New York*) and currently tours as a performance artist.

Felicia Hardison Londre

Felicia Hardison Londre received a B.A. with high honors from the University of Montana, an M.A. from the University of Washington, and a Ph.D. from the University of Wisconsin—Madison. She is the Curators' Professor of Theatre at the University of Missouri—Kansas City and dramaturg for the Missouri Repertory Theatre. She is also dramaturg for Nebraska Shakespeare Festival and dramaturg/honorary cofounder for Heart of America Shakespeare Festival. She is the author of *Duse and D'Annunzio,* an opera composed by Gerald Kemner, as well as plays, translations, and articles on French and Russian theater. In 1991, Professor Londre was the keynote speaker for a ten-day symposium in Los Angeles on "Shakespeare in the Non-English-Speaking World," which led to a 1992 lecture tour of Hungary, where she spoke on "The Questionable

Life of Shakespeare" from an Oxfordian perspective. She has also been a Fulbright professor at the Université de Caen and visiting foreign professor at Hosei University in Tokyo. Her books include *Tennessee Williams, Tom Stoppard, Federico Garcia Lorca*, and *The History of World Theater: From the English Restoration to the Present*.

Deanne Lundin

Deanne Lundin received a master of music from the Eastman School of Music at the University of Rochester and an M.A. and a C.Phil. from the University of California, Los Angeles. She is currently completing a dissertation on American poetry at UCLA, where she also teaches. Her poetry has been awarded a number of prizes, including the first annual Battrick Poetry Fellowship at UCLA and her work has appeared most recently in the *Jacaranda Review*.

Stephen J. Lynch

Professor Lynch received a B.A. from the State University of New York at Albany and an M.A. and a Ph.D. from Indiana University. He is assistant professor of English at Providence College. He has published articles on Shakespeare and Renaissance literature in journals such as *Shakespeare Studies, Philological Quarterly*, the *Upstart Crow*, and *South Atlantic Review* and is currently writing a book on Shakespeare's transformations of his source materials.

Douglas S. Mack

Professor Mack received an M.A. with second class honors in English language and literature from the University of Glasgow, an associate degree of the Library Association from the University of Strathclyde, and a Ph.D. from the University of Stirling. He is a lecturer in the Department of English Studies at the University of Stirling. He has also been research assistant at the National Library of Scotland and assistant librarian at the University of St. Andrews and University of Stirling.

Loralee MacPike

Professor MacPike received a B.A. in Russian from Bryn Mawr College, an M.A. in English from California State University—Hayward, and a Ph.D. from the University of California, Los Angeles. She is professor of English at California State University, San Bernardino, where she has taught Victorian literature, children's literature, and women's studies. She has also taught at the University of Hawaii and is the author of *Dostoevsky's Dickens* and "The New Woman, Childbearing, and the Reconstruction of Gender, 1880–1900" (*NWSA Journal*). She edited *There's Something I've Been Meaning to Tell You*.

Joel Marks

Professor Marks received a B.A. in psychology from Cornell University and a Ph.D. in philosophy from the University of Connecticut. He is associate professor of philosophy at the University of New Haven. His areas of special interest are ethics, emotion, Asian thought, and Gerard Hoffnung. Professor Marks has taught perception and psychology of art and was director of Liberal Studies at the Portland School of Art and Philosophy at the University of Connecticut, St. John Fisher College, and the University of Rochester. His articles have been published in *Philosophy East and West, American Association of Philosophy Teachers News, Teaching Philosophy, Connecticut Journal of Science Education, Metaphilosophy, Emotion: Philosophical Studies*, and *American Philosphical Association Newsletter on Teaching Philosophy*. He is editor of *The Ways of Desire: New Essays in Philosophical Psychology on the Concept of Wanting*.

Brian McCrea

Professor McCrea received a B.A. from Kalamazoo College and an M.A. and a Ph.D. from the University of Virginia. He is professor of English at the University of Florida. He is the author of *Henry Fielding and the Politics of Mid-Eighteenth-Century England* (1981) and *Addison and Steele Are Dead: The English Department, Its Canon, and the Professionalization of Literary Criticism*, and co-author of *College Writing*.

Victoria E. McLure

Professor McLure received a B.A. in English/history and an M.A. in English from Texas Tech University, with study at the International Graduate Summer School, Exeter College, Oxford University, and a thesis on P.G. Wodehouse. She teaches at South Plains College and she has taught at Texas Tech University.

Elgin W. Mellown

Professor Mellown received an M.A. and a Ph.D. from the University of London. He is professor of English at Duke University, and he has also taught at the University of Alabama. He has published many essays and books on British literature, among them *Edwin Muir* and *Jean Rhys: A Descriptive and Annotated Bibliography of Works and Criticism*.

David Mesher

Professor Mesher received B.A.'s in English and Near Eastern languages from the University of Washington, an M.A. from the University of Victoria, and a Ph.D. from the University of Washington. He is assistant professor of English at San Jose State University. Professor Mesher has also taught at Tel Aviv University, the Hebrew University of Jerusalem, the University of Victoria, and the University of Washington. Scores of his reviews and articles have been published in various journals, including *Modern Fiction Studies* and *San Jose Studies*, and in the *Jerusalem Post*.

Edmund Miller

Professor Miller received a B.A., summa cum laude, from Long Island University (C.W. Post Campus), an M.A. from Ohio State University, and a Ph.D. from the State University of New York at Stony Brook. He is professor of English and deputy chairman at the C.W. Post Campus of Long Island University. He is the author of *Drudgerie Divine: The Rhetoric of God and Man in George Herbert* and of a number of essays on Lewis Carroll and Edward Lear, and he is the editor of *Like Season's Timber: New Essays on George Herbert*.

Gwendolyn Morgan

Professor Morgan received a B.A. from McGill University and an M.A. and a Ph.D. from the University of South Florida. She is professor of English at Montana State University, where she teaches Old and Middle English literature, language and grammar, and British literature. She has also taught at the University of South Florida. Professor Morgan is the author of *Medieval Balladry and the Courtly Tradition* and has authored a number of critical articles dealing with early English literature, including publications in the *St. James Reference Guide to English Literature*, *In Geardagum*, *Journal for the Fantastic in the Arts*, and *The Explicator*. She contributed to *Masterplots II: Juvenile and Young Adult Fiction*, *Cyclopedia of Literary Characters*, and *Heroines of Popular Culture*. She is currently involved in producing a collection of imitative translations of the shorter Anglo-Saxon poems with poet Brian McAllister, the first of which, "The Ruin," appeared in the Fall 1991 issue of the *Northwest Review*.

Merritt Moseley

Professor Moseley received a B.A. from Huntingdon College and an M.A. and a Ph.D. from the University of North Carolina at Chapel Hill. He is professor of English at the University of North Carolina—Asheville. Professor Moseley is the author of *David Lodge: How Far Can You Go?* and contributed to the *Encyclopedia of American Humorists*. His publications include humorous articles in the *New Yorker* and articles on American literature and recent English literature in other journals; he is currently working on a book about Kingsley Amis.

Alexandra Mullen

Professor Mullen received a B.A. from St. John's College, Annapolis, and a Ph.D. in English literature from Columbia University. She teaches Victorian literature at Providence College. Her primary areas of interest are Victorian and modern British literature.

Don L.F. Nilsen

Don L.F. Nilsen received a B.A. in French from Brigham Young University, an M.A. in applied linguistics from American University, and a Ph.D. in linguistics from the University of Michigan. He is professor of English linguistics at Arizona State University. He has also taught at the University of Northern Iowa, the University of Michigan, Kabul University in Afghanistan, Eastern Michigan University, State University of New York at Oswego, and the University of Pittsburgh. Professor Nilsen is the executive secretary of the International Society for Humor Studies and the Newsletter Editor of *HUMOR: International Journal of Humor Research*. With his wife, Alleen Pace Nilsen, he is coeditor of six volumes of *WHIMSY* (World Humor and Irony Membership Serial Yearbook), and he is the author of *Humor Scholarship: A Research Bibliography* and *Humor in American Literature*. With Ann-Marie Laurian, he is the coeditor of a special issue of *Meta: Translators' Journal* on "Humor and Translation." With Alleen, he is also the coauthor of *Language Play, An Introduction to Linguistics*. He is a member of the advisory board of the Wayne State Series on "Humor in Life and Letters" and a member of the editorial board of *Metaphor and Symbolic Activity*.

Marjorie J. Oberlander

Professor Oberlander received a certificate from the American Academy of Dramatic Arts, a B.A. in English and B.S. in education from Syracuse University, an M.Phil. in comparative literature from Columbia University, and an M.A. with honors in humanities from Manhattanville College. She is professor of English at Touro College. She has taught at Rutgers University, Mercy College, the New York Institute of Technology, and Iona College. Her features, articles, interviews, and theater/book reviews have been published by UPI and in *Other Stages, Stages, Marlowe Society Newsletter, Broadside—Theatre Society Newsletter, Singles Unlimited, Shakespeare Bulletin, Backstage*, and *Critics Quarterly*. Professor Oberlander is cofounder and editor of *Stages*, editor of 'Cyclopedia of Literary Characters II*, and author of *Masterplots II: Drama*. Her Off-Broadway production of David Mamet's *Edmond* at Provincetown Playhouse won two Obies.

Robert O'Connor

Professor O'Connor received a B.A. from Cornell University, an M.A. from the State University of New York at Binghamton, and a Ph.D. from Bowling Green State University. He is associate professor in the English department at North Dakota State University, and he also taught at Southwest Texas State University. Professor O'Connor has published an edition of Henry William Bunbury's *Tales of the Devil*. He has published reference articles on numerous subjects pertaining to his primary areas of interest, Gothicism and British Romantic literature, and his critical essays have appeared in *Notes on Contemporary Fiction*, the *Lamar Journal of the Humanities*, and the *Wordsworth Circle*.

Jill Tedford Owens

Professor Owens received a B.A. from the Mississippi University for Women, an M.A. from Auburn University, and a Ph.D. from the University of Mississippi. She is assistant professor at Southwestern Oklahoma State University. Professor Owens has also taught at Louisiana State University, Louisiana Tech University, and the University of Houston. Her articles and book reviews related to British literature of the period 1890–1920 have appeared in *English Literature in Transition, University of Mississippi Studies in English*, the *Henry James Review*, and *Publications of the Mississippi Philological Association*.

Ruth Panofsky

Professor Panofsky received a B.A. with honors from Carleton University, Ottawa, and an M.A. and a Ph.D. from York University, Toronto, with a dissertation on Thomas Chandler Haliburton. She is a postdoctoral fellow and sessional lecturer in the department of English at the University of Toronto. She has also taught at York University and Centennial College and is a member of the Social Sciences and Humanities Research Council of Canada. Professor Panofsky is the author of *Adele Wiseman: An Annotated Bibliography*, has contributed to the *Dictionary of Literary Biography*, and had reviews published in *Papers of the Bibliographical Society of Canada*,

Religious Studies Review, *Essays on Canadian Writing*, and *Canadian Literature*. She was awarded the Tremaine Fellowship by the Bibliographical Society of Canada in 1990 and is working on a publishing history of Mazo de la Roche. Her research interests include Canadian literature and bibliography.

Louis J. Parascandola
Professor Parascandola received a Ph.D. in English from the City University of New York, where his dissertation was on Captain Marryat. He is an adjunct associate professor of English at Long Island University. He also works for the New York Public Library. He has contributed to a number of other works, including *An Encyclopedia of British Women Writers* and the *Dictionary of Literary Biography*.

P.B. Parris
Professor Parris received a B.F.A. from the University of Nebraska/Lincoln and an M.A. and D.A. from Drake University. She is a member of the literature and language faculty of the University of North Carolina at Asheville. Her work has appeared in a number of journals, including the *Southern Review* and the *Kenyon Review*. Professor Parris has published a first novel, *Waltzing in the Attic*, and her second novel—which had its beginnings in her research at Oxford on George Du Maurier—is forthcoming. She is also currently compiling an extensive annotated bibliography on Du Maurier.

George E.C. Paton
Professor Paton received a B.A. with honors in sociology and an M.A. in applied social science from the University of Nottingham. He is a lecturer in sociology at Aston University, Birmingham, England, and he has also taught at the University of Strathclyde, Glasgow, Scotland. He is coeditor of *Humour in Society*: *Resistance and Control*.

Alan Pratt
Alan Pratt received a B.A. and an M.A. from the University of West Florida and a Ph.D. from Florida State University. He is an assistant professor of humanities at Embry-Riddle Aeronautical University, Daytona Beach Campus. He is editor of *Black Humor*: *Critical Essays*, and his interests are in the areas of satire, black humor, riddles, and Woody Allen's films.

Robert A. Prescott
Robert Prescott received a B.S. in biochemistry and an M.A. and a Ph.D. in English from the University of Illinois at Urbana–Champaign. He is assistant professor of English at Bradley University, and he has also taught at the University of Maine and Lakeland College.

Jean Raimond
Jean Raimond received his doctorate from the École Normale Supérieure and the Sorbonne (Paris), where he defended his doctoral thesis in 1968, and is professor of English literature of the nineteenth and twentieth centuries at the University of Rheims Champagne—Ardenne. Raimond was chairman of the French Societé des Anglicistes de l'Enseignement Supérieur from 1986 to 1990 and president of the University of Rheims Champagne—Ardenne from 1987 to 1992. He is the author of *Robert Southey, L'homme et son temps, l'oeuvre, le rôle* and *Visages du romantisme anglais*, and coauthor of *Le preromantisme anglais* (with P. Arnaud) and *Le roman anglais au XIXe siècle* (with P. Coustillas and J.P. Petit). He is coeditor (with J. R. Watson) of *A Handbook to English Romanticism* (St. Martin's Press, 1992). He is currently working on a French edition of Kipling's works for la Pléiade, Gallimard.

Martha Rainbolt
Professor Rainbolt received a B.A. from Baldwin-Wallace College and an M.A. and a Ph.D. from the University of Missouri—Columbia. She is associate professor of English at DePauw University, where she specializes in eighteenth-century British literature and in composition. She has coauthored a composition textbook and has published on Jane Austen.

Betty Richardson

Betty Richardson is professor of English at Southern Illinois University, Edwardsville, where she has been the chair of the department of English. She is the author of three books: *Sexism in Higher Education*, *John Collier*, and a local history of firefighting, *Serving Together*. Her articles, reviews, and review essays have appeared in *Papers on Language and Literature*, *Clues*, *AAUP Bulletin*, *Victorian Studies*, *Victorian Britain*, and *British Literary Journals*, as well as in other periodicals and reference works.

Terrance Riley

Professor Riley received a B.A. in philosophy from the University of Michigan and an M.A. and a Ph.D. in English from Michigan State University. He is assistant professor of English at Bloomsburg University, and he has also taught at Rutgers University.

Frances Mayhew Rippy

Professor Rippy received an A.B. from Texas Christian University and an A.M. and a Ph.D. from Vanderbilt University; she has also studied at Birkbeck College of the University of London. She is professor of English and director of Ph.D. studies in English at Ball State University. She has also taught at Vanderbilt University, Texas Christian University, and Lamar State University, and as a visiting professor at Sam Houston State University and the University of Puerto Rico. For over twenty years she has been editor of the *Ball State University Forum*. She is senior adviser to the *Steinbeck Quarterly*. A specialist in Restoration and eighteenth-century British literature and in literary criticism, Professor Rippy has written and published eleven articles or chapters and thirty-four reviews, which have appeared in *Non Solus: A Publication of the University of Illinois Library Friends at Urbana-Champaign*, *New Mexico Quarterly*, *Beaumont Journal*, *Descant: The Texas Christian University Literary Journal*, and the *Writer*, *Studies in Medieval, Renaissance, American Literature: A Festschrift*. She has served as president of the Indiana College English Association and has held a Lilly Library Research Grant, a Danforth Summer Research Grant, and a Fulbright Scholarship to London and was named in 1973 as one of the Outstanding Educators of America.

Jeffrey Ritchie

Jeffrey Ritchie received an M.A. in English from West Virginia University. He is an adjunct professor of English at the University of Cincinnati and Northern Kentucky University.

Bonnie J. Robinson

Bonnie J. Robinson received a B.A. from Wesleyan University and an M.A. and a Ph.D. from the University of Virginia. She is a professor of English at the University of Miami. She specializes in late Victorian literature and the Aesthetic Movement and has written several articles and presented papers on Oscar Wilde's role within this movement. She is assistant editor of the journal *Turn-of-the-Century Women*.

David Rosen

Professor Rosen received a B.A. from Haverford College and a Ph.D. from the Johns Hopkins University. He is associate professor of English and drama at the University of Maine at Machias. Professor Rosen teaches and writes about Renaissance literature and is the author of *The Changing Fictions of Masculinity*. A practicing humorist, he was "DR. WAC," a writing-across-the-curriculum expert who published his tips in biweekly broadsides.

Joseph Rosenblum

Joseph Rosenblum received a B.A. from the University of Connecticut and a Ph.D. from Duke University. He is professor of English at the University of North Carolina at Greensboro, and he has also taught at Duke University and High Point University [*sic*]. In addition to contributing to various journals, Rosenblum has edited *The Plays of Thomas Holcroft* and compiled *Shakespeare: An Annotated Bibliography*.

Rebecca Rovit

Professor Rovit received a B.A. from Bucknell University, an M.A. from the University of Virginia, and a Ph.D. in theater from Florida State University. She is a professor in Indiana University's department of political science, and she has taught theater courses at Florida State University and Illinois State University. Her publications include essays in *American Theatre* and *The Drama Review* (the latter on contemporary productions of Jewish theater in Germany). She contributed to *Theatre in the Third Reich: The Peace Years*.

G. Ross Roy

Professor Roy received a Ph.D. in comparative literature from the University of Paris (Sorbonne) as well as a Ph.D. in English from the University of Montreal. He is Distinguished Professor Emeritus at the University of South Carolina. He has also taught at the Royal Military College, the University of Alabama, the University of Montreal, and Texas Tech University. He is the author of many books and articles, principally in the fields of comparative literature and Scottish literature, especially the works of Robert Burns. He is the founding editor of *Studies in Scottish Literature*, the oldest publication in this field, and serves on the editorial boards of several scholarly serials and editions. He edited the letters of Robert Burns. He is the only American Honorary Life President of the International Burns Federation.

Susan Rusinko

Professor Rusinko received a B.A. from Wheaton College and an M.A. and a Ph.D. from Pennsylvania State University. She is chair of the English department at Bloomsburg University and conducts theater study trips to Stratford, Ontario, and London. She is the author of *Terence Rattigan, Tom Stoppard, British Drama, 1950 to the Present: A Critical History*, articles and reviews in *Modern Drama*, the *Shaw Review*, *World Literature Today*, *Dictionary of Literary Biography*, and the *Critical Survey* series, and forthcoming articles on David Storey and Alan Ayckbourn in Garland's casebook series.

Peter J. Schakel

Peter J. Schakel received a B.A. from Central College, an M.A. from Southern Illinois University, and a Ph.D. from the University of Wisconsin. He is the Peter C. and Emajean Cook professor of English at Hope College. In addition to writing two books and editing two others on C.S. Lewis, Professor Schakel is author of *The Poetry of Jonathan Swift* and numerous articles on English literature of the Restoration and eighteenth century.

Laurence Senelick

Laurence Senelick is Fletcher Professor of Drama at Tufts University. His many books include *British Music-hall, 1840–1923: A Bibliography and Guide to Sources* and *The Age and Stage of George L. Fox*. He has edited and translated the two-volume series *Cabaret Performance: Europe, 1890–1940*.

Pamela K. Shaffer

Professor Shaffer received a B.A. from Fort Hays State University and an M.A. and a Ph.D. from the University of Arkansas. She is assistant professor of English at Fort Hays State University, where her specialty is medieval literature. She has published articles on William Dunbar in *Fifteenth Century Studies* and *Studies in Scottish Literature*.

Jason B. Shaw

Jason Shaw is an attorney and independent scholar. He graduated from Drake University Law School in May 1995.

L. Moody Simms, Jr.

Professor Simms received a B.A. in history from Millsaps College and an M.A. and a Ph.D. from the University of Virginia, where he was a Woodrow Wilson fellow and concentrated on American history. He is professor of history and former chairman of the department at Illinois State

University. Professor Simms has published widely on the social, cultural, and intellectual history of the South, on southern literature and art, and on American popular culture in *American Humor*, *Mississippi Quarterly*, *Southern Studies*, *Resources for American Literary Study*, *American Literary Realism*, *1870–1910*, and *Mid-South Folklore*. He has contributed essays on Joseph Glover Baldwin and H. Allen Smith to the *Dictionary of Literary Biography*: *American Humorists*, *1800–1950*. His essays on Robert Benchley, Charles Augustus Downing, Corey Ford, Montague Glass, Sam Levenson, A. J. Liebling, Phyllis McGinley, Jean Shepherd, Charles Henry Smith, and William Tappan Thompson appear in the *Encyclopedia of American Humorists*.

John S. Slack

John S. Slack did his undergraduate work at Lehigh University. He has a Masters and a Ph.D. in English from the University of Miami. His dissertation on Joyce is entitled "Games/Joyce: Literary and Cultural Aspects of Games and Play from *Dubliners* through *Ulysses*." He has published articles in the *North Dakota Quarterly* and in *Aethlon: The Journal of Sport Literature*; he has also coauthored reviews for the *James Joyce Quarterly* and the *James Joyce Literary Supplement*. He is currrently a lecturer in English at the University of Miami in Coral Gables, FL.

Bobby L. Smith

Professor Smith received a B.A., an M.A., and a Ph.D. from the University of Oklahoma. He is professor of English at Kent State University. Professor Smith has written extensively on O'Casey; he is the author of *Sean O'Casey's Satiric Vision* and a wide variety of articles on O'Casey, W.B. Yeats, and D.H. Lawrence.

Elton E. Smith

Professor Smith received a B.S. from New York University, a B.D. from Andover Newton Theological School, an M.A. and a Ph.D. from Syracuse University, and an honorary D.D. from Linfield College. He is professor of British literature and Bible at the University of South Florida. He has also been a visiting lecturer at the University of Algiers, Mohammed V University of Rabat, the University of Paris, and London University. Professor Smith is the author of volumes of literary criticism on Tennyson, Godwin, MacNeice, Auden, Day Lewis, Spender, and Reade.

Esther M.G. Smith

Professor Smith received a B.A. from Linfield College and a Ph.D. in British literature from the University of Florida. She has taught on both the high school and college levels and is the author of *Mrs. Humphry Ward* and *The Cascade Empire*. With Elton E. Smith, she coauthored *William Godwin* and, with M.L. Sutton, she coauthored *The Last Eight Days*.

Chris Snodgrass

Professor Snodgrass received a B.A. from Wabash College and a Ph.D. from the State University of New York at Buffalo. He is professor of English at the University of Florida. A specialist in late Victorian literature and art, Professor Snodgrass has numerous published articles on Swinburne, Wilde, Dowson, Symons, and Beardsley, among others. He has recently completed a book, *Aubrey Beardsley: Dandy of the Grotesque*, analyzing Beardsley's art and its significance in the Victorian decadence.

Laura Snyder

Professor Snyder received a B.S. and an M.A. from Ball State University and is pursuing a doctorate in modern and contemporary British and American literature at Loyola University of Chicago. She is an instructor of English at Ball State. Her articles have been published in *College Teaching* ("Student Videos Capture the Big Picture") and *Modern Drama* ("Learn to Play the Game: Learning and Teaching Strategies in Ann Jellicoe's *The Knack*").

Donald R. Swanson

Professor Swanson received a B.A. from Washington and Jefferson College, an M.A. from the University of Connecticut, and a Ph.D. from Rutgers University. He is professor of English and director of graduate studies at Wright State University. He was vice president of the Greater New York Regional College English Association, and later served as treasurer of the national College English Association, a member of its board of directors, and chairman of its Publications Committee. Professor Swanson was for some years editor of University Monographs, and was the acting director of the Wright State University Press, for which he still serves as a member of the Editorial Board. He is the author of *Three Conquerors: Character and Method in the Mature Works of George Meredith* and articles on nineteenth- and twentieth-century English and American literature.

John Timpane

Professor Timpane is a member of the faculty of Lafayette College, and he has also taught at Stanford University, Rutgers University, and the University of Southampton. His major interests are composition, Renaissance literature, and the theory of comedy. Professor Timpane has coauthored a composition textbook, *Writing Worth Reading*, and is currently completing a book on Renaissance humor. He has also written extensively for medical and scientific publications.

Charles Trainor

Professor Trainor received a B.A. from Dartmouth, an M.A. from Cambridge, and a Ph.D. from Yale University. He is department head and associate professor of English at Siena College, and he has also taught at Illinois College. Professor Trainor's publications include *The Drama and Fielding's Novels* and several articles on Fielding and other authors.

Eugene Trivizas

Professor Trivizas received an LL.B. and a B.Sc. from the University of Athens and LL.M. and Ph.D. from the University of London. A barrister-at-law and a criminologist, he teaches international and comparative criminology at the University of Reading in England. Professor Trivizas has also previously lectured at the Polytechnic of Central London and is a visiting professor at the Pantion University of Athens. As a criminologist, Professor Trivizas has published widely on deviance, censorship, hooliganism, and collective violence. One of Greece's leading humorous writers for children, he has produced more than thirty books and has been named the winner of fourteen national and international literary prizes and awards. Much of his work has been transferred to the stage and serialized for television. His first humorous book for children published in the English language (*The Three Little Wolves and the Big Bad Pig*) reached the second place in the American best seller list and has won many distinctions (including A.L.A. Notable Book and A.S.L.J. Best Book) and has been translated into seven languages.

Glyn Turton

Professor Turton received a B.A. from Oxon and an M.A. and a Ph.D. from Warwick. He is head of English literature at Chester College, Chester, England, and he has also taught at Birmingham Polytechnic. He is the author of *Turgenev and the Context of English Literature*.

Gene Washington

Professor Washington received a B.A., an M.A., and a Ph.D. from the University of Missouri. He is professor of English at Utah State University. Professor Washington's articles on Swift, Pope, Fielding, and Sterne have been published in scholarly journals such as *The Scriblerian*, *Swift Studies*, and the *Explicator*. He has also published some 20 short stories in journals such as *Nexus*, *New Mexico Humanities Review*, *Weber Studies*, and *Acta Victoriana*.

Edwin W. Williams

Professor Williams received a B.A. from Millsaps College, an M.Div. from Duke University, and a Ph.D. from the University of North Carolina at Chapel Hill; he also studied at the University of Edinburgh and the University of Hong Kong. He is professor of English at East Tennessee State University, where he specializes in Victorian literature and the twentieth-century British novel. He has also taught at Brevard College. Professor Williams has published articles on Alfred Lord Tennyson, James Joyce, W.D. Snodgrass, E.M. Forster, Tennessee Williams, and Clifford Odets.

Deborah Wills

Deborah Wills received a B.A. from the University of British Columbia and an M.A. from Moorhead State University as well as M.A.'s from North Dakota State University and the University of Iowa. She is reference librarian at Wilfrid Laurier University in Ontario. She has taught composition at North Dakota State University and has been humanities librarian at the University of Windsor in Ontario.

Natalie Joy Woodall

Professor Woodall received Ph.D.'s from the State University of New York at Albany (Classics) and from Syracuse University (English), where she is a member of the faculty. She has taught in public schools and at the State University of New York at Oswego. Professor Woodall's bibliography includes articles on Petronius, Milton, Griselda Gambaro, and nineteenth-century British women writers. She is currently editing a book on Latin American literature and culture.

Christopher G. Worth

Professor Worth received an M.A. from Oxford and a Ph.D. from the University of London. He is a lecturer in the department of English and in the Centre for Comparative Literature and Cultural Studies at Monash University, Clayton, Australia. He teaches narrative and literary theory as well as theater studies programs. Professor Worth has coedited *Postmodern Conditions* with Andrew Milner and Philip Thomson; *Discourse and Difference: Post-Structuralism, Feminism and the Moment of History* with Andrew Milner; and *Literature and Opposition*. He has published articles on Jerrold, Walter Scott, and narrative. He is currently working on a book on Walter Scott, Scottish drama, and the Edinburgh Theatre in the early nineteenth century.

Index

Aaron's Rod (D.H. Lawrence), 329
Abbey Theatre (Dublin), 104, 787–89, 792, 793
Abbey Theatre Company, 120
Abbot, Jack, 121
Abbott, Bud, xxxix, 387
Abbott, Charles D., 54 n
ABC, 254, 820
"Abide With Me," 125
Abinger Harvest (Forster), 390
Abner, Li'l, 54
About the House (Auden), 48, 51
!Abracadabra! (Mankowitz), 714, 715, 718
"Absalom and Achitophel" (Dryden), 334–35
Absent Friends (Ayckbourn), 68, 69–70
Absurd Person Singular (Ayckbourn), 69
"Abt Vogler" (Robert Browning), 163
Academie Française, 588
Account and Character of the Times, An (John Hall), 499
Achilles (Gay), 437, 438, 439
Acis and Galatea (Gay), 434, 437
Ackerley (Peter Parker), 6 n
Ackerley, J[oel] R[andolph]
    biography, 3–4
    editor, *The Listener*, 3
    literary analysis, 4–6
Act Without Words: A Mime for One Player (Beckett), 109
Acting Exercise (Barnes), 78
Acton, Harold, 474, 776
Acts, 628
Adam, 414
"Adam Pos'd" (Finch), 367
Adams, Douglas (Noel)
    biography, 6–7
    literary analysis, 7–10
    script editor, *Dr. Who*, 7
Adams, Williams, 585, 590–91
A.D.C. *See* Cambridge Amateur Dramatic Club
Addams, Charles, 294
"Addenda to 'Profile'" (Auden), 53
Addison and Steele Are Dead (McCrea), 13

Addison, Joseph, xxxvi, xxxviii, 59–60, 206, 208, 352, 360, 453, 866, 869
    biography, 10
    contributor to *Spectator*, 10–14
    contributor to *Tatler*, 10–14
    literary analysis, 11–14
    parodied by Alexander Pope, 10
    wrote preface for *Georgics* (Virgil, trans. John Dryden), 11
Additional Poems (Housman), 547
Address on the Present Condition, Resources and Prospects of British North America, Delivered by Special Request at City Hall, Glasgow, on the 25th March, 1857, An (Haliburton), 496
Adelphi, 414, 416, 808, 814
Adelphi Theatre (London), 447, 863
Admirable Bushville, The (Shaw), 207
Admirable Crichton, The (Barrie), 85, 86, 89
Adrian, Arthur, 654 n, 655 n
Advancement of Learning, The (John Hall), 501
Adventure of Lady Ursula, The (Hope), 544
Adventure of Mommy and Daddy, The (Isherwood), 560
Adventures of Father Brown, The (Boucher), 246–47 n
A.E. Housman: A Critical Biography (Page), 547
A.E. Housman: Collected Poems and Selected Prose (Rich), 547
Aeneid (Virgil), 639, 720, 868
Aeschylus, 162
"Aesthetic Point of View, The" (Auden), 53–54
African Queen, The, 262
After Dark, 83 n
After the Funeral (Barnes), 81
After Many a Summer Dies the Swan (Huxley), 554
"Against Commerce which is the Corruption of Mankind" (D'Israeli), 315
Age of Anxiety, The (Auden), 46, 48, 51, 52
Agnew, 171
Aids to Reflection (Coleridge), 258
Aissa Saved (Cary), 220–21

Alan Ayckbourn (Billington), 71
"Alan Ayckbourn Takes Manhattan"
    (Raymond), 68
"Alan Coren" (Clive James), 275
Alan, Terence. *See* Mulligan, Spike
Albee, Edward, 256
Alchemist, The (Jonson), 38, 39, 597, 599, 602–03
Aldington, Richard, 330, 387
Aldwych Theatre (London), xxxix, 414, 685,
    848, 849
Alfred Hitchcock Presents, 262
Ali, Noureddin. *See* Armstrong, John
Alice (Carroll), 647, 649, 653
Alice and Thomas and Jane (Bagnold), 74
"Alice Is at It Again" (Coward), 282
Alice's Adventures in Wonderland (Lewis Carroll),
    89, 208, 214, 215–17
Alice's Adventures under Ground
    (Lewis Carroll), 214
All Dressed Up and Nowhere to Go: The Poor
    Man's Guide to the Affluent Society
    (Bradbury), 152, 153
All Except the Bastard (Coren), 275–76
All Fools (George Chapman), 223, 225
All For Love (Dryden), 437
All My Little Ones (Ewart), 345
All Roads Lead to Calvary (Jerome), 574
All That Fall (Beckett), 109
All the Conspirators (Isherwood), 558, 561
All the Year Round, 309
"All You Need to Know About Europe"
    (Coren), 276
Allen, Adrienne, 286
Allen, Elizabeth, 482 n
Allen, Glen, 394
Allen, Roland. *See* Ayckbourn, Alan
Allen, Walter, 15, 20 n, 479
Allen, Woody, 171
Alma: or, The Progress of the Mind (Prior), 878,
    879, 881, 883, 884
Allot, Robert, 223
Allsop, Kenneth, 20 n
All's Well That Ends Well (Shakespeare), 38, 375
Alone (Norman Douglas), 331
Alonzo the Brave; or, Faust and the Fair Imogene
    (Burnand), 169
Alphabetical Order (Frayn), 399, 400
Alps and Sanctuaries (Samuel Butler), 187
Alphonsus, King of Aragon (Robert Greene), 488
Altangi, Lien Chi. *See* Goldsmith, Oliver
Alteration, The (Kingsley Amis), 18, 19
Amelia (Carey), 208
Amelia (Fielding), 359, 362
Amendments of Mr. Collier's False and Imperfect
    Citations (Congreve), 266
Amenities of Literature (D'Israeli), 316, 317
American Academy of Arts and Letters, 46, 74
American Literary Expatriates in Europe: 1815
    to 1950 (Bradbury), 152
American National Institute of Arts and
    Letters, 559

American Notes (Dickens), 308
American Tail 2: Fievel Goes West, An
    (Spielberg), 256
Amin, Idi, 275
Amis, Kingsley, 152, 153, 371, 695, 818
    biography, 14–15
    influenced by W.H. Auden and Robert
        Graves, 18
    literary analysis, 15–22
    parodied Henry James, 17
    pseudonym, Robert Markham, 19
Amis, Martin Louis, 15, 91, 121, 617
    biography, 22–23
    contributor to *Independent on Sunday*
        and *Observer*, 23
    editorial assistant, assistant literary editor,
        Times Literary Supplement, 22
    literary analysis, 23–26
    literary editor, *New Statesman*, 22
An Giall (Behan), 119
Ancient Mysteries Described (Hone), 532
And Even Now (Beerbohm), 115
Andersen, Hans Christian, 87
Anderson, Alan, 299 n
Anderson, Lindsay Gordon, 32 n
    biography, 26–27
    contributor to *Encore*, 26, 29
    contributor to *Observer, Sight and Sound,*
        The Times, 26
    director, *The Changing Room, The Contrac-*
        tor, Home, In Celebration, Life Class,
        This Sporting Life (David Storey), 26, 27
    director, *The Long and the Short and the Tall*
        (Willis Hall), 26
    director, *Wakefield Express*, 26
    director, *The Waiting of Lester Abbs*
        (Kathleen Sully), 26
    director, *The Whales of August*
        (David Berry), 27
    director, *What the Butler Saw* (Joe Orton), 27
    founder and editor, *Sequence*, 26
    literary analysis, 27–35
    producer and actor, *Pleasure Garden* (James
        Broughton) 26
"Andrea del Sarto," 161
Andreae, Johann Valentin, 499
Andreas, James R., 237
Andreyev, Leonid, 123
Androcles and the Lion (George Bernard Shaw), 88
Andronicus, 600
"Ane Ballat of the Fenyeit Freir of Tungland"
    (Dunbar), 341
"Anecdotes of Errata (D'Israeli), 316
Anecdotes of the Late Samuel Johnson, LL.D.
    (Thrale), 586, 590
Anelida and Arcite (Chaucer), 229
Angel and the Author—and Others, The (Jerome),
    574, 577
Anger and After (John Russell Taylor), 569
Angry Decade, The (Allsop), 20 n
"Angry Young Men," 16, 17, 121, 153, 681, 685

Angus, Ian, 493
Animal Farm (Orwell), 811, 813, 815–816, 818, 820, 821
Animal Farm and Nineteen Eighty-Four (Jenni Calder), 808, 811, 814, 817, 820
Annals of Horsemanship (Bunbury), 166, 168
Anne Finch and Her Poetry: A Critical Biography (Barbara McGovern), 365
"Anne Finch, Countess of Winchilsea: An Augustan Woman Poet" (Katharine M. Rogers), 368 n
Anne Finch, Countess of Winchilsea: Selected Poems (Denys Thompson), 368 n
Annotated Bibliography of Jane Austen Studies, An (Barry Roth), 64 n
Annual Anthology (Coleridge), 259
Another Mexico (Graham Greene), 475
Another Time (Auden), 46, 49
Anouilh, Jean, 413, 414
Ansell, Mary
    acted in *Walker, London*, 85
Anstey, F.
    biography, 35
    contributor to *Harper's Weekly*, 35
    contributor to *Punch*, 35
    contributor to *The Travelling Companion*, 37
    literary analysis, 35–38
Answer to the Grand Politick Informer (John Hall), 500
Answer to the Scots Declaration, An (John Hall), 500
Anthenaeum (Calverley), 204
Anthony John (Jerome), 514
Anti-Death League, The (Kingsley Amis), 18
Anti-Tami-Cami-Categoria (Melville), 523
Antic Hay (Huxley), 553
Antoinette Perry Award, 848, 849, 850, 937
Antonioni, Michelangelo, 28
Antonio's Revenge (Marston), 729–30, 731
Antony and Cleopatra (Shakespeare), 95, 334
Aoesdana (Irish Academy of Arts), 404
APH: His Life & Times (Herbert), 521
A.P. Herbert (Reginald Povad), 518, 520
Ape and Essence (Huxley), 554
Apes of God, The (Wyndham Lewis), 672, 676, 677, 678, 679
Aphra Behn, 352, 366
Apocryphal New Testament (Hone), 532
Apollo Theatre, 414
Apologia pro Vita Sua (Newman), 158
Apology for the Middle Class: The Dramatic Novels of Thomas Deloney (Lawlis), 305
Apostles, 389
"Apparition, The" (Hood), 539
Arbuthnot, John, 434, 879
Arcadia (Philip Sidney), 93, 95, 303, 304
Arcadian, 540
Archer, William, 36
Archetypes of Literature, The (Northrop Frye), 419
Architectural Review, 147
"Ardelia's Answer to Ephelia" (Finch), 367–68

Arden, John, 77
"Are You Too Late Or Was I Too Early?" (John Collier), 263
D'Argens, Marquis, 453
Argosy (London), 296, 297, 298
Ariosto, 199
Aristocrats (Friel), 406
Aristophanes, 94, 182, 372, 374, 567 n, 646, 658
Aristophanes' Apology (Robert Browning), 158
Aristotle, xxxv, 155, 266, 252, 361, 439
Armageddon (Christopher Fry), 410
Armin, Robert, 622
    acted in *All's Well That Ends Well, As You Like It, Much Ado about Nothing, Twelfth Night, Troilus and Cressida* (Shakespeare), 38
    acted in *When You See Me, You Know Me*, 40
    biography, 38–39
    literary analysis, 39–41
    pseudonyms, Clonnico de Curtanio Snuffe, Clonnico del mondo Snuffe, 39
    wrote preface, *A Brief Resolution of the Right Religion* (Dugdale), 38
Armstrong, John
    biography, 41–42
    influenced by Lord Shaftesbury and Abbe Morvan de Bellagarde, 43
    literary analysis, 42–45
    pseudonyms, Lancelot Temple, Esq. and Noureddin Ali, formerly of Damascus, 43
    pseudonym, Noureddin Ali, 45
Armstrong, Tom, 338
Arnim, Elizabeth von, 82
Arnold, Malcolm, 526
Arnold, Matthew, 61, 147, 158, 182, 553, 554, 680
    parodied by Hankin, 513
Around the World in Eighty Days, 284
Arrabel, Fernando, 286
"Art of Fiction, The" (Henry James), 383
Art of the Gawain Poet (Davenport), 433
Artaud, Antonin, 77
Arthur and the Bellybutton Diamond (Coren), 275
Arthur the Kid (Coren), 275
Arthur's Last Stand (Coren), 275
Arts Theatre (London), 69, 412, 414, 685, 686
Arts Theatre Club (London), 848. *See also* Arts Theatre
As I Am (Neal), 294
As We Are: A Modern Review (Benson), 136
As We Were: A Victorian Peep-show (Benson), 133, 136
As You Like It (Shakespeare), 38
Ascent of F6, The (Auden and Isherwood), 45, 559
Ascent of Mount Ventoux (Petrarch), 433 n
Ask No Questions? (Jerrold), 582
Asolando (Robert Browning), 158
Aspects of the Novel (Forster), 390, 393–94
"Assumption" (Beckett), 100
Astaire, Fred, 283
Astonished Heart, The (Coward), 285

"At a Lunar Eclipse" (Hardy), 516
At Bay in Gear Street (Frayn), 399
At Last, the 1948 Show (Cleese), 252, 253
"At the Eleventh Hour," 274
"At Twickenham" (D'Arcy), 298
At Swim-Two-Birds (O'Nolan), 798, 799, 800, 801
Athenae Oxonienses (ed. Bliss), 500
Athenaeum, 535, 538, 579
"Atilla the Hun Show, The" (Cleese), 254
Atlantic Monthly, The, 275
Attache; or, Sam Slick in England, The
    (Haliburton), 497
Attenborough, Richard, 482 n, 803
Auber, Daniel François, 446
Auctor Ludens: Essays on Play in Literature
    (Guinness and Hurley), 471 n
Auden Group, 47, 54
Auden's Poetry (Replogle), 54 n
Auden, W.H., 3, 115, 146, 147, 345, 346, 558, 559
    biography, 45–47
    collaborated with Chester Kallman, 46
    collaborated with Isherwood, 559
    commissioned by T.S. Eliot, 45
    influence on Kingsley Amis, 18
    "Introduction," *Oxford Book of Light
        Verse*, 51
    literary analysis, 47–59
    member, editorial board, *Decision*, 46
    works published in *Oxford Poetry*, 45
    wrote for *Criterion*, 45
Audience (Frayn), 401
Auguste (Gray), 467
*Augustus Carp, Esq. By Himself, Being the
    Autobiography of a Really Good Man*
    (Bashford), 90–91
Auld Licht Idylls (Barrie), 85
"Auld Lichts" (Burns), 180
"Auld Reikie" (Fergusson), 356
Austen, James, 60, 703
Austen, Jane, 152, 175, 176
    biography, 59–60
    literary analysis, 60–66
Austen, L.F., 296
Authoress of the Odyssey, The (Samuel Butler), 188
Author's Farce, The (Fielding), 360, 362
Autobiography (Chesterton), 243, 244, 246
Autobiography (Jerdan), 537
Awdley, John, 551
Ayckbourn, Alan, 402
    acted in *Bell, Book and Candle*, 67
    acted in *Waiting for Godot, A Man for All
        Seasons, Rainmaker, Two for the Seasaw,
        Mr. Whatnot, Xmas vs. Mastermind*, 68
    actor and assistant stage manager, *The Strong
        Are Lonely*, 67
    artistic director, Library Theatre, 68
    association with Stephen Joseph, 67
    biography 66–68
    collaborated with Stephen Joseph, 67
    literary analysis, 68–72
    pseudonym, Roland Allen, 67

Ayes Have it, The (Herbert), 519
Aylmer, Felix, 75

"Bab Ballads" (Gilbert), 446, 450
"Bab" Ballads, The (Gilbert), 447
Baboo Jabberjee, B.A. (Anstey), 37
Bacall, Lauren, 482 n
Bachardy, Don, 559–60
Bachelor, The (Gibbons), 443
Backscheider, Paula R., 382 n
Bacon, Francis, 87, 500, 587, 869
Bacon, Roger, 588
Bad Child's Book of Beasts, The (Belloc, ill.
    Blackwood), 131
Bagnold, Enid Algerine
    biography, 73–74
    co-edited *Hearth and Home, Modern
        Society*, 73
    cooperation with Irene Selznick, 75
    literary analysis, 74–76
    published in *English Illustrated, New Age,
        New Statesman*, and *Nation*, 73
Bair, Deirdre, 99, 100, 101, 104
Bakhtin, Mikhail, 611
Bakker, Jim, 32
Bakker, Tammy Faye, 32
Balcony, The (Genet), 81, 124
Ball, Lucille, 255
Ball State University Forum, 237
"Ballad" (Calverley), 204
Balmoral (Frayn), 399, 400
"Banker's hours" (Grahame), 458
Bankhead, Tallulah, 286
"Bar on the Piccola Marina, A" (Coward), 283
Barabbas (Lagerkvist), 414
Barber, C.L., 224
Bardot MP? (Herbert), 520
Barham, R.H. Dalton, 542
Barish, Jonas, 600
Barker, Howard, 77
Barnaby Rudge (Dickens), 308
Barnardo, John, 411
Barnes People II (Barnes), 78, 80
Barnes, Peter
    biography, 77
    directed *Hard Times* (Dickens), 82
    film critic for Greater London Council, 77
    literary analysis, 77–85
    story editor for Warwick Films, 77
Barrett, Elizabeth. *See* Browning, Elizabeth Barrett
Barrie, James Matthew, 411, 577, 660, 756
    apprentice on *Journal* (Nottingham), 85
    biography, 85–86
    collaborated with Arthur Conan Doyle, 85
    literary analysis, 86–89
    portrayed in "The Blind Man" (Lawrence), 85
Barth, John, 363, 617
Bartholomew Fair (Jonson), 597, 599, 600, 603
Bartlett's Familiar Quotations, 248, 866
Bartók, Béla, 526
Barzun, Jacques, 246 n

Baseless Biography (E.C. Bentley), 138
Bashford, Sir Henry Howarth
    biography, 89–90
    literary analysis, 90–92
    pseudonym, Peter Harding, 90
Bassett (Gibbons), 443
Bates, Alan, 466, 470, 849
Bateson, Frederick W., 208
"Battle of Malden, The," 143
Baudelaire, Charles, 558
Bayard from Bengal, A (Anstey), 37
Bayle, Pierre, 10
Bayley, John, 549
BBC (British Broadcasting Corporation), xxxvii,
    xxxviii, 3, 7, 68, 79, 82, 117, 119, 147,
    250, 251, 252, 253, 254, 274, 399, 413,
    415, 416, 443, 444, 474, 526, 527, 663,
    673, 684, 685, 711, 763, 767, 810, 847
BBC-TV, 83 n
Beach, Sylvia, 610
Beardsley, Aubrey, xxxviii, 115, 296
"Beast in the Jungle, The" (Henry James), 162
Beat Generation and the Angry Young Men, The
    (Walter Allen), 15, 16, 20 n
Beattie, James, xxxv, xxxvi, 42, 210, 250
Beauclerk, Lady Diana, 166
Beaumont, Francis, 372, 373, 374–75, 377 n
    biography, 92–94
    collaborated with Ben Jonson, 93
    collaborated with John Fletcher, 93–97, 372–73
    literary analysis, 94–99
Beaumont, John, 93
Beaux' Stratagem, The (Farquhar), 353–54, 355,
    357, 456
Beaverbrook, Lord, 50, 147
"Beckett by the Madeleine" (Driver), 111 n
Beckett, Samuel, xxxvii, xl, 123, 170, 286, 387,
    414, 419, 610, 615, 617, 681, 685
    biography, 99–102
    influenced Harold Pinter, David Mamet,
        and Vaclav Havel, 110
    literary analysis, 102–14
    translated (with Peron) *Finnegan's Wake*
        (Joyce), 100
"Bedfastness of Molly Bloom, The" (Herring), 617 n
Bedfordshire Times, 410
Bee, The, 452, 453, 454
"Beer" (Calverley), 204
Beerbohm, Max, 139, 244, 666
    biography, 114–15
    contributed to *Chap-Book, Daily Chronicle,*
        Daily-Mail, Savoy, and *Parade,* 114
    contributed to *The Yellow Book,* 114, 115
    critic for *Saturday Review,* 115
    literary analysis, 115–18
    parodied Henry James, 116
Beerbohm's Literary Caricatures (Riswald), 117 n
"Beerbohm's Seven Men and the Power of the
    Press" (Mener), 117 n
Beethoven, Ludwig von, 178
Beggar's Bush, The (Fletcher and Massinger), 372

Beggar's Opera, The (Gay), 70, 207, 354, 414,
    434, 435, 436, 437–38, 439, 864
Behan, Brendan, 131, 684
    appeared on *Panorama,* 119
    biography, 118–20
    broadcaster for Radio Eirann, 119
    literary anlaysis, 120–28
    pseudonym, Emmet Street, 119
Behn, Aphra, 352
Behrman, S.N., 115, 117 n
Beichner, Paul, 234
"Being Took Queer: Homosexuality in Simon
    Gray's Plays" (Clum), 471 n
Bell, Anne Olivier, 137 n
Bell, Book and Candle, 67
Bell, Clive, 389
Bellagarde, Abbe Morvan de, 43
Bellamy, Edward, 577
"Belle Dame sans Merci, La " (John Keats), 214
Belloc, Joseph Peter René Hilaire, 139, 143, 492,
    494 n, 773
    biography, 128–30
    founded *New Witness* (with Cecil
        Chesterton), 129
    literary analysis, 130–32
    wrote for *Land and Water,* 129
"Bells and Pomegranates" (Robert Browning), 157
Belushi, John, 254
Benchley, Robert, 170, 276
Benefactor, The (Ford), 384
Benefactors (Frayn), 399, 401, 402
Bennett, Arnold, 18, 116, 459, 567 n, 672
Benny, Jack, 171
Benson, Arthur Christopher, 133
Benson, E[dward] F[rederic], 91
    biography, 132–34
    literary analysis, 134–38
Benson, Maggie, 133
Benson, Mary, 136 n
Benson, R.H., 369
Bentley, Edmund Clerihew, 130, 131, 243
    biography, 138–39
    literary analysis, 139–42
    parodied Dorothy Sayers, 138–39
    wrote for *Speaker* and *Daily News, Daily*
        Telegraph, 138
Bentley, Gerald Eades, 372
Bentley, Nicholas, 131, 138, 139, 308, 764
Bentley, Richard, 138
    published *Bentley's Miscellany,* 138
    Bentley's Miscellany, 138, 651
Beowulf, 142–46
Beowulf Poet, xxxiv, xxxvii
    biography, 142
    literary analysis, 142–46
Beppo, A Venetian Story (Byron), 194–95
Berlin Memorandum, The. See Quiller
    Memorandum
Bergson, Henri, xxxv, 107, 155, 186, 232, 290,
    553, 671, 681, 852
Berkeley, Bishop, 586

Berkenhead, John, 94
Berliner Ensemble, 124
Berners, Lord, 369
Berry, David, 27
Besant, Annie, 574
Bespoke Overcoat, The (Mankowitz), 715, 716, 717
Bessinger, J.B., 230
Best of Alan Coren, The (Coren), 276
"Best of Betjeman, The" (Betjeman), 146
Best of Enemies, The (Fry), 415
Best of Mr. Punch: The Humorous Writings of Douglas Jerrold, The (ed. Kelly), 581
Betjeman, Sir John, 17, 18, 45, 279–80, 347, 776, 778
    assistant editor, *Architectural Review*, 147
    biography, 146–48
    book critic *Daily Telegraph*, 147
    co-edited *Cherwell*, 147
    columnist for *Spectator*, 147
    contributed to *The Draconian*, 146
    established *Heretick*, 146
    film critic, *Evening Standard*, 147
    literary analysis, 148–51
Betti, Ugo, 286
Betty or The Country-Bumpkins (Carey), 208
Bewitched, The (Peter Barnes), 78, 80
Bey, Pilaff. *See* Douglas, Norman; Orioli, Giuseppe
"Beyond the Fringe," 91, 766, 777
BFG, The (Dahl), 293
Bhagavad-Gita (translated by Isherwood), 559
Bibesco, Antoine, 74
Bible, 103, 106, 230, 409, 416, 628, 636
Bible: In the Beginning, The (Griffin), 415
Big Ben (Herbert and Ellis), 522
Bigsby, Christopher, 156 n
Bildungsroman, Paul Kelver (Jerome), 574
Billington, Michael
    Alan Ayckbourn, 69, 70
"Billy and Me" (Barnes), 79
Billy Budd (Britten)
    Forster's libretto for Benjamin Britten's opera, 390
Billy Liar (Waterhouse), 30
Bin Ends (Coren), 276
Biographia Literaria (Coleridge), 258, 259, 260, 635
Biography for Beginners (E.F. Benson, ill. G.K. Chesterton), 138
Bird Man of Alcatraz, The (Anderson), 30
Birkenhead, Earl of, 149
"Birth of the Squire, The" (Gay), 486
Birthday (Frayn), 399
Birthday Party, The (Pinter), 848, 849, 852, 854, 857
"Bishop of Screwe, The" (Frayn), 599
"Bishop Orders His Tomb, The" (Robert Browning), 160
Bishop's Dilemma, The (D'Arcy), 296, 299
Bitter Sweet (Coward), 280, 284, 285–86
Black and Silver (Frayn), 400

"Black and White Question, The" (Hood), 539
Black Ey'd Susan (Jerrold), 579, 580
Blackfriars, 565
Blackfriars Theatre, 93, 96
Blackmore, R.D., 279, 830
Blackwood, Lord Basil, 131
Blackwood's Edinburgh Magazine, 64 n, 296, 319 n, 530, 536, 579
Blades, John, 613, 617 n
Blair, Eric Arthur. *See* Orwell, George
Blake, William, 30, 221, 467
Blaydes, Sophia, 467
Bleak House (Dickens), 308
Bless the Bride (Herbert and Ellis), 522
Blessing, The (Mitford), 776, 777–78
Blind Beggar, The (George Chapman), 223, 224
Bliss, Philip, 500
Blithe Spirit (Coward), 285, 850
Blood, Marjorie, 90
Bloom, Claire, 412, 414, 417
Bloomfield, Morton, 235
Bloomsbury Group, 389, 672, 676
Blot in the 'Scutcheon, A (Robert Browning), 157
Blue Angel (Soto), 291
"Blue Cross, The" (Chesterton), 245
Boardman, Gwenn R., 480
Boat That Mooed, The (Fry), 415
Boccaccio, Giovanni, 228, 230, 433 n, 611
Bodley Head, 115, 296, 475, 476, 479
Body Language (Ayckbourn), 71
Boece (Chaucer), 229
Boethius, 230, 430
Bogdanovich, Peter, 399
Boileau-Despreaux, Nicolas, 455, 881
Boitani, Piero, 230
Bolitho, Walter, 280
Bolton, Guy, 283
Bon-Mots of Charles Lamb and Douglas Jerrold (ed. Walter Jerrold), 582, 583
Bond, Donald, 12
Bond, Edward, 77
Book News, 339
Book of Ballads, A (Herbert), 522
Book of Caricatures, A (Beerbohm), 115
Book of Common Prayer, 533
"Book of Genesis" (Morley), 76 n
Book of Nonsense, A (Lear), 645, 646–47
Book of the Duchess (Chaucer), 229, 230, 236–37
"Book of the Machines" (Butler), 187
Bookman, The, 90
Books and Persons (Arnold Bennett), 567 n
"Books within Books" (Beerbohm), 117
Boom, 285
Booth, Connie, 252
Borges, Jorge Luis, 102
Borstal Boy (Behan), 119, 120–22, 124, 126
Boswell, James, 60, 379, 380, 453, 456, 586, 590, 591
Boswell's Life of Johnson (Hill and Powell), 379, 382 n. *See also Life of Johnson*
"Bottle Party" (John Collier), 263–64

Boucher, Anthony, 246 n
Boucicault, Dion, 309, 787, 789, 799
Boulting, John, 482 n
Bowen, Stella, 383
Bowen, Zack, 615
Boy and the Magic, The
    (Colette, trans. Fry), 414
Boy & the Magic, The (Ravel), 527
"Boy Riding upon a Pig, A" (Bunbury), 165
Boy: Tales of Childhood (Dahl), 294, 295
Boy with a Cart, The (Fry), 411, 413
Bradbury, Malcolm Stanley
    biography, 151–52
    collaborated with David Lodge, 152
    contributed to *Nottinghamshire Guardian*, 152
    literary analysis, 152–57
    wrote for *Punch*, 151
"Braid Claith" (Fergusson), 357–58
Braine, Dennis, 526
Braine, John, 16, 121
Branagh, Kenneth, 253
Brant, Sebastianus, 551
Brass Bottle, The (Anstey), 36
"Brave Alum Bey" (Gilbert), 451
Brave New World (Huxley), 554, 577, 818, 819
Breath (Beckett), 102
Brecht, Bertoldt, 30, 77, 124, 355
Brendan (Ulick O'Connor), 126 n
Brendan Behan's Island (Behan), 119, 125
Brendan Behan's New York (Behan), 119, 125
Brenton, Guy, 26
Brenton, Howard, 77
Brever, Lee, 102, 110 n
Brian Friel (Maxwell), 407 n
"Bridge of Sighs, The" (Hood), 537, 539
Brief Encounter (Coward), 284, 285
Brief Resolution of the Right Religion, A
    (Dugdale), 38
Bright, Mary Chavelita Dunne, 299
Brightfield, Myron, 541
Brighton Rock (Graham Greene), 475, 479
Brissender, R.F., 61
Britannia Hospital (Anderson, McDowell, and
    Sherwin), 27, 31–32
*British Authors Before 1800: A Biographical
    Dictionary* (Haycraft and Kunitz, eds.),
    209 n
British Broadcasting System. *See* BBC.
British Library, 42
British Magazine, 453
British Museum, 77
British Museum Is Falling Down, The (Lodge),
    692, 693, 694–95
Britten, Benjamin, 46, 390
Bromley, Walter, 496
Bronne, Charles Farrar, 497
Bronson, Bertrand, 234
Brontë, Anne, 415
Brontë, Emily, 61, 308
Brontës of Haworth, The (Fry), 415, 416
Brook, Peter, 413

Brooks, Hillary, 482 n
Brophy, Brigid, 369
Brown, Ford Madox, 383
Brown, Julia Prewitt, 64 n
Brown Man's Servant, The (Jacobs), 567
Brown Owl, The (Ford), 383
Brown, Pamela, 412, 413, 417
Brown, Richard, 7, 9
Brown, William, 93
Browne, Hablot Knight, 170, 654
Brownie of Bodsbeck, The (Hogg), 530
Browning, Elizabeth Barrett, 157, 204
Browning, Robert, 204, 210, 212, 347, 513, 631
    biography, 157–58
    literary analysis, 158–64
    parodied by Charles Stuart Calverley, 204–05
Bruno, Gordano, 611
Bryden, Ronald, 80
Bubbles of Canada, The (Haliburton), 496
Bubbles of the Day (Jerrold), 580
Buckingham, Lord, 360
Budgen, Frank, 610
Bulwer-Lytton, Edward, 169, 186, 308, 725
Bumf (Coren), 276
Bunbury, Henry William, 167
    biography, 164–65
    collaborated with Captain Francis Grose, 166
    literary anlaysis, 165–68
    parodied Matthew Gregory "Monk" Lewis,
        Robert Southey, Walter Scott, and
        Samuel Taylor Coleridge, 166
Bunny Lake Is Missing, 285
Bunyan, John, 30, 138, 211, 347, 409, 410, 636, 639
Buonapartephobia (Hone), 533
Burger, Gottfried August, 166, 835
Burgess, Anthony, 90, 91
"Burglars, The" (Grahame), 459, 460
Burke, Edmund, 452, 586
Burke's Landed Gentry, 369
Burkman, Katherine, 466, 471 n
Burlase, William, 605
"Burlesque Tradition and *Sir Gawain
    and the Green Knight*" (Owen), 432
*Burlesque Tradition in the English Theatre after
    1660, The* (Clinton-Baddeley), 209 n
Burnand, Francis Cowley, 37, 653, 654
    biography, 168–69
    collaborated with W.S. Gilbert and Arthur
        Sullivan, 169
    contributed to *Fun* and *Punch*, 169
    edited *Catholic Who's Who and Year
        Book*, 169
    edited *Punch*, 171
    founded Cambridge Amateur Dramatic
        Club, 169
    literary analysis, 169–72
Burnett, Carol, 399
Burney, Charles, 172
Burney, Frances "Fanny," 43, 44, 60, 165
    biography, 172–73
    literary analysis, 173–77

Burney, Sarah, 173
Burns, Robert, 209, 356, 357
    biography, 177–79
    contributed to *The Scots Musical Museum*
        (James Johnson) and *Select Collection*
        of Original Scotish Airs (George
        Thomson), 178
    literary analysis, 179–85
    parodied by Hankin, 513
"Burnt Norton" (Eliot), 471
Burnt-Out Case, A (Graham Greene), 476,
        477–78, 479, 490
Burton, Richard, 411, 482 n
Burton, Robert, 412
Busch, Wilhelm, 527
Bussy D'Ambios (George Chapman), 223
Busy Day, A (Frances "Fanny" Burney), 175
Butler, Samuel, 6, 740, 883
    biography, 185–86
    influence on Robert Graves, 188
    literary analysis, 186–190
    translated *Iliad* and *Odyssey*, 187–88, 189
    wrote for *Examiner*, 187
    wrote for *Press*, 186
Butley (Gray), 465, 466–67, 471, 849
Butt, John, 434
Bye Bye Columbus (Barnes), 82
Byron, Lord George Gordon, 28, 52, 116, 147,
        150, 163, 258, 276, 315, 317, 346, 347,
        466, 541, 745, 766, 835, 837, 838
    biography, 190–92
    influenced by Horace, John Dryden,
        and Alexander Pope, 192
    literary analysis, 192–202
    parodied by Charles Stuart Calverley, 204
    parodied by Hankin, 513
Byron, Robert, 4, 776
Byron, Thomas, 642, 643, 649
"Byting Satyres" (Joseph Hall), 503

Caesar and Pompey (George Chapman), 224
Cabaret (Van Druten), 559, 562
Cain (Lord Byron), 200
Caine, Michael, 399
Calamities of Authors (D'Israeli), 316, 317
Calder, Jenni, 808, 811, 814, 817, 820–821
Calendar of the Year (Auden), 46
"Caliban on Setebos" (Robert Browning), 162
Caliph's Design: Architects! Where Is Your
        Vortex?, The (Wyndham Lewis), 672
Calisto 5 (Ayckbourn), 71
Call, A (Ford Madox Ford), 384
Call Me Jacky (Bagnold), 75
"Call, The" (John Hall), 501
Calverley, Charles Stuart, 459, 547
    biography, 203–04
    literary analysis, 204–05
    parodied Longfellow, Byron, Tupper,
        and Ingelow, 204
    parodied Virgil and William Morris, 205
    parodied Tennyson and Browning, 204–05

translated Theocritus and Virgil, 204
Calvino, Italo, 617
Cambridge Amateur Dramatic Club (A.D.C.)
    founder Francis Cowley Burnand, 169
Cambridge Chaucer Companion, The (ed. Piero
    Boitani and Jill Mann), 230
Cambridge Circus. See Clump of Plinths, A
Cambridge Footlight Players, 371
Cameron, John. *See* Macdonell, Archibald Gordon
Camilla, or A Picture of Youth (Francis "Fanny"
    Burney), 173, 175, 176
"Campaign, The" (Addison), 10
Campbell, O.J., 506
Campbell, Thomas, 150, 838
"Campbells are Coming, The" (Burns), 183
"Camping Out" (Crisp), 291
"Can the Ayckbourn Curse Be Broken?"
    (Nightingale), 70
Can You Find Me: A Family History (Fry), 415–16
Canaans Calamitie: Jerusalems Misery
    (Deloney), 302
Candida Plays, 415
Candide (Voltaire), 30, 74, 80, 198, 221, 460
Cannan, Denis, 414
Cannan, Gilbert, 85
"Canonization, The" (Donne), 236
Canon's Tale (Chaucer), 232
Canterbury Tales, The (Chaucer), 229, 230, 234,
    325, 436
"Canterbury Tales II: Comedy, The" (Pearsall), 230
Cape, Jonathan, 558
Capote, Truman, 4, 284
Capri: Materials for a Description of the Island
    (Norman Douglas), 330
Captain & the Enemy, The (Graham Greene), 477
Captive and the Free, The (Cary), 221
Captives, The (Gay), 434, 437
Capuchin, The (Foote), 379
Caretaker, The (Pinter)
    film script, 848–49, 853, 856, 857
Carey, Henry
    biography, 206
    literary analysis, 206–09
Carey, John, 310
Carfax Gallery, 115
Caricatures of Twenty-Five Gentlemen
    (Beerbohm), 115
Carlyle, Thomas, 86, 297, 309, 358, 754
    biography, 209–10
    contributed to *London Magazine*, 536
    influenced by Coleridge, 258
    influenced by Laurence Sterne, Daniel Defoe,
        and Jonathan Swift, 211
    literary analysis, 210–12
    parodied in *Punch*, 212
Carpenter, Humphrey, 521 n
Carroll, Lewis, 35, 87, 205, 371, 449, 547, 615,
        647, 649, 653, 771, 773
    biography, 213–14
    influenced by John Keats, Alfred Lord
        Tennyson, and Samuel Coleridge, 214

literary analysis, 214–19
parodied G.W. Langford, 215
pseudonym of Charles Lutwidge Dodgson, 213
wrote for *The Rectory Umbrella, Whitby Gazette,* and *Mischmasch,* 214
Carte, Richard D'Oyly, 447–48, 451
Cartwright, William, 94
Cary, Joyce
   biography, 219–20
   contributed to *Saturday Evening Post,* 220
   literary analysis, 220–22
   pseudonym, Thomas Joyce, 220
Case Is Altered, The (Jonson), 595
Cassils Engagement, The (Hankin), 513
Caste (Robertson), 513
Castle Corner (Cary), 219
Catalogue of Crime, A (Barzeen and Taylor), 246 n
Catastrophe (Beckett), 102
Caterpillar Stew (Ewart), 347
Catholic Who's Who and Year Book (Burnand), 169
Catiline (Jonson), 93, 597
Cato (Addison), 10
Cautionary Tales for Children (Belloc), 131
Cavalcade (Coward), 279, 284, 285
Cazamian, Louis, xxxiii, xxxiv, xxxvii, xxxviii, xli
CBS, xxxiii n, 255, 739
Cecilia, or, Memoirs of an Heiress (Frances "Fanny" Burney), 173, 174–75
"Celebration of Charis, A" (Jonson), 605
Celebrity, The (Jerome), 577
Century Magazine, 296, 299, 338, 339
Century of Parody and Imitation, A (Walter Jerrold and R.M. Leonard), 204
Cervantes, Miguel de, xxxvi–xxxvii, 96, 140, 198, 199, 361, 373, 439, 490, 505, 611, 756, 869
Chabot (George Chapman), 224
Chalk Garden, The (Bagnold), 74, 75
Chamber Music (Joyce), 609, 611
Chambers Dictionary (Ewart), 347
Champion, The, 359, 360
Chances, The (Fletcher), 315
"Change of Treatment, A" (Jacobs), 566
Changed Man and Other Stories, A (Hardy), 516
Changing Places: A Tale of Two Campuses (Lodge), 692, 694, 696–98
Changing Places (Bradbury), 152
Changing Room, The (Storey), 26
Chap-Book, 114
Chapman, George, 93, 134, 801
   biography, 223–24
   literary analysis, 224–27
   poems in *The English Parnassus* (Robert Allot), 223
   translated *Iliad* and *Odyssey* (Homer), 223
Chapman, Graham, 253, 254, 377 ñ
   member *Monty Python,* 252
"Character of Holland, The" (Marvell), 734, 735, 736
Characters of Vertues and Vices (Joseph Hall), 504, 505, 507

"Charivaria" (Burnand), 171
Charlie and the Chocolate Factory (Dahl), 294
Charlie Hammond's Sketch Book (Fry), 416
Charley Is My Darling (Cary), 220
Charlot, Andre, 411
Charlotte Brontë (Benson), 134, 136
Charmers, The (Gibbons), 443, 444
Charney, Maurice, 110
Chartism (Carlyle), 210
"Chaser, The" (John Collier), 263
Chater, Geoffrey
   actor in *If . . . ,* 28. *See also* Anderson, Lindsay Gordon
Chatten, Elizabeth N., 380, 381, 382 n
Chaucer, Geoffrey, xxxiv, xxxvii, xl, xli, xli n, 12, 134, 179, 341, 343, 434, 582, 611, 746
   biography, 228–29
   literary analysis, 229–43
Chaucer Review, 240, 241, 242, 243
Chaucerian Play: Comedy and Control in the Canterbury Tales (Kendrick), 231
"Chaucer's Creative Comedy: A Study of the *Miller's Tale* and the *Shipman's Tale*" (Thro), 232
Chaudhuri, Nirad C., 630
Cheers, 252
Chekhov, Anton, 70, 123, 399, 400, 402, 403, 406, 468, 569, 656
Cherry Orchard, The, 406, 468
Cherwell, 147
Chesterfield, Earl of, 42
Chesterfield, Lord, 581
Chesterton, Cecil, 129
Chesterton, Edward, 139
Chesterton, Cecil, 244
Chesterton, G[ilbert] K[eith], 15, 129, 138, 139, 140, 141, 143, 567 n
   assistant to Redway and Fisher Unwin, 243
   biography, 243–44
   edited *The New Witness,* 244
   founded *G.K.'s Weekly,* 244
   illustrated *Biography for Beginners* (E.F. Benson), 138
   illustrated *Emmanuel Burden* and *The Hedge and the Horse* (Joseph Peter René Hilaire Belloc), 130
   illustrated *The First Clerihews* (with Edward Chesterton, Bentley, Oldershaw, d'Avigdor, and Solomon), 139
   literary analysis, 244–48
   wrote for "English Men of Letters," 244
Chichester Festival Theatre, 415
"Child and the Man in Max Beerbohm, The" (Roger Lewis), 117 n
Childe Harold's Pilgrimage (Lord Byron), 191, 192–93, 194, 197, 198
Children's Hour, 412
"Child's Angel, The" (Lamb), 87
Chimes, The (Dickens), 308
"Chinese Letters" (Goldsmith), 452
Chinese Prime Minister, The (Bagnold), 75

Chitty Chitty Bang Bang (Fleming), 295
Chorus of Disapproval, A (Ayckbourn), 70
"Christabel" (Coleridge), 257, 158
Christie, Agatha, 466
Christmas Carol, A (Dickens), 308, 309, 539
Christmas Eve and Easter Day (Robert
    Browning), 158
Christmas Garland, A (Beerbohm), 115, 116
Christopher and His Kind (Isherwood), 558,
    560–61
Christopher Isherwood (Alan Wilde), 562
Christopher Isherwood (Summers), 560
Chronicles of Narnia (C.S. Lewis), 664,
    665, 666
Chrononhotonthologos (Carey), 206, 207, 208
Churchill, Charles, 42
*Churchill Reader: The Wit and Wisdom of Sir
    Winston Churchill, A* (Coote), 249
Churchill, Winston, 116, 283, 518, 519, 819
    biography, 248–49
    literary analysis, 249–52
    wrote for *Morning Post*, 249
Cibber, Colly, 352, 869
Circle of Chalk, The (Laver), 412
"Circuit of Apollo, The" (Finch), 366, 367
Citizen of the World, The (Goldsmith), 452, 453,
    455, 456
Citizens House Theatre (Bath), 410
City Without Walls (Auden), 48
Clap Hands (Barnes), 82
Clarissa (Richardson), 17, 636
Clark, Kenneth, 3
"Classics of Humor" (Sutton), 444
Clay, Frederic, 447
Cleanness (Gawain/Pearl Poet), 430, 433
Cleaver, Eldridge, 121
Cleese, John, xxxvi, xxxix, xl, 767
    acted in *An American Tail 2: Fievel Goes
        West* (Spielberg), *The Screwtap Letters*
        (C.S. Lewis), and *Time Bandits*
        (Gilliam), 256
    acted in *Mary Shelley's Frankenstein*
        (Branagh), 253
    acted in *The Taming of the Shrew*
        (Shakespeare), *Cheers*, and *The Great
        Muppet Caper*, 252
    biography, 252–53
    created *Monty Python's Flying Circus*, 252
    emceed "Spot the Brain Cell," 254
    literary analysis, 253–56
    wrote for *That Was The Week That Was*
        (Frost), *The Frost Report* (Frost), and
        Comedy Machine (Feldman), 252
Clemens, Samuel L., *See* Twain, Mark
"Cleon" (Robert Browning), 162
"Clergyman, A" (Beerbohm), 116
Clerk's Tale (Chaucer), 230, 235, 236
Clinton-Baddeley, V.C., 207, 209 n
*Clockmaker; or The Sayings and Doings of Samuel
    Slick, of Slickville, The* (Haliburton),
    496–97, 498

Clockwise (Cleese), 256
Clockwise (Frayn), 399
Close of Play (Gray), 470, 850
Clouds (Frayn), 399, 400, 402
Club, The, 452
"Club in Ruins, A" (Beerbohm), 116
Clubbe, John, 536, 539, 540 n
Clum, John, 471 n
Clump of Plinths, A (Cleese), 252
Clutterbuck (Levy), 656, 657–58, 659, 660
Coal Face (Auden), 46
Cochrane, Charles, 522
"Cock and the Bull, The" (Calverley), 204, 205
Cock Lorel's Boat, 551
Cockpit Theatre Club (London), 569
Cocktail Party, The (Eliot), 416
Codd's Last Case (Herbert), 520
Cogswell, Fred, 496
Cohn, Ruby
    Samuel Beckett: The Comic Gamut, 106
Cold Comfort Farm (Gibbons), 441–42, 444
Coleridge, Samuel Taylor, 13, 88, 116, 167, 192,
    195, 196, 197, 214–19, 362, 449, 530,
    635, 637, 638, 640, 725, 746, 835,
    837–39

    biography, 256–58
    collaborated with William Wordsworth,
        257–58
    contributed to *Monthly Magazine*, 258
    contributed to *Morning Post*, 259
    influence on Hood, 539
    influence on Hook, 542
    influence on John Keats, R.W. Emerson, Walter
        Scott, Thomas Carlyle, James Fenimore
        Cooper, and William Hazlitt, 258
    literary analysis, 214–19, 258–62
    parodied G.W. Langford, 215
    pseudonym, Silas Tomkyn Comberbache, 257
    wrote for *The Rectory Umbrella*, *Whitby
        Gazette*, and *Mischmasch*, 214
Colette, Sidonie, 414
Collected Bulletins of Idi Amin (Coren), 275
*Collected Essays, Journalism and Letters of George
    Orwell: As I Please, 1943–1945, The*
    (George Orwell, ed. Sonia Orwell and
    Ian Angus), 822
Collected Ewart, 1933–1980, The (Ewart), 345, 346
Collected Letters of a Nobody, The
    (Waterhouse), 493
Collected Plays (O'Casey), 790, 791, 792, 793–94
Collected Poems (Auden, ed. Edward Mendelson),
    54 n
Collected Poems (Betjeman), 147, 148
Collected Poems, 1980–1990 (Ewart), 345
Collected Poems (Ford), 383
Collected Poems (Joyce), 610
Collected Poems of John Betjeman (comp. Earl
    of Birkenhead), 149
Collected Stories (Graham Greene), 477
Collected Works of Oliver Goldsmith (Goldsmith,
    ed. Friedman), 453, 454, 455

Collier, Jeremy, 158, 268, 352
Collier, John Henry Noyes
    biography, 262
    co-authored *Just the Other Day: An Informal History of Great Britain Since the War*, 262–63
    influenced by Sterne, Smollett, and Fielding, 264
    literary analysis, 262–64
    wrote for *Playboy, Esquire, New Yorker,* and *Alfred Hitchcock Presents*, 262
Collier, Vincent, 262
Collins, William, 75, 590, 591
Colmain (Gray), 465
"Cologne" (Coleridge), 259
Colonel Sun, 19
Columbia University Forum IV, 110 n
Comberbache, Silas Tomkyn. *See* Coleridge, Samuel Taylor
Comedians, The (Graham Greene), 476, 479, 490
Comedies and Tragedies (Francis Beaumont, John Fletcher, and Philip Massinger), 94
Comedy and Culture! England, 1820–1900 (Henkle), 493
Comedy High and Low: An Introduction to the Experience of Comedy (Maurice Charney), 110
Comedy Machine (Marty Feldman), 252
Comedy of Language, The (F.M. Robinson), 105
Comedy Opera Company, 447
Comic Annual (Hood), 537
Comic Faith: The Great Tradition from Austen to Joyce (Polhemus), 616
Comic Tales of Chaucer, The (T.W. Craik), 231–32, 235
Coming from Behind (Howard Jacobson), 155 n
Coming Race, The (Edward Bulwer-Lytton), 186
Commentaries of the Life and Reign of Charles I (D'Israeli), 316
Common Pursuit, The (Gray), 465, 468–69, 471, 850
Communicating Doors (Ayckbourn), 71
Communication Cord (Friel), 405–06
Comparatist, The, 237
"Complaint of Chaucer to His Purse, The" (Chaucer), 237
Complaisant Lover, The (Graham Greene), 478, 479
Complete Clerihews of E.C. Bentley, The (Bentley), 138, 140
Complete Collected Stories, The (Pritchett), 891, 892, 893
Complete Little Ones, The (Ewart), 348
Complete Plays, The (Behan), 123–25
Complete Poems of Thomas Hardy, The (Hardy), 516
Complete Poetry and Prose of Geoffrey Chaucer (Chaucer, ed. John H. Fisher), 229
"Compline" (Auden), 52
Compton-Burnett, Ivy, 75
    influenced by Firbank, 371
Concerning the Eccentricities of Cardinal Pirelli (Firbank), 370

"*Concerto for Hosepipe and Strings*" (Hoffnung), 526
Condor and the Cows, The (Isherwood), 559
Conference at Cold Comfort Farm (Gibbons), 442–43
Confessions of an Irish Rebel (Behan, ed. Rae Jeffs), 119
Confidential Agent, The (Graham Greene), 475
Confusion Confounded (John Hall), 500
Congreve, William, 10, 96, 134, 174, 256, 334, 352, 354, 360, 376, 455, 755, 869, 875
    biography, 264–66
    literary analysis, 266–74
Conley, John, 430, 433 n
Connaught Theatre Repertory Company (Worthington), 67
Connery, Sean, 295, 414
Connolly, Cyril, 370, 559, 813
Conquest of Granada, The (Dryden), 334
Conrad, Joseph, 116, 121, 329, 330, 332, 383, 396, 725, 727
Conspiracy and Tragedy of Byron, The (George Chapman), 224
Constant Couple, or the Trip to the Jubilee, The (Farquhar), 351, 352, 354–55
Constructions (Frayn), 399
Contemporary Authors, 275
Contemporary Novelists (ed. James Vinson), 20
Continual Dew: A Little Book of Bourgeois Verse (Betjeman), 147, 150
Contractor, The (Storey), 26
Contrivances: or More Ways than One, The (Carey), 206, 208
Conversation with a Cat, A (Belloc), 13
Conversation with an Angel, A (Belloc), 129
Conversations with Ayckbourn (Watson), 67
Cook (Jerome), 574
Cooke, T.P., 580
Cooper, James Fenimore
    influenced by Coleridge, 258
Cooper, William, 16
Coote, Colin, 249
Copland, Aaron, 526
Copland, Robert, 551
Coppard, Audrey, 811, 813, 815, 819, 820
"Copyright and Copywrong" (Hood), 539
Corelli, Marie, 574
Coren, Alan
    biography, 274, 275
    edited *The Listener*, 274
    edited *Punch*, 274, 275
    edited *The Punch Book of Kids*, 274
    literary analysis, 275–78
    wrote for "That Was the Week That Was," "Not So Much a Programme," "At the Eleventh Hour," and "The Punch Review," 274
    wrote for *The Times, The Mail on Sunday, Daily Mail,* and *Evening Standard*, 274
Cornhill Magazine, 338, 829
Corona, La (Donne), 321

Corsican Brothers, The
    actor Kean, 446
Costa, Richard Haur
    "Graham Greene," 479
Costello, Lou, xxxix, 387
"Cottar's Saturday Night" (Burns), 356
Cotten, Joseph, 482 n
    The Third Man (with Welles), 475
Cottle, Joseph, 258
Coucy, Sire de, 433 n
"Count Gismond" (Robert Browning), 161
"Counterweight," 276
Court Theatre, 512
Covent Garden Theatre (London), 175, 207, 379,
    446, 453, 579, 863
Covent-Garden Journal, The, 359, 360
Covent-Garden Tragedy, The (Fielding), 360
Coward, Sir Noel Pierce, 88, 482 n, 656, 657,
    660, 739
    acted in *Around the World in Eighty Days*,
        284, 285
    acted in *Hearts of the World, The Italian Job*,
        and *Bunny Lake*, 285
    acted in *Peter Pan* (Barrie), 88, 279
    acted in *The Scoundrel*, 285
    acted in *Meet Me Tonight, Our Man in
        Havana, Surprise Package, Paris When
        it Sizzles*, and *Boom*, 285
    biography, 278–80
    collaborated with Esme Wynne, 284
    hosted "Ninety Years On," 251
    literary analysis, 280–89
    wrote for *Tails Up!* 284
Cowardy Custard (Coward), 283
Cowasjee, Saros, 4
Cowper, William, 60, 150, 883, 885
Cox and Box (Sullivan), 447
Coxcomb, The (Beaumont and Fletcher), 93
Cozeners, The (Foote), 381
Crabbe, George, 150
Craik, Henry, 525
Craik, T.W.
    The Comic Tales of Chaucer, 231–32, 235
Crane, Stephen, 298
Crest-Jewel of Discrimination (Shankara), 559
Crick, Bernard, 811, 813, 815, 819, 820
Crick, Monte, 411
Cricket on the Hearth (Dickens), 308
Cricklewood Diet, The (Coren), 276, 277
Crime of the Century, The (Kingsley Amis, pseud.
    Robert Markham), 19
Crisp, Quentin, 283
    acted in *The Importance of Being Ernest*, 290
    biography, 289–90
    literary analysis, 290–92
"Cristina" (Robert Browning), 161
Criterion, 45, 610
Critical Quarterly, 153
Critical Writings, The (Joyce), 609
Critique of Judgment (Carlyle), 210
Croker, John Wilson, 176 n

Crome Yellow (Huxley), 553
Cromwell, Oliver, 500, 734, 880
Crossman, Richard, 45
Crowden, Graham, 31
Cruikshank, George, 533, 534
    pseudonym, Phiz, 748
Cruise of the "Nona," The (Belloc), 130
Cruiskeen Lawn (O'Nolan), 799, 801–02
"Cuisine de la Poste, La" (Bunbury), 165
Cukor, George, 482 n
Cumberland, Richard, 455
Cupid's Revenge (Beaumont), 93, 95
Curiosa Mathematica, Part 1 (Lewis Carroll), 214
Curiosa Mathematica, Part 2 (Lewis Carroll), 214
Curiosities of Literature (D'Israeli), 315–16, 317
Currie, James, 178
Curtain Theatre, 39, 96
Curtis, Jamie Lee, 256
Curtmantle (Fry), 410, 414
Cusak, Cyril, 482 n
Cushman, Robert, 80
Custom of the Country, The (Fletcher
    and Massinger), 372
Cuts: A Very Short Novel (Bradbury), 152, 155
Cyder (John Philips), 435, 746, 846
Cynthia's Revels (Jonson), 595, 597, 601
*Cyrano de Bergerac: A Heroic Comedy in Five
    Acts* (Rostand), 420

Dad's Tale (Ayckbourn), 67
"Daft Days, The" (Fergusson), 356
Dahl, Roald, 264
    adapted *You Only Live Twice* (Fleming) and
        Chitty Chitty Bang Bang (Fleming), 295
    biography, 293–94
    literary analysis, 294–96
Daily Chronicle, 114
Daily Express, 526
Daily-Mail, 114, 274
Daily News, 138
Daily Telegraph, 138, 147
Dali, Salvador, 216
Dalkey Archive, The, 799, 800–01
Damer Hall (Dublin), 119
Dance of Death, The (Auden), 45
Dancing at Lughnasa (Friel), 404, 405, 406
Dancing Faun, The (Fair), 301
Dane, Henry J., 206
Dane, Joseph, 230–31
Daniels, Stan, 27
D'Annunzio, Gabriele, 611
Danny: The Champion of the World (Dahl), 295
"Dante . . . Bruno . . . Vico . . . Joyce" (Beckett), 100
Dante Alighieri, 99, 100, 103, 110, 116, 195, 199,
    228, 230, 260, 542, 612
    Inferno, 612
"Danvers" (Hook), 541
D'Arcy, Ella
    biography, 296
    contributed to *Argosy* (London), 296,
        297, 298

contributed to *Century Magazine*, 296, 299
contributed to *Good Words* and *Blackwood's
        Edinburgh Magazine*, 296, 297
literary analysis, 296–302
stories in *Temple Bar* and *The English
        Review*, 296
sub-edited *The Yellow Book*, 296, 298, 299
Dark Is Light Enough, The (Fry), 414, 417, 418–19
Darkwater Hall Mystery, The (Kingsley Amis), 19
Darwin, Charles, 186, 187
Darwin, Erasmus, 187
Daughters of Queen Victoria (E.F. Benson),
        134, 136
Davenport, W.A., 431
David Copperfield (Dickens), 169, 308, 754
Davidge's Coburg Theatre, 579
Davie, Donald, 17, 516
Davies, Sir John, 93. 499, 500
d'Avigdor, W.P.H., 139
Davis, H.W.C.
        Dictionary of National Biography
                (with Weaver), 492
Day of the Dog, The (Frayn), 399
"Day of the Rabblement, The" (Joyce), 609
"Dead, The" (Joyce), 609, 612
Dead Babies (Martin Amis), 23, 24
Deal Boatman (Burnand), 169
Dear Brutus (Barrie), 85, 86, 88
"Dear Old Village, The" (Betjeman), 150
"Death and Doctor Hornbook" (Burns), 181
"Death Bed, The" (Hood), 537
Death Fish II (Cleese), 252
"Death Is a Kind of Love" (Fry), 415
Death of a Hero (Aldington), 387
Death of a Teddy Bear (Gray), 465
Death of Jesus Christ, The (William McGill), 180
"Death of the Lion, The" (Henry James), 299
Decision, 46
Declaration, 16
Decline and Fall of the Roman Empire (Edward
        Gibbon), 249
"DeCoverley Papers, The," 12
        See also Addison, Joseph; *Spectator*
"Dedication" (Byron), 195–96
Defense of Conny Catching, The (Greene), 303
"Defense of Cosmetics" (Beerbohm), 116
"Defense of Detective Stories, A" (Chesterton),
        246, 246 n
Defoe, Daniel, 305
        influence on Thomas Carlyle, 211
        Review, 11
"Deformed X.R." (John Hall), 501
Defy the Foul Fiend (John Collier), 263
Degnan, James P., 294
Deighton, Bell, and Company, 203
"De'il's awa wi' th' Exciseman, The" (Burns), 181
"Dejection: An Ode" (Coleridge), 257, 260
Dekker, Thomas, 302, 507, 304, 595, 731
Deloney, Thomas
        biography, 302–03
        literary analysis, 303–07

Delta Magazine, 465
Dennis, John, 317
Deor's Lament, 142
Derry down Derry. *See* Lear, Edward
Descartes, René, 100
Deschamps, Eustache, 229
"Description of an Author's Bedchamber, The"
        (Goldsmith), 455
Deserted Village, The (Goldsmith), 452–53, 455
Design for Living (Coward), 280, 283, 285
Desperate Remedies (Hardy), 515
"Destructors, The" (Graham Greene), 477
"Development" (Robert Browning), 158
"Devil, George and Rosie, The" (John Collier), 263
Devil is an Ass, The (Jonson), 597, 603
Devil Upon Two Sticks, The (Foote), 329, 381
Devine, George, 26
Devitis, A.A., 475
"Devonshire Roads" (Coleridge), 258
Devotions upon Emergent Occasions (Donne), 321
Dialstone Lane (Jacobs), 566–67
Diary of a Nobody, The (George and Walter
        Weedon Grossmith), 492–93, 830
Diary of a Pilgrimage, The (Jerome), 577
Diary of Virginia Woolf (Bell), 137 n
Diary Without Dates (Bagnold), 73, 74
Dickens, Charles, xxxvi, xl, xli, 82, 134, 136, 152,
        210, 211, 212, 291, 304, 305, 468, 498,
        567 n, 579, 581, 611, 631, 642, 646,
        651, 688, 715, 725, 726, 739, 748, 754,
        766, 809, 820, 839
        biography, 307–09
        contributed to *All the Year Round*, 309
        edited *Bentley's Miscellany*, 138
        edited *Household Words*, 308–09
        influence on Hood, 539
        influence on Hook, 542
        literary analysis, 309–15
        reported for *Morning Chronicle*, 308
        story in *The Times*, 308
Dickinson, Thorold, 26
Dickinson, William
        engraved "Richmond Hill" (Bunbury), 165
Dictionary (Samuel Johnson), xxxiii, 586,
        588–89, 591
"Dictionary of Biography" (E.C. Bentley), 139
Dictionary of Canadian Biography
        (ed. Halpenny), 496
Dictionary of Literary Biography, 348 n, 479
Dictionary of National Biography, The, 42, 134,
        136, 479, 492, 494 n, 542, 654
Dietrich, Marlene, 291
Difficulties With Girls (Kingsley Amis), 18
Dione (Gay), 434, 437
Dirk Gently's Holistic Detective Agency (Douglas
        Adams), 7, 8, 9
"Discourse Upon Comedy, A" (Farquhar),
        351, 352
"Discovery in Astronomy, A" (Hood), 537–38
*Discovery of a New World, The. See Mundus Alter
        et Idem* (Joseph Hall)

Disjecta (Beckett), 102
D'Israeli, Isaac
    biography, 315–16
    literary analysis, 316–19
    "Against Commerce which is the Corruption
        of Mankind," 315
Distressed Wife, The (Gay), 437, 438, 439
Diversions of the Morning, The (Foote), 379
Divine Comedy, The (Dante), 195, 612, 675
Dixon, Ella Hepworth, 296
Dmytryk, Edward, 482 n
Do Not Adjust Your Set (Palin and Jones), 253
Dobson, Dennis
    O Rare Hoffnung; A Memorial Garland
        (with Hoffnung), 525
"Doctor—" (Robert Browning), 159
Doctor Criminale (Bradbury), 152, 153, 154, 155
Doctor Fischer of Geneva, or the Bomb Party
    (Graham Greene), 477, 479, 480
"Doctor No will see You Now" (Coren), 277
Doctrine and Discipline of Divorce
    (Milton), 353
Dodgson, Charles. *See* Carroll, Lewis
Dodo (Benson), 133, 136
Dog Beneath the Skin, The (Auden), 45
Dog Beneath the Skin, The; or, Where Is Francis?
    (Isherwood), 559
Dog It Was That Died, The (Coren), 275
Doing It with Style (Crisp), 291
Dolly Dialogues, The (Hope), 543, 544–45
Don Juan (Byron), 192, 193, 194, 195, 196–200,
    450, 560
Don Quixote (Cervantes), xxxvi–xxxvii, 96, 361,
    373, 439
Don Quixote in England (Fielding), 360
Donbey and Son (Dickens), 308
Donkeys' Years (Frayn), 399, 400
Donne, John, xl, 93, 260, 466, 504, 507, 508, 523,
    705, 706
    biography, 319–21
    literary analysis, 321–29
"Don't Let's Be Beastly to the Germans"
    (Coward), 283
Don't Put Your Daughter on the Stage, Mrs.
    Worthington (Coward), 280
Don't Tell Alfred (Mitford), 776, 777, 778
Doody, Margaret, 174, 176 n
"Doors of Perception" (Huxley), 553
Dostoyevsky, Feodor, 121, 276, 674
Double Dealer, The (Congreve), 174, 265, 266,
    268–69, 270
Double Disguise, The (Madden), 540
Double Harness (Hope), 544
Double Man, The (Auden), 46
"Double Transformation: A Tale, The"
    (Goldsmith), 455
Doughty, Charles, 329
Douglas, Lord Alfred, 133, 286
Douglas, Norman, 4
    assistant editor, *English Review*, 330
    biography, 329–31

collaborated with Elizabeth Louisa
    Fitzgibbon, 330
collaborated with Guiseppe Orioli, 330
literary analysis, 331–33
pseudonym, Normyx, 330
pseudonym (with Orioli), Pilaff Bey, 329
Douglas, Sir James, 183
Down and Out in Paris and London (Orwell), 808,
    809, 813
Down There on a Visit (Isherwood), 560, 562
Downing, Jack. *See* Smith, Seba
Dowson, Ernest, 150
Doyle, [Sir] Arthur Conan, 86, 462, 574
    collaborated with James Matthew Barrie, 85
D'Oyly Carte Opera Company, 448
Dr. Who, 7
Draconian, The, 146
Dragon of Wantley, The (Carey), 206, 207, 208
Dragoness, A Burlesque Opera, The (Carey),
    207–08
Drama: The Quarterly Theatre Review, 32, 400
Dramatic Works of Wycherley, Congreve,
    Vanbrugh, and Farquhar (Hunt), 353
Dramatis Personae (Robert Browning), 158
Dramatists of Today (Trewin), 286
Draper, Muriel, 329
Drawcarisir, Sir Alexander. *See* Fielding, Henry
Drayton, Michael, 93, 303
"Dream Children: A Reverie" (Lamb), 87,
    636, 640
Dream Days (Grahame), 459, 461
Dream of Eugene Aram, the Murderer, The
    (Hood), 536, 537, 539
Dream of Fair to Middling Women
    (Beckett), 100
"Dregy of Dunbar Maid to King James the Fowrth
    being in Strivilling, The" (Dunbar), 342
Dreiser, Theodore, 284, 738
Driver, Tom F., 109, 111 n
Drummer, The (Addison), 10
Drums of Father Ned, The (O'Casey), 788,
    793, 795
Drury Lane Theatre (London), 191, 351, 352, 379,
    579, 580, 586, 833, 835, 863
Dryden, John, 11, 53, 94, 265, 266, 268, 269,
    365, 366, 373, 374, 455, 507, 587, 598,
    679, 682, 734, 845, 866, 875, 876, 879,
    881, 885
    biography, 333–34
    influence on George Gordon Byron, 192
    literary analysis, 334–37
Du Jardin, Edouard, 617 n
"Du Maurier and London Society" (James), 339
Du Maurier, Daphne, 338
Du Maurier, George, 653, 654
    biography, 337–38
    contributed to *Illustrated London News,*
        Once a Week, Cornhill Magazine,
        and *Century Magazine*, 338
    contributed to *Punch*, 338, 339, 340
    illustrator of *Punch*, 170, 171

literary analysis, 339–340
  satirized Whistler, 340
Du Maurier, Gerald, 338, 702
Dublin University Magazine, 498
Dubliners (Joyce), 609, 611, 612, 613
Duel of Angels (Fry), 414
Duffell, Peter, 482 n
Dugdale, Gilbert, 38
*Dulcimara, or the Little Duck and the Great
  Quack* (Gilbert), 447, 865
Dukore, Bernard F., 83 n
Dunbar, William, 179, 182
  biography, 340–41
  literary analysis, 341–44
Dunciad, The (Pope), 10, 192, 866, 868–70
Dunsany, Lord, 264
D'Urfey, Thomas, 437
Durrenmatt, Friedrich, 110
Duryea, Dan, 482 n
"Dusky Night Rides Down the Sky, The"
  (Fielding), 360
Dutch Courtezan, The (John Marston), 94,
  729, 731
Dutch Uncle (Gray), 465, 466
Dwarfs, The (Pinter), 848, 850
Dyce, Alexander, 372
Dyer's Hand, The (Auden), 46, 54 n
Dyer's Hand and Other Essays, The (Auden),
  47, 50
Dynasts, The (Hardy), 514, 516–17

"Ear, Believed Genuine Van Gogh, Hardly Used,
  What Offers?" (Coren) 276
Earl of Rochester. *See* Wilmot, John
"Earl Widgeon" (Bunbury), 167
Earle, John, 13, 94
"Early Electric" (Betjeman), 149
Easthope, Antony, 820
Eastward Ho (Jonson, Chapman, and Marston),
  223, 596
Eating People Is Wrong (Bradbury), 151, 152, 153
"Ecce Puer" (Joyce), 610
Ecclesiastes, 160, 507
Echo's Bones (Beckett), 101
"Eclogue, An" (Fergusson), 357
Eclogues (Virgil), 204, 435
Economist, The, 407 n, 408
Ed Sullivan Show, The, 252
Edgeworth, Maria, 60
Edinburgh Review, 834
Edinburgh University Press, 531
Edward 1 (Peele), 843
Edwards (Barry Pain), 830
Edwy and Elgiva (Frances "Fanny" Burney), 175
Egerton, George. *See* Bright, Mary Chavelita Dunne
Eggs 'n Gravy (Barnes), 83
"Ego darling Me" (Isherwood), 559
Egoist (Pound), 609
Egoist, The (Meredith), 298, 755, 756
Eh? (Livings), 685, 686–688
8 a.m. News. *See 8 Orai ujsag*

Einstein's Monsters (Martin Amis), 22, 25
Elder Brother, The (Fletcher and Massinger),
  376–77
Elderton, William, 303
"Election, The" (Fergusson), 357
"'Elegie,' The" (D'Arcy), 297–98
"Elegy on the Death of a Mad Dog, An" (Gold-
  smith), 454
"Elegy on the Death of Mr. David Gregory"
  (Fergusson), 356
"Elegy on the Glory of her Sex, Mrs. Mary Blaize,
  An" (Goldsmith) 454
"Elegy 6: The Perfume" (Donne), 325, 326
Elegy Written in a Country Churchyard (Gray),
  588, 590, 591, 794
"Elephant and the Bookseller, The" (Gay), 436
Elephant's Work (Bentley), 139
Eleutheria (Beckett), 102
Elia. *See* Lamb, Charles
Elinor and Marianne (Austen), 60, 61
Eliot, George, 212, 308, 891
  influenced by Fielding, 362
Eliot, T.S., 45, 47, 51, 54, 146, 147, 150, 337, 409,
  412, 414, 416, 417, 419, 466, 516, 523,
  553, 611, 662, 671, 722, 758, 811, 880
Eliza (Barry Pain), 830–31
Eliza Getting On (Barry Pain), 830
Elizabeth I, Queen, 39
Eliza's Husband (Barry Pain), 830
Eliza's Son (Barry Pain), 830
"Ella D'Arcy: A Commentary with a Primary
  and Annotated Secondary Bibliography"
  (Fisher), 299 n
"Ella D'Arcy Reminisces" (Fisher), 299, 301 n
Elliot, Denholm, 399, 482 n
Ellis, Vivien
  collaborated with Herbert, 522
Elliston's Surrey Theatre, 579
Ellman, Richard, 614
"Elusive Birds and Narrative Nets: The Appeal
  of Story in C.S. Lewis' Chronicles
  of Narnia" (Schakel), 667 n
*Emblems with Elegant Figures: Sparkles of Divine
  Love, The* (John Hall), 500
Emerson, Ralph Waldo, 182, 210
  influenced by Coleridge, 258
Emilia in England (George Meredith), 754
Emilia Wyndham (Marsh-Caldwell), 582
Emma (Austen), 60, 64 n
Emmanuel Burden (Belloc, ill. Chesterton), 130
Empedocles on Etna (Arnold), 158
En Attendant Godot (Beckett). *See Waiting
  for Godot*
Enchanted April (von Arnim), 82
Enchanted Flood, The (Auden), 46
Enchanted Places, The (Christopher Milne), 771
Encore (Maugham), 26, 29–30, 739
Encounter, 476, 482 n, 630
Encounter Pamphlet, 819
Encyclopedia Britannica, xxxiii, xxxiv, 277, 685
Encyclopedia of British Humorists (Gale), 416

End of the Affair, The (Graham Greene), 479
Endgame (Beckett), 102, 105, 108–09, 387
Ending Up (Kingsley Amis), 18
Eneados (Norman Douglas), 182
Engaged (Gilbert), 447
"Engagement, An" (D'Arcy), 300
Engel, Elliot, 541
England, Your England and Other Essays (Orwell),
    811–12, 821
"English Aristocracy, The" (Mitford), 776, 778
"English Bards and Scotch Reviewers" (Byron),
    191, 192, 193, 195
English Cities and Small Towns (Betjeman), 147
English Comic Drama (Bateson), 208, 209
English Girl, An (Ford Madox Ford), 384
English Humor (Priestley), xxxiii, 492
English Illustrated, 73
English in America, The (Haliburton), 496
English Literature in the Sixteenth Century Excluding
    Drama (C.S. Lewis), 505, 506, 663, 665
English Literature in Transition, 117 n, 299 n
"English 'Maupassant School' of the 1890's: Some
    Reservations, The" (George Worth),
    297, 301 n
"English Men of Letters" (Chesterton), 244
English Opera House, 579
English Parnassus, The (Allot), 223
English Prose Selections (Craik), 505
English Review, The, 296, 330, 383, 671, 890
English Romantic Writers (Perkins), 260 n
English Stage Company, 26
Englishman in Paris, The (Foote), 380
"Enoch Soames" (Beerbohm), 117
Enola Gay, 25
Enquiry into the Present State of Polite Learning
    in Europe, An (Goldsmith), 452
Ensemble Company, 414
"Entertaining Intellect, The" (Nightingale), 398,
    399, 400
Entertaining Mr. Sloane (Orton), 803–04, 805
"Entertainments" (Greene), 19
"Enthusiast, The" (Warton), 13
Epicoene, or the Silent Woman (Jonson), 93, 597,
    599, 601, 602
"Epigram on the Court Pucell" (Jonson), 605
Epigrammes (Jonson), 597, 598, 604–05
"Epistle" (Jonson), 605
"Epistle of Karshish the Arabian Physician, The"
    (Robert Browning) 162
"Epistle to a Friend, An" (Jonson), 605
"Epistle to a Godson" (Auden), 50
Epistle to a Godson and Other Poems (Auden),
    48, 50
"Epistle to Dr. Arbuthnot" (Pope), 10, 13
"Epistle to Elizabeth, Countess of Rutland"
    (Jonson), 595
Epistles in Six Decades (Joseph Hall), 504, 505
Erasmus, xxxvii, 506, 508, 587, 551
Erewhon (Butler), 577
Erewhon, or Over the Range (Butler), 186–87,
    188, 189

Erewhon Revisited Twenty Years Later (Butler),
    186, 188, 189
Ernest Pontifex, or The Way of All Flesh (Butler),
    185, 186, 188 189, 740
Erpingham Camp, The (Orton), 803, 805
"Espousal, The (Gay), 436
Esquire, 262
Essay for the Abridging of the Study of Physick,
    An (Armstrong), 43
Essay on Comedy, An (Meredith), 754–56
Essay on Criticism, An (Pope), 366, 866
Essay on Laughter and Ludicrous Composition
    (Beattie), xxxv, 210, 250
Essay on Man. Epistle 1, An (Pope), 589, 866
Essay on the Literary Character, An (D'Israeli),
    316, 317
"Essay on the Theatre; or, a Comparison between
    Laughing and Sentimental Comedy,
    The" (Goldsmith), xxxv–xxxvi, 455
Essays (Goldsmith), 452
Essays, Articles and Reviews of Evelyn Waugh
    (Waugh, ed. Gallagher), 492
Essays by Divers Hands (Irvine), 280
Essays in Divinity (Donne), 321
Essays of Elia (Lamb), 575
"Essence of Parliament: The Diary of Toby M.P."
    (Lucy), 171
Essential Wyndham Lewis: An Introduction
    to His Works (Lewis, ed. Symons),
    676, 677, 679
E.T. (Spielberg), 88
Etherege, Sir George, xxxviii, 265, 352, 875
Etruscan Places (Lawrence), 153
Euclid and His Modern Rivals (Carroll), 214
Eulenspiegel. *See* Howleglas
"Eunuch, An" (John Hall), 501
Euphuese (Lyly), 486
Euripides, 162
Europe and the Faith (Belloc), 130
Evan Harrington (George Meredith), 754–55
Evangeline, A Tale of Acadie (Longfellow), 496
Evans (publisher), 171
Evans, Dame Edith, 75, 354, 414, 417
Evelina, or, A Young Lady's Entrance into the
    World (Frances "Fanny" Burney),
    173–74, 176
Evening News (London), 526
Evening Standard, 75, 102, 147, 274, 441,
    685, 848
Evening with Quentin Crisp, An (Crisp), 290
Every-Day Book, The (Hone), 532, 534
Every Day Except Christmas (Anderson), 26
Every Man in His Humour (Jonson), xxxiii, 595,
    601, 622, 748
Every Man Out of His Humour (Jonson),
    595, 601
Evidence for the Resurrection of Jesus Christ
    (Samuel Butler), 186
Evolution, Old and New (Butler), 187
Ewart, Gavin
    biography, 345

introduction to *The Complete Clerihews* (Edmund Clerihew Bentley), 140
literary analysis, 345–49
Ex Voto (Butler), 187
Examiner, The, 11, 187, 748, 834, 878
"Execration" (Jonson), 598
"Execration Upon Vulcan" (Jonson), 605
Except the Lord (Cary), 221
Exeter Book, xxxvii, 143
Exiles (Joyce), 609, 849
Exit Eliza (Barry Pain), 830
Expedition of Humphrey Clinker, The (Smollett), 497
"Experience of Critics, An" (Fry), 414, 417
"Experiment" (Coward), 283
"Experiments" (Kingsley Amis), 19
Explorer, The (Maugham), 739
Eyton, Frank, 411

Faber & Faber, 45, 46, 811
Faber Popular Reciter (Kingsley Amis), 19
Fables (Gay), 434, 436, 439
Fables, Ancient and Modern (Dryden), 334
Factory Girl, The (Jerrold), 580
Fair Haven, The (Butler), 186
Faith Healer (Friel), 406
Faithful Shepherd, The (Fletcher), 93
Faithful Shepherdess, The (Fletcher), 372, 374
"Faithless Nelly Gray" (Hood), 536, 539
"Faithless Sally Brown" (Hood), 536, 539
"Fall of the Mogul" (Maurice), 745
Fallen Angels (Coward), 279
Fallen Idol, A (Anstey), 36
False Alarm, The (Wilkes), 590
Families and How to Survive Them (Cleese and Skynner), 252
"Fan, The" (Gay), 434, 435, 436
Fanny and the Servant Problem (Jerome), 577
Fanny Burney (Simons), 176 n
Far from the Madding Crowd (Hardy), 514–15
Faraday, Michael, 214
"Farmer's Ingle, The" (Fergusson), 356
Farquhar, George, xxxviii, 376, 455, 456
biography, 351
literary analysis, 351–55
Farr, Florence, 301
"Fashion and Her Bicycle" (Beerbohm), 116
Fasternis Evin in Hell (Dunbar), 342
"Fat Contributor" (Thackeray), 170
Father Brown Omnibus, The (Chesterton), 245–46
Father Stafford (Hope), 543
Fathers and Sons (Turgenev), 406
Faulkner, William, 284, 611
Faust (Goethe), 169, 182
Faustus Kelly (O'Nolan), 799
Fawlty Towers (Booth and Cleese), xxxix, 252, 255, 256
Fawn, The (Marston), 729, 731
Feldman, Marty, 252, 253
Felltham, Owen, 735, 737 n
Female Tatler, 11

femmes savantes, Les (Molière), 174
Fenelon, François, 199
Fergusson, Robert, 179, 180, 182, 351
biography, 355–56
literary analysis, 356–58
Ferishtah's Fancies (Robert Browning), 158
Ferrer, Jose, 415
Festival Theatre, 415
Few Crusted Characters, A (Hardy), 514
Few Late Chrysanthemums, A (Betjeman), 147, 149, 150
"Few Remarkable Adventures of Sir Simon Brodie, A" (Hogg), 531
Feydeau, Georges, 465–66
"Field Day in London: Through Irish Eyes" (Maxwell), 407 n
Field Day Theatre Company, 404, 405, 407
Field, Lila, 279
Field, Nathan, 93, 372
Fielding, Henry, xxxvi, xxxviii, xl, 11, 16, 60, 61, 152, 176, 198, 199, 205, 305, 377 381, 454, 611, 846
biography, 358–59
edited *The Champion*, 359, 360
edited *The Covent-Garden Journal*, 359, 360
influence on Firbank, 371
influence on John Collier, 264, 304
influence on Scott, Thackeray, and Eliot, 362
literary analysis, 359–65
parodied Richardson, 359
pseudonym, Scriblerus Secundus, 362
pseudonym, Sir Alexander Drawcansir, 360
satirized Walpole, 361
wrote for *The True Patriot* and *The Jacobite's Journal*, 359, 360
Fifine at the Fair (Robert Browning), 163
Fifteen Years of a Drunkard's Life (Jerrold), 580
Fifth Queen, The (Ford Madox Ford), 383
Fifth Queen Crowned, The (Ford Madox Ford), 384
Fifth Queen, Privy Seal, The (Ford Madox Ford), 384
Fifty Bab Ballads (Gilbert), 447
Fifty Caricatures (Beerbohm), 115
Fifty Years of Peter Pan (Roger Green), 88
Figaro in London (Mayhew), 747, 748
Figaro, Le, 475
Figures in Modern Literature (Priestley), 567 n
File on Ayckbourn (Page), 68, 70
Fillinger, Johan, 415
Film (Beckett, Ionesco, and Pinter), 101
Fin, La (Beckett), 101
Fin de Partie (Beckett). See *Endgame*
Final Edition (Benson), 133, 136
Finch, Anne
biography 365–66
literary analysis, 366–69
Finch, Peter, 482 n
"Finding of the Princess, The" (Grahame), 459
Finkelpearl, Philip, 730
Finnegan's Wake (Joyce), 100, 216, 610, 611, 615–16

Firbank, Ronald
    biography, 369–70
    influence on Ivy Compton-Burnett, 371
    influenced by Sterne and Fielding, 371
    literary analysis, 370–71
Firesign Theater, 766, 767
First and Last (Frayn), 399
First and Second Anniversaries (Donne), 504
First Clerihews, The (Bentley, Oldershaw,
    d'Avigdor, ill. Chesterton), 139
First Folio (Shakespeare), 39
First Impressions (Austen), 60
"First Principles" (Spencer), 514
First Year in Canterbury Settlement, A (Butler), 186
Firstborn, The (Fry), 409, 412
Fish Called Wanda, A (Cleese), xl, 253, 255–56
Fisher, Benjamin F., IV, 301 n
Fisher, John, 229
Fisher, Leona Weaver, 655 n
Fisher Unwin, 243
Fisherman's Progress (Bashford), 90
"Fit of Rhyme Against Rhyme, A" (Jonson), 605
Fitzgeffrey, Charles, 782
Flammulae Amoris S.P. Augustini (Hoyer), 500
Flatte, Bob, 442
Flaubert, Gustave
    influence on Ford Maddox Ford, 383–84, 385
Flayed, The (Flatte), 442
"Flea, The" (Donne), 323–24
"Fleckno, an English Priest at Rome" (Marvell),
    734–35
Fleming, Ian, 295
Fleming, Peter, 4
Fletcher, Giles, 372
Fletcher, John, 93, 97, 758
    biography, 371–73
    literary analysis, 373–78
    collaborated with Field and Rowley, 372
    collaborated with Francis Beaumont, 93–97
    collaborated with Massinger, 372
    collaborated with Shakespeare, 372, 374
    influence on Shirley, 377
    influenced by Aristophanes, 372, 374
    influenced by Shakespeare, 375
Fletcher, Phineas, 372
"Flight of the Duchess, The" (Robert Browning), 161
*Flim-Flams! Or the Life and Errors of My Uncle
    and the Amours of My Aunt* (D'Israeli),
    316, 317–18
Flower Beneath the Foot, The (Firbank), 370, 371
Fly Leaves (Calverley), 205
Foggerty's Fairy and Other Tales (Gilbert), 448
Folks Who Live on the Hill, The (Kingsley
    Amis), 18
Fontaine, Jean de la, 436
"Fool as Hero: Simon Gray's *Butley and Otherwise
    Engaged, The*" (Burkman), 471
Foole upon Foole (Armin), 38, 39–40
Foote, Samuel
    biography, 378–79
    literary analysis, 379–82

Footfalls (Beckett), 99, 109
For Services Rendered (Maugham), 739
For the Honour of Wales (Jonson), 604
"For the Time Being" (Auden), 46
Forbidden Laughter (Draitser), 822
Ford, Ford Madox, 330, 331, 370, 611
    biography, 382–83
    literary analysis, 383–89
    pseudonym, Fenil Haig, 383
Ford Foundation, 47
Ford, John, 28
Ford Madox Ford (Hoffman), 384–85, 386
Ford Madox Ford (Stang), 385
Ford Madox Ford and the Voice of Uncertainty
    (Snitow), 385, 386–87
Ford, Paul, 482 n
Forester, C.S., 293
Forewords and Afterwords (Auden), 47
"Forgiveness, A" (Robert Browning), 162
Forrest, The (Jonson), 545, 604–05
Forster, E[dward] M[organ], 3, 4, 6, 37, 152,
    389–91, 391–98, 459, 559, 811
    biography, 389–91
    influenced by Samuel Butler, 188
    literary analysis, 391–98
Forster, John, 232, 234, 235, 237
Fortnightly Review, 309–10, 609
Fortress, The (Hook), 541
Forum for Modern Language Studies, 432
Foster, Edward, 232, 234, 235, 237
"Four Ages of Poetry, The" (Peacock), 833,
    837–38
Four Letters (Nashe), 781–83
Four Letters Confuted (Nashe), 38
Four Men: A Farrago, The (Belloc), 130, 131
Four Month Elegy (Fry), 412
"Four Quartets" (Eliot), 471
"Fragment of Greek Tragedy" (Housman), 547
Frances Burney: The Life in the Works (Doody), 176 n
Frank Hauser's Oxford Theatre, 67
Frankenstein (Mary Shelley), 31
Franklin's Tale (Chaucer), 230, 235, 236
Franz, Arthur, 482 n
Fraser, Lovat, 73
Fraser's Magazine, 210, 211, 834
Fraternity of Vagabonds (Awdley), 551
Frayn, Michael
    biography, 398–99
    influenced by Russell and Wittgenstein, 399
    literary analysis, 399–404
Free Holder, The (Addison), 10
Free Inquiry into the Nature and Origin of Evil, A
    (Jenyn), 589
Freedom of the City, The (Friel), 404
French Revolution (Carlyle), 210
Frere, John Hookham, 194, 196
Freud, Sigmund, xxxvi, 54, 155
Friar Bacon and Friar Bungay (Robert Greene),
    488–89
Friar's Tale (Chaucer), 230, 232
"Friday" (Gay), 435–36

Friedman, Arthur
    edited *Collected Works of Oliver Goldsmith*, 453, 454
Friedman, Richard, 820
Friel, Brian
    biography, 404
    literary analysis, 404–07
Friend, The (Coleridge), 257
Friendship's Offering (Coleridge), 259
Frightful Hair; or Who Shot the Dog? The (Burnand), 169–70
Frohman, Charles, 85
Froissart, Jean, 230
"From Ballybeg to Broadway" (Gussow), 407 n
From Sleep and Shadow (Barnes), 79
From Studio to Stage (Walter Weedon Grossmith), 492
"Frost at Midnight" (Coleridge), 257
Frost, David, 252
Frost in the Flower, The (O'Casey), 787
Frost Report, The (Frost), 252
Froude, James Anthony, 210
Fry, Christopher, 419–28
    biography, 409–16
    literary analysis, 416–19
Fry, Roger, 829
Frye, Northrop, 419
Frye, Roger, 389
Fun, xxxviii, 169, 446–47, 449, 451
Funeral Games (Orton), 803, 805–06
"Funeral, The" (Gay), 436
Funeral, The (Steele), 352
"Fungi on Toast" (Hoffnung), 526
Furnivall, F., 458
Furniss, Harry, 171
Further Bulletins of Idi Amin (Coren), 275
Fuseli, Henri, 42
Fyler, John, 230
Fyvel, T.R., 820

Gable, Clark, 441
Gagg to Love's Advocate, A; or, an Assertion of the Justice of the Parliament in the Execution of Mr. Love (John Hall), 500
"Gags for God—it's not funny" (Roy Porter), 81
Gaiety Theatre, 447
Gale Research Company, 204
Gallagher, Donat, 492, 494
Galsworthy, John, 383
Galt, John, 357
Game at Cheese, A (Middleton), 758
Game of Logic, The (Carroll), 214
Games Authors Play (Peter Hutchinson), 471 n
Gammer Gurton's Needle, 542
Gannet, Lewis, 75
"Garden Fancies" (Robert Browning), 158
Garden, The (Bagnold), 74, 75
Gardner, Thomas, 145
Gargantua and Pantagruel (Rabelais), 551
Garland, Judy, 281, 282
Garland of Good Will, The (Deloney), 302
Garland, Patrick, 280

Garrick Club, 763
Garrick, David, 165, 173, 354, 379, 381, 445, 586, 591
Garrick Theatre, 448
Garth, Sir Samuel, 845, 869
Gascoigne, George, 505, 782
Gaskell, Elizabeth, 338
Gathorne-Hardy, Jonathan, 28
Gaudier-Brzeska, Henri, 73
Gauguin, Paul, 739
Gaumont-British films, 559
Gavin Ewart: Selected Poems, 1933–1988 (Ewart), 345
Gavin Ewart Show: Selected Poems, 1939–1985, The (Ewart), 345
Gawain/Pearl Poet, 429, 430–34
Gawain-Poet, The (Savage), 433 n
Gay, John, xxxvi, 42, 70, 174, 207, 268, 354, 368, 845, 879
    biography, 434
    literary analysis, 434–40
Gay, Peter, 13
Gay's Trivia: or, The Art of Walking the Streets of London (Gay), 436
Gem, The, 535
Gemini (John Collier), 262
General Description of Nova Scotia, A (Haliburton), 496
"General John" (Gilbert), 450
Genesis, 199
Genet, Jean, 77, 81, 121, 124
Genius of the Thames, The (Peacock), 833
"Genius, Talent, and Failure: The Brontës" (Fry), 416
Gentle Craft, The (Deloney), 304
Gentleman in the Parlour, The (Maugham), 742
Gentleman Usher, The (Chapman), 223
Gentleman's Magazine, 588
"Geoffrey Gambado, Esquire" (Bunbury), 166
"George Du Maurier: English and American Criticism on His Life and Works," 339
George Du Maurier (Kelly), 339
George, Lloyd, 518
George Orwell: An Annotated Bibliography of Criticism (Jeffrey Meyers and Valerie Meyers), 821
George Orwell (L.H. Meyers), 821
Georgics (Virgil, trans. Dryden), 11, 435–36, 846
"Get Out and Push!" (Anderson), 26
"Get There if You Can" (Auden), 49
Geulincx, Arnold, 100
Ghastly Good Taste: A Depressing Story of the Rise and Fall of English Architecture (Betjeman), 147
Gibbon, Edward, 210, 248, 249, 586
Gibbons, Stella Dorothea, 440–45
Gielgud, John, 412, 413, 850
Gilbert: A Century of Scholarship and Commentary (Pearson), 446
Gilbert Gurney (Hook), 541
Gilbert, John, 170, 654, 865
Gilbert, Sandra M., 368 n

Gilbert, Stuart, 610
Gilbert, Sir William Schwenk, 169, 204, 253, 283, 346, 445–47, 448–52, 492, 512, 547, 863
Gildon, Charles, 265
Gilliam, Terry, 252, 254, 256
Gingold, Hermione, 67
Giraudoux, Jean, 414–16
Girl, 20 (Kingsley Amis), 18
Girl Who Came to Dinner, The (Coward), 284
Girl's Journey (Bagnold), 76
Gish, Lillian, 482 n
Gissing, George, 756
Gittings, Robert, 411
Giveaway, The (Jellicoe), 571, 572
G.K.'s Weekly, 244
Glaspell, Susan, 290
Glenville, Peter, 482 n
Gleyre, Charles, 338
Globe Theatre, 39, 93, 412–13, 595, 622, 623, 834
Glory! Glory! (Anderson), 32
"Glove, The" (Robert Browning), 159
God in the Car, The (Hope), 543
"God the Known and God the Unknown" (Butler), 187
"God Save the King" (Carey), 206
"God Save the Queen," 206
God's Chillun (Auden), 46
Godwin, William, 635, 636, 638, 640, 835
Goethe, Johann Wolfgang von, 60, 116, 169, 182, 210, 211, 212, 454, 756
Gogol, Nikolai, 611
"Going Back to School" (Beerbohm), 116
"Going Out for a Walk" (Beerbohm), 116
"Going Out in New York" (Crisp), 291
Going Solo (Dahl), 295
"Gold Hair" (Robert Browning), 159–60
Gold in the Sea, The (Friel), 404
Gold, Jack, 482 n
Golden Age, The (Grahame), 459–61
Golden Age of Science Fiction, The (Kingsley Amis), 19
Goldyn Targe, The (Dunbar), 341
Goldsmith, Oliver, xxxv–xxxvi, xxxviii, xl, 11, 37, 60, 134, 165, 354, 586–87, 883
    biography, 452–53
    contributed to *British Magazine*, 453
    contributed to *Public Ledger*, 452
    contributed to *The Bee*, 452–54
    contributed to *Westminster Magazine*, 455
    influenced by Boileau-Despreaux, 455
    influenced by Farquhar, 456
    influenced by Montesquieu, Lyttleton, and D'Argens, 453
    literary analysis, 453–56
    pseudonym, Lien Chi Altangi, 453–54
Goldsmith: The Critical Heritage (G.S. Rousseau), 454, 456 n
Goldwyn, Samuel, 559
Golfing for Cats (Coren), 276
Gollancz, Victor, 809
Gondoliers (Gilbert and Sullivan), 448

Good and Faithful Servant, The (Orton), 803–05
"Good Man of Alloa, The" (Hogg), 531
"Good Morrow, The" (Donne), 326
Good Natur'd Man, The (Goldsmith), 452–53, 455–56
Good Soldier, The (Ford Madox Ford), 331, 383–86, 388
Good Words, 296–97
Goodbye to Berlin (Isherwood), 558–59, 561–62
Goodbye to the Mezzogiorno (Auden), 51–52
Goodman Theatre, The (Chicago), 81
Goon Show, The (Milligan), xxxviii, 253, 766–67
Goons, 767
Gopaleen, Myles na. *See* O'Nolan, Brian
Gordon, Neil. *See* Archibald Macdonell
Gorer, Geoffrey, 16
Gorki, Maxim, 133, 660
Gorman, Herbert, 610
Gosse, Edmund, 36, 115
"Gossips' Corner" (Jerome), 573
"Goute and the Spider, The" (Finch), 367
Gower, John, 229, 341
Gowling, W. Aylmer, 573
"Grace" (Joyce), 612
Graeme and Cyril (Barry Pain), 830
"Graham Greene" (Costa), 479, 484
Graham Greene (De Vitis), 475, 484
Graham Greene (Pryce-Jones), 479, 485
Graham Greene (Spurling), 477, 485
Graham Greene: The Aesthetics of Exploration (Boardman), 484
Graham Greene the Entertainer (Wolfe), 478, 485
Grahame, Kenneth, 771
    biography, 458–59
    contributed to *National Observer*, 459, 460
    contributed to *St. James's Gazette*, 459
    literary analysis, 459–64
Grammar Lecture (Beaumont), 93
"Grammarian's Funeral, A" (Robert Browning), 161
"Grand Oul' Dame Britannia, The" (O'Casey), 788
Grant, Robert, 220
Granta, 770, 829
Granville-Barker, Harley, 512
Graves, Robert
    influence on Kingsley Amis, 18
    influenced by Samuel Butler, 188
Gray, Simon, 152
    biography, 465
    edited *Delta Magazine*, 465
    literary analysis, 465–73
Gray, Thomas, 588, 590–91, 794
"Great Automatic Grammatisor, The" (Dahl), 294
Great Divorce, The (C.S. Lewis), 664–66
Great Expectations (Dickens), 308
"Great Mogul's Company of English Comedians, The" (Fielding), 359
Great Muppet Caper, The, 252
Greater London Council, 77
"Greedy Night" (Bentley), 139
Green Carnation, The (Hitchens), 299
Green Cow, The (O'Casey), 793–94

"Green Grow the Rashes, O" (Robert Burns), 182
Green, Gwendolyn, 481 n
Green Man, The (Kingsley Amis), 19
Green, Peter, 459, 464 n
Green, Roger, 88
Greenblatt, Stephen Jay, 825
Greene, Ellen, 32
Greene, Graham, 19, 121, 329, 330, 693, 695
    biography, 474–77
       contributed to *Oxford Chronicle*, 474
       contributed to *Weekly Westminster*, 474
       literary analysis, 477–85
Greene, Marion, 481 n
Greene, Robert, 303, 305, 485–86, 487–90,
    781–83
Greenless, Ian, 330
Gregory, Lady, 788
Grey, J. David, 64
Grey, Thomas, 60
Greybeards at Play (Chesterton), 243
Grieninger, Johannes, 550
Grierson, John, 45–46
Grierson, Sir Herbert, 523
Grigson, Geoffrey, 346, 412
"Grim, King of the Ghosts" (Bunbury), 167
"Grimsby Ghost, The" (Hood), 539
Groatsworth of Wit Bought with a Million of
    Repentance (Robert Greene), 486, 490
Groddeck, Georg, 54
Grose, Captain Francis, 166
Grossmith, George, 91, 491–94, 830
    acted in *Patience and Iolanthe*, 492
    acted in *The Sorcerer*, 491
    biography, 491–92
    literary analysis, 492–94
Grossmith, Walter Weedon, 91, 491–94, 830
    biography, 491–92
       contributed to *Punch*, 492
    literary analysis, 492–94
Group of Noble Dames, A (Hardy), 516
Group Theatre, 45
Grumbler, The (Goldsmith), 453
Gryll Grange, 834, 839–40
Grylls, David, 36
Guardian, 399
Guardians and Angels (Grylls), 36
Gubar, Susan, 368 n
Guerre de Troie n'aura pas lieu, La
    (Giraudoux), 414
Guilpin, Edward, 503–04, 622
Guinness, Alec, 222, 466, 482 n
Guinness, Gerald, 471 n
Gulliver's Travels (Swift), 14, 362, 665,
    815, 820
Gun for Sale (Graham Greene), 474–75
Gunn, Thom, 17
Gurney Married (Hook), 541
Gussow, Mel, 404, 406, 407 n
Guthrie Theatre (Minneapolis), 404
Guthrie, Thomas Anstey. *See* Anstey, F.
Guthrie, Tyrone, 404

Gypsies Metamorphosed, The (Jonson), 598, 604

Hackney, Alan. *See I'm All Right, Jack*
Hadas, Moses, 204
Hagerty, Julie, 399
Hagmann, Stuart, 28
Haig, Fenil. *See* Ford, Ford Madox
Half Moon, The (Ford Madox Ford), 384
Haliburton, Thomas Chandler
    biography, 495–96
       contributed to *Dublin University*
        Magazine, 498
       contributed to *Nova Scotian, or Colonial*
        Herald, 496
       influenced by Seba Smith, 497
       influenced by Smollett, 497
    literary analysis, 496–99
Halifax, Lord, 44
Hall, Adrian, 81
Hall, John
    biography, 499–500
       edited *In aliquot Sacrae Paginae loca*
        Lectiones (Hegge), 499
       influence on Samuel Butler, 501–02
    literary analysis, 500–02
       pseudonym J. de la Salle, 500
       pseudonym J.H., 499
       pseudonym N.LL., 499, 500
       translated Andreae, 499
       translated Longinus, 500–01
       translated Procopius and Maierus, 500
Hall, Joseph
    biography, 503–05
    literary analysis, 505–11
Hall, Kay, 249
Hall, Sir Peter, 78, 848, 849
Halliwell, Leslie, 285
"Hallow-Fair" (Fergusson), 180, 356
Halprin, John, 64 n
Hamilton, Clive, *See* Lewis, C.S.
Hamilton, Marie Padgett, 433 n
Hamlet (Shakespeare), 31–32, 95,
    451, 490, 864
"Hamlet's Aunt," 477
Hammond, Emma Louise Lowe Fry, 409
Hand of Ethelberta, The (Hardy), 515
Hand Witch of the Second Stage, A (Barnes),
    79–80
Handel, George Frideric, 262, 434
Handful of Authors, A (G.K. Chesterton), 567 n
Handful of Dust, A (Evelyn Waugh), 519
Hands, Terry, 83 n
"Hanging, A" (Orwell), 808–09, 821
Hanging and Marriage (Carey), 208
Hankin, St. John
    biography, 511–12
       contributed to *Punch*, 511–13
       contributed to *The Times*, 511–12
    literary analysis, 512–13
       parodied Pinero, 512
       parodied Shakespeare, 512

parodied Taylor and Robertson, *The Last of the DeMullins*, 513
parodied Wordsworth, Byron, Shelley, Burns, Tennyson, Browning, Rossetti, Swinburne, and Arnold, 513
Hans Carvel (Prior), 881, 882, 883
Happiest Man in England, The (Hood), 539
Happy Days (Beckett), 109
Happy Foreigner, The (Bagnold), 74
Happy Hypocrite (Beerbohm), 115, 117
"Happy Thoughts" (Burnand), 170, 171
Hard Life, The (O'Nolan), 799–800
Hard Measure (Joseph Hall), 504
Hard Times, (Dickens), 82, 83 n, 212, 308
Harding, Peter. *See* Bashford, Sir Henry Howarth
Hardy, Oliver, xxxix, 105
Hardy, Thomas, 147, 301, 308, 338, 347, 756
  biography, 513–14
  influenced by Spencer and Swinburne, 514
  literary analysis, 514–18
"Hare and many Friends, The" (Gay), 436
Hare, David, 77
"Hark, the Voice of Jesus Crying" (Housman), 547
Harland, Henry, 114, 115, 296, 299
Harper's Weekly Magazine, 35, 153, 340
Harris, Frank, 73
Harris, John, 165, 645
"Harrison Bergeron" (Vonnegut), 577
Harrison, Rex, 283
Harte, Bret, 829
Harvest Festival, The (O'Casey), 787
Harvey, Frank. *See I'm All Right, Jack*
Harvey, Gabriel, xxxiv, 303, 486, 781, 783, 784, 843
Harvey, Laurence, 77
Harvey, Richard, 781, 784
Hasan, Noorul, 514
Haste to the Wedding (Gilbert and Grossmith), 492
Haunch of Venison, The (Goldsmith), 455
Hauptmann, Gerhard, 611
Have with You to Saffron-walden. Or, Gabriell Harveys Hunt Is Up (Nashe), 782, 784
Havel, Vaclav
  influenced by Samuel Beckett, 110
Hawking, Stephen, 7
Hawkins, Jack, 412, 482 n
Hawkins, Sir John, 591
Hay Fever (Coward), 279, 283, 285
Haycraft, Howard, 209 n, 681
Haydn, Joseph, 178
Haymarket Theatre, 379, 381, 447
Hayworth, Rita, 740
Hazlitt, William, xxxv, xxxvii, xxxviii, 195, 250, 258, 454, 635, 637, 640
  contributed to *Examiner*, 11
  contributed to *London Magazine*, 536
  contributed to *Morning Chronicle*, 11
  influenced by Coleridge, 258
Head to Toe (Orton), 803
Headlong Hall (Peacock), 833, 835–36
Heard, Christopher, 740

Heard, Gerald, 553–54, 559
Heart of Darkness, The (Conrad), 383
Heart of Princess, The (Hope), 543
Heart of the Matter, The (Graham Greene), 475, 479
Hearth and Home, 73
Hearts of the World, 285
Heaven's Blessing (Barnes), 82
Hecht, Anthony, 141
Hedge and the Horse, The (Belloc, ed. Chesterton), 130
Hegge, Robert, 499
Height of Eloquence, The (John Hall), 500–01
Heine, Heinrich, 280, 756
Heinemann, 474
Hemans, Felicia Dorthea, 204
Hemingway, Ernest, 249, 276, 725
Henceforward (Ayckbourn), 71
Henkle, Roger B., 493, 494 n
Henley, W.E., 458, 830
Henn, T.R., 632
Henry VIII (Fletcher and Shakespeare), 372, 847
Henry IV (Shakespeare), 50, 354
"Henry James" (Beerbohm), 116
Henryson, Robert, 179, 182
Henslowe, Philip, 595
Herbert, A[lan] P[atrick], 37
  biography, 518–20
  collaborated with Ellis, 522
  contributed to *Punch*, 518–21
  literary analysis, 520–22
Herbert, George, 260, 895
  biography, 522–23
  literary analysis, 523–25
Here Be Dragons (Gibbons), 443, 444
Here Comes Charlie (Barnes), 82
Here I Come (Friel), 406
Heretick, 146
"Heretic's Tragedy, The" (Robert Browning), 159
Heritage Press, 204
Hero and Leander (Marlowe), 223, 720, 784
Herrick, Robert, 502, 646
Herring, Philip, 617 n
Herself Surprised (Cary), 221
"Hey for a Lass wi' a Tocher" (Burns), 181
"Hiawatha" (Ewart), 347
Hibbard, G.R., 781
Hichens, Robert, 299
Hick Scorner, 551
Hicks, Granville, 294
Hidden Laughter (Gray), 465, 470–71
Hierocles (John Hall), 500
Hierocles upon the Golden Verses of Pythagoras; Teaching a Vertuous and Worthy Life (John Hall), 500
High and Low (Betjeman), 150
Highland Fling (Mitford), 775, 776, 777
Highway to the Spittal House (Copland), 551
Hildreth, Richard, 496
Hill, Brian, 189 n

Hill, Christopher, 504, 507, 508
Hill, G.B.
    editor with Powell, *Boswell's Life
        of Johnson, The*, 379
Hill of Devi, The (E.M. Forster), 4 n
"Hind and the Panther, The" (Dryden), 336, 337
    burlesqued by Montague and Prior, 876
Hind, C.L., 830–31
Hindoo Holiday (Ackerley), 3–4, 6
"His Evening Out" (Jerome), 574
"His Majesty's Most Gracious Speech to Both
        Houses of Parliament" (Marvell), 734
His Monkey Wife (John Collier), 262, 263
*Historical and Statistical Account of Nova Scotia,
        An* (Haliburton) 496
Historical Register for the Year, The (Fielding),
        359, 360
History Man, The (Bradbury), 152, 154, 155
History of Antonio and Mellida, The
        (Marston), 729
*History of England, from The Earliest Times
        to the Death of George II, The*
        (Goldsmith), 453
"History of England from the Reign of Henry IV
        to the Death of Charles the First, by a
        Partial, Prejudiced, and Ignorant
        Historian, A" (Austen), 60
History of Madon, King of Britain, The
        (Beaumont), 93
History of Parody (Hone), 532
History of PUNCH, A (R.G.G. Price), 171, 521,
        654 n
History of "Punch," The (Spielmann), 171
History of St. Giles and St. James, The
        (Jerrold), 581
History of the English-Speaking Peoples
        (Churchill), 249
History of the Royal Society (Sprat), 11
History of the Two Maids of More-clacke, The
        (Armin), 39, 40
History of the United States of America, The
        (Hildreth), 496
Histriomastix, or the Player Whipt (Marston), 595,
        729, 730
Hitchhiker's Guide (Adams), 7, 8, 9
Hitchhiker's Guide to the Galaxy, The (Adams), 7
HMS Pinafore (Gilbert, Sullivan, and Carte),
        447–48, 451, 864
Hobbes, Thomas, 500
Hobhouse, John Cam, 834
Hochwalder, Fritz, 67
Hodgson, Ralph, 73
Hoffman, Charles G., 384–86
Hoffman, Dustin, 88, 685
Hoffnung Companion to Music, The
        (Hoffnung), 527
Hoffnung, Gerard, xxxviii
    biography, 525–26
    contributed to *Daily Express* and *Evening
        News*, 526
    contributed to *Lilliput*, 526

    contributed to *Punch*, 526
    literary analysis, 526–29
Hoffnung Music Festival, The (Hoffnung), 527
Hoffnung Symphony Orchestra, The
        (Hoffnung), 527
Hoffnung's Acoustics (Hoffnung), 527
Hoffnung's Encore (Hoffnung), 527
Hoffnung's Musical Chairs (Hoffnung), 527
Hogarth, George, 308
Hogarth, William, 165, 168, 362, 672
Hogg, James
    biography, 529–30
    contributed to *Blackwood's Edinburgh
        Magazine*, 530
    contributed to *Royal Lady's Magazine*, 531
    literary analysis, 530–31
Holiday, Henry, 214
Hollander, John, 141
Holloway, John, 16, 17
Holmes, Oliver Wendell, 297, 883, 885
    influenced by Hood, 537
Holy Deadlock (Herbert), 520
"Holy Fair, The" (Burns), 180–81
Holy Sonnets (Donne), 321
Holy Terror, The (Gray), 465
Holy Terror and Tartuffe, The (Gray), 470–71
"Holy Willie's Prayer" (Burns), 179–80
Homage to Catalonia (Orwell), 810, 814
Homage to Clio (Auden), 48
Home Chimes, 573, 575, 577
Home (Storey), 26
"Home Thoughts from Abroad" (Robert
        Browning), 513
"Home Thoughts from at Home" (Hankin), 513
Homecoming, The (Pinter), 849, 856, 857
Homer, 116, 187–88, 189, 195, 223, 613
Hone, William
    biography, 531–32
    contributed to *The Times*, 532
    literary analysis, 532–34
    subedited *The Patriot*, 532
Honegger, Peter, 550
Honest Whore, The (Marston), 731
Honest Yorkshire-Man, The (Carey), 208
Honeys, The (Dahl), 295
Honorary Consul, The (Graham Greene), 476, 480
Honour of the Garter, The (Peele), 841
Hood, Thomas, 167, 205, 639, 654
    biography, 535
    collaborated with Reynolds, 536
    contributed to *Athenaeum and Literary
        Chronicle*, 535, 539
    contributed to *Hood's Magazine*, 537
    edited *Fun*, 447
    edited *London Magazine*, 535–36, 539
    edited *New Monthly Magazine*, 535
    edited *The Gem*, 535
    influence on Holmes, Whittier, Longfellow,
        and Lowell, 537
    influenced by Coleridge, 539
    influenced by Dickens, 539

influenced by Keats, 537, 539
influenced by Poe, 539
influenced by Shelley, 537
influenced by Sterne, 538–39
literary analysis, 534–40
Hood, Tom
  edited *Fun*, 447
Hood's Own (Hood), 537
Hook (Spielberg), 88
Hook, Theodore Edward
  biography, 540–41
  edited *Monthly Magazine*, 541
  influenced by Dickens, Thackeray, Trollope,
    and Coleridge, 542
  literary analysis, 541–43
"Hook, Theodore Edward" (Garnett), 542
Hooked (Kael), 284
Hope, Anthony
  biography, 543–44
  contributed to *Westminster Gazette*, 544
  literary analysis, 544–46
Hopkins, Anthony, 482 n
Hopkins, Gerard Manley, 53
Hopkinson, Tom, 808–10, 813–15, 819
"Hop-Picking" (Orwell), 813
Horace, 44, 205, 505, 587, 866, 870, 875, 883
  influence on Lord Byron, 192
Horae Vacivae (John Hall), 499
Hordern, Michael, 482 n
Horne, R.C., 730
Hornsby, Leslie. *See* Twiggy
Horse's Mouth, The (Cary), 221–22
"Hospodar, The" (Bunbury), 167
Hostage, The (Behan), 119, 124, 125
"Houdini's Heir" (Barnes), 79
Hours of Idleness (Byron), 191, 192
House at Pooh Corner, The (Milne), 771–73
House by the River, The (Herbert), 518, 520
House of Children, A (Cary), 219, 220
House of Fame, The (Chaucer), 229, 230, 236,
    237, 432
House of Quiet, The (Benson), 133
"House of Teeth, The" (Spike Milligan), 766
Household Words (Dickens), 11, 308–09
Housman, A[lfred] E[dward], 147
  biography, 546–47
  literary analysis, 547–50
Housman, Laurence, 547, 549
Housman's Poems (Bayley), 549
How Far Can You Go? (Lodge), 692, 694, 696,
    697–98
"How Free Was the *Beowulf* Poet?" (Gardner), 145 n
How It Is (Beckett), 109
"How It Strikes a Contemporary" (Robert
    Browning), 161–62
"How Lost, How Amazed, How Miraculous We
    Are" (Christopher Fry), 414
How the Other Half Loves (Ayckbourn), 68, 69
How to be a Brit (Mikes), 764
How to be an Alien (Mikes), 763
How to Be Inimitable (Mikes), 764

"How to Be Run Away With" (Bunbury), 166
How to Become a Virgin (Crisp), 290, 291
How to Lose Customers Without Really Trying
    (Cleese), 252
"How to Lose Your Way" (Bunbury), 166
"How to Recognize Different Parts of the Body"
    (Cleese), 254
How to Scrape Skies (Mikes), 764
"How to Travel Upon Two Legs in a Frost"
    (Bunbury), 166
Howard, Daniel F., 188
Howard, Douglas, 382 n
Howard, Trevor, 354, 482 n
Howard, William K., 482 n
Howards End (Forster), 389–90, 392–93
How-Do Princess (Novello), 411
Howe, Irving, 818
Howe, Joseph, 496
Howleglas
  biography, 550
  literary analysis, 550–52
Howleglas, 550–52
How's That for Telling 'Em, Fat Lady? (Simon
    Gray), 469
Hoyer, Michael, 500
Hudibras (Butler), 501–02, 883
Human Age, The (Wyndham Lewis), 672, 673,
    675–76, 680, 681
Hueffer, Ford Hermann. *See* Ford, Ford Madox
Hueffer, Francis, 382
Hughes, Thomas, 28
Hughes-Hallet, Penelope, 64, 65, 66
Hugo, Victor, 170
Human Factor, The (Graham Greene), 476–77,
    478–80
Human Shows (Hardy), 516
*Humble Motion to the Parliament of England
    Concerning the Advancement
    of Learning and Reformation of
    Universities, An* (John Hall), 500
Hume, David, 210
"Humor in the Knight's Tale" (Edward Foster),
    232, 235, 327
Humor of Samuel Beckett, The (Topsfield),
    106, 109
Humorous Day's Mirth, An (Chapman), 223,
    224–25
Humorous Lieutenant, The (Shirley), 377
"Humor's Death" (Coren), 274
Hunt, Holman, 214, 644
Hunt, Leigh, xxxvi, 353, 366, 638, 735
Hunting of the Snark, The (Carroll), 214, 215, 216
Huntley, Frank Livingstone, 507
Hurley, Andrew, 471 n
"Hurried Love" (Ewart), 346
Hurry on Down (Wain), 15
Hutchinson, A.S.M., 830
Hutchinson, Peter, 471 n
Hutchinson, Sarah, 257
Huttar, Charles A., 667 n
Huxley, Aldous, 577, 559, 662, 741, 818, 819–20

biography, 552–53
    influenced by Samuel Butler, 188
    literary analysis, 553–55
"Huxley Hall" (Betjeman), 150
Huxley, Julian, 553
Huxley, Leonard, 555
Huxley (Robert Calder), 818
Huxley, T[homas] H[enry], 162, 553–54
Hydaspes (Mancini), 12
Hyde, Douglas, 788
Hymenaei (Jonson), 596
"Hymn to God My God, in My Sickness" (Donne),
    321, 327
"Hymn to God the Father, A" (Donne), 321, 327

I Am a Camera (Van Druten), 559, 562
I Like It Here (Kingsley Amis), 16, 17, 18, 20
I Love Lucy, 255
I Want It Now (Kingsley Amis), 18
I Wonder What Happened to Him (Coward), 280
Ibsen, Henrik, 36, 415, 611, 738, 741, 892
    translated by Jellicoe, 569
"Ibsen's New Drama" (Joyce), 609
"Ichabod" (Beerbohm), 116, 117
Iceman Cometh, The (O'Neill), 124
Idle, Eric, xl, 252, 253, 254
Idle Ideas in 1905 (Jerome), 574, 577
"Idle Thoughts" (Jerome), 573, 577
Idle Thoughts of an Idle Fellow (Jerome), 575–76
Idler, The, 565, 574, 590
If . . . (Anderson and Sherwin), 26–30, 31, 32
If I Were a King (Milne), 773
Ignatius His Conclave (Donne), 321
Iliad (Homer), 187, 223, 866, 868
    translation by Pope, 879
"I'll Follow My Secret Heart" (Coward), 283
I'll Leave It to You (Coward), 279, 284, 286
"I'll See You Again" (Coward), 283
Ill Seen Ill Said (Beckett), 102
Illuminated Magazine, 579, 581
Illustrated London News (Lemon), 296, 338, 651
Illustrated Times, 446
*Illustrious Evidence: Approaches to English Litera-
    ture of the Early Seventeenth Century*
    (Miner), 507
I'm Sorry, I'll Read That Again (Cleese), 252, 766
"I.M. Walter Ramsden" (Betjeman), 149
*Imagining a Self: Autobiography and Novel in
    Eighteenth-Century England* (Spacks),
    176 n
"Imitation of Milton, An" (John Philips), 845
"Importance of Being Earnest, The" (Ewart), 347
Importance of Being Earnest, The (Wilde), 86, 266,
    287, 290, 513, 545
"Importance of Being Hoffnung, The"
    (Hoffnung), 525
In a Canadian Canoe (Barry Pain), 830
"In a Gondola" (Robert Browning), 161
In aliquot Sacrae Paginae loca Lectiones
    (Hegge), 499
In Celebration (Storey), 26, 27

"In Defense of Cosmetics" (Beerbohm) 115
"In Memoriam Sir John Betjeman (1906–84)"
    (Ewart), 347
In Memoriam (Tennyson), 158, 214
"In Memory of W.B. Yeats" (Auden), 46
In Search of Chaucer (Bronson), 234
"In Secreit Place" (Dunbar), 342
In the Beginning (Norman Douglas), 330
In the Belly of the Beast (Abbot), 121
"In the Room of the Bride-Elect" (Hardy), 516
In Time of War (Auden), 49
"In Westminster Abbey" (Betjeman), 148
"In which a house is built at Pooh Corner for
    Eeyore" (Milne), 773
"In which it is shown that Tiggers don't climb
    trees" (Milne), 772
"In which Rabbit has a busy day and we learn
    what Christopher Robin does in the
    mornings" (Milne), 772
"In which Tigger comes to the Forest and has
    breakfast" (Milne), 773
In Which We Serve (Coward), 284, 285
"Incident of the French Camp"
    (Robert Browning), 161
Incompleat Angler, The (Burnand), 170
Inconstant, The (Farquhar), 351
Indefinite Articles (Milligan), 767
"Independence" (Milne), 773
Independent Member (Herbert), 519
Independent on Sunday, 23
Independent Stage Society, 36
"Index of Psychology, Mentality and Other Things
    Frequently Noted in Connection with
    Genius" (Bentley), 140
Indian Daily News, 511
"Indian Trinities" (Maurice), 745
Indiscretion in the Life of an Heiress, An
    (Hardy), 515
"Infamous Brigade, An" (Beerbohm), 116
Inferno (Dante), 612
Influence of a Bad Temper in Criticism
    (D'Israeli), 317
Ingelow, Jean
    parodied by Charles Stuart Calverley, 204
Inheritors, The (Ford and Conrad), 383
Inishfallen, Fare Thee Well (O'Casey), 793
Inn Album, The (Robert Browning), 163
Innocence of Father Brown, The (Chesterton), 245
Innocents Abroad (Clemens), 391
L'Innommable (Beckett), 102
Inns of Court, 265
*Inquiry Into the Literary and Political Character
    of James the First* (D'Israeli), 316
Insect Play, The (O'Nolan), 799
"Inside the Coach" (Coleridge), 258
Inside the Whale (Orwell), 815
"Interlace Structure of *Beowulf*, The"
    (Leyerle), 145
Interlude of Youth, 551
"Interview" (Pinter), 848, 849, 852
Intimate Exchanges (Ayckbourn), 68

"Invisible Man, The" (Chesterton), 245
Iolanthe (Gilbert), 448, 492
Ionesco, Eugene, 101, 110, 286
Iphigenia (Peele), 841
Irene (Samuel Johnson), 586, 587
Irish Academy of Letters, 404
Irish Masque, The (Jonson), 604
Irish Times, 119, 799, 801
Irish Worker, 788
"Irremediable" (D'Arcy), 298, 299
Irrepressible Churchill: A Treasury of Winston Churchill's Wit (Halle), 249
Irvine, St. John, 280
Irving, Edward, 532
Irving, Washington, 451, 454, 725
Isherwood, Christopher, 3, 4, 6, 45, 46, 50, 53, 740
    biography, 557–60
    collaborated with Auden, 559
    collaborated with Bachardy, 559–60
    contributed to *Oxford Outlook*, 558
    literary analysis, 560–64
    translated *Bhagavad-Gita*, 559
Isle of Dogs, The (Dekker, Nashe, and Jonson), 595, 782, 784
Italian Job, The (285)
Italian Tailor's Boy, The (Armin), 39
Ives, Burl, 37, 482 n

"Jabberwocky" (Carroll), 215
Jack: C.S. Lewis and His Times (Sayer), 662
"Jack and Alice" (Austen), 63–64
Jack Brag (Hook), 541
Jack of Newberry (Deloney), 304, 305
Jack, R.D.S., 89
Jack Straw (Maugham), 739
Jacke Drums Entertainment (Marston), 729–30
Jack's Horrible Luck (Livings), 684
Jackson, Holbrook, 830
Jacob Faithful (Marryat), 726
Jacob, Giles, 265
Jacobi, Derek, 482 n
Jacobite's Journal, The, 359, 360
Jacobs, W[illiam] W[ymark]
    biography, 565
    contributed to *Blackfriars*, 565
    contributed to *The Idler*, 565, 574
    contributed to *To-day* and *Strand Magazine*, 565
    literary analysis, 565–68
Jacobson, Howard, 152, 155 n
Jail Journal, or Five Years in British Prisons (Mitchel), 121
Jake's Thing (Kingsley Amis), 18, 19–20
James and the Giant Peach (Dahl), 294
James, Clive, 275
James, Edward, 147
James IV (Robert Greene), 488, 489
James, Henry, 133, 162, 211, 297, 299, 301, 338, 339, 383–84, 626, 693, 695, 697, 756
    parodied by Kingsley Amis, 17
    parodied by Max Beerbohm, 116
    influence on Ford, 388
James Joyce: A Portrait of the Artist as a Young Man (Blades), 613
James Joyce: His First Forty Years (Gorman), 610
James Joyce and the Making of "Ulysses" (Budgen), 610
James Joyce (Ellman), 614
James, King, 39
James, Mary. See Worley, Irene
Jameson, Frederic 675–76, 681–82
Jamie's on a Flying Visit (Frayn), 399
Jane Austen: Bicentenary Essays (Halprin), 64 n
Jane Austen: The Critical Heritage (ed. Southam), 64 n
Jane Austen's Beginnings: The Juvenilia and Lady Susan (ed. Grey) 64
Jane Austen's Emma: A Casebook (ed. Lodge), 692
Jane Austen's Novels: Social Change and Literary Form (Brown), 64 n
Jane Shore (Rowe), 366
Japhet, in Search of a Father (Marryat), 726
Jarrolds Publishing, Ltd., 656
Jealous God, The (Levy), 656, 660
Jeffrey, Francis, 835
Jeffrey, Lloyd N., 538–39, 540 n
Jeffs, Rae, 119, 125
Jellicoe, Patricia Ann, 686
    biography, 568–69
    literary analysis, 569–73
    translated Ibsen and Chekhov, 569
"Jenkens Papers" (Jerrold), 581–82
Jennings, Elizabeth, 17
Jennings, Humphrey, 28
Jenyn, Soame, 589
Jerdan, William, 260 n, 537
    edited *Literary Gazette*, 537
Jerome, Jerome, K[lapka], xxxviii, 91, 829–30
    biography, 573–74
    contributed to *Home Chimes*, 573, 575, 577
    contributed to *The Play*, 573
    edited *The Idler*, 574
    literary analysis, 574–79
Jeronimo, 600
Jerrold, Douglas, 170, 653, 747, 748
    biography, 579
    contributed to *Athenaeum, New Monthly Magazine,* and *Blackwood's Edinburgh Magazine*, 579
    contributed to *Punch*, 580, 582–83, 652
    edited *Bon-Mots of Charles Lamb and Douglas Jerrold*, 582
    edited *Illuminated Magazine*, 579, 581
    literary analysis, 579–85
Jerrold, Walter, 204, 535, 540
Jest Book, The (Lemon), 652
Jew of Malta, The (Marlowe), 720, 722–23
Jews: Are They Human?, The (Wyndham Lewis), 673
Jocoseria (Browning), 158
John, 212
"John Anderson" (Burns), 182

John, Augustus, 369, 671
John Bull, 540
John Gay: Poetry and Prose (ed. Dearing), 435
John Halifax, Gentleman (Mulock), 754
John Ingerfield and Other Stories (Jerome), 574
Johnson, Claudia L., 64
Johnson, James, 178
Johnson, Lionel, 459
Johnson, Samuel, xxxiii, 11, 13, 60, 116, 173, 249,
    334, 357, 379–81, 445, 452–53, 455,
    745, 881
  biography, 585–86
  contributed to *Gentleman's Magazine*, 588
  contributed to *Rambler*, 586, 588, 590
  contributed to *The Idler*, 590
  literary analysis, 586–94
"Johnsoniana" (Hood), 538
Joking Apart (Ayckbourn), 68, 70
Jolas, Eugene, 610
Jolas, Maria, 610
"Jolly Beggars, The" (Burns), 181–82
Jonathan Wild (Fielding), 361–62
Jones, D.A.N., 819
Jones, Edward T. 674, 680
Jones, Henry Festing, 185, 186
Jones, Inigo, 598
Jones, James Earl, 482 n
Jones, Terry, 252, 253, 254
Jonson, Ben, xxxviii, 13, 32, 38, 39, 80, 94, 95,
    134, 223, 377 n, 507, 622, 646, 729–30,
    735, 747, 758, 764, 782, 875, 883
  biography, 594–99
  collaborated with Francis Beaumont, 93
  collaborated with Inigo Jones, 598
  influenced by Martial, 604
  literary analysis, 598–608
Joseph Andrews (Fielding), 16, 359, 361, 362,
    363, 454
Joseph, Michael, 67
Joseph, Stephen, 67
Joseph's Library Theatre, 67
Journal (Nottingham), 85
Journal of a Voyage to Lisbon (Fielding), 359, 362
Journal of English and Germanic Philology, 430
Journal to Stella (Swift), 366, 878
Journaux Intimes (Baudelaire), 558
Journey from This World to the Next, The
    (Fielding), 361
Journey to a War (Auden and Isherwood), 46, 559
Journey to the Western Isles of Scotland (Samuel
    Johnson), 586
Joyce and Dante: The Shaping Imagination
    (Reynolds), 612
Joyce Cary: A Preface to His Novels (Wright), 221
Joyce, James, xl, 100, 101, 136, 188, 212, 215,
    216, 370, 383, 396, 561, 671, 676–78,
    680–81, 693–95, 756, 802
  biography, 608–11
  contributed to *Fortnightly Review*, 609
  contributed to *Little Review*, 610
  contributed to *Time*, 610

influenced by Samuel Butler, 188
literary analysis, 611–20
Joyce, Thomas. *See* Cary, Joyce
Jud (Livings), 685
Jude the Obscure (Hardy), 514, 516
Judith: A Tragedy in Three Acts (Christopher
    Fry), 414
Julius Caesar (Shakespeare), 88
Jung, Carl, 101
Juno and the Paycock (O'Casey), 787–90, 792
Just Between Ourselves (Ayckbourn), 68, 70
*Just the Other Day: An Informal History of Great
    Britain Since the War* (John Collier),
    262, 263
Justified Sinner (Hogg), 530
Juvenal, 505–06, 587

Kael, Pauline, 284
Kafka, Franz, 158, 216, 818, 821
Kahn, Florence, 115
Kallman, Chester, 46, 47
Kant, Immanuel, xxxvi, 13, 210, 250, 318, 856
Karl, Frederick, 821
Kathleen and Frank (Isherwood), 557, 560
"Kathleen: Maid of All Work" (D'Arcy), 297
Kean, Charles, 446
Keaton, Buster, xxxix, 101
Keats, John, 17, 214, 370, 635, 637, 638, 642, 801
  influence on Hood, 537, 539
Keene, Charles, 170–71, 338, 339, 653, 654
Keep the Aspidistra Flying (Orwell), 809, 814
Kelly, Hugh, 455
Kelly, Kenny, 81
Kelly, Richard, 339–40, 581, 583 n
Kelly's Eye (Livings), 685
Kempe, William, 38, 39, 40, 303
  biography, 611
  literary analysis, 611–24
Kemps Nine Dales Wonder (Kempe), 622, 623, 624
Kendrick, Laura, 231
Kennedy, George, 482 n
"Kensington Minor" (D'Arcy), 297
Kenyon Review, 294, 480
Kermode, Frank, 476
Kerouac, Jack, 284
Kerr, Deborah, 75
Kettlebrand, Florence Winifred, 764
Keynes, Geoffrey, 189 n
Keynes, John Maynard, 3, 389
Keynotes Series (Lane), 301
Kid for Two Farthings, A (Mankowitz), 715, 716
Kidwelly, Davies of, 500
Kierkegaard, Søren, 50, 54, 54 n
Kiley, Dan, 88
"Kill John Bull With Art" (Wyndham Lewis), 671
Killigrew, Anne, 365
Killing no Murder (Hook), 541
Kim (Kipling), 627, 630–31
Kindness of the Celestia, The (Barry Pain), 830
King and No King, A (Beaumont and Fletcher), 93
King Edward VII (E.F. Benson), 134, 136

King George's Middy (Gilbert), 447
"King George the Fourth" (Beerbohm), 116
King, Margaret, 541
King of Cadonia, The (Lonsdale), 702
"'Kingdom at Sixes and Sevens': Politics and the Juvenilia, The" (Johnson), 64
"King's Birth-Day in Edinburgh" (Fergusson), 356, 357
King's Men, 93, 94, 372, 758
King's Mirror, The (Hope), 544
"King's Prophecie or Weeping Joy, The" (Joseph Hall), 504
Kingsley Amis: An English Moralist (McDermott), 16, 17, 20
"Kingsley Amis—the Writer and the Symbol" (Silverlight), 20
Kingsley, Charles, 410
Kinkaid, James, 310
Kinsayder, W. *See* Marston, John
Kipling, [Joseph] Rudyard, 15, 28, 30, 116, 147, 249, 250, 347, 574
    biography, 624–28
    literary analysis, 628–34
Kirkpatrick, D., 718 n
"Kirk's Alarm, The" (Burns), 180
Knack, The (Jellicoe), 569–71, 72
Knight of the Burning Pestle, The (Beaumont and Fletcher), 93, 95, 96–97, 372–73
Knight, Richard Payne, 835
Knight's Tale (Chaucer), 230, 232, 234, 235
Knipper, Olga, 656
Koestler, Arthur, xli n, 763, 821
Koppel, Ted, 820
Koran, 722
Korda, Alexander, 702
Kovacs, Ernie, 482 n
Krapp's Last Tape (Beckett), 109
Krause, David, 789
Krishnamurti, G., 296, 301 n
Krokodil, 822
"Kubla Khan" (Coleridge), 257, 258
Kubrick, Stanley, 30
Kunitz, Stanley J., 209 n, 681, 711
Kyd, Thomas, 97, 720, 729

La Nausée (Lafourcade), 681
La Rochefoucauld, François, Duc de, 199
La Vie Généreuse, 551
Labiche, Eugene, 37
"Laboratory, The" (Robert Browning), 160
Lacey, James, 379
Ladies and Gentlemen (Belloc, ill. Nicolas Bentley), 131
Ladies Whose Bright Eyes (Ford Madox Ford), 384
"Ladle, The" (Prior), 877, 882, 883
"Lady Appledore's Mesalliance" (Firbank), 369
Lady Chatterley's Lover (Lawrence), 390
Lady Frederick (Maugham), 738, 739, 741
Lady from Stalingrad Mansions, The (Coren), 276, 277
Lady of the Barge, The (Jacobs), 567

Lady Susan (Austen), 60
Lady's Not for Burning, The (Christopher Fry), 412–13, 415, 417–18
Lafourcade, Bernard 678–81
Lagerkvist, Par, 414
"Lake District" (Betjeman), 150
Lake Poets, 195
Lamarck, J.B., 187
Lamb, Charles, 11, 87, 459, 536, 575, 636
    biography, 635–36
    literary analysis, 636–42
    pseudonym Elia, 639
Lament for Armenians and Grey Viruses (Barnes), 80–81
"Lamia" (Hood), 537
Lancelot Temple, Esq. *See* Armstrong, John
Lancet, The (Bashford), 90
Land and Water, 129
Land of the Rising Yen, The (Mikes), 764
Landing on the Sun, A (Frayn), 399, 400
Lane, John, 115, 117, 296, 301, 459
Lang, Andrew, 35, 625
Lang, Fritz, 482 n
Langbaine, Gerard, 265
Langford, G.W., 215
Langland, William, 53
Langridge, Richard, 93 n
Language of Fiction: Essays in Criticism and Verbal Analysis of the English Novel (Lodge), 691
Laodicean, A (Hardy), 515
Lara (Byron), 193
Lark, The (Anouilh), 414
Larkin, James
    influenced O'Casey, 787
Larkin, Phillip, 15, 17, 149, 345, 347, 895
Last Battle, The (C.S. Lewis), 664, 666
"Last Chance to See" (Douglas Adams), 7
Last Chance to See (Douglas Adams), 7, 9
Last Essays of Elia, The (Lamb), 636, 639–40
"Last Instruction to a Painter, The" (Marvell), 734–35
Last Joke (Bagnold), 75
"Last Man, The" (Hood), 536, 538
Last of Mr. Norris, The (Isherwood), 561
Last of Mrs. Cheyney, The (Lonsdale), 702–03
Last of the DeMullins, The (Hankin), 513
Last Poems (Housman), 546–48
Last Post, The (Ford Madox Ford), 383
"Last Things, The" (Ewart), 346
Late John Wilkes's Catechism, The (Hone), 532
Late Lyrics and Earlier (Hardy), 516
Late Pickings (Ewart), 345
"Late Victorian to Modernist: 1870–1930" (Bergonzi), 681
Latter-Day Pamphlets (Carlyle), 210
Laugh Till You Cry (Mankowitz), 715
"Laughing Song" (trans. Gilbert), 446
Laughter (Bergson), 290, 681
Laughter! (Barnes), 78, 81
Laurel, Stan, xxxix, 105
Laver, James, 412

Lawless Roads, The (Graham Greene), 473, 475, 481 n
Lawlis, Meritt E., 305
Lawrence, D.H., 85, 136, 153, 329, 332, 383, 390, 396, 463, 516, 553, 611, 682, 725
Lawrence, Gertrude, 286
"Lawrence of Arabia" (Coward), 281
Lawson, Michael, 400, 403 n
"Lay of the Labourer, The" (Hood), 537, 539
Lay Sermons (Coleridge), 258
Laye, Evelyn, 284
Le Calmant (Beckett), 101
Leacock, Stephen, 91, 170
Lear, Edward, 131, 449, 547
    biography, 642–46
    literary analysis, 646–50
    pseudonym, Derry down Derry, 645
Learned Dissertation on Dumpling, A (Carey), 208
Learned Hippopotamus, The (Ewart), 347
Leavis, F.R., 468
Led Zeppelin, 255
Leech, John, xxxvii, 338–39, 581, 653
Leech, Michael T., 80
LeFlon, Robert, 28
LeGallienne, Richard, 115
Legend of Good Women (Chaucer), 229
Legends of Number Nip, The (Lemon), 651
Legouve, Ernest, 309
Lehman, David, 246 n
Lehmann, John, 559
Lehmann, Liza, 829
Lehmann, Rudolf, 829
Leibniz, G.W., 10
Leicester Galleries, 115
Leigh Hunt's London Journal, 651
Leigh, Percival, 653
Leigh, Vivien, 414, 417
Leishman, J.B., 321
"Leith Races" (Fergusson), 356
Lemon, Dickens, and Mr. Nightingale's Diary (Leona Weaver Fisher) 655 n
Lemon, Mark, 37, 537, 581, 650–56, 748
    biography, 650–52
    founding editor *Punch*, 169, 170, 537
    literary analysis, 652–56
L'Enfant et les Sortilèges (Colette), 414
L'Enfant et les Sortilèges (Ravel), 527
Lennon, John, 766, 767
"Lenore" (Burger), 166, 835
"Lenvoy de Chaucer a Bukton" (Chaucer), 237
Leonard, R.M., 204
"Les Saltambiques" (Wyndham Lewis), 671
Lesley, Cole, 279
"Let's Fake an Opera" (Hoffnung), 526
Letter to a Gentleman in the Country, Touching the Dissolution of the Late Parliament (John Hall), 500
Letter to Lord Byron (Auden), 51
Letters (Chesterfield), 581
Letters from Iceland (Auden and MacNeice), 46

"Letters of Mephibosheth Stepsure" (McCulloch), 497
Letters to Malcolm: Chiefly on Prayer (C.S. Lewis), 663
Lettres Chinoises (D'Argens), 453
Lettres Persans (Montesquieu), 453
"Leucenia" (John Hall), 499
Lévi-Strauss, Claude, 162
Levine, Robert T. 699 n
Levy, Benn Wolfe
    biography, 656
    literary analysis, 656–61
Lewes, George, 61
Lewis, Cecil Day, 3, 45, 54, 147
Lewis, C[live] S[taples], xxxiii, 147, 256, 505–06
    biography, 661–62
    literary analysis, 662–70
    pseudonym Clive Hamilton, 662
    pseudonym N.W. Clerk, 662
Lewis, L.N., 678
Lewis, Matthew Gregory "Monk," 166, 834
    parodied by Henry William Bunbury, 166
Lewis, Naomi, 295
Lewis, (Percy) Wyndham
    biography, 671–73
    literary analysis, 673–84
"Lewis, Percy Wyndham" (Bertram), 383, 681
"Lewis, (Percy) Wyndham" (Daiches), 675
Lewis, Roger, 115, 475
Lewis, Sinclair, 678
"Lewis's Prose Style" (McCluhan), 682 n
L'Expulsé (Beckett), 101
Leyerle, John, 145
Leyton Hall and Other Tales (Lemon), 652
Liber Vagatorum (Luther), 551
Library of Literary Criticism: Modern British Literature, A (Sharve-Taylor), 137 n
Library Theatre, 68
Life, 475
Life and Letters, 412
Life and Letters of Dr. Samuel Butler, The (Butler), 188
Life and Remains of Douglas Jerrold, The (Jerrold), 581–82
Life and Remains of Theodore Edward Hook, The (Barham), 542
"Life and Works of Henry Carey, The" (Dane), 206
Life and Writings of Major Jack Downing of Downingville, Away Down East in the State of Maine, The (Seba Smith), 497
Life Class (Storey), 26
Life of Addison (Samuel Johnson), 590
Life of Brian, The (Cleese), 252, 255
Life of George Herbert (Walton), 523
Life of Grahame Greene, Volume 1: 1904–1939, The (Sherry), 473–74
Life of Hilaire Belloc, The (Speaight), 129, 130
Life of Johnson (Boswell), 379–80, 453, 456 n, 592–93. See also *Boswell's Life of Johnson*
Life of Milton (Samuel Johnson), 590
Life of Noel Coward, The (Lesley), 279

Life of Pope (Samuel Johnson), 589–90
Life of Richard Nash, The (Goldsmith), 452
Life, the Universe, and Everything
      (Douglas Adams), 7
Life's Little Ironies (Hardy), 516
"Ligeia" (Poe), 316
Light Freights (Jacobs), 566
"Light Woman, A" (Robert Browning), 159
"Lightheartedness in Rhyme" (Coleridge),
      259, 260
Like It Or Not (Ewart), 347
"Lillibullero" (Gay), 438
Lillie, Bea, 285
Lilliput, 526
Lilly, William, 500
Lincoln, Abraham, 251
Lincoln's Inn Fields, 265, 351
Lindeman, Ralph D., 330
Lindley Kays (Barry Pain), 830
"Lines: to a Comic Author, on an Abusive Review"
      (Coleridge), 260
Lindsay Anderson (Sussex), 26
Linton, Elizabeth Lynn, 574
L'Invitation au Chateau (Anouilh), 413
Lion and the Unicorn: Socialism and the English
      Genius, The (Orwell), 815
Lion, the Witch and the Wardrobe, The
      (C.S. Lewis), 664
Lions and Shadows (Isherwood), 558–61
Lippincott, H.F., 39
Listener, The, 3, 274–75, 414, 673
Litany, A (Donne), 321
"Literary Allusion as Satire in Simon Gray's
      Butley" (Blaydes), 67, 471 n
Literary Chronicle (London), 535, 538
Literary Gazette, 537
Literary Remains, A Memoir (Calverley, ed.
      Sendall), 204–05
Literary Reminiscences (Hood), 538
Literaturnaya Gazette, 537
Little Dorrit (Dickens), 208, 311, 312
"Little Grey Man, The" (Bunbury), 166
"Little Learning, A" (Coren), 276
Little Less than Gods, A (Ford Madox Ford), 387
Little Minister (Barrie), 85
Little Mrs. Foster Show, The (Livings), 685
Little Portia (Gray), 465
Little Review, 610
Little Theatre, 360
Little White Bird, The (Barrie), 86
Littlewood, Joan, 119, 124, 684
Lives and Characters of the English Dramatic
      Poets, The (Langbaine) 265
Lives of the Poets: Dryden (Johnson), 334
Lives of the Poets (Johnson), 11
Living Together (Ayckbourn), 69
Livings, Henry
      biography, 684–85
      literary analysis, 685–90
Liza of Lambeth (Maugham), 738–41
LL., N. *See* Hall, John

"Loafing" (Grahame), 459
Lobo, Father Jerome, 585
Locke, John, 10, 269–70, 352, 869, 875, 877, 880
"Locksley Hall" (Tennyson), 205
Lodge, David, 152
      biography, 691
      literary analysis, 691–701
Lodge, Thomas, 305, 505
Loiterer, 60
London Evening Standard, 69
London Fields (Martin Amis), 24–25
London Girls' Friendly Society, 412
London, Jack, 776
London Journal, 170, 654
London Labour and the London Poor
      (Mayhew), 748
London Magazine, 11, 535–36, 539, 636, 639
London Mercury, 711
London Morning (Coward), 284
London Observer, The, 83 n
London Review, 834
London (Samuel Johnson), 587–88
London Times. *See Times, The* (London), 339,
      444, 537
London Weekly, 712
Londoners (Ewart), 345
Loneliness of the Long-Distance Runner, The
      (Sillitoe), 121
Long and the Short and the Tall, The (Hall), 26
Long Dark Tea-Time of the Soul, The (Douglas
      Adams), 7, 8–9
Longest Journey, The (Forster), 389
Longfellow, Henry Wadsworth, 163, 204, 496
      influenced by Hood, 537
Longinus, 500–01
Lonsdale, Frederick
      biography, 701–02
      literary analysis, 702–04
Look Back in Anger (Osborne), 15, 16, 27, 77
Look Look (Frayn), 399, 401–02
Look, Stranger! (Auden), 46
Looking Back (Norman Douglas), 329
Looking Backward (Maugham), 739
Looking Backwards (Bellamy), 577
Loot (Orton), 803
Lord Admiral's Men, 223
Lord Chamberlain's Men, 38, 39, 621, 623
Lord Chando's Men, 39
Lord Jim (Conrad), 383
Lord Ormont and His Aminta (Meredith), 755
Lord Randolph Churchill (Churchill), 249
Lord Rochester's Monkey (Graham Greene), 476
Lords and Masters (Archilbald Macdonell), 712
Lorna Doone (Blackmore), 279
Lorre, Peter, 482 n
Lorris, Guillaume de, 230
Los Angeles Times, 444
Loser Takes All (Graham Greene), 476–78
"Losing Myself" (Barnes), 79
"Lost Centaur, The" (Graham), 459
Lost Childhood, The (Graham Greene), 473–74

Lost Masterpieces and Other Verses (Hankin), 511–13
Lost Ones, The (Beckett), 102–03
"Lost, The" (Isherwood), 562
Lottie Dundass (Bagnold), 75
Love after All (Ayckbourn), 67
Love and a Bottle (Farquhar), 351, 352
Love and Fashion (Frances "Fanny" Burney), 175
Love and Friendship (Austen), 60
"Love and Lethe" (Beckett), 103–04
"Love and Liberty—A Cantata" (Robert Burns), 181
Love and Pride (Hook), 541
Love for Love (Congreve), 265, 266, 269–70, 271
Love in a Cold Climate (Mitford), 776–78
"Love in a Valley" (Ewart), 347
Love In a Wood (Wycherley), 352
Love in Several Masques (Fielding), 358–59, 360
Loved and Envied, The (Bagnold), 74, 75
Loved at Last (Lemon), 652
Lovelace, Richard, 499
    biography, 704–05
    literary analysis, 705–09
"Lovers, and a Reflection" (Calverley), 204
"Lovers' Quarrel, The" (Fry), 410
Love's Cure (Beaumont and Fletcher, rev. Massinger), 93
Love's Labours Lost (Shakespeare), 621, 657
Love's Last Shift (Cibber), 352
Lowell, James Russell, 163
    influenced by Hood, 537
Lower Depths, The (Gorki), 660
Lowry, Malcolm, 476
"Loyal Scot, The" (Marvell), 735
Lucan, 720
Lucas, Sir Jocelyn, 559
Lucasta (Lovelace), 705
Lucasta Posthume Poems (Lovelace), 705
"Lucasta, taking the waters at Tunbridge" (Lovelace), 707
Lucia in London (E.F. Benson), 134, 135–36
Lucian, xxxvii, 19, 360, 506
Luck or Cunning (Butler), 187
Lucky Jim (Kingsley Amis), 15, 16–17, 18, 19, 20, 695
Lucubrations of Sir Isaac Bickerstaff Esq., The (Addison and Steele), 10
Lucy, Henry, 171
Ludgate Magazine, The, 829
"Lullaby" (Auden), 49
Lulu (Wedekind), 82
Lunn, Arnold
Lunts, Alfred, 285
"Lusish Satis" (Grahame), 460
Lusus Senus; or, Serious Passe-Time (Malerus), 500
Luther, Martin, 199, 551
Lyceum Theatre (London), 446, 863
"Lycus the Centaur" (Hood), 537
Lydgate, John, xxxiv, 341
Lyly, John, 373, 486, 781
Lynch, Bohun, 115
Lyre and Lancet (Anstey), 37

Lyric Theatre (Hammersmith), 414, 848
Lyric Theatre (London), 252
Lyrical Ballads (Coleridge), 257, 259
Lysistrata (Aristophanes), 372, 374, 658
Lyttleton, Lord, 453

Mabou Mines, 102
Mac Flecknoe (Dryden), 366, 845
Macauley, Robie, 386
Macaulay, Thomas Babington, 13, 248, 249
McCarthy, Desmond, 280
McCarthy, Patrick A., 616, 617 n
Macbeth (Shakespeare), 67, 97, 856
McCluhan, Marshall, 680
MacCool, Finn, 801
McCrea, Brian, 13, 14
McCulloch, Thomas, 497
McDermott, John, 20 n
MacDonald, Donald, 234
MacDonell, Annie, 514
Macdonell, Archibald Gordon
    biography, 711
    literary analysis, 711–14
McDowell, Malcolm, 27, 30, 30 n
Macey, Samuel L., 206, 208 n
McGill, William, 180
McGovern, Barbara, 365
McGowen, Alec, 482 n
MacHaggis: A Farce in Three Acts, The (Jerome), 577
Machaut, 230
Machiavel. *See* Machiavelli, Niccolò
Machiavelli, Niccolò, 199
MacKellan, Ian, 402
MacKenzie, Compton, 133
Macklin, Charles, 379
McLean, Thomas, 645
McMahon, Frank, 120
MacNeice, Louis, 45, 46, 54
Macready, Charles, 157
Macready, W.R., 309
Mad Dogs and Englishmen (Coward), 280, 283
Mad World My Masters, A (Middleton), 760–61
Madame Bovary (Zola)
    stage adaptation by Levy, 656
"Madame Zenobia" (Barnes), 79
Madden, Miss
    pseudonym of Mrs. James Hook, 540
Made for Man (Herbert), 520
"Madman and the Lethargist, The" (Coleridge), 259
Madonna, 23
Maestro, The (Hoffnung), 526–27
Magic Cabinet of Professor Smucker (Mankowitz), 716, 718
Magic Christian, The (Cleese and Chapman), 252
Magic Mirror, The (Gilbert), 446, 447
Magician's Nephew, The (C.S. Lewis), 664
Magnall's Questions, 642
Magnetic Lady, The, 598

Mahogany Tree: An Informal History of PUNCH, The (Prager), 654 n
Maid Marian (Peacock), 833, 838–39
Maid of the Mountain, The (Lonsdale), 702
Maid's Tragedy, The (Beaumont and Fletcher), 93, 372
Maierus, Michael, 500
Mail on Sunday, The, 274
Mailer, Norman, 819
Mainly on the Air (Beerbohm), 115
Major Barbara (G.B. Shaw), 660
Make and Break (Frayn), 400
Make Me an Offer (Mankowitz), 714–15, 716–17
Make Way for Lucia (E.F. Benson), 134
Making a Film (Anderson), 26
Making History (Friel), 404–05
Malcontent, The (Marston), 730–31
Male Impersonator, The (E.F. Benson), 136
Malign Fiesta (Wyndham Lewis), 673, 675
Mallett, David, 42
Malone Dies (Beckett), 102, 105, 106
Malone Meurt (Beckett). *See Malone Dies*
Malthus, Thomas, 835
Mamet, David
    influenced by Samuel Beckett, 110
Mamillia (Robert Greene), 486–87, 489
Man and Superman (G.B. Shaw), 375, 675, 660
Man Could Stand Up, A (Ford Madox Ford),
    383, 387
Man for All Seasons, A (Robert Shaw), 68
Man From Blankley's, The (Anstey), 37
Man in the Moon, The (Hone), 533–34
Man Made of Money, A (Jerrold), 581
Man of Character (Jerrold), 581
Man of Law's Tale (Chaucer), 235–36
Man of Mark, A (Hope), 543
Man of the Moment (Ayckbourn), 68, 71
Man Who Was Thursday: A Nightmare, The
    (Chesterton), 245
Man With Red Hair, A (Levy), 660
Man Within, The (Graham Greene), 474
Mancini, Francesco, 12
"M'Andrews' Hymn" (Kipling), 626
Maner, Martin, 117 n
Manet, Edouard, 221
Manfred (Byron), 192–94, 198
Mankowitz, Wolf
    biography, 714–16
    literary analysis, 716–19
Mann, Jill, 230
Mann, Klaus, 46
Manners from Heaven (Crisp), 290–91
Mannes, Marya, 441, 444 n
Manning, 638
Manon Lescaut (Prevost), 446
"*Mansfield Park*: Freedom and the Family"
    (Brissender), 64 n
Mansfield Park (Austen), 60–61, 63
Manton, Jo, 415
Manwayring, Arthur, 265
Many and the Few, The (Bradbury), 155
Many Cargoes (Jacobs), 565–66

Many Inventions (Kipling), 626
Mapp and Lucia (E.F. Benson), 136
Marat Sade (Weiss), 77
Marcus, Leah, 604
Marcuse, Herbert, 30
Margaret Ogilvy (Barrie), 86
"Marginalia" (Grahame), 459
Mariana (Tennyson), 214
Mark Lemon: First Editor of "Punch" (Adrian),
    654 n, 655 n
"Mark of Frayn, The" (Lawson), 403 n
Markham, Robert. *See* Amis, Kingsley
Marlborough: His Life and Times (Churchill), 249
Marlowe, Christopher, 223, 488, 636, 784
    biography, 719–21
    literary analysis, 721–24
"Marriage, A" (D'Arcy), 299, 300
Marriage à La Mode (Dryden), 334
Marriot, R.B., 80
Marryat, Frederick
    biography, 725
    literary analysis, 725–28
Marsden Case, The (Ford Madox Ford), 386
Marsh-Caldwell, Anne, 582
Marshall, John, 646
Marston, John, 80, 93–95, 503–04, 595–96, 758
    biography, 728–29
    literary analysis, 729–33
    pseudonym W. Kinsayder, 729
Martial, 412
    influence on Jonson, 604
Martian, The (Du Maurier), 340
Martin Beck Theatre, 413
Martin Chuzzlewit (Dickens), 308
Martin, Mary, 88
Martyr of Antioch, The (Milman), 448
Marvell, Andrew, 366
    biography, 733–34
    literary analysis, 734–38
Marx Brothers, 107, 767
Marx, Groucho, 54, 255, 470, 853
Mary Rose (Barrie), 85
Mary Shelley's Frankenstein (Branagh), 253
"Mary's Ghost" (Hood), 538
Masefield, John, 244
Masque of Blackness (Jonson), 596
Masque of the Inner Temple and Gray's Inn
    (Beaumont), 93
"Masquerade, The" (Fielding), 361
Massacre at Paris, The (Marlowe), 720
Massey, Daniel, 82
Massinger, Philip, 93
    collaborated with Fletcher, 94, 372
Master Humphrey's Clock (Dickens), 539
"Master Humphrey's Code" (Dickens), 308
Master of Mrs. Chilvers, The (Jerome), 577
Master Sings, The (Coward), 283
Masterman Ready (Marryat), 727
Matchmaker, The (Gibbons), 443, 444
Materer, Timothy, 678
Matilda, Anna, 204

Matter of Gravity, A (Bagnold), 75
Matthews, A.E., 284
Maugham, W[illiam] Somerset, 16, 282, 702
    biography, 738–39
    influenced by Maupassant and Voltaire, 740
    literary analysis, 739–44
Maupassant, Guy de, 297, 301 n
    influence on Maugham, 740
Maurice (Forster), 389–90, 395–96
Maurice, Thomas
    biography, 744–45
    literary analysis, 745–47
Max in Perspective (Lynch), 117 n
Maxwell, D.E.S., 405, 407 n
Maxwell (Hook), 541
May Day (Chapman), 223
May Lord, The (Jonson), 597
"May of the Moril Glen" (Hogg), 531
May, Phil, 171
*May We Borrow Your Husband? And Other
    Comedies of the Sexual Life* (Graham
    Greene), 476, 479
Mayhew, Henry
    biography, 747–48
    co-founded *Punch*, 579
    literary analysis, 748–52
Mayhew, Horace, 653
Mayor of Casterbridge, The (Hardy), 515
Mayor of Garratt, The (Foote), 379, 380–81
Meaning of Life (Cleese), 252, 254, 255
"Meaning of the Wild Body, The" (Wyndham
    Lewis), 672
"Mechanics of Comedy in Chaucer's *Miller's Tale,
    The*" (Dane), 230–31
"Medal of John Bayes, The" (Shadwell), 336
"Medal, The" (Dryden), 335, 336
*Medieval Studies in Honor of Lillian Herlands
    Hornstein* (ed. J.B. Bessinger and R.
    Raymo), 230
Meditations (Joseph Hall), 504
Medley, Robert, 45
Meet Me Tonight, 288
Meet My Father. See Relatively Speaking
Meeting by the River, A (Isherwood), 560, 562–63
"Meeting, The" (Ewart), 347
Meisel, Martin, 583 n
Melincourt (Peacock), 833, 836–37
Melon (Gray), 465, 470–71
Melville, Andrew, 523
Melville, Herman, 284, 725
Member of Gaza, The (Levy), 656
Memento Mori (Spark), 18
Memoir of the Bobotes (Cary), 220
Memoirs of Constantin Dix (Barry Pain), 830
Memoirs of Dr. Burney (Frances "Fanny"
    Burney), 176
Memoirs of Percy Bysshe Shelley (Peacock), 834
Memorial, The (Isherwood), 557, 559, 561
Memories and Notes (Hope), 544
Men and Women (Robert Browning), 158
Men Without Art (Wyndham Lewis), 672, 679–80

Menander, 94
Menaphon (Robert Greene), 485, 487–88
    preface (Nashe), 781–82
Mendelman Fire, The (Mankowitz), 715, 716
Mendelson, Edward, 54 n
Mendelssohn, Moses, 316
Merchant of Venice (Shakespeare), 30, 621
Merchant's Tale (Chaucer), 230, 234
Mercier and Camier (Beckett), 102, 103, 107
Mercurius Britannicus (John Hall), 500
Mere Christianity (C.S. Lewis), 662–63
Meredith, George, xxxvi, 116, 211, 212, 250,
    298, 834
    biography, 752–53
    influenced by Carlyle, 754
    influenced by Peacock, 755
    literary analysis, 753–57
Meredith, H.O., 389
"Merriments of the men of Goteham, in receiving
    the King into Goteham" (Kempe),
    622–23
*Merry Muses of Caledonia; A Collection of
    Favourite Scots Songs, Ancient and
    Modern, The* (Burns), 182
Merry Wives of Windsor, The (Shakespeare), 651
Messenger, Ann, 366
Metamorphoses (Ovid), 726, 882
*Metamorphosis of Pigmalions Image and Certaine
    Satyres, The* (Marston), 729–30
Metamorphosis of Tobacco, The (Beaumont), 93
Metcalf, John, 717
Methuen, 461, 559, 560
Metro-Goldwyn-Mayer, 557, 559
Metropolitan Magazine, 725
"Metropolitan Railway, The" (Betjeman), 149
Metscher, T., 682
MGM. *See* Metro-Goldwyn-Mayer
Meune, Jean De, 230
Meyers, Jeffrey, 680, 821
Meyers, L.H., 810, 821
Meyers, Valerie, 821
Middleton, John, 80
Middleton, Thomas, 637
    biography, 757–58
    literary analysis, 758–63
Midnight Oil (Pritchett), 890–92
Midsummer Night's Dream, A (Shakespeare), 39,
    88, 621, 623
Midwest Quarterly, 467
Mikado, The (Gilbert and Sullivan), 448–49
Mikes, George
    biography, 763
    literary analysis, 763–64
Mikhaylov, Mikhail
    translated by Hook, 537
Mildonay, The (Marryat), 725–26
Milic, Louis, 14
Milk and Honey (Mikes), 764
Milk Train Doesn't Stop Here Anymore, The
    (Tennessee Williams), 285
Mill, James, 833–34

Mill, John Stuart, 158, 210, 211, 754, 834
Millais, Sir John Everett, 170, 214, 309, 644, 654
Milland, Ray, 482
Millar, Andrew, 591
Miller, Arthur, 284
Miller, Henry, 697
Miller's Tale (Chaucer), 230–32, 234
Milligan, Alphonso, 764
Milligan, Spike, xxxviii, 253, 371
    biography, 764–65
    literary analysis, 765–70
Milligan's War (Spike Milligan), 767
Milliken, E.J., 171
Millionairess, The (G.B. Shaw)
    film version by Mankowitz, 715
Mills, Haley, 75
Mills, John, 75, 482 n
Milman, H.H., 448
Milne, A.A., 37, 763
    biography, 770–71
    literary analysis, 771–75
Milne, Christopher (Robin), 771
Milton, John, 11, 13, 42, 44, 53, 88, 150, 163,
    193, 195, 353, 435, 466, 500, 504,
    523, 548, 590, 663, 734–46, 844–46,
    866, 870
Miner, Earl, 507
Minin, Dick, 590
Ministry of Fear, The (Graham Greene), 475,
    477–78
Ministry of the Scottish Border (Hogg), 530
Minor, The (Foote), 379, 380
"Miracle of St. Jubanus, The" (Kipling), 629
Miracles (C.S. Lewis), 663
"Mirth and Marriage in *The Parliament of
    Fowles*" (Francis J. Smith) 237
Mirror for Magistrates, The (Lydgate), 665
*Mirror in My House: The Autobiographies of Sean
    O'Casey* (O'Casey) 787
Miscellaneous Poems (Marvell), 734
Miscellanies (Fielding), 361
*Miscellany Poems on Several Occasions
    Written by a Lady* (Finch), 366
Mischmasch (Carroll), 214
Miser, The (Fielding), 360
Misfortunes of Elphen, The (Peacock), 834,
    838–39
Misleading Cases in the Common Law (Herbert),
    518–19, 520–22
"Miss Gee" (Auden), 52
Miss Hobbs (Jerome), 577
Miss Linsey and Pa (Gibbons), 443, 444
"Miss Maniac" (Lear), 642
Miss Mapp (E.F. Benson), 134, 135, 136
Missa Luba, 29
Mitchel, John, 121
Mitchell, Giles, 221
Mitchell, Keith, 415
Mitford, Nancy
    biography, 775–76
    literary analysis, 776–79

Mock Doctor, The (Fielding), 360
"Model Music Hall Songs" (Anstey), 35
Modell of a Christian Society, A (Andreae), 499
Modern Criticism and Theory (Lodge), 692
"Modern Gallantry" (Lamb), 635
"Modern Incident, A" (D'Arcy), 298
Modern Instances (D'Arcy), 298
Modern Language Notes, 299 n, 502
Modern Movement, The (John Gross), 675–76
Modern Philology, 145
Modern Society, 73
Modern Times, 686
*Modes of Modern Writing: Metaphor, Metonymy,
    and the Typology of Modern Literature*
    (Lodge), 691
"Modest Proposal" (Ewart), 345–46
Modest Proposal, A (Swift), 19
Mohocks, The (Gay), 434, 436
Mokeanna, or the White Witness (Burnand), 170
Mokeanna, or the White Witness (Lemon), 654
Molière, Jean Baptiste, 35, 37, 71, 174, 352, 360,
    416, 611, 755–56
Molloy (Beckett), 102, 105–06
Moments of Vision (Hardy), 516
Monarch of Wit, The (Leishman), 321
"Money Box, The" (Jacobs), 566
Money (Martin Amis), 23, 24
"Monkey who had seen the World, The" (Gay), 436
"Monkey's Paw, The" (Jacobs), 567
Monks of St. Mark, The (Peacock), 834
Monk's Tale (Chaucer), 229, 230
Monochromes (D'Arcy), 297, 298, 299, 301
"Monody on a Tea Kettle" (Coleridge), 258
Monsell, Thomas, 71
Monsieur d'Olive (Chapman), 223, 226
Monsieur Thomas (Fletcher), 377
Monsignor Quixote (Graham Greene), 477, 479,
    480–81
Monstre Gai (Wyndham Lewis), 673, 675–76
Montaigne, Michel de, xxxvii, 94, 636, 880
Montesquieu, Charles Louis de Secondat de, 453
Montgomery, Field Marshal Bernard, 518
Month in the Country, A (Turgenev), 406
    stage adaptation by Simon Gray, 465
Monthly Magazine, 258, 541
Monthly Mirror, 319 n
Monthly Review, 452, 883
Monty Python and the Holy Grail (Cleese),
    252, 255
Monty Python's Flying Circus, 7, 31, 91, 252,
    253–55, 256, 371, 766–67
Moon and Sixpence, The (Maugham), 739–40
Moondog Rogan and the Mighty Hamster
    (Barnes), 79
Moore, Dudley, xxxix, 767
Moore, George, 459, 617 n
Moore, Thomas, 150, 194, 838, 883
Moral Alphabet, A (Belloc), 131, 132
"Moral of Punch, The" (Lemon), 651, 653
More Bab Ballads (Gilbert), 447
More Beasts for Worse Children (Belloc), 131

More (Beerbohm), 115
More Frightened than Hurt (Jerrold), 579
"More Happy Thoughts" (Burnand), 171
More, Henry, 501
More Like Old Times (Coren), 277
More Misleading Cases (Herbert), 520
More Nonsense (Lear), 645–47
More Peers (Belloc), 131
More Poems (Housman), 547
More Pricks Than Kicks (Beckett), 100, 103, 104
More Than a Touch of Zen (Barnes), 82
More, Thomas, 19, 508
Morley, Christopher, 74, 76 n
Morley, Sheridan, 81, 82, 83 n
Morning Chronicle, 11, 308, 748
Morning Post, 249, 259, 581–82, 639
Morris, Mowbray, 309–10
Morris, William, 205, 577, 671
Morrison, Blake, 155, 156 n
Mortal Passion (Mikes), 764
Mortimer, John, 656
Mortimer, Raymond, 776
"Mortmere" (Isherwood), 558
Morton, J.B., 712
Moryson, Fynes, 550
Moseley, Humphrey, 93, 94
Mostly Harmless (Douglas Adams), 7
"Mote in the Middle Distance, The"
      (Beerbohm), 116
Motion, Andrew, 345, 348 n
Mount Zion (Betjeman), 147
Mountain Bard, The (Hogg), 580
Mountain Beast, The (Gibbons), 441
Mourning Bride, The (Congreve), 265, 272
Mozart, Wolfgang Amadeus, 16
Mr. Apollo (Ford Maddox Ford), 384
Mr. A's Amazing Maze Plays (Ayckbourn), 71
Mr. Flight (Ford Maddox Ford), 384
Mr. Foot (Frayn), 400
"Mr. Greene's Eggs and Crosses" (Kermode), 476
Mr. H—(Lamb), 636
"Mr. Harrington's Washing" (Maugham), 740
"Mr. Henry James revisiting America"
      (Beerbohm), 116
Mr. Midshipman Easy (Marryat), 727
Mr. Nightingale's Diary (Dickens and Lemon), 651
Mr. Norris Changes Trains (Isherwood), 559, 561
Mr. Paul Pry (Jerrold), 579
Mr. Punch's Dramatic Sequels (Hankin), 511, 512
"Mr. Punch's Fancy Ball" (Leech), 653
Mr. Punch's Pocket Ibsen (Anstey), 36
*Mr. Punch's Young Reciter: Burglar Bill and Other
      Pieces* (Anstey) 35–36
"Mr. Sludge, 'the Medium'" (Robert
      Browning), 161
Mr. Smirke, or The Divine in Mode (Marvell), 734
"Mr. Thomas Hardy composing a lyric"
      (Beerbohm), 116
"Mr. W.B. Yeats, presenting Mr. George Moore
      to the Queen of the Fairies"
      (Beerbohm), 116

Mr. Witt's Widow (Hope), 543
"Mrs. Battle's Opinions on Whist" (Lamb), 638–39
"Mrs. Caudle's Curtain Lectures" (Jerrold), 170,
      579, 582
Mrs. Dot (Maugham), 739
Mrs. Moonlight (Levy), 660
Mrs. Murphy (Barry Pain), 830
Mrs. Pooter's Diary (Waterhouse), 493
Mrs. Warren's Profession (G.B. Shaw), 741
MTV, 254
Mucedorus, 97
Much Ado about Nothing (Shakespeare), 38, 95,
      354, 621
"Muckle-mouth Meg" (Robert Browning), 159
Mud and Treacle (Levy), 660
"Mud-king, or Smedley's Ghost, The"
      (Bunbury), 167
Muggeridge, Malcolm, 119, 714
"Mulholland's Contract" (Kipling), 630
Mulock, Dinah, 754
Muncher's and Guzzler's Diary, The
      (Armstrong), 44
Mundus Alter et Idem (Joseph Hall), 504–07
Mundy Scheme, The (Friel), 404
"Murder of Nancy, The" (Dickens), 309
Murdock, Iris, 15, 154, 155
Murphy (Beckett), 100–01, 104
Murray, John, 61, 147, 150
"Museé des Beaux Arts" (Auden), 46, 49
"Museum Piece, A" (Zelazny), 264
Mushrooms and Toadstools (Livings), 685
Music at Midnight (Draper), 329
"Music" (Coleridge), 258
Mutiny on the Nore, The (Jerrold), 580
"Mutual Complaint of Plainstones and Causey"
      (Fergusson), 357
"M.W. the Great Eater" (John Hall), 501
My American (Gibbons), 443–44
My Brother, A.E. Housman (Laurence
      Housman), 547
My Dear Cassandra: The Letters of Jane Austen
      (Hughes-Hallet, ed.) 64, 65 n
My Discovery of England (Leacock), 91
My Dog Tulip (Ackerley), 4–5
My Early Life (Churchill), 249
My Fair Lady, 283–84
My Father and Myself (Ackerley), 3
"My Last Duchess" (Robert Browning), 160–61
My Life and Times (Jerome), 574
"My Maiden Brief" (Gilbert), 450
"My Mistress' Eyes" (Shakespeare), 707
"My New Cat Ashlar" (Kipling), 628
My Old Man's a Dustman (Mankowitz), 715–17
"My Own Epitaph" (Gay), 434–35
"My Picture Left in Scotland" (Jonson), 605
My Relations with Carlyle (Froude), 210
My Scotland (Archibald Macdonell), 712
My Secret (Petrarch), 432
My Strange Quest for Mensonge (Bradbury),
      152, 154
"Myfanwy" (Betjeman), 148

"Myfanwy at Oxford" (Betjeman), 148
Mystery of Edwin Drood, The (Dickens), 309

Nabokov, Vladimir, 153, 215, 617
Naked Civil Servant, The (Crisp), 290
"Namby Pamby" (Carey), 208
Name and Nature of Poetry, The (Housman), 546–47
Name of Action, The (Graham Greene), 474
Napoleon and His Marshals (Archibald Macdonell), 712
Napoleon of Notting Hill (Chesterton), 244–45
Narrative Poems (C.S. Lewis), 663
Narizzano, Silvio, 803
Nash, Ogden, 36, 347
Nashe, Thomas, 38, 303, 485–86, 622
  biography, 781–82
  literary analysis, 782–86
Nashe's Lenten Stuffe (Nashe), 782, 784
Nathan, George Jean, 417
Nation, 73
National Arts Foundation, 46
National Book Committee, 47
National Endowment for the Arts, 46
National Film Theatre, 26
National Observer (Graham), 459–60, 829
National Tales (Hood), 537, 539
National Theatre (London), 68, 70, 353, 850
National Velvet (Bagnold), 74–75, 76
"Nationality in Drinks" (Robert Browning), 158
"Natural Theology" (Kipling), 630
Nature and Human Nature (Haliburton), 497
Nature of the Crime, The (Ford and Conrad), 383
Naulahka (Balestier and Kipling), 626
Naval Officer: or, Scenes and Adventures in the Life of Frank Mildonay, The (Marayat), 725, 726
NBC, 88, 117
Neal, Patricia, 293, 294
Neame, Ronald, 75, 222
"Nearly Fifty Years of *Punch*" (Burnand), 169
Necessary and the Contingent, The (Bradbury), 155
"Necessitarians, The" (Kipling), 629
Never Put Off to Gomorrah (Frayn), 399
New Age, 73
New American Mercury, 417
New Atlantis (Bacon), 87
New Bats in Old Belfries (Betjeman), 147, 149
New Cautionary Tales (Belloc), 131, 138
New Ewart Poems 1980–1982, The (Ewart), 345
New Humpty-Dumpty, The (Ford), 384
New Inn, The, 598
New Lamps for Old (Jerome), 573, 577
New Men and Old Acres (Taylor), 513
New Monthly Magazine, xli n, 579
New Oxford Book of Light Verse, The (Kingsley Amis), 18–19
New Road, 412
"New Simile. In the Manner of Swift, A" (Goldsmith), 455

New Sporting Magazine, 651
New Statesman, 23, 73, 295, 891
New Times, The, 533
"New Utopia, The" (Jerome), 577
New Verse (Grigson), 346
New Way to Pay Old Debts, A (Massinger), 372
"New Wing at Elsinore, The" (Hankin), 513 n
New Witness, 129, 244
New Year Letter (Auden), 54 n. See also *Double Man, The*
New York Herald Tribune, 75
New York Post, 83 n
New York Shakespeare Festival, 110 n
New York Times, 70, 71, 294, 444 n, 657, 850
New York Times Magazine, 398–400, 403 n, 404, 406–07, 441, 444
New York World, 280
New Yorker, The, xxxix, 117 n, 262, 293, 404, 527, 849
Newberry, John, 452
Newman, John Henry, 158
Newman, William, 653
News from Nowhere (Morris), 577
News from the New World Discovered in the Moon (Jonson), 604
Newsweek, 153
Newton, J.F., 835, 837
Nice Work (Lodge), 692–93
Nicholas Nickleby (Dickens), 308, 310–11, 575
Nicolson, Harold, 559
Nietzsche, Friedrich, 86, 155
"Nigger Question, The" (Carlyle), 210
Night of the Party, The (Weedon Grossmith), 492
Night of the Simhat Torah, The (Barnes), 79
"Night, Youth, Paris and the Moon" (John Collier), 264
Nightingale, Benedict, 70, 71, 398–99, 400, 403 n
Nightline, 820
Nightmare Abbey (Peacock), 833–34, 837
Nil Carborundum (Livings), 685–86
"Nina" (Coward), 283
Nine Daies Wonder (Kempe), 303
Nineteen Eighty Four (Orwell), 664, 808, 811, 817–20, 822
"Ninety Years On" (Rattigan), 251
No Cards (Gilbert), 447
No Enemy (Ford Madox Ford), 387
No More Parades (Ford Madox Ford), 383
"No. 2: The Pines" (Beerbohm), 116
Noble Gentleman, The (Beaumont or Fletcher), 93
Noblesse Oblige (Mitford), 776, 778
Nobody Here But Us Chickens (Barnes), 8
"Nocturnal Reverie, A" (Finch), 366
Noel Coward at Las Vegas (Coward), 283
Noel Coward in New York (Coward), 283
Noises Off (Frayn), 399, 401–02
Non Mi Ricordo! (Hone), 533
Nones (Auden), 46
Noonan, Christine, 30
Nonsense and Wonder: The Poems and Cartoons of Edward Lear (Byron), 649

Nonsense Songs, Stories, Botany and Alphabets (Lear), 645, 648
Norman Conquests, The (Ayckbourn), 68, 69
Norman Douglas (Lindeman), 330
Normyx. *See* Douglas, Norman
Northanger Abbey (Austen), 60, 61–62, 63, 64 n
Norton, C.E., 629
"Nose, The" (Coleridge), 258
Nostromo (Conrad), 383
Not as Bad as They Seem (Barnes), 82
Not Honour More (Cary), 221
Not I (Beckett), 110
"Not So Much a Programme," 274
Note-Books of Samuel Butler, The (Butler), 186
"Notes for a Preface" (Anderson), 32 n
Notes on the Acting of a Fairy Play (Barrie), 88
"Notes on the Comic" (Auden), 50, 52–53, 54 n
"Nothing Can Last Forever" (Coward), 283
Notorious Mrs. Ebbsmith, The (Pinero), 512
Nottingham Playhouse, 415
Nottinghamshire Guardian, 152
Noureddin Ali, formerly of Damascus. *See* Armstrong, John
Novascotian, or Colonial Herald, 496
Novelist at the Crossroads, and Other Essays on Fiction and Criticism, The (Lodge), 691
Novello, Ivor, 411
Novels and Novelists: A Guide to the World of Fiction (ed. Seymour-Smith), 676, 680
"Novels by Eminent Hands" (Thackeray), 170
"Novels of Jane Austen, The" (Lewes), 61, 64 n
Now You Know (Frayn), 399, 400
Now We Are Six (Milne), 771
Noyes, Alfred, 831
Nude with Violin (Coward), 284
Nun's Priest's Tale (Chaucer), 230, 231, 232, 234
"Nutcrackers and the Table and the Chair, The" (Lear), 648

O'Brien, Flann. *See* O'Nolan, Brian
Observer, 22, 26, 76 n, 399, 447, 569, 711
O'Casey, Sean
    biography, 787–88
    literary analysis, 788–98
    influenced by Larkin, 787
    influenced by Boucicault, 789
O'Connor, Ulick, 125, 126 n
O'Connor, William Van, 221
O Coward! (Coward), 283
O Dreamland (Anderson), 26
O Lucky Man! (Anderson, McDowell, and Sherwin), 27, 30–32
O Rare Hoffnung: A Memorial Garland (Hoffnung and Dobson), 525
Octave of Claudius, The (Pain), 830
Odd Craft (Jacobs), 566
"Ode ad Henricum St. John" (John Philips), 845
Ode for St. Cecilia's Day (Samuel Johnson), 590
"Ode to a Chinaman" (Lear), 642
"Ode to a Nightingale" (Keats), 637
"Ode to H. Bodkin, Esq." (Hood), 538

"Ode to Himself" (Jonson), 598
"Ode to the Gowdspink" (Fergusson), 356
"Ode to Tobacco" (Calverley), 204
O'Dea, Jimmy, 799
Odes and Addresses to Great People (Hood), 536, 539
Odyssey (Homer), 187–88, 189, 613, 866
Oeconomy of Love, The (Armstrong), 42, 43
OED. *See* Oxford English Dictionary
Oedipus Tyrannus (Maurice), 745
Of Human Bondage (Maugham), 739–41
"Of Literary Filchers" (D'Israeli), 316
"Of Pleasing; an Epistle to Sir Richard Temple" (Congreve), 266
"Of Smoking" (Grahame), 459
"Of Stage Tyrants" (Carey), 208
Of the Advantageous Reading of History (John Hall), 500
"Of the Implements for Walking the Streets, and Signs of the Weather" (Gay), 436
"Of Walking the Streets by Day" (Gay), 436
"Of Walking the Streets by Night" (Gay), 436
"Office Friendships" (Ewart), 346
"Oh Lyric Love" (Robert Browning), 158
O'Hara, Maureen, 482 n
O'Henry, 264, 294
Ohio Impromptu (Beckett), 102, 103, 110
Old Batchelor, The (Congreve), 265, 266–68
Old Calabria (Norman Douglas), 330
Old Curiosity Shop, The (Dickens), 308
"Old Devils, The* (Kingsley Amis), 15, 18
"Old Familiar Faces, The" (Lamb), 637
Old Judge; or, Life in a Colony, The (Haliburton), 498
Old Lights for New Chancels (Betjeman), 147, 148, 150
Old School Tie: The Phenomenon of the English Public Schools, The (Gathorne-Hardy), 28
Old Vic Theatre (London), 415, 850
Old Wives' Tale, The (Bennett), 18
Old Wives' Tale, The (Peele), 842–43
Oldershaw, L.R.F., 139
Oldham, John, 587
Oldsey, Bernard, 479
Oliver Twist (Dickens), 308, 309, 311
Olivier, Sir Laurence, 286, 354, 413
Ollier's Literary Miscellany, 833
"Olympians, The" (Grahame), 459, 460
"Olympic Girl" (Betjeman), 148
On (Belloc), 130
"On a Volunteer Singer" (Coleridge), 260
"On an Hour-Glass" (John Hall), 501
On Anything (Belloc), 130, 132
On Approval (Lonsdale), 703
"On Being Hard Up" (Jerome), 576
On Comedy and the Uses of the Comic Spirit (Meredith), xxxvi, 250
"On Dress" (Goldsmith), 453
"On Gut" (Jonson), 604
On Everything (Belloc), 130

On Heroes and Hero-Worship (Carlyle), 210
"On Imitation" (Coleridge), 258
"On Irony" (Belloc), 132
"On My Joyful Departure from the Same City" (Coleridge), 259
On Nothing (Belloc), 130
"On Seeing a Butterfly in the Street" (Fergusson), 357–58
On Something (Belloc), 130
"On Stories" (C.S. Lewis), 663–64
"On the Abuse of Satire" (D'Israeli), 316
"On the Artificial Comedy of the Last Century" (Lamb), 638
On the Constitution of the Church and State (Coleridge), 258
"On the Death of the Right Honourable***" (Goldsmith), 454
On the Frontier (Isherwood), 559
"On the Gate, a Lowbrow Commentary" (Purefoy), 629–30
"On the Gate, a Tale of '16,'" 629–30
On the Grounds and Reasons of Monarchy Considered (John Hall), 500
"On the Idea of Comedy and the Uses of the Comic Spirit" (Meredith), 754–55
On the Outskirts (Frayn), 399
On the Stage—and Off (Jerome), 573, 575
On the Subjection of Women (John Stuart Mill), 755
"On the Tragedies of Shakespeare" (Lamb), 637
"On Wit and Humour" (Hazlitt), xxxv, 250
On with the Dance (Coward), 279
Once a Week, 338
"Once I Put It Down, I Could Not Pick It Up Again" (Coren), 276
One Before, The (Barry Pain), 830
One Day in the Life of Ivan Denisovich (Solzhenitsyn), 121
One Fat Englishman (Kingsley Amis), 17–18
"One Minute Please" (Hoffnung), 526
One of Our Conquerors (Meredith), 755
"One of the Family" (Auden), 117 n
One Thing More (Christopher Fry), 409, 416
One Touch of Venus (Anstey)
    screenplay by S.J. Perelman and Ogden Nash, 36
"One Word More" (Robert Browning), 158, 162
O'Neill, Eugene, 124, 281, 284, 656
O'Nolan, Brian, 125, 371
    biography, 798–99
    literary analysis, 799–803
    pseudonym, Flann O'Brien, 799, 801
    pseudonym, Myles na Gopaleen, 799, 801
"Open Boat, The" (Crane), 298
Open Door (Fry), 411
Opera Comique, 447–48
Opie, Amelia, 835
O'Prey, Paul, 477
Orai Ujsag (Mikes), 763
Orators, The (Auden), 45, 49, 50, 51, 53
Orators, The (Foote), 381

Ordeal of Richard Feverel, The (George Meredith), 754
Orgel, Stephen, 603
Oriental Express (Graham Greene), 474
Origin of Harlequin, The (Barrie), 87
Origin of Species (Darwin), 186
"Origin of the English Language, The" (D'Israeli), 317
Original Letters of Sir John Falstaff (James White), 635
Original Plays (Gilbert), 447, 448
Original Poetry of Victor and Cazire (Percy Bysse Shelley and Elizabeth Shelley), 167
Orioli, Giuseppe, 329, 330
Orlando (Woolf), 122
Orlando Furioso (Robert Greene), 488
Orton, Joe, 27, 77, 110, 402, 849
    biography, 803
    literary analysis, 803–07
Orwell, George, 493, 505, 664
Orwell, Sonia, 493
Osborne, John, 15, 16, 27, 77, 419, 656
O'Shea, Milo, 803
Osorio (Coleridge), 258
Ossian, 591
O'Terrall, George Moore, 482 n
Othello (Shakespeare), 95
Other People (Martin Amis), 24
Other People's Clerihews (Ewart), 347
"Other Town, The" (Isherwood), 558, 561
Otherwise Engaged (Gray), 468, 471, 850
O'Toole, Peter, 77
Ouida, Marie Louise de la Ramée, 170
Our Basic Concerns (Christopher Fry), 415
Our Betters (Maugham), 741
Our Country's Good (Wertenbaker), 355
Our Exagmination Round His Factification for Incamination of Work in Progress (Joyce), 610
Our Family (Hood), 539
"Our Lady of Antibes" (D'Arcy), 299
Our Man in Havana (Greene), 285, 476–77, 478–79, 490
Our Mutual Friend (Dickens), 308, 310, 646
Ousley, Ian, 494 n
"Out of Town" (Burnand), 170
Out of the Shelter (Lodge), 691–94
Out of the Silent Planet (C.S. Lewis), 663–65
Outsider, The (Wilson), 16
Over to You: Ten Stories of Flyers and Flying (Dahl), 293
Overbury, Sir Thomas, 13, 507
Ovid, 230, 325, 720, 726, 875, 882
Ovid's Epistles (Dryden), 334
Owen, D.D.R., 433 n
Owen, Robert, 432, 839
Owen, Wilfred, 53, 387
"Owl and the Pussy-Cat, The" (Lear), 645, 647–48
"Owl Describing Her Young Ones, The" (Finch), 367
"Owl Writes a Detective Story, The" (Ewart), 347
Oxford Book of Light Verse (Auden), 51, 54 n

Oxford Chronicle, 474
Oxford English Dictionary, xxxiv, 49, 130, 139, 347
"Oxford in the Vacation" (Lamb), 635
Oxford Outlook, 558
Oxford Poetry, 45
Oxford Repertory Players, 412
Oxford Sausage, The (Maurice), 745
Oxford Times, 711
Oxford University Chest, An (Betjeman), 147
Oxford University Press, 139, 204, 412
"Oxonian, The" (Maurice), 745–46

"Pacchiarotto" (Robert Browning), 162
Pagan Papers (Grahame), 459, 461
Page, Malcolm, 68, 70
Page, Norman, 547, 549 n
Page of Plymouth (Dekker and Jonson), 595
Pain, Barry Eric Odell, 565
      biography, 829–30
      literary analysis, 830–32
"Pains of Sleep, The" (Coleridge), 258
Pair of Blue Eyes, A (Hardy), 515
"Palace of Art, The" (Lear), 646
Palace of Truth, The (Gilbert), 447
Palin, Michael, 252, 253, 254
Pall Mall Gazette, 447, 645
Palmer, John, 638
Palmer, Mary, 734
Palmer, Samuel, 642
Pamela (Richardson), 359, 361
Pandosto (Robert Greene), 487
Paper Money Lyrics (Peacock), 834, 838
Paracelsus (Robert Browning), 157
Parade's End (Ford Madox Ford), 383–84, 386–88
Paradise Lost (Milton), 44, 193, 195, 262, 590, 845
      imitation by Maurice, 745
      opera version by Fry, 416
Paradise News (Lodge), 692, 693–94
Paradoxes (John Hall), 500
Paradoxes and Problems (Donne), 320
Parasitaster (Marston), 729
Pardoner's Tale (Chaucer), 234
Pariah, The (Anstey), 35
Parker, Dorothy, 283
Parliament of Fowles (Chaucer), 229, 236–37, 341
Parnell, Charles Stuart, 613
Parnell, Thomas, 434
Parson's Daughter (Hook), 541
Partners (Gray), 468
Partridge, Bernard, 171, 576
Pasquin (Fielding), 359, 360
Passage to India, A (Forster), 390, 393, 394–95, 396
"Passion and Principle" (Hook), 541
"Passion Vaincue, La" (Finch), 367
Past and Present (Carlyle), 210, 211–12
Pater, Walter, 611, 830
Path to Rome, The (Belloc), 129, 130–31
Patience (Gawain/Pearl Poet), 430, 432
Patience (Gilbert and Sullivan), 448, 492

Patriot, The, 532
Paul Pry (Jonson), 748
Pauline (Robert Browning), 157
Peacock, Thomas Love, 152, 167, 318, 331, 553, 755
      biography, 832–34
      literary analysis, 834–41
Peanut Papers, The (Coren), 275
Pearl (Gawain/Pearl Poet), 429, 430–31
Peele, George, 781–82
      biography, 841
      literary analysis, 841–44
"Pelican Chorus, The" (Lear), 649
Penguin Book of Light Verse, The (Ewart), 345
Penguin Books, 147, 329
Penultimate Poems (Ewart), 345
"Peppering Roads" (Lear), 642
Pepys, Samuel, 346, 376
Percival Keene (Marryat), 727
Peregrine Bunce (Hook), 542
Perelandra (C.S. Lewis), 664, 666
Perelman, S.J., 36, 170, 275, 276, 284
"Perils of Hypergamy, The" (Gorer), 20 n
Peron, Alfred, 100, 101
Perrot, Mary Louis, 511
"Persecution of Bob Pretty" (Jacobs), 566
Persian Letters (Lyttleton), 453
Persius, 505–06
Persuasions (Austen), 60, 62, 63, 175
Pestell, Thomas, 94
Peter Ibbetson (Du Maurier), 338, 339–40
Peter Ibbetson (Grahame), 460
Peter Pan (Barrie), 85, 86–88, 89, 279
Peter Simple (Marryat), 726
Petrarch, Francesco, 228, 230, 432, 433 n
"Phallus in Wonderland" (Ewart), 346
Phantasmagoria (Carroll), 214
"Phantom of Funkingberg, The" (Bunbury), 167
Phantom Rickshaw, The (Kipling), 625
"Pharaoh's March" (Fry), 409
Philadelphia (Friel), 406
Philaster (Beaumont and Fletcher), 93, 95, 372
Philipon, Charles, 653
Philips, Ambrose, 435, 845
Philips, John, 42, 43, 435, 745–46
      biography, 844–45
      literary analysis, 845–47
Phillips, Ambrose, 206, 208
Philological Quarterly, 506, 507
"Philosopher and the Pheasants, The" (Gay), 436
Philosophy of Mclancholy, The (Peacock), 833
Phiz. *See* Cruikshank, George
Phiz. *See* Browne, Hablot Knight
Phoenix Too Frequent, A (Fry), 412–13, 417
Phogey! Or, How to Have Class in a Classless Society (Bradbury) 151–52
Phroso (Hope), 543
Piano and I (George Grossmith), 492
Picaresque Saint, The (R.W.B. Lewis), 475
"Pictor Ignotus" (Robert Browning), 161
Picture of Dorian Gray, The (Wilde), 117, 283

Picturegoers, The (Lodge), 692
Pictures of English Society (DuMaurier), 339
Pie-Eating Contest (Livings), 685
Piece of Monologue, A (Beckett), 102
Pierce Penilesse his Supplication to the Divell
    (Nashe), 781, 783–84
Piers Plowman, 505
Pigeon Pie (Mitford), 776
Pike Theatre (Dublin), 119
Pilgrim's Progress (Bunyan), 30, 211, 410,
    639, 656
"Pilgrim's Progress, The" (Ewart), 347
Pilgrim's Regress, The (C.S. Lewis), 662, 665
Pinero, Arthur Wing, 512
Pinorman (Aldington), 330
Pinter, Harold, 77, 101, 286, 419, 466, 685
    influenced by Samuel Beckett, 110
Pioneer, 625
Pippa Passes (Robert Browning), 157
Pirates of Penzance, The (Gilbert), 446,
    448–49, 451
Plain Dealer, The (Wycherly), 266
Plain Tales from the Hills (Kipling), 625, 629
Plato, 199, 248, 395
Platonov (Chekhov), 399
Plautus, 94, 95, 758
Play, The, 573
Play Parade (Coward), 285
Playboy, 262, 294
Playboy of the Western World, The (Synge), 788
Playgoer, The (Jerome), 576
Plays and Players, 69
Plays of Henry Carey (Macey), 206, 208 n, 209 n
Plays: One (Frayn), 400, 402
Plays: One (Gray), 466, 470
Playthings and Parodies (Barry Pain), 830
Plea of the Midsummer Fairies, The (Hood),
    537, 539
"Pleasant Plays" (Shaw), 577
Pleasure Garden (Broughton), 26
"Pleasure Pilgrim, The" (D'Arcy), 300, 301
Pleasure Reconciled to Virtue (Jonson), 598, 604
Plough and the Stars, The (O'Casey), 787–93
PMLA, 235, 394, 439 n
Pnin (Nabokov), 153
"Pobble Who Has No Toes, The" (Lear), 649
Poe, Edgar Allen, 297, 316, 536, 539, 715
Poems (Auden), 45, 49
Poems (C.S. Lewis), 663
Poems (Fergusson), 356
Poems (John Hall), 499
Poems and Lyrics of the Joy of Earth
    (Meredith), 755
Poems and Songs (Ewart), 345
Poems by Four Authors (Ackerley), 3
Poems, Chiefly in the Scottish Dialect (Burns), 178
Poems in the Porch (Betjeman), 147
Poems. Minor Poets of the Caroline Period
    (Saintsbury), 501
Poems of Alexander Pope: A Reduced Version of
    the Twickenham Text (Butt), 434

Poems of Anne, Countess of Winchilsea
    (Myra Reynolds), 365, 366, 368 n
Poems of the Past and the Present (Hardy), 516
Poems on Several Occasions (Gay), 434, 436
Poems on Several Subjects (Coleridge), 635
Poems on the Death of Priscilla Farmer
    (Lloyd), 635
Poems on Various Subjects (Coleridge), 257
"Poet, A" (Hardy), 517 n
Poetaster (Jonson), 595, 601, 729
Poetic Mirror, The (Hogg), 530
Poetical Register (Jacob), 265
Poetry: Direct and Oblique (Tillyard), 230
Poetry of the Present (Grigson), 412
Poets at Work (Abbott), 54 n
Poet's Heart, The (Levy), 660
Point Counter Point (Huxley), 553
Polhemus, Robert, 616
Political House That Jack Built, The (Hone), 533
Political Litany, The (Hone), 532
Political Showman-At Home! The (Hone), 534
"Politics and the English Language" (Orwell), 818
Politics and the Novel (Howe), 818
"Politics vs. Literature" (Orwell), 815
"Politeness" (Milne), 773
"Pollio" (Virgil), 436
Polly (Gay), 434, 437–39
Polyhymnia (Peck), 841
Pomes Penyeach (Joyce), 610
"Pompey's Ghost" (Hood), 538
Pongo Plays (Livings), 688
Poole, John, 579
Poole, Thomas, 257
"Poor Cousin Louis" (D'Arcy), 300
Poor Jack (Marryat), 727
"Poor Little Rich Girl" (Coward), 283
Poor Man and the Lady, The (Hardy), 515
Poor Mouth, The (Patrick Power), 799, 801
Pope, Alexander, 10, 13, 14, 53, 60, 167, 174, 183,
    192, 204, 265, 267, 271, 316, 317, 334,
    362, 366, 368, 434–36, 455, 505, 508,
    587 679, 682, 734, 845
    influence on Lord George Gordon Byron, 192
"Pope and his Miscellaneous Quarrels"
    (D'Israeli), 317
"Porphyria's Lover" (Robert Browning), 160,
    162–63
Porter, Cole, 283
Portrait of Max (Behrman), 115, 117
"Portrait of Samuel Beckett, the Author
    of the Puzzling *Waiting for Godot*, A"
    (Shenker), 110 n
"Portrait of the Artist, A" (Joyce), 609
Portrait of the Artist as a Young Man, A (Joyce),
    560, 609, 612–13, 693
Portrait, The (Ford Madox Ford), 384
"'Posh-school' Science Fiction" (Brown), 7, 9
Possessed, The (Dostoyevsky), 121
Posthumous Papers of the Pickwick Club, The
    (Dickens), 308, 309, 310, 497, 574–75,
    577, 726, 820

Potoker, E.M., 370
Potter, Beatrix, 467
Pound, Ezra, 115, 147, 150, 383, 516, 609–11, 662, 671
Pound, Reginald, 518–20
Pour Lucrece (Giraudoux), 414
Powell, Anthony, 17
Powell, L.F., 379, 382 n
Power and the Glory, The (Graham Greene), 475–76
Power in Men (Cary), 221
Power of Satire, The (Robert Elliot) 682 n
Prager, Arthur, 170, 171, 654 n
"Praise of Chimney Sweepers, The" (Lamb), 635, 640
Praise of Folly, The (Erasmus), 551
"Praise of this Book" (Belloc), 131
Prancing Nigger (Firbank), 370
Prancing Novelist: In Praise of Ronald Firbank (Brophy), 369
Prater Violet (Isherwood), 559, 562
Pratt, Denis. *See* Crisp, Quentin
Precious Five (Auden), 48
"Predicting 1984: How Did Orwell Do?— Don't Ask" (Richard Friedman) 820
Preface to Paradise Lost, A (C.S. Lewis), 663
Prefaces, Biographical and Critical to the Works of the English Poets (Samuel Johnson), 586
Prelude, The (Wordsworth), 88, 149
Premier Amour (Beckett), 101
Pre-Raphaelite Brotherhood, The (Ford), 383
Present and Ireland, The (O'Casey), 788
Present State of Wit, The (Gay), 434
Press (Christchurch), 186
"Prevailing Forms of English Satie, The" (Campbell), 506
Prevost, Abbe, 446
Price, Alan, 30
Price, Martin 435, 439 n
Price, R.G.G., 170, 171, 521, 654 n
Price, Uvedale, 835
Pride and Prejudice (Austen), 60, 61, 62–63
Priestley, J.B., 474, 492, 567 n, 660, 712, 763
Prima Donna (Dickens), 309
Prince Caspian (C.S. Lewis), 664, 666
Prince Hohenstiel-Schwangau (Robert Browning), 162
Princess Ida (Gilbert and Sullivan), 448
"Princess, The" (Lear), 646
Princess, The (Tennyson), 148
Princess Toto (Gilbert), 447–48
Prior, Matthew, 53, 199
Prisoner of Chillon, The (Byron), 192
Prisoner of Grace (Cary), 221
Prisoners of War, The (Ackerley), 3, 4
Prisoner of Zenda, The (Hope), 461, 543–55
Pritchett, V.S., 329, 330
Pritchard, William H. 677
Private Life of Don Juan, The (Lonsdale), 702
Private Lives (Coward), 280, 281, 285, 286, 657

Private Memoirs and Confessions of a Justified Sinner, The (Hogg) 530
Privates on Parade (Cleese), 253
Problem of Pain, The (C.S. Lewis), 663
Procopius, 500
Proctor, B.W., 636, 638
Prometheus Unbound (Shelley), 833
"Propagation of a Lie, The" (Bunbury), 165, 168
"Prophetic Qualities of Rudyard Kipling's Works, The" (Esther Smith), 628
Prose and Verse (Lemon), 652
Proust (Beckett), 100, 103
Proust, Marcel, 153, 772
"Proverbial Philosophy" (Calverley), 204
Provok'd Wife, The (Vanbrugh), 354
Pryce, Jonathan, 402
Pryce-Jones, David, 479
Psalm in C (Fry and Tippett), 411
Pseudo-Martyr (Donne), 321
Public and Confidential (Levy), 656, 660
Public Ledger (Newberry), 452–53
Puck of Pook's Hill (Kipling), 627
Puckoon (Spike Milligan), 767
Pudding and Dumpling Burnt to Pot, or, A Compleat Key to the Dissertation on Dumpling (Carey), 208
Pulci, Luigi, 194, 196
Punch, 35, 49, 83 n, 151, 168, 170, 171, 212, 214, 274, 275, 276 277, 336, 338, 340, 346, 391, 441, 446, 449, 511–13, 518–21, 526, 537, 545, 575–77, 579, 580–83, 651–54, 714–15, 747–48, 770, 829
Punch Book of Kids, The (Coren, ed.), 274
"Punch Review, The," 274
Punch's Complete Letter Writer (Jerrold), 579, 581
Punch's Letters to His Son (Jerrold), 579, 581
"Pupil, The" (James), 162
Purefoy, A.E., 629–30
Purple Dust (O'Casey), 789–90, 794–95
"Purple William or, The Liar's Doom" (Housman), 547
Pursuit of Love, The (Mitford), 776–78
Pye, Henry J., 166
Pygmalion and Galatea (Gilbert), 447
Pynchon, Thomas, 617

Q5 (Milligan), 253
Quad (Beckett), 102
Quare Fellow, The (Behan), 119, 122–23, 124, 125, 684
Quarrels of Authors (Dickens), 316, 317
Quarterly Review, 61, 64 n, 176 n
Quartermaine's Terms (Gray), 465–66, 468–69, 471
Quartet (Maugham), 739
Quartette (Kipling), 625
Queen Is Crowned, The (Fry), 414
Queen Lucia (E.F. Benson), 135, 136
Quennell, Peter, 680
Queen's Matrimonial Leader, The (Hone), 533
Queen's Theater, 351

Queen's Wake, The (Hogg), 530–31
Queer Book, A (Hogg), 531
"Queries in Natural History" (Hood), 539
"Question, The" (Auden), 49
Questions at the Well, The (Ford), 383
"Quia Imperfectum" (Beerbohm), 116
Quiet American, The (Greene), 121, 475, 693
Quiller-Couch, Arthur, 458
Quintana, Ricardo, 502
Quintero, Jose, 119
Quips upon Questions (Armin), 38, 40

"Rabbi Ben Ezra" (Robert Browning), 163
Rabelais, François, 131, 505–06, 551, 591, 611
Rachel Papers, The (Martin Amis), 22, 23
Racine, Jean Baptiste, 334
Radical Imagination and the Liberal Tradition, The
    (Zeigler and Bigsby), 156 n
Radio Eirann, 119
Radio Prune Crew, 371
Rae, Stephen, 405
"Rain" (Maugham), 739–40
Rainmaker, The, 68
Raj, 280
Ralegh, Sir Walter, 44, 223, 597
Rambler (Johnson), 11, 586, 588, 590
Ramsay, Allan, 179, 182
Randall, Tony, 37
Rape of the Belt, The (Levy), 656, 658–59
Rape of the Lock, The (Pope), 366
Raspberry Reich (Mankowitz), 715, 718
Rasselas (Samuel Johnson), 454, 586, 589, 591
Rates of Exchange (Bradbury), 152, 153, 154
Rattigan, Terence, 251, 286, 660
Rattel (Livings), 685
Ravel, Maurice, 414, 527
Raymo, R., 230
Raymond, Gerard, 68
Raymond, William B., 161
Razor's Edge, The (Maugham), 282, 740–41
Reade, Charles, 148, 309
Reader's Guide to Graham Greene, A
    (O'Prey), 477
"Reading" (Calverley), 205
Reading, Peter, 348 n
Real Adventures of Robinson Crusoe, The
    (Burnand), 170
Real Long John Silver and Other Plays, The
    (Barnes), 81
Rear Column, The (Gray), 465
Reasons for Flying, The (Livings), 685
Rebel Art Centre, 671
"Recantation" (Coleridge), 259
"Recessional" (Kipling), 626
"Recollections of Nova Scotia" (Haliburton), 496
Records and Reminiscences (Burnand), 169
Recruiting Officer, The (Farquhar), 351, 352–53,
    354, 355
Rectory Umbrella, The, 214
Red Bull Theatre, 96
Red Noses (Barnes), 78, 81

Red Roses For Me (O'Casey), 788, 790, 793–94
Redgrave, Michael, 414
Redway, 243
Reed, Carol, 482 n
Reed, E.T., 171
Reeve, Christopher, 399
Reeve's Tale (Chaucer), 230, 231, 232
"Reflections off the City Angels" (Crisp), 291
Reflections on the Psalms (C.S. Lewis), 663
Reformist's Register (Hone), 532
Reggel, 763
Rehearsal, The (Villiers), 335, 360
Rehearsal at Goatham, The (Gay), 437–39
Rehearsal Transpos'd, The (Marvell), 734
Reid, J.C., 535–37
Reinhardt, Gottfriend, 559
Reinhold, Judge, 36
Reisz, Karel, 26
Relapse, The (Vanbrugh), 353
Relatively Speaking (Ayckbourn), 68, 69
"Relic, The" (Beerbohm), 117
"Religio Laici" (Dryden), 335, 336–37
Religious Comedy, A (Levy), 660
"Relique, The" (Donne), 323
"Reluctant Dragon, The" (Grahame), 461
"Remaining Christmas, A" (Belloc), 129
Remick, Lee, 803
"Rennaissance Influences in Hall's *Mundus Alter*
    et Idem" (Salyer) 506–07
Rent Day, The (Jerrold), 579–80
Rent Man, The (Livings), 685
Reply to the Report of the Earl of Durham
    (Haliburton), 496
"Reproof and Reply, The" (Coleridge), 259
Repton, Humphry, 835
"Reputation of Richard Steele: What Happened?
    The" (Milic), 14
Restaurant at the End of the Universe, The
    (Douglas Adams), 7
Retaliation (Goldsmith), 453, 455
Return of A.J. Raffles, The (Graham Greene), 476
Return of the Native, The (Hardy), 514, 515
Return to Tyassi (Levy), 656
"Reveille" (Housman), 547
Reverie at the Boar's-head-tavern in Eastcheap, A"
    (Goldsmith), 453
Revenge for Love, The (Wyndham Lewis), 672
Revenge of Bussy, The (Chapman), 223
Revengers' Comedies, The (Ayckbourn), 68, 71
Revenger's Tragedy, The (Tourneur), 637
    possible attribution to Middleton, 756
Review (Defoe), 11
Revolutionary Witness & Nobody Here But Us
    Chickens (Barnes), 82
"Revolver in the Corner Cupboard, The"
    (Graham Greene) 473–74
Reynolds, Eileen Carey, 788
Reynolds, John Hamilton, 536
Reynolds, Mary T., 612
Reynolds, Myra, 365–66, 368 n
Reynolds, Sir Joshua, 165, 445, 452, 586

Rewards and Fairies (Kipling), 627
"Rhetoric of Chaucerian Comedy: The Aristotelian
    Legacy, The" (Andreas), 237
Rhineland Journey (Fry), 413
Rhinestones as Big as the Ritz, The (Coren),
    276, 277
Rhodaphne (Peacock), 833
Rhodes, Cecil, 627
Rhyme? Reason? (Carroll), 214
Rich, Christopher, 547
Richard Crookback (Jonson), 595
Richard III (Shakespeare), 639
Richard's Cork Leg (Behan), 120
Richards, I.A., 47
Richardson, Charles, 527
Richardson, Dorothy, 617 n
Richardson, Ralph, 482 n
Richardson, Samuel, 11, 17, 60, 173, 305, 359,
    361, 636
Richardson, Tony, 26
"Richmond Hill" (Bunbury), 165
Richter, Paul, 210, 211
Rickles, Don, 846
Riddles of "Finnegans Wake," The (Patrick
    McCarthy), 616, 617 n
Ridge, Pett, 830
Rifle Volunteer, The (Livings), 685
"Right and Wrong as a Clue to the Meaning
    of the Universe" (C.S. Lewis), 662
Right Hand of Christian Love Offered, The
    (Andreae), 499
Right Playmate, The (Hoffnung), 526, 527
Right Time and Place, The (Barnes), 79
Rightful Heir, The (Bulwer-Lytton), 169
"Rime of the Ancient Mariner The" (Coleridge),
    167, 214, 257, 536 638
Ring and the Book, The (Robert Browning), 158,
    159, 161, 205
Ring Round the Moon: A Charade with Music
    (Fry), 413, 415
Rire, Le (Bergson), 681. *See also Laughter*
"Rising of the Session, The" (Fergusson), 357
Ritson, Joseph, 838
Ritter, John, 399
River War, The (Churchill), 249
Riverside Chaucer, The (Fyler), 230
Riverside Villas Murder, The (Kingsley Amis),
    15, 19
"Road to Strome, The" (Barnes), 79
*Road to the Never Land: A Reassessment of J.M.
    Barrie's Dramatic Art, The* (Jack), 89
Road to Wigan Pier, The (Orwell), 809, 814
Roaring Queen, The (Wyndham Lewis), 672
"Roast Beef of Old England, The" (Fielding), 360
Robert Browning (Chesterton), 243
Robert of Sicily: Opera for Children (Tippett), 412
Robert II King of Scots (Dekker and Jonson), 595
Roberts, Julia, 38
Robertson, T.W., 513
Robin. *See* Blood, Marjorie
Robinson, E. Kay, 625

Robinson, Fred Miller, 105, 106
Robinson, Henry Crabb, 635
Robinson, Lennox, 788
Robinson, Michael, 110 n
Robinson, Robert, 90
Rockabye (Beckett), 109
Rockwell, Norman, 846
Roderick Random (Smollett), 198
Rogers, Katherine M., 366–67, 368 n
Rogers, Paul, 482 n
"Rolling English Road, The" (Chesterton), 246
"Roman and English Comedy Considered
    and Compared" (Foote), 379
Roman de la Rose (De Meun), 230
Romance (Ford and Conrad), 383
"Romance of the Road, The" (Grahame), 459
Romances (D'Israeli), 316
Romantic Adventures of a Milkmaid, The
    (Hardy), 515
Romantic History of Robin Hood
    (Barry Pain), 830
Romaunt of the Rose (Chaucer), 229
Romeo and Juliet (Shakespeare), 67, 621
Ronald Firbank (Potoker), 370
Room at the Top (Braine), 16
"Room with a View, A" (Coward), 283
Room with a View, A (Forster), 37, 389, 391–92
Roosevelt, Teddy, 249
*Root and Sky: Poetry from the Plays
    of Christopher Fry*, 415
Rose Theater, 223
Rosenkrantz and Guildenstern (Gilbert), 447,
    448, 451
Ross, Alan, 778
Ross, Jean W., 291
Rossetti and His Circle (Beerbohm), 115, 116
Rossetti, Dante Gabriel, 214, 513
Rossetti, William, 644
Rossiter, Leonard, 31
Rostand, Edmond, 45
Roth, Samuel, 610
Rothenstein, William, 114, 115
Rothermere, Lord, 50
Rotting Hill (Wyndham Lewis), 673, 681
Round and Round the Garden (Ayckbourn), 69
Round Table, The (Peacock), 833
Rousseau, G.S., 454, 456 n
Rousseau, Jean Jacques, 86, 199, 315, 316,
    317, 835
Routledge, George, 512
Routledge, Warne and Routledge, 645, 647
Rover, The (Behn), 352
"Row Us Out From Desenzano" (Tennyson), 649
Rowe, Nicholas, 366
Rowlandson, Thomas, 165
Rowley, Samuel, 40
Rowley, William, 372, 758
Rowse, A.L., 474
Royal Academy, 165
Royal Court Theatre, 26, 78, 355, 685
Royal Lady's Magazine, 531

Royal Shakespeare Company (London), 78, 83 n, 88, 685
Royale Theatre (New York), 413
Royalty Theatre, 447
Rude Assignment: A Narrative of My Career Up-to-Date (Wyndham Lewis), 673
Ruddigore (Gilbert and Sullivan), 448
Ruddiman, Thomas, 356
Rudyard Kipling (Seymour-Smith), 627
Ruffian on the Stair (Orton), 803–04
Ruggiers, Paul, 230
Rule a Wife and Have a Wife (Fletcher), 372
Ruling Class, The (Barnes), 77, 81
Rumour at Nightfall (Graham Greene), 474
Running, Jumping, Standing Still Film, The (Sellers and Milligan) 253
Runyon, Damon, 716
Rupert of Hentzau (Hope), 543
"Rural Sports" (Gay), 434–35
Ruskin, John, 210, 212, 214, 384, 393, 645, 725, 830
Russell, Bertrand, 399, 553
Russian Interpreter, The (Frayn), 399, 400
Ryan, C. Paul, 32

Sacred Flame, The (Maugham), 739, 742
Sad Shepherd, The (Jonson), 599
"Sad/Funny Man" (Spike Milligan), 767
Sadleir, Michael, 137 n
"Saga of the Seas, A" (Grahame), 461
Sail Away (Coward), 280
St. Jacques, Raymond, 482 n
St. James Gazette (Grahame), 459, 511–13
St. James Theatre, 702
St. John, Oliver, 734
"St. Patrick's Day in the Morning" (O'Casey), 793–94
Saintsbury, George, 501
Saki, 264, 294, 460
Salle, J. de la. *See* Hall, John
"Sally Brown" (Hood and Reynolds), 536
"Sally in Our Alley" (Carey), 206, 208
"Sally Simpkin's Lament" (Hood), 538
Salmacis and Hermaphroditus (Beaumont), 93, 94
Salted Almonds (Anstey), 37
Salyer, Sanford, 506–07
Sam Foote, Comedian, 1720–1777 (Trefman), 382 n
Sam Slick's Wise Saws and Modern Instances: or, What He Said, Did or Invented (Haliburton), 497
Samuel Beckett: A Biography (Bair), 99, 100, 101, 104, 110 n
Samuel Beckett: The Comic Gamut (Cohn), 106
Samuel Butler: A Biography (Raby), 189 n
Samuel Butler's Note Books (Keynes and Hill), 189 n
Samuel Foote (Chatten), 380–81, 382 n
Samuel Taylor Coleridge (Radley), 260 n
Sanditon (Austen), 60, 64
Sandra Belloni (George Meredith), 754
Sanity Inspector (Coren), 274, 276

Santal (Firbank), 370
Sardou, Victorien, 309
Sartor Resartus (Carlyle), 210–11, 212, 754
Sartre, Jean Paul, 216, 563, 681
Satire Against Presbytery, A (John Hall), 500
"Satire and Fiction" (Wyndham Lewis), 672, 676, 679
"Satire: The English Tradition, the Poet and the Age" (Hallett Smith), 503
Satires of Circumstance (Hardy), 516
Satiromastix (Dekker), 595
Saturday Evening Post, 220, 293
Saturday Night and Sunday Morning (Sillitoe), 16, 985–88
"Saturday Night at The Rose and Crown" (Coward), 283
Saturday Night Live, 254, 766
Saturday Review, 115, 511
Saturday Review of Literature, 74
Saucer of Larks, The (Friel), 404
Savage, Eliza Mary Ann, 185
Savage, Fred, 36
Savage, Henry L., 433 n
Savage, Richard, 586
Savonarola, Girolamo, 140
Savoy, The, 114, 574
Savoy Operas, 492
Savoy Theatre, 448
Savrola (Churchill), 249
Sayer, George, 662
Sayers, Dorothy, 138–39
Sayings and Doings (Hook), 541
"Scaffolding of Rhetoric, The" (Churchill), 249
Scarborough Theatre-in-the-Round Company, 70
Scarperer, The (Behan), 119
Scenes from Provincial Life (Cooper), 16
Schell, Maria, 482 n
Schenker, Daniel, 675, 677, 678, 680
Scheps, Walter, 233–34
Schiller, Johann, 210
"Schir Thomas Norny" (Dunbar), 342
Schlesinger, Arthur, Jr., 819
Scholars, The (Lovelace), 705
Schönberg, Arnold, 526
School for Scandal, The (Sheridan), 354, 412
"School of Night" (Ralegh), 223
Schoolboy Lyrics (Kipling), 625
"Schoolboy, The" (Maurice), 745–46
"School-Mistress Abroad: An Extravaganza" (Hood), 539
Schopenhauer, Arthur, 210–11
Scienza Nuova (Vico), 616
Scoggan, John, 552
Scoop (Evelyn Waugh), 155
Scornful Lady, The (Beaumont and Fletcher), 93, 94, 374–75
Scotch Gentleman, The (Hogg), 530
Scots Musical Museum (James Johnson), 178
Scott, Captain Robert, 85
Scott, John 639
Scott, Sir Walter, 60, 61, 495, 530, 835, 838

Scoundrel, The, 285
Scourge of Villanie, The (Marston), 729–30
Screwtape Letters, The (C.S. Lewis), 256, 663, 666
Scribe, Augustin, 309
Scriblerus Club, 434, 437
Scriblerus Secundus. See Fielding, Henry
"Scrutinie, The" (Lovelace), 705–06
Sea and the Mirror, The (Auden), 51
"Seafarer," 143
Seaman, Owen, 171, 518
Sean (Eileen Reynolds), 788
Season-Ticket, The (Haliburton), 498
Season's Greetings (Ayckbourn), 70
Secker, Martin, 831
Secombe, Harry, 766
Second Jungle Book, The (Kipling), 626
Second Mrs. Tanquery, The (Pinero), 512
Second Nun's Tale, The (Chaucer), 229, 230, 232–33, 235, 236
"Second Rate Woman, A" (Kipling), 629
Second Shepherd's Play (Wakefield Master), 432
Second World War, The (Churchill), 249
Secret Agent, The (Conrad), 121
Secret Battle, The (Herbert), 518
Secret Diary of Adrian Mole, The (Townsend), 493
Secret History (Procopius), 500
Secret People (Dickinson), 26
Secret Policeman's Other Ball, The (Cleese), 252
Secret Policeman's Private Parts, The (Cleese), 252
Seems Like Old Times: A Year in the Life of Alan Coren (Coren), 277
Seinfeld, 255
Sejanus (Jonson), 595–97
Select Collection of Original Scotish Airs (Thomson), 178
Selected Literary Essays (C.S. Lewis), 663
Selected Poems (Betjeman), 150
Self Condemned (Wyndham Lewis), 673
Sellers, Peter, 252, 253, 371, 766
Selznick, Irene, 75
Semele (Congreve), 272
Sendall, Walter J., 204
Sense and Sensibility (Auden), 60, 61, 62
"Sentimental Journey from Islington to Waterloo Bridge, in March 1821" (Hood), 538
Sentimental Journey through France and Italy by Mr. Yorick (Sterne), 538
Sentimental Tommy (Barrie), 86
"September 1, 1939" (Auden), 46
Sequence, 26
Serena Blandish (Bagnold), 73, 76
Serious Epistle to Mr. Prynne (John Hall), 500
Seven at a Stroke: A Play for Children (Fry and Tippett), 412
Seven League Boots, The (Gilbert), 447
Seven Men (Beerbohm), 117
Seven Seas, The (Kipling), 626–30
Seven Who Were Hanged, The (Andreyev), 123
"Sex and the Single Bed" (Crisp), 291
"Sex Revolution" (Spike Milligan), 767

Seymour-Smith, Martin, 627, 676, 680, 682
"Shades of Night Were Falling Fast, The" (Housman), 547
Shadow of a Gunman, The (O'Casey), 787–93
Shadow of a Sorcerer, The (Gibbons), 444
Shadowlands (C.S. Lewis), 662
Shadwell, Thomas, 236, 265
Shaftesbury, Lord, 43
Shakespeare Murders, The (Archibald Macdonell), 711
Shakespeare, William, 30, 31–32, 38, 39, 40–41, 50, 59, 61, 64, 67, 88, 93, 94, 95, 97, 106, 109, 116, 153, 158, 175, 182, 188, 252, 266, 268, 272, 276, 334, 345, 354, 372–73, 377, 411, 416, 466, 470, 479, 486, 488, 490, 514, 517, 521, 539, 586, 589–92, 594–95, 599–611, 621, 622, 631, 637–39, 640, 646, 651, 657, 680, 684, 707, 720, 722, 723, 730–31, 758, 766–67, 787, 820, 843, 846
Shakespeare's Sisters: Feminist Essays on Woman Poets (Sandra Gilbert and Susan Gubar), 368 n
Shakespeare's Sonnets Reconsidered (Butler), 188
Shall We Join the Ladies? (Barrie), 85
Shamela (Fielding), 359, 361
Shankara, Aparokshanubhuti, 559
Sharp, Evelyn, 301
Shaughraun, The (Boucicault), 787, 789
Shaw, George Bernard, 36, 77, 86, 88, 89, 115, 116, 187, 207, 243 281, 284, 286, 355, 375, 407, 411, 574, 577, 656, 657, 658, 660, 661, 679, 739, 741, 830
Shaw, Martin, 412
She Shall Have Music (Frankan, Fry, and Charlot), 411
She Stoops to Conquer (Goldsmith), 354, 453, 455–56
Sheares, William, 729
Shelden, Michael, 810
Shelley, Elizabeth, 167
Shelley, Mary, 31
Shelley, Percy Bysshe, 163, 167, 370, 638, 640, 833–34, 837
Shenker, Israel, 100, 110 n
Shenstone, William, 53
Shepherd's Week, The (Gay), 434–35, 439
Sheppey (Maugham), 739
Sheridan, Richard Brinsley, 60, 286, 354, 412, 541, 789
Sherlock Holmes Society, 711
Sherry, Norman, 473–74
Sherwin, David, 26–27
Shield of Achilles, The (Auden), 46, 48
Shifting of the Fire, The (Ford Madox Ford), 383
Ship of Fools (Brant), 551
Shipman's Tale (Chaucer), 231, 233, 234
Shirley, James, 377
Shoemaker's Holiday (Dekker), 303
"Shoemaker's Holiday" (Deloney), 304
"Shooting an Elephant" (Orwell), 808

Shooting an Elephant, and Other Essays (Orwell), 811, 820–21
"Shop" (Robert Browning), 159
Short Cruises (Jacobs), 566
"Short Happy Life of Margaux Hemingway, The" (Coren), 276
Short View of the Profaneness and Immorality of the English Stage, A (Jeremy Collier), 268, 352
Shropshire Lad, A (Housman), 546–49
Shumlin, Herman, 482 n
Shuttlecock (Livings), 685
Sibylline Leaves (Coleridge), 258, 259
Sidney, Sir Philip, 93, 95, 303–04, 782
Siege (Fry), 411
Sigh No More (Coward), 284
Sight and Sound, 26
"Signs of the Times" (Carlyle), 210
Sillitoe, Alan, 16, 121
Silver Bridges (Barnes), 79
Silver Chair, The (C.S. Lewis), 664, 665
Silver Tassie, The (O'Casey), 788, 793–94
Silverlight, J., 20
Simon Gray: A Casebook (Burkman), 471 n
"Simon Gray and the Pedagogical Erotics of the Theatre" (Roof), 471 n
"Simon Sniggle" (Bunbury), 167
Simons, Judy, 175, 176 n
Simple Life Limited, The (Ford Madox Ford), 384
Simple People (Gray), 465
Simpson, Alan, 119, 120
Simpson, N.F., 686
Sinecurist's Creed, The (Hone), 532
Single Man, A (Isherwood), 560, 562, 563
Sir Gawain and the Green Knight (Gawain/Pearl Poet), 429–30, 431–32
Sir Giles Goosecap (Chapman), 223, 225–26
Sir Harry Wildair (Farquhar), 351, 352
Sir Hornbook (Peacock), 833
"Sir Julian Garve" (D'Arcy), 298–299
"Sir Plausible" (Finch), 368
Sir Proteus (Peacock), 833, 835
"Sir Thopas: The Bourgeois Knight, the Minstrel and the Critics" (Scheps), 233–34
Siren Land (Norman Douglas), 330
Sister Dora (Manton), 415
    television script by Fry, 415
Sisterly Feelings (Ayckbourn), 68
"Sitting of the Session, The" (Fergusson), 357
Sitwell, Osbert, 569, 676
"Six-Mark Tea-Pot, The" (Du Maurier), 339
Skelton, John, 316, 505, 551
Sketches and Eccentricities of Col. David Crockett of West Tennessee, 497
Sketches by Boz (Dickens), 308, 581
Sketches or Essays on Various Subjects (Armstrong), 43, 44
Skipper's Wooing, The (Jacobs), 567
Skynner, Robin, 252
Slap at Slop, A (Hone), 533
Slattery's Sago Saga (O'Nolan), 799

"Slaughterman" (Barnes), 79
Sleep of Prisoners, A (Fry), 413, 415
"Slough" (Betjeman), 150
Small Family Business, A (Ayckbourn), 68, 70
Small World (Bradbury), 152
Small World (Lodge), 692, 694, 696, 698–99
Smith, Charlotte, 60
Smith, Esther M.G., 628
Smith, Francis J., 237
Smith, Hallett, 503
Smith, Harold Llewellen, 45
Smith, Maggie, 354, 482 n
Smith, Seba, 497
Smock Alley Theatre (Dublin), 267
Smollett, Tobias, 11, 42, 43, 44, 152, 198, 199, 354, 497, 567 n, 725
    influence on Collier, 264
Sneeze, The (Frayn), 402
Snitow, Ann Barr, 385–87
Snooty Baronet, The (Wyndham Lewis), 672, 678, 679, 681
"Snowbound" (Grahame), 459
So Long and Thanks for All the Fish (Adams), 7
"So We'll Go No More A-Roving" (Byron), 347
Social Pictorial Satire (Du Maurier), 338, 339
Society Clown, A (George Grossmith), 492
Socks Before Marriage (Frayn), 401
Socrates, 13, 837
Soldier of Humor, A (Wyndham Lewis), 681
Soldier, The (Lovelace), 705
Soldiers Three (Kipling), 625
"Soliloquy of the Spanish Cloister, The" (Robert Browning), 159
Solomon, 199
Solomon, Maurice, 139
Solzhenitsyn, Alexander, 121
"Some Day I'll Find You" (Coward), 283
Some Do Not (Ford Madox Ford), 383, 386–87
"Some Persons of 'the Nineties'" (Beerbohm), 116
Someone Like You (Dahl), 293
Somersaults (Barnes), 78
"Somerset Maugham Theatre," 739
Something for the Weekend (Coren), 276, 277
Something of Myself (Kipling), 628
"Song" (Donne), 326
Song at Twilight, A (Coward), 286
Song of Songs (Song of Solomon), 507
"Song of the English, The" (Kipling), 626
Song of the Shirt, The (Hood), 537, 654
Songs and Sonets (Donne), 320, 322, 326
"Songs for the Sentimental" (Lemon), 652
Songs From Books (Kipling), 628
Songs of a Savoyard (Gilbert), 448
"Sonnet: Afterwards" (Ewart), 346
"Sonnets Attempted in the Manner of Contemporary Writers" (Coleridge), 285, 260
Sophocles, 162
Sophy of Kravonia (Hope), 543
Sorcerer, The (Gilbert and Sullivan), 447, 491
Sordello (Robert Browning), 157

Sorrows of Young Werther (Goethe), 212
Sort of Life, A (Greene, Graham), 473, 476
Soto, Donal, 291
Soul on Ice (Cleaver), 121
Souls and Bodies (Lodge), 692
South Wind (Norman Douglas), 4, 329, 330, 331–32
Southerne, Thomas, 265
Southey, Robert, 195, 257, 638, 834–35, 838
    parodied by Henry William Bunbury, 166
Spacks, Patricia M., 173, 176 n
Spain (Auden), 49, 54 n
"Spain, 1937" (Auden), 46
Spanish Pistol, The (Archibald Macdonell), 712
Spanish Tragedy, The (Kyd), 97, 729
Spark, Muriel, 18
Sparrow, John, 150
Speaight, Robert, 129, 130
"Speak Gently" (Langford), 215
"Speak Roughly to Your Little Boy" (Carroll), 215
Speaker, 138
Spearing, A.C., 433 n
Specimens of the English Dramatic Poets Who Lived about the Time of Shakespeare (Lamb), 635, 637, 640
Spectator, The (Steele), 4, 6 n, 10–14, 147, 265, 295, 453, 454
"Speculations of a Naturalist" (Hood), 549
Speculum, 234
"Speech According to Horace" (Jonson), 605
Speech of the Hon. Mr. Justice Haliburton, M.P. in The House of Commons, on Tuesday, the 21st of April 1860, on the Repeal of the Different Duties on Foreign and Colonial Wood (Haliburton), 496
Spencer, Gabriel, 595
Spencer, Herbert, 514
Spender, Stephen, 3, 4, 16, 45, 50, 54, 345, 348 n, 558
Spenser, Edmund, 372, 506, 663, 699, 746, 782
Spenser's Images of Life (C.S. Lewis), 663
Spielberg, Steven, 88, 256
Spielmann, M.H., 171, 653, 654–55
Spirit of Man & More Barnes' People, The (Barnes), 78, 79, 83 n
Spirits in Bondage (C.S. Lewis), 662
Splendid Shilling, The (John Philips), 435, 745–46, 844–46
Spoiled (Gray), 465–66
Sport of My Mad Mother, The (Jellicoe), 569
Sport Royal (Hope), 543
"Spot the Brain Cell," 254
Sprat, Thomas, 11
Springtime for Henry (Levy), 656, 657, 658
Spurling, John, 477
Spurzheim, J.K., 835
Square Cat, The (Ayckbourn), 67
"Squares and Oblongs" (Auden), 54
Squire (Bagnold), 75, 76
Squire, J.C., 494 n

Squire, Sir John, 37, 712
"Sredni Vashtar" (Saki), 264
"Stage and Television Today, The" (Marriot), 80
Stage Society, 512
Stage Struck (Gray), 466
Stage-Land (Jerome), 576–77
Stalky and Co. (Kipling), 28
Stamboul Train (Graham Greene), 474–76
"Stand Up! Stand Up!" (Anderson), 26
"Standard Novels" (Bentley), 834
Standing Room Only (Ayckbourn), 67
Stanford, Derek, 412
Stang, Sondra, 385
Stanislavsky, Konstantin, 684
Stanley and the Women (Kingsley Amis), 18
"Stanzas for Music" (Byron), 193–194, 200
Staple of News, The (Jonson), 598
Star Over Bethlehem (Fry), 416
Star Turns Red, A (O'Casey), 788–89, 793
Starlight (Gibbons), 444
"Stately Homes of England, The" (Coward), 283
Steele, Richard, 10–14, 265, 352, 354, 360, 437, 453
Steinberg, Saul, 527
Stephen Hero (Joyce), 515, 609, 611–13
Stephen, Sir Leslie, 542
Stephens, J.K., 205, 794
"Stepping Eastward" (Morrison), 156 n
Stepping Westward (Bradbury), 152, 153–54
Sterne, Laurence, 183, 198, 205, 211, 212, 370, 454, 538–39, 611, 678
Stevenson, Lionel, 675, 676, 677, 679, 682
Stevenson, Robert Louis, 85, 87, 459, 473, 725, 756, 820
Still More Misleading Cases (Herbert), 520
"Still Out There Pushing: Lindsay Anderson in Interview" (Ryan) 32 n
"Stinker of a script plagues Goodman's 'Red Noses'" (Weiss), 81
Stoddart, John, 533
Stones of Venice (Ruskin), 393
Stop It, Whoever You Are (Livings), 685–686
Stoppard, Tom, 110, 402
Storey, David, 26, 27, 123
Stories and Interludes (Barry Pain), 830
Story of a Feather, The (Jerrold), 581
Story of a Modern Woman, The (Dixon), 296
Story of the Gadsbys, The (Kipling), 625
Story of the Irish Citizen Army, The (O'Casey), 788
Story of the Malakand Field Force, The (Churchill), 249
Storyteller (Chesterton), 245
Strachey, Lady, 644
Strachey, Lytton, 389
Straehan, Alan, 660, 661
Strafford (Robert Browning), 157
Strand Magazine, 711
Strange Case of Dr. Jekyll and Mr. Hyde (Robert Louis Stevenson) 820

Strange Histories of Kings, Princes, Dukes, Earls, Lords, Ladies Knights, and Gentlemen (Deloney), 303
Strange Newes, of the Intercepting certaine Letters (Nashe), 781 783–84
"Strange Ride of Marrowbie Jukes, The" (Kipling), 625
Strand Magazine, 445, 565
Strand Theatre, 447
Stratford, Philip, 481 n, 482 n
Strauss, Richard, 286
Stravinsy, Igor, 46, 526
Strawberry Statement, The (Hagmann), 28
Streatfeild, R.A., 188
Street, Emmet. *See* Behan, Brendan
Stritch, Elaine, 77
Strong Are Lonely, The (Hochwalder), 67
Strong, L.A.G., 221
"Structure, Symbol, and Theme in *A Passage to India*" (Allen), 394
Studies in Medieval and Renaissance Literature (C.S. Lewis), 663
"Subaltern's Love-Song" (Betjeman), 148
Sublime and the Ridiculous, The (Bradbury), 155
"Subversive, Radical and Revolutionary Traditions in European Literature between 1300 and the Age of Bunyan" (Metscher), 682
Success (Martin Amis), 24
Such, Such Were the Joys (Orwell), 821
Suckling, John, 466, 883
    biography, 1080–81
    literary analysis, 1081–84
"Suffer Little Children" (Coren), 276
Sullivan, Barry, 482 n
Sullivan, Sir Arthur, 169, 204, 446–51, 491–92, 512, 575, 627
Summers, Claude, 560
Summers Last Will and Testament (Nashe), 782–83
Summing Up, The (Maugham), 742
Summoned by Bells (Betjeman), 147, 149
Summoner's Tale (Chaucer), 230, 231, 232, 234
"Sun Rising, The" (Donne), 326
Sunday Times, 278, 475, 776, 778
Sunsets and Glories (Barnes), 82
"Supper Superstition, The" (Hood), 538
"Supplimentary Notice" (Peacock), 834
Surprise Package, 285
Surprised by Joy (C.S. Lewis), 662, 665
Sutcliffe Ltd. of Wakefield, 26
Sully, Kathleen, 26
Summoned by Bells (Betjeman), 147
Sutherland, Graham, 251
Swaggart, Jimmy, 32
Swanson, Gloria, 740
Sweet Dreams (Frayn), 400
"Sweet Hussy, The" (Hardy), 516
Sweethearts (Gilbert), 447
Swift, Jonathan, 10, 13, 14, 19, 91, 131, 174, 186, 199, 205, 208, 211, 212, 265, 310, 360, 362, 366, 434–36, 438, 455, 505, 508, 611, 665, 676, 677, 679, 682, 735, 741, 815, 820–21, 835–36, 845
Swinburne, Algernon Charles, 116, 244, 514, 611
Swinburne, Arnold, 513
Sword of Honor (Waugh), 387
Sykes, Christopher, 147
Sylvia Scarlett, I Am a Camera (John Collier), 262
Sylvie and Bruno (Carroll), 214, 216
Sylvie and Bruno Concluded (Carroll), 214, 216
Symbolic Logic (Carroll), 214
Symons, Julian, 672, 675, 676, 677, 678, 679
Symphonic Pathetique (Tchaikovsky), 396
Symposium (Plato), 395
Synge, J.M., 788

Table Book, The (Hone), 532, 534
Table Manners (Ayckbourn), 69
Tabley, Lord de, 642
Tactical Exercises (Evelyn Waugh), 1191
Taffeta Petticoat, The (Lemon), 652
Tailor's Britches, The (Livings), 685
Tails Up! 284
Take a Girl Like You (Kingsley Amis), 17, 20
Taking Steps (Ayckbourn), 68
Tale of a Tub, A (Swift), 131, 211, 362, 598
Tale of Mejnoun and Leila, a Persian Romance (D'Israeli), 316
Tale of Rosamund Gray, A (Lamb), 636–37
Tale of Sir Thopas (Chaucer), 233, 234, 342
"Tale of Terror, A" (Hood), 539
"Tale of the Great Plague, A" (Hood), 539
Tale of Two Cities, A (Dickens), 308
Tales of Terror (Bunbury), 166–67, 168
Tales of the Devil (Bunbury), 167, 168
Tales of the Unexpected, (Dahl), 295
Tales of the Wars of Montrose (Hogg), 531
Tales of Wonder (Matthew Gregory "Monk" Lewis), 166
Talking Horse, The (Anstey), 36
"Tam o' Shanter" (Burns), 182, 183, 531
Tamburlaine (Marston), 488, 729
Tamburlaine the Great, I (Marlowe), 720, 721–722, 723
Taming of the Shrew, The (Shakespeare), 252, 372–74, 622, 947
"Tank in the Stalls: Notes on the 'School of Anger'" (Holloway), 16
Tarlton's Jests (Armin), 38, 39
Tarlton, Dick, 38–39, 40, 551, 621, 623
Tarr (Wyndham Lewis), 672, 674, 681
Taste: An Epistle to a Young Critic (Armstrong), 44
"Taste Be Damned" (Crisp), 291
Taste (Foote), 380
Tatler, 10, 269, 441
Tatling Harlot, 11
Taxation No Tyranny (Samuel Johnson), 590
"Tay Bridge Disaster, The," 928
Taylor, Cecil P., 929 n
Taylor, Elizabeth, 74, 285
Taylor, J.P., 778
Taylor, Jeremy, 412

Taylor, John Russell, 569, 639, 685
Taylor, Tom, 171, 513, 653
Taylor, Wendell Hertig, 246 n
Taylor, William, 166, 835
Tchaikovsky, Peter, 396
"Tea Party" (Pinter), 848, 849
Tea Table Talk (Jerome), 577
"Tea-Table, The" (Gay), 436
Teddy Bear (A.A. Milne), 773
Tekeli (Hook), 541
Tempest (Christopher Fry), 411
Tempest, The (Shakespeare), 175, 946, 948
Temple Bar, 296
Temple, Shirley, 475
Temple, The (Herbert), 523–25
Ten Times Table (Ayckbourn), 70
Tenant of Wildfell Hall, The (A. Brontë), 415
        adapted by Fry, 415
Tenducci, Giusto, 356
Tenniel, John, 171, 214, 653
Tennyson, Alfred Lord, 15, 147, 148, 150, 158,
        159, 163, 210, 212, 214, 298, 346–47,
        414, 513, 642, 644–45, 649, 953, 1210
        parodied by Charles Stuart Calverley, 204
Tennyson, Hallam, 853
Tentamen (Hook), 540
Teraminta (Carey), 208
Terence, 758
"Terence, this is stupid stuff" (Housman), 548–49
Ternan, Ellen Lawless, 308
Terror of St. Trinian's, The (Willans), 1208
Terrors of the Night, The (Nashe), 782
Terry, Ellen, 959
Terry-Thomas, 874
"Tesment of Maister Andro Kennedy"
        (Dunbar), 342
Tess of the d'Ubervilles (Hardy), 516
Thackeray, William Makepeace, 140, 169, 170,
        204, 308, 338, 454, 542, 579, 581,
        653, 712, 725, 739, 747, 754, 834,
        883, 885, 958
        influenced by Fielding, 362
Thacred Nit (Livings), 685
Thais (Anatole France), 696
Thames Television, 290
Thank You, Fog (Auden), 48
That Hideous Strength (C.S. Lewis), 664, 665–666
That Singular Person Called Lear (Chitty), 643
That Time (Beckett), 103, 109
That Uncertain Feeling (Kingsley Amis), 15, 17
That Was the Week That Was, 931
That Was The Week That Was (Frost), 252, 274
"That's All" (Pinter), 848, 849
"That's Entertainment," 80
"That's Your Trouble" (Pinter), 848, 849
Theater Week, 68
Theatre Journal, 466
Theatre of Peter Barnes, The (Dukore), 83 n
Theatre Quarterly, 850
Theatre Royal (Dublin), 958
Theatre Royal (Stratford), 119, 265, 414, 684
Theatre Workshop, 124
"Theatre: Young Man Named Fry" (Nathan), 417
Theobald, Lewis, 869
Theocritus, 204
Theocritus Translated into English Verse
        (Calverley), 204
Theodore Hook and His Novels (Brightfield), 542 n
"Theologian's Dream, The" (Bertrand Russell), 911
*Theological Discourse on the Lamb of God and
        His Enemies* (Richard Harvey), 781
"There Are Bad Times Just Around the Corner"
        (Coward), 283
"There Was a Sick Man of Tobago" (Lear), 646
Thespis (Gilbert and Sullivan), 447–48, 451
"They" (Kipling), 627
"They Flee From Me That Sometime Did Me Seek"
        (Wyatt), 341
They Went (Norman Douglas), 330
"Thief and the Cordelier, A Ballad, The"
        (Prior), 882
Thief's Journal (Genet), 121
Third Man, The (Welles–Cotten), 475
"Third Mrs. Tanquery, The" (Hankin), 512
Third Policeman, The (O'Nolan), 799, 800–01
Thirst (O'Nolan), 799
"Thirties Novels, The" (Symons), 672, 678
This Gun for Hire. See Gun for Sale.
This Happy Breed (Coward), 285
This Is Sylvia? (Sandy Wilson), 1213
This Island (Auden). *See Look, Stranger!*
This Jockey Drives Late Nights (Living), 685
"This Lime-Tree Bower My Prison" (Coleridge),
        257, 640
This Sporting Life (Storey), 26
This Woman Business (Levy), 656, 657, 658
This Year of Grace (Coward), 284
Thistle and the Rose, The (Dunbar). *See The
        Thrissill and the Rois*
"Thomas Hobbes" (Wood), 500
*Thomas of Reading; or the Sixe Worthie Yeomen
        of the West* (Deloney), 303, 304
Thomas, Brandon, 1213
Thomas, Dylan, 17, 405, 926
Thomas, Richard, 32
Thompson, Denys, 368
Thomson, George, 178, 181
Thomson, James, 42
Thor, with Angels (Fry), 413
Thorndike, Sybil, 959
Those Barren Leaves (Huxley), 553
Those Days (E.C. Bentley), 138, 139, 140
Thoughts and Adventures (Churchill), 249
Thrale, Hester, 586, 590–91
Thread of Gold, The (A.C. Benson), 133
Three Books of Satyres (Marston), 729
"Three Dialogues with George Duthuit," 110 n
Three Hours After Marriage (Gay, Pope, and
        Arbuthnot), 174, 434, 437
Three Men in a Boat (Jerome), 91, 573,
        576–77, 1197
Three Men on the Bummel (Jerome), 577

Three Perils of Man, The (Hogg), 530
Three Plays (Ayckbourn), 69
Three Plays by Noel Coward (ed. Albee), 286
3 Return from Parnassus, 622
Three Sisters (Chekhov), 406
"Three Strangers, The" (Hardy), 516
Three Sunsets and Other Poems (Carroll), 214
Three Visions, The (Barnes), 78, 81
Threepenny Opera, The (Brecht), 124
Thrissill and the Rois, The (Dunbar), 341
Thro, A. Booker, 232
Through the Looking-Glass and What Alice Found There (Carroll), 214, 215
Throwback, The (Sharpe), 951, 954
Thursday's Child: A Pageant (Fry and Shaw), 412
Thursday's Children (Anderson and Brenton), 26
"Thus I Refute Beelzy" (John Collier), 264
Thwaite, Anthony, 345, 348 n, 953, 954
Tickell, Thomas, 883
Ticky (Gibbons), 443–44
Tiddles (Livings), 685
Tiger at the Gates (Fry), 414–16
Till We Have Faces (C.S. Lewis), 664–665, 666
Tillers of the Sand (Seaman), 925
"Tilling Society," 133
Tillotson, Louis G. Locke, 199
Tillyard, E.M.W., 230
Time, 413, 477, 479, 610, 1208
Time and Tide (Bagnold), 75, 673
Time and Western Man (Wyndham Lewis), 681
Time Bandits (Gilliam), 256
Time of the Barracudas, The (Barnes), 77
Time Vindicated to Himselfe and to His Honours (Jonson), 604
Time Works Wonders (Jerrold), 581
Time's Arrow (Martin Amis), 25
"Time's Laughing Stocks" (Hardy), 514, 516
Times Literary Supplement, 7, 9, 22, 76, 90, 153, 156 n, 233–34, 504, 507–08, 849, 875, 926, 951, 1208, 1215
Times, The (London), 26, 211, 274, 277, 308, 318, 339, 382, 474, 511–12, 519–20, 532, 575, 626, 748, 954
Times Weekly Review (London), 1215
Timor Mortis conturbat me (Dunbar), 341
Tin Men, The (Frayn), 399–400
Tinted Venus, The (Anstey), 36
Tinykin's Transformations (Lemon), 651
Tippett, Michael, 411, 412
Tissues for Men (Coren), 276, 277–78
Tit for Tat, 11
Titus Andronicus (Shakespeare), 515, 723
"To a Child of Quality of Five Years Old" (Prior), 884
"To a Lady" (Pope), 367
"To a Louse, On Seeing One on a Lady's Bonnet at Church" (Burns), 179
"To a Mountain Daisy" (Burns), 179
"To a Mouse" (Burns), 179
"To a Plum-Colored Bra Displayed in Marks & Spencer" (Ewart), 346

"To a Young Gentleman in Love. A Tale" (Prior), 877
To Be a Pilgrim (Cary), 221
"To Caroline" (Byron), 192
"To my Auld Breeks" (Fergusson), 357–358
"To Penshurst" (Jonson), 597, 605
"To Pertinax Cob" (Jonson), 604
"To Rosemounde" (Chaucer), 237
To Sea in a Sieve (Fry), 411
"To the Honourable Charles Montague, Esq." (Prior), 876
"To the Nightingale" (Finch), 366
To the Palace of Wisdom (Martin Press), 439 n
"To the Principal ad Professors of the University of St. Andrews, on their superb treat to Dr. Samuel Johnson" (Fergusson), 357
"To the Tron-kirk Bell" (Fergusson), 357
Toad of Toad Hall (Kenneth Grahame), 771
"Tobermory" (Saki), 920
"Toccata of Galuppi's, A" (Robert Browning), 158
To-Day, 565, 829, 958
"Toilette, The" (Gay), 436
Tolkien, J.R.R., 662, 663
Tolstoy, Leo, 402, 617 n
Tom Brown's Schooldays (Hughes), 28, 1209
Tom Jones (Fielding), 198, 359, 362, 363
"Tom May's Death" (Marvell), 734–35
Tom Moody's Tales (Lemon), 652
Tom Thumb (Fielding), 359, 360
Tom Thumb (Livings), 685
Tomkins, J.M., 632
Tomlin, Eric Walter Frederick, 681
Tommy and Grizel (Barrie), 86
Tom's A-Cold (John Collier), 263
Tonight Is Ours (Coward), 285
Tono-Bungay (Wells), 1198
Tonson, Jacob, 876
Tony Award. *See* Antoinette Perry Award
"Toothlesse Satyrs" (Joseph Hall), 503
Topper (Thorne Smith), 9
Topsfield, Valerie, 106, 107, 109
Topsy MP (Herbert), 519
Tough at the Top (Herbert and Ellis), 522
Tourist in Africa, A (Evelyn Waugh), 1191
Tourmalin's Time Cheques (Anstey), 36
Tourneur, Cyril, 637, 758
Tourney, Leonard D., 507
Towards the End of the Morning (Frayn), 400
Tower, The (Fry), 412
Townsend, Sue, 493
Townshend, F.H., 171
"Toy-Drawer Times, The" (Isherwood), 557
Toys of Peace, The (Saki), 919
Tracy, Spencer, 482 n
Tractatus Theologico-Politicus, 276
Traffics and Discoveries (Kipling), 627
Tragedy of Antony and Cleopatra, The (Shakespeare), 946
Tragedy of Edward II (Marlowe), 720, 723, 724
Tragedy of Hamlet, The (Shakespeare), 512
Tragedy of Macbeth, The (Lamb), 637

Tragedy of Romeo and Juliet, The
    (Shakespeare), 946
Tragedy of Tragedies: or The Life and Death
    of Tom Thumb the Great, The
    (Fielding), 360
Tragic Comedians, The (Meredith), 755
Tragical History of Dr. Faustus (Marlowe), 720,
    723–724
Transatlantic Review, 383, 610
"Transcendentalism: A Poem in Twelve Books"
    (Robert Browning), 161
Transition, 110 n, 610
Translations (Friel), 404–05
Translations into English and Latin
    (Calverley), 204
Trapeze (Mankowitz), 715
Traveler, The (Goldsmith), 590
Traveller, The (Gilbert), 452–53, 455
Travelling Companion, The, 37
Travels with My Aunt (Graham Greene), 476–77,
    479–80, 490
Travolta, John, 850
Treasure Island (Robert Lewis Stevenson), 87
Treatise of the Two Married Women
    and the Widow, The (Dunbar).
    See Tretis of the Tua Mariit Wemen
    and the Wedo, The
"Treatise on the Passions, so far as they regard
    the Stage" (Foote), 379
"Trebetherick" (Betjeman), 150
Tree, Herbert Beerbohm, 114
Trefman, Simon, 379, 382 n
Trembling of a Leaf, The (Maugham), 740
Trent Intervenes (E.C. Bentley), 139
Trent's Last Case (E.C. Bentley), 138, 139, 141
Trent's Own Case (E.C. Bentley), 139
Tretis of the Tua Mariit Wemen and the Wedo
    (Dunbar), 342–43
Trewin, J.C., 286
"Trial By Jury" (Gilbert), 446–47, 451
Trial of Man, The (Wyndham Lewis), 675
Trial of Socrates (Barnes), 82
Trial, The (Kafka), 216, 818
"Tribe of Ben" (Jonson), 598, 605
Tribune, 661, 954
Trick of It, The (Frayn), 400
Tricke To Catch the Old One, A (Middleton), 761
Trilby (George Du Maurier), 340
Trilling, Lionel, 821
Trilogy (Beckett), 106
Trinity Rep, The (Providence), 81
Trio (Maugham), 739
Trip to Calais, The. See The Capuchin (Foote)
Tristan and Isolde (Wagner), 958
Tristram Shandy (Sterne), 454, 678
Trivia (Gay), 434, 439
Troilus and Cresseda (Shakespeare), 38
Troilus and Criseyde (Chaucer), 229, 235, 432
Trojan War Will Not Take Place, The (Jean
    Giraudoux), 850. *See also Guerre*
    de Troie n'aura pas lieu, *La*

Trollope, Anthony, 212, 308, 542, 739, 1219
Trouble for Lucia (E.F. Benson), 136
"Trouble in the Works" (Pinter), 848, 852
True Patriot, The, 359, 360
"True-Born Englishman, A" (Barnes), 79
Trumpet Major, The (Hardy), 515
Truth About the Truth, The (Levy), 656
"Truth and Falshood. A Tale" (Prior), 882
Tuba Concerto (Williams), 526
Tunbridge Wells, Repertory Players, 411
Tune, Tommy, 1213
Tupper Martin Farquar, 298
    parodied by Charles Stuart Calverley, 204–05
Turgenev, Ivan, 406
Turner, Reginald, 114
"Turtle and the Sparrow, The" (Prior), 879,
    882, 883
Turtle Diary (Russell Hoban), 850
"Turtle Soup" (Carroll), 215
Tushingham, Rita, 482 n
"Twa Herds: or The Holy Tulzie, The"
    (Burns), 180
Twain, Mark, 143, 249, 251, 300–01, 391, 574,
    712, 891
Twelfth Night (Shakespeare), 38, 40, 684, 947
Twentieth Century, 848
Twentieth Century Authors: A Biographical
    Dictionary of Twentieth-Century
    Authors (Kunitz and Haycraft), 684
Twentieth Century Authors (Orwell), 810
Twentieth Century Fox, 475
Twentieth Century Literary Criticism (Lodge), 692
Twenty Orders of Callets or Drabs, The, 551
Twenty Orders of Fools, The, 551
Twice Brightly (Secombe), 928
Twiggy, 1213, 1216
Twin Rivals, The (Farquhar), 351, 354–55
"Twinkle, Twinkle, Little Bat" (Carroll), 215
Two Cheers for Democracy (Forster), 390–91
Two Faces of Dr. Jekyll, The (Mankowitz), 715
Two for the Seesaw (William Gibson), 68
"Two Gallants" (Joyce), 612
Two Gentleman of Verona, The (Shakespeare),
    489, 621, 947
"Two Lives" (Kipling), 625
Two Mr. Wetherby's, The (Hankin), 512–13
Two Noble Kinsmen, The (Fletcher
    and Shakespeare), 372, 374
Two of Us, The (Frayn), 400
Two on a Tower (Hardy), 514
"Two People in a Room: Playwriting"
    (Pinter), 849
Two Plays (Vaclav Havel), 850
Two Treatises on Government (Locke), 269–70
Two Witnesses (Gwendolyn Greene), 481 n
Tylney Hall (Hood), 539
Tynan, Kenneth, 76 n, 685, 848
Tyro: A Review of the Arts of Painting, Sculpture
    and Design, The (Wyndham Lewis), 672
"Tyros and Portraits" (Wyndham Lewis), 672
Tyson, Cicily, 482 n

"U and Non-U: An Essay in Sociological
        Linguistics" (Alan Ross), 778
Uber Alles (Mikes), 763
Ulysses (Joyce), 212, 609–10, 613–16, 681,
        694, 695
"Ulysses" as a Comic Novel (Bowen), 615
Uncle Baby (Gilbert), 446
"Uncle Harry" (Coward), 283
Uncle Vanya (Frayn), 402
Uncommon Law (Herbert), 520–21
Unconscious Memory (Butler), 187
Under the Deodars (Kipling), 625, 629
Under the Greenwood Tree (Hardy), 514–15
Under the Volcano (Lowry), 476
Underhill, Francis, 299
Undertaker, The (Hood), 539
Underwood, The (Jonson), 604
"Unforgettable," 81
"Unfortunate Mr. Ebbsmith, The" (Hankin),
        512–13
*Unfortunate Traveller, Or, the Life of Jacke Wilton,
        The* (Nashe), 782–85
Ungathered Verse (Jonson), 604
University Wits, 781
"Unlocking the Potting Shed" (Stratford), 481 n,
        482 n
Unnamable, The (Beckett), 103, 105, 106
Unnatural Pursuit and Other Pieces, The
        (Gray), 469
University of Toronto Quarterly, 145
Unprofessional Tales (Norman Douglas), 330
"Unqualified Assistance" (D'Arcy), 297, 298
*Unsent Letters: Irreverent Notes from a Literary
        Life* (Bradbury), 152, 155
Up Against It (Orton), 803
Up and Down the London Streets (Lemon), 651
"Up the Rhine" (Hood), 537, 539
"Upon Appleton House" (Marvell), 734
"Upon the King's Great Porter" (John Hall), 501
"Upon T.R., a Very Little Man, But Excellently
        Learned" (John Hall), 501
Usk, Thomas, 229
Ustinov, Peter, 36 482 n
Utopia (More), 507
Utopia Limited (Gilbert), 448
*Utterly, Utterly Merry Comic Relief Christmas
        Book, The* (Adams), 7

Vagabonds in Perigord (Bashford), 90
Valiant Welshman, The (Armin), 39
Vallone, Raf, 482 n
Valmouth (Firbank), 370
Vanbrugh, Sir John, 10, 352, 353, 354, 455
Vanity of Human Wishes, The (Samuel Johnson),
        586–89
Variable Lengths (Livings), 685
Vaurien, or Sketches of the Times (D'Israeli), 316,
        317, 318
Vedrenne, J.C., 512
Venture of a Rational Faith, The
        (Maggi Benson), 133

Venus in the Kitchen (Norman Douglas
        and Guiseppe Orioli), 329, 330
Venus Observed (Fry), 410, 413, 417–18
Verses and Translations (Calverley), 203, 204
Version of the Truth, A (Nicholas Bentley), 139
Very Private Life, A (Frayn), 400
Vicar of Wakefield, The (Goldsmith), 452–54, 456
Vice Versa (Anstey), 35, 36
Vickers, Hugo, 711
Vico, Giambattista, 616
"Victor" (Auden), 52
Victoria Theatre, 68
Victorian Age in Literature, The
        (Chesterton), 244
Victorian Forerunner (Clubbe), 539
Viertel, Berthold, 559
"View on the Pont Neuf at Paris" (Bunbury), 165
Views in Rome (Lear), 645
Vigo, Jean, 28
Viking Book of Aphorisms (Auden), 50
Vile Bodies (Evelyn Waugh), 776
"Villa Lucianne, The" (D'Arcy), 299 n
Village Coquettes, The (Dickens), 308
"Village Like Yours, A" (Mankowitz), 716
"Village that Voted the Earth Was Flat, The"
        (Kipling), 629
Village Wooing (Christopher Fry), 411
Villiers, George, 335
Villon, François, 303
Vinson, James, 17, 494 n, 660, 718 n
Vintage London (Betjeman), 147
Violent Moment (Barnes), 77
Virgidemiarum (Joseph Hall), 503, 505–07
Virgil, 11, 12, 110, 195, 204, 205, 230, 435–36,
        639, 720, 846
        translated by Dryden, 337
"Virgil, Dryden, Gay, and Matters Trivial"
        (Sherbo), 439 n
"Virtuoso, The" (Busch), 527
Vision of Judgement (Byron), 200
Visit to America, A (Archibald Macdonell), 712
"Vital Theatre?" (Anderson), 26, 32 n
Vive Le Roy (Ford Madox Ford), 387
"Vocabulary for Chaucerian Comedy:
        A Preliminary Sketch, A" (Ruggiers), 230
Voces Populi (Anstey), 36
Vogue, 280, 441
Volpone (Jonson), 93, 598–99, 601–03
Voltaire, François, 30, 74, 80, 198, 210, 221, 315,
        316, 317, 460, 505, 740
Vonnegut, Kurt, 8, 577
Vortex, The (Coward), 279, 286
Voyage of the "Dawn Treader," The (C.S. Lewis),
        664, 665, 666
Voyage to Abyssinia (Lobo), 585

Wadsworth, Charles, 415
Wadsworth, Jean, 415
Wagner, Geoffrey, 680, 682
Wain, John, 15, 16, 17, 821
Wait for the End (Lemon), 652

Waiting for Godot, (Beckett), 68, 102, 106, 107–08, 387
Waiting in the Wings (Coward), 286
Waiting of Lester Abbs, The (Sully) director Lindsay Gordon Anderson, 26
Wakefield Express, Lindsay George Anderson, director, 26
"Walk, The" (Hardy), 516
Walker, London (Barrie), 85, 86
Wallace, David, 231
Wallace, Hazel Vincent, 67
Walpole, Horace, 43, 60, 165, 208
Walpole, Hugh, 660, 741
Walpole, Sir Robert, 359, 360, 438, 587 satirized by Fielding, 361
"Walrus and the Carpenter, The" (Carroll), 215
Walt Disney Company, 87, 88
"Walt Whitman, inciting the bird of freedom to soar" (Beerbohm), 116
Walton, Isaak, 508, 523, 636, 638
Wanderer, or Female Difficulties, The (Frances "Fanny" Burney), 173, 175–76
"Wanderers" (Calverley), 204
Wandering Minstrel, The (Mayhew), 747
War: A Fleet in Being, The (Kipling), 631
War Lord, The (John Collier), 262
Warburg, Fredric, 819
Ward, Artemus. *See* Browne, Charles Farrar
Ward, Mrs. Humphrey, 553
Warden, The (Trollope), 212
Warner, David, 685
Warrilow, David, 102, 103
Warton, Joseph, 13
Warwick Films, 77
Waste Land, The (Eliot), 47, 418
"Watcher in Spanish, The" (Isherwood), 558
Watchman, The (Coleridge), 257
Water Babies (Kingsley), 410
Water Gipsies, The (Herbert), 520
Waterhouse, Keith, 30, 121, 493
Watson, Ian, 67
Watson, Thomas, 720
Watsons, The (Austen), 60
Watt (Beckett), 101, 104–05, 108, 681
Watts, Richard, 80
Waugh, Alec, 565, 712
Waugh, Auberon, 692
Waugh, Evelyn, 4, 16, 17, 147, 152, 155, 371, 387, 492, 519, 678, 692, 776, 778
Way of the World, The (Congreve), 265, 266, 270, 352
Way Upstream (Ayckbourn), 70
Ways of Escape (Graham Greene), 474–77, 479
We Think the World of You (Ackerley), 4, 5, 6
We Were Dancing (Coward), 285
"We Were Two Pretty Babes" (Lamb), 637
We (Zamyatin), 818–819
Weather at Tregulla, The (Gibbons), 443–44
Weaver, J.R.H., 492
Webb, Allan Bourne, 441
Webb, Clifton, 282

Weber, Andrew Lloyd, 284
Webster, John, 507
Wedekind, Frank, 82
"Wednesday" (Gay), 435
Wee Willie Winkie (Kipling), 475, 625
Weekly Magazine or Edinburgh Amusement (Ruddiman), 356
Weekly Westminster, 474
Weill, Kurt, 30
Weimer, Michael J., 688
Weiss, Hedy, 81
Weiss, Peter, 77
Welles, Orson, 475, 482 n
Wells, H.G., 31, 116, 383, 459, 554, 739, 770
Wertenbaker, Timberlake, 355
Wesker, Arnold, 77, 686
Wesley John, 199
Wessex Tales (Hardy), 515, 516
West, W.J., 821
Westminister Gazette, 544
Westminister Magazine, 455
Westminister Review, 511, 834
Westward Ho (Beckett), 102
Westwood (Gibbons), 443–44
W.H. Auden: A Biography (Humphrey), 49
W.H. Auden (Carpenter), 54 n
Whales of August, The (Berry), 27
"What can a Young Lassie do wi' an auld man?" (Burns), 181
"What *Did* Aunt Ada See?" (Mannes), 441, 444 n
What D'Ye Call It, The (Gay), 434, 437, 439
"What I Believe" (Forster), 391
"What Is Love?" (Coward), 282
What the Butler Saw (Orton), 27, 803, 806
What Every Woman Knows (Barrie), 85, 86, 88
"What of soul was left, I wonder, when the kissing had to stop?" (Robert Browning), 158–59
What Were (Beckett), 102
What You Will (Marston), 595, 730–731
Whately, Bishop Richard, 65 n
Wheeler, Stephen, 625
"When Earth's Last Picture Is Painted" (Kipling), 626
"When Lovely Woman Stoops to Folly" (Goldsmith), 454
"When Princes and Prelates" (Burns), 182
When We Were Very Young (Milne), 771
When You See Me, You Know Me (Rowley), 40
Where Angels Fear to Tread (Forster), 389
Whims and Oddities (Hood), 536, 539
Whims and Oddities, Second Series (Hood), 536
Whistlecraft (Byron), 194
Whistler, James McNeill, 338, satirized by George Du Maurier, 340
"Whistler's Writing" (Beerbohm), 116
Whitby Gazette, 214
White Bus, The (Anderson), 29
White Fang (Jack London), 776
White, James, 635
"White Magic" (D'Arcy), 299

White Sand and Grey Sand (Gibbons), 443
White, William Anthony Parker.
    See Boucher, Anthony
"White Wine Election, The" (Herbert), 521–22
"Whitewashed Uncle, A" (Graham), 459
Whittier, John Greenleaf, 537
Who Do You Think You Are? (Bradbury), 154–55
Whoroscope (Beckett), 100
Who's Who, 411, 711
Why Come To Slaka? (Bradbury), 154
"Why Do the Wrong People Travel?"
    (Coward), 282
"Why Does Life Get in the Way So?"
    (Coward), 282
"Why I Write in Verse" (Fry), 414
"Why Is It the Woman Who Pays?" (Coward), 282
Why Must the Show Go On? (Coward), 280, 282
"Why Verse?" (Fry), 414
Wicked World, The (Gilbert), 447
Widow Club, 12
Widow's Tears, The (Chapman), 223, 226–27
Wife, A (Overbury), 507
Wife of Bath, The (Gay), 434, 436–37
Wife of Bath's Tale (Chaucer), 230, 232–33,
    235, 236
Wigs on the Green (Mitford), 776
Wild Body, The (Wyndham Lewis), 672
Wild Goose Chase, The (Fletcher), 372, 375–76
Wild Honey (Frayn), 399, 402
Wild Knight, The (Chesterton), 143
"Wildboy" (Wyndham Lewis), 679
Wilde, Alan, 562
Wilde, Oscar, 77, 86, 99, 114, 117, 133, 134,
    266, 280, 281, 287, 290, 291, 299, 300,
    317, 347, 369–70, 396, 409, 411, 463,
    469–70, 513, 545, 611, 702, 740, 741,
    742, 829
Wilder, Thornton, 115
Wildest Dreams (Ayckbourn), 71
Wilkes, John, 590
Wilks, Robert, 351, 352, 353
William McGonagall Meets George Gershwin
    (Spike Milligan), 767
Williams, Charles, 412
Williams, Orlo, 677
Williams, Robin, 88
Williams, Tennessee, 285
Williams, Vaughan, 526
Williams, William Carlos, 383, 610
"Willie Wastle and his Dog Trap" (Hogg), 530–31
Willman, Noel, 75
Willy Wonka and the Chocolate Factory
    (Dahl), 295
Wilmay (Barry Pain), 830
Wilson, Angus, 694
Wilson, Colin, 16
Wilson, Edmund, 115
Wind in the Willows, The (Grahame), 459,
    461–63, 771
Windham, William, 678
Window in Thrums (Barrie), 85

Wine (Gay), 434–35
Wing, George, 310
Winnie-the-Pooh (Milne), 771
Winter Woods (Hardy), 516
Winter's Tale, The (Shakespeare), 413, 487
Wisdom of the Ancients, The (Bacon), 87
"Wissenschaft File, The" (Bradbury), 152, 155
Wise Child (Gray), 465–66
Wit and Mirth: or, Pills to Purge Melancholy
    (D'Urfey), 437
{*Wit and Opinions of Douglas Jerrold, The*
    (Jerrold), 582
Wit and Wisdom of Quentin Crisp, The
    (Crisp), 290
Wit Without Money (Fletcher), 376–77
Witch of Edmonton, The (Oekker), 637
"Witch of Fife, The" (Hogg), 531
Wither, George, 636
Within the Gates (O'Casey), 793–794
Witlings, The (Frances "Fanny" Burney),
    173, 174
Wittgenstein, Ludwig, 399
Wittig, Susan, 230
Wizard of Oz, 89
Wodehouse, P.G., 16, 19, 170, 283, 346, 377,
    666, 712
Wolfe, Peter, 478
Wolfit, Sir Donald, 67
"Wolf-King; or Little Red-Riding-Hood, The"
    (Bunbury), 167
Wolves Were in the Sledge, The (Stella Gibbons),
    443–44
Woman Hater, The (Beaumont), 93, 94, 95, 96
Woman Hater, The (Frances "Fanny" Burney),
    175, 372–73
Woman in Mind (Ayckbourn), 68, 70
Woman with a History, A (Weedon
    Grossmith), 492
"Woman's Constancy" (Donne), 326, 706
Woman's Prize, or The Tamer Tamed, The
    (Fletcher), 372–74
Women Beware Women (Middleton), 758
Wonderful Tennessee (Friel), 406
Wood, Anthony à, 500
Wood, Christopher, 559
Wood, David, 29
Wood, Frederick T., 208, 209 n
Wood, Murray, 573
Woodbarrow Farm (Jerome), 577
Woodcock, George, 822
Woodlanders, The (Hardy), 515
Woolf, Leonard, 389, 559
Woolf, Virginia, 3, 122, 136, 370, 389, 396, 559,
    561, 611, 672, 676, 695, 725, 726,
    727, 756
    influenced by Samuel Butler, 188
Worcester's Men, 623
Word and Story in C.S. Lewis (Schakel
    and Huttar), 667 n
Word from Our Sponsor, A (Ayckbourn), 71
Words and Music (Coward), 284

Wordsworth, William, 87, 88, 147, 149, 195, 196,
    197, 204, 259, 347, 366, 513, 590, 638,
    643, 746, 835, 837, 838
  collaborator with Coleridge, 257–58
Work Is a Four Letter Word (Livings), 685
"Worker's Bag is Deepest Red, The" (Coren), 276
Workes (Jonson), 595, 597
*Working with Structuralism: Essays and Reviews
    on Nineteenth and Twentieth-Century
    Literature* (Lodge), 691
Works (Joseph Hall), 504
Works (Lamb), 636
Works of Douglas Jerrold, The (Jerrold), 581
Works of Douglas Jerrold, The (Richard Kelly),
    583 n
Works of Max Beerbohm, The (Beerbohm), 115
*Works of Robert Burns; with an Account of his
    Life, and a Criticism of his Writings. To
    which are Prefixed, some Observations
    on the Character and condition of the
    Scottish Peasantry, The* (Currie), 178
Works of Virgil (Dryden), 334
World, The, 625
World as Will and Idea, The (Schopenhauer),
    210–11
World Crisis (Churchill), 249
World in the Evening, The (Isherwood), 559, 562
Worley, Irene, 67
Worms (Barnes), 78–79
Wright, Andrew, 221
Write On: Occasional Essays, 1965–1985
    (Lodge), 691
Writers in Exile, PEN, 763
Writer's Notebook, A (Maugham), 742
"Written After a Walk Before Supper"
    (Coleridge), 258
"Written at Cambridge" (Lamb), 637
Wyatt, Sir Thomas, 327, 347
Wycherley, William, 96, 265, 266, 352, 376
Wyndham, George, 130
*Wyndham Lewis: A Portrait of the Artist as the
    Enemy* (Geoffrey Wagner), 680, 682
"Wyndham Lewis and Vorticism" (Wyndham
    Lewis), 673
Wyndham Lewis and Western Man (Ayers), 681
"Wyndham Lewis as Imaginative Writer"
    (Seymour-Smith), 682 n
"Wyndham Lewis" (Edward Jones), 674, 680
"Wyndham Lewis" (Tomlin), 681
Wyndham Lewis (William Pritchard), 677
Wyndham Lewis: Religion and Modernism

(Schenker), 675, 677
Wynne, Esma, 284

"X" (Belloc), 132
Xmas vs. Mastermind, 68

"Yank My Doodle, It's a Dandy" (Barnes), 78
"Yankee Doodle," 208
Yard of Sun, A (Fry), 415, 417, 419
"Yarn of the 'Nancy Bell,' The" (Gilbert), 450
Year Book, The (Hone), 532, 534
Year in Cricklewood, A (Coren), 277
Years Between, The (Kipling), 629–30
Yeats, John Butler, 47
Yeats, W.B., 516, 609, 787, 788, 792, 793
"Yellow" (Beckett), 104
"Yellow Book Celebrities" (D'Arcy), 299
Yellow Book, The, 114, 115, 296, 298, 299,
    300, 574
Yeomen of the Guard, The (Gilbert
    and Sullivan), 448
Yeoman's Tale (Chaucer), 232
Yes, Minister, 712
Yesterday and After, 675
Yet Again (Beerbohm), 115
York, Michael, 482 n
"You Are Deceiv'd" (Lovelace), 707
You Only Live Twice (Fleming, adapted
    by Dahl), 295
"Young Adam Cupid" (Grahame), 459
"Young and the Old Self, The" (Beerbohm), 116
Young Charles Lamb 1775–1802 (Courtney), 641
Young George du Maurier, The (Daphne
    Du Maurier), 338
Young Madame Conti (Levy), 656, 660
Young Pobble's Guide to His Toes, The
    (Ewart), 345
You're Free (Livings), 685
Youth, 551

Zabriskie Point (Antonioni), 28
Zamyatin, Evgeny, 818
Zangwill, Israel, 574
Zapolya (Coleridge), 258
Zehr, David Morgan, 808, 810, 811, 813, 817, 818
Zeigler, Heide, 156 n
Zelazny, Roger, 264
Zero de Conduite (Vigo), 28
"Zigeuner" (Coward), 283
Zola, Emile, 297
Zuleika Dobson (Beerbohm), 115, 117